COMPREHENSIVE EVALUATIONS

COMPREHENSIVE EVALUATIONS:

CASE REPORTS FOR PSYCHOLOGISTS, DIAGNOSTICIANS, AND SPECIAL EDUCATORS

Edited by

NANCY MATHER

LYNNE E. JAFFE

WILEY

John Wiley & Sons, Inc.

Published by John Wiley & Sons, Inc., Hoboken, New Jersey.

Published simultaneously in Canada.

For general information on our other products and services please contact our Customer Care Department within the U.S. at (800) 762-2974, outside the United States at (317) 572-3993 or fax (317) 572-4002.

Wiley also publishes its books in a variety of electronic formats. Some content that appears in print may not be available in electronic books. For more information about Wiley products, visit our website at www.wiley.com.

Library of Congress Cataloging-in-Publication Data:

Comprehensive evaluations : case reports for psychologists, diagnosticians, and special educators / edited by Nancy Mather and Lynne E. Jaffe.
p. cm.
Includes bibliographical references and index.
ISBN 978-0-470-61791-5 (pbk.); 978-0-470-88194-1 (ePDF); 978-0-470-88195-8 (eMobi); 978-0-470-88196-5 (ePub)
1. Autism—Case studies.   I. Mather, Nancy.   II. Jaffe, Lynne, 1946–
RC553.A88C673 2011
616.85'882—dc22

2010013511

Printed in the United States of America
10 9 8 7 6 5 4 3 2 1

This book is dedicated to Dr. Richard W. Woodcock, a visionary in the field of cognitive and academic measurement. He has always understood, and has helped others to understand, the role and the importance of comprehensive evaluations in identifying the factors that underlie a student's problems in learning and behavior.

N. M.
L. J.

Contents

Acknowledgments

We would not have been able to bring this book to publication without the encouragement and contributions of our friends and colleagues. We are sincerely grateful

- To our colleagues, who generously responded to our requests for reports and for their willingness to share their expertise regarding students with diverse special needs.
- To Kathy Gardner, who graciously accepted the onerous task of obtaining multiple permissions for the use of copyrighted material. Without her help, we would still be sending out forms.
- To Erin Katz, for her help in formatting the reports and gathering information for the appendices during the initial stages of this project.
- To Isabel Pratt, our project director at John Wiley & Sons, for her enthusiasm, encouragement, and friendship as she guided us through the publication process.

- To Kim Nir, our production editor, for her attention to detail. She oversaw the design, copyediting, typesetting, and proofreading stages of a long and complex manuscript.
- To our life partners, Michael and Brian, who have tolerated our writing of yet another book with minimal complaint and plenty of love, encouragement, and support.
- To each other, for finishing this book and still remaining the best of friends.

Finally, we raise our glasses in a toast to Dr. John Willis for his ability to connect clinical knowledge with cognitive theory, and his skill in explaining controversial issues in the field with both eloquence and wit. We are grateful for his willingness to take time from his busy schedule to write the foreword to this book.

List of Contributors

Bashir Abu Hamour, Ph.D.
Mu'tah University
Jordan

Vincent C. Alfonso, Ph.D.
Professor and Associate Dean
Graduate School of Education
Fordham University
New York, NY

Dale A. Bailey, M.A., CCC-SLP
Speech-Language Pathologist
Special Education Consultant
Fort Kent, ME

Sherry Mee Bell, Ph.D.
Associate Professor
Special Education
Nashville, TN

Virginia W. Berninger, Ph.D.
Professor of Educational Psychology
University of Washington
Seattle, WA

Thomas M. Brunner, Ph.D.
Clinical, Forensic, & Consulting Psychology
San Rafael Professional Offices
Tucson, AZ

Mary N. Camarata, M.S., CCC-SLP
Assistant Professor Hearing & Speech Science
Vanderbilt University School of Medicine
Nashville, TN

Stephen M. Camarata, Ph.D., CCC-SLP
Professor Hearing & Speech Science
Vanderbilt University School of Medicine
Nashville, TN

Gail Cheramie, Ph.D.
Associate Professor and Director
School Psychology Program
University of Houston-Clear Lake
Houston, TX

Chris Coleman, M.A.
University of Georgia
Athens, GA

Lisa Coyner, Ph.D.
School Psychologist
Arizona State Schools for the Deaf and the Blind
Tucson, AZ

James M. Creed, M.Ed.
JCreed Consulting
Leominster, MA

Sean Cunningham, M.S.
University of Utah
Salt Lake City, UT

Milton J. Dehn, Ed.D.
Schoolhouse Educational Services
Stoddard, WI

Ron Dumont, Ed.D.
Director of School Psychology
Fairleigh Dickinson University
Teaneck, NJ

Krystle Edwards, B.A.
Warner Pacific College
Portland, OR

Colin D. Elliott, Ph.D.
Gevirtz Graduate School of Education,
University of California, Santa Barbara
Newbury Park

Steven Feifer, D.Ed.
School Psychologist
Frederick, MD

Catherine A. Fiorello, Ph.D.
Associate Professor and Coordinator of School
   Psychology
Temple University
Philadelphia, PA

Dawn P. Flanagan, Ph.D.
Professor of Psychology
Director, School Psychology Programs
St. John's University
Jamaica, NY

Elaine Fletcher-Janzen, Ed.D.
American Board of Pediatric Neuropsychology
Professor of School Psychology
Chicago School of Professional Psychology
Chicago, IL

Sarah Gaines, Psy.S., NCSP
School Psychologist
Arizona State Schools for the Deaf and the Blind
Tucson, AZ

John M. Garruto, D.Ed., NCSP
School Psychologist
Oswego City School District
Fulton, NY

Brigid Garvin, M.Ed.
School Psychology Program
Temple University
Philadelphia, PA

Michael E. Gerner, Ph.D., P.C.
Consulting Psychologists
Flagstaff, AZ

Marshall Andrew Glenn, Ph.D.
Oklahoma City University
Norman, OK

Sam Goldstein, Ph.D.
Neurology, Learning, and Behavior
Salt Lake City, UT

Lisa A. Hain, Psy.D., NCSP
School Psychologist
Adjunct Faculty

Department of Psychology
Philadelphia College of Osteopathic Medicine

James B. Hale, Ph.D.
Associate Professor of Clinical Neuropsychology
University of Victoria
Victoria, BC, Canada

Joel S. Hanania, Ph.D.
School Psychologist, Washington School District
Kid Assist, Director
Cave Creek, AZ

Jim Hanson, M.Ed.
School Psychologist
Portland, OR

Frances Ingram, M.A.
School Psychologist
Stern Center for Language and Learning
Williston, VT

Lynne E. Jaffe, Ph.D.
Learning Disabilities Consulting and Evaluation
Adjunct Assistant Professor
University of Arizona
Tucson, AZ

Randy Kamphaus, Ph.D.
Dean and Distinguished Research Professor
Georgia State University
College of Education
Atlanta, GA

Nadeen L. Kaufman, Ed.D.
Child Study Center
Yale University School of Medicine
New Haven, CT

Melissa M. King, M.Ed.
Educational Consultant
Learning Curve, LLC
Essex Junction, VT

Judith M. Kroese, Ph.D.
Pediatric Neuropsychologist
Southern Arizona Neuropsychology Associates
Tucson, AZ

Toby Laird, Ph.D.
Consulting Psychologists
Flagstaff, AZ

Elizabeth O. Lichtenberger, Ph.D.
Clinical Psychologist
Carlsbad, CA

Sally J. Logerquist, Ph.D.
Psychologist
Scottsdale, AZ

Nancy Mather, Ph.D.
Professor, Learning Disabilities
University of Arizona
Tucson, AZ

R. Steve McCallum, Ph.D.
Professor and Head
Educational Psychology and Counseling
Knoxville, TN

George McCloskey, Ph.D.
Professor and Director of School Psychology Research
Philadelphia College of Osteopathic Medicine
Philadelphia, PA

Jane McClure, Ph.D.
Psychologist
McClure, Mallory & Baron
San Francisco, CA

Kelly Kathleen Metz, M.Ed.
Measurement and Evaluation
Teacher for the Deaf and Hard of Hearing
Arizona State Schools for the Deaf and Blind
Phoenix, AZ

Robert Misak, M.Ed., M.A.
Licensed Specialist in School Psychology
Victoria Independent School District

Kimberly Morris, Ph.D., NCSP
School Psychologist
Tucson, AZ

Richard Morris, Ph.D.
Meyerson Distinguished Professor of Disability and
    Rehabilitation
Professor and Director, School Psychology Program
University of Arizona
Tucson, AZ

Jack A. Naglieri, Ph.D.
Professor of Psychology
George Mason University
Senior Research Scientist
The Devereux Foundation
Centreville, VA

Christopher J. Nicholls, Ph.D.
Clinical/Pediatric Neuropsychologist
The Nicholls Group
Scottsdale, AZ

Samuel O. Ortiz, Ph.D.
Professor of Psychology
St. John's University
New York, NY

Tulio M. Otero, Ph.D.
Associate Professor
Departments of Clinical & School Psychology Programs
Chicago School of Professional Psychology
Chicago, IL

Linda Hernandez Parks, M.A.
University of Houston-Clear Lake
Houston, TX

Mitchel D. Perlman, Ph.D.
Forensic Neuropsychologist
San Diego, CA

Blanche Podhajski, Ph.D.
President, Stern Center for Language and Learning
Clinical Associate Professor of Neurology
University of Vermont College of Medicine
Williston, Vermont

Eva M. Prince, Ed.S.
School Psychologist
Tucson, AZ

Tara C. Raines, Psy.S.
School Psychologist
Atlanta, GA

Cecil Reynolds, Ph.D.
Emeritus
Professor of Educational Psychology
Professor of Neuroscience
Distinguished Research Scholar
Texas A&M University
Bastrop, TX

Deborah Rhein, Ph.D., CCC-SLP
Assistant Professor
Communication Disorders Program
New Mexico State University
Las Cruces, NM

Gale H. Roid, Ph.D.
Warner Pacific College
Portland, OR

Janice R. Sammons, Ph.D.
Southern Arizona Neuropsychology Associates
Tucson, AZ

Ashley Schuler, M.A.
University of Houston-Clear Lake
Houston, TX

Ed Schultz, Ph.D.
Assistant Professor
Midwestern State University
Wichita Falls, TX

Andrew Shanock, Ph.D.
Associate Professor of Psychology
College of Saint Rose
Schenectady, NY

Donna Rury Smith, Ed.D.
Independent Consultant
Fort Worth, TX

Annmarie Urso, Ph.D.
Assistant Professor
State University of New York at Geneseo
Geneseo, NY

Christina M. Vasquez, Ed.S.
School Psychology Program
University of Arizona
Tucson, AZ

Barbara J. Wendling, M.A.
Woodcock-Munoz Foundation
Dallas, TX

Mary C. Wright, M.A.,
School Psychologist
Learning Curve, LLC
Essex Junction, VT

Aimee Yermish, Psy.D.
Educational Therapist
da Vinci Learning Center
Stow, MA

Foreword

John O. Willis

If you don't know where you are going, you will probably end up somewhere else.

—Laurence J. Peter

Comprehensive Evaluations: Case Reports for Psychologists, Diagnosticians, and Special Educators clearly and informatively answers in the affirmative the question: "Do we need comprehensive psychoeducational evaluations of children with disabilities?"

A passion for parsimony, efforts to save time and control costs, and complacency about offering nothing more than diagnoses with only minimal, vague, generic, or one-size-fits-all recommendations often lead to evaluation reports that are neither very comprehensive nor especially helpful to examinees, parents, teachers, therapists, and other consumers of our reports. Perhaps the most extreme pressure for oversimplification of reports has been with evaluations for children with specific learning disabilities (SLD).

The Individuals with Disabilities Education Improvement Act (IDEA) (1990, 1997, 2004) and its predecessor, the Education of All Handicapped Children Act (EHA, 1975) have always used the following definition for SLD with minor word changes: "a disorder in one or more of the basic psychological processes involved in understanding or in using language, spoken or written, which disorder may manifest itself in the imperfect ability to listen, think, speak, read, write, spell, or do mathematical calculations."

That definition seems clear enough, with "a disorder in one or more of the basic psychological processes" being the defining characteristic of the disability. However, since the original Education of All Handicapped Children Act (1975), the regulations implementing the laws have never operationalized or even required the assessment of basic psychological processes as part of the legal identification

of SLD. Instead, the requirements focused on ruling out sensory or motor impairments, intellectual disability, emotional disturbance, or disadvantage as primary causes of the child's learning problems, and—until 2004—on establishing a "severe discrepancy" between levels of achievement and intellectual ability. Based on myriad complaints about severe discrepancy (e.g., Bijou, 1942; Bradley, Danielson, & Hallahan, 2002; Cronbach, 1957; Donovan & Cross, 2002; Fletcher, Denton, & Francis, 2005; Hoskyn & Swanson, 2000; Kavale, 2002; Reschly, Tilly, & Grimes, 1999), the 2006 regulations for the 2004 reauthorization of IDEA (Assistance to States, 2006) fundamentally altered the operational definition of specific learning disability. Critics referred to the "severe discrepancy" criterion as a "wait to fail" model. Under the new (2006) regulations, the states could still allow, but could no longer require, a severe discrepancy between ability and achievement as a criterion for identifying SLD. Instead, states were required to permit a Response to Intervention (RtI) approach as part of the process for identifying SLD and could also permit the use of other, undefined research-based methods of identification. Explaining these regulations in more detail, the criterion for low achievement was expanded: "The child does not achieve adequately for the child's age or to meet state-approved grade-level standards." In addition, the criteria for identifying a child as having SLD through the RtI process were explained: "The child does not make sufficient progress to meet age or state-approved grade-level standards in one or more of the areas identified in paragraph (a)(1) of this section when using a process based on the child's response to scientific, research-based intervention." The more confusing alternative, use of undefined research-based methods, was described: "The child exhibits a pattern of strengths and weaknesses in performance, achievement, or both, relative to age, state-approved grade level standards, or intellectual development, that is determined by the group to be relevant to the identification of a specific learning disability, using appropriate assessments, consistent with §§ 300.304 and 300.305."

Subsequently, partly in response to the regulations and partly to minimize educational spending, special education programs often attempt to limit the number of comprehensive psychoeducational assessments that are conducted or, in the case of SLD, eliminate them altogether in the belief that documented failure to respond to scientific, research-based interventions, plus a vision and hearing screening, and a review of the student's history, including school-wide and state-wide assessments, would constitute a sufficiently comprehensive evaluation to identify SLD.

The addition of and preference for RtI for the purpose of identifying specific learning disabilities has caused consternation in the field (see, for example, Mather & Kaufman [2006a, 2006b]). A superficial reading of the regulations might suggest that there is no longer any place for traditional psychoeducational evaluations. However, the commentary in the 2006 regulations (Assistance to States, 2006) includes such observations as "An RtI process does not replace the need for a comprehensive evaluation, and a child's eligibility for special education services cannot be changed solely on the basis of data from an RtI process" (p. 46648) and "RtI is only one component of the process to identify children in need of special education and related services. Determining why a child has not responded to research-based interventions requires a comprehensive evaluation" (p. 46647). I think they got that part right.

Identification of other disabilities under EHA (1975) and IDEA (1990, 1997, 2004) has always required surprisingly little psychoeducational information about the student. Unlike SLD, which has its very own sections for detailing evaluation methods, the other disabilities have no specific guidance for evaluation other than the definition of each disability and the general guidelines for all evaluations in Evaluations and Reevaluations (IDEA 2004, § 614). Yet, it is often a referral for academic difficulties and the subsequent *comprehensive* evaluation that provides a different perspective on the difficulty the student is having, as well as a non-SLD diagnosis, that lead to the most appropriate treatment recommendations. For these students (e.g., with

severe anxiety, autism, intellectual disability), "watching them fail" the RtI interventions just postpones the help they need. "Watch them fail" does not seem to be much of an improvement over "wait to fail."

Thus, for students who do not respond completely satisfactorily to attempted interventions in an RtI model, the questions should become *why* does the student have such difficulty and, once we understand the *why*, *how* can we help the student succeed? If we do not fully understand the problem, we are unlikely to stumble across the solution. I believe that this is the reason that the IDEA definition of a specific learning disability still specifies "a **disorder** in one or more of the basic psychological processes" as the core of the disability. Similarly, the definition of emotional disturbance specifies that it is "a **condition** exhibiting one or more of the following characteristics over a long period of time and to a marked degree that adversely affects a child's educational performance" [emphasis supplied] (Assistance to States, 2006, § 300.8 (c) (4) (i)). If we understand, for example, the nature of the "disorder" or the "condition," then we have a fighting chance of figuring out what to do to help the student succeed. The above examples are drawn from federal laws and regulations pertaining to two disabilities in schoolchildren, but the same considerations are equally important for evaluations of all disabilities and concerns with both children and adults. If we cannot explain the mechanism whereby the disability impairs the examinee's functioning, we have little hope of offering useful suggestions. An unexplained and unexplored diagnosis or IDEA category leaves us closing our eyes and blindly sticking pins into books of remedial techniques, such as provided in Mather and Jaffe (2002) or Wendling and Mather (2009).

As just one example (Beal, Dumont, & Willis, 2003), let us consider how many different ways you can fail to read the word "cat." These 21 possibilities do not exhaust all reasons for reading difficulty, are listed in no particular sequence, and include difficulties with auditory perception, memory span and working memory, long-term storage and retrieval, sequencing, oral vocabulary, and other issues.

1. You do not know the sounds represented by each of the three letters.
2. You know the sounds but cannot recall them.
3. You know the sounds and can eventually recall them, but not quickly enough to finish sounding out the word.
4. You cannot blend the three sounds into a single, spoken word.

5. You can blend the sounds but not quickly enough to finish sounding out the word before you forget what you are doing.

6. You do not recognize the spoken word "cat" as containing three distinct sounds.

7. You appreciate the three distinct sounds but do not recognize them as /k/, /ă/, and /t/.

8. You do not process the three sounds in correct sequence ("act," "tac").

9. You sound out the word flawlessly, but do not know the spoken English word "cat."

10. Your working memory cannot handle all three sounds at once.

11. Your working memory cannot handle two possible sounds for c, four (or more) possible sounds for a, and one more sound for t.

12. Your processing speed is too slow for your memory.

13. Your memory span is too limited for your processing speed.

14. Your visual acuity is insufficient to discern the letters correctly.

15. Your visual perception or orthographic ability causes you to confuse t with f.

16. Your auditory acuity impairs your ability to hear the spoken word "cat."

17. Your auditory perception impairs your ability to perceive the spoken word "cat."

18. You have not had enough whole-language experience with rich literature involving cats.

19. You cannot guess a word without seeing it in context.

20. There is a social or emotional barrier to your reading progress.

21. English is not your first language.

Given even this incomplete list of reasons a student might encounter difficulty with a simple reading task, it should be obvious that we sometimes need more than a record of responses to intervention to determine and remediate the causes of school difficulty. In many instances, a careful, thoughtful consideration of the student's history will suggest an intervention that will be completely effective in resolving the student's school difficulties. However, in others, the record of interventions will be like the ship whose bridge was swamped by a rogue wave that destroyed all navigational equipment except the speedometer. The captain announced, "We have no idea where we are and no clue where we might be headed, but we do know we are making record time."

"Explaining" the failure to read with a diagnosis of mental retardation, learning disability, emotional disturbance, or some other disability really does not, by itself, tell us how to help the student. We still need to understand why the student cannot read (or do math or get along with other students or pay attention in class or succeed in the job for which she or he was trained), and we need to understand how all of the cognitive, personality, sensory, motor, social, academic, and other issues interact. In short, we need a comprehensive evaluation.

We see far too many evaluations that focus on an overall intelligence score and one or more diagnoses. Although they may be admirably parsimonious, I find such evaluations of little value in helping plan remediation and rehabilitation. More than 40 years ago, John McLeod commented that "A respect for the law of parsimony is a characteristic of science, but educational psychology's penchant for simple answers to questions of complex human behavior, particularly in the area of learning disability, has tended toward paucity rather than parsimony of explanation" (1968, p. 97). Sadly, McLeod's lament still holds true far too often.

My shelves sag under the weight of excellent texts telling me how to select, administer, score, and interpret psychological and educational tests. Many of my best books even tell me how to write reports and recommendations with specific strategies, and some even include helpful case studies. A few are devoted to carefully constructed philosophies and frameworks for rationally planning and organizing assessments. The special virtue of *Comprehensive Evaluations: Case Reports for Psychologists, Diagnosticians, and Special Educators* is that it provides us with complete models of a variety of actual assessments, not just instructions and a few examples.

The case reports in this book dramatically illustrate the value and the importance of providing genuinely comprehensive evaluations when referral questions are complex and perplexing and when other approaches to solving the problems have failed. The reports employ a variety of approaches and instruments to explore different concerns and different types of disabilities for both children and adults. The unifying theme is that complex and difficult problems require carefully planned, very thorough, goal-directed, comprehensive evaluations that will guide the examinees, parents, teachers, and other professionals in fully understanding the student's strengths and needs as a basis for planning interventions that will ameliorate the problems and lead to improved functioning.

The evaluations in this book go well beyond simply using intelligence tests to measure overall, global intellectual ability or *g*. Global intellectual ability is probably the best single predictor of academic achievement and other important things (see, for example, Sternberg & Grigorenko, 2002), but it is not, by itself, much help in understanding the nature of complex learning problems, nor in designing effective interventions. These evaluations use test, observation, interview, and historical data in a variety of ways, all resulting in concrete plans for remediation. The cases are all real evaluations done with real (albeit disguised) persons; they offer insights into the methods, instruments, and—most important—the thinking of the evaluators. Far better than a textbook *explaining* what can be done, this compendium of evaluations *shows* both what can be done as well as how it can be done. I plan to refer to these reports frequently in my teaching and in planning my own evaluations.

REFERENCES

Assistance to States for the Education of Children With Disabilities, 34 C.F.R. Part 300 (2006).

Beal, A. L., Dumont, R., & Willis, J. O. (April 2003). *Guide to identification of learning disabilities.* Paper presented at the meeting of the National Association of School Psychologists, Toronto, Ontario.

Bijou, S. W. (1942). The psychometric pattern approach as an aid to clinical assessment—A review. *American Journal of Mental Deficiency, 46,* 354–362.

Bradley, R., Danielson, L. & Hallahan, D. P. (Eds.) (2002). *Identification of learning disabilities: Research to practice.* Mahway, NJ: Erlbaum.

Cronbach, L. J. (1957). The two disciplines of scientific psychology. *American Psychologist, 12,* 671–684.

Donovan, M. S., & Cross, C. T. (2002). *Minority students in special and gifted education.* Washington, DC: National Academy Press.

Education of All Handicapped Children Act, 20 U.S.C. § 1400 ff. (1975).

Fletcher, J. M., Denton, C., & Francis, D. J. (2005). Validity of alternative approaches for the identification of LD: Operationalizing unexpected underachievement. *Journal of Learning Disabilities, 38,* 545–552.

Hoskyn, M., & Swanson, H. L. (2000). Cognitive processing of low achievers and children with reading disabilities: A selective meta-analytic review of the published literature. *The School Psychology Review, 29,* 102–119.

Individuals with Disabilities Education Improvement Act, 20 U.S.C. § 1400 ff. (1990).

Individuals with Disabilities Education Improvement Act, 20 U.S.C. § 1400 ff. (1997).

Individuals with Disabilities Education Improvement Act of 2004, 20 U.S.C. § 1400 ff.

Kavale, K. (2002). Discrepancy models in the identification of learning disabilities. In R. Bradley, L. Danielson, & D. P. Hallahan (Eds.). *Identification of learning disabilities: Research to practice* (pp. 370–371). Mahwah, NJ: Erlbaum.

Mather, N., & Jaffe, L. (2002). *Woodcock-Johnson III: Recommendations, reports, and strategies* (with CD). Hoboken, NJ: John Wiley & Sons.

Mather, N., & Kaufman, N. (Guest Eds.) (2006a). Special Issue, Part 1: Integration of cognitive assessment and response to intervention. *Psychology in the Schools, 43(7).*

Mather, N., & Kaufman, N. (Guest Eds.) (2006b). Special Issue, Part 2: Integration of cognitive assessment and response to intervention. *Psychology in the Schools, 43(8).*

McLeod, J. (1968). Reading expectancy from disabled readers. *Journal of Learning Disabilities, 1,* 97–105.

Reschly, D. J., Tilly, W. D., & Grimes, J. P. (1999). *Special education in transition: Functional assessment and noncategorical programming.* Longmont, CO: Sopris West.

Sternberg, R. J., & Grigorenko, E. L. (Eds.) (2002). *The general factor of intelligence: How general is it?* Mahwah, NJ: Lawrence Erlbaum.

Wendling, B. J., & Mather, N. (2009). *Essentials of evidence-based academic interventions.* Hoboken, NJ: John Wiley & Sons.

If these tests will give us a basis from which we can start to understand a child's difficulties, they will have justified the time spent on them. Anything which helps educators or parents to *understand* any phase of development or lack of development is of immeasurable value.

Stanger & Donohue, 1937, p. 189

Introduction

COMPREHENSIVE EVALUATIONS: CASE REPORTS FOR PSYCHOLOGISTS, DIAGNOSTICIANS, AND SPECIAL EDUCATORS

This book contains a wide variety of reports written for the purpose of explaining the reasons for an individual's school-related difficulties. The reports come from different disciplines within psychology and education, and reflect different theoretical perspectives and paradigms. The subjects of these case reports range in educational level from preschool to postsecondary. Similarly, the evaluators who contributed their reports represent multiple professions, but all related, in some way, to the education of individuals with exceptional needs. They include authors of the tests frequently used; educational and cognitive researchers; university faculty responsible for training school psychologists and specialists in special education; clinical psychologists, school psychologists, diagnosticians, special education teachers, and speech-language therapists working in public schools or private practice.

Although the content, style, and format of these reports vary considerably, they all illustrate that informative, clearly written psychological and educational evaluations play an essential role in describing and explaining an individual's abilities and disabilities, and provide the basis on which effective interventions and accommodations are developed.

The reports in this book were selected to represent the usual questions that accompany a referral, the cognitive and educational problems that typically and not so typically confront evaluators, an assortment of writing styles, and different levels of information analysis and methods of interpretation. Throughout, however, these reports answer the referral question through carefully selected tests; provide appropriate interpretation of the scores and other key information (e.g., history, observations, interviews, qualitative analysis); and propose logical and knowledgeable solutions for intervention.

PURPOSES OF THE BOOK

In the current educational and political climate, some researchers and practitioners have questioned the value of comprehensive evaluations for students suspected of having specific learning disabilities (SLD), arguing that monitoring of a student's performance and response to varying instructional approaches can provide sufficient information to make a disability diagnosis and determine effective interventions. Comprehensive evaluations, however, are both beneficial and necessary for truly understanding the reasons *why* a student is struggling in school and for designing interventions that are tailored to the cognitive and academic profile of that student. A child who appears to have a learning disability may, in fact, have an intellectual disability. A language impairment could be confused with autism, learning disability, or inattention. Behaviors suggestive of emotional disturbance may really stem from the school failure and low self-esteem that accompanies learning disabilities. Sometimes, the problem is not a disability at all, but rather a case of "dyspedagogia," or inadequate teaching (Cohen, 1971). The interventions for these different types of problems can differ considerably and the sooner a student can receive effective interventions, the better. Otherwise, the learner continues to be confronted by evidence of his or her "inability" to learn,

What is a comprehensive evaluation? IDEA 2004 Regulations regarding evaluation procedures mandate that an evaluation for disability includes "all areas related to the suspected disability, including, if appropriate, health, vision, hearing, social and emotional status, general intelligence, academic performance, communicative status, and motor abilities." It further states that "… in evaluating each child with a disability … the evaluation is sufficiently comprehensive to identify all of the child's special education and related services needs, whether or not commonly linked to the disability category in which the child has been classified" (Assistance to States, 2006). Although well-planned, problem-focused Response to Intervention (RtI) is an appropriate pre-referral intervention and may reduce the number of comprehensive evaluations that are needed, RtI should not be used as the sole method for diagnosing the existence of a disability.

People who write comprehensive evaluations often think: "I wonder how others write their reports?" The purposes of this book are therefore twofold: (a) to provide models of psychological and educational reports using a variety of different tests and approaches, and (b) to illustrate the value of comprehensive evaluations for understanding an individual's unique learning abilities and disabilities. In building a new skill or polishing a frequently used one, models are often helpful. Rather than "starting from scratch," one may adopt what fits and adapt what does not. By reading and studying these diagnostic reports, practitioners may:

- Increase their understanding of the usefulness of comprehensive evaluations;
- Expand their knowledge of possible interpretations of assessment results;
- Expand their familiarity with widely used test instruments;
- Enhance their understanding of test scores;
- Increase their understanding of common childhood disorders and how these, treated or untreated, manifest in adults;
- Improve their ability to tailor written reports to the purposes of the evaluation;
- Improve their abilities to translate assessment results into meaningful treatment recommendations; and
- Recognize the differences in what evaluators from various school districts and agencies consider to be a comprehensive evaluation.

TYPES OF CASES

The diagnostic reports in this book are authentic, but for the sake of confidentiality, all names and identifying information have been changed. The reports illustrate: (a) varied reasons for referral (e.g., academic, behavioral);

(b) different ages, backgrounds, medical histories, and educational situations; (c) the use of a variety of evaluation materials (e.g., standardized tests, curriculum-based measures, classroom work samples, rating scales); (d) the use and interpretation of different types of scores; and (e) a range of different diagnoses from clear-cut cases to those that are extremely complex. The reader may also observe how different clinical perspectives and the choice of assessment instruments have influenced the interpretation of results.

Some reports are follow-ups based on a referral from another evaluator for a more specialized evaluation; other reports contain recommendations for further testing from a specialist in another field regarding a suspected comorbid or underlying disability (e.g., language impairment, Attention-Deficit/Hyperactivity Disorder, or clinical depression). To help a reader locate specific types of reports, the Table of Reports (see Appendix A) lists key characteristics of each report, including the name and age of the examinee, the diagnosis, the tests used, and the examiners.

COMPONENTS OF REPORTS

A comprehensive, individualized assessment may include an assessment of cognitive and metacognitive processes, such as executive function; language development and processing; academic performance; and social-emotional functioning and behavior. It will also include the student's background, including information provided by parents and teachers.

The types of information provided in a report often correspond with the sections of the report. These typically include:

- Reason for referral
- Background information
- Tests administered and assessment procedures used
- Behavioral observations
- Results of cognitive and academic testing
- Results of social/emotional/behavioral testing
- Interpretation of results
- Conclusions
- Recommendations

Appendix B provides guidelines regarding the types of components typically included in comprehensive evaluations. Further guidelines for report writing can be found in other sources (e.g., Lichtenberger, Mather, Kaufman, & Kaufman, 2004; Sattler, 2008). Appendix C provides a list of the acronyms for the tests that were used within the current evaluations.

Ultimately, the quality and validity of the results of a comprehensive evaluation depend on the skill of the evaluator in: (a) selecting and administering the tests; (b) evaluating the validity of individual test scores in light of possible interfering factors (e.g., fatigue, inattention, motivation, cultural differences, sensory impairments); (c) interpreting and integrating test results; (d) analyzing error patterns; (e) discerning the person's strengths, strategies, and compensations; and (f) selecting appropriate recommendations and interventions.

REASONS FOR THE EVALUATION

Evaluations may be requested for a variety of reasons, leading to different types of assessments and recommendations. For a child or adult without a previous diagnosis, a full battery of tests may be administered, including cognitive, language, and academic assessments. If a concern exists regarding social functioning, emotional stability, or behavior that interferes with learning, social-emotional and behavior rating scales—and possibly projective tests—may be added to the battery. Reports of delayed motor development may generate a further evaluation by an occupational therapist. Such reports tend to be quite complicated and lengthy, especially if recommendations are added for the home and for each area in which the individual needs intervention, accommodations, or more information.

When an evaluation of this type is requested, vision and hearing problems should be the first to be ruled out, prior to any testing, to avoid a misdiagnosis. For example, at one clinic, a complete developmental history of a child was not taken prior to testing. The child was nonresponsive to auditory tests, attended better to visual stimuli, and had trouble following verbal directions. He received a diagnosis of severe auditory processing disorder. Subsequently, when the parents took the child for a long-overdue pediatric checkup, they found that he had a severe hearing impairment.

Other evaluations can be brief. For example, if continued eligibility for special education services is the primary issue, administration of a standardized achievement test, supplemented by informal testing, curriculum-based measurement, and work samples, may be sufficient. Similarly, if the evaluation is solely for documentation of progress in academic skills, the evaluator might decide to administer only progress monitoring procedures, such as CBM, and review classroom work samples.

LEVEL OF DETAIL AND REPORT WRITING STYLE

The purpose for an evaluation may also influence the levels of information sought through testing and interpretation, as well as the amount of detail included in the report. A lengthy report with detailed information does not necessarily signal the complexity of the case, although a person with many difficulties and/or an atypical background may certainly warrant a more extensive evaluation and a more complex report. Alternatively, a lengthy and detailed report—or a brief overview of what was done and the conclusions—may also be a reflection of the writer's personal style.

All of the information included in a report should help answer the referral question. This might include developmental, medical, and educational history that would assist the writer in confirming or ruling out specific disabilities.

Some evaluators prefer to describe all of the tasks used in the testing process, the individual's response, and the scores achieved. Others write an entire report as if it were the summary and conclusions. Still others offer a couple of sentences explaining the skill or ability that is measured by the test, a verbal descriptor of range in which the score fell, and the practical application of the ability in relation to the student's functioning in the classroom. In schools, practicality may dictate less time for testing, error analysis, and report writing; the teachers, who are the ultimate readers, often do not have time to read a lengthy report. A psychologist or diagnostician in private practice might be able to devote more time to the process of assessment and analysis, and include more detail, recognizing that the report is likely to be read by physicians, therapists, other specialists, and teachers, as well as the parents or the individual.

The two most important features of a report are that it is accurate and comprehensible to the readers for whom it is intended. Thus, it is important to omit professional jargon and use terms and examples that people who do not have training in psychology, cognitive sciences, or even the terminology of academics, will understand. Lichtenberger and Kaufman found their way around this difficulty by writing two forms of the same report—one for the parents and teachers, and another, simplified but with a practical focus, for the teenage client.

REPORTING SCORES

Depending on the purpose of the evaluation and the specific information offered within the report, evaluators use, emphasize, or report different types of test scores. Some evaluators embed scores in the narrative; some place partial score tables throughout the results section (e.g., reading scores above the section in which reading performance is discussed); and some include a notation stating, "All test scores are attached to the end of this report." Although the scores were not included in all cases within this book because of space constraints, many of the case reports do include the full set of obtained scores. Individuals who are new to report writing may want to read the background information, study the score tables, and formulate their own hypotheses and conclusions before reading the interpretation of scores presented within the report.

Score Ranges and Verbal Classifications

Most tests provide verbal classifications, or descriptors, for given sets of score ranges. The width of the score ranges may differ from test to test; many tests label standard scores from 90 to 109 as Average but a few use 85 to 115. Within each test or test battery, ranges of scaled scores and percentiles will be set to match the standard score ranges. Each test or test battery may use its own verbal classifications as well. For example, standard scores from 80 to 89 may be described as Low Average or Below Average. So that the verbal classifications do not change with each test the evaluator is discussing, it is important to select one classification scheme to use for all of the tests discussed in the report.

Other types of scores also have verbal descriptors for score ranges (e.g., relative proficiency index [RPI]). When using these descriptors, the writer must ensure that it is clear to the reader what type of score is being described. For example, verbal descriptors for the levels of proficiency based on the RPI ranges include: Very Advanced, Advanced, Average to Advanced, Average, Limited to Average, Limited, Very Limited, and Negligible. These descriptors are specific to the RPI, not to the standard score ranges. The delineation must be clear.

Willis and Dumont (1998) presented the following example to illustrate the different verbal classification systems used.

There are 200 &s.
Each && = 1%.

```
                                        &&    &&
                                     &&&&&&  &&&&&&
                                     &&&&&&  &&&&&&
                               &&    &&&&&&  &&&&&&   &&
                            &&&&&&    &&&&&&  &&&&&&  &&&&&&
                            &&&&&&    &&&&&&  &&&&&&  &&&&&&
                     &      &&&&&&    &&&&&&  &&&&&&  &&&&&&  &&&&&   &
                  &&&&&&    &&&&&&    &&&&&&  &&&&&&  &&&&&&  &&&&&&  &&&&&&
       & & & &   &&&&&&    &&&&&&    &&&&&&  &&&&&&  &&&&&&  &&&&&&  & & & &
```

Percent in each	2.2%	6.7%	16.1%	50%	16.1%	6.7%	2.2%
Standard Scores	< 70	70–79	80–89	90–110	110–120	121 – 130	> 130
Scaled Scores	1 2 3	4 5	6 7	8 9 10 11	12 13	14 15	16 17 18 19
Percentile Ranks	< 03	03 – 08	09 – 24	25 – 74	75 – 90	91 – 97	> 97
Woodcock-Johnson Classification	Very Low	Low	Low Average	Average	High Average	Superior	Very Superior
PRO-ED Classification	Very Poor	Poor	Below Average	Average	Above Average	Superior	Very Superior
KTEA-II Classification	Lower Extreme	Below Average 70–84		Average 85 115		Above Average 116–130	Upper Extreme

Source: Willis, J. O., & Dumont, R. P. (1998). *Guide to identification of learning disabilities* (New York State ed.) (Acton, MA: Copley Custom Publishing, p. 27). Also available at: http://alpha.fdu.edu/psychology/test_score_descriptions.htm.

In discussing the score ranges used on the Stanford-Binet Intelligence Scales (SB5), Roid (2003) stated:

> Other reasonable systems for dividing scores into qualitative levels do exist, and the choice of the dividing points between different categories is fairly arbitrary. When the situation requires exact comparisons of scores across tests, it is more effective to contrast scores rather than category designations. It is also unreasonable to place too much importance on the particular label...used by different tests that measure the same construct.... The important concern is to describe the examinee's skills and abilities in detail, going beyond the label itself. (2003, p. 150)

On a stylistic note, some evaluators capitalize the verbal classifications of score ranges and others do not. If these are capitalized, however, it indicates to the reader that these are terms with a specific meaning rather than just an informal description.

LEVELS OF INTERPRETATION AND USE OF SCORES

In almost all tests, three levels of interpretive information are available: qualitative, level of development, and relative standing in a group; a few tests also provide an additional level, proficiency (Woodcock & Mather, 1989). When interpreting a person's performance on a test, it is helpful to investigate all of the levels of interpretive information available and to move from the global to the specific.

Relative Standing in a Group

Scores that indicate a person's relative standing in a group, such as standard scores, percentile ranks, T scores, and z scores, are commonly used for purposes of diagnosis and determination of eligibility for special education services. They describe the *ordinal position* of an individual's raw score (or other foundational score, such as the W score), based on the standard deviation, within the range of scores obtained by the comparison group (same age/grade peers) in the norming sample.

Peer-comparison scores do not describe proficiency or the level of task difficulty an individual can manage. For example, Jason obtained a raw score (number correct) that was just below the mean for his age-peers in the norm sample. Because very little variation occurred among the scores (on that test) for his age group in the norm sample, his score is lower than that of 75% of his age-peers;

consequently, although his score is very close to the mean, it falls at the 25th percentile. It is just as possible, however, that his score would be very far below the mean (indicating considerable difficulty in the task) and still be at the 25th percentile if there is a great amount of variation in his peer group.

Standard scores are most often used for comparison with the norm group, to decide if the person's performance represents a normative strength or weakness. They are also used for intra-individual comparison, to consider the differences between a person's performance on different tasks, representing different abilities. These comparisons represent relative strengths and weaknesses within the individual. When using standard scores to ascertain whether or not a difference is "significant," one should ask three questions:

1. Are the differences statistically significant? If the confidence bands around the two scores overlap, the difference might be due to chance. The higher the level of confidence chosen (e.g., 90% rather than 68%), the wider the bands will be and the higher the likelihood that they will overlap.

2. How unusual is the difference in the population (base rate)? It is possible that a statistically significant difference, at the confidence interval chosen, is reasonably common in the population. Consequently, the evaluator must consider whether or not this difference signals an important difference.

3. Regardless of statistical significance and the base rate, is the difference educationally significant? Even though two scores differ significantly, the evaluator must determine the educational relevance (or irrelevance). For example, a low score in phonological awareness may have great significance for a child just learning to read, but little significance for a student entering vocational training.

Proficiency

Proficiency scores indicate the quality of a person's performance on criterion tasks at a given difficulty level. Typically, the criterion level is that which their age/grade peers have mastered. Examples of scores that describe proficiency are the W score and RPI on the Woodcock-Johnson III, the growth scale value on the Kaufman Test of Educational Achievement, Second Edition, and the change-sensitive score of the Stanford-Binet Intelligence

Scales, Fifth Edition. These scores are based on the distance of an individual's score (the foundational score, transformed from the raw score for placement on an equal-interval scale) from an age or grade reference point. For example, on the WJ III, the reference point for the RPI is the difficulty level on the W scale at which 50% of one's grade/age peers have passed an item. Proficiency scores are not subject to the standard deviation and thus, always show how far a person's current performance (ability) is from the median level of performance of the comparison group.

Development

Examples of scores that indicate level of development are age and grade equivalents. For many tests, the age and grade equivalents simply tell what age- or grade-group in the norm sample had a median score that was the same as the examinee's raw score.

Grade and age equivalents might be used to report an approximate level of instructional materials to be used for a specific task. Although grade equivalent scores do not equate with the level of instructional materials, they do show a person's developmental standing within the normative sample. The performance level of the examinee's grade-peers, however, may not match the level of performance of their peers in the norm sample. Considering the variability of schools and individual classes across the nation, a third-grade child could receive a grade equivalent score one year below his or her actual grade level (in the norm sample), but be performing exactly as expected within that school. Moreover, different instructional materials intended for a certain grade level may vary considerably from each other in the initial level of student skill and knowledge assumed.

Qualitative Analysis

Qualitative information is not based on a score, but it is a critical component for understanding and interpreting all of the scores an individual obtained. Often, the way in which a student obtains a score is as important as the score itself—or more so. Qualitative information may be gained from three sources: the behavior of the student being tested, analysis of the task used, and analysis of the student's responses.

The student's behaviors and comments may indicate the reasons why tasks are perceived as particularly difficult or easy. For example, on seeing a page of 80 single-digit math problems, 12-year-old Leo stated,

"These are the kind of tests I really dislike. I look at the test and think there are 5,000 problems." His comment suggested one way that his weakness in processing speed affected his math functioning and the fact that covering part of a page, either of math problems or print (tried later, informally) helped him to avoid being visually distracted by the rest of the page. Eight-year-old Katrina stated: "I hate math and so does my teacher!" Seven-year-old Kevin, while listing the names of animals "as fast as you can," said, "dog, monkey, lions, tigers, and bears—oh my." Although his response was clever, he was obviously not very cued in to the "fast as you can" instruction. Other similar comments ruined the test as a fluency measure but gave insight into his ability to concentrate. Another student, age 14, pretended to be asleep whenever he was confronted with a test that required reading or writing. These types of behaviors are both suggestive of problems that might be affecting the student—and suggestive of other formal or informal assessments that might further investigate or document the underlying problems.

The two other sources of qualitative analysis interact with each other; they are analysis of the task demands and analysis of the student's response patterns. Analysis of the task demands means answering the question "What specific skills and knowledge are needed—cognitive, linguistic, and academic—to succeed on this test at the level of peers?" For example, spelling requires many skills in all three domains, such as understanding the alphabetic principle and skills in phonemic segmentation, phonics (letter-sound correspondence), orthography (common letter patterns that may or not be phonically regular), fine-motor coordination, and handwriting. Analysis of the student's responses indicates which of these skills is presenting difficulty. Christina, in fourth grade, spelled all of her words phonetically, so that anyone could decipher what the word was supposed to say, but they were not correct spellings. For example, she spelled "might" as *mit*, and "walked" as *wokt*. Clearly she could perceive all of the sounds in the words, so her phonemic awareness appeared adequate, but she did not remember the orthographic features of words she had doubtlessly seen hundreds of times. Consequently, one area of cognitive ability, orthographic processing and retrieval, appears weak. To confirm this, the evaluator would look for better nonsense word reading and spelling than irregular word reading and spelling, as well as slow perceptual speed, and slow rapid automatized naming, which are often corollaries of weak orthography.

Qualitative interpretation provides four major benefits:

1. It extends the usefulness of a test by allowing the evaluator to discover qualities of a student's skills/abilities other than that which the test was designed to measure (e.g., spelling is designed to assess spelling but can be used to assess all of the skills involved in the task of spelling).

2. It helps ascertain not only the level at which a student is performing in cognitive, linguistic, and academic areas but also the reasons. This information helps one select effective interventions.

3. It can help to account for significant discrepancies between test scores within a factor, cluster, composite, or index.

4. It generates insights not obtainable from test scores alone. These can prompt a shift in perspective regarding the student's abilities and difficulties, prompting a new hypothesis, which may better fit the characteristics of the problem.

An in-depth comprehensive evaluation, then, will not only be broad in scope of the areas of possible disability (e.g., cognitive, academic, motor, social-emotional), but also in the depth of analysis of the information available for interpretation. In the report, under the appropriate subsection of Test Results and Interpretation, each level of information can be described and integrated with the other levels (i.e., standard scores and/or percentile ranks; proficiency scores; grade and age equivalents), with an explanation of how the more detailed levels either support or contradict the more global levels.

RECOMMENDATIONS

Reports might also differ in scope and specificity of recommendations. In some reports, whether private or school-based, recommendations may be written to cover all areas: cognitive, academic, and behavioral. Other reports might include recommendations only for areas seen as critical for immediate intervention and then organize recommendations by the major areas of concerns that are addressed (e.g., math, oral language, behavior, self-advocacy). Reports may include general interventions or suggestions for specific techniques and materials.

Before making recommendations, evaluators first consider the referral question or questions, review any important background information, analyze the results of

diagnostic testing, and assess the specific needs of a student within the educational setting. The goal is to select specific modifications and interventions to enhance an individual's opportunities for success. For some reports, the recommendations are written directly to a student or client, such as: "You should arrange appointments with each of your teachers at the beginning of each semester." Or, a recommendation may be made to the student's teacher, parents, or counselor, such as: "Help Tobias arrange appointments with his teachers at the beginning of each semester." In a few of the reports, it is noted that recommendations will be made by the educational team when the evaluation results are discussed.

CAUTIONS FOR NEW REPORT WRITERS

Comprehensive evaluations are difficult to write and many include several errors. The following list, although not exhaustive, provides examples of errors that are most commonly observed.

Use of the Scores and Confidence Bands

When choosing the standard error of measurement (SEM) for the obtained scores, consider:

- When the confidence bands of the subtests within a composite overlap, there is a chance that the scores for each are not significantly different; thus, it is reasonable to discuss the composite score as representing the broader ability. When the confidence bands do not overlap, it is not defensible or good practice to interpret the composite score as though it were representing the broader ability. John Willis explains that his doctor just doesn't buy it when John maintains that if one averages his below-average height and above-average weight, his Full Scale Body Quotient is dead average (Dumont & Willis, 2001). Do not ignore the subtests, however; interpret them as narrow abilities and analyze them for patterns of strengths and weaknesses.

- Recognize the effect of your choice of confidence bands. Wider bands (e.g., 90% or 95%), albeit accurate, have two disadvantages. One is that the band can be so wide as to be meaningless. What is the implication for performance in related tasks if the person's true score is somewhere between 73 and 91? It's an assurance that the person's ability, compared with peers, is in the

Low, Low Average, or Average range. Although this is accurate, it is not very helpful. Second, and more to the point, the wider the bands, the more likely it is that they will overlap, allowing the evaluator to view the composite score as validly representing a broad ability, which, in fact, may obscure some important differences between the narrower abilities. Valuable information might be overlooked with the consequence that the resulting diagnosis is incorrect.

Missing or Misused Information

- Observe and report a child's test-taking behaviors and comments and, when interpreting all of the levels of available information, consider if the student's behaviors and comments would either support or contradict any likely hypotheses.

- When considering test-taking behavior, consider the effect, negative or positive, on the student's score on particular tests and explain it. For example, Kevin's low score on rapid retrieval of words did not actually reflect a problem in retrieval; he was just not well focused on the task. That has other implications but it would be incorrect to report and use Kevin's score as though it measured his ease and speed of word retrieval.

- Do qualitative analysis (see above) to help both develop and confirm possible hypotheses regarding the student's difficulties.

- Use great caution in "testing the limits." Testing the limits is a way of following up on an observation about a student's strategy in doing a task or finding out more about what part of the task is giving the student difficulty. Typically, the evaluator completes the test, then has the student repeat some of the items in a different way or with different directions. Consider, for example, a situation in which the examiner administers the WJ III ACH Spelling of Sounds test and questions whether or not the student has perceived the sounds accurately. When the test was completed, the evaluator might replace the student's response book with a blank sheet of paper, and play each word again, having the student repeat each word before writing it. In doing so, the evaluator is able to judge whether the student heard the words correctly and if repeating them made a difference regarding spelling accuracy. When testing the limits, the evaluator must *never* instruct the student or change the task in such a way as to give the student an advantage

the next time he or she takes the test. This would be an unethical use of testing the limits and invalidate any future use of that particular test. The evaluator may be able to create an informal test that addresses or further explores the concern.

- When using computer scoring programs for tests, make sure to state in the report the version of the scoring program that was used and the norms—grade or age. This information becomes critical if someone tries to compare scores on a test taken earlier or later.

Selecting the Tests

- Prior to selecting the tests to use, review the student's records (including previous evaluations); conduct parent, teacher, and student (if appropriate) interviews; and observe the student in the classroom. Ask the teacher, parent, and student what each would like to see come out of this evaluation. Use this information to decide what tests would be most likely to help answer the questions and explain the student's difficulties. Do not limit yourself to a specific test or tests just because you are most comfortable with them.

Writing for an Audience

- Who are you expecting will have to read and understand your report, not only now, but in the future as well—parents, teachers, student, or other psychologists? Many reports contain professional jargon, such as "ideational fluency" or "auditory processing" without an explanation that would make sense to an accountant, a lawyer, a teacher, or, indeed, an adult student. Some reports explain every test task in detail, rather than doing so just when necessary to give an example of a student's behavior and its significance. It is, in fact, quite difficult to translate the jargon and explain what has been assessed in such a way that a "layperson" will understand it and not be overwhelmed by the amount of information. Many well-written reports have not found a way around this, but ideally, reports are most useful when they are both clearly written and easy to understand.

Verbal Descriptors for Score Ranges

- Prior to reporting test performance, include a table that lists the verbal descriptors that will be used for score ranges and the associated score ranges for each, including each type of score you use. This table might include the list of descriptors and across from each, the standard score ranges, scaled score ranges, and *T* score ranges. If you have used scores other than peer-comparison scores, use a different set of descriptors for them.

Writing Composition 101

- Each time you write and distribute a report, it is a reflection of your professional knowledge and your writing skill. The most common errors seen in reports involve poor sentence structure, grammar, punctuation, capitalization, and even spelling. Spell-checkers do not detect homonyms (e.g., principals vs. principles). Within sentence structure, the most frequently seen errors are multiple clauses within a sentence that are not parallel, misplaced modifiers, and incorrect transition words that obscure rather than clarify the relationship among the clauses or sentences. Although it is not an incorrect structure, passive voice is more difficult to understand than active voice, and the *Publication Manual of the American Psychological Association, Sixth Edition,* advises against its use. Regarding grammar, verb tenses fluctuate, subject-verb agreement is often incorrect, and singular pronouns are used to refer to plural nouns (or vice versa).

- With the use of computers, and the increasing use of shells for report writing, evaluators must be particularly careful as well not to have another name for a student or school within the report or use incorrect pronouns to describe the student's gender.

- There are specific rules for words that should be capitalized and those that should not. Some professions add to these rules for their own purposes, such as capitalizing the verbal descriptors for score ranges. It is good practice to learn the rules of capitalization and, when you find yourself about to capitalize a word that does not fit within the rules, reflect on the reason why it should be capitalized. One question that consistently arises is whether or not names of disabling conditions should be capitalized, such as bipolar disorder, attention-deficit/hyperactivity disorder, and dyslexia. The first two are frequently capitalized in reports, and the third, hardly ever. Yet these terms are not capitalized on medical and professional web sites. In addition, most writers capitalize test and subtest names, so that they can be distinguished from the general ability (e.g., his performance on the Spelling subtest, versus his performance on the weekly spelling test). Thus, writers should have rationales for capitalizing the words they do.

- Although it is traditional for reports to be written in the third person (e.g., the evaluator), some writers prefer to use the first person (i.e., I). Either is acceptable as long as its use is consistent throughout the report.

IN CONCLUSION

Throughout this book, the various reports illustrate the role and importance of clinical judgment, the integration and interpretation of information from multiple sources, the rationales for the selection of certain assessment instruments, and the determination of appropriate accommodations and instructional recommendations. Each evaluator has contributed a short introduction to draw attention to specific features in the report that may be of interest to the reader.

Comprehensive evaluations play a vital role in planning appropriate instruction for students enrolled in school. As noted by Johnson and Myklebust (1967):

> The single most important factor in planning for a child with a learning disability is an intensive diagnostic study. Without a comprehensive evaluation of his deficits and assets, the educational program may be too general, or even inappropriate. The diagnostic study should include an evaluation of sensory acuity, intelligence, language (spoken, read, written), motor function, educational achievement, emotional status, and social maturity (p. 50)… The implication is that it is necessary to have immediate access to all diagnostic findings because it is from these that the educational approach must be evolved. Sometimes teachers are required to begin remediation without adequate knowledge of the deficits and integrities. Although information can be obtained from personal contact with the child, precise planning is possible only when these observations are supplemented by detailed diagnostic information. (p. 51)

Thus, the overarching goal of this book is to illustrate the value of comprehensive evaluations for understanding the reasons that a student is struggling in school, and most importantly, formulating a plan for the best ways to help. As noted by the famed British scientist, Lord Kelvin: "If you cannot measure it, you cannot improve it."

A Note about Formatting and Attachments in this Book

The formatting of the reports in this book is not intended as a model. For the purpose of presenting multiple reports, the formatting (e.g., headings) and style (e.g. capitalization of verbal descriptors of score ranges) of the original reports have been changed for consistency. Additionally, many reports include references to attachments (e.g., strategies, graphs, supplementary reports). Due to space considerations, these attachments are not included in this book, although the author's reference to them has been retained. Score pages have been included for some but not all reports. Other report features that were removed were: letterhead that included the names of clinics and agencies; the signature lines, signatures, and titles at the end of the report; and the word "confidential" written at the top of the report.

REFERENCES

American Psychological Association. (2010). *Publication manual of the American Psychological Association* (6th ed.). Washington, DC: Author.

Assistance to States for the Education of Children With Disabilities, 34 C.F.R. Part 300 (2006).

Cohen, S. A. (1971). Dyspedagogia as a cause of reading retardation: Definition and treatment. In B. Bateman (Ed.), *Learning Disorders* Vol. 4 (pp. 269–291). Seattle, WA: Special Child.

Dumont, R., & Willis, J. O. (April 2001). Guide to the identification of learning disabilities. Pre-conference workshop at the annual conference of the National Association of School Psychologists, Washington, DC.

Johnson, D. J., & Myklebust, H. R. (1967). *Learning disabilities: Educational principles and practices.* New York: Grune & Stratton.

Kaufman, A. S. (1994). *Intelligent testing with the WISC-III.* New York: John Wiley & Sons.

Lichtenberger, E. O., Mather, N., Kaufman, N. L., & Kaufman, A. S. (2004). *Essentials of assessment report writing.* Hoboken, NJ: John Wiley & Sons.

Mather, N., & Woodcock, R. W. (2001). *Examiner's manual: Woodcock-Johnson III tests of cognitive abilities.* Rolling Meadows, IL: Riverside Publishing.

Roid, G. H. (2003). *Stanford-Binet intelligence scales, fifth edition: Examiner's manual.* Rolling Meadows, IL: Riverside.

Sattler, J. M. (2008). *Assessment of children: Cognitive foundations* (5th ed.). La Mesa, CA: Author.

Stanger, M. A., & Donohue, E. K. (1937). *Prediction and prevention of reading difficulties.* New York: Oxford University Press.

Woodcock, R. W., & Mather, N. (1989). WJ-R tests of achievement – Standard and supplemental batteries: Examiner's manual. In R. W. Woodcock & M. B. Johnson (Eds.), *Woodcock-Johnson psycho-educational battery-Revised.* Rolling Meadows, IL: Riverside.

COMPREHENSIVE EVALUATIONS

Assessment of Individuals with Autism: Procedures and Pitfalls

Sally Logerquist

The diagnosis of an Autistic Disorder is complicated by many factors, such as variability in interpretation of autistic characteristics among psychologists, and a lack of awareness within the schools as well as the general public as to how autism manifests differently in one case to another. The variability in interpretation of autistic characteristics among psychologists is due to the qualitative nature of the behaviors and a lack of instruments with good psychometric properties to measure autism. The two instruments used in this case, the Autism Diagnostic Inventory-Revised (ADI-R) and the Autism Diagnostic Observation Schedule (ADOS) are considered the gold standard in the field of autism (Klin, Sparrow, Marans, Carter, & Volkmar, 2000). These instruments are being used widely in research studies on autism, but they are not widely used among clinicians due to their cost and the additional training requirements (Klin et al., 2000). The ADOS and ADI-R have standardized procedures for test administration. The ADOS is a series of situations that are developed to elicit behaviors associated with autism. During the administration the evaluator has the opportunity to probe a wide array of behaviors. The evaluator who is not trained in these instruments uses checklists, parent reports, and/or observation. These techniques do not include the probing for autism characteristics that occurs during the ADOS administration or standardized administration. Often, a psychologist is left with his or her own clinical judgment, hence the variability in interpretation.

Autism is not a widely understood diagnosis. Limited understanding of this disorder within the schools may impact how the report is written. This report is written to all of the possible consumers (e.g., schools, state agencies). It is much easier for school personnel to respond to findings of the report when the conclusions are clearly supported by the data. To differentiate between the autism characteristics of Erik and another individual with the same diagnosis, it is helpful to describe specific behaviors (e.g., echolalia) in addition to the category of behaviors (e.g., communication). In addition, parents want to know what specific behaviors resulted in a diagnosis of autism. To aid in their understanding, clinicians should identify the behaviors that the child exhibits that are associated with autism, as well as those that are not. This is also very important for school personnel as they need an accurate description of the child to ensure that the interventions match their needs.

The diagnostic category of Autistic Disorder is more appropriate for Erik than the diagnostic category of Asperger's Disorder. The criteria for Asperger's Disorder are similar to Autistic Disorder with regard to impairment in social interactions and restricted repetitive and stereotyped patterns of behavior, interests, and activities. The criteria for these disorders are different with regard to cognition and aspects of communication. Asperger's Disorder is not associated with either a communication or a cognitive delay, whereas an Autistic Disorder is associated with a communication delay and may be associated with a cognitive delay. Erik did not use oral language until the age of 3. Whereas he compensated effectively with sign language, historically and currently he presents with communication impairments (as measured by the ADI-R and ADOS). Based on a documented communication delay, Autistic Disorder is the appropriate diagnostic category.

MULTIDISCIPLINARY TEAM REPORT

Name:	Erik Templeton
Date of Birth:	10-26-2006
Age:	3 years, 11 months
Parents:	Lisa and Seth Templeton
Grade:	Shadow Rock Preschool
Evaluation Dates:	September 28 and 30, 2010
Evaluator:	Sally Logerquist, Ph.D.

REASON FOR REFERRAL

Erik, a 3-year, 11-month-old boy, was referred by his preschool teacher and his parents for a comprehensive evaluation to rule out an Autism Spectrum Disorder. Erik has been experiencing some difficulty transitioning from his parents' and grandparents' homes to the preschool classroom. His reluctance to go to school increases in the beginning of the school year and following school breaks. Erik is awkward in his social approach with peers; however, he has strong language skills and is comfortable with familiar adults. He is typically a happy, caring, cooperative child, but at times has intense tantrums and demonstrates oppositional behavior. Although these tantrums are infrequent, they are of concern to the family. Erik has a supportive family and extended family members who are eager to understand his behavior and provide the appropriate interventions.

BACKGROUND INFORMATION

Erik resides with his biological mother and father; his grandmothers provide his daycare. Mrs. Templeton reported that her pregnancy progressed without complications. During labor, however, because Erik did not drop in the birth canal and pushing decreased his heart rate, he was delivered by cesarean section. His weight and height were 8 pounds, 6 ounces and 20.5 inches, respectively. As an infant, Erik was content, was easy to feed and hold, and slept easily. He met his motor milestones at the usual times; he crawled at 10 months and walked at 12 months. Erik did not use oral language until he was 3 years old and the use of phrases soon followed. He did, however, understand oral language and use sign language effectively to communicate his wants and needs. Sign language was introduced by his mother when oral language did not emerge within the expected time frame. By the age of 18 months he had an American Sign Language (ASL) vocabulary of 175 words. When Erik began to speak, he reversed pronouns (e.g., using *I* for *you* and *you* for *I*), referred to himself in the third person, and demonstrated echolalia (repetition of what is said by other people as if echoing them). All of these language errors have decreased but have not been eliminated at this time. His only significant medical history was the development of fluid under the skin of his forehead at 8 weeks and croup with a high fever at 32 months. At his last annual checkup with his pediatrician, Dr. Andrew Moore, his vision and hearing were both normal.

EDUCATIONAL HISTORY AND SCHOOL BEHAVIOR

Erik currently attends Shadow Rock Preschool 3 to 4 times a week for 6.5 hours per day. His teacher, Ms. Jeanette Spaulding, reported that he will cry and protest when his parents or grandparents drop him off at school, especially at the beginning of each school year and after school breaks. He does not cry for long as Ms. Spaulding quickly redirects his attention to an activity. Ms. Spaulding reports that Erik "barks" and demonstrates self-stimulating behaviors. Erik demonstrates the self-stimulating motor movements of flapping and the self-stimulating verbal behaviors of echolalia.

Ms. Spaulding reported that Erik possesses language and reasoning skills "way beyond his years" and that he is often preoccupied by a special interest. His current interest is volcanoes. He draws volcanoes and talks about them at great length every day. He is able to provide information on volcanoes, such as the cause and effect of a volcanic eruption including details, such as the temperature of the lava.

ASSESSMENT FINDINGS

The Autism Diagnostic Inventory-Revised (ADI-R) was administered in an interview format with Erik's parents. This instrument relies primarily on descriptions of an individual during the early years. The strengths of this approach lie in its objectification of symptoms that are unique to the diagnosis of autism, and the developmental course an individual shows during the early years. The limitations of this approach are that it is primarily interview based, and relies on parental reports. The ADI-R is structured so as to assess the presence or absence of the American Psychiatric Association's *Diagnostic and Statistical Manual's* (*DSM-IV*) definition of autism. Questions are grouped into three sections addressing: Language and Communication Functions, Social Development and Play, and Interests and Behaviors. Parental responses are coded in each area and cut-off scores are assigned to reliably differentiate the presence or absence of autism.

The Autism Diagnostic Observation Schedule (ADOS) was administered in direct assessment. The ADOS is a comprehensive, semi-structured instrument covering most developmental and behavioral aspects of autism. Information is obtained by presenting activities designed to illicit behaviors associated with autism. The scoring criteria are consistent with *DSM-IV* criteria for an Autism Disorder. The scoring system is as follows:

0 = behavior (associated with autism) is NOT present

1 = behavior is present but not clear, severe, or frequent

2 = behavior is present and meets criteria for autism

Mr. and Mrs. Templeton report that they have been concerned about Erik's behavior since he was 2 years old. The behaviors of concern include:

- Lining up toys
- Tantrums, biting and flapping his arms when frustrated
- Referring to himself in the third person
- Late acquisition of oral expressive language
- Echolalia that began at age 3, when he began to use oral language, which is still present
- Reluctance to enter a conversation or play situation with a same-age peer
- Not including others in his conversation or play

QUALITATIVE IMPAIRMENTS IN SOCIAL INTERACTIONS

The Templetons noticed impairments in social interactions at age 2 when Erik entered preschool. He was awkward in social situations with same age peers in contrast to his ease in conversing with adults. The Templetons report that he is still awkward in conversing with peers. When he does talk to peers, his interchanges are focused on his interests with little or no awareness of whether the listener is inter-ested. While this is not uncharacteristic for a 3-year, 11-month old child, the lack of awareness of others is also evident in group interactions (not taking turns) and in play (parallel play).

During the direct administration of the ADOS, Erik used eye contact; however, he did not use eye contact to regulate social interactions (i.e., looking in the direction he wants the listener to look). He shared his enjoyment of the activities with his father by directing smiles toward him; he did not indicate shared enjoyment with either smiles or words with the evaluator. He did respond to his name the first time it was used by the evaluator. Erik seldom initiated conversation with the evaluator; when he did, the topics were related to his interests or to gain assistance.

Erik's ADI-R score of 6 did not meet the cutoff of 10 for autism. Erik's ADOS score of 10 exceeded the cutoff of 6 for autism. Based on the results of parent interview (ADI-R) and direct assessment (ADOS), Erik meets the DSM-IV criteria for an Autistic Disorder in the area of qualitative impairments in social interactions. Despite his impairment, he demonstrates many positive behaviors in this area that are not characteristic of autism, such as:

- He demonstrates appropriate speech fluctuation, rate, and pitch of speech and is capable of modulating the volume to be appropriate to the setting.
- He has a full range of facial expressions that are appropriate for a variety of situations.
- Erik demonstrates empathy and seems to care about other people and their needs.
- He is very thoughtful with regard to his family.
- He does initiate sharing, more with adults than peers.

Qualitative Impairments in Communication

Erik did not acquire oral expressive language until he was 3 years old. Prior to that time he understood the oral language of others (receptive language). He also compensated for his expressive language delay by using ASL. By the age of 18 months, he knew 175 ASL signs. Once he developed oral language at age 3, phrase speech soon followed. Language errors were observed as soon as he began speaking, such as reversed pronouns, reference to himself in the third person, and echolalia. All of these language errors have decreased but have not been eliminated at this time. Echolalia is only observed now when he is excited (e.g., a birthday party) or anxious (e.g., entering a new situation).

Currently, he has strong language skills; he uses sentences of five or more words including adverbs, adjectives, prepositions, and proper plurals. This was reported by parents and observed by the evaluator. Erik can maintain a conversation if the topic is of his choice. His communication style is one directional (in which he reports facts) rather than two directional (the back and forth of a reciprocal conversation). His verbal discourses continue without requesting input from the listener. His parents report that he recently began to bring others into his conversations by directing their attention, verbally or by pointing, to something of his interest (joint attention). At this time, the majority of Erik's interactions are for the purpose of directing others toward things that he wants or areas of his interest rather than socially sharing. The Templetons report that Erik will use the gestures, such as head nodding, head shaking, shrugging, and pointing for nonverbal communication.

During the ADOS administration, Erik did not show an interest in interacting with the evaluator except to share his knowledge about volcanoes. He showed no interest in entering into imaginative play. For example, he was offered toys (e.g., dolls, rocket, dog) to see if he would pretend they were animate and have them interact with each other. He did not. When asked to make up a story, he responded, "I don't know a story." The evaluator initiated imaginative play to see if he would join in but he did not. The only imaginative play that was observed during the ADOS was to load up a toy truck and dump it.

In the category of qualitative impairments in communication, Erik's ADI-R score of 10 exceeded the cut-off of 8 for autism. Erik's ADOS score of 7 exceeded the cut-off of 5 for autism. Based on the results of parent interview (ADI-R) and direct assessment (ADOS), Erik meets the *DSM-IV* criteria for an Autistic Disorder in the area of qualitative impairments in communication. Despite his impairment, he demonstrates many positive behaviors in this area that are not characteristic of autism, such as:

- Erik does not engage in use of inappropriate questions or make inappropriate statements (with a few exceptions that are consistent with his developmental level).
- He does not use made-up words or idiosyncratic language.
- Erik imitates the actions of others; for example, when his father sits down to watch TV, he postures himself in a similar manner.

- Erik demonstrates appropriate fluctuation in tone to match his emotions, such as louder and faster speech when he is excited.

Restricted, Repetitive, and Stereotyped Patterns of Behavior

Erik's parents and teacher reported that he is restricted in his play and conversations. His preoccupations have changed over time with his current special interest being volcanoes. This was observed during the ADOS administration. He did not want to talk about any of the topics presented by the evaluator, and he only wanted to talk about volcanoes. Volcanoes came up in other contexts; sometimes it was appropriate; sometimes it was not. For example, in one activity, he was asked to describe what he saw on a pictured map. He focused on areas with volcanoes, which was appropriate, but resisted redirection to any other area on the map. In another activity, the evaluator set up a pretend birthday party and invited Erik to participate. During this activity, he made the play dough into a volcano rather than a cake. The evaluator praised his work and then redirected him to the birthday activity but he informed the evaluator that he was not interested in the birthday party. He did not explore toys that were provided for free play; he used a truck, blocks, and puzzles but his play often included lining up blocks and puzzle pieces.

The Templetons report that in the past, Erik engaged in the repetitive motor movements of flapping his arms; however, these have been greatly reduced. He continues to have temper tantrums in highly anxious situations (e.g., going into a new classroom). These are infrequent (less than once a month), but intense in that they may last for hours. The tantrum behaviors include refusal, withdrawal, and yelling.

In the category of restricted, repetitive, and stereotyped patterns of behavior, Erik's ADI-R score of 3 matched the cutoff of 3 for autism. Erik scored a 1 on the ADOS but there is not a cutoff score in this area. Based on the results of parent interview (ADI-R) and direct assessment (ADOS), Erik meets the *DSM-IV* criteria for an Autistic Disorder in the area of restricted, repetitive, and stereotyped patterns of behavior. Despite his impairment he does not demonstrate some of the negative behaviors commonly associated with autism. For example, he is not aggressive to others or himself with the current exception of biting his nails and hitting his arm when he was very young. He does not engage in hyperventilation and has never had a seizure.

SUMMARY

Erik's scores on the ADI-R indicate that history and present behaviors meet or exceed the diagnostic criteria for Autism in 3 of 4 categories. Erik's scores on the ADOS indicate that his present behaviors meet or exceed the *DSM-IV* diagnostic criteria for Autistic Disorder in three of three categories:

1. Qualitative impairments in social interactions
2. Qualitative impairments in communication
3. Restricted, repetitive, and stereotyped patterns of behavior

Erik qualifies for consideration as a child with an Autistic Disorder. In the school setting, the appropriate category of eligibility would be autism. Autism, as defined by IDEA-2004, is a developmental disability that:

- Significantly affects verbal and nonverbal communication and social interaction
- Is generally evident before the age of 3
- Affects educational performance

Evidence is provided in this report to address items 1 and 2. The multidisciplinary team, which includes Erik's parents, will need to identify the effect on educational performance and make the final determination of eligibility.

RECOMMENDATIONS

Educational Programming

1. Erik's parents are encouraged to share the current evaluation with the school psychologist at the school he will attend for kindergarten. Initially, it is recommended that a district individual, knowledgeable in the current research and practice in autism, be consulted to assist the team in developing appropriate accommodations. The nature and degree of the appropriate accommodations will depend on: Erik's age, the task demands of the classroom, and the ability of the general education teacher to provide appropriate accommodations (taking into consideration the composition of the class, teacher's knowledge in this area, etc.).
2. Children with neurodevelopmental disorders (such as autism) learn best when they are provided with clear and predictable learning environments. Attention should be directed to the physical environment (reduction of distractions, sequencing of activities, and duration of activities) so as to not overwhelm or overstimulate Erik.
3. The National Research Council has endorsed the inclusion of children with neurodevelopmental disorders with age-mates in all areas of educational and non-educational instruction, to the extent that it promotes the ongoing development of educational goals. To this end, Erik's school team is encouraged to explore the potential for him to continue to be in the mainstream environment, with special education support, as needed. It will be important for Erik's teachers to receive instruction and education in effective strategies for teaching children with autism.

Qualitative Impairment in Social Interactions

1. Erik appears bright and verbally skilled beyond his years, which may result in his using language that is more mature than that of his peers. He is also interested in concepts and material that may be less interesting to his peers. While his vocabulary and understanding of special interest (volcanoes, for example) are characteristics that appeal to adults, these behaviors will not help him relate to other children. Assist him in being aware of the tone and content of his communication. Currently he is saying, "I am sorry, did you think I was talking to you?" While this may sound precocious now (at almost 4 years old), as he gets older it may be considered disrespectful. Start now to shape the communication that will serve him well in the future.
2. Erik will need support to facilitate social interactions. Adults in his environment may need to determine first if he understands whether his behavior is appropriate or inappropriate in social situations. As he does not seem to read the facial messages and body language of his peers, he may not gain the feedback in the natural environment that tends to shape our social behavior. In the absence of this feedback, it may be beneficial for adults to teach appropriate behavior explicitly in the form of a social story. See http://www.thegraycenter.org/ for information on the use of social stories to promote social skill development.
3. In the future, Erik would benefit from social skills education, training, and participation in a structured group setting. A social skills group will serve as a safe environment to learn and practice core skills, with supportive feedback from others. Such a setting should also bolster his confidence and increase his willingness to take risks in initiating social contact.

Qualitative Impairments in Communication

Erik does not present with expressive or receptive language impairment at this time. However, he does seem to be impaired in nonverbal communication, specifically sending and receiving nonverbal messages. Parents and teachers are encouraged to promote eye contact as a source of nonverbal information. Suggest to Erik that the information that is provided by the eyes and the mouth are clues to uncovering information about other people. The book *Teaching Your Child the Language of Social Success* (Nowicki, 1996) is a valuable tool for teaching these skills. Parents and teachers are encouraged to point out to Erik (privately) when he has not correctly detected a social cue. For example, if another child's body language suggests irritation, pull Erik aside and show him the body posture that indicates "I'm irritated."

Restricted, Repetitive, and Stereotyped Patterns of Behavior

1. At times Erik has difficulty transitioning from one activity to another. Adults are encouraged to provide consistent prompts to cue him to move in "X" amount of time. It will be beneficial if the cues for prompting are consistent at home and school. For example, 5 minutes prior to the end of the activity the adult would provide a prompt. This may be in the form of a verbal prompt ("5 minutes to finish") and/or visual prompt (egg timer). At first it may be necessary to provide both verbal and visual prompts. When the time is up, the adult must insist that the activity end. If this results in avoidance, noncompliance, or a meltdown, the adult will need to stay calm and consistent. Continue to provide him with the visual and/or verbal prompt to calm down.

2. Anytime that Erik has a meltdown, it will be necessary for an adult to be available to stay with him until the incidence is resolved. This may take quite awhile at first; however, it is very important that this process be completed prior to moving on to the next activity. While he is angry, adults are encouraged to provide only the prompt to calm down. If he has problems processing words when he is angry, then provide a visual cue of a calm face. An alternative is to take a picture of him when he is calm and use this to prompt him to resume that state. There should be no discussion of any topic while he is upset.

Make sure he is calm before attempting to discuss the incidence. Once he is calm, the adult can assist him in problem solving by using the following 3-step process:

   a. Stop, take a deep breath, and count to 3

   b. Think about your choices and the consequences of each choice

   c. Make a decision and act on it

3. Arrange for Erik to be allowed to choose "time out" when he feels overwhelmed or overstimulated, and arrange for an area to which he can retreat for a short period of time to regroup. Actively teach progressive muscle relaxation, deep breathing, and positive self-statements as positive stress management strategies. Have him practice these skills when he is calm so they may be used in stressful situations.

Thank you for the opportunity to work with your child.

PSYCHOMETRIC SUMMARY

Autism Diagnostic Inventory-Revised

Scale	Diagnostic Cutoff	Erik's Score
Qualitative Impairment in Reciprocal Social Interaction	10	6
Communication	8	10
Repetitive Behaviors and Stereotyped Patterns	3	3
Abnormality of Development Evident At or Before 36 Months (score of 1 = delay was reported, score of 0 = no delay)	1	1

Autism Diagnostic Observation Schedule

Scale	Diagnostic Cutoff	Erik's Score
Reciprocal Social Interaction	6	10
Communication	5	7
Communication + Social Interaction	12	17
Stereotyped Behaviors and Restricted Interests	No cutoff score	1

The scoring system for the Autism Diagnostic Observation Schedule and Autism Diagnostic Interview-Revised is as follows:

0 = behavior (associated with autism) is NOT present

1 = behavior is present but not clear, severe, or frequent

2 = behavior is present and meets criteria for autism

A score that meets or exceeds the diagnostic cutoff indicates that the individual has met the *DSM-IV* criteria for Autistic Disorder in that area.

REFERENCES

Duke, M. P., Nowicki, S. Jr., & Martin, E. A. (1996). *Teaching your child the language of social success.* Atlanta, GA: Peachtree Publishers.

Klin, A., Sparrow, S. S., Marans, W. D., Carter, A., & Volkmar, F. R. (2000). Assessment issues in children and adolescents with Asperger Syndrome. In A. Klin, F. R. Volkmar, & S. S. Sparrow (Eds.), *Asperger syndrome* (pp. 309–339). New York: Guilford Press.

CASE 2

Neuropsychological Evaluation of a Young Child with a Seizure Disorder

Marshall Andrew Glenn

This evaluation of a child with a seizure disorder bears significance for several reasons: the effects of seizure disorders on early neurological development, the long-term effects of antiepileptic drugs (AEDs) and their attendant side effects on neuropsychological functioning, and the need for close monitoring and periodic reevaluation. Sometimes the control of seizures comes with significant consequences on neuropsychological functioning, which may be the case here. This report addresses not only the implications of the effects of seizure disorders on development, but also the possible deleterious (iatrogenic) effects of medications on current functioning. The other issues addressed in this evaluation are the importance of collecting a thorough medical history and adhering to the Lurian principle of documenting supporting qualitative behaviors during assessment and not relying strictly on psychometric results in arriving at a diagnosis.

PSYCHOLOGICAL REPORT

Name:	Susie Waterhouse
Date of Birth:	06/25/2006
Age:	4 years, 3 months
Parents:	Bill and Esther Waterhouse
School:	Robert F. Kennedy Preschool
Grade:	Preschool
Date of Evaluation:	09/20/2010
Evaluator:	Marshall Andrew Glenn, Ph.D.

REASON FOR REFERRAL

Susie was referred for an evaluation to assess her current neuropsychological functioning at the request of her epileptologist. Susie was given a developmental screening from the Department of Health on 08/02/2010. The Ages and Stages Questionnaire assessed Susie's skills in the areas of communication, gross motor, fine motor, problem solving, and personal-social. Suzie fell within the at-risk range in all areas.

Mrs. Waterhouse, Susie's mother, reported that Susie had more than 200 seizures last year. She described these seizures as being grand mal; however, her medical report indicated a diagnosis of complex partial seizure disorder. Her mother reported that Susie becomes frustrated easily, acts out aggressively, is experiencing some problems with memory recall, and complains of fatigue in her legs. Susie is currently attending Robert F. Kennedy Preschool. Although school has only been in session for 3 weeks, her teachers have already noted problems in learning and behavior.

In an interview, Mrs. Waterhouse described her concerns regarding Susie's problems in communication.

- Susie cannot retain information such as colors, numbers, or letters. One day she asked me to write numbers, so I wrote 1–9. She asked repeatedly for me to draw a 5 then she'd ask me to point to the 5 in the row of numbers. When I asked her to point to the 5, she never could figure out which one the 5 was.

- When I take a shower, Susie stays in the bathroom with me. I tell her that if the doorbell rings, she is to stay in the room with me. We go over this at least three times a week. Last week I said, "Susie, now what do you do if the doorbell rings while we're in here?" She said, "Papa."

- She was disruptive in school twice, pushing a child out of line one day and pinching a girl the next. I said, "Susie what's something you can do tomorrow when you are mad instead of pinch?" She said, "10."

- When people ask her what she did in school she can't provide an answer until yes or no questions are presented, and then she'll say, "Oh, yeah, I do that" to everything you ask her.

- She said, "Mommy, what's Megan and Mary (two children she plays with)?" I asked, "What's Megan and Mary's what, Susie?" because her question didn't make sense, and she nodded her head and said, "Yeah, you're right, Mommy."

- She asked me what letter her name starts with, so I wrote S's and practiced with her (she could only draw a line) for 2 days. On the third day at dinner she said, "Daddy, my name starts with L." She became extremely frustrated when he corrected her, and she kept yelling, "It's an L, it's an L" repeatedly.

- She didn't know her first name was Susie until this month, and still doesn't recognize that Waterhouse is her last name.

- Susie broke something in her brother's room. I asked her what she had broken, and she kept saying, "I broke Harold's …" Finally I asked her, "You broke Harold's what, Susie?" and she said, "I just can't think the name of it, Mommy."

Based on Mrs. Waterhouse's recent observations, Susie is having symptoms related to aphasia, that is, word retrieval difficulties or problems finding the words she needs to express herself along with memory problems. Thus, her language output is often confused and confusing to her as well. These behaviors describe clinically significant symptoms that should be seriously considered in the context of her results on neuropsychological tests.

BRIEF LITERATURE REVIEW

According to Williams and Sharp (2000), epilepsy is the most common neurological condition of childhood, with higher occurrence in males. Prevalence statistics are 4.3 to 9.3 per 1,000 children. The authors noted that antiepileptic drugs (AEDs) are successful in controlling approximately 70% to 80% of seizures in children.

The authors further noted that remission over 5 years occurs in approximately 70% of children with epilepsy, and approximately 75% who have been seizure-free for at least 2 years can be successfully taken off AEDs.

Susie's medical reports indicated a diagnosis of complex partial seizures, which involves an alteration of consciousness, accompanied later by confusion, memory loss, and fatigue. Other reports mentioned primary generalized tonic/clonic seizures, suggesting that Susie's seizures may be complex partial with secondary generalization. In as much as Susie's presenting concerns are language-related, it is important to note that seizures affecting the language cortex may result in several types of language impairments (Ho-Turner & Bennett, 1999). Children with seizure disorders may exhibit variability in cognitive processes, and periodic reexamination is warranted (Arzimanoglou, Guerrini, & Aicardi, 2004).

BACKGROUND INFORMATION

According to information provided by her parents, Susie's first seizure occurred in January 2007 at 6 months of age. It was a one-sided seizure involving the right side of her body; the duration was approximately one-and-a-half hours. While she was in the emergency room, efforts to intervene with medication were unsuccessful. She was later given phenobarbital, but it was not entirely successful in controlling her seizures and she continued to have episodes every month or two. Between the ages of 6 months and 3 years, Susie had seizures at varying intervals, from none to several within a month. She has been prescribed Keppra, Trileptal, and Zonegran at different times and in different combinations and dosages. Throughout, EEGs, MRIs, and CT scans have shown normal brain activity.

In September 2009, Susie spent three weeks in the Epilepsy Monitoring Unit (EMU) at Arlington Children's Hospital. During her stay, she had 12 seizures and her medication was changed to Depakote. Subsequent evaluation with MRI and PET tests again were normal. Her performance on a neuropsychological examination, administered on September 7, 2009, was reportedly affected by an IV splint on her right-dominant hand; additionally, some of the tasks could not be completed. The report noted that the test results "may be an underestimate of her abilities due to being in an unfamiliar environment during testing and the immobility caused by her hand splint.…" On the Wechsler Preschool and Primary Scale of Intelligence-III (WPPSI-III), Susie earned a Full Scale score of 107, based on a Verbal IQ of 97 and Performance IQ of 117, with no outstanding pattern of strengths or weaknesses. Subtest scores were not reported. Susie was also administered the NEPSY. Results indicated below average memory, poor ability to organize and name body parts, average phonological processing, and ability to follow instructions at the lower end of average. Results of the WPPSI-III suggested average receptive and expressive vocabulary and average to above average visual-spatial abilities. The report noted that although language and nonverbal abilities were average relative to her age, her frequent seizures placed her at risk for developmental delays. Since complex problem solving and memory skills are developing, an annual evaluation was recommended.

Susie is currently taking Topamax, 100 mg in the morning and 125 mg in the evening. A review of the literature on side effects of Topamax included sedation, weight loss, and *language disturbance* (Williams & Sharp, 2000).

BIRTH AND DEVELOPMENTAL HISTORY

Developmental history indicated that Susie was the product of a full-term pregnancy. She was placed in the neonatal care unit due to fluid in her lungs. Susie accomplished developmental milestones within normal limits. She rolled back-to-front at 3 to 4 months, was able to sit up without support at 5 months, was able to pull herself up at 9 to 10 months, and was able to walk at 13 months. She was able to construct two-word sentences around 1 year of age.

Family Background

Susie lives with her biological mother and father and her 5-year-old brother, Harold. A review of information provided by the parents indicated a family history for depression, anxiety, and bipolar disorder in distant relatives. Mrs. Waterhouse also reported a history of having two seizures, one in infancy and one at 14 years of age.

Temperament and Behavior

With regard to temperament and behavior, it was reported that Susie has some incidents of inappropriate disruptive behaviors. Alistella Grace, RN, has observed Susie in a church program since August 2009. According to Ms. Grace, Susie often engaged in "disruptive, nonviolent behavior" attributed in part to inattention and hyperactivity caused by the side effects of her medication. During these episodes, Susie has to be removed from the room. Ms. Grace said that Susie's seizure disorder has had an adverse effect on her education and class participation because she frequently has to be removed from the room. Her mother reported that Susie does not consider the consequences of her actions and often appears unremorseful.

CURRENT ASSESSMENT INSTRUMENTS AND PROCEDURES

Miller Neuropsychological Processing Concerns Checklist (Neuropsychological Checklist) (for baseline qualitative observations of behaviors)

Wechsler Preschool and Primary Scale of Intelligence, Third Edition (WPPSI-III)

NEPSY (a developmental neuropsychological assessment)

Behavior Assessment System for Children, Second Edition (BASC-2), Parent Rating Scale – Child

OBSERVATIONS

Rapport with Susie was established quickly and she seemed to put forth the effort necessary to elicit valid test results. At times she did not seem to understand what was required of her or the nature of a question. She simply remained quiet with a rather vacant stare, at which point she was redirected as allowed by standardization. Overall, she appeared immature relative to her chronological age. Additional test observations are noted below under each cognitive area assessed.

TEST RESULTS

Intellectual Functioning

WPPSI-III

Susie's scores on the current administration of the WPPSI-III were lower than those on the previous administration (9/09) at Children's Hospital, despite the restriction of the IV splint at that time. Her current Verbal IQ score was 88 (compared to 97), her Performance IQ score was 98 (compared to 117), and her Full-Scale IQ was 91 (compared to 107).

NEPSY

The NEPSY provides neuropsychological measures in five domains: Attention/Executive Function, Language, Sensorimotor, Visuospatial, and Memory and Learning. The NEPSY addresses diagnosis of primary deficits, those underlying a particular domain (e.g., sensorimotor), and secondary deficits, impairments arising from a primary deficit. The NEPSY is therefore designed to assess subcomponents of complex functioning. For the sake of achieving optimal comparisons for pre-post testing purposes, the NEPSY was readministered in favor of the NEPSY-II. Given that Susie's performance may have been affected by her limited right-dominant hand mobility due to her IV splint, it is important to see how she performs on the same instrument without this handicap.

Attention

Presenting Concerns

According to the Neuropsychological Checklist, Susie's parents noted that Susie becomes absorbed in what she's doing (e.g., playing with puzzles) and has difficulty moving to another task. She is easily frustrated with difficult tasks and often does not attempt to complete them. Problematic behaviors that they attributed to her included the following.

Focused Attention

- Becomes easily distracted by sounds, sights, or physical sensations (moderate problem)
- Is inattentive to details or makes careless mistakes (moderate problem)
- Does not know where to start when given a task (mild problem)

Sustained Attention

- Has difficulty paying attention for long periods of time (moderate problem)
- Mind appears to go blank or loses train of thought (moderate problem)
- Seems to lose place in an academic task (moderate problem)

Shifting Attention

- Has difficulty stopping one activity and starting another (severe problem)

- Gets stuck on one activity (severe problem)
- Applies a different set of rules or skills to an assignment (mild problem)

Divided Attention

- Has difficulty attending to more than one thing at a time (moderate problem)
- Does not seem to hear anything else while watching TV (moderate problem)
- Easily becomes absorbed into one task (severe problem)

Attentional Capacity

- Stops performing tasks that contain many details (severe problem)
- Seems overwhelmed with difficult tasks (severe problem)

NEPSY	Scaled Score
Visual Attention	9

Visual Attention

Susie was given the NEPSY Visual Attention subtest. This is a time-restricted test in which she has to scan multiple rows of pictures to find and mark specific ones. Her performance was in the Average range (SS 9). This test assesses attention to visual detail as well as perceptual speed. She held her pencil with a high, light pencil grip and marked her targets with a light-trace mark. She randomly scanned the pages, rather than systematically proceeding from left to right in pursuing targets. The Neuropsychological Checklist indicated attention problems that may likely manifest on neuropsychological measures when she is older and can be assessed in more depth.

Executive Functions

Presenting Concerns

According to the Neuropsychological Checklist, Susie's parents noted that she is slow to grasp concepts and learn, but "once she understands, she excels." They also reported that Susie does not consider the consequences of her actions and often is unremorseful. She has hit her brother many times. In the first few weeks of preschool, she was removed from class because she threw toys and pushed other children. Problematic behaviors attributed to her regarding executive functioning were as follows.

Problem Solving, Planning, and Organizing

- Has difficulty learning new concepts or activities (mild problem)
- Has difficulty solving problems that a younger child can do (moderate problem)
- Makes the same kinds of errors over and over (severe problem)
- Quickly becomes frustrated and gives up easily (severe problem)

Behavioral-Emotional Regulation

- Appears to be undermotivated to perform or behave (moderate problem)
- Has trouble getting started with tasks (moderate problem)
- Demonstrates signs of impulsivity (severe problem)
- Has trouble following rules (moderate problem)
- Demonstrates signs of irritability (moderate problem)
- Lacks common sense judgment (severe problem)
- Cannot empathize with feelings of others (moderate problem)

Summary of Executive Functions

Because of Susie's young age, executive functions are not reliably assessed, but her parents have expressed several concerns regarding her problem-solving, planning, organization, and self-regulation abilities.

Sensory and Motor Functions

Presenting Concerns

On the Neuropsychological Checklist, Susie's parents noted that she "will sit down and say she can't walk because her legs are too tired"; she has trouble with fine motor skills such as copying a line drawn on a paper and using scissors properly.

Motor Functioning

- Muscle weakness or paralysis-bilateral (mild problem)
- Clumsy or awkward motor movements (mild problem)

- Walking posture difficulties (mild problem)
- Involuntary or repetitive movements—taps feet while standing (moderate problem)
- Poor fine-motor skills (mild problem)

Tactile/Olfaction Functioning

- Overly sensitive to touch, light, or noise (mild problem)
- Complains of loss of sensation (e.g., numbness) bilaterally in arms and legs (severe problem)

Auditory Functioning

- Does not like loud noises (severe problem)

NEPSY	Scaled Score
Imitating Hand Position	9
Visuomotor Precision	12

Summary of Sensorimotor Functioning

Susie's performance on subtests that measure sensorimotor skills was within the Average range. She was able to plan motor activities, reproduce hand positions, and use a pencil to execute a maze-like task under speeded conditions. Notice that her mother has reported bilateral muscle weakness and awkward movements, which may require additional follow-up with her pediatrician. Susie's pencil grip is rather high and as a result she draws with very light, rather wisp-like marks. Pencil grip is a learned skill and she may need some instruction to give her more control of the pencil and the marks she makes.

Visual-Spatial

Presenting Concerns

The Waterhouses' response to the Neuropsychological Checklist indicated that Susie experiences the following problems.

Visual-Spatial Functioning

- Drawing or copying difficulties (severe problem)
- Difficulty with puzzles (mild problem)
- Confusion with direction (moderate problem)

WPPSI-III	Scaled Score
Block Design	7
Matrix Reasoning	12
Picture Concepts	10
Picture Completion	7
NEPSY	
Design Copying	9
Block Construction	10

Summary of Visual-Spatial Functioning

Susie's performance on subtests that measure visual-spatial skills showed variability ranging from Below Average to Average. Her overall nonverbal reasoning as reflected by her Performance Index on the WPPSI-III was within the Average range. She showed relative weakness in nonverbal spatial reasoning on the Block Design and Picture Completion subtests. Both subtests of the NEPSY were within the Average range.

Language

Presenting Concerns

In responding to the Neuropsychological Checklist, Susie's parents noted concerns about Susie's receptive language.

"She has difficulty answering questions. She appears unable to process the meaning of questions at times and her responses do not make sense. For example, if you ask what she did in school, she'll say 'yes' or if you ask who she played with she'll say 'blocks'. She recognizes when her answers don't make sense, but can't provide the correct information. She is intelligent in that she attempts to compensate for missed information, so people don't realize that she does not understand. She is still learning to say her first and last name."

Articulation

- No problems noted

Phonological Processing

- Difficulty blending individual sounds to form words (mild problem)

Receptive Language

- Trouble understanding what others are saying (moderate problem)
- Does not do well with verbal directions (moderate problem)

Expressive Language

- Difficulty finding the right word to say (moderate problem)
- Unusual language or vocal sounds (mild problem)

WPPSI-III	Scaled Score
Vocabulary	10
Word Reasoning	7
Comprehension	8
Similarities	6
NEPSY	
Body Part Naming	4
Phonological Processing	12
Comprehension of Instructions	8
Verbal Fluency	9
Core Domain Score	88 (SS)

BASC-2	T Score
Functional Communication	26

Summary of Language Functioning

Susie's language scores show uneven development. She has good skills in naming common pictures and describing familiar objects as indicated by her average WPPSI-III Vocabulary score; however, she was rather dysnomic on Body Part Naming. She does not do as well on language tasks that call for more abstract skills such as figuring out the correct word when an object is described. She had great difficulty when asked to retrieve words or to describe the attributes in a picture. She did well on a phonological processing task in which she matched a spoken phoneme to one of three pictures.

Language comprehension was more challenging for her. On the WPPSI-III Comprehension subtest, her score was at the lower end of the Average range (SS 8). On this task, she had to answer an opened-ended question. She looked perplexed and often replied, "I don't know." On the Comprehension of Instructions subtest (NEPSY), she also earned a scaled score of 8. On this task, she was to identify the picture that matched a set of multiple modifiers (e.g., "Show me the one that is blue and happy"). She was able to do so for sentences with two modifiers but not for three (e.g., "Show me the one that is blue, big, and happy").

On the Similarities subtest, she had extreme difficulty answering how two things are alike, such as red and yellow, despite ample training prior to starting this subtest. Taken together, these findings suggest that while she has some fundamental knowledge of word meanings when the words are presented in isolation, she has trouble reasoning with language and engaging in spontaneous expression. Her relative weakness in comprehension of language appears to match the behaviors described by her mother. Mrs. Waterhouse has observed that Susie is sometimes aware that she has expressed herself incorrectly but then she does not know how to correct it. Additionally, Susie has been observed to have significant word finding problems both in the classroom and in the home.

Memory and Learning

Presenting Concerns

According to the Neuropsychological Checklist, Susie's parents expressed concerns about her lack of retention of information, poor comprehension, and limited recall. They reported that she answers questions incorrectly, such as 'How was your day?' or 'What did you do?' and if you ask her about an upcoming activity or event, she will say she has already done it.

Short-Term Memory

• Frequently asks for repetitions of instructions/explanations (moderate problem)
• Seems not to know things right after they are presented (moderate problem)
• Has trouble following multiple step directions (severe problem)

Active Working Memory

• Loses track of steps/forgets what they are doing amid tasks (moderate problem)

Long-Term Memory

• Has difficulty answering questions quickly (severe problem)
• Forgets what happened days or weeks ago (moderate problem)

General Learning

• Has difficulty with verbal, visual, and integrating both (moderate problem)

Current Levels of Functioning

WPPSI-III	Scaled Score
Information	7
NEPSY	
Narrative Memory	8
Sentence Memory	9

SUMMARY OF MEMORY FUNCTIONING

According to the subtests measuring memory, Susie's long-term recall of basic facts was Below Average. Note that her mother reported that Susie still struggles with the recall of her own first and last name, a task that is within expectations for her age. She is also struggling with learning and recalling the names of colors, letters, and numbers. Her performance on Narrative Memory (NEPSY), which requires her to listen to a short story and recall the essential details, was within the lower limits of the Average range. Short-term auditory memory, assessed by listening to sentences and repeating them verbatim, was Average, an improvement from her previous score. When one examines her mother's observations of her memory problems, however, along with the fact that memory functions are frequently adversely impacted for children with severe seizure disorders, her current scores may belie a more serious and emerging memory deficit. One must consider also the implications of memory on language. Susie appears to do better on rote memory tasks such as sentence repetition. She has considerably more difficulty attending to and performing a mental operation on information she has been given, such as listening to a story and answering questions, a complex task requiring integration of language.

Social-Emotional Functioning

Behavior Assessment System for Children-2

The BASC-2 assesses emotional and behavioral disorders in children and can be used to develop intervention plans. Susie's overall Behavior Symptom Index of 72 fell within the Clinically Significant range, indicating serious problems in socio-emotional functioning that require intervention. Please refer to the separate report in her confidential file for more detailed information.

SUMMARY OF FINDINGS

According to the results of this evaluation, although Susie is functioning within the Average range of intellectual functioning, the effects of her seizure disorder appear to have adversely impacted neuropsychological functioning, particularly manifested in areas of language and memory.

RECOMMENDATIONS

Further Evaluation and Monitoring

1. Susie has symptoms of a subclinical mixed receptive-expressive language disorder that should be evaluated by a pediatric speech-language pathologist. Diagnostically, the difficulties in language processing described by Mrs. Waterhouse are equal in importance to the scores and help to put them in context. Susie would benefit from intensive speech/language therapy focusing on word retrieval and receptive and expressive language abilities.

2. It would also be advisable to have an occupational therapist conduct further fine-motor assessment to design a program to help Susie develop her fine-motor and visual-spatial skills.

3. The complexity of Susie's medical condition warrants close and frequent monitoring by her pediatric neurologist and by periodic neuropsychological reevaluation. Side effects of AEDs should be thoroughly researched and carefully observed. Also, her mother has reported bilateral muscle weakness and awkward movements, which should be disclosed to Susie's pediatrician.

For School

1. Refer Susie for special education under the category of Developmental Delay.

2. Keep in close contact with Susie's parents to facilitate a coordinated support system for Susie's learning.

3. To improve selective/focused attention:
   a. Reduce auditory and visual distracters that may unnecessarily compete with her attention.
   b. Teach Susie how to keep her desk organized and free of unnecessary objects that could distract her.
   c. Maximize the high interest material and visual cues in assignments. She may profit from having a visual depiction of what she is expected to do.
   d. Make sure you have Susie's attention before giving her oral instructions.
   e. Allow for breaks throughout the day as needed to reduce fatigue, and divide large assignments into manageable units.

4. To alleviate memory difficulties:·
   a. Deliver oral instructions at a slow pace in a brief and concrete format, and accompanied by visual reinforcement when possible.
   b. When giving brief instructions, keep in close physical proximity while maintaining eye contact. Then have her repeat what she is expected to know.
   c. As Susie grows older, teach memory strategies such as using daily schedules, organizers, and hand-held recorders.
   d. When introducing new skills, provide Susie with pictures to visualize and form associations regarding what is being learned.

5. To alleviate behavior problems:
   a. Susie may benefit from behavioral therapy to alleviate problems she is having with getting along with peers.
   b. Provide positive feedback on instructions and assignments. Given her sensitivity, she should be reinforced for her effort along with the quality of her work.

REFERENCES

Arzimanoglou, A., Guerrini, R., & Aicardi, J. (2004). *Aicardi's epilepsy in children* (3rd ed.). Philadelphia, PA: Lippincott, Williams & Wilkins.

Ho-Turner, M., & Bennett, T. (1999). Seizure disorders. In S. Goldstein & C. Reynolds (Eds.), *Handbook of neurodevelopmental and genetic disorders in children* (pp. 499–524). New York: Guilford.

Williams, J., & Sharp, G. (2000). Epilepsy. In K. Yeates, M. Ris, & H. Taylor (Eds.), *Pediatric neuropsychology: Research, theory, practice* (pp. 47–73). New York: Guilford.

CASE 3

Language Assessment of a Sibling of a Child with Autism

Dale Bailey

Given the increase in the incidence of autism over the last decade, much attention has been given to comprehensive language assessment during a youngster's early years of life (age 5 and younger). Likewise, an increase in the incidence of autism has resulted in a greater number of assessment instruments being developed for this population. Most notable is the increase in the number of assessment instruments available to evaluate language pragmatics.

Comprehensive assessment of language and greater resources devoted to early childhood language assessment have resulted in two significant outcomes. First, children with autism have benefited significantly because instruments that are more sensitive to language differences caused by autism and/or pervasive developmental delays are more readily available and used. This results in a more accurate diagnosis, as well as the provision of early intervention.

Second, children without autism have benefited because these same instruments are also used with children without autism. Some of the children evaluated do not carry an autism diagnosis, but they are the siblings of children with autism.

This is the case of Anthony Oscar who was referred for a speech-language evaluation prior to the age of 2. Anthony has an older brother who has autism (diagnosed before the age of 3). Anthony's parents, who learned about autism through their older son's diagnosis, became concerned when Anthony was demonstrating delayed receptive oral language skills (i.e., listening) and delayed expressive oral language skills (i.e., speaking).

The speech-language evaluation report that follows details Anthony's developmental history, including his speech-language evaluation history to age 5 years. Significant throughout the years is that Anthony demon-strated a fairly stable language profile over the course of 3 years. That is, with minimal intervention provided (i.e., language therapy at a frequency of 1x/week), Anthony's language delay did not markedly increase over time, as would be likely with a child with autism. Review of Anthony's receptive oral language skills, in fact, shows that progress occurred during the 3-year time frame.

By age 5, through both observation and language sampling, it became clear that Anthony enjoyed playing and interacting with others and was developing relatively good pragmatic language skills.

Through standardized assessments, however, Anthony's specific language deficits became clear as well. By the age of 5, it was clear that Anthony's receptive language skills were low average to mildly delayed and that his expressive syntax was most problematic.

Following this evaluation, Anthony went off to kindergarten in September and was referred by the school for a psychological evaluation "to identify possible Attention-Deficit/Hyperactivity Disorder of unknown type" and to obtain "assistance in developing a plan to help Anthony succeed and focus/stay on task." He was 5 years, 1 month at the time of the psychological evaluation. A Child Symptom Inventory (CSI), ADHD Rating Scale-IV, BASC-2, IVA+, and WISC-IV (selected subtests) were administered and the diagnostic impressions were a "provisional" diagnosis of ADHD-Predominantly Inattentive Type, "problems with primary support group," and "academic problems." The evaluator explained "for better future comparisons, test selection included two tests that were beyond Anthony's age range by two months."

Several recommendations for improving behavior(s) were made in the psychological evaluation report. There was also discussion of "environmental disconnection" that is "common in the siblings of special needs children." The evaluator went on to say that Anthony "does demonstrate an immature level of ability suggesting that he will likely be able to develop proficiency in the right environment, given effective modeling." In contrast to the conclusions of the school evaluation, the results of the following evaluation suggest that Anthony's behavioral and attentional challenges may be more attributable to his language delays.

SPEECH-LANGUAGE PATHOLOGY REEVALUATION REPORT

Name:	Anthony Oscar
Date of Birth:	12/10/04
Age:	5 years, 1 month
Parents:	John and Donna Oscar
Address:	423 Tangram Avenue Parker, Idaho
Dates of Evaluation:	1/10, 1/11, & 1/17/10
Physician:	Dr. Jeremy Murphy
Evaluator:	Dale A. Bailey, M.A., CCC-SLP

SIGNIFICANT INFORMATION

Anthony is a 5-year, 1-month-old boy who lives with his parents and older brother in Parker, Idaho, and attends the pre-kindergarten program at Parker Elementary School. Anthony was originally referred for a speech-language evaluation just prior to turning 2 years old. There were no significant pre- or postnatal challenges. Labor was induced at 40 weeks' gestation and Anthony's birth weight was 7 pounds, 1 ounce. There is no history of frequent middle ear infections. This reevaluation is occurring at this time to determine Anthony's progress in language therapy.

A history of speech-language delays exists on both sides of the family. In addition, Anthony's older brother, Matthew, was diagnosed with autism after an interdisciplinary evaluation, when he was 2½ years of age. Matthew is currently a fifth grader and requires the services of a 1:1 aide throughout his school day. Although he is verbal, he is considered to have severe autism.

Mr. and Mrs. Oscar are both high school graduates. Mrs. Oscar remains home to care for the family and Mr. Oscar owns an air-conditioning business. Anthony's parents have consistently attended his speech-language sessions, as has his maternal grandmother who is also active in the treatment plan. English is the only language spoken in the home.

Anthony's initial evaluation indicated mildly delayed receptive oral language, mildly delayed expressive oral language, and moderately delayed overall oral language. Regular/weekly speech-language therapy was recommended (at a frequency of 1–2x/week) and was provided, but mostly at a frequency of 1x/week.

Anthony's speech and language were reevaluated in January of 2008 (at age 3 years, 1 month). Results of that evaluation indicated moderately delayed receptive language, mildly delayed expressive language, and moderately delayed overall language. An attempt was made to assess oral vocabulary; however, this was unsuccessful because Anthony's responses were considered unreliable and inconsistent. Continued speech-language therapy was recommended and subsequently provided at a frequency of 1x/week. Given that Anthony's receptive language was more delayed than his expressive language, more emphasis was placed on the development of receptive language in therapy. Anthony made good progress on his speech-language goals through June of 2008 so extended school year (ESY) services were not recommended. Anthony did not receive speech-language therapy during the summer of 2008 and therapy commenced in September of 2008; he also began participating in a Head Start program in the fall of 2008.

A speech-language reevaluation was conducted in January of 2009. Results of that evaluation indicated at least average receptive and expressive vocabulary, mildly delayed receptive language, moderately delayed expressive language, and moderately delayed overall language. Continued speech-language therapy was recommended and subsequently provided at a frequency of 1x/week. ESY services were provided during the summer of 2009 that included speech-language therapy. Services continued into the fall of 2009 at a frequency of 1x/week. The current reevaluation is being conducted to determine Anthony's present status and progress, as well as to address Anthony's parents' concern that his slow language development may be indicative of autism.

TESTS ADMINISTERED/METHODS USED

Test of Language Development-Primary, Fourth Edition (TOLD-P:4)

Comprehensive Assessment of Spoken Language (CASL)

Language Sample/Observation of Play

File Review

TESTS/RESULTS

General Behavior

Although Anthony was mostly cooperative and compliant throughout the course of this evaluation, completion of standardized tests typically successfully used with 5-year-old children was challenging. Specifically, Anthony repeatedly attempted to turn the tasks into a game. Although reinforcing activities were used intermittently (between tests) to increase participation, Anthony did not appear to enjoy more structured tasks, such as naming pictures. As such, his somewhat limited engagement should be taken into account when considering whether the results are representative of his actual level of speech-language functioning.

Oral-Peripheral, Speech/Articulation, and Voice and Speech Fluency

No significant deviations were present in the structure or function of the oral-peripheral area and mechanism. Anthony's oral-peripheral mechanism is considered structurally and functionally adequate for speech production purposes. Speech articulation is considered to be within normal limits. Anthony's speech is easily understood. For this reason, speech articulation was not assessed. Voice and speech fluency characteristics observed during this evaluation were judged to be within normal limits. No speech fluency behaviors were noted or suspected.

Language

The Test of Language Development-Primary, Fourth Edition (TOLD-P:4) was administered in order to evaluate Anthony's oral language skills. The TOLD-P:4 is a standardized assessment instrument consisting of six subtests that are combined into composites. These composites provide information about an individual's receptive, expressive, and overall oral language skills, language organization, language form (grammar), and language content (semantics). Only five of the six subtests of the TOLD-P:4 were administered because only the listening, speaking, and grammar composites were warranted. Information about Anthony's performance on the TOLD-P:4 follows. Descriptions of the TOLD-P:4 subtests are found in the Appendix.

The following table illustrates the verbal descriptors used in this report to describe the score ranges:

Standard Score	Verbal Descriptor
<70	severely delayed
70–77	moderately delayed
78–84	mildly delayed
85–115	average
116–122	above average
123–130	significantly above average
>130	superior

TOLD-P:4 Performance

Subtests	Standard Score (mean 10; SD 3)	Percentile
Picture Vocabulary	7	16
Oral Vocabulary	6	9
Syntactic Understanding	8	25
Sentence Imitation	3	1
Morphological Completion	7	16

Composites	Quotient (mean 100; SD 15)	Percentile
Listening	85	16
Speaking	79	8
Grammar	74	4

A review of Anthony's performance on the TOLD-P:4 indicates that his receptive language skills are in the low average to mildly delayed range and that his expressive language skills are mildly delayed. The Picture Vocabulary and Syntactic Understanding subtests combine to derive the Listening composite. The Oral Vocabulary and Morphological Completion subtests combine to derive the Speaking composite. Anthony's grammar skills (i.e., language form, including morphology and syntax) are considered moderately delayed. The Syntactic Understanding, Sentence Imitation and Morphological Completion subtests combine to derive the Grammar composite. Review of Anthony's subtest performances within the area of language form indicates that expressive syntax is most problematic.

On the Sentence Imitation subtest, Anthony often shortened sentences by omitting words, including pronouns, and/or by omitting phrases, such as prepositional phrases. Anthony also transposed words within sentences. An example of a word reversal is repeating "the dogs chased the boy" as "the boy chased the dogs."

Given Anthony's performance in the area of syntax, his frequent use of short phrases, his occasional use of "stock phrases," and an autism diagnosis in a sibling, additional measures of syntax and a measure of language pragmatics were warranted. Syntax refers to sentence form (including length and complexity), whereas language pragmatics refers to the purpose and function of language. This was the purpose of administering the Comprehensive Assessment of Spoken Language (CASL). Information about the CASL tests administered and about Anthony's performance on the CASL follows. Descriptions of the CASL tests are presented in the Appendix.

CASL Performance

Tests	Standard Score	Percentile
Antonyms	76	5
Syntax Construction	67	1
Paragraph Comprehension	84	14
Pragmatic Judgment	75	5

Review of the above indicates mildly delayed receptive language (see Paragraph Comprehension), moderate delays in vocabulary (see Antonyms) and language pragmatics (see Pragmatic Judgment), and a severe delay in syntax/sentence formulation (see Syntax Construction). On the Paragraph Comprehension test, Anthony had difficulty listening to short paragraphs (five to eight sentences) and responding to *what*, *which*, and *when* questions with multiple choice options provided for answers (represented by pictures). On the Antonyms test, Anthony had difficulty providing opposites for common prepositions, nouns, and adjectives.

On the Pragmatic Judgment test, Anthony had trouble indicating what he would do or say in common/everyday social scenarios. It is possible (and likely) that Anthony's delayed receptive and expressive oral language impacted his performance on this test.

On the Syntax Construction test, Anthony had difficulty repeating short (four-word) sentences and using prepositional phrases in isolation (in response to a question/prompt). He also had difficulty completing sentences requiring present tense verbs, plural, and singular present progressive tense verbs. Because these four tests are the core tests for children Anthony's age, they can be combined to form a composite measure of overall language.

Anthony's performance on this composite was a standard score of 71 and a percentile rank of 3, indicating that, although Anthony demonstrates only mildly delayed receptive language, his overall language is considered to be moderately delayed.

Language Sample

During our time together, the following samples of Anthony's language were obtained using a toy model of a kitchen that was equipped with utensils and dishes.

The Evaluator said:	Anthony said:
Have you ever played with a toy kitchen before?	I didn't play that a long time. (Hands evaluator a fork)
Thank you.	You welcome.
Let me know when you're done (making a pretend meal).	Try this—it's ready.
Aw, can I have a bigger piece?	I tease you.
Look what I have (showing cups).	Aw…
Where have you played with a toy kitchen before?	At my grandma house.
Do you sometimes go to your grandma's house?	Yes.
Where is your grandma's house?	It's in Petersburg.
I have red on my shirt (from dropped food).	Uh-oh! Do you have green?
(Evaluator tastes some pretend food)	Is it hot?
Wow! I guess it's hot!!	It's bad.
What should we do with this?	That go in the garbage.
(Evaluator "cleans up")	I take them.
Can I do that?	I do it.
I'll put the dishes away.	I do the dishes.
Do I have to pay? (for my meal)	Not for real.
Look what I found (showing money).	How you got that?
I usually have to pay.	Where you got your computer?
Right here (bringing out a pretend cash register)	Is that a computer?
	I don't do that at school.
Here's some money.	I can have it?
Well…	I wanna do a trick.
I know a trick…it's the disappearing hot dog trick.	Oh.

While Anthony demonstrated many important language skills through language sampling, including good language pragmatics, such as turn-taking and conversation, his sentences were all relatively short and errors in language form were also evident. Overall, the results of language sampling are considered consistent with the results of standardized testing.

SUMMARY AND DIAGNOSTIC IMPRESSIONS

Anthony is a 5-year, 1-month-old boy in preschool who lives with his parents and older brother in Parker, Idaho. A speech-language evaluation conducted just prior to Anthony turning 2 years old indicated mild receptive and expressive language delays, and moderately delayed overall language. Since then, Anthony has had weekly speech-language therapy and has participated in Head Start and then a public preschool. This reevaluation was conducted at this time to determine Anthony's present status in language development and address his parents' concerns regarding the possibility of autism.

Standardized testing indicates low average to mildly delayed receptive language and moderately delayed expressive language with expressive syntax being most problematic (severely delayed). Overall language is considered moderately delayed. Language sampling conducted during the course of this evaluation is consistent with the results of standardized testing.

Despite Anthony's low performance on a test measuring pragmatic judgment, his language is not considered typical or consistent with that of a child with autism for a number of reasons. As indicated above, it is likely that Anthony's delayed receptive and expressive oral language delays impacted his performance on the CASL Pragmatic Judgment test. In addition, language sampling suggests that Anthony demonstrated several (pragmatic) language skills that are typical of children without autism.

Specifically, Anthony referenced the past on at least two occasions and referenced teasing and "tricking" others. His language was neither perseverative with regard to topic nor atypical with regard to intonation. He also answered and asked questions, sustained conversation, and managed rapid topic changes well. Eye contact (with the evaluator/during play) and body posture (facing the evaluator/not turning his back toward the evaluator) were also behaviors that are considered consistent with that of typically developing children. Finally, Anthony's engagement in imaginative play (with a toy kitchen set) was consistent with behaviors seen in typically developing children. He

handed the evaluator a fork, "stirred" (pretend) food in a pot, and "sipped" (pretend) liquid from a cup during play.

RECOMMENDATIONS

Given Anthony's current level of speech-language functioning, the following recommendations are provided to the Individualized Education Plan (IEP) team for consideration.

1. Continued language therapy is recommended. Given interventions to date (including weekly therapy and preschool programming) and given Anthony's language status, an increase of sessions to two per week is advised.

2. Continued participation in a preschool program is recommended. Efforts to support both receptive and expressive oral language skill development (in a preschool setting) should be undertaken.

3. Efforts to support social language skill development in the classroom setting would be appropriate. When feasible, gain Anthony's attention prior to speaking to him. Break multistep directions into component steps (and provide the next step after Anthony has completed the previous step). Determine Anthony's understanding by asking him to repeat what was said.

4. Teach/provide visual cues that will help Anthony transition from one activity to the next. An example would be gaining his attention and showing him a snack box or cup when it is time for snack. Use these types of cues when Anthony appears lost or confused.

5. Further develop Anthony's listening skills by providing lots of opportunities to listen to stories and answer questions about them. As Anthony's listening skills develop, provide longer stories (i.e., more sentences, longer sentences, and/or more complex sentences within the story). Also, as Anthony's listening skills develop, increasingly vary the questions (e.g., who, what, when, where) so as to put an increased demand on his listening and reasoning skills.

6. Provide opportunities to listen to spoken language and demonstrate an understanding of language through games. For example, keep an object out of Anthony's view, verbally describe it, and then ask Anthony to try to guess what it is. Then, have Anthony take a turn and have a partner or adult guess the object.

7. As his listening skills develop, read stories aloud to Anthony and ask him to make predictions about what may happen next.

8. To increase Anthony's expressive syntax, ask him to repeat spoken sentences. At first, use visuals (e.g., circles drawn on paper, wooden blocks) to represent the spoken words. Increase sentence length and complexity as Anthony's skills develop. Also, reinforce Anthony's use of grammatically correct (short) phrases (e.g., prepositional phrases) in response to questions, as well as his ability to speak in complete sentences. For a multisensory approach to building and correcting syntax, consider using "Sentence Builders, Word Shapes" from The ARK Institute of Learning (www.arkinst.org/resources). Each part of speech is represented by a tile of a different shape and color.

9. Anthony would benefit from parent participation during therapeutic activities (such as those described above). Additional home activities to support Anthony's language development could include: providing story telling/listening opportunities while traveling in the car, at bedtime, during bath time, etc. Play games such as "guess what's for lunch/dinner" or "guess what I'm describing." During such interchanges, provide Anthony with additional verbal information or pictures so that he can guess what is being described. Then, have Anthony take a turn.

Should any questions arise regarding the content of this report, please contact me.

APPENDIX: SUBTEST DESCRIPTIONS

Test of Language Development—Primary, Fourth Edition: Subtests

- **Picture Vocabulary** measures the extent to which a child understands the meanings of spoken English words; this subtest is administered with pictures.

- **Oral Vocabulary** is an associative task that measures a child's ability to understand and orally express the relationships between two spoken words; this subtest is administered without pictures.

- **Syntactic Understanding** assesses the ability to comprehend the meaning of sentences; this subtest is administered with pictures.

- **Sentence Imitation** measures the ability to imitate English sentences (spoken by the evaluator); this subtest is administered without pictures.

- **Morphological Completion** assesses the ability to recognize, understand, and use common English morphological forms; this subtest is administered without pictures.

Comprehensive Assessment of Spoken Language: Tests

- **Antonyms** measures an aspect of word knowledge (the ability to identify words that are opposite in meaning) and an aspect of language expression (the ability to retrieve, generate, and produce a single word when its opposite is given as a stimulus); this test is administered without pictures.

- **Syntax Construction** measures the ability to generate sentences using a variety of morphosyntactic rules; this test is administered with pictures.

- **Paragraph Comprehension** measures the comprehension of syntax by means of a series of spoken narratives; this test is administered with pictures.

- **Pragmatic Judgment** measures the knowledge and use of pragmatic rules of language by having to judge the appropriateness of language used in specific environmental situations or by actually using language appropriate to given environmental conditions; this test is administered with pictures when administered to young children (to age 9).

CASE 4

Cognitive and Achievement Correlates of Language Disorders

Stephen Camarata and Mary Camarata

A language disorder is a relatively high incidence condition described in the *Diagnostic and Statistical Manual of Mental Disorders—Fourth Edition TR (DSM-IV-TR)*. Although it is the second most prevalent disability condition served in schools (the first being learning disability), school psychologists, special educators, and teachers may not be cognizant of the potential impact of this disorder on learning. Conversely, speech-language pathologists serving these children may not be aware of the broader educational implications of the disorder. The purpose of this report is to illustrate the importance of integrating information on language, achievement, and cognitive abilities for cases of students with language disorders. Co-normed instruments such as the Woodcock-Johnson III are particularly useful because meaningful relative performance can be examined across a range of narrow abilities in both the cognitive and achievement domains. Because eligibility and service delivery personnel may be relatively specialized, the educational impact of language disorder may not be readily recognized unless information from the language assessment and the psychological assessment are integrated and interpreted. For example, low language ability can easily be mistaken for global cognitive deficits (intellectual disability), as a form of autism spectrum disorder (ASD), or Attention-Deficit/Hyperactivity Disorder (ADHD) – inattentive type, when the impact of the disorder is not properly evaluated and understood. Differential diagnosis is crucial in order to obtain proper intervention services and to ensure eligibility under the correct special education classification.

Key elements of the assessment include expressive language ability, receptive language ability, speech (pronunciation), and social language skills (pragmatics). Important cognitive abilities include processing speed, fluid reasoning, and auditory processing. Auditory working memory, short-term memory, and long-term retrieval are particularly important. Diagnostic and educational considerations. Word retrieval and visual-spatial abilities should also be examined because these broad abilities are often relative strengths and, in fact, are usually intact in children with language disorders. In the current case, fluid reasoning and visual-spatial thinking were strong but retrieval was questionable.

In the achievement arena, depending on the age of the child, the evaluation should include tests of reading decoding and comprehension and writing ability. Oftentimes, there is considerable individual variation among the skills within reading or writing achievement. In young children, at least the pre-academic skills should be assessed. Although math skills are often a relative academic strength, usually math computation is much stronger than applied math because math problem solving involves oral language abilities. This was also evident in the test results for this case; computation was much higher than math problem solving.

Moreover, a clinician must think through the educational ramifications of the weaknesses in expressive and/or receptive language. Because so much of education, particularly in preschool and in elementary years, relies so heavily on auditory abilities and listening comprehension, teachers must be made aware of the special needs of these children. It is often useful to discuss patterns of strengths and weaknesses in cognitive and achievement abilities so that a teacher may gain insight into effective compensatory strategies needed for assuring that the student understands and learns educational concepts. Because key aspects of several cognitive abilities are relatively intact, educational programs designed for students with global cognitive impairments are not appropriate for children with language disorders. This case included superior fluid reasoning and high average visual-spatial thinking. Similarly, because children with language disorders do not show reductions in motivation for social interaction or the compulsive or stereotypic behaviors that are core elements of ASD, programs designed for autism are likely to be ineffective.

With regard to impact on psychological assessment, language disorders can potentially confound seemingly independent tests. For example, a child with severe expressive-receptive language disorder may receive a low score on the Wechsler Preschool and Primary Scale of Intelligence (WPPSI-III). A relatively high proportion of the overall WPPSI-III "IQ" score is derived from items that directly or indirectly measure language comprehension ability (especially the lower extension of the WPPSI-III). For example, completion of areas such as perceptual organization requires substantial language comprehension, so that an "IQ" from cognitive tests of this nature may in fact be a proxy for receptive language ability. The functional consequence of this is that estimates of general intellectual ability that are dependent on receptive language ability may inadvertently underestimate learning potential.

Finally, many children with language disorder may be misidentified as having Attention-Deficit/Hyperactivity Disorder (ADHD), particularly the inattentive type. This happens because in educational situations that require high auditory comprehension, the child will have difficulty attending to the instructions. A parallel can be seen in bilingual populations; it is not surprising that an ESL child's attention may waver when verbal instructions far exceed the comprehension level. The key differential diagnostic marker for this is that the "inattentive" behaviors diminish or disappear altogether when verbal instructions that are at or below the child's functional comprehension level are delivered. Unlike those with receptive language disorder, in cases of ADHD-inattentive type, distracters will capture and deflect the child's attention even in very low verbal or even nonverbal contexts.

This case presentation illustrates how language disorders may relate to other aspects of development and education, and ultimately have an impact on psychometric assessment. The case also demonstrates the need for integrating and coordinating information gained by speech pathologists, school psychologists, special educators, and teachers to accurately diagnose and properly serve these children.

SPEECH AND LANGUAGE EVALUATION

Name:	Brandon Weiss
Date of Birth:	12/26/2004
Age:	5-8
Date of Evaluation:	09/17/10
Clinicians:	Stephen Camarata, Ph.D., CCC-SLP and Mary N. Camarata, M.S., CCC-SLP

REASON FOR REFERRAL

Brandon was referred by his parents and by school personnel with a concern about delayed speech and language. The purpose of the evaluation was to examine speech and language abilities for the purpose of determining special education eligibility and to evaluate this performance relative to cognitive abilities and initial academic achievement.

BACKGROUND

Brandon's parents completed a case history form. Comprehensive medical information can be reviewed in Brandon's permanent medical file. Mrs. Weiss reported "excellent" health during her pregnancy, with one hospitalization due to dehydration from flu. Brandon was delivered normally at 36.5 weeks, gestation. He had postnatal complications including jaundice and some feeding difficulties. He met all developmental milestones, with the exception of speech articulation and language, within typical age ranges. Brandon said his first word at 14 months (ball); named people and objects at 2 years, 4 months; began to use 2-word phrases at 2 years, 9 months; and started speaking in sentences at 3 years, 3 months. His health has been generally good.

A hearing assessment was performed by an audiologist at the University of Charleston Hearing Clinic. Because Brandon refused to wear headphones, hearing in each ear could not be tested separately. Consequently, sound field testing indicated normal hearing in at least one ear but a unilateral hearing loss could not be ruled out. Impedance was within normal limits bilaterally. This indicates that both ear drums were moving and suggests that both middle ears were clear of fluid.

Brandon lives at home with both parents and has a younger sister, age 1 year, 2 months. She has begun using single words and evidently is typically developing thus far. Brandon's parents are both college graduates; his mother is an accountant and his father is an intensive care nurse. Brandon's mother reportedly talked late and his father received speech-articulation therapy in the first grade to correct a distorted "r." He also reported having private tutoring for reading in middle school, but generally did well academically. Brandon's mother evidently caught up on her own, did not receive services for speech or language, and could not recall any particular difficulties in school. She realizes that Brandon is at risk for academic difficulty so she plays number and letter games with him and he has a variety of toys that incorporate numbers and letters. Additionally, she has a set of Dolch Basic Sight Word cards and motivates him to work with her on them by giving him a dime for each word he reads correctly. She or Brandon's father reads to him nightly before bedtime, and although they make a point of tracking the words with a finger as they read, Brandon is more attentive to the pictures.

Brandon's mother indicated that she became concerned when he did not learn new words as quickly as peers when he was a toddler. Although his first words did start on time (14 months), he progressed slowly and did not use 2-word combinations until well beyond his second birthday. In addition, the early words he used were difficult to understand and primarily included only "m" and "b" consonants and a few vowels. Both parents reported that he behaved as if he didn't understand when they spoke to him, particularly when they used longer sentences. For example, his father reported: "If I ask him to pick up the blocks and put them in the toy box, he may pick up some of them but then he'll come to me with his arms full, as if asking what to do with them. He never seems to understand more than one thing at a time." Because of these concerns, Brandon was enrolled in a special education blended (mixed typical and special students) preschool at age 3 and attended three times weekly. He also received speech therapy twice weekly for 30 minutes. The preschool focused on language enrichment and school readiness, including pre-academic skills. The speech therapy focused on vocabulary, grammar, speech discrimination, and articulation. Brandon's parents reported that he seemed to be progressing well but still seemed to have trouble saying and understanding long sentences. They reported that he primarily uses short phrases and does not always respond correctly to "wh" questions, especially "why" and "when."

Both parents attended the evaluation session, which was completed over a 4-hour period with a lunch break. Brandon cooperated well with the testing and appeared to readily attend to most items. Because of this, we were able to complete a large number of tests with only short play breaks and minimal prompting. He responded especially eagerly to the Leiter-R and other tests that had a low verbal load. Unlike some other children with language disorders who will only respond when they are certain of the correct answer, Brandon responded readily, albeit sometimes slowly, even when it was clear that he was unsure of the answer.

TEST MEASURES AND SCORES REPORTED

Autism Diagnostic Observation Scale (ADOS)

Childhood Autism Rating Scale (CARS)

Leiter International Performance Scale, Revised (Leiter-R)

Preschool Language Scale, Fourth Edition (PSL-4)

Test of Auditory Comprehension of Language, Third Edition (TACL-3)

Woodcock-Johnson III Tests of Cognitive Ability (WJ III COG): selected tests

Woodcock-Johnson III Tests of Achievement (WJ III ACH): selected tests

Spontaneous speech and language sample (SS/LS)

Parent Interview

All standardized test results are reported as percentile ranks (PR). Percentile ranks do not describe Brandon's proficiency on a task but rather the percentage of children his age whose scores were the same as or below his.

For the tests of the Woodcock-Johnson III (WJ III), Relative Proficiency Indexes (RPI) are also reported. The RPI is derived from a mathematical calculation of probability based on the norms. The RPI predicts Brandon's proficiency on tasks similar to those of the test, at a difficulty level at which typical children of his age (age-peers) would be 90% successful. Ninety percent is the level of success that generally represents mastery of a skill or ability. Descriptive labels for the RPI ranges are provided in the table below. Proficiency is used for academic achievement; developmental labels are used for cognitive and language abilities. The implications describe how the child would perceive a similar task at an age-appropriate level of difficulty. For example, Brandon's RPI of 95/90 on the Visual-Spatial Thinking cluster indicates that on tasks such as reorienting objects in space and recalling details of pictures, at a level of difficulty at which the typical child of age 5–8 would be successful 90% of the time, Brandon would be successful 95% of the time. His development in this ability is age-appropriate to advanced and he is likely to perceive tasks similar to those administered as easy.

	Proficiency	Development	Implications
100/90	very advanced	very advanced	extremely easy
98/90 to 100/90	advanced	advanced	very easy
95/90 to 98/90	average to advanced	age-appropriate to advanced	easy
82/90 to 95/90	average	age-appropriate	manageable
67/90 to 82/90	limited to average	mildly delayed to age-appropriate	difficult
24/90 to 67/90	limited	mildly delayed	very difficult
3/90 to 24/90	very limited	moderately delayed	extremely difficult
0/90 to 3/90	negligible	severely delayed	impossible

Adapted from: Schrank, F. A., & Woodcock, R. W. (2002). Manual and Checklists. *Report writer for the WJ III.* Itasca, IL: Riverside Publishing.

Within this report, examples of Brandon's responses use invented items similar to the actual test items, which are confidential.

Complete score tables are appended to this report.

AUTISM ASSESSMENTS

Brandon's parents completed the Autism Diagnostic Observation Scale (ADOS) and the Childhood Autism Rating Scale (CARS). The results indicated that Brandon does not have characteristics of Autism or Autism Spectrum Disorder as he fell below the ASD cut-off score on the ADOS and below the mild autism cut-off on the CARS.

ORAL LANGUAGE

Spontaneous Speech and Language (SS/LS)

A spontaneous speech and language sample (SS/LS) was collected and analyzed. This placed Brandon in Brown's Stage V of linguistic development with his mean length of utterance (MLU) of 4.10 morphemes corresponding to his level of grammar use. His MLU fell below the typical range for his chronological age. Brandon produced the following grammatical forms accurately:

- Noun plurals
- Verbs: Present progressives, past tense, copulas, and early modals (e.g., can, will); third person forms (e.g., walks) and auxiliaries (e.g., is walking) were produced with above 75% accuracy
- Reverse question forms (e.g., Are we going now?) and *what, who,* and *where* questions (e.g., Where is the ball?)
- Complex syntax was emerging and evident in 7% of Brandon's sample, including simple infinitives (e.g., She likes *to play*) and conjoined syntactic forms (e.g.,She walks *and* runs).

Speech intelligibility was above 80% (i.e., another person would be able to understand his speech when he is referring to a context that is not shared).

Important developmental errors were noted, and Brandon's phonemic repertoire was immature for a 5-year, 8-month-old child, including fronting of velars (e.g., saying "dum" instead of "gum") and stopping of fricatives (e.g., "pour" for "four"). Brandon also produced some phonemically advanced phonemes such as /l/ and consonantal blends.

Brandon does have a language learning style of note, referred to as an "expressive" learner. Children who use this pattern of language learning learn by assembling language information and making inferences about meaning. They tend to produce utterances that sound like jargon with an occasional word in the string. They also repeat lines from movies and verbally "script," but this is qualitatively different than echolalia because the child changes a word or several words in the "script." As their language continues to develop, more and more intelligible words become apparent within the utterance. It is hypothesized that this learning style includes "bootstrapping" meaning from partial knowledge of all the words in the elaborated sentence. New words and new language continue to become apparent within the vocalization string and eventually the string is a complete utterance. On the surface this may seem "backwards" because the child is producing long vocalization strings and learning simpler, shorter forms, however this is the case in children with this profile.

Brandon's pragmatic skills were not grossly atypical. Brandon is at first cautious in new situations. Trust must be established. After he is comfortable and secure in the environment, interaction is much more comfortable.

Brandon freely demonstrated visual referencing and shared enjoyment, which concurs with the negative finding for autism on the ADOS and the CARS. He was willing and able to be directed (e.g., to do tasks, follow simple instructions, change his focus of attention) both via language and contextual cueing. He also directed the attention of others. Brandon displayed appropriate affect in a variety of situations ranging from fun and enjoyable to less preferred activities, and disappointment. He smiled, showed shared enjoyment, and readily looked to his name.

Brandon played appropriately with the toy sets present. He was observant and quick to figure out how various toys worked. He demonstrated reciprocal play and enlisted both the clinician and his mother into his play. Brandon's attention was appropriate; he maintained meaningful play and was not distracted or inattentive in this context. He also focused well during testing. Brandon was cautious at first and had his preferences, though they were not outside the range expected in five-and-a–half-year-olds. His parents reported that he may remain insistent on returning to an activity that has been denied, but with gentle boundaries, Brandon can get over his disappointment and happily move on to the available alternatives. Brandon was a delightful, perceptive little boy with age-appropriate play and, within the limits of his receptive language disorder, appropriate social use of language.

Within the SS/LS, Brandon's functional understanding of spoken language was below normal limits, as per the TACL-3 and the PLS-4, and this result was consistent with observations made during the SS/LS.

Test of Auditory Comprehension of Language, Third Edition (TACL-3)

The TACL-3 is a measure of receptive oral language that requires the child to point to one of three pictures in response to a clinician prompt, indicating listening comprehension. The prompts include vocabulary (single words), grammatical morphemes (e.g., plural, possessive, negation, and past tense markers), and elaborated sentences (e.g., "The boy ate cookies while watching TV"). Brandon's performance on each of the three subtests did not show any significant strengths. His overall score was below the 1st percentile, indicating that less than 1% of 6-year-olds would score as low as or lower than he did. His comprehension of spoken language is significantly weak.

Preschool Language Scale, Fourth Edition (PLS-4)

The Auditory Comprehension subscale of the PLS-4 was used to further assess Brandon's language comprehension and skills that are considered important precursors for language development. Brandon paid attention to the examiner when alerted to do so and used toys appropriately, but his comprehension of vocabulary, language concepts, and grammatical markers was similar to his results on the TACL-3. Again, his test results indicated that his language comprehension is significantly delayed; his overall performance was in the 3rd percentile.

The Expressive Communication subscale measures a child's skills and efficacy in communicating with others. Although limited by vocabulary, grammar, and syntax, Brandon's social use of language and recognition of social roles was appropriate. His vocabulary, grammar, and syntax were consistent with the information provided in the language sample. Brandon's overall performance on this subscale was in the 2nd percentile.

Observations made during the SS/LS indicated Brandon's understanding of spoken language was below normal limits, consistent with the results of the TACL-3 and the PLS-4.

Woodcock-Johnson III Tests of Cognitive Ability (WJ III COG) and Tests of Achievement (WJ III ACH)

Consistent with his scores on the TACL-3 and the PLS-4, Brandon's performance on all of the WJ III language-based tests was significantly weak. His RPIs indicated mildly delayed development of the language abilities assessed.

Knowledge

Brandon was administered two tests of general world knowledge. At his age, the questions addressed information a child would be likely to acquire incidentally, through experience and language, such as "What is the person called who helps to heal sick people?" and questions about where common objects would be found and what they are used for (e.g., Where would you find a fish? What would one do with a plate?). Based on his Knowledge cluster RPI of 24/90 (PR 2), Brandon's level of general knowledge is moderately delayed.

Receptive Language

Brandon's performance on two tests of receptive language were similarly low. The Oral Comprehension test (RPI 52/90, PR 14) required him to supply the last word in an orally presented sentence. For the first three items, Brandon did not grasp the concept of analogy. For example, when told "A cow moos, a duck …," Brandon responded, "doesn't moo." He completed other sentences with associations; given "A young cat is called a …," he said, "Fluffy." Fluffy is Brandon's cat. On the Understanding Directions test (RPI 54/90, PR 4), he was given oral instructions regarding objects to point to within a picture and the order in which to do so. He was able to point to up to two objects, in the order of mention (e.g., "Point to the house and then the dog") and a few statements incorporating two objects and a preposition (e.g., "Point to the truck near the house"). He was not able to respond correctly to three critical elements when one was an adjective (e.g., "Point to the black horse and then to the fence") and did not attend to negation (e.g., "Point to the ducks that are not in the lake." He pointed to those in the lake). Brandon demonstrated a mild delay on all of these language skills, indicating that he will find similar tasks at age-appropriate levels very difficult.

Expressive Language

On the WJ III expressive language tests, Brandon had significant difficulty on both vocabulary tests: Picture Vocabulary (RPI 54/90, PR 14) required him to name pictures; Verbal Comprehension (RPI 59/90, PR 8) required him to name pictures, supply antonyms and synonyms for given words, and complete simple analogies. Based on these measures, his expressive vocabulary is mildly delayed. Brandon's best performance, albeit still low, was on Story Recall (RPI 72/90, PR 5), retelling details in stories that had just been told to him. As the stories increased in length, he omitted details. It is likely that he has benefited from having his parents read books to him every night. Still, his developmental level in retelling is mildly delayed to age-appropriate. When other 5-year-olds would be 90% proficient in retelling a brief, simple story, Brandon would be 72% proficient and would find the task difficult.

Phonemic Awareness

Phonemic awareness is the ability to perceive the individual sounds in spoken words, such as the three sounds in "cat" and the four sounds in "fox" and mentally reorder them. Phonemic awareness is a critical basis for learning to read and spell using letter-sound associations. Brandon's performance on the Phonemic Awareness cluster indicated that he is mildly delayed in these skills (RPI 59/90, PR 5).

COGNITIVE ABILITIES

Leiter International Performance Scale – Revised (Leiter-R)

The Leiter-R is an individually administered test that estimates global nonverbal intellectual abilities based on the performance of complex nonverbal mental processes involving conceptualization, visualization, and inductive reasoning. Brandon obtained a Brief Intelligence Quotient of 137, in the Superior range, and a Fluid Reasoning Quotient of 112, in the High Average range.

Woodcock-Johnson III Tests of Cognitive Abilities (WJ III COG)

General Intellectual Ability (Extended Battery)

Brandon's General Intellectual Ability (GIA) standard score of 89 cannot be considered representative of his overall intelligence or his general aptitude for learning due to the tremendous discrepancy among the test scores from which it is derived. Not only do they vary over 3.5 standard deviations, but of the 14 tests that make up the GIA, 9 are at least partially language-based. The difference between Brandon's GIA of 89 and his Leiter-R Brief IQ score of 137, which is based solely on nonverbal measures, highlights the extensive weakness of his language skills.

Fluid Reasoning and Visual-Spatial Thinking

Brandon demonstrated significant strengths in fluid reasoning, the ability to use both inductive and deductive reasoning to solve problems one has not previously encountered. In this case, Brandon's strength was somewhat surprising. Although the problems in these tests are represented by series of colored geometric shapes and the problem solving is nonverbal, the verbal directions are initially simple, but increase in complexity along with the problems. However, once Brandon understood the general concept of the task, he seemed to understand the progression of the drawings and what was required *despite* the instructions. Additionally, as these are controlled learning tasks, if Brandon was correct, he was told so, and if he was not, he was told the correct answer. Brandon seemed quite engrossed in both of these tests, as though he were challenging himself to figure out each problem, and then looking to the examiner for confirmation. Brandon's Fluid Reasoning RPI of 99/90 indicated that when others his age would be 90% successful on similar reasoning tasks, Brandon would be 99% successful and would find such tasks very easy. His percentile rank indicates that his score was as high as 95% of children of his age.

Brandon demonstrated average to advanced proficiency in thinking with visual-spatial information, such as solving puzzles, mentally reorienting forms in space, and remembering details of pictures (Visual-Spatial Thinking, RPI 95/90, PR 81). Consequently, he is likely to benefit from visual information such as bar graphs, pictures, and webs to help him understand concepts and acquire new information that is being explained verbally.

Brandon's results on both of these factors were consistent with the results of the Leiter-R, which also measures fluid reasoning and visual-spatial thinking.

Memory

Brandon had significant difficulty on all of the WJ III COG measures requiring memory (Short-Term Memory, RPI 53/90, PR 18; Working Memory, RPI 51/90, PR 15). His RPIs indicated a mild delay in memory span (i.e., the amount of unrelated information that he can hold in immediate awareness) and in working memory (i.e., his ability to work with information while holding it in memory). He was only able to repeat three words in the order presented, and two digits in reverse order. Based on test results, Brandon's associative memory (i.e., the ability to create, store, and retrieve a symbol-word association over a period of a few minutes) was also mildly delayed (RPI 59/90, PR 4). These skills are critical for acquiring vocabulary such as names of shapes, colors, letters, and numbers, letter-sound associations, and math facts. The effects of these memory weaknesses are already evident in Brandon's low vocabulary. Soon, working memory will be critical for learning basic skills in school, such as blending individual sounds into a word and regrouping in addition.

Word Retrieval

Rapid retrieval is the ability to recall information that is stored in long-term memory quickly and efficiently. The faster one can retrieve data, the easier it is to use it to work with other information held in short-term memory or, simply, to answer questions. Brandon was given two tests of rapid word retrieval; both were time-limited. Retrieval Fluency required him to name as many words as he could in each of three categories (e.g., articles of clothing). His RPI of 84/90 indicates that his ability to do so was age-appropriate; however, the categories on the test are frequently used for teaching the concept of categories and facilitating word retrieval in language therapy and this was true for Brandon. After given the instructions for one segment of the test, he commented, "School Plays this game." Consequently, his score may be an over estimation of his developmental level.

The other test given was Rapid Picture Naming, a task requiring Brandon to name pictures of common objects as fast as he could. His RPI of 60/90 (PR 11) indicates that when attempting to retrieve words from memory, even ones that he knows well, he will need plenty of time, as he is likely to be only 60% successful when his age peers are 90% successful. For some items, he gave the wrong name, said "no," and then gave the correct word; on others, he was just silent, apparently thinking, before responding. When the test was completed, he was asked to name the pictures again, without a time limit. He did so, indicating that his difficulty on this test was due to his rate of retrieval and not his limited vocabulary.

Considering the difference between Brandon's performance on these two tests, it's likely that Brandon does have difficulty with word retrieval but that teaching him new and known vocabulary within categories (e.g., food, transportation, colors), and with plenty of practice, will help him develop more efficient retrieval, at least of the words taught.

Processing Speed

Processing speed, as assessed on the WJ III COG, is the ability to quickly scan and recognize visual symbols, designs, or pictures. These tests are time-limited. Although Brandon's responses were accurate on both tests, his scores were significantly different. His performance was age-appropriate when identifying the two digits that were the same, presented within rows of other digits (Visual Matching, RPI 92/90, PR 56). In contrast, his performance was just at the top of the mildly delayed range when asked to find the two pictures in a row that were most alike (Decision Speed, RPI 67/90, PR 9). One difference between the two tasks is that digits can be matched purely visually, whereas picture matching is conceptual. With Brandon's strong performance on the fluid reasoning tests, better performance on picture matching would be a reasonable expectation, so the likely critical difference would be his speed in considering the concepts represented in the pictures.

Although he has discrepant scores on the two tests within each cluster requiring speed of response, it would, at this time, be safe to assume that Brandon needs considerably extra time than other children of his age to express his thoughts, to generate answers to questions, and to recognize and organize visual information (e.g., pictures, letters, designs).

ACADEMIC SKILLS

Letter-Word Identification

Based on the results of the WJ III ACH, Brandon's proficiency in identifying letters and sight words is advanced (RPI 99/90, PR 72). To achieve these scores, however, he had only to recognize letters (e.g., point to *M*), name some letters, and "read" four primary-level sight words. His high performance is likely a result of his mother's focus and time spent with Brandon on letter games and practicing sight words. Consequently, this performance should not be considered indicative of his ease of future learning.

Spelling

Brandon was able to make some marks, trace some shapes, and write 5 uppercase letters. He was not able to spell a 2-sound, phonetically regular word. Although Brandon's scores would indicate that his spelling proficiency is delayed (RPI 36/90, PR 17), one should consider that Brandon just started kindergarten.

Calculation

Brandon does seem to be familiar with numbers and their meaning. His proficiency was advanced on the Calculation test (RPI 100/90, PR 99). He answered 10 items correctly, all but one of which were single-digit arithmetic facts—adding 1 or 2 to numbers of 6 or under, and subtracting 1 or 2 from numbers of 5 or under. He also solved one addition fact with a sum above 10. He counted on his fingers for almost all of the problems but used the concepts of adding-on for addition and counting up for subtraction.

Applied Problems

The earliest items of this test provide pictures to support addition and subtraction. Brandon was able to count up to four objects but was unable to mentally subtract from a set of objects. The subtraction problems were phrased as "if-then" questions, such as "If you gave away 3 of these cookies, how many would you have left?" He also missed a question that used a negative, such as, "How many dogs are not near the car," which he had also done on the Understanding Directions test. Brandon's RPI of 27/90 (PR 13) placed him near the lower end of mildly delayed, although language comprehension did seem to be involved in the errors he made on this test.

SUMMARY AND CONCLUSIONS

At the time of this evaluation, Brandon's expressive and receptive language performance fell significantly below expected limits on all standardized language measures so that he meets the *Diagnostic and Statistical Manual-IV-TR* criteria for mixed expressive-receptive language disorder. Brandon's functional language skills in real context, as per the SS/LS, supported these findings.

Autism and autism spectrum disorder can be ruled out at this time, which is in accord with the results of the ADOS and the CARS. Children with receptive language disorder do have difficulty with conversation because of the limited nature of auditory comprehension. This weakness in conversational ability can be mistaken as a symptom of Autism Spectrum Disorder, but in this case, the lack of response is a result of comprehension deficits rather than a reduced motivation for social communication (as seen in ASD). Brandon demonstrated appropriate social use of language and interaction within the limits of his language disorder. In the general education classroom, if Brandon is not able to understand the language used during instruction and during class discussions, his attention may certainly wane, leading his teachers to question whether or not he has a primary attentional deficit. He does not. Nonverbal cognitive performance was well above the typical range on the Leiter-R. In addition, estimates of fluid reasoning and visual-spatial thinking on both measures of cognitive abilities indicate that these aspects of cognitive ability are strong, so that global intellectual deficits can be ruled out.

Brandon does display significant weaknesses in some broad cognitive abilities including all aspects of memory assessed, phonemic awareness, and general knowledge, with probable significant weaknesses in word retrieval and processing speed. The confluence of these weaknesses will certainly cause him difficulty in many areas of learning, but most immediately, he is likely to have difficulty learning, retaining, and retrieving all information typically learned by rote, including letter-sound associations and math facts. He is also likely to have difficulty with blending and segmenting the sounds in words, as necessary for applying phonics to reading and spelling. With slow processing speed and word retrieval, he may have difficulty acquiring new sight words and automatizing all basic skills for use in higher-level academic applications. Because Brandon has good pragmatics and fluid reasoning, the severity of difficulty he is likely to have may be puzzling to his teachers despite knowledge of his language disorder. It is critical for them to be aware of these possibilities so that they will recognize that these difficulties are effects of his already diagnosed cognitive weaknesses and require immediate, specialized intervention.

With regard to special education eligibility, he continues to be eligible for services under the "speech and language disorders" criteria. As well, he will certainly require learning disability services for specialized instruction in reading and spelling, and possibly math.

RECOMMENDATIONS

Educational Placement

Educational placement should be in the general education classroom with special education services for both speech articulation and language disorders, and with consultative services of a learning disabilities specialist.

Oral Language

1. Brandon's parents should be instructed in recast techniques to continue to support Brandon's speech and language development within the home and other environments typical to Brandon's day. A recast is a response to a child's verbal initiation that adds grammar to his utterance. For example, if Brandon says "I want go store," a recast response could be "Oh, you want to go to the store now." Recasts affirm a child's immature verbal attempt and add in the deleted forms (in this case, an infinitive marker, a preposition, and an article). Brandon's atypical receptive language skills, above average nonverbal cognitive performance, and good pragmatic skills are all positive prognostic indicators.

2. Brandon's continued language development should be monitored periodically via the analysis of a spontaneous speech and language sample (SS/LS) every four to six months for a period of one year, and follow-up testing should be completed in one year.

3. Brandon's teachers should be apprised of the educational implications of his language disorder and the relative strengths and weaknesses in his cognitive and academic profile. They must be made aware that his performance is above average in some respects while simultaneously being significantly limited in other areas.

For the Teachers: Acquisition of Academic Concepts and Skills

General

1. When calling on Brandon in class, provide him with as much time as necessary to organize his thoughts and formulate a response. He may know the answer but need extra time to find the words. Privately, alert Brandon to this plan so that he does not feel pressured to come up with answers quickly.

2. In all learning, impaired memory is a concern. Brandon will be able to remember any new learning more effectively if he clearly understands the underlying concepts. This is true in math, reading, writing, and content areas.

3. When presenting information verbally, use accompanying visual images such as pictures, graphics (e.g., webs, charts, graphs), and videotapes. Enhancing auditory information may be as simple as drawing a sketch on the board to illustrate concepts such as contrasts, similarities, levels of importance, and cause-effect.

Phonemic Awareness, Reading, and Spelling

1. Initiating the following recommendations now will avoid failure, the accompanying problems in self-esteem, and the need to catch up later.

2. When introducing new phonological or phonemic awareness concepts, use real objects or manipulatives, and then pictures, before starting oral activities without the support of visual aids.

3. Brandon would gain optimal benefit from an instructional program in basic reading and spelling skills that is multisensory and systematic in introduction, practice, and reinforcement of phonemic awareness skills, phoneme-grapheme relationships, sight words, syllabication rules, structural analysis, and spelling rules. In a systematic program, skills are presented in graduated steps, from simple to complex, with students achieving mastery before the next skill is introduced. Practice assignments on the current skill incorporate previously learned skills, providing opportunities for the student to develop automaticity. Reading and spelling skills are taught simultaneously, so that the student learns how to spell every phonics generalization and word structure that he learns how to read. This type of program is called multisensory structure of language (MSSL). An example of such a program for young, beginning readers is Wilson Fundations, which also includes training

in handwriting. [See Appendix: Multisensory Structure of Language.] Other possible programs would include: S.P.I.R.E and Sounds Sensible (www.epsbooks.com), Phono-Graphix (www.readamerica.net), Sound Partners (www.sopriswest.com), or the Road to Reading (www.brookespublishing.com).

4. Do not use separate lists for reading and spelling. Focus Brandon's spelling practice on the phonics patterns he is learning within the reading program. Use a whole-word approach to teach spelling *only* for high-frequency sight words, and only as they come up in the systematic reading program. For whole-word spelling, use a multisensory method such as the Modified Fernald Technique to incorporate visual, oral/aural, and kinesthetic-tactile components. [See Appendix: Fernald Method for Reading and Spelling – Modified.]

5. With the possibility that Brandon has low processing speed, he would benefit from supplementary techniques to help him automatize orthographic skills such as recognizing common letter patterns and whole words. One technique offered here is reading speed drills, using any word elements on which Brandon requires extra practice as they come up in his reading program (e.g., sight words, syllable structures, letter patterns, and phonic elements). [See Appendix: Speed Drills for Reading Fluency and Basic Skills.]

Math

1. Demonstrate new concepts and ones that you are re-teaching with manipulatives and, to the extent possible, highlight any visual-spatial aspect. For example, one would teach regrouping in addition by using Base Ten Blocks on a place value mat to "trade up," and then introduce the digits associated with each column.

2. When Brandon has to memorize rote information, such as units of measurement, help him to create visual-auditory associations as memory aids. For example, 12 inches in a foot could be drawn as a footprint of a bare foot with 12 inchworms end to end crawling across it. Three feet to a yard is illustrated as a fenced lawn with three footprints across it.

Attachments

Multisensory Structure of Language

Speed Drills for Reading Fluency and Basic Skills

Fernald Method for Reading and Spelling—Modified

Addition Fact Memorization: Organizational Structures

Addition and Multiplication Facts: Instructional Sequence

SCORES

Standard scores have a mean of 100 and a standard deviation of 15.

Scaled scores have a mean of 10 and a standard deviation of 3.

Leiter International Performance Scale—Revised

Quotient	Standard Score
Brief	137
Fluid Reasoning	112

Autism Diagnostic Observation Scale

Communication Total	2
Social Interaction	2
Communication + Social Interaction	4

Childhood Autism Rating Scale: Total score: 17 (non-autistic range)

Test of Auditory Comprehension of Language, Third Edition

Subtest	Percentile Rank	Scaled Score	Standard Score
Vocabulary	5	5	
Grammatical Morphemes	1	3	
Elaborated Phrases and Sentences	2	4	
TACL-4 Quotient	<1		61

Preschool Language Scale, Fourth Edition

	Percentile Rank	Standard Score
Auditory Comprehension	3	72
Expressive Communication	2	68
Total Language	2	70

Table of Scores

Woodcock-Johnson III Normative Update Tests of Cognitive Abilities and Tests of Achievement
(Form A), WJ III NU Compuscore and Profiles Program, Version 3.0
COG norms based on age 5–8; ACH norms based on age 5–9

Bolded clusters indicate that the component tests have overlapping bands; consequently, the cluster may be interpreted as a unitary ability.

CLUSTER/Test	Raw	W	AE	Proficiency	RPI	SS (68% Band)	PR
GIA (Ext)	–	464	5–1	lmtd to avg	81/90	89 (87–91)	23
Analysis-Synthesis	18–D	487	7–8	advanced	99/90	124 (119–128)	94
Concept Formation	18–E	488	8–0	advanced	99/90	120 (117–124)	91
Spatial Relations	58–D	495	8–0	avg to adv	97/90	114 (110–118)	83
Picture Recognition	21–B	487	6–5	average	93/90	106 (98–114)	65
Visual Matching	15–2	460	5–10	average	92/90	102 (98–106)	56
Numbers Reversed	4	435	5–3	limited	61/90	92 (88–97)	31
Memory for Words	10	447	4–2	limited	45/90	87 (83–91)	19
Retrieval Fluency	19	487	4–3	average	84/90	85 (77–92)	16
Verbal Sound Blending	7	466	3–10	limited	57/90	84 (79–89)	14
Comprehension	–	444	3–10	limited	59/90	79 (71–86)	8
Decision Speed	5	458	4–2	limited	67/90	79 (74–84)	9
Visual-Auditory Learning	57–D	463	3–5	limited	59/90	74 (70–78)	4
Auditory Attention	14	466	3–5	limited	55/90	73 (67–78)	3
General Information	–	437	3–0	limited	29/90	72 (66–78)	3
VERBAL ABILITY (Ext)	**–**	**441**	**3–3**	**limited**	**43/90**	**72 (67–77)**	**3**
COMP-KNOWLEDGE (Gc)	**–**	**441**	**3–3**	**limited**	**43/90**	**72 (67–77)**	**3**
Verbal Comprehension	–	444	3–10	limited	59/90	79 (71–86)	8
General Information	–	437	3–0	limited	29/90	72 (66–78)	3
COG EFFICIENCY (Ext)	–	450	5–0	lmtd to avg	70/90	86 (83–90)	18
Visual Matching	15–2	460	5–10	average	92/90	102 (98–106)	56
Numbers Reversed	4	435	5–3	limited	61/90	92 (88–97)	31
Decision Speed	5	458	4–2	limited	67/90	79 (74–84)	9
Memory for Words	10	447	4–2	limited	45/90	87 (83–91)	19
L-T RETRIEVAL (Glr)	**–**	**475**	**3–8**	**lmtd to avg**	**73/90**	**72 (67–76)**	**3**
Visual-Auditory Learning	57–D	463	3–5	limited	59/90	74 (70–78)	4
Retrieval Fluency	19	487	4–3	average	84/90	85 (77–92)	16
VIS-SPATIAL THINK (Gv)	**–**	**491**	**7–1**	**avg to adv**	**95/90**	**113 (107–119)**	**81**
Spatial Relations	58–D	495	8–0	avg to adv	97/90	114 (110–118)	83
Picture Recognition	21–B	487	6–5	average	93/90	106 (98–114)	65
AUDITORY PROCESS (Ga)	–	466	3–7	limited	56/90	75 (71–80)	5
Auditory Attention	14	466	3–5	limited	55/90	73 (67–78)	3
Sound Blending	7	466	3–10	limited	57/90	84 (79–89)	14
FLUID REASONING (Gf)	**–**	**487**	**7–10**	**advanced**	**99/90**	**124 (121–127)**	**95**
Concept Formation	18–E	488	8–0	advanced	99/90	120 (117–124)	91
Analysis-Synthesis	18–D	487	7–8	advanced	99/90	124 (119–128)	94

(continued)

CLUSTER/Test	Raw	W	AE	Proficiency	RPI	SS (68% Band)	PR
PROCESS SPEED (Gs)	–	459	5–2	average	82/90	91 (87–94)	27
Decision Speed	5	458	4–2	limited	67/90	79 (74–84)	9
Visual Matching	15–2	460	5–10	average	92/90	102 (98–106)	56
SHORT-TERM MEM (Gsm)	**–**	**441**	**4–11**	**limited**	**53/90**	**86 (82–91)**	**18**
Numbers Reversed	4	435	5–3	limited	61/90	92 (88–97)	31
Memory for Words	10	447	4–2	limited	45/90	87 (83–91)	19
PHONEMIC AWARE	**–**	**468**	**3–8**	**limited**	**59/90**	**75 (70–81)**	**5**
Sound Blending	7	466	3–10	limited	57/90	84 (79–89)	14
Incomplete Words	7	471	3–6	limited	61/90	76 (68–83)	5
WORKING MEMORY	–	439	4–10	limited	51/90	85 (79–90)	15
Numbers Reversed	4	435	5–3	limited	61/90	92 (88–97)	31
Auditory Working Memory	1	442	<4–8	limited	42/90	79 (71–88)	9
KNOWLEDGE	**–**	**433**	**3–3**	**limited**	**24/90**	**68 (64–73)**	**2**
General Information	–	437	3–0	limited	29/90	72 (66–78)	3
Academic Knowledge	–	429	3–7	v limited	21/90	73 (69–78)	4
ORAL LANGUAGE (Ext)	**–**	**458**	**3–9**	**limited**	**59/90**	**77 (74–81)**	**7**
Oral Comprehension	4	445	3–7	limited	52/90	83 (78–89)	14
Understanding Directions	–	453	4–0	limited	54/90	75 (69–80)	4
Story Recall	–	478	3–1	lmtd to avg	72/90	76 (65–86)	5
Picture Vocabulary	12	456	3–11	limited	58/90	84 (79–90)	14
BRIEF MATH	–	435	6–2	avg to adv	97/90	110 (106–114)	75
Calculation	10	472	7–7	v advanced	100/90	134 (130–139)	99
Applied Problems	10	398	4–5	limited	27/90	83 (80–87)	13
ACADEMIC SKILLS	–	416	6–2	advanced	98/90	111 (108–113)	76
Letter-Word Identification	19	388	6–3	advanced	99/90	109 (106–112)	73
Spelling	9	389	5–0	limited	36/90	86 (81–91)	17
Calculation	10	472	7–7	v advanced	100/90	134 (130–139)	99
PRE-ACADEMIC (Ext)	–	412	5–0	limited	59/90	86 (84–89)	18
Letter-Word Identification	19	388	6–3	advanced	99/90	109 (106–112)	73
Spelling	9	389	5–0	limited	36/90	86 (81–91)	17
Applied Problems	10	398	4–5	limited	27/90	83 (80–87)	13
Picture Vocabulary	12	456	3–11	limited	58/90	84 (79–90)	14
Academic Knowledge	–	429	3–7	v limited	21/90	73 (69–78)	4
Concept Formation	18–E	488	8–0	advanced	99/90	120 (117–124)	91
Analysis-Synthesis	18–D	487	7–8	advanced	99/90	124 (119–128)	94
Spatial Relations	58–D	495	8–0	avg to adv	97/90	114 (110–118)	83
Picture Recognition	20–B	484	5–10	average	91/90	101 (94–109)	53
Verbal Comprehension	–	444	3–10	limited	59/90	79 (71–86)	8
General Information	–	437	3–0	limited	29/90	72 (66–78)	3
Visual-Auditory Learning	57–D	463	3–5	limited	59/90	74 (70–78)	4
Retrieval Fluency	21	488	4–7	average	86/90	89 (81–96)	23
Auditory Attention	14	466	3–5	limited	55/90	73 (67–78)	3

CLUSTER/Test	Raw	W	AE	Proficiency	RPI	SS (68% Band)	PR
Sound Blending	7	466	3–10	limited	57/90	84 (79–89)	14
Incomplete Words	7	471	3–6	limited	61/90	76 (68–83)	5
Numbers Reversed	4	435	5–3	limited	61/90	92 (88–97)	31
Auditory Working Memory	1	442	<4–8	limited	42/90	79 (71–88)	9
Memory for Words	10	447	4–2	limited	45/90	87 (83–91)	19
Decision Speed	5	458	4–2	limited	67/90	79 (74–84)	9
Visual Matching	15–2	460	5–10	average	92/90	102 (98–106)	56
Rapid Picture Naming	43	458	3–11	limited	60/90	82 (80–84)	11
Oral Comprehension	4	445	3–7	limited	52/90	83 (78–89)	14
Understanding Directions	–	451	3–10	limited	49/90	72 (66–78)	3
Story Recall	–	478	3–1	lmtd to avg	72/90	76 (65–86)	5
Picture Vocabulary	12	456	3–11	limited	58/90	84 (79–90)	14
Letter-Word Identification	19	388	6–3	advanced	99/90	109 (106–112)	73
Spelling	9	389	5–0	limited	36/90	86 (81–91)	17
Calculation	10	472	7–7	v advanced	100/90	134 (130–139)	99
Applied Problems	10	398	4–5	limited	27/90	83 (8087)	13
Academic Knowledge	–	429	3–7	v limited	21/90	73 (69–78)	4

VARIATIONS	STANDARD SCORES			VARIATION		Significant at + or – 1.50 SD (SEE)
	Actual	Predicted	Difference	PR	SD	
Intra-Cognitive (Ext)						
COMP-KNOWLEDGE (Gc)	**72**	**94**	**–22**	**2**	**–1.98**	**Yes**
L-T RETRIEVAL (Glr)	**72**	**94**	**–22**	**1**	**–2.28**	**Yes**
VIS-SPATIAL THINK (Gv)	**113**	**93**	**20**	**94**	**+1.55**	**Yes**
AUDITORY PROCESS (Ga)	75	95	–20	5	–1.66	Yes
FLUID REASONING (Gf)	**124**	**85**	**39**	**> 99.9**	**+3.45**	**Yes**
PROCESS SPEED (Gs)	91	94	–3	41	–0.23	No
SHORT-TERM MEM (Gsm)	**86**	**93**	**–7**	**29**	**–0.54**	**No**
PHONEMIC AWARE	**75**	**95**	**–20**	**6**	**–1.57**	**Yes**
WORKING MEMORY	85	93	–8	24	–0.70	No

DISCREPANCIES	STANDARD SCORES			DISCREPANCY		Significant at – 1.50 SD (SEE)
	Actual	Predicted	Difference	PR	SD	
Intellectual Ability/Achievement Discrepancies*						
ORAL LANGUAGE (Ext)	**77**	**90**	**–13**	**7**	**–1.48**	**No**
ORAL EXPRESSION	**79**	**92**	**–13**	**12**	**–1.19**	**No**
LISTENING COMP	**78**	**91**	**–13**	**9**	**–1.33**	**No**
ACADEMIC KNOWLEDGE	**73**	**91**	**–18**	**6**	**–1.54**	**Yes**
BRIEF MATH	110	92	18	95	+1.65	No

*These discrepancies compare WJ III GIA (Ext) with Broad, Basic, Brief, and Applied ACH clusters.

(*continued*)

DISCREPANCIES	STANDARD SCORES			DISCREPANCY		Significant at − 1.50 SD (SEE)
	Actual	Predicted	Difference	PR	SD	
Oral Language/Achievement Discrepancies*						
ACADEMIC KNOWLEDGE	73	83	−10	20	−0.83	No
BRIEF MATH	110	89	21	94	+1.52	No
*These discrepancies compare Oral Language (Ext) with Broad, Basic, and Brief ACH clusters.						

DISCREPANCIES	STANDARD SCORES			DISCREPANCY		Significant at + or − 1.50 SD (SEE)
	Actual	Predicted	Difference	PR	SD	
Predicted Achievement/Achievement Discrepancies*						
ORAL LANGUAGE (Ext)	77	97	−20	4	−1.72	Yes
ORAL EXPRESSION	79	95	−16	10	−1.27	No
LISTENING COMP	78	98	−20	3	−1.86	Yes
ACADEMIC KNOWLEDGE	73	85	−12	17	−0.97	No
BRIEF MATH	110	95	15	90	+1.31	No
*These discrepancies compare predicted achievement scores with Broad, Basic, Brief, and Applied ACH clusters.						

DISCREPANCIES	STANDARD SCORES			DISCREPANCY		Significant at + or − 1.50 SD (SEE)
	Actual	Predicted	Difference	PR	SD	
GIA Std/Cognitive						
COMP-KNOWLEDGE (Gc)	72	94	−22	1	−2.22	Yes
L-T RETRIEVAL (Glr)	72	94	−22	1	−2.40	Yes
VIS-SPATIAL THINK (Gv)	113	96	17	90	+1.31	No
AUDITORY PROCESS (Ga)	75	95	−20	3	−1.81	Yes
FLUID REASONING (Gf)	124	93	31	>99.9	+3.27	**Yes**
PROCESS SPEED (Gs)	91	96	−5	34	−0.42	No
SHORT-TERM MEM (Gsm)	86	94	−8	21	**−0.81**	**No**
PHONEMIC AWARE	75	95	−20	5	**−1.66**	**Yes**
WORKING MEMORY	85	94	−9	16	−0.98	No

Woodcock-Johnson III Strengths and Weaknesses Comparison—Based on Relative Proficiency Indexes

CLUSTERS/Tests		
Delayed	**Age Appropriate**	**Advanced**
KNOWLEDGE	VISUAL-SPATIAL THINK	FLUID REASONING
SHORT-TERM MEMORY		BASIC READING SKILLS
LONG-TERM RETRIEVAL		
VERBAL ABIL/COMPRE-KNOWLEDGE		
PHONEMIC AWARENESS		
ORAL LANGUAGE		
Verbal Comprehension	Spatial Relations	Concept Formation
General Information	Picture Recognition	Analysis-Synthesis
Visual-Auditory Learning	Retrieval Fluency	
Auditory Attention		
Sound Blending		
Incomplete Words		
Numbers Reversed		
Auditory Working Memory		
Memory for Words		
Decision Speed	Visual Matching	
Rapid Picture Naming		
Oral Comprehension		
Understanding Directions		
Story Recall		
Picture Vocabulary		
Spelling		Letter-Word Identification
Applied Problems		Calculation

CASE 5

Comorbidity and Cumulative Effects of Inattention, Poor Emotional Control, and Language Problems on Academic Achievement in Early Childhood

Randy Kamphaus and Tara Raines

The report of Clara Mays illustrates the psychoeducational assessment of a student who is demonstrating social-emotional challenges, issues regarding attention, and a language impairment. She recently transferred from another school district with an established declaration of special education eligibility. In her case, as with many school-based psychological evaluations, obtaining important, specific background information was a challenge. Although Clara was identified as a student with disabilities impacting her educational performance, access to previous psychological reports, medical history, and developmental information was limited at the time of the evaluation. This lack of data occurs often in school psychology practice. As with Clara, her mother was also transient as a child, spending much of her childhood in the custody of various family members. To compensate for this absent information, the psychologist selected a battery of assessment methods that provided information regarding the student's global functioning within the scope of the referral, anticipating that additional testing could then be conducted. Assessment instruments were selected to ensure that important domains of functioning were covered including cognitive, social-emotional, and academic achievement. Second, the instruments had accumulated a body of consistent evidence to support the validity of score inferences for children with a history of ADHD.

Overall intellectual integrity was seen as necessary to assess (hence the Kaufman Assessment Battery for Children, Second Edition [KABC-II]) in order to rule out significant cognitive impairment that may be adversely affecting Clara's academic achievement. Due to her history of emotional and behavioral problems, the Behavior Assessment System for Children, Second Edition (BASC-2), the most comprehensive of such diagnostic tools available, was chosen to assess

her adjustment across a variety of contexts. Portions of the Children's Self-Report Projective Inventory (CSRPI) were administered to obtain additional information regarding Clara's self-perceptions and perceptions of others, rather than assess her intrapsychic (i.e., defense mechanisms, conflicts, and other constructs associated with psychodynamic theory and the "projective hypothesis" that emanates from this theoretical perspective) adjustment per se. Additionally, instruments were selected because they are both visually engaging and stimulating when compared to other batteries that are used to assess similar constructs and processes. This battery was selected by the psychologist in order to avoid Clara reaching her frustration level and to maximize her engagement throughout the session.

Both Clara's cognitive development and academic achievement results are considered tentative, and potentially variable, depending on the context, at this time, given the apparent effects of her attention problems. It was deemed advisable, given that emotional and behavioral problems are paramount, to assess cognitive development and academic adjustment in the everyday context of her learning at school, by recommending further classroom academic testing across curriculum area, time of day, and other variables. This information will be prerequisite to formulating an aggressive educational intervention plan.

Observations, diagnostic impressions, and parent accounts of developmental, social, and medical history were all considered in making diagnostic decisions. Due to limited background information, information from the BASC-2 and school personnel reports was used as primary data for making the *DSM-IV-TR* diagnostic decisions.

Reading this report should not only assist evaluators in developing the rationale for various interventions when a limited history is available, but also in developing proper justification for a more detailed, comprehensive assessment in such cases. Additionally, the report is written at a readability level that allows parents and teachers easy access and understanding of the information provided. The recommendations are formatted in a manner that will allow school-based teams to integrate them easily into Clara's educational plan, monitor her progress, and foster collaboration across home and school settings.

PSYCHOLOGICAL REPORT

Name:	Clara Mays
Date of Birth:	1/2/2004
Age:	6-4
School:	Lincoln Elementary School
Grade:	Kindergarten
Dates of Evaluation:	5/4, 5/6/2010
Psychology Intern:	Tara C. Raines, Psy.S.
Psychologist:	R. W. Kamphaus, Ph.D.

INSTRUMENTS ADMINISTERED

Kaufman Assessment Battery for Children, Second Edition (KABC-II)

Developmental Test of Visual-Motor Integration, Fifth Edition (Beery VMI)

Kaufman Test of Educational Achievement, Second Edition (KTEA-II)

Behavior Assessment System for Children-2-Parent Rating Scale-C (6-11) (BASC-2-PRS-C)

Behavior Assessment System for Children-2-Teacher Rating Scale-C (6-11) (BASC-2-TRS-C)

Behavior Assessment System for Children-2-Self-Report-C (6-7) (BASC-2-SRP-I)

Children's Self-Report and Projective Inventory (CSRPI)

Review of records

Interview

CONSULTATIONS

Teacher: Mrs. Eklund

Parent: Ms. Miller

REFERRAL REASON

Clara was referred for a psychological evaluation to help determine her eligibility for special education services. Clara recently moved from California to Georgia, where she received special education services under the categories of Developmental Delay and Speech-Language Impairment.

BACKGROUND INFORMATION

Information was gathered from a review of records and an interview with Clara's mother, Ms. Bridget Miller. Clara is a 6-year-old Caucasian female who currently lives with her mother and brother, age 12. According to Clara's mother, she only dated Clara's biological father for a brief period of time and thus has little information about him. Clara just moved into her mother's household 6 months ago, after previously living with her maternal grandparents in California who were granted court-appointed custody for approximately 2 years. Ms. Miller provided appropriate documentation of custody and declined to discuss the circumstances of Clara's placement with her grandparents. Ms. Miller described Clara's relationships with her and her older brother as optimal at the present time.

Ms. Miller reports Clara was the product of an uncomplicated pregnancy and delivery. As an infant, Clara suffered from colic, frequent ear infections, and feeding difficulties. Developmental history suggests that milestones were met within normal time limits. Available medical history indicates Clara has a previous diagnosis of Attention-Deficit/Hyperactivity Disorder (ADHD), and currently takes Adderall (dosage unknown). Ms. Miller reported that a diagnostic evaluation resulting in special education placement was done while Clara was in the custody of her grandparents. She was unable to provide previous psychological reports. Additionally, Clara suffers from seasonal allergies and takes medication for these as needed.

Clara's educational history includes some preschool experience in California. However, her mother reported that Clara cried for hours at preschool so she stopped making her go. Clara's mother also reported that she has moved approximately nine times since Clara's birth. Ms. Miller reports that she and Clara's brother have both been diagnosed with Bipolar Disorder.

Clara began kindergarten in California in August 2009. She entered the San Diego Unified School District in

November 2009, where she enrolled at San Pedro Elementary School. She transferred to Lincoln Elementary School in Atlanta in February 2010. Clara's current kindergarten teacher reported that Clara has difficulty maintaining focus, requires frequent redirection to complete tasks, and has difficulty controlling impulses. On days when she has not taken her medication, she hits, kicks, growls, and crawls under the table. When engaging in these behaviors, she sometimes remarks that she is pretending to be a dog. Clara is unable to attend to instruction and does not comply with teacher requests when her behavior is this severe. Both her mother and current teacher agree that these behaviors interfere with Clara's learning, and as a result, she has made very little to no progress in all academic areas.

Clara passed the school district vision screening on March 4, 2010. However, she failed the hearing screening because she replied "no" every time a tone was played. Clara was tested again on March 6, 2010, by the audiologist who determined that Clara's hearing was within normal limits and sufficient for educational and psychological evaluation.

TEST BEHAVIOR AND OBSERVATIONS

Clara was assessed in two sessions. She readily accompanied the psychologist to the testing area each time. She appeared to be relaxed and comfortable in the testing environment as evidenced by her relaxed posture in the chair and by the ease at which she entered into, initiated, and maintained conversation with the examiner. During a rapport building interview, when asked about her favorite food, Clara indicated that she likes corn dogs with syrup. She also told the examiner she enjoys watching television and playing with her Barbie doll. Rapport with Clara was easily established and effectively maintained throughout both assessment sessions.

Clara attended to oral instructions and was able to carry out tasks as instructed such as pointing to items, drawing, or completing pencil-and-paper tasks. She responded without hesitation to items that were less challenging, and when faced with more challenging tasks, she would, at times, respond impulsively, apparently without due deliberation. At other times, she would take considerable time to formulate her response. During easier tasks, Clara sang and bounced in her seat. When presented with more difficult items, Clara made frequent somatic complaints, claiming that her arms were getting tired from pointing, and that her legs, stomach, and toe hurt. Clara also rubbed her eyes and said, "Do I have to do another one?" on one

task and that she was "too starving" to continue during another portion of the testing. However, with verbal praise and encouragement from the examiner, Clara was able to complete all test items.

According to her teacher, these types of behaviors are typical for Clara. Therefore, overall test results are considered to be an accurate estimate of current functioning.

TEST RESULTS AND INTERPRETATION

Cognitive

Intelligence, for purposes of this report, refers to an individual's developed cognitive abilities, meaning that Clara has acquired a certain level of cognitive ability that serves as one set of competencies that is important for school success, others being motivation, quality of schooling, and so on. Although estimates of intelligence are relatively stable, some individuals do show significant changes over the course of development. In addition, although not common, some individuals are able to achieve at high levels, beyond what would be expected based on their intelligence test results. Thus, these results should be viewed as merely suggestive of future potential while realizing that prediction is always fallible.

The KABC-II is an individually administered measure of intelligence and processing for children and adolescents ages 3 to 18. The KABC-II is organized into three age levels yielding from one to five scales. In Clara's case, the KABC-II measures a range of abilities including Sequential Processing (short-term memory), Simultaneous Processing (visual processing), Learning (long-term storage and retrieval), and Knowledge, which, combined, make up an overall Fluid/Crystallized Index (FCI).

Range of Standard Scores	Descriptive Category
131 or greater	Upper Extreme
116–130	Above Average
85–115	Average
70–84	Below Average
69 or less	Lower Extreme

According to this administration of the KABC-II, Clara's FCI of 90 is within the Average range. This score falls at the 25th percentile for her age. This estimate of overall cognitive ability is within normal expectations for her chronological age. Overall, the various scores yielded by this measure suggest average intelligence.

Index scores are presented as standard scores (SS) with a mean of 100 and a standard deviation of 15. Approximately two thirds of the population obtains scores between 85 and 115 and about 95 percent obtain scores between 70 and 130. Percentile ranks (PR) have a mean of 50. Percentile ranks between 15 and 84 are in the Average range.

Kaufman Assessment Battery for Children, Second Edition

KABC-II Indexes	Index Score	PR	Classification
Sequential	80	9	Below Average
Simultaneous	91	27	Average
Learning	94	34	Average
Knowledge	107	68	Average

Sequential processing involves solving problems by arranging information in a step-by-step, sequential or serial fashion. Subtests composing this index involve short-term memory and the use of auditory and/or visual information. Clara's score on the Sequential Index was in the Below Average range.

Simultaneous processing refers to solving problems by integrating several pieces of information at once and conceptualizing it as a whole. It also involves perceiving, storing, manipulating, and thinking with visual stimuli. Subtests within this index also measure visual-spatial reasoning. Clara's score on the Simultaneous Index was in the Average range.

The Learning Index measures the ability to efficiently store, retrieve, and recall information. Clara's score on the Learning Index was in the Average range.

The Knowledge Index provides a measure of accumulated information including factual knowledge and verbal concepts. Clara's score on the Knowledge Index was in the Average range.

Graphomotor

Visual-motor functioning, as measured by the Developmental Test of Visual-Motor Integration-5, a paper-and-pencil measure of visual-motor skills, was in the Low range for Clara's chronological age (SS = 71, PR = 3). Clara's difficulty on this task seemed primarily to be the result of a haphazard and impulsive approach to the tasks involving attention-concentration factors, as well as inadequate integration of perceptual and fine-motor skills.

Academic

The Kaufman Test of Educational Achievement, Second Edition (KTEA-II), was administered to assess Clara's current level of academic knowledge. Scores on this instrument are presented in terms of standard scores with a mean of 100 and a standard deviation of 15. The achievement testing yielded the following results.

Kaufman Test of Educational Achievement, Second Edition

	SS	Composite	PR
Letter & Word Recognition	95	–	37
Math Concepts & Application	85	–	16
Math Computation	81	–	10
Math Composite	–	80	9
Written Expression	108	–	70
Listening Comprehension	99	–	47
Oral Expression	82	–	12
Oral Language Composite	–	88	21
Comprehensive Achievement	–	100	50

Clara performed in the Average range in the areas of letter and word recognition, written expression, and listening comprehension, and in the Below Average range in the areas of mathematics and oral expression. However, Clara's performance in the classroom is significantly below expectations based on the current measures of intelligence and academic achievement. Clara's teacher reported that she has difficulties with blending individual sounds to read one-syllable words and problems applying phonics skills when reading words and sentences. Clara has difficulties retelling stories and remembering important events in a story. In mathematics, Clara has difficulty sequencing steps for problem solving and continues to struggle with one-to-one correspondence. Her numbers are inadequately spaced and formed incorrectly. Clara also has problems communicating her ideas in writing. She is unable to write complete sentences, use appropriate punctuation or capitalization, or read her own written work.

Social-Emotional

Social-emotional assessment is the evaluation of an individual's social relations, behavioral problems, behavioral competencies, coping strategies, and self-perceptions. The present assessment is based on information gathered from teacher and parent reports, individual personality assessment, self-report measures, and interview.

Rating Scales: Behavior Assessment System for Children, Second Edition (BASC-2)

The BASC-2 is a multimethod, multidimensional system used to evaluate the behavior and self-perceptions of children and young adults aged 2 to 25 years. Rating scales are available for completion by teachers, parents, and/or students themselves. Scores are reported in terms of T scores with a mean of 50 and a standard deviation of 10.

The Teacher Rating Scale (TRS) is a comprehensive measure of both adaptive and problem behaviors observed in the school setting. The TRS evaluates the broad domains of Externalizing Problems, Internalizing Problems, and School Problems, and also measures Adaptive Skills. The TRS has two scales (Learning Problems and Study Skills) that are not measured by the Parent Rating Scale and are relevant only to the school setting.

The PRS is a comprehensive measure of adaptive and problem behaviors observed by parents at home and in the community. The PRS assesses most of the clinical and adaptive skills domains that the TRS measures. In addition, the PRS includes a scale (Activities of Daily Living) that the TRS does not measure.

The Self-Report of Personality (SRP) is a personality inventory completed by children, adolescents, and young adults themselves on forms appropriate for their age level.

This report is based on their perceptions of their personality, their behavior, and the ways in which they believe others regard them.

The following chart is provided as a guide to T score interpretation:

Clinical Scales		Adaptive Scales	
70+	Clinically Significant	70+	Very High
60–69	At-Risk	60–69	High
41–59	Average	41–59	Average
31–40	Low	31–40	At-Risk
30 and below	Very Low	30 and below	Clinically Significant

Based on observations and related information presented in this report, which supports the presence of maladaptive behaviors, it is likely that Clara's teachers and parent were being forthright and candid in describing observations of Clara's behavior and that the ratings represent an accurate assessment of Clara's social-emotional functioning.

Clara's mother reported clinically significant scores in the areas of hyperactivity, anxiety, depression, somatization, atypicality, and activities of daily living, and scores in the At-Risk range in the areas of aggression and attention problems. Clara's previous teacher rated her behavior in the clinically significant range in the areas of hyperactivity, somatization, attention problems, learning problems, and school problems, and rated her behavior in the At-Risk range in the areas of atypicality, adaptability, social skills, leadership, and study skills. Scores for Conduct Problems,

BASC-2 Scales	Description	Parent	Teacher 1	Teacher 2
Behavioral Symptoms Index	Overall rating of the individual's behavior	86**	88**	63*
Externalizing Problems		85**	86**	55
Hyperactivity	Tendency to be overly active, rush through work, and act w/out thinking	96**	87**	70*
Aggression	Tendency to act in a hostile manner (either verbal or physical) that is threatening to others	68*	82**	45
Conduct Problems	Tendency to demonstrate rule-breaking behavior	–	–	49
Internalizing Problems		87**	60*	58
Anxiety	Tendency to be nervous, fearful, or worried about real/imagined problems	76**	55	43
Depression	Feelings of unhappiness, sadness, stress that may result in an inability to carry out everyday activities	85**	75**	53
Somatization	Tendency to be overly sensitive to and complain about relatively minor physical problems or discomforts	73**	44	73**

(*continued*)

BASC-2 Scales	Description	Parent	Teacher 1	Teacher 2
School Problems				76**
Attention Problems	Tendency to be easily distracted and unable to concentrate more than momentarily	69**	75**	71**
Learning Problems	The presence of academic difficulties, particularly understanding or completing work	–	–	76**
Additional Clinical Scales				
Atypicality	Tendency to behave in ways that are considered strange, such as being disconnected from or unaware of normal surroundings	93**	89**	69**
Withdrawal	Tendency to evade others to avoid social contact	51	64*	55
Adaptive Skills				
Adaptability	The ability to readily adapt to changes in the environment	34*	30*	36*
Social Skills	Skills needed to interact successfully with peers/adults in home, school, and community settings	41	35*	37*
Leadership	The skills associated with accomplishing academic, social, or community goals, including the ability to work with others	–	–	36*
Functional Communication	The ability to express ideas and communicate in ways others can easily understand	31*	29**	40*
Activities of Daily Living	The skills associated with performing basic, everyday tasks in an acceptable and safe manner	26**	–	–

**Indicates areas of clinical significance
*Indicates areas at risk

Learning Problems, and Leadership are not reported because Clara was 5 years old at the time of the first behavior ratings, and these scales are not included in the assessment of 5-year-olds. Clara's current teacher rated her behavior in the clinically significant range in the areas of somatization, attention problems, and learning problems, and in the At-Risk range in the areas of hyperactivity, atypicality, adaptability, social skills, leadership, study skills, and functional communication. Although some disagreement exists between Clara's teachers, overall the ratings of Clara's behavior from her mother and teachers indicate that she has significant difficulty maintaining self-control and becomes easily upset, angry, or frustrated. She has a tendency to react negatively to changes in her environment and has difficulty controlling her behavior and emotions. Clara also has problems with social skills and communication, which may impact her relationships with peers and adults.

Clara was assessed using the BASC-2 Self-Report of Personality Interview for Children. She rated herself in the At-Risk range for Attitude to Teachers and Atypicality and in the Clinically Significant range for Social Stress, Anxiety, and Depression. Although Clara perceives herself in the Average range for Attitude to School (i.e., she likes coming to school) and Interpersonal Relations (i.e., she gets along

BASC-2 Scales – SRP	Description	Self-Report
Emotional Symptoms Index	Overall indicator of current emotional adjustment	69*
Attitude to School	General opinion of the usefulness of school, along with comfort level with school-related matters	56
Attitude to Teachers	Perception of teachers as being uncaring, unfair, or overly demanding	69*
Atypicality	Unusual thoughts, perceptions, and behaviors	62*
Social Stress	The level of stress experienced by children in relation to their interactions with peers and others	71**
Anxiety	Feelings of nervousness, worry, and fear; the tendency to be overwhelmed by problems	73**
Depression	Feelings of loneliness, sadness, and inability to enjoy life	72**

well with peers), her responses on the scales for Attitude to Teachers and Social Stress indicate that she often perceives that others are making fun of her or are "out to get her," and often feels lonely or left out. This is likely to impact Clara's ability to make and maintain friendships in the classroom. Clara also reported frequent feelings of anxiety and depression (she "worries a lot" and feels sad most of the time), which are likely to interfere with her concentration and impact her performance in the classroom.

Children's Self-Report and Projective Inventory

Clara also completed portions of the Children's Self-Report and Projective Inventory. The examiner was unable to complete administration of this instrument due to Clara's limited attention to the tasks. One task on this instrument required Clara to color her feelings using various color crayons she was explicitly taught represented a particular feeling. Clara was asked to explain her use of color during this activity; she stated that her head makes her mad and she worries about "being bad all the time." Clara also expressed that she is sad when she does "something bad." When asked to use the colors to describe how she feels around others, she indicated she feels mad when her mom yells at her. When using the red crayon to express this anger, Clara used more pressure than on her other colorings. She volunteered that she was drawing her mother "dark" because she is "really angry." She also stated that she is nervous that people will see her with her mom. However, she used the indicator for "happy" to describe the majority of her feelings toward her mother. In contrast, she used only the color indicated for anger to describe her feelings for her teacher, Ms. Eklund, and her brother. Clara indicated that Ms. Eklund takes her to the principal's office too much and that she never believes her. Clara also explained that her brother hates her and tortures her. She was unable to explain what she meant by "torture" when probed.

In addition, as a part of this instrument, Clara was asked to draw herself in the rain. She stated that she wanted to "start with the background." She then proceeded to impulsively draw long strokes of rain and struck the paper with the tip of the pencil lead making dots between the strokes. Then she inserted a stick figure with no face and traced the outline of the stick figure. She indicated that the figure was her and the outline was her raincoat. When asked to draw a picture of her family doing something together, Clara hastily drew two faceless stick figures sitting. She indicated that it was her and her brother playing video games in the basement. She then drew a horizontal line to divide the page and drew four faceless stick figures on top of the line. She stated that those figures represent her mom, her mom's boyfriend, Pat, and Bill in the kitchen drinking beer. She revealed that Pat and Bill were neighbors who often come over to her home.

During the sentence completion portion of this instrument, Clara reported that her biggest problem is "mean people" and that she gets "sad" when her mother yells at her. She also said that she gets "mad" because people tease her at school. After some hesitation, Clara stated that one thing she does not do well is "being quiet," she does not understand why she has to obey teachers, and her life would be better if she had a new Barbie doll.

CONCLUSIONS AND RECOMMENDATIONS

Clara is a 6-year-old kindergarten student referred for a school-based psychological evaluation. Clara moved to Georgia from California where she received special education services for significant developmental delays in social-emotional development and speech-language impairment. She currently lives with her mother and 12-year-old brother.

With regard to cognitive abilities, Clara's overall level of development is within the average range. Clara's performance was also in the average range on standardized measures of academic achievement; however, teacher report and analyzed work samples suggest she is currently performing below grade level in the classroom. Based on functional behavioral assessments and data collected throughout this evaluation, it is evident that Clara's emotional state and her ability to pay attention and control her behavior interfere with her ability to learn in the classroom. Clara's difficulty with inhibiting behavioral responses impacts her ability to develop and maintain satisfactory relationships with peers and adults. Additionally, Clara consistently displays behavior problems that are outside the normal range compared to same-age peers.

The previous diagnosis of Attention-Deficit/Hyperactivity Disorder, Combined Type was confirmed by this evaluation.

DSM-IV-TR Diagnostic Impressions

Axis I: 314.01 Attention-Deficit/Hyperactivity Disorder, Combined Type
Axis II: 799.9 Diagnoses Deferred
Axis III: None

Axis IV: Mother and brother diagnosed bipolar

Axis V: GAF = 35 (current)

Given these results, the following recommendations are made:

1. The results of this evaluation, and additional educational data, should be reviewed by the special education eligibility team to determine if Clara meets the Georgia criteria for special education services.

2. Provide Clara with competing responses to negative thoughts or behaviors. For example, if she says, "I'm afraid I'll start crying in class," ask her, "If you start to feel sad, what can you do before you start to cry? Can you read something that makes you laugh or distracts you from your sadness? Is there somewhere you can go if you feel the urge to cry?"

3. Use a consistent deescalation procedure already familiar to school staff. For example, when worried, Clara will: (a) take 10 breaths, (b) identify how a preferred "hero" would handle the situation, (c) access designated staff, (d) do alternative, less stressful work, (e) do reading for 5 minutes in a designated area (corner of room, library), then answer questions.

4. Provide an alternative focus to distract Clara from somatic symptoms. For example, if Clara complains of a recurrent headache without medical etiology, provide her with a phrase to think of ("These never last long, I will feel better soon") or an activity (doing three problems then standing up, 10 problems then walking to the fountain). Another method for distracting Clara from excessive concern about her state of wellness is to teach her to hold a stress ball and practice squeezing and relaxing her arm while breathing in and out at an even pace.

5. Identify a hierarchy of safe places for Clara to deescalate emotionality symptoms. Some examples are: to stay at her desk, to move to another part of the classroom, to go to the edge or outside of class, or to go to a designated room (other classroom, library, office). Reward Clara's use of lower-level places, such as her desk or another part of the classroom, and more time staying on task, by allowing her to eat with a peer or help the teacher with a special task.

6. Identify safe, comfortable staff with whom Clara can discuss traumatic events, flashbacks, or triggering events, and establish a procedure for accessing those staff when needed. Identify a hierarchy of staff (counselor, aide, coach) and places (guidance office, hall next to office, gym) Clara can access if she cannot focus on academics and instead needs to discuss a traumatic event. While at school, Clara may reduce anxiety by drawing pictures, writing her thoughts in a journal, or bouncing a ball in the gym.

7. Reward successive approximations of a desired behavior. For example, when Clara begins on her work, teachers can immediately praise her for sitting quietly and getting started on her work.

8. Develop social skills that focus on increased peer interactions by teaching communication skills aimed at developing friendships. Use a structured learning curriculum to teach the social behaviors identified as problematic for Clara. The components of a structured learning curriculum are modeling, role-playing, feedback, and transfer of training.

9. Provide these results to Clara's treating physician and arrange a meeting to coordinate school and home medical treatments.

10. Clara's response to these interventions, medication, and other treatments should be systematically monitored via teacher ratings at 1 month intervals at a minimum. The BASC-2 Progress Monitor (PM) Externalizing/ADHD form is recommended to assess changes in symptomatology and the Adaptive Skills form is recommended for tracking success with behavioral and emotional skill building. These results should also be provided to her treating physician.

11. Clara is showing some risk for the development of co-occurring depression and anxiety problems. Consequently, screening for these problems is recommended at least annually. The Behavioral and Emotional Screening System (BESS) parent and teacher forms are measures that could be used for this purpose.

12. It is also recommended that Clara's mother complete the parent-child interaction training with the parent center staff at her school.

CASE 6

How a Weakness in Attention Can Mask True Learning Capabilities and Achievement Gains

Eva Prince

No teacher enjoys having a child miss recess, but educators often feel they must resort to such a tactic to ensure that the child keeps up with classmates. An inattentive youngster who lags behind his or her peers in task completion too often experiences this "opportunity to make up their work." While there is no doubt of the extreme importance that focused attention bears on school success, a sound review of multidisciplinary data can serve to spare a student of the demoralizing reactions of others to a student's weak attentional abilities.

The opportunity to use data-driven decisions in response to instructional concerns can assist a diagnostic team in developing specific interventions to promote academic behaviors without depriving a student of social and recreational opportunities. This multisource, psychoeducational report offers a perspective on the different types of behavioral options available for promoting a student's academic success without compromising his or her social-emotional development.

COGNITIVE EVALUATION

Name:	Trevor Martinelli
Date of Birth:	07/27/2003
Age:	6 years, 6 months
Ethnicity:	Caucasian
School:	Las Sierras Elementary, first grade
Date of Testing:	02/08/2010
Evaluator:	Eva M. Prince, Ed.S.

REASON FOR REFERRAL

According to teacher report, Trevor is having difficulty keeping pace with the first-grade curriculum. Similar concerns were expressed during Trevor's matriculation into the Las Sierras Elementary kindergarten program. The Child Study Team reviewing his educational records requested that additional data be collected regarding his cognitive abilities. In addition to his struggles in handling grade-level expectations, staff expresses concern regarding Trevor's ability to maintain his focus during efforts to complete daily work. At times, he must miss recess to complete the morning's academic tasks. His teacher believes that Trevor is aware that he is unable to keep up with his classroom peers and his mother reports that he expresses his dislike of school to his family.

BACKGROUND INFORMATION

Trevor lives with his mother, father, and one older brother in Las Sierras, Colorado. He has attended Las Sierras Elementary since kindergarten and did not attend any preschool program. Trevor is young for his grade as he became eligible for enrollment into kindergarten just a few weeks before the beginning of the school year. Trevor's mother reports that he was with a Spanish-speaking caregiver for the first 2 years of his life.

According to a developmental history form completed by Mrs. Martinelli, Trevor sat at 7 months, walked at 1 year of age, began speaking at 2 years, and was toilet trained at 3 years of age. Although some of these developmental milestones are outside of normal limits, the family does not express any developmental concerns at this time. His mother reports that Trevor was on a trial of medication for Attention-Deficit/Hyperactivity Disorder (ADHD) but stopped the medication after 2 weeks as she noted deterioration in his behavior at home and no reported benefit was conveyed from the school's perspective. Mrs. Martinelli reports that she has experienced an attention disorder throughout her school years and continues to be a very active adult. She related that Mr. Martinelli works at a much slower pace and demonstrates a high level of inattentiveness. Mrs. Martinelli observes that Trevor enjoys mathematics and is willing to work on sight word development through family reading activities. He does not like to read independently as he does not have the patience to work through difficult words, even when he has the skills to sound the words out. Trevor often arrives home from school unhappy and on some mornings resists going to school.

On the day of the evaluation, Trevor was observed briefly in his first-grade classroom. He was working independently at his desk with a hands-on activity. He demonstrated good fine-motor skills in his use of the scissors and followed the teacher's directions. When it was time to transition to the next activity, Trevor was a bit unorganized in his manner of collecting his materials, clearing his work space, and getting to the next expected activity. He appeared to be more interested in attending to the activities of others in the class but eventually found his way to doing the task without too great a delay.

Trevor accompanied the evaluator to the test setting without hesitation and engaged in friendly conversation along the way. He was attentive to each of the test activities and never asked when the session would end or if he could rejoin his group. When he was dismissed for lunch and was asked to return right after the lunchtime recess, Trevor returned early to the test setting and was eager to begin again. As the tasks became more difficult, he persevered without hesitation or expression of self-doubt. Overall, Trevor would be categorized as an "enthusiastic" test participant in the one-to-one setting.

Previous Assessments

Trevor was administered the Wechsler Individual Achievement Test-III (WIAT-III) by Ms. Murphy, the special education teacher, at Las Sierras Elementary

several weeks before this cognitive evaluation. A review of those scores indicated that Trevor is performing at an expected level in comparison to his age-level peers in most achievement areas. In addition, the two benchmarks obtained by his school district with the Dynamic Indicators of Basic Early Literacy Skills (DIBELS) First-Grade Benchmark Assessment in August 2009 and February 2010 indicated clear gains in his basic reading skills.

Margaret Parsons, speech-language pathologist from Las Sierras Elementary, conducted a speech and language evaluation with Trevor in the fall of 2009 to address concerns expressed by his kindergarten teacher and his non-passing score on a preschool screening measure. Her assessment results indicated that Trevor displayed a moderate articulation delay characterized by sound substitutions and blend reduction. Overall receptive and expressive language skills were measured to be within the low normal range with many of his weaknesses being related to weak preacademic skills in the area of quantitative, sequential, and phonemic awareness activities. Trevor received articulation therapy to remediate his speech delay, and it was recommended that both educational and home settings should work in unison to address his delays within the natural context in which they occur.

Trevor passed the hearing and vision screenings administered at Las Sierras at the start of the academic year.

TESTS ADMINISTERED

Stanford-Binet Intelligence Scales, Fifth Edition (SB5): Full-Scale Battery

Conners' Parent Rating Scales – Revised: Long Version

How SB5 Scores Are Reported

The scores show how well Trevor performed compared to a group of children of the same age from across the United States. Scores from 85 to 115 are Average. A percentile rank is also given that shows a child's rank in the national comparison group. If the percentile rank were 45, for example, it would mean that he scored as high or higher than approximately 45 out of 100 children his age.

IQ and Factor Index Score Results

	Standard Score*	Percentile	95% Confidence Interval		Descriptive Classification
			Standard Score	Percentile	
IQ Scores					
Full-Scale IQ (FSIQ)	98	45	94–102	34–55	Average
Nonverbal IQ (NVIQ)	97	42	91–103	27–58	Average
Verbal IQ (VIQ)	98	45	92–104	30–61	Average
Abbreviated IQ (ABIQ)	94	34	87–103	19–58	Average
Factor Index Scores					
Fluid Reasoning (FR)	103	58	95–111	37–77	Average
Knowledge (KN)	97	42	89–105	23–63	Average
Quantitative Reasoning (QR)	100	50	92–108	30–70	Average
Visual Spatial (VS)	108	70	99–115	47–84	Average
Working Memory (WM)	83	13	77–93	6–32	Low Average
*Standard Scores have a mean of 100 and a standard deviation of 15.					

Full-Scale Score

Trevor earned a Full-Scale IQ (FSIQ) score of 98 on the Stanford-Binet Intelligence Scales, Fifth Edition (SB5). His current overall intelligence is classified as Average and is ranked at the 45th percentile. There is a 95% probability that his "true" FSIQ is between 94 and 102. When considering Trevor's performance on the FSIQ, his Nonverbal IQ (NVIQ) of 97 is commensurate with his Verbal IQ (VIQ) score of 98. The FSIQ is considered a reliable measure of general ability to reason, solve problems, and adapt to the cognitive demands of the environment. It measures more than acquired knowledge from schooling; it also measures the sum of five major facets of intelligence, including reasoning, stored information, memory, visualization, and the ability to solve novel problems.

Nonverbal IQ

The SB5 NVIQ is based on the nonverbal subtests of the five-factor index scales. It measures skills in solving abstract, picture-oriented problems; recalling facts and figures; solving quantitative problems shown in picture form; assembling designs; and recalling sequences. Trevor's "true" NVIQ is expected to lie between 91 and 103 with 95% confidence. His nonverbal reasoning skills are classified as Average and are ranked at the 42nd percentile among his age-peers.

The NVIQ measures the general ability to reason, solve problems, visualize, and recall information presented in pictorial, figural, and symbolic form, as opposed to information presented in the form of words and sentences (printed or spoken). The NVIQ does require a small degree of auditory skill to understand brief examiner-spoken directions.

Verbal IQ

The SB5 VIQ provides a composite of all the cognitive skills required to solve the items in the five verbal subtests. Trevor's "true" VIQ of 98 is expected to lie between 92 and 104 with 95% confidence. Trevor's current verbal reasoning abilities are classified as Average and are ranked at the 45th percentile for his age.

The VIQ measures general ability to reason, solve problems, visualize, and recall important information presented in words and sentences (printed or spoken). Additionally, the VIQ reflects the student's ability to explain verbal responses clearly, present rationale for response choices, create stories, and explain spatial directions. The VIQ subtests require the examinee to understand the examiner's spoken directions and then clearly vocalize responses to questions. General verbal ability, measured by VIQ, is one of the most powerful predictors of academic success because of the heavy reliance on reading and writing in school programs.

FACTORS

Fluid Reasoning

Fluid Reasoning is the ability to solve verbal and nonverbal problems using inductive or deductive reasoning. In the test activities presented to Trevor, he was required to inspect pictures depicting human activities and deduce the underlying problem or situation by telling a story. These testing tasks require attention to visual cues, prompt the production of creative answers, and encourage an individual to use a trial-and-error strategy to devise an accurate response. Trevor's Fluid Reasoning abilities are solidly within the Average range in comparison to his age-level peers, according to this evaluation measure (Fluid Reasoning Index score = 103; 58th percentile rank).

Knowledge

Knowledge is a person's accumulated fund of general information acquired at home, school, or work. This ability involves learned material, such as vocabulary, that has been acquired and stored in long-term memory. Trevor's Knowledge Index standard score is 97 indicating Average abilities (Knowledge Index score = 97; 42nd percentile rank).

Quantitative Reasoning

Quantitative Reasoning is an individual's skill with numbers and numerical problem solving. Activities in the Quantitative Reasoning tasks emphasize applied problem solving more than specific mathematical knowledge acquired through school learning. Compared to other individuals his age, Trevor presented with Average abilities and earned a standard score of 100, indicating performance at the 50th percentile rank.

Visual-Spatial Processing

Visual-Spatial Processing measures an individual's ability to see patterns, relationships, spatial orientations, or the gestalt (whole) among diverse pieces of a visual display. Testing activities involved moving geometric pieces to copy a pictured design and to work with a collection of position and direction items. Visual-Spatial Processing was identified as the highest Factor Index score in Trevor's profile. His earned standard score of 108 represents an area of relative strength for Trevor. He may find tasks requiring this ability easier, and such strengths may suggest a preferred learning style. Compared to other individuals, this score would be described as Average.

Working Memory

Working Memory represents Trevor's ability to acquire and store various information in short-term memory, to "transform" or "sort" this information, and to present it in a new format. Working Memory represents Trevor's poorest area of performance. Trevor will likely find tasks that require this ability to be more challenging. Working Memory is proven to be of great importance in school learning and general problem solving. Compared to other individuals, Trevor's standard score of 83 would be described as Low Average.

Information about SB5 Subtests

Nonverbal	Scaled Scores*	%ile	Verbal	Scaled Scores	%ile
Fluid Reasoning	9	37	Fluid Reasoning	12	75
Knowledge	10	50	Knowledge	9	37
Quantitative Reasoning	10	50	Quantitative Reasoning	10	50
Visual-Spatial	11	63	Visual-Spatial	12	75
Working Memory	8	25	Working Memory	6	9
*Scaled Scores have a mean of 10 and a standard deviation of 3.					

No significant differences were found between the Full-Scale IQ subtests and the average of all 10 FSIQ subtests, indicating a balanced cognitive ability profile for Trevor.

Verbal Working Memory was found to be significantly and practically lower than the average of the 10 FSIQ subtests. This may show that Trevor is relatively less proficient in recalling sentences or portions of information presented orally.

Academic Achievement Evaluation Discussion

The testing data gathered by Ms. Murphy at Las Sierras Elementary through the use of the Wechsler Individual Achievement Test – Third Edition (WIAT-III) indicated that Trevor is performing at expected levels in comparison to his age peers. When compared to others, Trevor appears to be acquiring the beginning principles of reading, written language, and math at a pace comparable to that of most 6-year-olds/first graders.

The WIAT-III testing information provided to this evaluator did not include any observations that might have been made during the administration of this testing measure. Therefore, comments regarding Trevor's outward behaviors or attitude to the testing task cannot be offered. However, a review of Trevor's educational records indicates that he does his best work when in a one-to-one educational situation, which is what individualized testing provides. Therefore, Trevor's performance on this assessment may indicate what he is able to perform well in academic areas when provided with support from an adult. This is not indicative of the "real life" of the educational world, as students learn in groups.

Conners' Teacher Rating Scales, Revised; Long Version

Behavior Area	T Scores (mean = 50; SD: 3)
Oppositional	45
Cognitive Problems/Inattention	72*
Hyperactivity	55
Anxious-Shy	64
Perfectionism	56
Social Problems	45
Conners' ADHD Index	72*
Conners' Global Index: Restless-Impulsive	66
Conners' Global Index: Emotional Lability	58
Conners' Global Index: Total	66
DSM-IV: Inattentive	74*
DSM-IV: Hyperactive-Impulsive	62
DSM-IV: Total	70*
*Score is: Moderately Atypical.	

Conners' Rating Scales–Revised: Teacher Form, Long Version

The Conners' Rating Scale – Revised was used as part of a screening procedure to address teacher concerns regarding Trevor's ability to pay attention to learning tasks. Both the Parent Rating Scale and the Teacher Rating Scale were distributed but only the teacher form was returned.

Rating Scale Interpretations

Attention is a complex construct and extremely important to success in school. Attention can be viewed as the foundation of all other higher-order processing. In order to regulate thinking and to complete tasks of daily living, such as school work, it is necessary to be able to attend to both auditory and visual stimuli in the environment.

According to his teacher's observations, Trevor's behaviors at school indicate that he is presenting with a high level of inattention that may be impacting his ability to benefit fully from his daily classroom instruction.

Research shows a strong link between early elementary attention problems and subsequent academic difficulties, particularly in the area of reading. Though there are few research-based interventions that consistently show positive results in improving attention in youngsters, a multimodal approach is believed to be most effective. This approach should incorporate behavior management at both school and home to promote attention, and social skills training to improve self-awareness. When considering Trevor's inattentive behavior, it is important to differentiate between problem behaviors that are intentional and within his control and those that are secondary to weak self-regulation. Do not punish Trevor for behaviors that are symptoms of the disability (e.g., poor self-regulation, lack of organization, poor listening) until you have established a behavioral program that delineates and supports expected behavior and clearly spells out the consequences ahead of time for not meeting the expectations as agreed on between student and teacher. Additional recommendations are included at the conclusion of this report.

SUMMARY

Trevor is a 6-year, 6-month-old boy attending first grade at Las Sierras Elementary School. He is noted as a friendly boy who gets along well with classmates and performs best when afforded one-to-one interaction with a teacher or other adult. Trevor is noted to lack self-confidence and requires additional time to keep pace with classroom activities.

The testing session was deemed valid for obtaining an accurate representation of Trevor's current level of functioning. His current overall intellectual functioning is classified as Average and is ranked at the 45th percentile. Trevor's nonverbal and verbal reasoning skills are comparably developed; however, he demonstrates a relative strength in his ability to see patterns, visual relationships, and to work with activities that rely on his knowledge of spatial orientation. His weakest area was in verbal working memory, indicating that he is less proficient in working with oral information while holding it in memory.

According to the Conners' Teacher Rating Scale, Trevor's level of inattention is noted to be elevated and above expected levels in comparison to his age peers. To keep pace in the classroom, a student must be able to maintain focus; remain alert for new directions, instructions, and verbal information; and have the internal organization to decide which "learning tools" to use in various situations. Trevor's behaviors suggest a need for a classroom behavior management plan to increase his understanding of the need to maintain his focus and his ability to do so. He also requires accommodations to promote self-esteem and self-confidence while improving his academic performance.

Trevor's academic skills are uniformly developed in comparison to his age peers according to testing conducted by Ms. Murphy. When assessed in the one-to-one test setting, he is able to demonstrate an average level of academic achievement. However, due to his high level of inattention in the general education classroom, he may not be able to demonstrate the same level of achievement. It is heartening to realize, however, that although the educational staff may feel that they are not getting through to Trevor in their instructional attempts, he has clearly profited from instruction.

APPROACHES TO MANAGEMENT

Trevor would benefit from interventions designed to help him improve his ability to focus and sustain attention in order to access the important instruction provided in these formative school years. Both home and school interventions should be used to help increase him improve his ability to attend.

School Interventions

1. Structure the environment to minimize auditory and visual distracters. Small group learning settings are preferable over full-class instruction.
2. Make sure you have Trevor's attention before giving him oral instructions. Keep oral instructions as short and simple as possible.
3. Provide immediate feedback. Incorporate computer programs that rely on sustained-controlled attention and that provide instantaneous feedback.
4. When Trevor enters the classroom, have a "Rules for Readiness" card on his desk. The card should have written on it (with picture support if necessary) the few things that he has to do to be ready to begin class (e.g., 1. Get book from shelf; 2. Get notebook, pencil, and homework from backpack; 3. Sit down and look at teacher). If Trevor is not following the directions, an overt verbal reminder does not need to be given but

rather the teacher can point to the instruction that he is missing and rely on Trevor to comply with the expectation independently.
5. As Trevor's difficulty with sustained attention interferes with his efficiency, allow him extended time to complete in-class assignments. Inform him ahead of time that this will be allowed so as to reduce anxiety while he is working. Trevor may benefit from a small countdown clock to be within his view so that he can self-monitor how much time remains before he is expected to complete the task.

Home Interventions

1. Share this report with Trevor's pediatrician and explain the problems that he experienced with the previous medication. Many medications are available for ADHD and each may have different target effects and side effects on a person. You might ask the physician to refer you to a developmental/behavioral pediatrician who specializes in disabilities affecting behavior.
2. Limit the amount of television viewing that Trevor engages in, as watching TV does not require him to demonstrate that he is registering information or to engage in two-way communication that is more likely to promote thinking, reasoning, and problem solving.
3. Monitor home chores and self-care activities to ensure that Trevor is completing all necessary steps and is doing so in a timely manner. The sequential steps of home living can be important building blocks for demonstrating to children the sequence of events in life's activities and the importance of sustained focus to complete those events. Have Trevor make a list of duties and check off the tasks as they are completed.
4. Ensure that Trevor develops an island of competence. He needs to have one or more areas where he is accomplished, admired, and rewarded for his knowledge and talents.
5. Trevor's family may enjoy working with him through books on tape/CD that allow Trevor to "read along" as the story is read aloud. This format provides a sound to inform Trevor when it is time to turn the page and to keep the reading process going. This listening-while-reading format will reduce the frustration in decoding that Trevor demonstrates at home while encouraging his focused attention to the story.

6. There are programs available that are designed to enhance the reading skills in younger children while promoting the development of visual-auditory attention. One example is Earobics (designed for ages 4 to 7; Earobics II for ages 7 to 10). This computer program published by Cognitive Concepts is designed to develop effective listening comprehension skills, phonological awareness, and auditory processing skills.

7. Stress and perceived failures can affect a person's ability to learn. Provide Trevor with a safe and secure climate and environment to exercise his individual learning, while praising his successes and strengths.

CASE 7

Associative Memory Disorder

An Unexpected Struggle Resulting in Difficulty with Basic Skill Acquisition

James Creed

Normative scores are important when reporting the results of a formal evaluation for learning problems. They are useful in comparing a student to his own age or grade peers and to illustrate his own learning strengths and weaknesses. However, including the reports from multiple sources can be invaluable in validating and communicating the information to others. The comments from parents, teachers, and others who have observed the child in different settings help to corroborate the results of the formal test performance. Providing descriptions of a student like Isaac, using his own words and actions, can also be an effective means to illustrate the struggles he is having every day in the classroom. If those who have been or will be working with the student see their own comments amidst others with similar observations, it helps to show how their thoughts and observations compare. It may help the team members come to a consensus regarding how to make the most positive changes in that student's life.

EDUCATIONAL EVALUATION

Name:	Isaac Hartman
Date of Birth:	01/18/2003
Age:	6 years, 11 months
School:	Brigham Elementary
Teacher:	Mrs. Wright
Grade:	1.4
Dates of Testing:	12/14/2009, 12/15/2009, 12/19/2009
Examiner:	James M. Creed, M.Ed.

REASON FOR REFERRAL

Isaac was referred for an evaluation by his parents at the urging of his pediatric neurologist, Alan Nikles, M.D., because of their continuing frustration with their son's difficulty in learning basic academic skills despite tutorial help given both at school and at home. His parents did not predict these school-related difficulties due to his good oral language and other strong abilities, and consulted Dr. Nikles for an evaluation. Dr. Nikles has ruled out birth or developmental issues and is considering the possibility that an attentional difficulty may be the cause or at least a contributing factor to Isaac's school problems. Isaac has seen a speech-language pathologist for some time for some minor articulation issues.

TESTS ADMINISTERED

WJ III Tests of Cognitive Abilities (administered on 12/14/2009)

WJ III Tests of Cognitive Abilities—Diagnostic Supplement (administered on 12/15/2009)

WJ III Tests of Achievement (administered on 12/19/2009)

CURRENT SCHOOL PERFORMANCE

Isaac's teachers at Brigham Elementary and his parents were asked to comment on his skill levels, learning strengths/weaknesses, behavior/attitude, and motivation/

effort. Responses were gathered from his first-grade teacher, Mrs. Wright, his speech-language therapist, Mrs. Manning, and his parents, Mr. and Mrs. Hartman. The following information is summarized from their written reports.

Isaac's skill levels vary. His grade 1 readiness skills, including his fine- and gross-motor skills, were described as adequate. His cognitive ability, vocabulary, and general language development were described as grade appropriate, if not above. His knowledge of letters and their corresponding sounds, however, was below grade level; he can say the alphabet in sequence but does not recognize all of the individual letters in print. His writing (penmanship) is grade appropriate and his letters are precise and well formed, but he often needs a visual model to remember how to make some of them. His mother reported that he is especially good at building things with Legos and singing. She also reported that his speech production has improved greatly with the therapy he has received.

Isaac has both learning strengths and weaknesses. He is a cooperative class member, plays well with others, and enjoys the social aspects of the classroom. He has a good grasp of concepts, especially in math, when he is engaged in the learning activity. He is not, however, always engaged, which all the observers see as a weakness. He was described as easily distracted, needing directions broken into smaller steps, and frequently needing reminders to refocus, even when in a small group. He does not work well independently, or complete work on his own. His difficulties in attending cause him to miss information, which, in turn, causes him increasing frustration as the curriculum becomes more advanced.

Isaac's social behavior and attitude were generally described as positive. He is a well-intentioned young boy who clearly understands right and wrong. At times he may need reminders about the rules, but he is responsive and cooperative when guided to make better choices. He shows interest in learning, but he can lose concentration, have difficulty organizing his work and materials, and be distracted by his peers or objects in his environment. At times, he can become frustrated or overly emotional and fail to assume full responsibility for his actions.

Isaac's motivation and effort were described as variable, depending on what he is doing. He is described as eager to learn, especially with "preferred" activities like playing games. He puts effort into the learning process and tries to listen and produce careful work, but his inability to stay engaged interrupts his learning. He doesn't seem able to stick to things; his effort wanes on lengthy tasks. His

mother reported that he needs constant reminding, and that it is rare for him to remember beyond the moment. Lately he has seemed more easily frustrated, and with at least one of the respondents, he is resisting help. This resistance is beginning to become a concern as she sees his motivation and effort starting to wane.

In summary, the respondents see Isaac as a bright, personable, endearing child who has the ability to succeed when he is focused and attentive. Isaac has many strengths, but his short attention span and tendency to get distracted have significantly affected his progress in acquiring academic skills, despite much help from various adults.

TEST SESSION OBSERVATIONS AND DIAGNOSTIC IMPRESSIONS

Isaac was evaluated on three different days in sessions ranging from 2 to 3 hours in length with breaks. He displayed good conversational language and an open, likeable, engaging personality. He was cooperative some of the time, eagerly displaying his knowledge and problem-solving abilities. He was somewhat uncooperative at other times, appearing fidgety or restless, asking, "Can we play a game now?" He appeared comfortable during the testing, but he seemed distracted also, wanting to know about the different games on the shelf behind him or wanting to tell the examiner a joke, such as: "What do you have if you have five ducks and one cow? Don't know? Okay, milk and quackers!" He preferred to sit or kneel on the edge of his chair, sometimes also leaving his seat and standing right next to the examiner and asking: "What are you writing now?" He did respond to directions to return to his seat, only to be up again later. He responded promptly to questions and other task demands during testing, generally persisting with more difficult items, but taking opportunities between activities to try to shift the focus away from the testing toward a more "preferred" activity.

Isaac had the most difficulty on one of the tests in the Woodcock-Johnson III Tests of Cognitive Abilities (WJ III COG), Visual-Auditory Learning (VAL). It is a test of long-term storage and retrieval, specifically associative memory, requiring the person to learn, store, and retrieve a series of visual-auditory associations. Isaac was asked to learn and recall words for rebuses (pictographic representations of words). Most students learn, store, and retrieve the names of the first rebuses and are able to successfully "read" the early stories with few, if any, mistakes. Usually when students begin to struggle, it is when the rebuses become more numerous and the stories more lengthy. This was not the case for Isaac. He struggled with the very first rebus, and learned, stored, and retrieved the names of only two out of six rebuses in the second story. When he made a mistake, he was immediately told the correct name, which he often repeated to himself. Most students make use of the corrective feedback and improve performance. Isaac profited very little from the feedback and made similar mistakes the next time the rebus was presented. He substituted the article "a" for the article "the" 13 times during the test even though he was corrected each time. In the formal testing situation, Isaac demonstrated what his teachers and parents reported they see when Isaac attempts to learn letters/sounds, numbers, and other basic skills. This difficulty in learning, storing, and retrieving through association was the only ability measured in the WJ III COG in which Isaac's score fell below the average range.

This poor performance prompted more investigation into this area. On a subsequent day Isaac was given a test from the WJ III COG Diagnostic Supplement (DS) that measures the same narrow ability as VAL, associative memory. This test required Isaac to learn the names of space creatures and then, when given a name, pick the correct one out of a lineup of other space creatures. His performance was similar to that of VAL; he struggled to remember the second space creature when asked to point to both the second and first on a page of nine others. More than once he said, "I don't remember him" and "I remember the name but not which one he is." These two tests combine to form the Associative Memory cluster, the only cluster in Isaac's cognitive performance that fell below the average range.

Isaac seemed to know that he should be better at some writing skills. When asked to write his full name on his Achievement Student Response Booklet, he wrote three letters, "Hrd," and said, "My name's got a lot of letters; it's kinda hard to write, you know." When asked to write his full name on the Cognitive Response Booklet at the next session, he wrote three letters, "Har," then looked up and asked the examiner, "Can you write the rest …'cause you know it, right?" When solving a math problem, he responded, "I know 2 + 2 = 4, but I don't know how to make a four. Is it like this one?" Here he pointed to a printed four on the test page and looked for a reaction from the examiner. When told to give his best answer, he guessed that the printed four was a good choice to copy, saying as he copied it, "It's like that one, I think." When asked to print a lower case e, he asked, "Now what's a lowercase e look like? … I

think I don't remember." When presented with some (to him) difficult words to spell, he responded, "I know a lot of first letters. If I only had the words. Mrs. Wright has piles of words with rubber bands around them that I look at in my folder to help me. It's right in my folder or in her folder."

Isaac expressed some personal opinions about reading. When asked about reading, he volunteered, "I read with Mrs. Wright sometimes because she helps me. I read books by myself sometimes, too." When asked which he liked better, he responded, "With Mrs. Wright helping me because I need a lot of help. It's pretty hard, you know." Later, when testing his knowledge in subject matter, he said he would like to be a scientist. When asked why, he responded, "A scientist doesn't have to read stuff." When asked if he thought that was always true, he added, "Well, he might sometimes, but not too much." Another time, when testing his knowledge of vocabulary, he was asked for the name of a picture of a pyramid; he responded, "I don't know the name, but I know it's an ancient tower that mummies lived in, and it's Egyptian." Although he did not receive credit (the test is a measure of vocabulary knowledge), the examiner was curious as to how he knew so much about the subject. When asked, he responded that he didn't know, but he was very sure "it wasn't by reading about it."

SUMMARY

Isaac is a 6-year, 11-month-old first-grade student at Brigham Elementary School in Center City. He was referred for an evaluation by his parents at the urging of his pediatric neurologist, Dr. Nikles, who is in the process of evaluating him for attentional issues. Isaac's teachers and his parents report that he has generally appropriate first-grade readiness skills with one large exception, his knowledge of his letters and the corresponding sounds. Both his teachers and parents report that he is not always fully engaged in the learning process, is easily distracted, and needs frequent refocusing. This difficulty in attending causes Isaac to miss information, frustrating him. They see him beginning to develop a negative attitude toward learning, which they all wish to avoid.

Isaac's General Intellectual Ability, an overall estimate based on performance on tests that measure seven different cognitive abilities, is within the average range. When all of his cognitive and achievement scores are compared, Isaac demonstrated a significant strength in fluid reasoning (i.e., the ability to reason, form concepts, and solve problems using unfamiliar procedures) and a significant weakness in the narrow ability of associative memory (i.e., the process of learning, storing, and retrieving information through visual-auditory associations), which is necessary for learning letters' names and sounds. Isaac's lowest academic areas were basic reading and writing skills and reading comprehension.

When Isaac's achievement is compared to his own scores for the cognitive abilities most related to each achievement area, his achievement is significantly lower than predicted in both broad reading and writing, showing his significant difficulty in developing phoneme-grapheme knowledge. Also, his broad reading, basic reading skills, reading comprehension, written language, and basic writing skills are significantly lower than would be predicted by his level of oral language development.

RECOMMENDATIONS

Attention

This report should be forwarded to Dr. Nikles for his use in evaluating Isaac for attentional issues. Observations of Isaac's behavior at formal testing sessions and at home and at school suggest that poor attention is a factor affecting his performance.

Reading and Writing

Isaac's performance on those measures that are directly related to early reading and writing skill acquisition (phonemic awareness, processing speed, general language development, listening comprehension, rapid automatic naming, and working memory) are all within the average range. His difficulty in learning these basic skills (phoneme-grapheme relationships) seems to be directly related to his difficulty with forming the associations between symbol and name, and then symbol and sound, the knowledge base he has to acquire so he can be successful in reading and writing. He shows such difficulty in making the associations that it will take a concerted effort from all involved (teachers, specialists, parents) to teach Isaac his letters and sounds. The following recommendations are made as suggestions to be added to what has already been discovered to work for Isaac:

1. Isaac would benefit from carefully sequenced, explicit, systematic, multisensory instruction that teaches sounds and letters. Examples of appropriate interventions include: Fundations (Wilson), Zoo Phonics, or Road to the Code. Fundations provides keywords and pictures to aid in making letter-sound associations and incorporates continuous reinforcement, letter formation, and spelling along with reading.

2. Have Isaac use gross-motor movements to help him visualize and remember his letter forms. For example, have him stand up straight and stick both arms out to form the letter "T." Let him be creative trying to form other letters as long as he is accurate and consistent.

3. Use visual imagery of concrete objects to help Isaac remember letter forms, their spatial orientations, and their sounds. For example, teach Isaac that a *b* looks like a bat and a ball, but the bat comes first; an *m* (compared to an *n*) has more mountains (two humps); an *s* is a snake. If one of the instructional systems above is used, however, incorporate strategies for making and retaining these associations.

4. Help Isaac make raised letters to use in tracing. Write a letter with a colored marker on an index card and have Isaac write over it with Elmer's glue. Once the card has dried, have Isaac trace over the letter with his finger, as he says the name (or the sound). As letters are mastered, create new cards.

5. Have Isaac use the software program *Read, Write, & Type*. This software program, designed for ages 6 to 8, teaches typing, as well as beginning literacy skills. The sequential curriculum provides instruction and games with all 40 speech sounds while students learn to use the keyboard. The program involves several steps: (a) learning each sound; (b) identifying beginning, middle, and ending sounds in words; (c) building words by typing sounds; (d) reading and writing simple stories; (e) creating stories; and (f) writing messages. Companion CDs and additional reading materials are also available (http://www.talkingfingers.com).

Games to Play at Home or in the Classroom

Note that the following activities are intended to reinforce what Isaac is learning and to make practice fun. They are not a substitute for a systematic instructional program.

1. Letter Matching Concentration: Make two sets of alphabet cards, two each of both uppercase and lowercase letters. Objective is to visually match the letters.

Game 1

Spread all uppercase cards face-up and out of order.
Match 26 pairs, working with a partner.

Switch to lowercase cards and match 26 pairs.

Game 2

Spread out one set uppercase and one set lowercase cards, face-up and out of order.

Match uppercase to lowercase cards.

Game 3

Spread all uppercase or lowercase cards face-down.

Play a game like Concentration.

Players take turns turning letters over trying to make matches.

2. Get an alphabet wall chart at teacher's store and place it in a central area of house. Use it throughout day. For instance, say to Isaac: "Show me the 'K' before you eat your lunch."

3. Use play dough to make the letters from the wall chart or letter cards.

4. Salt/sand tray: Pour table salt or sand on a plate. Wet the salt and then trace the letters.

5. Label everything in the house that you can (table, television, refrigerator). Underline the beginning letter.

It has been a pleasure working with Isaac. A thank you is extended to the professional staff at the Brigham Elementary School for providing invaluable information for this assessment.

Table of Scores

Woodcock-Johnson III Tests of Cognitive Abilities (including Diagnostic Supplement) and Tests of Achievement Compuscore for the WJ III, Version 3.0

COG norms based on grade 1.3; DS norms based on grade 1.4; ACH norms based on grade 1.4

CLUSTER/Test	Raw	GE	EASY to DIFF		RPI	PR	SS (68% BAND)	AE
GIA (Ext)	–	1.4	K.5	2.7	91/90	55	102 (100–104)	7–1
VERBAL ABILITY (Ext)	–	1.8	K.9	2.9	94/90	68	107 (102–111)	6–10
THINKING ABILITY (Ext)	–	2.0	K.8	4.7	94/90	72	109 (106–111)	7–6
COG EFFICIENCY (Ext)	–	1.7	1.0	2.4	94/90	66	106 (102–110)	7–0
COMP-KNOWLEDGE (Gc)	–	1.8	K.9	2.9	94/90	68	107 (102–111)	6–10
L-T RETRIEVAL (Glr)	–	K.1	<K.0	1.6	78/90	9	80 (77–83)	5–0
VIS-SPATIAL THINK (Gv)	–	4.1	1.2	10.9	96/90	88	118 (113–122)	9–3
AUDITORY PROCESS (Ga)	–	1.8	K.5	6.1	93/90	62	105 (99–110)	7–10
FLUID REASONING (Gf)	–	2.8	1.8	4.3	98/90	87	117 (113–121)	8–1
PROCESS SPEED (Gs)	–	1.5	1.0	2.2	93/90	62	104 (101–108)	7–0
SHORT-TERM MEM (Gsm)	–	1.9	1.1	2.9	95/90	66	106 (100–113)	7–0
PHONEMIC AWARE	–	1.3	K.1	4.7	90/90	51	100 (94–107)	7–1
PHONEMIC AWARE 3	–	1.5	K.5	3.2	90/90	52	101 (96–105)	7–0
WORKING MEMORY	–	1.6	K.8	2.4	93/90	60	104 (98–109)	6–9
COGNITIVE FLUENCY	–	1.9	K.8	3.2	94/90	67	107 (104–109)	7–2
KNOWLEDGE	–	1.9	1.0	3.1	94/90	68	107 (102–111)	7–0
ASSOCIATIVE MEMORY	–	<K.0	<K.0	K.5	62/90	0.3	58 (53–63)	4–6
ORAL LANGUAGE (Ext)	–	2.1	K.8	3.9	94/90	70	108 (104–112)	7–8
ORAL EXPRESSION	–	2.1	K.4	4.6	93/90	65	106 (101–111)	7–8
LISTENING COMP	–	2.1	1.0	3.5	95/90	70	108 (103–113)	7–8

(continued)

CLUSTER/Test	Raw	GE	EASY to DIFF		RPI	PR	SS (68% BAND)	AE
BROAD READING	–	<K.8	<K.8	K.9	20/90	5	75 (71–79)	5–10
BROAD MATH	–	1.1	K.7	1.7	84/90	34	94 (90–98)	6–5
BROAD WRITTEN LANG	–	K.5	K.1	K.9	45/90	6	76 (69–84)	5–10
BASIC READING SKILLS	–	K.8	K.6	1.0	30/90	12	82 (76–88)	6–2
READING COMP	–	<K.7	<K.7	K.9	29/90	10	81 (77–85)	5–9
MATH CALC SKILLS	–	1.1	K.6	1.7	83/90	33	93 (88–98)	6–4
MATH REASONING	–	1.0	K.6	1.5	78/90	31	93 (89–96)	6–3
BASIC WRITING SKILLS	–	<1.2	<1.2	<1.2	55/90	10	81 (75–87)	6–3
WRITTEN EXPRESSION	–	K.9	<K.0	1.4	73/90	18	86 (75–98)	5–11
ACADEMIC SKILLS	–	K.7	K.4	K.9	29/90	5	75 (72–79)	6–1
ACADEMIC FLUENCY	–	<K.8	<K.8	1.2	67/90	7	78 (67–89)	5–8
ACADEMIC APPS	–	K.8	K.5	1.1	56/90	18	86 (83–89)	6–0
ACADEMIC KNOWLEDGE	–	1.4	K.6	2.4	90/90	49	100 (95–104)	6–7
PHON/GRAPH KNOW	–	K.4	<K.0	K.8	23/90	5	75 (68–83)	5–10
Verbal Comprehension	–	1.2	K.4	2.1	89/90	46	99 (94–104)	6–3
Visual-Auditory Learning	65-E	<K.0	<K.0	K.6	60/90	6	76 (74–79)	4–7
Spatial Relations	61-D	3.7	1.0	9.7	96/90	78	111 (107–116)	8–9
Sound Blending	15	1.4	K.4	4.0	90/90	52	101 (93–108)	7–4
Concept Formation	17-D	2.7	1.8	4.0	98/90	81	113 (109–117)	8–0
Visual Matching	22-2	1.4	1.0	1.8	92/90	54	102 (97–106)	6–11
Numbers Reversed	6	1.0	K.5	1.6	84/90	43	97 (92–103)	6–1
Incomplete Words	16	1.2	<K.0	5.7	90/90	49	100 (93–106)	6–8
Auditory Working Memory	12	2.6	1.5	3.9	97/90	79	112 (107–118)	8–2
Vis-Aud Learn—Delayed	65	<K.0	<K.0	1.4	76/90	4	74 (68–80)	4–9
General Information	–	2.6	1.5	3.8	97/90	84	115 (109–122)	7–6
Retrieval Fluency	34	1.2	<K.0	8.5	90/90	48	99 (94–105)	6–3
Picture Recognition	46-D	4.4	1.5	12.8	97/90	83	114 (109–119)	9–10
Auditory Attention	34	2.6	K.7	12.3	94/90	71	108 (102–114)	8–6
Analysis-Synthesis	19-D	2.8	1.7	4.7	98/90	86	116 (111–121)	8–1
Decision Speed	19	1.9	1.0	2.8	95/90	68	107 (102–111)	7–3
Memory for Words	16	3.9	2.3	6.0	99/90	81	113 (106–120)	9–0
Rapid Picture Naming	85	2.1	1.2	3.2	96/90	63	105 (103–107)	7–4
Memory for Names	27-C	<K.0	<K.0	<K.0	67/90	4	73 (68–78)	4–3

Form A of the following achievement tests was administered:								
CLUSTER/Test	Raw	GE	EASY to DIFF		RPI	PR	SS (68% BAND)	AE
Letter-Word Identification	15	K.7	K.5	K.9	15/90	10	81 (77–85)	6–0
Reading Fluency	0	<K.8	<K.8	<1.0	–	–	–	<5–10
Story Recall	–	4.0	K.5	>18.0	95/90	83	114 (105–124)	9–6
Understanding Directions	–	1.5	K.4	2.9	91/90	52	101 (95–106)	7–2
Calculation	5	1.2	K.9	1.6	83/90	39	96 (90–102)	6–6
Math Fluency	5	K.5	<K.2	2.3	84/90	9	79 (70–89)	5–10
Spelling	11	K.3	K.1	K.5	7/90	3	71 (65–76)	5–8

CLUSTER/Test	Raw	GE	EASY to DIFF			RPI	PR	SS (68% BAND)	AE
Writing Fluency	0	<K.0	<K.0		<1.5	–	–	–	<5–6
Passage Comprehension	6	K.6	K.3		K.8	14/90	12	82 (78–86)	5–9
Applied Problems	21	1.2	K.8		1.7	85/90	42	97 (92–101)	6–5
Writing Samples	4-A	K.9	K.4		1.3	70/90	23	89 (82–96)	6–2
Story Recall—Delayed	–	1.7	<K.0		8.1	91/90	54	102 (87–116)	6–9
Word Attack	3	1.0	K.7		1.2	50/90	23	89 (79–99)	6–3
Picture Vocabulary	19	1.6	K.3		3.1	91/90	54	101 (96–107)	7–1
Oral Comprehension	15	2.6	1.6		3.9	97/90	76	110 (105–115)	8–3
Editing	2	1.7	1.3		2.2	95/90	69	107 (100–115)	6–10
Reading Vocabulary	–	<K.7	<K.7		<1.2	–	–	–	<5–11
Quantitative Concepts	–	K.8	K.3		1.3	69/90	25	90 (86–94)	6–0
Academic Knowledge	–	1.4	K.6		2.4	90/90	49	100 (95–104)	6–7
Spelling of Sounds	2	<K.0	<K.0		<K.0	8/90	0.3	59 (52–67)	5–2
Sound Awareness	24	1.5	K.9		2.4	92/90	56	102 (98–106)	6–11
Punctuation & Capitalization	5	K.2	<K.0		K.5	22/90	0.4	61 (52–69)	5–9

VARIATIONS	STANDARD SCORES			DISCREPANCY		Significant at + or − 1.50 SD (SEE)
	Actual	Predicted	Difference	PR	SD	
Intra-Individual						
COMP–KNOWLEDGE (Gc)	107	97	10	84	+0.99	No
L-T RETRIEVAL (Glr)	80	99	−19	7	−1.51	Yes
VIS-SPATIAL THINK (Gv)	118	98	20	91	+1.36	No
AUDITORY PROCESS (Ga)	105	98	7	69	+0.50	No
FLUID REASONING (Gf)	117	97	20	95	+1.65	Yes
PROCESS SPEED (Gs)	104	98	6	67	+0.44	No
SHORT-TERM MEM (Gsm)	106	98	8	74	+0.65	No
PHONEMIC AWARE	100	98	2	57	+0.17	No
PHONEMIC AWARE 3	101	98	3	62	+0.31	No
WORKING MEMORY	104	98	6	69	+0.50	No
BASIC READING SKILLS	82	99	−17	4	−1.76	Yes
READING COMP	81	99	−18	3	−1.91	Yes
MATH CALC SKILLS	93	99	−6	33	−0.44	No
MATH REASONING	93	98	−5	30	−0.53	No
BASIC WRITING SKILLS	81	99	−18	6	−1.59	Yes
WRITTEN EXPRESSION	86	99	−13	14	−1.09	No
ORAL EXPRESSION	106	98	8	76	+0.70	No
LISTENING COMP	108	97	11	84	+0.97	No
ACADEMIC KNOWLEDGE	100	98	2	56	+0.14	No
ASSOCIATIVE MEMORY	58	99	−41	0.5	−2.59	Yes
KNOWLEDGE	107	98	9	82	+0.92	No

(*continued*)

| DISCREPANCIES | STANDARD SCORES | | | DISCREPANCY | | Significant at |
	Actual	Predicted	Difference	PR	SD	+ or – 1.50 SD (SEE)
Oral Language/Achievement Discrepancies*						
BROAD READING	75	104	–29	1	–2.30	Yes
BASIC READING SKILLS	82	104	–22	4	–1.80	Yes
READING COMP	81	104	–23	2	–1.98	Yes
BROAD MATH	94	104	–10	21	–0.80	No
MATH CALC SKILLS	93	103	–10	23	–0.75	No
MATH REASONING	93	105	–12	17	–0.95	No
BROAD WRITTEN LANG	76	104	–28	2	–2.09	Yes
BASIC WRITING SKILLS	81	103	–22	4	–1.74	Yes
WRITTEN EXPRESSION	86	103	–17	9	–1.31	No
ACADEMIC KNOWLEDGE	100	105	–5	32	–0.46	No

*These discrepancies compare Oral Language (Ext) with Broad, Basic, and Applied ACH clusters.

| DISCREPANCIES | STANDARD SCORES | | | DISCREPANCY | | Significant at |
	Actual	Predicted	Difference	PR	SD	+ or – 1.50 SD (SEE)
Predicted Achievement/Achievement Discrepancies*						
BROAD READING	75	96	–21	3	–1.92	Yes
BASIC READING SKILLS	82	96	–14	11	–1.25	No
READING COMP	81	96	–15	8	–1.38	No
BROAD MATH	94	98	–4	36	–0.36	No
MATH CALC SKILLS	93	97	–4	37	–0.33	No
MATH REASONING	93	99	–6	28	–0.58	No
BROAD WRITTEN LANG	76	96	–20	4	–1.72	Yes
BASIC WRITING SKILLS	81	96	–15	9	–1.37	No
WRITTEN EXPRESSION	86	98	–12	17	–0.95	No
ORAL LANGUAGE (Ext)	108	97	11	84	+1.00	No
ORAL EXPRESSION	106	97	9	77	+0.74	No
LISTENING COMP	108	98	10	82	+0.91	No
ACADEMIC KNOWLEDGE	100	99	1	54	+0.10	No

*These discrepancies compare predicted achievement scores with Broad, Basic, and Applied ACH clusters.

| DISCREPANCIES | DISCREPANCY | | Significant at | |
	PR	SD (or z)	+ or – 1.50 SD (SEE)	Interpretation
Measures of delayed recall*				
DELAYED RECALL	46	–0.09	No	Within normal limits
Vis-Aud Learn—Delayed	71	+0.54	No	Within normal limits
Story Recall—Delayed	18	–0.92	No	Within normal limits

*These discrepancies based on predicted difference between initial and delayed scores.

CASE 8

Evaluation of a Bilingual Student with a History of Language Delay

Differentiating Between a Language Impairment and Second Language Learning

Brigid Garvin

The following case study of Alondra provides one model for conducting bilingual evaluations. This particular case addresses important topics that are frequently confronted in evaluations of individuals acquiring a second language. The evaluation addresses issues such as: native language loss; the appropriate selection of test measures; the qualitative, as well as quantitative, interpretation of results; and the importance of a thorough investigation of background and developmental history.

Alondra's case presents the additional element of a history of native language delay and prior consideration of the diagnoses of Pervasive Developmental Disorder-NOS and Autism. Each of these possibilities is further investigated in light of a long history of previous evaluations. In addition, the importance of a culturally sensitive form of data collection from multiple sources (e.g., teachers, parents, and caregivers) is made apparent.

This evaluation may be of particular interest to students and clinicians working with English language learners, specifically those who have the additional factor of prior diagnoses of disability in their native languages. Furthermore, while the author seeks to emphasize the importance of a thorough investigation of prior diagnoses, it is vital to keep in mind the careful interpretation of previous assessments. When working with individuals with complicated diagnostic histories who are also English language learners, the assumption that there is *not* a disability becomes even more important—with the burden on the evaluator to prove that there is.

As students acquire a second language they may experience the loss of their native language because of a lack of continued exposure to the more complex concepts in that language and because the second language is introduced before the first language is fully developed. Native language loss may still occur even though the native language is still being spoken in the home, especially if the native language is not used in school. Alondra's limited cognitive academic proficiency in Spanish suggests that she may be experiencing the loss of her native Spanish while still in the process of acquiring proficiency in English.

BILINGUAL PSYCHOEDUCATIONAL EVALUATION

Name:	Alondra Torres
Date of Birth:	06/15/2002
Age:	7-9
Parents:	George and Maritza Torres
School:	Collier Elementary School
Teacher:	Delia Fernandez
Grade:	3
Evaluation Dates:	03/20, 21, 23/10
Date of Report:	04/1/10
Examiner:	Brigid Garvin, M.Ed.

REASON FOR REFERRAL

Alondra was referred for a psychoeducational evaluation by her mother, Mrs. Torres, at the recommendation of Alondra's pediatrician, Dr. Alfonso. Mrs. Torres's concerns included Alondra's difficulties with oral language, specifically expressive language, as well as academic difficulties, particularly reading. Mrs. Torres requested a comprehensive evaluation in order to clarify previous diagnoses and concerns including an auditory processing disorder, poor working memory, a language delay, a diagnosis of Pervasive Developmental Disorder (PDD), and general concerns regarding autism spectrum disorders. Mrs. Torres was also concerned about Alondra's social-emotional difficulties including her high levels of anxiety and worry, as well as her limited social relationships.

BACKGROUND INFORMATION

The information presented in this section was obtained from background information and an interview provided by Alondra's mother that was conducted in Spanish. Academic records and previous evaluations were also reviewed; some were in Spanish and others in English.

Alondra is an 8-year-old female of Puerto Rican nationality. She is currently in the third grade at Collier Elementary School in Philadelphia. She lives with her younger sister and biological mother and father. Alondra's grandmother also lives with the family; however, she frequently returns to Puerto Rico for weeks at a time. Alondra lived with her family in Puerto Rico until the age of 6, when she came with her mother and younger sister to the Philadelphia area.

Mrs. Torres's pregnancy and Alondra's birth are significant for increased blood sugar levels, weight gain, and hypertension experienced by Mrs. Torres during the final month of pregnancy. Mrs. Torres underwent a Cesarean section with no reported complications. Alondra was given formula as an infant due to difficulties with breast-feeding.

Alondra's health history is significant for a diagnosis of asthma at 1 year, a ruptured appendix at 2 years, and a possible febrile seizure resulting from a high fever prior to the appendectomy. Mrs. Torres reports that Alondra's developmental history is significant for a language delay and difficulties feeding due to Alondra being a very fussy eater.

At 3 years, Alondra was enrolled in a Head Start program where she was administered yearly psychological, speech and language, and occupational therapy evaluations. According to evaluations by the Department of Education of Puerto Rico, Alondra was found eligible for special education services as a result of a language delay. The preliminary evaluation by Head Start (8/2004) reported that Alondra performed at the Average to Low Average range on the Leiter International Performance Scale-Revised. She was also performing in the Moderately Low to Low range on the Vineland Adaptive Behavior Scales, Second Edition. Alondra was also administered the Childhood Autism Rating Scales (CARS), and the results indicated she did not fall within the autistic range. Prior to her entrance into the

Head Start program, Alondra lived with her grandmother and had very little social contact with children her age. Alondra communicated mostly with signals and gestures, but also produced some isolated words and had recently begun to use short phrases.

This initial evaluation raised the possibility of Pervasive Developmental Disorder (PDD) based on evidence of a severe language delay. Subsequent yearly evaluations by the Head Start program in Puerto Rico (6/2005, 5/2006) reported that Alondra scored in the High Average range (6/2005) and in the Superior range (5/2006) on the Leiter International Performance Scale-Revised. The latter evaluation noted that Alondra had begun to use short phrases and sentences as well as to address others by their names when speaking to them (6/2005). In a speech and language reevaluation through Head Start (1/2006), Alondra scored in the Moderately Low range on the Peabody Picture Vocabulary Test-IV. It was also noted that Alondra had difficulty articulating and differentiating specific phoneme sounds. This evaluation maintained that Alondra had a specific phonological language delay and recommended speech and language therapy twice weekly for 40-minute intervals. Alondra's social skills seemed to improve during her time in the Head Start program. Both Head Start evaluations indicated that Alondra expressed interest in others, shared and played with other children, and displayed some evidence of imaginative and cooperative play (6/2005, 5/2006). The final psychological report by Head Start (5/2006) considered the possibility of ruling out a diagnosis of PDD. These evaluations were completed in Spanish using the appropriate Spanish language versions of the testing measures.

In September 2008, Alondra was enrolled in the second grade at Collier Elementary School in Philadelphia. Shortly after beginning second grade, Alondra was evaluated at the University Medical Center, where she was administered a speech and language evaluation in Spanish (10/2008). This evaluation concluded mild/moderate expressive language and articulation difficulties. A completed evaluation from the Center for Autism (10/2008) reports a history of speech delay, isolation, and difficulty relating to peers consistent with a diagnosis of an autism spectrum disorder. However, the evaluation concluded with ruling out the following: pervasive developmental disorder, not otherwise specified (PDD-NOS), Attention-Deficit/Hyperactivity Disorder (ADHD), and depression. Instead, the following diagnoses were made: mixed receptive-expressive language disorder, phonological disorder, and mild mental retardation. An additional occupational therapy evaluation by the University Medical Center (11/2008) concluded that

Alondra had decreased balance with challenging postures, visual-motor integration concerns, poor scissor skills needed for success in school tasks, decreased motor planning, and limited ability to follow directions. It was also noted that Alondra had a sensitivity to certain fabrics and enjoyed being barefoot, so often avoided wearing shoes. Furthermore, it was explained that she often displayed an unusual need for touching people and objects.

Alondra was also evaluated by the School District of Philadelphia in December 2008. According to this report, most tests were administered in English. There was no indication if the evaluation was conducted by a Spanish-speaking psychologist. Results of this evaluation included a score in the Low Average range on the Wechsler Intelligence Scale for Children – Fourth Edition (WISC-IV). Of note was a significant discrepancy between superior nonverbal skills and borderline verbal skills. It was concluded that Alondra should receive services for a language-based Specific Learning Disability. Furthermore, Alondra was said to demonstrate weaknesses in oral reading and comprehension, written expression, and reasoning. As part of this evaluation, Alondra was also administered the Beery Buktenica Developmental Test of Visual Motor Integration-Fifth Edition, on which she received a standard score of 83. It was noted that Alondra required extra time to complete tasks.

In April 2008, Alondra under went a comprehensive biopsychosocial evaluation by a private psychologist following a referral from the Philadelphia Mental Health Center. This evaluation concluded with elevated scores on both the Childhood Autism Rating Scale (CARS) and the Autism Treatment Evaluation Checklist (ATEC). The evaluator suggested the diagnosis of Pervasive Developmental Disorder, NOS, and recommended weekly therapy in her home and in the community with the goals of enhancing social reciprocity and communication skills.

In October 2008, a reevaluation by the Center for Autism was conducted although no specific measures were administered. This reevaluation reviewed the previous biopsychosocial evaluation and with that information concluded a diagnosis of PDD, NOS, and "Borderline Intellectual Functioning." In January 2009, a second reevaluation by the Center for Autism was conducted with the same results.

Mrs. Torres also mentioned a number of concerns regarding Alondra's social, emotional, and behavioral issues. She explained that Alondra has difficulty sleeping in her own room. Alondra seems to express a great deal of worry about certain things and displays generally high levels of anxiety. Mrs. Torres also expressed concern for Alondra's ability to make friends and socialize with her peers. She explained that Alondra tends to be very "selective" with her friends and does not like to engage socially with children who are too loud.

Mrs. Torres explained that Alondra's maternal grandmother and maternal aunt both suffer from emotional problems that may relate to bipolar disorder. Mrs. Torres also explained that she has experienced anxiety/panic attacks in the past and previously received therapy for these issues.

CLASSROOM OBSERVATION

Alondra was observed at Collier Elementary School on the afternoon of March 29, 2010, in her general education classroom. The classroom was arranged with long tables placed together lengthwise in three rows, and the teacher's desk was located at the back right-hand corner of the room. Alondra was seated at the left corner of the back table. There were 28 students in the class, including 16 girls and 12 boys. The classroom was neatly organized with a variety of colorful posters and designated activity areas; materials were placed for easy access for all students. The classroom rules were posted in clear view on the front wall. On the front chalkboard was a daily schedule written out in chronological order. Also posted on the front wall was a behavioral consequence system consisting of color-coded levels ranging from "Warning" to "Out of the Room Time Out." Students were assigned a clothespin with their name written on it which was to be placed at a specific level as a result of inappropriate behavior. There was a clothespin for "Room 201" which was placed at the "Warning" level when the students became too noisy.

On the afternoon of the observation, students were engaged in a variety of activities including correcting a reading worksheet, participating in a shared reading activity with a question-and-answer session, a journal activity, and free time where the students played board games in small groups. During the teacher-led worksheet activity, Alondra was consistently following along, paying attention, and making the appropriate corrections to her own work. At 1:40 P.M., during this worksheet activity, a 10-minute time sample of Alondra's on-task and off-task behavior was taken. Alondra was observed to be on-task and engaged in her work 93% of the observed time and off-task only 6% of the time. Alondra, as well as the rest of the class, was very efficient in her transitions from one activity to the next. During one of these transitions, Ms. Fernandez verbally noted Alondra's efficient transitioning and commented that "I can see Alondra is ready for the next activity."

At approximately 1:55 P.M., students were led in a shared reading activity in which Ms. Fernandez read a few pages from a story about the life of President Barack Obama. Following the reading, Ms. Fernandez conducted a brief question-and-answer session about the reading. Alondra followed directions and appeared engaged but did not raise her hand to participate.

This activity was followed by 5 to 10 minutes in which the students were asked to work independently to complete a workbook page and write a few sentences in their journals. It was noted that Alondra worked very diligently, independently, and was not distracted even when some of the other students at the table were talking amongst themselves. In fact, for the majority of the observation period, Alondra seemed to be more on task than most of her classmates. Upon completion of this workbook activity, students were allowed to break into small groups and have free time where they were able to play a variety of board games that Ms. Fernandez had available in her classroom. When Alondra finished her assignment, she was asked by another classmate to go choose a board game to play with her. The two girls, along with two other students, went to one corner of the room to play the board game "Sorry." Alondra seemed to play well with her classmates and it was observed that she demonstrated appropriate turn-taking behavior and seemed to abide by the general rules of the game.

At the end of the free time, students were asked to return to their seats so that homework books could be passed around. When Ms. Fernandez asked for two volunteers to pass out the homework books, Alondra quickly raised her hand. Ms. Fernandez called on Alondra and another student, and they proceeded to pass out the homework composition books to their classmates.

At the end of the observation period, students were called on in groups to retrieve their belongings from the closet and get ready to transition to the school yard for dismissal. It was noted that Alondra made efficient transitions including getting her belongings from the closet and lining up at the front door for dismissal. Ms. Fernandez explained that this was a typical day for Alondra and seemed to provide an adequate representation of Alondra's behavior.

TEACHER INTERVIEW

Alondra's teacher, Ms. Fernandez, was interviewed on the afternoon of February 26, 2010. Ms. Fernandez explained that this was her second consecutive school year as Alondra's teacher. She reviewed Alondra's daily schedule, which begins with ESOL (English as a Second Language) class from 8:30 to about 9:45 A.M. Alondra then attends the Resource Room for both reading, from 10:00 to about 10:30, and math, from 11:10 to 12:00. Ms. Fernandez also noted that Alondra receives speech and language therapy on Thursdays from 2:00 to 2:45 P.M.

Ms. Fernandez explained that Alondra is an attentive and cooperative student, good at routines, and a good helper. She said that Alondra is easy to get along with so she can put her anywhere in the class and be assured that she will not have any problems working with or sitting near any other child. Ms. Fernandez also noted that while Alondra has to leave the classroom multiple times during the mornings to attend ESOL classes and the resource room, she is always able to transition well into any activity or assignment that the rest of the class is working on.

Ms. Fernandez explained that academically, Alondra is performing at the basic level as compared to the rest of her class and that while certain activities may be challenging for Alondra, she is able to complete most of her assignments in a timely manner. At the times when Alondra is in the general education classroom for guided reading, Ms. Fernandez usually places her with the most basic reading level group, and Alondra often ends up helping her peers follow along with the reading. Ms. Fernandez also noted that Alondra's English language fluency has greatly improved since last year; while Alondra was previously restricted to one- or two-word phrases, this year she has begun to use complete sentences in a more reciprocal and conversational discourse.

BEHAVIORAL OBSERVATIONS DURING TESTING

Alondra came to each testing session with her mother. On each occasion, Alondra was dressed neatly and comfortably. Upon greeting Alondra, the examiner questioned her regarding which language she preferred to speak. Alondra indicated that she would rather speak Spanish. Once Alondra and the examiner were situated in the testing room, rapport was established with a general discussion of Alondra's interests, friends, family, pets, and favorite activities at school. Alondra explained that she enjoyed school and playing with her friends in class. She was able to engage in reciprocal conversation with the examiner and demonstrated appropriate social skills.

Throughout the first testing session, Alondra remained focused and on task. She completed test items with great care and used self-correction strategies, such as rethinking incorrect answers and arriving at the correct answer after further consideration. Alondra stated that she particularly liked math and was excited when math tasks were presented. During subsequent testing sessions, it was slightly more difficult to motivate her. During the third testing session, a schedule was used that included the opportunity for reinforcers on completion of certain tasks, and this motivated Alondra to complete the activities.

Alondra seemed to become particularly frustrated with writing tasks and reading tasks that focused on phonological processing skills such as deletion, segmentation, and reading nonsense words. These tasks required significantly more motivating prompts than other test items.

Most of the general conversation during testing sessions was in Spanish. However, Alondra would sometimes mix English words into conversations. Alondra seemed comfortable answering questions presented to her in English when she was able to actually see the question in written form. During listening comprehension tasks, she often asked to see the question that the examiner was reading, explaining that she could understand it better by reading it. Alondra often asked for verbally presented questions in English to be repeated. However, when questions were presented in Spanish, she was most often able to respond on the first try. While Alondra was able to demonstrate appropriate use of grammar skills in conversational Spanish, at times she mispronounced some words, such as saying "bificil" instead of the correct Spanish word for difficult, "dificil."

Overall, Alondra responded well to verbal prompts to increase motivation and was able to stay on task and cooperate. While she required more prompts, breaks, and reinforcers during the last two testing sessions, Alondra was generally attentive and able to complete each task.

Alondra's performance on the various tests administered should provide a valid representation of her abilities.

TESTS ADMINISTERED

Universal Nonverbal Intelligence Test (UNIT)

Woodcock-Johnson III Tests of Cognitive Abilities (WJ III COG)

Batería III Woodcock-Muñoz (Batería III)

Wechsler Intelligence Scale for Children-Integrated, Fourth Edition (WISC-IV Integrated)

Kaufman Test of Educational Achievement, Second Edition (KTEA-II)

Curriculum Based Measures, Math and Reading (CBM)

Oral and Written Language Scales (OWLS)

Kinetic Family Drawing (KFD)

Behavior Assessment System for Children, Second Edition (BASC-2) (Teacher Rating Scales)

Roberts Apperception Test for Children and Adolescents, Second Edition-Hispanic/Latino Cards (Roberts-2)

Childhood Autism Rating Scale (CARS)—completed by Mrs. Torres

Autism Treatment Evaluation Checklist—Spanish Version (ATEC)

TEST INTERPRETATION

Within the body of the report, Alondra's levels of performance are referred to by verbal descriptors. The standard score ranges and descriptors and listed below:

Standard Score Range	Descriptor
130 and up	Significantly above average
120–129	Well above average
116–119	Above average
110–115	High average
90–109	Average
85–89	Low average
80–84	Below average
70–79	Well below average
69 and below	Significantly below average

All tests, observations, and interviews were administered by a clinician fluent in both English and Spanish.

Cognitive Abilities

Intellectual Ability

Alondra's overall intellectual ability was assessed with the Universal Nonverbal Intelligence Test (UNIT), Batería-III Woodcock-Muñoz (Batería-III), Woodcock-Johnson III Tests of Cognitive Abilities (WJ III COG), and two subtests from the Wechsler Intelligence Scale for Children-Integrated, Fourth Edition (WISC-IV Integrated). On the UNIT, Alondra's overall ability was in the Average range, with a score of 100, where she performed as well as or better than 50% of her same-aged peers. On subtests from the WJ III COG, Batería-III, and the WISC-IV Integrated, Alondra's abilities varied from Well Below Average to Well Above Average.

These tests were selected to create a comprehensive battery according to the tenets of the cross-battery approach. The cross-battery approach seeks to measure cognitive ability according to the research-based Cattell-Horn-Carroll theory of cognitive ability (CHC theory). The specific results of Alondra's performance are presented in Appendix A. A chart with each specific cognitive ability score according to the CHC theory can be found in Appendix B of this report. Appendix C contains the analysis of the effects of learning a second language and culture on test results.

Higher-Level Processing

Higher-level processing and reasoning skills, which can be thought of as "thinking abilities," are used in tasks that require problem solving or information processing. They involve the ability to process and retain new information, as well as the ability to retrieve previously learned concepts and apply them to new tasks and situations. The cognitive abilities within this area are: fluid reasoning, long-term storage and retrieval, auditory processing, and visual processing. Auditory processing is discussed under Oral Language.

Fluid Reasoning Fluid reasoning, or novel reasoning and problem solving, is minimally dependent on cultural knowledge and prior schooling. It is related to school achievement, particularly in math and science, as it encompasses the ability to use reasoning and problem-solving skills when encountering new information in the classroom. Tests in this area assessed two components of fluid reasoning, induction and general sequential reasoning, otherwise known as deduction. Induction is the ability to discover a rule or concept that governs a problem, while general sequential reasoning is the ability to start with stated rules and engage in one or more steps to solve a novel problem. On tasks of fluid reasoning, Alondra's scores fell within the Average range.

Long-Term Storage and Retrieval Long-term storage and retrieval is the ability to store information in long-term memory and fluently retrieve it later through association. Long-term retrieval is related to basic reading skills, such as sound-symbol associations and word recognition. It is also related to fluent calculation skills in mathematics, such as recall of basic math facts. Learning new information requires the ability to store information in long-term memory and retrieve it fluently at a later time. Two components of long-term storage and retrieval were assessed. One component of long-term storage and retrieval to be examined was Alondra's ideational fluency, or her ability to rapidly produce a series of known words related to a particular concept or object. This task allows the flexibility to respond with any words as long as they fit the category specified. Alondra provided words for each category in both Spanish and English. Her performance was in the Average range. She performed in the Well Below Average range on a separate task of long-term storage and retrieval that assessed her ability to rapidly produce names for pictured objects. While most of her responses were accurate (and given in both English and Spanish), Alondra's response rate was slow, which impacted her score. A lower score on this subtest may be the result of Alondra's somewhat limited proficiency in both English and Spanish. This task differed from the previous one in that it required Alondra to retrieve *specific* names for objects, involving a significant amount of processing and therefore more time than for her monolingual peers.

Visual Processing Visual processing can be described as the ability to analyze and synthesize visual information and to perceive or discriminate between visual shapes. Alondra was administered a number of tasks of visual processing ability. These tasks were all part of a nonverbal test battery. On these tasks, Alondra performed in the Average ability range.

Automatic Processing

Automatic or low-level processing is the ability to process information quickly and efficiently, without conscious thought, and is used for both recall and rapid processing of information. Automatic processing is the foundation of higher-level processing skills, because the amount of energy one can commit to higher-level processes is inversely related to the energy demands necessary to carry out these lower-level activities. The cognitive abilities within the area of automatic or low-level processing are short-term memory and processing speed.

Short-Term Memory Short-term memory, or the ability to hold information in immediate awareness and use it within a few seconds, is related to reading and math achievement and impacts an individual's ability to follow directions and learn. It includes memory span and working memory. Memory span is the ability to attend to and recall temporally ordered elements immediately in the correct order after a single presentation. Working memory is the capacity to manipulate information while holding it in immediate awareness, such as repeating a sequence of numbers in reverse order. On one task of memory span, which required Alondra to repeat a sequence of tapped blocks in the same order as demonstrated by the examiner, she scored in the Average range. On a task of working memory, requiring Alondra to repeat the sequence of tapped blocks in the reverse order, she performed in the Well Above Average range, demonstrating a relative strength in this ability.

Processing Speed Processing speed, or the ability to perform automatic cognitive tasks quickly, is composed of speed of reasoning and perceptual speed, and is related to academic achievement in reading and math. On tasks of processing speed, Alondra performed in the Average range.

Oral Language

Oral language involves listening comprehension (receptive language) and oral expression (expressive language). Alondra's listening comprehension and oral expression skills were assessed using both the KTEA-II and the OWLS.

Listening Comprehension

Listening comprehension, or the ability to understand spoken information, was first measured by subtests from the KTEA-II. On these subtests, Alondra performed in the Well Below Average range. Alondra often asked for questions or passages to be repeated, which is not permitted on this test. She also frequently asked to see the questions in written form as opposed to just hearing the test items, explaining that she can "understand them better when she sees them." All of the items in the area of listening comprehension from the KTEA-II were presented in English. While it was clear that Alondra was unable to understand many of the verbally presented items in English, she demonstrated a significant amount of effort when attempting to provide answers for these items. The listening comprehension items on this subtest are presented on a CD and therefore the spoken rate at which the items were presented maintained a quick and steady pace, which may have been a bit too quick for Alondra to comprehend.

In order to further investigate Alondra's listening comprehension abilities, she was administered the listening comprehension subtest from the OWLS. This test was initially presented in English, and Alondra had some difficulties. In order to minimize the effects of Alondra's limited English proficiency, items that were originally incorrect when presented in English were informally readministered in Spanish. Alondra was able to answer most of these items when presented in Spanish.

Oral Expression

Oral expression, or the ability to organize and verbally communicate fluently and in a coherent manner, was measured using subtests from the KTEA-II and the OWLS. On the KTEA-II subtests, Alondra performed in the Well Below Average range. Items from this subtest were administered only in English. While Alondra was able to interpret and respond to easier items, she had difficulty understanding and subsequently responding to more difficult items.

The oral expression subtest from the OWLS was also administered in order to determine her overall oral expressive ability. Alondra was instructed to answer the test items in whichever language she felt most comfortable. Furthermore, when it was evident that Alondra did not understand the question in English, the question was then repeated in Spanish. Alondra answered most of the items in Spanish; however, when asked to attempt these answers in English, Alondra was able to provide content-relevant answers that conveyed the main idea or theme for most items. While Alondra was able to provide grammatically correct and coherent answers in Spanish, many of her answers in English had grammatical errors that are common among English language learners, such as subject-verb agreement and adjective-noun reversal.

As noted in the introduction, it is important to interpret Alondra's performance on these two subtests of verbal comprehension with consideration for the process of acquiring a second language.

Acquired Knowledge

Acquired knowledge is information that has been learned through previous exposure. It represents an individual's breadth and depth of culture-specific knowledge and the ability to apply this type of knowledge. One aspect of acquired knowledge is crystallized intelligence, which is composed primarily of language-based knowledge and tends to predict an individual's academic success. Alondra was administered tasks of crystallized ability measuring verbal comprehension from the English and Spanish versions of a test battery (WJ III COG and Batería-III). Alondra performed similarly on both versions of these tasks, with scores falling in the Well Below Average range. It is important to note that these tasks have high language and cultural demands.

Cognitive Academic Language Proficiency

Scores of Alondra's cognitive academic language proficiency (CALP) were obtained for verbal comprehension subtests in both English and Spanish. CALP is the basis for a student's academic success and is highly dependent on previous schooling, age, and cultural experiences. CALP can, many times, take 5 to 7 years to develop and represents higher levels of processing including analysis, synthesis, and evaluation. Alondra's CALP scores on both the English and Spanish verbal comprehension subtests from the WJ III COG and the Batería-III fell in the limited range. It is important to note that while CALP scores are normally used to describe the extent to which a student has acquired a second language, Alondra's CALP score on the Spanish verbal comprehension subtest indicates that her Spanish academic proficiency level is also in the limited range.

Academic Achievement

Academic achievement represents all the skills and information acquired through schooling and explicit instruction, including reading, mathematics, and written language. Alondra's test scores are presented in Appendix A.

The tests of academic achievement were administered in English, with some variation in the area of oral language ability. Due to Alondra's progress in English language acquisition over the past school year as reported by her teachers, it is important to evaluate Alondra's academic abilities in the English language in order to have a better understanding of her progress and current ability levels. Such an evaluation will provide important information for Alondra's educational programming, as well as assist in monitoring her academic progress throughout the next few school years.

Reading

Alondra's basic reading skills and reading comprehension skills were assessed using the KTEA-II and CBM reading probes. Alondra was able to identify all the letters of the English alphabet and most of the letters of the Spanish alphabet.

Alondra was administered reading-related subtests from the KTEA-II. On a test of phonological awareness, Alondra performed in the Well Below Average range. While she was able to complete a rhyming task with ease, tasks requiring her to identify and segment individual phonemes within a word and delete individual phonemes were difficult for Alondra. This is consistent with concerns identified in previous evaluations conducted in Spanish.

Alondra's word recognition skills were found to be in the Below Average range when compared to her same-aged peers. She made an effort to sound out some of the more difficult words; however, she tended to recognize the initial letters and then guess a familiar word with the same initial sounds. Her word recognition fluency was at a similar level, in the Below Average range.

Alondra was also administered word recognition curriculum-based measurement (CBM) probes of varying difficulty. She was able to identify familiar words at a rapid pace and with ease. She correctly identified 97% and 88% of words at the Pre-primer and Primer levels, respectively. At the first-, second-, and third-grade levels, she was able to identify most of the words at a somewhat rapid pace with 78%, 75%, and 72% accuracy, respectively.

On a task of nonsense word decoding from the KTEA-II, Alondra performed in the Below Average range. When she was asked to decode fluently, Alondra experienced greater difficulty and performed in the significantly Below Average range. Alondra had particular difficulty reading nonsense words (i.e., letter combinations that represent phonetically correct made-up words). She attempted to read many of these words as real words with similar initial and final letter sounds. Although she made some attempt to sound out the nonsense words, she had difficulty generating sounds for letter combinations that were unfamiliar to her.

Alondra was also administered CBM oral reading fluency probes in English. She was able to read passages at the first-grade level with an "instructional" proficiency level, at a rate of 56 words per minute (wpm) with three errors per minute. At the second-grade level, Alondra read at a rate of 44 wpm with nine errors per minute. Although her rate fell in the "instructional" range, her error rate placed her performance in the "frustration" range. At the third-grade level, Alondra read at a rate of 42 wpm with seven errors, placing her again in the "frustration" range. It is evident that Alondra has received a good amount of instruction and practice with English language reading skills. Her performance on these reading tasks, in conjunction with information regarding her progress provided by her teachers, seems to demonstrate that Alondra is benefiting from the intense instruction in not only the ESOL classes but in her reading groups as well.

The examiner attempted to assess Alondra's word recognition skills and oral reading fluency in Spanish. Alondra seemed hesitant to attempt these tasks, explaining that she wasn't good at reading in Spanish. She read with 19% accuracy on the Spanish word recognition probes and was unable to read a passage.

On the KTEA-II, Alondra performed in the Below Average range in reading comprehension. Alondra used some contextual clues to answer questions; however, it was evident that she was unable to pronounce many of the English words. Many times, Alondra, rather than answering a question orally, pointed to a word or phrase in the text. Her difficulty with reading unfamiliar words seemed to affect her ability to answer most of the reading comprehension questions at the level of her same-aged peers.

Written Language

Written language is composed of both the basic writing skills required to produce written text, including spelling ability, and the ability to effectively communicate ideas in written words. Alondra performed in the Average range on a spelling task from the KTEA-II.

Alondra was also administered a written expression task from the KTEA-II and seemed to have difficulty with most of the items on this subtest. Many of her errors were structural and grammatical errors typically made by English language learners, such as improper subject-verb agreement and adjective-noun order reversal. Alondra demonstrated some knowledge of punctuation, including capitalization of initial words in a sentence and titles (Mr. and Mrs.).

Alondra had difficulty understanding many of the probes from this task and required repetition of most items. She became frustrated easily, specifically with a section requiring a written summary of the story read previously. Alondra was not able to complete the written summary, but when asked to verbally summarize the story, she captured most of the main ideas and some details, expressing them in a combination of English and Spanish. Due to the great amount of difficulty with this subtest and a failure to complete the final summary, an overall score was not calculated for the written expression subtest.

To further assess Alondra's writing ability, she was administered a CBM writing probe. During a 3-minute writing task with a story starter provided, Alondra was able to produce two well-thought-out sentences in English that contained minimal grammatical errors. Alondra needed, however, a significant amount of prompting and incentives to complete this task. Here, also, written tasks seemed to cause a great deal of frustration for Alondra.

Mathematics

Tests of mathematics and quantitative knowledge assess computation and the ability to reason with numbers. On the KTEA-II, Alondra performed in the Average range on computation and on tasks involving mathematical concepts and applications. Her mathematical skills were age appropriate and she was also able to differentiate between skills that she had and had not learned yet. Alondra seemed to thoroughly enjoy mathematics-based tasks and seemed eager and motivated, self-correcting and reasoning well when she attempted more difficult tasks.

On CBM probes that target math fluency in grade-level math skills, Alondra performed in the "instructional" range for second-grade probes, which included addition of two-digit numbers. Although Alondra performed in the "frustration" range on a third-grade-level probe, including both addition and subtraction, many of her errors were inconsistent and a result of her failure to recognize the correct operational sign or her failure to complete the entire problem. Although Alondra seems to demonstrate age-appropriate skills, her performance in the "frustration" range indicates that she has not yet mastered them. Thus, Alondra seems to be performing at a level similar to her same-aged peers in mathematics skills as measured by the KTEA-II subtests; however, she may have some difficulty with mixed addition and subtraction problems on timed tasks.

Overall, Alondra seems to demonstrate strengths in the areas of spelling, math computation, math concepts, and math application. Alondra seemed to enjoy these tasks and demonstrated good use of strategies to attempt more difficult problems. While she is able to complete timed tasks at the second-grade level with ease, similar tasks involving mixed skills at the third-grade level proved to be more difficult for her.

While Alondra's oral reading fluency and word recognition skills seem to be improving (as noted by her teachers), and fall just below grade level (as assessed by CBM probes and KTEA-II subtests), Alondra had significant difficulty with phonemic awareness tasks and difficulty as well with word attack and word identification. Alondra will require specific instruction in basic reading skills.

Social-Emotional and Behavioral Functioning

Information regarding Alondra's social-emotional functioning was obtained from an interview with Mrs. Torres, observations, a teacher interview, the Behavior Assessment Scale for Children, Second Edition (BASC-2)—Teacher

Form, and the Roberts Apperception Test for Children (Roberts-2).

During the initial interview, Mrs. Torres indicated concern regarding Alondra's social interactions with other children her age. She explained that Alondra tends to be very "selective" when approaching or interacting with other children and tends to cling to her mother in social situations. Alondra tends to be bothered when other children are particularly loud. Ms. Fernandez had reported that Alondra works well with all of her peers and is able to approach and socialize with her classmates in an age-appropriate manner. During the classroom observation, Alondra engaged in reciprocal social conversation with her peers and demonstrated appropriate turn-taking behavior when playing a board game with three other students. Ms. Fernandez also noted that while Alondra works well with routines, she also responds appropriately to change.

Mrs. Torres expressed concern over her daughter's tendency to worry about age-inappropriate things such as the family's financial situation. She also noted that Alondra is frightened when she hears an ambulance or fire truck and sometimes worries about accidents such as fires in their home although there is no history of such incidents. Mrs. Torres is concerned about Alondra's overall levels of anxiety and worry. She also noted that Alondra has trouble sleeping alone in her own room and frequently asks her mother to lie down with her until she falls asleep. Mrs. Torres also expressed concern over Alondra's eating habits. She explained that Alondra is a very fussy eater and is extremely selective about what she will and will not eat.

Alondra's responses to the Roberts-2 conveyed a general theme of sadness resulting from not performing well in school. Many of her responses regarding apparent sadness of the characters in the pictures referred to poor school performance: "Mom and dad upset because she didn't do well on spelling;" "She's very sad because she didn't do well on her test."

Ms. Fernandez was asked to complete the BASC-2-Teacher Rating Scale. The BASC-2 is an objective rating scale system used to diagnose emotional and behavior disorders in children. Ms. Fernandez's responses regarding Alondra's social, emotional, and behavioral functioning placed her at the Average or expected level, indicating that she is functioning at a similar level as her same-aged peers. No areas of concern were indicated.

Although Ms. Fernandez's responses on the BASC-2 and in the interview indicated that Alondra is generally positive and displays appropriate affect in school, Alondra's concerns indicate that she may need more or a different type of instructional support, and may need counseling to help understand the reasons for her current level of performance. Further, Mrs. Torres's concerns regarding Alondra's tendency to worry and her fears might warrant further investigation. Finally, the reference to Alondra's overly picky and fussy eating habits is an area that should be investigated regarding a nutritional program and general physical health.

OBSERVATIONS AND DATA REGARDING AUTISM/ DEVELOPMENTAL DISORDER DIAGNOSES

Due to previous diagnoses of Pervasive Developmental Disorder and concern for the possibility of an autism spectrum disorder, an examination of many aspects of these disorders was undertaken to explore relevant behaviors and to clarify the diagnoses.

Mrs. Torres and Ms. Fernandez were asked to complete the Childhood Autism Rating Scales (CARS), which addresses a wide variety of behaviors associated with diagnoses on the autism spectrum. Mrs. Torres completed this through an interview with the examiner. The CARS distinguishes children with autism in the mild to moderate range from children with autism in the moderate to severe range. This rating scale contains questions about behaviors seen in students diagnosed with autism that include relating to other people; imitation; emotional response; body use; object use; adaptation to change; visual response; listening response; taste, smell, and touch response; fear or nervousness; verbal communication; nonverbal communication; activity level; and intellectual response.

Both Ms. Fernandez and Mrs. Torres's responses to the CARS items place Alondra in the Non-Autistic range. Ms. Fernandez expressed no concern regarding behaviors associated with autism spectrum disorders. Mrs. Torres's responses indicated slight concern with Alondra's emotional responses, or the tendency to display exaggerated or inappropriate emotional reactions to certain situations, her difficulty with adapting to changes in routines, and a moderately abnormal level of fear or nervousness.

Mrs. Torres was asked to complete the Autism Treatment Evaluation Checklist – Spanish Version (ATEC). Since this measure is generally used to evaluate the efficacy of autism treatment plans, Mrs. Torres's responses were interpreted qualitatively and were used to create a better understanding of Alondra's functioning and areas of concern. The ATEC addresses four general areas of functioning, including Speech/Language/Communication, Sociability, Sensory/Cognitive Awareness, and Health/Physical Awareness. In the Speech/Language area, Mrs. Torres's responses indicated concerns regarding Alondra's "somewhat" limited ability to use appropriate language to explain what she wants, ask meaningful questions, and communicate in an age-appropriate manner. Regarding sociability, Mrs. Torres expressed concerns regarding Alondra's tendency to sometimes avoid eye contact and her lack of friends. Furthermore, she expressed concern that Alondra is not very imaginative and does not have an inquisitive nature about certain things. Most of her concerns, however, were in the area of Health/Physical Awareness, again noting her difficulty with sleeping alone, her limited diet and interest in certain foods, her tendency to be sad or cry frequently, sensitivity to certain noises or sound, and high levels of fear or nervousness about certain situations.

Information provided in the interviews with Mrs. Torres and Ms. Fernandez, results of questionnaires, a classroom observation, and observations during testing sessions were reviewed in consideration of previous diagnoses, as were the previous evaluations, including evidence of a significant language delay. However, current observations and the information provided by Mrs. Torres and Ms. Fernandez do not indicate that Alondra presents as a child with an autism spectrum disorder.

SUMMARY

Alondra is an 8-year-old female referred to the psychoeducational clinic by her mother at the recommendation of Alondra's pediatrician, Dr. Alfonso. Mrs. Torres referred Alondra for a comprehensive evaluation with specific concerns regarding Alondra's difficulties with oral language and academics. Mrs. Torres also wanted to clarify previous diagnoses, including an auditory processing deficit, a weakness in working memory, a language delay, Pervasive Developmental Disorder (PDD), and possible autism spectrum disorder (ASD). Mrs. Torres was also concerned about Alondra's lack of social relationships and emotional difficulties, including anxiety.

Alondra was first evaluated in her native Puerto Rico, where concerns of a language delay surfaced around the age of 2, when Alondra was brought to her pediatrician by Mrs. Torres for a hearing exam. Through the Department of Education of Puerto Rico, Alondra was evaluated on numerous occasions, including speech and language, occupational therapy, and psychoeducational. Results indicated a severe phonological language delay, the possibility of PDD, and Average to High Average cognitive abilities. As a result of these findings, Alondra became eligible for special education services, where she attended a Head Start program until the age of 5. Alondra also received speech and language therapy and occupational therapy throughout preschool and kindergarten.

In 2007, Alondra's family moved to Philadelphia, where Alondra was evaluated by the school district and St. Christopher's Hospital, resulting in another finding of phonological awareness problems. Mrs. Torres also had Alondra evaluated through the Center for Autism, due to persisting concern of ASD. Their initial evaluation did not identify ASD, but a second evaluation, conducted through interview, did.

Alondra is in the third grade at Collier Elementary School. She receives daily ESOL services and attends the resource room for both math and reading instruction. She receives speech and language therapy once a week in school, as well as additional speech-language and occupational therapy through St. Christopher's Hospital. Alondra also attends Sylvan Learning Center weekly for additional instruction and receives homework help in math and reading as well as weekly home/community therapy for social skills.

During a classroom observation, Alondra demonstrated high levels of on-task behavior, cooperation, and attentiveness. She engaged in appropriate reciprocal social interactions with her peers, and according to her teacher, gets along well with her classmates and is a great helper in class.

To better understand Alondra's current functioning, a comprehensive evaluation was completed across multiple sessions. The evaluation was conducted by a bilingual clinician and, while most conversations were in Spanish, many standardized and nonstandardized tests were administered in English as well. During these sessions, Alondra was cooperative and able to remain on task and required few verbal prompts and rewards. In order to increase motivation for particularly frustrating tasks during the second and third test sessions, a schedule and reward system were established. Alondra responded well to rewards (e.g., stickers) and short breaks after completion of academic tasks.

Alondra's Full Scale score on a nonverbal battery of cognitive abilities fell within the Average range. Her scores on individual subtests indicate a broad range of abilities ranging from Well Below Average to Well Above Average.

Fluid reasoning, working memory, visual processing, processing speed, and ideational fluency represent relative strengths for Alondra. Ability areas that have a high dependence on English language skills and American cultural knowledge are relative weaknesses. She had significant difficulty on verbal comprehension tasks (i.e., vocabulary and analogies) in both Spanish and English. Her overall cognitive academic language proficiency in both English and Spanish fell in the limited range, indicating that tasks requiring higher-level language processing will be difficult for Alondra.

Information provided in interview sessions with Mrs. Torres and Ms. Fernandez indicate that while Alondra has progressed significantly in English language acquisition over the past year and a half, understanding some verbal instructions and use of correct grammar remain challenging. Mrs. Torres also expressed concern regarding Alondra's anxiety levels. Information regarding Alondra's social, emotional, and behavioral functioning provided by Ms. Fernandez revealed several strengths, including good cooperation, attention, and interpersonal skills, and no areas of concern.

Alondra's overall academic achievement was assessed in the areas of mathematics, reading, written expression, listening comprehension, and oral expression. Alondra's performance in the areas of math computation and application indicate she is performing at grade level. She also demonstrated a relative strength in spelling. Alondra demonstrated many areas of academic difficulty including phonemic awareness, word recognition, reading comprehension, and written expression in English. As a phonologically based language disorder was first diagnosed in Puerto Rico, her difficulty in phonemic awareness seems to be independent of her limited English proficiency and instead demonstrates an innate weakness in phonological processing skills. Alondra's oral language abilities were assessed formally and informally in both English and Spanish. While Alondra had difficulty understanding more complex verbal directions in English, when these were repeated more slowly or presented in Spanish, Alondra usually understood and responded appropriately. Alondra also demonstrated appropriate expressive language in Spanish and the ability to provide contextually correct responses in English.

Checklists and questionnaires administered to Mrs. Torres and Ms. Fernandez did not indicate ASD. Furthermore, observations and interviews with Mrs. Torres and Ms. Fernandez indicate that Alondra is functioning at appropriate social and cognitive levels and when given the opportunity, demonstrates good use of reciprocal interpersonal skills.

Continued opportunities to practice English and increase American cultural knowledge are important considerations for Alondra. Her progress in English shows that she possesses the potential to achieve at grade level in many academic skills. She also demonstrates strong social skills and would most likely benefit from additional opportunities to practice these social skills, along with her increasing English language skills.

Strengths

- Math computation
- Math concepts and applications
- Spelling
- Fluid reasoning
- Ideational fluency
- Visual processing
- Short-term memory
- Processing speed
- Cooperation and attention
- Social skills

Challenges

- English grammar
- English writing skills
- Increased frustration with language-loaded academic tasks
- Basic reading skills
- Word identification
- Reading fluency
- Phonological awareness
- Sleeping issues—sleeping alone
- Anxiety and worry

RECOMMENDATIONS

The following recommendations may benefit Alondra and her family.

Recommendations for the School

1. The multidisciplinary team should review this report and integrate the findings and recommendations into her educational program. Her overall cognitive scores,

as well as the significant academic weaknesses identified in this evaluation, should be considered when making decisions about providing her with necessary classroom services and accommodations.

2. Alondra needs direct instruction in the development of basic reading skills, which can be provided in the resource room. Alondra would benefit from participating in *Corrective Reading*, a program designed to promote reading accuracy (decoding), fluency, and comprehension skills of students in third grade or higher who are reading below their grade level. The first focus of instruction should be on developing her word-level reading skills. This program can be implemented in small groups of four to five students or in a whole-class format. Instruction should be provided in 45-minute lessons four to five times a week.

3. Alondra's performance on mathematics achievement tasks indicates that she is performing at, or only slightly below, grade level. It is recommended that Alondra spend only half of the time of the math instructional block in the resource room so that she is able to benefit from some time in the general education classroom for math instruction.

4. Alondra's participation in the general education classroom for math instruction should prevent her from falling behind in the appropriate grade-level math skills instruction. She is capable of grade-level math skills when task expectations are clearly presented to her. Use Alondra's time in the resource room to reinforce the material and math skills presented in the general education classroom.

5. Due to Alondra's limited proficiency with the English language, she may benefit from specific accommodations for certain academic tasks in the general education classroom. These accommodations could include:

a. Extended time for written assignments.

b. Repeated presentations of instructions or test items administered orally in English.

c. Presentation of instructions or test items in writing. (Alondra demonstrated that she understand English direction better when she is able to read them.)

6. Alondra should continue with her daily intensive ESOL classes. Her progress over the past year and a half indicates that she is greatly benefiting from consistent English language instruction. Alondra's enrollment in the ESOL program during summer vacation is also strongly recommended, with instruction focused on the following: English writing, conversational English, English grammar, and phonemic awareness.

7. Alondra should participate in after-school programs or clubs. Because currently school is the only place where Alondra is exposed to spoken English, participation in nonacademic social groups and activities will provide important opportunities to practice English, gain cultural experiences, and develop peer social interactions. These activities could include the Museum on the Go Program, a nutrition program, or Project Pride.

8. As Alondra's word identification skills improve, provide additional reading instruction that focuses on evidence-based practices for increasing oral language skills in English language learners. An example of these types of practices is Dialogic Reading – Reading Rockets Program (http://www.readingrockets.org). Dialogic reading can be used to help ELLs build abstract language and to acquire the second language. Skills such as inferencing, prediction, and identifying main ideas build comprehension skills.

a. The PEER Sequence: The fundamental reading technique in dialogic reading is the PEER sequence. This is a short interaction between a child and the adult. The adult:

Prompts the child to say something about the book.

Evaluates the child's response.

Expands the child's response by rephrasing and adding information to it.

Repeats the prompt to make sure the child has learned from the expansion.

b. Types of Prompts: Five types of prompts that are used in dialogic reading to begin PEER sequences. You can remember these prompts with the word CROWD.

Completion prompts: You leave a blank at the end of a sentence and get the child to fill it in. These are typically used in books with rhyme or books with repetitive phases. For example, you might say, "I think I'd be a glossy cat. A little plump but not too _____," letting the child fill in the blank with the word "fat." Completion prompts provide children with information about the structure of language that is critical to later reading.

Recall prompts: These are questions about what happened in a book a child has already read. Recall prompts work for nearly everything except alphabet books. For example, you might say, "Can you tell me what happened to the little blue engine in this story?" Recall prompts help children in understanding story plot and in describing sequences of events. Recall prompts can be used not only at the end of a book, but also at the beginning of a book when a child has been read that book before.

Open-ended prompts: These prompts focus on the pictures in books. They work best for books that have rich, detailed illustrations. For example, while looking at a page in a book that the child is familiar with, you might say, "Tell me what's happening in this picture." Open-ended prompts help children increase their expressive fluency and attend to detail.

Wh- prompts: These prompts usually begin with what, where, when, why, and how questions. Like open-ended prompts, wh- prompts focus on the pictures in books. For example, you might say, "What's the name of this?" while pointing to an object in the book. Wh- questions teach children new vocabulary.

Distancing prompts: These ask children to relate the pictures or words in the book they are reading to experiences outside the book. For example, while looking at a book with a picture of animals on a farm, you might say something like, "Remember when we went to the animal park last week. Which of these animals did we see there?" Distancing prompts help children form a bridge between books and the real world, as well as helping with verbal fluency, conversational abilities, and narrative skills. Distancing prompts and recall prompts are more difficult for children than completion, open-ended, and wh-prompts.

Virtually all children's books are appropriate for dialogic reading. The best books have rich detailed pictures.

9. Use repeated reading to help Alondra increase her fluency. Repeated reading is a group or individual activity in which students read a text with a fluent reader and then reread the text alone until they can read it at a steady rate, with normal prosody. Repeating passages helps the reader develop confidence, fluency, and word prediction ability.

   – Stories should be read with a fluent reader the first time in order to achieve comprehension. This way, each additional time the student reads the story, they can concentrate on reading quickly.

   – Passages should be 50 to 200 words long and at the student's independent reading level, as this activity is intended to build speed rather than word attack or word identification skills.

A handout with specific steps on how to implement repeated reading is attached.

10. Alondra's performance on English writing tasks demonstrates that she lacks appropriate writing skills. A portion of Alondra's time in the resource room should be devoted to increasing these skills as well as her overall writing fluency skills.

11. Alondra can be administered Curriculum-Based Measures (CBM) probes in writing, which provide a quick assessment of her writing progress.

   a. CBM probes include a "Starter Sentence" such as "At school, my favorite thing to do is…." or "When I get home from school, the first thing I do is…."

   b. Students are then given 1 minute to plan what they are going to write. Alondra should be taught how to plan a well-thought-out composition including a main idea sentence and subsequent supporting detail sentences, and then a concluding sentence.

   c. Students are then given 3 minutes to write.

   d. Scoring procedures can be found at www.interventcentral.com

   e. Writing skills probes can be used in a daily journal writing system, where Alondra is rewarded at the end of the week for completing her five journal entries.

Recommendations for the Parents

1. Reevaluate Alondra's after-school schedule to provide more time for involvement in social activities and groups. Provide Alondra with ample opportunities to engage in peer social interactions while at the same time practicing important English language skills and gaining appropriate cultural knowledge.

2. Due to Mrs. Torres's concern with Alondra's picky eating habits, implement a choice system to encourage Alondra to independently make a decision between two healthy food choice options.

   – Mrs. Torres can offer Alondra two food choices at mealtimes and indicate that while there are only the two options, Alondra can choose between the two.

   – Alondra can also take part in making her school lunches. This way, Alondra will be able to decide foods she likes to eat and perhaps be more inclined to finish her school lunches.

– Alondra should be offered healthy options for meals. Although Mrs. Torres indicated that Alondra tends to opt for more unhealthy foods such as Doritos and sodas, make it clear that healthy foods are the only options for meals and that only if a meal is finished can a dessert be chosen.

3. The following are recommendations for parents of English language learners to help reinforce the acquisition of the second language as well as maintain native language skills in the home. For more information regarding the process of second language acquisition, please see the handouts that are available from the National Association of School Psychologists.

English Version (A Spanish Version Was Provided to Alondra's Parents)

What parents can do …

1. In the United States it is important for parents to actively participate in the education of their children. This may involve attending meetings to discuss your child's progress, offering suggestions in planning your child's school program, asking how you can help at home, volunteering at school, and getting involved in school improvement and advisory activities. Collaborate with the school in planning your child's educational program.

2. Ask about school programs and teaching strategies designed to meet the needs of your child. Make sure your child is actually receiving the services she is eligible for at school, such as English for Speakers of Other Languages (ESOL), English as a Second Language (ESL), or bilingual programs.

3. Find out about the assessments used to measure your child's progress and school requirements for promotion and graduation.

4. Make sure your child has access to a dual language dictionary in English and Spanish both at home and at school.

5. Ask for feedback on your child's growth and progress in second language acquisition.

6. Ask about obtaining the services of bilingual school personnel or interpreters if your English skills are limited.

7. Continue to use your native language when communicating with your child. Proficiency in the first language makes second language learning easier.

8. Teach your child about the advantages of being bilingual, including increased opportunities in the job market.

9. Show an interest in your child's schoolwork and encourage your child to share information about the school day with you on a regular basis.

10. Establish a structured time and place for your child to complete homework.

11. Read and tell stories to your child beginning when they are very young. Once your child begins to learn to read, provide materials suitable for her current reading level. Books are available for checkout at school and community libraries.

12. Set aside a special time to spend with your child on non-school-related activities that your child enjoys. This type of positive interaction can enhance communication skills, increase self-esteem, and help you bond with your child.

13. Provide support and encouragement to your child to reduce frustration and stress.

14. Learn as much as you can about the second language process and about programs and resources available within the school system and community to support your child's learning and adjustment.

APPENDIX A

Universal Nonverbal Intelligence Test (UNIT)

Scale	Standard Score	Percentile Rank	Confidence Interval (95%)
Memory Quotient	95	37	88–104
Reasoning Quotient	104	61	94–112
Symbolic Quotient	102	55	93–111
Nonsymbolic Quotient	97	42	88–106
Full Scale	100	50	93–107

Subtest	Scaled Score	Area	Scaled Score
Symbolic Memory	12	Cube Design	12
Spatial Memory	8	Analogic Reasoning	11
Object Memory	8	Mazes	9

Woodcock-Johnson III Tests of Cognitive Abilities (WJ III COG)

Test	Standard Score	95% Confidence Interval	CALP Score*	Percentile Rank	Level
Verbal Comprehension	75	66–85	3	5	Well Below Average

*CALP – Cognitive Academic Language Proficiency

Batería-III Woodcock Muñoz

Test	Standard Scores	95% Confidence Interval	Percentile Rank	CALP Score	Level
Habilidad Verbal (Verbal Comprehension)	76	67–85	5	3	Well Below Average
Fluidez de recuperación (Retrieval Fluency)	109	97–121	72		Average
Rapidez en la decisión (Decision Speed)	104	93–115	61		Average
Rapidez en la identificación de dibujos (Rapid Picture Naming)	78	74–83	8		Well Below Average
Cancelación de pares (Pair Cancellation)	107	103–111	67		Average
Análisis-Síntesis (Analysis-Synthesis)	103	92–114	58		Average

Wechsler Intelligence Scales for Children, Fourth Edition—Integrated (WISC-IV Integrated)

Subtest	Standard Scores	Level
Spatial Span Forward	100	Average
Spatial Span Backward	125	Well Above Average

Kaufman Test of Educational Achievement, Second Edition (KTEA-II)

Subtests	Standard Score	Percentile	95% Confidence Interval	Level
Reading	**80**	**9**	**76–84**	**Below Average**
Letter & Word Recognition	83	13	79–87	Below Average
Reading Comprehension	81	10	75–87	Below Average
Phonological Awareness	78	7	67–89	Well Below Average
Nonsense Word Decoding	80	9	73–87	Below Average
Word Recognition Fluency	81	10	71–91	Below Average
Decoding Fluency	66	1	57–75	Significantly Below Average
Math	**91**	**27**	**85–97**	**Average**
Math Concepts & Applications	91	27	84–98	Average
Math Computation	95	37	88–102	Average
Written Language	*	*	*	*
Written Expression	*	*	*	*
Spelling	92	30	86–98	Average
Oral Language	**70**	**2**	**60–80**	**Well Below Average**
Listening Comprehension	78	7	66–90	Well Below Average
Oral Expression	70	2	57–83	Well Below Average

*Unable to complete subtest

CBM—Mathematics

Skill	Digits Correct Per Minute	Proficiency Level
2 × 2–Addition, (2nd grade)	15.5	Instructional
Mixed Skill Add./ Subt. (3rd grade)	6.5	Frustration

Curriculum Based Measurements (CBM)—Oral Reading Fluency (ORF)—English

Grade Level	Correctly Read Words Per Minute	Errors Per Minute	Proficiency Level
1	56	3	Instructional
2	44	9	Frustration*
3	42	7	Frustration
*Although the reading rate places her at the Instructional level, the high error/minute rate falls in the frustration level.			

CBM—Word Recognition—English

Level	Errors	Percent Correct
Pre-Primer	1	97
Primer	4	88
Grade 1	7	78
Grade 2	8	75
Grade 3	9	72

CBM—Word Recognition—Spanish

Grade 1	26	19

Childhood Autism Rating Scale (CARS)

The CARS is a 15-item behavioral rating scale developed to identify children with autism. It further distinguishes children with autism in the mild to moderate range from children with autism in the moderate to severe range. The total CARS score may range from a low of 15, obtained when the child's behavior is rated as falling within normal limits on all 15 scales, to a high of 60, obtained when the child's behavior is rated as severely abnormal on all 15 scales. Scores below 30 are categorized as Non-Autistic while those with scores between 30 and 36.5 are categorized as Mild to Moderately Autistic, and scores between 37 and 60 are considered Severely Autistic.

Completed by Ms. Fernandez

Total Score	Diagnostic Category	Descriptive Level
15.5	Nonautistic	Nonautistic

Completed by Mrs. Torres (in interview format with the examiner, translated to Spanish)

Total Score	Diagnostic Category	Descriptive Level
19.5	Nonautistic	Nonautistic

APPENDIX B

Test Interpretation Using the Cattell-Horn-Carroll Model

	Factor	Test	Subtest Name	Subtest Score	Conv. Score	Avg. Score	Level of Performance
Higher-Level Processing and Reasoning	**Fluid Reasoning**	UNIT	Analogic Reasoning	11	105	104	Average
		Batería III	Análisis-Síntesis	103	103		
	Long-Term Retrieval	Batería III	Rapid Pic Naming	78	78	78	Well Below Average
		Batería III	Retrieval Fluency	109	109	--------- 109	--------------- Average
	Visual Processing	UNIT	Cube Design	12	110	99	Average
		UNIT	Object Memory	8	90		
		UNIT	Spatial Memory	8	90		
		UNIT	Symbolic Memory	12	110		
		UNIT	Mazes	9	95		
Automatic Processing	**Short-Term Memory**	WISC-IV Integrated	Spatial Span Forward	10	100	100 --------------	Average --------------------
		WISC-IV Integrated	Spatial Span Backward	15	125	125	Well Above Average
	Processing Speed	Batería III	Decision Speed	104	104	106	Average
		Batería III	Pair Cancellation	107	107		
Acquired Knowledge and Achievement	**Crystallized Ability (verbal reasoning, language ability, and general knowledge)**	WJ III COG	Verbal Comprehension	75	75	75	Well Below Average
		Batería III	Comprehension Verbal	76	76	----------- 76	-------------------- Well Below Average
	*Conv. Score refers to subtest scores converted to a common scale. Only converted scores can be averaged. **Scores not averaged due to significant discrepancy (+/– 1)						

APPENDIX C

Analysis of Effects of Language and Culture on Assessment Results (Cognitive Abilities Tests)

		Language Ability		
		Low	Medium	High
American Cultural Knowledge	Low	Spatial Memory (UNIT), **90.** Cube Design (UNIT), **110.** Mazes (UNIT), **95.**		Análisis y Síntesis (Batería-III), **103.**
		Cell average = 98		Cell average = 103
	Medium	Symbolic Memory (UNIT), **110**	Rapidez identificación de dibujos (Batería-III), **78.**	Rapidez en la decisión (Batería-III), **104.**
		Cancelación de pares (Batería-III), **107.**	Fluidez de recuperación (Batería-III), **109.**	
		Cell average = 109	Cell average = 94	Cell average = 104
	High	Object Memory (UNIT), **90.** Analogic Reasoning (UNIT), **105.**		Verbal Comprehension (WJ III COG) **75**
				Comprehensión Verbal (Batería-III), **76**
		Cell average = 98		Cell average = 76

CASE 9

Twice-Exceptional

A Gifted Child with Concomitant Learning Disabilities

Aimee Yermish

Most of the people I evaluate for possible learning disabilities are like Rebekah, bright-to-gifted individuals whose struggles are at times inexplicable or invisible to those around them. Frequently, those who are twice-exceptional find that both their high intelligence *and* their learning disabilities go unrecognized, because the learning disabilities bring down the broad-based cognitive scores, and their strong cognitive abilities enable them to at least partially compensate for their weaknesses. I have often seen children who can barely decode nevertheless score in the average range on reading tests.

Although Rebekah's case is more clear cut than many, evaluations are often quite a detective process. In planning the evaluation, I have to strategically choose diagnostic tests that will enable me to see both strengths and weaknesses, while still being at least reasonably efficient in terms of how I use my time. I tune in carefully not just to what the scores were, but how the individual managed to get them, and I try to present some of this information in the report. Because I began my professional life as a scientist, I like to stay very close to the test data, the background information, and the behavioral observations. Often, that is where I will find the clues that help me find and support a coherent understanding.

I also feel that recommendations should be tailored specifically to the individual, should present information and ideas beyond what might be easily found on a routine Internet search, and should be concrete enough that a parent or teacher would know how to implement them. This may lead to a longer report, but my clients have generally said that they welcome the direction.

PSYCHOEDUCATIONAL EVALUATION

Name: Rebekah Washington
Date of Birth: March 25, 2002

Age: 7-10
Parents: Sage and Samuel Washington
School: Home-school
Grade: Nominally 2nd grade
Dates of Evaluation: February 2–3, 2010
Evaluator: Aimee Yermish, Psy.D.

REASON FOR REFERRAL

Rebekah's parents referred her for assessment for three main reasons. First, because they home-school her, they wish to have an objective measurement of how she is progressing in the various curricular areas so as to guide their future curriculum delivery. Second, because they have observed that she has a great deal of difficulty expressing herself orally and in writing, whether about her own ideas or about what she has read, they are concerned about possible expressive language difficulties. Finally, her parents have observed some "tuning-out" behaviors, possibly consistent with auditory processing or attentional problems, and wish to have these possibilities investigated.

BACKGROUND

Rebekah is the elder of two children in an intact family. Her father is a software engineer; her mother is a home-maker and provides home-school instruction for Rebekah and her brother. Rebekah's mother provided the following background information.

Rebekah's gestation and birth were unremarkable. Her development of gross-motor, fine-motor, and graphomotor control has been within normal limits. Her social-emotional development has also been satisfactory. She makes friends easily, interacting well with both adults and with children of various ages. She has a wide range of interests in athletics, music, and art.

Rebekah's initial oral language development was markedly advanced. Her mother reports that she spoke early and communicated her needs effectively. She enjoyed language and actively sought to increase her vocabulary, asking about unfamiliar words and their usage. However, in recent years, she has experienced considerably more difficulty when she is asked to use language in more sophisticated ways, such as being asked to discuss something she has read or experienced, or to express her feelings. Her speech is often filled with long pauses while she struggles to figure out how to say what she wants to say or possibly to find the words to express her thoughts. When asked to summarize or recount something she has read, she tends to politely demur, suggesting that the adults should read the material themselves.

Rebekah spontaneously taught herself to read at age 3, and reads avidly on an upper-elementary and middle-school level. She demonstrates strong conceptual understanding of mathematics and real-world problem solving, although rote facts and procedures are more challenging for her. She enjoys learning new information in all content areas. She learns the rules of language mechanics readily, but her written production is slow and inadequate.

Rebekah has been educated at home since early childhood, spending one day per week with a local home-school cooperative. Both she and her parents are happy with this arrangement.

Rebekah's mother's concerns about attentional problems arise from Rebekah's tendency to lose herself in a book or in her own thoughts, particularly when she is trying to avoid a situation. No other symptoms of difficulty in attention or executive functioning were reported.

Rebekah was tested at age 4–9 with the Wechsler Preschool and Primary Scales of Intelligence – Revised. Her Full Scale IQ was measured at >149, with significant ceiling effects, and no significant discrepancies between the Verbal and Performance scales. Rebekah's only relative weaknesses on that testing were on the Comprehension and Similarities subtests, where the tester reported that her responses were correct but not well-enough elaborated to receive full credit.

TESTING OBSERVATIONS

Rebekah presented as an engaging and relatively mature child; she was focused and personable both during initial interviews and during the testing sessions. She appeared to be giving her best effort, even when tasks were too easy or too difficult; none of the reported "checking out" or other resistant or inattentive behaviors were observed during testing. She implemented a variety of visual, auditory, and kinesthetic strategies throughout testing, flexibly managing different task demands. Her self-monitoring was consistently strong; she was well aware of when she was guessing or making mistakes, and she was able to spontaneously self-correct many errors. These results are considered to be a valid assessment of Rebekah's performance.

CLINICAL INTERVIEW

An interview was conducted in Rebekah's home. During this informal discussion, her weaknesses in expressive language were evident. Her speech was slow and labored; her sentences were complex and grammatically correct but came out a phrase or a clause at a time, with very long latent periods (often 5–10 seconds) between them. She appeared to have a great deal of difficulty finding words to express her ideas. For example, when trying to explain that she liked multiple-choice questions better than short-answer ones, even with prompting, she was unable to create an explanation that would have made sense to a naïve listener, and never used words that reflected selecting among choices.

Similarly, when describing her pleasure reading, she had no trouble identifying her interests and naming specific books of a middle-school reading and interest level. She had enormous difficulty, however, in both recounting and summarizing the plots, as well as in answering specific questions. Her language tended to be vague, and she often used verbatim recall of phrases from the book in her answers and explanations. When given neutral choices and primed with appropriate language, she was able to effectively answer questions about plot, characters, motivations, and actions.

Rebekah's responses to routine questions about her hobbies and activities were slow enough that most adults and other children might have assumed that she was not going to answer at all.

COGNITIVE TESTING

Rebekah was administered a number of different tests of cognitive ability and academic achievement. These tests assess a wide variety of different cognitive factors and academic skills, providing the opportunity to ascertain her strengths and weaknesses compared with others of her age.

The tests used in this evaluation provide standard scores (SS) with a mean of 100 and a standard deviation of 15, scaled scores (ScS) with a mean of 10 and a standard deviation of 3, and relative proficiency indexes (RPI). The RPI is a mathematical prediction, based on the norms, of Rebekah's expected proficiency on a task at a difficulty level at which a typical age-peer would be 90% successful. For example, when the average child of age 7–10 would be 90% successful in pronouncing a list of age-appropriate words, Rebekah's RPI of 100/90 indicates that she would be 100% successful. RPIs can often show a weakness in actual performance that may not be evident from standard scores. The following verbal labels represent standard score and scaled score ranges:

SS Range	Verbal Label	ScS Range
< 69	Very Low	1–3
70–79	Low	4–6
80–89	Low Average	7
90–110	Average	8–12
111–120	High Average	13
121–130	Superior	14–16
>130	Very Superior	17–19

The following verbal descriptors represent relative proficiency index levels:

RPI Range	Level of Proficiency
0–3	Negligible
3–24	Very limited
24–67	Limited
67–82	Limited to Average
82–95	Average
95–98	Average to Advanced
98–100	Advanced
100	Very Advanced

In following tables, those scores marked with an asterisk (*) indicate that Rebekah completed the test before reaching discontinuation criteria (i.e., an extremely high raw score in a test with cutoffs). These scores may be lower than her theoretical "true" score, the score she would have achieved if the test had contained more difficult items. Clusters containing these scores should also be considered as potential underestimates of her ability or achievement.

Parentheses around a cluster score indicate that the cluster is composed of tests with widely varying scores; consequently, the cluster score is not a meaningful representation of her ability and achievement in these areas.

Woodcock-Johnson III NU Tests of Cognitive Abilities and Diagnostic Supplement to Woodcock-Johnson III Tests of Cognitive Abilities

Cluster/Test	Standard Score[a]	Percentile Rank	Relative Proficiency Index
Fluid Reasoning (Gf)	*148	>99.9	100/90
Concept Formation	*138	99.5	100/90
Analysis-Synthesis	*149	>99.9	100/90
Short-Term Memory (Gsm)	(131)	(98)	(100/90)
Numbers Reversed	108	69	96/90
Memory for Words	139	99.5	100/90
Auditory Memory Span	151	>99.9	100/90
Memory for Words	139	99.5	100/90
Memory for Sentences	147	>99.9	100/90
Working Memory	(133)	(99)	(100/90)
Numbers Reversed	108	69	96/90
Auditory Working Memory	149	>99.9	100/90
Cognitive Fluency	(89)	(22)	(77/90)
Retrieval Fluency	69	2	76/90
Decision Speed	94	35	82/90
Rapid Picture Naming	94	35	73/90
Oral Language	141	99.7	99/90
Story Recall	144	99.8	99/90
Understanding Directions	*134	99	100/90
Auditory Attention (not in cluster)	121	92	97/90
[a]Mean = 100, Standard Deviation = 15, Norms used: age			

Rebekah's performance on cognitive testing was consistent with her performance on previous testing. The domain of Fluid Reasoning, the ability to think through novel problems in a flexible and logical fashion, was extremely high for her age. She was able both to infer rules from given information and to apply given rules to solve puzzles. In both inductive and deductive formats, she was able to use rules flexibly and in combination, trying different possibilities and monitoring her success. Her near-flawless performance rivaled that of many adults.

Rebekah's short-term and working memory were assessed, in order to consider the possibility that difficulties in summarizing text might be related to difficulties with holding the material in memory for the length of time needed for her to come up with appropriate language to describe it. Again, her performance was excellent. She was able to repeat sequences of six unrelated words, and when meaningful context was added, she was able to repeat 20-word sentences perfectly; both performances were in the Very Superior range for her age. On a test of working memory, however, requiring her to repeat a sequence of digits in reverse order, she had considerably more difficulty, scoring in the Average range. She used a variety of strategies; most notably, she subvocally rehearsed the stimulus repeatedly, in the order given, for almost a full minute, before responding. On a different test of working memory, however, she performed far above the mean. Possibly, because this test required sorting by category, but not reordering the items within the category, her strong verbatim memory was more helpful. Because Rebekah did demonstrate a variety of information-handling strategies that would have been appropriate in real-world situations when she was permitted to choose her own strategies, and because she showed no difficulties in handling large amounts of information in memory, the evidence seems to be more supportive of the hypothesis that her short-term and working memory are functioning at a level commensurate with her other cognitive abilities, and not causing significant impairment.

Rebekah had considerably more difficulty in the area of cognitive fluency, where she was asked to perform relatively simple tasks under time pressure. She had particular difficulty with tasks that required verbal responses. When asked to come up with words quickly to fit into particular semantic categories (e.g., articles of clothing), she was unable to generate effective strategies (such as using a recent experience, or hierarchical information) to do so; she produced fewer than half the number of responses typical for a child her age, resulting in a standard score in the Very Low range. On a test requiring automatic recall of the names for common objects, content typically overlearned long before school age, her performance was slow and labored, and her standard score was in the lower end of the Average range. The Decision Speed test requires rapid identification of two pictures in a row of seven that are the most similar conceptually (e.g., two animals among a variety of other objects), without overt verbal processing. Despite her very superior abstract reasoning, she found this task quite difficult, scoring again in the lower end of the Average range. When examining her RPIs in cognitive fluency, her limited-to-average proficiency indicates that she struggles with tasks her peers would find quite manageable. While average-range standard scores might not raise concern regarding other children, the extreme contrast between Rebekah's powerful reasoning abilities and her more fundamental skills, automatic in others, suggests a significant problem for her. Unless lower-level cognitive skills are automatic, even simple tasks are likely to require significant effort, using up attentional resources that should be available for more complex or higher-level processes.

Many children appear at times not to be paying attention, for a variety of cognitive or motivational reasons. Therefore, it is important to explore the possibility that there is a difficulty in receptive language, executive functioning, or auditory processing. In Rebekah's case, these do not appear to be problematic. She was able to produce near-verbatim recall of meaningful stories, performing in the Superior range for her age. Unlike many children her age, she was also able to maintain the sequential logic of each story, suggesting an additional strength. She was able to follow complex multistep directions, including conditional and sequential information, without apparent difficulty. Her performance near the ceiling of the test supports the hypothesis that her working memory and attention are intact. Finally, Rebekah was able to consciously focus on auditory stimuli in the presence of increasing levels of background noise, suggesting that auditory figure-ground discrimination is not a problem for her.

Woodcock-Johnson III Tests of Achievement, Form A

Cluster/Test	Standard Score	Percentile Rank	Relative Proficiency Index
Broad Reading	**143**	**99.8**	**100/90**
Letter-Word Identification	141	99.7	100/90
Reading Fluency	136	99	100/90
Passage Comprehension	128	97	100/90
Broad Written Language	**142**	**99.8**	**100/90**
Spelling	140	99.6	100/90
Writing Fluency	124	95	99/90

(continued)

Cluster/Test	Standard Score	Percentile Rank	Relative Proficiency Index
Writing Samples	133	99	99/90
Handwriting (not in cluster)	90	25	–
Broad Math	**(145)**	**(99.9)**	**(100/90)**
Calculation	138	99.5	100/90
Math Fluency	103	58	91/90
Applied Problems	150	>99.9	100/90

Rebekah demonstrated very strong phonics-based reading skills; she was able to sound out unfamiliar polysyllabic words that would be challenging for average adults. The automaticity of her reading and her comprehension of simple content were also robust. At times, on the Reading Fluency test, she slowed down to consider alternate possibilities and technicalities, as many gifted children will. Even with these delays, however, her score remained in the Very Superior range for her age, indicating that she can gather information from simple text with very little difficulty. When she was asked to read higher-level, albeit brief, content and use context clues to fill in a missing word, without time pressure, she again performed well into the Superior range. She was able to understand passages up to approximately a middle-school reading level, similar to what she reads for pleasure and in home-schooling. As the passages approached a challenging reading level, she clearly needed significant time to retrieve a suitable word but was still able to do so effectively.

Rebekah's strong phonics skills and good long-term memory for rules and exceptions also helped her in writing. She was able to spell a broad range of both regular and irregular words, and to make reasonable guesses at unfamiliar words, scoring well into the Very Superior range. She maintained this level of spelling when writing words in context. Her grammar and punctuation, although not scored separately, were also very strong; she correctly used commas, periods, question marks, and quotation marks. Her ability to maintain attention to different aspects of writing simultaneously speaks to her strong attentional and executive resources.

When given target words and the instruction to write short sentences as rapidly as possible, her scores were in the Superior range, but her sentences were at times awkward and only barely grammatical, particularly if the words needed to be used in a different order from the way in which they were given. On the untimed Writing Samples test, which required her to write single-sentence responses to a variety of oral and written prompts, although her overall score was in

the Very Superior range, her responses were of inconsistent quality. She often showed an extremely long wait period, well over a minute, before beginning her response. When the prompt allowed it, she effectively used verbatim repetition of parts of the prompt in constructing her responses. When it did not, her responses tended to be brief and unelaborated, often receiving only partial credit. If the structure of the prompt did not immediately suggest a sentence construction (for example, where she was given only a topic and a target phrase to use), she experienced significant difficulty, and on one item was completely unable to produce a response.

Rebekah's handwriting was assessed by comparing her responses on the untimed Writing Samples test to standardized handwriting samples and to a checklist of criteria. She used both cursive and print. Although she appeared to prefer printing, her handwriting was more consistent and legible in cursive. In both handwriting forms, she demonstrated inconsistent letter slant, with the problems more prominent in print. In print, she also showed inconsistent spacing between letters and words, letter heights, use of baseline, and letter formation; some of these errors interfered with legibility.

In the area of mathematics, Rebekah's performance was inconsistent. On the untimed Calculation test, she scored in the Very Superior range, demonstrating a range of solid elementary arithmetic skills, including adding and subtracting multiple-digit numbers with regrouping, multiplication, and simple operations with fractions. She was unfamiliar with division and negative numbers. Similarly, when she was asked to apply mathematical reasoning to real-world problems (again untimed), her logical and abstract reasoning skills were evident in her extremely strong performance. She was consistent in her ability to determine salient details from among distracters, devising appropriate mathematical models to solve a wide range of problems involving time, money, measurement, rate, geometry, and some simple percentage and proportion problems. She showed appropriate use of pencil-and-paper techniques.

In contrast, on the 3-minute Math Fluency test, where she was required to give the answers to single-digit arithmetic facts as rapidly as possible, her performance was much more labored. She completed only 36 problems, never reaching the level of sums above 10, or multiplication. Even problems involving zero were no quicker for her than more difficult problems. Rebekah's slow speed of retrieval of verbal information appears to have made this task considerably more difficult for her than expected. Although her score was in the Average range, it was 2 to 3 standard deviations below her scores on the other math tests.

Test of Narrative Language (TNL)

Cluster/Subtest	Standard Score	Scaled Score	Percentile Rank
Narrative Language Ability Index	(124)		(95)
Narrative Comprehension		*18	>99
Oral Narration		10	50

As noted above, Rebekah shows a marked discrepancy between her ability to understand language and her ability to spontaneously produce spoken language to express the depth and complexity of her ideas. The TNL, administered to explore this problem further, alternates between a receptive task, requiring her to recall details from orally presented stories, and an expressive task, in which she was to use these stories as models for retelling or creating narratives of her own. In the Narrative Comprehension subtest, Rebekah's ability to recall detailed information was nearly perfect; she missed only two items on the entire test, and gave most responses verbatim.

The Oral Narration subtest proved much more difficult for her, with an overall score in the Average range. She earned points primarily on the first item, which allowed her to use verbatim recall to retell a story she had just heard. Even this retelling was marked by long pauses, however—often 4 to 9 seconds of silence in the middle of a phrase—while she struggled to think of the words to use. For the other two items, she was asked to make up stories based on picture prompts; scores were based on language use, depth of content, and maturity of narrative. Her performance on these two items was quite low, both because she used very little of the information provided in the pictures, and because her narratives were incomplete and incoherent, with poor use of detail and narrative flow. She used a sentence from one of the Narrative Comprehension stories almost verbatim to provide an ending for her second story, even though the ending was not appropriate in the situation described. On the last item, without the support of a provided sequence and a clearly implied story, she floundered in trying to create a logical and internally consistent narrative of her own; she mixed together two very different ideas, without a clear conflict or solution. As before, her speech was marked with long pauses and somewhat unusual phrasings. It is important to note that most children Rebekah's age do not read as well or as extensively as she does, and thus do not have the exposure to the high level of mature narrative that she experiences in her pleasure reading. Most children at a similar cognitive level to Rebekah are able to produce far more detailed and coherent narratives, with considerably more oral language fluency. This marked discrepancy between her ability to understand narratives and her average to below-average ability to create her own is interpreted as indicating a considerable weakness in oral expression.

SUMMARY

Rebekah is a highly gifted 7-year-old girl who shows strengths in fluid reasoning, short-term and working memory, executive functioning, and receptive language. She is able to consider alternatives, is flexible in generation and use of strategies, and shows a level of comfort with abstract thought that is unusual even among adults.

In contrast, her speed of information retrieval and response is exceedingly slow by comparison, causing a significant impediment to her use of expressive language. When she is pressed for time, or when she is not able to use verbatim recall as a scaffold, she has extreme difficulty in quickly finding the words and constructing the sentences she needs to express her ideas.

Rebekah's academic achievement is consistent with her cognitive abilities. She showed excellent skills and reasoning abilities in reading, writing, and arithmetic, and is likely to continue to do well. The only exceptions to this were handwriting and fluency of basic math facts, both tasks that require automatic recall and execution; in both cases, her performance was average for her age. These lower-level but less automatic skills may increase the burden on her attentional resources as she moves to higher levels of the curriculum.

In the one-on-one testing situation, Rebekah demonstrated strengths in the areas of attention, concentration, and direction following. The real world of the home and the classroom do present more distractions and fewer specific directions to attend to instruction, but it is likely that her "tuning out" represents a common childhood attempt to avoid a task, or deep involvement in a current activity, such that she does not notice the attempt to get her attention.

RECOMMENDATIONS

General

1. As a twice-exceptional learner, Rebekah is at risk for having both her giftedness and her difficulties in processing speed and expressive language go unrecognized.

Most people regard quickness and high levels of verbal expression as the most obvious signs of giftedness. Furthermore, the very nature of Rebekah's difficulties will make it challenging for her to advocate for herself as she matures and considers returning to conventional school environments. Adults who work with Rebekah should educate themselves about giftedness and twice-exceptionality; the website www.hoagiesgifted.org contains a wide variety of articles and links.

2. Rebekah is also at risk for coming to regard herself as likely to fail, feeling that she must avoid tasks that are difficult for her. Help her learn to celebrate and build on her considerable strengths, as well as to understand that her areas of weakness are focal rather than global in nature, and amenable to change over time. Carol Dweck's book *Mindset* offers an excellent description of this approach.

3. Support Rebekah's sense of autonomy and self-efficacy by engaging her as a partner in the learning process. With guidance, she can use her strong abstract reasoning skills to help adults identify why specific tasks may be difficult for her, devise effective strategies, and create methods for improving her performance over time.

4. In general, for Rebekah to be able to perform well orally or in writing, she needs to be given ample time. In evaluating her work, emphasis should be placed on the quality of the work rather than its quantity. Meeting this need may require allowing her extra time, or reducing the amount of work. The exact accommodations should be selected based on an analysis of the specific tasks, to ensure that she is able to engage in enough drill and practice to master the relevant skills without being overwhelmed by the workload.

Expressive Language

1. While it appears from this evaluation that Rebekah's difficulties are focused around the areas of word-finding and sentence formulation, it would be beneficial to have her evaluated by a speech and language pathologist. This professional should provide additional specific recommendations for helping to improve Rebekah's expressive language, likely including language therapy.

2. A formal program to assist Rebekah in word-finding, the Word-Finding Intervention Program, is available from PRO-ED, www.proedinc.com. Other useful information can be found on www.wordfinding.com.

3. Teach her to recognize when she is having trouble finding a word, and use semantic networks (e.g., related words, synonyms, antonyms, and context) to help her talk about the meaning she is trying to retrieve. Additionally, using phonological hooks, such as providing Rebekah with the initial sounds of a word that she is trying to recall (e.g., say "sp" when she is trying to recall "splendid"), can help her with word retrieval.

4. The most important thing to give Rebekah when she is struggling to express herself is time. Adults and other children, out of impatience or a desire to help, are likely to jump in to provide hints or to speak for her. This practice will only fuel a sense of helplessness and teach her to let others speak for her.

5. Provide opportunities for Rebekah to paraphrase both oral and written material. At first begin with familiar stories and events. Gradually, progress to having her summarize more complex events.

6. For complex reading and writing tasks, provide Rebekah with advance organizers (e.g., outlines, concept maps, question lists). Each key point should contain a question about the reading that, when answered, and in combination, will create an organized set of notes. Encourage her to take notes on the organizer while reading or shortly afterwards. When asking her about her reading, use the same questions as in the organizer. These organizers can then be used to scaffold the writing process.

Automatic Recall

1. When Rebekah needs to learn simple factual or procedural information that must be recalled rapidly, she will benefit from regular structured repetition and review. Limit the amount of new information being learned at any given time. Make sure that Rebekah has thoroughly mastered the content before gradually adding more, and continue to practice timed retrieval of the old information on a regular basis, gradually fading the reinforcement over a long period of time. Emphasize the goal of improving her personal best. Most children enjoy seeing their progress on a graph; when improvement reaches a plateau, increase the difficulty of the task slightly.

2. Because she has strong verbatim recall, teach Rebekah by using consistent scripts and keywords. When she has difficulty remembering something, cue her recall by using those keywords, rather than providing the answers. For example, when teaching multistep procedures for solving mathematical problems, use instructions with consistent phrasing, and assign a keyword to each step. Have her repeat the keyword as she implements each step. Later, if

she has trouble remembering what to do, cue her recall of the next step by using its keyword. Only if that is insufficient should she be reminded of the entire instruction.

3. Rather than using nonsense-word mnemonic techniques, such as acronyms or one-bun-two-shoe pegword techniques, teach content area vocabulary and concepts in ways that tap into fluid reasoning and sense-making, emphasizing cause and effect, process analysis, comparison/contrast, and the like. For example, rather than creating a nonsense word mnemonic for the parts of the digestive system, help her understand the process by which food is progressively broken down and nutrients are absorbed.

4. Rebekah may find learning a foreign language to be particularly challenging due to her difficulty in retrieving words from long-term storage and formulating sentences; consequently, she may need to have foreign language requirements waived or reduced, should she reenter formal school situations requiring them. If she has difficulty in learning spoken languages, American Sign Language, with its kinesthetic focus, may be a good option for her. Alternatively, a classical language such as Latin, where she can use her strong understanding of rule-based systems and there is less demand for rapid oral expression, may be more appropriate.

Attention and Following Directions

1. Recognize that the usual behavioral and motivational strategies (sticker charts and the like) are often ineffective or counterproductive when used with gifted children; the children often subvert or manipulate the system, or derive self-esteem by being able to resist adult control. It will be much more effective to work collaboratively, helping her decide on goals she values (even if one of those is to "not get nagged so much") and then providing her with strategies to reach them.

2. Orient her prior to giving instructions. Simply saying, "Rebekah, look at me," and then waiting until she does so, may be sufficient. Have her do the task as soon as you give her the instructions, watching her as she gets up to begin (e.g., "I need you to take out the garbage now"). If the task is to be done sometime later, set a timer to ring at the time she is to start. When the instructions are first given, have her repeat them and ask any questions that she might need to clarify the expectations. Use point-of-performance reminders, cues that are visible at the time and place when Rebekah needs to act on them. For example, a list of items that need to be

brought to the home-school cooperative would be best placed either on the door to the garage or written on a tag attached to the backpack. Similarly, create checklists for routine tasks.

3. The most effective means of reinforcement is praise. Provide sincere and specific praise frequently and promptly, even for tasks that you might think "should already be routine." A sincere statement expresses honest appreciation; specificity identifies and reinforces the behavior. An example of sincere and specific praise is "You carried your own plate to the kitchen. That makes the cleanup so much easier. Thanks."

4. For more concrete advice on talking to children in ways that support the growth of self-regulation, the book *How to Talk So Kids Will Listen and Listen So Kids Will Talk*, by Adele Faber and Dorothy Mazlich, is excellent, as is the classic *Between Parent and Child*, by Haim Ginott.

Reading

1. In general, it appears that Rebekah's basic and advanced reading skills are well in line with her cognitive ability. The information seems to be going in; her difficulties in summarizing and recounting appear to be more connected with getting the information back out again in a form others can understand. Recognize that a response from her that includes significant verbatim material may not necessarily indicate that she has not understood; she may simply be using the language from the text because it is easier for her than formulating the sentences she needs to express her own ideas.

2. When asking her to summarize, recount, or explain what she has read, phrase the questions so that the words she may need are present in the question. That is, rather than asking, "What did Jane use to solve her problem?" ask, "How did Jane use the X to do Y?" Use questions to support her recall, asking for information one piece at a time rather than in large integrated chunks.

3. Teach Rebekah pre-reading strategies such as scanning, examining headlines, captions, and topic sentences, predicting what the passage will be about and what questions she might have answered by it, and activating prior background knowledge about the topic. Additionally, use these strategies as opportunities to trigger the retrieval of relevant vocabulary and phrases, so that Rebekah will have an easier time retrieving the needed language to demonstrate her comprehension afterwards.

Writing

1. Rebekah's handwriting, while appropriate to her age, represents a relative weakness that may lead to frustration as she learns to write essays and stories at a level congruent with her high intelligence. Because handwriting appears to require conscious effort for her, reducing the attention available for thinking about what she wants to say and how to say it, teach her how to keyboard. Choose a typing software program that is appealing to Rebekah so that she will be willing to practice regularly. Additionally, encourage her to use the computer for informal high-interest communication (e.g., letters to friends), while maintaining the expectation that she use correct spelling and grammar.

2. Rebekah also needs to increase her fluency and legibility in handwriting. At present, her cursive writing is more consistent and legible, but she appears to prefer printing for speed. Many students find that "italic" or "manu-cursive" handwriting—a hybrid with the smooth, continuous lines of cursive and the simple letter forms of printing—to be an excellent compromise. Barchowsky Fluent Handwriting (www.bfhhandwriting.com) and the Getty-Dubay system (www.cep.pdx.edu) are both examples of this type of instructional system.

3. At first, it is more important to emphasize legibility over speed, using constant daily practice for short time periods. Once Rebekah gains proficiency and consistency, have her engage in daily 2-minute timed writings where she copies from a simple but interesting text, so that there is no cognitive load other than the handwriting itself. Count the number of well-formed letters, to encourage legibility rather than pure speed, and graph her progress over time, encouraging her to improve her personal best.

4. Provide her with banks of words or phrases relevant to the topic she is writing about, to draw on as she composes her thoughts.

5. For the use of concept maps, investigate Inspiration software (www.inspiration.com). Consider using Inspiration, which has fewer distractions than Kidspiration, the child version. She may also like working with the open-source mind-mapping program Freemind (freemind. sourceforge.net), which provides for more flexible reorganization of ideas.

Arithmetic Fact Fluency

Rebekah demonstrates strong mathematical and logical reasoning but struggles with the automatic recall of math facts. As she progresses through the curriculum, this weakness is likely to become increasingly problematic, because it will slow her down and use up attentional resources needed to practice more complex skills.

1. Assess Rebekah's knowledge of math facts in an untimed format to ascertain if her difficulty with fact retrieval is lack of knowledge of the math facts or difficulty retrieving the information. If unsure whether or not she knows the answer or is counting mentally (or on her fingers) to find the answers, ask her. She is likely to be aware of which facts she knows and which she has to figure out. Focus on teaching those she needs to figure out. For those she already knows, focus on developing rapid retrieval.

2. Leverage Rebekah's strong fluid reasoning to help her organize math facts in memory and facilitate retrieval. For example, using the commutative property ($A + B = B + A$, $A \times B = B \times A$) halves the number of facts to learn. Identity rules ($N + 0 = N$, $N \times 1 = N$), the multiplicative property of 0 ($N \times 0 = 0$), and the use of rote-counting to facilitate problems of the form $N + 1$, $N - 1$, $N + 10$, and $N - 10$ can help her move more quickly.

3. For the remaining facts, organize them into a sequence, beginning with those that are easiest to learn, and adding more as she masters each group. Start with doubles ($N + N$, $2 \times N$), and progress to those involving adding 9 ($N + 10 - 1$), multiplying by 5, multiplying by 9, and perfect squares ($N \times N$). The remaining facts should be learned in groups with the same operation; for example, all of the facts of the form $N \times 6$ should be mastered before she goes on to those of the form $N \times 7$.

4. As an incentive, have Rebekah keep a chart of the math facts she has learned to automaticity (i.e., correct response within 3 seconds), using standard addition and multiplication charts. When she has gained mastery of a fact, have her color it in on the chart.

5. Once Rebekah has learned addition and multiplication facts, teach her to use inverse operations to transform subtraction facts into addition facts ($9 - 4 = ?$ should become $4 + ? = 9$) and division facts into multiplication facts ($21 \div 3 = ?$ should become $3 \times ? = 21$), so that these do not need to be learned separately.

6. Because she shows a strength in verbatim recall, have her memorize the facts as a consistent set of verbal scripts, rather than varying the language used. The Schoolhouse Rock songs (available on DVD from www.amazon. com) associate each set of times tables with a different animation and musical style, giving each set of numbers

a more distinct "personality." Additionally, she may find it helpful to create a story or picture for each fact; one such approach, covering the 6 through 9 times tables, is available from www.triggermemorysystems.com.

7. As Rebekah increases her knowledge of math facts, drill her on math facts by giving her a page of all of the math facts you are sure she knows. Tell her to take all the time she needs to respond to all of the facts. Monitor the number of minutes she takes. Figure out the number of seconds per problem and chart it. Slowly, through daily drills, without pressure, her time will decrease. Add new facts only after you are sure she knows the answer.

8. Worksheets of varying levels of difficulty can be generated online at a number of web sites, including www.aplusmath.com and www.edhelper.com. The Flashmaster (www.flashmaster.com) is a standalone toy that allows the difficulty level to be adjusted. There are also numerous applications for mobile phones or other handhelds, such as Math Drills for the iPhone; choose one that allows specific sets of facts to be focused on, and, ideally, a per-problem pace to be set.

9. Games, both commercial ones such as Equate and Prime Pak (both available from www.conceptualmathmedia.com), and ones Rebekah and her parents create using dice and cards (consider using polyhedra dice from www.rpgshop.com and stickers to change the numbers as needed), can be a way to make practice more fun.

Mathematics: Problem Solving

1. While Rebekah is learning her math facts, it is also crucial not to ignore her strengths in abstract reasoning and problem solving. Build on these strengths and encourage her to enjoy learning math at a high level. She will probably learn well using an inductive approach. Present a challenge, let her explore, encourage her to figure out general rules from her specific observations, state the rules explicitly, test them in new situations, and then practice them to mastery.

2. Note that when Rebekah is solving a conceptually challenging problem, it may be difficult for her to verbally explain her reasoning. Teach her to divide the page vertically, working the problem on the left and jotting down notes about her thought process on the right. This will help her remember what she was thinking about later on.

3. Consider supplementing the traditional elementary curriculum with materials that will engage and extend her reasoning skills. Key Curriculum Press (www.keypress.com) publishes a book on techniques for solving nonroutine problems, called *Crossing the River With Dogs*. Ed Zaccaro's *Challenge Math* books present a graded series of applications of the traditional curriculum. Don Cohen's books (www.mathman.biz) offer advanced topics in a conceptual fashion that is both appealing and understanding to children. Harold Jacobs's classic *Mathematics: A Human Endeavor* may have been written for math-phobic college students but is also very effective enrichment for young gifted children. Dale Seymour has authored a number of books presenting in-depth explorations of mathematical concepts.

Future Directions

1. When Rebekah is working with other adults in academic environments, particularly when she is ready to transition to a more conventional classroom, it will be crucial to educate them about the nature of her difficulties with expressive language and how they can cope with her long response time. People often underestimate the intelligence of those who do not express themselves with verbal fluency. Besides participation in classroom discussion, Rebekah will likely have difficulty with test taking, note taking, and other common classwork formats.

2. To prepare for a smooth transition, prior to the transition, share this report with the school principal, the school psychologist, and Rebekah's teachers. Schedule a meeting, with the request that all will have read the report prior to the meeting, to ensure that they understand Rebekah's strengths and needs, and to discuss appropriate accommodations.

3. As she grows older, it will become more and more important for her to learn to advocate for herself. Teach her to recognize situations that play to her weaknesses, to find ways to bring her strengths to bear on them, and to speak appropriately and effectively to adults about her needs. Because the very nature of her difficulties will make it challenging for her to express herself, help her plan ahead with behavioral and verbal scripts for approaching teachers, and with specific proposals to help solve the problems. Teachers generally take students far more seriously when they are able to make their own needs known, rather than relying on parents to speak for them, and when they come with some ideas for solutions, rather than simply stating problems.

If you have any further questions about this evaluation or these recommendations, please do not hesitate to call. It was a pleasure to be able to assist in ascertaining and explaining Rebekah's educational needs.

APPENDIX: INFORMATION AND CAUTIONS REGARDING TESTING AND SCORES

Although these tests provide scores that are generally considered to have strong reliability and validity, it is important to understand that no test is perfect in the way it defines intelligence, achievement, or any other construct, or in the way it measures these. The real world encompasses many different kinds of functioning, not all of which can be measured effectively on a single test. Many different aspects of a test, such as the question formats and specific items used, can affect a child's scores. Similarly, many different events that are not test related, such as whether the child had a good breakfast or was comfortable in the testing situation, can also affect the scores. Rather than defining some permanent characteristic of the child, a test is best understood as a snapshot of the way this specific child did on these specific tasks on that specific day. Test results must be considered in the context of a child's real-world functioning.

These tests provide scores based on a normative comparison to other children of the same age. Standard scores of 100 and scaled scores of 10 represent average performance; scores are distributed on a normal curve, as shown below. As one moves outward from the mean, scores that are more distant represent progressively more unusual levels of functioning. Approximately 50% of the population receives standard scores between 90 and 110 (scaled scores of 8–12), which is considered to be the "average" range.

In considering percentile scores, it is important to remember that these do not reflect "percent correct," but rather the percentage of the population who performed below the level that this child did. It is also important to note that percentile scores are compressed toward the middle of the normal curve, so that what might look like large differences between percentile scores in the average range may not be clinically relevant, while what might look like small differences between percentile scores on the "tails" of the curve may be more significant. Scaled scores are more linear and can thus be compared to each other more meaningfully; for this reason, these scores are the ones that are discussed in this report.

To understand Rebekah's performance, it may be helpful to refer to this image of the normal curve and the various types of scores.

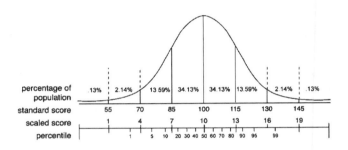

Some of the tests used in this evaluation also include Relative Proficiency Index (RPI) scores. These scores are similar to the scores on a traditional eye chart, comparing the child's performance to that of an average child of the same age. So, for example, a child with an RPI of 70/90 would be predicted to be 70% proficient on tasks similar to those tested, at a level of difficulty on which her age-peers would be 90% proficient. These scores can often show a weakness in actual performance that may not be evident from standard scores.

CASE 10

An Elementary School Student with a Specific Learning Disability in Reading

Use of the DAS-II to Generate and Test Causal Hypotheses

Colin Elliott

Children with difficulties in learning to read are frequently referred for psychoeducational evaluations. They often pose difficult, sometimes intractable, problems for their teachers and parents. Because reading disability is so heterogeneous and varied in its causes, these types of cases also present challenges to psychologists and diagnosticians in determining the nature of the underlying deficits in cognitive processing, where these exist.

This report provides an example of using a cognitive ability test battery—in this case, the Differential Ability Scales, Second Edition (DAS-II)—in an exploratory way in order to uncover a possible pattern of strengths and weaknesses in a student's cognitive abilities. Converging evidence about the nature of this pattern is obtained, not only from the DAS-II findings, but also from teachers' reports and observations, and from achievement test results from the Wechsler Individual Achievement Test, Third Edition (WIAT-III).

The child has a specific difficulty in acquiring reading skills; his math progress at school is average. The problem in his acquisition of reading skills appears to be related to a specific difficulty in integrating complex auditory-verbal and visual information, while being able to process purely verbal and visual tasks at an average level for his age. The DAS-II is able to provide unique information in comparing and contrasting a child's ability to handle tasks in single modalities with his or her ability to integrate complex visual and verbal information. This should be an important characteristic in any cognitive assessment battery because of the nature of the reading process, and because psychoeducational examiners are so often asked to evaluate children who are having difficulty in learning to read. The nature of reading is that it presents a visual code that must be translated into single words and ultimately into meaningful language—this process requires complex integration of visual and verbal information.

The assessment results lead us to a strong hypothesis about the nature of the child's underlying difficulties. The intervention plan at the end of the report is targeted at the child's cognitive strengths and weaknesses and contains various suggestions that could well be supplemented by experienced teachers and clinicians.

Cognitive assessment is a process in which information is unfolded piece by piece. As this happens, hypotheses are raised about a child's cognitive processing and his or her strengths and weaknesses. As more tests are given, the hypotheses are supported or need to be modified. For you, the reader, to understand the development of hypotheses and the thinking behind the tests, I have put comments in boxes at various points in the report.

PSYCHOLOGICAL EVALUATION

Name:	Ralph Benigno
Date of Birth:	2/11/2002
Age:	7 years, 11 months
School:	Sycamore Elementary
Grade:	2
Date of Evaluation:	1/11/2010
Date of Report:	1/18/2010
Evaluator:	Colin D. Elliott, Ph.D.

REASON FOR REFERRAL

The Student Assistance Team referred Ralph for a comprehensive psychoeducational evaluation to determine why he has not responded to the reading interventions provided as part of his instructional program. The team would like to be able to identify additional targeted instructional recommendations as a result of the evaluation.

RELEVANT BACKGROUND INFORMATION

Ralph is in second grade at Sycamore Elementary School. His language appears appropriate for his age. He uses complete sentences to describe his experiences and chooses words that convey his ideas. During math activities, he frequently raises his hand to answer the teacher's questions. When working with small groups of classmates on math, he takes on a leadership role. However, Ralph does not display the same enthusiasm for reading. During reading activities, his teacher frequently reminds him to lift up his head from his desk and turn to the appropriate page in his book. His teacher is concerned that his reading skills are lower than the skills of the majority of his classmates. She has observed that Ralph struggles to recall high-frequency words. He attempts to use segmentation and blending to pronounce unfamiliar words but he reads fewer words correctly within a minute than the other children in his second-grade class.

In an effort to improve his reading, his teacher and the reading specialist provided supplemental instruction focused on segmentation and blending of simple consonant-vowel-consonant words. Ralph demonstrated minimal improvements in the number of words read correctly based on these interventions. The Student Assistance Team reviewed Ralph's progress and decided to request additional assessment of Ralph's reading skills.

The school psychologist, as a member of the Student Assistance Team, administered several subtests from the Process Assessment of the Learner–Second Edition (PAL-II). These subtests provided information about Ralph's skills on auditory and visual components of reading and about his ability to name aloud stimuli quickly and accurately. The results on the subtests Syllables, Phonemes, Rimes, Pseudoword Decoding, Receptive Coding, RAN-Letters, RAN-Words, and RAN-Digits indicated the following:

- He named few whole words quickly and accurately.
- He struggled to segment spoken words into syllables and into phonemes.
- He performed significantly below expectations in naming the portion of the syllable that is left (e.g., *end*)

when the initial phoneme (e.g., b) or phonemes (e.g., *bl*) of the syllable is/are omitted.

- In using phonological decoding skills to read nonsense words, he named simple consonant-vowel-consonant words with short vowel sounds.
- He did well on tasks that required him to name quickly and accurately single letters and simple letter groups and single-digit and double-digit numbers.

Based on this information, the members of the Student Assistance Team requested a comprehensive psychoeducational evaluation in an effort to identify targeted interventions to improve Ralph's reading achievement.

TESTS ADMINISTERED

Wechsler Individual Achievement Test, Third Edition (WIAT-III)

Differential Ability Scales, Second Edition (DAS-II)

RESULTS

The examiner administered several tests to evaluate Ralph's cognitive ability and academic achievement. The WIAT-III was administered first to assess his achievement of skills in reading, written expression, and mathematics. The DAS-II was administered to assess Ralph's ability to receive, perceive, process, and remember information.

Academic Achievement

The WIAT-III was administered to assess Ralph's achievement of skills in reading, writing, and mathematics. His scores on the WIAT-III subtests and composites are shown in Table 1. Consistent with teacher observations, Ralph performed better on mathematics subtests than on reading and writing subtests. His standard score of 100 for mathematics was within the Average range and equaled or exceeded the scores of approximately 50% of others his age in the standardization sample. He earned a standard score of 106 for Numerical Operations, which required him to solve written mathematics problems. His score was 96 on Mathematics Problem Solving, which assessed his ability to reason mathematically when problems were presented with verbal and visual prompts. His score was 104 on Math

Fluency-Addition and 100 on Math Fluency-Subtraction, which measured speed and accuracy of solving written addition and subtraction problems. Although he performed within the Average range on all of the mathematics subtests, it is noteworthy that Ralph's score was slightly lower on Mathematics Problem Solving, which required processing of both auditory and visual information.

On the Reading Composite, Ralph earned a standard score of 69. Within the Extremely Low range, this score equaled or exceeded the scores of approximately 2% of others his age in the standardization sample. Put another way, his performance is in the lowest 2 percent of children his age.

His best performance in reading was on Pseudoword Decoding, which required him to pronounce nonsense words that are phonetically correct. Although his score was Below Average on this task, he was able to sound out unfamiliar letter combinations, following regular rules of phonemic analysis, and blend the segments together to pronounce the words. His score was significantly lower on Word Reading, which on the lower items required him to identify beginning and ending sounds, blend two word parts he heard to name a word, and point to a letter symbol based on a letter sound said by the examiner. Word Reading also contains irregularly spelled words that require visual memory and a sight vocabulary, in contrast to the phonetically regular decoding task in Pseudoword Decoding. For Reading Comprehension, he struggled to read sentences even when given picture clues. His performance is consistent with information from the PAL-II, referred to earlier.

Ralph's score for Written Expression was within the Low Average range. He scored in the Average range on Sentence Composition, which required him to generate a sentence using a prescribed word and to combine multiple sentences into one meaningful sentence. In contrast, he scored within the Borderline range in Spelling, which measures written spelling of letter sounds and single words. This is consistent with weaknesses in segmentation identified on earlier assessments.

Ralph achieved a GCA score of 97 on the DAS-II (see Table 1). On the basis of that score, his WIAT-III scores for all composites and subtests were predicted to be 98. All of his reading scores were highly significantly below the predicted score ($p < .01$). The same is true for his Written Expression composite and his Spelling subtest score. Ralph's discrepancy of 29 points between his actual (69) and predicted (98) Reading score is also highly unusual: Fewer than 1% of all children show a difference of this size.

Table 1 Ralph's WIAT-III Scores

Wechsler Individual Achievement Test-Third Edition			
Composite/Subtests	Standard Score (M = 100; SD = 15)	Percentile Rank	Significant Ability/ Achievement Discrepancy?*
Total Reading	**69**	**2**	**Yes**
Word Reading	58	0.3	Yes
Pseudoword Decoding	86	18	Yes
Reading Comprehension	72	3	Yes
Written Expression	**83**	**13**	**Yes**
Spelling	79	8	Yes
Sentence Composition	90	25	No
Mathematics	**100**	**50**	**No**
Numerical Operations	106	66	No
Mathematics Problem Solving	96	39	No
Math Fluency	**102**	**55**	**No**
Addition	104	60	No
Subtraction	100	50	No

*($p < .01$) Based on the difference between Ralph's actual WIAT-III scores and those predicted from his DAS-II GCA score of 97.

Assessment of Cognitive Abilities

Complex Mental Processing: On the DAS-II, Ralph was given a number of "core" subtests to assess his ability to perform complex mental processing involving conceptualization and transformation of information. These subtests yield three cluster scores measuring Verbal Abilities, Spatial Abilities, and Nonverbal Reasoning. Ralph's scores on these subtests and composites are shown in Table 2.

Verbal Ability Cluster

Ralph's score of 102 was within the Average range and equal to or better than those of approximately 55% of his same-age peers in the standardization sample. Ralph's performance was consistent on the two subtests that assessed verbal ability. He was able to define words presented orally by the examiner (Word Definition

T score = 52) and identify the common concept linking three words (Verbal Similarities *T* score = 50). Note that these tasks are purely verbal and require no visual processing.

Spatial Ability Cluster

Ralph's score of 102 shows that he is also within the Average range on tasks that required complex visual-spatial processing. Once again, his score was equal to or better than the scores of approximately 55% of others his age in the standardization sample. His performance also was consistent on the two subtests that assessed visual-spatial ability. He performed within the Average range on a task that measured his ability to recall briefly exposed abstract designs by drawing them with pencil and paper (Recall of Designs *T* score = 51). His performance was also within the Average range on a task that measured his ability to use blocks to construct patterns demonstrated by the examiner or presented in a picture (Pattern Construction *T* score = 52). Note that these are purely visual-spatial tasks and require no verbal processing.

Nonverbal Reasoning Cluster

In contrast with Ralph's average performance on verbal and visual-spatial tasks, he performed in the Below Average range on tasks that measured Nonverbal Reasoning Ability (standard score = 89). This score equaled or exceeded the scores of approximately 23% of others his age in the standardization sample. On the two subtests assessing nonverbal reasoning, his performance was comparable. His ability to perceive and apply relationships among abstract figures (Matrices *T* score = 43) and to perceive sequential patterns (Sequential and Quantitative Reasoning *T* score = 44) was at the low end of the Average range. The items for both tasks are presented visually with little verbal instruction. Nevertheless, internal verbal mediation of the problems is an important component enabling the child to determine the correct solution.

The 13-point differences between Verbal and Nonverbal Reasoning and between Spatial and Nonverbal Reasoning are statistically significant. Although each of these differences, taken individually, occurred in over 15% of children Ralph's age in the standardization sample, only 6% of children of his age showed both Verbal and Spatial abilities at 13 points or more above Nonverbal Reasoning.

Given that these differences are relatively infrequent (and that there are no differences between the subtests within each cluster), we have a hypothesis that Ralph's lower nonverbal reasoning abilities represent a relative weakness in integrating visual and verbal information in these complex tasks. We now look for further confirmatory evidence supporting this hypothesis.

Note:

The reasoning behind this interpretation is as follows:

- If there had been significant differences between subtests within any cluster, we would need to modify our interpretation based on the specific characteristics of each subtest. However, where there are no significant differences between them, we may interpret the cluster score with confidence.
- The Verbal and Spatial clusters represent two distinct independent systems of information processing that tend to be localized in the left and right cerebral hemispheres, respectively.
- For normal cognitive functioning, the auditory-verbal and visual-spatial systems operate in an integrated fashion. Integration of these systems is always required when problems are presented in visual form, but the individual has to encode the picture or figure verbally and then use internal verbal mediation to solve the problem. The Nonverbal Reasoning cluster has these characteristics and measures fluid reasoning (Gf), according to CHC theory. The best tests of Gf require that integrative process.
- Therefore, because of Ralph's lower scores on the Nonverbal Reasoning subtests, we have the hypothesis that he has difficulty in integrating verbal and visual information in complex tasks.

See further discussion on ability constructs and neurological structures in Elliott (2007), pp. 14–16, and Elliott (2005), pp. 402–405.

Because Ralph's Nonverbal Reasoning Ability score is significantly lower than his scores on the Verbal and Spatial clusters, his overall General Conceptual Ability score of 97 (Average range) does not give a complete picture of his abilities in complex mental processing.

Table 2 Ralph's DAS-II Core Subtest Scores

Differential Ability Scales-Second Edition (DAS-II)			
Composite/Cluster/Core Subtest	Standard Score (Mean = 100)	*T* score (Mean = 50)	Percentile Rank
General Conceptual Ability	97		42
Verbal Ability	102		55
Word Definitions		52	58
Verbal Similarities		50	50
Nonverbal Reasoning Ability	89		23
Matrices		43	24
Sequential and Quantitative Reasoning		44	27
Spatial Ability	102		55
Recall of Designs		51	54
Pattern Construction		52	58

Table 3 Ralph's DAS-II Diagnostic Subtest Scores

Differential Ability Scales-Second Edition (DAS-II)			
Cluster/Diagnostic Subtest	Standard Score (M = 100; SD = 15)	*T* score (M = 50; SD = 10)	Percentile Rank
Working Memory	93		32
Recall of Sequential Order		40	16
Recall of Digits Backward		52	58
Processing Speed	89		23
Speed of Information Processing		51	54
Rapid Naming		38	12
Other Diagnostic Subtests			
Recall of Objects—Immediate		40	16
Recall of Objects—Delayed		41	18
Recall of Digits Forward		53	62
Recognition of Pictures		54	66
Phonological Processing		45	31

Other Diagnostic Ability Tests

To further assess Ralph's abilities to receive, perceive, process, and remember information, the "diagnostic" subtests from the DAS-II were administered. Results are shown in Table 3.

Working Memory Cluster

Ralph earned a standard score of 93 on this cluster. Although this score suggests that Ralph's ability to process information that is temporarily being held within short-term memory is within the Average range, the score does not completely summarize his working memory ability. This is because his performance was significantly better on the subtest Recall of Digits Backward (*T* score = 52) than on Recall of Sequential Order (*T* score = 40).

Both tasks required Ralph to listen to a list of verbally presented words and/or numbers and to hold the list in short-term memory while the list is worked on and put in a different order. Recall of Digits Backward is an entirely verbal task. However, on the Recall of Sequential Order subtest, the examiner presents lists of the names of body parts verbally and in random order. However, the child needs to visualize the body in order to recall the body parts in correct sequence (upper to lower). Ralph's

Below-Average score on this subtest suggests that, while he can adequately handle purely verbal working memory tasks, he may have more difficulty with tasks that require the integration of verbal and visual-spatial information. This low subtest score is consistent with Ralph's somewhat Below-Average score on the Nonverbal Reasoning cluster.

Processing Speed Cluster

Ralph also earned a score in the Below Average range (standard score = 89), suggesting on first sight that he is relatively slow in processing information. Once again, however, we need to be cautious about such an interpretation because there was a statistically significant difference between his scores on the two subtests that form the cluster.

His performance was Average for his age on the Speed of Information Processing subtest (*T* score = 51). This task assesses the speed of children in scanning a page to make visual, quantitative comparisons, and is entirely nonverbal. Responses consist of brief marks made with a pencil on a test booklet.

However, Ralph's score on the Rapid Naming subtest (T score = 38) was in the Below Average range. The tasks on this subtest require the child to retrieve names of colors and animals as quickly as possible. The tasks are visually presented, but require a verbal response from the child, who names the colors and the animals in the pictures. This subtest therefore requires some degree of integration of visual and verbal processing.

It is noteworthy that Ralph performed better on Rapid Naming when the task required him to perform simple mental operations such as naming the colors only, or naming the animals only (T score = 40). His performance was significantly weaker on a more complex task that required him to look at pictures of colored animals (for example, red dog, blue cow) and name the color first, and then the name of the animal (T score = 32). We conclude that Ralph has particular difficulty with a complex naming task requiring verbal-visual integration. Once again, the pattern of Ralph's scores on the Processing Speed subtests is very consistent with his scores on the Nonverbal Reasoning and Working Memory clusters.

> **Note:**
>
> According to recent versions of CHC theory, tests of rapid automatized naming are characterized as measuring the factor of long-term retrieval ability (Glr). The DAS-II Rapid Naming subtest clearly clusters with Speed of Information Processing in measuring the Processing Speed factor (see Elliott, 2007, pp. 153–162), and there is no evidence that it clusters with the Recall of Objects subtest to form a Glr factor. The Rapid Naming subtest may perhaps be best characterized as a measure of speed and accuracy of lexical access and retrieval.

Further support for this hypothesis about Ralph's difficulties came from the Recall of Objects—Immediate subtest. Twenty colored pictures are presented on a card for 45 seconds, and after that period the child is asked to name as many pictures as he or she can. There are two further trials, with briefer presentations of the same pictures, and a delayed trial follows later. Successful performance requires verbal encoding, rehearsal, and retrieval strategies as well as visualization of the array of pictures—in other words, integration of visual and verbal information. His scores were within the Below Average range on Recall of Objects—Immediate (T score = 40) and Recall of Objects—Delayed (T score = 41). His score on Recall of Objects—Immediate was significantly lower than the mean of his T scores on the "core" subtests, indicating a probable specific cognitive weakness. The Recall of Objects subtest measures visual-verbal memory.

> **Note:**
>
> According to CHC theory, the Recall of Objects subtest measures the factor of long-term retrieval ability (Glr). Elliott (2007) would prefer to call this factor "visual-verbal short-term memory," because tests measuring Glr typically have both visual and verbal components.

On two diagnostic subtests presenting tasks within a single sensory modality, Ralph achieved average scores for his age. The first of these is Recall of Digits Forward (T score = 53), a measure of short-term auditory sequential recall. No visualization is required on this subtest. The second is Recognition of Pictures (T score = 54), which requires the child to remember and recognize visual images. This subtest measures short-term visual recognition rather than visual recall and requires detailed discrimination. No verbalization is required on this subtest. We conclude from these subtests, together with Ralph's average scores on the Verbal cluster and on the Spatial cluster, that whenever he is required to process information within one sensory modality (verbal or visual), he performs at an average level for his age.

Ralph's score on the Phonological Processing subtest was also within the Average range (T score = 45). This subtest consists of four tasks measuring Rhyming, Blending, Deletion, and Phoneme Identification and Segmentation. Analysis of his performance on these tasks indicates Ralph did well both on rhyming (e.g., tell me a word that rhymes with **bake**) and in blending syllables (e.g., *Mon–day*) and phonemes (e.g., *o–n*). He had difficulty with the deletion task (e.g., say *Mon–day* without *Mon*), and on this task he scored significantly below the level of his scores on rhyming and blending. This may reflect a weakness in analytic skill that indicates if he has an "ear" for sounds within words. He also struggled to name beginning phonemes (e.g., tell me the first sound in *fish*) and segments of words he heard (e.g., tell me all the sounds in the word *cat*). Segmentation of orally presented words is a fundamental skill needed for spelling.

Summary of Cognitive Assessment

In processing information, Ralph responds effectively when tasks are presented verbally and when the tasks require a verbal response. He is able to hold verbal information in short-term memory and repeat or transform the information. Similarly, he responds effectively when tasks are presented visually and when he is asked to recall information he saw or organize visual information and objects in space. In comparison, he struggles to respond effectively on tasks that require integration of visual and verbal processing. This probably impacts his performance on reading tasks which require him to translate printed words (visual modality) into spoken words (verbal modality).

OVERALL SUMMARY AND RECOMMENDATIONS

Ralph is a 7-year, 11-month-old student in the second grade at Sycamore Elementary School. His achievement in mathematics is at the expected rate and is consistent with his GCA score of 97 on the DAS-II. On the WIAT-III, he scored within the Average range for mathematics. However, he is performing significantly below grade-level expectations in reading, and his scores for reading and written expression are substantially lower than would be expected given his average intellectual ability. Following interventions in the classroom, the Student Assistance Team referred Ralph for a comprehensive psychoeducational evaluation.

Ralph's achievement in reading and writing is affected by weaknesses at the acquisition phase of learning. In collecting information, he demonstrated weaknesses in auditory-visual information processing. He struggles to allocate attention when information is presented visually and requires verbal processing. This weakness affects the accuracy of the information he stores in his memory and the accuracy of the information he retrieves. There is evidence that an increase in the complexity of tasks has a large impact on his ability to respond efficiently. Overall, he struggles with tasks that demand integration between verbal and visual processing.

RECOMMENDATIONS

The Individualized Education Program Committee will make decisions regarding Ralph's eligibility and need for direct specialized instruction. Regardless of the setting, instruction for Ralph must focus on improving his basic skills in reading and writing. In providing instruction, his teachers will consider his ability to perform effectively when tasks are presented either verbally or visually and his lowered performance on tasks that require integration of verbal-visual processing. A multisensory approach to reading instruction should be considered for Ralph. See, for example, books by Judith Birsh (2005) and by Janet Townend and Martin Turner (2000).

Here are some immediate recommendations for teaching:

1. To improve Ralph's phonological awareness, focus on syllables. Ask him to:
   a. Find a word hidden in a longer word. For example, "Say *ball*. Is the word *ball* hidden in *baseball? ballgame? cowboy? bolt?*"
   b. Ask for the syllable missing from a word he hears. For example, "Say *forgotten*. Now say *gotten*. What part is missing?"
   c. Say a word without a part of the word. For example, "Say *destiny*. Now say it without *des*."
   d. Say a new word by substituting a given syllable for another. For example, "Say *sunshine*. Now don't say it with *shine*—say it with *day*."

2. To improve reading and spelling, provide explicit instructions on translating printed words into spoken words (Berninger, V. W. [1998b] *Talking letters: Teacher guide and student desk cards in PAL Intervention Kit*). Ask Ralph to look at a sheet with letters and pictures that begin with each letter. The teacher points to the letter, names the letter and asks Ralph to repeat this. Then the teacher names the picture and makes the sound at the beginning of the picture. Use this strategy to teach Ralph to sound out words and to listen for the sounds in dictated words.

3. Use the Looking Game to focus his attention on each letter in a word by sweeping your finger under the word from left to right. Cover up the word with a blank card and ask him to spell the word. If he does not spell the word correctly, show the word and point out the letters he missed. Begin with simple consonant-vowel-consonant patterns (e.g., *bat, nap, jet, kid, cot, but*).

4. Use the Sound Game to focus his attention on the number of phonemes in a word. For example, ask Ralph to say *bed*. Then ask him to "say it again but don't say /b/." Use blocks or chips to identify the number of phonemes in a word. For example, for *bed*, place three blocks horizontally in front of Ralph. As you say each phoneme, point to the corresponding block. Then remove the block

corresponding to the deleted phoneme and pronounce the remaining sounds pointing to the corresponding block as you say the phoneme. For these and other suggested interventions, see Berninger (1998c).

REFERENCES

Berninger, V. W. (1998a). *Process assessment of the learner—Second edition*. San Antonio, TX: The Psychological Corporation.

Berninger, V. W. (1998b) *Talking letters: Teacher guide and student desk cards in PAL intervention kit*. San Antonio, TX: The Psychological Corporation.

Berninger, V. W. (1998c). *Process assessment of the learner: Guides for reading and writing intervention*. San Antonio, TX: The Psychological Corporation.

Birsh, J. R. (Ed.) (2005). *Multisensory teaching of basic language skills* (2nd ed.). Baltimore, MD: Paul H. Brookes.

Elliott, C. D. (2005). The differential ability scales. In Flanagan, D. P., & Harrison, P. L. (Eds.), *Contemporary intellectual assessment: Theories, tests, and issues* (2nd ed.) (pp. 402-405). New York, NY: Guilford Press.

Elliott, C. D. (2007). *Differential ability scales, Second edition: Introductory and technical handbook*. San Antonio, TX: Harcourt Assessment.

Townend, J., & Turner, M. (2000). *Dyslexia in practice: A guide for teachers*. New York: Kluwer.

CASE 11

Using a Pattern of Strengths and Weaknesses Approach in a Complex Case

James Hanson

Sabrina's report is an example of how current laws regarding examining patterns of strengths and weaknesses allow school psychologists to identify learning disabilities using valid cognitive constructs. The report follows the guidelines in the Oregon School Psychologists Association Technical Assistance Paper for SLD evaluations using a Pattern of Strengths and Weaknesses (PSW) approach (www.ospaonline.org, PSW Toolkit).

ORGANIZATION

The report is organized according to the six possible comparison areas under Pattern of Strengths and Weaknesses (PSW): (a) achievement relative to age, (b) performance relative to age, (c) achievement relative to state grade-level standards, (d) performance relative to state grade-level standards, (e) achievement relative to intellectual development, and (f) performance relative to intellectual development. In a PSW approach, achievement is measured by scores on standardized tests, and performance is measured by classroom performance of acquired knowledge.

One major feature of the report is that the academic narrative is replaced by a state standards rubric. IDEA 2004 requires that teams examine achievement and performance related to grade-level standards. For a student who has not taken state tests, the team can only provide a measure of performance based on the state standards and using data from norm-referenced achievement tests, teacher tests, and progress monitoring. The rubric allows collaboration among report writers on the team because relevant data

Note: The author would like to thank Dr. Elaine Fletcher-Janzen for her help in case conceptualization.

from cognitive and language testing (e.g., phonological awareness) are found within the state reading standards. The rubric provides an easy guide to developing appropriate Individualized Education Plan (IEP) goals. Another major feature of the report is that the narrative regarding cognitive abilities is organized by the relationships of the cognitive abilities to the academic referral questions regarding reading and writing.

Choice of Instruments

Sabrina's report calls attention to the need for a comprehensive evaluation. It also argues for the importance of measuring all cognitive abilities related to the referral question, not just a few. The WJ III COG was chosen because it measured several abilities that the WISC-IV had not: Associative Memory and Rapid Naming. The community-based evaluation had recommended that Sabrina be classified as a student with a learning disability based on a Full-Scale IQ/achievement discrepancy. It did not identify a disorder in one of the basic psychological processes relevant to her academic problem. With the additional information from the WJ III COG, the team could explain to the parent, the teacher, and the student what her strengths were and why she was struggling to retain information.

The team also used the Cross Battery Data Management and Interpretive Assistant from *Essentials of Cross-Battery Assessment, Second Edition* (Flanagan & Ortiz, 2007) and the WJ III ACH to supplement the results from the WIAT-II. The use of these instruments was essential. In alignment with cross-battery assessment (CBA) principles, we used at least two tests to measure each construct, preventing a frequent mistake of using only one test to determine a disability. The team relied on the information provided by the WJ III ACH Relative Proficiency Index, which provided more relevant information than the standard scores regarding the seriousness of Sabrina's academic deficits. The team also used the BRIEF, teacher records/interviews, and observations in order to ascertain that the hypotheses generated by the cognitive tests were observable in the classroom.

Decision Making

Often, a school psychologist has more access to students in their learning environment, their teachers, and their developmental and educational history than a private clinician does. In Sabrina's case, this information was crucial to team decision making and intervention. The family needed to address several health factors in order to rule out educational disabilities. The more comprehensive school-based report documented ADHD symptoms that also needed to be addressed medically. Finally, in contrast to their information from the community evaluation, the parents understood the reasons that Sabrina was struggling with reading and what could be done about it. From that information, the team was able to prioritize interventions effectively.

PSYCHOEDUCATIONAL EVALUATION

Name:	Sabrina Jones
Date of Birth:	10/16/01
Age:	8-1
Parents:	Dylan Jones, Gyllian Peters
School:	Barkley Primary
Teacher:	Elizabeth Moorehouse
Grade:	3.2
Date:	11/14/2009
Examiner:	James Hanson, M.Ed.

REASON FOR REFERRAL/REVIEW OF INFORMATION

Sarah Cole, Sabrina's second-grade teacher, referred Sabrina for an evaluation of special education eligibility and learning needs in early June 2009, when Sabrina had failed to respond to supplemental reading instruction. Ms. Cole

reports that on the Spokane Public Schools (SPS) first- and second-grade K-3 literacy assessments, Sabrina performed below age and class expectations. Ms. Cole reported that Sabrina appeared very bright and creative, but she was concerned with Sabrina's focus and attention. She noted that Sabrina had a low frustration level and a high level of anxiety.

DEVELOPMENTAL AND SCHOOL HISTORY

Sabrina is an only child. Her parents both graduated from college. There is a history of mild learning disabilities on her father's side of the family. Her uncle and her father both received reading tutoring when they were in elementary school. Her mother reports that Sabrina met developmental milestones within normal time parameters. Sabrina's hearing and vision were tested in March 2009 and found to be normal. Sabrina's mother reports that Sabrina's current health is generally good; however, Sabrina has mild asthma. She rarely uses an inhaler but has one with her at all times. Sabrina has had some difficulty falling asleep, sleeping soundly, and waking up easily.

Sabrina attended preschool and most of first grade in Spokane. Her family moved to Nebraska in December of her first-grade year and returned in early February of her second-grade year. Upon her return, Ms. Cole reported that based on her assessment, Sabrina learned her alphabet letters well by name and sound but didn't progress to fluent letter blending, word identification skills, or reading comprehension strategies. Based on her teacher's report and schoolwide Dynamic Indicators of Basic Early Literacy Skills (DIBELS) screening, Sabrina was placed in a supplemental reading group with three other children in early March 2009. The certified teaching assistant/tutor used the Slingerland method of instruction twice a week for 40 minutes during the afternoon elective time in the general education classroom. Slingerland is a multisensory approach to basic reading skills that emphasizes mastery level of sound-symbol relationships and frequent review of concepts. Fidelity to the curriculum was documented by three 10-minute observations using the Slingerland script checklist. Sabrina's instructor remarked that Sabrina sometimes had difficulty paying attention in the small group setting. Sabrina was also on a behavioral modification (charting and reward) program for respectful listening skills during class meeting times. Ms. Cole writes that

Sabrina did a good job of making choices at large group time with the extra support.

CLASSROOM OBSERVATION, DATE: 11/14/2009

During the instructional period, students worked in large and small groups on the following reading skills: phonological awareness, the alphabetic principle, reading fluency, vocabulary, and concepts of print. Explicit instructions in reading comprehension skills were not given as a part of this lesson but have been observed repeatedly in the classroom at other times.

During phonological instruction, students read a poem aloud from the board. After reading the poem the first time, the students clapped to discover how many syllables each word contained. The teacher asked the students to listen for the words that began with the *st* consonant blend and words that ended with the long *e* sound. Sabrina came in at the end of this instruction. She looked sleepy; her eyelids began to close. The class then moved to large group phonics instruction. This session lasted from 9:25 to 9:52. Before the lesson began, the teacher reviewed the consonant digraphs *ch* and *th*. The children had studied these digraphs the previous week. The teacher began the day's lesson with stating the objective: learning *r*-controlled vowels, the diphthongs *ou* and *ow*, and the rule for *ou* when it's followed by *r*. Examples of *r*-controlled vowels were written and hung on the clothesline. The students responded approximately 6 to 8 times per minute. Their accuracy rate was over 90%. The teacher told Sabrina that she would be calling on her in a minute for an *O-R* word and to be ready. Sabrina gave a correct answer twice. Sabrina was praised twice for correct behavior, once for raising her hand and once for respectful listening. Sabrina was positively corrected (redirected) twice, once for talking to another student ("Put your hands like this") and once for not looking at instruction ("Put your eyes where my red pen is").

During group instruction in the alphabetic principle, Sabrina was on task 24% of the time. She spent the rest of the time looking at other students, looking out the window, or attempting to talk to a peer. A comparison female student was on task 100% of the time. When students were told to pair up to perform a practice exercise, Sabrina found a friend easily and began work. Students were instructed to find examples of two-syllable words in a short passage. During this 3-minute period, Sabrina was on task 100%

of the time. She listened and counted syllables as her peer read the passage.

PROGRESS MONITORING DATA

Appropriate Instruction

Sabrina's classroom teacher is employed by Spokane Public Schools and therefore by district policy is considered to be highly qualified to deliver instruction. Sabrina's literacy curriculum is not research based; however, the instruction has been observed repeatedly throughout the year for adherence to the Five Big Ideas of Reading (phonemic awareness, phonics, fluency, vocabulary, and comprehension) and the principles of effective instruction (explicit, intensive, scaffolds, high response rate, praise, and correction). Over 90% of students in the class are meeting Dynamic Indicators of Basic Early Literacy Skills (DIBELS) benchmarks.

Progress Monitoring/Repeated Assessments

During her second-grade year, Sabrina's class was administered the DIBELS screening measures. The Barkley team used the Oral Reading Fluency (ORF) measure to determine group placement. In February 2009 Sabrina's oral reading fluency rate was 5 correct words per minute. In May, Sabrina's oral reading fluency rate was 25 correct words per minute. At the end of second grade, students should have 90 correct words per minute. During the time that Sabrina was in supplemental instruction, her progress was monitored every week with the DIBELS Nonsense Word Fluency (NWF) measure. This measure was most closely aligned with her phonics instruction. In early March, Sabrina's NWF score was 21, indicating a deficit. Her scores improved weekly; however, they did not improve rapidly enough to meet her learning target. At the end of the 10-week intervention, Sabrina's NWF score was 45.

PATTERN OF STRENGTHS AND WEAKNESSES

Achievement Relative to Age

Standardized, individually administered tests of academic achievement were used to determine Sabrina's achievement relative to age.

WJ III ACH Form B Date: 11/1/2009, Examiner: James Hanson

Composite or Test	SS	RPI	PR	GE
Broad Reading	**73**	**10/90**	**4**	**<K.8**
Basic Reading Skills	**84**	**22/90**	**14**	**K.6**
Letter Word Identification	79	5/90	8	K.3
Reading Fluency	82	55/90	11	1.2
Word Attack	92	63/90	29	1.0
Reading Comprehension	**74**	**14/90**	**4**	**<K.7**
Passage Comprehension	71	2/90	3	<K.0
Reading Vocabulary	85	27/90	15	K.8
Broad Written Language	**86**	**68/90**	**18**	**K.6**
Spelling	93	69/90	33	K.6
Written Expression	**81**	**67/90**	**10**	**K.7**
Writing Fluency	84	66/90	13	1.3
Writing Samples	86	66/90	17	K.7
Handwriting (not in cluster)	80	NA	9	<K.0

For academic purposes, standard scores between 90 and 110 are considered average. Scores below 90 are considered normative weaknesses. Scores above 110 are considered normative strengths. Grade equivalents are approximations and should not be used for analysis of strengths and weaknesses. The team is strongly encouraged to examine Sabrina's scores on the Relative Proficiency Indexes (RPI). RPI scores indicate the level of mastery on age-level academic tasks. The average student demonstrates 90/90, or 90% mastery. This level of mastery on tasks falls within students' proximal zone of academic development and indicates that students will profit from exposure to age-level academic materials. Students that score 96/90 or above (96% mastery) will find most age-level academic tasks easy, and enrichment activities might be considered. Students that demonstrate RPI scores of 75/90 and below (75% mastery) will find most age-level academic tasks difficult and might require accommodations within general education curriculum, modifications to work, or supplemental instruction in order to master age-level academic material. All of Sabrina's academic scores fall below an RPI of 75/90.

WIAT-II Date: 3/12/2009, Examiner: Private Evaluator

Composite or Test	SS	PR	AE
Reading Composite	**81**	**10**	
Word Reading	83	13	5.2
Reading Comprehension	82	12	5.7
Pseudoword Reading	86	18	5.8
Reading Speed	Quartile: 1		
Spelling	88	21	6.8

Quartile scores indicate the bottom (first); lower-middle (second); upper-middle (third); and upper (fourth) 25% ranges for each grade level.

Performance Relative to Age

Sabrina's report card from the first quarter of third grade (last week) was used to determine her performance relative to age. Students are scored on skill levels: beginning, developing, and proficient on end of third-grade material.

Basic Reading Skills

Sabrina is at a "beginning" level in the following four basic reading skills: reading third-grade material with 90% to 100% accuracy, using many strategies to read, recognizing common words with irregular spelling patterns, and reading independently for 20 to 30 minutes daily. Sabrina is at a "beginning" level in reading fluently with flow and phrasing.

Reading Comprehension

Sabrina is at a "developing" level in five reading comprehension skills. She identifies the main idea, uses information and context for reading comprehension, infers what is meant by what is said, compares two or more texts, and evaluates/analyzes/draws conclusions about text. Sabrina is at a "beginning" level on reading independently for pleasure or information. Ms. Moorehouse writes, "Sabrina works hard and her oral comprehension is good. The reading and writing process is still a struggle for her. She needs a lot of one-on-one support to be successful academically."

Written Expression

Sabrina is at a "beginning" level in seven of eight writing skills: writing in a variety of modes including persuasive essays and narratives; writing a main idea with some supporting details; organizing ideas into beginning, middle, and end with some transitional words; using fluent and varied sentences; writing legibly; using grammar, capitalization, and punctuation appropriate to grade; and spelling using phonics, word patterns, and frequently used words. Sabrina is at a "developing" level in using the writing process (brainstorming, writing, editing).

Area	Oregon State Standard	Present Level of Performance	Measure	Priority 0 = meets 5 = needs
Decoding/Word Recognition	Read regular multisyllabic words.	Sabrina's word reading skills are at the 8th to 13th percentile for her age.	WJ III ACH WIAT-II	5
Decoding/Word Recognition	Use letter-sound correspondence to sound out unknown words.	Sabrina's decoding of regularly spelled words and nonsense words is at the 18th to 29th percentile for her age.	WJ III ACH WIAT-II	3
Decoding/Word Recognition	Recognize and use knowledge of spelling patterns (such as cut/cutting, slide/sliding, and the vowel sound "oy" in boy) when reading.	Sabrina does not change words into the present progressive without assistance. She answered questions on vowel digraphs with 100% accuracy when forewarned, but her teacher reports that her accuracy in oral reading is poor. She answered 3/15 prompts for vowel digraphs and diphthongs on group screening tests.	K-3 Literary Assessments, observations DIBELS ORF	4
Decoding/Word Recognition	Apply knowledge of basic syllabication rules when reading (e.g., VCV su-per, VCCV sup-per).	Sabrina decodes simple CVC words with 80% accuracy. She has not learned syllabication rules.	CBM K-3 Literacy Assessment	3
Decoding/Word Recognition	Recognize and correctly read and use regular and irregular plurals.	Sabrina recognizes and reads regular plurals with 75% accuracy and irregular plurals with 20% accuracy.	DIBELS ORF	4
Decoding/Word Recognition	Recognize common abbreviations (e.g., Jan., Sun., Mr., St.).	Sabrina recognizes Mrs., Mr., and Ms.	Teacher observation	3
Fluency	Read aloud grade-level text fluently and accurately with appropriate intonation and expression using cues of punctuation to assist.	Sabrina's oral reading fluency in September 2009 was 30 correct words per minute. The beginning of third-grade benchmark is 93. Sabrina's reading fluency is at about the 11th percentile for her age.	DIBELS ORF WJ III ACH WIAT-II Report Card	5
Comprehension	Listen to, read, and understand a wide variety of grade-level information and narrative text including children's magazines, dictionaries, reference materials, online information, and poetry.	Sabrina's reading comprehension is at the 4th to 12th percentile for her age. Sabrina participates in classroom activities including online and reference materials and poetry. She comes late to class for some activities.	WJ III ACH WIAT-II Observation Attendance	4
Comprehension	Demonstrate listening comprehension of more complex text through discussions.	Sabrina is on task 66% of the time during listening times and participates in classroom discussions.	Teacher report	2
Comprehension	Draw on a variety of comprehension strategies as needed (re-reading, self-correcting, summarizing, class and group discussion).	Sabrina self-corrected very often during assessments. She did not re-read or summarize for meaning.	WIAT-II K3 Literacy Assessment	4
Comprehension	Read voluntarily for interest and own purposes.	Sabrina does not read for pleasure.	Parent/teacher report	3
Comprehension	Read informational texts for answers to specific questions.	Sabrina shows an interest in special topics but uses pictures for information.	Teacher report	2
Comprehension	Recall facts and details in the text to clarify and organize ideas.	Sabrina recalled stated facts from text on 50% of such questions.	WIAT-II	3
Comprehension	Pose possible answers to how, why, and what-if questions.	Sabrina participates in discussions but does not read selections.	Teacher report	3
Comprehension	Retell the sequence of a story.	Sabrina recalled the sequence in stories on 75% of such questions.	WIAT-II	2
Comprehension	Identify and describe the plot, setting, and characters in a story.	Sabrina accurately identifies these elements when she hears a story read aloud.	Teacher report K3 Literacy Assessment	1
Comprehension	Make and confirm predictions about what will happen next.	Sabrina answered 25% of outcomes questions.	WIAT-II	3

(Continued)

Area	Oregon State Standard	Present Level of Performance	Measure	Priority 0 = meets 5 = needs
Comprehension	Recognize the use of rhyme, rhythm, and alliteration by a poet and discuss its use.	Sabrina accurately counts for rhythm. She rhymes words well.	Observation WJ III ACH	1
Comprehension	Take part in creative responses to texts such as dramatizations and oral presentations.	Sabrina takes part in plays and in science activities that demonstrate what the class has studied.	Teacher report	1
Vocabulary	Understand, learn, and use new vocabulary that is introduced through stories and informational texts.	Sabrina's oral vocabulary is at the 99th percentile for her age. Her reading vocabulary is at the 15th percentile.	WISC-IV WJ III ACH	0
Vocabulary	Know and explain common antonyms and synonyms.	Sabrina's verbal reasoning is at the 98th percentile.	WJ III COG	0
Vocabulary	Know the meaning of simple prefixes and suffixes.	Sabrina identifies -ing and -ed.	K3 Literacy Assessment	4
Vocabulary	Determine meanings of words by using a dictionary or glossary.	Sabrina developed a personal dictionary and uses the dictionary with assistance.	Teacher report	2

Math Calculation Skills: Sabrina is at a "developing" level in four of four math calculation skills: reading and writing numbers to 999; counting by 2s, 3s, 4s, 5s, and 10s; understanding and using simple fractions like ½, ¼, and ¾; and knowing addition and subtraction facts to 18.

Math Reasoning

Sabrina is at a "developing" level in 9 of 10 math reasoning skills: using appropriate operations to solve word problems; generalizing about patterns to solve problems; recognizing, describing, and continuing number patterns; recognizing and naming 2- and 3-dimensional shapes; describing math terms such as *symmetry* and *parallel*; using common and metric measures of length, weight, and volume; estimating measurements; demonstrating understanding of a variety of graphs and charts; communicating mathematical thinking in a variety of ways; and adding sums of money to 10 dollars and making change. Sabrina is at a "beginning" level at telling time to the minute.

Summary of Performance Relative to Age

Sabrina's pattern of strengths and weaknesses in performance relative to age indicate strengths or relative strengths in oral language skills, reading comprehension skills, and some math reasoning. Sabrina's weaknesses include basic reading skills and written expression.

Achievement Relative to State Grade-Level Standards

Sabrina has not yet taken state grade-level standards tests.

Performance Relative to State Grade-Level Standards

The team used a state standards rubric to determine Sabrina's performance on state standards.

Achievement Relative to Intellectual Development

Standardized, individually administered tests of intellectual development/cognitive abilities were used for determination.

WISC-IV   Date: 3/12/2009   Examiner: Private Evaluator

WJ III COG   Date: 5/22/2009   Examiner: Private Evaluator

NEPSY   Date: 5/22/2009   Examiner: Private Evaluator

WJ III COG   Date: 10/29/2009   Examiner: James Hanson, M.Ed., School Psychologist

KABC-II   Date: 10/29/2009   Examiner: James Hanson, M.Ed., School Psychologist

Composite/Test	Test	SCS/SS	90% CI	PR
Comprehension-Knowledge (Gc)	EXBA-2*	**128**	Not Reported	**98**
Vocabulary	WISC-IV	16 (130)	Not Reported	99
Similarities (VL, LD)	WISC-IV	15 (125)	Not Reported	95
Long-Term Retrieval (Glr)	WJ III COG	Limited usefulness due to difference between narrow ability scores		
Associative Memory (MA)	EXBA-2	**86**	Not Reported	**19**
Visual Auditory Learning (MA)	WJ III COG	89	84–93	23
Visual Auditory Learning Delayed (MA)	WJ III COG	82	78–87	12
Atlantis (MA)	KABC-II	85	81–90	16
Retrieval Fluency (IF)	WJ III COG	114	107–120	82
Rapid Automatic Naming	EXBA-2	**108**	Not Reported	**69**
Rapid Picture Naming (NA)	WJ III COG	111	109–114	77
Speeded Naming (NA)	NEPSY	11 (105)	Not Reported	63
Visual-Spatial Reasoning (Gv)	EXBA-2	**115**	Not Reported	**85**
Perceptual Reasoning	WISC-IV	**125**	Not Reported	**95**
Block Design (SR, Vz)	WISC-IV	14 (120)	Not Reported	91
Picture Completion (CF)	WISC-IV	14 (120)	Not Reported	91
Picture Recognition (MV)	WJ III COG	110	102–118	75
Fluid Reasoning (Gf)	WJ III COG	**119**	**115–125**	**92**
Concept Formation (I)	WJ III COG	113	106–121	82
Analysis/Synthesis (RG)	WJ III COG	125	116–133	95
Phonemic Awareness (PA)	WJ III COG	**116**	**109–122**	**87**
Auditory Processing (Ga)	WJ III COG	**120**	**114–127**	**91**
Sound Blending (PC-S)	WJ III COG	105	98–111	63
Incomplete Words (PC-A, PC-S)	WJ III COG	119	112–127	90
Auditory Attention (US/U3, UR)	WJ III COG	121	115–127	92
Sound Awareness (PC-A, PC-S)	WJ III COG	114	107–120	82
Processing Speed (Gs)	EXBA-2	**106**	Not Reported	**65**
Coding (R9)	WISC-IV	15 (125)	Not Reported	95
Decision Speed (RE)	WJ III COG	111	106–117	77
Pair Cancellation (P)	WJ III COG	100	98–102	50
Short-Term Memory (Gsm)	EXBA-2	**108**	Not Reported	**72**
Working Memory (MW)	WISC-IV	**110**	Not Reported	**75**
Digit Span (MS, MW)	WISC-IV	12 (110)	Not Reported	75
Letter-Number Sequencing (MW)	WISC-IV	12 (110)	Not Reported	75
Auditory Working Memory (MW)	WJ III COG	103	97–108	57
Memory for Words (MS)	WJ III COG	117	111–123	89

*Scores were derived from the Cross Battery Data Management and Interpretive Assistant from *The Essentials of Cross Battery Assessment–Second Edition.*

The following is a list of the abilities that are related to reading. The most important are listed first. The second list contains abilities that are less related to reading (fluid reasoning and visual-spatial thinking).

- *Verbal Ability: (Strength)* Sabrina's verbal ability is within the superior range.

- *Phonemic Awareness/Auditory Processing: (Strength)* Sabrina's overall Phonemic Awareness and Auditory Processing scores are within the high average range.

- *Working Memory: (Strength)* Sabrina's working memory is within the high average range.

- **Rapid Automatic Naming: (Relative Strength)** Sabrina's Rapid Automatic Naming (RAN) scores are within the average range.
- **Processing Speed: (Relative Strength)** Sabrina's processing speed is within the average range.
- **Associative Memory: (Weakness)** Sabrina's associative memory is at the 19th percentile for her age and within the low average range. Sabrina does not form "paired associations" between visual and auditory materials well. Her associative memory pairings degrade more rapidly than others students' do. Sabrina will tend to forget the pairings she has learned over time, and in the time between learning sessions. Sabrina's associative memory scores indicate a disorder in one of the basic psychological processes that has a research-based link to achievement in early reading and math.

This pattern indicates that Sabrina might have difficulty learning and remembering phonics skills. Children with associative memory deficits often have to exert extra effort in remembering the mechanics of basic skills, which can result in fewer attention resources available for using their higher-level comprehension strategies. These results help explain why Sabrina has had difficulty moving from letter identification to fluent identification of consonant blends, vowel digraphs and diphthongs, *r*-controlled vowels, syllables, and whole words.

Children with associative memory deficits may need extra, explicit teaching in breaking the reading and math "codes." They may profit from instruction that emphasizes multisensory techniques, uses warm-up exercises that review previous concepts, uses explicit links between old and new material, requires a high response rate and mastery of new material before moving on, and offers frequent and repeated review of new material across situations. Practice on fluency skills for reading and math is often profitable.

- *Fluid Reasoning: (Strength)* Sabrina's fluid reasoning skills are within the high average range. Fluid reasoning is related to math reasoning achievement and higher-level reading comprehension skills. It is not related to basic reading skills.
- *Visual Reasoning: (Strength)* Sabrina's visual-spatial thinking skills are within the high average range. Visual-spatial skills are not related to academic achievement at Sabrina's age.

Performance Relative to Intellectual Development

The Behavior Rating Inventory of Executive Function (BRIEF), a standardized behavioral checklist, and work samples were used for determination.

BRIEF, Date: 11/12/2009, Respondent: Elizabeth Moorehouse, Teacher

Index/Scale	*T* Score	PR	90% CI
Inhibit	62	89	57–67
Shift	47	54	41–53
Emotional Control	66	91	61–71
Behavioral Regulation Index (BRI)	**62**	**89**	**59–65**
Initiate	62	89	55–89
Working Memory	66	91	61–71
Plan/Organize	75	97	70–80
Organization of Materials	66	91	61–71
Monitor	58	80	52–64
Metacognition Index	**68**	**94**	**65–71**
Global Executive Composite (GEC)	**65**	**89**	**63–67**

BRIEF

T scores between 35 and 65 are within the expected range and indicate average performance. *T* scores above 65 indicate areas of significant difficult for students. Sabrina's overall index, the GEC, was within the expected range for her age. The Behavioral Regulation Index (BRI) was somewhat elevated. The Metacognition Index (MI) was elevated.

Her teacher's rating of Sabrina's behavior in the classroom indicates that Sabrina exhibits difficulty with some aspects of executive function. Concerns are noted with Sabrina's ability to control her emotions, sustain working memory, organize her tasks and materials, and plan and organize problem-solving approaches. Sabrina is not rated as having significant problems inhibiting impulsive responses, making adjustments to routine or new task demands, monitoring her own behavior, or initiating activities. Children with similar elevation on the Working Memory scale but without significant elevations in the Behavioral Regulation scales are often described as generally inattentive. Without appropriate working memory, their ability to sustain focus for adequate lengths of time may be reduced. This profile is often seen in children with learning disabilities, language disorders, and mild attention disorders. The Negativity and

Inconsistency scales were acceptable, indicating that the teacher's responses are likely valid.

Work Sample Analyses and Observations

Sabrina often has trouble concentrating and is easily distracted by other children or things in the environment. She'll often start to spell a word and then forget the word she was trying to spell. She has good ideas but can't put them on paper. Her sense of time isn't very good, and she doesn't plan ahead. "Messy" characterizes her work style, even though she is always well dressed and clean. When she sounds out words, she doesn't identify them on the next page.

Assessments Related to Social/Emotional Status

BASC-2, Date: 11/12/2009

Overall, Sabrina's adaptive skills are within the average range on her mother's rating and within the at-risk range on her teacher's rating. Overall, Sabrina's Emotional Symptoms Index score is within the at-risk range on both ratings. Her scores are *somewhat similar* to the scores of students who have been diagnosed with emotional disturbances. Sabrina's teacher's rating indicates a high level of aggressive behaviors, such as teasing others, arguing, and annoying other children on purpose. Sometimes Sabrina loses her temper and bullies, threatens, and calls people names. Sabrina's score on inattention is within the at-risk range on her mother's rating and within the clinically significant range on her teacher's rating. Sabrina's teacher's rating indicates the team might wish to consider possible Generalized Anxiety Disorder. Ms. Cole reports that Sabrina almost always worries about things, and worries about things that cannot be changed. Appropriate goals based on assessment include working independently, taking turns, developing conflict resolution skills, managing anger/disappointment, ignoring distractions, and issuing invitations at appropriate times.

CRS-R, Date: 11/14/2009

The Conners' Rating Scale-Revised is a questionnaire that measures behaviors associated with Attention-Deficit/Hyperactivity Disorder. Sabrina's ADHD Index score of 89 based on her teacher's ratings falls within the markedly atypical range. This score indicates possible or probable significant problems associated with ADHD-Combined Type. In addition, the team might consider if

Sabrina's behaviors are indicative of Oppositional Defiant Disorder (ODD).

SUMMARY AND RECOMMENDATIONS

Sabrina Jones is an 8-year-old third-grade student at Barkley Primary. Sabrina has many strengths, including her intelligence, creativity, social skills, enthusiasm, and love of science. Her math development was not listed as a referral concern. Ms. Cole, Sabrina's second-grade teacher, was concerned with her lack of focus and her poor academic skills. She was also concerned with Sabrina's seemingly high anxiety level. Sabrina's family history includes mild learning disabilities. Sabrina's hearing, vision, and health are generally good, and she met most developmental milestones at normal times. Sabrina has asthma and must occasionally use her inhaler (about two days a month). She isn't sleeping well, has difficulty waking up easily, and comes to school late about one day in five.

Because of these concerns, Sabrina's parents initiated an evaluation at a private evaluation center, and then at school. Testing results indicated that Sabrina has superior overall cognitive abilities and verbal reasoning skills. Sabrina has high average abilities in fluid reasoning, visual-spatial thinking, and phonological awareness. Rapid naming and processing speed scores are average. However, Sabrina's associative memory scores are below average. This deficit in a basic psychological process that is relevant to reading has been observed within the classroom. Sabrina has difficulty pairing visual with auditory stimuli, such as pairing a sound with a pattern of letters. This pattern of strengths and weaknesses is reflected in Sabrina's reading and spelling scores: Sabrina's word identification scores are within the low average range. Because Sabrina struggles to sound out words, her reading comprehension and reading fluency are within the low average range. This pattern is seen in Sabrina's performance of the skills that reflect Oregon state second-grade-level standards and Spokane Public School third-grade report cards.

Results of assessment and observation suggest that Sabrina might learn best in smaller literacy groups that stress mastery of basic skills as they are framed in higher-level comprehension and analysis tasks, tasks that take advantage of Sabrina's exceptional intellectual strengths. Although Sabrina's math skills appear to be developing, the team will wish to closely monitor her math progress and consider interventions if appropriate. The team will also examine opportunities for Sabrina to pursue her academic and extracurricular interests and passions.

Behavioral checklists, family history, and interviews suggest that one of the reasons for Sabrina's lack of academic progress might be Attention-Deficit/Hyperactivity Disorder-Combined Type. The team might consider further evaluation for Oppositional Defiant Disorder (although oppositional behaviors occur more frequently at school and not at home). However, the team might also consider that children with sleep problems and allergies sometimes demonstrate ADHD-like symptoms. Sabrina's parents might want to consider the benefits of consulting with her pediatrician on sleep and allergies.

Although ADHD and sleep issues might be the largest presenting problems for Sabrina, the team is also concerned with possible anxiety and depression. Sabrina has the tendency to take things hard and not recover as well from setbacks as many children her age do. Many children with learning challenges experience feelings of frustration and sadness; therefore, even if the primary causes of Sabrina's possible emotional upset are ADHD, lack of sleep and lack of ease in learning academic skills, further evaluation and/or interventions for mood might be considered.

Finally, although deficits in associative memory can co-exist with ADHD and be considered a pattern of weaknesses in "executive functioning," and although temporary lower scores can be found in associative memory when a student is depressed or anxious, Sabrina's lower associative memory performance has been observed for some time, and might therefore be considered as relevant to a specific learning disability.

Despite her challenges, Sabrina possesses many of the characteristics that bode well for her future. These include her outstanding intelligence, her awareness of her environment, her exposure to good instruction, and her emotionally supportive and capable parents. The team will continue to work with Sabrina and her parents to provide the most appropriate instruction and enhanced educational experiences. In addition, once Sabrina has learned phonics well and can identify common sight words, she should progress rapidly in reading comprehension skills.

REFERENCE

Flanagan, D. P., & Ortiz, S. O. (2007). *Essentials of cross-battery assessment* (2nd ed.). New York, NY: Guilford Press.

CASE 12

Learning Is the Best Therapy
The Emotional Consequences of a Learning Disability

Lynne Jaffe

Dakota was 8 years old and heading into second grade when he was referred to me for a psychoeducational evaluation. He was a slight, angelic-looking, emotional mess of a kid who had repeated kindergarten (an effort at "remediation by retention") and had acquired virtually no reading or spelling skills by the end of first grade. Since his second kindergarten year, Dakota's increasing behavior problems interfered with his own learning and that of his classmates. He acted silly; bothered other children; refused to do assignments; was prone to tears; and, if urged to do something he did not want to do, had a full-blown tantrum, crying, yelling, and throwing whatever was in reach. He regularly threatened to blow up the school. He wasn't very popular.

Mid-first grade, the school psychologist tested him; all of his cognitive processing scores—other than the tests he refused—were in the higher end of the average range or above. Consequently, he did not qualify for services as a child with a specific learning disability (SLD). Subsequently, he was diagnosed with Tourette Syndrome and Attention-Deficit/Hyperactivity Disorder (ADHD), and he became eligible for special education under the classification of OHI. He spent the majority of his day in the cross-categorical classroom with 12 other students whose disabilities included emotional disorder, moderate mental retardation, and cerebral palsy. The students with learning disabilities were served in the LD resource room. At the initiation of medication for ADHD, Dakota's attention improved, but his anger, tears, and refusal of work did not.

Testing took 10 test sessions because Dakota was so emotionally fragile and self-protective that he dissolved into tears and anger, or closed his eyes and shut down, at any task that he perceived as challenging, any perceived

offense, or even the sound of the cicadas outside. I became wondrously creative in developing incentives to keep him stable and on task, and, in every session, had the opportunity to learn a whole new level of patience and to practice maintaining a neutral tone of voice and facial expression. In over 30 years of working with children with a myriad of learning and behavioral difficulties, Dakota was the indisputable winner of the "most difficult" category.

Periodically, when testing was going nowhere, I attempted to get Dakota to tell me why he was so resistant. As Dakota knew that the plan was for me to tutor him in reading once the assessment was completed, I explained that the assessment would help me find out how to teach him to read so that it was easier for him.

"That's complicated," he said.

"What's complicated?"

"Reading's complicated," he said, matter-of-factly. I assured him that it was, but that if he would work cooperatively with me, he *would* learn. He put his forehead on the table for a few seconds, then looked up and, with tears sliding down his face, said, "It's too late."

Puzzled, I asked, "What's too late?"

"It's too late to learn to read. My learning disability is too severe."

Finally, the assessment was completed. Dakota unquestionably had some severe learning disabilities, and I designed an instructional plan based on the Wilson Reading System. Through tutoring for the first 6 to 8 months, his self-protective, angry, accusative, and avoidance behaviors continued, and I got to practice new levels of patience and creativity. Many sessions had 10 minutes of instructional time, some less, some none. His behaviors did not fit TS or ADHD or, I thought, learning disabilities. Over the months, it became clear that with the specialized instruction, Dakota *was* learning to read and spell, albeit slowly, but his emotional lability and avoidance behaviors were now clearly the major obstacles. Convinced that he had some other deep-seated psychological problem, I suggested to his mother that therapy for Dakota would be a better use of the family's limited funds, and that he could return to tutoring—and make considerably faster progress—when he was more stable. His mother—wiser than I—refused, saying that slow as his progress was, for the first time since starting school, he *was* learning to read, and she would not jeopardize that.

In November of his second-grade year, Dakota's special education classification was changed to SLD and, at his mother's insistence, he was scheduled into LD resource and out of the cross-categorical classroom, to be used only as a safe place when he was out of control. Given materials, the resource specialist reinforced Dakota's Wilson instruction. Difficult behaviors continued, but not so often in the resource room.

Very slowly, over the summer before third grade, Dakota allowed more of our tutoring time to be devoted to straight instruction, albeit with frequent task changes, a well-learned procedure for each, and a variety of materials. Based on his cognitive strengths and weaknesses, I incorporated supplementary instructional techniques, as needed.

Dakota started third grade. Ms. Haley, his teacher, is both kind and firm, and has "learning aids" in place for any child in the classroom who needs them. Any child can take noise-canceling headphones or listen to an assigned story on a CD while following along in the book. Dakota's spelling list comes from the most frequently seen words in print and words that match the syllable and spelling structures he learns in tutoring and which are still reinforced in LD resource. For language arts, a special education aide works with Dakota and three of his classmates in the classroom.

About 3 months ago, I realized that instead of feeling huge relief each time we got through a whole lesson, I was now expecting to get through a whole lesson. When I open the door for Dakota, he walks in purposefully, dragging his rolling backpack behind him. He walks ahead of me into my office and rummages in his backpack for his homework. Along with his Wilson homework, I give him "chapter books," albeit still at quite a low level, that he

uses for his Accelerated Reader (AR) tests. Nobody reads his AR books to him anymore. He has no temper tantrums in school, does the assigned work (modified when needed), only occasionally tears up, and has friends in his class.

In tutoring, we continue with our regular work, but now that he understands the structure of words and how phonics works, he is acquiring and retaining some phonics skills and reading concepts taught in school. As much as possible, we incorporate them into our work. Dakota is witty and brings a surprising level of general knowledge to our lessons. Word retrieval, short-term memory, working memory, and perceptual speed are still very weak, but he is developing a base of automatic skills that ease the burden on these processes when they are called into play.

Dakota did not have an undiagnosed psychological/emotional disorder. His central problem was that he couldn't learn to read, spell, or write and he couldn't stand it. His belief that his failure would be with him for the rest of his life tainted almost every aspect of his daily functioning. Every day in school reinforced this belief, further degrading his self-esteem.

I was fortunate in that I not only did Dakota's assessment but—mainly—had the opportunity to observe his behavioral changes as his *belief* in his ability to learn to read was transformed by his *experience* of learning. Of course I knew that an unidentified learning disability, an incorrectly identified learning disability, and/or inadequate treatment for a learning disability have serious emotional ramifications that can be lifelong—but when you're distanced from it, it becomes theoretical. Consequently, it is easy to forget how serious a learning disability can be—and assume that a child's depression, inattention, or opposition are the primary causes of his learning problems, rather than the effect.

PSYCHOEDUCATIONAL EVALUATION

Name:	Dakota Briones
Date of Birth:	May 7, 2002
Age:	8-3
Parents:	Alda and Darren Briones
School:	Randolph Heights Elementary
Grade:	2.0
Testing Dates:	July 7–August 20, 2010
Evaluator:	Lynne E. Jaffe, Ph.D.

REASON FOR REFERRAL

Dakota's mother initiated this evaluation to identify the reason for his extremely limited progress in reading and determine an effective instructional method for reading and spelling.

BACKGROUND INFORMATION

Dakota is a rather slight 8-year-old boy from an intact family. He lives with his mother, Alda Briones, his father, Darren Briones, his brother, Ezekial, 18 months, and two step-siblings from his father's previous marriage, Trevor, 15, and Patrice, 16. Dakota's father designs computer programs and his mother does not work outside the home. Mrs. Briones reports a family history of intellectual giftedness. Mr. Briones' family includes a brother with bipolar disorder, borderline personality disorder, and difficulty with impulse control; Mr. Briones and his father have been diagnosed with depression. He is not aware of any learning problems in his family history and reportedly taught himself to read at age 3. Trevor has been diagnosed with Oppositional Defiant Disorder but has no learning problems. Patrice had some problems learning to read and is still somewhat delayed in her reading but achieves well in school through strong effort.

   Dakota's mother provided the following information. She reported that Dakota was born about 1½ months premature, slightly jaundiced, and with a club foot. Surgery was performed at age 6 months and Dakota's lower leg was in a cast until his first birthday. He walked as soon as the cast was removed. All developmental milestones were within normal limits except language, which seemed advanced, and toilet training, which is still a problem. Until last February, Dakota both urinated and defecated in his pants, at home and school, with no identifiable medical reasons.

   During the summer before first grade, Mrs. Briones took Dakota to see multiple mental health professionals due to inattention, anger, and defiance at school and at home, behaviors that appeared to interfere with his reading/writing development and social interactions. Dr. Candace Steinfeld, pediatric psychiatrist, diagnosed him with Tourette Syndrome (TS) and Attention-Deficit/Hyperactivity Disorder (ADHD). In late February, Dakota started taking Strattera for the symptoms of ADHD, at which time he stopped defecating in his pants; he still wets his pants occasionally during the day and more often during sleep. Until last week, Dakota was often awake and wandering around the house during the night. This week, Mrs. Briones began giving him his Strattera at night and has noticed that he seems to sleep better and is more rested during the day. Other benefits have been reduced time getting him ready for school in the morning and for bed at night, but he still has a violent and unpredictable temper. He is a picky eater and, during mealtimes, wanders around, bothers family members, and refuses to eat anything except chicken nuggets or peanut butter and jelly sandwiches. Dakota's health is good. He passed the school vision and hearing screenings on September 11, 2009.

EDUCATIONAL HISTORY AND EVALUATIONS

The following information is based on the interview with Mrs. Briones and a review of school records. Dakota could not attend preschool because he was not toilet trained. He has attended school at Randolph Heights Elementary in the Meridian Unified School District (MUSD) since age 5. In kindergarten, he enjoyed story time and hands-on science and math but hated activities related to reading and writing. He did not complete his work and often missed outdoor playtime because of it. He did not make or maintain friendships easily. School reports noted his kindergarten teacher's concerns that he "learns slowly; displays attention problems; is below grade level in reading, writing, math; and has difficulty acquiring, retaining, manipulating information." His teacher suggested that he repeat kindergarten due to immaturity. During his second kindergarten year, his teacher reported that he was actively disruptive during reading and writing activities and had difficulty maintaining focus and completing work. In April 2009, a Functional Behavioral Assessment and a Behavioral Intervention Plan were completed. At the end of the year, the plan was assessed as "partially effective." His teacher noted that he had retained "almost nothing" and an evaluation was recommended.

   Dakota's first-grade teacher reported that he was articulate and participated in class discussions but was noncompliant in tasks he did not want to do, was quick to become angry or cry, and distracted others by acting silly, moving around, and touching others. He refused to cooperate with reading and writing activities but was willing to engage in one-on-one situations in which he could use manipulatives.

She stated that his handwriting showed a lack of control and his spelling was "semi-phonetic" (i.e., included a few sounds in the word) but that he required continual individual help and needed to be made to work.

Amanda White, school psychologist, evaluated Dakota in September 2009. She administered the Reynolds Intellectual Assessment Scales (RIAS) and noted that he refused to attempt the verbal memory tests that involved listening to and retelling brief stories. Results of the RIAS indicated that Dakota's overall intelligence and verbal ability were in the higher end of the Average range with nonverbal ability and nonverbal memory Above Average. Results of the Beery-Buktenica Developmental Test of Visual-Motor Integration, Fifth Edition, were in the Low range, indicating weak visual-motor coordination.

Results of the Behavior Assessment System for Children, Second Edition, indicated that Dakota's mother and teachers observed significant problems in the areas of hyperactivity, attention, aggression, adaptive behaviors, and atypical behaviors. The teachers also noted signs of depression and anxiety. Dakota was evaluated by the MUSD Autism Spectrum Disorder (ASD) evaluation team. Results indicated that his behaviors were not characteristic of ASD. As part of this evaluation, Dakota was administered selected tests of the Woodcock-Johnson III Tests of Achievement (WJ III ACH) and the Young Children's Achievement Test (YCAT). His reading, writing, and math scores were all in the Very Low and Low ranges.

Dakota was provided special education services and an Individualized Education Plan (IEP) under the category of Other Health Impaired (OHI) based on his Tourette Syndrome diagnosis. His current IEP, amended last January, provides for a health aide for assistance with toileting, dressing, and cleanliness 15 minutes a day, and reinforcement of goals in socialization, impulse control, and redirection for 30 minutes a day. In actuality, Dakota does not get this service. The IEP also provides for occupational therapy on a consultation basis, including a sensory diet, adaptive physical education, and counseling once a week. According to his special education teacher, he does not receive the counseling either. His special education services include instruction in the cross-categorical classroom for 4½ hours per day and in the general education classroom for 1½ hours per day. He also is taken to the cross-categorical classroom to calm down when he is having a temper tantrum and, consequently, spends most of his day there. He has goals in the areas of reading, math, written language, social skills and emotional stability, and motor skills.

BEHAVIORAL OBSERVATIONS

Dakota demonstrated extreme emotional fragility and self-protectiveness. Testing was completed in 10 sessions of 1 to 2 hours each with a great deal of time spent preventing or dealing with Dakota's repeated emotional "meltdowns" and resistance. At most testing sessions, Dakota initially refused to come into my office, lying face-down on a couch and pretending to sleep. During testing, when encouraged to do something he did not want to do, he often put his head down on the table, began to cry, or just got up and walked out of the room, closing the door behind him. Frequently, I reminded him that the tests were developed for a wide range of ages so that when he had difficulty, he was probably working on items intended for older children. Occasionally this worked. He was considerably more comfortable and less resistant to tests that incorporated pictures. Depending on the test, if he thought that he did not know the answer, he wouldn't guess. Had he been willing to do so, some test scores might have been higher. Although an incentive program did help considerably (he earned a piece of a multiple-part construction kit for each test completed with reasonable cooperation), his cooperation and willingness to attempt tasks remained variable and unpredictable. His mood was likely to deteriorate from laughing at his own joke to anger or tears at what was to me an unidentifiable provocation. If I could not coax him to focus on a test with reasonable confidence that his performance was representative of his ability, I switched tests. Once we had started a test, I was usually able to coax him to finish it with good effort. This, however, required an unfailingly calm and patient demeanor; calm denial of Dakota's accusations that I was "mean," "annoying", and "irritating"; readiness to change tests according to his mood; and willingness to discontinue a session with little accomplished. One session was discontinued when Dakota dissolved in tears after being unable to name any of the people he knows. Crying, he said, "I don't know any 'cause I maybe haven't had my pill. It keeps me unthinking faster and everything faster." Subsequently, I re-administered the tests given that day. No scores changed by more than one raw score point.

Frequently, Dakota takes an exceedingly long time to process a question, such that one would assume that he didn't hear it or was ignoring it. Repeating or rephrasing the question, however, interrupts his thought process. For example, between tests, I asked Dakota if he would like a glass of water. I waited a few seconds and then began to set up the next test. After about 10 seconds, he said, "Yes."

When I introduced a reading test in which Dakota was asked to give the sounds of letters and read nonsense words, he said that the print was too small. I retyped the words on the computer using a similar font (Times New Roman) but allowed Dakota to choose the size. He chose 72 point. He explained that he had trouble seeing smaller print due to "little dots that I see everywhere." He described these as colored, mostly green, moving fast, and interfering with his ability to see small print. I recommended that Dakota see an ophthalmologist prior to any more testing. He did so and I received a report that his visual acuity and visual functioning were normal. During our diagnostic teaching sessions, when instruction was disguised as games, he was comfortable with 28-point print.

For now, considering Dakota's behavioral manifestations of his emotional and attentional problems, the results of this evaluation are probably a good representation of Dakota's cognitive and linguistic abilities and academic achievement as he currently functions. When Dakota develops a level of stability, focus, and self-confidence, he should be reevaluated. I suspect that the results will indicate a higher level of functioning than he is currently demonstrating.

TESTS ADMINISTERED

Woodcock-Johnson III Tests of Cognitive Ability (WJ III COG)
Woodcock-Johnson III Tests of Cognitive Ability, Diagnostic Supplement (WJ III DS)
Woodcock-Johnson III Tests of Achievement (WJ III ACH), Form A
Comprehensive Test of Phonological Processing (CTOPP)
Comprehensive Assessment of Spoken Language (CASL)
Phonological Awareness Test 2 (PAT-2)
Qualitative Reading Inventory, Fifth Edition (QRI-5)
Interview with mother
Review of school records
Eight diagnostic teaching sessions

INFORMATION REGARDING TESTS AND SCORES

All standardized tests were scored according to age norms. Dakota's performance on the abilities measured by the WJ III, CTOPP, CASL, and PAT-2 are described as percentile ranks (PR), standard scores (SS), and standard score ranges created by 68% confidence bands. The standard score ranges and the associated verbal labels are:

SS Range	< 69	70–79	80–89	90–110	111–120	121–130	> 130
Verbal Label	Very Low	Low	Low Avg	Average	High Avg	Superior	Very Sup.

For the tests of the WJ III, Relative Proficiency Indexes (RPI) are sometimes reported. Whereas the SS and PR indicate the rank order of Dakota's score within his age group, the RPI is a norm-based, criterion-referenced score that predicts his proficiency on tasks similar to the ones used on the test and at a level of difficulty that typical age-peers would manage with 90% success. For example, Dakota's RPI of 51/90 on the Applied Problems test indicates that on similar tests of math problem solving, whereas a typical 8-year-old would be 90% successful, Dakota's expected proficiency would be 51%. This indicates that his math problem-solving proficiency is limited and that he will find age-level tasks very difficult. RPI ranges, the verbal descriptors, and implications regarding one's ability to manage age-appropriate tasks are provided in the following table.

Reported RPIs	Proficiency	Implications
100/90	Very Advanced	Extremely Easy
98/90 to 100/90	Advanced	Very Easy
95/90 to 98/90	Average to Advanced	Easy
82/90 to 95/90	Average	Manageable
67/90 to 82/90	Limited to Average	Difficult
24/90 to 67/90	Limited	Very Difficult
3/90 to 24/90	Very Limited	Extremely Difficult
0/90 to 3/90	Negligible	Impossible

Adapted from: Schrank, F. A., & Woodcock, R. W. (2002). Manual and Checklists. *Report writer for the WJ III*. Rolling Meadows, IL: Riverside Publishing.

All of the tests administered were appropriate for Dakota's ethnicity and primary language. The following were considered and ruled out as primary contributing factors to the referral concerns: a visual, hearing, or motor disability; cultural factors; environmental or economic disadvantage; and limited English proficiency.

Test items presented as examples within the report are representative of the test items but are not the actual test items, which are confidential.

COGNITIVE ABILITIES

Dakota's General Intellectual Ability (GIA) standard score (SS) of 90 cannot be considered representative of his overall intelligence or his general aptitude because the test scores from which it is derived vary over 3.6 standard deviations and include the processing weaknesses that contribute to his academic problems. Based on his test scores, however, his overall intelligence is at least in the Average range.

Strengths

Dakota demonstrated strengths in logical reasoning—both inductive and deductive—and processing of visual-spatial information. His general knowledge and academic knowledge were typical of a child of his age.

Visual-Spatial Abilities

Dakota performed in the Superior range in visual-spatial abilities. These represent a variety of abilities involved in thinking with visual patterns, including mentally visualizing images and objects from different perspectives, mentally integrating parts of a design or object to make a whole, storing the details of pictures in memory for later retrieval, and figuring out what object is pictured when only parts are shown. In primary school, visual-spatial abilities are mostly used in art and in hands-on learning. Later, these abilities are necessary for courses such as geometry, physics, and technical classes. (SS 123, PR 93, RPI 97/90)

Fluid Reasoning

Dakota performed in the High Average range in fluid reasoning. The Fluid Reasoning tests assess the ability to use inductive and deductive reasoning and to form concepts and solve problems that often involve unfamiliar information or procedures. Academically, these abilities are strongly related to mathematical reasoning, understanding scientific concepts and procedures, and higher-level reading comprehension. (SS 114, PR 82, RPI 97/90)

Knowledge

Dakota demonstrated an Average fund of general knowledge typically acquired through school instruction, reading, and life experience. (SS 99, PR 48, RPI 89/90)

Weaknesses

Dakota exhibited varying memory capabilities depending on the type of information he was expected to retain. He had no difficulty retaining visual-spatial information (e.g., pictures) or verbal information that was presented in a meaningful linguistic context (e.g., stories). This is discussed further under Oral Language. Dakota demonstrated significant weaknesses when required to retain or retrieve specific words or sounds rather than the meaning of what he has heard. The difference might be thought of as information from which the meaning can be extracted (e.g., narrative, expository) versus information that must be memorized (i.e., rote). Dakota also demonstrated severe weaknesses in perceptual speed and in rapid naming.

Short-Term Memory and Working Memory

Dakota's performance bordered the Low to Low Average ranges in both of these clusters. These tests incorporate the type of information that must be memorized, for example repeating a series of unrelated words, and hearing a series of digits and objects (e.g., cat, table) and giving them back in a different order. Short-term memory allows one to hold information in immediate awareness for a few seconds. Working memory can be thought of as an agent that works with short-term memory and long-term memory to do the more complex work related to learning or the activities of daily living. Working memory involves holding information or ideas in immediate awareness while working with it mentally and/or transforming it in some way. We use working memory to place new or transformed information in long-term memory, and to search for and retrieve specific information from long-term storage to be used in mental processes. Working memory has a limited capacity in terms of the amount of information it can hold and the length of time it can hold it. When the capacity or time limit is exceeded, the information begins to deteriorate.

Dakota's RPIs indicate that classroom tasks such as memorizing letter names and sounds, dates, math facts, or a set of instructions that is not related to something he is already doing or has done previously would be very difficult for him. In such tasks, whereas a typical age-peer might be 90% successful, Dakota would be approximately 50% successful. On many of the oral language tests in which the items were not presented in a meaningful context, he frequently asked for repetition. For example, on the CASL Synonyms test, he was told a word, then told four more words from which to choose a synonym for the first one. He requested repetition on 8 of the first 16 items. (Short-Term Memory: SS 83, PR 13, RPI 51/90; Working Memory: SS 79, PR 8, RPI 48/90)

Associative Memory

Associative Memory represents the ability to form an association between previously learned pairs of items (paired-associate learning)—in this case a visual item and a word. These tests are presented as controlled-learning tasks in which the individual is told the correct answer each time he gives an incorrect answer, thus giving him repeated opportunities to learn the association. Dakota was required to learn familiar words for abstract symbols and nonsense names for pictures of odd-looking creatures. Asked to "read" a story using the symbols, he had difficulty recalling the associated words. In contrast, he performed significantly better on the test where he was told the name of a creature and had to point to the correct picture from a set including all he had seen previously. The difference in his performance appeared to be that in the second test, he did not have to retrieve a word, just identify the associated picture. (WJ III COG Visual-Auditory Learning: SS 71, PR 3, RPI 58/90; Memory for Names: SS 93, PR 33, RPI 86/90)

Retrieval Fluency

Retrieval Fluency represents the ability to rapidly retrieve information stored in long-term memory. Dakota scored in the Very Low range on this cluster. Asked to name familiar items in a given category (e.g., different pieces of clothing) within a limited time, initially he was simply unable to respond. When I encouraged him to try, he silently got up, left the room, and lay face-down on a sofa. Willing to try this test on another day, he scored as low as or lower than 999 in 1,000 children his age. He usually had a 5- to 6-second pause before each response and could not refrain from making side comments about his responses, which added to his time. This revealed not only his difficulty retrieving well-known words quickly, but also his tendency to become distracted by tangential thoughts (WJ III COG Retrieval Fluency: SS 51, PR <0.1, RPI 70/90)

Rapid Automatized Naming (RAN)

RAN refers to the speed with which a person can recognize and name familiar visual images such as letters, digits, and pictures of objects. Because Dakota has difficulty recalling letter names, he was given tests incorporating only pictures and colors. Based on current research in reading disabilities, RAN is related to the ability to immediately identify letters, common letter patterns, and words as familiar visual patterns—skills necessary for recognizing common word parts (e.g., *at, ing, tion, ed*) and acquiring sight words.

Dakota demonstrated great difficulty on all of the RAN tests but did not appear worried about them, possibly because he perceived them as easy. Nevertheless, he obtained scores in the Very Low range. In fact, on the CTOPP tests, Dakota's time in naming all of the items was almost twice as long as the time associated with the lowest possible score for 8-year-olds. On the WJ III COG Rapid Naming test, Dakota scored lower than 999 out of 1,000 8-year-olds. During all of the tests, he had pauses of up to 15 seconds before naming a color or a common object such as a chair. (CTOPP Alternate Rapid Naming: SS 46, PR < 1; WJ III COG Rapid Picture Naming: SS 46, PR < 0.1, RPI 5/90)

Perceptual Speed

Dakota's performance indicated a weakness in perceptual speed. Perceptual speed is the ability to rapidly scan visual symbols, such as letters or numbers, and identify similarities and differences based solely on visual appearance. Even the higher of his two scores, in the Low Average range, indicated difficulty on this type of task. In contrast, Dakota displayed average ability to rapidly scan a row of pictures and match them based on their conceptual similarities (e.g., Which two are most alike?

Low perceptual speed and rapid naming have been shown to interfere with a person's ability to recognize common letter patterns as "chunks" (e.g., word parts, whole words, syllable patterns) and retrieve the sounds associated with them, even when memory is not impaired. Whereas many children learn to recognize sight words before or while they learn phonics, these deficits are likely the reason that Dakota has been unable to do so. It was only 2 weeks ago that he learned to recognize and spell "the" (using a multisensory method) and still requires frequent review to solidify it in long-term memory. (Cross Out: SS 84, PR 14, RPI 74/90; Visual Matching: SS 63, PR 1, RPI 37/90)

Visual-Motor Integration

When discussing writing, visual-motor integration is the ability to plan and execute small-muscle movements according to a visual image. Formal testing was not done, but Dakota's writing of letters and numbers was slow and awkward. On the Math Fluency test, Dakota took more time to write each digit than to solve the problem. Since then, in diagnostic teaching, with direct instruction and ample supervised practice, he has shown that with focused effort he can form individual letters neatly. However, if he has to focus to form a letter within the context of a more complex task, such as spelling a word, his letters and numbers are shaky and poorly formed. These findings are consistent with Dakota's performance on the Developmental Test of Visual Motor Integration given by the MUSD school psychologist.

Oral Language

According to the scores on the language tests, Dakota's comprehension is significantly stronger than his language expression. The size of the discrepancy between Dakota's receptive and expressive language scores would be found in only 1% of 8-year-olds. Qualitative analysis of Dakota's responses, however, indicated that his expressive language may not be as low as the test scores suggest. The reason for this is that his performance on each test was considerably affected by the response mode, his understanding of the task, and his willingness to guess. His best scores were on tests that required no word retrieval and tests that were focused on language meaning rather than form. For example, although the CASL tests of Synonyms and Antonyms both assess word meaning, his score on Synonyms was significantly higher than his score on Antonyms. On Synonyms, the examiner gives four choices and the individual picks one, whereas on Antonyms, the individual has to retrieve a word from long-term memory. Furthermore, on these tests and others, Dakota's scores may have been reduced by his unwillingness to guess. (CASL Synonyms: SS 109, PR 73; Antonyms: SS 87, PR 19)

Language Comprehension

Comprehension and recall of language presented within a meaningful context, such as a narrative, was clearly Dakota's strength, with scores within the mid-Average to High Average range. These tests assessed comprehension of complex syntax, of concepts, of story details, and of nonliteral language (e.g., figurative language, indirect requests) within passages comprising multiple sentences that were presented orally or on CD. He indicated comprehension by selecting a picture in response to a question, by orally filling in the missing word, by retelling key details of a brief story, and by explaining what someone really meant within the context of a given situation (e.g., "Don't you think it's cold in here?" means "Turn on the heat.")

Similar to his response to a similar task on the RIAS, retelling stories was most threatening to him, and after listening to the first story (two short sentences), he said he couldn't remember anything. Encouraged to try, he teared

up and stated, "Well, I guess this is a failure." We moved on to another test. During a subsequent session, I played a "game" with him, allowing him to earn a magnet piece each time he made an attempt to repeat a brief sentence after me. Rewards were not tied to success, which received no comment—only to an honest effort. After very few tries, Dakota realized that he was able to do the task. Later, when I reintroduced the test, he simply went ahead with it without comment. His performance was solidly in the Average range. (As the first story had been given in the previously failed attempt, the first set of stories was not included in the scoring.) Five days later, he was asked to retell what he remembered about each story. His recall of the story details exceeded 99% of 8-year-olds whose initial score was the same as his. (CASL Paragraph Comprehension: SS 114, PR 82; WJ III ACH Oral Comprehension: SS 105, PR 62, RPI 94/90; Story Recall: SS 100, PR 49, RPI 90/90; Story Recall-Delayed: SS 123, PR 94, RPI 96/90; CASL Nonliteral Language: SS 99, PR 47)

In contrast, Dakota had significant difficulty on a test in which he had to listen to syntactically complex directions, then follow them by pointing to different parts of a picture (e.g., "If there are three horses together, point to the star farthest to the right, but only if there is a man standing near the river"). This test requires good syntactic comprehension, which is a strength, but also strong short-term and working memory, which are weaknesses. He could not hold on to all of the details and the items could not be repeated. (WJ III ACH Understanding Directions: SS 80, PR 10, RPI 67/90)

Expressive Grammar and Syntax

Dakota also had difficulty on tests of grammatical knowledge and usage (e.g., verb tense, subject-verb agreement). All of these required an understanding of metalinguistics, the ability to think about the form of language (i.e., how it is conveyed) rather than its meaning (e.g., what is conveyed). Dakota did not understand this aspect of the tests. For example, when asked to complete analogies that would show recognition of grammatical structures, such as "bug is to bugs as child is to ....," he might answer "capture," going for a conceptual association, rather than the plural form of the word. Similarly, he performed in the lower end of the Average range on a test of syntax usage, losing points, again, because he did not understand the task, not because he could not use proper syntax. In his spontaneous speech, Dakota's syntax and grammar are usually correct and, often, quite complex (e.g., "I have three TVs in my house but one is not usable because it's not connected").

(Grammatical Morphemes: SS 89, PR 23; Syntax Construction: SS 93, PR 32)

Word Retrieval and Expressive Vocabulary

In addition to his difficulty on tests specifically assessing retrieval, Dakota demonstrated problems with word retrieval in other tests and in his spontaneous speech. For example, asked what a bar of soap is used for, he gestured washing his hands but could not remember the word. When asked to name a picture of a door knob, he said, "a thingy for pulling the door, a puller." When asked his first-grade teacher's name, he responded, "I don't remember her name anymore because I haven't been to her again and again and again and again," rather than saying, "in a long time." It took him about 30 seconds to remember the name of his school. As well, Dakota has some oddities in his speech, inserting "even," "of course," and "only" when they are not appropriate.

Dakota's scores on expressive vocabulary were in the Average range; however, this may be an underestimate of his ability, as the response mode for almost all of these tests required good word retrieval. In conversation, Dakota demonstrated some unexpected linguistic maturity. For example, when answering a question that most children answer with "volcano," Dakota responded, "On a volcanic island." He described a picture of a partially collapsed building as "a ruin of a building." (WJ III ACH Picture Vocabulary: SS 97, PR 43, RPI 87/90; WJ III COG Verbal Comprehension: SS 93, PR 31, RPI 81/90; CASL Antonyms: SS 87, PR 19)

Language Processing Speed

As explained under "Behaviors," Dakota frequently needs a great deal of time, far more than usual, to process a question or verbal information. This was true during testing and is seen during his diagnostic teaching sessions. Teachers and other school staff need to be aware of this and allow Dakota extra time so as not to interfere with his thinking process.

Phonemic Awareness

Phonological awareness is the understanding that a stream of speech can be broken down into smaller units such as words, syllables, and sounds. At the level of individual sounds, it is called phonemic awareness. These skills are critical for learning fundamental reading and spelling skills and can be trained. Dakota's performance on the WJ III COG Phonemic Awareness cluster was solidly in the Average range. His scores within the composites of the

Phonological Awareness Test, however, were varied. Subtest scores and qualitative analysis of his responses indicated that Dakota had a solid grasp of some of the most important skills but did not understand the tasks at a metalinguistic level. He could not judge whether or not a pair of words rhymed but could produce a correct rhyme for a given word every time. He did not know the difference between words and syllables but segmented words into syllables accurately and segmented three-sound words into individual sounds (e.g., What are the sounds in *sock*? /s/ /o/ /k/). He was able to isolate the initial and final sounds of words (e.g., What is the beginning sound of *box*?) but not the middle sound, although he pronounced it correctly when segmenting the word. He correctly blended up to four syllables into words and up to three sounds into words. It is likely that he has had training in these skills. Nevertheless, at this point, good phonemic awareness skills are not helping him acquire reading skills.

Academic Achievement

Dakota's test results indicated severe weaknesses in all reading and spelling skills.

Reading and Spelling

In contrast to his average oral language abilities and phonemic awareness skills, all of Dakota's reading skills were severely impaired. His performance on tests of word attack, sight word identification, and passage comprehension were all in the Very Low range. His percentile rank indicates that in a group of 1,000 students of his age, his scores would be within the lowest 5. His RPI indicates that in overall reading ability, his likelihood of success in reading age-appropriate text would be 0% when a typical age-peer would be 90% successful. The practical implication of this is that he will perceive age-level reading and spelling tasks to be impossible, and he does. (WJ III ACH Brief Reading: SS 56, PR 0.2, RPI 0/90; Basic Reading Skills: SS 61, PR 0.5, RPI 0/90)

Dakota could not write his last name; could not say or write the entire alphabet; and did not know all of the names or the primary sounds for the consonants, consonant digraphs (e.g., *sh, th*), or the short sounds for the vowels. He could not sound out any words and recognized only three sight words. On the QRI-5, he recognized 6 of the 20 words on the pre-primer word list but was not able to read the pre-primer passage. He had lots of ideas about what it should have said ("It would be better if it said…").

Handwriting

Although the final shape of some of Dakota's letters and numbers is correct, his formation of them and his sequence of strokes is incorrect and does not follow a top-to-bottom, left-to-write flow. Many of his letters and numbers are reversed. Additionally, the cognitive attention required by the mechanical act of writing then is less available for use regarding the content of his writing. As described below, in a simulated test, when he dictated his responses to simple math facts rather than writing them, he was able to complete considerably more items.

Math

Math Calculation Skills

The Math Calculation Skills cluster includes math computation and retrieval of simple math facts. Test results indicated that Dakota's computation of arithmetic problems is in the Low Average to Average range. His RPI indicates that he will find age-appropriate calculation difficult. In informal testing, when counting tokens, Dakota was unsure what came after 12, then what came after 20. He counted on his fingers to solve single-digit low-level addition and subtraction problems, indicating that he has not yet memorized his math facts. He recognized the addition and subtraction signs but pointed to a multiplication sign and asked, "What is it? Plus or take-away?"

The Math Fluency test assesses efficiency in solving or retrieving math facts. When Dakota took the test, he was so slow and awkward in writing his answers that the writing took considerably longer than figuring out the answer. In a subsequent test session, I gave him a math facts test I had created, containing only single-digit addition and subtraction problems and had him write his answers. He had 3 minutes. At the end of the session, I gave him a clean copy of the test and had him tell me his answers, so as to eliminate writing mechanics as an interfering factor. His number correct increased from 15 to 24, an increase of 60%. Consequently, his score on the Math Fluency test underestimates his knowledge of addition and subtraction, but still, his knowledge of math facts is not automatic.

Math Reasoning includes applying math skills to practical situations and knowledge of math concepts. Although Dakota performed in the Low Average range on this test, his RPI indicated that when typical age-peers would be 90% proficient in application of math skills, Dakota would be 51% proficient. He was able to do simple addition and subtraction based on pictures but when asked how many would be left if five objects were taken away from seven, he said, "I don't know because I can only use one hand. The other one is bothering me." I rubbed his hand and when it felt better, he covered five of the objects with one hand and counted those left with the other. He was able to identify a dime and a quarter but did not know their value. He was able to tell time to the hour on an analog clock face. The subsequent items required use of 2-digit numbers and he could go no further.

SUMMARY

Academic Achievement

At the time of the evaluation, test results indicated that Dakota's achievement in reading and spelling was significantly deficient. His relative proficiency indexes on all of the reading tests indicated that his likelihood of success in age-level reading tasks was negligible. Dakota could not say the alphabet all the way through. His performance on the WJ III ACH reading tests was the same as or lower than 995 of 1,000 age-peers. On the QRI-4, he was unable to read at the pre-primer level. He could recognize a few sight words but could not spell them. It is possible that his emotional fragility during testing might have prevented him from demonstrating some reading skills that he has already acquired, but this is unlikely that this would have made a significant difference.

Although Dakota's standard scores on basic math skills were in the Low Average to Average range, his RPIs place his proficiency in computation and speed of recalling/figuring basic math facts in the Limited-to-Average range and his ability to apply his math skills, Limited. Dakota counted on his fingers to answer 1-digit addition and subtraction problems. As the test was time-limited, slow, effortful number formation also lowered his score. Spelling and handwriting were so difficult for Dakota, and his emotional reaction so negative, that tests of written expression were not attempted.

Oral Language

Test scores and qualitative analysis indicate that Dakota has Average to somewhat Advanced oral language comprehension and at least Average language expression. His ability to retain information that is presented in a meaningful language context, such as a narrative, is also strong. Currently, Dakota's fund of general and academic knowledge is typical for a child of his age. He does demonstrate, however, two specific language problems that require attention. First, he demonstrates exceedingly slow word retrieval, the ability to quickly come up with the word he intends to use when speaking. When he cannot find a word, it interferes with his sentence formulation, resulting in incorrect syntax or imprecise/immature word usage, such as "thingy." Second, he frequently needs an excessively long time to process and respond to a question. If given that time, he does come up with a response or asks for a repetition of the question.

Cognitive Abilities

Test results indicate that Dakota has both a normative and an intrapersonal strength in fluid reasoning (i.e., logical reasoning for problem solving). Research into the nature of intelligence often points to fluid reasoning as the cognitive ability that is most representative of general intelligence. He also demonstrated superior performance in visual-spatial abilities, including memory for visual images. In contrast, Dakota's score of 90 on the WJ III COG General Intelligence Ability (GIA) cluster is likely to be a gross underestimation of his actual intellectual ability because it includes scores that reflect his specific disabilities. The GIA score is *not* representative of his aptitude for learning; it is reported here *only* because the school district requires it for the provision of learning disabilities services.

Dakota demonstrated significant weaknesses in all aspects of memory for verbal information that is not presented within a meaningful context—information that depends on rote memory (e.g., letter names as opposed to a story). Dakota had difficulty holding this type of information in short-term memory, using it in working memory, and rapidly retrieving it from long-term memory. To a large extent, primary school instruction is focused on this type of information, such as the names and sounds of letters, the sequence of the alphabet, and math facts. Additionally, Dakota displayed severe deficits in perceptual speed (i.e., the ability to rapidly perceive similarities and differences in visual symbols) and in rapid naming (i.e., the ability to see and rapidly retrieve from memory the names of very familiar items, such as letters or numbers).

Although a weakness in any of these processes would be expected to cause considerable difficulty in learning basic academic skills, their interaction produces a significantly more severe interference. Information can be retained in short-term or working memory for only seconds before it deteriorates. Processing the information refreshes it, allowing it to be retained long enough to either come up with a result, such as the solution to a math problem, or to embed it in long-term memory. Even with normal memory capacity, if processing is slow, the information deterio-

rates before it can be fully processed. Combining impaired memory function with slow processing multiplies the difficulties rather than adding them.

An example may help clarify, using the process of sounding out a word. To sound out a word, such as *dig*, a beginning reader must first have established the sounds of the three letters in long-term memory. This requires paired-associate learning and memory, a weakness for Dakota. Next, he must retrieve the sound of the *d* from long-term memory and hold onto it while he retrieves the sound of the *i*, then do it again for the *g*. He must recognize each letter and recall its sound quickly enough so that the sounds do not deteriorate in working memory before he can blend them. Dakota's perceptual speed, and thus his ability to recognize each letter, however, is slow, as is his ability to retrieve their sounds; consequently, each sound held in working memory is likely to begin to disintegrate as he works on the next letter/sound pair. Next, he must hold all of these sounds in working memory while he blends them into a word. Finally, he must retain that word while he searches his long-term memory for an oral word that matches it to see if it makes sense. If it does, he can start the process all over again with the next word. For most children, these processes are automatic; they require no conscious thought. For Dakota, none of these processes are automatic; they all require too much time and cognitive effort. Fortunately, Dakota has good phonemic awareness skills so that the acts of sound blending and sound segmenting in themselves come fairly easily to him—at least for words of up to three sounds.

The type of information that Dakota has difficulty holding on to is the information that is the foundation for developing basic reading, writing, and math skills—the skills that must be acquired before he can use his strong reasoning and language abilities at the higher levels—the purposes for which these skills are intended—reading comprehension, written expression, and math reasoning. In contrast, Dakota would be expected to have no difficulty remembering information such as stories, historical events in context, and classroom rules.

CONCLUSIONS

Dakota's identified cognitive weaknesses in short-term memory, working memory, and retrieval for noncontextual verbal information, perceptual speed, and rapid naming appear to be the major factors contributing to his difficulty in learning basic reading, spelling, and math skills. These weaknesses are especially concerning given his strong higher-order reasoning, oral language, and visual-spatial abilities and his good phonemic awareness skills. Dakota is as proficient as his age-peers in learning and retaining general world knowledge generally taught in school and from his own experience as long as this information is presented orally and/or visually (other than in print), and in a narrative or expository language context rather than as a list of isolated facts.

From fourth grade on, reading becomes the major vehicle for learning new information and for acquiring new vocabulary. Consequently, a child who does not read the same quantity of material and at the same level as his age-peers falls behind in oral vocabulary development as well as in world knowledge. In turn, limited oral vocabulary and knowledge make it more difficult for the child to recognize new words in print, read fluently, and comprehend text. As reading becomes harder, the child reads less, and a negative spiral develops. It is critical that Dakota receive intensive instruction in reading to close this gap, and that during this process, he is provided, through oral language, videos, and visual displays, the same vocabulary and academic information as the other children learn through reading so that his knowledge and language development keep pace with that of his peers.

Dakota has specific learning disabilities that affect his acquisition of basic reading skills, basic writing skills, and basic math skills. These weaknesses in cognitive abilities that cause significant difficulty in acquiring reading and spelling skills constitute the core symptoms of dyslexia.

Dakota's difficulty with acquiring basic academic skills is undoubtedly magnified by the behaviors associated with his Tourette Syndrome and ADHD, including his inability to focus on activities that are not of intrinsic interest to him, his impulsive behavior, which interrupts both his learning and the work of others, and his extreme emotional fragility, which manifests in tears and/or refusal of tasks. These behaviors, however, are not the primary reason for his learning difficulties.

Consideration of Eligibility for Special Education Services as a Child with Specific Learning Disabilities

Federal guidelines for IDEA 2004 allow the following three procedures in determining eligibility for learning disabilities services:

1. The child exhibits a pattern of strengths and weaknesses in performance and/or achievement or intellectual de-

velopment that is determined to be indicative of specific learning disability, using appropriate assessments.
2. The child does not demonstrate an adequate response to scientific, research-based intervention (Response to Intervention).
3. The child demonstrates a severe discrepancy between aptitude (intellectual ability) and academic achievement.

The results of this assessment indicate that Dakota meets the federal guidelines as a child with a Specific Learning Disability under procedure #1 above. This evaluator did not have data pertinent to qualification under procedure #2, RTI. Dakota's school district requires that he meet the criteria under procedure #3, a severe discrepancy between aptitude and achievement.

Although Dakota's WJ III GIA-Std standard score of 90 is likely an underestimate of his aptitude for learning, a severe discrepancy does exist between the GIA score and his reading achievement. The WJ III Intellectual Ability/Achievement Discrepancy table indicates that only 0.3 percent (3 in 1,000) of Dakota's age-peers would have a discrepancy of this magnitude between the GIA and the Basic Reading Skills cluster score, and less than 0.1 (less than 1 in 1,000) would have a discrepancy of this magnitude between the GIA and the Brief Reading cluster (Letter-Word Identification and Passage Comprehension) score.

RECOMMENDATIONS FOR THE PARENTS

Medical/Health/Emotional Stability

1. Request that all of Dakota's teachers help you ascertain the level of the effectiveness of Dakota's medication in school by having them complete a behavior rating chart. The chart should include a few ADHD-related behaviors that are problems for Dakota in the classroom and in less structured situations and that should be responsive to medication (e.g., pays attention while teacher is talking, socializes only when appropriate, work shows appropriate level of thought). Have the teachers chart Dakota's behaviors for 1 week and share the results with Dr. Reichmann. If the ratings indicate a need for a change in medication, request that the teachers continue charting until the optimal dosage and dosage times are established.
2. Make sure that Dakota understands the reason for his medication, what effect it is expected to have (e.g.,

allow him to pay attention if he tries to do so), what it cannot do (e.g., make him pay attention if he does not try), and the possible side effects. Make sure that he understands that he still has responsibility for his behavior and that he, not the medication, gets credit for any improvements in his behavior and learning. The medication is not "working"; he is using it well.

School Planning/Scheduling

1. Before the end of each school year, meet with the school principal or counselor to discuss Dakota's general and special education teachers for the next year. Students with learning disabilities and/or disorders with behavioral characteristics such as Tourette Syndrome and ADHD generally do well with calm and well-organized teachers who use daily routines and positive, consistent behavior management techniques, who are comfortable accommodating individual needs, who can correct without being critical, and who are knowledgeable or willing to learn about the behavioral characteristics associated with Tourette Syndrome and ADHD and with specific learning disabilities.

2. Before the beginning of each school year, meet with Dakota's teacher(s) to explain his learning disabilities, how these affect his reading and writing skills, and the effect this has had on his current self-concept. Include information regarding Tourette Syndrome, his ADHD behaviors, any obsessive-compulsive behaviors that might show up at school, and the situations in which the problem behaviors are most likely to occur. Discuss with the general education teacher his/her key role as a member of the treatment team and solicit cooperation in working with you and with any outside professionals in establishing accommodations and interventions as needed.

Homework and Organization of Materials

1. Before beginning nightly homework, help Dakota review all assignments, estimate the time each will take, prioritize them, and then list them in order on an index card. As he finishes an assignment, have him cross it off the list.

2. Use a timer to help Dakota stay on task. Set the timer for the amount of time you think he can work before taking a break and have him work until the timer rings. Set the timer for a 5-minute break, and have him return to work when it rings.

3. Ask the teacher how long she expects the other children to work on each homework assignment and to write the amount of time on the top of each worksheet or e-mail you with the information. Solicit an agreement with her that Dakota will work for the amount of time that others are expected to work. She will grade/mark only the amount of work he was able to complete and will not penalize him for that which he was not able to complete.

Supporting Academics with Computer Software

Buy or find on the Internet computer software that Dakota will enjoy that also gives him drill and practice in the academic skills that he knows already but needs to practice. In reading, at this point, this would include sounding out and spelling three-sound, closed syllable words and the sight words "the" and "is." In math these would provide drill and practice in basic addition and subtraction. It would be especially helpful if the program allows you to program it with the current skills he is working on, such as addition facts to a sum of 5 and the related subtraction facts.

RECOMMENDATIONS FOR SCHOOL

General Instruction

When presenting information verbally, use accompanying visual images such as pictures, graphics (e.g., webs, charts, graphs), and videotapes. Enhancing auditory information may be as simple as drawing a sketch on the board to illustrate concepts such as contrasts, similarities, levels of importance, and cause-effect.

Accommodations

1. Do not ask Dakota to read aloud in class unless he volunteers.
2. Do not require Dakota to work under time pressure. Replace timed tests with alternative evaluation procedures. Place the emphasis in evaluation on accuracy rather than speed.

Self-Concept

Poor self-concept, emotional problems, and anxiety are common effects of learning disabilities if they are not treated appropriately and early. While remediation is provided to alleviate these problems, school staff can help reduce the negative effects by giving frequent acknowledgement of actual improvement in skills or demonstration of knowledge. Make praise specific and meaningful. "Good job" may be meaningful, but it does not tell Dakota exactly what he did that was good. "You sharpened your pencil nicely" is specific but wouldn't really matter to Dakota in terms of self-concept. "I noticed that you tried to sound out the words you didn't know rather than just guessing at them" is both specific and meaningful.

Word Retrieval and Speed of Language Processing

1 Request that a speech-language pathologist assess further for the level of word retrieval problems that Dakota has and provide therapy if necessary.

2. When calling on Dakota in class, provide him with as much time as necessary to organize his thoughts and formulate a response. He may know the answer but need extra time to find the words. Privately, alert Dakota to this plan so that he does not feel pressured to come up with answers quickly.

Reading and Spelling

Instruction

1. Dakota needs an instructional program in basic reading and spelling skills that is systematic in introduction, practice, and reinforcement of phonemic awareness skills, phoneme-grapheme relationships, sight words, syllabication rules, structural analysis, and spelling rules. In a systematic program, skills are presented in graduated steps, from simple to complex, with students achieving mastery before the next skill is introduced. Practice assignments on the current skill incorporate previously learned skills, providing opportunities for the student to develop automaticity. Reading and spelling skills are taught simultaneously so that the student learns how to spell every phonics generalization and word structure that he learns how to read. This type of program is called multisensory structure of language (MSSL). An example of such a program is the Wilson Reading System, which is currently being used in private tutoring with good results. Within this program, Dakota will need individual, intensive, daily instruction from a learning disability specialist trained to teach such a program.

2. Due to Dakota's low perceptual speed, he will need supplementary techniques to help him automatize

orthographic skills such as recognizing common letter patterns and whole words. One technique offered here is reading speed drills using any word elements on which Dakota requires extra practice as they come up in his reading program (e.g., sight words, syllable structures, letter patterns, and phonic elements) [See Addendum: Speed Drills for Reading Fluency and Basic Skills.]

3. Do not use separate lists for reading and spelling. Focus Dakota's spelling practice on the phonics patterns he is learning within the reading program. Use a whole-word approach to teach spelling only for high-frequency sight words, and only as they come up in the systematic reading program. For whole-word spelling, use a multisensory method such as the Modified Fernald Technique to incorporate visual, oral/aural, and kinesthetic-tactile components. [See Addendum: Fernald Method for Reading and Spelling—Modified.]

4. Supplement Dakota's phonics instruction with decodable books that he can read during free reading time and at home. Decodable text is reading material that comprises the phonics and sight words he has already learned. Reading decodable text provides the opportunity for application of newly learned skills, reinforcement of sight words, and transitioning skills learned in isolation to practical use. At his current skill level, reading aloud is best. One good option would be books from Flyleaf's Publishing Authentic Decodable Literature Series. These books are attractive, interesting, colorful, and decodable.

5. If teaching reading comprehension strategies (e.g., paraphrasing the main idea, supporting details), teach them orally and at Dakota's oral language level, not his decoding level. As his word identification level increases, guide him to apply the listening comprehension skills to the reading material.

Handwriting

Provide explicit instruction and supervised practice in writing both upper- and lowercase letters and numbers. Make sure that Dakota starts each letter/number on the proper line, and forms the strokes properly and in the correct sequence. He will need to be supervised in his practice so that he continues to follow this sequence rather than regressing to his current habit of forming them incorrectly and/or reversed. He will need much more practice than most children in order that the letter and number formations become automatic while retaining correct form.

Math

1. When teaching addition and subtraction facts, use strategies to help Dakota organize them mentally. Teach subtraction facts as a reformulation of addition facts and later, division as the inverse of multiplication (but not until he has mastered addition and subtraction). Continue fact practice even when he seems to know them automatically. [See Addendum: Addition Fact Memorization: Organizational Structures; Addition and Multiplication Facts: Instructional Sequence.]

2. Build math fact fluency by using programs such as Great Leaps Math (www.greatleaps.com) and/or computer games that provide math fact drill. Effective computer programs will allow the teacher to program for the specific facts or algorithms the student needs to practice and automatically monitor and document his success and errors.

3. When Dakota has to memorize rote information, such as units of measurement, help him to create visual-auditory associations as memory aids. For example, 12 inches in a foot could be drawn as a footprint of a bare foot with 12 inchworms end to end crawling across it. Three feet to a yard is illustrated as a fenced lawn with three footprints across it.

Homework Accommodations

1. Reduce the amount of work in each area assigned for homework so that Dakota can complete his assignment in approximately the same amount of time other students are expected to spend. Examples of modified assignments are: solving the odd-numbered math problems instead of all the items, reading a few pages of a book with decodable text that coincides with the reading skills he has learned, and dictating a report into a tape recorder rather than writing it. When grading a reduced assignment, consider the reduced amount of work to represent 100%. This emphasizes the quality of his work rather than the quantity.

2. For now, do not expect Dakota to copy his homework assignments from the board into his assignment book. He is unlikely to be able to read it later, it will require excessive time, and he is likely to refuse. At this point, the most time efficient way for him to get his homework assignments would be for the teacher to write the assignments on an index card before class (with the amount of time expected for each) and hand it to Dakota to place in the pocket of his homework folder. A system in which teachers post the homework daily on a school web site would be better, if available.

I hope this report proves helpful in establishing an effective and comprehensive educational program for Dakota. Please do not hesitate to contact me if you have any questions about this report.

Attachments

Speed Drills for Reading Fluency and Basic Skills
Fernald Method for Reading and Spelling – Modified
Addition Fact Memorization: Organizational Structures
Addition and Multiplication Facts: Instructional Sequence

STANDARDIZED ASSESSMENT RESULTS

Comprehensive Test of Phonological Processing

Subtest*	Age Equivalent	Grade Equivalent	Percentile Rank	Standard Score
Rapid Color Naming	<5-0	<K.0	<1	1
Rapid Object Naming	<5-0	<K.0	<1	1
COMPOSITE				
Alternate Rapid Naming	—	—	<1	46

*Subtest standard score mean = 10, Standard deviation = 3
**Composite standard score mean = 100, Standard deviation = 15

Phonological Awareness Test

Skill/subskill	Age Equivalent	Percentile Rank	Standard Score
Rhyming	6-0	17	91
Discrimination	BN*	6	63
Production	AN*	73	109
Segmentation	7-2	33	93
Sentences	5-7	7	76
Syllables	8-0	47	104
Phonemes	AN*	49	98
Isolation	6-5	12	84
Initial	6-1	27	98
Final	AN*	80	110
Medial	6-1	3	63

(Continued)

Phonological Awareness Test (cont'd)

Skill/subskill	Age Equivalent	Percentile Rank	Standard Score
Deletion	BN*	<1	<45
Compound Words & Syllables	5-3	4	72
Phonemes	BN*	<1	<41
Substitution	BN*	<2	<58
With Manipulation	BN*	<5	<66
Sound Substitution	BN*	<3	<69
Blending	6-1	5	73
Syllables	BN*	58	106
Sounds	6-0	5	67
*BN: Below norms AN: Above norms			

Comprehensive Assessment of Spoken Language

Domain/Test	AE	PR	SS	68% Conf. Band
Lexical/Semantic				
Antonym		19	87	81-93
Synonym	9-2	73	109	102-116
Sentence Completion		37	95	88-102
Syntactic				
Syntax Construction		32	93	87-99
Paragraph Comprehension	9-10	82	114	109-119
Grammatical Morphemes		23	89	84-94
Supralinguistic				
Nonliteral	8-0	47	99	92-106
Pragmatic				
Pragmatic Judgment		12	82	78-86

Comprehensive Assessment of Spoken Language

Mode/Test	AE	PR	SS	68% Conf. Band
Comprehension				
Synonyms	9-2	73	109	102–116
Paragraph Comprehension	9-10	82	114	109–119
Expression				
Antonyms		19	87	81–93
Syntax Construction		32	93	87–99
Grammatical Morphemes		23	89	84–94
Primarily Comprehension				
Nonliteral Language	8-0	47	99	92–106
Primarily Expression				
Sentence Completion		37	95	88–102
Pragmatic Judgment		12	82	78–86
Retrieval				
Antonyms		19	87	81–93
Sentence Completion		37	95	88–102
World Knowledge				
Nonliteral Language	8-0	47	99	92–106
Pragmatic Judgment		12	82	78–86

Woodcock-Johnson III Normative Update Tests of Cognitive Abilities (including Diagnostic Supplement) and Tests of Achievement (Form A)

COG/ACH norms based on age 8-2; DS norms based on age 8-3

Bolded cluster headings indicate that the confidence bands of the individual tests within the cluster overlap; thus the cluster can be considered to represent a unitary ability.

CLUSTER/Test	AE	Proficiency	RPI	SS (68% Band)	PR
GIA (Std)	7–2	Lmtd to Avg	81/90	90 (88–93)	26
VERBAL ABILITY (Ext)	**7–6**	**Average**	**83/90**	**94 (90–98)**	**35**
COMP-KNOWLEDGE (Gc)					
Verbal Comprehension	7–5	Lmtd to Avg	81/90	93 (88–97)	31
General Information	7–9	Average	86/90	96 (90–102)	40
FLUID REASONING (Gf)	10–3	Avg to Adv	97/90	114 (110–117)	82
Concept Formation	12–0	Advanced	99/90	117 (113–121)	87
Analysis-Synthesis	9–1	Average	94/90	106 (100–112)	65
VIS-SPATIAL THINK (Gv)	**11–9**	**Avg to Adv**	**96/90**	**115 (110–120)**	**84**
Spatial Relations	10–11	Average	95/90	109 (104–114)	73
Picture Recognition	12–11	Avg to Adv	96/90	114 (108–120)	82
PROCESS SPEED (Gs)	6–6	Limited	65/90	75 (72–79)	5
Visual Matching	5–11	Limited	37/90	63 (59–68)	1
Decision Speed	7–6	Average	85/90	93 (87–98)	31
PERCEPTUAL SPEED	**6–4**	**Limited**	**55/90**	**69 (64–74)**	**2**
Visual Matching	5–11	Limited	37/90	63 (59–68)	1
Cross Out	7–0	Lmtd to Avg	74/90	84 (75–92)	14
AUDITORY MEM SPAN	**6–4**	**Limited**	**66/90**	**86 (81–91)**	**17**
Memory for Words	6–7	Lmtd to Avg	68/90	90 (83–97)	26
Memory for Sentences	6–0	Limited	65/90	85 (79–90)	15
SHORT-TERM MEM (Gsm)	**6–3**	**Limited**	**51/90**	**83 (77–88)**	**13**
Memory for Words	6–7	Lmtd to Avg	68/90	90 (83–97)	26
Numbers Reversed	6–1	Limited	33/90	82 (75–88)	11
WORKING MEMORY	**6–3**	**Limited**	**48/90**	**79 (74–85)**	**8**
Numbers Reversed	6–1	Limited	33/90	82 (75–88)	11
Auditory Working Memory	6–7	Limited	63/90	85 (80–91)	17
ASSOCIATIVE MEMORY	**5–11**	**Lmtd to Avg**	**74/90**	**77 (73–81)**	**6**
Memory for Names	6–10	Average	86/90	93 (89–98)	33
Visual-Auditory Learning	5–6	Limited	58/90	71 (67–75)	3
L-T RETRIEVAL (Glr)	**4–11**	**Limited**	**64/90**	**58 (53–63)**	**0.3**
Visual-Auditory Learning	5–6	Limited	58/90	71 (67–75)	3
Retrieval Fluency	3–11	Lmtd to Avg	70/90	51 (41–61)	<0.1
PHONEMIC AWARE	**7–9**	**Average**	**89/90**	**98 (92–104)**	**44**
Sound Blending	8–3	Average	90/90	100 (94–107)	51
Incomplete Words	7–2	Average	86/90	95 (89–102)	37
COGNITIVE FLUENCY	4–6	Limited	47/90	50 (47–54)	<0.1
Retrieval Fluency	3–11	Lmtd to Avg	70/90	51 (41–61)	<0.1
Rapid Picture Naming	2–9	V Limited	5/90	46 (44–49)	<0.1
Decision Speed	7–6	Average	85/90	93 (87–98)	31
COG EFFICIENCY (Ext)	6–4	Limited	58/90	78 (74–83)	7
Visual Matching	5–11	Limited	37/90	63 (59–68)	1
Decision Speed	7–6	Average	85/90	93 (87–98)	31
Numbers Reversed	6–1	Limited	33/90	82 (75–88)	11
Memory for Words	6–7	Lmtd to Avg	68/90	90 (83–97)	26

(Continued)

CLUSTER/Test	AE	Proficiency	RPI	SS (68% Band)	PR
KNOWLEDGE	**8–1**	**Average**	**89/90**	**99 (95–103)**	**48**
General Information	7–9	Average	86/90	96 (90–102)	40
Academic Knowledge	8–5	Average	92/90	102 (96–108)	56
ORAL LANGUAGE (Ext)	7–8	Average	87/90	96 (92–99)	39
Story Recall	8–1	Average	90/90	100 (89–110)	49
Picture Vocabulary	7–9	Average	87/90	97 (92–103)	43
Oral Comprehension	8–9	Average	94/90	105 (99–110)	62
Understanding Directions	6–4	Limited	67/90	80 (75–86)	10
ORAL EXPRESSION	**7–10**	**Average**	**89/90**	**98 (92–103)**	**44**
Story Recall	8–1	Average	90/90	100 (89–110)	49
Picture Vocabulary	7–9	Average	87/90	97 (92–103)	43
LISTENING COMP	7–7	Average	85/90	94 (90–99)	35
Oral Comprehension	8–9	Average	94/90	105 (99–110)	62
Understanding Directions	6–4	Limited	67/90	80 (75–86)	10
PHON/GRAPH KNOW	5–11	Negligible	3/90	63 (56–69)	1
Word Attack	6–1	Negligible	1/90	69 (61–78)	2
Spelling of Sounds	5–4	V Limited	8/90	44 (36–53)	<0.1
BASIC READING SKILLS	**6–0**	**Negligible**	**0/90**	**61 (57–66)**	**0.5**
Word Attack	6–1	Negligible	1/90	69 (61–78)	2
Letter-Word Identification	5–10	Negligible	0/90	60 (58–63)	0.4
BRIEF READING	**5–11**	**Negligible**	**0/90**	**56 (53–58)**	**0.2**
Letter-Word Identification	5–10	Negligible	0/90	60 (58–63)	0.4
Passage Comprehension	5–11	Negligible	1/90	57 (52–61)	0.2
MATH CALC SKILLS	7–5	Lmtd to Avg	78/90	87 (81–92)	19
Calculation	7–7	Lmtd to Avg	78/90	91 (85–98)	28
Math Fluency	6–8	Lmtd to Avg	78/90	74 (69–79)	4
BRIEF MATH	**7–5**	**Limited**	**66/90**	**87 (83–92)**	**20**
Applied Problems	7–3	Limited	51/90	87 (82–91)	19
Calculation	7–7	Lmtd to Avg	78/90	91 (85–98)	28
BROAD MATH	7–4	Lmtd to Avg	71/90	85 (81–89)	16
Calculation	7–7	Lmtd to Avg	78/90	91 (85–98)	28
Applied Problems	7–3	Limited	51/90	87 (82–91)	19
Math Fluency	6–8	Lmtd to Avg	78/90	74 (69–79)	4
ACADEMIC SKILLS	6–3	Negligible	1/90	59 (56–62)	0.3
Calculation	7–7	Lmtd to Avg	78/90	91 (85–98)	28
Letter-Word Identification	5–10	Negligible	0/90	60 (58–63)	0.4
Spelling	5–8	Negligible	0/90	56 (51–61)	0.2
ACADEMIC KNOWLEDGE	8–5	Average	92/90	102 (96–108)	56
Academic Knowledge	8–5	Average	92/90	102 (96–108)	56
BRIEF ACHIEVEMENT	6–1	Negligible	1/90	58 (55–61)	0.3
Applied Problems	7–3	Limited	51/90	87 (82–91)	19
Letter-Word Identification	5–10	Negligible	0/90	60 (58–63)	0.4
Spelling	5–8	Negligible	0/90	56 (51–61)	0.2

DISCREPANCIES	STANDARD SCORES			DISCREPANCY		Significant at −1.50 SD (SEE)
	Actual	Predicted	Difference	PR	SD	
Intellectual Ability/Achievement Discrepancies*						
BASIC READING SKILLS	61	94	−33	0.3	−2.78	Yes
BROAD MATH	85	94	−9	23	−0.73	No
MATH CALC SKILLS	87	95	−8	28	−0.59	No
ORAL LANGUAGE (Ext)	96	93	3	63	+0.32	No
ORAL EXPRESSION	98	94	4	63	+0.34	No
LISTENING COMP	94	93	1	54	+0.11	No
ACADEMIC KNOWLEDGE	102	93	9	78	+0.78	No
BRIEF READING	56	94	−38	<0.1	−3.29	Yes
BRIEF MATH	87	93	−6	31	−0.50	No
*These discrepancies compare WJ III GIA (Std) with Broad, Basic, Brief, and Applied ACH clusters.						

DISCREPANCIES	STANDARD SCORES			DISCREPANCY		Significant at ±1.50 SD (SEE)
	Actual	Predicted	Difference	PR	SD	
Oral Language/Achievement Discrepancies*						
BASIC READING SKILLS	61	98	−37	0.2	−2.92	Yes
BROAD MATH	85	98	−13	17	−0.96	No
MATH CALC SKILLS	87	99	−12	21	−0.81	No
ACADEMIC KNOWLEDGE	102	97	5	71	+0.54	No
BRIEF READING	56	98	−42	<0.1	−3.39	Yes
BRIEF MATH	87	98	−11	23	−0.75	No
*These discrepancies compare Oral Language (Ext) with Broad, Basic, and Brief ACH clusters.						

DISCREPANCIES	STANDARD SCORES			DISCREPANCY		Significant at ±1.50 SD (SEE)
	Actual	Predicted	Difference	PR	SD	
GIA Std/Cognitive						
COMP-KNOWLEDGE (Gc)	94	93	1	56	+0.16	No
L-T RETRIEVAL (Glr)	58	93	−35	<0.1	−3.51	Yes
VIS-SPATIAL THINK (Gv)	115	95	20	93	+1.45	No
FLUID REASONING (Gf)	114	92	22	99	+2.30	Yes
PROCESS SPEED (Gs)	75	95	−20	6	−1.57	Yes
SHORT-TERM MEM (Gsm)	83	93	−10	17	−0.96	No
PHONEMIC AWARE	98	94	4	61	+0.28	No
WORKING MEMORY	79	93	−14	10	−1.30	No
COGNITIVE FLUENCY	50	96	−46	<0.1	−3.30	Yes
ASSOCIATIVE MEMORY	77	93	−16	8	−1.39	No
AUDITORY MEM SPAN	86	94	−8	26	−0.65	No

DISCREPANCIES	DISCREPANCY		Significant at ±1.50 SD (SEE)	Interpretation
	PR	SD (or z)		
Measures of delayed recall*				
Story Recall-Delayed	99	+2.54	Yes	Above expected recall
*These discrepancies based on predicted difference between initial and delayed scores.				

CASE 13

Difference Versus Disorder

Nondiscriminatory Assessment of an English Learner Suspected of Learning Disability

Samuel Ortiz

An effective psychoeducational assessment report accomplishes four things: (a) it identifies and describes the significant elements in the student's learning environment that relate to the observed academic difficulties; (b) it describes the present status of the student's functioning in those areas suspected of being problematic; (c) it offers an opinion regarding the possible reasons for the student's learning problems; and (d) it links assessment results with specific instructional strategies and educational modifications that guide the educational decision-making process and program development.

In order to accomplish these goals and to provide information that is helpful in understanding the nature of and reasons for an individual's current functioning in school, this report uses straightforward, plain English, minimizing irrelevant information and technical terms. The language and format of this report are designed to provide information in a manner that is useful to anyone involved in making educational decisions in this case. Accordingly, the results are given in summary form using functional descriptions of proficiency so that they present a coherent and easily understandable view of Maria's functioning in all evaluated areas. In addition, test scores and other results, designed to facilitate the meaning and significance of Maria's scores, may be found in the Appendix.

The report uses headings with slightly different wording, such as "experiential factors" instead of "background information." This is intended to reinforce that all information is important and central to the purpose of the evaluation, especially when there are cultural or linguistic differences. This case is a relatively typical one where an English language learner (ELL) is referred because of increasing difficulties in language arts, particularly writing. It highlights the degree to which an ELL can demonstrate apparent academic and cognitive deficits when in fact his or her abilities are quite normal

but attenuated due to the influence of cultural and linguistic variables. The report includes descriptions of these issues and provides an explanation regarding how they have affected academic achievement. Such issues are not easy to explain, or easily understood. Nevertheless, the report is intended to serve as a model for nondiscriminatory evaluation where a learning disability was ruled out in favor of cultural/linguistic issues.

PSYCHOEDUCATIONAL ASSESSMENT-FOR-INTERVENTION REPORT

Name:	Maria Ayala
Date of Birth:	08/19/2001
Age:	8-4
Ethnicity:	Spanish/ Mexican
School:	George Washington Elementary
Grade:	3rd
Language of Instruction:	English
Native Language:	Spanish
Evaluation Dates:	12/21/09–1/6/10
Report Date:	1/8/10
Evaluator:	Samuel O. Ortiz, Ph.D.

REASON FOR AND PURPOSE OF ASSESSMENT

Maria was referred for evaluation by her teacher, Ms. Contino, who expressed concerns regarding Maria's academic performance. Ms. Contino reported that Maria is behind academically in most subjects, especially in her writing and written language skills. Maria's reading seems to be alright, but Ms. Contino has observed some problems at times with comprehension. Ms. Contino has begun to wonder if the underlying cause of Maria's learning difficulties might be some kind of learning disability. Therefore, this assessment was conducted specifically to evaluate the nature of Maria's apparent learning problems and determine whether they may be due to a disability. Results from this assessment will be used to guide the decision-making process in developing recommendations and intervention strategies, as may be necessary and appropriate in this case, regardless of the reasons for or cause of Maria's apparent difficulties.

DESCRIPTION OF PROCEDURES

This assessment was conducted in a systematic manner by first collecting information from multiple sources such as a review of records, interviews, actual work samples, general health screening results, and informal testing. This information helped in finding out whether any environmental or experiential factors were present that could be the cause of the reported difficulties. Because there was some concern regarding schoolwork, additional procedures were also employed to evaluate Maria's ability to learn and benefit from instruction. Formal testing, including scales, questionnaires, and standardized tests and batteries, was conducted in order to generate additional information with which to assess the specific nature of Maria's learning problems. Overall, this process helps generate specific and relevant information while avoiding needless, invasive, and redundant testing.

STATEMENT OF VALIDITY OF ASSESSMENT RESULTS

The ecological methods and procedures used in the course of this assessment are specifically intended to enhance patterns seen in the data as well as reduce potential bias and discrimination inherent in the "interpretation" of any single test score or combination of scores. In general, the following steps were used to increase the validity of the findings: (a) testing was conducted in English with consideration regarding exposure or experience with a second language; (b) norm-referenced measures with the most appropriate norms were selected; (c) tests that provide information on both specific cognitive constructs and general function-

ing were utilized; (d) whenever possible less culturally and linguistically biased assessment methods were used; (e) results were interpreted within the context of Maria's unique cultural and linguistic background; and (f) conclusions were based on multiple sources of information and not any single score or procedure.

In Maria's case, the area most subject to bias involves the use of standardized, norm-referenced tests due to the concern that the norms of such assessment tools may not adequately represent Maria's linguistic background and cultural experience. As such, the validity of interpretations made on the basis of such test results may be questionable, and the obtained scores may not be reliable estimates of Maria's true functioning. To evaluate the validity of the test results and enhance the validity of interpretations, three approaches were used: (a) information about how other children like Maria typically perform on such tests was used as one basis for comparison; (b) the extent of the difference between Maria's unique cultural and linguistic background and experiences and those of the individuals in the norm sample was determined; and (c) the Culture-Language Interpretive Matrix (C-LIM) was used to evaluate the impact of cultural and linguistic variables on specific test performance. In this manner, the conclusions and opinions offered regarding Maria's functioning are believed to be as valid and as nondiscriminatory as possible.

EVALUATION OF EXPERIENTIAL FACTORS

Careful examination of cultural/linguistic difference, environmental or economic disadvantage, level of acculturation, and educational experiences indicates that Maria's reported difficulties can be at least partially attributed to one or more of the following factors: (a) neither Maria nor her parents are native English speakers, (b) they have roots in a culture different from the U.S. mainstream, and (c) Maria's parents have limited education themselves. During an informal interview, Maria's mother indicated that since birth Maria has learned Spanish primarily at home, as her native language. She also reported that she tries to encourage the use of more English at home, but because neither she nor her husband speak English very well, Spanish remains the most frequently spoken language in the household. Similarly, Maria's mother reports that although the family has adopted some of the cultural customs of the U.S. mainstream (e.g., dressing up for Halloween, decorating the outside of the house at Christmas, watching English language programs on television), the majority of the experiences in the home are rooted in their native Mexican culture and heritage, including their food, religious holidays, and various values, expectations, and attitudes. Maria's mother states that she wishes she could do more to help Maria in school but that because she and her husband both work, they do not have the time to make sure that she has the necessary materials and the ability to complete her schoolwork. Maria is often left on her own to get her work done. Maria's father works in the local agricultural industry as a greenhouse attendant and her mother is employed as a house cleaner.

The information from Maria's parents indicates that Maria's cultural and linguistic experiences are "moderately different" than that of other native English-speaking students of the same age and grade. This difference is sufficient to be a primary factor in the difficulties reported by Maria's teacher. For example, because her parents are not native English speakers and have minimal education, although Maria was born in the United States., her language development in English is not at the level expected of children of her age. The same can be said regarding her cultural development—that is, her knowledge and familiarity with U.S. mainstream objects, concepts, and values are not comparable to average classmates who are fully acculturated to the mainstream. Because Maria entered school with minimal English language development, compared with other kindergarteners, her initial school time was spent learning to speak and comprehend English. At the same time, her peers who were competent in English were receiving instruction at a level that could not benefit Maria due to her limited English comprehension skills. Now, in third grade, Maria is able to understand classroom instruction reasonably well but still misses many of the subtle linguistic or cultural nuances. More importantly, she lacks the solid academic skill and knowledge foundation that her classmates have built because she remains developmentally behind them—a condition due to circumstances, not disability. As such, this "developmental difference" is evident in school achievement and grades, as well as in formal academic testing. In addition, Maria is immersed in English-only instruction. Although this type of instruction promotes acquisition of conversational skills in English, it is not sufficient to foster the age- or grade-appropriate proficiency necessary to be competitive in school at any grade level. Therefore, it seems reasonable that Maria's current difficulties in the classroom are likely due, at least to some degree, to her linguistic and cultural differences.

EVALUATION OF HEALTH AND DEVELOPMENTAL FACTORS

According to the information provided by Maria's mother, the results of Maria's vision and hearing tests at school and in her pediatrician's office were normal. Ms. Ayala indicated that there were no problems or concerns with her pregnancy and that labor and delivery were normal. In addition, Maria met her developmental milestones (e.g., walking, talking, toilet training, feeding/bathing self) within normal limits. In general, health or developmental factors do not account for the educational problems that have been reported in this case.

OBSERVATION OF CURRENT BEHAVIOR AND PERFORMANCE

Observation of Maria's performance during informal assessment revealed no unusual or significant issues or problems. She actively engaged in all tasks, including academic ones, with relative enthusiasm and attention. In addition, Maria appeared to have a good grasp of factual knowledge regarding numbers and the alphabet. When asked to draw a picture of her family, Maria carefully drew a picture showing her family playing soccer that was developmentally appropriate for her age and grade. During conversations, Maria expressed that she was feeling a little worried about school because she was finding it harder and harder to do well in her work. Maria stated that she knows she is not doing very well in her assignments, especially writing and "a little in mathematics too." She also stated that her inability to do better seems to disappoint her teacher so much that she feels Ms. Contino is beginning to dislike her. Maria reports that her teacher has sometimes become upset with her about her schoolwork and this makes her feel very anxious and nervous.

In general, Maria's performance during formal testing was consistent with the academic problems noted by Ms. Contino. For example, during a test on mathematics, Maria appeared to handle computation (adding, subtracting, multiplying) reasonably well, although at times she worked too quickly and made simple errors. She had significantly more difficulty on math reasoning tests in which she had to read questions on her own or listen to spoken instructions. At times, Maria did not seem to fully comprehend what the question was asking and responded incorrectly. During a reading vocabulary subtest Maria took a considerable amount of time on several words, frequently sounding them out. She occasionally confused the sounds of letters (e.g., *t/d*). Maria seemed to do better on nonverbal tests—those that did not require much cultural knowledge or language skills. She struggled more on tests that required her to rely on her language skills and factual knowledge. For example, she was unable to recognize certain pictures of objects and was not able to clearly articulate her thoughts in response to some questions, although it seemed that she understood them. After testing was completed, conversation in Spanish with Maria revealed that she might have been able to respond correctly to a few items in Spanish but not many. The fact that she has not been provided native language instruction, coupled with the limited education of her parents, suggests that her overall academic development has been adversely influenced and that formal native language testing would not have resulted in significantly different performance. Many of these observations are consistent with behaviors and characteristics of individuals who are in the process of acquiring English as a second language and who are culturally different, particularly those who have not been provided with formal, native-language instruction.

CLASSIFICATION OF TEST SCORES

The results obtained from evaluation of Maria's academic and cognitive abilities using standardized, norm-referenced tests were interpreted using a classification system that describes her performance compared to peers in a functional manner. This type of classification is used to highlight Maria's current levels of performance and identify areas of instructional need. The classification categories are as follows:

Category—Description	Relative Proficiency Index	Percentile Rank	Standard Score
Highly Proficient—excellent functioning, needs very little help	95/90 or above	76th or higher	111 or higher
Proficient—consistent functioning, occasionally needs help	82/90 to 95/90	25th to 75th	90 to 110
Emergent—inconsistent functioning, often needs help	67/90 to 82/90	9th to 24th	80 to 89
Problematic—difficulty in functioning, always needs help	67/90 or below	8th or less	79 or less

EVALUATION OF ACADEMIC ACHIEVEMENT

Maria's overall academic performance was variable. In general, her broad math and reading skills were within the proficient range, whereas her general writing skills were within the problematic range. A closer look at her performance suggests that she did more poorly on tasks that tapped into advanced language abilities, such as reading comprehension and all forms of written expression, than on tasks that relied primarily on direct instruction, such as math calculation and letter-word identification. For example, Maria did better in basic math computation than she did when solving math word problems. Similarly, she was able to decode words correctly, but her comprehension of written text was low. She displayed the most significant difficulties in writing, a task in which her performance was consistently in the problematic range.

Ordinarily, such findings might be indicative of a disability. In this case, however, they are believed to be a reflection of Maria's linguistic and cultural differences. For example, her problems were more pronounced on the academic skills that rely most heavily on language development and experience. Language arts skills, particularly reading comprehension, basic writing skills, and written expression, frequently lag behind grade- and age-level expectations in English language learners because their acquisition of English begins considerably later than that of their peers whose native language is English. Consequently, they simply have not had sufficient development or experience in using English to have acquired age- or grade-expected vocabulary and concepts. In contrast, she does well on tasks that are explicitly taught in school including math computation and learning the sounds that letters of the alphabet make. Although Maria appears to have difficulties with many tasks, overall she seems to be performing at about the level that would ordinarily be expected of age- and grade-peers with the same linguistic and cultural background, especially considering that she has received all instruction in English only. Given the pattern of performance represented in the test results, the primary factor contributing to Maria's learning difficulties is most likely limited English language development rather than a learning disability.

EVALUATION OF COGNITIVE PROCESSES AND INTELLECTUAL FUNCTIONING

Maria's overall cognitive and intellectual functioning showed similar variability as that found in her academic performance. For example, whereas Maria's ability to process and work with visual information was in the proficient range, her knowledge of cultural information and her language abilities were much lower, within the problematic range. The rest of Maria's cognitive abilities and processes were within the emergent range. Ordinarily, her general intellectual ability would be reflected in the broadest available score, which in this case is within the emergent range. But before we can accept this and her other scores as good estimates of her true ability, we must be certain that the scores are valid—that is, that they measured what they were supposed to be measuring and not something else. In Maria's case, this means ensuring that the test results were accurate estimates of her ability or knowledge and not the result of cultural or linguistic differences. To this end, the Culture-Language Interpretive Matrix (C-LIM) was used to systematically evaluate the possible effects of limited English proficiency and lack of acculturation. Within this framework, Maria's test results reveal a pattern of decline that is typical of other individuals with similar cultural and linguistic backgrounds, suggesting that apparent weaknesses in her test performance were influenced by cultural and linguistic factors rather than lack of ability. Accordingly, these test results cannot be considered valid and are not interpretable from a strict psychometric standpoint. However, as the pattern is consistent with performance that is typical of nondisabled, culturally and linguistically diverse individuals with average ability, we can reasonably conclude that Maria's abilities are also within the average range and do not support the presence of a learning disability.

The C-LIM Matrix and Graph, in the Appendix, summarize the results described in this section and compare them with that of other children of the same age. They illustrate Maria's difficulties as a reflection of her linguistic and cultural differences rather than as a disability.

OPINIONS AND IMPRESSIONS

This evaluation sought to answer the question of whether Maria's classroom difficulties were the result of a learning disability. Within the context of Maria's unique experiential background, including cultural and linguistic factors that demonstrate at least a "moderate" difference from the mainstream, nondiscriminatory analysis of the patterns seen across all the data collected during this assessment suggests that Maria does not have a learning disability. The areas where Maria has difficulty are those where developmentally appropriate language proficiency is necessary. The interruption in Maria's native language development, and its replacement with English when she started school, has placed her in a situation where she does not possess the same level of English language development as her native English speaking peers. Thus, it is unreasonable to expect Maria to perform at the same level as her age- and grade-level peers, especially in skills that rely heavily on language development, such as writing. However, Maria's current lack of development in language arts is not due to any disability. Rather, it is a common, albeit unfortunate, result in children who are not given the benefit of instruction in the heritage language. The data collected in the course of this evaluation, including the pattern of test results, demonstrate that Maria's potential for school success is probably within the average range and that she is capable of performing academically with reasonable expectations considering her educational history and her cultural and linguistic background.

RECOMMENDATIONS FOR INTERVENTION AND REMEDIATION

Although Maria does not appear to have a learning disability, she is significantly below age expectations regarding her academic skills. Instructional modifications are necessary in order to increase her academic success. Her cultural and linguistic difference should be the most significant factor in designing appropriate instruction and interventions. The following suggestions may be considered in the planning of Maria's educational program:

1. Present all types of verbal information accompanied by visual stimuli that clearly illustrate the concept being taught. Examples are pictures, charts, graphs, semantic maps, and videotapes. The visual information will help Maria understand and retain new concepts and new vocabulary.

2. Do not assume that Maria has prior knowledge or previous experience of the words or information you are using to teach new concepts.

3. Be aware of the linguistic complexity of the language you use in instructions, questions, and test items.

4. Directly teach Maria to request repetition or rephrasing of instructions, questions, or statements when necessary. Additionally, encourage her to ask you to paraphrase test questions when needed. She may know the content but not understand the question.

5. If possible, arrange for Maria to spend time with an adult who will expose her to a wide variety of experiences, explain what is happening, name objects and actions, and answer questions.

6. Reteach Maria those skills and concepts that she is missing in academic areas, specifically oral vocabulary, reading comprehension strategies, spelling, English syntax, and interpreting math word problems. This might be done through classroom ability grouping, an after-school tutoring program, or the school's Title 1 program.

7. Preview and review key concepts within tasks and assigned readings in Spanish and English whenever possible.

8. If possible, pair Maria up with a bilingual peer who is performing adequately and who can help her understand classroom instructions and assignments.

9. Be aware of your use of colloquialisms, metaphors, and idioms and explain their meaning.

10. Recommend to Ms. Ayala to continue to converse with Maria in Spanish so that Maria continues to develop proficiency in her native language.

APPENDIX

The following table of scores, compiled from the Woodcock-Johnson III Tests of Cognitive Abilities and Tests of Achievement (Form A), was generated by the WJ III NU Compuscore and Profiles Program, Version 3.0.

Table 1

Norms based on age 8-4

Name: Ayala, Maria   DOB: 08/19/2001

Date of Testing: 01/06/2010

CLUSTER/Test	Raw	W	AE	EASY to DIFF		RPI	SS (68% Band)	PR
GIA (Ext)	–	480	6–7	5–7	7–11	70/90	80 (78–82)	9
COMP-KNOWLEDGE (Gc)	–	469	6–2	5–3	7–2	50/90	77 (73–82)	7
General Information	–	467	5–11	4–10	7–1	48/90	77 (71–84)	7
Verbal Comprehension	–	470	6–5	5–7	7–4	52/90	80 (75–85)	9
LONG-TERM RETRIEVAL (Glr)	–	492	6–11	5–0	11–4	84/90	86 (82–90)	18
Retrieval Fluency	38	496	7–1	3–11	16–2	87/90	90 (83–97)	24
Visual-Auditory Learning	26–E	489	6–11	5–7	9–4	80/90	88 (83–92)	20
VISUAL-SPATIAL THINK (Gv)	–	494	7–11	5–9	12–8	89/90	97 (92–102)	43
Spatial Relations	60–D	497	8–8	6–1	14–1	91/90	101 (97–106)	53
Picture Recognition	41–D	492	7–5	5–6	11–4	86/90	95 (90–100)	37
AUDITORY PROCESSING (Ga)	–	487	6–3	4–10	8–5	76/90	81 (75–88)	11
Auditory Attention	31	491	6–9	5–3	10–1	81/90	87 (79–95)	19
Sound Blending	13	483	5–9	4–7	7–6	68/90	83 (76–90)	13
FLUID REASONING (Gf)	–	480	7–1	6–2	8–3	74/90	88 (84–92)	21
Analysis-Synthesis	18–E	486	7–8	6–8	9–4	85/90	95 (90–100)	37
Concept Formation	11–C	474	6–6	5–8	7–6	59/90	85 (81–90)	16
PROCESSING SPEED (Gs)	–	483	7–6	6–5	8–10	82/90	89 (85–93)	24
Decision Speed	17	480	6–8	5–5	8–3	74/90	81 (76–87)	11
Visual Matching	30–2	486	8–1	7–1	9–4	88/90	97 (92–102)	42
SHORT-TERM MEMORY (Gsm)	–	473	6–5	5–10	7–4	56/90	84 (79–89)	14
Memory for Words	13	470	5–9	5–0	6–8	42/90	83 (76–89)	12
Numbers Reversed	8	476	6–11	6–3	8–0	68/90	91 (85–96)	27
BROAD READING	–	472	7–9	7–4	8–4	75/90	92 (90–94)	30
Letter-Word Identification	44	480	8–8	8–4	9–2	96/90	104 (102–107)	61

(*Continued*)

CLUSTER/Test	Raw	W	AE	EASY to DIFF		RPI	SS (68% Band)	PR
Reading Fluency	10	475	7–1	5–1	8–0	70/90	84 (79–89)	14
Passage Comprehension	17	462	7–0	6–9	7–4	32/90	82 (79–86)	12
BRIEF READING	–	**471**	**7–11**	**7–7**	**8–5**	**77/90**	**95 (93–97)**	**37**
Passage Comprehension	17	462	7–0	6–9	7–4	32/90	82 (79–86)	12
Letter-Word Identification	44	480	8–8	8–4	9–2	96/90	104 (102–107)	61
BROAD WRITTEN LANGUAGE	–	**462**	**6–11**	**6–7**	**7–3**	**35/90**	**71 (68–75)**	**3**
Writing Samples	9–B	460	6–10	6–7	7–1	26/90	75 (71–80)	5
Writing Fluency	4	470	6–11	<5–4	7–8	58/90	79 (72–86)	8
Spelling	20	456	7–0	6–8	7–4	24/90	81 (77–85)	10
BRIEF WRITING	–	**458**	**6–11**	**6–8**	**7–2**	**25/90**	**77 (74–80)**	**6**
Writing Samples	9–B	460	6–10	6–7	7–1	26/90	75 (71–80)	5
Spelling	20	456	7–0	6–8	7–4	24/90	81 (77–85)	10
WRITTEN EXPRESSION	–	**465**	**6–10**	**6–6**	**7–3**	**41/90**	**75 (70–79)**	**4**
Writing Samples	9–B	460	6–10	6–7	7–1	26/90	75 (71–80)	5
Writing Fluency	4	470	6–11	<5–4	7–8	58/90	79 (72–86)	8
BROAD MATH	–	**479**	**7–10**	**7–2**	**8–8**	**82/90**	**93 (89–96)**	**31**
Calculation	13	486	8–7	7–10	9–4	93/90	104 (96–112)	60
Math Fluency	33	488	7–9	5–6	10–1	87/90	91 (87–95)	27
Applied Problems	25	462	7–5	6–11	7–11	55/90	88 (84–92)	21
BRIEF MATH	–	**474**	**7–11**	**7–4**	**8–6**	**80/90**	**93 (89–97)**	**32**
Calculation	13	486	8–7	7–10	9–4	93/90	104 (96–112)	60
Applied Problems	25	462	7–5	6–11	7–11	55/90	88 (84–92)	21
MATH CALC SKILLS	–	**487**	**8–4**	**7–5**	**9–6**	**90/90**	**100 (95–105)**	**50**
Calculation	13	486	8–7	7–10	9–4	93/90	104 (96–112)	60
Math Fluency	33	488	7–9	5–6	10–1	87/90	91 (87–95)	27
Verbal Comprehension	–	470	6–5	5–7	7–4	52/90	80 (75–85)	9
Visual-Auditory Learning	26–E	489	6–11	5–7	9–4	80/90	88 (83–92)	20
Spatial Relations	60–D	497	8–8	6–1	14–1	91/90	101 (97–106)	53
Sound Blending	13	483	5–9	4–7	7–6	68/90	83 (76–90)	13
Concept Formation	11–C	474	6–6	5–8	7–6	59/90	85 (81–90)	16
Visual Matching	30–2	486	8–1	7–1	9–4	88/90	97 (92–102)	42
Numbers Reversed	8	476	6–11	6–3	8–0	68/90	91 (85–96)	27
General Information	–	467	5–11	4–10	7–1	48/90	77 (71–84)	7
Retrieval Fluency	38	496	7–1	3–11	16–2	87/90	90 (83–97)	24
Picture Recognition	41–D	492	7–5	5–6	11–4	86/90	95 (90–100)	37
Auditory Attention	31	491	6–9	5–3	10–1	81/90	87 (79–95)	19
Analysis-Synthesis	18–E	486	7–8	6–8	9–4	85/90	95 (90–100)	37
Decision Speed	17	480	6–8	5–5	8–3	74/90	81 (76–87)	11
Memory for Words	13	470	5–9	5–0	6–8	42/90	83 (76–89)	12
Letter-Word Identification	44	480	8–8	8–4	9–2	96/90	104 (102–107)	61
Reading Fluency	10	475	7–1	5–1	8–0	70/90	84 (79–89)	14
Calculation	13	486	8–7	7–10	9–4	93/90	104 (96–112)	60
Math Fluency	33	488	7–9	5–6	10–1	87/90	91 (87–95)	27
Spelling	20	456	7–0	6–8	7–4	24/90	81 (77–85)	10
Writing Fluency	4	470	6–11	<5–4	7–8	58/90	79 (72–86)	8
Passage Comprehension	18	465	7–1	6–10	7–6	41/90	85 (81–88)	15
Applied Problems	25	462	7–5	6–11	7–11	55/90	88 (84–92)	21
Writing Samples	9–B	460	6–10	6–7	7–1	26/90	75 (71–80)	5

Name	**Maria**	Grade	**3**	Evaluator	**Samuel O. Ortiz, Ph.D.**
Age	**8.4**	Date	**1/6/2010**		

DEGREE OF LINGUISTIC DEMAND

	LOW			MEDIUM			HIGH	

Cultural-Linguistic Interpretive Matrix showing a 3×3 matrix. Rows represent DEGREE OF CULTURAL LOADING (LOW, MEDIUM, HIGH), columns represent DEGREE OF LINGUISTIC DEMAND (LOW, MEDIUM, HIGH).

LOW cultural loading row:

LOW linguistic demand:
- WJ III Spatial Rel. (Gv) — Score 101 | 101
- Cell Average = **101**

MEDIUM linguistic demand:
- WJ III Num. Reversed (Gsm) — 91 | 91
- WJ III Visual Matching (Gs) — 97 | 97
- Cell Average = **94**

HIGH linguistic demand:
- WJ III Analysis Synthesis (Gf) — 95 | 95
- WJ III Aud. Working Mem. (Gsm)
- WJ III Concept Form. (Gf) — 85 | 85
- Cell Average = **90**

MEDIUM cultural loading row:

LOW linguistic demand:
- WJ III Pair Cancellation (Gs)
- WJ III Picture Recognition (Gv) — 95 | 95
- WJ III Planning (Gv)
- Cell Average = **95**

MEDIUM linguistic demand:
- WJ III Del.Recall-Vis.Aud.Lear.(Glr)
- WJ III Rapid Pic. Naming (Glr)
- WJ III Retrieval Fluency (Glr) — 90 | 90
- WJ III Visual-Aud. Learn.(Glr) — 88 | 88
- Cell Average = **89**

HIGH linguistic demand:
- WJ III Aud. Att. (Ga) — 87 | 87
- WJ III Decision Speed (Gs) — 81 | 81
- WJ III Incomplete Words (Ga)
- WJ III Mem. for Words (Gsm) — 83 | 83
- WJ III Sound Blending (Ga) — 83 | 83
- Cell Average = **84**

HIGH cultural loading row:

LOW linguistic demand:
- Cell Average =

MEDIUM linguistic demand:
- Cell Average =

HIGH linguistic demand:
- WJ III General Information (Gc) — 77 | 77
- WJ III Verbal Comp. (Gc) — 80 | 80
- Cell Average = **79**

Figure 1   Cultural-Linguistic Interpretive Matrix

This graph was generated using the XBA Data Management and Interpretive Assistant v1.0 by Elizabeth O. Lichtenberger and included on the CD-ROM from *Essentials of Cross-Battery Assessment*, 2nd Edition, by Flanagan, Ortiz, & Alfonso, © 2007, John Wiley & Sons, Inc.

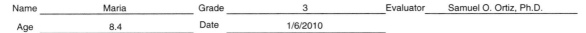

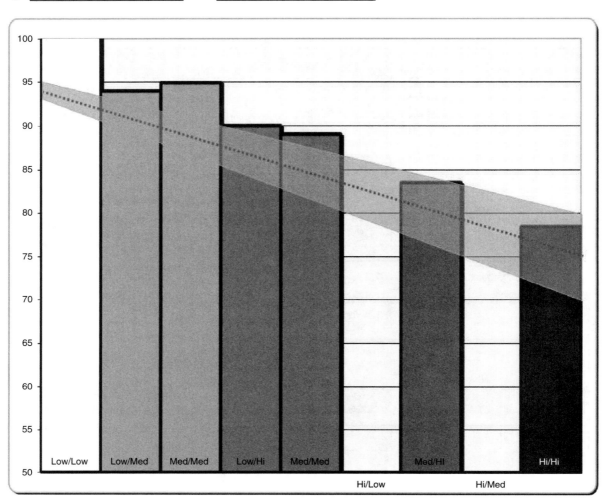

Figure 2   Cultural-Linguistic Interpretive Graph

This graph was generated using the XBA Data Management and Interpretive Assistant v1.0 by Elizabeth O. Lichtenberger and included on the CD-ROM from *Essentials of Cross-Battery Assessment*, 2nd Edition, by Flanagan, Ortiz, & Alfonso, © 2007, John Wiley & Sons, Inc.

Using the PASS Theory to Uncover Disorders in Basic Psychological Processes

An Example of Specific Learning Disability

Jack Naglieri

The purpose of this case example of Ben is to describe how the Planning, Attention, Simultaneous, Successive (PASS) theory as measured by the Cognitive Assessment System (CAS) can be used within the context of IDEA 2004 to identify a child who has a specific learning disability. In this illustration, I present only the essential information (additional data would of course be included in a full report) that forms the basis of the eligibility determination; this includes (a) evidence for a disorder in one or more of the basic psychological processes and (b) academic failure. This approach is referred to as a discrepancy/consistency model (Naglieri, 1999) and is based on the concept that a child with a specific learning disability shows significant evidence of variability in academic and cognitive test scores. This variability results in a significant discrepancy between poor academics and good PASS scale scores (as well as other academic areas) and a consistency between the low PASS score(s) and low academic score(s). In this case the child has two disorders (this is unusual) (see Naglieri, 2000) that underlie his academic failure. The low Planning and Successive scores on the CAS provide reliable and valid evidence of these disorders, which pose a considerable challenge for the child. Additionally, reading decoding and math problems are particularly critical because Ben has difficulty working with information in order (which requires successive processing) and has limited ability to figure out how to do better (which requires planning). The resulting academic failure that is associated with these cognitive weaknesses forms the basis of diagnosis as well as treatment planning.

PSYCHOLOGICAL EVALUATION

Name:	Ben
Date of Birth:	November 1, 2001
Age:	8-5

Parents:	Marie and Tony Tarantino
School:	East Lake Elementary Tarantino
Grade:	2
Date of Evaluation:	April 5, 2010
Evaluator:	Jack A. Naglieri, Ph.D.

REASON FOR EVALUATION

Ben was referred for this evaluation by his teacher, Anna Parsons, who was concerned about his difficulties with reading, handwriting, and memory. Ben is currently in the second grade at East Lake Elementary; his teacher reported that he is progressing slowly in arithmetic, spelling, and reading but is making adequate progress in reading comprehension. His teacher also described him as a student who has difficulty understanding what he hears and remembering multiple-step directions. Similarly, Ben's mother reported that he had trouble learning to tie his shoelaces, forming letters properly, and completing homework. When asked questions about his homework, Ben's responses indicated that he has problems organizing what he has to do to get his work done.

TESTS ADMINISTERED

Cognitive Assessment System (CAS)

Kaufman Test of Educational Achievement, Second Edition (KTEA-II)

TESTING OBSERVATIONS

Ben was cooperative and appeared to put forth good effort on every task given to him during the testing sessions. He often, however, impulsively blurted out an answer, reached for objects to play with, or amused himself by running his fingers along the edges of the table. Ben occasionally restated the instructions to the tests before responding, sometimes doing so in the wrong order, and, consequently, responded incorrectly. On multiple-choice items, he frequently chose an answer without carefully considering all of the options.

During the testing, Ben showed little foresight when answering the questions. For example, on those tasks designed to measure planning, Ben did not use any strategies to complete the test. On one of the Planning tests, he filled out the page in a left to right, top to bottom manner when the task is more efficiently completed by column. Toward the end of the time limit, he realized this and said, "Oh, I could have done it this way" (pointing down the column), but then he failed to utilize a similar strategy (completing the page on the diagonal) on the next item.

Ben's behavior during testing suggested that he had trouble remembering information. During administration of one of the Successive processing tests that required him to repeat words in the order spoken by the examiner, he made statements such as "I stink at this!" and "I just can't remember." Importantly, Ben's performance on the tests on this scale showed that he could remember the words but not in the correct order. He often lost credit because he reversed the order of two words or got confused when the meaning of a sentence was based on the order of the information given. In these instances he gave answers that were conceptually accurate but the details, which were based on the order of information, were incorrect.

TEST RESULTS AND INTERPRETATION

Ben earned scores on various measures of ability and achievement that fell within the Average (e.g., 90–109) to Below Average (70–79) ranges (see Figure 1). He earned a Cognitive Assessment System (CAS) Full-Scale score of 82, which is within the Low Average classification and is ranked at the 12th percentile. This means that his performance was equal to or greater than 12% of those obtained by children his age in the standardization group. There is a 90% probability that Ben's true Full-Scale score is within the range of 78 to 88. This score is consistent with Ben's Comprehensive Achievement Composite score of 88 (90% confidence range of 84 to 92) on the Kaufman Test of Educational Achievement (KTEA-II), which fell at the 21st percentile rank.

There was important variation within Ben's PASS cognitive ability scores. These four cognitive processing abilities measure a person's ability to develop and use strategies for

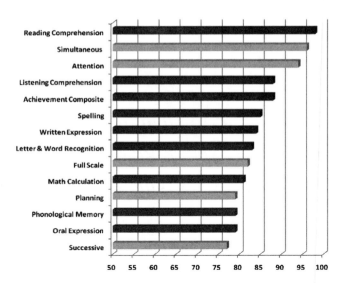

Figure 1 Comparison of Assessment Results by Standard Scores

solving problems (Planning), focus and resist distraction (Attention), work with information as a whole (Simultaneous), and work with information in a specific order (Successive). Ben earned low scores on the Planning and Successive processing scales of the CAS with a significant strength on the Simultaneous processing scale. This means that the Full Scale of 82 does not adequately describe each of the four ability scores included in the CAS. The differences among the PASS processing scales also have important implications for understanding Ben's current academic successes and difficulties, as well as for instructional planning.

Ben earned a CAS Simultaneous processing scale standard score of 96, which is within the Average classification and is ranked at the 39th percentile (90% confidence interval of 90 to 103). Ben's Simultaneous processing ability score was significantly higher than his average PASS score, indicating that he performed well on tests that required him to relate parts into a group or whole, understand relationships among pictures and words, and work with spatial relationships. There was no significant variation among the three subtests on this scale. Ben appeared to use his strength in Simultaneous processing to read words when taking the KTEA-II Reading Comprehension subtest. For example, he looked at each word as a whole, even though he sometimes substituted a similar-looking word that also made sense in the paragraph. His ability to see the whole also helped him understand the meaning of written text; he earned a KTEA-II Reading Comprehension score of 98 (45th percentile).

Ben's attention was measured by tests that required him to focus on specific features of the stimulus material and resist reacting to distracting parts of the tests. He earned an Attention scale standard score of 94, which is within the

Average classification and is ranked at the 34th percentile (90% confidence interval of 87 to 102). Not only does his score on the Attention Scale reflect his ability to focus his cognitive activity on an important dimension of the materials, but also his ability to modulate his concentration over time. There were no significant variations among the three subtests on this scale.

Ben's Planning processing scale score reflects his ability to make decisions about the best way to complete the test items, use strategies, control behavior, self-monitor, and self-correct. Ben earned a CAS Planning scale standard score of 79, which is within the Below Average classification and is ranked at the 8th percentile (90% confidence range of 74 to 89). He had considerable difficulty on the tasks that make up this scale because he did not develop or use good strategies and attempted to apply the same strategy even as the demands of the task changed. For instance, one subtest required that he find the same two numbers in a row containing eight numbers. As the numbers increased in digit length, Ben used the strategy of scanning the row for a match, which became a less-effective method. He failed to realize that this strategy was not working and he failed to develop a more effective way to find a match. Ben's weakness in planning underlies his difficulty organizing and finishing schoolwork, as well as with written composition. In fact, Ben earned a score of 84 on the Written Expression subtest of the KTEA-II (14th percentile), a task that involves considerable Planning ability. Ben did not appear to have a strategy for completing the sentences or filling in missing words as required. He had particular trouble deciding what he wanted to say in the paragraph on the essay portion of the test. Ben's weak Planning ability also underlies some of his problems in Math Calculation, a subtest on which he earned a standard score of 81 (10th percentile). During this test he did not notice his mistakes in basic math facts, did not check his work, and had difficulty completing problems that required regrouping. These academic problems are all related to the child's ability to determine the best way to get tasks done, monitor the success of that strategy, and develop new strategies as needed. This was not, unfortunately, his only low area of cognitive processing.

Ben's Successive processing score was also significantly lower than his average PASS score and well below the average range. This indicates that he has a cognitive weakness in two basic psychological processes (Planning and Successive abilities) which are very important for academic success. Ben earned a CAS Successive scale standard score of 77, which is within the Below Average classifica-

tion and is ranked at the 6th percentile (90% confidence interval of 72 to 85). Ben's score on the Successive scale reflects his difficulty working with information in a specific linear order and understanding the syntactic organization of language. For example, questions on this scale required him to comprehend sentences when the meaning was based on word order and to remember the order of words presented orally. He could only repeat up to three words in proper order, even though he could remember more than three words. Ben's difficulty working with information that is arranged in a specific order had considerable influence on his achievement tests, which also require working with sequential information.

Ben earned low scores on academic tasks that demanded working with information in a specific order. He earned a KTEA-II standard score of 85 in Spelling (16th percentile), 83 (13th percentile) in Letter & Word Recognition, and 79 (8th percentile) on the Oral Expression subtest. On these subtests, Ben's errors involved difficulty recalling and/or using information in the correct sequence. Similarly, Ben also earned a score of 88 (21st percentile) on the Listening Comprehension subtest because he did not adequately recall the specific order of the details of the story. Finally, Ben earned a low standard score of 79 (8th percentile) on the Phonological Memory scale of the CTOPP, which required repeating strings of digits in order and repeating nonsense words (such as *fob-rube*) in a specific order. These scores are also commensurate with reports of problems remembering multiple-step directions, difficulty with tying shoelaces, and adequately forming letters with a pencil, all of which demand Successive processing ability.

SUMMARY

Ben is an 8-year-old who is experiencing substantial academic problems. The findings of this evaluation indicate that he has a disorder in two basic psychological processes (Successive score of 77 [6th percentile] and Planning score of 79 [8th percentile]), accompanied by significant academic failure. Importantly, Ben's Attention and Simultaneous processing ability scores are in the Average range, illustrating wide variation among his abilities. His average Simultaneous and Attention scales with very low Planning and Successive processing and low achievement scores suggest that Ben should be considered for special education services as an individual with a specific learning disability. These processing and academic findings also have important instructional implications, which are provided in the Recommendations section following.

RECOMMENDATIONS

1. The present assessment results yielded considerable evidence that Ben has average ability on the Simultaneous and Attention scales of the CAS but a disorder in the basic psychological areas of Planning and Successive processes, along with academic failure consistent with these processing disorders. The multidisciplinary team should consider that he meets eligibility for special education services for children with specific learning disabilities.

2. Ben has cognitive processing strengths of which he, his parents, and teachers need to be aware. The attached handouts from Naglieri and Pickering (2010) entitled "Attention Processing Explained" and "Simultaneous Processing Explained" provide explanations of these abilities. Understanding Ben's strengths (and weaknesses) will allow his parents and teachers to structure assignments and tasks to best meet his needs. The handouts from Naglieri and Pickering (2010) that are particularly relevant are described below:

    a. Ben has a strength in simultaneous processing that should be used to help in areas of academic weaknesses. Use the handout "Word Sorts for Improving Spelling" to help Ben use his relative strength in simultaneous processing to improve his spelling skills.

    b. Encourage Ben to use methods like the one entitled "Graphic Organizers for Connecting and Remembering Information." This approach will help Ben better organize and remember information because it capitalizes on his strength in simultaneous processing.

3. Ben and his teachers need to understand the nature and implications of his cognitive processing weaknesses. Have Ben and his teachers review the attached handouts "Successive Processing Explained" and "Planning Processing Explained" (Naglieri & Pickering, 2010).

    a. Ben's weakness in Successive processing needs to be managed using strategies for working with serial information.

    - For spelling, use the strategies summarized in the handouts "Mnemonics for Spelling," "Strategies for Spelling," and "Chunking for Spelling."

    - For calculation, use the handout that describes the alternative to counting on one's fingers entitled "Touch Math."

    - For math facts, use the handout "Number Squares for Math Concepts." This will help Ben use his simultaneous processing strength to learning math facts by seeing the patterns the numbers form.

    - For writing composition, use the handout "Story Grammar for Writing" to help Ben understand the sequential elements of writing a well-organized story.

    b. Address Ben's weakness in planning by teaching him specific strategies and plans for completing any task. First, Ben must be made aware of the importance of being strategic when trying to accomplish any goal. He needs to be taught what the intervention is, why it is being used, and how it can be helpful to him. His parents and teachers should only provide as much help as necessary so that he can begin to develop his own strategies. Use the following planning-based handouts:

    - To help Ben become an active participant in the generation of strategies and in monitoring their effectiveness, use the handouts "Teaching Self-Awareness" and "Teaching Good Thinking Skills."

    - Use the handouts "Strategies for Improving Organization" and "Making a Plan for Organizing" to help Ben improve his organizational skills.

    - Use the handouts "Planning Facilitation for Math Calculation" and "Part-Whole Strategy for Math Calculation" to help Ben learn to use efficient plans for solving math problems.

    - For written composition, use the handouts "Plans for Writing," "Planning by Writing Sentence Openers," and "Planning to Write" to help Ben write more clearly and in a well-organized manner.

    - Use the handouts "Strategies for Multiple Choice, Matching, and True-False Tests" to help Ben develop better strategies for completing multiple-choice tests.

REFERENCES

Naglieri, J. A. (1999). *Essentials of CAS assessment*. Hoboken, NJ: John Wiley & Sons.

Naglieri, J. A. (2000). Can profile analysis of ability test scores work? An illustration using the PASS theory and CAS with an unselected cohort. *School Psychology Quarterly, 15,* 419–433.

Naglieri, J. A., & Pickering, E. (2010). *Helping children learn: Intervention handouts for use in school and at home* (2nd ed.). Baltimore: Paul H. Brookes.

CASE 15

Neuropsychological Evaluation of a Child with a Brain Injury at Birth

Sam Goldstein and Sean Cunningham

The following evaluation exemplifies the complexities of developmental and behavioral problems experienced by children who suffer from a brain injury. At birth David suffered from a frontal lobe stroke and multiple organ failure. He subsequently had corrective heart surgery. Typically when assessments are completed, cause or etiology are not a major focus. However, it is important for readers to understand and appreciate that the diagnoses typically used are based on children studied within a generally normal population. Thus, applying these diagnoses to children who otherwise genetically and developmentally might have been normal but now are not due to their trauma may lead to a misunderstanding of the child's current presentation, future development, and most importantly, current needs. This evaluation also exemplifies the often perplexing set of scores children with brain injury can present.

NEUROPSYCHOLOGICAL EVALUATION

Name:	David Sylvester
Date of Birth:	May 15, 2001
Age:	8-11
Parents:	Kimberlee and Cory Sylvester
Address:	Salt Lake City, Utah 84117
Grade:	2.7
Date of Evaluation:	April 14, 2010
Psychology Technician:	Sean Cunningham, M.S.
Evaluator:	Sam Goldstein, Ph.D.

REASON FOR EVALUATION

Subsequent to a traumatic birth history, David was diagnosed with a combination of psychiatric and behavioral problems. Due to the nature and extent of the problems David is experiencing at school and at home, this evaluation was requested for clarification of his diagnoses, for further information regarding his cognitive, academic, and behavioral strengths and difficulties, and for treatment recommendations.

BACKGROUND INFORMATION

David's mother provided an overview of his history and development. David is the youngest of her three children. Sally, age 10, has not experienced developmental or adjustment problems. Bradley, age 13, has a history of anxiety. Ms. Sylvester, an entrepreneur with a master's in business administration, stated that she had a history of attention problems and, during high school, was disinterested in school. Mr. Sylvester completed college and is employed in medical sales. He reported no personal history of learning or adjustment problems. The family has recently moved here from Arizona.

David was the product of full-term pregnancy and induced labor. He was born with a congenital heart defect, no thyroid gland, poorly developed lungs, and an abnormally thick tongue. At birth, he suffered a frontal lobe stroke and multiple organ failure, and was hospitalized for 2½ months. At 18 days of age, he had corrective heart surgery. Until David was 5 years old, he received state-funded medical support services. Currently, he experiences ongoing medical problems associated with his lack of a thyroid gland.

David was late in meeting all developmental milestones although his motor skills appeared normal until approximately 24 months of age. David's mother reported that as an infant, David had difficulty nursing and later drooled excessively. As a toddler, he was generally happy and adapted well to new situations. Although she described him as somewhat underactive, he was easily distracted and "constantly into things." Once, he swallowed pills and had to have his stomach pumped. Currently, David's appetite is poor. At bedtime, he has trouble settling down but once asleep, he sleeps through the night without disruption. He is nocturnally enuretic and wears a diaper. His fine-motor coordination is also poor. David does not understand verbal directions well and does not "read" situations well. Intellectually, he appears below average and his mother estimates that his academic skills are at a first-grade level. He is repeating second grade. Last year in Arizona, David had an aide part-time in his classroom and received special education services.

Socially, David wants to play with other children and seeks them out but does not know how to engage them or maintain a play activity. He has complained that children do not want to play with him. Within the home setting, David can be persistent and affectionate although he demonstrates significant behavioral problems. He is fidgety, has trouble remaining seated, seems to have boundless energy, and has difficulty playing quietly. He appears to "love aggressive, violent play" and is sometimes aggressive with his siblings, failing to appreciate that they do not enjoy it. David continues to be easily distracted and has difficulty following through on instructions and paying attention during tasks or activities. Similarly, he often shifts from one incomplete activity to another. Although he can work for short-term rewards, he is less successful with long-term rewards. David often does not listen to what is being said, interrupts or intrudes on others, and does not wait his turn well. He does not reason well, frequently demonstrates poor judgment, and loses his temper when he cannot get his way. He does not seem to learn from experience, and no particular form of discipline has been effective.

Previously, David was diagnosed with Asperger disorder and obsessive/compulsive disorder (OCD), although he does not experience typical compulsions. Primarily he is very rigid and inflexible and, in the past, displayed some superstitious behavior. He has an excessive interest in guns and capes. David's current medications are Synthroid, Risperdal, Vyvanse, and Lexapro. Prior medications were Lithium and Daytrana.

Previous Evaluation

Wechsler Intelligence Scale for Children—IV (2/09)

Composite	*SS
Verbal Comprehension	67
Perceptual Reasoning	67
Working Memory	88
Processing Speed	59
Full Sale I.Q.	62
*Standard Score: mean = 100, SD = 15	

Woodcock Johnson III—Tests of Cognitive Abilities (2/5/09)

Cluster	*SS
GIA	71
Verbal Ability	64
Comprehension Knowledge	64
Thinking Ability	80
Cognitive Efficiency	71
Long-Term Retrieval	73
Visual-Spatial Thinking	73
Fluid Reasoning	64
Processing Speed	60
Short-Term Memory	88
Phonemic Awareness	95
Cognitive Fluency	56
Knowledge	63
*Standard Score: mean = 100, SD = 15	

Woodcock-Johnson III—Tests of Achievement (1/10/09)

Cluster	*SS
Oral Language	70
Oral Expression	80
Listening Comprehension	74
Broad Reading	87
Broad Math	81
Basic Reading Skills	99
Reading Comprehension	82
Math Calculation Skills	82
Math Reasoning	75
Academic Skills	92
Academic Application	83
Academic Knowledge	69
*Standard Score: mean = 100, SD = 15	

Vineland-II Teacher Rating Form (2/10/09)

Composite	*SS
Communication	69
Daily Living Skills	60
Socialization	67
Motor Skills	60
Adaptive Behavior Composite	63

Vineland-II Parent Survey (2/13/09)

Composite	*SS
Communication	88
Daily Living Skills	100
Socialization	104
Motor Skills	72
Adaptive Behavior Composite	95
*Standard Score: mean = 100, SD = 15	

Test of Language Development—I (1/9/09)

Composite	*SS
Listening	67
Organizing	73
Speaking	74
Grammar	68
Semantics	69
Spoken Language	65
*Standard Score: mean = 100, SD = 15	

Goldman Fristoe Test of Articulation (1/9/09)
Standard Score: 49

CURRENT ASSESSMENT PROCEDURES

Conners Comprehensive Behavior Rating Scales (CBRS)—Parent

Conners Comprehensive Behavior Rating Scales (CBRS)—Teacher

Home Situations Questionnaire

Social Attributes Checklist (parent and teacher forms)

Teacher Observation Checklist

Elementary School Situations Questionnaire

Peabody Picture Vocabulary Test, Fourth Edition (PPVT-4)

Expressive Vocabulary Test-2 (EVT-2)

Wechsler Intelligence Scale for Children—IV (WISC-IV)

Test of Memory and Learning-2 (TOMAL-2)

Cognitive Assessment System (CAS)

Gordon Diagnostic System

Purdue Pegboard Test

Motor-Free Visual Perception Test

Beery-Buktenica Developmental Test of Visual Motor Integration, 5th Edition

Human Figure Drawing Test

Letter and Number Writing Sample

Woodcock-Johnson III Tests of Achievement (WJ III ACH)

Clinical Interview

ASSESSMENT RESULTS AND INTERPRETATION

Adaptive Functioning

The Conners Comprehensive Behavior Rating Scales (CBRS) was completed by David's parents and teachers. The CBRS includes the Content Scales and the *DSM-IV-TR* Scales, both of which incorporate behaviors indicative of a variety of disorders. For comparative purposes, *T* scores for both of these scales appear below. Elevated scores indicate problems. A score of 61–65 indicates that the behavior is possibly a significant problem; scores of 66 and above indicate a significant problem. The CBRS also contains Validity Scales; these scales indicate if the respondent's responses are negative or positive to the extent that the ratings may be invalid.

Conners Comprehensive Behavior Rating Scales (CBRS)

Content Scales	*T scores		
	Parent	Teacher Special Ed.	Teacher Gen'l Ed.
Emotional Distress	75+	57	75+
Upsetting Thoughts	75+	59	64
Worrying	75+	45	61
Social Problems	75+	53	75+
Aggressive Behavior	75+	65	75+
Academic Difficulty	75+	75+	75+
Language	75+	75+	75+

(Continued)

		*T scores	
Content Scales	**Parent**	**Teacher Special Ed.**	**Teacher Gen'l Ed.**
Math	75+	75+	73
Hyperactivity/Impulsivity	75+	75+	68
Separation Fears	75+	75+	75+
Perfectionist & Compulsive Behaviors	75+	45	65
Violence Potential	75+	75+	75+
Physical Symptoms	75+	45	45
*T scores: mean = 50, SD = 10			

		*T scores	
***DSM-IV-TR* Scales**	**Parent**	**Teacher Special Ed.**	**Teacher Gen'l Ed.**
ADHD Inattentive Type	75+	75+	72
ADHD Hyperactive-Impulsive Type	75+	75+	66
Conduct Disorder	75+	52	75+
Oppositional Defiant Disorder	75+	73	75+
Major Depressive Episode	75+	75+	75+
Manic Episode	75+	75+	75+
Generalized Anxiety Disorder	75+	75	75+
Separation Anxiety Disorder	75+	53	61
Social Phobia	75+	50	75
Obsessive/Compulsive Disorder	75+	45	75+
Autistic Disorder	75+	75+	75+
Asperger Disorder	75+	75+	75+
*T scores: mean = 50, SD = 10			

Results of the Validity Scales suggest that Ms. Sylvester's positive impressions of David appear valid but that her descriptions of his negative behaviors may be exaggerated. The same pattern was observed to a slightly less degree in the general education teacher's responses. Based on their responses, David would appear to have symptoms of many of the disorders listed above in the Content and *DSM-IV-TR* scales. Overall, David appears to be somewhat more comfortable and in control of his behavior in school than at home and more so in the special education classroom than in the general education classroom.

On the Home Situations Questionnaire, Ms. Sylvester's responses indicated that David has problems to a moderate degree when playing alone and with others, at meals, and when visitors are in the home. She also noted that there were often problems when in public places.

On the Social Attributes Checklist, an informal scale developed by McClellan and Katz (1992), Ms. Sylvester noted that David is rarely in a positive mood and does not often display humor. In social situations, he sometimes approaches others in a positive manner and, at times, can express his wishes and preferences clearly. Typically, however, he does not assert his rights and needs appropriately, nor does he express frustration and anger effectively. David has difficulty joining a group and is rarely invited to do so. He rarely shows empathy or interest in others and is usually unsuccessful in entering a conversation, taking turns, negotiating, and compromising.

School Functioning

David's classroom and special education teachers also completed the Social Attributes Checklist, Teacher Observation Checklist, and Elementary School Situations Questionnaire. The teachers noted that thus far in the second grade year, David demonstrates weak academic self-concept and limited interest in classroom activities. His vocabulary and oral language skills are inconsistent, and he demonstrates significant problems with gross-motor, fine-motor, and perceptual abilities. His reading skills are more advanced than his math skills. David is dependent and seems lost in new situations, often seeking assistance. His approach to problems is inexact, careless, and disorganized. He can follow simple instructions but often needs individual help. David learns slowly and works very slowly. He frequently displays below average frustration tolerance and often demands attention. In the general education classroom, David is rarely problem free. The teacher noted moderate to significant problems during individual work, small-group activities, free time, recess, lunch, and in the hallways. Mild problems were noted in other settings. This pattern is also observed in the special education room.

David's classroom teacher noted that at times he is in a positive mood and displays humor but often draws inappropriate attention to himself. He sometimes expresses his wishes and preferences clearly, asserts his rights and needs appropriately, and expresses anger and frustration effectively. He typically does not approach others in a positive manner and does not enter a conversation, negotiate, compromise, or take turns well. He does not demonstrate empathy or show interest in others. The teacher observed that David is not sought out by peers and seems to be quite lonely. He is often intimidated and is quite dependent on adults.

David's current Individualized Education Plan (IEP), dated December 10, 2009, provides a classification of Intellectual Disability. His IEP goals address the need for improvement in reading, writing, math, functional skills, motor skills, and communication.

Behavioral Observations

David had received his psychiatric medications on the day of the evaluation. He was seen for two assessment sessions with a lunchtime break, meeting with this evaluator in the morning and with Mr. Cunningham in the afternoon. His behavior during both sessions was similar. David easily greeted the examiners in the waiting room and quickly made conversation. Eye contact was appropriate. David was talkative but his conversation was often tangential. He demonstrated weak receptive and expressive language skills and often spoke in incomplete sentences. He had difficulty following a conversation and understanding instructions.

Throughout the sessions, David smiled appropriately, related well to the examiners, and generally appeared emotionally comfortable. Despite his developmental impairments, it was not especially difficult to establish a working relationship with him. David demonstrated a markedly overactive pattern of behavior and was extremely fidgety. His level of concentration varied considerably and he was occasionally distracted. With prompting and support, he attempted all tasks presented, but as tasks became difficult, his effort quickly waned. It was difficult to assess his level of self-confidence.

Some of the tests used in this evaluation were administered recently in a school-based assessment. This may lead to some practice effect, primarily for perceptual- and motor-based activities.

Vocabulary

The Peabody Picture Vocabulary Test (PPVT-4) was administered as a measure of one-word receptive vocabulary. David completed this test with a standard score of 61, below the 1st percentile. The Expressive Vocabulary Test-2, which required David to provide a synonym for a given word, was administered as a measure of expressive vocabulary. David completed this test with a standard score of 46, again below the 1st percentile. David's receptive and expressive vocabulary skills appear to be similar to that of a child of 4½ to 5 years old.

Intellectual

The fourth edition of the Wechsler Intelligence Scale for Children was administered as an overall screening of intellectual ability and achievement.

Wechsler Intelligence Scale for Children—IV

Index/Test	*Sc S
Verbal Comprehension	
Similarities	6
Vocabulary	5
Comprehension	6
Information	5
Word Reasoning	5
Perceptual Reasoning	
Block Design	3
Picture Concepts	4
Matrix Reasoning	5
Working Memory	
Digit Span	10
Letter-Number Sequencing	6
Processing Speed	
Coding	2
Symbol Search	4
*Scaled scores: mean = 10, SD = 3	

Index	*SS	**SS 90% CI	***PR
Verbal Comprehension	75	71–82	5
Perceptual Reasoning	63	60–72	1
Working Memory	88	83–93	21
Processing Speed	62	59–74	1
Full Scale	65	62–70	1

*Standard score: mean = 100, SD = 15
**Standard score confidence interval
***Percentile rank: mean = 50

Learning and Working Memory

The Test of Memory and Learning-2 was administered as an overall screening.

Test of Memory and Learning, Second Edition

Verbal Subtests	*ScS
Memory for Stories	5
Word Selective Reminding	3
Object Recall	2
Digits Forward	10
Paired Recall	8
Nonverbal Subtests	
Facial Memory	3

(Continued)

Nonverbal Subtests	*ScS
Visual Selective Reminding	5
Abstract Visual Memory	5
Visual Sequential Memory	6
Memory for Location	7
Delayed Recall Scores	
Memory for Stories	2
Facial Memory	5
Word Selective Reminding	4
Visual Selective Reminding	7
*Scaled scores: mean = 10, SD = 3	

Index	*SS
Verbal Memory Index	70
Nonverbal Memory Index	67
Composite Memory Index	67
Delayed Recall Index	63
*Standard score: mean = 100, SD = 15	

Executive/Neuropsychological Skills

The Cognitive Assessment System was administered as a neuropsychological screening. Age-adjusted scaled scores appear in the subsequent table.

Cognitive Assessment System

Subtest	
Matching Numbers	6
Planned Codes	5
Nonverbal Matrices	6
Verbal-Spatial Relations	7
Expressive Attention	6
Number Detection	4
Word Series	12
Sentence Repetition	13
*Scaled scores: mean = 10, SD = 3	

Composite	SS	SS 90% CI	PR
Planning	74	70–86	4
Simultaneous	79	74–89	8
Attention	71	67–84	3
Successive	114	106–120	82
Full Scale	78	73–89	7
*Standard score: mean = 100, SD = 15			

David demonstrated markedly impaired planning, simultaneous processing, and attention abilities. In contrast, his ability to work with information in sequence appeared above average. These tasks required rote memory without higher-level processing of meaningful information, a pattern observed across all tasks administered. David's strength in this area may well represent his initial developmental potential absent the trauma experienced at birth and the absence of a thyroid.

Attention

The Gordon Diagnostic System was administered as a computerized measure of David's ability to sustain attention and inhibit impulsive responding. On the Delay tasks he was well below average for correct responding and significantly above average for impulsive responses. David could not understand the 8-year-old version of the Vigilance task so the 6-year-old version was administered. Even for that task, his correct responses were abnormal.

Motor/Perceptual

David held a pencil in his right hand with a pincer grip. Casual observation did not indicate any marked gross motor problems. However, David's manipulation of a pencil reflected significant motor/perceptual problems.

David's motor speed and coordination, based on the Purdue Pegboard Test performance, appeared below the 10th percentile. On the Motor Free Visual Perception Test, David's performance was also below the 1st percentile, an ability level equivalent to a child of age 4 to 7. David's reproductions of the figures on the Developmental Test of Visual Motor Integration yielded a standard score of 72, equivalent to the 3rd percentile. David's human figure drawings appear at right. His drawings are consistent with a 4- to 5-year-old level of ability.

Academic

The Woodcock-Johnson III Tests of Achievement was administered as an assessment of academic abilities and fluency.

Woodcock-Johnson III NU Tests of Achievement

Norms based on Age 8-11

Cluster/Test	*SS	Cluster/Test	*SS
Oral Language	55	**Phoneme-Grapheme Knowledge**	108
Story Recall	78	Word Attack	114
Understanding Directions	49	Spelling of Sounds	95
Broad Reading	89	**Broad Math**	61
Letter/Word Identification	99	Calculation	53
Reading Fluency	86	Math Fluency	76
Passage Comprehension	79	Applied Problems	73
Basic Reading Skills	106	**Math Calculation Skills**	56
Word Attack	114	Calculation	53
Letter/Word Identification	99	Math Fluency	76
Broad Written Language	85	**Total Achievement**	76
Spelling	92	Academic Skills	86
Writing Samples	90	Academic Fluency	77
Writing Fluency	79	Academic Application	74
Written Expression	84		
Writing Samples	90		
Writing Fluency	79		
*Standard Score: mean = 100, SD = 15			

David was able to write the alphabet and the numbers 1 through 20 in sequence. His writing sample follows in reduced size.

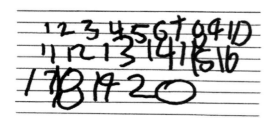

David demonstrated average basic reading skills with low to low average comprehension. His ability to spell and write simple phrases and sentences was in the low average to average range although he has difficulty generating and writing simple sentences quickly. His achievement in basic reading and writing skills is consistent with his strong sequential processing abilities, including rote memory and sound blending (based on the school's testing). David's pattern of scores in the math tests indicated that

although he can figure out or has memorized some basic addition and subtraction facts, he does not know how to apply these to computation or practical problems. David's markedly impaired math skills are consistent with his very poor planning ability. David's performance on all of the oral language tests suggested that his current levels of language comprehension and expression are in the very low and low ranges. Generally, a person's level of oral language is considered his potential for developing comprehension of text; consequently, David will need specialized instruction in improving his comprehension of oral language if he is to improve his reading comprehension. Generally, David's academic abilities mirror his cognitive abilities in that he has developed those skills that are based on the more rote and lower-level cognitive abilities. He has not, however, developed the academic skills that depend on complex working memory, higher-level reasoning abilities, and self-monitoring of one's own comprehension and problem solving. Nevertheless, David's success with tasks requiring sequential processing, including basic reading and spelling skills, indicates that he is not a child with a global intellectual disability, but rather a child experiencing marked impairments secondary to brain damage caused by his perinatal stroke.

Emotional/Personality

The examiner did not have very much success interviewing David. He described feeling happy when he gets "a new gun," being sad "when someone takes stuff from me," and angry "when someone punches me." David acknowledged that he had difficulty "keeping my hands to myself" at school but could not explain the reason he got into so much trouble. He spoke positively about his parents but noted that he disliked his siblings because "they punch me in the face and kick me." David acknowledged that he created problems at home because he kicks, punches, and hits. He spontaneously told the examiner about his "beautiful girlfriend, Bailey" and that when he grows up he wants to be a baseball coach. He then asked the examiner if baseball coaches have whistles. When the examiner suggested they did not, David then responded he wanted to be a basketball coach "because they have whistles."

On the basis of history, presentation, and current test data, David presents as a child with inconsistent, immature thought processes but generally adequate psychological grounding in reality. Significant psychological or emotional problems do not appear to be responsible for David's marked impairments.

DIAGNOSTIC IMPRESSIONS

David suffered a frontal lobe stroke at birth, multiple organ failure, and problems associated with a heart defect and absence of the thyroid. This examiner did not have the opportunity to review medical records, although this history would suggest that David likely suffered a significant brain injury at birth. David has since demonstrated delayed development. He has taken a number of different psychiatric medications; currently he is taking an antipsychotic, a psychostimulant, and an antidepressant. He has been diagnosed in the past with obsessive/compulsive disorder and Asperger syndrome. He displays aggressive and disruptive behavior, poor attentional capacity, and impaired interpersonal skills, patterns reported at school and at home. Previous school assessment suggested marked delays in development, which led to a classification, for special education purposes, of Intellectual Disability.

Data generated during the course of this assessment suggest that while David's language, perceptual, perceptual-motor, and reasoning abilities are markedly impaired, his strength in sequential processing, leading to average basic reading and spelling skills, argue strongly that David's presentation is the result of a brain injury rather than a global developmentally driven intellectual disability. David demonstrates language and perceptual abilities similar to that of a 4½- to 5-year-old child. Neuropsychological processes appear to be between the 3rd and 8th percentile for planning, simultaneous processing, and attention but at the 82nd percentile for sequential processing. Rote, short-term verbal memory appears intact but other memory functions, including verbal and nonverbal working memory, are markedly impaired as well. Further, testing indicated significant difficulty with sustained attention and a strong tendency for impulsivity.

David's patterns of disruptive behavior are likely part of his organic brain syndrome. It is also likely that he resorts to aggressive and noncompliant behavior in the face of failing to understand the behavior and motives of others. There are no indications to suggest that David is a child with a serious emotional or psychiatric disorder. Current assessment data provide no support for any type of pervasive developmental disorder or cycling mood disorder. The patterns of atypical behavior David presents are most likely part of his organic brain syndrome and cognitive disorder caused by his perinatal stroke.

RECOMMENDATIONS

1. It is strongly recommended that David's educational team review the current evaluation. Although his cognitive and behavioral presentation is similar to that of a child with a traumatic brain injury, he does not meet the IDEA-2004 definition of that classification. Consequently, the current classification of Intellectual Disability (termed "mental retardation" under IDEA-2004 guidelines) will continue to qualify him for special education services. The team, however, should recognize his cognitive strength in sequential processing when designing instruction. David would be best served in a self-contained placement for children with global developmental and behavioral impairments. This examiner is prepared to consult further with David's educational team.

2. David's parents would benefit from additional strategies and resources to increase David's compliance and improve his behavior at home. This examiner is prepared to consult with the Sylvesters regarding behavior management.

3. It is particularly important that David participate in one or more activities in which he is successful and feels comfortable. David's educational team and David's parents should investigate possibilities.

4. David is likely to require significant services throughout school as well as assistance transitioning into adult life. Results of the current evaluation suggest that if he is to enter the competitive workforce and live semi-independently, he will require significant transitional programming.

5. It is recommended that David's psychiatrist review the current evaluation. Should adjustments be made in his current medications, this examiner is prepared to assist in the collection of behavioral data at home and at school to monitor its effectiveness.

6. Given the extent of David's language and perceptual-motor difficulties, his parents should consider obtaining community-based services, particularly speech/language and occupational therapy. This examiner is prepared to make referrals to providers.

7. It is recommended that David be reevaluated during his fifth-grade year.

REFERENCE

McClellan, D., & Katz, L. G. (1992). Assessing the social development of young children: A checklist of social attributes. *Dimensions of Early Childhood, 21(1),* 9–10.

CASE 16

Missing Out on Early Intervention
The Delay of Appropriate Services for a Child with SLD

Nancy Mather

This case report illustrates a situation of a child who needed help learning to read beginning in kindergarten, but services were never provided. Despite the fact that Tanya has advanced oral language, the first intervention was retention in kindergarten, which did not result in any improvement. Although her teachers noted that Tanya was behind her peers in literacy development, they stated that she was not yet sufficiently delayed to be eligible for any type of help. Feeling frustrated with the lack of support, the Rubens decided to homeschool Tanya, even though both parents had full-time jobs and four young children. Thus, the grandmother, a former fifth-grade teacher, assumed the task of homeschooling Tanya. After several months, the Rubens realized that Tanya was still not making adequate progress. In addition, Tanya was complaining about missing her friends at school. The Rubens decided to finish the year with homeschooling and then reenroll Tanya in school for third grade.

Based on the results of the present assessment, the evaluator made a strong recommendation to the Rubens to have Tanya begin summer tutoring as soon as possible and an appropriate, highly trained tutor was located. In spite of several phone calls and e-mails by the tutor and evaluator, the Rubens never followed through and the summer just passed by. In the fall, Tanya would begin third grade with no special services or supports. Ideally, in a school with an effective RTI model, Tanya would have started receiving extra support in kindergarten and would not now be faced with the challenge of entering third grade significantly behind her peers in all academic subjects: reading, writing, and mathematics.

Sometimes, evaluations are conducted and specific recommendations are offered, but no one follows through and then the child does not get appropriate help in a timely fashion.

DIAGNOSTIC EVALUATION REPORT

Name:	Tanya Rubens
Date of Birth:	6/26/2001
Age:	8 years, 11 months
Parents:	Josh and Laura Rubens
School:	Homeschooled
Grade:	2.8
Test Dates:	4/28, 5/12/2010
Evaluator:	Nancy Mather, Ph.D.

REASON FOR REFERRAL

Tanya was referred for an evaluation by her grandmother, Ms. Alice Garrigus, a former fifth-grade teacher. Her main concern was trying to understand why Tanya has had such difficulty learning in school when she seems capable in so many ways. She has struggled since kindergarten with the acquisition of basic reading, writing, and math skills. Both the mother and grandmother report that Tanya has trouble concentrating and just seems to get lost in her thoughts at times. The purposes of this evaluation were to determine what specific factors are affecting Tanya's academic progress, as well as what instructional methodologies would be most effective for addressing her educational needs.

BACKGROUND INFORMATION

Tanya lives at home with her mother and father and three siblings: Bart, 4; Angela, 6; and Jeanne, 11. Her father is a fireman and her mother is a dentist. Tanya began kindergarten at Marston Elementary School in Keeling Unified School District. Because she was having such difficulty learning simple things, such as the names of the letters of the alphabet, it was recommended that she repeat kindergarten. Her kindergarten teacher said that Tanya's reading and writing were more like that of a preschool child and she suggested that the Rubens write a letter requesting retention. At first, Tanya found her second year of kindergarten to be easy, but midway through the year she confided to her mother that it was a "big mistake" and she was not learning anything new. At this point, the Rubens requested that school provide a comprehensive evaluation, but they were informed that Tanya was too young and it was likely that she would grow out of her difficulties.

The family then moved to the Aberdeen School District and Tanya attended Ridgewood Elementary for first grade and the first half of second grade. By the middle of second grade, her teacher reported that Tanya was falling farther and farther behind on school benchmarks, but there was nothing that they could do because she still was not far enough behind to be eligible for special help. Her teacher suggested she attend a reading and math intersession camp, and Tanya did so. Although Tanya enjoyed the camp, she did not seem to make much progress. In mid-second grade, when the Rubens requested additional support for Tanya, they were told again that she did not rank low enough to receive special help. During this period, Mr. Rubens noted that Tanya would often spend over three hours a night trying to complete the homework, and that little was accomplished unless one parent sat with her the entire time.

Frustrated by Tanya's lack of progress and the lack of school support, Ms. Rubens decided it would be best to homeschool Tanya so that she could receive more intensive help geared to her present performance levels. She removed Tanya from Ridgewood in December 2008. After several months of homeschooling, Ms. Rubens realized that Tanya still was not making adequate progress, and Tanya was complaining that she missed being with her friends.

The family has recently moved to the Pine River School District and plans to enroll Tanya in the third grade in the fall. In contrast to her academic skills, language and science have always been areas of strength and interest. Tanya loves the outdoors and can spend hours observing plants, bugs, and animals. She loves to conduct experiments and engage in hands-on activities. She is very excited that the family may get a Cocker Spaniel sometime in the near future. Tanya is a very social child and loves being with other children.

TESTS ADMINISTERED

Woodcock-Johnson III Tests of Cognitive Ability (WJ III COG) Standard (Tests 1–7) and Extended (Tests 9, 11, 16, 17, 18)

Woodcock-Johnson III Tests of Achievement (WJ III ACH) Standard (Tests 1–11) and Extended (Tests 13, 14, 15, 20) (a complete set of WJ III scores is included at the end of this report).

Test of Orthographic Competence (TOC): Sight Spelling and Homophone Choice

Test of Silent Word Reading Fluency (TOSWRF)

Behavior Assessment System for Children, Second Edition (BASC-2), Parent Rating Scales

BEHAVIORAL OBSERVATIONS

Testing was conducted in two 2-hour sessions. Tanya was polite and engaged during all of the testing. She was cooperative in both sessions, but her ability to sustain attention was quite variable. In the first session, which was conducted at a patio table outside, Tanya was highly engaged and had little difficulty concentrating. On occasion she would talk about environmental factors, such as a bird she observed eating or the sound of the water in the pool, but she was then easily redirected to the task. She commented about how much she loved the outdoors.

During the second session, which was conducted inside her grandmother's home at a dining room table, Tanya had extreme difficulty concentrating and sustaining attention. Directions had to be repeated on several occasions, and she had to be reminded numerous times about what she was supposed to be doing. Although she tried to do her best, she smiled and apologized several times for her lack of focus and concentration.

TEST RESULTS

The WJ III COG and WJ III ACH were scored according to age norms. Because these two batteries are co-normed, direct comparisons can be made among her cognitive and achievement scores. These comparisons can help determine the presence and significance of any strengths and weaknesses among her abilities. These tests provide measures of Tanya's specific cognitive and oral language abilities, as well as her academic achievement.

On the WJ III, Tanya's performance is compared to that of her age-peers using the following standard score (SS) ranges:

SS Range	<69	70–79	80–89	90–110	111–120	121–130	>130
Verbal Label	Very Low	Low	Low Average	Average	High Average	Superior	Very Superior

Her proficiency on specific tasks is described by Relative Proficiency Index (RPI) levels. The RPI indicates the difficulty level a student would be expected to be able to manage in tasks similar to those used in the test. The numerator indicates the expected level of success on a task when a typical age-peer would be 90% proficient. For example, Tanya's RPI of 9/90 on the Word Attack test predicts that when the average student of age 8-11 would be 90% successful in sounding out unfamiliar but phonetically regular words, Tanya would be only 9% successful, indicating very limited proficiency.

RPI Range	Level of Proficiency
0–3	Negligible
3–24	Very Limited
24–67	Limited
67–82	Limited to Average
82–95	Average
95–98	Average to Advanced
98–100	Advanced
100	Very Advanced

Percentile ranks and standard scores are provided for the TOC and TOSWRF. At-risk and clinically significant ratings from the BASC-2 are also presented.

Cognitive Abilities

Based on the tests of the WJ III COG, Tanya's overall intellectual ability, as measured by the General Intellectual Ability-Standard (GIA-Std) was average. Significant strengths and weaknesses, however, were found among her abilities; thus a global measure of intelligence does not provide an adequate description of her abilities. In general, Tanya's proficiency in language use and comprehension, as well as her general knowledge and vocabulary, were advanced. Tanya could easily define words, repeat back stories she had just heard, and answer questions involving general information and world knowledge. In fact, her oral language abilities fall in the Superior range. In contrast, her cognitive efficiency, a combination of processing speed and working memory, was limited. Cognitive efficiency is the ability to quickly recognize visual symbols (e.g., letters and numbers), hold them and related information in memory, and work with them to solve a problem or come up with an end product. This ability underlies much skill-learning, but especially basic reading, spelling, and math skills. In this regard, Tanya had the most difficulty on tests of processing speed (requiring the rapid processing of symbols), as well as tests involving memory for noncontextual information (e.g., lists of unrelated items rather than stories) and for visual symbols, such as letters and numbers. She had difficulty reversing the order of digits (Numbers Reversed, RPI = 57/90; SS 87). She was also confused when directions involved pointing to the right or pointing to the left.

Academic Achievement

Tanya's academic performance was assessed in reading, writing, and math using selected tests of the WJ III ACH. In addition, her performance was analyzed on the TOC and TOSWRF. Currently, Tanya's present proficiency with all academic areas (reading, writing, and math) is very limited.

Reading

On reading tasks, Tanya had difficulty applying phonics skills, recognizing common sight words (e.g., *there, when*), and reading simple sentences quickly. As words increased in length, she tended to guess at their pronunciations by using the initial consonant (e.g., reading *sentence* as "science").

WJ III ACH Cluster/Tests	RPI	Proficiency	SS(±1 SEM)
BROAD READING	31/90	Very Limited	77 (75–80)
Letter-Word Identification	4/90	Very Limited	79 (77–82)
Reading Fluency	78/90	Limited to Average	88 (83–93)
Passage Comprehension	36/90	Limited	82 (79–86)

Tanya also scored significantly below average on the TOSWRF with a percentile rank of 10 and a standard score of 81. These findings suggest that Tanya has difficulty recognizing common words appropriate for her age level and will read much more slowly than her average age-peers.

Written Language

Tanya's lowest performance was in basic written language skills. The Spelling test measured her ability to spell simple to more complex spelling patterns. Although she was able to represent the sounds in many of the words, she did not recall the correct letter sequences (e.g., spelling "were" as *wree*, and "girl" as *gril*. When spelling a phonically regular nonsense word that began with a /k/ sound, Tanya began the word with the letters 'ck,' an orthographic pattern that never starts an English word.

In contrast, on the Writing Fluency test, given three words and a picture, Tanya was able to formulate and write simple sentences quickly. On Writing Samples, a test that measures skill in formulating and writing sentences or phrases in response to a variety of demands, Tanya wrote complete sentences but her spelling was so poor that many words were not recognizable, which lowered her overall score. (Spelling errors are not penalized on Writing Fluency and Writing Samples as long as the intended word is recognizable.) Tanya has an unusual pencil grip that makes it difficult for her to form letters easily and results in her putting too much pressure on her thumb.

WJ III CLUSTER/Tests	RPI	Proficiency	SS(±1 SEM)
BROAD WRITTEN LANGUAGE	23/90	Very Limited	64 (60–68)
Spelling	4/90	Very Limited	67 (62–71)
Writing Fluency	81/90	Limited to Average	92 (85–99)
Writing Samples	14/90	Very Limited	66 (61–72)

Tanya was also administered two subtests from the TOC, Sight Spelling and Homophone Choice. Her percentile rank was 3 and her standard score was 73 with a descriptive term of "poor." Tanya had considerable difficulty spelling the irregular words. Specifically, she had difficulty recalling the word parts that must be memorized visually because they are not spelled as they sound (e.g., words such as *was* and *said*). She also had difficulty recognizing which one of two or three homophones matched a given picture (e.g., picture of a flower with the spellings "flower" and "flour").

Mathematics

In basic math skills, Tanya could only complete simple calculations. She was able to add and subtract single digits by counting on her fingers. She was unable to complete two-digit addition and subtraction problems with or without regrouping. On several problems, she failed to notice the operation sign. Her proficiency on the Math Fluency test, solving single-digit addition and subtraction problems, was Average. Tanya had difficulty solving simple

story problems and counting change below a dollar. She was, however, able to count accurately with pictures, add and subtract using pictures, identify the names of coins, and identify the time on a clock to the hour.

WJ III CLUSTER/Tests	RPI	Proficiency	SS(±1 SEM)
BROAD MATH	42/90	Limited	72 (68–76)
Calculation	43/90	Limited	77 (70–84)
Math Fluency	82/90	Average	83 (79–86)
Applied Problems	10/90	Very Limited	74 (69–78)

Clinical Clusters

On both the Academic Skills and the Academic Applications clusters, Tanya's proficiency was very limited. These clusters measure basic skills and practical application of those skills across academic areas (basic skills: word identification, computation, and spelling; application: reading comprehension, math application, written expression). Tanya's limited academic skills are likely the major reason for her difficulty with the higher-level academic applications. Her proficiency was Limited to Average on the Academic Fluency cluster, indicating that she has somewhat less difficulty in the speed with which she reads and writes simple sentences and solves math facts.

Tanya's proficiency on each of the two tests of the Phoneme-Grapheme cluster was significantly different. On the Word Attack test, her proficiency was very limited (RPI 9/90), whereas on the Spelling of Sounds test, her proficiency was Limited to Average (RPI 81/90). Tanya found it easier to spell phonically regular nonsense words (made-up words that conform to common English spelling patterns) than to read them.

WJ III Variation and Discrepancy Procedures

On the WJ III, intraindividual variations are computed to show the likelihood of a person obtaining a particular score, given the average of her other cognitive and achievement cluster scores. Large variations indicate areas of significant strength and weakness. Tanya's verbal ability was a significant strength, whereas her cognitive efficiency was a significant weakness.

Additionally, based on her General Intellectual Ability-Standard score (GIA-Std), as well as her Oral Language-Extended scores, all of Tanya's academic scores were significantly below the predicted expectations. Her overall verbal and reasoning abilities were significantly higher than her current levels of reading, writing, and math performance. When her Oral Language-Extended score is used to predict her reading, writing, and math performance, only 1 person out of 100 would have such large discrepancies. When her Oral Language-Extended score is compared to her Broad Written Language score, only 1 out of 1,000 students with her predicted score would have a standard score as low. This means that Tanya's verbal abilities are significantly higher than her current academic performance levels.

BASC-2: Parent Ratings

Mrs. Rubens completed a BASC-2 rating scale regarding her perceptions of Tanya's temperament and behaviors. The Clinical level of behavior indicates behaviors that are significantly more frequent and/or severe than in others of the same age, and suggest a high level of maladjustment, usually warranting follow-up. The At-Risk level of behavior may identify a significant problem that may not be severe enough to require formal treatment or may identify a potential problem that needs careful monitoring. On the scales of Externalizing Problems, Internalizing Problems, Behavioral Symptoms Index, and Content (except Resiliency) higher scores indicate higher levels of concern. On the Adaptive scales and Resiliency (BSI), lower scores indicate higher levels of concern. The score ranges are described below in the following table. Mrs. Rubens's ratings of Tanya's behaviors resulted in At-Risk or Clinically Significant classifications on the scales for externalizing problems, internalizing problems, and behavioral symptoms.

Scale	T score[a]	Percentile Rank	Level[d]	Description of Scale as Related to Tanya
Externalizing Problems	**66**	**93**	**A-R**	
Hyperactivity	74	97	C	Engages in many disruptive, impulsive, and uncontrolled behaviors.
Aggression	64	91	A-R	Sometimes displays aggressive behaviors such as being argumentative, defiant, and/or threatening to others.
Conduct Problems	56	80	N	Demonstrates rule-breaking behavior no more than age-peers.
Internalizing Problems	**58**	**81**	**N**	
Anxiety	60	85	A-R	Sometimes displays behaviors stemming from worry, nervousness, or fear.
Depression	66	93	A-R	Sometimes seems withdrawn, pessimistic, and/or sad.
Somatization	44	33	N	Complains of health-related problems to about the same degree as age-peers.
Behavioral Symptoms Index[c]	**71**	**96**	**C**	
Atypicality	73	96	C	Engages in behaviors that are considered strange or odd, and generally seems disconnected from her surroundings.
Withdrawal	51	63	N	Does not avoid social situations and appears capable of developing and maintaining friendships with others.
Attention Problems	69	96	A-R	Has difficulty maintaining necessary levels of attention at school.
Content Scale				
Anger Control	62	88	A-R	Tends to become irritable quickly and has difficulty maintaining self-control when faced with adversity.
Bullying	59	84	N	Does not tend to act in an intrusive or threatening manner.
Developmental Social Disorders	58	79	N	Has social and communication skills typical of others her age.
Emotional Self-Control	73	97	C	Tends to become easily upset, frustrated, and/or angered in response to environmental changes.

Scale	T score[a]	Percentile Rank	Level[d]	Description of Scale as Related to Tanya
Executive Functioning	74	98	C	Has difficulty controlling and maintaining her behavior and mood.
Negative Emotionality	69	96	A	Tends to react negatively when faced with changes in everyday activities or routines.
Resiliency[b]	39	13	A-R	Has difficulty overcoming stress and anxiety.
Adaptive Skills[b]	**38**	**11**	**A-R**	
Adaptability	35	7	A-R	Has difficulty adapting to changing situations; takes longer than others to recover from difficult situations.
Social Skills	48	42	N	Possesses sufficient social skills and generally does not experience debilitating or abnormal social difficulties.
Leadership	40	17	A-R	Sometimes has difficulty making decisions, lacks creativity, and/or has trouble getting others to work together effectively.
Activities of Daily Living	34	7	A-R	Has difficulty performing simple daily tasks in a safe and efficient manner.
Functional Communication	40	17	A-R	Demonstrates poor receptive and expressive communication skills and has difficulty seeking out and finding information on her own.

a. Unless noted (b), T scores of 60-69 indicate an At-Risk level of behavior; T scores of 70 and above indicate a Clinical level.
b. T scores of 31–40 indicate an At-Risk level of behavior; 30 and below indicate a Clinical level.
c. Also includes Hyperactivity, Aggression, and Depression.
d. Levels: A-R is At-Risk, C is Clinical.

Behavior Assessment Scale for Children—2

In general, findings from the Parent Report of the BASC-2 indicate that Tanya is easily distracted and has difficulty maintaining attention and self-control. She has difficulty working independently and completing tasks. She becomes upset and frustrated easily when faced with homework and challenging tasks, worries about making mistakes, and has sudden mood changes. She tends to be argumentative when she does not get her own way. These difficulties with behavior and maintaining attention most likely affect her academic performance at home and in school.

In contrast, Tanya makes friends easily, compliments and shows interest in others, shares easily, and always encourages others to do their best. She enjoys social situations, has good communication skills, and does not engage in rule-breaking behaviors. She is kind, considerate, and enjoys social interactions with both adults and other children.

CONCLUSIONS

Tanya will be entering third grade in the fall. She was referred for an evaluation by her grandmother because of concerns regarding her academic progress and ability to pay attention. Tanya's verbal ability (acquired knowledge and language comprehension) is advanced when compared to her age-peers. In contrast, her processing speed and memory were both significantly lower. Presently, her overall proficiency in reading, writing, and mathematics skills is very limited.

DIAGNOSTIC IMPRESSIONS AND RATIONALE

Specific Reading Disability (Orthographic Dyslexia)

Tanya has extreme difficulty recognizing common words quickly and easily and in learning phonics skills so that she can sound words out. She has similar difficulty visualizing words and their spellings. She tends to rely on the way that words sound, rather than the way that they look. She confuses letters with similar appearance (e.g., b and d) and transposes the order of letters when writing (e.g., *hre* for *her*). Given her high level of verbal competence, her supportive grandmother, her retention in kindergarten, and her individualized homeschooling for five months, one would predict much higher levels of academic performance.

Attention-Deficit/Hyperactivity Disorder (ADHD)

Tanya has extreme difficulty concentrating in situations demanding sustained attention, such as sitting in a classroom or trying to complete homework. Symptoms of ADHD were observed in the past by school staff, as well as by her parents and this evaluator. The results of the BASC-2 indicate clinically significant behaviors consistent with the symptoms of ADHD.

EDUCATIONAL RECOMMENDATIONS

School Programming

Eligibility for learning disabilities (LD) services should be explored as soon as Tanya returns to school. Tanya has severe discrepancies between her cognitive abilities and her academic achievement, and has not made sufficient academic progress in school.

1. As she enters third grade, Tanya will require specific accommodations in the classroom, such as extended time on assignments and shortened homework assignments. Tanya would benefit from sitting at the front of the classroom so as to maximize attention.

2. Until her academic performance improves, Tanya will need adjustments in the difficulty level in school and homework assignments. Although she is entering third grade, her performance levels are significantly below her age-peers.

3. When possible, break Tanya's in-class assignments into smaller, more manageable chunks. Give her one part at a time, with instructions to hand in each as it is completed and pick up the next. Each time she hands in a portion of the work, provide reinforcement for completed work and time on task. Using this technique, she is likely to stay on task and complete assignments.

4. Tanya has very advanced language skills, as well as considerable knowledge about the world. Provide her with opportunities, such as oral reports and science projects (hands-on rather than written), so that she can use her strengths and excel in certain school subjects.

Parents

1. To make progress, Tanya requires specialized academic instruction from a teacher with expertise in teaching children with attention and learning difficulties. Ideally, intensive private tutoring should be provided during this summer for an hour three to five times a week.

2. Tanya's parents are encouraged to meet with their pediatrician to discuss the possibility of Attention-Deficit/Hyperactivity Disorder (ADHD) and medications that may be beneficial for increasing her focus and ability to concentrate.

3. Many of the behaviors that Tanya exhibits result from her problems with attention, learning, and memory. Keep in mind that her difficulties do not stem from a lack of effort or caring. Tanya wants to do well, but too often the expectations and academic demands are too high for her present skill levels.

4. Keep in mind also that attention is necessary as a foundation for storing information and learned skills in memory and, subsequently, retrieving it when needed. Tanya's difficulties on the processing speed and memory tests (e.g., Visual Matching and Numbers Reversed) of this evaluation might have been exacerbated by difficulties maintaining her concentration. Similarly, the interference of poor attention on memory might be making it more difficult for Tanya to learn and retrieve basic academic skills.

Initial Tutoring Goals

1. Provide Tanya with an intensive synthetic phonics program that will teach her phoneme-grapheme relationships directly. She will also require instruction that increases her recognition of common letter patterns, builds her understanding of spelling rules, and shows her how to use structural analysis. Reading and spelling instruction will be most effective if the patterns taught for reading are taught for spelling at the same time.

2. To build speed and accuracy in pronunciation of sight words and phonetically irregular words, use one-minute speed drills. Tanya should be timed daily on reading lists of common, irregular words, as quickly as she can but with accuracy as the primary goal. Her daily performance should be recorded and displayed on some type of graph. She should also practice spelling these words. The same type of speed drills can be used to help her learn to automatically recognize certain syllable patterns (e.g., closed vs. vowel-consonant-*e*) and common letter

combinations (e.g., *tion, ing, igh*). (See Speed Drills for Reading Fluency and Basic Skills in the Appendix.)

3. Teach Tanya basic math skills including addition and subtraction facts and the algorithms for adding and subtracting two-digit numbers without regrouping. When these are mastered, progress to problems involving regrouping. If Tanya is unable memorize math facts, or while she is doing so, teach Touch Math as a bridge to learning the facts and as a well-structured procedure for learning the algorithms.

4. Provide practice in math facts using fun video games. Many of these can be found on www.coolmath.com. When she is ready to learn multiplication facts, a good resource is "Timez Attack" which can be played on the Internet: www.bigbrainz.com/indexc.php.

5. Provide instruction in learning the value of coins and how to add them together and make change.

6. Tanya will feel frustrated by her attention and learning difficulties. Try to minimize her frustration by providing short periods of instruction (e.g., 10 to 15 minutes) that are followed by rewards or some type of engaging activity, such as a game. Alternatively, she may stay on task for longer periods of time if she is rewarded throughout the activity (e.g., chips, Monopoly money) for correct answers, for good reasoning related to the task, or for a short period of good attention and cooperation.

Table of Scores

Woodcock-Johnson III Normative Update Tests of Cognitive Abilities and Tests of Achievement (Form A)
WJ III NU Compuscore and Profiles Program, Version 3.
Norms based on age 8-11

WJ III Tests of Cognitive Abilities

CLUSTER/Test	Raw	W	AE	Proficiency	RPI	SS (68% Band)	GE
GIA (Std)	–	494	8–6	Average	88/90	97 (94–99)	3.2
THINKING ABILITY (Std)	–	499	9–4	Average	91/90	102 (99–106)	4.0
VERBAL ABILITY (Ext)	–	507	11–2	Advanced	98/90	116 (112–120)	5.8
COMP–KNOWLEDGE (Gc)	–	507	11–2	Advanced	98/90	116 (112–120)	5.8
Verbal Comprehension	–	503	10–6	Avg to adv	96/90	111 (105–116)	5.1
General Information	–	511	11–9	Advanced	99/90	120 (114–127)	6.3
COG EFFICIENCY (Ext)	–	478	6–11	Limited	61/90	79 (75–83)	1.6
Visual Matching	22–2	472	6–9	Limited	48/90	69 (65–74)	1.5
Decision Speed	20	485	7–6	Lmtd to avg	78/90	85 (80–91)	2.2
Numbers Reversed	8	476	6–11	Limited	57/90	87 (82–93)	1.6
Memory for Words	14	478	6–7	Limited	56/90	87 (80–94)	1.3
PROCESSING SPEED (Gs)	–	479	7–0	Limited	64/90	75 (71–78)	1.7
Visual Matching	22–2	472	6–9	Limited	48/90	69 (65–74)	1.5
Decision Speed	20	485	7–6	Lmtd to avg	78/90	85 (80–91)	2.2
SHORT OF TERM MEMORY (Gsm)	–	477	6–9	Limited	57/90	84 (78–89)	1.5
Numbers Reversed	8	476	6–11	Limited	57/90	87 (82–93)	1.6
Memory for Words	14	478	6–7	Limited	56/90	87 (80–94)	1.3
WORKING MEMORY	–	486	7–9	Lmtd to avg	77/90	91 (86–95)	2.4
Auditory Working Memory	15	495	8–10	Average	90/90	100 (95–104)	3.5
Numbers Reversed	8	476	6–11	Limited	57/90	87 (82–93)	1.6
ADDITIONAL TESTS							
Rapid Picture Naming	85	487	7–6	Lmtd to avg	81/90	92 (90–95)	2.2
Visual-Auditory Learning	15–E	497	8–9	Average	89/90	99 (94–104)	3.4
Concept Formation	22–E	496	9–1	Average	91/90	101 (97–105)	3.8

(continued)

CLUSTER/Test	Raw	W	AE	Proficiency	RPI	SS (68% Band)	GE
Spatial Relations	61–D	498	9–0	Average	90/90	100 (96–105)	3.6
Sound Blending	19	503	10–7	Average	94/90	106 (99–112)	5.2

WJ III Tests of Achievement

CLUSTER/Test	Raw	W	AE	Proficiency	RPI	SS (68% Band)	GE
ORAL LANGUAGE (Ext)	–	503	10–11	Avg to adv	96/90	114 (110–118)	5.6
Story Recall	–	508	>20	Avg to adv	96/90	124 (118–130)	>13.3
Picture Vocabulary	28	513	12–9	Advanced	99/90	116 (111–121)	7.3
Understanding Directions	–	494	8–11	Average	90/90	101 (95–106)	3.6
Oral Comprehension	19	499	9–9	Average	95/90	106 (101–111)	4.4
ORAL EXPRESSION	–	510	13–6	Advanced	98/90	122 (117–127)	8.0
Story Recall	–	508	>20	Avg to adv	96/90	124 (118–130)	>13.3
Picture Vocabulary	28	513	12–9	Advanced	99/90	116 (111–121)	7.3
LISTENING COMP	–	496	9–5	Average	93/90	104 (100–109)	4.0
Understanding Directions	–	494	8–11	Average	90/90	101 (95–106)	3.6
Oral Comprehension	19	499	9–9	Average	95/90	106 (101–111)	4.4
BROAD READING	–	462	7–4	Limited	31/90	77 (75–80)	2.0
Letter-Word Identification	31	434	7–3	V limited	4/90	79 (77–82)	2.0
Passage Comprehension	19	469	7–2	Limited	36/90	82 (79–86)	1.9
Reading Fluency	20	482	7–8	Lmtd to avg	78/90	88 (83–93)	2.4
BRIEF READING	–	451	7–3	V limited	14/90	78 (75–80)	1.9
Letter-Word Identification	31	434	7–3	V limited	4/90	79 (77–82)	2.0
Passage Comprehension	19	469	7–2	Limited	36/90	82 (79–86)	1.9
BASIC READING SKILLS	–	443	7–1	V limited	6/90	77 (75–80)	1.8
Word Attack	5	452	6–10	V limited	9/90	79 (75–83)	1.5
Letter-Word Identification	31	434	7–3	V limited	4/90	79 (77–82)	2.0
PHON/GRAPH KNOW	–	472	7–0	Limited	39/90	82 (79–86)	1.7
Spelling of Sounds	21	491	7–9	Lmtd to avg	81/90	91 (85–97)	2.5
Word Attack	5	452	6–10	V limited	9/90	79 (75–83)	1.5
BROAD WRITTEN LANG	–	461	6–10	V limited	23/90	64 (60–68)	1.6
Writing Fluency	10	484	8–1	Lmtd to avg	81/90	92 (85–99)	2.7
Spelling	17	442	6–7	V limited	4/90	67 (62–71)	1.3
Writing Samples	8–B	456	6–9	V limited	14/90	66 (61–72)	1.4
BRIEF WRITING	–	449	6–8	V limited	7/90	65 (61–68)	1.4
Spelling	17	442	6–7	V limited	4/90	67 (62–71)	1.3
Writing Samples	8–B	456	6–9	V limited	14/90	66 (61–72)	1.4
WRITTEN EXPRESSION	–	470	7–1	Limited	46/90	74 (70–79)	1.8
Writing Fluency	10	484	8–1	Lmtd to avg	81/90	92 (85–99)	2.7
Writing Samples	8–B	456	6–9	V limited	14/90	66 (61–72)	1.4
BROAD MATH	–	468	7–1	Limited	42/90	72 (68–76)	1.8
Calculation	9	467	7–4	Limited	43/90	77 (70–84)	2.0
Math Fluency	30	487	7–7	Average	82/90	83 (79–86)	2.3
Applied Problems	22	449	6–9	V limited	10/90	74 (69–78)	1.5

CLUSTER/Test	Raw	W	AE	Proficiency	RPI	SS (68% Band)	GE
BRIEF MATH	–	458	7–0	V Limited	22/90	72 (68–76)	1.7
Calculation	9	467	7–4	Limited	43/90	77 (70–84)	2.0
Applied Problems	22	449	6–9	V Limited	10/90	74 (69–78)	1.5
MATH CALC SKILLS	–	477	7–5	Limited	65/90	77 (71–82)	2.0
Calculation	9	467	7–4	Limited	43/90	77 (70–84)	2.0
Math Fluency	30	487	7–7	Average	82/90	83 (79–86)	2.3
ACADEMIC SKILLS	–	448	7–1	V Limited	10/90	72 (69–74)	1.7
Letter–Word Identification	31	434	7–3	V Limited	4/90	79 (77–82)	2.0
Spelling	17	442	6–7	V Limited	4/90	67 (62–71)	1.3
Calculation	9	467	7–4	Limited	43/90	77 (70–84)	2.0
ACADEMIC APPS	–	458	6–11	V Limited	18/90	68 (65–71)	1.6
Passage Comprehension	19	469	7–2	Limited	36/90	82 (79–86)	1.9
Writing Samples	8–B	456	6–9	V Limited	14/90	66 (61–72)	1.4
Applied Problems	22	449	6–9	V Limited	10/90	74 (69–78)	1.5
ACADEMIC FLUENCY	–	484	7–10	Lmtd to Avg	80/90	86 (81–90)	2.5
Reading Fluency	20	482	7–8	Lmtd to Avg	78/90	88 (83–93)	2.4
Writing Fluency	10	484	8–1	Lmtd to Avg	81/90	92 (85–99)	2.7
Math Fluency	30	487	7–7	Average	82/90	83 (79–86)	2.3
BRIEF ACHIEVEMENT	–	442	6–11	V Limited	5/90	69 (66–71)	1.6
Letter–Word Identification	31	434	7–3	V Limited	4/90	79 (77–82)	2.0
Spelling	17	442	6–7	V Limited	4/90	67 (62–71)	1.3
Applied Problems	22	449	6–9	V Limited	10/90	74 (69–78)	1.5

VARIATIONS	STANDARD SCORES			VARIATION		Significant at + or – 1.50 SD (SEE)
	Actual	Predicted	Difference	PR	SD	
Intra-Cognitive (Std)						
VERBAL ABILITY (Std)	111	94	17	93	+1.51	Yes
THINKING ABILITY (Std)	102	96	6	72	+0.59	No
COG EFFICIENCY (Std)	79	104	–25	3	–1.84	Yes

VARIATIONS	STANDARD SCORES			VARIATION		Significant at + or – 1.50 SD (SEE)
	Actual	Predicted	Difference	PR	SD	
Intra-Achievement (Std)						
BROAD READING	77	84	–7	22	–0.79	No
BROAD MATH	72	87	–15	8	–1.39	No
BROAD WRITTEN LANG	64	89	–25	1	–2.49	Yes
ORAL LANGUAGE (Std)	111	80	31	99	+2.53	Yes

(continued)

DISCREPANCIES	STANDARD SCORES			DISCREPANCY		Significant at − 1.50 SD (SEE)
	Actual	Predicted	Difference	PR	SD	
Intellectual Ability/Achievement Discrepancies*						
BROAD READING	77	98	−21	4	−1.75	Yes
BASIC READING SKILLS	77	98	−21	4	−1.75	Yes
BROAD MATH	72	98	−26	2	−2.14	Yes
MATH CALC SKILLS	77	98	−21	6	−1.54	Yes
BROAD WRITTEN LANG	64	98	−34	0.3	−2.72	Yes
WRITTEN EXPRESSION	74	98	−24	3	−1.83	Yes
ORAL LANGUAGE (Ext)	114	97	17	96	+1.70	No
ORAL EXPRESSION	122	98	24	98	+2.03	No
LISTENING COMP	104	98	6	73	+0.60	No
BRIEF READING	78	98	−20	4	−1.77	Yes
BRIEF MATH	72	98	−26	2	−2.14	Yes
BRIEF WRITING	65	98	−33	0.4	−2.64	Yes

*These discrepancies compare WJ III GIA (Std) with Broad, Basic, Brief, and Applied ACH clusters.

DISCREPANCIES	STANDARD SCORES			DISCREPANCY		Significant at − 1.50 SD (SEE)
	Actual	Predicted	Difference	PR	SD	
Oral Language/Achievement Discrepancies*						
BROAD READING	77	108	−31	0.5	−2.56	Yes
BASIC READING SKILLS	77	107	−30	1	−2.41	Yes
BROAD MATH	72	107	−35	1	−2.54	Yes
MATH CALC SKILLS	77	105	−28	3	−1.94	Yes
BROAD WRITTEN LANG	64	107	−43	<0.1	−3.26	Yes
WRITTEN EXPRESSION	74	106	−32	1	−2.38	Yes
BRIEF READING	78	108	−30	1	−2.49	Yes
BRIEF MATH	72	107	−35	0.5	−2.57	Yes
BRIEF WRITING	65	107	−42	<0.1	−3.18	Yes

*These discrepancies compare Oral Language (Ext) with Broad, Basic, Brief, and Applied ACH clusters.

DISCREPANCIES	STANDARD SCORES			DISCREPANCY		Significant at + or − 1.50 SD (SEE)
	Actual	Predicted	Difference	PR	SD	
Predicted Achievement/Achievement Discrepancies*						
BROAD READING	77	95	−18	4	−1.72	Yes
BASIC READING SKILLS	77	96	−19	4	−1.73	Yes
BROAD MATH	72	91	−19	4	−1.70	Yes
MATH CALC SKILLS	77	87	−10	20	−0.86	No
BROAD WRITTEN LANG	64	92	−28	1	−2.41	Yes
WRITTEN EXPRESSION	74	93	−19	6	−1.53	Yes
ORAL LANGUAGE (Ext)	114	98	16	92	+1.41	No
ORAL EXPRESSION	122	100	22	95	+1.68	Yes
LISTENING COMP	104	97	7	72	+0.60	No

DISCREPANCIES	STANDARD SCORES			DISCREPANCY		Significant at + or – 1.50 SD (SEE)
	Actual	Predicted	Difference	PR	SD	
BRIEF READING	78	97	–19	3	–1.83	Yes
BRIEF MATH	72	93	–21	3	–1.83	Yes
BRIEF WRITING	65	93	–28	1	–2.50	Yes
*These discrepancies compare predicted achievement scores with Broad, Basic, Brief, and Applied ACH clusters.						

DISCREPANCIES	STANDARD SCORES			DISCREPANCY		Significant at + or – 1.50 SD (SEE)
	Actual	Predicted	Difference	PR	SD	
GIA Std/Cognitive						
COMP-KNOWLEDGE (Gc)	116	97	19	98	+1.97	Yes
PROCESS SPEED (Gs)	75	98	–23	3	–1.87	Yes
SHORT-TERM MEM (Gsm)	84	98	–14	11	–1.25	No
WORKING MEMORY	91	97	–6	27	–0.62	No

CASE 17

Learning Disabilities and Mathematics
A School Psychological Framework

Steven Feifer

At face value, reading and math seem diametrically opposed. For instance, reading uses the language of words whereas math uses the language of numbers. Also, when students are engaged in reading text, they are traditionally taught to read from left to right. Conversely, when learning basic problem solving techniques in math, students are taught to start on the right side of the problem, in the ones column, then work toward the left. However, math and reading still share a final common destination: to develop *fluency*. Students who have a strong fundamental understanding of phonological properties in reading ultimately develop rapid and automatic word recognition skills, and eventually become fluent. Russell (1999) defined mathematical fluency in terms of a compilation of three foundational skills: efficiency, accuracy, and flexibility. *Efficiency* is the ability to carry out steps easily and in a reasonable amount of time. *Accuracy* implies that the method used yields a correct solution. Finally, *flexibility* requires the student approach a problem through a variety of different means. It stands to reason that fluency in mathematics is only achieved when all three components are present.

The following case illustrates the importance of developing mathematical fluency in children by promoting *number sense*. It is helpful for students to discover and explore patterns in numbers in order to foster mathematical fluency skills. The specific recommendations offered are geared toward developing *number sense*, and not simply a collection of gadgets and tricks designed to promote fact acquisition. This case also highlights how relatively unimportant full-scale intelligence scores have become in diagnosing a learning disability. Simply put, the study of mathematics disorders from a brain-behavioral perspective involves comprehending the various cognitive attributes that facilitate calculation and other mental operations. Furthermore,

the reader should be aware of the inherent value of a true diagnostic mathematical test such as the PAL-II, which helps to analyze problematic areas in mathematical skill building. In summary, this case may also give insight into the dynamic properties of a learning disability and the many ways in which it can manifest to hinder the academic development of children in school.

PSYCHOLOGICAL REPORT

Name:	Brianna Zimmerman
Sex:	Female
Date of Birth:	02/12/2001
Age:	9 yrs. 0 months
School:	Jackson Road Elementary School
Grade:	3rd
Teacher:	Mrs. James
Test Dates:	02/03/09, 02/17/2010
Examiner:	Steven G. Feifer, D.Ed.

REASON FOR REFERRAL

Brianna was referred for a psychological assessment due to her continued difficulties in mathematics. This assessment was administered in order to determine her present educational needs.

TESTS ADMINISTERED

Wechsler Intelligence Scale for Children, Fourth Edition (WISC-IV)

Developmental Test of Visual-Motor Integration: Fifth Edition (Beery VMI)

Gray Oral Reading Test: Fourth Edition (GORT-4)

Process Assessment of the Learner: Mathematics, Second Edition (PAL-II)

Parent questionnaire

Records review

DEVELOPMENTAL HISTORY

Brianna is a 9-year-old child who resides with both parents and her older sister. Brianna was born full term and weighed 7 pounds, 5 ounces at birth. No medical concerns were reported with either the pregnancy or delivery, and most early developmental milestones were reached within normal limits. There is no history of learning disabilities in the family. Her mother described Brianna as being a happy, loving, and caring child who enjoys music and sports. Her only concern regarding Brianna's academic development was her difficulties with mathematics. Her mother indicated that Brianna frequently transposes numbers, has difficulty telling time, and often avoids homework involving math. Brianna indicated she enjoys music, shopping, and school, particularly her science class. She also wants to play on a soccer team this year.

EDUCATIONAL HISTORY

Brianna attended pre-kindergarten, although she was absent for 26 days. She has attended Jackson Road Elementary School since kindergarten. In kindergarten, Brianna was reported as not mastering early benchmark skills in mathematics. She received numerous interventions for language arts and mathematics in first grade, including participation in the school reading support program and in the Numbers World math intervention program. Last year, Brianna received reading intervention services in the Early Success reading program, had Targeted Math intervention services, and had an Individual Learning Plan (ILP) for both reading and mathematics. According to her third-grade teacher, Mrs. James, Brianna has extremely weak number sense and has difficulty reading a "hundreds chart"; she often transposes numbers, struggles to count forward and backward from points on a number line, and is lacking many basic numeric concepts and number

identification skills. Mrs. James indicated Brianna has not met most third-grade benchmark standards in mathematics and that her skills were on approximately a first-grade level. Currently, Brianna is receiving resource services from the math intervention specialist. Brianna's mother questioned the value of this service because Brianna is becoming increasingly frustrated by her limited progress. Mrs. James described Brianna as being more confident and working closer to grade level in reading and language arts. Brianna's teachers have no concerns regarding behavior or attention, and they describe Brianna as being a highly motivated student who puts forth her best effort each day.

BEHAVIORAL OBSERVATIONS

Brianna was evaluated on two separate occasions. She warmed up quickly to the assessment process. She responded to questions at an appropriate pace, was attentive and well focused throughout the evaluation, and had little difficulty comprehending test directions on their initial presentation. She was polite and respectful, although she spoke in a quiet, timid voice. No emotional or behavioral issues were evident at this time. Brianna demonstrated good general problem-solving skills, although she had significant difficulty on most visual-perceptual types of tasks. For instance, she tended to rotate her paper when drawing or copying shapes, and had extreme difficulty when working with most math-related activities. Brianna worked somewhat slowly when engaged in most nonverbal problem-solving measures and had a tendency to become quickly discouraged. In contrast, she approached most language-related measures in a more confident style and exhibited more persistence on these tasks. In summary, Brianna put forth an excellent effort throughout both testing sessions, and the following test results should be a valid measure of her skills and abilities.

TEST RESULTS AND INTERPRETATION

Test results are described as standard scores (SS), scaled scores (ScS), verbal labels corresponding to standard scores and scaled scores, and percentile ranks (PR). The standard score confidence interval was set at 95%. The verbal labels are as follows:

SS	ScS	Verbal Label
>130	17–19	Extremely High
121–130	15–16	Well Above Average
111–120	13–14	Above Average
90–110	8–12	Average
80–89	6–7	Below Average
70–79	4–5	Well Below Average
<70	1–3	Extremely Low

Cognitive Measures

Brianna was administered the WISC-IV in order to assess her overall level of cognitive functioning. This test measures four basic styles of information processing and problem solving. The Verbal Comprehension Index (VCI) assesses a student's verbal reasoning and comprehension, as well as general language development skills. The Perceptual Reasoning Index (PRI) assesses nonverbal reasoning and visual pattern recognition skills. The Working Memory Index (WMI) measures the ability of a student to hold information in mind while problem solving. Lastly, the Processing Speed Index (PSI) measures speed of performance on several timed paper-and-pencil tasks. All four constructs combine to yield an overall or Full Scale measure of cognitive functioning.

Cautionary Note:

It should be cautioned that intelligence tests do not necessarily measure important attributes for learning such as creativity, motivation to learn, or personality styles. Furthermore, test score performance can be altered by cultural background, preexisting learning conditions, and environmental factors.

Index	Composite Score	Confidence Interval	Range	Percentile Rank
Verbal Comprehension	93	87–100	Average	32
Perceptual Reasoning	69	64–79	Lower Extreme	2
Working Memory	80	74–89	Well Below Average/ Below Average	21
Processing Speed	88	80–98	Below Average/ Average	7

Brianna's Full Scale IQ was 78, which was in the Well Below Average to Below Average range of functioning, and at the 7th percentile compared to peers. This score should be interpreted with caution given the large variability among her cognitive domain scores. Her specific subtest scores were as follows:

Verbal Comprehension		
Core Subtests	Scaled Score	Ability Range
Similarities: A measure of abstract verbal reasoning skills, as pairs of words are presented orally in order to determine common relationships.	10	Average
Vocabulary: The child defines words read aloud on a page. Measures overall word knowledge and general vocabulary skills. Influenced by education and cultural factors.	9	Average
Comprehension: Students respond to questions pertaining to social rules and regulations. Measures verbal reasoning, and the ability to use past experiences to solve practical problem-solving situations.	7	Below Average
Note: Mean = 10, Standard deviation = 3		

Brianna's Verbal Comprehension Index was 93, which was in the Average range of functioning, and at the 32nd percentile compared to peers. She performed well when defining individual vocabulary words (Vocabulary), and when determining common relationships between pairs of words (Similarities). Stronger scores in these areas often suggest good development of verbal concepts. Brianna had mild difficulty when responding to "wh" questions pertaining to everyday facts and events (Comprehension), suggesting a weaker understanding of social and cultural situations. Still, no significant weaknesses were apparent.

Perceptual Reasoning		
Core Subtests	Scaled Score	Ability Range
Block Design: The child assembles colored blocks to form various patterns as seen on a stimulus card. Measures visual-spatial reasoning skills and visual pattern recognition.	5	Well Below Average
Picture Concepts: A visual-verbal reasoning task, as students select from a series of pictures those that share common characteristics.	4	Well Below Average
Matrix Reasoning: The student selects from a series of pictures the one that best illustrates the missing portion of a figure, or best completes a matrix or analogy. Measures visual pattern recognition skills and abstract reasoning skills.	6	Below Average
Note: Mean = 10, Standard deviation = 3		

Brianna's scores indicated a significant weakness in perceptual reasoning, as she scored 69, which was in the Lower Extreme range, and at the 2nd percentile compared to peers. She had extreme difficulty solving most visual-spatial problems. For instance, she had difficulty assembling colored blocks to duplicate pictures of abstract designs (Block Design) and identifying common characteristics among familiar pictures (Picture Concepts). Brianna also had difficulty with matching basic patterns among groups of pictures (Matrix Reasoning).

Working Memory		
Core Subtests	**Scaled Score**	**Ability Range**
Digit Span: A series of orally presented digits that the child repeats back in order and reversed. Measures auditory short-term memory, sequencing skills, and attention.	7	Below Average
Letter-Number Sequencing: The child hears a sequence of letters and numbers and must recall the numbers in ascending order and the letters in alphabetical order. Measures auditory working memory, sequencing, mental manipulation, and attention.	6	Below Average
Note: Mean = 10, Standard deviation = 3		

Brianna's Working Memory Index was 80, which was in the Well Below Average to Below Average range of performance and at the 9th percentile compared to peers. She had difficulty repeating a series of digits presented by the examiner (Digit Span), especially when required to repeat them in reverse order. Also, Brianna struggled with repeating both letters and numbers in their correct sequence (Letter-Number Sequencing) which may be due to her poor visual-perceptual skills and difficulty visualizing numbers and letters in the "mind's eye."

Processing Speed		
Core Subtests	**Scaled Score**	**Ability Range**
Coding: A timed subtest requiring students to copy various symbols. Measures visual-motor speed, short-term memory, visual-motor coordination, and motivation to the task at hand.	8	Average
Symbol Search: A timed task requiring the child to scan a group of pictures to determine if they match a target stimulus. Measures visual processing speed, visual-motor coordination, sustained attention, and concentration.	8	Average
Note: Mean = 10, Standard deviation = 3		

Lastly, Brianna's Processing Speed Index was 88, which is at the lower end of the Average range of performance

and at the 21st percentile compared to age-peers. She performed adequately on a timed paper-and-pencil task requiring her to copy various shapes (Coding), and when visually scanning groups of symbols to determine a match (Symbol Search). In summary, Brianna's overall cognitive profile suggested good development of verbal concepts, adequate processing speed, and significant weaknesses in solving most types of visual-perceptual problems.

Visual-Motor Integration

On the Beery VMI, a test of visual perceptual skills requiring students to copy various geometric designs, Brianna's performance was in the Average range with a standard score of 92, at the 30th percentile. This score indicated little difficulty with visual-motor integration skills. Brianna is left-handed and demonstrated an adequate pencil grip. She often tried, however, to rotate the paper when drawing more complicated designs. Often, students with difficulties on visual-perceptual tasks and visual-motor integration struggle on most paper-and-pencil tasks, and may struggle with handwriting as well, but in Brianna's case, no weaknesses were observed.

Academic Measures

Reading

Brianna was administered the Gray Oral Reading Test – 4 to assess her ability to read with speed and accuracy and to evaluate her comprehension skills. This was a timed (but not time limited) reading measure. Her oral reading quotient was 103 (+/–6), which was in the Average range and at the 58th percentile compared to age-peers. Her score corresponded to approximately a late third-grade to early fourth-grade reading level. Brianna's oral reading was fluent, although she often used her finger to keep her place. Still, she had little difficulty automatically recognizing words and applied decoding strategies to unfamiliar words. Brianna demonstrated adequate reading comprehension skills and had little difficulty answering questions about each passage. She obtained the following scaled scores:

Gray Oral Reading Tests – 4	Standard Score	Range	Grade Equivalent
Rate Score	10	Average	3.7
Accuracy Score	11	Average	4.7
Fluency Score	10	Average	4.2
Comprehension Score	11	Average	4.2
Oral Reading Quotient	103	Average	
Note: Mean = 10, Standard deviation = 3			

Mathematics

Brianna's overall development of basic mathematical processes was assessed using selected subtests from the Process Assessment of the Learner – Second Edition: Diagnostic Assessment for Math (PAL-II). This test examines core math-related processes such as oral counting, computational processing, spatial working memory, multistep problem solving, and math fact retrieval. Her overall scores were as follows:

PAL-II Math Subtests	Scaled Score	Percentile Rank	Range
Numeric Coding—The child views a set of numerals, then a second set, and decides whether the second set is the same as the first. In Task B, the child views a set of numerals and then must write them from memory.	9	37	Average
Finding the Bug—Assesses the ability to detect computational or fact retrieval errors. The child must determine which math operational problem among four choices is incorrect.	4	2	Well Below Average
Fact Retrieval: Look and Write			
Fact Retrieval: Addition—The child has 60 seconds to solve as many written addition problems as possible.	5	5	Well Below Average
Fact Retrieval: Subtraction—The child has 60 seconds to solve as many written subtraction problems as possible.	3	1	Extremely Low
Fact Retrieval: Mixed Addition & Subtraction—The child has 60 seconds to solve as many written addition and subtraction problems as possible.	3	1	Extremely Low
Fact Retrieval: Multiplication—The child has 60 seconds to solve as many written multiplication problems as possible.	4	2	Well Below Average
Fact Retrieval: Division—The child has 60 seconds to solve as many written division problems as possible.	n/a		
Fact Retrieval: Listen and Say			
Fact Retrieval: Addition—The child has 60 seconds to solve as many oral addition problems as possible.	5	5	Well Below Average
Fact Retrieval: Subtraction—The child has 60 seconds to solve as many oral subtraction problems as possible.	5	5	Well Below Average

PAL-II Math Subtests	Scaled Score	Percentile Rank	Range
Fact Retrieval: Mixed Addition & Subtraction—The child has 60 seconds to solve as many oral addition and subtraction problems as possible, presented in mixed order.	4	2	Well Below Average
Fact Retrieval: Multiplication—The child has 60 seconds to solve as many oral multiplication problems as possible.	6	9	Below Average
Fact Retrieval: Division—The child has 60 seconds to solve as many oral division problems as possible.	n/a		
Fact Retrieval: Mixed Multiplication & Division—The child has 60 seconds to solve as many oral multiplication and division problems as possible, presented in mixed order.	n/a		
Working Memory Tasks			
Quantitative Working Memory—The child hears a number then is asked to perform a mathematical operation mentally, and then recall the original number.	8	25	Average
Spatial Working Memory Location—The child is shown pictures of dominoes and asked questions requiring revisualization of the number patterns.	6	9	Below Average
Spatial Working Memory Drawing—The child is shown pictures of dominoes, and once it is removed, must draw a picture of the domino pattern.	4	9	Below Average
Note: Mean = 10, Standard deviation = 3			

Brianna's mathematical processing abilities were extremely limited, as most of her skills were in the Well Below Average to Extremely Low range of functioning. Her overall number sense and knowledge of basic number relationships were somewhat weak. For instance, she had difficulty retrieving facts when calculating math equations, as well as when attempting to solve problems presented orally. Brianna was able to answer only a few single-digit addition and subtraction facts and was unable to solve two-digit computation problems. In addition, she was unable to solve problems involving single-digit multiplication or division and was confused with mixed addition and subtraction facts. Lastly, Brianna had significant difficulty on a multiple-choice task requiring her to identify which of four math problems was incorrect (Find the Bug).

Regarding working memory for numbers, Brianna was able to solve basic math equations in her head when provided enough time (Quantitative Working Memory). In addition, she worked well on a visual short-term memory task requiring her to recall and write numbers flashed before her (Numeric Coding). She had difficulty, however, on a spatial working memory task that required her to hold an array of dots in mind, and reproduce them.

Overall, Brianna's math skills were extremely limited; she had memorized relatively few facts, did not understand multiplication or division concepts, had difficulty holding a mental array of symbols in her head, and exhibited a poor understanding of number relationships.

SUMMARY AND RECOMMENDATIONS

Brianna is a 9-year-old, third-grade student who was referred for a psychological assessment due to continued difficulty with mathematics. Brianna has not met most third-grade benchmarks in mathematics, and her skills were reported as being on approximately a first-grade level. Conversely, Brianna was described as working closer to grade level in language arts. Brianna has received numerous academic interventions in reading and math. No concerns exist regarding behavior or attention.

Current testing revealed her overall cognitive abilities were in the Well Below Average range of functioning (FSIQ = 78). This score should be interpreted with caution given the large variability among her cognitive domain scores. Brianna demonstrated good development of verbal concepts and significant weaknesses on most visual-perceptual reasoning tasks. Further testing noted significant visual processing difficulties as Brianna often rotated her paper when writing and often used her finger reading aloud. Brianna's overall math skills were extremely limited. She has memorized relatively few facts, does not understand multiplication or division concepts, has difficulty holding a mental array of symbols in her head, and exhibits a poor understanding of number relationships. In summary, test results and observations indicate that Brianna has a specific learning disability related to mathematics. In light of these results, the following recommendations are offered.

RECOMMENDATIONS

1. Brianna should be considered for special education services under the category of Specific Learning Disabilities due to her marked limitations in mathematics.

2. Evaluate Brianna's understanding of the concepts underlying addition and subtraction in a variety of situations and with a variety of materials. She may not understand that numbers represent the quantity of objects (or any other type of entity) within a set, that addition is the combining of sets, and that zero also represents a set that has nothing in it (the null set). Before Brianna will be able to make sense of the basic arithmetic facts, she must understand sets and how they can be combined.

Instructional Approach

1. Brianna may have to be retaught preacademic arithmetic concepts and then progress into the use of numbers. Throughout this process, use a highly structured, sequential program for teaching preacademic and then basic arithmetic skills that includes teacher-directed instruction, hands-on activities to develop a clear understanding of arithmetic concepts, continuous review and integration of previously learned skills, and ongoing evaluation.

2. Teach all new concepts and extensions of known concepts first with concrete materials, making sure that Brianna has a chance to experiment with the materials and understands the new concept before moving to the next level of abstractness. For example, when teaching addition, use a variety of materials to represent the sets to be combined. Make sure she understands or learns the related terminology (e.g., addition, plus, added to, total, all together) by having her talk about what she is doing with the materials. Provide plenty of practice in manipulating the materials to solve problems. Then present similar types of problems using pictures and requiring her to draw pictures to represent the problems posed. When she has mastered this step, associate these materials with numbers. If necessary, tallies may be used as a level between pictures and symbols. The last step is to use numbers alone to represent new concepts. [Adapted from Principles and Standards for School Mathematics, National Council of Teachers of Mathematics, 2000.]

Number Sense and Numeration

Engage Brianna in guided activities to develop the concept of sets, including what makes a set, the empty set, naming sets by attributes (classification), and representing sets by the amount of items (number). A suggestion for the sequence of concepts to be taught follows.

1. The members of a set may or may not contain objects/pictures that have a common attribute (e.g., a star, a ball, and a tree may all share membership in a set just because they are described as such). Teach this concept with real objects—the concrete level.

2. Sets in which members have a common attribute may be named for that attribute (e.g., a group of colored objects may be sorted into a red set and a green set).

3. A set with no members is still a set, represented by the number zero.

4. At the semi-concrete level, items in sets may be represented by pictures.

5. At the semi-abstract level, items in sets may be represented by a tally mark. The instructional objective is that sets can be represented by the number rather than the other characteristics of the items in the set.

Counting and One-to-One Correspondence

1. Teach Brianna to count to 10 and provide practice in activities that will highlight their use in daily living. For example, have Brianna count the students ordering milk, pass out a certain number of books, or play board games that involve moving a marker according to a number on a chosen card or spinner.

2. Teach Brianna that when items are counted, the order in which the numbers are counted does not matter and the last number named represents the number of the set.

3. Engage Brianna in activities to develop the concept of one-to-one correspondence. This is a prerequisite to understanding addition and subtraction.

4. Teach Brianna to use one-to-one correspondence to compare quantities and teach the associated vocabulary. For example, have her match each member of one set with a member in another set. Help her verbalize if one set has the same number as the other set or not. Gradually, introduce comparative terms such as *more, less, same, equal* and have her use these terms in statements describing the relationship between the sets (e.g., "There are more shoes than stars;" "There are the same number of shoes as stars.")

5. When using numerals in simple addition, some students do not "count on" because they still don't understand that the quantity of a group of objects in a set is invariable (as long as nothing is done to it). To help Brianna understand the process of counting on, have her count all the objects in two sets and write the answer. Then guide her in counting on and in comparing the answers. She may need to practice this many times to understand the validity and efficiency of the latter approach.

Using Numerals

1. Use games to reinforce the idea of numbers representing a set and rapid recognition of the number of items in a set. For example, play a version of Bingo in which the teacher holds up a card with a set of dots on it and the students cover the corresponding number on their Bingo cards. To reinforce rapid recognition of item amounts up to 5, the teacher can show the cards for decreasing intervals of time.

2. After Brianna understands that addition is the combining of two sets to form a new set, have her give each of the addend sets a number (in writing or with number tiles). Then have her count the items in the combined set and give that a number. Show that combining the numbers of items in both sets makes a new number that represents both sets together.

3. Counting up on a number line means adding a new set to the current set, but doing it one by one.

4. Use objects or pictures to teach Brianna that sets may be broken up into a variety of subsets. For example, a set of five objects contains: five subsets of one member each; one subset of two and one subset of three; one subset of four and one subset of one; or one subset of five and one subset of zero. These correspond to the addition facts.

5. As a conceptual basis for subtraction, use manipulatives or pictures to teach Brianna that one subset of a set may be removed from the set, leaving the other subset(s).

Math Fact Learning and Retrieval

1. Do not require Brianna to memorize facts until her understanding of the underlying concepts are firmly established. Then, have her memorize the math facts as each operation is introduced.

2. Continuously reinforce previously learned facts interspersed with practice of more recently learned facts. Continue fact practice even when Brianna seems to know them automatically.

3. While teaching addition facts, help Brianna to develop flexibility and a deeper understanding of number relationships by working with addition sentences (e.g., 2 + 5 = 7). This will reinforce the addition facts while

increasing readiness to learn the subtraction facts. Provide a variety of guided activities with addition sentences in which one of the numbers or relational signs is omitted. Have Brianna figure out the number or sign that would make the sentence true and explain how she did so. Use the fact groups Brianna is studying for the arithmetic sentences. As she develops facility in filling in the missing element, she will be able to come up with the related subtraction facts. The ability to complete $6 + 2 = \square$, $6 + \square = 8$, $\square + 6 = 8$, $2 \square 6 = 8$ and $2 \square 6 = 8$ facilitates comprehension and acquisition of $8 - 2 = 6$ and $8 - 6 = 2$.

Motivation

1. To increase motivation, teach Brianna how to monitor her progress in automaticity of math facts by using a chart with each math fact in each square. As she learns each fact to an automatic level, allow her to highlight the square. If she understands the commutative property, she may fill in two squares for each fact learned.

2. Use computer programs to motivate drill and practice, but do not let it replace regular monitoring of fact knowledge through oral response to flash cards and written timed math probes.

Problem-Solving Instruction

1. Do not teach Brianna "tricks" for solving math problems, such as identifying cue words (i.e., how many or altogether means addition). Instead draw attention to understanding the language of the problems.

2. Ensure that when Brianna is asked to solve story problems, the computation involved is not difficult. This will allow Brianna to concentrate on understanding the language of the problem.

3. Provide Brianna with extensive guided practice in reading addition word problems, setting them up with manipulatives and then as computation problems, and solving them. Use problems that incorporate many types of objects (e.g., pencils, nickels, miles, minutes). Try to use situations that would be familiar to her as well as practical (e.g., paying for her family to see a movie at $7.50 each). When she is learning subtraction, switch to subtraction word problems, then a series of problems in which addition and subtraction are mixed so that she has to consider the language of the word problem carefully to decide which operation to use.

Homework

1. Before Brianna takes home math assignments, make sure that she understands the directions and process for solving the problems. Work the first few problems with Brianna at school.

2. Request that Brianna's parents put a check next to those items completed with their assistance. In this way, the teacher can monitor the types of problems with which Brianna is having difficulty.

Resources

1. For a valuable resource for teaching mathematics from readiness skills through algebra and geometry, especially in developing conceptual foundations, the teacher is referred to *Today's Mathematics: Concepts, Methods, and Classroom Activities, 12th Edition* (Heddens, Speer, & Brahier, 2009, John Wiley & Sons). This book and the accompanying CD provide comprehensive and detailed information regarding national math standards, a graded scope and sequence for curriculum expectations, developmental levels within strands of mathematics, explanation of and instructional approaches in developing mathematical concepts and procedures from readiness through beginning high school math, and integration of technology, as well as specific activities and suggestions for classroom instruction.

2. Encourage Brianna's parents to play math games with her to increase her confidence, conceptual understanding, and automaticity in basic math facts. A good resource for games and activities is *Playing With Math ... The Name of the Game!* (Horne & Feifer, 2007, School Neuropsych Press).

3. The web site of the National Council of Teachers of Mathematics provides the Principles and Standards for School Mathematics with instructional principles, ideas, and examples (www.nctm.org).

REFERENCE

Russell, S. J. (1999). *Relearning to teach arithmetic: Addition and subtraction: A teacher's guide.* Lebanon, IN: Dale Seymore Publications.

CASE 18

The Cognitive Assessment System and the Wechsler Intelligence Scale for Children-IV in a Neuropsychological Context

Tulio Otero and Jack Naglieri

This report illustrates how the Cognitive Assessment System (CAS) can be used within a neuropsychological context for a child with a history of problems despite average IQ scores. The report also emphasizes the importance of considering brain-behavior relationships in the evaluation process. The case informs the reader as to the limitations of using a general intelligence approach in a complex situation such as this one and further demonstrates how a referral for academic achievement difficulties may in fact suggest an underlying neurocognitive deficit. In particular, in cases such as Sara's, the cerebellum and its development are very frequently affected, especially in posterior regions.

The posterior regions of the brain are associated with cognitive function, but there is also a secondary representation of certain sensory-motor functions in two posterior lobules. If the cerebellum is considered as regulating the force, rate, and rhythm of cognition, sensory, motor, and behavioral functions (Koziol & Budding, 2009), then these behavioral observations are consistent with difficulties also at the cortical-subcortical level. Sara's history and presentation suggest poor fine articulatory control, hypersensitivity to sound, and rambling verbal responses. Her WISC-IV scores are unremarkable and may only suggest that Sara's cerebral cortex is working relatively well. Test results from the CAS Planning and Attention scales implicate difficulty with the frontal lobe and executive functions and illustrate the importance of assessing this construct that is not assessed by the WISC-IV. Although it is difficult to rule out abnormal prefrontal cortex-basal ganglia circuitry, the cortex (or certain regions of it) may be receiving inaccurate information from the cerebellum.

PSYCHOLOGICAL EVALUATION

Name:	Sara Post
Date of Birth:	January 15, 2001
Age:	9-2
Parents:	Miriam and Samuel Post
School:	Monte Vista Elementary
Grade:	4.7
Dates of Evaluation:	March 18–19, 2010
Evaluators:	Tulio Otero, Ph.D.
	Jack A. Naglieri, Ph.D.

REASON FOR REFERRAL AND BACKGROUND INFORMATION

Sara is a 9-year-old, fourth-grade student who was referred for a multidisciplinary evaluation due to a history of low math achievement. Her current teacher described her behavior as "odd." Sara uses glasses for astigmatism and is left-handed. Review of medical records was noteworthy for birth history of prematurity. Sara was born by emergency C-section in the seventh month, at 1 lb. 5 oz., due to placenta abruptio (pulling away of the placenta from the uterine wall). Sara required resuscitation, intubation, a ventilator, and blood transfusions. She was in a neonatal intensive care unit for 1 month followed by 2 months at a local hospital. Complications included a blood clot on the brain, which resolved. Due to problems related to her prematurity, she received occupational, physical, and speech therapies as an infant.

Sara's family history is positive for muscular dystrophy; however, Sara has not developed any symptoms and is being monitored by her physician. She receives weekly speech-language services for targeted articulation goals. Sara's teacher reported that she intermittently displays weak production of the nonemphasized syllable in multisyllabic words. She was able to correct errors in speech sounds when provided with a model and multiple cues. Overall speech intelligibility was considered good, depending on context, rate of speech, and volume. She currently demonstrates age-appropriate skills in the areas of receptive and expressive language, although she does have mild-to-moderate articulation delays. Speech-language interventions will be continued for the rest of the school year. The occupational therapist who evaluated Sara for low muscle tone and possible sensory processing difficulties noted that Sara has difficulties with distractibility.

BEHAVIORAL OBSERVATIONS

Sara was friendly and cooperative during this examination. She tended to walk very fast, gave adequate eye contact, and put forth good effort. Her mood and affect were unremarkable. Her speech was intelligible with few articulation errors. When answering questions, she tended to provide too much information, whereas most children her age would likely answer in one or two sentences. On occasion, she needed to be told to limit the amount of her verbal output in order to move the session along. Sara was distracted by the visual input in the room and by children walking in the hall. She was distracted repeatedly by the music from the adjacent music room and required redirection to tasks. Many of her selections on paper-and-pencil or motor-free tasks appeared to be impulsive, with inconsistent self-monitoring and variable focus of attention to several portions of the test stimuli. Sara tended to verbalize "all right" before every test item. This seemed to be an automatic tic-like response and, at the time, she had no conscious awareness of it. Once made aware, she was able to suppress it only for a short time and then the behavior resumed. Sara did not show obvious signs of fatigue during the evaluation.

TEST RESULTS AND INTERPRETATION

General Ability

Sara attained an average Full-Scale score (FSIQ = 107) on the Wechsler Intelligence Scale for Children, Fourth Edition (WISC-IV). The separate indices of Verbal Comprehension, Perceptual Reasoning, and Processing Speed were well within the Average range with Index scores of 108, 103, and 97, respectively. Working Memory was at the lower end of the Average range, as evidenced by an Index score of 92, but was not significantly lower than the average of these four scales. There was no significant subtest scatter within the profile. These scores did not suggest any significant weaknesses in general ability when measured using verbal or nonverbal tests.

Cognitive Processing

Sara earned a Cognitive Assessment System (CAS) Full-Scale score of 82, which is within the Low Average classification and is ranked at the 12th percentile. The Full Scale comprises four separate processing abilities, of which three out of four were below the Average range. She obtained the following PASS scale scores: Planning, 85; Simultaneous, 100; Attention, 77; and Successive, 86. The Simultaneous processing scale was significantly higher than the average of her PASS scale scores and is considered a cognitive processing strength.

Sara's Planning score of 85 is equivalent to a 16th percentile and falls in the Low Average range. Although Sara's Planning score was not significantly lower than her the average of her PASS scale scores, it is considerably below the normative mean of 100, suggesting performance that is well below what is expected for her age. Planning is part of the executive function system subserved by the frontal cortex. Planning helps one to achieve goals through the development of strategies necessary to accomplish tasks for which a solution is required. Therefore, planning is an essential ability for all activities that demand that the child figure out how to solve a problem. This includes self-monitoring and impulse control as well as making, assessing, and implementing a plan. Thus, planning allows for the generation of solutions and discriminating application of knowledge and skills, as well as control of attention and simultaneous and successive processes.

Sara earned a CAS Simultaneous scale score of 100, which is within the Average classification and is ranked at the 50th percentile. The ability to recognize patterns as interrelated elements is made possible by the parieto-occipital-temporal brain regions. Due to the substantial spatial characteristics of most simultaneous tasks, there is a visual-spatial dimension to activities that demand this type of process. Conceptually, the examination of simultaneous processing is achieved using tasks that could also be described as involving visual-spatial reasoning. But simultaneous processing is not limited to nonverbal content. It also plays an important role in the grammatical components of language and comprehension of word relationships (as measured by the CAS Verbal Spatial Relations subtest), prepositions, and inflections.

Attention was measured by tests that required Sara to focus on specific features of the material and resist reacting to distracting stimuli. Sara's score on the Attention Scale reflects how well she is able to attend, concentrate, and resist distractions. She earned a CAS Attention scale standard score of 77, which is within the Below Average classification and is ranked at the 6th percentile. Attention is a cognitive process that is closely connected to the orienting response and is subserved by the reticular formation and other medial subcortical structures, allowing one to focus selective attention toward a stimulus over a period of time without the loss of attention to other, competing stimuli. The longer attention is needed, the more that activity necessitates vigilance. Intentions and goals mandated by the planning process control attention, while knowledge and skills also play an integral part in the process.

Sara earned a CAS Successive scale standard score of 86, which is within the Low Average classification and is ranked at the 18th percentile. Successive processing is typically an integral element involved with the serial organization of sounds, such as learning sounds in sequence and early reading. Furthermore, successive processing has been conceptually and experimentally related to the concept of phonological skills. Difficulty following directions and comprehending what is being said when sentences are too lengthy are also related to low successive processing. Teachers and parents may often misinterpret this weakness as a failure to comprehend or remember, or as a problem of attention. Although, Sara's Successive score was not significantly lower than the average of her PASS scale scores, it is considerably below the normative mean of 100, again suggesting performance that is well below what is expected for her age.

Sara's Below Average scores on the scales of Attention, Planning, and Successive Processing are consistent with several of the behavioral observations previously mentioned, particularly distractibility, impulsivity, vocal-motor (vocal-tic), verbosity, and variable self-monitoring. Difficulties in math have been related to poor planning and successive processing, a profile that certainly fits for Sara.

Sara's academic achievement within the reading and writing domains as measured by the WJ III ACH reflects performance that is within the Average range. This finding is consistent with the classroom teacher's report that

Sara is not experiencing difficulties in all academic areas, just math. In fact, Sara's performance in brief math is Low Average, as evidenced by her standard score of 83. Both math calculation and math reasoning are within the Low Average range.

SUMMARY

Sara's measured ability is within the Average range across domains on the WISC-IV. When her cognitive ability is measured within a neurocognitive model using the CAS, a pattern of strengths and weaknesses is noted, with attention being her weakest area followed by planning and successive processing. Simultaneous processing is within the Average range.

RECOMMENDATIONS

Sara received the following interventions from the classroom teacher in consultation with the school psychologist:

- Sara was first taught about planning using the "Teaching Students about Planning" and "Attention" guidelines (Naglieri & Pickering, 2010) followed by the specific interventions "Seven-Step Strategy for Word Problems" and "Plans for Basic Math Facts." Each of these strategies was selected because of Sara's low performance on the CAS Planning and Attention scales. The intent of the instruction is to help Sara discover and use strategies, monitor her performance, think about how a strategy can be used in different situations, develop an awareness of the importance of strategies, and achieve self-regulated strategy use. In essence, the goal is to help Sara become thoughtful, planful, and evaluative.

- Sara was also taught about what attention is. Teaching Sara about attention will encourage her to self-monitor her level of attention, make her aware of when she is distracted so that she can attend more consistently, and learn that her learning requires attention to detail and resisting distractions. Sara's classroom teacher recently reported that Sara is making fewer errors on both calculation and math reasoning tasks. For example, daily math quizzes for the last 2 weeks have shown 90% accuracy rate versus 65–75% accuracy prior to intervention. The teacher expects Sara will continue to make progress, albeit slowly. Schoolwide academic testing to

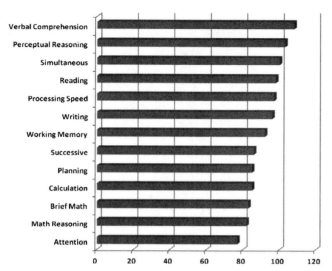

Figure 1 Sara's Standard Scores for WISC-IV, CAS, & WJ III.

measure academic progress in 6 weeks will serve as an additional measure of how Sara is progressing in math.

For the remainder of this academic school year, Sara will continue to receive speech and language therapy and occupational therapy.

REFERENCES

Koziol, L., & Budding, D. (2009). *Subcortical structures and cognition: Implications for neuropsychological assessment.* New York: Springer.

Naglieri, J. A., & Pickering, E. (2010). *Helping children learn: Intervention handouts for use in school and at home: Second edition.* Baltimore: Paul H. Brookes.

CASE 19

Reestablishing Eligibility and Reevaluation Post Natural Disaster

Tara Raines and Cecil Reynolds

The report of Fulanito Fulano illustrates the psychoeducational assessment of a student who is suffering both social/emotional and cognitive impairment, and is transferring from another district with a declaration of eligibility already in place. In the case of Fulanito, as with many school-based psychoeducational evaluations, obtaining important specific background information was a challenge. Although Fulanito was identified as a student with disabilities impacting his educational performance, previous psychological reports, records of psychiatric treatment, medical history, and developmental information were not available at the time of the evaluation. While this phenomenon occurs too often in school psychology practice, many schools were overwhelmed with students in this situation following Hurricane Katrina. Fulanito, his mother, and his brother left New Orleans just prior to the storm and they have moved several times since. To compensate for this absent information, the evaluators selected a battery that provided information regarding the student's global functioning within the scope of the referral, with the hope that additional testing could then be conducted or obtained as the need was revealed. As you will see, additional assessment was recommended but at the time of this writing, not yet authorized. Assessment instruments administered were chosen for their sound psychometric properties and their ability to indicate areas of intervention that seemed most pressing. These instruments were also selected for the purpose of evaluating the need for follow-up assessment once Fulanito had been integrated into the current program and had experienced some relief from his emotional issues. The goal of this evaluation was to investigate Fulanito's current functioning and report on available history.

Overall intellectual integrity was seen as necessary to assess, hence the use of the Reynolds Intellectual Assessment Scales (RIAS), and with Fulanito's history of emotional and behavioral issues, the Behavior Assessment System for Children, Second Edition (BASC-2), the most comprehensive of such diagnostic tools, was selected. Due to the history of head injury, neuropsychological screening was conducted via the Comprehensive Trail-Making Test (CTMT). The CTMT is extremely sensitive to central nervous system damage and dysfunction so if results of testing with this instrument are normal, neuropsychological problems are unlikely. Additionally, readers should attend to the instruments selected. It may be noted that they are shorter in administration time when compared to other batteries used to assess similar constructs and processes. This battery was selected in an effort to minimize the interference of the attention disorder and to avoid Fulanito reaching his frustration threshold.

Results did reveal some issues with memory, as well as academic skills, and appropriate follow-up assessments were subsequently recommended. However, it seems best in this case, as it will in others where emotional and behavioral issues are paramount, to await treatment and improvement on this front prior to exploring additional cognitive and academic issues. His emotional state may lead to false positive findings on additional cognitive and academic testing at this time, or at least confound accurate interpretation of the results.

Observations, diagnostic impressions, and parent account of psychiatric history were all considered in making diagnostic decisions. Due to the limited nature of background information, information from the BASC-2 and school personnel reports were used to make the *DSM-IV TR* diagnostic decisions.

Reading this report should not only assist in developing the rationale for various interventions when a limited history is available but also in developing proper justification for a more in-depth, comprehensive assessment in such cases. Additionally, the report is written at a readability level that ensures that parents and teachers can access and understand the information provided. The recommendations are formatted in a manner that will allow school-based teams to integrate them easily into Fulanito's educational plan and monitor his progress, and they can be generalized across home and school settings.

PSYCHOLOGICAL REPORT

Name: Fulanito Fulano
Date of Birth: 1/10/2001
Age: 9-2
Parent: Michelle Fulano
Address: 123 Palm Drive
School: Ingleside Elementary School
Grade: 3
Test Date: March 24, 2010
Psychologists: Tara C. Raines, Psy.S., Cecil Reynolds, Ph.D.

REFERRAL REASON

Fulanito has recently moved to this city from Nashville in the aftermath of Hurricane Katrina. As his records include an active IEP and eligibility for an Emotional and Behavioral Disorders placement, he was referred for an evaluation by the Ingleside Elementary School reevaluation team in an effort to gather additional information to assist with his educational planning. Classification issues were not a concern of the referring team.

BACKGROUND INFORMATION

Background information was gathered from a parent interview and the parent information form. Previous psychological reports should be reviewed for an in-depth developmental history. Fulanito is a 9-year-old male who currently lives with his biological mother, Michelle Fulano, and younger brother, Samuel (age 6). Fulanito's mother and the two boys recently relocated to Waycross, Georgia, from the Nashville, Tennessee, area. Mrs. Fulano reports that the family has had a difficult time with the transition and indicated that her relationship with Fulanito has recently become strained due to his behavioral difficulties.

Ms. Fulano's report indicated that Fulanito was the product of a typical pregnancy and delivery. Previous psychological reports suggested speech and toileting milestones were met later than expected; Fulanito began speaking at the age of 4. Ms. Fulano reports that Fulanito has been treated by psychiatrists on several occasions resulting from crisis mental health placements. Ms. Fulano also divulged that in the past Fulanito has been prescribed medications to "help him calm down and not hear voices" but she discontinued the medications at the advice of her friends. She does not recall the names of the medications but stated they were prescribed while Fulanito was being treated at a psychiatric hospital in May 2007 for 6 days. Although requested, these records were not made available.

Social and family histories provided by the mother are positive for learning disabilities, intellectual disability mental illness and emotional disturbance of an unspecified nature, and birth defects (but with details unrecalled by Ms. Fulano). Ms. Fulano additionally reported that she and Fulanito were involved in a car accident during Fulanito's infancy and he was thrown from the car, sustaining a head injury. She was not able to recall Fulanito's exact age at the time of the accident nor any specifics about the injuries sustained. Ms. Fulano reports that the family was living in New Orleans at the time of Hurricane Katrina. She and her sons fled the storm to Tennessee, while Fulanito's father stayed behind and has been reported as missing since.

Educational history indicates that Fulanito has attended several elementary schools; however, Ms. Fulano was unable to provide the names of all of them. The most recent eligibility report available is from March 2008 when it was determined that Fulanito would benefit from the support of special education services. Since being found eligible, Fulanito has received special education services in the general education setting with resource support, as well as in a self-contained setting for students served under the category of Emotional and Behavior Disorders. It was reported that in the self-contained setting, the student-to-teacher ratio was 11:2. When they become available, previous Individualized Education Plans (IEPs) and psychological reports should be reviewed for additional information.

Since his enrollment at Ingleside Elementary School, Fulanito's special education teachers have continued to honor his most recent IEP. Additionally, in the general education classroom, the teacher uses a daily behavior folder and the "1, 2, 3 Magic" behavior management system. Functional Behavior Analysis suggests periods of crisis or tantrums typically stem from a teacher request or redirection. When these episodes occur, it is difficult to calm or console Fulanito and redirect him to appropriate behavior. There are also occasions on which Fulanito will have major disruptive episodes with no known antecedent. Often, these are rapid episodes of unpredictable rage and he calms quickly. Teachers report Fulanito is overactive and inattentive in the classroom. It is often difficult to redirect him to a nonpreferred task. Teacher reports suggest Fulanito has struggled to initiate and maintain relationships with his classmates.

In February 2010, Fulanito passed the school vision and hearing screenings.

INSTRUMENTS ADMINISTERED

Reynolds Intellectual Assessment Scales (RIAS)

Behavior Assessment System for Children, Second Edition, Parent Rating Scale-C (6-11) (BASC-2-PRS-C)

Behavior Assessment System for Children, Second Edition, Self Report of Personality-C (6-11) (BASC-2-SRP-C)

Comprehensive Trail-Making Test (CTMT)

Children's Apperception Test (CAT)

Records review

Interview

CONSULTATIONS

Teacher: Susan McElroy
Parent: Michelle Fulano

TEST BEHAVIOR AND OBSERVATIONS

Fulanito willingly accompanied the examiner from the classroom for the evaluation. He appeared well-groomed and was dressed in the style of his peers. As the examiner asked rapport-building questions and tried to engage Fulanito in conversation, he looked around the room uneasily. He was offered the opportunity to take a break and get water. Upon returning, Fulanito smiled but continued to glance around the room. When asked his birth date, he provided the correct month and day. When asked the year, Fulanito replied "I think Friday." Fulanito was able to

answer easily other rapport-building questions. He said that his favorite food is pepperoni pizza and his favorite movie is "Spy Kids 3." Rapport with Fulanito was adequately established for the purposes of assessment.

Fulanito attempted all items presented and was cooperative. However, he required frequent redirection to tasks. He became visibly discouraged and initially refused to answer when presented with difficult items. He responded to verbal praise and, with encouragement, attempted the tasks. It is believed that his limited attention and anxiety level negatively impacted his performance on some measures; however, his behavior during the assessment is consistent with teacher reports of his performance. Therefore, results are believed to be an accurate estimate of Fulanito's current functioning.

TEST RESULTS AND INTERPRETATION

Cognitive

Intelligence refers to a person's ability to receive information through various perceptual modalities, retain information in memory, and organize it meaningfully through various cognitive processes (i.e., concept formation, comprehension, reasoning, judgment, planning, information processing, working memory, and problem solving). Simply put, intelligence is how well you think, problem-solve, and process information.

The Reynolds Intellectual Assessment Scales (RIAS) is an individually administered intelligence test that is appropriate for individuals ages 3 to 94. The RIAS includes a two-subtest Verbal Intelligence Index (VIX) and a two-subtest Nonverbal Intelligence Index (NIX). Scores from the four subtests are combined to form the Composite Intelligence Index (CIX), which provides a summary estimate of global intelligence. Two additional subtests may be administered to produce a Composite Memory Index (CMX), which provides an estimate of verbal and nonverbal memory functions.

In the chart below, T scores reflect performances on individual subtests. Each T score has a mean of 50 and a standard deviation of 10. Approximately two thirds of the population earn T scores between 40 and 60.

Index scores are presented as standard scores with a mean of 100 and a standard deviation of 15. Approximately two thirds of the population obtain scores between 85 and 115, and about 95 percent obtain scores between 70 and 130. The Index scores are categorized within the following descriptive ranges:

69 or below	Significantly Below Average
70–79	Moderately Below Average
80–89	Below Average
90–109	Average
110–119	Above Average
120–129	Moderately Above Average
130 and above	Significantly Above Average

	RIAS Subtest Scores/Index Summary Age-Adjusted *T* Scores				
	Verbal	Nonverbal			Memory
Guess What (GWH)	55				
Odd-Item Out (OIO)		51			
Verbal Reasoning (VRZ)	28				
What's Missing (WHM)		55			
Verbal Memory (VRM)					40
Nonverbal Memory (NVM)					43
Sum of *T* Scores	83	+	106	=	189	83

RIAS Indexes	VIX	NIX	CIX	CMX
	89	106	96	85

Percentile Rank	23	66	39	16
	Verbal Intelligence Index	Nonverbal Intelligence Index	Composite Intelligence Index	Composite Memory Index

According to this administration of the RIAS, Fulanito's skills appear to be unevenly developed with a clear pattern of strengths and weaknesses. Overall, these results are similar to estimates of his ability on previous evaluations, which likewise demonstrated lower verbal than nonverbal skills. During the assessment, Fulanito was easily distracted and his thought processes appeared disjointed.

It is likely that this negatively impacted his performance on some parts of this assessment, particularly the memory subtests.

On testing with the RIAS, Fulanito earned a Composite Intelligence Index (CIX) of 96. This level of performance falls within the range of scores designated as average and exceeds the performance of 39% of individuals of Fulanito's age. The chances are 90 out of 100 that Fulanito's true CIX falls within the range of scores from 91 to 101. Individuals at this level of overall functioning may be expected to demonstrate overall cognitive skills that are within expectation for this chronological age.

Fulanito earned a Verbal Intelligence Index (VIX) of 89, which falls within the Below Average range of verbal intelligence skills and exceeds the performance of 23% of individuals Fulanito's age. The chances are 90 out of 100 that Fulanito's true VIX falls within the range of scores from 84 to 95. Skills measured by the Verbal Intelligence Index (VIX) include the ability to deduce or infer relationships and the ability to apply knowledge to problem solving using words and language skills. The VIX provides a measure of verbal reasoning ability with primary emphasis on crystallized intelligence functions (i.e., the application of knowledge to problem solving). Fulanito's VIX score of 89 indicates mild deficits in the development of verbal intellect relative to others of Fulanito's age. However, due to the variance in his performance on the "Guess What" subtest (*T* score 55) and the Verbal Reasoning subtest (*T* score 28), the VIX might not be an accurate reflection of his verbal abilities if his attentional difficulties were better controlled. Fulanito demonstrated considerable difficulty sustaining attention during Verbal Reasoning despite the brevity of the items. His limited attention may have negatively impacted his performance. Generally, verbal ability is important for virtually every aspect of activity because language is key to nearly all areas of human endeavor. Verbal ability also is the foundation for linguistic knowledge, which is necessary for many types of learning, especially school learning.

Fulanito earned a Nonverbal Intelligence Index (NIX) of 106, which falls within the average range of nonverbal intelligence skills and exceeds the performance of 66% of individuals Fulanito's age. The chances are 90 out of 100 that Fulanito's true NIX falls within the range of scores from 100 to 111. Skills measured by the Nonverbal Ability Index (NIX) include the ability to perceive, manipulate, or transform accurately the image of spatial patterns into other visual arrangements. The NIX provides a measure of nonverbal reasoning ability with primary emphasis on fluid intelligence functions (i.e., the ability to solve problems with no prior knowledge required).

Although Fulanito's CIX is a good estimate of his general intelligence, a statistically significant discrepancy exists between his NIX of 106 and VIX of 89, demonstrating generally better-developed nonverbal intelligence or spatial abilities. A pattern of VIX < NIX is consonant with the existence of difficulties in school learning and raises suspicions regarding the presence of a specific learning disability as well. Although this discrepancy represents a real difference in his abilities in these two intellectual domains, the actual frequency of occurrence of a difference of this magnitude is relatively common, occurring in 26% of the general population. Therefore, this difference may or may not be indicative of the presence of a psychopathological condition, depending on the results of other clinical assessments.

Fulanito earned a Composite Memory Index (CMX) of 85, which falls within the Below Average range of working memory skills. This exceeds the performance of 16% of individuals Fulanito's age. The chances are 90 out of 100 that Fulanito's true CMX falls within the range of scores from 80 to 91. Skills measured by the Composite Memory Index (CMX) include the ability to attend to a stimulus, register the stimulus in immediate memory, and then recall or recognize the stimulus. Fulanito's performance indicates mild difficulties with recall of verbal and visual-spatial information relative to others Fulanito's age. This may cause mild problems and some consternation for Fulanito, in learning new academic material, but is unlikely to disturb most functions of day-to-day living. Fulanito's CMX falls significantly below his measured level of general intelligence. This result indicates that he is able to engage in intellectual problem solving and general reasoning tasks significantly better than he can use immediate recall and working memory functions. Although the size of the observed difference is reliable and indicates a real difference in these two cognitive domains, the magnitude of the difference observed is relatively common, occurring in 50% of the population. Therefore, this difference may or may not be indicative of the presence of a psychopathological condition, depending on the results of other clinical assessments.

The RIAS subtest scores are reported as T scores. The Guess What subtest measures vocabulary knowledge in combination with reasoning skills that are predicated on language development and acquired knowledge. This subtest requires the student to deduce an object or concept from a set of two to four verbal clues. Fulanito earned a T score of 55 (average) on Guess What. This score contributes to the Verbal Intelligence Index with particular emphasis on vocabulary knowledge.

Verbal Reasoning measures analytical reasoning abilities within the verbal domain. This subtest requires the student to provide a response to complete a verbal analogy. English vocabulary knowledge is also required. Fulanito earned a T score of 28 (Significantly Below Average) on Verbal Reasoning. Verbal Reasoning contributes to the Verbal Intelligence Index with particular emphasis on verbal-analytical reasoning. Fulanito's performance in this area would suggest a personal weakness in his ability to deduce abstract relationships in the verbal domain.

The Odd-Item Out subtest requires the student to identify which of five to seven pictures does not belong with the group. Odd-Item Out measures analytical reasoning abilities within the nonverbal domain. On testing with the RIAS, Fulanito earned a T score of 51 (Average). Odd-Item Out contributes to the Nonverbal Intelligence Index with particular emphasis on spatial ability and attention to visual imagery.

The What's Missing subtest measures spatial and visualization abilities and requires the student to identify the missing element in a picture. Fulanito earned a T score of 55 (Average). What's Missing contributes to the Nonverbal Intelligence Index with particular emphasis on nonverbal reasoning and attention to visual detail.

The Verbal Memory subtest requires the student to recall a series of verbally presented sentences or stories. Verbal Memory measures the ability to encode, briefly store, and recall information in the verbal domain. English vocabulary knowledge also is required. Fulanito earned a T score of 40 (Below Average) on Verbal Memory. Verbal Memory contributes to the Composite Memory Index with emphasis on the ability to encode, store, and immediately recall verbal material presented in a meaningful context.

The Nonverbal Memory subtest requires the student to identify a target picture, displayed for 5 seconds, from a group of similar pictures presented subsequently. Fulanito earned a T score of 43 on Nonverbal Memory. Nonverbal Memory contributes to the Composite Memory Index with emphasis on the ability to encode, store, and immediately recognize pictorial stimuli presented without meaningful context. Nonverbal Memory measures the ability to encode, briefly store, and recall information in the nonverbal and spatial domains.

Based on observations of attention and memory issues as well as the VIX-NIX split and Fulanito's history, additional screening for signs of neuropsychological dysfunction was undertaken. On the Comprehensive Trail-Making test, a measure extremely sensitive to brain injury and other CNS disturbance, Fulanito earned a T score of 40 (Below Average), which is one standard deviation below the mean and fell at the 25th percentile compared to age mates. Little variation was seen in his performance across the five Trails. This finding is generally consistent with his mild attention and memory deficits and also is in the score range that is common among children with mild learning problems. Children of this age who have more significant neuropsychological problems commonly earn much lower scores on the CTMT.

Academic

Selected subtests of the Kaufman Tests of Educational Achievement-II were administered in a recent school assessment to measure Fulanito's current academic functioning in reading and math. The KTEA-II scores are presented as standard scores (SS) with a mean of 100 and a standard deviation of 15. Testing yielded the following results.

Kaufman Tests of Educational Achievement, Second Edition

	SS
Letter & Word Recognition	72
Reading Comprehension	71
Reading Composite	**70**
Math Computation	52
Math Concepts and Applications	66
Math Composite	**60**

Results of academic testing suggest Fulanito's academic abilities are significantly below average and substantially lower than estimates of his intellectual functioning based on the current assessment. Teacher reports suggest Fulanito's academic performance in the classroom has been difficult to assess, as his behavioral disturbances have hindered his ability to perform in the classroom thus far.

Social-Emotional

Social-emotional assessment involves the evaluation of an individual's social relations, coping strategies, and self-perceptions. The assessment is based upon information obtained from a variety of sources, which can include evaluations by teachers and parents, as well as through individual personality testing.

Behavior Assessment System for Children, Second Edition (BASC-2)

The BASC-2 is a multimethod, multidimensional system used to evaluate the behavior and self-perceptions of children and young adults aged 2 to 25 years. Rating scales are available for completion by teachers (TRS), parents (PRS), and/or students themselves (SRP). Scores are reported in terms of T scores with a mean of 50 and a standard deviation of 10.

The Parent Rating Scale (PRS) is a comprehensive measure of adaptive and problem behaviors observed by parents at home and in the community. The PRS assesses most of the clinical and adaptive skills domains that the TRS measures. In addition, the PRS includes a scale (Activities of Daily Living) that the TRS does not.

The Self-Report of Personality (SRP) is a personality inventory completed by children, adolescents, and young adults themselves on forms appropriate for their age level. This report is based on their own perceptions of their personality, behavior, and the ways in which they believe others regard them.

The following chart provides a T score interpretation for the BASC-2:

Clinical Scales		Adaptive Scales	
70+	Clinically Significant	70+	Very High
60–69	At-Risk	60–69	High
41–59	Average	41–59	Average
31–40	Low	31–40	At-Risk
30 and below	Very Low	30 and below	Clinically Significant

The Parent Rating Scale yielded the results shown in Figure 1.

Based on observations and related information presented in this report, which support the presence of maladaptive behaviors, it is likely that Ms. Fulano was candid in describing

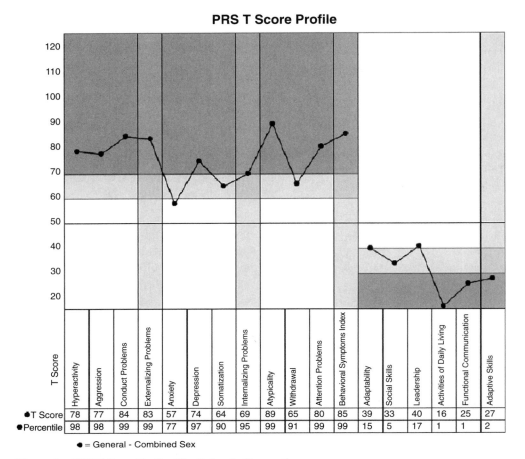

Figure 1 PRS T Score Profile: Ms. Fulano's Observations

observations of Fulanito's behavior and that the ratings represent a valid assessment of his social-emotional functioning.

Results suggest Fulanito is demonstrating clinically significant behaviors in the areas of Hyperactivity, Aggression, Conduct Problems, Depression, Atypicality, Attention Problems, Activities of Daily Living, Functional Communication, and Adaptive Skills. The BASC-2 Scales are described in the following chart.

BASC Scales	Description	Parent
Behavioral Symptoms Index	Overall rating of the individual's behavior	78
Externalizing Problems		81
Hyperactivity	Tendency to be overly active, rush through work, and act without thinking	83
Aggression	Tendency to act in a hostile manner (either verbal or physical) that is threatening to others	77
Internalizing Problems		69
Anxiety	Tendency to be nervous, fearful, or worried about real/imagined problems	57
Depression	Feelings of unhappiness, sadness, or stress that may result in an inability to carry out everyday activities	74
Somatization	Tendency to be overly sensitive to and complain about relatively minor physical problems or discomforts	64
School Problems		
Attention Problems	Tendency to be easily distracted	66

BASC Scales	Description	Parent
Additional Clinical Scales		
Atypicality	Tendency to behave in ways that are considered strange, such as being disconnected from or unaware of normal surroundings	89
Withdrawal	Tendency to evade others to avoid social contact	65
Adaptive Skills		
Adaptability	The ability to readily adapt to changes in the environment	39
Social Skills	Skills needed to interact successfully with peers/adults in home, school, and community settings	33
Functional Communication	The ability to express ideas and communicate in ways others can easily understand	25
Activities of Daily Living	The skills associated with performing basic, everyday tasks in an acceptable and safe manner	16

It is suggested that specific interventions to address the elevated areas of concern be developed and implemented to promote his overall success.

Fulanito was administered the Self-Report of Personality which yielded the results in Figure 2.

Based on these results, Fulanito's self-assessment suggests that he has concerns regarding interpersonal relationships, relationships with his parents, and attention problems. Following completion of the questionnaire, the examiner queried Fulanito's response to some questions. Fulanito indicated he

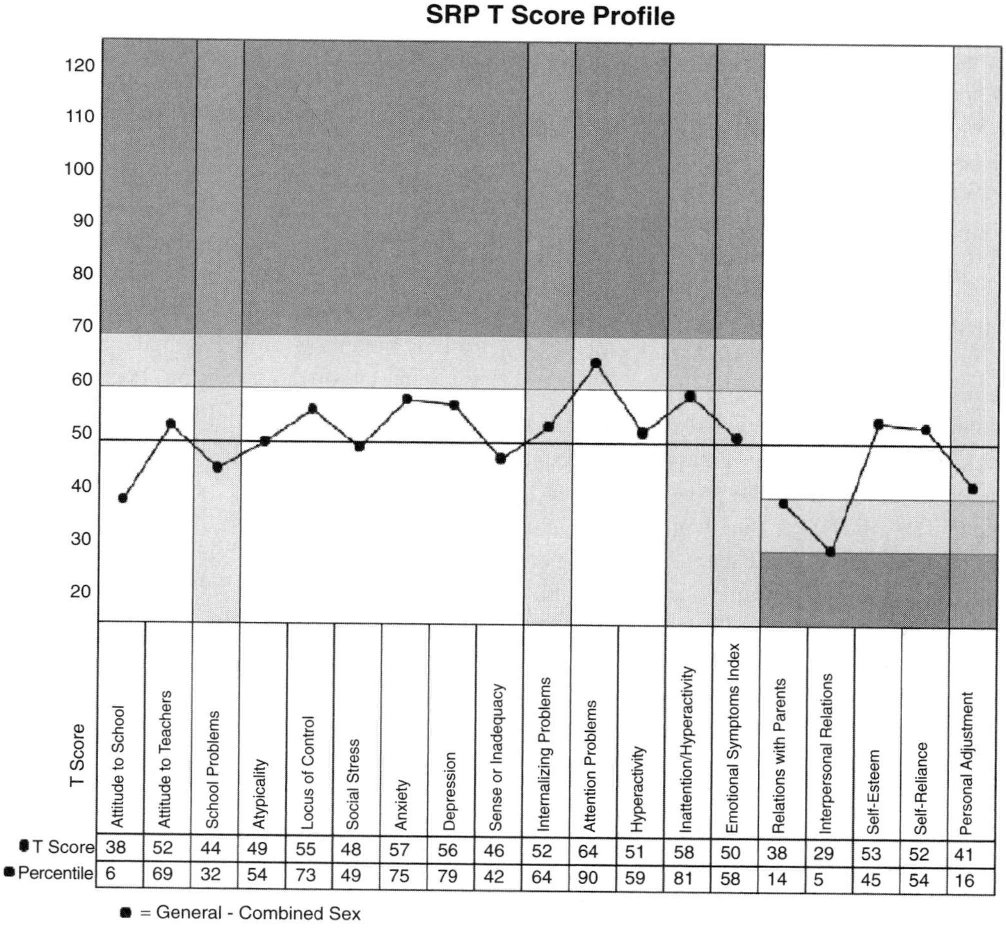

SRP T Score Profile

	Attitude to School	Attitude to Teachers	School Problems	Atypicality	Locus of Control	Social Stress	Anxiety	Depression	Sense or Inadequacy	Internalizing Problems	Attention Problems	Hyperactivity	Inattention/Hyperactivity	Emotional Symptoms Index	Relations with Parents	Interpersonal Relations	Self-Esteem	Self-Reliance	Personal Adjustment
T Score	38	52	44	49	55	48	57	56	46	52	64	51	58	50	38	29	53	52	41
Percentile	6	69	32	54	73	49	75	79	42	64	90	59	81	58	14	5	45	54	16

● = General - Combined Sex

Figure 2   SRP *T* Score Profile: Fulanito's Self-Assessment

feels he wants to hurt himself when people "make him mad" and that at times he wants to kill himself by "jumping off a building." School personnel and Fulanito's mother were both made aware of these responses.

Personality assessment is accomplished through the administration of tests designed to evaluate an individual's self-perceptions, social relations, and coping strategies. During this evaluation, story-telling tests and self-interview were used to assess personality. Fulanito was exposed to selected cards from the Children's Apperception Test (CAT) and was asked to make up a story to describe the scene. Information obtained from this assessment of personality suggests Fulanito has a difficult time with story topic maintenance; he was often distracted by details of the picture and changed the story midstream. Recurring themes on the CAT included punishment and characters in the story feeling "sad." When queried about the feelings of the characters, on more than one occasion, Fulanito shook his head to indicate he did not want to answer.

Additionally, as part of rapport-building activities, Fulanito was asked to draw a picture of his family. He spent several minutes meticulously drawing stairs. He then drew his mother and brother on the bottom portion of the stairs. He stated they were going downstairs to cook and watch television. He drew himself last in a box at the top of the stairs that he indicated was his room. When asked why he was in his room, he said he was lying down because he was "tired and it's too hot [down] there." He also stated that when in his room, he "likes to look for him," and when queried, explained that he looks out his bedroom window waiting for his father to "find him." He believes that his father is still at his house in Louisiana.

During the initial student interview, Fulanito appeared to have a difficult time distinguishing fantasy from reality. When asked about the activities of the previous weekend, Fulanito indicated he saw the Easter Bunny in his house and he chased him out of the house but caught his tail. When asked if there was a person in a costume at his house, Fulanito denied this and reiterated that it was a real rabbit that "broke into" his house to leave gifts. He also struggled to maintain the topic of conversation and his thoughts appeared disjointed. He told the examiner that he often gets "so mad" that he feels like he is "catching a heart attack" and his brain is "just going crazy." He made this statement abruptly in the midst of a conversation about classwork. While making these statements, Fulanito stared away from the examiner and balled his fists. The examiner called Fulanito's name several times to regain his attention and then suspended the interview session to take a break and get water.

Overall assessment of Fulanito's social and emotional functioning indicates areas of concern that suggest behavioral and emotional differences that are affecting Fulanito's ability to make satisfactory academic progress.

CONCLUSIONS

Fulanito is a 9-year-old male who lives with his mother and younger brother. Reports indicate he was the product of a typical pregnancy and delivery. Developmental milestones were reported as delayed in some areas. Fulanito's family recently relocated to Georgia from Tennessee after having left Louisiana to avoid Hurricane Katrina. Fulanito was deemed eligible for special education services in Tennessee under the category of Emotional and Behavioral Disorders and currently has an active IEP. Diagnostic impressions below were obtained from Fulanito's most recent IEP and the current evaluation results.

Results of this assessment suggest Fulanito possesses an unevenly developed cognitive profile. He is demonstrating weaknesses in both memory and verbal ability. He is demonstrating below average academic skills, which is consistent with previous findings. Additionally, Fulanito is exhibiting social and emotional functioning that is of great concern. He has reported the desire to hurt himself, and his mother indicates that Fulanito has a history of psychiatric crisis placements. At this time, it appears both emotional and behavioral factors continue to impair Fulanito's ability to make satisfactory progress in the general education setting. It is recommended that the information presented in this report be used in combination with information provided by other school personnel for the determination of continued eligibility for special education services.

Results of the current evaluation are consistent with the following *DSM-IV-TR* diagnostic impressions:

Axis I:	309.3 Adjustment Disorder with Disturbance of Conduct
	314.01 Attention-Deficit/Hyperactivity Disorder, Combined Type
	315.9 Learning Disorder NOS
Axis II:	799.9 Diagnoses Deferred
Axis III:	none
Axis IV:	Educational adjustment and family conflicts due to behavior, recent move
Axis V:	GAF 47

RECOMMENDATIONS

Medical

1. Encourage Fulanito's mother to share this report and to discuss his psychiatric history with his current health care provider. Further, she should request a referral to a pediatric psychiatrist. Fulanito's diagnosis or diagnoses should be clarified and appropriate medication discussed. It is important that she understand the reasons for the medication, the intended effects, the behavioral improvements she and the teachers should be seeing, and possible negative side effects. Moreover, it is important that she understand that any consideration of discontinuing the medication be discussed with the psychiatrist beforehand.

2. If at any point Fulanito is scheduled to start a trial of medication, prior to this, initiate teacher/staff completion of a rating chart composed of a few behaviors that are problems in the classroom and that are likely to respond to medication (e.g., pays attention while teacher is talking, socializes only when appropriate, ignores mild distractions, work shows appropriate level of thought, stays in seat without excessive fidgeting), a question about time of the day when medication benefits appear to have worn off, and comments. Have the teacher and other school staff continue to chart behaviors, sharing results with the student's parents and physician, until the optimal dosage and dosage times are established.

Further Testing

1. **Comprehensive evaluation.** Once Fulanito's emotional and behavioral difficulties have improved significantly, a comprehensive assessment of cognitive abilities and academic skills should be undertaken to further ascertain the presence of learning disabilities and/or related problems that might require additional modifications of his instructional environment. Include a language evaluation, especially in the areas of vocabulary and verbal reasoning.

2. **Memory.** One area that should receive particular attention in the reevaluation is memory. One cannot remember information unless one has first paid attention to it. Consequently, it is possible that Fulanito's memory, if he is focused on the task at hand, is better than his current test scores indicate. As well, because performance on memory tests is typically quite variable, depending on even small changes in task demands, Fulanito should be given a comprehensive battery of memory tests. The two most comprehensive batteries available are the Test of Memory and Learning – Second Edition (TOMAL-2) and the Wide Range Assessment of Memory and Learning – -Second Edition (WRAML-2). More detailed information regarding Fulanito's difficulties in memory tasks (if any) will facilitate the selection of memory strategies and academic interventions.

3. **Reading.** The present assessment was not sufficient to analyze specific areas of weakness regarding Fulanito's reading skills but clearly reading interventions are needed immediately. The following assessment can be done by the classroom teacher. Administer an informal reading inventory and tape-record Fulanito's oral reading of the passages for in-depth analysis and to obtain a baseline measure of reading speed and fluency. Record mispronunciations and substitutions verbatim. Analyze the types of errors he makes regarding letter-sound correspondence, phonics rules, and immediate identification of whole words (both regular and irregular) and common word parts (e.g., *re, com, tion*). Plan appropriate instruction for the development of decoding and word identification skills.

Memory

1. Limit the length and complexity of all instructions to Fulanito and state them in the same order he is to do them.

2. If Fulanito has difficulty remembering instructions for in-class assignments, set up a buddy system for him. Seat him next to a responsible student with permission to ask the student for help if he forgets instructions. Prior to doing so, ask the other student privately if he would be willing to help in this way and ask Fulanito privately if he would like this type of help to be available. Then work out any rules and ways to implement this system in private with both children. It is important that Fulanito not be embarrassed by being singled out in front of the class.

3. Understanding facilitates memory. Ensure that Fulanito understands the concept underlying any new information or skill, as well as how each aspect of the new information is related to every other part. As much as possible, provide Fulanito with multisensory learning experiences. Present content and skill instruction using combinations of visual, auditory, tactile, and kinesthetic input or experience.

4. Present all types of verbal information accompanied by visual stimuli that clearly illustrate the concept being taught. Examples are: pictures, charts, graphs, semantic maps, and videotapes. This will improve both comprehension and retention of information.

5. For all skill learning, provide intensive repetition, practice, and review. Then provide reinforcement activities (for content learning as well) at frequent, regular intervals. Gradually increase the intervals between reinforcement to less frequent and intermittent.

6. Teach memory strategies to the entire class. Select each strategy to be taught along with new information or topics that will correspond to its use (e.g., using an acrostic to memorize the names of the four oceans: "I Am A Porpoise" for Indian, Arctic, Atlantic, Pacific). This will be helpful to the entire class and Fulanito will not be singled out. It is likely that he will need extra guidance to actually learn the strategy and to recognize the situations in which its application would be appropriate.

Attention, Hyperactivity, and Anxiety

Fulanito evidences clear difficulties with attention and hyperactivity consistently across environments. The use of Contingency Management and Cognitive Behavioral Therapy is strongly recommended to help Fulanito learn to increase his self-regulation of attention and activity level. The evaluator can provide information and instructions for implementing these behavior management strategies in school.

1. Fulanito is likely to function best in a class placement incorporating the following components:

   • A highly organized teacher with a structured and systematic teaching style and calm, respectful manner of interacting with students

   • A behavioral program with clear rules, frequent and immediate positive reinforcement for target behaviors, and immediate consequences for specified negative behaviors

   • A consistent schedule so that areas of academic instruction, recess, and routines (e.g., passing out daily work, assigning homework) are done in the same manner and order daily

   • A morning review of each day's schedule (with the student given a copy of his schedule for that day)

   • A minimum of classroom noise and confusion (visual and auditory)

   • A system in which students are aware that a transition is coming, when the current activity will end, what will happen next, and what they are expected to do to be ready

   • An emphasis on interactive and participatory instructional activities in which students have minimal wait time

2. Because Fulanito is unlikely to be able to read a daily schedule, provide a pictorial schedule for him. This can be made by finding (or taking) pictures to represent the usual activities the class does throughout the week (e.g., morning calendar, reading, math, recess, lunch, P.E.), pasting each on a piece of cardboard backed by a small piece of Velcro, and placed in the order for the day on a small board with a vertical strip of the opposing side of the Velcro. Each day, the pictures can be rearranged to match the order of activities for the day. Such a schedule is likely to reduce Fulanito's anxiety and help him move through transitions, as he will always know what is happening next and what his whole school day will look like.

3. As children with ADHD and anxiety often respond poorly to changes in routine, warn Fulanito ahead of time, privately if possible, about any upcoming change and how it will affect him.

4. If you use some of the following sequence of steps for whole group instructions, it is likely that Fulanito will pay attention without having to be singled out:

   a. Decide on a signal to let students know you want their attention. Use the same signal consistently. Examples are ringing a bell, tapping a triangle, turning the lights off and on, turning on a music tape, and saying, "Attention, please." Another way of getting students' attention is to tell them to make some physical movement (e.g., "Put your hands on top of your heads"). The students who are not paying attention notice the others doing this and look to see what is happening. Signals other than voice are easier for students to differentiate from background noise.

   b. Do not speak until all students are quiet and looking at your face. (Be aware that in some cultures, making eye contact with an elder or authority figure is considered rude.)

   c. Establish helping behaviors to guide students in helping each other to turn their attention to you. [See Behavioral Interventions for the Whole Class in the Appendix.]

   d. Give instructions briefly, clearly, and in the same sequence as they are to be followed.

   e. Write instructions on the board as backup or for students who process information more slowly or have poor memory.

   f. If a transition will follow the instructions, teach students that nobody moves until all instructions have been given and the teacher gives the transition signal. [See Transitions Between Activities in the Appendix.]

5. Seat Fulanito close to the teacher so that she may help him to remain on task or to return to task. The proximity of the teacher will help him stay involved in teacher-directed and interactive tasks and make it easier for the teacher to make frequent contact and provide feedback during independent work.

6. Provide a visually quiet, nondistracting place in the classroom where Fulanito can go when he needs or wants to work in a more isolated environment (e.g., a desk away from others, facing the wall). Explain to him that you are aware that sometimes he needs a quiet place, away from other students to help him concentrate on his work better. Describe the chosen area as "his special place" (not a punishment place), to which he may go whenever the class is doing seatwork and he feels that he could work better there.

7. When the classroom or environmental noise level is particularly distracting, or at any time it might be helpful, allow Fulanito to listen to quiet music or white noise (e.g., water sounds, Native American flute music, classical guitar) with a headset while he does his work.

8. Divide Fulanito's in-class assignments into smaller, more manageable chunks. Give him one chunk at a time with instructions to hand each in as it is completed and pick up the next. Each time Fulanito hands in a portion of the work, provide reinforcement for completed work and for time on task. Examples for dividing the work are: Cut apart the major sections of a worksheet and give the student one section at a time to complete; place a piece of "sticky" paper over the bottom half of a worksheet; put a sticker on the bottom of every two pages of a story.

9. To increase Fulanito's time on task, teach him to use a beeper tape/CD. This recording provides a sound at varying time intervals, cuing the student to ask himself, "Am I on task?" If he is, he places a check on a chart. If not, he resumes work. Build in positive reinforcement for increasing the number of checks he accumulates within a work session. You might set a lower number of checks necessary for a reward in tasks in which his attention is significantly challenged (e.g., writing a paper) and raise the limit in tasks in which his attention is not so challenged (e.g., watching a video).

10. Find ways for Fulanito to take frequent breaks from seatwork or if needed, from the classroom. For example, give him an errand to do, have him hand out materials, or send a note to another teacher in a sealed envelope. The note can simply say, "Fulanito needed a break from the classroom. Please just thank him and send him back to class." Alternatively, provide occasional breaks in the work schedule for exercise (e.g., using light weights for 2 minutes when work is completed, using stretch Therabands, doing sit-ups). Fulanito may do exercises individually when he completes a task or the teacher may direct a whole class exercise break.

11. Allow Fulanito to move in and around his seat as long as he is not disruptive to others.

12. As often as possible, praise specific behaviors in Fulanito that you want to encourage. For example, stop by his desk and say quietly, "You're concentrating well on this assignment," or, after the activity, say to the class, "Many of you really stayed focused on this assignment," with a smile at Fulanito so he knows he is included. This technique will help make him aware of the behavior and encourage him to continue it and repeat it at a later time. Make sure, however, that all praise is specific and legitimate. Clearly state the behavior to be reinforced and only praise behaviors that matter (e.g., "Good job" may be legitimate but is not specific. "You're the best pencil sharpener in the class" is specific but not legitimate).

Anxiety

1. If possible, designate a place and person, such as the school counselor, or even a secretary in the school office, to whom Fulanito can go when he is feeling "so mad" but before he feels that he is "catching a heart attack" or that his "brain is going crazy." Work out a plan regarding how he is to let the teacher know that he needs a break and how the designated person will be contacted to ensure he/she is available. The person does not have to interact with Fulanito, just be there to make sure he has a safe place to calm down, and then return him to class. Make sure his mother knows and approves of this plan.

2. Teach Fulanito how to practice positive self-talk. For example, introduce positive "scripts" to practice in anxiety-provoking situations, such as "I have done this many times, so now I'll just start by doing one problem, then checking to see if it's correct."

3. Teach Fulanito a relaxation ritual, such as taking three deep breaths, or tensing his fingers or toes for five seconds, and then relaxing. It will also be necessary to work with Fulanito to help him recognize when he needs to use the relaxation ritual.

Instructional Approaches and Accommodations

1. Detailed instructional recommendations for reading and math cannot be made until more specific information is available regarding his areas of need. However, it is critical to start individualized reading and math instruction (individual or small group) as soon as in-depth reading and math evaluations can be completed and appropriate approaches designed or selected. As Fulanito continues to experience himself as "not learning," he is likely to translate this into "unable to learn" and use negative behaviors to avert attention from his failings.

2. Reduce the amount of work Fulanito is required to do during independent assignments so that he is more likely to complete his work in school. When figuring the grade, the reduced amount assigned is considered as 100%. Do not send unfinished class work home for homework.

3. Provide Fulanito with content area textbooks and assigned literature on CD so that he can learn the material that he is not able to read and will be able to participate in classroom discussions. If a comprehensive evaluation finds that he has a specific reading disorder, books on CD may be ordered from Recordings for the Blind and Dyslexic (www.rfbd.org).

Psychoeducational Assessment of a Child with High-Functioning Autism Using a Problem-Solving Approach

Joel Hanania

The request for Brayden's charter school to assess his cognitive and academic functioning stemmed from a routine request from a physician who had recently diagnosed Brayden with autism and Attention-Deficit/Hyperactivity Disorder (ADHD). The report illustrates the importance of not limiting an evaluation to the initial referral questions and including procedures designed to screen for other areas of disability, as well as obtaining data directly from teachers, parents, and caregivers who know the child best. In this case, an evaluation limited to reporting the results of cognitive and achievement testing would not have revealed the extent of Brayden's social-behavioral problems, which were having a significant adverse impact on his educational performance.

To assess for possible learning problems, the Differential Ability Scales-II (DAS-II) is an ideal instrument due to its breadth of coverage of the cognitive processes that constitute the CHC model of cognitive abilities. Using cognitive and academic instruments with linked norms is considered by many to be best practice; thus, the WIAT-III was an appropriate choice to use with the DAS-II in this case. Conducting additional assessments for autism and ADHD was not deemed necessary as there was sufficient evidence supporting these diagnoses from direct observations, as well as from parent and teacher descriptions of Brayden's behavior.

The organization of the report follows a traditional sequence. This sequence closely mirrors the order in which the evaluation data come to the psychologist with elements of the clinician's problem solving appearing throughout the report. Test scores, explanations of test scores, and explanations of tests are not included in the body of the report, as these do not add to the reader's understanding of the child's problems. The report leads the reader to the point where they understand the nature of the child's difficulties,

with the solutions offered more likely to be accepted and implemented with fidelity. It is imperative for the reader to know not only what they need to do to meet the child's needs, but also why they need to do it. To accomplish this, Brayden's report does not include an enumerated list of highly specific interventions. Rather, the report presents recommendations in a way that explains Brayden's problems followed by solutions that connect logically to these problems.

PSYCHOEDUCATIONAL EVALUATION

Name:	Brayden Moats
Date of Birth:	1/5/2001
Age:	9-3
Parents:	Alice and Jerry Moats
Ethnicity:	Caucasian
Primary Language:	English of Child and Home
School:	Ashville Elementary Phoenix, AZ
Grade:	3.7
Date of Evaluation:	4/10/2010
Evaluator:	Joel S. Hanania, Ph.D.

REASON FOR REFERRAL

Mrs. Moats requested an updated psychoeducational evaluation based on a recommendation from a recent developmental pediatric evaluation that described Brayden as a child with autism and Attention-Deficit/Hyperactivity

Disorder (ADHD). Brayden is currently receiving speech-language therapy and occupational therapy in school under the classification of Speech and Language Impairment. The purpose of the present evaluation was to determine Brayden's current educational programming needs and to suggest ways to address his behavioral challenges at school.

DEVELOPMENTAL, MEDICAL, EDUCATIONAL, AND SOCIAL HISTORIES

The following information was obtained from a review of records and from a social and developmental history form completed by Mrs. Moats.

Brayden lives with both parents, a 9-year-old twin brother, and a 4-year-old sister. The siblings were reported to be developing typically. Although Mrs. Moats reported an uncomplicated pregnancy, Brayden and his twin were born 2 weeks prematurely and weighed only 3 lbs., 8 oz. Brayden spent 10 days in intensive care due to difficulties breathing. Brayden's motor milestones were achieved within normal age expectations until approximately age 4, when motor coordination problems became apparent. All of Brayden's language skills were delayed. Brayden has been healthy with the exception of seasonal allergies for which he takes Zyrtec. No other medications are prescribed at the present time. Brayden passed vision and hearing screenings on 9/9/09 and 9/22/09, respectively.

Brayden began his education at Mountain View preschool at the age of 3 and since kindergarten has been continuously enrolled at Ashville Elementary School. He has never repeated a grade or received any failing grades, and his attendance was reported to be excellent.

Socially and emotionally, Brayden was described as displaying an easy-going disposition along with a high activity level. He becomes angry in response to stress or frustration, and changes to daily routines may cause some slight agitation. Brayden reportedly gets along well with his parents and siblings, but not as well with his peers. His mother reported the following behavioral difficulties at home: lack of motivation, disorganization, short attention span, distractibility, and impulsivity. Brayden is currently participating in group therapy at the Scheffel Child Study Center to improve his social interactions with peers.

At the present time, Mrs. Moats is most concerned about Brayden's difficulties with sensory processing, socializing with peers, paying attention, and completing tasks in class.

Brayden underwent a Comprehensive Developmental Assessment completed by the Sunnydale School District on 2/8/06 when he was 5 years old and a student at Mountain View preschool. Using the Differential Ability Scales, Brayden's overall nonverbal cognitive ability fell within the upper half of the Average range. His nonverbal reasoning and visual-spatial perceptual skills were High Average, whereas his performance on a copying task was Low Average, suggesting significantly weaker visual-motor coordination skills.

Language assessments indicated Low Average receptive and expressive language abilities. Significant delays were also reported in the adaptive behavior areas of daily living and socialization. The results of the Behavior Assessment System for Children (BASC) completed by his mother showed mostly normal functioning across the clinical scales but mild problems on the Attention Problems and Atypicality scales, which fell at the lower limits of the At-Risk range. The Atypicality scale measures the presence of peculiar behaviors, many of which are associated with Pervasive Developmental Disorder (PDD). Weak social skills were also indicated. Specific behaviors of concern included: perseverating on particular topics in conversation, problems transitioning between activities, and difficulty interacting with peers. Both his gross- and fine-motor skills were within normal limits, but sensory processing problems were reported. Although Brayden was found to be eligible for special education services under the category of Preschool Moderate Delay, no recommendations were written for school-aged special education eligibility for the following school year.

As noted above, Brayden underwent a recent developmental and behavioral pediatric evaluation completed by Dr. Barry Gibbs at the McCaslin Child Study Center. The resulting diagnoses included Autism and ADHD-Combined type, along with mild anxiety symptoms. Behavior ratings using the Achenbach Child Behavior Checklist parent and teacher report forms showed consistent problems in the area of Thought Problems, a scale that is sensitive to problems associated with PDD. Problems with inattention, hyperactivity, and impulsivity were seen across both parent and teacher ratings on various items, but the ratings were not always consistent.

Brayden took the TerraNova group achievement test last spring and demonstrated moderate to high levels of mastery across the areas of reading, language, and mathematics, with the exception of low mastery in one math area involving patterns, functions, and algebra.

Based on Brayden's history, economic, environmental or educational disadvantages, or cultural differences could not be considered to be a primary cause of his educational difficulties.

PROCEDURES ADMINISTERED[1]

Differential Ability Scales-II (DAS-II)
Wechsler Individual Achievement Test-III (WIAT-III)
Student Progress Report Form
Review of records

BEHAVIORAL OBSERVATIONS

Brayden was cooperative when leaving his classroom for the assessment and throughout the evaluation. He displayed adequate levels of attention and concentration in the one-to-one situation and appeared to handle failure and challenging tasks well. He did not make eye contact and did not appear to be socially connected in his interaction with the psychologist. Brayden occasionally demonstrated echolalia (immediate repetition of the examiner's words) and tended to use exaggerated intonation in his voice when speaking. He chattered almost constantly while performing both verbal and nonverbal tasks—audible verbal mediation reflecting his thinking processes. During nonverbal tasks, he assigned verbal labels to shapes and designs and once, when he could not come up with a label, he asked the psychologist for help.

During the assessment, Brayden suddenly asked the time and then stated with some agitation, "I missed snack. And it's reading!" Permitting him to go back to his classroom to retrieve his snack and giving him a good reason for why he needed to miss reading today were sufficient for keeping Brayden on track.

The results of the current evaluation are considered a valid representation of Brayden's cognitive functioning and academic achievement.

EVALUATION FINDINGS

Cognitive/Intellectual Functioning

Brayden's overall level of cognitive/intellectual ability fell within the Average range of functioning. Fairly even levels

---

[1] All assessment instruments were chosen, administered, and interpreted with consideration of the child's cultural and ethnic background.

of development were demonstrated across the Core areas of cognitive processing assessed by the DAS-II, with his Verbal, Nonverbal Reasoning, and Visual-Spatial abilities all falling within average age expectations. Among the Core subtests, Brayden demonstrated a significant weakness on Pattern Construction, a task in which he needed to use cubes with different patterns on each side to create a match for a given design. His performance on this task, near the lower limit of the Average range, was weaker than his overall level of cognitive ability. A similar level of ability was demonstrated on the other visual-spatial task administered, Recall of Designs, in which he had to draw geometric designs from memory. These findings indicate that Brayden has some difficulty with analyzing, constructing, and recalling visual-spatial patterns and designs.

Working Memory, the ability to hold information in one's mind, manipulate it, and then retrieve it, and Processing Speed, the ability to perform relatively simple tasks quickly and fluently, were also in the Average range. Brayden's abilities in the areas of immediate short-term recall and long-term retention were also assessed. The assessment of long-term retention involves the ability to learn new material and then retrieve it after a longer period of time than what is typically used to assess working and short-term memory (this is not the same as long-term memory). While his long-term retention skills fell within average expectations and were very consistent with his other cognitive abilities, his immediate recall ability was Above Average. This latter skill was assessed by having Brayden repeat increasingly longer strings of random digits.

Academic Functioning

With the exception of listening comprehension, Brayden's levels of academic achievement across the areas of reading, mathematics, and written language all ranged from the Average to Superior range. While some statistically significant differences existed between some of the broad composites yielded by the WIAT-III, none were considered to be unusually large.

Reading and Writing

Brayden's word reading, nonsense word decoding, oral reading fluency, and reading comprehension were fairly evenly developed. Compared to age-peers, his scores ranged from the Average to High Average range. He demonstrated a relative strength in decoding and was able to sound out nonsense words with ease. A similar level of overall achievement was seen in the area of written language where his skills fell within the Average range. Brayden's ability to spell words accurately fell within the Average range, as did his abilities to compose sentences and to express himself in an essay.

Math

Brayden's strongest academic area was mathematics. His overall achievement fell within the High Average range. While his math reasoning skills fell within the Average range, his calculation and math fluency skills bordered on the High Average and Superior ranges. Brayden's ability to solve simple computations quickly (addition, subtraction, and multiplication) fell in the Superior range. His calculation skills, however, were somewhat scattered. Brayden did not consistently use regrouping procedures with subtraction, although he seemed to know the procedure. He was able to add with regrouping, solve 2-digit by 1-digit multiplication problems, and answer simple division and long division problems. Brayden was unable to work a 3-digit by 3-digit multiplication problem. He was able to multiply two simple fractions but was not able to solve addition and subtraction of simple fractions with like and unlike denominators.

Oral Language

Brayden's overall oral language skills were commensurate with his levels of cognitive ability and academic achievement. The oral language measures of the WIAT-III yielded interesting results. An extremely large disparity existed between Brayden's listening comprehension and oral expression abilities. Listening comprehension was an area of significant weakness and fell in the Well Below Average range. In contrast, his overall oral expression abilities were strong and fell within the Superior range. This strength was primarily due to Brayden's superior ability to repeat back sentences that were read to him. This discrepancy between oral expression and listening comprehension is not surprising for children with autism spectrum disorders, as listening comprehension, an aspect of receptive language, requires the individual to attend to other people, an inherent weakness among children with these disorders. One of the tasks of the WIAT-III (Receptive Vocabulary) involved pointing to one of four pictures that best matched a sentence read to him. Brayden had particular difficulty interpreting pictures depicting people in various situations. He confused male and female figures and ignored people in the pictures. On another task (Listening Comprehension), Brayden was asked to listen to different things, such as stories and conversations, and then was asked a question.

On several items, instead of trying to answer the question, Brayden would just repeat a part of the question.

Social/Behavioral Functioning

Brayden's two classroom teachers completed a Student Progress Report Form to provide information regarding his daily classroom functioning. Brayden is generally receiving passing grades, although some areas were graded as "needs improvement." Ratings of his typical classroom behavior ranged from extremely poor to average, with day-to-day variation. Difficulties were noted with regard to task completion in class. One teacher noted that frequently Brayden is not focused on the assigned task; the other reported that Brayden often completes only the first half of an assignment. In math, his level of class participation was rated as poor. Sometimes he performs his work adequately and at others, he reads books instead or walks around the room flapping his hands repetitively. His teacher reported that Brayden often needs to be prompted to join in activities and "pulled away from the books." In reading, his teacher stated that Brayden can usually provide a correct answer when he is called on, but again, he is not always focused on the lesson. Additionally, he makes impulsive comments that are disruptive and often negative or comical. She reported that his organizational skills are adequate, that he hands in almost all of his homework, and that it is completed satisfactorily. The math teacher rated his organizational skills as below average, noting that although he completes his homework, he often forgets to bring it, as well as needed supplies, from his homeroom class. Many of these behaviors are consistent with his diagnosis of ADHD.

Not surprisingly, the teachers rated Brayden's ability to relate to his peers as extremely poor to below average. The math teacher noted that Brayden typically does not initiate interactions but does respond to peers who initiate interactions with him. The reading/home room teacher reported some inappropriate behaviors with the girls in his class including kissing the top of their heads, kissing the name tags on their desks, and patting their bottoms. The teacher noted that she did not feel these behaviors were sexual in nature and that Brayden appears not to realize these behaviors are inappropriate.

The reading teacher also reported that Brayden is beginning to resist longer writing assignments and that writing tasks appear to be physically difficult for him. The reader is referred to his occupational therapy evaluation report for more information in this area.

CONCLUSIONS AND RECOMMENDATIONS

Brayden demonstrates average cognitive abilities. His one evident weakness in visual-spatial perception does not appear to be interfering with his academic learning but may contribute to his difficulties with interpreting pictures and with motor skills. His academic achievement in reading, math, and written language all fell within the Average or Above Average range and were commensurate with expectations based on his assessed level of general cognitive ability. Therefore, there was no evidence of any learning disabilities in these areas. Brayden demonstrated a significant weakness, however, in comprehension of oral language, which is consistent with his diagnoses of autism and speech and language impairment.

Behaviors observed during this evaluation and reported by his teachers are consistent with Brayden's recent diagnosis of Autism. Brayden is demonstrating some behavioral challenges in school that are associated with both his Autism and ADHD and require accommodations as well as a behavior intervention plan to support him in the regular classroom.

Most of Brayden's challenging behaviors are associated with his need to adhere to schedules or to engage in activities or thinking related to his preoccupations. These behaviors led to an event just before the winter break that involved Brayden becoming very upset and angry at his teachers, resulting in an out-of-school suspension. Many of Brayden's episodes of agitation can probably be linked to events proceeding in a different manner than he expects. It is as if Brayden has a predetermined plan of how the universe is supposed to function, and if events do not proceed according to his preconceptions, he experiences anxiety and becomes agitated. His subsequent behaviors reflect his attempts to get his world back on track to reduce his anxiety. To ensure that Brayden's perceived plan for the day matches those of his teachers, provide a visible schedule of the day in each of his classrooms and, at the beginning of each period, write on the board and explain an outline of activities or topics for the current class. Provide a warning 2 minutes (and, if possible, 5 minutes) before any transition. Brayden demonstrated some anxiety when a stopwatch was used during the evaluation so using a timer to signal these warnings is probably not a good idea. To improve compliance and reduce agitation at times when changes are unavoidable, provide him a legitimate reason why he needs to follow the current plan and, if possible, provide warnings, as above. Be mindful to state

demands pleasantly but directly rather than by using requests in the form of questions (e.g., "Brayden, please line up now," rather than "Brayden, could you please line up now?").

Brayden's poor listening comprehension can also be a source of behavioral challenges, as he may not understand the directions given. Recognize that when Brayden does not follow verbal directions, his behavior may not indicate willful noncompliance but rather inattention, or attending to something else intently at the time the direction was given, or misunderstanding what was said. Before giving instructions, make sure that Brayden is ready to receive a direction and, when possible, provide additional visual cues. For example, when explaining the directions for a worksheet, project it on an overhead projector and point to the areas you are explaining. Brayden's speech-language therapist may be able to provide additional ways to improve Brayden's attention to and comprehension of verbal information.

There will be times when episodes of agitation cannot be avoided. At those times, Brayden needs a place to go that he considers safe. Encourage Brayden to recognize and ask when he needs to remove himself, as well as to comply when adults make the request. One possible safe place at his school is the chairs by the front reception area. It needs to be stressed that this is not a disciplinary procedure and Brayden needs to understand that he is not in trouble. Using positive reinforcement to promote attention to task and task completion in class should prevent Brayden from taking advantage of this intervention.

Although Brayden's frequent chattering may be annoying to others in the classroom, he is not being intentionally disruptive. Some of this chatter is Brayden's thinking out loud, whereas at other times it is due to impulsivity. Brayden needs to be taught how to subvocalize his thinking and modulate the volume of his voice. Techniques such those described in *The Incredible 5-Point Scale* (Buron & Curtis, 2003), as well as providing him prompts and feedback, would be beneficial. Self-monitoring techniques can also be helpful. For example, give Brayden a chart for his desk on which he is to keep track of how many times he gets out of his seat or calls out during class. Provide reinforcement for frequencies of these behaviors that are below baseline levels. Gradually reduce the criterion for receiving a reward so that less frequent monitoring is needed. A sample chart for this purpose is included in the Appendix. When Brayden leaves his seat to ask or tell the teacher something, say,

"Brayden, you're out of your seat without permission. Return to your seat, raise your hand, and I will be happy to call on you."

Social stories are a useful technique for teaching children with autism spectrum disorders appropriate social behaviors for specific situations. These can be devised after an event to teach Brayden appropriate alternative behaviors. Social stories can also be used to help Brayden understand that kissing and certain types of touching are inappropriate. Weekly school-based counseling services would be appropriate for this purpose. Interventions such as using peer helpers in the classroom might also be considered.

Both of Brayden's teachers reported problems with task completion, and one teacher reported that he frequently does not bring the appropriate materials when he switches classes. To help Brayden remember his books and homework assignments, he would benefit from either a prompt before leaving his homeroom for other classes or having what he needs in an identifiable folder that he routinely takes to math. Additionally, Brayden should respond to a positive reinforcement program that focuses on task completion as the major target behavior. A program where he is given positive feedback and tangible rewards whenever he completes a task adequately will increase his rate of task completion. Allow him to earn stickers, marks on a chart, or the like, that he can then exchange for a reinforcing activity. Brayden's behavior of completing only the first half of an assignment indicates a need to break down longer tasks into smaller components. This will not only increase on-task behavior, it will also provide more opportunities for Brayden to receive positive feedback from teachers.

Brayden's inattention, impulsive verbalizations, and inappropriate touching of others are due, at least in part, to his ADHD. The parents are encouraged to meet with the developmental pediatrician who made this diagnosis and discuss the possible benefits of medication to increase Brayden's ability to regulate his own behavior.

Brayden needs to learn about his disability so he understands his learning and behavioral differences. Given his love of books, bibliotherapy would be very helpful. Some examples of appropriate books include: *I Am Utterly Unique: Celebrating the Strengths of Children with Asperger Syndrome and High-Functioning Autism* by Elaine Marie Larson (2006, Autism Asperger Publishing Company) and *Andy and His Yellow Frisbee* by Mary Thompson (1996, Woodbine House).

REFERENCES

Buron, K. D., & Curtis, M. (2003). *The incredible 5-Point Scale: Assisting students with autism spectrum disorders in understanding social interactions and controlling their emotional responses.* Shawnee Mission, KS: Autism Asperger Publishing Company.

Larson, E. M. (2006). *I am utterly unique: Celebrating the strengths of children with Asperger Syndrome and high-functioning autism.* Shawnee Mission, KS: Autism Asperger Publishing Company.

Thompson, M. (1996). *Andy and his yellow Frisbee.* Bethesda, MD: Woodbine House.

PSYCHOMETRIC SUMMARY[2]

Differential Ability Scales-II: *Core Battery*

Core Cluster and Composite Scores and Indexes

Cluster/ Composite	Standard Score	Percentile Rank	90% Confidence Interval	Qualitative Description
Verbal	98	45	91–106	Average
Nonverbal Reasoning	106	66	100–112	Average
Spatial	97	42	92–102	Average
General Conceptual Ability	101	53	96–106	Average
Special Nonverbal Composite	102	55	97–107	Average

Verbal Ability Cluster Subtest Scores Summary

Subtests	Item Set	Ability Score	T Score	Percentile	Age Equiv.
Verbal Similarities	16–26	109	52	58	9:3
Word Definitions	5–18	98	46	34	8:7

Note: These scores are provided for professional use only, by persons trained in psychological tests and measurements. A significant risk of misinterpretation of these scores exists. Please refer to the body of the report for interpretive information Standard Scores: ≥130 = Very Superior; 120–129 = Superior; 110–119, Above Average; 90–109 = Average; 80–89 = Below Average; 79 and below = Well Below Average. Standard Scores: Ave = 100, SD = 15; Scaled Scores: Avg = 10, SD = 3; *T* scores: Avg = 50, SD = 10

Nonverbal Reasoning Ability Cluster Subtest Scores Summary

Subtests	Item Set	Ability Score	T Score	Percentile	Age Equiv.
Matrices	20–41	99	56	73	11:3
Sequential and Quantitative Reasoning	9–35	115	52	58	9:9

Spatial Ability Cluster Subtest Scores Summary

Subtests	Item Set	Ability Score	T Score	Percentile	Age Equiv.
Recall of Designs	4–16	94	52	58	10:3
Pattern Construction	20–28	207	45	31	8:1

Differential Ability Scales-II: Diagnostic Battery

Diagnostic Cluster Scores and Indexes

Cluster	Standard Score	Percentile	90% Confidence Interval	Qualitative Description
Working Memory	104	61	99–109	Average
Processing Speed	95	37	88–103	Average

Working Memory Cluster Subtest Scores Summary

Subtests	Item Set	Ability Score	T Score	Percentile	Age Equiv.
Recall of Sequential Order	1–20	122	51	54	9:9
Recall of Digits—Backward	1–30	117	53	62	10:9

Processing Speed Cluster Subtest Scores Summary

Subtests	Item Set	Ability Score	T Score	Percentile	Age Equiv.
Speed of Information Processing	7–12	132	49	46	9:3
Rapid Naming	1–3	138	46	34	7:7

Diagnostic Subtest Scores Summary

Subtests	Item Set	Ability Score	T Score	Percentile	Age Equiv.
Recall of Objects—Immediate	1–60	162	50	50	9:3
Recall of Objects—Delayed	1–20	9	46	34	8:4
Recall of Digits—Forward	1–38	189	62	88	17:3

Summary of WIAT-III Subtest Scores (Age-Based)

Subtest Score Summary									
Subtests	Raw Score	Standard Score	95% Confidence Interval	Percentile Rank	Normal Curve Equiv.	Stanine	Age Equiv.	Grade Equiv.	Growth Score
Listening Comprehension	–	78	66–90	7	19	2	5:10	1.1	457
Reading Comprehension	34*	105	92–118	63	57	6	11:0	5.2	515
Math Problem Solving	45	107	96–118	68	60	6	9:8	4.6	531
Sentence Composition	–	114	104–124	82	70	7	12:6	7.2	520
Word Reading	45	108	104–112	70	61	6	10:0	5.0	551
Essay Composition	–	98	88–108	45	47	5	8:8	3.7	504
Pseudoword Decoding	36	112	108–116	79	67	7	13:0	8.1	553
Numerical Operations	30	118	109–127	88	75	7	10:4	5.2	572
Oral Expression	–	127	116–138	96	88	9	15:9	9.9	559

(Continued)

Subtests	Raw Score	Standard Score	95% Confidence Interval	Percentile Rank	Normal Curve Equiv.	Stanine	Age Equiv.	Grade Equiv.	Growth Score
Oral Reading Fluency	154*†	102	94–110	55	53	5	9:4	4.0	507
Spelling	23	103	96–110	58	54	5	9:4	4.2	537
Math Fluency—Addition	35	121	108–134	92	79	8	12:4	7.2	647
Math Fluency—Subtraction	30	120	110–130	91	78	8	11:8	6.7	650
Math Fluency—Multiplication	22	117	108–126	87	74	7	10:4	5.2	624

– Indicates a subtest with multiple raw scores (shown in the Subtest Component Score Summary).
* Indicates a raw score that is converted to a weighted raw score (not shown).
† Indicates that a raw score is based on a below grade level item set.

Supplemental Subtest Score Summary

Subtests	Raw Score	Standard Score	95% Confidence Interval	Percentile Rank	Normal Curve Equiv.	Stanine	Age Equiv.	Grade Equiv.	Growth Score
Essay Composition: Grammar and Mechanics	50	107	94–120	68	60	6	10:4	5.6	N/A
Oral Reading Accuracy	126*	106	94–118	66	58	6	10:4	4.9	N/A
Oral Reading Rate	49*	110	100–120	75	64	6	11:0	5.8	N/A

* Indicates a raw score that is converted to a weighted raw score (not shown).

Subtest Component Score Summary

Subtest Component	Raw Score	Standard Score	Percentile Rank	Normal Curve Equivalent	Stanine	Qualitative Description
Listening Comprehension						
Receptive Vocabulary	7	80	9	22	2	Below Average
Oral Discourse Comprehension	9	82	12	25	3	Below Average
Sentence Composition						
Sentence Building	22	108	70	61	6	Average
Sentence Combining	16	117	87	74	7	Above Average
Essay Composition						
Word Count	50	97	42	46	5	Average
Theme Development and Text Organization	5	98	45	47	5	Average
Oral Expression						
Expressive Vocabulary	11	114	82	70	7	Average
Oral Word Fluency	35	119	90	77	8	Above Average
Sentence Repetition	24	128	97	89	9	Above Average

Composite Score Summary							
Composites	**Sum of Subtest Standard Scores**	**Standard Score**	**95% Confidence Interval**	**Percentile Rank**	**Normal Curve Equiv.**	**Stanine**	**Qualitative Description**
Oral Language	205	102	93–111	55	53	5	Average
Total Reading	427	107	102–112	68	60	6	Average
Basic Reading	220	110	107–113	75	64	6	Average
Reading Comprehension and Fluency	207	104	95–113	61	56	6	Average
Written Expression	315	106	99–113	66	58	6	Average
Mathematics	225	114	106–122	82	70	7	Average
Math Fluency	358	122	114–130	93	81	8	Above Average
Total Achievement	1069	109	105–113	73	63	6	Average

Differences Between Composite Standard Scores				
Comparison	**Difference**	**Critical Value (Significance Level .01)**	**Significant Difference Y/N**	**Base Rate**
Oral Language vs. Total Reading	−5	12.15	N	>15%
Oral Language vs. Basic Reading	−8	11.74	N	>15%
Oral Language vs. Reading Comprehension and Fluency	−2	14.47	N	>15%
Oral Language vs. Written Expression	−4	14.07	N	>15%
Oral Language vs. Mathematics	−12	13.18	N	>15%
Oral Language vs. Math Fluency	−20	13.71	Y	>15%
Total Reading vs. Basic Reading	−3	7.24	N	>15%
Total Reading vs. Reading Comprehension and Fluency	3	11.13	N	>15%
Total Reading vs. Written Expression	1	10.61	N	>15%
Total Reading vs. Mathematics	−7	9.40	N	>15%
Total Reading vs. Math Fluency	−15	10.12	Y	>15%
Basic Reading vs. Reading Comprehension and Fluency	6	10.68	N	>15%
Basic Reading vs. Written Expression	4	10.13	N	>15%
Basic Reading vs. Mathematics	−4	8.85	N	>15%
Basic Reading vs. Math Fluency	−12	9.62	Y	>15%
Reading Comprehension and Fluency vs. Written Expression	−2	13.20	N	>15%
Reading Comprehension and Fluency vs. Mathematics	−10	12.24	N	>15%
Reading Comprehension and Fluency vs. Math Fluency	−18	12.81	Y	>15%
Written Expression vs. Mathematics	−8	11.77	N	>15%
Written Expression vs. Math Fluency	−16	12.36	Y	>15%
Mathematics vs. Math Fluency	−8	11.33	N	>15%

Note. A negative difference indicates that the second composite has a higher score than the first composite listed in the comparison.

Ability-Achievement Discrepancy Analysis

Date of Ability Testing: 4/10/2010

Ability Score Type: GCA

Ability Score: 101

Predicted-Difference Method

	Predicted Score	Actual Score	Expected Difference	Critical Value	Significant Difference Y/N	Base Rate
WIAT-III Subtests						
Word Reading	101	108	−7	6.37	Y	
Reading Comprehension	101	105	−4	7.79	N	
Pseudoword Decoding	101	112	−11	6.03	Y	
Numerical Operations	101	118	−17	9.73	Y	
Math Problem Solving	101	107	−6	6.15	N	
Spelling	101	103	−2	8.02	N	
Sentence Composition	101	114	−13	10.09	Y	
Essay Composition	101	98	3	6.20	N	
Listening Comprehension	101	78	23	13.83	Y	1–2%
Oral Expression	101	127	−26	11.48	Y	
Composites						
Total Reading	101	107	−6	5.93	Y	
Mathematics	101	114	−13	7.98	Y	
Written Expression	101	106	−5	8.18	N	
Oral Language	101	102	−1	10.65	N	
Total Achievement	101	109	−8	6.37	Y	

Statistical Significance (Critical Values) at the .05 level
Base Rates are not reported when the achievement score equals or exceeds the ability score.

CASE 21

RTI Data and Cognitive Assessment Are Both Useful for SLD Identification and Intervention Planning

Dawn Flanagan and Vincent Alfonso

This report illustrates the need for a comprehensive evaluation of academic and cognitive abilities and processes, as well as exclusionary factors when a child fails to respond to quality instruction and intervention. In this case study, Thomas, a fourth grader, experienced academic difficulties in reading and writing, despite having been exposed to quality instruction and intervention over a prolonged period of time (i.e., grades 1 through 3). Because Thomas did not make progress in the school's response to intervention program (RTI), it was necessary to gather additional data through a comprehensive evaluation. Specifically, the evaluation was conducted to gain more information about how Thomas learns and his cognitive strengths, as well as to determine the specific nature of any weaknesses in cognitive abilities and information processing. An understanding of Thomas's strengths and weaknesses is necessary to assist in understanding why learning is exceedingly difficult, why the interventions that were tried did not lead to appreciable academic gains, and what Thomas's teachers can do differently in the future that may prove more effective.

This case study also illustrates the fact that data from a comprehensive evaluation are necessary for differential diagnosis. Thomas's evaluation was conducted within the context of Flanagan and colleagues' operational definition of specific learning disability (Flanagan, Ortiz, Alfonso, & Mascolo, 2006) and demonstrated that he met SLD criteria consistent with this definition. Specifically, the data demonstrated that Thomas's difficulties in reading and writing could not be explained by global cognitive impairment, social-emotional problems, cultural and linguistic differences, sensory-motor difficulties, lack of motivation, environmental disadvantage, or health-related impairments. Rather, Thomas exhibited specific weaknesses in cognitive areas that are known to be related to difficulties in reading and writing, namely working memory, retrieval ability, and phonological processing.

Therefore, whereas Thomas has the ability to think and reason like most children his age, as demonstrated by his performance in the cognitive areas of reasoning, knowledge, and visual-spatial thinking, he possesses specific and related cognitive and academic deficits that are consistent with a diagnosis of SLD. The recommendations suggested for Thomas demonstrate how some of his difficulties can be remediated, whereas others need to be compensated for or accommodated. It is expected that Thomas will be able to achieve grade-level performance, as long as he is provided with targeted reading and writing interventions, explicit instruction in how to compensate for memory difficulties, and continued accommodations in the classroom.

CONFIDENTIAL PSYCHOEDUCATIONAL REPORT

Name:	Thomas MacAloon
Date of Birth:	1/25/2001
Age:	9-8
Parents:	Harry and Marge MacAloon
School:	Yantacaw Elementary
Teacher:	Ms. Sharon Conti
Grade:	4
Dates of Evaluation:	9/28, 29/2010
Evaluators:	Dawn Flanagan, Ph.D.
	Vincent Alfonso, Ph. D.

REFERRAL CONCERNS

Thomas's fourth-grade teacher referred him to the Child Study Team (CST) due to continued concerns with his academic performance, primarily in the areas of reading and

197

writing. According to information contained in his school records and from interviews with his teacher and parents, Thomas has had difficulty learning to read and write since entering school. Initially, the problems were minimal; it was believed that he might be slow in his maturation and that with time, his skills might improve. As he progressed through the grades, however, Thomas has fallen steadily behind his same-age and grade peers in the development of literacy skills.

Given the level of support Thomas received in the second and third grades, including evidence-based interventions in reading, coupled with a "tremendous amount" of home support, his failure to meet grade-level benchmarks in both reading and writing by the end of third grade was unexpected. As such, the CST requested a complete psychoeducational evaluation to explore the possibility of a specific learning disability.

BACKGROUND INFORMATION

Educational and Family History

Thomas was born in northern New Jersey, where his family has resided for several generations. Thomas's ethnic heritage is Anglo-American. At this time, there are no indications of economic hardship in Thomas's family. Thomas's parents indicated that the only language spoken in the home is English and that he has had no exposure to a second language in the home or community. Thomas's father is a local real estate agent, and his mother teaches at a junior high school in a neighboring school district. He has two older siblings, a brother in the seventh grade and a sister in the tenth grade, both of whom are reported to be "average" students. Thomas has a good relationship with the members of his family and is well liked by his peers.

Thomas attended a local preschool at ages 3 and 4 prior to beginning his education at Yantacaw Elementary at the age of 5, where he is still enrolled. In second grade, Thomas received instruction that used an Open Court and Saxon Phonics combination program. Although Thomas made progress, he did not meet second-grade benchmarks and, therefore, this instruction continued into the third grade. In the second half of third grade, based on the results of a district-wide language arts test, Thomas qualified for additional academic intervention services in the language arts lab. This supplementary service focused on developing Thomas's reading and writing skills. For the remainder of the year, he received small-group instruction with eight children for one 45-minute period, three days per week.

Additional strategies to help Thomas were also implemented at home and in the classroom. Thomas's parents hired a tutor to assist him with study skills and work with him on more involved class projects (e.g., science projects and book reports). In school, Thomas's teacher paired him with a "peer buddy." He could ask his buddy questions if he did not understand or remember an in-class assignment or the teacher's directions. Thomas's progress was monitored closely and he made only minor improvement in his reading and writing skills in the third grade. Thomas's fourth-grade teacher, Ms. Conti, referred him to the Child Study Team to discuss his continued difficulties.

Thomas's teacher also described him as having word retrieval problems. She stated that, quite often, while he is speaking, he pauses for an extended period of time, apparently trying to come up with a word, then continues. Frequently, when he pauses, he describes the meaning of the word he is trying to find rather than recalling the word itself (e.g., "You know, the bowl with holes in it that mom uses to drain the spaghetti in"). When reading, although Thomas is reportedly able to indentify several high-frequency words, Ms. Conti described his decoding of unknown words and reading comprehension skills as weak. She reported that Thomas also has difficulty with spelling and written expression. Despite his struggles acquiring basic reading and writing skills, Thomas has always performed well in math.

Developmental/Health History

Developmental history revealed that Thomas was the product of a normal pregnancy and birth. Developmental milestones were reportedly met within normal limits. Other than two asthma attacks, specific ENT-related procedures (bilateral myringotomies at age 4 years), and a single hospitalization due to a chronic respiratory infection, Thomas's health history is unremarkable and he is currently reported to be in good health. Information from the school nurse revealed that Thomas's most recent physical exam was unremarkable and his vision and hearing are within normal limits. Overall, there appear to be no current physical or health factors that might be related to Thomas's educational difficulties.

TESTS ADMINISTERED AND EVALUATION PROCEDURES

Behavior Assessment System for Children – Second Edition, Parent Rating Scales – Child (BASC-2, PRS-C)

Kaufman Test of Educational Achievement, Second Edition (KTEA-II; selected subtests)—09/28/10

Woodcock Johnson III Tests of Cognitive Abilities (WJ III COG; selected tests)—09/29/10

Woodcock Johnson III Tests of Achievement (WJ III (ACH; selected tests)—09/28/10

Teacher interview

Parent interview

Classroom observation

Records review

Work sample/Permanent product reviews

Standard Score Range	Percentile Range	Classification
< 70	< 2nd	Lower Extreme
70–84	2nd to 14th	Well Below Average/Normative Weakness
85–89	16th to 23rd	Low Average*
90–110	25th to 75th	Average*
111–115	77th to 84th	High Average*
116–129	86th to 97th	Well Above Average/Normative Strength
>130	> 97th	Upper Extreme
*Within Normal Limits (range in which most people perform)		

BEHAVIORAL OBSERVATIONS

Thomas was cooperative throughout testing and appeared to put forth consistent effort on all tasks. Rapport was easily established and maintained throughout the evaluation. Although Thomas found some of the items administered to be "hard," he responded well when encouraged to try his best. At times, Thomas asked for a previously read instruction to be repeated and sometimes questioned the exact requirements of a task. Interestingly, after giving an initial response to a question, Thomas sometimes asked, "What did I just say?" before settling on a final answer. Thomas also often paused or talked around a response prior to giving a final answer. These test behavior observations are consistent with the examiner's observations of Thomas in the classroom. Overall, the current test results appear to represent a reliable and valid estimate of Thomas's academic and cognitive functioning.

ASSESSMENT FINDINGS: ACADEMIC PERFORMANCE

Thomas demonstrated academic strengths and weaknesses on standardized measures of academic achievement, including the WJ III ACH and KTEA-II. His performance on these measures was consistent with teacher and parent reports, progress monitoring data, work samples, and the examiner's classroom observations. Thomas's performance on each test is described below using the following classification system.

Basic Reading and Reading Fluency

Thomas's performance in the areas of basic reading and reading fluency skills reflect his ability to identify real words, apply phonics strategies to decode nonsense words, and read words and simple sentences fluently. In terms of basic reading skills, Thomas was required to identify a series of letters and words presented in isolation (WJ III ACH Letter-Word Identification, SS = 90 [88–93], Average), as well as to decode a series of nonsense words (WJ III ACH Word Attack, SS = 84 [81–87], Well Below Average). Thomas demonstrated a normative weakness on the latter task, indicating that most children his age (about 85%) performed better than he did on this task. His poor performance on Word Attack is likely the result of a deficit in phonetic coding (which is discussed in the "cognitive performance" section).

In the area of reading fluency, Thomas scored in the Average range when required to quickly read a series of short statements and determine if they were true or false (WJ III ACH Reading Fluency, SS = 92 [90–94]), but scored in the Well Below Average range when required to rapidly decode a list of nonsense words (KTEA-II Decoding Fluency, SS = 79 [75–83]). Thomas demonstrated a normative weakness on this latter task, which is consistent with his performance on WJ III ACH Word Attack. Overall, it appears that while Thomas is developing a basic sight word vocabulary that assists him in recognizing many words automatically (thus allowing him to perform in the lower end of Average range on the WJ III ACH Letter-Word Identification and Reading Fluency tests), his phonetic decoding skills are severely limited and significantly hamper his ability to figure out words that he does not recognize already. Thomas's Reading Fluency score in the lower end of the Average range was also affected by his difficulty reading the words although it is likely that the meaning of the sentences helped him to figure them out.

Reading Comprehension

Thomas's reading vocabulary and reading comprehension, as assessed, were both in the Well Below Average range and represent normative weaknesses for him, meaning that his performance in this area is significantly below that of same-age peers from the general population. The WJ III ACH Reading Vocabulary test (SS = 83 [81–86]) required Thomas to provide synonyms and antonyms for a series of printed words and to complete analogies. Thomas had a variety of difficulties in the synonyms and antonyms subtests; sometimes he read the word wrong or just said, "I don't know that word," and so could not come up with a response. On some words, his response was correct but was the second or third response he gave, saying, "no" between each attempt. Additionally, his responses on all three subtests were notably slow, sometimes up to 15 seconds. As the Analogies subtest is read silently (only the response is given aloud), this type of task analysis was not possible. The KTEA-II Reading Comprehension test (SS = 80 [76–84]) required Thomas to answer a series of literal and inferential questions based on a previously read passage.

Summary of Reading Performance

Overall, when faced with words that are part of his sight vocabulary, Thomas reads them relatively automatically. When faced, however, with words that should be familiar but are not, Thomas does not have sufficient skills to analyze them phonetically. Additionally, Thomas's performance on an oral vocabulary test (discussed below) indicated that he performed as well as or better than only 25% of his age-peers. This may also negatively affect his phonetic decoding because even if he sounds out a word correctly, if it is not in his oral vocabulary, he will not recognize that he has done so. Additionally, it is difficult to understand the meaning of a passage if one does not know the meaning of key words in it. Consequently, difficulties with phonetic coding and, to some extent, vocabulary knowledge, adversely affect his ability to comprehend what he reads. Thomas's reading difficulties affect his academic performance broadly and significantly.

Mathematics Calculation and Problem Solving

On a task requiring Thomas to solve basic computational problems (WJ III ACH Calculation, SS = 114 [109–120]) his performance was High Average compared to that of same-age peers. Thomas's performance on a task requiring him to quickly add, subtract, and multiply a series of single-digit numbers (WJ III ACH Math Fluency, SS = 118 [115–121]) was Well Above Average and represented a normative strength for him as compared to his age peers. Thomas performed as well as or better than 83% and 88% of same-age peers from the general population on these math tasks, respectively. These results demonstrate that Thomas excels in math calculation.

Thomas's performances on tests of math reasoning (WJ III ACH Applied Problems, SS = 106 [102–110]) and understanding numerical concepts and operations (WJ III ACH Quantitative Concepts, SS = 104 [98–109]) were Average. Thomas's overall problem-solving skills are well developed and commensurate with expectations for an individual of his age. In accordance with standardized procedures, all math problems were read to Thomas. Reading to Thomas allowed him to focus on the computational aspects of the problems without having to allocate attentional resources to the decoding of words contained in the word problems.

Written Language

Thomas's performance in the area of writing represents his quality of written expression as well as his fluency of written production. His performance in writing was variable. Specifically, Thomas demonstrated Average performance when required to quickly write simple sentences (WJ III ACH Writing Fluency, SS = 100 [95–105]). Noteworthy is the fact that the Writing Fluency test included contextual cues (i.e., pictures and words) and spelling errors were not penalized. When presented with a task that contained less contextual support and required Thomas to generate written text in response to a variety of demands, his performance was Low Average (WJ III ACH Writing Samples, SS = 85 [78–91]). Thomas's performance was similar when he was presented with a test that contained even less contextual support and required him to compose lengthier amounts of text (KABC-II Written Expression, SS = 82 [76–88]; Well Below Average). On both tests of written expression, Thomas's sentences were simple, lacked detail, and contained minor grammatical errors. Although spelling is usually not penalized on these tests, some of his spellings were so far from their phonetic representations as to be indecipherable, thus costing him points.

Analysis of three classroom writing samples revealed that Thomas's performance on the KABC-II Written Expression test was most consistent with his performance on classroom writing tasks. Furthermore, this analysis showed errors in the mechanics of writing (i.e., punctuation, capitalization, and spelling). These observations were consistent with Thomas's performance on the WJ III ACH Basic Writing Skills cluster, which was Well Below Average, indicating significant difficulty with the mechanics of writing (Basic Writing Skills, SS = 82 [79–85]; Spelling, SS = 83 [81–86]; Editing, SS = 84 [81–87]).

ASSESSMENT FINDINGS: COGNITIVE PERFORMANCE

In order to determine whether Thomas's academic difficulties are related to delays or weaknesses in cognitive ability, he was administered a select set of tests from the WJ III COG. This test battery provides estimates of cognitive functioning in seven broad areas, including: Comprehension-Knowledge, Long-Term Retrieval, Visual-Spatial Thinking, Auditory Processing, Fluid Reasoning, Processing Speed, and Short-Term Memory. A description of Thomas's performance in each of these domains follows.

Comprehension-Knowledge

Comprehension-Knowledge refers to an individual's breadth and depth of knowledge, including verbal communication, general information, and reasoning using the relationship among word meanings. Thomas's ability in this domain was assessed through tasks that required him to name pictures of objects, provide synonyms or antonyms for words presented by the examiner, and complete verbal analogies. Taken together, these tasks provide a measure of Thomas's vocabulary knowledge as well as his ability to reason using lexical knowledge (Verbal Comprehension, SS = 90 [85–95]; Average). Additionally, Thomas was required to respond to a series of questions in which he had to identify where he would find specific objects (e.g., a wall) and, later, what he would do with specific objects (e.g., a shovel) (General Information, SS = 91 [86–97]; Average). This latter task primarily assessed Thomas's fund of general (verbal) knowledge. Overall, Thomas obtained a Comprehension-Knowledge standard score of 91 (87–94), which is classified as Average compared to same-age peers

from the general population. Although Thomas's Comprehension-Knowledge score falls in the Average range, it equals or exceeds that of only 27% of age peers, suggesting that he would benefit from explicit and direct instruction in building word knowledge, especially in an effort to facilitate the development of reading skills.

Long-Term Retrieval

Long-Term Retrieval involves an individual's ability to store information efficiently and retrieve it later through association. Thomas's Long-Term Retrieval was assessed through tasks that required him to learn and recall a series of rebuses (i.e., pictographic representations of words) and translate these rebuses into a series of orally read sentences (Visual-Auditory Learning, SS = 75 [70–79]; Well Below Average) as well as name as many examples as possible from a series of three categories (e.g., things we wear, things that make sounds, types of fruit) within a 1-minute time period (Retrieval Fluency, SS = 88 [81–94]; Low Average). Thomas's performance on the tasks composing the Long-Term Retrieval domain was variable. An examination of his performance on each task suggests that his efficiency in retrieving stored information may be partly dependent on the degree of specificity required in the retrieval demands of the task. Thomas's weak performance on Visual-Auditory Association might have been due to difficulty storing the new information (picture-word associations) in long-term memory, retrieving the specific word for each picture, or both. In contrast, Retrieval Fluency allowed considerable flexibility in responses (as long as they fit the given category) and produced a higher score. Another test, Rapid Picture Naming, was similar to Retrieval Fluency in that both required him to retrieve information previously stored in long-term memory within a time limit. Rapid Picture Naming, however, required Thomas to retrieve a *specific* word to match each of a series of familiar pictured objects, without any flexibility. Thomas had significantly more difficulty on this test (SS = 68 [66–69], 2nd percentile), scoring in the Lower Extreme. An error analysis of Thomas's performance on this task revealed that he produced an accurate response for most items; however, he could only provide a general response for some (e.g., Thomas said "person" when shown a picture of a soldier and "bowl" when shown a picture of a colander).

Overall, Thomas's Long-Term Retrieval performance appears to be related to how well information is stored in long-term memory as well as the specific retrieval demands of the task and the time parameters involved. In general, Thomas's performance on Long-Term Retrieval tasks was Within Normal Limits when broad parameters were involved in the task (i.e., a variety of responses were acceptable, no time limit); however, when more stringent parameters were present (i.e., a specific word was required), Thomas's performance declined significantly. Finally, Thomas's performance was most adversely impacted when he was required to generate specific responses under strict timed conditions. Because retrieval plays an important role in relating new knowledge to prior knowledge, as well as in expressing one's knowledge (both of which are important in reading and writing), attempts to compensate for or accommodate long-term retrieval difficulties should play an essential role in developing educational interventions for Thomas.

Visual-Spatial Thinking

Visual-Spatial Thinking includes spatial orientation, the ability to analyze and synthesize visual stimuli, and the ability to hold and manipulate mental images. Thomas's ability in Visual-Spatial Thinking was assessed through tasks that required him to identify two or three pieces that formed a complete target shape (Spatial Relations, SS = 117 [111–123]) and recognize a subset of previously presented pictures within a field of distracting pictures (Picture Recognition, SS = 117 [110–123]). These tasks assessed Thomas's ability to perceive and manipulate visual patterns as well as his visual memory of objects or pictures, respectively. Thomas obtained an overall Visual-Spatial Thinking cluster of 122 (116–128), which is ranked at the 93rd percentile and is classified as Well Above Average. Thomas's Visual-Spatial Thinking ability is very well developed and may be useful in helping him to compensate for weaknesses in other cognitive and academic domains.

Auditory Processing

Auditory processing involves the ability to discriminate, analyze, and synthesize auditory stimuli. Thomas's auditory processing was assessed through a task that required him to listen to a series of separate syllables or phonemes and blend the sounds into a complete word (e.g., *f-a-th-er* is *father*) (Sound Blending, SS = 80 [74–86]; Well Below Average), as well as a task that required Thomas to discriminate among similar sounding words (e.g., *cat* and *cap*) in the presence of increasing background noise (Auditory Attention, SS = 102 [95–110]; Average). While the former task primarily measured Thomas's skill in synthesizing

speech sounds to produce a whole word (phonetic coding), the latter task provided an estimate of Thomas's speech discrimination ability.

On another task of phonetic coding, Thomas was required to listen to a series of words with missing phonemes and provide a complete word (e.g., *g-ape-f-uit* is *grapefruit*) (Incomplete Words SS = 80 [73–87]; Well Below Average). Both tests of phonetic coding make up the Phonemic Awareness cluster. Thomas obtained a Phonemic Awareness cluster score of 74 (68–80; 4th percentile; Well Below Average), which indicates that he has a normative weakness or deficit in phonetic coding. The considerable difficulty Thomas has with analyzing and synthesizing speech sounds directly impairs his ability to learn phonics skills, a prerequisite for many children in learning to read and spell. Given that there was significant variability in Thomas's performance on Auditory Processing tasks, an analysis of task components was conducted. Thomas's highest score in the area of Auditory Processing was on Auditory Attention. This test involved the use of visual stimuli (e.g., pictures of common objects or concepts). Perhaps because Thomas had visual support on Auditory Attention, which was not available on the phonetic coding tests, he was able to perform in the Average range. Moreover, the words used in the Auditory Attention test were presented as whole words, unlike the phonetic coding tasks, wherein the words were either missing phonemes or were presented as word parts (e.g., syllables, individual sounds) with pauses between them. As such, the blending tasks placed demands on Thomas's short-term memory to a greater extent than did the Auditory Attention task. It seems clear that Thomas's performance on academic tasks may vary quite substantially as a function of the qualitative features of the task (e.g., visual or auditory; time requirements; memory demands). Therefore, it is important to consider those features that facilitate Thomas's performance prior to selecting or developing interventions.

Fluid Reasoning

Fluid Reasoning involves the ability to reason and solve problems that often involve unfamiliar information or procedures. Fluid Reasoning is generally manifested in the reorganization, transformation, and extrapolation of information. Thomas's Fluid Reasoning ability was assessed through tasks that required him to derive rules for a set of presented stimulus items (Concept Formation, SS = 116 [112–120]; Well Above Average) and analyze the parts of an incomplete logic puzzle to identify the missing parts (Analysis-Synthesis, SS = 110 [104–116]; Average Range). These two tests make up the Fluid Reasoning cluster. Thomas obtained a Fluid Reasoning cluster of 115 (111–119), which is ranked at the 84th percentile and is classified as High Average, suggesting that his ability to solve novel problems using reasoning and exercising forethought is well developed. Thomas's ability in this domain can facilitate his performance on academic tasks that require him to make inferences and draw conclusions based on visual information (e.g., making predictions using visual stimuli, such as graphs and charts).

Processing Speed

Processing Speed involves the speed and efficiency in performing automatic or very simple cognitive tasks. Thomas's Processing Speed ability was assessed through tasks that required him to quickly locate and circle two identical numbers in a row of six numbers (Visual Matching, SS = 105 [100–110]; Average) and quickly locate the two pictures in a row of pictures that are most conceptually similar (Decision Speed, SS = 99 [95–104]; Average). These two tests make up the Processing Speed cluster. Thomas obtained an overall Processing Speed cluster of 103 (99–107), which is ranked at the 58th percentile and classified as Average.

Short-Term Memory

Short-Term Memory is the ability to hold information in immediate awareness and then use it within a few seconds. Thomas's Short-Term Memory ability was assessed through tasks that required him to repeat a series of increasingly lengthy number chains in reverse order (Numbers Reversed, SS = 88 [83–94]; Low Average) and repeat lists of unrelated words verbatim (Memory for Words, SS = 86 [82–93]; Low Average). Noteworthy is the fact that Thomas was able to recall many of the words presented to him but often did not recite them in the order presented and sometimes omitted or inserted words in the initial portions of the word list. Thus, although Thomas demonstrated adequate free recall ability in most instances, when additional demands were added (retaining the proper sequence in mind), he had increased difficulty. Thomas obtained a Short-Term Memory cluster score of 86 (81–90; 17th percentile; Low Average).

SOCIAL-EMOTIONAL AND BEHAVIORAL FUNCTIONING

To assess Thomas's social-emotional and behavioral functioning in the home setting, his mother was asked to complete the Behavior Assessment System for Children, Second Edition Parent Rating Scales – Child (BASC-2, PRS-C). These scales assess externalizing and internalizing behavior problems, school problems, and adaptive skills and provide an index of overall social-emotional adjustment, called the Behavioral Symptom Index (BSI), which was within normal limits. Mrs. MacAloon's ratings of Thomas's behavior in all areas indicate that Thomas is well adjusted relative to his same-age peers. Moreover, based on these ratings, teacher reports, and the examiner's observations and interactions with Thomas, it seems clear that his academic difficulties are not the result of social-emotional or behavioral difficulties.

SUMMARY AND DATA INTEGRATION

Thomas was referred for a psychoeducational evaluation at the request of his school's Child Study Team. The academic and cognitive measures administered indicated that Thomas's performances in both domains ranged from Well Below Average to Well Above Average, suggesting a number of strengths and weaknesses relative to same-age peers. Based on this evaluation, it appears that Thomas's academic difficulties are the result of specific cognitive weaknesses in the domains of short-term memory, long-term retrieval, and phonological processing. There is no evidence of global or pervasive cognitive dysfunction, as Thomas's performance in the cognitive domains of Fluid Reasoning, Comprehension-Knowledge, Visual-Spatial Thinking, and Processing Speed were all well within normal limits or higher.

Overall, Thomas's weaknesses in short-term memory, ability to store visual-auditory associations (associative memory), rapid retrieval of specific words, and phonetic coding help to explain his difficulties in basic reading and writing skills. More specifically, Thomas may not have learned all of the letter-sound associations, may have difficulty retrieving those he knows, and/or may have difficulty retaining the complete phonemic sequence in mind prior to blending it into a complete word. Additionally, it is easier to decode a word that is in one's oral vocabulary than one that is not; accordingly, Thomas's relatively low oral vocabulary knowledge may further impede his word attack skills. It is likely that Thomas's reading comprehension is low because he does not recognize most of the words and does not have the skills to sound them out. It is possible, however, that Thomas's oral language abilities are also somewhat low. If so, difficulty with reading comprehension could be ongoing even after his decoding skills have improved.

Thomas's nonphonetic spelling errors suggest that he is not perceiving the individual sounds of words and/or does not know how to represent these sounds with letters. This supposition is supported by his low phonetic coding skills. The cognitive attention necessary for him to attempt to figure out how to spell the words he wants to use to express his thoughts may be diverting the attention needed to focus on the higher-level thoughts he wants to express. Furthermore, his difficulty with short-term memory and retrieval may interfere with his ability to retrieve the specific words to articulate his thoughts and to hold in mind what he wants to say while he struggles to get it down on paper. Although Thomas may have a sufficient amount of information available to him in terms of general information and word knowledge (Comprehension-Knowledge), albeit in the lower end of the Average range, his ability to access this information (Long-Term Retrieval) may be compromised, leading to difficulties with idea generation, topic expansion, and insufficient application of descriptive terms and other writing conventions (e.g., imagery, figurative language) that would add depth and "richness" to his writing.

A recurring theme throughout this evaluation was that Thomas's performance varied as a function of specific task parameters (e.g., time limits, specificity of response, and availability of supports). Therefore, variability in performance may be evident in Thomas's academic work (e.g., he may appear to perform well on one occasion and not another or one type of task and not another). Individuals working with Thomas should be careful not to ascribe variable performance to noncognitive factors (e.g., motivation, laziness), but rather should examine whether qualitative differences exist in task demands. If such differences exist, tasks should be adapted in a manner that would maximize Thomas's performance (e.g., add contextual cues, provide more structure).

DIAGNOSTIC IMPRESSIONS

Thomas's academic difficulties in reading and writing have persisted despite being exposed to quality instruction and intervention over a prolonged period of time. These difficulties could not be explained by global cognitive impairment, social-emotional problems, cultural and linguistic differences, sensory-motor difficulties, lack of motivation, environmental disadvantage, or a health-related impairment. Rather, Thomas exhibited specific and circumscribed weaknesses in cognitive areas that are known to be related to difficulties in reading and writing, namely short-term memory, retrieval ability, phonological processing, and possibly associative memory. Thus, while Thomas has the ability to think and reason like most children his age, as demonstrated by his performance in the cognitive areas of Fluid Reasoning, Comprehension-Knowledge, and Visual-Spatial Thinking, he possesses specific and related cognitive and academic deficits that are consistent with a diagnosis of Specific Learning Disability (SLD).

RECOMMENDATIONS

Based on his unique patterns of strengths and weaknesses, the following types of instructional strategies and interventions may prove to be more effective for Thomas than those that have been used in the past. The list is not exhaustive, but contains examples of a few strategies that may be used.

Word Retrieval and Memory

1. Due to Thomas's reported and observed problems with word retrieval, it would be beneficial to have his language abilities evaluated by a speech-language pathologist, both to investigate the possibility of other areas of language weaknesses and to offer strategies for facilitating word retrieval.

2. To strengthen Thomas's ability to retrieve words, use a visually based technique for continued vocabulary development. One technique, which would capitalize on Thomas's strength in visual processing, involves the use of vocabulary cartoons. These cartoons pair a new word with mnemonics and visual stimuli to help create meaningful associations. The book *Vocabulary Cartoons: Kids Learn a Word a Minute and Never Forget It* (Burchers, Burchers, & Burchers, 1998) is available from New Monic Books (www.vocabularycartoons.com) or Amazon.com.

3. To facilitate Thomas's ability to retrieve and use any new vocabulary, make sure that he learns to visualize the spelling of the words (to use their initial letters as a "hook" for retrieval) and that he is required to use the word in speech and writing frequently.

4. Because Thomas's memory is weak, teach him a variety of strategies (e.g., chunking, use of mnemonic devices, visualization) to increase the likelihood that he will recall specific information.

5. Whenever possible, use recognition-type test formats (e.g., multiple-choice, matching) as opposed to retrieval-based formats (e.g., fill-in-the-blank questions) to assess Thomas's knowledge in specific content domains.

6. On content-based essay tests (e.g., science, social studies) allow Thomas to use a list of relevant vocabulary words when formulating his written responses. A listing of such terms will likely lessen the impact of his retrieval weaknesses.

7. Continue to provide Thomas an "instruction buddy," a peer with whom he is comfortable, to answer questions about in-class assignments.

Reading

1. Because of his low reading skills, Thomas is likely to require extended time on exams and projects requiring lengthy reading, and/or a reduction in the number of pages assigned.

2. Allow Thomas to take all content area tests that depend on reading and writing orally. He will not be able to demonstrate his knowledge if he must attempt to read the questions and write the answers himself.

3. As Thomas is particularly weak in both word attack skills and the phonological skills that support phonics learning, provide individualized or small-group instruction in a highly explicit, multisensory decoding and spelling program that directly teaches sound blending and segmenting, and all the basic reading and spelling skills in a step-wise fashion. It is critical that Thomas stay on each skill level until he has mastered it for both reading and spelling, before moving on to the next. Instructional methods that typically meet these criteria are called Multisensory Structure of Language programs. They include, but are not limited to, Wilson Reading System, Orton-Gillingham Approach, SPIRE, Alphabetic Phonics, and Sonday System.

4. As Thomas's skill in decoding improves and the focus of instruction shifts to multisyllabic word pronunciation, you might be able to move into a faster-paced program such as Just Words (www.wilsonlanguage.com). The Just Words program provides a year-long curriculum for accelerated Wilson study of word structure through mastery of the six English syllable types.

5. To circumvent the impact of his reading difficulties, Thomas may benefit from using specific reading supports (e.g., books on tape or CD) when presented with texts that are too difficult for him to read (e.g., texts focusing on specific content areas, such as social studies and science, or assigned novels). This technology can provide Thomas with the opportunity to process information in multiple modalities as well as provide him with a model to follow when he is attempting to decode difficult words.

6. For other reading assignments (e.g., class reading selections), pair Thomas and his peer-buddy in a choral repeated reading activity, which will build fluency and sight word vocabulary, as well as expose Thomas to proper pronunciation of unknown words.

Writing

1. Thomas is likely to require additional time on exams and projects requiring writing. In addition, he should not be penalized for spelling errors on any assignments that are not spelling tests.

2. Provide direct instruction and ample practice in the use of punctuation and capitalization rules. As Thomas masters one rule, continue to reinforce it while moving on to others. Without frequent reinforcement, which can gradually be reduced to intermittent practice, Thomas is likely to forget it. Continue to reinforce and monitor his application of previously taught rules until the reuse is automatic.

3. Provide Thomas with an opportunity to correct errors in writing mechanics by identifying the specific error (e.g., highlighting an incorrectly spelled word in a written essay) and its nature (e.g., *sp* written above it). Gradually limit feedback by identifying only the nature and location of the error (e.g., "missing punctuation on line 5"). Eventually, identify only the nature and number of errors contained within his written work (e.g., "5 spelling errors, 2 punctuation errors") and require Thomas to locate the error independently.

4. Provide Thomas with an editing checklist that he can refer to upon completion of writing activities (e.g., Are words beginning each sentence capitalized? Is there a period at the end of each sentence?). One useful mnemonic strategy is SCOPE, which incorporates the following questions:

S   Is my *spelling* correct?

C   Are the first words of sentences proper names and nouns *capitalized*?

O   Is the syntax or word *order* correct?

P   Are there *punctuation* marks where needed?

E   Does the sentence *express* a complete thought? Does the sentence contain a noun and a verb?

5. Provide Thomas with an electronic spell-checker, such as the Franklin Spelling Ace, to use during writing assignments. He will have to make an effort to spell words phonetically in order for the program to provide a list of spelling possibilities. If Thomas uses a word processing program for writing assignments, encourage the use of the "spell-check" function.

6. Thomas may benefit from and enjoy using a software program to help him record and organize his thoughts before writing an assignment such as an essay, book report, or research report. An excellent program for creating graphic webs is Kidspiration, the lower-level version of Inspiration (www.inspiration.com).

REFERENCES

Burchers, S., Burchers, B., & Burchers, M. (1998). *Vocabulary cartoons, elementary edition: Kids learn a word a minute and never forget it.* Punta Gorda, FL: New Monic Books.

Flanagan, D. P., Ortiz, S. O., Alfonso, V. C., & Mascolo, J. (2006). *The achievement test desk reference (ATDR)— second edition: A guide to learning disability identification.* Hoboken, NJ: John Wiley & Sons.

CASE 22

Specific Learning Disability Report
The Importance of Professional Judgment
Edward Schultz

Professional judgment can be defined as "the reasoned application of clear guidelines to the specific data and circumstances related to each unique individual. Professional judgment adheres to high standards based on research and informed practices established by professional organizations or agencies" (Iowa Department of Education, 2006). This report illustrates several features of this definition and illustrates many of the concepts and trends of contemporary assessment. The following summary will highlight specific areas of the report including: (1) selective assessment strategies, (2) determining a pattern of strengths and weaknesses, (3) importance of cognitive assessment, and (4) the use of professional judgment.

Selective Assessment Strategies

Using selective assessment procedures instead of administering a standard battery is dependent on the examiner receiving a focused referral question, complete and thorough documentation of the academic history, and data-based documentation of formative assessment completed during the pre-referral process. These data allow the examiner to work within a problem-solving model and select assessment instruments that will maximize the information obtained during the evaluation. In this report, the referral question was clearly math-related. As previously collected data regarding other academic skills showed satisfactory progress, the examiner used only measures related to math. For example, the Number Matrices test was added as a measure of fluid intelligence for the purpose of comparing measures *underlying* math learning with one that directly *involves* the use of math knowledge. Measures of long-term retrieval were included to provide information as to why Olivia appears to forget information that she seemed

to understand previously. The purposeful selection of tests in this case maximized both the time and usefulness of the information.

Olivia's cognitive profile was obtained using the SLD Assistant Volume 1 and the Cross-Battery Data Management and Interpretive Assistant (CBDMIA). The SLD Assistant Volume 1 helps the examiner determine if overall cognitive functioning is within normal limits. A *g-value* greater than 1 indicates overall cognitive functioning within normal limits. Olivia's scores indicate a *g-value* of 1.20, indicating her scores will be interpreted within an "otherwise normal profile" and the majority of her cognitive abilities are within normal limits. The CBDMIA (Flanagan, Ortiz, & Alfonso, 2007) helps the examiner organize individual ability scores into clusters, obtain a student profile, and assist in interpretation. This program allows one to create clusters from tests different than those provided in the WJ III, if the tests measure the same cognitive ability (abilities) as the original tests. For example, in this assessment, the Long-Term Retrieval cluster includes Retrieval Fluency and Memory for Names, with Visual-Auditory Learning used to confirm an apparent weakness.

Pattern of Strengths and Weaknesses

In contemporary assessment and policy, a pattern of strengths and weaknesses (PSW) is not always clearly defined. In practice, data analyzed via a PSW evaluation should be used to: (a) understand the learner, (b) predict future performance, and (c) develop meaningful interventions. This report describes the overall learning profile of the student from a cognitive, academic, and social perspective. The prediction inherent in this report is based on the numerous data points collected over time, essentially stating that if Olivia's education continues as is, she will continue to fail to make adequate progress. Further, meaningful interventions were developed that were directly related to the assessment data obtained.

Importance of Cognitive Assessment

Many states no longer require the use of cognitive assessment to determine eligibility for learning disability services. This report, however, clearly illustrates the use of cognitive assessment not only for determining eligibility for special education but to further our understanding of the learner and, subsequently, develop effective interventions. While the Response to Intervention (RTI) process was able to establish that Olivia needed math intervention, the cognitive assessment enabled the evaluator to identify the cognitive processes involved in her failure to respond to the interventions provided and to develop other, likely more effective interventions. Without a cognitive assessment and the subsequent development of math interventions tailored to Olivia's needs, the student support team would not be able to meet Olivia's unique needs.

Professional Judgment

As mentioned, selecting tests, integrating data, and matching interventions require professional judgment. Additionally, professional judgment is required for using item analysis to "look beyond" the scores when scores were in the borderline Average range. The integration of a variety of assessment tools and strategies also requires professional judgment. Consideration of behavioral observations, such as Olivia's nonuse of paper and pencil for computation, requesting information from Olivia, such as why she did not do so, and taking into account information from other sources, such as her teacher's comment about her "forgetting how to do her work at home," helped the examiner select additional cognitive tests and develop more specific interventions.

Final Comments

While this report provides a comprehensive description of Olivia, the effectiveness of this report is enhanced with graphic information such as the progress monitoring data. Much of the data reported were collected over time via the RTI process with the involvement of Olivia's parents throughout. The report was written in a style intended for educational diagnosticians, teachers, and parents. The use of technical language, acronyms, and other abbreviations is limited, and explanations are provided when possible confusing terms are used.

FULL INDIVIDUAL EVALUATION REPORT

Name:	Olivia Firek
Date of Birth:	01/22/2000
Age:	9-9
Gender:	Female
Ethnicity:	Caucasian
Parents:	Thomas and Claudia Firek
Address:	300 Main Street
School:	Fain Elementary School
Teacher:	Davis
Grade:	4
Date of Report:	11/23/09
Evaluator:	Edward Schultz, Ph. D.

REASON FOR REFERRAL

Olivia has difficulty with mathematics, specifically division and word problems involving division. Despite 12 weeks of targeted interventions, Olivia has been unable to meet the fourth-grade math standards. The student support team suspects a specific learning disability (SLD) affecting mathematics.

BACKGROUND INFORMATION

Olivia is a 9-year-old child who lives with her mother, father, and younger sister, Samantha (age 5). According to the parent information, Olivia met all of her developmental milestones and is reported to be in good health. She has had no major childhood illnesses and has not required any surgery. Olivia's hearing and vision were recently screened by the school nurse (10/29) with normal results. Olivia's parents reported that she is a "sweet and caring" daughter who gets along well with her younger sister. Her parents report she is responsible, completes her chores, and is rarely noncompliant. Reportedly, there are no apparent physical factors that might affect her educational progress. The Fireks reported no economic hardship, and Olivia is not eligible for free or reduced lunch.

Olivia has attended Fain Elementary school since kindergarten. School records indicate regular attendance through this year and in prior years. Olivia's behavior both in and out of school do not appear to influence her learning or to interfere with her ability to learn or to follow the school's disciplinary rules. According to the reports of four teachers, she is "friendly," "outgoing," and well liked by her classmates.

Although Olivia speaks Spanish, English is the primary language used in the home and instructionally in school. Formal testing was administered in English, Olivia's dominant language. Current information indicates there are no significant speech or language problems, receptively or expressively. During testing, Olivia demonstrated oral language abilities that appeared commensurate with her overall level of intellectual ability.

Olivia's adaptive behavior appears to be within normal limits for her age and is not a factor in educational programming. Her teachers do not indicate that she has any difficulty functioning within age-level expectations in the areas of personal independence and social responsibility. Olivia's adaptive behavior appears to be consistent with her intellectual functioning.

Olivia's limited progress in math is not attributable to or primarily the result of a visual, hearing, or motor impairment, emotional disturbance, cultural factors, or environmental or economic hardship.

TESTS ADMINISTERED

Informal Data Collected

School records

Teacher reports

Parent reports

Classroom observation

Vision and hearing screenings

Speech and language evaluation

Formative Assessment Data

CBM data (AIMSweb®)

Current work samples

In-class tests

Benchmark testing

Formal Data

Woodcock-Johnson III Tests of Achievement (WJ III ACH): Selected tests

Woodcock-Johnson III Tests of Cognitive Abilities (WJ III COG): Selected tests

Woodcock-Johnson III Tests of Cognitive Abilities Diagnostic Supplement (WJ III COG DS): Selected tests

CLASSROOM OBSERVATIONS (11-11-09)

Olivia was observed in both her math class and math tutoring session. In her math class, she sat with three other students in a cluster of desks near the front of the classroom. The students were learning about probability using coins and dice. Olivia was actively engaged in this cooperative activity and was assigned to be the "recorder" of the group. The classroom appeared well organized, inviting, and engaging.

Olivia was also observed for 30 minutes during RTI Tier 2 small-group instruction with four other students. She spent 10 minutes reviewing multiplication and division facts and the rest of the period receiving direct instruction on comparing fractions. The teacher was using a "think aloud" strategy to work through the steps of comparing fractions. Olivia remained on task.

OBSERVATIONS DURING ASSESSMENT

During both test sessions, Olivia accompanied the examiner and entered the test room willingly. Rapport was established and testing began promptly. She was friendly and polite, and seemed to put forth her best effort throughout the cognitive and achievement testing. She followed instructions well and attempted all tasks.

During the math tests, Olivia rarely used paper and pencil to help her solve complex problems, and when she did, her problem-solving strategy was unsuccessful. When testing was completed, the examiner asked her if she used paper and pencil in class to set up problems. She replied, "My teacher taught us how, but I forgot."

SCHOOL HISTORY

Olivia is reported by both teachers and parents to be a good student who has a positive attitude toward school. A review of school records indicated passing grades with As and Bs in most subjects. Olivia's reading score on the Texas Assessment of Knowledge (TAKS) (Spring 2009) exceeded the minimum passing standard. She failed to meet the standard in math. According to her score report, she answered only 3 of 10 questions correctly on Objective 1 (Numbers, Operations, and Quantitative Reasoning). Her other errors were evenly dispersed throughout the other five objectives. Olivia has acquired some basic skills in math including number concepts, number recognition, and addition. Previous math grades were Bs and Cs. According to her third-grade teacher, she did very well on some concepts, specifically addition and subtraction of whole numbers, measurement, and geometry. She recalled that Olivia needed a little more support with multiplication and a great deal of support for division. According to her teacher, Olivia has outstanding work habits and does well in her other subjects: social studies, science, PE, and music.

Evidence of Prior Instruction, Intervention, and Progress

During the current school year (2009–2010), Olivia has been served via the general education program and has received standards-based math instruction 45 minutes a day, primarily delivered in a whole-group format. While her class grades reflect a C average, her grades on weekly tests have declined. Her teacher stated that she received the third-lowest grade on the district benchmark assessment administered in October 2009. In addition to her standards-based instruction, she has received supplemental math instruction for 45 minutes weekly (using the district-approved Success Maker® program) with the basic skills teacher. This is the standard protocol for Fain students who do not meet state standards on end-of-year tests. Olivia also received math tutoring in a small group for 45 minutes twice a week over 12 weeks as part of the school's Response to Intervention (RTI) system. Specific strategies involved the use of manipulatives to support conceptual understanding and direct teaching of word problem-solving strategies. According to her basic math skills teacher, Olivia has made little progress. She reported that Olivia seems to understand the concept at the time it is taught but cannot do similar problems on her homework. She has particular difficulty with multistep problems; when dividing, she can do the first and second steps of the algorithm but forgets what to do next. In addition to her instruction at school, her parents report that they spend at least 1 hour each night working with her on math homework.

Data-Based Documentation of Repeated Assessments of Achievement at Reasonable Intervals, Reflecting Formal Evaluation of Student Progress during Instruction

The Success Maker® scores were used to measure Olivia's progress on the district's standard protocol for students who did not meet state standards in prior-year state assessments. Her baseline score was 2.85 and, after 12 weeks, her scores improved slightly to 2.89. This growth is considerably lower than expected.

Her 12 weeks of RTI data also indicated very little growth. Her baseline score and progress monitoring data were collected using AIMSweb® CBM probes and norms. Her baseline score was 16 correct digits. This score is in the 10th percentile when compared to students in her grade. After 12 weeks of small-group instruction, she obtained 19 correct digits for a rate of growth of .25 digits per week. Despite targeted interventions, she remains in the 10th percentile when compared to peers. These data reflect a rate of growth considerably lower than expected. Figure 1 depicts her growth in correct digits over the intervention period.

Goal Statement

In 11.0 weeks, Olivia Firek will achieve 33 Correct Digits from grade 4 Mathematics Computation. The rate of improvement should be 1.55 Correct Digits per week. The current average rate of improvement is 0.19 Correct Digits per week.

Date	08/29	09/04	09/11	09/18	09/25	10/02	10/09	10/16	10/23	10/30	11/06	11/13
Correct Digits	16	15	17	17	14	18	15	15	16	17	18	19

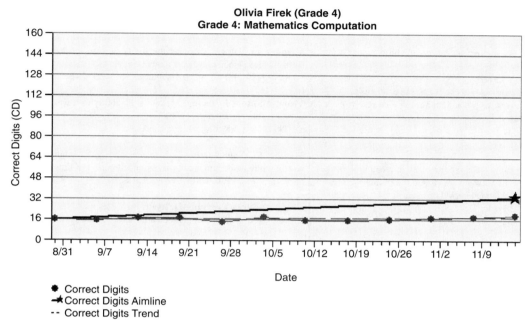

● Correct Digits
★ Correct Digits Aimline
-- Correct Digits Trend

Figure 1   Progress Monitoring Improvement Report for Olivia

COGNITIVE PROCESSES

Olivia's cognitive abilities were formally evaluated using selected tests of the Woodcock-Johnson III Tests of Cognitive Abilities (WJ III COG) and the WJ III COG Diagnostic Supplement (WJ III COG DS). These batteries are designed to measure general and specific cognitive functions. The results are presented in the following table.

Note that the Long-Term Retrieval cluster, which was created via the Cross-Battery Data Management and Interpretive Assistant (Flanagan et al., 2007), substituted Memory for Names for Visual-Auditory Learning. Score information includes the standard score (SS), the standard score 68% confidence interval, and the percentile rank (PR).

Cognitive/Psychological Process Clusters: Broad Abilities and Narrow Abilities (norm-referenced measures)	Individual Tests and Scores (Confidence Interval 68%)
Crystallized Intelligence (Comprehension-Knowledge): A person's level of acquired knowledge, including knowledge obtained through life experiences, school, and work. SS 97 (92–102), PR 42 ☐ Normative weakness (<84) ☒ Within normal limits (85–115) ☐ Normative strength (>116)	**Verbal Comprehension:** Measures language development and vocabulary. SS 96 (91–101), PR 39 Within normal limits. **General Information:** Measures general knowledge. SS 98 (93–103), PR 42 Within normal limits.
Fluid Reasoning 3: The type of thinking an individual may use when faced with a relatively new task that cannot be performed automatically; the ability to solve problems using deductive and inductive logic. SS 77 (72–82), PR 6 ☒ Normative weakness (<84) ☐ Within normal limits (85–115) ☐ Normative strength (>116)	**Concept Formation:** Measures categorical reasoning based on the principles of inductive logic. SS 91 (86–96), PR 27 Within normal limits. **Analysis-Synthesis:** Measures general sequential reasoning. SS 78 (73–83), PR 7 Normative weakness. **Number Matrices:** Measures the ability to use inductive and deductive reasoning with concepts involving mathematical relations. SS 76 (71–81), PR 5 Normative weakness.

(Continued)

Cognitive/Psychological Process Clusters: Broad Abilities and Narrow Abilities (norm-referenced measures)	Individual Tests and Scores (Confidence Interval 68%)
Long-Term Retrieval: Ability to learn, store, and retrieve information. **Cluster score:** Not interpretable at broad ability level **Narrow Ability Clusters** **Associative Memory:** Ability to learn, store, and use associations between words and unfamiliar pictures/symbols over a few minutes. SS 82 (78–86), PR 11 Normative weakness **Associative Memory—Delayed:** Ability to recall previously learned associations between words and unfamiliar pictures/ symbols after an extended period of time. SS 74 (70–78), PR 4 Normative weakness ☒ Normative weakness (<84) ☐ Within normal limits (85–115) ☐ Normative strength (>116)	**Retrieval Fluency:** Measures fluency of retrieval from stored knowledge. SS 100 (95–105), PR 50 Within normal limits. **Memory for Names:** Measures the ability to learn, store, and later recognize word-picture associations over a few minutes. SS 84 (79–89), PR 14 Borderline normative weakness. **Visual-Auditory Learning:** Measures the ability to learn, store, and later retrieve word-symbol associations over a few minutes. SS 79 (74–83), PR 8 Normative weakness. **Memory for Names-Delayed:** Measures ability to recognize previously learned word-picture associations after an extended period of time. SS 77 (73–81), PR 6 Normative weakness. **Visual-Auditory Learning-Delayed:** Measures the ability to retrieve previously learned word-symbol associations after an extended period of time. SS 70 (66–75), PR 2 Normative weakness.
Short-Term Memory: The ability to apprehend and hold information in one's mind and then use it within a few seconds. Cluster includes working memory (ability to attend to, process, and respond to information). SS 92 (87–97), PR 30 ☐ Normative weakness (<84) ☒ Within normal limits (85–115) ☐ Normative strength (>116)	**Numbers Reversed:** Measures working memory and/or attentional capacity. SS 90 (85–95), PR 25 Within normal limits. **Memory for Words:** Measures memory span. SS 94 (89–99), PR 34 Within normal limits.
Visual-Spatial Thinking: The ability to perceive, analyze, synthesize, and think with visual patterns, including the ability to store and recall visual representations. SS 104 (99-109), PR 61 ☐ Normative weakness (<84) ☒ Within normal limits (85–115) ☐ Normative strength (>116)	**Picture Recognition:** Measures recognition memory of pictures. SS 102 (97–107), PR 55 Within normal limits. **Spatial Relations:** Measures the ability to visualize spatial relationships. SS 106 (101–111), PR 66 Within normal limits.
Processing Speed: The ability to fluently and automatically perform simple cognitive tasks, especially when under pressure to maintain focused attention and concentration. SS 90 (85–95), PR 25 ☐ Normative weakness (<84) ☒ Within normal limits (85–115) ☐ Normative strength (>116)	**Decision Speed:** Measures the ability to make correct conceptual decisions rapidly. SS 88 (83–92), PR 21 Within normal limits. **Visual Matching:** Measures the ability to discriminate visual symbols quickly. SS 92 (87–97), PR 30 Within normal limits.
Auditory Processing: The ability to perceive, analyze, and synthesize and discriminate speech sounds. SS 94 (89–99), PR 34 ☐ Normative weakness (< 84) ☒ Within normal limits (85–115) ☐ Normative strength (> 116)	**Auditory Attention:** Measures the ability to detect and discriminate speech sounds and to overcome auditory distortion when listening. SS 96 (91–101), PR 40 Within normal limits. **Sound Blending:** Measures the ability to synthesize (blend) speech sounds. SS 92 (87–97), PR 30 Within normal limits.

Cognitive Profile Summary

The scores on six clusters were unitary (i.e., the scores on all of the tests within the group, or cluster, were similar) and interpretable (i.e., the cluster score could be used to represent the particular ability). Based on these, Olivia demonstrated a relative strength in the area of visual-spatial thinking, abilities in the average range for crystallized intelligence, auditory processing, processing speed, and short-term memory, and a normative weakness in fluid reasoning.

Olivia's long-term retrieval was initially interpreted based on the individual tests, or measures of narrow abilities. As the results of the two initial tests constituting the cluster were significantly different (Retrieval Fluency, Memory for Names), the cluster could not be considered as measuring a unitary ability; consequently, the cluster score could not be used to represent Olivia's general ability to learn, store, and retrieve information from long-term memory. Since this cognitive ability is directly related to the referral concern as well as to be-havior observed during testing (i.e., not being able to recall her problem-solving method), an additional measure (Visual-Auditory Learning) was administered to confirm her apparent difficulty in one of the narrow abilities, associative memory. Associative memory is the ability to learn new associations between words and visual information, such as symbols or pictures, retain them, and subsequently use them over a period of a few minutes. The resulting Associative Memory cluster score indicated that, indeed, associative memory is a considerable weakness. To explore this cognitive weakness further, Olivia was administered versions of both associative memory tests later, to see how well she could retain the same information over a longer period of time. Her performance was relatively weaker, indicating that not only does she forget newly learned associations relatively quickly, but what she has retained deteriorates somewhat more over time. In contrast, her average performance on the Retrieval Fluency test indicates that Olivia has no difficulty retrieving information that is well-established in memory.

Broad Abilities (norm-referenced measures)	Individual Tests and Scores 68% Confidence Intervals
Mathematic Calculation: Refers to the application of mathematical operations (i.e., addition, subtraction, multiplication, division). **Basic Math Skills*** Understanding of basic math facts and rules. SS 85 (80–90), PR 16 ☒ Normative weakness (< 84) ☒ Within normal limits (85–115) ☐ Normative strength (> 116)	**Calculation*:** Measures the ability to perform mathematical computations. SS 86 (81–91), PR 18 **Math Fluency*:** Assesses knowledge and automatic retrieval of math facts within a 3-minute time limit. SS 84 (79–89), PR 14
Mathematics Problem Solving Refers to the ability to apply knowledge of basic math operation and rules to set up, reason, and solve problems using quantitative concepts. **Math Reasoning*** SS 84 (79–89), PR 14 ☒ Normative weakness (< 84) ☒ Within normal limits (85–115) ☐ Normative strength (> 116)	**Quantitative Concepts*:** Measures mathematical vocabulary, concepts, and quantitative reasoning. SS 85 (80–90), PR 16 **Applied Problems*:** Requires the comprehension of both picture and word problems and the ability to apply the appropriate computation to solve them. SS 84 (79–89), PR 14
Broad Math SS 85 (80–90), PR 16 ☒ Normative weakness (≤ 84) ☒ Within normal limits (85–115) ☐ Normative strength (≥ 116)	
*Borderline between normal limits and normative weakness.	

EDUCATIONAL PERFORMANCE

Reading Summary: Consistency Analysis/ Data Integration

Olivia's overall reading abilities are within normal limits as indicated by her grades; her TAKS scores, which exceeded the state standard; universal screenings (Oral Reading Fluency of 112 words per minute, AIMSweb®); and progress toward fourth-grade standards on district benchmark tests.

Written Expression Summary: Consistency Analysis/Data Integration

Olivia's overall writing abilities are within normal limits as indicated by her grades, work samples, universal screenings (25 Correct Word Sequences, AIMSweb®), and progress toward fourth-grade standards on district benchmark tests.

Mathematics Summary: Consistency Analysis/ Data Integration

Olivia's overall math abilities are below both age- and grade-level standards by several measures, including classroom performance, scores on state assessments, and RTI data. The current norm-referenced assessments indicate her quantitative knowledge is between normal limits and a normative weakness. An item analysis revealed that Olivia is able to perform addition, subtraction, and multiplication tasks but has difficulty with division, fractions, and multistep problems involving multiplication and division.

The overall pattern of math weaknesses, based on borderline standardized test scores and classroom difficulties, can be logically and empirically related to deficits in fluid reasoning, the ability to use inductive and deductive reasoning to solve problems. These processes are critical for mathematical reasoning and learning. In addition, a significant weakness in associative memory has likely interfered with her ability to recall and apply previously learned algorithms (computational procedures).

CRITERIA AND CONCLUSIONS

Multiple data sources and an integrated model for SLD determination were applied in this case. According to state (Texas) and federal regulations, a student with SLD is one who:

1. Has been determined through a variety of assessment tools and strategies to meet the criteria for a specific learning disability (SLD) as stated in 34 CFR, §300.8(c)

(10), in accordance with the provisions in 34 CFR, §§300.307–300.311.

The basic psychological processes critical to math calculation and problem solving are fluid intelligence, especially inductive and general sequential reasoning. Olivia demonstrates below average to average inductive reasoning and weaknesses in both qualitative reasoning and general sequential reasoning. Also critical to math and other school tasks is the ability to retrieve information in an accurate and consistent manner. Olivia has a normative weakness in the narrow ability of associative memory as part of her long-term retrieval system, which may interfere with her ability to recall mathematical operations and math problem-solving techniques. Thus, Olivia meets this criterion for SLD in mathematical calculation and math problem solving.

2. Does not achieve adequately for the child's age or meet state-approved grade-level standards in oral expression, listening comprehension, written expression, basic reading skill, reading fluency skills, reading comprehension, mathematics calculation, or mathematics problem solving when provided appropriate instruction.

Olivia is not achieving adequately for her age, nor does she meet state-approved grade-level standards in mathematical calculations and mathematic problem solving as evidenced by her borderline norm-referenced overall math scores and test item analysis. Her failure to pass the previous year's state assessment and her limited progress this year in her standards-based general education curriculum are further evidence of meeting this criterion.

3. Does not make sufficient progress when provided a process based on the child's response to scientific, research-based intervention (RTI).

Olivia has not made sufficient progress when provided a process based on RTI, as indicated by her Success Maker® scores and progress monitoring data collected via AIMSweb® CBM probes and norms. It should be noted that Olivia has received intensive support at both school and home. Her lack of progress despite being provided intensive intervention satisfies this criterion.

4. Exhibits a pattern of strengths and weaknesses in performance, achievement, or both relative to age, grade-level standards, or intellectual ability, as indicated by significant variance among specific areas of cognitive function, such as working memory and verbal

comprehension, or between specific areas of cognitive function and academic achievement.

Olivia's evaluation indicates a pattern of strengths and weaknesses in performance. She demonstrates a relative pattern of strengths in the areas of reading (both classroom and state assessments), writing, and other subjects. She also demonstrates strengths socially as she gets along well with peers and adults. Her pattern of weaknesses centers on tasks involving math. She has a history of math failure on state assessment measures, has made inadequate RTI progress, and obtained borderline math scores with norm-referenced measures. Whereas most of her cognitive processes are within the Average range, she exhibits a relative strength in visual-spatial thinking (Gv). Two of her cognitive abilities represent normative weaknesses and are directly related to the referral concern regarding math performance. Thus, Olivia meets this criterion as well.

ELIGIBILITY STATEMENTS

Olivia is a fourth-grade student who was referred for testing by the Student Support Team due to continuing difficulty in math. Current testing indicated that Olivia exhibited a pattern of strengths and weaknesses in performance and achievement relative to age, grade-level standards, and intellectual ability, as indicated by significant variance among specific areas of cognitive function and between specific areas of cognitive function (fluid intelligence, long-term retrieval) and academic achievement (math calculation and math problem solving). Olivia meets the Texas Education Agency criteria to be identified as a student with a specific learning disability. Olivia's disability significantly impairs her performance in the area of mathematics, and she requires specialized instruction and classroom accommodations in order to make adequate progress in the general education program. This finding will be reviewed by the IEP Committee for eligibility determination.

IMPLICATIONS FOR EDUCATION

Implications of Olivia's learning disability in mathematics and strategies for increasing the rate of her learning are as follows:

1. Olivia should continue to have access to the full range of the general education mathematics curriculum and general education services. She will benefit from spe-cially designed instruction with tasks involving division and problem solving.

2. Use her strengths in visual processing by having her draw or act out word problems, and use graphic organizers such as flowcharts and decision charts to help her learn algorithm sequences (computational procedures).

3. Allow her to continue through the math curriculum even if she is not able to rapidly compute her division facts on her own. Provide a division chart, but encourage her to try to think of the answer before referring to it. This will give her immediate reinforcement and/or immediate correction.

4. To assist Olivia in retrieving instructions and problem-solving procedures, provide recorded instructions to help her remember the procedures when she is doing assignments at home. This will help her practice the skills using the appropriate procedure, thus increasing the opportunity that she will both learn and be able to recall problem-solving steps when needed.

5. Olivia should have access to and be allowed to use a calculator. She needs this accommodation to progress through the math curriculum especially as she encounters more difficult and higher-level problems.

6. Teach Olivia how to use visual association or mental imagery strategies to enhance the retrieval of information. For example, the information that there are 3 feet in a yard can be illustrated by a picture of a grassy yard with 3 large feet taking up the space from one fence to another.

7. After giving multistep instructions to Olivia, it may be necessary for her to repeat them to facilitate encoding and storage of information.

8. Provide math instruction using the concrete-representational-abstract (CRA) approach. See the following web site for details: http://www.k8accesscenter.org/training_resources/CRA_Instructional_Approach.asp

Assistive Technology

Assistive technology needs were considered, and based on the previously addressed competencies, testing, and observations, such devices and services are not recommended for Olivia at this time. While it is recommended that Olivia have access to and be able to use a calculator, it should be considered as a needed accommodation and part of the usual classroom instruction.

ASSURANCES

- Tests and evaluation materials used for this evaluation were selected and administered so as not to be racially or culturally discriminatory.

- Standardized tests were validated for the specific purpose for which they were used.

- Standardized tests were administered by trained personnel in accordance with the instructions provided by the producer of the test.

- More than one procedure was used for determining whether the student has a disability and for determining an appropriate educational program for the student.

- The student did not have any sensory or physical impairments so that selecting tests and materials that would not be influenced by these was not a factor. (Tests were selected and administered so as to best ensure that if a test were administered to a child with impaired sensory, manual, or speaking skills, the test results accurately reflect the student's aptitude or achievement level or other factors the test purports to measure, rather than reflecting the student's impaired sensory, manual, or speaking skills [unless those skills are the factors that the test purports to measure].)

- Technically sound instruments were used to assess the relative contribution of cognitive and behavioral factors, in addition to physical or developmental factors.

- The evaluation provides relevant information that directly assists persons in determining the educational needs of the student.

- As the student's primary language was English and she was fluent in English, selection of materials and procedures that would not disadvantage a student with limited English proficiency was not a factor. (Materials and procedures used to assess a student with limited English proficiency were selected and administered to ensure that they measure the extent to which the student has a disability and needs special education, rather than measuring the student's English language skills.)

- Information has been drawn from a variety of sources including aptitude and achievement tests, parent input, teacher recommendations, physical condition, social or cultural background, and adaptive behavior.

This report is respectfully submitted for use by the IEP team in reaching educational decisions concerning Olivia. The findings and judgments expressed here are believed to be an accurate reflection of her current performance levels.

REFERENCES

Flanagan, D. P., & Ortiz, S. O. (2007). *Essentials of cross-battery assessment, second edition.* New York: Guilford Press.

Iowa Department of Education. (2006). *Special education eligibility standards.* Retrieved December 10, 2008, from: http://www.aea10.k12.ia.us/divlearn/specialeducation/docs/spedeligstandardsjuly2006.

CASE 23

Integrating RTI with an Individual Comprehensive Assessment to Identify a Specific Learning Disability in Reading

Donna Rury Smith

With the advent of the Response to Intervention (RTI) model, a struggling student would ideally be identified in the primary grades as being at risk and begin receiving some form of intervention, through general education, immediately. Only after increasing levels of interventions that have been implemented with fidelity fail to close the achievement gap would referral be made to consider a possible learning disorder. Unfortunately, as some students move through the tiers of increasingly more intensive instruction, little objective data are collected to inform how instruction should be delivered so as to meet the specific student's needs. Frequently, every at-risk student is placed in the same intervention "program," resulting in success for some and more failure for others. This case study illustrates how Maggie, a fourth-grade student, failed to respond to intervention over a period of more than 2 years, in part because information that could have changed the focus of instruction was not obtained. The case also illustrates a common misunderstanding that all reading disorders are primarily phonemic in nature. The wait-to-fail model appears to still exist even in the world of RTI, and for Maggie the delay has contributed to a significant achievement gap.

In addition to timeliness, the focus of the individual comprehensive assessment must move beyond mere eligibility to providing an explanation of why Adequate Yearly Progress (AYP) has not occurred and what might be interfering with the student's ability to respond to empirically validated interventions. This case demonstrates that although eligibility is of major concern, it was not the most important question to answer. Whether she qualifies for special education services or not, Maggie will continue to receive some form of instruction somewhere.

Ideally, the individual comprehensive assessment will provide essential guidance as to the form and focus of that instruction.

Finally, Maggie was referred with a reading-specific question and ample evidence was provided that her other academic skills were grade appropriate. For this reason, the focus of her assessment was solely on reading. This case demonstrates how a focused reading evaluation that includes both measures of cognitive abilities and academic skills can direct the educational plan, as well as provide evidence of a specific learning disability. The specific pattern of Maggie's cognitive and achievement strengths and weaknesses provides a better understanding of why she has been unsuccessful. The examiner, however, must go beyond test scores and interpret what they represent instructionally. In Maggie's case, adequate referral information including the specifics of interventions, careful attention to behaviors during classroom observation and testing sessions, and a detailed skills and error analysis were used in an integrated fashion to identify instructional recommendations.

PSYCHOEDUCATIONAL EVALUATION

Name:	Maggie Moore
Date of Birth:	April 14, 2000
Age:	9-10
Grade:	4
Report Date:	February 18, 2010
Examiner:	Donna Rury Smith, Ed.D.

REASON FOR REFERRAL

Maggie was referred by the Student Assistance Team (SAT) at Williams Elementary School following a history of academic difficulty in reading. The focus of the evaluation was specific to reading to determine: (1) why Maggie is not making Adequate Yearly Progress, (2) why she has not responded to interventions, (3) if there is evidence of a specific learning disability, and (4) what additional or different interventions are recommended to close her achievement gap.

BACKGROUND INFORMATION

Maggie is the youngest in a family of three children. Her older brother is a high school senior; her older sister is a seventh grader. Both are honor students and active in sports in school and the community. Mr. Moore is a salesman, and his wife works intermittently as a substitute teacher. Both parents attended but did not graduate from college. English is the home language and Maggie's only language. Mr. and Mrs. Moore completed a questionnaire about their daughter's medical and developmental history. They reported no difficulties during pregnancy or birth, and that she met developmental milestones at about the same pace as her siblings. She has no medical history of serious illness or injury, or chronic health conditions other than seasonal allergies. Her parents described her as athletic, eager to please, sensitive, and empathetic. They believed that she likes school but often complains that she "hates to read." When she was younger, her parents took turns reading to her at bedtime but discontinued the practice when she began school. Maggie has a desk in her room for homework, and her parents provide help when asked. At the request of her teacher, Mrs. Moore listens to Maggie read from a book of her choice for about 10 minutes most evenings.

Maggie has been a student at Williams Elementary since kindergarten. She has never repeated a grade, although she did attend summer school between the third and fourth grades. She has maintained good attendance. Vision and hearing screenings were conducted recently and no problems were identified by the school nurse.

According to school records, Maggie began to experience problems related to reading in first grade. She barely met the cutoff on the district reading screening assessment and had difficulties learning sight words and blending sounds. Her teacher placed her in a smaller reading group and provided an additional 5 to 10 minutes of phonics instruction per day. Mrs. Samuels, Maggie's third-grade teacher, made the initial referral to the SAT in January 2009, when Maggie's scores on the grade-level benchmark reading test fell below the cutoff point in the areas of fluency and comprehension for the second consecutive time. In addition, her scores in reading real and nonsense words were below expectation. Her math benchmark scores were high to above average. The SAT determined that Maggie was at risk for continued academic difficulty in reading and recommended placement in the after-school tutoring program. She attended tutoring in a small group with four other third graders, twice weekly, for 30 minutes per session, for the next 6 weeks.

Her tutor, Miss Jamison, another third-grade teacher on campus, focused on reteaching the phonics lessons that were not mastered by the students in their classes that week. She monitored Maggie's response to intervention by administering 1-minute oral reading prompts on a weekly basis and tracking her performance using AIMSweb. At placement, Maggie was able to read 60 words per minute on a grade-level passage. The average score for mid-year third graders is 107 wpm. After 6 weeks of tutoring, she improved her oral reading by 10 more words per minute; however, the average gain for her tutorial group was 15 words per minute. Not only was she not responding at the same pace as her peers but, at this rate of learning, she was not on track to meet target by the end of the school year. The SAT met in late February and recommended that tutoring be increased to 3 days per week. Weekly progress monitoring continued to show slow but steady progress, and by May, Maggie had increased her oral reading by an additional 10 words per minute; however, the average gain for her tutorial group was 16 words per minute. Her performance placed her in the bottom 15% when compared to other third graders. In spite of intervention, Maggie continued to acquire reading skills at a slow pace and remained a dysfluent reader with considerable reading comprehension deficits. In March, Maggie took the statewide test of basic skills, and did not show adequate proficiency in reading. She passed both the math and writing sections. At the recommendation of her teacher, she attended summer school for 4 weeks where remediation focused on her lowest scores on the statewide exam. No progress monitoring data were reported for summer school.

Maggie was described by her fourth-grade teacher, Ms. Young, as a "hard-working student who persists on task even when the work is difficult for her." She reported that Maggie's weakest academic skill is still in reading comprehension, that she performs much better in math class than in reading, and that her writing is filled with good ideas but many spelling errors. She most often misspells words the way they sound, rather than the way they look. Her teacher further reported that Maggie has a good vocabulary, is knowledgeable about many topics in science and social studies, and participates in class discussions and cooperative learning groups. She prefers to tell rather than write about what she knows and has occasionally taken written tests orally. Ms. Young is concerned that Maggie recognizes few words by sight, often decoding unfamiliar words in a laborious fashion. As a result, her reading is typically dysfluent, and her comprehension is poor. Since late September, Ms. Young has been working with Maggie and one other student for 30 minutes on a daily basis before school. She is currently using a code-based reading program to build Maggie's phonemic skills. She noted that one of her goals is for Maggie to be able to read silently without whispering to herself. On the mid-year reading benchmark, Maggie scored in the bottom 25% of students in her class.

TESTS ADMINISTERED

Review of school records

Interview with Maggie

Questionnaire completed by Mr. and Mrs. Moore

Interviews with third-grade teacher, Mrs. Samuels, and fourth-grade teacher, Ms. Young

Classroom observation

Wechsler Individual Achievement Test-Third Edition (WIAT-III): Reading Comprehension, Word Reading, Pseudoword Decoding, Oral Reading Fluency, and Spelling subtests

Test of Silent Word Reading Fluency (TOSWRF)

Differential Ability Scales, Second Edition (DAS-II)

BEHAVIORAL OBSERVATIONS

During a classroom observation, Maggie was in a group with four other students completing a reading task. The assignment was to read silently an article from the local newspaper, discuss three comprehension questions as a group, and then individually write a letter in response to the article. When asked to read silently, Maggie looked down or peeked to see what others were doing but did not

appear to be actively engaged in reading. When the group discussion began, she made several on-topic comments, but they were not specific to the article. As other students began to write their letters, Maggie got up to sharpen her pencil, stopped by the teacher's desk to ask an unrelated question, then looked through her desk for another sheet of paper. Her avoidant behavior limited her writing time on task. After several minutes, she began to write, covering her paper with her arm. She erased several times but did not ask for assistance from her teacher or peers. At the end of the activity, Maggie had written about one-third of a page. Her writing was on topic but difficult to read and included several spelling errors. She was able to include a basic understanding of the article but did not demonstrate inferential comprehension. For example, she included reasons why children should want to help others in crisis (general knowledge) but could not specify why responding to the crisis identified in the article should be done in a timely manner.

Maggie was tested on two separate occasions. For the first testing session she was talkative, engaged in the tasks, and eager to know about her performance. She noted that she especially enjoyed doing the "word tests" in reference to the DAS-II Verbal Similarities and Word Definitions subtests. She also commented that the visual memory tasks were difficult, but she had tried her best. For the second test session, Maggie appeared to be more anxious and frustrated, especially when asked to read aloud or spell; nonetheless, she typically persisted on the task. She frequently corrected herself and repeated words or phrases she had already read. While attempting to read the fourth-grade level passage aloud, she noted, "It is too hard; I can't do this," but persevered until stopped by the examiner. She was less frustrated once she was moved to the third-grade reading passages on both the Oral Reading Fluency and Reading Comprehension subtests. During the Spelling subtest, Maggie typically whispered the word to herself several times, wrote the word, erased it, and then rewrote it. While reading words and nonsense words from the page, she used her finger to keep her place, whispered possible pronunciations to herself prior to responding, and laboriously sounded out each word, phoneme by phoneme.

STUDENT INTERVIEW

A brief interview was conducted after the second testing session. Maggie described herself as a poor student except in math. She commented that fourth grade was very difficult, and that she was fearful of retention at the end of the school year. She reported that she had several friends both in and out of school, that she played soccer on a community league, and that she wanted to make good grades like her brother and sister. When asked, "What would you like your teacher to do more often?," she replied that she would like more time to finish her work, easier materials to read, and less homework.

TEST RESULTS AND INTERPRETATION

WIAT-III

The Wechsler Individual Achievement Test-Third Edition (WIAT-III) is an individually administered measure of achievement. Four reading subtests and the spelling subtest were administered following standardized procedures. Maggie's scores are reported in the tables following this narrative. The WIAT-III yields standard scores at both the composite and subtest levels (a mean of 100, with the average range being 85–115). Based on the subtests administered, Basic Reading, Reading Comprehension, and Fluency, Total Reading composite scores are reported. Individual subtest scores are reported for the Word Reading, Pseudoword Decoding, Oral Reading Fluency, Reading Comprehension, and Spelling subtests. In addition, Maggie's actual achievement scores are compared to her predicted scores (using a .05 level of significance) based on the General Conceptual Ability (GCA) score from the DAS-II. This analysis was considered to establish unexpected underachievement, which may be relevant to the identification of a specific learning disability.

Maggie's Basic Reading Composite score was 81, which placed her at the 10th percentile ranking in the Below Average range. The score is based on her performance on two subtests, namely Word Reading and Pseudoword Decoding. The Word Reading subtest required her to read aloud from a list of words of increasing difficulty. An analysis of her errors revealed her difficulties with Vowels that had short, schwa, or irregular sounds, and silent consonants. She read words slowly, trying to sound them out by phonemes. Once she began to misread words, she commented on their difficulty and started to whisper her responses, but persisted until the test was discontinued. Her Word Reading subtest score was 79, placing her at the 8th percentile, which falls in the Below Average range. The Pseudoword Decoding subtest score was based on Maggie's ability

to decode nonsense words, which required her to apply her phonics skills. Her subtest score of 83 placed her at the 13th percentile, also within the Below Average range. Maggie made similar errors when reading nonsense or real words and also approached this task by trying to decode individual phonemes. She had difficulty with single short vowels (*e, i*), the schwa vowel sound for *u*, the diphthong *oy*, the r-controlled vowel in *ur*, and the consonant blend *ft*. Once the words became difficult, Maggie began to respond with "I don't know" rather than attempt decoding. Overall, Maggie's below average word level reading skills and her inability to read whole words with automaticity place her at considerable risk in being able to read grade-level text with fluency and comprehension. At the same time, she does show some benefit from code-based instruction as evidenced by her decoding strategy.

The composite score for Reading Comprehension and Fluency, based on the Reading Comprehension and Oral Reading Fluency subtests, was 76. This score places her at the 5th percentile ranking in the Below Average range. The Reading Comprehension subtest required her to read a grade-level passage and answer aloud several questions about what she had read. Maggie chose to read the passages silently. It must be noted, however, that she was unable to read the fourth-grade level passage with the required comprehension and was redirected to the third-grade set. The score reflects her comprehension on below-grade-level text. While reading silently, her eyes frequently left the page, she squirmed in her seat, put her head on her hand, and sighed loudly. She answered questions with little confidence and often sought reassurance. Although the majority of the questions she missed required inferential comprehension or "reading between the lines," she also missed items directed at specific details (e.g., questions related to who, what, when, where, and how). In addition, her reading was slow, she subvocalized or whispered as she read, and showed signs of fatigue and frustration.

Perhaps her most noteworthy performance was on Oral Reading Fluency where Maggie read passages aloud. Both her reading rate and her accuracy in reading words within text were evaluated. Once more, she began reading at grade level but was unable to meet the completion time requirement; therefore, she was administered the two third-grade-level passages. Her Oral Reading Fluency Rate score was 70, which falls at the bottom of the Below Average range (2nd percentile), and her Oral Reading Fluency Accuracy score was 74 (4th percentile). Her overall Oral Reading Fluency, which includes both rate and accuracy, was 79 (8th percentile). Again it must be noted that this score is based on below-grade-level text. This subtest was difficult for Maggie and she demonstrated considerable anxiety and frustration. She was unable to maintain any fluency as she typically re-read words or phrases and self-corrected misread words. She laboriously decoded unfamiliar words with mixed results and guessed at some words after looking at the initial and/or ending letters. She did not recognize high-frequency words that should be read automatically. Her prosody (i.e., the use of tone of voice, pauses, and emphasis while reading to increase understanding) was so choppy that she was unable to garner meaning from the words she read. In fact, she missed the comprehension question following both passages. Of special concern is Maggie's dysfluent reading of text, which no doubt negatively impacts her reading comprehension. It is likely that her lack of fluency is as problematic when she reads silently as when she reads aloud.

Her Total Reading composite score was 78 (7th percentile) which falls in the Below Average range. There was little difference, and no statistical discrepancy, among the subtests contributing to the composite; therefore, the Total Reading composite score appropriately represents her overall reading skills.

Maggie was also given the Spelling subtest to determine if her decoding difficulties were evident on an encoding task. Whereas when reading words she went from symbol (i.e., letters) to sound, it was necessary for her to move from sound to symbol when spelling. Her subtest score was 73 (4th percentile ranking), which falls in the Below Average range. She misspelled words containing silent consonants, irregular vowel sounds, consonant blends (*mp, ct*), and -*ive* word endings. Her error pattern when spelling was similar to that when decoding, and she revealed difficulty with morphological characteristics of words (e.g., prefixes, suffixes, plurals, possessives). Although Maggie was not referred with a suspected writing disorder, she is certainly at risk and the development of her writing skills should be monitored closely.

TOSWRF

The Test of Silent Word Reading Fluency (TOSWRF), which measures the ability to recognize printed words accurately and efficiently was also administered. Maggie was presented with rows of words, ordered by reading difficulty with no space between the words. She was given 3 minutes to draw lines between the boundaries of as many words as possible. In contrast to many of

the reading tests that she has taken, which focus on phonology (i.e., learning the alphabet principle or code for decoding written words into spoken words), the TOSWRF measures rapid recognition of whole words and orthographic patterns. This is more than just reading "sight" words, as recognizing whole words quickly is a necessary component of fluent reading. Her standard score of 72 placed her at the 3rd percentile, in the Below Average range. She worked slowly and often self-corrected her markings. She failed to identify several high-frequency words (e.g., *each, much, under,* and *above*) and became agitated as time passed. This was a very difficult task for Maggie, and she was visibly upset by her performance.

Maggie's achievement scores are consistent with her academic history of reading difficulties, but they do not adequately explain why she has failed to respond to intervention. Of particular concern is the amount of time that has been spent primarily on phonics instruction without expected reading improvement. An analysis of her cognitive processing abilities was conducted to better understand what factors have interfered with her success in making adequate yearly progress and provide direction in designing a more differentiated intervention plan.

DAS-II

The Differential Ability Scales, Second Edition (DAS-II), an individually administered battery of cognitive subtests, was selected for Maggie because of the variety of distinct areas of cognitive functioning measured. Further, the DAS-II provides a sound basis for interpreting a profile of relative strengths and weaknesses to direct interventions. The battery required Maggie to perform tasks such as define words, name pictured objects, complete visual patterns, repeat information she had just heard or seen, and reproduce designs she had seen. The DAS-II yields a *composite score*, the General Conceptual Ability score (GCA), which focuses on reasoning and conceptual abilities, lower-level composite scores called *cluster scores*, and specific-ability measures, which provide *subtest scores*. The results for each of these types of scores appear in tables at the end of the report. They can also be plotted on a bell curve to view their relationships to each other. The GCA and the cluster scores are reported as standard scores with a mean of 100 (the average range being 90–109). The subtest scores are reported as *T* scores with a mean of 50 (the average range being 43–56).

The GCA measured Maggie's overall, general intellectual ability and is based on a combination of the lower-level composite scores. Her GCA standard score of 100 falls right in the middle of the Average range and places her at the 50th percentile rank in comparison with children her same age. It is highly likely (90% confidence interval) that her true GCA score lies somewhere between 95 and 105. Although Maggie has better developed verbal and nonverbal reasoning abilities than spatial abilities, there is not a statistically significant difference between the scores, and her pattern of performance is not exceptionally unusual for her age. For this reason, the GCA is a sufficiently meaningful descriptor of her overall abilities and will be analyzed in comparison to her academic achievement scores; however, a closer look at her cluster level scores provides additional understanding about her cognitive strengths and weaknesses.

Maggie's Verbal Ability standard score of 106 also falls within the Average range (range of 98–113, at 90% confidence level), at the 66th percentile ranking. This score is based on two subtests, Verbal Similarities and Word Definitions, which Maggie described as her favorites. On Verbal Similarities she was given three words and asked how they go together or how they are alike. Maggie's subtest T score of 56 falls at the 73rd percentile ranking, near the top of the Average range, and her subtest T score of 51 on Word Definitions places her at the 54th percentile ranking. On the later subtest, she was asked to tell what a word means. Her performance on these subtests as represented by the Verbal Ability cluster score demonstrates her relative strength in acquired verbal concepts, her level of vocabulary development, her retrieval of information from long-term verbal memory, and her fund of general knowledge. In the classroom this ability has enabled Maggie to participate in class discussions, share her experiences and knowledge with others, and orally demonstrate what she has learned. Because of her strengths in verbal reasoning, it may be puzzling why she has so much difficulty with reading comprehension. However, it is not unusual for children with specific reading disorders to show a similar pattern of high verbal abilities.

Two diagnostic subtests, Recall of Digits Forward and Recall of Digits Backward, provided additional information about Maggie's verbal learning abilities. When asked to repeat a series of orally presented digits of increasing length, she performed better than 76% of children her age (T score of 57), indicating a relative strength in verbal short-term memory, which supports long-term memory.

On Recall of Digits Backward, a more difficult task requiring her to rearrange information that is being held in short-term verbal memory, Maggie's T score was 55, placing her at the 69th percentile ranking. Her Above Average Digits Forward score and her Average Digits Backward score suggests that she is able to get verbal information into short-term memory, as well as to manipulate and retrieve it. Many children are able to hang on to verbal information longer or manipulate it better by visualizing what they have heard. Based on other information learned about Maggie, it is likely that she primarily relies on her stronger short-term verbal memory skills instead. This also explains her tendency to verbally mediate difficult tasks and to whisper as she reads.

Maggie's Nonverbal Reasoning Ability (standard score of 103 with a range of 97–109 at 90% CI) also falls within the Average range and places her at the 58th percentile ranking. Two subtests, Matrices and Sequential and Quantitative Reasoning, contribute to this cluster score. Her Matrices T score of 54, at the 66th percentile, was based on her ability to visually process a matrix of 4 to 9 cells, all but one of which contain a picture or design. She had to select among alternatives but not verbally explain the picture that correctly completed the matrix. On the Sequential and Quantitative Reasoning test, her T score of 50, at the 50th percentile, was based on her ability to perceive sequential patterns in geometric figures or common rules in numerical relationships. Maggie talked her way through both of these subtests and was able to benefit from her stronger verbal reasoning abilities to complete the tasks. This level of performance indicates that she is able to engage in inductive and analytical reasoning and achieve visual-verbal integration by applying her verbal strengths to visual reasoning tasks. It is likely that these abilities support her stronger math performance in the classroom and should be more helpful to her in the area of reading. Although she was able to visually scan items and use higher-order reasoning to direct her selections, she worked slowly and relied heavily on verbal mediation.

Maggie's Spatial Ability cluster standard score was 90, which places her at the 25th percentile ranking (with a range of 85–96 at 90% CI). Two subtests, Recall of Designs and Pattern Construction, contribute to this score. The Recall of Designs subtest required her to examine and reproduce pictured designs after a 5-second exposure. The subtest is a measure of visual-spatial ability and immediate visual memory. Verbal encoding is more difficult because of the complexity of the designs and the quick exposure time, and verbal mediation was less likely. Maggie talked to herself during the task and was visibly disturbed by the short exposure time. She did not have difficulty with the required motor output demand but erased several times and asked to start again on another piece of paper for one design. Her incorrect responses were both inaccurate and incomplete. Her subtest T score was 43, placing her at the 24th percentile slightly below the Average range when compared to peers. On the Pattern Construction subtest, she was asked to reproduce pictured designs using two- and three-dimensional bi-colored foam or blocks. Her T score of 46 placed her at the 34th percentile ranking within the Average range. Pattern Construction, which measures visual-perceptual ability, problem-solving ability, and spatial orientation, can also be supported by verbal encoding strategies. Once more, Maggie talked her way through the task. She worked methodically, using trial and error and recognized when her design was incorrect, but she was unable to correct errors on the more difficult items within the time limit. It is important to note that she continued to have some difficulty on visual-spatial tasks even when the memory requirement was removed.

Additional diagnostic subtests were administered to better understand the relationship between her identified difficulties on visual encoding, visual-spatial, and short-term visual-memory tasks and her strengths on verbal encoding and short-term verbal-memory tasks relative to her reading difficulties. First, another measure of visual processing, Recognition of Pictures, was administered. On this subtest she was asked to find among a group of pictures one or more pictures that were previously shown to her. She achieved a T score of 45 (31st percentile, within the Average range). This subtest measures short-term visual recognition memory, but it is based on her ability to recall meaningful visual images. Once more, Maggie called on verbal rehearsal to improve her performance. She focused on the display of pictured items for the entire time and whispered the name of each. It is likely that her better performance on this subtest in comparison to Recall of Designs and Pattern Construction is related to the meaningful stimuli and her ability to attach a verbal label to each.

She was also given two subtests that measured her ability to integrate visual and verbal encoding and retrieval—Recall of Objects-Immediate and Recall of Objects-Delayed. Maggie was asked to look carefully at a card containing the pictures of 20 common objects. After 45 seconds she was given another 45 seconds to name as many of the objects as she could recall. She was only shown the same

card twice more but for a period of 20 seconds each with recall limited to 40 seconds. Again she was asked to name all of the objects she could remember. She was then asked to do two nonverbal subtests (taking about 15 minutes), and without prior warning or being shown the picture card again, she was asked to recall the objects on the card. This subtest assesses short-term verbal memory, short-term visual memory, or a combination of the two. On the initial trial, Maggie recalled 8 of 20 objects; on the second trial she recalled 10, and on the third trial she recalled 12. She seemed to benefit from repetition (practice) and ended up with an average T score of 47 (38th percentile) on Immediate Recall. She responded quickly and it was obvious that she was verbally rehearsing the list from trial to trial. She did not appear to group objects, relying instead on list order for retrieval. Typically, once an item was recalled on a list, it remained on subsequent lists. After the time delay and interfering tasks, she was able to recall only seven of the objects. Unlike her previous performance, she responded slowly, repeated some objects, and became frustrated. Her Delayed Recall T score of 38 (12th percentile) placed her in the Below Average level. Although the difference in scores is not statistically significant, it is worthy of noting because of the change in her strategy and behavior.

Maggie was successful in recalling information only when she was able to pair her weaker visual short-term memory with her stronger verbal short-term memory. When she was unable to continue verbal rehearsal because of interfering activities, she stored considerably less information in long-term memory. Maggie's verbal learning strengths have helped her be more successful in learning the phonological aspects of reading, specifically how to identify decodable words phoneme by phoneme; however, her visual encoding and retrieval deficits have made the orthographic requirements of reading whole words extremely difficult for her. Further, the instructional emphasis on phonology has had limited effect on her overall reading proficiency because she also needs remediation in orthography and morphology. Maggie also lacks strategies for learning new information and relies heavily on verbal mediation or rehearsal.

Two diagnostic subtests contribute to the Working Memory composite score: Recall of Sequential Order and the previously discussed Recall of Digits-Backward. Working memory, the ability to hold information in short-term memory as it is manipulated in some fashion, underlies many cognitive abilities but should be tested directly. On both of these subtests, Maggie had to hold verbal information in short-term memory as she manipulated the list and put it into the requested order. On the Recall of Sequential Order subtest, Maggie heard a list of the parts of the body in random sequence and was asked to order the list from highest to lowest position. The more difficult items required her to remember one or two additional words that are not parts of the body. The task began with a picture of a child in front of her, but the picture was later removed. Her subtest T score was 47 (38th percentile), which falls within the Average range. When paired with her T score of 55 on Recall of Digits-Backward, she earned a Working Memory composite score of 102 (55th percentile), which falls well within the Average range. As previously observed, Maggie relied heavily on verbal rehearsal, repeating the list over and over as she reordered it. This strategy was successful, but it resulted in slower response time.

One additional diagnostic subtest, Rapid Naming, was given because of its relationship to reading fluency. On this subtest, Maggie was presented with an array of colors, pictures, and colored pictures, which she was to name as quickly as possible. This is a measure of processing speed paired with automatic lexical access. In other words, could she retrieve the labels for the colors and pictures automatically? This task also requires integrated visual and verbal processing as stored information is retrieved, but the stimuli represent overlearned information. Her T score of 48 (42nd percentile) placed her in the Average range. Maggie's lack of reading fluency is more likely related to poor encoding of paired visual and verbal information rather than simple retrieval.

SUMMARY

Maggie is a fourth-grade student who has struggled in learning to read almost from the time she started school. Her willingness to put forth extra effort has been instrumental in the gains she has made primarily in learning to decode words, but in spite of interventions, the gap between her reading performance and that of her peers has continued to widen. One purpose of this evaluation was to determine if Maggie has a specific learning disability.

Although a discrepancy between ability and achievement is no longer considered to be a requirement for a specific learning disability, it does indicate the presence of unexpected underachievement. There are statistically significant gaps between Maggie's academic skills and her cognitive abilities. In comparison to the GCA from the DAS-II, her Basic Reading Composite score was 22 points lower than predicted. This difference is unusual in that it occurred in only 1% to 5% of the standardization sample. The difference between her achieved Word Reading and GCA scores was 21 points, also a rare occurrence found in only 1% to 5% of the sample. Similarly, the difference between her actual Pseudoword Decoding and GCA scores was 17, which occurred in no more than 10% of the standardization sample. When her Reading Comprehension score was compared to her DAS-II GCA score, the difference was both statistically significant and unusual in that it occurred in only 5% to 10% of the standardization sample.

The difference between her actual Oral Reading Fluency score and the GCA score was also statistically significant, occurring in no more than 5% of the sample. Likewise, her Oral Reading Accuracy and her Oral Reading Rate scores, when compared to the GCA, were both statistically significant and occurred in 1% to 5% and less than or equal to 1% of the sample, respectively. When Total Reading is compared to the GCA score from the DAS-II, the statistically significant difference was identified in only 1% to 5% of the standardization sample. Her predicted Spelling score fell 26 points below her actual score. A significant difference of that magnitude occurred in only 1% to 5% of the standardization sample.

Maggie also demonstrates a pattern of cognitive processing strengths in verbal reasoning and short-term verbal memory paired with processing weaknesses in short- and long-term visual memory, most notably when information is more abstract or cannot be paired with verbal mediation for encoding. When Maggie's educational history, teacher and parent reports, behavioral observations, and test results are all taken into consideration, there is compelling evidence to support a diagnosis of a specific learning disability (SLD). Further, educational need for additional intervention is warranted based on her failure to respond to interventions prior to referral.

A second purpose of this assessment was to identify why Maggie has not responded as expected to interventions. By and large, the intervention she has received has focused on the phonological aspect of reading. Instruction has been somewhat generic and designed to meet the needs of a group of students rather than differentiated based on Maggie's specific skill deficits. She has learned to decode words by sounding them out, and has had some success in part because of her strengths in verbal processing. Nonetheless, decoding words, although necessary, is not sufficient for fluent reading with comprehension. Moving forward, intervention must be more focused, explicit, and systematic. It should be closely monitored using objective measures to ensure steady progress is being made.

The third purpose of testing was to make recommendations for future intervention, which follow in the next section.

RECOMMENDATIONS

1. The information contained in this report should be shared with the multidisciplinary team, including her parents, in consideration of eligibility as a student with SLD. The team will address whether special education services are appropriate.

2. Whether provided in special education or through general education, Maggie needs a more balanced reading program. Interventions should include direct, explicit, and systematic instruction in the phonological, orthographic, and morphological aspects of word reading. Intensive interventions such as Read Naturally, Read 180, or Soar to Success, supplemented by the Process Assessment of the Learner Orthographic Awareness training (Berninger, 1998), address each of these skills in an integrated fashion and have demonstrated effectiveness.

3. Encourage Maggie to read high-interest materials with controlled vocabulary to practice reading fluently. Other fluency-based interventions such as choral reading or partner reading can be helpful in increasing comprehension as she hears herself read aloud.

4. Teach Maggie effective learning strategies to improve her encoding of visual information so that she can rely less on verbal mediation. For example, use color-coding to teach word parts so that she can "see" prefixes and suffixes or underline the irregular spellings within words to aid quicker word recognition (e.g., *sight, fight, night, light*). Enhance a phonics lesson by color-coding onset-rimes (i.e., word families such as *-am, -ile*). Words need to be more visually enhanced for her.

5. Closely monitor Maggie's writing skills as the demands for written language increase. Her difficulties with spelling contribute to her frustration in demonstrating what she knows in a written form. When appropriate, provide her the opportunity to supplement her written work verbally. Do not assume she doesn't have the knowledge just because she cannot write it down. Teach specific

writing strategies such as those found in *Powerful Writing Strategies for All Students* (Harris, Graham, Mason, & Friedlander, 2008) to proactively deal with potential writing problems.

6. Sharing ongoing progress monitoring data with Maggie and her parents will be important so that intervention effectiveness can be closely monitored. Feedback will also be important to encourage Maggie to take ownership of her learning and to keep her engaged in the remediation process.

7. Presently, Maggie is discouraged by her poor reading performance. It is important that Maggie continue to participate in activities in and out of school where she experiences success. Intervention/remediation activities should be provided during the school day to the extent possible.

DAS-II TEST RESULTS

Core Cluster and Composite Scores and Indexes

Cluster/ Composite	Sum of T Scores	Standard Score	Percentile	90% Confidence Level	Qualitative Description
Verbal	107	106	66	98–113	Average
Nonverbal Reasoning	104	103	58	97–109	Average
Spatial	89	90	25	85–96	Average
GCA	300	100	50	95–105	Average

Verbal Ability Cluster Subtest Scores Summary

Subtests	Raw Score Total	T Score	Percentile
Verbal Similarities	6	56	73
Word Definitions	10	51	54

Nonverbal Reasoning Ability Cluster Subtest Scores Summary

Subtests	Raw Score Total	T Score	Percentile
Matrices	19	54	66
Sequential and Quantitative Reasoning	22	50	50

Spatial Ability Cluster Subtest Scores Summary

Subtests	Raw Score Total	T Score	Percentile
Recall of Designs	11	43	24
Pattern Construction	28	46	34

Differences between Cluster Standard Scores

Discrepancy Comparisons	Score 1	Score 2	Diff.	Critical Value	Sig. Diff. Y/N	Base Rate
Verbal-Nonverbal Reasoning	106	103	3	13	N	>15%
Verbal-Spatial	106	90	16	12	Y	10–15%
Nonverbal Reasoning – Spatial	103	90	13	10	Y	10–15%
Base Rate by Overall Sample Statistical Significance (Critical Values) at the .05 level						

Differences between Subtest T Scores within Clusters

Discrepancy Comparisons	Score 1	Score 2	Diff.	Critical Value	Sig. Diff. Y/N	Base Rate
Word Definitions— Verbal Similarities	51	56	−5	12	N	>15%
Matrices—Sequential and Quantitative Reasoning	54	50	4	9	N	>15%
Recall of Designs— Pattern Construction	43	46	−3	8	N	>15%
Base Rate by Overall Sample Statistical Significance (Critical Values) at the .05 level						

Differences between Subtest T Scores and the Mean T Score of the Core Subtests

Strengths and Weaknesses	Subtest T Score	Mean Core T Score	Diff.	Critical Value	H/L	Base Rate
Word Definitions	51	50	1	7		>15%
Verbal Similarities	56	50	6	8		>15%
Sequential and Quantitative Reasoning	50	50	0	6		
Matrices	54	50	4	7		>15%
Pattern Construction	46	50	−4	5		>15%
Recall of Designs	43	50	−7	7	L	15%
Mean Core T Score = 50, Scatter = 13, Base Rate = >25% Statistical Significance (Critical Values) at the .05 level						

Diagnostic Cluster Scores and Indexes

Cluster	Sum of T Scores	Standard Score	Percentile	Qualitative Description
Working Memory	102	102	55	Average

Working Memory Cluster Subtest Scores Summary

Subtests	Raw Score Total	T Score	Percentile
Recall of Sequential Order	14	47	38
Recall of Digits—Backward	16	55	69

Processing Speed Cluster Subtest Scores Summary

Subtests	Raw Score Total	T Score	Percentile
Rapid Naming	36	48	42

Diagnostic Subtest Scores Summary

Subtests	Raw Score Total	T Score	Percentile
Recall of Objects—Immediate	30	47	38
Recall of Objects—Delayed	7	38	12
Recall of Digits—Forward	24	57	76
Recall of Digits—Backward	16	55	69
Recognition of Pictures	7	45	31
Recall of Sequential Order	14	47	38
Rapid Naming	36	48	42

Differences between Subtest T Scores within Diagnostic Clusters

Discrepancy Comparisons	Score 1	Score 2	Diff.	Critical Value	Sig. Diff. Y/N	Base Rate
Recall of Sequential Order—Recall of Digits Backward	51	56	−5	12	N	>15%
Base Rate by overall sample Statistical Significance (Critical Value) at the .05 level						

Differences between Diagnostic Subtest T Scores and the Mean T Score of the Core Subtests

Strengths and Weaknesses	Subtest T Score	Mean Core T Score	Diff.	Critical Value	H/L	Base Rate
Recall of Objects— Immediate	47	50	−3	9		>15%
Recall of Digits— Forward	57	50	7	7	H	>15%
Recognition of Pictures	45	50	−5	13		>15%
Recall of Sequential Order	47	50	−3	7		>15%
Speed of Information Processing	45	50	−5	7		>15%
Recall of Digits— Backward	55	50	5	7		>15%
Rapid Naming	48	50	−2	10		>15%
Statistical Significance (Critical Values) at the .05 level						

Differences between Subtest T Scores for Digits Forward versus Digits Backward

Discrepancy Comparisons	Score 1	Score 2	Diff.	Critical Value	Sig. Diff. Y/N	Base Rate
Recall of Digits Forward—Recall of Digits Backward	57	55	2	8	N	>15%
Base Rate by overall sample Statistical Significance (Critical Value) at the .05 level						

Differences between Subtest T Scores for Recall of Objects Immediate versus Recognition of Pictures

Discrepancy Comparisons	Score 1	Score 2	Diff.	Critical Value	Sig. Diff. Y/N	Base Rate
Recall of Objects Immediate— Recognition of Pictures	47	45	2	14	N	>15%
Base Rate by overall sample Statistical Significance (Critical Value) at the .05 level						

Differences between Subtest T Scores for Recall of Objects Immediate versus Recall of Objects Delayed

Discrepancy Comparisons	Score 1	Score 2	Diff.	Critical Value	Sig. Diff. Y/N
Recall of Objects Immediate—Recall of Objects Delayed	47	38	9	11	N
Statistical Significance (Critical Value) at the .10 level					

WIAT-III TEST RESULTS

Grade-Based Composite Score Summary

Composite	Sum of Subtest Standard Scores	Standard Score	Percentile	Qualitative Description
Total Reading	323	78	7	Below Average
Basic Reading	162	81	10	Below Average
Reading Comprehension and Fluency	161	76	5	Below Average

Grade-Based Subtest Scores Summary

Subtests	Raw Score Total	Weighted Raw Score	Standard Score	Percentile	Growth Scale Value
Reading Comprehension	17*	45*	82*	12*	398
Word Reading	23		79	8	434
Pseudoword Decoding	14		83	13	457
Oral Reading Fluency	54*	30*	79*	8*	477
Oral Reading Accuracy	190*	73*	74*	4*	
Oral Reading Rate	350*	74*	70*	2*	
Spelling	12		74	4	395
Results are based on a lower than grade placement item set					

Grade-Based Cumulative Percentages Associated with Raw Scores for Word Reading and Pseudoword Decoding Speed

Subtest Speed Score	Raw Score	Cumulative Percentage
Word Reading Speed	21	10%
Pseudoword Reading Speed	10	10%

Ability-Achievement Discrepancy Analysis Using DAS-II GCA Score and Grade-Based Composite Scores

WIAT-III Composite	DAS-II GCA Score	WIAT-III Score		Difference	Critical Value (.05)	Base Rate
		Predicted	Actual			
Total Reading	100	100	78	22	6.37	1–5%
Basic Reading	100	100	81	19	5.34	5–10%
Reading Comprehension and Fluency	100	100	76	24	9.06	1–5%

Ability-Achievement Discrepancy Analysis Using DAS-II GCA Score and Grade-Based Subtest Scores

WIAT-III Subtest	DAS-II GCA Score	WIAT-III Score		Difference	Critical Value (.05)	Base Rate
		Predicted	Actual			
Reading Comprehension	100	100	82	18	11.5	5–10%
Word Reading	100	100	79	21	6.19	1–5%
Pseudoword Decoding	100	100	83	17	5.91	10%
Oral Reading Fluency	100	100	79	21	8.40	<5%
Oral Reading Accuracy	100	100	74	26	12.69	1–5%
Oral Reading Rate	100	100	70	30	8.49	<1%
Spelling	100	100	74	26	7.30	1–5%

TOSRWF RESULTS

Standard Score 72

Percentile Rank 3

Descriptive Range: Poor

REFERENCES

Berninger, V. (1998). *Process Assessment of the Learner (PAL). Guides for intervention. Reading and Writing.* San Antonio, TX: The Psychological Corporation.

Harris, K. R., Graham, S., Mason, L.H., & Friedlander, B. (2008). *Powerful writing strategies for all students.* Baltimore, MD: Paul H. Brookes.

CASE 24

Assessing a Child with a Nonspecific Pervasive Development Disorder
Can a Nonverbal Cognitive Measure Help?

Steve McCallum

When a child appears to be at risk for academic or social problems, parents and teachers want answers to questions about his or her condition (e.g., etiology, diagnosis, prognosis, possible interventions). A psychoeducational report should provide some answers, and should ultimately make a positive impact on the examinee's life. In the case below it is obvious that Marty's behaviors were inconsistent with a straightforward diagnosis (e.g., inconsistent pattern of academic, language, and social skills). Previous evaluations had been inconclusive, and there were questions about the prognosis and optimal interventions. This case illustrates how historical, medical, and developmental data can be integrated into current findings from nontraditional assessment tools (e.g., a nonverbal cognitive battery and a neuropsychological test) to generate a reasonable tentative diagnosis and (some) treatment option(s) that might have been unavailable, or at least not as obvious, using more traditional measures.

CONFIDENTIAL PSYCHOLOGICAL REPORT

Name:	Marty Vinson
Date of Birth:	11/20/1999
Age:	9-11
Grade:	4
Evaluation date:	10/20/2009
Examiner:	R. Steve McCallum, Ph.D.

REASON FOR REFERRAL AND BACKGROUND INFORMATION

Marty's parents requested an evaluation to determine his current levels of cognitive functioning, and to determine a diagnosis regarding his academic, language, and social skills. Previous evaluations have yielded inconclusive findings. In addition, Marty's parents were interested in obtaining some ideas for interventions.

A review of records revealed a long history of speech and language delay. Marty has received speech and language services through Cox County schools and the local university Hearing and Speech Center for the past 4 years. In 2005, Marty was determined to be eligible for special education services under the category of Developmentally Delayed, and delays were noted in fine-motor skills, receptive language, expressive language, social-emotional development, and adaptive behavior. On the evaluation conducted in the local school system in 2005, the following scores were obtained:

Stanford-Binet Intelligence Scale-IV (M = 50, SD = 8)

Pattern Analysis	58 (+1.00 SD)
Vocabulary	36 (−1.75 SD)

Peabody Picture Vocabulary Test-III (M = 100, SD = 15) SS 77, PR 6

Wechsler Individual Achievement Test-II (M = 100, SD = 15)

Word Reading	SS 104, PR 61
Math Reasoning	SS 89, PR 23
Spelling	SS 94, PR 34

Receptive and expressive language skills were described as borderline.

For the school system evaluation, Marty's parents completed the Conners' Parent Rating Scale – Revised. All subscale scores (Oppositional, Cognitive Problems/Inattention, Hyperactivity, and Conners' ADHD Index) were in the average range when compared to same-aged male peers. Results suggested no problems with attention or activity level. The Oppositional subscale score indicates that Marty follows rules, complies with authority, and is not easily angered.

One of Marty's teachers completed the Vineland Adaptive Behavior Scales–II; adaptive skills were reported to be significantly weak in the areas of communication, daily living, socialization, and motor skills. A follow-up evaluation 2 years later (2007) confirmed significant speech and language delays and noted borderline autistic characteristics. On the Childhood Autism Rating Scale (CARS), completed by Marty's second-grade teacher, his score fell between the "nonautistic" and "mildly to moderately autistic" range. Autism was not, however, ruled in or out. Following this assessment, Marty was referred to Dr. Josie Mueller, a neurologist, to rule out neurological impairment. Dr. Mueller's notes, dated January 2006, indicated a "congenital hypotonia, associated with developmental lag." A brain MRI was conducted and the results were within normal limits.

In November 2007, Marty participated in a central auditory processing evaluation conducted by personnel at the local university Hearing and Speech Center. A mild-to-moderate central auditory processing disorder was reported. Difficulties in binaural integration (processing two different signals at the same time), binaural separation (separating two different signals occurring at the same time), and phonemic decoding were noted.

Marty currently attends the fourth grade at Posey Elementary. When the local school implemented the RTI process last year, he was receiving special education services already based on the previous diagnosis. He now receives 4 hours per week of resource assistance, focusing primarily on building reading comprehension skills, and 1 hour per week of speech and language therapy. He also receives tutoring twice a week. He is currently making Cs in reading and As and Bs in all other subjects. Marty achieved the following percentiles last year on the end-of-year group achievement test:

Test	Percentile	Test	Percentile
Reading	15	Math	53
Word Analysis	7	Science	12
Spelling	34	Social Studies	32
Language	32		

Marty's mother currently reports concerns regarding his peer relations. She reports that Marty will play with a friend for a little while but does not seem to understand the rules of reciprocity; he loses interest in interacting easily. Often he prefers to play alone. In the past, Marty has expressed interest in playing sports, such as basketball and football, but when given the opportunity, he quickly loses interest. Most recently, he has expressed an interest in swimming. Marty's mother has requested that the tutor help Marty develop social skills. The tutor is providing some limited help in this area (e.g., role-playing activities, verbal mediation training). Even though Ms. Vinson is still concerned about his social skills and passive nature, she reported that his social skills have improved, as well as his reading and math, as a result of the special education services and targeted tutoring and social skills training.

ASSESSMENT PROCEDURES AND INSTRUMENTS

UNIT: Universal Nonverbal Intelligence Test

NEPSY-II: A Developmental Neuropsychological Assessment

Records review

RELEVANT TEST BEHAVIORS

Marty accompanied me to the testing room willingly on request and rapport was easily established and maintained. He worked diligently throughout the tests and complied readily with my requests. His speech was sometimes difficult to understand and he consistently mispronounced sounds, such as the *r* and *k* sounds. During conversations, Marty often hesitated when asked a question; he appeared to have difficulty understanding the question and/or formulating his response. Other than the speech articulation problems, no physiological problems were noted. Marty is approximately average in height and weight for his chronological age with short blond hair, bangs, bright blue eyes, a round face, and a ready smile. He appeared happy and seemed to enjoy most tasks, although he also seemed reserved and reluctant to engage in new tasks. In response to specific requests, he put forth good effort and appeared motivated to do well. His activity level was normal for his age, and there were no indications of attention problems. The following results should be considered a valid estimate of Marty's current levels of functioning.

ASSESSMENT RESULTS

UNIT

The UNIT is a nonverbal test of intelligence. One of the purposes of the UNIT is to provide an overall estimate of intellectual ability for examinees with language impairments. On the UNIT, Marty achieved the following scores. The range of scores from 92 to 104 is believed to capture Marty's true score with 90% confidence.

	ScS	SS		ScS	SS
Memory Scale		100	**Symbolic Scale**		95
Symbolic Memory	10		Symbolic Memory	10	
Object Memory	9		Object Memory	9	
Spatial Memory	11		Analogic Reasoning	8	
Reasoning		98	**Nonsymbolic Scale**		104
Analogic Reasoning	8		Spatial Memory	11	
Cube Design	11		Cube Design	11	
Mazes	10		Mazes	10	
Full Scale IQ		98			

Standard scores (SS) have a mean of 100 and a standard deviation (SD) of 15.
Scaled scores (ScS) have a mean of 10 and a standard deviation of 3.

Marty displayed relatively little variability on the non-verbal cognitive tasks. He performed somewhat stronger (a little more than half a standard deviation) on nonsymbolic versus symbolic tasks. There was no meaningful difference in his performance on reasoning versus short-term memory tasks. The slight relative strength in nonsymbolic versus symbolic abilities is consistent with Marty's deficits in language, as language requires strong symbolic thinking. Results of the UNIT indicate average cognitive abilities overall. His scores are higher on this instrument than those obtained previously on language-loaded tests. In Marty's case, language does not provide a "window on the intellect" as is the case for most of his peers; in fact, his poor language skills limit his ability to communicate and express his knowledge.

NEPSY-II

The NEPSY-II is a comprehensive instrument that was designed to assess neuropsychological development. The name, NEPSY-II, is an acronym that was formed from the word neuropsychology. NEPSY-II assesses the development of neuropsychological functioning. The following five domains were assessed: Attention/Executive Functioning, Language, Sensorimotor, Visuospatial Processing, and Memory and Learning.

On the NEPSY-II, Marty's domain scores from highest to lowest were: Visuospatial Processing, Attention/Executive Functioning, Sensorimotor, Language, and Memory and Learning. However, as is obvious from the subtest scores, Marty's performance was variable. The lowest scores occurred on subtests that assess memory for meaningful auditory content; his highest score was in the area of visuospatial/kinesthetic functioning. Visuospatial processing is complex and involves multiple distinct but interrelated subcomponents: the ability to synthesize elements into a meaningful whole and represent objects mentally; the ability to discriminate between objects, judge the orientation line in angles, and distinguish between left and right; the ability to understand the relationships among objects and space; and the ability to copy a model or reproduce it using a pencil and paper. These skills were all well developed for Marty.

Scale/Subtest	ScS	PR	Scale/Subtest	ScS	PR
Visuospatial Processing			**Language**		
Design Copying	13	84	Phonological Processing	7	16
Arrows	11	63	Speeded Naming	7	16
			Comprehension of Instructions	1	1
Attention/Executive Functioning			**Memory and Learning**		
Animal Sorting	8	25	Memory for Faces	6	9
Auditory Attention & Response Set	8	25	Memory for Names	5	5
Clocks	10	50	Narrative Memory	2	1
Sensorimotor					
Finger Tapping	8	25			
Imitating Hand Positions	5	5			
Visuomotor Precision	8	25			

Scaled scores (ScS) have a mean of 10 and a standard deviation of 3.

Typically, performance within the other domains assessed by the NEPSY-II is below the level demonstrated within the visual-spatial domain. In general, these areas are relatively weaker for Marty and are weak relative to chronological age mates. Marty's second-highest domain, Attention/Executive Functioning, assesses areas central to neuropsychological processing. According to developmental neuropsychologists, executive functioning is a label describing the ability to plan and to engage flexible strategies; the ability to adopt, maintain, and shift cognitive set; to use and organize search strategies; to monitor performance and correct errors; and to resist or inhibit the impulse to respond to salient but irrelevant aspects of a task. Overall, this area of functioning was slightly below average for Marty and represents a weakness compared to peers. The one subtest score that was average within this domain (Clocks, PR 50) contains a strong visual-spatial element, already described as a relative strength.

Marty's next-highest domain of functioning was the sensorimotor area. Traditionally, sensorimotor abilities have been viewed as markers of normal physiological development or as indicators of atypical development and/or dysfunction. These abilities are assumed to mediate functions within a goal-oriented complex system through which knowledge is acquired, problems are solved, and intent or purpose is communicated. Much of what children learn and do requires a coordination of multiple systems that mediate production of smooth and efficient limb and body movements and dexterous movements of the hands and fingers. The subtests within this area are below average for Marty, relative to his peers.

Marty's next-highest area of functioning, Language, is also central to neuropsychological skill development. Components include phonological processing, naming, receptive language comprehension, understanding of the syntactic structure of language, and ease of linguistic production. Capacity to analyze the phonological elements of words is an essential component of reading. Speed of naming is an important subcomponent of language and reflects automaticity with which information and semantic memory can be accessed. In general, poor readers seem to be slower relative to good readers on tasks of rapid automatized naming. Marty's performance was Low Average on phonological skills and naming speed, and significantly lower on comprehending instructions. Marty performed very poorly on the subtest Comprehension of Instructions, which requires understanding and responding to multistage oral directions.

Marty's performance on the Memory and Learning domain was a relative and normative weakness, and is impacted by his limited ability to remember visual and auditory stimuli that have meaningful content. Moreover, the subtests do not just require short-term rote memory, but more intermediate or long-term memory. As is obvious from the UNIT scores above, his ability to remember visual content over a short period of time is a relative strength. His weakest area of memory involved recall and expression of a story that was read aloud to him. Performance was stronger (though still somewhat weak) on visual and visual-auditory memory tasks. In general, he is much less capable of remembering auditory content than visual.

SUMMARY AND RECOMMENDATIONS

Marty is 9 years old and in the fourth grade; he has a history of speech and language delay and was identified as Developmentally Delayed by the Cox County school system in 2005 and again in 2007. Based on current assessment results, combined with previous assessments and history, the diagnosis of Pervasive Developmental Disorder Not Otherwise Specified (*DSM-IV-TR* 299.80) appears to be appropriate. Results from this assessment, the MRI, and the autism checklist help confirm this diagnosis. Importantly, Marty exhibits some of the characteristics of autism (most notably language delay), but he does not exhibit others (e.g., according to his parents he has always been affectionate and seems to enjoy physical contact such as cuddling).

Marty's performance on the NEPSY-II is consistent with the pattern of scores obtained by a group of children diagnosed with autistic spectrum disorders reported in the NEPSY-II literature. That is, his highest score was in the area of visual-spatial functioning and his lowest score in the area of memory/language. Auditory memory was significantly weaker than visual memory and visual-auditory memory combined. Although his language functioning is relatively low, his general cognitive ability, as assessed by the UNIT, was within the Average range. Previous cognitive tests that showed depressed scores were heavily language dependent. Individuals with patterns of scores similar to the ones that Marty obtained on this assessment and previous assessments often have difficulty interacting successfully with peers, likely due to their limited facility with language. If somewhat impulsive, these individuals sometimes learn to express themselves primarily via gross motor behaviors and are characterized as behaving like a "bull in a china shop." On the other hand, some are characterized as excessively shy and become tentative, and as a result, are sometimes ignored. Marty has adopted the latter strategies.

RECOMMENDATIONS

Marty should be reevaluated by the local university's Speech and Hearing Clinic for an updated language assessment and auditory processing evaluation. Information from such an assessment can help determine if Marty would benefit from specialized interventions such as an auditory trainer in the classroom. The language assessment should also provide comprehensive recommendations regarding language development. Continued speech/language therapy is indicated, as well as social skills training and the continuation of individualized tutoring.

In addition, the following recommendations are offered:

1. Continue special education services. A combination of special education pullout and general education services will likely be most beneficial for Marty.

2. Because Marty has good general cognitive ability, he will likely benefit from social skills training with a strong visual-motor component (e.g., role-playing, use of gestures, facial expressions). He should benefit from extra practice in understanding and following both oral and written directions.

3. To increase comprehension and retention of new information, use visual aids (e.g., graphic organizers, semantic mapping) as much as possible, and limit lecture-style environments. Marty has difficulty understanding and processing fast-paced narrative material, presented orally. He may need directions repeated and assignments broken down into smaller steps or components (relative to peers). Marty may need to have assignment and test modifications, especially when complex verbal material is involved.

4. Use sight-word flash cards as a strategy to increase speed of word recognition. In addition, it may be helpful to practice unfamiliar words prior to reading new material, as well as to use/teach comprehension strategies, such as making predictions and finding the main ideas in passages.

5. Because he exhibits slow processing speed on many unfamiliar tasks that require intermediate or long-term memory, Marty will benefit from extended time on assignments and tests.

6. Carefully plan Marty's transition to middle school. His progress will need to be followed closely in middle school where he will have a variety of teachers. His schedule will need to be planned to ensure opportunities for success without being overwhelmed.

7. As Marty gets older, more of the academic content will be presented in lecture format. He will need support in developing strategies to compensate. Older students sometimes profit from the use of handheld recorders. Because his attention/executive functioning is somewhat depressed relative to peers, he will benefit from the training in the use of metacognitive (learning to learn) strategies, typically taught by a tutor or special educator (pacing, prioritizing, self-checking).

CASE 25

Difficulty Versus Disability?
A Student Struggling with Math

John Garruto

School psychologists are frequently called on to conduct psychoeducational evaluations. Unfortunately, training programs have so much to teach (e.g., assessment, counseling, consultation) in such a short period of time, that it becomes challenging to keep expanding one's toolbox. Some have even joked that once upon a time, the answer to every problem could have been answered with "A WISC, a WRAT, and a Bender." Furthermore, in this era where the importance of the use of cognitive and neuropsychological assessment has been called into question (e.g., Reschly, 2008; Reschly & Ysseldyke, 2002 and that outside of auditory processing these measures offer little benefit (Gresham, Restori, & Cook, 2008), school psychologists may feel dissuaded from conducting comprehensive evaluations.

This case serves as a reminder that school psychologists must strive to answer the referral question and carefully choose the tools from his or her toolbox not only to facilitate diagnosis, but also to plan an appropriate intervention. From the RTI perspective, we know one thing about the child referred for evaluation—what *didn't* work. By simply saying that this child failed to respond to intervention, we would have missed some salient information. The truth for Lupita is that her math skills are below average, but other concerns exist, as well. These included difficulty with sustaining attention (related to executive function control), as well as anxiety. She may not have been eligible as a student with a disability but certainly she has learning challenges and requires intervention.

As is often the case for school psychologists, many do not tend to hear of students after they have evaluated them. During the year of the problem-solving team process, Lupita failed three out of four quarters. The year of the evaluation, she did improve; she not only passed her math class, but was one point away from "meeting the standards" on the state test. Lupita is still earning passing grades in her math class, but she continues to struggle. Continuing to keep a close eye on her progress and providing best-practice instruction in math will be important for Lupita. Her difficulties with information processing (cognitive fluency, rapid retrieval from long-term memory, and shifting set) could only have been detected by using several different assessment instruments.

PSYCHOLOGICAL REPORT

Name:	Lupita Thalgott
Date of Birth:	6/8/2000
Age:	10-3
School:	Wayside Academy
Teacher:	Betty Meyers
Grade:	5
Dates of Evaluation:	9/10/10, 9/17/2010
Date of Report:	9/20/2010
Examiner:	John M. Garruto, D.Ed., NCSP

REASON FOR REFERRAL

Because of difficulties with math problem solving, Lupita was referred to the school problem-solving team by her fifth-grade teacher, Ms. Betty Meyers. In the preceding school year, from February until June, Lupita received targeted intervention to improve her ability to solve one-step story problems. Despite having the information broken down and having a math helper in the classroom, Lupita continued to struggle with math. The purposes of this evaluation are to determine whether or not she has a learning disability in mathematics and to recommend appropriate interventions.

BACKGROUND AND OBSERVATIONS

Lupita is a quiet and polite 10-year-old girl who currently lives at home with her mother, her mother's significant other, and his 8-year-old daughter, Zoe. Lupita is currently attending the fifth grade at Wayside Academy. Ms. Thalgott was interviewed regarding developmental history and provided the following information. Lupita was the result of an uncomplicated pregnancy and delivery. She met her developmental milestones early, walking at 7 months and talking at 8 months. Ms. Thalgott recalled that Lupita was a bit "busy and bossy" as a young child. She also noted that when there were changes in family or home dynamics, Lupita's grades seemed to be affected. She experienced good progress at a Head Start preschool and in kindergarten at Valley View. She then transferred to first grade at Wayside Academy. Although her teachers have always expressed minor concerns regarding her educational performance, significant concerns over her progress only emerged in third grade. Past teacher reports indicated that Lupita has difficulty with both listening comprehension and math problem solving. Teachers also indicated that Lupita needs "wait time" to process information before answering. Lupita has passed the third- and fourth-grade state tests in Language Arts, but has not passed the third- or fourth-grade math tests. (Her score on both indicated "partially meeting the standards.") Lupita has not had any significant illnesses or injuries and is currently not on any medications.

Lupita was observed in her classroom on September 10, 2010. She participated appropriately in a math activity and responded to help by the two teachers who were present. She seemed to show some difficulty with number sense, as she did not seem to know that if she kept counting by twos, she would eventually reach the number 36. When she finished her math activity, she started reading independently.

ASSESSMENT PROCEDURES

Behavior Assessment System for Children, Second Edition (BASC-2): Parent and Teacher forms, and Self-Reports

Delis Kaplan Executive Function System (D-KEFS): selected subtests

KeyMath – Revised (KeyMath-R)

Process Assessment of the Learner, Second Edition: Diagnostics for Math (PAL-II Math)

Woodcock-Johnson III Tests of Cognitive Abilities (WJ III COG)

Woodcock-Johnson III Tests of Achievement (WJ III ACH)

The scores of the D-KEFS, KeyMath-R, PAL-II, WJ III COG, and WJ III ACH are appended to this report. Age norms were used. For score reports of the BASC-2: SRP-C, TRS-C and PRS-C, please see the confidential file.

Descriptors	Standard Scores (SS)	Scaled Scores (ScS)	Percentiles
Deficient	< 70	1	< 2
Well Below Average	70 to 79	4 to 5	2 to 8
Below Average	80 to 89	6 to 7	9 to 24
Average	90 to 109	8 to 12	25 to 74
Above Average	110 to 119	13 to 14	75 to 90
Well Above Average	120 to 129	15 to 16	91 to 97
Very Superior	130+	17 to 19	98 and above
Standard scores (SS) have mean of 100 and a standard deviation of 15. Scaled scores (ScS) have a mean of 10 and a standard deviation of 3.			

BEHAVIORAL OBSERVATIONS

Lupita was cooperative and persistent and was willing to engage with the examiner in conversation. At times, she appeared inattentive, even in the controlled environment of the testing room, and would stare out the window. During administration of the KeyMath-R, Lupita seemed more concerned about whether her scrap paper looked orderly than attending to the problems. She admitted that she does better when she pays better attention. The examiner asked if she had difficulty focusing in the classroom, to which Lupita indicated that she does daydream quite a bit.

Lupita's performance during the assessment can best be described as inconsistent. As indicated earlier, at times she seemed to only be partially attending to the tasks. Lupita was able to get challenging items correct, yet would miss easier items. When engaged in the sorting task of the D-KEFS, although she was shown how to do the sorting (both by the words on the cards [verbal sorts] and by the way the cards actually were shaped [perceptual sorts]), she only attended to perceptual sorts. When asked why she did not attend to the words, she seemed bewildered that she only focused on the shape of the cards. Lupita seemed to misunderstand some directions or the nature of the tasks, yet when she had things explained more clearly, she met with more success. Given the inconsistency of her performance, the results of this assessment should be interpreted cautiously.

ASSESSMENT FINDINGS

Cognitive Development

Although Lupita's overall cognitive profile was within the Average range, strengths and weaknesses existed. Lupita's overall verbal ability was within the Average range. Thinking ability (intentional cognitive processing) was within the Average range, as was cognitive efficiency (how effectively Lupita processes information). Discrepancies existed, however, among the tests within each area.

Comprehension-Knowledge

Lupita's Comprehension-Knowledge, which reflects her overall fund of knowledge, including general information about her environment and vocabulary, was within the Average range. Lupita's ability to give synonyms and antonyms, and complete analogies was in the Low Average range. When coming up with synonyms and antonyms, she sometimes chose words that were close but their meanings did not quite fit. Lupita also had considerable difficulty with analogies as well, indicating some difficulty in language tasks involving reasoning. In contrast, she obtained a High Average score in her ability to state the location and function of everyday objects, such as a frying pan. Furthermore, given various teacher reports that Lupita had difficulty with content information (science and social studies), she was given the WJ III ACH Knowledge test. Her academic knowledge was also in the Average range.

Long-Term Storage and Retrieval

The tests that measure long-term storage and retrieval abilities were significantly discrepant. Lupita's ability to learn new information was measured by an associative learning task in which she was taught words to match numerous small drawings and then was asked to "read" sentences "written" with the drawings. Lupita performed within the High Average range, showing facility with learning visual-auditory associations. When asked to read sentences "written" in the drawings later, Lupita performed within the

Average range, indicating that she retained many of the newly learned associations.

Lupita's ability to retrieve information, specifically words, from long-term memory was assessed by an ideational fluency task and a rapid naming task. Lupita was given a category and was asked to name as many things as she could within that category in 1 minute (e.g., articles of clothing). This task was repeated with two other categories. Her score was between the Low Average and Average ranges, and significantly weaker than her ability to encode new information. Analysis of her responses, many of which were repeated, suggests that she may not have information well organized in long-term memory. She also scored in the Low Average range when asked to name pictures of common objects as fast as possible. Although she was accurate, she was slow to come up with the name. Slow retrieval may have contributed to her difficulty with the verbal comprehension tasks, as she seemed to have some difficulty pulling words from memory. It appears that although Lupita has facility to learn new information, it takes her time to retrieve well established in memory information. This fits very well with past teachers' observations regarding the importance of providing Lupita with sufficient time to respond.

Visual-Spatial Thinking

Visual-spatial thinking measures one's ability to perceive spatial relationships and mentally manipulate objects. Lupita's abilities with visualization and spatial relation skills were within the Average range. Lupita also presented with Average visual memory skills. Overall, her visual-spatial skills are adequately developed.

Auditory Processing

Auditory processing measures how well Lupita can process information that she hears. Her overall auditory processing skills also fell within the Average range. The tasks on this assessment include phonetic coding (synthesis) and an auditory figure ground task. Lupita performed within the Average range on the auditory synthesis task, as evidenced by her ability to hear individual sounds and then blend them into a word. Lupita also performed within the Average range on the auditory figure ground task, showing that she can discriminate speech sounds even in the presence of distracting noise. Overall, her auditory processing skills are adequately developed.

Fluid Reasoning

Fluid reasoning is the ability to use deductive and inductive reasoning to solve problems that one has not encountered before or that cannot be solved in a simple manner. Lupita's overall reasoning was in the Low Average range with no difference in her performance on the two tests. Both tests are controlled-learning tasks; she was told if her answer was right and given the correct answer if hers was wrong.

Deductive reasoning is the ability to use given rules to move step-by-step toward a resolution of the problem. On this test, she was given a key displaying how colored squares could be combined to make other colors. She was then to use the key to figure out the missing color in new combinations of colored squares.

Inductive reasoning measures one's ability to use multiple observations or examples and come up with a generalization that holds true for all of the elements (e.g., a pineapple, apple, banana, and watermelon are all fruits). On this controlled-learning task, she was required to look at two forms that could differ in a variety of characteristics and generate the "rule" that described how they were different. For each incorrect response, she was given corrective feedback. Lupita was able to figure out the "rules" for the basic puzzles, but when they became more complex, she had more difficulty.

Lupita was also administered inductive reasoning tasks on the D-KEFS. She was required to sort cards into groups based on their physical characteristics and on the categories represented by the words on the cards. Lupita's performance was in the low end of the Average range. Next, the examiner sorted the cards and Lupita was asked to state the concept by which he had grouped them. Her performance was Below Average. An interesting observation was that Lupita sorted the cards based on how they looked, forgetting about the verbal information available. Lupita seemed to "get lost" when trying to decipher what a problem is asking of her. However, with minimal guidance, she was able to "get back on track." This has implications for her math ability, discussed later.

Short-Term Memory and Working Memory

Lupita's performance on the Short-Term Memory and Working Memory clusters of the WJ III COG was the same, at the upper end of the Average range. The three tests composing the two clusters assess memory span and working memory. Memory span measures how much information one can hold in memory for a few seconds (such as hearing and immediately repeating a series of words). Working memory is the ability to hold information in memory and then add to it, work with it, or change it in some way. Overall, Lupita's memory abilities are well developed.

Processing Speed/Perceptual Speed

Processing speed is the ability to automatically and fluently perform easy or overlearned tasks, especially when mental efficiency is required. Lupita's performance on the two tests was different. She performed in the Low Average range on a task that required her to rapidly scan and circle the two identical numbers in rows of numbers. Her performance was in the Average range when required to look at rows of pictures and determine which two were "most alike." Lupita seems to be faster in identifying conceptual similarities than purely visual similarities.

Perceptual speed is the ability to rapidly search, compare, and identify visual elements. Lupita performed in the Low Average range on both tests within this cluster. She was accurate, but slow, indicating that she has some difficulty with speed for this type of comparison.

Executive Functioning

In addition to various cognitive skills assessed, Lupita's executive function abilities were assessed with the D-KEFS. Executive functioning has many facets. One way of conceptualizing it concerns how we use thought to direct purposeful action. Examples include: planning (e.g., "If I do all of the easy ones first, I may get a better score"); inhibition (e.g., "I want very much to answer that question, but if I shout out, I may get in trouble"); working memory (e.g., "I need to perform the second task first, the third task second, and the first task last"); cognitive flexibility (e.g., "There must be another way to solve this task" or "My way may not be the only way to look at it"); set shifting (e.g., "I've been adding, but now the problem has changed to subtracting"); and allocation of attentional resources (e.g., "I need to be attending to what the teacher is saying, not on the snow falling outside"). Lupita was administered a variety of tasks that measure executive functioning.

Lupita was administered three time-limited sequencing tasks. The first two required her to find and identify numbers in sequence from a set placed in random order; the second was a similar task using the alphabet. She demonstrated Average skill in rapid scanning and sequencing. The third task required her to set-shift, constantly switching between sequencing the numbers and letters. On the set-shifting task, her performance was in the Deficient range. This indicates that although her sequencing abilities are well developed, Lupita has difficulty when required to "switch gears" in the middle of a task.

Another executive function measured set-shift within an ideational fluency task. Lupita performed in the Average range when asked to name as many items as she could that began with a certain letter. However, she scored in the Below Average range when required to name items within a given category, consistent with her performance on the similar task on the WJ III COG, suggesting she has difficulty with a rapid systematic search for semantic information in long-term memory. Lupita also scored in the Below Average range when she was required to do this task again, this time alternating between two categories of items (e.g., alternating between names of vegetables and names of toys). This suggests that the added burden of set shifting makes her search for information more difficult. Furthermore, as noted previously, Lupita was slow on the retrieval tasks of the WJ III COG (Below Average/Average), suggesting that it may take her longer to retrieve words and find information that is in long-term memory.

On the D-KEFS, Lupita was also administered a timed inhibition task. She was presented with a page of color words, with each word printed in a different color than the word's meaning (e.g., the word "red" was written in blue letters). Lupita was required to scan across the page, naming the color of the word rather than reading the text. Lupita's performance was in the low end of the Average range regarding the amount of time it took her to complete the task but was Below Average in regard to the number of errors she made. Lupita always self-corrected her errors, indicating that she recognized the correct answer but had difficulty inhibiting the more automatic response, which is reading the word. Surprisingly, Lupita performed competently (in regard to speed and errors), when required to alternate between reading the word and the color. This performance contrasts with other test findings that indicated that Lupita had difficulty with set shifting. However, a key difference with this task is that Lupita did not have to either visually or cognitively "search" for the answer—it was right there in front of her. Her greater success with inhibition could also have resulted from the practice employed on the earlier task.

Finally, as described earlier, Lupita's concept formation skills were assessed when required to sort cards. Again, she attended more to what she saw rather than the meaning of the words printed on the cards.

ORAL LANGUAGE

Because those who work with Lupita have noted that she seems to get lost with directions, two oral language tasks were administered. The first was a measure of lis-

tening comprehension and recall; she was to listen to a story and then retell it (WJ III ACH Story Recall). Lupita performed within the Average range. On the second test, she was given a detailed picture to review. She was then given multiple-step directions regarding objects to point to in the picture and the order in which to point to them (e.g., "Point to the tree if you see a train, otherwise point to a bird" [WJ III ACH Understanding Directions]). Lupita performed within the Average range on this task also. Her performance on these tests is noteworthy given that Lupita is reported to have a history of difficulty with language comprehension, and her difficulty was also observed in this assessment on tasks such as oral counting. However, a key difference between the oral counting task and Understanding Directions is that on the latter test, Lupita had a picture to use. Again, having meaningful visual information to reference appears to help Lupita.

ACADEMIC ACHIEVEMENT

Math Achievement

In math, Lupita was assessed on computation, math fluency, and math reasoning. Math Computation assesses how well students can complete basic math operations, including addition, subtraction, multiplication, and division. Lupita's performance varied based on the test that was administered. Although Lupita tended to perform in the Below Average range across tasks, her skills fluctuated across the different operations. Lupita was able to add and subtract with regrouping. She demonstrated an understanding of the concept underlying multiplication but has not yet memorized her multiplication facts. She was able to multiply 2-digit numbers by a 1-digit number. Lupita is beginning to understand the steps to division but cannot yet carry them out. Interestingly, her performance on the PAL-II division problems was markedly better than on the KeyMath-R, although both were significantly weak. This change in performance was most likely the result of several sessions of tutoring by the math specialist on division concepts during the week between the two test sessions. Although her division skills are much weaker than her skills on other operations, she seems to be making progress.

Math fluency is the ability to retrieve math facts from long-term memory automatically. Lupita performed within the Below Average range but was accurate, indicating that she has difficulty related to the automaticity with which she can retrieve math facts.

Math problem solving is the ability to solve word problems and understand concepts such as time and money. Lupita's performance across different tasks ranged from Below Average to the lower end of the Average range. Interestingly, Lupita sometimes missed easy problems but answered more difficult ones correctly. She sometimes appeared overwhelmed when problems required multiple steps.

Lupita was also given tasks that assessed basic math processes. She demonstrated Average ability with numeral writing. She had significant difficulty with oral counting, obtaining a score in the Very Deficient range. However, Lupita's problem was not so much the nature of the task as that she was confused by the directions. For example, when she was asked to count forward by 5s starting at 10, Lupita counted by 10s. However, given a more challenging counting task, counting by 7s starting at 7, Lupita was successful because she started with the 7. This is an important theme throughout Lupita's difficulty with math skills. Although her math skills present as an area of difficulty, she may also be confused by task directions.

SOCIAL-EMOTIONAL ADJUSTMENT

Lupita, her teacher, and her mother completed the Behavior Assessment System for Children, Second Edition (BASC-2). All three rating scales had satisfactory scores on the validity, consistency, and response pattern indexes and thus were considered valid representations of Lupita's social-emotional behaviors and feelings. Lupita's social-emotional status was assessed on a broad range of characteristics. According to her teacher, Lupita does not demonstrate any at-risk or clinically significant concerns (although the "attention problems" factor was nearly at-risk). According to Lupita's mother, Lupita demonstrated at-risk concerns with attention problems and activities of daily living. In contrast, Lupita's self-report reflected at-risk concerns related to locus of control, hyperactivity, and self-reliance. She rated clinically significant concerns in the areas of atypicality, depression, anxiety, and attention problems.

The contrast is noteworthy. This suggests that although Lupita is not exhibiting many behavioral problems, she is experiencing emotions associated with depression and anxiety, and difficulty with attention. Those who work with Lupita note that she is sometimes hesitant to take risks, which may be a reflection of her concern regarding "being incorrect." An interview with Lupita confirmed her concerns. Furthermore, when asked if she was interested in receiving counseling services, Lupita agreed that she was interested.

Concerns regarding attention were noted by Lupita, her mother, and, to a lesser extent, her teacher. When asked about her concerns, Lupita indicated that she daydreams a lot. This was also noted throughout the assessment (e.g., looking out the window). Thus, the possibility of Attention-Deficit/Hyperactivity Disorder (ADHD) should be explored.

Although there were some social-emotional concerns raised in this assessment, Lupita also has adaptive strengths. She is cooperative and well-behaved, with no history of discipline referrals. Furthermore, Lupita's candid discussion of her social-emotional concerns, as well as high interest in doing well in school, reflect that she is a goal-directed individual who strives to do her best.

SUMMARY AND CONCLUSIONS

Lupita is a 10-year-old girl who was referred due to concerns regarding her math problem-solving skills. Cognitively, Lupita performs within the Average range, although significant differences exist among her abilities. Her abilities were in the upper end of the Average range to the Above Average range in short-term memory and working memory, visual-spatial thinking, auditory processing, and general information. Her oral language abilities in recalling narratives and following complex oral directions were also Average, although her performance in a test of expressive vocabulary was Low Average due to her difficulty with word retrievals.

Test results indicated that Lupita has Low Average abilities in fluid reasoning, cognitive fluency, perceptual speed, and rapid naming. Except for fluid reasoning, the tests for these abilities all required rapid performance, which does seem to present some difficulty for her. Lupita's attention throughout the test sessions was notably inconsistent although she seemed motivated to do well.

Lupita's demonstration of math skills was highly inconsistent as well. Sometimes she missed very easy items but completed more complex items correctly. And on the KeyMath-R computation, although her multiplication, division, and mental computation scores spanned the Below Average to Deficient ranges, her math applications were primarily solidly average. Over the week between test sessions, Lupita had three sessions of tutoring on division with the math specialist. At the next session, albeit on another test, her multiplication and division skills were notably higher.

Lupita does appear to have some difficulty with both computation and math problem solving. Her math difficulties may stem, in part, from somewhat weak cognitive abilities, and may be compounded by attentional difficulties. Presently, however, her difficulties do not seem sufficiently consistent or severe to qualify as a learning disability. At this time, no special education classification is recommended, but Lupita should continue receiving the additional classroom support and tutoring from the math specialist. Her progress should be carefully monitored and if she fails to show growth, or her performance begins to decline, she should be referred back to the Committee on Special Education.

Although Lupita has some adaptive strengths and is clearly motivated to succeed in school, she rated herself as having serious emotional concerns and attentional problems, and expressed an interest in counseling. These issues require immediate attention.

RECOMMENDATIONS

Further Evaluation

Lupita's self-identified emotional and attentional problems require a psychological evaluation to rule out or confirm a primary attentional disorder and to make recommendations regarding Lupita's anxiety, depression, and low self-esteem.

Self-Esteem

1. Capitalize on instructional activities in which Lupita is successful. For example, have Lupita participate in a cross-age tutoring program in a structured setting where she teaches a younger student the skills that she has recently mastered. Alternatively, she can teach any other skill she knows to other students in her class.

2. One of the strongest factors in improving a student's self-concept and effecting the personal changes secondary to improved self-concept is a strong, positive relationship with a teacher who likes and enjoys the student as a person. Ideas for showing acceptance are:

   • Demonstrate to Lupita that you like and approve of her by providing frequent positive reinforcements, such as a smile, a positive comment on a paper, special privileges, or rewards.

   • Watch for situations where Lupita is doing something correctly or behaving appropriately. Make a positive comment to her in front of others regarding the behavior.

   • Assign Lupita a classroom task that she would enjoy, such as watering the plants or collecting homework assignments. Express gratitude after she has completed the task.

   • Create opportunities to ask Lupita what she thinks about certain things. Make it apparent that you are sincerely interested in her opinion.

Attention

1. Teach Lupita to use a beeper tape to remind her to stay on task. This tape provides a sound at varying time intervals, cueing Lupita to ask herself, "Am I on task?" If she is, she places a check on a chart. If not, she resumes work. Build in positive reinforcement for increasing the number of checks she accumulates within a work session. You might set a lower number of checks necessary for a reward in tasks in which her attention is significantly challenged and raise the limit in tasks in which her attention is not so challenged.

2. Divide Lupita's in-class assignments into smaller, more manageable chunks. Give her one chunk at a time with instructions to hand each in as it is completed and pick up the next. Each time she hands in a portion of the work, provide reinforcement for completed work and for time on task. Examples for dividing the work are: Cut apart the major sections of a worksheet and give her one section at a time to complete, place a piece of "sticky" paper over the bottom half of a worksheet; put a sticker on the bottom of every two pages of a story.

Instructions

1. Make sure you have eye contact with Lupita before speaking to her or giving oral instructions.

2. Encourage Lupita to ask for clarification and repetition of instructions.

3. Explain all the instructions clearly before allowing Lupita to start any assignment. Methods for helping to clarify the instructions for Lupita and the group include: having Lupita or another student repeat the instructions to the group; modeling the activity before having students start; or pretending to model the activity and asking the students to try and catch you in mistakes. Make mistakes deliberately, and, when caught, ask, "What did I do wrong? What was I supposed to do?"

4. Prior to giving complex verbal instructions, write them on the board. This will avoid the need for repetition as Lupita needs to see the organizational structure to grasp it.

Response Speed

1. When calling on Lupita in class, provide her with as much time as necessary to organize her thoughts and formulate a response. She may know the answer but need extra time to find the words. Privately, alert Lupita to this plan so that she does not feel pressured to come up with answers quickly.
2. Except when the focus is to increase or monitor speed, do not have Lupita do timed tests, written or oral. Provide her as much time as she needs to complete a test. If extra time cannot be made available, reduce the number of problems she is expected to do.

Math: General

1. When teaching Lupita any new process or skill, provide slow, step-by-step instruction. Use manipulatives and concrete objects whenever possible to illustrate the concepts.
2. Reinforce Lupita for persevering on tasks when they become more challenging.

Math Fluency

1. Lupita will require additional time, or fewer problems on timed math tasks.
2. An easy-to-use program to help Lupita increase her speed of retrieval of the basic facts, including addition, subtraction, multiplication, and division, is *Great Leaps Math* (www.greatleaps.com).
3. To help Lupita increase her speed in math operations, drill her on math facts using visual stimuli such as flash cards, computer programs, and, when she can respond to a math fact within 3 seconds, worksheets. Eventually, move to timed tests.

Math Problem Solving

1. Teach Lupita a specific math problem strategy to use for solving story problems. [See the Supplementary Appendix, which includes a more in-depth description of a math problem-solving strategy.]

2. When Lupita has difficulty with the computation involved in a story problem, have her substitute smaller numbers so that she can understand the operation(s) involved and then calculate the problem a second time using the original numbers.
3. Teach Lupita how to plan what she needs to do to solve a problem. Different techniques, such as the following, may be called for by the type of question asked:

- Decide what operation(s) to use (e.g., Harry weighed 250 pounds. He weighed 72 more pounds than James. How much did James weigh?)
- Make a table, graph, or chart of the information provided (e.g., Hansel and Gretel went to the witch's house every day except Sunday. On Mondays and Thursdays, Hansel went twice. On Wednesday, Gretel went in the morning, at noon, and once after Hansel was in bed. Who traveled to the witch's house more times in a month?)
- Make a drawing of the information provided (e.g., Mehitabel planted a square garden with 12 garlic plants on each side to keep the snails away. How many garlic plants did she plant?)
- Make inferences and logical deductions (e.g., The Carsons went to Jack-in-the-Bag and spent $20.75 for lunch. An adult meal costs $4.95 and lunch for a child costs $2.95. How many people are in the family? How many of them are children?)

SCORES

Scores based on age 10-3.

KeyMath-R

Composite/Subtest	SS/ScS	Percentile
Basic Concepts	**87**	**19**
Numeration	7	
Rational Numbers	9	
Geometry	8	
Operations	**82**	**12**
Addition	8	
Subtraction	11	
Multiplication	7	
Division	1	
Mental Computation	5	
Applications	**90**	**25**

Composite/Subtest	SS/ScS	Percentile
Measurement	9	
Time and Money	7	
Estimation	9	
Interpreting Data	9	
Problem Solving	9	

PAL-II: (Subtest scores from 8–12 are within the Average range)

Subtest	ScS	Subtest	ScS
Automatic Legible Numeral Writing	13		
Legible Numeral Writing	14		
Total Time	10		
Oral Counting	1		
Numeric Coding	5		
Look and Write—Addition	12	Listen and Say—Addition	6
Look and Write—Subtraction	4	Listen and Say—Subtraction	4
Look and Write—Mixed Addition and Subtraction	5	Listen and Say—Mixed Addition and Subtraction	4
Look and Write—Multiplication	9	Listen and Say—Multiplication	7
Look and Write—Division	4	Listen and Say—Division	6
Look and Write—Mixed Multiplication and Division	4	Listen and Say—Mixed Multiplication and Division	6

D-KEFS

Trail Making Test:		Verbal Fluency Test:	
Condition 1: Visual Scanning	9	Condition 1: Letter Fluency	10
Condition 2: Number Sequencing	11	Condition 2: Category Fluency	7
Condition 3: Letter Sequencing	9	Condition 3: Category Switching (Correct)	6
Condition 4: Number-Letter Switching	3	Condition 4: Category Switching (Accuracy)	7

D-KEFS Sorting Test

Condition 1: Free Sorting	ScS
Confirmed Correct Sorts	9
Free Sorting Description	8
Condition 2: Sort Recognition	
Sort Recognition Description	7
Combined Description Score	**8**

D-KEFS Color-Word Interference Test

Subtest	ScS
Condition 1: Color Naming	11
Condition 2: Word Reading	12
Condition 3: Inhibition	8
Condition 3:-Errors	7
Condition 4: Inhibition/Switching	11
Condition 4:-Errors	11

Behavior Assessment System for Children, Second Edition

Reporting only At-Risk and Clinically Significant Scores

Scale	Lupita	Mother	Teacher
Attention		67	59
Hyperactivity	65		
Inattention/hyperactivity	**74**		
Locus of Control	62		
Atypicality	**79**		
Depression	**70**		
Anxiety	**80**		
Sense of inadequacy	**77**		
Adaptive Scales			
Activities of daily living		39	
Self-Reliance	38		

At Risk = *T* scores from 60–69; Clinically Significant scores 70 and above
Adaptive scales: At Risk = 31–39; Clinically Significant = 30 and below

Table of Scores

Woodcock-Johnson III Normative Update Tests of Cognitive Abilities and Tests of Achievement (Form A)

WJ III NU Compuscore and Profiles Program, Version 3.0

Norms based on age

CLUSTER*/Test	RPI	SS (68% Band)	PR
GIA (Ext)	89/90	98 (95–100)	44
THINKING ABILITY (Ext)	89/90	99 (95–102)	46
COGNITIVE EFFICIENCY (Ext)	92/90	104 (99–109)	61
Numbers Reversed	99/90	114 (109–120)	83
Memory for Words	93/90	103 (96–110)	57
Visual Matching	75/90	85 (79–91)	16
Decision Speed	87/90	96 (91–101)	40
COMPREHENSION-KNOWLEDGE (Gc)	87/90	97 (93–102)	43
VERBAL ABILITY (Ext)	87/90	97 (93–102)	43
General Information	96/90	111 (105–118)	77
Verbal Comprehension	64/90	84 (79–89)	14
LONG-TERM RETRIEVAL (Glr)	93/90	108 (102–114)	71
Visual-Auditory Learning	96/90	114 (107–121)	82
Retrieval Fluency	88/90	90 (84–97)	26
Vis-Aud Learn – Delayed	91/90	103 (98–108)	58
VISUAL-SPATIAL THINKING (Gv)	92/90	103 (99–108)	59
Spatial Relations	93/90	105 (100–109)	62
Picture Recognition	90/90	101 (95–106)	52
AUDITORY PROCESSING (Ga)	93/90	106 (100–112)	66
Sound Blending	93/90	104 (98–110)	61
Auditory Attention	92/90	106 (97–114)	64
FLUID REASONING (Gf)	74/90	88 (84–92)	22
Concept Formation	72/90	90 (85–94)	24
Analysis-Synthesis	76/90	90 (85–96)	26
PROCESSING SPEED (Gs)	82/90	88 (84–93)	22
Decision Speed	87/90	96 (91–101)	40
Visual Matching	75/90	85 (79–91)	16
PERCEPTUAL SPEED	74/90	83 (78–88)	13
Visual Matching	75/90	85 (79–91)	16
Cross Out	73/90	86 (78–93)	17
SHORT-TERM MEMORY (Gsm)	97/90	110 (105–116)	75
Numbers Reversed	99/90	114 (109–120)	83
Memory for Words	93/90	103 (96–110)	57
WORKING MEMORY	97/90	111 (107–116)	77

CLUSTER/Test	RPI	SS (68% Band)	PR
Numbers Reversed	99/90	114 (109–120)	83
Auditory Working Memory	93/90	104 (99–109)	61
COGNITIVE FLUENCY	82/90	85 (82–89)	16
Decision Speed	87/90	96 (91–101)	40
Retrieval Fluency	88/90	90 (84–97)	26
Rapid Picture Naming	65/90	84 (81–86)	14
KNOWLEDGE	94/90	106 (101–110)	65
General Information	96/90	111 (105–118)	77
Academic Knowledge	90/90	100 (95–105)	50
ORAL LANGUAGE (Std)	90/90	99 (93–105)	47
Story Recall	91/90	104 (95–113)	60
Understanding Directions	87/90	97 (91–103)	41
BROAD MATH	70/90	84 (80–88)	14
Calculation	74/90	89 (82–95)	22
Applied Problems	55/90	88 (84–92)	21
Math Fluency	79/90	82 (79–85)	12
MATH CALCULATION SKILLS	77/90	84 (78–89)	14
Calculation	74/90	89 (82–95)	22
Math Fluency	79/90	82 (79–85)	12
MATH REASONING	68/90	89 (86–93)	24
Applied Problems	55/90	88 (84–92)	21
Quantitative Concepts	79/90	93 (87–98)	31
ACADEMIC KNOWLEDGE	90/90	100 (95–105)	50
Academic Knowledge	90/90	100 (95–105)	50

*Bolded clusters contain tests with over lapping confidence bands.

REFERENCES

Gresham, F. M., Restori, A. F., & Cook, C. R. (2008). To test or not to test: Issues pertaining to response to intervention and cognitive testing. *Communique, 37(1)*, 5–7.

Reschly, D. J. (2008). School psychology RTI paradigm shift and beyond. In A. Thomas & J. Grimes (Eds.), *Best practices in school psychology V* (5th ed., pp. 3–15). Bethesda, MD: National Association of School Psychologists.

Reschly, D. J., & Ysseldyke, J. E. (2002). Paradigm shift: The past is not the future. In A. Thomas & J. Grimes (Eds.), *Best practices in school psychology IV* (4th ed., Vol. 1, pp. 3–20). Bethesda, MD: National Association of School Psychologists.

CASE 26

Psychoeducational Assessment of a Student with a Visual Impairment Using the Woodcock-Johnson III Tests of Achievement – Braille Adaptation

Kimberly Morris

The following report is the result of a unique reevaluation of a student with a visual impairment who was referred by his teacher of students with visual impairments (TVI) due to concerns regarding his limited academic progress. The case was complex in that the student is completely blind and has other complicating medical issues such as agenesis of the corpus callosum, a rare birth defect in which there is complete or partial absence of the corpus callosum. At this time, no comprehensive test batteries exist that have been specifically designed to assess the cognitive abilities of people who are blind. Consequently, several different measures were used. Further, until the recent publication of the Woodcock-Johnson III Tests of Achievement – Braille Adaptation (WJ III ACH-Braille), no academic achievement test batteries were available that were specifically adapted for students who are blind. The WJ III ACH-Braille was used for this evaluation.

This report reflects a true multidisciplinary team approach to a psychoeducational evaluation. The team members included a school psychologist, a learning disabilities specialist with knowledge of visual impairments, and a TVI. Much of the valuable information gained from the evaluation was not gained from the standardized scores, but rather from observations during the testing process. Although the standardized scores are presented and discussed in the report, it was the examination and discussion of the student's test behaviors by the team members, each sharing her own expertise and perspectives, that resulted in a far more accurate account of the student's learning potential and useful interventions. Based on observations during the testing, the team followed up with informal assessment to gain additional information. The results of the evaluation revealed several areas of strength and learning strategies that the student used spontaneously on which to build,

especially if the TVI were provided regular sessions for collaboration with other specialists within the educational system.

The report reflects a multidisciplinary approach to evaluating a child who is unable to participate in a traditional assessment and reveals the ultimate benefits of observations and discussion between team members in order to obtain the most accurate account of a student's learning potential and educational needs.

PSYCHOLOGICAL EVALUATION

Name:	Aaron Demers
Date of Birth:	03/15/1999
Age:	10 years, 8 months
Parents:	Mark and Sandra Demers
School:	Carlsbad Elementary
Grade:	4
Evaluation Date:	12/15/2009
Evaluator:	Kimberly Morris, Ph.D., NCSP
Primary Language:	English
Home Language:	English
Vision Screening:	Visually Impaired—legally and functionally blind
Hearing Screening:	Passed
Assistive Devices Required:	None
Causal Factors:	Educational Disadvantage: Ruled out

Cultural Disadvantage:	Ruled out
Economic Disadvantage:	Ruled out
Environmental Disadvantage:	Ruled out
Primary Language Disadvantage:	Ruled out

REASON FOR REFERRAL

Aaron was referred for a reevaluation by Catherine Antonelli, teacher of students with visual impairments (TVI), due to concerns regarding his limited academic progress. Aaron currently receives special education services due to a visual impairment. His teacher requested a reevaluation to determine current levels of cognitive and academic functioning, to determine if he would qualify for additional services, and to develop a more appropriate Individualized Education Program (IEP).

BACKGROUND INFORMATION

Health and Developmental History

Aaron currently lives with his mother, father, and older brother. Aaron and his family moved to Phoenix, Arizona, in 2004 from Albuquerque, New Mexico. Aaron is totally blind. He is diagnosed with congenital bilateral micropthalmos and optic nerve hypoplasia. Micropthalmos refers to abnormally small eyeballs and optic nerve hypoplasia is a congenital abnormality referring to small optic discs. Aaron was also born with a congenital birth defect called agenesis of the corpus callosum (ACC), which refers to the partial absence of the corpus callosum, the part of the brain responsible for communication between the two hemispheres. On the Student Developmental History form, Aaron's mother also noted that the septum pellucidum, which separates the lateral ventricles of the brain, is absent. Aaron's mother did not note any complications during her pregnancy; however, at birth Aaron received oxygen and he was born with fused eyelids. At approximately 2 months of age, Aaron had surgery to repair an esophageal stricture and subsequently, had several dilations of the esophagus. Aaron achieved the majority of his developmental milestones within normal ranges such as crawling at 7 months, walking at 14 months, and speaking his first word at 11 months. Toilet training was delayed and began at the age of 4 years.

Overall, Aaron has been a healthy child. He broke his arm when he was 2 years old but has not experienced any other significant illnesses or injuries. More recently Aaron has worn conformers and expanders to help shape the orbits of his eyes.

Educational History

A review of records indicates that Aaron received home-based early intervention services including speech and occupational therapy through the Albuquerque Infant/Toddler Program from April 1999 to September 2002. He also attended a toddler group once per week between July 2001 and August 2002 and Red Rock Center Preschool two to three times per week from September 2002 to August 2004. Services provided in these settings included vision therapy; orientation and mobility; and occupational, physical, speech, and music therapy. After his family moved to Phoenix, Aaron began attending the Foundation for Blind Children preschool. Records also indicated that Aaron repeated preschool and entered kindergarten at age 6. Aaron transferred to Carlsbad Elementary at the beginning of his first-grade year. He has remained in special education throughout school and receives services from a TVI as well as a classroom aide to help him access the curriculum when he is included in the general education classroom. Aaron received speech services through May 2009, when he was dismissed for adequate progress. He continues to receive occupational therapy, orientation and mobility training, and adaptive physical education. Aaron's TVI requested the current evaluation to determine current levels of cognitive and academic functioning. She reported that he is significantly below his grade-level peers and feels that an evaluation may provide information on instructional interventions and strategies that may help Aaron improve his academic achievement.

Review of Standardized Testing

Arizona Instrument to Measure Standards (AIMS) (March 2009)

Reading—Approaches the Standard
Mathematics—Falls Far Below the Standard

Review of Previous Evaluations

Aaron was previously evaluated in May 2005 as part of his transition from preschool to kindergarten.

Slosson Intelligence Test, Revised

Standard Score	70
95% Confidence Interval	61–79
Percentile Rank	3

Adaptive Behavior Assessment System, Second Edition (ABAS-II)—Parent Rating

Composite	95% Confidence Interval	Percentile Rank	Qualitative Range
Global Adaptive Composite	50–58	0.1	Extremely Low
Conceptual	52–66	0.3	Extremely Low
Social	49–63	0.2	Extremely Low
Practical	54–68	0.5	Extremely Low

Adaptive Behavior Assessment System, Second Edition (ABAS-II)—Teacher Rating

Composite	95% Confidence Interval	Percentile Rank	Qualitative Range
Global Adaptive Composite	59–67	1	Extremely Low
Conceptual	71–81	5	Low
Social	55–67	0.5	Extremely Low
Practical	54–70	1	Extremely Low

CURRENT EVALUATION

Measures

Wechsler Intelligence Scale for Children, Fourth Edition (WISC-IV): Verbal Subtests

Reynolds Intellectual Assessment Scales (RIAS): Verbal Subtests

Differential Ability Scales, Second Edition (School Age Battery, DAS-II): Verbal Subtests

Woodcock-Johnson III NU Tests of Achievement— Braille Adaptation (WJ III ACH-Braille)

Vineland-II Adaptive Behavior Scales (Vineland-II)

Classroom performance

District-wide standardized assessments

Teacher input

Parent input

The racial/ethnic background of this student has been considered prior to the selection of psychometric instrumentation and prior to interpretation of test data. Consistent with Arizona Administrative code R7-2-401, the language proficiency of this student was reviewed prior to the evaluation and interpretation of test data. The student's primary language was English and all measures were presented in English.

The results of the current evaluation should be interpreted with caution for several reasons. First, the cognitive assessment measures used were standardized on a sighted population. Only the verbal subtests were administered, which may not provide a complete or accurate representation of Aaron's true cognitive abilities. Additionally, on occasion, standardized administration of the Woodcock-Johnson III Tests of Achievement – Braille Adaptation (WJ III ACH-Braille) were altered, when the evaluators perceived that Aaron would be able to do the task presented but was not able to understand the standardized instructions. These alterations are discussed in this report.

Testing Observations

Aaron was extremely cooperative throughout the testing process. Due to the nature of the assessments, there were multiple testing sessions that lasted several hours. Breaks and snack times were provided in an effort to maintain Aaron's focus and interest. Aaron let the evaluators know when he required a break, as he became restless or overstimulated, shaking his head from side to side, flapping his hands, or bouncing in his seat. During these times he often chose to swing on the playground for several minutes to help him refocus. Squeezing a ball or Theraputty also helped him keep his hands relatively quiet so that he could attend better. Aaron was polite and engaged in appropriate conversation. He did not appear easily distracted by external stimuli even when excessive noise was present from adjacent classrooms.

Aaron required repetition of directions frequently as well as repetition of the item prompt, such as "tell me the opposite of…" on each item given. If the administrator dropped the item prompt when it was assumed he understood the directions, Aaron would often provide an unrelated answer. If the item was administered again with the prompt, he was often able to respond correctly. Thus, the examiner continued to provide the item prompts each time to ensure he understood what was being asked. Several other factors may have affected Aaron's performance. For example, Aaron typically uses double-spaced braille, but the WJ III ACH-Braille uses single-spaced braille. Ms. Antonelli, Aaron's TVI, often redirected his fingers to the correct placement on the page to ensure he was attending to the correct item. On the Passage Comprehension test, Aaron was expected to read a sentence and then supply the missing word. This format was unfamiliar to Aaron and had to be explained several times. Although Aaron was cooperative and patient throughout, the unfamiliarity with the testing materials, wording of the directions, and length of administration may have negatively impacted his performance and should be considered in the interpretation of the results.

Classroom Observations

Aaron was observed during instruction provided by his aide. Initially, Aaron was completing a braille worksheet on which he was expected to place pushpins on all of the vowels that were interspersed with consonants. His aide explained that Aaron often skips over the vowels when reading and the worksheet was intended to reinforce his ability to identify these letters when randomly placed among an entire sheet. He then completed a spelling worksheet on his braille writer. Aaron was working on simple three- to four-letter words and at times reversed the order of letters, such as spelling "god" for "dog." Occasionally, Aaron got excited, but at redirection from his aide, was Aaron able to compose himself and continue with the task.

Aaron was also observed during reading instruction provided by Ms. Antonelli. Aaron completed a short reading passage and was asked questions by his teacher. Aaron had to read the passage two additional times before answering a literal question, the answer to which was specifically stated in the passage. Aaron was then asked to develop two questions he could ask his mother about the passage when he got home. Although he required some prompting from his teacher to develop appropriate questions, he was able to compose general questions related to the topic. This task was followed by timed reading to assess his fluency skills. Aaron's final task was a braille worksheet. He was given sentences to write on his braille writer. He typically made one to three errors per line and was asked to correct them before moving on to the next sentence. Errors included forgetting to put in a space, transposing letters, and adding spaces where they were not needed. Throughout the observation, Aaron was cooperative and completed all tasks expected of him. He was able to move about and find needed materials within his workspace with some minimal direction or prompting from his teacher. Aaron was able to earn "scratch and sniff" stickers for his work completion, which he placed on his sheets to take home and show to his mother.

Intellectual Assessment Results

Score Ranges and Classifications Used in this Report*

Standard Score (SS)	Scaled Score (ScS)	T Score	Percentile Rank (PR)	Classification
130 and above	17–19	70 and above	98 and above	Significantly Above Average
120–129	15–16	63–69	92–98	Well Above Average
110–119	13–14	57–67	77–91	Above Average
90–109	8–12	43–56	25–75	Average
80–89	6–7	37–42	9–23	Below Average
70–79	4–5	30–36	2–8	Well Below Average
69 and below	1–3	29 and below	<1–2	Significantly Below Average

*Standard scores have a mean of 100 and a standard deviation of 15. Scaled scores have a mean of 10 and a standard deviation of 3. *T* scores have a mean of 50 and a standard deviation of 10. Percentile ranks have a mean of 50. Standard deviations do not apply.

Wechsler Intelligence Scale for Children, Fourth Edition (WISC-IV)

The WISC-IV assesses a child's current cognitive abilities in both verbal and nonverbal areas. The Verbal Comprehension subtests assess the child's ability to process verbal material and to use language to reason and express ideas. The ability to hold auditory information in memory while working with it is assessed by Working Memory subtests. The subtests of the Perceptual Reasoning and Processing Speed Indexes were not given, as they require vision.

WISC-IV Results

Index/Subtest	Scaled Score	Standard Score	Confidence Interval	Percentile Rank	Classification
Verbal Comprehension Index		91	85–98	27	Average
Similarities	6				Below Average
Vocabulary	14				Above Average
Comprehension	5				Well Below Average
(Information)	5				Well Below Average

Index/Subtest	Scaled Score	Standard Score	Confidence Interval	Percentile Rank	Classifi- cation
(Word Reasoning)	7				Below Average
Working Memory Index		56	52–67	0.2	Signif. Below Average
Digit Span	1				Signif. Below Average
Letter- Number Sequencing	4				Well Below Average
Mean = 100; SD = 15					

The results of the WISC-IV indicate Aaron's verbal abilities are within the Average range with a score of 91 (91st percentile). These results should be interpreted with caution, however, as Aaron's subtest scores all fell within the Below Average and Well Below Average ranges with the exception of the Vocabulary subtest, which was within the Above Average range. The large discrepancy between these subtest scores may indicate an inflated Verbal Comprehension score. On the Vocabulary subtest, Aaron often provided answers that were too vague regarding the defining feature of the word asked. Asked for more information, he named physical characteristics rather than supporting his first answer. As words became more difficult, Aaron often used the stimulus word in his response without providing additional detail. For example, Aaron was asked to state what the word *manners* means and he responded, "Someone with good manners" and "not bad manners." On the Similarities subtest, Aaron provided appropriate answers on items that were similar, such as *cat* and *mouse*, but struggled to identify an overall similarity on items that were different, such as *happy* and *sad*. Aaron also had difficulty on the Word Reasoning subtest; it appeared he did not listen to the complete clue and provided responses that would be reasonable if changed slightly or if a word were removed. An example of this is when Aaron responded that "fish" could make food taste better and could be found in the ocean. Aaron scored significantly lower on the Working Memory Index (56; 0.2 percentile) than on the Verbal Comprehension Index, indicating abilities within the Significantly Below Average range. On the Digit Span subtest, Aaron recalled a string of two digits in sequence but was not able to reverse a sequence for any items. The directions were repeated several times using the sample items; however, Aaron continued to repeat the numbers in the order given.

When given more meaningful information on the Letter-Number Sequencing subtest, Aaron recalled a string of three letters and numbers. He often did not provide the numbers first followed by the letters, as instructed, but he was able to recall all items within the trial, which is considered a correct response. Thus, it appears that Aaron is able to recall information but has difficulty manipulating it, which resulted in the low score.

Reynolds Intellectual Assessment Scales (RIAS)

The RIAS is an individually administered test of intelligence appropriate for ages 3 through 94 years, which includes a co-normed, supplemental measure of memory. Three subtests were administered: the two that make up the Verbal Intelligence Index (VIX) and the verbal subtest from the Working Memory Index (CMX). The VIX assesses verbal intelligence by measuring verbal problem solving and verbal reasoning where acquired knowledge and skills are important. The Verbal Memory subtest provides a basic, overall measure of short-term memory skills (e.g., working memory, short-term memory, learning) and assesses recall in the verbal domain. The three other subtests of the RIAS require vision.

RIAS Results

	T Score	SS	PR	95% Confidence Interval	Clasification
Verbal Intelligence Index		55	0.1	51–64	Signif. Below Average
Guess What (GWH)	10				Signif. Below Average
Verbal Reasoning (VRZ)	31				Well Below Average
Verbal Memory (VRM)	35				Well Below Average

Aaron received a Verbal Intelligence Index standardized score of 55 (0.13 percentile) on the RIAS. He was administered two verbal subtests, Guess What and Verbal Reasoning. On the Guess What subtest, Aaron received a T score of 10, which is four standardized deviations below the mean. Similar to word Reasoning, Aaron often provided responses that made sense if part of the item clue were removed, as if he did not consider all of the information provided. Aaron scored much higher on the Verbal Reasoning subtest, with a T score of 31. The majority of Aaron's responses fit appropriately within the second part of the item presented but at times were not analogous to the first part of the statement. Aaron was able to recall several specific aspects of a short story read aloud to him. His Verbal Memory *T* score of 35 indicates that Aaron may have adequate knowledge of items or concepts as well as the ability to recall specific facts but may struggle with reasoning tasks and integrating the information to develop the most appropriate response.

Differential Ability Scales, Second Edition (DAS-II)

The DAS-II is a comprehensive, individually administered, clinical instrument for assessing the cognitive abilities that are important to learning.

DAS-11 Results	SS/ T Score	PR	95% Confidence Interval	Classification
Verbal Ability (Core subtests)	73	4	67–85	Well Below Average
Word Definitions	*34*	5		Well Below Average
Verbal Similarities	*33*	4		Well Below Average
Diagnostic Subtests				
Recall of Digits Forward	*25*	1		Signif. Below Average
Recall of Digits Backward	*10*	<0.1		Signif. Below Average

On the DAS-II, Aaron received a Verbal composite standard score of 73, which places him within the 4th percentile relative to similar-aged peers. The Verbal composite is designed to measure verbal concepts, vocabulary development, expressive language ability, and a general knowledge base. His *T* scores on the two verbal subtests were commensurate with each other and indicate functioning in the Low range. As he did on previous tests, when asked to give a definition for a word, Aaron's response included the word he was asked to define, without additional elaboration. Additional instruction was provided by requesting that Aaron respond without using the word provided by the examiner; however, the pattern continued. On the Verbal Similarities subtest, Aaron required frequent repetition of the instructions as he began to repeat the three items rather than saying how they were similar. In order to compare his working memory abilities to the subtests administered on the WISC-IV, Aaron was administered the Recall of Digits Forward and Recall of Digits Backward subtests. Aaron was able to recall a string of five digits in a forward sequence, using a chunking strategy. For example, 2-3-7-6-9 was recalled as twenty-three seven sixty-nine. This significantly improved his performance compared

with the same task on the WISC-IV. Aaron continued to demonstrate difficulty understanding the Recall of Digits Backward. He recalled all strings in forward sequence even when continually prompted to recall the digits in reverse order. These test results indicate a significant weakness in his ability to manipulate and recall information.

Language and Academic Achievement

Woodcock-Johnson III NU Tests of Achievement – Braille Adaptation

The WJ III ACH-Braille is a battery of individually administered tests, each designed to measure different aspects of academic achievement and skill. Measures are obtained in the areas of oral language, reading, math, and basic writing skills. The WJ III ACH-Braille is an adaptation of the Woodcock-Johnson III NU Tests of Achievement that was specifically developed for blind individuals. In collaboration with the Woodcock-Munoz Foundation, items and tests were substituted where necessary to reduce the visual bias and a Compuscore and Profiles program was created to incorporate these changes. The norms provide a comparison of Aaron's academic achievement and language abilities to the (sighted) WJ III ACH norm sample. The tests were scored according to age norms. The WJ III ACH-Braille was administered and interpreted by an examiner team, the psychologist and the TVI, who had both been trained on this instrument.

Some test results are described by relative proficiency indexes (RPI). These are mathematical predictions, based on the norms, that indicate the level of difficulty the individual would be able to manage when his same-age or same-grade peers would be 90% successful—in other words, had attained mastery—in a task similar to the one used in the test. For example, Aaron's RPI of 2/90 on the Oral Vocabulary test indicates that when other 10-year-olds would be 90% proficient in spelling, Aaron would be 2% proficient.

Oral Language

The WJ III ACH-Braille Oral Language cluster is designed to measure linguistic competency, listening ability, and oral comprehension. Aaron demonstrated oral language abilities within the Low range (SS 73, PR 4). One of the reasons his score is so low is that Aaron had considerable difficulty understanding the tasks on two of the tests. On the Oral Comprehension test, he gave some multiple-word answers although he was consistently asked for a one-word answer. As well, it was sometimes apparent that he understood the sentence but was not able to come up with the correct word to complete it. A few of these errors might have been due to his visual impairment, as when he used the word "mountains" rather than "islands" to describe a place that others his age would typically have seen on a map. And on some items, his answer just did not make sense. On the Vocabulary test, he was unable to understand the concept of synonyms but did understand antonyms. He also managed a few simple verbal analogies, but then seemed to lose the concept. Aaron scored just below the Average range on the Story Recall test, demonstrating the ability to recall specific facts of an orally presented narrative. Although not part of the Oral Language Cluster, Aaron's highest test score was on Story Recall-Delayed (SS 120; PR 90). His ability to recall details of the stories told the day before was higher than 90% of his age peers. Despite the low Oral Language score, Aaron's oral language skills revealed an area of significant strength relative to his reading and math achievement scores. The discrepancy in scores between the Oral Language cluster and the Broad Reading cluster would be expected in only 0.1 percent of the population (1 out of 1,000 people); the same discrepancy existed between the Oral Language cluster and the Broad Math cluster.

Reading

Aaron's reading was assessed using uncontracted braille. All of Aaron's reading test scores fell in the Significantly Below Average range (Total Reading cluster, SS 45, PR <0.1). His RPIs of 0/90 and 1/90 indicated that his proficiency is negligible in sounding out unfamiliar words, word identification, reading comprehension, and reading vocabulary as compared to same-age peers, and that he will find all of these tasks impossible when attempting to read age-appropriate material. Reading braille typically takes longer than reading print, due solely to the reading medium, but in this case, Aaron's speed and comprehension of simple sentences was his strongest performance, with an RPI of 33/90. Although this task represented his strongest proficiency, it still means that when reading simple sentences to himself and simply recognizing if each is true or false, Aaron would be successful on 33% of them compared with his peers' 90% success.

Some of Aaron's reading errors stemmed from incorrect braille-reading technique. Ms. Antonelli pointed out that Aaron moves his hands back and forth over the braille cells (which make up letters) rather than moving his hands systematically from left to right; consequently, he often reads words with the letters transposed, such as "father" for *after*. Another braille error was his inconsistent confusion of the

letters *h* and *f*, making it impossible to sound out words with *wh*, *th*, and *ch* digraphs, such as *then* (he read out the letters as t-f-e-n). Ms. Antonelli only recently started working with Aaron and noted that trying to correct bad braille-reading habits is much more difficult now than it would have been when he first started to learn braille. She also pointed out that many of the words he read were only one letter off in their pronunciation, such as *mouth* for *month*, and that he does not know the sounds of the vowels, other than the short sound of *a*. Aaron made similar errors when spelling real words and nonsense words on the Spelling and Spelling of Sounds tests. Aaron did demonstrate the use of some reading strategies such as sounding out words letter-by-letter and reading sentences a second time for additional understanding.

On the Reading Fluency test, Aaron skipped three of only six items attempted during the 3-minute period provided. The items he attempted, he answered correctly. His lowest reading cluster, Reading Comprehension, resulted in a standard score of 28 (RPI 1/90). His difficulty on the Passage Comprehension test was a combination of difficulty reading the words and understanding the task (i.e, to fill in the blank). Similarly, it was clear that Aaron had difficulty understanding the tasks of the Reading Vocabulary test, and his score reflects this difficulty, as well as his low reading ability and limited vocabulary when tested in this format (i.e., synonyms, antonyms, analogies).

Aaron's Reading Comprehension cluster score (SS 28, RPI 1/90) was significantly lower than his performance on the Oral Comprehension cluster (SS 71, RPI 31/90). This discrepancy indicates that although Aaron has significant difficulty understanding oral language, there is considerable room for his reading skills to advance before he reaches what is often considered one's potential reading level, the level of oral comprehension.

Aaron's performance on the Phonemic Awareness – Braille cluster indicated solidly average ability to blend individual sounds into familiar words but significantly deficient ability in other phonological awareness skills such as rhyming, sound deletion, and sound reversal. His good blending ability reflects Ms. Antonelli's direct instruction of that skill while teaching him phonics skills.

Mathematics

Aaron also scored in the Significantly Below Average range on all of the math tests, which, on the WJ III ACH-Braille, are written in Nemeth code. His performance on tests of rapid recall of math facts, computation of number problems, solving word problems, and understanding of math concepts was such that only 1 in 1,000 students of his age would score as low as or lower than he did. Difficulty reading Nemeth code appeared to account for some of his errors in the Calculation and Math Fluency tests, as he read some of the numbers incorrectly (e.g., he read 6 + 1 as 8 + 1) and read all operation signs as addition. On the Math Fluency test, Aaron answered only one item correctly in the 3 minutes provided. Although he attempted several others, he read most incorrectly and failed to answer most of the problems he read.

In this adaptation of the WJ III ACH, all of the pictures in the Applied Problems and Quantitative Concepts tests are represented by raised graphics of geometric shapes (i.e., square, rectangle, circle, triangle). Consequently, prior to administration of these tests, Aaron was given a test called Shape Recognition, an informal test intended to ensure that an individual can tactually recognize all of the shapes used in Applied Problems and Quantitative Concepts. Aaron was familiar with the shapes but had poor technique in tracing them, requiring substantial help from Ms. Antonelli to ensure accurate recognition. Nevertheless, poor tracing led to two errors in simple counting of shapes. Aaron was able to answer some addition problems that used tactile graphics (e.g., If you had 3 apples and someone gave you 2 more, how many apples would you have?) but no subtraction problems (e.g., Jim had 5 apples and gave 2 to Sam. How many did Jim have left?). He did understand word problems posed in negative terms (e.g., How many balls are not in the bowl?). He demonstrated an understanding of the concepts of *largest* and *smallest*, and *first* and *last*, but could not identify a shape in the *middle* of a row, the number of pennies in higher-value coins, how to continue a simple number pattern, and how to read a tactile graphic calendar. Aaron had an abacus but used it on only one math fact (2+2). Ms. Antonelli indicated that they had only recently introduced it in their lessons.

Adaptive Behavior, Vineland Adaptive Behavior Scales, Second Edition (Vineland-II)

The Vineland-II is an individually administered measure of personal and social skills used for everyday living. Measurements are obtained in the areas of Communication, Daily Living Skills, Socialization, and Motor Skills. This assessment provides critical data for the diagnosis or evaluation of a wide range of disabilities, including intellectual disability, developmental delays, functional skills impairment, and speech/language impairment.

Teacher Rating Form Results

Domain	Standard Score	Percentile Rank	Adaptive Level
Communication	74	4	Moderately Low
Daily Living Skills	63	1	Low
Socialization	69	2	Low
Adaptive Behavior Composite	66	1	Low

Parent/Caregiver Rating Form Results

Domain	Standard Score	Percentile Rank	Adaptive Level
Communication	70	2	Low
Daily Living Skills	73	4	Moderately Low
Socialization	64	1	Low
Adaptive Behavior Composite	67	1	Low

Aaron's mother and Ms. Antonelli completed the Vineland-II rating scale in order to assess his adaptive skills. As with the other assessments administered during this evaluation, the results must be interpreted with caution, as many of the items on the Vineland-II refer to sight, resulting in a score that may underestimate his abilities. The results of the rating scales indicate similar impressions of Aaron's adaptive skills with scores in the Low to Moderately Low range. The largest discrepancy between scores was present in the Daily Living Skills Domain in which Aaron's mother rated his skills higher than his teacher did. Within the Daily Living Skills Domain, the parent rates the child on domestic skills while the teacher rates the child on academic skills. These areas resulted in the largest discrepancy in scores indicating that Aaron's mother observes higher domestic skills than predicted while his teacher observes lower academic skills than predicted. The results indicated that Aaron is functioning below his expected age level and demonstrated significantly delayed behaviors; however, his visual impairment and other medical conditions must be considered in the interpretation of these results.

SUMMARY AND RECOMMENDATIONS

Aaron is a 10-year, 8-month-old Caucasian male currently attending the fourth grade at Carlsbad Elementary School. Aaron was referred for an evaluation by his TVI due to concerns regarding his academic progress. Aaron currently receives special education services under the category of

Visual Impairment due to his diagnosis of congenital bilateral micropthalmos and optic nerve hypoplasia. Aaron has also been diagnosed with partial absence of the corpus callosum. He received numerous early interventions services including vision therapy; orientation and mobility; and occupational, physical, speech, and music therapy. Aaron repeated kindergarten and began attending Carlsbad Elementary in first grade. He receives services from a TVI as well as a classroom aide to help him access the general curriculum, in addition to continued occupational therapy, orientation and mobility, and adaptive physical education. Aaron's teacher for the visually impaired requested the current evaluation to determine current levels of cognitive and academic functioning. She reported that, although he is a year older than his grade-level peers, he is significantly below them in academic achievement. She hoped that an evaluation would provide information on strategies that would help Aaron improve his academic achievement. Additionally, she requested consultation from a learning disabilities specialist.

The results of the current evaluation should be interpreted with caution as, due to Aaron's visual impairment, only the verbal subtests of the cognitive assessments were administered. Language and academic achievement testing was done with the Woodcock-Johnson III NU Tests of Achievement – Braille Adaptation. Aaron's work ethic and level of cooperation were outstanding during both the testing sessions and classroom observations.

The results of the current evaluation indicate Aaron's cognitive abilities are most likely within the Well Below Average range with areas of significant strengths and weaknesses. Aaron demonstrated average abilities during vocabulary reasoning as he was able to provide detailed information regarding specific words. He struggled, however, in relating word meanings to one another and in reasoning when provided multiple pieces of information. Memory tasks revealed that Aaron is able to remember information when it is presented orally and in a context that is sequential or meaningful. He demonstrated a significant weakness, however, when asked to hold that information in memory and simultaneously work with it. This difficulty may be related to his diagnosed agenesis of the corpus callosum, as the two hemispheres of his brain are unable to communicate with each other to accomplish this task.

Aaron demonstrated strengths in oral comprehension and sound blending as compared to academic tasks. His reading and math skills are significantly below grade level as well as significantly below the level expected given his oral language and cognitive abilities. Based on his RPIs,

skills were negligible compared to same-age peers in basic reading skills, reading fluency, reading comprehension, math calculation skills, and math reasoning skills. Aaron demonstrated several strategies during the testing process that further support his ability and willingness to learn, such as sounding out words, chunking pieces of information, and reviewing text to clarify information or gather new information. Continuing services for special education will be determined by the Multidisciplinary Education Team; however, it is apparent to the current examiner that Aaron continues to qualify for services based on his visual impairment. The results of the testing process did not reveal evidence of intellectual disability given his broad range of cognitive scores. In addition, although his adaptive skills were rated as Low to Moderately Low, it is believed these are an underestimate of his true abilities due to his visual impairment. There is evidence, however, that Aaron may qualify for additional services in the area of Specific Learning Disability due to the weaknesses in memory and the discrepancies among his oral language, cognitive, and academic scores. Aaron may benefit from additional support and consultation from a learning disability specialist to improve his basic academic skills.

RECOMMENDATIONS

1. Ms. Antonelli should be provided with the opportunity to collaborate with a learning disabilities specialist on a regular basis. Aaron requires specialized instructional techniques that are not within the training of a TVI. These techniques will need to be adapted for use with a person who is blind, and for braille and Nemeth code. These are areas in which a learning disabilities specialist is typically not trained. Consequently, Aaron's instructional needs will best be served through a collaboration of the TVI and the LD specialist.

2. Aaron's TVI should also be provided with the opportunity to collaborate with a speech-language pathologist on a regular basis. Although Aaron's oral language abilities are considerably above his academic skills, they are severely delayed compared with his age-peers. Ms. Antonelli and Aaron's parents would benefit from the consultation of a speech-language pathologist to help them plan a language development program for him and to guide them in following that program. Again, Ms. Antonelli's expertise will be necessary to ensure that the plan takes into account Aaron's lack of sight, excitability, and general level of comprehension.

3. Until the recommended collaborations start, the following recommendation is offered regarding reading instruction. Provide Aaron with an instructional program in basic reading and spelling skills that is systematic in introduction, practice, and reinforcement of phonemic awareness skills and phoneme-grapheme relationships, and irregular words that are included in the a list of 200 words most frequently used in English text. Skills should be presented in graduated steps, from simple to complex, with Aaron achieving mastery before the next skill is introduced. Practice assignments on the current skill need to incorporate previously learned skills, providing opportunities for Aaron to develop automaticity. Teach reading and spelling skills simultaneously, so that Aaron learns how to spell every phonics generalization and word structure that he learns to read. Whatever program is chosen will need to be combined with the braille program being used—or it may be possible for Ms. Antonelli to use the reading program to help structure her teaching of braille.

4. Supplement Aaron's phonics instruction with simple, decodable books that he can read during free reading time and at home. Decodable text is reading material comprised of the phonics and sight words he has already learned. Reading decodable text provides the opportunity for application of newly learned skills, reinforcement of sight words, and transitioning skills learned in isolation to practical use. At his current skill level, reading aloud is best. It is possible that these books will have to be brailled at school, depending on the availability of phonics-based books in braille. Print series that might be considered include Steck-Vaughn Phonics Readers (Steck-Vaughn), SRA Reading Series (SRA/McGraw-Hill), Decodable Books (The Wright Group), J & J Language Readers (Sopris West), Phonics-Based Chapter Books (High Noon), and Scholastic Phonics Readers.

5. If teaching reading comprehension strategies, teach them orally and at Aaron's oral language level, not his decoding level. As his word identification level increases, guide him to apply the listening comprehension skills to the reading material.

6. As Aaron does seem to understand numeracy, in math, focus on the recognition of numbers in Nemeth code and the value of money. These seem to be the most immediate needs.

7. Generally, focus on proper braille reading techniques and efficient tracing of tactile graphics.

Table of Scores

Woodcock-Johnson III Normative Update Tests of Achievement – Braille Adaptation

WJ III NU Compuscore and Profiles Program – Braille Adaptation, Version 1.0

Norms based on age 10-8

Braille format used: Uncontracted

CLUSTER/Test	Raw	W	GE	Proficiency	RPI	SS (68% Band)	PR
TOTAL ORAL LANG-BRAILLE	–	479	1.5	limited	51/90	73 (68–77)	3
Oral Comprehension	11	471	1.2	limited	30/90	74 (69–79)	4
Oral Vocabulary	–	471	1.5	limited	31/90	72 (66–78)	3
Story Recall	–	495	2.6	average	86/90	88 (74–103)	22
Story Recall-Delayed	–	509	>17.8	avg to adv	96/90	119 (105–134)	90
ORAL LANGUAGE COMP	–	471	1.4	limited	31/90	71 (66–75)	2
Oral Comprehension	11	471	1.2	limited	30/90	74 (69–79)	4
Oral Vocabulary	–	471	1.5	limited	31/90	72 (66–78)	3
TOTAL READING	–	438	1.1	negligible	1/90	45 (41–49)	<0.1
Word Attack	3	423	K.8	negligible	0/90	56 (45–66)	0.2
Letter-Word Identification	27	419	1.6	negligible	0/90	62 (59–65)	1
Passage Comprehension	3	437	1.1	negligible	1/90	52 (48–57)	<0.1
Reading Fluency	3	468	1.2	limited	33/90	61 (52–70)	0.5
Reading Vocabulary	–	442	<K.7	negligible	1/90	40 (32–47)	<0.1

CLUSTER/Test	Raw	W	GE	Proficiency	RPI	SS (68% Band)	PR
BROAD READING	–	441	1.3	negligible	2/90	48 (45–51)	<0.1
Letter-Word Identification	27	419	1.6	negligible	0/90	62 (59–65)	1
Passage Comprehension	3	437	1.1	negligible	1/90	52 (48–57)	<0.1
Reading Fluency	3	468	1.2	limited	33/90	61 (52–70)	0.5
BRIEF READING	–	428	1.4	negligible	0/90	53 (50–56)	<0.1
Letter-Word Identification	27	419	1.6	negligible	0/90	62 (59–65)	1
Passage Comprehension	3	437	1.1	negligible	1/90	52 (48–57)	<0.1
BASIC READING SKILLS	–	421	1.2	negligible	0/90	53 (47–59)	<0.1
Word Attack	3	423	K.8	negligible	0/90	56 (45–66)	0.2
Letter-Word Identification	27	419	1.6	negligible	0/90	62 (59–65)	1
READING COMP	–	439	K.9	negligible	1/90	28 (23–34)	<0.1
Passage Comprehension	3	437	1.1	negligible	1/90	52 (48–57)	<0.1
Reading Vocabulary	–	442	<K.7	negligible	1/90	40 (32–47)	<0.1
PHON/GRAPH KNOW	–	453	1.0	v limited	4/90	61 (53–68)	0.4
Word Attack	3	423	K.8	negligible	0/90	56 (45–66)	0.2
Spelling of Sounds	16	482	1.6	limited	52/90	72 (66–78)	3
BROAD MATH	–	432	<K.0	negligible	1/90	9 (3–15)	<0.1
Calculation	1	413	K.3	negligible	0/90	7 (1–18)	<0.1
Math Fluency	1	477	<K.0	limited	51/90	52 (40–63)	<0.1
Applied Problems	12	407	<K.0	negligible	0/90	39 (35–43)	<0.1
BRIEF MATH	–	410	<K.0	negligible	0/90	7 (1–13)	<0.1
Calculation	1	413	K.3	negligible	0/90	7 (1–18)	<0.1
Applied Problems	12	407	<K.0	negligible	0/90	39 (35–43)	<0.1
MATH CALC SKILLS	–	445	K.2	negligible	3/90	2 (1–13)	<0.1
Calculation	1	413	K.3	negligible	0/90	7 (1–18)	<0.1
Math Fluency	1	477	<K.0	limited	51/90	52 (40–63)	<0.1
MATH REASONING	–	419	<K.0	negligible	0/90	34 (31–37)	<0.1
Applied Problems	12	407	<K.0	negligible	0/90	39 (35–43)	<0.1
Quantitative Concepts	–	431	<K.0	negligible	0/90	35 (30–39)	<0.1
BRIEF ACHIEVEMENT	–	423	1.1	negligible	0/90	38 (35–41)	<0.1
Letter-Word Identification	27	419	1.6	negligible	0/90	62 (59–65)	1
Spelling	10	442	1.3	negligible	2/90	61 (57–66)	0.5
Applied Problems	12	407	<K.0	negligible	0/90	39 (35–43)	<0.1
ACADEMIC SKILLS	–	424	1.1	negligible	0/90	37 (33–41)	<0.1
Letter-Word Identification	27	419	1.6	negligible	0/90	62 (59–65)	1
Spelling	10	442	1.3	negligible	2/90	61 (57–66)	0.5
Calculation	1	413	K.3	negligible	0/90	7 (1–18)	<0.1
PHON AWARE-BRAILLE	–	477	1.0	limited	48/90	69 (63–74)	2
Sound Awareness	8	454	<K.0	v limited	9/90	42 (36–48)	<0.1
Sound Blending	18	500	4.1	average	90/90	99 (92–107)	48
Oral Comprehension	11	471	1.2	limited	30/90	74 (69–79)	4
Oral Vocabulary	–	471	1.5	limited	31/90	72 (66–78)	3

(Continued)

CLUSTER/Test	Raw	W	GE	Proficiency	RPI	SS (68% Band)	PR
Story Recall	–	495	2.6	average	86/90	88 (74–103)	22
Story Recall-Delayed	–	509	>17.8	avg to adv	96/90	119 (105–134)	90
Sound Awareness	8	454	<K.0	v limited	9/90	42 (36–48)	<0.1
Sound Blending	18	500	4.1	average	90/90	99 (92–107)	48
Word Attack	3	423	K.8	negligible	0/90	56 (45–66)	0.2
Letter-Word Identification	27	419	1.6	negligible	0/90	62 (59–65)	1
Passage Comprehension	3	437	1.1	negligible	1/90	52 (48–57)	<0.1
Reading Fluency	3	468	1.2	limited	33/90	61 (52–70)	0.5
Reading Vocabulary	–	442	<K.7	negligible	1/90	40 (32–47)	<0.1
Spelling of Sounds	16	482	1.6	limited	52/90	72 (66–78)	3
Spelling	10	442	1.3	negligible	2/90	61 (57–66)	0.5
Calculation	1	413	K.3	negligible	0/90	7 (1–18)	<0.1
Math Fluency	1	477	<K.0	limited	51/90	52 (40–63)	<0.1
Applied Problems	12	407	<K.0	negligible	0/90	39 (35–43)	<0.1
Quantitative Concepts	–	431	<K.0	negligible	0/90	35 (30–39)	<0.1

VARIATIONS	STANDARD SCORES			VARIATION		Significant at + or – 1.50 SD (SEE)
	Actual	Predicted	Difference	PR	SD	
Intra-Reading						
BASIC READING SKILLS	53	57	–4	30	–0.52	No
READING COMPREHENSION	28	67	–39	<0.1	–3.41	Yes
PHON/GRAPH KNOWLEGE	61	61	0	48	–0.05	No
READING FLUENCY	61	66	–5	28	–0.59	No

DISCREPANCIES	STANDARD SCORES			DISCREPANCY		Significant at + or – 1.50 SD (SEE)
	Actual	Predicted	Difference	PR	SD	
Oral Language/Achievement*						
BASIC READING SKILLS	53	85	–32	0.5	–2.60	Yes
READING COMPREHENSION	28	79	–51	<0.1	–4.55	Yes
BRIEF READING	53	83	–30	0.5	–2.58	Yes
BROAD READING	48	83	–35	0.1	–3.03	Yes
MATH CALC SKILLS	2	90	–88	<0.1	–6.01	Yes
MATH REASONING	34	85	–51	<0.1	–4.36	Yes
BRIEF MATH	7	85	–78	<0.1	–6.34	Yes
BROAD MATH	9	86	–77	<0.1	–6.15	Yes

*These discrepancies compare Total Oral Language – Braille to achievement clusters.

DISCREPANCIES	DISCREPANCY		Significant at + or − 1.50 SD (SEE)	Interpretation
	PR	SD (or z)		
Measures of delayed recall*				
Story Recall-Delayed	>99.9	+3.26	Yes	Above expected recall
*These discrepancies are based on the predicted difference between initial and delayed scores.				

CASE 27

Differential Diagnosis
ADHD, Emotional Disturbance, or Asperger's Syndrome?

Elaine Fletcher-Janzen

When providing reports for publication, there is a temptation to try and create a perfect report—but the reality on the job is that busy school psychologists get to the heart of the matter in a report with as much efficiency and diplomacy as possible. Therefore, in the interests of representing a real-world case, this report has not been polished for publication.

This report about Page Smith-Wesson reflects a common situation where a school psychologist is asked to review a case where the diagnosis and special education labels have never seemed to quite fit. A file review yields multiple diagnoses, assessments, and interventions that have never really led to much progress and have left everyone frustrated. In this case, Page was about to move up to middle school and his teachers were worried about letting him go to face the academic and social challenges without having a good plan to support what lay ahead.

This report also reflects another common situation facing school psychologists, and that is to deliver a new diagnosis to the Individualized Education Plan (IEP) team. In this case, the team knew that Page was exhibiting something different than ADHD or emotional disturbance, but they just did not know exactly what. The nuances of differential diagnosis with Page were difficult indeed and compounded by the fact that several members of the school team had strong opinions about what was really affecting Page. Therefore, the report was kept terse, to the point, and with very few behavioral observations that might lead readers to interpret the scores for themselves.

The report was also framed in a way that might lessen the "pathology" of behaviors being observed. It was important that the parents could read the report and think that there was a fair reason as to why others thought of Page as odd or eccentric. Indeed, the assessment result was called

Asperger's Syndrome as opposed to Asperger's Disorder. The latter was likely to create more of a picture of something wrong, when really, Page was just fine as he was and was not going to change per se. The family and school team needed to accept his way of functioning as "normal for him." Sometimes, school psychologists have the job of modeling for the team that the child is doing well, that the child needs everyone to accept him as he is, and help him accept himself as he goes forward to form a sense of identity. The issue of intervention, in this case, had to shift from diagnosis/cure to maximizing quality of life.

COMPREHENSIVE PSYCHOLOGICAL ASSESSMENT

Name:	Page
Date of Birth:	5/5/1999
Age:	10-11
Parents:	Donald Wesson and Donna Smith-Wesson
School:	Independence Elementary
Grade:	5.8
Date of Report:	4/9/2010
Evaluator:	Elaine Fletcher-Janzen, Ed.D.

REASON FOR REFERRAL

The central reason for referral was that the Admission, Review, and Dismissal (ARD) committee feels that a psychological evaluation is needed in order to further explore Page's attentional and behavioral difficulties.

DEVELOPMENTAL, MEDICAL, AND FAMILY HISTORY

Please refer to the full special education chart for detailed academic and family history. No major illnesses, accidents, or trauma were noted in the case file, and all developmental milestones were passed within normal limits. Page is currently in the gifted and talented program, receives excellent grades, and passed his Texas Assessment of Knowledge Skills (TAKS) with a commendation this past spring.

Page was diagnosed as having Attention-Deficit/Hyperactivity Disorder (ADHD) at age 8 by Frederick Burnstein, M.D., in April 2007 and was found to be eligible, because of behavioral issues, for special education under the category of Emotional Disturbance (ED). Subsequently, in December 2007, Page was assessed by school personnel and declared ineligible for special education under the category of ED but eligible under Other Heath Impaired as a child with ADHD. At the present time, Page is not taking any medications.

CLASSROOM OBSERVATION

Page was observed during his reading class and during a test in math lab. During the reading class, Page had his head down on his desk for over 10 minutes and did not participate in the discussion. He was the last student to reach the math lab and to start his test. He was on task for the entire period, asked one or two questions, but did not finish the test although he was aware that he would have to stay in at recess to do so. Page was compliant and socially appropriate during both observations.

TEST ADMINISTRATION OBSERVATIONS

Page came to testing in a calm and cooperative manner and, on the second testing occasion, seemed to be pleased to see the examiner. Page was pleasant, asked questions as to why we were testing, and was appropriate throughout both testing sessions. Page did take excessive time to complete drawing tasks, and his processing time for the whole session was very protracted.

TESTS ADMINISTERED

Reynolds Intellectual Assessment Scale (RIAS)
Bender Visual-Motor Gestalt Test, Second Edition (Bender-Gestalt II)

Behavior Rating Inventory of Executive Function (BRIEF)
Teacher Form and Parent Form
Behavior Assessment System for Children-2 (BASC-2)
Teacher Form and Parent Form
Kaufman Test of Educational Achievement-II (KTEA-II)
3 Wishes Test
Kinetic Family Drawing (KFD)
Draw-A-Person Test
Children's Color Trails Test (CCTT)
Krug Asperger's Disorder Index
Asperger Syndrome Diagnostic Scale
Gilliam Asperger's Disorder Scale
Mental Status Examination

TEST INTERPRETATION

Reynolds Intellectual Assessment Scale (RIAS)

The RIAS is a brief measure of intellectual ability and is composed of three indexes assessing verbal ability, nonverbal ability, and overall intellectual ability. On the Verbal Index of the RIAS, Page obtained a standard score of 108, placing him in the Average range. On any given occasion, there is a 90% chance that his score will range between 102 and 113. On the Nonverbal Index of the RIAS, Page obtained a standard score of 112, which is in the Average to Above Average range. On any given occasion, there is a 90% chance that he will score between 106 and 117. On the Composite Intelligence Index (CIX) that measures overall ability, Page scored in the Average to Above Average range with a standard score of 113. On any given occasion, there is a 90% chance that he will score between 108 and 117.

This brief measure was given to see if his previous scores were still valid. One prior testing Page showed a distinct difference between verbal and nonverbal abilities (in favor of nonverbal), and this appears to be consistent, albeit not significant, with the current scores.

Kaufman Test of Educational Achievement-II (KTEA-II)

Page's achievement scores were as follows:

Math Concepts and Applications	107
Math Computation	93

Spelling	123
Written Expression	107

The reading tests on the KTEA-II were not administered because Page received a commendation on the reading section of the TAKS, indicating above average reading ability.

Behavior Rating Inventory of Executive Function (BRIEF)

Executive functions are cognitive processes that organize, plan, and prioritize information and actions in everyday life. The BRIEF Teacher Report measures these functions based on the observations of school staff who interact with Page on a daily basis.

The results of the BRIEF completed by Page's general education teacher indicate that he has significant problems in executive functions at school. Compared with other children of his age, he has clinically significant problems with inhibition (controlling impulsivity), shifting his focus, emotional control, getting started on work, working memory, planning and organizing materials, and self-monitoring. A graph of the numerical scores and results can be found in Figure 1.

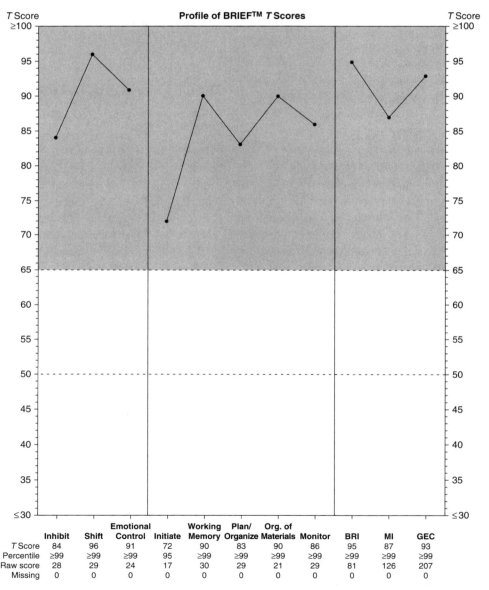

	Inhibit	Shift	Emotional Control	Initiate	Working Memory	Plan/ Organize	Org. of Materials	Monitor	BRI	MI	GEC
T Score	84	96	91	72	90	83	90	86	95	87	93
Percentile	≥99	≥99	≥99	95	≥99	≥99	≥99	≥99	≥99	≥99	≥99
Raw score	28	29	24	17	30	29	21	29	81	126	207
Missing	0	0	0	0	0	0	0	0	0	0	0

Figure 1   BRIEF Teacher Report: General Education Teacher's Observations

Bender Visual-Motor Gestalt Test, Second Edition

On the Bender-Gestalt II, the evaluator presents multiple cards, one at a time, each with a geometric design that the child has to copy onto one piece of paper. Page's performance on this test indicates that he has age-appropriate visual-motor skills with no deficits in visual-motor coordination or visual-motor organization.

Children's Color Trails Test (CCTT)

The CCTT is a brief measure of attention and working memory. Page's standard scores on the CCTT were below 55. Page exhibited very slow processing speed and poor working memory on this test compared to his peers. These scores are Significantly Low and suggest that it is very difficult for Page to stay on task and complete work.

Behavior Assessment System for Children-2 (BASC-2)

The BASC-2 is an integrated system of scales that is designed to facilitate the differential diagnosis and classification of a variety of emotional and behavioral disorders in children.

Two teachers filled out the Teacher Rating scales of the BASC-2 and their results were very similar, lending support to consistent observations in different classroom settings. Both teachers were in agreement regarding their observations of Clinically Significant behaviors of aggression, depression, atypicality, withdrawal, and learning and attention problems. Both teachers also see At-Risk or elevated problems with hyperactivity, conduct problems, anxiety, somatization, school problems, poor adaptability, a lack of resilience, and poor adaptive skills. The atypical items that were endorsed suggest that Page is seen as having odd or eccentric behaviors and thoughts. He is also withdrawn, and the withdrawal appears to be egosyntonic in that he is quite happy to be in his own world and absorbed in his own ideas most of the time, as opposed to being externally focused and engaged with children his own age.

In general, Page's mother sees similar problems but to a lesser degree. This lends support to teacher observations and also probably reflects less intense demands at home than at school. All three raters agree that Page has age-appropriate functional communication and social skills. A graph of the numerical results of the BASC-2 appears in Figure 2.

In summary, the results of the BASC-2 indicate that Page is experiencing significant attentional problems and psychic distress, which is affecting his ability to meet the demands of everyday living and his ability to be resilient. His profile on the BASC-2 could be indicative of Asperger's Syndrome, as it concurs with group profiles of children with this disorder. High scores on the Atypicality and Withdrawal scales along with poor resiliency are the areas of concern on this profile. Attentional problems are also indicative of the profile, as are hyperactivity and aggression.

Kaufman Test of Educational Achievement-II

The reading subtests of the KTEA-II were not given due to his obtaining a commendation on his fifth-grade reading TAKS. On the Math Concepts and Applications subtest, Page scored in the Average range with a standard score of 107. On the Math Calculation subtest, he scored 93, which is in the Average range, but significantly lower than his overall intellectual ability as measured by the RIAS (SS 113). On the Spelling subtest, he obtained a Standard Score of 123, indicating an Above Average score in this area.

3 Wishes

When asked about what he would like if given three wishes, Page asked:

1. For his cousin to come back to life. (He died from cancer in 2009.)
2. To be famous.
3. To have his dog, Lucky, back.

Kinetic Family Drawing and Draw-A-Person Test

Page took excessive time to draw two family members and the examiner discontinued the test. Of note, the drawings were age appropriate, in great detail, and imaginative in content. Also of note, Page drew the pictures of people from the objects that they were holding first, to the torso next, and the person's head last. This system of drawing is unusual and exceptional. It may be representative of poor object relations and unique cognitive processing suggestive of fragmentation of thought.

ASPERGER MEASURES

Krug Asperger's Disorder Index

The results of three raters (principal, general education teacher, special education teacher) on the Krug Asperger's Disorder Index averaged out to a standard score of 86,

Multi-Rater *T* Score Profile

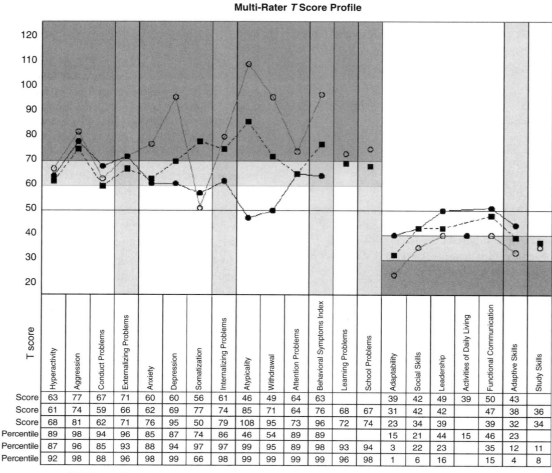

	Hyperactivity	Aggression	Conduct Problems	Externalizing Problems	Anxiety	Depression	Somatization	Internalizing Problems	Atypicality	Withdrawal	Attention Problems	Behavioral Symptoms Index	Learning Problems	School Problems	Adaptability	Social Skills	Leadership	Activities of Daily Living	Functional Communication	Adaptive Skills	Study Skills
Score	63	77	67	71	60	60	56	61	46	49	64	63			39	42	49	39	50	43	
Score	61	74	59	66	62	69	77	74	85	71	64	76	68	67	31	42	42		47	38	36
Score	68	81	62	71	76	95	50	79	108	95	73	96	72	74	23	34	39		39	32	34
Percentile	89	98	94	96	85	87	74	86	46	54	89	89			15	21	44	15	46	23	
Percentile	87	96	85	93	88	94	97	97	99	95	89	98	93	94	3	22	23		35	12	11
Percentile	92	98	88	96	98	99	66	98	99	99	99	99	96	98	1	6	16		15	4	8

● = PRS-C, 04/04/2008, Rater: Teacher 1
■ = PRS-C, 04/04/2008, Rater: Teacher 2
○ = TRS-C, 04/04/2008, Rater: Mother

Figure 2   BASC-2 Results: Two Teachers' and Mother's Observations

which indicates the possibility that Page has Asperger's Syndrome as "somewhat likely." Items that were endorsed by all three raters were fixating on ideas or activities, conversationally talks about single subject excessively, makes naïve remarks (unaware of reaction produced in others), interprets language literally (uses concrete meaning of words), and "expresses opinions to strangers inappropriately." Other items that were endorsed by all three raters described Page as being intelligent and verbally fluent, using pronouns correctly, and having college potential.

Asperger's Syndrome Diagnostic Scale

On this scale, responses of the same three raters resulted in a standard score of 82, suggesting the probability of Asperger's Syndrome being present as "possibly." On the

Cognitive Scale, the raters endorsed the following items: displaying above average intelligence, extreme or obsessive interest in a narrow subject, lacking organizational skills, lacking common sense, and oversensitivity to criticism.

Gilliam Asperger's Disorder Scale

The averaged results of two raters for this test was a standard score of 102, indicating a higher probability of Asperger's Syndrome—in the "high/probable" range. The profile indicates problems mostly with social interaction and pragmatic skills. The items on this scale were endorsed strongly and included items such as: has difficulty understanding what causes people to dislike him or her, has difficulty identifying when someone is teasing, fails to predict probable consequences in social events, demonstrates eccentric forms of behavior, seems unaware of social conventions or codes of conduct, needs an excessive amount of reassurance if things are changed or go wrong, and requires specific instructions to begin tasks.

Mental Status Examination

Page was oriented to time, place, and person. He denied homicidal and suicidal ideations and denied visual and auditory hallucinations. He exhibited a good sense of affective identification and variability about different topics. His mood was bright. Page chatted with the examiner about multiple subjects, seemed age appropriate, and denied any current distress. He said that he might want to start medication again because it helped him stay on task when he took it previously. Page was polite and pleasant throughout testing and seemed to have a dreamy/distant-like quality to his thoughts about friends, social relationships, and cause and effect in real life.

CLINICAL SUMMARY

Page Smith-Wesson is a 9-year-old Anglo male in fifth grade at Independence Elementary. He has exhibited clinically significant problems with attention, aggression, and eccentric thoughts and behaviors for several years. He has above average intelligence and participates in the gifted and talented program. While Page is engaging and verbally fluent with adults, he does have trouble making relationships with same-age peers. He has a broad range of interests but also has specific areas of intellectual interest that are unusual and could be considered obsessive. He frequently exhibits concrete thinking and socially inappropriate comments (literal and ill-timed) and appears to have attentional problems that are internally provoked as opposed to being due to external distracters.

At this time, the diagnostic profile that best fits Page's symptoms is High-Functioning Asperger's Syndrome. It should be noted that because Page is so pleasant and cooperative with adults these days, it would be easy to overlook the subtle deficits that, in the end, are leading to social isolation, poor self-esteem, withdrawal, and other behaviors that are representative of extreme distress. Therefore, the description of Asperger's Syndrome should always be placed in the "mild" or "very-high-functioning" category so the individuals around him will understand that there is a distinct syndrome present that is not easily recognized by laypersons. While Page does exhibit many symptoms of ADHD, it should also be noted that Asperger's Syndrome has unique attentional deficits inherent in the diagnosis and treating Page simply as an individual with ADHD does not serve his best interests. Treatment for Asperger's Syndrome is different than treatment for ADHD, and educational interventions and expectations must be adjusted accordingly.

RECOMMENDATIONS

1. Staff should continue to support Page with prompts to help with attentional issues. Prompts should be worked out ahead of time with him as to the type of prompts that will help him initiate work. Staff should offer a small amount of direct instruction at the beginning of each new task to help Page "get going." Staff should also work out a variety of prompts to help Page get back to the task when his mind wanders. Develop prompts in such a way that Page feels both supported and in a cooperative relationship with the teacher.

2. Counseling and related services are recommended for Page next year. Subjects of focus could be how to make friends, how to initiate conversations, how to compliment peers, how to play cooperatively, and education about Asperger's Syndrome.

3. At an appropriate time, Page should be introduced to Asperger's Syndrome online activities and informational sites. Chat groups with other children who have high-functioning capabilities could be helpful and a normalizing experience for him.

CASE 28

The Heterogeneity and Complexities of Children with Developmental Delays

Melissa King and Mary Wright

Lucy is an adopted child with a complex medical and developmental history. Children with intellectual disabilities of mild-to-moderate severity vary tremendously in their overall cognitive, social, emotional, and physical profiles. Lucy is a particularly charming and likable child. Her parents are caring professionals who questioned the comprehensiveness of Lucy's Individualized Education Plan (IEP), which was mainly written for the purpose of attaining educational standards set for all children in fourth grade. As difficult as it may be, it is essential to be honest about a child's potential or aptitude, and while one strives for normalcy, such as placing the child in the least restrictive environment, the evaluator must be honest about the different route that a child such as Lucy will have to take.

Lucy was originally diagnosed with autism for reasons that were not exactly clear, although it would appear that her poor language, "sensitivities" (e.g., to loud noises), and her atypical behavior and social development accounted for this diagnosis. As an 11-year-old, Lucy is highly social and likable; nevertheless, her global language and cognitive delays do contribute to awkwardness. These difficulties, however, should not be confused with the social deficits associated with autism. She is not "in her own world" and her ability to understand and express humor, as well as her empathy and warmth, are definite strengths.

Lucy had been evaluated twice before, with her Full-Scale IQ on the WISC-IV having declined significantly between the first and second administrations. Neither parents nor teachers could understand this; consequently, one of the referring questions was "Why the decline?" It is essential for evaluators to understand not only learning differences, but differences in learning rates. Furthermore, a child with intellectual disabilities, particularly mild to moderate, may at some point in his or her life have a mental

age that is fairly commensurate with same-age peers; however, as those peers mature, the disparity between mental and chronological age grows ever more disparate. As long as children with intellectual disabilities are compared to same-age peers, their abilities or skills are going to appear to diminish, when in fact they may still be making gains, albeit small ones, in the areas tested or in areas not measured by traditional cognitive and achievement assessments.

The inclusion of scores in the body of the report integrates the quantitative data alongside the narrative. The purpose, then, of the narrative is to make the quantitative data meaningful.

COMPREHENSIVE EDUCATIONAL EVALUATION

Name:	Lucille (Lucy) Miller
Date of Birth:	April 6, 1998
Age:	11-3
Parents:	Jim and Margaret Miller
Grade:	Completed 4th
Dates of Evaluation:	July 20 and 26, 2009
Evaluators:	Melissa M. King, M.Ed., and Mary C. Wright, M.A.

Choice of assessments was made based on our opinion that fine-motor output for writing and reading fluency were not being adequately addressed within Lucy's IEP. We wanted data to support our recommendation for a move toward assistive technology for writing at the very least.

The evaluation was driven by referral questions, and the report was written for parents, teachers, and other professionals in Lucy's life. Not only did we want to identify areas of need, but we also wanted to acknowledge her unique strengths so that these might be capitalized on to make her life as rich and rewarding as possible.

REASON FOR REFERRAL

Lucy was recently reevaluated at her public school in March of this year to review her current special education services. Mr. and Mrs. Miller sought additional testing through a private evaluation to help them answer a number of questions. Specifically, they wanted to know (a) the reason that the recent testing showed a 19-point decline in Lucy's intelligence quotient, (b) her strengths and weaknesses, (c) how to maximize Lucy's potential, (d) the strategies that would be most beneficial for Lucy, and (e) whether she has any unidentified learning disabilities.

BACKGROUND INFORMATION

Lucy's developmental history was obtained through a parent interview, previous reports, and a parent questionnaire.

Birth, Developmental, and Medical History

Lucy is the adopted daughter of Jim and Margaret Miller. She was born in Eastern Europe and adopted when she was 6 months old. A previous report identified myotonic syndrome at birth and a history of hydrocephaly. Myotonic syndrome is a genetic disorder characterized by generalized muscle weakness and atrophy commonly accompanied by absence of tendon reflexes and mental retardation. The Millers were told that Lucy's biological mother was approximately 20, but they were given no information regarding her prenatal care or delivery, Lucy's medical history, or her biological father.

Regarding her developmental milestones, Lucy sat alone at 12 months, walked and spoke her first words at 2, and was able to talk in complete sentences by the age of 5. She learned to cut with scissors at the age of 5, and could tie her shoes between the ages of 6 and 7. Lucy's mother reported a history of language delays. At 18 months and 29 months of age, Lucy underwent surgery for strabismus. Lucy also has a urological/genital anomaly that delayed toileting and has led to several surgeries and hospital visits. Her hearing

was described as "sensitive." The most recent assessments of Lucy's vision and hearing in 2009 produced normal results. Lucy has not been prescribed any medications.

Social and Behavioral History

Lucy lives at home with both parents and her 12-year-old adopted brother, Luke. Her interests include music, baseball, skiing, swimming, and drama. Her parents report that Lucy likes school and works very hard to succeed. She receives instruction in the resource room for math and reading. Most recently, Lucy met the special education criteria as a child with a Learning Impairment (intellectual disability or mental retardation), Autism, and Speech and Language Impairment. Her mother shared that she questions the Autism diagnosis and feels Lucy's early difficulties with language and sensory integration have improved and were most likely symptoms of her Learning Impairment.

Educational History

Lucy has attended Lake Country School since kindergarten. She does not have behavior problems but has always experienced difficulties learning. Lucy has the benefit of a para-educator and/or special educator for all subjects. Her current Individualized Education Plan (IEP) includes reading goals for decoding and comprehension, and math goals regarding number concepts and computation skills. Specific math objectives include: making change, following recipes, telling time, identifying and comparing fractions, and solving story problems. Goals for written expression were based on state standards. Language goals address listening comprehension, oral expression (including pragmatics), and personal development.

Current special education services include: (a) 1 hour of case management per month, (b) 30 minutes of reading and 45 minutes of math instruction daily with Ms. Jenkins, a para-educator, in the resource room, (c) 20 minutes of writing assistance daily from Ms. Jenkins, in the classroom, (d) 6½ hours of "personal care" daily from Ms. Jenkins, and (e) 30 minutes of speech and language services twice a week in a small group, and once a week, individually.

Services during the summer are (a) 30 minutes each of reading, writing, and math for 4 weeks from Mr. Mantell, a para-educator, and (b) 3 hours (total) of occupational therapy services, to include 1 hour of home consultation.

According to the IEP, Lucy will take the grade-level state assessment with the following accommodations:

help of a reader and scribe, individual administration, extended time, clarified directions, and a familiar test administrator.

Previous Testing

In preschool, the school psychologist administered the Wechsler Preschool and Primary Scale of Intelligence-Third Edition (WPPSI-III). Results indicated Below Average Verbal IQ, with a standard score (SS) of 83 and a percentile rank (PR) of 13, Performance IQ in the Well Below Average range (SS 72, PR 3), and a Full-Scale IQ also in the Well Below Average range (SS 73, PR 4). In second grade, Lucy was administered the Wechsler Intelligence Scale for Children – Fourth Edition (WISC-IV) by Dr. Jessamyn Richmond, a private clinical psychologist. On the four indices on the WISC-IV, Lucy demonstrated a relative strength in Verbal Comprehension, bordering the Below Average/Average ranges. Processing Speed was Below Average and both Perceptual Reasoning and Working Memory were Well Below Average. Her Full-Scale IQ was Well Below Average. (At that time, Lucy would have taken the Coding subtest for children under 8, a test considerably less complex than the one for older children. The 2009 test results revealed that this increase in task difficulty had a significant impact on her Coding performance.) Academic testing with the Woodcock-Johnson III Tests of Achievement (WJ III ACH) indicated Below Average performance in Broad Reading and Written Language and Well Below Average performance in Broad Math. Lucy was also administered the Comprehensive Test of Nonverbal Intelligence, Second Edition (CTONI-2) and obtained a Below Average score of (SS 87, PR 19). Overall results indicated that Lucy had significant difficulties in oral language, executive functioning, fine motor skills, and memory.

In March 2009, Lucy was readministered the WISC-IV by Dr. Donaldson, the school psychologist. All of her index scores were lower. Verbal Comprehension, Perceptual Reasoning, and Working Memory were all Extremely Below Average (PR 1 and below) and Processing Speed was Well Below Average (PR 5). Results of an adaptive behavior scale indicated "Extremely Low" functioning compared with others her age. Dr. Donaldson attributed the decline in Lucy's scores to her difficulties with word retrieval and verbal expression. He suggested that she might perform better on parts of the WISC-IV Integrated, which assesses some of the same skills using a multiple-choice format.

Results of testing with the WJ III ACH indicated Below Average basic reading skills (word recognition and fluency), with reading comprehension in the Well Below Average range. Lucy's skill in generating and writing phrases and sentences (with no penalties for spelling or minor grammatical errors) was Below Average, with her ability to generate and write simple sentences quickly somewhat lower. Her spelling was Extremely Below Average. Lucy's performance on paper-and-pencil math, rapid recall of math facts, and math problem solving were also Extremely Below Average. The drop in achievement results indicated that although Lucy might have been making some progress in academic skills, her rate of learning lagged behind that of her age-peers.

A speech and language evaluation, also conducted in March 2009 by Amanda Thompson, confirmed Extremely Below Average expressive language and memory capabilities. Ms. Thompson concluded that Lucy's receptive language was significantly stronger than her expressive language, as she obtained a Below Average score on the Peabody Picture Vocabulary Test-4 (PPVT-4), a test of single-word receptive vocabulary.

Eileen Muffitt, occupational therapist, assessed Lucy's fine-motor development and visual-motor and visual-perceptual skills. Lucy's visual-motor integration abilities were in the Extremely Below Average range. Noting Lucy's myotonic syndrome, Ms. Muffitt stated, "Handwriting is very difficult for Lucy and the team needs to accommodate her with alternatives to handwriting whenever possible."

ASSESSMENT PROCEDURES

Woodcock-Johnson-III NU Tests of Cognitive Ability, Third Edition (WJ III COG): Selected Tests

Wechsler Individual Achievement Test-Third Edition (WIAT-III), selected subtests

Gray Oral Reading Test-Fourth Edition (GORT-4), Form B

Informal assessments in alphabet writing and pseudo-word reading

Review of records

Different tests use different score ranges and verbal labels to refer to these ranges, making it somewhat difficult to compare a person's performance from test to test or over time. For the sake of consistency, the following standard score ranges and descriptors are used throughout this report, including results of previous testing:

>130	Extremely Above Average (EAA)
120–129	Well Above Average (WAB)
110–119	Above Average (AA)
90–109	Average (A)
80–89	Below Average (BA)
70–79	Well Below Average (WBA)
<70	Extremely Below Average (EBA)

BEHAVIORAL OBSERVATIONS

Lucy was seen on two separate occasions. She appeared as a happy, well-adjusted young girl who was inquisitive and conversed with ease. Occasional errors in syntax and grammar were noted, but her ability to express herself was seen as one of her relative strengths. Lucy's pragmatic language skills were less well developed. She sometimes stood too close when speaking and perseverated on topics. Overall, Lucy was cooperative, easy to redirect, and responded well to humor. In this one-to-one setting, she demonstrated excellent attention and concentration. She did become frustrated when tasks became difficult. For example, she often complained and asked, "How many more?" Lucy responded well to encouragement and positive feedback, but she did not have a great deal of persistence when presented with more cognitively complex tasks. Although higher-order reasoning and use of logic were weaknesses, Lucy was frequently quick with a humorous comment. Lucy's fine-motor skills were, as previously identified, weak, and she was accommodated in certain situations. She put forth great effort when fine-motor skills were required, even for such a simple task as circling numbers. Given Lucy's cooperation and task commitment, these results are deemed to be valid indicators of her present functioning.

EVALUATION RESULTS

Across all test batteries, standard scores (which are sometimes described as "composites," "clusters," or "quotients") have a mean of 100 and a standard deviation of 15. Scaled scores, often described as subtest scores, have a mean of 10 and a standard deviation of 3. Percentiles have a mean of 50. Relative proficiency indices (RPI) allow statements to be generated about a subject's predicted quality of performance on tasks similar to the ones tested. For example, an RPI of 70/90 is interpreted to mean that when others at the subject's age show 90% success on a certain task, the subject is predicted to show only 70% success on the same or similar tasks. The educational implication of an RPI of 82/90 or below is that age-appropriate tasks will be somewhere between difficult and impossible.

WJ III COG Results

Cluster/Test	Standard Score	Percentile Rank	Descriptor	RPI	RPI Educational Implications
GIA	57	0.2	EBA	21/90	
Verbal Ability (Ext)	82	12	BA	58/90	very difficult
Verbal Comprehension	86	17	BA	65/90	very difficult
General Information	80	9	BA	50/90	very difficult
Thinking Ability	74	4	WBA	61/90	very difficult
Visual-Auditory Learning	75	5	WBA	64/90	very difficult
Spatial Relations	84	15	BA	72/90	difficult
Sound Blending	87	18	BA	72/90	difficult
Concept Formation	79	8	WBA	32/90	very difficult
Cognitive Efficiency	36	<0.1	EBA	0/90	impossible
Visual Matching	38	<0.1	EBA	0/90	impossible
Numbers Reversed	46	<0.1	EBA	0/90	impossible
Long-Term Retrieval	64	1	EBA	71/90	difficult

(Continued)

Cluster/Test	Standard Score	Percentile Rank	Descriptor	RPI	RPI Educational Implications
Visual-Auditory Learning	75	5	WBA	64/90	very difficult
Retrieval Fluency	64	1	EBA	77/90	difficult
Visual-Spatial Thinking	**83**	**13**	**BA**	**75/90**	difficult
Spatial Relations	84	15	BA	72/90	difficult
Picture Recognition	89	24		78/90	difficult
Auditory Processing	**88**	**22**	**BA**	**81/90**	difficult
Sound Blending	87	18	BA	72/90	difficult
Auditory Attention	96	40	A	87/90	manageable
Processing Speed	**43**	**<0.1**	**EBA**	**1/90**	impossible
Visual Matching	38	<0.1	EBA	0/90	impossible
Decision Speed	60	0.4	EBA	5/90	extremely difficult
Phonemic Awareness	**79**	**8**	**WBA**	**71/90**	difficult
Sound Blending	87	18	BA	72/90	difficult
Incomplete Words	78	7	WBA	70/90	difficult
Working Memory	**49**	**<0.1**	**EBA**	**2/90**	impossible
Numbers Reversed	46	<0.1	EBA	0/90	impossible
Auditory Working Memory	72	3	WBA	22/90	extremely difficult

Cognitive Performance

The Woodcock-Johnson III Tests of Cognitive Abilities (WJ III COG) was administered to obtain another impression of her intellectual functioning. Results revealed an Extremely Below Average General Intellectual Ability (GIA) standard score of 57 (90% confidence range = 53–62; 0.2 percentile). Some of the clusters that contribute to this score, however, differ significantly from each other. For example, Lucy's Verbal Ability score was three standard deviations above her Cognitive Efficiency score. Consequently, it is more helpful and accurate to view Lucy's complex cognitive profile as a pattern of strengths and weaknesses to either be capitalized on or strengthened.

Lucy's scores were based on age norms. When no significant difference was found between the test scores within a cluster, only the cluster score is discussed. Lucy's performance on individual WJ III cognitive performance clusters (representing broad categories of cognitive abilities) is presented below.

Intra-Individual Strengths

Lucy's performance on the tests and clusters of the WJ III COG indicate that with one exception, all cognitive abilities tested are weak, albeit to varying degrees. Lucy's only Average score was in the ability to sustain attention to and discriminate between speech sounds despite competing noise.

Based on the Relative Proficiency Indexes, Lucy demonstrated strengths *relative to her other cognitive abilities* in three areas: phonemic awareness, long-term retrieval, and visual-spatial thinking. On tasks similar to those in the test, Lucy's likelihood of success is 71% to 75% compared with age-peers whose likelihood of success is 90%. Lucy demonstrated some facility in blending sounds into whole words. It is likely that she has had a good deal of instruction in this skill, a critical subskill of learning to read.

Lucy also had some success storing information in memory efficiently and retrieving it later through associations. Tasks requiring these skills include recalling the sounds associated with letters when reading, recalling words for objects, and retrieving previously learned math facts—tasks with which she has, in fact, demonstrated difficulty. Despite a standard score in the Extremely Below Average range, her RPI indicated that she is not quite *as* far behind her age-peers as her standard score implies.

Another relative strength for Lucy was visual-spatial thinking, the ability to mentally work with visual patterns/ designs (e.g., recognize similarities and differences, reassemble parts of a design) and to store and later retrieve visual representations (e.g., pictures). Learning and re-membering *visual* information, especially pictures of tangible objects, appeared to be easier for Lucy than tests that were purely verbal.

Although phonemic awareness, long-term retrieval, and visual-spatial thinking are *intrapersonal* strengths for Lucy, her standard scores bordered the Well Below Average to Below Average ranges and her RPIs indicated that age-level activities with similar task demands will be difficult for her.

Intra-Individual Variations

In terms of difficulty for Lucy, the next levels of cognitive skills are verbal ability and thinking ability; the latter incorporates inductive reasoning. Lucy's standard scores on the Verbal Ability and Thinking Ability clusters were in the Well Below Average and Below Average ranges, respectively; her RPIs (59/90 and 61/90) indicated that tasks requiring these skills will be "very difficult" for her. Verbal ability, as assessed, reflects a combination of abilities and knowledge, including receptive and expressive vocabulary, the ability to reason with the concepts represented by words (e.g., synonyms, antonyms, analogies), and knowledge about one's environment. Lucy's performance was consistent with her performance on the PPVT-4 in March.

Thinking ability represents an aggregate of the abilities that allow an individual to process information that has been placed in short-term memory but that requires deliberate, conscious thought. Within and critical to this ability is logical reasoning, assessed by Concept Formation, a test of inductive reasoning. Lucy was clearly frustrated as this task became more complex, requiring greater and greater higher-order reasoning ability. Lucy's RPIs on the broad ability, as well as the more specific test of logical reasoning, predict that tasks requiring deliberate, conscious thought and reasoning will be "very difficult" for her.

Test results indicated that Lucy's most severe difficulties were in the cognitive abilities of processing speed and working memory. Her performance on both was in the Extremely Below Average range. Her RPIs indicated that she will find similar age-level tasks "impossible." Almost all academic learning requires both working memory and processing speed. Working memory allows a person to hold information in immediate awareness while performing some mental process on it, such as reordering or transforming it in some way. Lucy was not able to do so on either of the tests given. On Numbers Reversed, when

asked to repeat a series of digits in reverse order, Lucy was not consistently able to do so with just two digits. She became frustrated quickly, saying, "I can't," and "I can only say the way it is" (in a forward sequence, as presented). On Auditory Working Memory, she was to reorder numbers and names of objects into two discrete categories. She was able to recall items from both categories only when each contained only one item. After that, she could recall only some of the items, usually the objects, which tend to be more meaningful and thus more memorable.

The tests of processing speed assessed the speed at which Lucy could do a simple, repetitive task, suggesting the rate at which lower-level skills can become automatic. Visual Matching required her to scan rows of numbers and circle the two identical numbers in each row. Decision speed required her to scan rows of pictures and circle the two that were the most conceptually similar (e.g., gloves, pen, cat, pencil). Lucy's performance on this cluster, however, may be spuriously low due to the impact of her myotonic syndrome on the mode of response. The "simple" motor task of circling the target item, intended to be fast and automatic, was, for Lucy, slow and labored. Consequently, her extremely low cluster score reflects her weak fine-motor skills, as well as her low processing speed.

Tests of processing speed and working memory combine to provide a measure of cognitive efficiency, or the capacity of the cognitive system to process information automatically. Cognitive efficiency is particularly important, as it allows a person to do certain mental tasks without conscious thought, leaving cognitive attention available for learning or thinking about new or more complex information or procedures. As with the component abilities, Lucy is expected to find tasks requiring cognitive efficiency "impossible."

Academic Performance

During some informal testing, Lucy was asked to write the alphabet and copy a nine-word sentence. Writing the alphabet, she wrote up to the letter *g* and said, "I don't remember the rest of the ABCs—there's the problem!" She was able to write the remaining letters from dictation. In both writing tasks, Lucy's handwriting was very legible and her words well spaced, although her letter formation was slow and labor intensive, and she had difficulty writing letters composed of circles and lines, such as *d* and *g*. Lucy also had trouble placing her letters on the lines; she put a good deal of pressure on her pencil and worked very slowly. These findings are in good agreement with previous measures of visual-motor integration.

Lucy was asked to read a list of nonsense words that conform to English spelling patterns for the purpose of assessing her phonics skills. Lucy struggled to read consonant-vowel-consonant patterns due to confusion over vowel sounds and voiced and unvoiced consonants, such as *b* and *p*. She was proficient in reading consonant digraphs (e.g., *th, sh*) and beginning and ending blends (e.g., *bl, nd*), but knew very few vowel digraphs (e.g., *ea, oo*). Lucy worked very slowly, carefully sounding out each new pattern. She was often able to segment a word into its constituent sounds but had difficulty blending the sounds into a word. Although her skill in blending when working only with sounds was a relative strength, it is likely that having to retrieve the sounds from letter prompts, one at a time, hold them in memory in sequence, and then blend them together put too much of a burden on her weak working memory.

GORT-IV Results

Subtest	SS	ScS	%	GE
Oral Reading Quotient	61		<1	
Rate		3	1	2.2
Accuracy		2	<1	1
Fluency*		1	<1	1
Comprehension		6	9	3
*Combination of Rate and Accuracy subtests				

To obtain an impression of Lucy's reading fluency, accuracy, and comprehension, the Gray Oral Reading Test-Fourth Edition (GORT-4) was administered. The GORT-4 presents graded reading passages with five multiple-choice comprehension questions for each. Lucy's reading accuracy, rate, and fluency (a combination of the rate and accuracy) were all at or below the 1st percentile. Her accuracy on the first passage placed her ability to read independently at about pre-primer level but hit her frustration level at first grade. On Story 2, Lucy reached her frustration level in terms of accuracy and she asked, "How many do I have to do?" Familiarity of content appeared to support her reading accuracy, as her reading was somewhat more accurate on the Level 3 passage, the topic of which was familiar to her, than on the Level 2 passage, which was not. Lucy's errors included omissions of whole words and suffixes and word substitutions on the smaller (function) words. Her self-corrections and her correct responses to comprehension questions on the first three passages indicate that she was reading for meaning. Lucy appeared to benefit from a multiple-choice format; her receptive language skills (listening and reading) were also clearly better developed than her expressive abilities. At this point, Lucy's weak decoding skills are the major impediment to her comprehension of text. Her future reading comprehension, however, will be limited by her comprehension of spoken language.

Mathematics

WIAT-III Math Subtests: Results

Subtest/Cluster	Standard Score	Percentile	Grade Equiv.
Numerical Operations	53	0.1	1.2
Math Problem Solving	60	0.4	1.9
Mathematics Composite	**49**	**<0.1**	

The results of the WIAT-III math subtests indicate that Lucy is severely lacking in basic math concepts and skills. Although she was able to add two-digit numbers with regrouping, she suddenly seemed confused about place value when confronted with a similar problem that included a three-digit number. She asked, "Does the 1 go there too because my number is 14?" She was not able to generalize the regrouping procedure from a two-digit to a three-digit problem. Subtraction with or without regrouping was difficult for her. She did not attempt any multiplication or division problems.

On Math Problem Solving, Lucy was asked to solve a variety of simple word problems, most of which involved pictures. Lucy could use whole numbers to describe quantities shown but physically covered up pictures when the problem involved subtraction. She could tell time to the hour and quarter hour and use a calendar to identify a day, if given the data. She could not determine how many weeks until a scheduled event when given a date in the middle of the month. Lucy was unable to read graphs, solve problems with money, or demonstrate an understanding of place value up to four digits. On one occasion Lucy confused "tallest" with "widest," indicating that she may need instruction in basic language concepts, which, in turn, may be interfering with her understanding of the language of math. Lucy's performance on the WIAT-III math tests was consistent with her performance on the WJ III ACH Applied Problems test that was administered in March.

SUMMARIES AND CLINICAL IMPRESSIONS

Cognitive Summary

Lucy was recently reevaluated for special education determination in March of this year. The Millers sought additional testing to learn the reason for the decline in Lucy's intelligence quotient on the most recent testing, her strengths and weaknesses, how to maximize her potential and the strategies to do so, and whether she has any learning disabilities. Lucy's school has qualified her for special education under the categories of Learning Impairment, Autism, and Speech and Language Impairment. Mrs. Miller questions the Autism diagnosis.

Results of the WJ III Tests of Cognitive Ability place Lucy's GIA of 57 in the Extremely Below Average range, consistent with WISC-IV Full-Scale score of 58, obtained in March. Whereas this score is in excellent agreement with Lucy's most recent WISC-IV score, significant intra-cognitive variations existed, as they did on the WISC-IV, making both Lucy's GIA and Full-Scale IQ less meaningful or useful as indicators of her ability to succeed in school. More meaningful and useful information can be obtained from considering Lucy's strengths and weaknesses for the purposes of educational planning.

Children with learning impairments learn differently from other children, and they learn at different rates. As individuals mature chronologically, the expectation in normal development is to acquire a greater and greater propensity for thinking and reasoning abstractly. As Lucy matures, her cognitive abilities are developing significantly more slowly than typical. This is not to say that Lucy is not learning, as she surely is; however, because she is now being compared to other 11-year-olds, as opposed to 7- or 8-year-olds, her cognitive abilities and, accordingly, the academic skills that depend on them, are more noticeably different than those of her same-age peers. This is why at age 11, her measured potential for school success is less robust than when she was assessed and compared to children age 7 years, 11 months.

Lucy's relative intra-individual strengths include her auditory processing of speech sounds, long-term retrieval, and visual-spatial thinking. Positive personal characteristics include her temperament, work ethic, attention, and sense of humor. Although these are intrapersonal strengths, it must be noted that her capacities in the cognitive abilities were significantly lower than those of her age-peers and that she will have difficulty with tasks requiring them.

Her intrapersonal weaknesses include abstract reasoning and problem-solving skills, the ability to process and produce complex oral language, working memory, processing speed, and fine-motor skills.

Academic Summary

Academically, Lucy's reading skills are at approximately a pre-primer level. Her sound-symbol associations are not sufficiently automatic to allow her to sound out words presented in print. Her limited decoding is, at this point, affecting her comprehension of text. Currently, the major impediments to her acquisition of decoding skills are slow processing speed and limited memory and retrieval. Prior knowledge of the content of a passage, activated prior to reading, supports her comprehension. Lucy can best demonstrate her comprehension when she is tested in a multiple-choice format.

Lucy's math skills appear to be limited to counting and addition, with some practical skills such as telling time and calendar use. She appears to lack the conceptual understanding of procedures that she has learned to use; consequently, she cannot generalize them. Math has a unique language and requires the fluent retrieval of facts and memory for algorithms that consistently challenge Lucy. Her math achievement is impacted by weaknesses in basic language concepts (e.g., tall, wide), slow processing speed, limited memory and retrieval, and low reasoning abilities.

When assessing writing, emphasis in this evaluation was on Lucy's grapho-motor output skills, as this seems to be understated in her present IEP. Lucy's willingness to cooperate and persevere, despite significantly delayed fine-motor skills that have a neurological basis, has perhaps delayed the introduction of technological alternatives to handwriting. While the cognitive and linguistic demands of written communication will pose challenges to Lucy, she is also significantly challenged by the physical act of writing and will need accommodations and the use of technology to allow her to express herself in writing.

Clinical Impressions

Lucy is a friendly girl who is tenacious, optimistic, and motivated, despite her learning challenges. She demonstrates a mild-to-moderate level of intellectual disability. The appropriate special education category is Learning Impairment with previously measured deficits in adaptive behavior. Adaptive behavior is "the effectiveness or degree with which individuals meet the standards of personal independence and social responsibility expected for age and cultural group." Lucy does not evidence any additional learning disabilities. She does not demonstrate behaviors or thought patterns that would indicate autism. Her speech and language development, which has heretofore been identified on her IEP, is congruent with her cognitive development.

While Lucy will be challenged by the cognitive and linguistic demands of school, she has many strengths to draw on, and as long as she is presented with appropriate instruction, learning experiences, and materials, will continue to grow and learn.

Lucy does have a comprehensive IEP. In meeting her goals and objectives, several methods and materials are suggested, along with a greater emphasis in addressing Lucy's fine-motor challenges and providing her the use of technology for learning.

RECOMMENDATIONS

Memory

1. Recognize that Lucy has difficulty on tasks that require her to manipulate information mentally. Provide strategies and accommodations to reduce the demands placed on working memory.
2. Provide intensive repetition, practice, and review in all learning activities. To promote retention, provide activities to reinforce the skills or content at frequent and regular intervals, gradually increasing the intervals to less frequent and intermittent.
3. In each teaching session, before introducing new information to Lucy, review previous information from the last lesson and check for mastery.

Higher-Order Reasoning

1. When teaching Lucy any new process or skill, provide slow, step-by-step instruction. Use manipulative and concrete objects whenever possible to illustrate the concepts. Lucy has difficulty recognizing similarities and differences as the basis for forming new concepts. Provide explicit instruction in the development of categorization skills, moving from concrete to abstract materials and from simple comparison to contrast based on multiple attributes.

Language

1. Use a collaborative approach for teaching language and academic skills. In this model, the speech and language pathologist (SLP) shares with the teacher the current focus of therapy and ways to integrate work toward the language objectives into classroom activities. The teacher shares the current units or skills being presented in class. Together, they can decide on modifications in activities, instructional techniques, or presentation styles that can be instituted in class and content-related vocabulary and concepts for the SLP to integrate into therapy activities. Such collaboration is most likely to facilitate Lucy's comprehension of classroom material and success on classroom tasks.
2. When teaching any new process or skill, provide systematic sequential instruction, ensuring mastery of each skill before moving on to a more complex level or new skill.
3. As much as possible, teach new concepts and vocabulary within thematic units so that new learning is interrelated conceptually. The thematic unit will provide a consistent framework and familiar context to introduce new concepts and vocabulary.

Visual-Motor Integration and Fine-Motor Skills

1. Use Shared Writing to ease the burden of writing challenges. A description of this procedure is provided in an appendix.
2. Lucy's parents are encouraged to visit the Vermont Parent Information Center in Williston to explore technology to facilitate word processing and writing skills. Software such as Co-Writer may be beneficial. Vermont Assistive Technology may also be of assistance. The goal, however, should be to get Lucy using the computer for writing as much as possible. Consult also with the occupational therapist, as she may have suggestions regarding the possible benefit of an adaptive keyboard, such as Intellikeys.
3. Reduce the amount of homework and the difficulty level of the work so that Lucy is not consistently spending more time on work at home than her peers.
4. Provide Lucy with periodic breaks when she is working on difficult material. Teach and model coping strategies. It is important to acknowledge Lucy's difficulties and assure her that she will be supported as she works to achieve.

5. Carefully monitor the amount of copying and writing Lucy is asked to do. Her teachers should reduce the quantity of work while maintaining appropriate standards for quality. Those who work with Lucy will need to strike a balance between accommodating her and "letting her off the hook." Lucy responds well to encouragement but will also often continue writing and copying when it is too difficult for her to do so.

Literacy

1. An essential aspect of Lucy's literacy instruction needs to include the development of her letter recognition and production skills. Provide multisensory instruction to aid in letter learning. When teaching Lucy to associate letters with their names, teach only one letter name at a time. To promote retention and attention, incorporate tactile-kinesthetic activities into instruction. Activities may include having Lucy trace glitter letters while saying the letter name, put letter forms into their proper place in a puzzle jig while reminding herself of its name, or working with another student, making the shape of the letter with their bodies while saying (shouting, singing) its name.

2. Teach Lucy D'Nealian handwriting or use *Handwriting without* Tears to reinforce letter formation and writing in general. These systems introduce letters in groups of similar formation, making the proper formation easier to remember and providing more practice in the required movement.

3. Lucy's IEP suggests a synthetic phonics approach to teaching decoding which, to date, has not been successful. Lucy's phonemic awareness is not sufficiently developed and she has not yet developed automaticity in letter-sound associations. When trying to sound out a word, she must retrieve the sound for each letter in succession, hold each in memory in sequence, and then blend them. This process places too much of a burden on working memory if the sound retrieval is not automatic. Consequently, the current focus must be on building automaticity in sound-symbol relationships and, while doing so, have her work on sounding out only words for which she has established this automaticity.

4. Reading-spelling programs that are based on the Orton-Gillingham principles of instruction incorporate the previous recommendation, are multisensory and highly systematic, continuously incorporate previous learning, teach spelling along with reading skills, and ensure that a student has mastered each subskill before moving on to the next. Many of these programs teach letter names and sounds simultaneously. Programs following these principles are called *multisensory structure of language* (MSSL) programs. This type of program, along with supplementary multisensory activities for extra reinforcement, is most likely to benefit Lucy. Specifically, the Lindamood Phonemic Sequencing (LIPS) reading program is recommended for establishing a strong foundation on which to build basic reading and spelling skills. Information on the effectiveness of LIPS may be found at the web site of the Florida Reading Research Center (www.fcrr.org). Further information on MSSL programs is provided in the supplementary appendix.

5. Use the attached Modified Fernald Method for learning to read and write irregular words as well as words that must be learned in advance of the skills that would allow it to be decoded. Use a Spelling Flow List to ensure retention. For spelling, include sight words either from Lucy's writing or from a basic sight word list.

6. Include 20 minutes a day of practice reading decodable text (i.e., text incorporating only the word structures that Lucy has learned) to increase automaticity in decoding.

7. Activate Lucy's prior knowledge before reading, and specifically teach her how to answer a variety of questions. Lucy does best with a multiple-choice format.

8. As Lucy's current decoding skills do not yet approach her comprehension of oral language, teach comprehension strategies orally. Later, help Lucy to apply them to her reading. One useful strategy for teaching her to think about the meaning of spoken language and text is the Directed-Reading-Thinking Activity. A description of this activity is attached.

9. Continue with *Framing Your Thoughts* if this is proving to be successful with Lucy. When teaching Lucy any skill, the teacher will need to always be cognizant of whether Lucy is likely to understand the language of instruction.

10. Given Lucy's cognitive, linguistic, and academic functioning, grade-level tests are inappropriate. It is, however, reasonable to give Lucy standardized tests that represent her general level of academic functioning. If this is not an option or considered valuable, then other, more relevant assessment (e.g., criterion-referenced assessments) should be used.

Mathematics

1. Lucy has difficulty with the procedural knowledge of math as outlined in the NCTM standards for children her age and grade because of her cognitive impairments. Review the Edmark company's offerings for teaching functional math skills, such as handling money, using clocks and calendars, and so forth.

2. Given Lucy's need for visual representation and hands-on experiences, use Math-U-See (www.mathusee.com), especially for teaching Lucy subtraction.

It has been a pleasure working with Lucy. Home-school coordination will be essential to Lucy's ongoing success, and this may include bi-monthly updates, with quarterly updates of IEP progress minimally. The examiners are available to answer questions about this report and/or provide further consultation regarding Lucy's educational program and progress.

CASE 29

Differential Diagnosis
Emotional Disturbance or Conduct Disorder?

Elaine Fletcher-Janzen

Evaluators are often called on to mediate between conflicting opinions between home and school. The report does not outline much of the case history because of the sensitivity of the individuals who were going to read it. In this case, Bobby's grandfather worked for the school district and had a great investment in procuring special education services for his grandson. If Bobby were found to be emotionally disturbed, then school services would be enhanced and "the problem" would be defined as belonging to Bobby. Bobby's parents were divorced and were still continually fighting. Also, Bobby's brothers had left his mother's house and gone to live with their father in another state. Bobby missed his brothers but had also experienced a great deal of abusive bullying from them in prior years. The politics of this case were, therefore, that the grandfather was trying to get his grandson the best help that was available, that his mother and father were uninterested in getting him any help, and that the school district administration did not want to identify this child as emotionally disturbed because they believed Bobby's behaviors to be situational and because, once identified as eligible for special education, general education consequences for his behaviors would not be available. As usual, the school psychologist's report was delivered in the middle of this interesting situation.

This case also illuminates the problems that school psychologists have in determining the difference between conduct disorder and emotional disturbance. Fortunately, in this case, Bobby had been in an alternative school and he showed no problems with conduct/emotions at all for an extended time. This showed that he did not have underlying pathology that was resulting in acting out. There is no doubt that in the general education setting he was oppositional, aggressive, and provocative, but the *Diagnostic and Statistical Manual for Mental Disorders-IV-TR*

indicates that if a youth meets the criteria for Conduct Disorder then the diagnosis stops there and does not extend to to Oppositional Defiant Disorder. For a diagnosis of emotional disturbance to be made, the pathology has to extend across settings. In this case, Bobby was a master at manipulation and managed to traverse the alternative setting notwithstanding similar class loads, rules, and regulations. He was very eager to get back to his general education class because of the end-of-school social activities that were coming up and he was aware of what he had to do to achieve this end.

This case also begs the question as to when personality disorders start to emerge. School psychologists do not tend to identify and treat personality disorders because much of formal identity development is done in the later adolescent years. However, Bobby exhibited classic prenarcissistic personality characteristics. Underneath the grandiose and disdainful acting out was a very sad child without a family that was willing to do the work necessary for him to get back on track.

This case also illustrates that even when the assessment is backed up by good instruments and clinical judgment, the school psychologist's report can be completely ignored! The Individualized Education Plan (IEP) team, at a later date, bowed to political pressure brought to bear by the grandfather (and an attorney) and found Bobby eligible for special education services under the category of "emotionally disturbed."

PSYCHOLOGICAL ASSESSMENT

Name:	Bobby Johnson
Date of Birth:	11/25/98
Age:	11-4

School:	Mountain Alternative School
Grade:	5
Date of Report:	4/02/10
Evaluator:	Elaine Fletcher-Janzen, Ed.D.

REASON FOR REFERRAL

Bobby was referred for evaluation of his eligibility for special education services.

DEVELOPMENTAL, MEDICAL, AND FAMILY HISTORY

Bobby is currently attending the Mountain Alternative program due to physical aggression against a teacher at Independence Elementary that resulted in her hand being slammed in a door. Depending on his behavior, he is due to go back to Independence Elementary on May 12. His parents filled out BASC-2 and BRIEF ratings but did not respond to repeated requests for an interview regarding early developmental and medical history.

CURRENT MEDICATIONS

Stimulant medication for Attention-Deficit/Hyperactivity Disorder (ADHD)

(Medication and dosage not received from parent)

CLASSROOM OBSERVATION

Bobby was observed in his classroom in the alternative school. He was working at his desk, which was separated from others by a study carrel. He appeared to be working consistently; he got up and asked for help from the teacher two times and was quiet and appropriate. The teachers in that classroom stated that he is compliant and quiet all of the time.

TESTS ADMINISTERED

Kaufman Assessment Battery for Children, Second Edition (KABC-II)

Bender Visual-Motor Gestalt Test, Second Edition (Bender Gestalt II)

Kaufman Test of Educational Achievement-II (KTEA-II)

Behavior Rating Inventory of Executive Function (BRIEF)—Teacher and Parent Forms

Behavior Assessment System for Children-2 (BASC-2)—Teacher and Parent Forms

3 Wishes Test

Kinetic Family Drawing (KFD)

Draw-A-Person Test (DAP)

Test Administration Observations

Bobby came with the examiner in a calm and cooperative manner. He was dressed in the school uniform of jeans and a white tee shirt and appeared well groomed. When Bobby and the examiner were walking by a classroom on the way to the testing room, a much older and larger student called to him and laughed. Bobby looked up and said "Shut up!" and continued to walk. The size differential between Bobby (slight build, small height) and the other student (nearly 6 feet tall, 180 pounds) was remarkable and yet Bobby took on the peer in a provocative manner without hesitation. Later, as Bobby and the examiner were returning to test after lunch, Bobby asked to go into the building through another door because "that kid was picking on" him.

At first, Bobby enjoyed the testing. He engaged with the materials and appeared to enjoy the challenge of the first few subtests of the KABC-II. In fact, he was socially appropriate and engaging. After some time, Bobby's attitude toward testing became guarded. At one point, toward the latter part of the KABC-II battery, Bobby started to fail simple questions on purpose. When the examiner asked him why he was doing this, he went into a long questioning/discussion period wherein he said that he did not agree with the purpose of testing, that he suspected that his peers did not have to test, and that he did not understand why his grandfather could not administer the test (even after ethical constraints had been explained). Therefore, Bobby's KABC-II test results are slightly lower on the Pattern Reasoning and Word Order subtests because of unwillingness to comply. Bobby's questioning took on an argumentative tone and it appeared that he had little respect for the examiner's or the test's credibility. Notwithstanding Bobby's shift in attitude, the results of the examination are deemed to be reasonable estimates of his current functioning levels because the majority of his test behavior showed authentic and good effort.

TEST INTERPRETATION

Kaufman Assessment Battery for Children, Second Edition (KABC-II)

The KABC-II is an individually administered measure of the processing and cognitive abilities of children and adolescents aged 3 through 18. It measures a range of abilities including sequential and simultaneous processing, learning, and reasoning that are relevant to understanding children who are having educational and/or psychological problems.

On the Sequential Scale of the KABC-II, which represents information that is processed in a step-by-step fashion along with visual and auditory short-term memory and working memory, Bobby performed in the Below Average range with a standard score of 85. On any given occasion, we can be 90% sure that his Sequential Scale score will range between 78 and 94. It is probable that his true score is more toward the upper limit of the range due to Bobby's slight negative attitude after the first few items of the test.

On the Simultaneous Scale of the KABC-II, Bobby scored in the Average range with a standard score of 94. On any given occasion, we can be 90% sure that his score will range from 86 to 102. The Simultaneous Scale measures visual problem solving and visual-spatial organization.

On the Learning Scale of the KABC-II, Bobby performed in the Average range. He obtained a standard score of 103. On any given occasion, we can be 90% sure that his score would range between 96 and 110. The Learning Scale is a dynamic measure of the child's ability to hold information in working memory and transfer it to long-term storage and retrieval. It is a demanding test that requires attention to task and willingness to engage with the materials.

On the Planning Scale of the KABC-II, Bobby performed in the Average range. He obtained a standard score of 85. On any given occasion, we can be 90% sure that his score would range between 75 and 95. It is probable that his true score is more toward the upper limit of this range due to his purposely failing the first few items of this test. In general, the Planning subtests are good measures of planning, problem solving, general intelligence, and executive functions.

The numeric results of the KABC-II are reported in Figure 1.

In summary, Bobby's cognitive and information-processing abilities (after adjusting for attitude) appear to be in the Average range without significant indications of processing weaknesses or strengths. Learning disabilities are not indicated. What is significant, however, is Bobby's guarded attitude toward testing and his argumentativeness about who should test him. An 11-year-old child challenging the veracity of the test and examiner and manipulating his performance is unusual and indicative of issues that may be affecting his ability to perform well not only on tests but within academic settings.

It should be noted that these results were obtained with Bobby on medication, the effects of which are difficult to assess because neither the type of medication nor the dosage are known.

Wechsler Individual Achievement Test (WIAT-III)

Age-based standard scores:

Total Reading	99
Mathematics	86
Written Expression	87

Bobby's academic functioning appears to be within the average range.

Behavior Rating Inventory of Executive Function (BRIEF)

Executive functions are cognitive processes that organize, plan, and prioritize information and actions in everyday life. The BRIEF also is a good measure of the child's ability to control emotions. Figure 2 displays numerical results of the general education teacher's observations of Bobby's executive functions. The profile indicates Clinically Significant problems with inhibition, emotional self-control, and self-monitoring; and At-Risk behaviors concerning shifting from one thought/activity to another, working memory, and planning/organization.

The teacher at the alternative school also rated Bobby's executive functioning during his 30-day stay at the school. The numerical results are charted in Figure 3 and indicate a marked difference in functions and behaviors. Indeed, this profile indicates age-appropriate functioning in all areas. This suggests that Bobby's executive function problems noted above are reactive to his environment and not due to an internal/organic disorder.

KABC-II Score Summary Table

Global Scale	Sum of Subtest Scores	Index (Standard Score)	90% Confidence Interval	Percentile Rank	Descriptive Category
Mental Processing Index (MPI)	69	**89**	**84–94**	**23**	**Average**

Scale	Sum of Subtest Scores	Index (Standard Score)	90% Confidence Interval	Percentile Rank	Descriptive Category	Normative Strength/ Weakness	Difference from Scale Mean	Personal Strength/ Weakness	Frequency of Difference
Sequential/Gsm	15	85	78–94	16	- - - - - - - - Not Interpretable (Range = 5) - - - - - - - -				
Simultaneous/Gv	18	94	86–102	34	- - - - - - - - Not Interpretable (Range = 6) - - - - - - - -				
Learning/Glr	21	103	96–110	58	Average	+11	PStr	>10%	
Planning/Gf	15	85	77–95	16	Average	−7			
Knowledge/Gc	- -			- -	- -	- -	- -	- -	- -

Mean Scale Index: 92

Bold denotes core subtests.

Subtest	Raw Score	Scaled Score	Percentile Rank	Age Equivalent	Additional Information
Sequential/Gsm					
Number Recall	12	10	50	11:4	
Word Order	15	5	5	6:0	
Simultaneous/Gv					
Rover	31	12	75	14:8	
Triangles	21	6	9	7:6	Scored w/o Time Points
Learning/Glr					
Atlantis	99	13	84	14:4	
Rebus	54	8	25	9:0	
Atlantis Delayed	16	9	37	7:3	
Rebus Delayed	30	8	25	8:9	
Planning/Gf					
Story Completion	17	9	37	10:0	Scored w/o Time Points
Pattern Reasoning	14	6	9	8:0	Scored w/o Time Points
Knowledge/Gc					
Verbal Knowledge	- -	- -	- -	- -	
Riddles	- -	- -	- -	- -	

Figure 1   KABC-II Results

Bender Visual-Motor Gestalt Test, Second Edition

The Bender Gestalt II presents cards with geometric designs on them that have to be copied onto a piece of paper by the child. Bobby's performance on this test indicates age-appropriate visual-motor coordination and visual-motor organization.

Behavior Assessment System for Children-2 (BASC-2)

The BASC-2 is an integrated system of rating scales that are designed to facilitate the differential diagnosis and classification of a variety of emotional and behavioral disorders in children. See Figure 4.

Bobby's teachers in the general education classroom settings (Reading, English, Math) appear to agree that they observe clinically significant externalizing problems including aggression, conduct problems, and hyperactivity. In addition, they concur that Bobby exhibits depressive symptoms, attention problems, and learning problems. Their ratings also indicated behaviors associated with bullying, poor ego strength, displaying of negative emotionality, and very poor resilience. While this profile is indicative of ADHD, it is also indicative of comorbid depression. The presence of these two conditions plus poor ego strength and

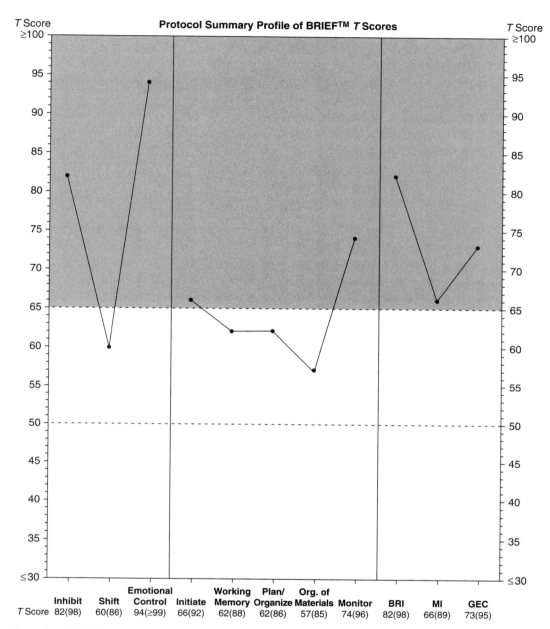

Figure 2   BRIEF Teacher Report: General Education Teacher's Observations

low resilience indicate that Bobby has experienced severe stress and poor coping skills for a long time. Unfortunately, his coping skills are currently compromised by his severe conduct problems.

An informative comparison between Ms. Oswald (general education teacher) and Ms. Payson (Mountain Alternative teacher) shows a marked difference in behaviors depending on the setting. The numerical results are charted

in Figure 5 and show a significant difference on internalizing and externalizing behaviors, and school learning and attention. (A similarity coefficient of −.13 indicates a significant difference.) Ms. Payson's profile (circle) indicates no problems and age-appropriate skills, whereas Ms. Oswald's profile (square) indicates marked aggression. The only area of functioning that both teachers agree is problematic for Bobby is At-Risk problems with social skills.

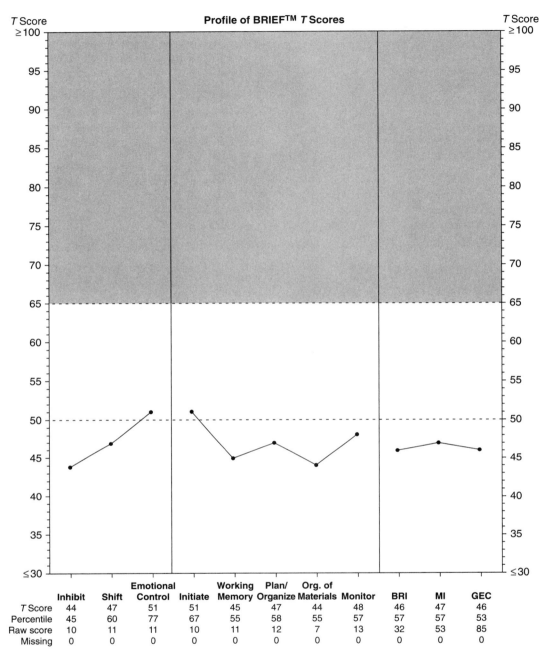

Profile of BRIEF™ *T* Scores

	Inhibit	Shift	Emotional Control	Initiate	Working Memory	Plan/ Organize	Org. of Materials	Monitor	BRI	MI	GEC
T Score	44	47	51	51	45	47	44	48	46	47	46
Percentile	45	60	77	67	55	58	55	57	57	57	53
Raw score	10	11	11	10	11	12	7	13	32	53	85
Missing	0	0	0	0	0	0	0	0	0	0	0

Figure 3   BRIEF Teacher Report: Alternative School Teacher's Observations

In summary, the BASC-2 results indicate that Bobby's acting-out behaviors are setting specific and suggest that he has age-appropriate skills (on a consistent basis) in one setting and a negative set of behaviors in the other. Therefore, control of his behaviors is probably due to a response to external factors and not internal psychopathology.

The results of the BASC-2 Parent Rating Form indicate that Bobby's mother observes behaviors that are generally At-Risk or Significant in externalizing, internalizing, and school problems. She also indicates poor adaptive functions. The numerical results are charted in Figure 6.

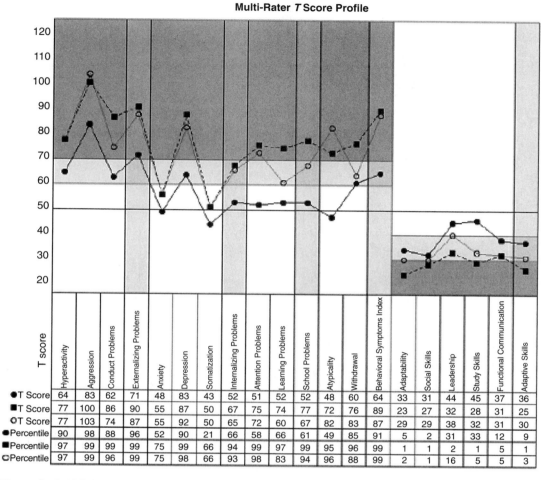

Figure 4   BASC-2 Rating Form: Multiple Observations

3 Wishes

When asked about what he would like if given three wishes, Bobby asked for:

1. An X-Box 360
2. A kitten
3. Five more wishes

These are age-appropriate answers.

Kinetic Family Drawing and Draw-A-Person Test

Bobby completed the drawings quickly and with little effort but the results are interesting and helpful. Bobby drew a picture of himself and his brothers playing basketball. There was no indication of adult family members or a family unit. His self-portrait seems to be of a large and ferocious-looking person. The footing of the person is very unsure, with multiple erasures.

Mental Status

Bobby was oriented to time, place, and person. He denied homicidal ideation but did admit that he wanted to hurt people from time to time. He then related a story about how "one time I did it" when a peer pushed him twice. He waited until gym class and struck the boy in the chest and the boy started crying. Bobby stated that every 5th grader that he hits cries, and that it is funny because although he is smaller, he can make bigger kids cry. He also explained the reason that he is at Mountain Alternative was because

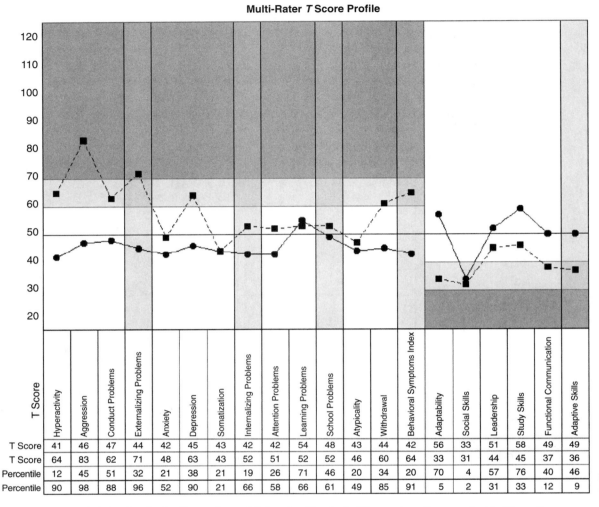

Figure 5   BASC-2 Teacher Rating Form: General Education Teacher's Observations Compared with Alternative School Teacher's

a "stupid retarded teacher slammed her own hand in a door and blamed me." The "retarded teacher was going to press charges" and that was "retarded because the whole thing was her fault." Bobby said that he was looking forward to seeing the "retarded" teacher when he was back at school because she would see him and be afraid and she would run away—and that would be "hilarious."

Bobby admitted to suicidal ideation "one time" about 2 years ago when he was grounded. He thought about cutting his arms and bleeding but then he thought that he was "too young to die." As for hallucinations, Bobby does "see things moving around." "I see things that look like shadows and I hear voices in the house that sound like they are whispering." These events occur about

twice a month and he has not told anyone except his brothers.

When asked what made him mad, Bobby said, "Some people calling me names or pushing me, so I hit them back." When asked what made him sad, he said, "People saying things about my dog who died at Christmas. One kid said, 'You killed your dog,' so I started pushing him. He is tall and I pushed him down and started punching him right there." When asked what made him scared, Bobby said, "Being in the house all alone and hearing voices and movement but there isn't anybody there." When asked what made him happy, he said, "Going shopping with my Grandma, spending time with my family, and talking to friends."

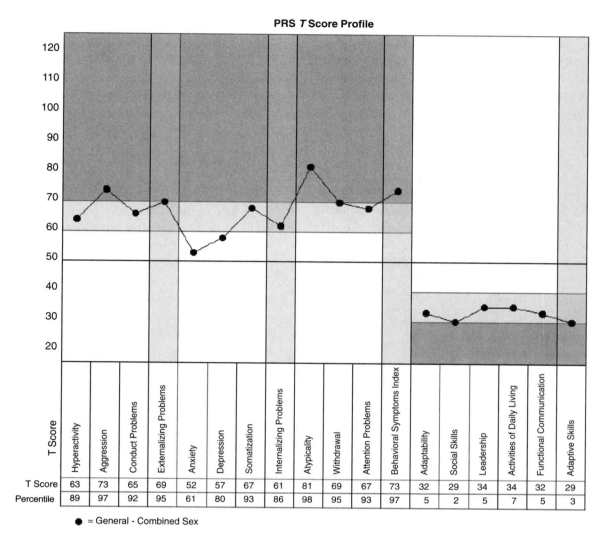

PRS *T* Score Profile

T Score	Hyperactivity	Aggression	Conduct Problems	Externalizing Problems	Anxiety	Depression	Somatization	Internalizing Problems	Atypicality	Withdrawal	Attention Problems	Behavioral Symptoms Index	Adaptability	Social Skills	Leadership	Activities of Daily Living	Functional Communication	Adaptive Skills
T Score	63	73	65	69	52	57	67	61	81	69	67	73	32	29	34	34	32	29
Percentile	89	97	92	95	61	80	93	86	98	95	93	97	5	2	5	7	5	3

● = General - Combined Sex

Figure 6 BASC-2 Parent Rating Form: Mother's Observations

CLINICAL SUMMARY

Bobby Johnson is an 11-year-old male student currently attending an alternative school instead of the regular 5th grade at Independence Elementary. Bobby has a long-stated history of ADHD, conduct problems, and aggression toward peers, adults, and property. The results of this evaluation indicate that Bobby's intellectual ability is solidly in the Average range with no indications of learning disabilities or executive function problems. His attitude toward compliance with testing procedures or examiner directives, however, could easily interfere with his performance. His attitude is one of superiority, a lack of empathy and respect for the examiner, and disdain for being forced to participate in an activity that he does not deem important.

Overall, adults in Bobby's school have concerns about significant externalizing behaviors, depression, attentional and learning problems, bullying, poor ego strength, and lack of resilience. These problems, in addition to a marked lack of empathy for others, refusal to take responsibility for incidents, disdain for older individuals, disdain for group rules, lack of remorse, distortion about his aggressive prowess, and self-aggrandizement, all point toward the beginnings of personality issues that will make him stand out and react in negative way.

At present, there seem to be two different Bobbys. One Bobby is a sweet, naïve, charming boy who loves to laugh, play, and be social; the other Bobby is a young man who is experiencing tremendous stress and grief about life events and covers up his continual psychic distress by trying to overpower and dominate others. In Bobby's mind, the only way to look important or superior is to make others look insignificant or inferior (by insult, aggression, or bullying).

Reliable and valid instruments measuring psychological functioning and executive functions indicate marked differences in performance depending on the setting. In the general education setting, Bobby has had conduct problems, and in the alternative setting, he has been a model student for over 30 days. This significant difference in functioning indicates that psychological disorders such as ADHD and executive function problems are not necessarily driving his behaviors. Therefore, at this time, Bobby is young enough to fit the pattern of characteristics associated with severe Conduct Disorder. It is clear that his acting out may become a way of life, internalized as a personality style that will help him maintain some semblance of control over life events. He is still young enough to benefit from intense treatment before his personality characteristics become set, which is likely to happen in adolescence and young adulthood. The impact of long-term family stress and separation should not be underestimated in this case. This child has had a great deal of distress in his life for which he has few coping skills and is therefore driven to act out his negative feelings against his own best interests and the best interests of others.

RECOMMENDATIONS

1. Bobby should continue to receive natural and logical consequences for his behavior. Counselors at school and attending adults should emphasize the relationship between his behavior and the undesirable results and also stress that "he is not bad" but that his behaviors are not appropriate or serving him well, and he can change them any time he wants to. On the other hand, those around him should emphasize positive feedback when Bobby is being responsible or thoughtful about others, explicitly drawing the relationship between good intentions and good results.

2. Exposing Bobby to school activities that will help him take responsibility and feel good about himself, such as helping the counselor conduct bully-proofing activities in kindergarten classrooms, will make him use his intellect toward responsible behavior and allow him to experience himself in a positive leadership position in front of others.

3. The family should consider exploring intense family therapy in a private setting to help reduce the chronic discord/distress that is affecting Bobby's conduct. The issues are private and not appropriate for the public school setting.

4. It is critical for Bobby's parents to contact his physician regarding his visual and auditory perceptual problems (potential hallucinations) in terms of medication management. These may require a change in medication or some other type of evaluation. Any new medication regime should be objectively monitored (by repeated measures of behavioral and academic functioning) because subjective accounts of his behavior in different settings do not represent medication effects adequately.

CASE 30

Integration of Post-Referral Progress Monitoring Data in a Specific Learning Disability Evaluation

Robert Misak

The case of John West illustrates a recent dilemma for practicing evaluators: How should one integrate standardized testing with Response to Intervention (RTI) data? While many states and schools have used RTI methods for years, there are just as many, if not more, that have only recently started to implement RTI policies and procedures. In addition, even in schools that are currently implementing RTI, there is little data regarding how to measure progress in areas other than basic reading skills. So, how does one determine if a student is responding to interventions if such data are not available at the time of referral? John West's case illustrates how to generate progress-monitoring data, if this type of information is not available at the time of the referral, and integrate it with more formal assessment data in the limited time allowed by special education regulations.

The data obtained during the course of the evaluation were gathered using readily available and inexpensive (if not free) sources in a manner that was time and labor efficient. John's case is also an example of the value of progress-monitoring data and how it can be used to shed additional light on difficult eligibility decisions. Additionally, in John's case, the use of progress-monitoring data helped school staff to recognize his lack of progress and see the implications more clearly (i.e., he was not catching up and would not catch up without a more focused and specialized intervention). The team also increased their awareness of the potential diagnostic and instructional benefits of progress monitoring.

FULL INDIVIDUAL EVALUATION: SPECIFIC LEARNING DISABILITY

Name: John West
Date of Birth: August 11, 1998

Age: 11-5
Parents: Robert and Barbara West
City: Central
State: Texas
School: Vera Elementary
Teacher: Laverne Park
Grade: 5.7
Student ID: 310360
Referral: Initial
Report Date: March 7, 2010
Evaluator: Robert Misak, M.A., M.Ed.

REASON FOR REFERRAL

John was referred for a Full Individual Evaluation to determine if a disability exists and, if so, whether it affects his school performance to such a degree that special education services are necessary. The Campus Review Committee (CRC) met at the end of last year (5/09) after John failed the math portion of the Texas Assessment of Knowledge and Skills (TAKS). Results of that meeting included recommendations for small-group intervention for 30 minutes daily and computer math tutoring for 1 hour daily. A second CRC meeting was held at the beginning of the current school year (9/2009); the committee recommended that small-group intervention be continued, to focus on specified math skills. The concern noted was "borderline performance without improvement." A third CRC meeting was held on 10/2009. The review indicated that although John had progressed in reading, he still required extra assistance with math. The committee recommended computer-based training four times per week for 30 minutes each and individual tutoring with a math teacher for 45 minutes daily.

Math tutoring would focus on math concepts and homework completion. Although the interventions did result in some improvement in math, they were not sufficient to permit John to function independently in the general education classroom.

SUMMARY AND CONCLUSIONS

This section provides professional advice given to the Admission, Review, and Dismissal (ARD) committee, which is charged with the legal responsibility for developing an educational program for John. The following conclusions and suggestions do not, however, represent the final decisions of the ARD committee.

Test Results

Despite 8 months of small-group, individual, and computer-based tutorial support in math, results of the Woodcock-Johnson III NU Tests of Achievement (WJ III ACH) placed John's performance in basic math skills and math reasoning skills in the Low Average range. These skills include automatic retrieval of basic math facts, computation, practical application of computation skills (e.g., word problems), understanding of math concepts, and analysis of number patterns. Of note, his lowest score was in rapid retrieval of basic facts; only 3% of his age peers would score as low as or lower than he did. Slow recall of facts was observed as well on the curriculum-based measures (CBM), or probes; he solved the problems he attempted correctly, but his extremely slow speed resulted in very few digits correct. Also on his CBM probes, the trend line of his progress indicated that without some other kind of intervention, he will not catch up with his classmates.

Also based on the results of the WJ III ACH, John's basic reading skills and reading comprehension were in the Low Average range. These include sight word recognition, word attack, reading fluency, reading vocabulary, and passage comprehension. John's teachers, however, have not reported reading as a problem for John and no referrals to the CRC committee have been made.

Effect of Cognitive Weaknesses on Academic Achievement

Slow processing means that John is slow to take in visual information and organize it cognitively. Once information is received by the cognitive system, it must be held in memory until it can be considered, worked on, and transferred to long-term memory. Memory does not have an unlimited capacity, however, and if active processing is not happening, the information in memory disintegrates. Consequently, this combination may prevent John from acquiring new information, especially information that is not within a meaningful context, or from processing it quickly enough to transfer into his long-term memory. Test results indicate, however, that John is able to quickly retrieve information that is already solidly stored in long-term memory.

Basic math and reading skills have, as a foundation, information that must be memorized by rote, such as math facts and letter-sound associations. If these are not learned well enough to be well organized in long-term memory and available for immediate retrieval, all higher-level skills are compromised. Regarding math, in addition to John's difficulty with learning math facts to an automatic level, his weakness in inductive reasoning and numerical reasoning make it more difficult for him to use logic to figure out computation and word problems. Similar problems exist with reading. Acquiring a store of sight words requires initial rapid processing of the letter patterns of the word so that it can be stored in memory and, subsequently, recognized when seen again. When words are not recognized quickly, fluency deteriorates, making it more difficult to comprehend the text. Particularly important to reading comprehension is crystallized intelligence. The broader one's stores of knowledge and vocabulary, the easier it is to match what you are reading to what you already know. John's relative weakness in crystallized intelligence is likely to reduce his understanding of what he reads even if he can read the individual words.

Consideration of Specific Learning Disability

A diagnosis of a Specific Learning Disability (SLD) would be indicated by academic difficulties in conjunction with disorders in basic psychological processes that have been shown to be related to the areas of academics that are weak. This evaluation attempted to determine if John exhibits a pattern of strengths and weaknesses in performance, achievement, or both, relative to age, grade-level standards, or intellectual ability that would meet the criteria of SLD. This pattern would be indicated by significant variability among specific areas of cognitive function or between specific areas of cognition and academic achievement. In order for the team to determine whether or not John qualifies for services as a student with a Specific Learning Disability, the following questions were considered. All questions must be answered affirmatively to qualify John for district special education services.

1. Does John have a significant normative academic deficit (below normal limits)?

Yes. John does have a significant normative academic deficit. While John was able to perform math reasoning tasks within the normal limits for his age (23rd percentile), albeit in the Low Average range, he had significant difficulties with knowledge of and automatic retrieval of basic math facts (3rd percentile).

2. Does he have a significant normative cognitive deficit?

Yes. John has cognitive deficits below normal limits. He demonstrated significant weaknesses in short-term memory (6th percentile), processing speed (7th percentile), and inductive reasoning (3rd percentile).

3. Have extraneous factors been ruled out as primary causes for these academic and cognitive deficits?

Yes. John has not had behavioral problems or any significant events within the past 3 years that would affect his learning. He has had excellent school attendance and English is the only language spoken at home. His vision and hearing have been tested with normal results.

4. Are there empirical and logical links between his cognitive disorders and his areas of academic deficit?

Yes. Research in math disabilities indicates that fluid reasoning, processing speed, memory span, and working memory (the latter two are assessed within the short-term memory factor) are frequently correlated with disabilities in math fact retrieval, computation, and math reasoning.

5. Do these cognitive deficits occur within an otherwise normal cognitive ability profile?

Yes. John demonstrated abilities within normal limits in auditory processing (54th percentile), visual processing (43rd percentile), long-term retrieval (36th percentile), and deductive reasoning (30th percentile). In addition, his performance on basic reading skills (28th percentile) and reading comprehension (21st percentile) were within normal limits, indicating that his academic and cognitive deficits are unexpected considering his other abilities.

6. Have these deficits resulted in significant or substantial academic failure or other restrictions/limitations in daily life functioning?

Yes. John's weaknesses in cognitive abilities have resulted in substantial academic failure. Despite 8 months of small-group, individual, and computer-based tutorial support, John has had consistently low grades in math and failed the math section of the fifth-grade TAKS. Although his test results in computation on this evaluation were within normal limits (22nd percentile), he was unable to add three multiple-digit numbers with regrouping or do higher-level arithmetic. Additionally, the results of the CBM monitoring indicated his learning slope was significantly below that of his same-grade peers, and predictions based on the two slopes indicated that the gap between them is increasing.

CONCLUSION

John appears to meet the criteria for a Specific Learning Disability in math calculation.

RECOMMENDATIONS

John had significant difficulties with short-term memory, processing speed, and math fluency. Because of these difficulties, John will likely benefit from the following interventions and accommodations.

Interventions

1. Use Precision Teaching to help John memorize his math facts. Have him complete daily timed drill activities where he competes against his own best score. [See Appendix: Precision Teaching.]
2. Use a program such as the Great Leaps Math Program (www.greatleaps.com) to build fluency in the basic facts, including addition, subtraction, multiplication, and division.
3. To help John increase his speed in math operations, provide drill on math facts using visual stimuli such as flash cards and computer programs. When he can respond to a math fact within 3 seconds, provide further practice with timed worksheets.

Other Accommodations

1. Because John has difficulty performing tasks rapidly, provide him with ample time to complete his work or shorten his assignments so that they can be accomplished within the time allotted.
2. John has difficulty on tasks that require him to manipulate information mentally. Provide strategies and accommodations to reduce the demands placed on working memory.

3. John is more likely to remember lecture content if he can devote his full attention to listening rather than dividing his attention between listening and note taking. To this end, provide him with a copy of the lecture notes or a copy of the notes of a student who is a particularly good note taker.

4. When giving directions for a task or assignment, write the steps on the board so that John can review directions as often as needed.

5. Whenever it is possible, use a game format for learning (e.g., reviewing for a test by playing Jeopardy with the target information). John will find it easier to attend to the information and hold it in his mind long enough to process it more effectively.

BACKGROUND INFORMATION

Cultural Background

Laverne Park, John's teacher, submitted a report (9/2009) providing information regarding John's family and sociological background. According to the report, John's cultural, linguistic, and experiential background have provided him with an environment conducive to the development of positive learning and behavioral patterns. For the current year, John has missed only 1 day of school. Before this year, he had no absences.

Medical and Developmental History

Jane Austin, RN, the school nurse, submitted a health history report in May of last year. John's history reveals no significant problems or events that would affect his ability to profit from educational opportunities. According to John's teacher, his gross-motor skills are age appropriate.

John's father, Robert West, provided the following information (1/2010). John's mother had complications during pregnancy, including anemia, emotional problems, and colds. Both John and his mother had high fevers at delivery and they both stayed at the hospital for 4 days. John met his developmental milestones within normal limits and has enjoyed good health.

Language and Communication Status

Ms. Park rated John's expressive and receptive language proficiency as average (12/2009) within the context of the classroom, such as participating in class discussions.

Emotional Status

Ms. Park (12/2009) indicated that characteristics of John's behavior in school and out of school do not appear to negatively influence his learning or affect his educational placement, programming, or discipline. She also noted that he shows empathy/compassion for others, exhibits organization in accomplishing tasks, and expresses feelings appropriately. She noted that "John seems very happy this year and somewhat more positive. He is actively participating in team group and whole class activities."

John's father provided the following information (1/2010) regarding social-emotional characteristics. He described John as "mostly a loner who sometimes displays passive/aggressive tendencies, but often craves and seeks affection and approval."

EVALUATION PROCEDURES

Test Conditions and Behaviors

Testing was conducted using standard procedures. Rapport was established and maintained adequately for testing. In general, John was cooperative and exerted an appropriate amount of effort. These results are considered to provide a valid estimate of John's current functioning.

All tests administered were scored according to age norms. Results of the WJ III are reported as standard scores, the 68% confidence intervals around them, and percentile ranks. The following verbal labels are associated with each standard score range:

SS Range	<70	70–79	80–89	90–110	111–120	121–130	>130
Verbal Label	Very Low	Low	Low Average	Average	High Average	Superior	Very Superior

The classification of Average encompasses the scores obtained by the middle 50% of the children in the norm sample of age 11 years, 5 months. Also reported is whether or not John's score fell within ±1 standard deviation of the mean, representing the middle 68% of the population. In this case, "within normal limits" indicates that John's score was between the standard scores of 85 and 115. Standard scores that are below 85 are considered to be a normative weakness. This distinction is intended to differentiate between scores that would be considered below average but within one standard deviation and those that fall significantly lower.

Evaluation of Educational Performance Levels

A formal academic evaluation was conducted to determine the presence of any significant educational weaknesses using the WJ III ACH, Form A.

Reading

Cluster	Test	Standard Score	Confidence Interval 68%	Percentile Rank	Classification
Basic Reading Skills		91	90–93	28th	Average
	Letter-Word Identification	89	87–92	24th	Low Average
	Word Attack	94	92–97	35th	Average
	Reading Fluency*	87*	87–92*	19th*	Low Average*
Reading Comprehension		88	85–91	21st	Low Average
	Passage Comprehension	86	83–90	18th	Low Average
	Reading Vocabulary	94	90–97	33rd	Average
*Not included in the cluster.					

The Basic Reading Skills cluster includes sight vocabulary and word attack skills. Letter-Word Identification required John to read words in lists, many of them with irregular pronunciations (e.g., *what, buoyancy*), and Word Attack required him to apply phonics, orthographic, and structural analysis skills in reading nonsense words (e.g, *glimp, franticious*). His performance on these tests was Low Average and Average, respectively, and within normal limits on both. In combination, John's overall basic reading skills are classified as being Average, and within normal limits. He was also given a measure of reading fluency that required him to quickly read simple sentences and decide if the statement was true or false. Although his performance was in the Low Average range, it is considered to be within normal limits.

Reading Comprehension includes reading vocabulary and the ability to comprehend connected discourse while reading. On the Passage Comprehension test, John was required to read a short passage and identify a missing key word that would make sense within the context. His score was Low Average and just within normal limits. On the Reading Vocabulary test, John was required to read words and provide synonyms, read words and provide antonyms, and read three words of an analogy and then provide the fourth word to complete the analogy. His performance on this test was in the Average range. John's overall reading comprehension skills are classified as Low Average range but within normal limits.

In January, Laverne Park, John's teacher, reported that in classroom reading tasks, John has mastered the following skills regarding narrative text: reading a short passage aloud with few errors, describing the setting of a story, describing the feelings and emotions of characters, and recalling details. In expository text, John has not mastered stating the main idea of a paragraph, arranging events in sequential order, or summarizing a selection.

Mathematics

Cluster	Test	Standard Score	Confidence Interval 68%	Percentile Rank	Classification
Math Calculation Skills		82	79–86	12th	Low Average
	Calculation	88	84–94	22nd	Low Average
	Math Fluency	72	69–75	3rd	Low
Math Reasoning		89	86–92	23rd	Low Average
	Applied Problems	90	87–94	26th	Average
	Quantitative Concepts	89	84–93	23rd	Low Average

Math Reasoning includes mathematical knowledge and reasoning. On these tests, John was required to analyze and solve practical mathematical problems (e.g., word problems), demonstrate knowledge of a variety of math-related concepts and applications (e.g., meaning of symbols and abbreviations, calendar use), and analyze number patterns. Results indicated that John's overall math reasoning is Low Average range, but within normal limits.

The Math Calculation cluster is composed of two tests: Calculation, a test of computation in graduated levels of difficulty, and Math Fluency, a test of knowledge and rapid recall of simple math facts. His performance of computation was in the Low Average range. He was able to subtract two 2-digit numbers with regrouping and perform simple addition and multiplication problems. He was unable to add multiple-digit numbers, multiply, or divide with regrouping. John counted on his fingers (surreptitiously, with his hand on his thigh) when he did addition or subtraction and used hatch marks for multiplication. John's automaticity with basic arithmetic facts was significantly lower than his already compromised computation skills. Only 3% of students his age would score as low as or lower than he did. His math fluency was in the Low range and considered a normative weakness.

A review of John's school math assessments was also included in this evaluation. Over the past 2 years, John's TAKS scores have been as follows:

Curricular Area	Items Correct/ Total	Scale Score	Met Standard?
Reading			
2009 (3rd)		2210	Yes
2010 (4th)	35/40 (87%)	2265	Yes
Math			
2009 (3rd)	29/40 (72%)	2124	Yes
2010 (4th)	23/42 (54%)	2005	No
Writing			
2010 (4th)	26/28 (92%)	2311 (C=2)	Yes

In addition, several curriculum-based measures (CBM) were used to further examine John's difficulties with his knowledge of and automaticity with basic math facts. CBM probes (algorithms, not applications) were generated based on the calculation requirements of the Texas Essential Knowledge and Skills (TEKS) at third-, fourth-, and fifth-grade levels. The probes were timed (3 minutes for third and fourth grade and 5 for fifth grade). When these probes were initially given to John, his correct digit scores (digits correct, DC) were 23, 12, and 17, respectively. His higher score on the fifth-grade probe than on the fourth-grade probe was likely due to the increase in time allowed at fifth grade (5 minutes rather than 3 minutes). A few days later, John and his fifth-grade math class took the fourth-grade math probe. John's DC was 15, the second-lowest in the class, compared with the class average of 39. Results of several additional probes are displayed in Figure 1.

Although John managed 39 DC on one probe, his scores are noticeably lower than those of his classmates, and the slope of his trend line does not show him catching up. On a subsequent class probe, the class average increased by 10 (to 49) and John's increased by 2 (to 17). On the previous class probe, the four lowest scores were 8, 15 (John), 15, and 22. In the later probe, the lowest four scores were 17 (John), 24, 26, and 30, indicating that the students who had previously scored similarly to John had made noticeable growth, whereas John did not. A review of John's performance of the CBM probes indicates that his low score was a result of a lack of automaticity with basic math facts and overall slow computation. Figure 1 reports John's digits correct (diamonds) across administrations along with

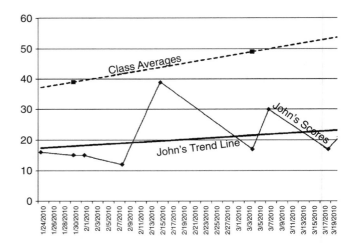

Figure 1   Comparison of John's Math Probe Scores with Class Average

the class averages over the two administrations (squares). The heavy line indicates the overall trend in his scores. Review of the data indicates that John's rate of improvement is lower than that of his peers.

INTELLECTUAL AND ADAPTIVE BEHAVIOR

Intellectual functioning was assessed using the Woodcock-Johnson III NU Tests of Cognitive Ability (WJ III COG), Woodcock-Johnson III NU Diagnostic Supplement (WJ III DS), and one test from the Wechsler Intelligence Scale for Children-Fourth Edition (WISC-IV).

Statistically and educationally significant discrepancies existed among John's strengths and weaknesses in cognitive abilities. Thus, the General Intellectual Ability (GIA) score does not represent a unitary factor and is not interpreted or reported here. Overreliance on this measure would ignore the fact that many of his abilities are within normal limits, whereas others are pronounced weaknesses. The reasoning for this decision is as follows.

People often think of intelligence as a single overall ability, whereas it is actually a combination of many different abilities. Most people perform different sorts of tasks at different levels. As an example, you may be able to put a jigsaw puzzle together expertly but totally unable to remember a phone number. You may be able to solve a complex calculus problem but incompetent at writing an essay comparing and contrasting the American and the French Revolutions. In some cases, a person is able to perform most types of cognitive tasks at levels similar to most other people of the same age (or grade). If just those types of tasks are considered, an overall estimate of cognitive ability—an IQ or GIA—can be interpreted. As an analogy, if a student has an A in all of his classes, you can safely say that he has an A average; if he has a C in all of his classes, he has a C average. But if he has an A in Math, a B in Language Arts, and an F in Reading, of what use is an overall average? Such an average misses the fact that he is performing well in Math, and that he is performing poorly in Reading. With that sort of student, what is important is how well he is doing in each class.

The following tests from the WJ III COG, WJ III DS, and WISC-IV were combined and interpreted using procedures and principles of Cattell-Horn-Carroll (CHC) Cross-Battery Assessment. The CHC Cross-Battery approach provides guidelines so that assessments can use multiple tests to measure a broader range of abilities than might be available on only one battery. This approach is based on current research evidence regarding the structure of human cognitive abilities and their interactions with academic abilities. This approach provides for an analysis of cognitive strengths and weaknesses that results in more focused interventions and accommodations.

Cluster	Test + (CHC ability code)	Standard Score	Confidence Interval 68%	Percentile Rank	Classification
Fluid Reasoning (Gf)		76	73–80	6th	Low
	Concept Formation (I)	71	67–75	3rd	Low
WISC-IV	Matrix Reasoning (I)	70	63–77	2nd	Low
	Inductive Reasoning (Gf-I) cluster*	71*	66–76*	3rd*	Low*
	Analysis-Synthesis (RG)	92	87–97	30th	Average
WJ DS	Number Series (RQ)	90	87–93	25th	Average
WJ DS	Number Matrices (RQ)	84	78–90	15th	Low Average
	Numerical Reasoning (Gf-RQ) cluster	85	81–89	16th	Low Average
Crystallized Intelligence (Gc)		82	79–86	12th	Low Average
	Verbal Comprehension (VL)	84	79–88	14th	Low Average
	General Information (K0)	83	77–88	13th	Low Average
Visual Processing (Gv)		97	93–102	43rd	Average
	Spatial Relations (Vz)	104	100–109	62nd	Average
	Picture Recognition (MV)	92	88–97	30th	Average
Auditory Processing (Ga)		101	96–107	54th	Average
	Sound Blending (PC:S)	101	96–107	53rd	Average
	Auditory Attention (US/U3)	101	93–109	53rd	Average
Short-Term Memory (Gsm)		76	71–81	6th	Low
	Memory for Words (MS)	75	69–81	4th	Low
	Numbers Reversed (MW)	84	79–89	14th	Low Average
Long-Term Retrieval (Glr)		95	90–100	36th	Average
	Visual-Auditory Learning (MA)	96	91–101	40th	Average
	Retrieval Fluency (FI)	95	89–102	38th	Average
Processing Speed (Gs)		78	75–81	7th	Low
	Visual Matching (P)	82	78–86	12th	Low Average
	Decision Speed (R9)	78	74–82	7th	Low

Unless otherwise noted, cluster and test scores were obtained from the WJ III Compuscore software.
*Score calculated by simple arithmetic mean.

Cognitive Strengths

The results of the WJ III COG and WJ III DS indicate that John's abilities in auditory processing, long-term retrieval, visual processing, and deductive reasoning are in the average range compared with age peers, and are within normal limits.

Auditory processing is the ability to analyze, synthesize, and discriminate auditory stimuli, including the ability to process and discriminate speech sounds that may be presented under distorted conditions. Visual processing is the ability to perceive, analyze, synthesize, and think with visual patterns, including the ability to store and recall visual representations. Visual processing as used here does not include processing speed (see below), which focuses on the speed at which visual information is processed. Long-term retrieval is the ability to store information efficiently and retrieve it later through association. Thus, although it is difficult for John to acquire certain types of information, once he has learned it and stored it in long-term memory, he is likely to be able to retrieve it when needed. Deductive reasoning is the ability to use given information and rules to move step by step through a process to solve a problem or come to a conclusion.

Relative Weaknesses

John had considerable difficulty on tasks that measured crystallized intelligence and numerical reasoning. Both were in the Low Average range and are considered normative weaknesses.

Crystallized intelligence represents the breadth and depth of language-based knowledge regarding one's culture, including the ability to verbally communicate that knowledge. John had some difficulty providing synonyms and antonyms for given words and completing analogies. He had similar difficulty telling what certain common objects are used for and where they are typically found (e.g., What do you do with a mop? Where would you find a stamp?). Only 12% of age peers would score as low as or lower than John.

Due to the referral concerns regarding John's math ability, the tests that make up the WJ III DS Numerical Reasoning cluster were also administered. These tests measure quantitative reasoning, the ability to reason with concepts involving mathematical relations and properties. The Number Series test is similar to the second subtest of the Quantitative Concepts test; John was required to look at a series of numbers, identify the pattern, and supply the missing number. On Number Matrices, he was given a two-dimensional matrix of numbers in which he was to analyze the relationships among the numbers in both rows and columns, and provide the missing number. On both tasks John used scratch paper to solve all of the problems. While this method seemed inefficient, at times he exhibited good problem-solving strategies. John's performance on the Numerical Reasoning cluster was in the Low Average range, similar to his performance on the Math Reasoning cluster. His score on Math Reasoning was within normal limits and his score on Numerical Reasoning, on the lower border. Only 16% of age peers would score as low as or lower than John.

Weaknesses

John had significant difficulty performing the tasks measuring processing speed, short-term memory, and inductive reasoning.

The Processing Speed factor represents John's ability to perform simple cognitive tasks rapidly, particularly when under pressure to maintain focused attention. Processing speed allows one to recognize and use visual information quickly and automatically, so that cognitive attention can be directed toward higher-level and more complex skills. John's processing speed was in the Low range, and is classified as a normative weakness. Only 7% of children his age would score as low as or lower than he did.

John also performed in the Low range on the Short-Term Memory factor, which represents John's ability to hold information in immediate awareness and use it within a few seconds, as well as his ability to work with or manipulate the information as it is held in memory. If one has a strong memory, it can help to compensate for slow processing; if one processes information quickly, it can help to compensate for a weak memory. Having a significant weakness in both, however, means that John is more likely to forget information as it is recognized and before it can be adequately processed.

Fluid Reasoning can be thought of as the ability to reason, form concepts, and solve problems using unfamiliar information or novel procedures. It consists of both inductive reasoning, the ability to discover the rule that underlies a specific problem or set of observations, or to apply a previously learned rule to the problem, and deductive reasoning, the ability to use given information and rules to move step by step through a process to solve a problem or come to a conclusion. John's deductive reasoning was in the Average range but his inductive reasoning was in the

Low range and considered a normative weakness. Consequently, the overall Fluid Reasoning cluster score contains two narrow abilities that differ significantly.

To better assess and understand John's functioning in inductive reasoning, a second measure was administered. On the WISC-IV Matrix Reasoning test, John was required to identify the pictures and designs needed to complete a series of matrices. His performance again was in the Low range. Thus, a narrow ability cluster was formed using Concept Formation and Matrix Reasoning. John's Inductive Reasoning cluster score was in the Low range, ranked at the 3rd percentile, and classified as a normative weakness.

Adaptive Behavior

John's adaptive behavior was assessed using informal measures. Results indicated that John's adaptive behavior is age appropriate with no significant weaknesses.

Assistive Technology Needs

Assistive technology needs were considered. Based on the previously addressed competencies, assistive technology devices and services are not recommended for John at this time.

ELIGIBILITY DETERMINATION: SPECIFIC LEARNING DISABILITY

YES ☒ NO ☐ When provided with learning experiences and instruction appropriate for his age or State-approved grade-level standards, he did not adequately meet age or State-approved grade-level standards in one or more of the required areas.

YES ☒ NO ☐ The findings of the group are not primarily the result of a visual, hearing, or motor disability; mental retardation; emotional disturbance; cultural factors; environmental or economic disadvantage; or limited English proficiency.

YES ☒ NO ☐ The group reviewed data that demonstrated that John was provided with appropriate instruction in reading (as described in 20 USC, §6368(3)), and/or mathematics within the general education setting delivered by qualified personnel and data-based documentation of repeated assessments of achievement at reasonable intervals, reflecting formal evaluation of his progress during instruction.

YES ☒ NO ☐ John has been determined through a variety of assessment tools and strategies to meet the criteria for a specific learning disability. He exhibits a pattern of strengths and weaknesses in performance, achievement, or both, relative to age, grade-level standards, or intellectual ability, as indicated by significant variance among specific areas of cognitive function or between specific areas of cognitive function and academic achievement.

ASSURANCES

The Multidisciplinary Team assures that:

1. A variety of assessment tools and strategies were used to gather relevant functional, developmental, and academic information.

2. No single measure or assessment was used as the sole criterion for determining whether John is a child with a disability.

3. Assessments and other evaluation materials used to assess John were selected and administered so as to not be discriminatory on a racial, cultural, or sexual basis; provided and administered in the language and form most likely to yield accurate information on what he knows and can do academically, developmentally, and functionally; were used for purposes for which the assessments or measures are valid and reliable; administered by trained and knowledgeable personnel; and administered in accordance with instructions provided by the producer of the assessments.

4. Assessments and other evaluation materials included those tailored to assess specific areas of educational need and not merely those that are designed to provide a single general intelligence quotient.

5. John was assessed in all areas of suspected disability.

6. Assessments and instruments were selected and administered so as to best ensure that the results accurately reflected his aptitude or achievement level or whatever factors the test purports to measure, rather than reflecting his impaired sensory, manual, or speaking skills.

7. The evaluation is sufficiently comprehensive to identify all of his special education and related service needs, whether or not commonly linked to the disability category in which he may have been classified.

8. Assessment tools and strategies that provide relevant information that directly assists persons in determining John's educational needs were provided.

9. The group that collected and/or reviewed evaluation data included his general education teacher and at least one person qualified to conduct individual diagnostic examinations of children.

10. John was observed in his learning environment.

Based on the data presented in this report, John appears to meet the disability condition criteria for Learning Disability.

Signature of Core Evaluation Team Members

	Agree	Disagree
_____	_____	_____
Signature of General Education Teacher		
_____	_____	_____
Signature of Person Trained/Certified in the area of Learning Disabilities		
_____	_____	_____
Signature of Assessment Specialist		

Note: If a team member disagrees with the conclusions reflected in the report, he/she must submit a separate statement presenting his/her objections.

CASE 31

Sweet Child (But Only When Not in School)

Mitchel D. Perlman

This assessment is an Independent Educational Evaluation referred by the current school district, which recognized its inability to provide a fair assessment of a child this complex. Using a Scientist-Clinician model, academic, special education, and medical files are reexamined and reinterpreted, through the blending of research knowledge, theoretical sophistication, and clinical expertise. As such, neuropsychological and psychodiagnostic issues are ruled in/out in a manner that promoted *buy-in* of the recommendations by both school district and parent. In fact, due to the comprehensive nature of the assessment, to the examiner's rapport with both the family and the district, and to both the district and parent clearly wanting what was appropriate for the child, the recommendations were implemented and the child's primary issues resolved.

NEUROPSYCHOLOGICAL/ PSYCHODIAGNOSTIC EVALUATION

Name:	Larry Robeson
Date of Birth:	May 2, 1998
Age:	11 years, 6 months
Grade:	5
Date:	November 19, 2009
Examiner:	Mitchel D. Perlman, Ph.D.

REASON FOR REFERRAL

Larry is a very sweet preadolescent who has been struggling at school with holding his emotions in check. This assessment was requested to determine how best to support him.

TESTS ADMINISTERED

Cognitive/Neurological

Kaufman Assessment Battery for Children, Second Edition (KABC-II)

NEPSY-II

- Language tasks: Phonological Processing, Speeded Naming
- Memory tasks: Narrative Memory

Delis-Kaplan Executive Function System (D-KEFS)

- Trail Making, Color-Word Interference, Twenty Questions, Tower

Rapid Automatized Naming & Rapid Alternating Stimulus Tests (RAN/RAS)

Test of Orthographic Competence (TOC)

Woodcock-Johnson III NU Tests of Cognitive Abilities (WJ III COG)

- Processing Speed tasks: Decision Speed, Visual Matching
- Memory tasks: Numbers Reversed, Auditory Working Memory

California Verbal Learning Test—Children's Edition (CVLT-C)

Achievement

Kaufman Test of Educational Achievement, Second Edition (KTEA-II)

- Written Language subtests: Reading Comprehension, Written Expression
- Oral Language subtests: Listening Comprehension, Oral Expression

Test of Written Language (TOWL-4)

Woodcock-Johnson III NU Tests of Achievement (WJ III ACH)

* Academic Fluency subtests: Reading Fluency, Math Fluency

Social/Emotional

Millon Pre-Adolescent Clinical Inventory (M-PACI)

Rorschach Inkblot Test (Rorschach)

DESCRIPTIVE CHARACTERISTICS

For the purpose of clarity and semantic continuity, I describe the descriptive labels used for the score ranges.

Labels Used in Describing Scores

Descriptors	Standard Scores (SS)	Scaled Scores (ScS)	Percentiles
Severely Deficient	<70	1	<2
Well Below Average	70 to 79	4 to 5	2 to 8
Below Average	80 to 89	6 to 7	9 to 24
Average	90 to 109	8 to 12	25 to 74
Above Average	110 to 119	13 to 14	75 to 90
Well Above Average (Superior)	120 to 129	15 to 16	91 to 97
Very Superior (Gifted)	130+	17 to 19	98 and above
Standard scores (SS) have mean of 100 and a standard deviation of 15. Scaled scores (ScS) have a mean of 10 and a standard deviation of 3.			

PERTINENT HISTORY

The information below was provided to me by Larry's parents and his school district. Primarily, I concentrated on the previous assessments where either standard scores or percentiles were provided. If they were not reported by previous examiners, I computed the standard scores and/or percentile ranks from the provided scaled scores.

Larry's mother reported that her pregnancy was unremarkable until about 4 weeks before the expected due date. Around that time, she developed high blood pressure, resulting in labor being induced 2 weeks early. A vaginal delivery with forceps occurred, whereupon it was discovered that the cord was wrapped twice around Larry's neck and shoulder, which caused him to be in distress. Still,

Larry was judged to be healthy at birth, weighing 4 lbs. 8 oz. and being 17¾ inches long. Based on the doctor's orders, Larry was fed every 3 hours for the first few months of his life.

Developmental milestones occurred at age-appropriate intervals. Larry crawled at 9 months, sat unassisted at 8 months, stood at 10 months, walked at 14 months, and spoke in sentences at 18 to 24 months. When Larry developed speech, he talked and constantly questioned "why" to just about everything. In fact, he still does. As an infant, Larry was extremely sensitive to sunlight. As a toddler, Larry was strong-willed, independent, and had an outgoing personality (he still does). Also, he disliked certain food textures; he didn't like wearing socks or shoes; and he would cry or have tantrums in response to loud noises. Today, he still suffers from these same sensitivities.

Larry attended the Weir Academy for 2 years of preschool and 1 of kindergarten. He continued to be strong-willed and inquisitive, and he was somewhat of a perfectionist. Regarding the latter, for example, when the students were learning how to write, Larry fixated on how well his letters looked. He erased and rewrote the letters until they were perfect, typically leaving holes in the paper. Larry got along well with other children, but only if he were the leader and made the rules.

After three-fourths of the kindergarten school year passed, his mother discovered that Larry was running from class—something that had started in preschool but had never been shared with her. By the end of the school year, Larry's mother and the staff at Weir Academy felt Larry was too emotionally immature to move on to first grade. Both academically and socially, Larry's kindergarten year was not successful. Larry's mother opted then to have him repeat kindergarten and receive tutoring for reading at the Paul Allen Learning Center.

Kindergarten (Repeat), 2004/2005 School Year

Larry repeated kindergarten the following year but transferred schools to the Van Diven Prep School (also a private school). He continued to be tutored at the Paul Allen Learning Center as well. About three-fourths of the way through the school year, Larry was asked not to return. The school believed Larry required supports that they could not provide.

Larry was assessed by Dr. Douglas, a child psychologist, in April 2005. The assessment was primarily by interview and by behavioral reports. Dr. Douglas noted that

Larry had difficulty with impulse control, attention, and cognitive flexibility. He made a list of recommendations for school-based behavioral interventions, many of which are still salient today (see prior report for detail).

Dr. Douglas also recommended that Larry be assessed further by his school district and by Dr. Watson, from the ADHD Solutions Center. Accordingly, Larry's mother requested that the school district assess Larry for learning disabilities, ADHD, sensory dysfunction, and organizational difficulties.

A special education referral form was completed. His teacher noted that Larry was hyperactive and impulsive, had poor anger control, and had already been suspended for making threatening remarks after a child had hit him.

A conference took place on April 19, 2005. Larry's teacher expressed concern over Larry's lack of self-control, his impulsive behaviors, and his use of inappropriate language. Additionally, he did not communicate in a positive manner with teachers or peers. No action plan was associated with that meeting.

Additional information was gathered from Larry's teacher on April 28, 2005. His teacher noted that Larry was performing at grade level in all academic areas. He was rated as being "Somewhat Below Grade Level" in Art and in PE, and as being "Far Below Grade Level" in Center and in Social Time. Additionally, Larry "often"

- Argued
- Was defiant and/or talked back to staff
- Was disobedient
- Disturbed others
- Disrupted class
- Was mean to others
- Had difficulty getting along with others
- Was impulsive
- Talked out of turn or too much
- Was inattentive
- Had difficulty following directions
- Broke school rules
- Had strange behaviors and strange ideas
- Was stubborn
- Felt hurt when criticized
- Had sudden changes in mood
- Was nervous or tense
- Couldn't get his mind off certain thoughts
- Was worried

- Was suspicious
- Screamed a lot
- Had temper tantrums
- Threatened others
- Was unusually loud
- Displayed explosive and unpredictable behaviors
- Demanded a lot of attention

District testing took place in early May and the report was prepared in early June. Through observations of Larry in class and during the assessment, the examiner noted that Larry had little regard for personal space and did not consider how his behavior affected others. Regarding the latter, though, the examiner noted that Larry did not appear to be either uncaring or oppositional.

While the initial testing session proceeded without incident, the sessions that followed were increasingly less fruitful. Larry became increasingly upset when he perceived he was not performing well; his thinking became increasingly rigid to the point that he demanded things proceed as he thought they should; and he refused to continue a task until the examiner told him whether or not he was correct on the item. Larry was so resistant to the TAPS-R when it was administered, that the examiner chose not complete all of the subtests.

To provide estimates of Larry's intelligence, the examiner administered a brief IQ test: the Kaufman Brief Intelligence Test (KBIT-2). Overall on the KBIT-2, Larry performed solidly Average (standard score of 102, 55th percentile). The best estimate of his intelligence on the KBIT-2, though, may have been from the Nonverbal Index, which was Above Average.

Kaufman Brief Intelligence Test (KBIT-2)

	SS	%ile		SS	%ile
Verbal	92	30	Nonverbal	111	77

Auditory processing was further assessed using the Test of Auditory Perceptual Skills—Revised (TAPS-R). Those results follow, for the most part suggesting Average auditory processing (Composite of 100, 50th percentile).

Test of Auditory Perceptual Skills (TAPS-R)

	SS	%ile		SS	%ile
Numbers Forward	102	55	Sentence Memory	110	75
Numbers Reversed	103	58	Interpret Directions	101	53
			Auditory Processing	85	16

Fine-motor skills were addressed using the Beery-Buktenica Developmental Test of Visual-Motor Integration, Fifth Edition (Beery VMI). Larry's performance was Below Average (standard score of 81, 10th percentile).

Academic achievement was estimated using the Woodcock-Johnson III NU Tests of Achievement (WJ III ACH). Larry's Reading was Below Average; his Writing, Average; and his Math, Above Average.

Woodcock-Johnson III Tests of Achievement (WJ III ACH)

	SS	%ile		SS	%ile
Reading			**Mathematics**		
Letter-Word Identification	89	23	Calculation	113	81
Passage Comprehension	80	9	Applied Problems	98	45
Written Language					
Spelling	97	42			

Social-emotional functioning was addressed by mother and teacher separately completing the BASC inventory (predecessor to the BASC-2). Both reported multiple areas of social-emotional concern.

Behavior Assessment Scale for Children (BASC)

Externalizing Problems	Mom Teacher	Internalizing Problems	Mom Teacher
Hyperactivity	** **	Anxiety	*
Aggression	** **	Depression	** **
Conduct	**	Somatization	* *
Adaptive Skills		**Additional Areas**	
Adaptability		Atypicality	** *
Social Skills		Withdrawal	
Leadership	*	Attention	
		Learning Problems	n/a

*At-Risk (*T* score 60–69)   **Clinically Significant (*T* score 70+)

The Individualized Education Plan (IEP) team met on June 21, 2005 to discuss the above assessment. The district (primarily school psychologist) did not believe that Larry met the eligibility requirements for special education. Oddly, the district's recommendation seemed to suggest that Larry would need to be placed in a public school program before they would consider qualifying (or reevaluating) him. The report concluded: "The team recommends a reevaluation if he is unsuccessful in a public school classroom."

On June 25, 2005, Larry was evaluated at La Paloma Therapy Services for Occupational Therapy with the test of visual perceptual skills (TVPS). The examiner did not believe Larry qualified for educationally based occupational therapy services.

In addition to the TVPS, the Beery VMI was readministered. Larry performed considerably higher on that instrument than he did when the district administered it less than 2 months earlier. Previously he performed Below Average; at the June administration, he performed Above Average (standard score of 119, 98th percentile). Larry performed quite well on the TVPS, as well, with half of his scores in the Superior to Very Superior ranges. Overall, in fact, Larry's Composite score was Superior (standard score of 122, 93rd percentile). Notably, the contrasting findings between the TAPS-R and the TVPS were consistent with Larry's differential performance on the Verbal and Nonverbal Indexes from the KBIT-2. Clearly, Larry excelled in nonverbal skills.

Test of Visual Perceptual Skills (TVPS)

TVPS Results

	SS	%ile		SS	%ile
Visual Discrimination	120	91	Visual Sequential	137	99
Visual Memory	104	61	Visual Figure Ground	108	70
Visual-Spatial Relations	113	81	Visual Closure	95	37
Visual Form Constancy	130	98			

Dr. Watson, at the ADHD Solution Center, officially diagnosed Larry with ADHD from a compilation of tests he took. Due to the severity of Larry's ADHD, she recommended Larry be tested at the Saddlebrook Clinic prior to a referral to a psychiatrist for a drug treatment regimen.

Larry was evaluated at the Saddlebrook Clinic on July 8, 2005. The examiner noted that, per mother's observations, Larry had always been extremely strong-willed and had a hard time accepting "No." Often, he became fixated on a certain notion or way of thinking and was unable to shift his perspective. In school, Larry became quickly frustrated, which led to emotional outbursts. He constantly misinterpreted the intentions/actions of his peers, which led to aggressive encounters. The examiner believed that Larry showed signs of both attention and mood disorders.

Larry's kindergarten report card suggested his academics were fine. He was rated less well, however, for Self-Control and for Sportsmanship (Larry struggled with losing).

First Grade, 2005/2006 School Year

A vision therapy evaluation took place on February 3, 2006, with Dr. Holmes. As part of that evaluation, the Beery VMI was readministered. Larry performed solidly Average (47th percentile). Dr. Holmes, though, found Larry to have deficiencies with eye-movement control, with focusing ability, with eye-teaming, with visual planning and sequencing, with motor development, with body schema, and with visual logic. An individualized program of vision therapy was recommended. The optometrist also recommended therapy by a registered occupational therapist specializing in sensory-motor integration. Larry was fitted with special glasses to compensate for his visual deficiencies. He also underwent 6 months of vision therapy, but he was resistant and little improvement resulted.

On February 10, 2006, Larry was evaluated by his school district for speech-language therapy. The speech-language pathologist (SLP) noted difficulties with articulation/phonology and recommended speech-language therapy.

A referral for a special education assessment was made on March 1, 2006. The referral noted that Larry's social skills impacted his peer relationships, and that he required rather high degrees of attention. Academically, Larry knew his phonics, but he was poor at applying phonics to reading and spelling. Larry continued his tutoring after school for reading at the Paul Allen Learning Center, and later at Sylvan.

To provide estimates of Larry's intelligence, the Wechsler Intelligence Scale for Children (WISC-IV) and the Naglieri Nonverbal Ability Test (NNAT) were administered. On the former, overall Larry performed solidly Average (standard score of 103, 58th percentile). Again, though, Larry performed higher on the nonverbal index (Perceptual Reasoning of 112, 79th percentile), which was consistent with the results from the NNAT (117, 87th percentile) and with the Nonverbal Index from the Kaufman Brief Intelligence Test, Second Edition (KBIT-2) (previously administered). At that time, then, Larry's intelligence could clearly be categorized as being Above Average.

Wechsler Intelligence Scale for Children – Fourth Edition (WISC-IV)

	SS/ScS	%ile		SS/ScS	%ile
Verbal Comprehension	100	50	**Perceptual Reasoning**	112	79
Similarities	9	37	Block Design	11	63
Vocabulary	11	63	Picture Concepts	11	63
Comprehension	11	63	Matrix Reasoning	14	91
Working Memory	88	21	**Processing Speed**	103	58
Digit Span	9	37	Coding	12	75
Letter/Number Sequence	7	16	Symbol Search	9	37

Visual processing was further addressed by the Motor-Free Visual Perception Test, Third Edition (MVPT-3), and by the Developmental Test of Visual Perception, Second Edition (DTVP-2). Larry performed Above Average on the former (110, 75th percentile), and Average to Superior on the latter. Those performances were consistent with Larry's performance on previous assessments of his visual processing.

Developmental Test of Visual Perception, Second Edition (DTVP-2)

	SS	%ile		SS	%ile
Eye-Hand Coordination	100	50	Visual Closure	115	84
Position in Space	120	91	Visual-Motor Speed	125	95
Copying	100	50	Form Constancy	105	63
Figure-Ground	100	50	VM Integration	115	84
Spatial Relations	120	91			

To address aspects regarding Larry's language processing, the Comprehensive Test of Phonological Processing (CTOPP) was administered along with the oral language subtests from the Wechsler Individual Achievement Test (WIAT-II). Larry performed about Average in each language area assessed: listening comprehension, oral expression, phonological awareness, phonological memory, and rapid automatized naming.

Comprehensive Test of Phonological Processing (CTOPP)

	SS/ScS	%ile			SS/ScS	%ile
Phonological Awareness	**100**	**50**	**Phonological Memory**		**103**	**58**
Elision	9	37	Memory for Digits		11	63
Blending Words	11	63	Nonword Repetition		10	50
Rapid Naming	**91**	**27**				
Rapid Digit Naming	9	37				
Rapid letter Naming	8	25				

Fine-motor skills were addressed using the Bender-Gestalt II and the Bruininks-Oseretsky Test of Motor Proficiency (Bruininks). Larry performed Above Average on the Bender Gestalt II (standard score of 116, 86th percentile). Standard scores and percentiles from the Bruininks were not reported, but Larry was at age level on both subtests administered.

Academic Achievement was addressed using the WIAT-II. For the most part, Larry's academic achievement was Average.

Wechsler Individual Achievement Test (WIAT-II)

	SS	%ile			SS	%ile
Reading	**87**	**19**	**Mathematics**		**95**	**37**
Word Reading	91	27	Numerical Operation		92	30
Reading Comprehension	92	30	Math Reasoning		101	53
Pseudoword Reading	87	19				
Written Language	**99**	**47**	**Oral Language**		**105**	**63**
Spelling	98	45	Listening Comp		103	58
Written Expression	103	58	Oral Expression		107	68

The BASC-2 (the renormed version of the BASC) was completed separately by mother and by teacher. Again, both noted several pertinent social-emotional issues (related to ADHD, problems with mood, conduct, related to social adjustment, and more).

Behavior Assessment Scale for Children (BASC-2)

Externalizing Problems	Mom	Teacher	Internalizing Problems	Mom	Teacher
Hyperactivity	**	*	Anxiety	*	**
Aggression	**	*	Depression	*	**
Conduct	**		Somatization		
Adaptive Skills	**Mom**	**Teacher**	**Additional Areas**	**Mom**	**Teacher**
Adaptability	*	**	Atypicality	**	*
Social Skills	*		Withdrawal		
Leadership	**		Attention	**	*
ADLs (home/school)	*		Learning Problems		
Functional Communication					

*At-Risk (*T* score 60–69)   **Clinically Significant (*T* score 70+)

The examiner noted Larry's social emotional struggles, many of which were evident empirically on the BASC-2, as well. The examiner, though, hesitated to qualify Larry for special education on the basis of having an emotional disability.

Larry was referred for a second opinion regarding whether he required vision therapy. Dr. Cohen evaluated Larry on May 1, 2006. He found many of the same difficulties that were evident on the earlier evaluation by Dr. Holmes and recommended a regimen of vision therapy, as well. The IEP team convened to discuss the above assessments on May 12, 2006. Larry was found eligible for special education under the category of Speech Language Impairment (SLI), for which he was offered 12 hours per year of speech-language therapy. Narratives of the initial progress reports suggested relatively good academic progress and relatively good behavior. Those progress reports, though, underreported Larry's behavioral difficulties, which were reflected on the report cards, below.

For a portion of the first trimester, Larry was in the Washington Union School District. Larry was rated as being Below Satisfactory in Reading, and as being Below Satisfactory in:

- Working well independently
- Working well collaboratively
- Talking at appropriate times
- Completing and returning class work on time
- Listening to and following directions

- Respecting the rights and property of others
- Accepting responsibility for his own actions
- Following classroom rules
- Using time wisely

Larry transferred to the Westin Valley Unified School District. No academic problems were reported, but "sometimes" Larry did not:

- Use time productively
- Follow directions
- Work cooperatively in a group
- Respect authority
- Respect others
- Demonstrate responsible behavior in classroom
- Demonstrate responsible behavior out of class

Larry again was compared to his peers by a behavior color chart. Mother noted that Larry was continually despondent at school, about his clip being in the red zone.

Second Grade, 2006/2007 School Year

Larry transferred to the Gibsonville School District during the second grade. He appeared to have performed well that school year (academics and behavior), with the exception of one incident of fighting that occurred on April 6, 2007. Larry was accepted into the GATE program, after scoring within the Gifted range on the previous district's testing.

Third Grade, 2007/2008 School Year

The IEP team convened on July 18, 2007, suggesting positive behaviors up until that point in that new school year. After, though, Larry was suspended on several occasions:

- On August 15, 2007, for "wishing a boy dead"
- On October 5, 2007, for running
- On November 1, 2007, for impeding a teacher's hand while she was trying to call the front office
- On November 21, 2007, for telling Dr. Hall he was leaving
- On February 13, 2008, for refusing to get out from underneath his desk
- On March 21, 2008, for running and being noncompliant
- On June 25, 2008, for throwing a chair

In fact, between August 5, 2007, and June 25, 2008, Larry was suspended for 17 days, and had three other disciplinary infractions for which he was not suspended. In addition to the suspensions, for the entire month of February 2008, the principal had Larry placed on half days to deescalate his behaviors. After-school tutoring continued at Sylvan for reading.

Larry was then evaluated at the Franklyn Behavioral Institute on November 19, 2007. For that evaluation, the Child Behavior Checklist (CBCL) and the Conners' Rating Scale – Revised (Conners') were completed. The Test of Variables of Attention (T.O.V.A.) (a computerized vigilance test for ADHD) was administered as well. Social-emotional difficulties were evident on the CBCL, and difficulties suggesting ADHD were evident on the Conners' and on the T.O.V.A. The examiner recommended neurofeedback to assist with attention. Larry completed the neurofeedback treatments and finished a 6-week course of Fast ForWord (an auditory/language processing program) without any observable benefits.

Child Behavior Checklist (CBCL)

Internalizing	**		Externalizing	**
Anxious/Depressed	*		Rule-Breaking Behavior	*
Withdrawn			Aggressive Behavior	*
Somatic Complaints	**			
Other				
Social Problems	*			
Thought Problems	**			
Attention Problems	**			
*At-Risk (*T* score 65–69) **Clinically Significant (*T* score 70+)				

A progress report was written on December 10, 2007. No academic difficulties were evident. Behaviorally, though, Larry exhibited the following behaviors:

- Did not follow directions
- Interrupted teacher and/or classmates
- Exhibited disrespectful behaviors toward self, peers, and/or teacher
- Showed lack of effort on assignments
- Had a poor attitude toward his learning

An assessment for special education took place in December 2007. Several incidents occurred during the evaluation, the observation, and the test administration. During the observation, the class was to take a test, and

Larry insisted that he be allowed to use his book. His teacher gave him his note cards, which Larry promptly tossed across the room. Larry disrupted the class for another 5 minutes before being escorted to the office by the assistant principal.

Things did not proceed smoothly with the assessment either. Each testing day became progressively more difficult. Larry eventually raged. When the examiner marked "don't know" to an item Larry did not know, Larry tried to erase what the examiner had written. He yelled and screamed statements such as "I despise you. Why can't you just listen? Just be quiet. I wish I could just rip your mouth off." Larry also threw objects, kicked chairs, and could not be soothed. Larry's behavior during the assessment, in concert with the results from the BASC-2 (Table 14), led the examiner to recommend Larry be qualified for special education under the category of ED (Emotional Disturbance).

To provide estimates about Larry's intelligence, the WISC-IV was readministered. Again, the Full Scale (102, 55th percentile) likely underestimated Larry's true intellectual ability. The Perceptual Reasoning Index (nonverbal) best estimated Larry's IQ, which again was Above Average (standard score of 117, 87th percentile).

Notably, at the previous assessment Larry performed Average in Processing Speed, but Below Average in Working Memory. At this latter assessment using the WISC-IV, the opposite occurred.

Wechsler Intelligence Scale for Children (WISC-IV)

	SS/ScS	%ile		SS/ScS	%ile
Verbal Comprehension	99	47	**Perceptual Reasoning**	117	87
Similarities	9	37	Block Design	10	50
Vocabulary	11	63	Picture Concepts	13	84
Comprehension	10	50	Matrix Reasoning	15	95
Working Memory	102	55	**Processing Speed**	80	9
Digit Span	11	63	Coding	7	16
Letter/Number Sequence	10	50	Symbol Search	6	9

Again Larry's social-emotional functioning was assessed using the BASC-2, and again multiple issues were noted (including issues related to ADHD and to a mood disturbance).

Behavior Assessment Scale for Children (BASC-2)

Externalizing Problems	Mom	Teacher	Internalizing Problems	Mom	Teacher
Hyperactivity	**	**	Anxiety	*	
Aggression	*	**	Depression	*	**
Conduct	**	*	Somatization		

Adaptive Skills	Mom	Teacher	Additional Areas	Mom	Teacher
Adaptability		**	Atypicality		
Social Skills		*	Withdrawal		
Leadership		*	Attention	n/a*	
ADLs (home/ school)		*	Learning Problems	n/a	
Functional Communication	*	*			

*At-Risk (*T* score 60–69)   **Clinically Significant (*T* score 70+)

A Behavior Support Plan (BSP) was written on December 13, 2007. The target related to Larry defying or bargaining with his teacher to achieve the outcome he wanted. As recorded, the behavior occurred two to five times per hour, and lasted as long as the activity that had initiated the behavior was still taking place (estimated to be between 5 minutes to 2 hours).

A privately funded speech-language evaluation took place on December 14, 2007. The Lindamood Auditory Conceptualization Test (LAC) and the Clinical Evaluation of Language Fundamentals (CELF-4) were administered. Larry performed well on the majority of the testing but also performed Below Average in a few areas from the CELF-4. Speech-language therapy was recommended. In fact, the Fast ForWord program was recommended specifically, which was odd as Larry did not perform poorly in the area typically addressed by that program.

Clinical Evaluation of Language Fundamentals (CELF-4)

Subtest	SS/ScS	%ile	Subtest	SS/ScS	%ile
Receptive Language	96	39	**Expressive Language**	98	45
Word Classes Receptive	7	16	Word Classes Expressive	7	16
Understanding Spoken Paragraphs	6	9	Expressive Vocabulary	6	9
Recalling Sentences	11	63	Formulated Sentences	11	63

The IEP team convened for its annual review on December 18, 2007. Larry was noted to be strong in Math, average in Reading, low in Written Language. It was his social-emotional functioning, though, that was believed to be impeding him from accessing the general education classroom without specialized support. Therefore, ED was listed as being his primary condition, and Specific Language Impairment (SLI) was listed as being secondary. Larry was offered

- Consultative support — 9 times per year — 20 minutes each
- Speech language therapy — 25 times per year — 30 minutes each

A referral for mental health services via AB-2726 was made, and a report by County Mental Health was written on April 15, 2008. Larry qualified for mental health services based on his problematic behaviors that interfered with his education. Group Therapy was recommended for a single 60-minute session weekly, which was later added onto Larry's IEP.

The Writing portion of the WIAT-II was administered on April 23, 2008. Larry obtained Average Spelling but Below Average Written Expression. That latter finding, especially, suggested a possible drop in this skill since the previous administration of that subtest in March 2006.

Wechsler Individual Achievement Test (WIAT-II)

	March 2006			April 2008	
	SS	%ile		SS	%ile
Spelling	98	45		94	34
Written Expression	103	58		86	18

The IEP team reconvened on June 5, 2008, and an addendum to the annual IEP was written. The team agreed that Larry needed an instructional assistant for up to 3 hours of his school day. That service was to begin the next school semester for a 45-day trial period.

Fourth Grade, 2008/2009 School Year

The IEP team reconvened with Larry's fourth-grade teacher on July 8, 2008. The meeting was to brainstorm ideas regarding how to minimize Larry's frustrations and meltdowns. As writing had historically been an area of frustration for Larry, a goal was written for writing, and he was offered resource room (RSP) services for a minimum of 20 minutes four times per week.

The IEP team reconvened on July 21, 2008, to add into the IEP the mental health services recommended. Complying with adults and not trying to bargain with them was added as being the goal. To assist, 16 sessions of group therapy (60 minutes each) were offered. The plan was to reevaluate continuing need after those sessions were completed.

The IEP team reconvened on September 3, 2008, to discuss Larry's services. The school psychologist noted that Larry required constant redirection. All services were retained.

Larry was suspended for 1 day for an incident that took place on November 26, 2008, for running, defiance, and not following directions. He received recess detention for 3 days for defiance and inappropriate language on December 4, 2008. The IEP team convened for its annual review on December 10, 2008. Notes reflect that the district's behavioral consultant would address Larry's issues. Larry's parents requested a functional analysis assessment (FAA). Larry continued to be eligible for special education under ED (primary) and SLI (secondary). The following services were offered:

Resource Specialist	99 times per yr.	20 min. each
Instructional Aide	15 hours per wk.	1 hr. each (3 hrs. per day)
Behavior Specialist	30 per wk.	5 days (6 hrs. per day)
County Mental Health	1 time per wk.	1 hr. each
Language Support, Consult	30 times per yr.	25 min. each

The IEP team reconvened on April 16, 2009, to discuss the FAA. On May 1, 2009, Larry called his teacher a name, for which he received a 2-day recess detention.

A school-based occupational therapy evaluation took place on June 19, 2009. Portions of the Bruininks were readministered. No difficulties were noted. The Sensory Profile, though, was completed, and numerous sensory issues were noted.

Bruininks-Oseretsky Test of Motor Proficiency (Bruininks)

Subtest	SS	%ile		Subtest	SS	%ile
Fine Manual Control	124	95		Manual Coordination	104	62

Larry's report card recorded his grades without behavioral ratings. He was lowest in Reading (C− to C+).

Fifth Grade, 2009/2010 School Year

The IEP team reconvened on July 24, 2009, to discuss the above occupational therapy results. Occupational therapy was added to the IEP (10 times per year, 30 minutes each session). The IEP team reconvened on September 8, 2009. The Behavior Support Plan (BSP) was revised, and County Mental Health added for individual counseling 1 hour per week.

On July 31, 2009, Larry was suspended for running. On September 4, 2009, he received an in-house suspension for noncompliance and for using inappropriate language.

On October 7, 2009, Larry perceived his classmates to be laughing at him when his teacher was correcting him for an assignment he had done incorrectly at home. Larry became defiant toward his teacher and made a threatening statement: "I'm going to murder everyone tomorrow." The police were called and they transported Larry from school to a psychiatric hospital. He was evaluated and released from that facility right away. For that incident, Larry was suspended for 5 days with a recommendation for expulsion. On October 14, 2009, the Manifestation Hearing determined the incident of October 7 to be a product of his disability. The recommendation for expulsion, therefore, was denied. Larry has not returned to school since, and has been on Home Hospital (i.e., instructed by a public school teacher in the home) pending the results of this current assessment.

Group-Administered Academic Achievement Tests

Group-administered achievement tests are typically administered to all students by private and public schools alike. At times, patterns of strengths and weaknesses can be determined from them by comparing performances between and across school years, and between and across subjects. A cautious approach, though, should be used when interpreting those scores, because group-administered testing cannot account for a variety of conditional possibilities, such as varying attention and differing environmental testing conditions.

Also, different mental processes are called on for academic success throughout elementary school years. For example, math computation does not call on sequential processing until computations require several steps, such as with borrowing and regrouping. Thus, a child may perform quite well on those tasks in kindergarten and first grade, but if that child is less adept at sequential processing, his/her scores on the math computation section may substantially decline thereafter.

Group testing results were available for grades 2 through 4. Larry typically performed well, although he was rated as being below proficient in English Language Arts (ELA) when he was last tested.

Group Achievement

	ELA	Math
2nd Grade	**	***
3rd Grade	**	***
4th Grade	*	**
* Basic **Proficient ***Advanced		

TEST RESULTS

Behavior Observations/Interviews

Larry is such a sweet boy that it is difficult to picture what has been described of him in the files. He was extremely respectful during the entire test administration, which took 3 hours on one day and 6 hours on another day. Not once did he complain or try to avoid completing a task, and his level of effort and motivation never wavered. It was clear, also, that Larry loved the one-on-one adult attention afforded by the testing setting. He was energetic, animated, curious, and engaged.

Larry did, though, appear to struggle when it became clear to him that he was not successful on several items in a row. He never shut down, however, in part because I was cautious to follow up rather quickly with tasks in which I predicted he would experience success.

In discussing Larry with his parents, it seemed to me that his greatest difficulties at school have occurred when strong emotions arise. When Larry feels overwhelmed (especially if he perceives he is being treated unfairly or is being misunderstood), it is extremely difficult for him to stop, to back away, to rethink the situation, and/or to make good choices for himself on how to respond (or not respond). Instead, he becomes exceptionally disagreeable, his tongue gets the best of him, and he bolts. Afterward Larry feels remorse, regret, and even embarrassment.

Interestingly, the behaviors seen at school are almost exclusively unique to that situation. At home Larry can be a handful, but he is always manageable. His mother explained that they use meaningful reinforcers that serve to motivate Larry to persevere over his challenges.

Cognitive Assessment

I administered several test batteries and a variety of specific tasks that are sensitive to neuropsychological issues and concerns. Those test batteries included the Kaufman Assessment Battery for Children (KABC-II) and selected tasks from the NEPSY-II, the Delis-Kaplan Executive Function System (D-KEFS), and the Woodcock-Johnson III Tests of Cognitive Ability (WJ III COG).

The KABC-II is grounded in two theoretical models: one that focuses on the integration of and interplay between the neuropsychological processes addressed by the Sequential, Simultaneous, Learning, and Planning Scales; and one that takes into account aspects of Crystallized and Fluid Intelligence, as well, by the inclusion of the Knowledge Scale. The former yields a Mental Processing Index (MPI); the latter a Fluid-Crystallized Index (FCI).

Grounded in developmental and neuropsychological theory, the NEPSY-II, in part, was developed to assess complex capacities and their basic subcomponents, so that deficiencies and proficiencies across various learning domains could be assessed. Those domains include Attention and Executive Function, Language, Memory and Learning, Sensorimotor, Visuospatial, and Social Perception. The D-KEFS measures various aspects specific to executive function, which is the ability to draw on fundamental (primary) cognitive skills for the purpose of generating higher levels of creative and abstract thought. The WJ III COG addresses a variety of very specific mental processes, depending on the specific clusters of tests administered.

Importantly, I did not alter the standardized test administration procedures to accommodate Larry in any way. Also, a working rapport was easily established and maintained, and Larry approached the tasks with consistent and sustained effort. Therefore, unless stated otherwise, the results that follow provide reliable estimates of his current processing skills and abilities. As several of the underlying processes from each of the scales and tasks relate to each other, results are presented in an integrative fashion, and grouped by area covered.

Intellectual Functioning

Estimates about Larry's intelligence had been ascertained on three previous occasions. On each, he performed within the Above Average range (even though the previous examiners may not have interpreted their data in that manner). For example, in April 2005, using the KBIT-2 the best estimate of Larry's intelligence was on the Nonverbal Index, which was 111 (77th percentile). In March 2006, using

the WISC-IV, the best estimate of Larry's intelligence was on the Perceptual Reasoning Index, which was 112 (79th percentile). Also in March 2006, the Naglieri Nonverbal Ability Test was administered, resulting in an Index score of 117 (87th percentile). In December 2007, using the WISC-IV, the best estimate of Larry's intelligence was again on the Perceptual Reasoning Index, which was 117 (87th percentile).

Using the KABC-II for this current assessment, Larry's intelligence was measured as being near-Gifted (Superior). His composite IQ (Mental Processing Index) of 127 was in the 96th percentile, meaning that less than 4 out of 100 children his age would outperform him. With few exceptions, Larry performed relatively evenly within and between each of the processing scales, suggesting that the Global Composite provides a reliable estimate of his true intelligence.

Kaufman Assessment Battery for Children, Second Edition

Subtest	SS/ScS	%ile	Subtest	SS/ScS	%ile
Sequential	115	25	Simultaneous	124	95
Word Order	12	75	Triangles	11	63
Number Recall	13	84	Rover	17	99
Learning	123	94	Planning	114	82
Atlantis	13	84	Story Completion	12	75
Rebus	15	95	Pattern Reasoning	13	84

To gain a more thorough understanding about one's intellectual strengths and weaknesses, it is often useful to compare that individual's effectiveness across multiple cognitive processes. Among others, the comparisons can include: sequential versus simultaneous processing, verbal versus nonverbal processing, and visual-scanning/discrimination versus visual-spatial processing. Where applicable to Larry, I provide those comparisons below.

Simultaneous Versus Sequential Processing

The nine-point difference between Larry's Sequential and Simultaneous Processing Index scores was not statistically significant. Also, his higher score on the latter occurred due to a divergently high score on one subtest. Larry's performance on the other subtest from that Index was consistent with his performance on the two sequential processing tasks. Overall, Larry's sequential and simultaneous processing abilities are relatively similar, with both being normative strengths. (Note: A personal strength or weakness is one that is relative to that individual's other processing abilities; a normative strength or weakness is one that is relative to the processing abilities of that individual's same-age peers.)

- Simultaneous processing is a mental process by which the individual integrates many features and details all at once. The essential feature of this process is that the answer is immediately able to be perceived through that integration.
- Sequential processing (Successive) is a mental process by which the individual integrates stimuli into a specific serial order that forms a chain-like progression. Things must follow in a prescribed order, and the answer is obtained only after working through a series of steps. Stimuli are not interrelated—as in simultaneous processing—rather, each element is related only to those that precede it.

Often, sequential processing relates more to math computation and to the phonemic blending involved when decoding unfamiliar words, whereas simultaneous processing is thought to be more involved in the understanding of math concepts (math applications) and in reading comprehension. At least from this processing perspective, then, and absent other mitigating processing differences and relative interest, Larry should be able to develop competence in each of the above areas.

From the Sequential Processing scale, the two core subtests were administered. The Number Recall subtest required Larry to listen to a series of single syllable numbers, then to repeat those numbers in the same order. Larry was able to inconsistently recall a series of seven digits. The Word Order subtest required Larry to listen to a series of words (e.g., house, star, key, cup), and demonstrate his ability to recall those words by pointing to the silhouettes of those words in the order presented to him. On this part of the task, with relative consistency, Larry was able to recall strings of five and six words (the maximum number of words on this part of the task). As the task increased in complexity, an interference condition was added, and Larry was able to advance to that level. After he listened to the word-series, he was to name specific colors. After about 5 seconds of the color naming, he was to touch the words I had spoken to him. In that condition, Larry was able to recall up to a four-word sequence.

From the Simultaneous Processing Scale, the two core subtests were administered. The Rover subtest required Larry to move a toy dog to a bone on a checkerboard-like grid that contained obstacles (i.e., rocks, weeds). The task required him to find the shortest route possible (i.e., the route that took the fewest number of moves). The Triangles subtest addressed nonverbal concept formation. Larry was required to match the printed 2D design, using rubber triangles.

Verbal Versus Visual Processing

Tasks involving simultaneous processing often involve visual stimuli, while tasks involving sequential processing often involve verbal stimuli. One might hypothesize, then, that Larry may be equally advantaged in the presence of visual and verbal cues. Of the tasks administered in this current evaluation, in general that hypothesis proved to be accurate. Larry's mother, in fact, has observed that Larry responds best to teaching methods that combine visual, verbal, and tactile cues.

Importantly, though, Larry was considerably weaker with visual-scanning/discrimination than he was with visual-spatial processing (below). Therefore, the hypothesis about Larry's visual and verbal processing abilities may be generally correct, but at the same time overly simplistic.

Visual Processing: Visual-Spatial Versus Visual Discrimination

Tasks involving visual processing can be separated into those that rely more on visual-spatial processing, and those that rely more on visual-scanning discrimination. Below, I recategorized the majority of the processing tasks administered that tended to capitalize on visual-scanning versus those tasks that tended to capitalize on visual-spatial processing. None of the tasks listed, though, should be taken as being pure measures of either process, which is why the tasks are further defined in other sections of this report.

Visual-spatial processing involves multiple distinct but interrelated subcomponents: (1) the ability to synthesize elements into a meaningful whole, (2) the ability to understand the relationships among objects in space (location and directionality), (3) the ability to adopt a variety of perspectives and rotate objects mentally, and (4) the ability to understand and interpret symbolic representations of external space (e.g., maps and routes).

Visual discrimination involves the ability to differentiate objects based on their individual characteristics. Visual discrimination is vital to the recognition of common objects and symbols and also refers to the ability to recognize an object as distinct from its surrounding environment.

Larry performed quite well in visual-spatial processing (Average to Very Superior). In contrast, he struggled on the single task administered that required visual-scanning/discrimination, and performed in the lower end of the Below Average range. Although a processing deficit cannot be determined by a single subtest, other evidence does suggest that visual-scanning/discrimination may hinder him academically. On the Math Fluency subtest, for example, all three of Larry's errors were due to his misreading the sign (+ as being a – or vice versa). With math word problems, I understand that Larry leaves out key words, causing him to become confused about what is being asked of him.

Importantly, Larry also performed relatively poorly on both of the Processing Speed tasks from the WISC-IV the last time it was administered. Both of those tasks also rely on visual-scanning/discrimination. His low performance on those tasks, then, is consistent with the results of this current testing.

Tasks Involving Visual-Scanning/Discrimination Versus Visual-Spatial Processing

Subtest	SS	%ile	Subtest	SS	%ile
Visual-Scanning			**Visual-Spatial**		
Visual Matching	82	12	*Triangles	105	63
			*Rover	135	99

*Task from the KABC-II, while the nonmarked items were from the WJ III COG.

Processing Speed

Processing Speed relates to the ability to perform automatic cognitive tasks, particularly when measured under pressure to maintain focused attention. Tasks of Processing Speed are typically quite easy, and most would get all items correct if the test were not highly speeded. To look at that process, I administered the two tasks from the WJ III COG.

Larry performed less well on both of the WJ III COG processing speed tests, with normative and personal weaknesses on that index overall (standard score of 88, 21st percentile). Still, Larry performed notably less well on the Visual Matching task that relies also on visual-scanning/discrimination, underscoring the probability of his having a deficit in that latter process.

Processing Speed Tests

Subtest	SS	%ile	Subtest	SS	%ile
Visual Matching	82	12	Decision Speed	98	45

The Visual Matching subtest required Larry to scan rows of numbers, with six single-digit numbers in each row. Larry merely had to find the two numbers in each row that matched (e.g., 5 3 9 3 1 4). The Decision Speed subtest measured Larry's ability to quickly process simple drawings and make conceptual decisions about them.

Executive Function: Attention

Together, tasks of Planning and Attention are considered to assess aspects about executive function: the ability to draw on fundamental (primary) cognitive skills for the purpose of generating higher levels of creative and abstract thought.

In general, attention is a mental process by which the individual selectively focuses on particular stimuli while inhibiting responses to competing stimuli presented over time. Importantly, though, attention is not a unified construct. Instead, it involves several key elements that combine to impact the effectiveness of many other cognitive processes as well. Attention, for example, involves: (a) alertness (i.e., a state of readiness to input, process, and/or retrieve information), (b) selective focus (i.e., distinguishing what's relevant from what is less relevant), (c) filtering (the ability to avoid becoming derailed/side-tracked), and (d) maintenance (the ability to sustain that alertness, and to sustain the selective focus).

To assess Larry's attention, I administered a task from the D-KEFS. I examined also the types and frequencies of errors made across various conditions from several tasks, as well. Larry did, in fact, demonstrate intermittent difficulties with attention.

The D-KEFS Color-Word Interference Test required Larry to rapidly identify the colors "red," "blue," and "green" randomized on a page. On the Color Naming condition, Larry merely had to name the colored patches as rapidly as he could. On the Word Naming condition, Larry merely had to read the word "red," "blue," or "green" as rapidly as he could. On the Inhibition condition, each word ("red," "blue," "green") was printed in a color that contradicted its label. Larry was to identify the color of the ink, as rapidly as he could, while simultaneously inhibiting the competing impulse to read the word.

On this task, the inhibition condition and the inhibition-switching condition (described elsewhere, below) are compared to the individual's performance on the other two conditions; a drop in performance may indicate an attentional issue. Larry did not have difficulty on this task.

Aspects of attention were also addressed by examining the quantity and types of errors made across several tasks administered: (a) omission errors involve failing to respond to the target, often resulting when self-monitoring is poor; (b) commission errors involve responding to the wrong target, suggesting either impulsivity, a susceptibility to becoming derailed (distracted) from task, and/or an inability to hold in awareness the task's demands; (c) sequencing errors involve responding out of order (e.g., numbers, letters), suggesting a poor ability to sustain attention with consistency; and (d) repetition errors involve repeating a target previously given, suggesting difficulty with self-monitoring.

Analysis of the combined results of the two tasks administered suggested intermittent difficulties with sustaining attention.

Executive Function: Planning

Planning is a mental process by which the individual determines, selects, applies, and evaluates solutions to problems. Success on tasks involving planning requires an individual to develop a plan of action, evaluate the value of the plan, monitor its effectiveness, revise or reject the plan as the task demands change, and control the impulse to act without careful consideration. To address planning, I administered the two planning tasks from the KABC-II and the Tower Test from the D-KEFS. Performing between the Above Average to Superior ranges, planning emerged as a normative strength. Importantly, in typical situations, Larry has considerable difficulty executing what has been planned, which is different from the above. For example, it is common for Larry to forget to bring home pertinent homework material.

Planning

Subtest	SS	%ile	Subtest	SS	%ile
Story Completion	110	75	*Tower Test	120	91
Story Completion	115	84			
*From the D-KEFS; the nonmarked tasks were from the KABC-II.					

- The Story Completion task required Larry to view a row of pictures that tells a story. One or more pictures from that story are missing, and he was to choose the missing ones, those that correctly completed the story, from the set provided to him.

- The Pattern Reasoning subtest required Larry to examine a series of printed objects (some meaningful, some involving geometric shapes) that formed a logical linear pattern, with one object from that pattern missing. From an array of four to six objects provided, he was to choose the one that completed/fit the pattern.

- The D-KEFS Tower Test required Larry to move single-colored disks of various sizes across three pegs to build a designated tower in the fewest number of moves possible. Only one disk could be moved at a time, and a larger disk could never cover a smaller disk. Larry was thus required to make advance predictions about his moves, and the consequences of each.

> **Note:**
>
> Importantly, on certain tasks of planning, children with ADHD often perform poorly. Perhaps due to their extraordinary focus on the here and now, children with ADHD often limit their focus to the moment without considering future effectiveness. The Tower Test, in fact, is especially sensitive to this issue, as refraining from fully assessing the task's demands before making an initial response has a greater consequence. On the Tower Test, those with attentional difficulties tend to come out of the starting gate too quickly and fail to increase their study time on the item before making a first move. As the task increased in complexity, Larry did tend to increase the amount of time he studied the items before making his first move. Additionally, at various intervals, he paused to reexamine his choices before he continued. That approach was rather consistent throughout the assessment, as on various tasks (e.g., the KTEA-II's Story Completion), Larry took his time to assess each item before beginning. Overall, the way Larry approached the Tower Test was not similar to those who carry a diagnosis of ADHD.

The above is not meant to discount the notion that Larry has ADHD. In a one-on-one setting with an adult, his impulsivity may be minimized and/or contained. Also, the tasks are both visual and tactile, which have been previously shown to help Larry organize his responses.

Executive Function: Abstract Reasoning (Problem Solving)

Another processing area related to higher cortical functioning is abstract reasoning. Abstract reasoning involves the ability to go beyond a specific instance. It involves the ability to understand qualities about an object, apart from the object itself. Abstract reasoning is involved in categorizing, in inferring, in understanding idioms and absurdities, and in understanding verbal or visual analogies.

Several tasks administered, at least in part, involved abstract reasoning for success. Larry performed quite well on those tasks (Average to Very Superior), suggesting Abstract Reasoning to be one of his stronger areas, as well, and as clearly being a normative strength.

Tasks Involving Abstract Reasoning

Subtest	SS	%ile	Subtest	SS	%ile
Riddles	100	50	*Initial Abstraction	145	>99
Pattern Reasoning	115	84	*Total Questions Asked	110	75
*Both conditions were from the D-KEFS Twenty Questions subtest.					

The D-KEFS Twenty Questions Test required Larry to deduce the object that I had chosen, from among the other objects that were also on the same page. He was to accomplish this deduction by asking me any question that I could answer with a "yes" or with a "no." The Initial Abstraction score relates to the level of abstraction obtained by the initial response to each item. At the most abstract level, one is able to eliminate one-half of the 30 items on the page. There are actually very few ways to do that, and each time Larry chose one of those ways. The score he obtained, then, was the highest one could obtain on that condition.

The Total Questions Asked relates to the number of questions asked before deriving the correct object. Although Larry had eliminated one-half of the items by his first question, he was unable to maintain that high level by his subsequent questions. Still, his overall performance on that condition was Above Average.

In some respects, this task (and especially the latter condition) relates to problem-solving abilities. Larry demonstrated rather high levels of problem solving on this task as well as on others. On the Atlantis subtest, for example, Larry talked his way through recalling the correct object (fish, plant, shell) by using deductive reasoning (e.g., "It can't be this one because …"). On the Rover subtest, Larry tried out several different approaches. When finding two approaches that resulted in the same number of moves, he'd say, "Hmmm, there must be a quicker way." On the Rebus Learning subtest, Larry actively (and spontaneously) tried to find a way to mentally associate the symbol with its word meaning.

Executive Function: Cognitive Flexibility

As a neuropsychological construct, cognitive flexibility (or shifting set) is considered to be one of the hallmarks of executive function (attributed primarily to the frontal lobes).

This ability allows an individual to abandon a previous response, in order to generate a novel response, an ability that is necessary for adaptive functioning. Individuals having difficulty in this area often have difficulty moving freely from one situation, activity, or aspect of a problem to another, as the circumstances demand.

The D-KEFS looks at cognitive flexibility by adding a switching component to several of the tasks in their batteries. I opted to administer two of the tasks having that component. Larry did not have difficulty with either. Historically, though, Larry has always struggled with being able to back away from emotionally laden situations and switch his frame of reference once he becomes upset. The test data suggest, then, that Larry's difficulty with cognitive flexibility likely relates more to an emotional source, rather than to a neuropsychological source.

As previously explained, the Color-Word Interference Test also involved several conditions, requiring Larry to rapidly identify the colors "red," "blue," and "green" randomized on a page. The inhibition-switching condition was similar to the inhibition condition previously described, with one added component. At random intervals, a word was enclosed in a box, and for those instances Larry was to read the actual word while rejecting the dissonant ink color. A drop in performance relative to the inhibition (non-switching) condition would suggest a possible deficit in cognitive flexibility. Larry's performance did not diminish on this condition.

The Trail Making Test involves several different conditions, with one of those conditions involving a switching component. Each condition required that Larry scan an 11 × 17 sheet of paper to complete the paper-and-pencil task that was asked of him.

- The visual scanning condition involved having Larry quickly find all of the circled 3s, among randomly placed circled numbers and circled letters on the same page.
- The number-sequencing condition involved having Larry connect 16 circled numbers in sequence (e.g., 1, 2, 3, 4…).
- The letter-sequencing condition involved having Larry connect 16 circled letters in sequence (e.g., A, B, C, D…).
- The switching condition required Larry to connect the circled numbers and circled letters in sequence, switching between a number and a letter (e.g., 1, a, 2, b, 3, c …). Larry's performance did not diminish on this condition.

Learning

Learning reflects an integration of several mental processes, placing a premium on selective attention, pairing and integrating the concurrent presentation of auditory and visual stimuli, the mediation of that stimuli via various aspects of sequential and simultaneous processing, and then the encoding and storage of information. As a child matures, learning also requires strategy generation (i.e., planning) to facilitate the efficient retrieval of the new associations from storage.

To address learning, I administered the California Verbal Learning Test-Children's version (CVLT-C) along with the two learning tasks from the KABC-II. In general, Larry's learning was Above Average; visual cues helped Larry recall information but both visual and verbal cues assisted him equally when it came to recognizing information.

Learning Tasks: Verbal Versus Verbal/Visual

Subtest	SS	%ile		Subtest	SS	%ile
Verbal				Verbal/Visual		
*Trial 5	107	68		Atlantis	115	84
*Long Delay Recall	93	32		Rebus	125	95
*Discriminability	115	84				
*Tasks were from the CVLT-C. Score on Discriminability was the highest one can obtain for Larry's age. Unmarked tasks were from the KABC-II.						

- The Rebus subtest from the KABC-II required Larry to be taught words associated with particular drawings/symbols. Larry's learning of those drawings/symbols was demonstrated by having him read sentences composed only of those drawings/symbols.

- The Atlantis subtest from the KABC-II required Larry to be taught nonsense names for fanciful pictures of fish, plants, and shells. Learning was demonstrated by having him point to the correct picture (from an array of many pictures) on request.

- The CVLT-C measures several strategies and processes involved in learning and recalling verbal material. It does so within the context of an everyday shopping list. Both recall and recognition of words are measured over a number of trials. For the first five trials, a 15-item list is read to the student; the requirement is to recall the words from the list immediately after each presentation. A second list is then presented, with the requirement to recall as many words as one can from that list. Immediately following, the student is to recall the words from the original list, but that original list is not repeated.

Immediate, multiple repetitions of the word list assisted Larry considerably. For example, he recalled 3 of the 15 words at trial 1, 9 words at trials 2 and 3, 12 words at trial 4, and 13 words at trial 5. He made his greatest amount of improvement on the first repetition (i.e., second trial), which is within typical standards.

Memory: Immediate

Immediate memory involves responses that are immediate, such as dialing a phone number right after hearing it from directory assistance. Immediate memory was addressed by the two tasks from the Sequential Processing Scale of the KABC-II, and by two conditions from the CVLT-C.

With immediate memory, Larry performed considerably better on the auditory sequential tasks than he did on the auditory nonsequential tasks. Larry appeared to have difficulty organizing the longer list (nonsequential) in a manner that would help him to recall it. He responded well, though, to the structure of having to recall the words/numbers sequentially (as well as to the fact that the list was shorter).

Immediate Memory Tasks

Subtest	SS	%ile		Subtest	SS	%ile
KABC-II: Auditory-Sequential				CVLT-C: Auditory Non-Sequential		
Word Order	110	75		List A – CVLT-C	70	2
Number Recall	115	84		List B – CVLT-C	93	32

Memory: Delayed Conditions

In addition to immediate memory, tasks/conditions were administered to address delayed memory in short delay and long delay conditions. The short delay condition occurred a few minutes after the task was initially administered, whereas the long delay condition occurred 20 minutes after that. On the CVLT-C, on the short delay condition Larry was able to recall 12 words, which was only one less than he recalled at the fifth trial. On the CVLT-C's long delay condition, Larry was able to recall nine words, a decrease of another three words (albeit, an average number of words).

The final condition from the CVLT-C involved recognition. On that condition, Larry was read 45 words containing the original 15 words from List A (targets) along with 30 distracter words not on that list (nontargets). Larry was to say "yes" if the word was from List

A and "no" if it were not. Larry correctly identified all 15 of the target words (6 more than he had recalled at the long delay condition); and he did not misidentify any of the distracter words, believing them to be targets when they were not. Taken together, the data suggest that Larry is able to adequately encode verbal information into memory, and adequately retrieve that information from memory. With verbal information, though, he may be better able to recognize that information than to recall it on his own.

Memory: Working Memory

As working memory is a processing component of reading comprehension, I opted to administer tasks addressing it. working memory is different from learning, immediate memory, and delayed memory. With working memory, information must be held in immediate awareness (kept active in one's consciousness) while other information is being gathered and/or worked with in some way. Working memory is required in everyday tasks, such as when performing calculations in one's head.

Working memory was addressed by the WJ III COG Auditory Working Memory and Numbers Reversed tests. Larry performed quite well on both tasks, overall suggesting Superior (standard score of 123, 94th percentile) working memory abilities.

Working Memory

Subtest	St Sc	%ile		Subtest	St Sc	%ile
Numbers Reversed	121	93		Auditory Working Memory	117	87

- The Auditory Working Memory subtest required Larry to listen to a series that contained digits and words, such as "dog, 1, shoe, 8, 2, apple." He was then required to tell that series back to me: first the objects in the order of delivery, then the digits in the order of delivery.

- The Numbers Reversed subtest required Larry to listen to a series of digits, and then to repeat those digits back to me in reverse order.

Language – Receptive/Expressive

Aspects of Larry's receptive and expressive language skills were addressed by one task from the KABC-II, one task from the KTEA-II, and one task from the NEPSY-II. Larry's receptive language was at least Average.

Language: Primarily Receptive

Subtest	SS	%ile		Subtest	SS	%ile
Verbal Knowledge	100	50		Listening Comprehension	112	79
				*Narrative Memory	100	50
*The Free Recall condition relied strongly on both Receptive and Expressive language.						

- The Verbal Knowledge subtest required Larry to select from an array of six pictures the one that illustrated the meaning of a vocabulary word or the answer to a general informational prompt. The task addresses both knowledge and vocabulary.

- The Listening Comprehension subtest from the KTEA-II was developed to assess the type of listening comprehension required in school. On that task, Larry was required to listen to passages played on a CD, and then to respond orally to questions asked by the examiner.

- The Narrative Memory subtest required Larry to listen to a story of a couple of paragraphs in length. He was then required to repeat the story back to me: first without prompts, then with prompts. Larry had no difficulty telling the story back to me without prompts, performing solidly in the Average range. His retelling of the story was orderly, and included most of the pertinent details targeted in the scoring criteria. The prompts later on did not assist him, and he recalled only a few additional details when they were provided.

Language Functioning – Primarily as It Relates to Reading Acquisition

Reading calls on the interplay of various cognitive processes. Two of those processes have been identified as being key when looking at issues related to classic dyslexia: phonemic awareness and speed of lexical access. Skills relating to phonemic awareness have been well known to relate to the decoding of unfamiliar words. Tasks addressing Rapid Automatized Naming (RAN) (also known as speed of lexical access or rapid serial naming) have been well known to relate to reading fluency and reading comprehension. The results indicate how fast the brain can integrate visual and language processes, and provide one of the best means of differentiating good and poor readers. That is, relative weaknesses on speeded naming tasks frequently predict relative weaknesses in reading fluency and comprehension.

Reading also involves working memory (discussed above) and orthography. Orthography refers to written language and the manner in which letters are used to form words. Components include letter patterns (graphemes), spelling (how letters and letter patterns are associated with speech sounds), punctuation, abbreviations, and special symbols (e.g., @, #, %). When looking at the results from all of the above processes related to reading, Larry had the most difficulty on the orthographic features of reading/writing. That is, in working memory, Larry performed Superior; in Phonemic Awareness, Larry performed Average; in Speed of Lexical Access, Larry primarily performed Average; but in Orthography, Larry primarily performed Below Average (primarily on tasks that were timed).

Processes Related to Reading

Subtest	SS	%ile	Subtest	SS	%ile
Phonemic Awareness			**Speed of Lexical Access**		
Phonological Processing	93	37	Color Naming*	95	37
			Word Naming	105	63
Orthography (TOC)			Objects	113	81
Punctuation	84	16	Colors	111	77
Abbreviations	75	5	Numbers	107	68
Letter Choice	80	9	Letters	102	55
Word Scramble	80	9	Letters/Numbers	102	55
Sight Spelling	100	53	Letters/Numbers/Colors	107	68
Homophone Choice	115	84			

Phonemic Awareness

The NEPSY-II Phonological Processing task required Larry to discriminate between word parts and phonemes. Primarily, the items involved elimination and substitution. An elimination example might include asking Larry to say the word *meat*, and then asking him to say it again without the /m/ sound (whereupon he was to respond with *eat*). A substitution example might involve asking Larry to say the word *bike*, and then asking him to say it again but to change the "i" sound for the "a" sound (whereupon he was to respond with *bake*).

Speed of Lexical Access

The Rapid Automatized Naming and Rapid Alternating Stimulus Tests (RAN/RAS) measure a person's ability to perceive a visual symbol (e.g., letter, color) and retrieve its name accurately and rapidly. The RAN/RAS includes five timed subtests in which Larry was asked to name pictured objects, colors, numbers, letters, and combinations of these as fast as possible.

Orthography

The Test of Orthographic Competence (TOC) reliably addresses many components of orthography. The TOC includes subtests assessing knowledge of punctuation, abbreviations, and letter orientation. Tasks include reordering strings of letters to make words (e.g., *lwal/wall*), filling in the missing letters in words with nonphonetic spellings (e.g., *w_ter*), and choosing among two or three homophones the one that correctly labels a picture (e.g., *you, ewe*).

Academic Achievement

While the above provides information about Larry's capacity to learn, along with the supporting mental processes used in learning, academic achievement quantifies aspects about what Larry has actually learned. To address aspects about Larry's academic skills, I administered portions of the Kaufman Test of Educational Achievement (KTEA-II), along with portions of the Test of Written Language (TOWL-4) and the WJ III ACH.

Relative to his intelligence, Larry's academic achievement scores were disappointing. Larry performed mainly within the Average range. Larry's reading fluency, though, was Below Average, which is consistent with his deficit in processing speed. Portions of his written expression were Above Average, which was better than he typically performs at school.

Academic Achievement

Subtest	SS	%ile	Subtest	SS	%ile
Reading (non-speeded)			**Reading (speeded)**		
Letter & Word Recognition	92	30	Word Recognition Fluency	90	25
Nonsense Word Decoding	96	39	Decoding Fluency	91	27
Reading Comprehension	105	63	*Reading Fluency	88	21
Mathematics			**Writing (TOWL-4)**		
*Math Fluency	97	42	Contextual Conventions	105	63
			Story Composition	115	84

*Tasks are from the WJ III ACH. Writing tasks are from the TOWL-4. Remainder of the tasks are from the KTEA-II.

Reading

Several aspects of Larry's reading skills were assessed in timed and untimed conditions, including reading decoding, word recognition, and reading comprehension. In the untimed conditions, Larry's reading was solidly Average. In the speeded conditions, Larry's reading was near or within the Below Average range.

- Larry's skills with recognizing familiar words (and decoding unfamiliar words) were addressed by the Letter & Word Recognition task and the Word Recognition Fluency task from the KTEA-II. That task required Larry to recognize and/or sound out individual words that increased in complexity.
- Larry's skills with decoding unfamiliar words were addressed by the Nonsense Word Decoding task and the Decoding Fluency task, which required Larry to apply phonic and structural analysis skills to made-up words such as "smuke" and "sleeg."
- Larry's reading comprehension skills were addressed by the Reading Comprehension task from the KTEA-II. Larry was required to read to himself passages of one to three paragraphs in length, and then to respond to several questions that followed. He was allowed to refer back to the text to answer those questions. As this task is not timed, Larry was not penalized for the length of time it took him to complete each item.
- The WJ III ACH Reading Fluency test required Larry to quickly read very simple sentences and then to circle the word "yes" or "no," depending on whether or not the sentence was true (e.g., "A bird can fly"). He was to complete as many sentences as he could within the 3-minute time limit.

Mathematics

I limited my assessment of Larry's math to fluency. The WJ III ACH Math Fluency test required Larry to rapidly complete single-digit addition, subtraction, and multiplication fact problems within a 3-minute time limit. Larry performed solidly within the Average range.

Written Language

Aspects about Larry's writing competence were addressed by the Spontaneous Format from the Test of Written Language (TOWL-4). Overall on that index, Larry's performance Above Average (standard score of 115, 84th percentile), suggesting a well-developed ability to incorporate good writing skills in a contextually meaningful composition.

The TOWL-4 is a comprehensive test of written language. It has a sound theoretical basis and employs both contrived and spontaneous formats to address conventional, linguistic, and cognitive components of writing. In the spontaneous format, the student is asked to compose an essay based on a picture scene. Contextual Conventions addresses the conventional and linguistic components mentioned earlier. Story Composition addresses the linguistic and cognitive components mentioned previously.

Social-Emotional Functioning

To quantify a variety of variables related to Larry's social-emotional functioning, I administered the Millon Pre-Adolescent Clinical Inventory (M-PACI) and the Rorschach Inkblot Test (Rorschach).

The Rorschach is individually administered. As it is process-driven and not content-driven, the Rorschach can provide pertinent information about how one thinks, but not about what one thinks. Also, unlike self-report inventories, the Rorschach is not readily susceptible to efforts at either concealing or exaggerating psychopathology.

The Millon Pre-Adolescent Clinical Inventory (M-PACI) is a multidimensional self-report clinical inventory designed to help predict and understand a broad range of psychological issues that are commonly seen in clinical settings among children 9 to 12 years old. There are 97 True/False questions, and I read each one to Larry to ensure comprehension. The M-PACI contains several validity indicators. Those indicators suggested that Larry responded in a frank and honest manner, not grossly underreporting or overreporting the issues queried.

Affect

Developmentally, it is appropriate for pre-teens Larry's age to begin struggling with issues about autonomy (including dependence versus independence). Larry's M-PACI profile, though, suggests his struggle to be more intense and profound, and to be marked by struggles between obedience and defiance, and between composure and unmodulated release. That is, while it is likely that Larry sincerely wants to exercise constraint, it has become increasingly difficult for him to restrain the strong emotions he feels. Accordingly, Larry's behaviors and moods are unstable, and they can be highly reactive to external stimuli. Periods of propriety and affability may quickly give way to reactive anger and a lack of control.

Given the above, it was not surprising to find that indices from the Rorschach indicated a vulnerability to mood disorders (anxiety/depression). That is, Larry may be disposed to the types of depressive disorders that may have a substantial impact on his ability to function effectively. Pessimism, self-reproach, and a sense of futility have begun to develop, to the point where Larry may have come to believe that good things that occur for him probably will not last. This can promote apathy and/or a sense of learned helplessness.

A cause and an outcome of the above is that Larry is hypersensitive to internal and external sources of criticism. While Larry can be self-reflective, he can also be extremely self-critical. The latter involves less of a psychologically healthy self-examination of strengths and weaknesses, and more of a psychologically damaging self-reproach. Additionally, he is sensitive to embarrassment.

One way Larry may attempt to ensure composure is to become emotionally blunted and/or withdrawn. That is, if he can shield himself from experiencing strong emotions altogether, then the odds of becoming out of control may be substantially reduced. The problem with adopting that posture, though, is that he must then refrain from participating in the kinds of everyday interactions that are necessary for normal development.

Frustration Tolerance

Consistent with the above, the development of a stable personal identity involves rubbing elbows with the world, where an appropriate amount of emotional risk has been taken along the way, and where interpersonal involvement has been sustained. In a determined effort to keep stressful experiences at a minimum, Larry may have restricted his social contacts and his activities. Avoiding challenging situations and limiting oneself to the familiar have reinforcing value. Each has the added benefit of reducing the possibility that Larry might be placed in affectively charged situations that produce anxiety, emotional discomfort, embarrassment, and/or self-reproach.

Larry's preference for avoiding potentially affectively charged situations may have been strong enough to cause him to opt out of participating in the typical emotionally charged situations that are part of a developing child's normal routine. Those experiences are pertinent, though, as they contribute to the building of a solid platform from which one's sense of self can be anchored.

An unfortunate finding about Larry's psychological profile, in fact, is that his internal resources are below the level he needs to cope with everyday stressors. This finding predicts, then, that Larry may have difficulty developing and maintaining adequate internal resources to cope with the combined demands of those he imposes on himself and those that are imposed on him. Larry, therefore, may:

- Have reduced abilities to persevere in the face of obstacles
- Have a low tolerance for frustration
- Be easily vexed and/or upset by trifles
- Have a vulnerability to impulsive actions that may be ill-advised
- Be easily provoked into unpredictable outbursts of anger/resentment
- Express momentary thoughts/feelings capriciously

The above concerns are in addition to Larry's mood disorder and ADHD. That is, even if an antidepressant medication were prescribed, its effectiveness may be circumscribed. Larry will require additional supports, as well (e.g., a structured environment filled with routine and predictability).

Sense of Self

Quite a bit of evidence within the testing suggests that Larry entertains self-persecutory thoughts and feels dissatisfied with himself. Larry's profile was also characterized by an internal conflict about dependence-independence. He experiences notable ambivalence about his continuing dependency needs and will vacillate between cooperation and compliance versus assertiveness and autonomy.

Still, that struggle between dependent acquiescence and assertive independence may have begun to intrude into his relationships at home and at school. It may very well be that his behavior keeps others on edge, not knowing if he will react in an agreeable, disconsolate, or irritable manner.

Social

Social situations are a cause of significant distress for Larry. Not only is he hypersensitive to criticism, but he also anticipates rejection by peers. That is, Larry is overly sensitive to comments and interactions that might be interpreted as rejection, contributing to his misperceptions and misinterpretations about the social situations he regularly finds himself in. Notably, also, Larry's moodiness almost guarantees the rejection that he anticipates.

Thoughts

At times Larry's thinking can also be problematic. While Larry certainly has the adaptive capacity to think logically and coherently, he can also have difficulty recognizing the obvious. As situations become more subtle, complex, or ambiguous, however, his ability to accurately size up and interpret what is going on around him decreases even further.

In part, the above occurs because Larry has the tendency to take in much more information than he can effectively and efficiently organize, and to examine situations more thoroughly than serves any reasonable purpose. In fact, he exhibited a marked tendency toward being excessively preoccupied with details, and to focus on what most would find to be irrelevant. Larry can even miss the obvious, let alone the more subtle nuances that typify daily interactions.

The above, then, suggests an impairment in Larry's social perception. Specifically, he is prone to perceiving events in an unconventional manner, forming inaccurate impressions of others, and misjudging their attitudes and intentions frequently. Very often, Larry may misperceive what is going on around him, form erroneous conclusions about those events, and then engage in ill-advised actions that may be totally misplaced until he is able to emotionally distance himself from the situation. Following an event, Larry is typically quite remorseful over how he conducted himself.

At other times, Larry does not really think about the situation at all. Alternatively, if he does, it is with minimal effort/investment. Instead, decisions are reached impulsively, and courses of action are taken without having given them much thought. Larry has difficulty with thinking before responding, anticipating the consequences of his own actions, and recognizing the boundaries of appropriate behaviors in various situations, making the adequacy of his social adjustment clearly in question.

SUMMARY

Larry is an 11-year, 6-month-old fifth grader, who I had the opportunity to spend about 9 hours testing across 2 separate days. He was extremely respectful during the entire test administration.

Cognitive Functioning

Estimates of Larry's intelligence had been ascertained on three prior occasions. On each, he performed within the Above Average range.

Using the KABC-II for this current assessment, Larry's Composite IQ (Mental Processing Index) was 127, which was in the 96th percentile, meaning that less than 4 out of 100 children his age would be expected to outperform him.

With few exceptions, Larry performed relatively evenly within and between each of the processing scales, suggesting the Global Composite to be a reliable estimate of his true intelligence.

In addition to the above, Larry's performance was at least Above Average in Simultaneous Processing, Sequential Processing, Learning, Planning, Abstract Reasoning, and Working Memory. His performance was Average in Receptive Language (Average to Above Average), Phonemic Awareness, and Speed of Lexical Access (Rapid Automatized Naming). His performance was Below Average in Visual-Scanning/Discrimination, Processing Speed (Below Average to Average), and Orthography (particularly on speeded measures).

It can be difficult to quantify Attention and Cognitive Flexibility using the above rubric. Larry did show intermittent difficulties with attention. He did not, however, show difficulties with cognitive flexibility. Regarding the latter, historically Larry has always struggled with being able to back away from emotionally-laden situations, and switch his frame of reference after he becomes upset. The test data suggest, then, that Larry's difficulty with cognitive flexibility likely relates more to an emotional source rather than a neuropsychological source.

Academic Achievement

Relative to his superior intelligence, the results from the achievement testing were disappointing, in that Larry performed mainly within the Average range. Larry's reading fluency, though, was Below Average, which is consistent with his deficit in Processing Speed. Portions of his written expression were Above Average, which was better than he typically performs at school.

Social-Emotional

To quantify a variety of variables related to Larry's social-emotional functioning, I administered the Millon Pre-Adolescent Clinical Inventory (M-PACI) and the Rorschach Inkblot Test (Rorschach). The results are summarized in an earlier section of this report.

RECOMMENDATIONS

Special Education Disability Category

Larry has been qualified for special education based on the classification of ED (Emotional Disturbance). At this juncture, ED continues to be the most accurate qualifier for Larry's difficulties. Clearly, Larry's emotional dyscontrol—not learning challenges—have been the deciding elements that have precluded him from being educated within the regular education environment without supports. Larry's ADHD, though, is a co-contributor.

Still, several previous examiners have hesitated to so qualify Larry, and I certainly can understand why. When Larry is not overwhelmed by his emotions, he truly is a very sweet, endearing child. He is not egocentric; he is not defiant; he does not even carry himself with a chip on his shoulder. In fact, Larry's general disposition is not at all similar to the population of children typically identified as having ED. Accordingly, placement for Larry needs to be judiciously considered. It is very doubtful, for example, that a classroom composed primarily of children with ED would be appropriate for Larry. Accordingly, I'd like to see the IEP notes reference this paragraph in my report.

Medication

I strongly recommend a trial of an antidepressant medication in conjunction with intensified psychotherapy and a specialized school environment (described below). The testing data suggested Larry may respond rather favorably to an antidepressant medication, but by itself that response may be insufficient.

One of the considerations that emerged, which may limit the breadth of an antidepressant's effect, was related to Larry's lack of internal resources to cope with everyday stressors. Larry has had persistent difficulty maintaining adequate internal resources to cope with demands either that he imposes on himself or that others impose on him.

Therapy

In conjunction with an antidepressant trial, I recommend intensified psychotherapy (twice weekly individual early on, which could be tapered to weekly and then to twice monthly). The therapist should be in regular contact with the school, as well, so that the interventions could be addressed ongoing with Larry, his therapist, and the appropriate school personnel. Programmatic changes need to be made immediately (with the therapist's approval), in lieu of waiting for the IEP team to reconvene.

Larry's therapist will need to assist him in developing insight into the following issues, and then develop a plan so that Larry can increase his ability to cope and respond (or not respond) more effectively/appropriately.

- Larry has an impairment in social perception. Specifically, Larry misperceives what is going on about him, he forms erroneous conclusions about those events; and then he engages in ill-advised actions that are totally out-of-step with the situation.
- Similarly, Larry is hypervigilant to comments and interactions that he misinterprets as being criticism and/or rejection.
- Larry's moodiness almost guarantees the rejection by peers that he anticipates. He needs to learn what it is that he does that either attracts or repels his peers.
- Larry needs a clear plan on how to problem solve social situations (i.e., addressing the difficulties with the spontaneous adaptation of his approach and responses to fit the needs and personalities of others in a constantly changing social milieu).
- Ultimately, Larry needs to be provided with an effective way that he might tolerate and control strong emotions when they emerge.

Consideration should also be given to having Larry join a social group (not necessarily formally therapeutic) and/or be provided with a social coach (who is trained specifically on how to work with Larry's difficulties), so that a corrective experience could be provided to Larry for the above areas.

Additionally, I have found that certain non-special education activity groups (some sports-related, some not sports-related) have been especially helpful in providing corrective experiences as well. Some of those groups—such as agricultural groups, 4-H clubs, wrestling, and marching band—involve in-school program changes, so that those students share many of the same classes. Where possible, Larry should be provided priority access to those groups/clubs. I understand, in fact, that Larry in the past has participated in Chess Club, and he currently rides horses. I encourage both of those activities.

School Placement

Larry's school placement should be carefully chosen, and the appropriate supports put in place before he is transferred from Home Hospital. At this time, Larry is an exceptionally emotionally fragile pre-teen. He is vulnerable to anxiety/depression, has a fairly low sense of self-worth, and has a low frustration tolerance. Care will need to be taken so that the school faculty responds to Larry in a manner that does not inadvertently exacerbate his social-emotional issues.

The placement chosen should include a good deal of structure and routine, yet be flexible enough to implement the specific supports that Larry will require. I'd rather those supports be worked out between Larry, a therapist, and the IEP team before he is transferred. Some of those supports will need to include a realistic plan:

- To assist Larry in monitoring of his emotional state (taking regular temperature readings, and breaks when needed)
- To provide Larry with a safe place to go when he feels overwhelmed and the need to escape the situation (e.g., the counselor's office)
- To review with his teacher, his social-coach (if provided), and other staff how to interact with Larry when he becomes distressed

Accommodations

Larry did display a weakness in processing speed and visual-scanning/discrimination, and its impact was apparent on speeded orthographic and reading tasks. It would not surprise me if writing speed were also adversely affected. I'd like to see Larry be accommodated for his processing speed weakness, by being provided with up to 50% additional extended time on tests and on in-class assignments.

Additional Assessments

Larry displayed a weakness/deficit in visual-scanning/discrimination, which appears to impact his orthographical awareness. The academic impact would be on reading speed/comprehension, writing, and alignment of the numbers and other symbols when computing math on paper.

Importantly, while the above may be pertinent, those deficits are not responsible for Larry's disparate emotional state. A referral for a vision therapy assessment may be warranted, but it should not be elevated to a priority status.

As always, I invite personal discussion about Larry Robeson with those individuals who have the appropriate releases and who have Larry's best interests in mind.

Psychoeducational Evaluation of a Bilingual Student with a Visual Impairment

Sarah Gaines

The following psychoeducational evaluation was conducted with a bilingual student with a visual impairment to determine the presence of a learning disability. In this case, the traditional assessment process for a learning disability was compounded by the presence of a visual impairment and two languages. To ensure an accurate and unbiased diagnosis, it was necessary to address the impact that her visual impairment and linguistic abilities would have on the results of testing while still recognizing her academic struggles.

As with all students with sensory impairments, examiners must be able to reflect on the accuracy and appropriateness of the assessment measures used. The availability of well-constructed cognitive tests in a tactual form or braille for individuals with visual impairments is virtually nonexistent. We are therefore left with assessing the individual's verbal abilities through the spoken verbal subtests of the assessment measure, which presents its own challenges. First and foremost, the test measure now depends solely on a student's auditory abilities. Secondly, verbal abilities such as vocabulary and related concepts can be reduced in an individual with a visual impairment when compared with that of a sighted person due to a lack of incidental learning opportunities that result from a lack of vision. Moreover, one must consider the degree of time involved in decoding braille or reading large print and the rate of becoming fatigued when accessing information in this medium. Finally, any results must be interpreted with caution because the measures used were not normed on the population that is being tested, and as such we are then comparing them to a typically functioning peer group.

Furthermore, very few standardized achievement tests are available for braille readers and only one has been specifically adapted and provided with a scoring system dedicated to it—the Woodcock-Johnson III NU Tests of Achievement-Braille Adaptation (WJ III ACH-Braille). Although it is now available, it has not been out long enough for someone to get pre- and post-tests on it. Regarding the assessment of academic abilities, we are able to attempt diagnostic teaching and testing with criterion-reference measures to find out what a child can and cannot do, but most examiners cannot do this alone. The certified Teacher of the Visually Impaired (TVI) will be the examiner's biggest ally in such situations. Even the WJ III ACH – Braille requires this team approach. The TVI can assist the examiner in knowing and understanding the impact of the student's sensory impairment, the student's abilities in comparison to what an individual with a visual impairment should be able to do at specific developmental levels, the student's access to appropriate education, and his or her preferred media (e.g., braille, enlarged print).

With a child like Anna, these aforementioned concerns are further compounded by the involvement of a second language issue. In these situations, examiners must ensure that the tasks presented are still measuring what they purport to measure after any accommodations, presentation in different media, and so forth. In this particular case, I addressed the assessment concerns with the addition of a bilingual ancillary examiner, consulted with specialists with educational backgrounds in visual impairments, and carefully interpreted the assessment data. The overall results were then based on a team decision-making process.

PSYCHOEDUCATIONAL EVALUATION

Name:	Anna Delgado
Date of Birth:	10/7/1998
Age:	11-8

Parents:	Oscar and Maria Delgado
Ethnicity:	Hispanic
Language of the Home:	Spanish
Language of Instruction:	English paired with braille
Educational Program:	California State Schools for the Deaf and the Blind Middle School for the Blind
Dates of Evaluation:	6/8, 6/10, 6/11, 6/15, 6/18, 6/19, & 7/9/10
Evaluators:	Sarah Gaines, Psy.S., NCSP School Psychologist

REASON FOR REFERRAL

Anna was referred for a psychoeducational evaluation to address possible learning disabilities in the areas of language and/or math. Anna's educational team expressed concerns related to her expressive language and her acquisition of mathematical concepts, as well as a general difficulty in processing and retaining information.

BACKGROUND INFORMATION

Anna Delgado is an 11-year-old female student currently attending the California State Schools for the Deaf and the Blind's Middle School for the Blind (CSDB) in Bakersfield, California. Anna has bilateral blindness secondary to Grade V Retinopathy of Prematurity (ROP), with complete bilateral retinal detachments. Anna has a history of corneal grafts bilaterally and keratoprosthesis in the left eye; the cornea in her right eye became opacified. Anna has no light perception.

Anna lives with her parents, Maria and Oscar Delgado, and her older sister in Bakersfield, California. Anna also has three older brothers who are married and no longer live in the home. Spanish is noted to be the primary language spoken in the home, although Anna's father and sister speak English. Anna's primary language of instruction is English. As documented in Anna's IEP, she will need braille and braille instruction in all subject areas based on her current and future reading and writing skills and needs. Anna is primarily a tactual learner, who also relies heavily on listening to get information. Her primary learning medium is braille and her secondary learning medium is auditory.

Mrs. Delgado's pregnancy was complicated by hypertension. Anna was born prematurely via Cesarean section at 25 weeks' gestation. She weighed 1 lb., 4 oz. at birth and remained hospitalized for 3 months with complications including cardiovascular and respiratory symptoms, nutrition concerns, anemia, and disseminated intravascular coagulation (a blood clotting disorder). While in the hospital, Anna received a blood transfusion. Due to problems with chronic lung disease, when Anna was sent home in April 1999 she was on oxygen; records indicate that the oxygen was discontinued by July of that year. Other significant health history includes the diagnosis of a modest sized atrial septal defect that was monitored but did not require medication and a large patent ductus arteriosus at birth that was closed with the use of Indomethacin.

Anna's developmental milestones were reportedly met within normal age ranges. She began walking and talking at 12 months. Other significant health history issues include an appendectomy at the age of 4 and a history of anemia from infancy. Anna is not currently taking any medications and is reported to be allergic to penicillin.

EDUCATIONAL HISTORY

Anna began receiving early intervention services at the age of 4 months through the Early Intervention program at the California State Schools for the Deaf and the Blind (CSDB). Services she received at this time included occupational therapy (OT), physical therapy (PT), and speech therapy. In 2003, Anna began attending the School for the Blind at CSDB Bakersfield's campus as a kindergarten student. Anna continues to attend CSDB and is currently enrolled as a sixth-grade student in the middle school. Educational records indicate Anna has a history of high absenteeism. When asked about this, Mrs. Delgado noted this occurred only during one school year due to Anna's feelings toward staff.

Anna currently receives OT services to address inefficiencies in gross motor activities, especially those requiring integration of the two sides of the body. Roz Corbett, M.A., OTR/L, noted that as of December 2009, Anna is behind her age-peers academically and experiences difficulties with organizing her thoughts in both English and Spanish. In addition, Anna receives Orientation and Mobility training, which is currently focued on learning to travel independently in residential and light business areas. At this time, Anna is unable to cross any street independently, and although her cane usage is adequate for on-campus travel, it is inadequate for unpredictable terrain. Anna is beginning to develop the skills to use cardinal directions and the sun for orientation, and is able to make accurate 90-degree turns in isolation.

According to teacher reports, Anna is working approximately 2 to 3 years below grade level in all subject areas, which is consistent with her April 2009 California Instrument for Measuring Standards testing results (Far Below the Standard for Math and Reading, Met the Standard for Writing). At times, Anna is noted to forget or confuse material she has already learned. In addition, educational staff has noted that Anna has difficulty organizing and expressing her thoughts orally and in writing. In spite of this, Anna seems to enjoy classroom writing activities. She is able to spell many one-syllable and high-frequency words correctly and is fairly successful on writing tasks, especially when using her BrailleNote, an electronic braille note taker that provides auditory feedback. Anna's instructional reading level is noted to be in the upper fourth- to fifth-grade level depending on the text. Kathleen Forsythe, her teacher from last year, noted that Anna has good decoding skills and can sound out many new multisyllabic words she encounters. Her overall level of reading comprehension is limited, however, due to her deficits in vocabulary. These deficits likely result from her visual impairment combined with a lack of English vocabulary. As of October 2009, Anna met her language arts goals.

All of Anna's teachers are concerned about her math performance. She has difficulties with numbers, addition, subtraction, and mathematical concepts. These difficulties do not appear to be language specific. In the area of math, Anna is currently working from a fourth-grade level text. Her teachers observed that she has difficulty understanding math concepts and retaining what she has learned. Her Present Levels of Performance as of her November 2009 IEP indicated that she is able to count, read, and write numbers to 999 with some help; count by 2s to 20, 5s to 100, and 10s to 100; perform addition and subtraction facts up to 20 using a finger counting method; and multiply by 0, 1, 2, 5, and 10 by using a counting by multiples method. In addition, she is able to add and subtract 2-digit numbers with assistance; count groups of assorted dimes, nickels, and pennies to $1.00; and understand simple word problems using addition and subtraction. Ms. Forsythe noted that at the time, a calculator had proven a valuable tool in speeding up the pace of Anna's math instruction and in helping her understand concepts when calculation became difficult. As of October 2009, Anna did not meet her math goal of solving four out of five word problems by dividing a number under 50 evenly by a single-digit number.

RESULTS OF PREVIOUS EVALUATIONS

Todd Hunter, NCSP, school psychologist for Bakersfield Unified School District (BUSD) evaluated Anna in February 2002. Mr. Hunter conducted the evaluation in Spanish and used the Battelle Developmental Inventory along with a review of Anna's performance as documented by her teachers on the Oregon Project for Visually Impaired/Blind Preschool Children. Results of the evaluation indicated that Anna's personal-social skills were within the expected ranges, whereas her adaptive skills were significantly delayed. Among her adaptive skills, Anna's greatest areas of challenge were: eating, dressing, personal responsibility, and toileting. At 3 years old, Anna was unable to independently perform tasks such as feeding herself, drinking from a glass, or dressing herself with even simple articles of clothing. Moreover, it was noted that Anna was not able to use the toilet independently and was still wearing diapers.

In February 2003, a physical and occupational therapy evaluation was conducted. The evaluators for BUSD, Sharon Ruef, P.T., and Christine Shenk, OTR/L, used observations along with a parent interview and a review of records. Results indicated that Anna's gross-motor skills were age appropriate and her fine-motor skills were developing well. Anna was able to walk, run, go up and down stairs (with adult assistance or railing), and ride toys. She was able to effectively use her hands to see and manipulate objects. It was recommended that Anna continue to be challenged with manipulatives (e.g., bottles with different tops, Velcro, zippers) to further develop her fine-motor skills.

In March and April 2005, Anna participated in an exit evaluation conducted by the California State Schools for the Deaf and the Blind's Visually Impaired Preschool Center. The evaluators, Vicki Morris, M.Ed., and Carla Vaughn, M.Ed., used the following measures in their assessment: Oregon Project for Visually Impaired/Blind Preschool Children, the Maxfield-Buchholz Social Maturity Scale for Blind Preschool Children (an adaptation of the Vineland Social Maturity Scale), and the Assessment of Braille Literacy Skills (ABLS). Results of the evaluation indicated that Anna demonstrated age-appropriate skills in all areas with the exception of cognitive skills. Anna presented with strengths in language (Spanish), socialization, and self-help skills. Furthermore, her fine-motor skills were noted to be within age-appropriate levels, although she did exhibit difficulty with tasks requiring hand and finger strength.

ASSESSMENT STRATEGY

The results of this present psychoeducational assessment are considered a valid estimate of Anna's current level of functioning and typical behavior patterns. It is important to note that the tests administered were not normed on the visually-impaired population and should be interpreted with some degree of caution. All tests were administered using spoken English paired with braille or standard tactile representations with the exception of the Batería III and portions of the Bilingual Verbal Ability Tests (BVAT) NU, which were conducted in Spanish via an ancillary examiner. Results from the Batería III will be interspersed throughout the discussion and interpretation of the testing as a whole; both English and Spanish testing results will be discussed under the broad ability area being measured (e.g., Oral Language). Careful attention was given to providing a testing environment that was both comfortable and free from distractions. Breaks were taken when needed, positive reinforcement and encouragement were used with Anna as necessary, and the examiner took care in ensuring that Anna understood all directions and task expectations.

Assessments Administered

Batería III Woodcock-Muñoz NU Pruebas de habilidades cognitivas, selected tests

Bilingual Verbal Ability Tests NU (BVAT)

Brigance Diagnostic Comprehensive Inventory of Basic Skills Revised, selected subtests (CIBS-R)

California Verbal Learning Test: Children's Version (CVLT-C)

Tactile Test of Basic Concepts (TTBC), a tactile version of the Boehm Test of Basic Concepts

Vineland Adaptive Behavior Scales, Second Edition (Vineland-II)

Survey Interview Form with Mrs. Delgado (in Spanish)

Teacher Rating Form completed by Isabel Duncan and Cathy Forsythe, Teachers of the Visually Impaired

Wechsler Intelligence Scale for Children-Fourth Edition (WISC-IV): Verbal Comprehension Index and Working Memory Index

Woodcock-Johnson III NU Tests of Cognitive Abilities including Diagnostic Supplement (WJ III DS), selected tests

Woodcock-Johnson III NU Tests of Achievement–Braille adaptation (WJ III ACH-Braille) selected tests

OBSERVATIONS

Anna was observed over multiple occasions during her participation in academic tasks such as writing, spelling, and mathematics. She participated in all of the classroom activities through answering questions, offering information, and appropriately interacting with her teacher and peers. During one language arts activity, Anna was using her braille writer to document the daily news (a classroom activity) and write stories. There were times when Anna was unsure of how to spell a word, how to word her idea, or even what to write. She knew, however, when to ask for assistance and would then commence working. It is likely that Anna's difficulties with putting her ideas into words are directly related to the fact that Spanish is her primary language. Anna was also observed during a math activity focusing on using graphs to track the number of gold medals obtained by the United States and China during the summer Olympics. She was able to count how many medals the U.S. team already had and with the help of classmates, determine how many to add to her graph. When asked the difference in the number of medals between China and the United States, Anna could identify that China had more, but was unable to perform mental math to compute the answer.

Anna was also observed during her Orientation and Mobility (O & M) lesson with Laquetha Rhein, Certified Orientation and Mobility Specialist. During this period, Anna was planning a route to two stores on a local street and then creating a map of the area. Using a tape recorder and a BrailleNote to document the details of the conversation, Anna called directory assistance to request the business's telephone number and then placed a call to the store to ascertain their exact address, the closest intersection, and any landmarks nearby. Although Anna was fairly independent in calling for information, she still needed some help with the process as this was only her third time planning a route. However, according to Ms. Rhein, Anna is already becoming more comfortable with the sequential steps of the process. When constructing the map, Anna required a greater amount of assistance from Ms. Rhein, especially when it came to orienting the streets (East-West, North-South), determining the block numbers, and figuring out if the street address was an even or an odd number. During the O & M session, it became apparent that Anna exhibited difficulties with concepts directly related to math. For example, when asked if Kenilworth Boulevard runs parallel or perpendicular to 4th Avenue, Anna continued to answer incorrectly, saying that it ran parallel. Also, after marking off sections to denote blocks, Anna was directed to begin counting to determine where a specific block was, such as the 400th block. She was unable to count out the blocks without assistance as she kept leaving out blocks (e.g., 900, 800, 500). Finally, Anna was asked to determine what side of the street a business would be on based on whether the street number was even or odd. Anna was unable to determine if a number was odd or even and therefore could not ascertain what side of the street the business was on.

Anna was a willing participant in all assessment activities during the testing that lasted several academic periods over multiple days within a 2-week span of time. She consistently put forth her best effort, and was noted to increase both her effort and focus on tasks that were challenging for her. Anna was eager to go with the examiner for each session and would participate in conversation on the way to and from testing. She presented as an inquisitive young lady who would ask questions about the day's activities and the date of the next session. Throughout the testing, Anna responded well to positive reinforcement. When presented with items she did not know, she was not easily discouraged. There were times during the English portions of the testing, however, that it was evident that Anna became unsure of herself. For example, she would give an answer, and then follow it with "I don't know" or "how am I going to say it?" It seemed that she was having difficulty accessing the English vocabulary to express her thoughts. She also demonstrated some phrasing which is likely a result of interference from her primary language such as "I don't have no ideas."

COGNITIVE ASSESSMENT FINDINGS AND INTERPRETATIONS

Verbal Comprehension

Anna's verbal reasoning abilities as measured by the WISC-IV Verbal Comprehension Index (VCI) are in the Very Low range and above those of approximately 1% of her sighted age peers (VCI=67; 90% confidence interval=63–75). The verbal reasoning tasks are designed to measure Anna's verbal reasoning and concept formation. It is important to note that Anna's Verbal Comprehension performance is based on her abilities in the English

language. Although Spanish is Anna's primary language and the primary language spoken in her home, English has been her language of instruction since entering early intervention services at 4 months of age. Examination of Anna's performance on the individual subtests provides additional useful information regarding her specific verbal abilities. Anna performed comparably on the verbal subtests contributing to the VCI, with all areas in the Very Low to Low range when compared to her same-age peers without a visual impairment, suggesting that these verbal cognitive abilities are similarly developed.

On tasks requiring Anna to use one primary idea to convey relationships among words (Similarities subtest), she demonstrated success when the questions elicited concrete, easily identifiable relationships (e.g., cat-mouse). However, Anna exhibited marked difficulties as the relationships between the items became less overt, requiring a greater degree of abstraction on her part (e.g., writer-artist). Her overall performance on this task was in the Low range, well below that of her sighted peers.

Anna was then presented with tasks requiring her to provide oral solutions to everyday problems and to explain the underlying reasons for these general principles (Comprehension subtest). These tasks assessed her understanding of social situations and judgment as well as her knowledge of conventional standards of behavior. On this task, she was able to provide solutions for situations such as returning lost items and appropriate courses of action to take in an emergency, but she demonstrated gaps in her knowledge of peer and community-related concepts. Again, Anna's performance indicated abilities in the Low range when compared to her same-age sighted peers.

Anna's verbal abilities were further examined with tasks requiring her to provide oral definitions for single words (Vocabulary subtest). Defining words provides a measure of Anna's fund of information, concept formation, and language development. Anna demonstrated her lowest verbal performance on these tasks, indicating deficits in her English language development, especially expressively.

Two additional, supplemental subtests of verbal comprehension were administered to gather more information regarding Anna's verbal abilities in her language of instruction. The first of the two subtests, Information, measures her knowledge of facts through answering questions on various types of content such as body parts, calendar information, and historical facts. Anna's factual knowledge appeared filled with gaps, with no specific pattern related to the information she did not know. Anna was also administered Word Reasoning, a subtest that provides a measure of her verbal reasoning, deductive reasoning, verbal abstraction, and ability to generate alternative concepts. With Word Reasoning, Anna was required to identify the common object or concept being described by an increasingly specific series of one to three clues. Anna's pattern of performance was comparable to her results on Similarities in that the overt, easily identifiable items were easier for her than those that required complex, deductive reasoning.

Dr. Ferraro, the ancillary examiner, assessed the depth of Anna's general verbal knowledge in Spanish via two tasks: identifying where objects are typically found and identifying what people usually do with an object (Batería III General Information test). In addition to her general verbal knowledge, this task also addresses her semantic memory and her ability to access declarative knowledge. Anna's performance was in the Low range when compared to her age peers without a visual impairment. Her abilities as measured by the Relative Proficiency Index (RPI) indicate that when average age peers would have 90% success in tasks of general knowledge, Anna is predicted to have only 30% success. In other words, Anna demonstrates limited proficiency in this area and is likely to find these types of tasks to be very difficult.

Retrieval

Anna was administered the test of Retrieval Fluency in both English and Spanish in order to examine the ease and speed of her ability to retrieve words from long-term memory. The Retrieval Fluency tasks required Anna to produce as many examples from a specific semantic category (e.g., names) as she is able to during a 1-minute interval. This requires retrieval from stored knowledge (long-term retrieval), recognition abilities, and oral production abilities. Anna's performance in Spanish was Low Average, whereas her performance in English was within the Average range of ability when compared to her age peers. These results indicate that Anna's quick retrieval of stored knowledge for basic concepts/facts will likely be a manageable task for her in either language. Anna's relative success on this task was likely a result of the task demands in that she was provided with a semantic cue to aid in the formation of her thoughts. This means that Anna will likely perform better on verbal tasks when she is given a prompt to organize her thoughts. Dr. Ferraro observed very little interchanging of Spanish and English, indicating that Anna separates her languages. This clear delineation of the boundaries between two languages is not common among bilingual children with backgrounds such as Anna's.

Linguistic Functioning

To gain a better understanding of Anna's linguistic abilities across both languages and to examine the differences, if any, between them, Anna was administered a number of tasks meant to focus on various components of language. First, Anna was given portions of the BVAT to determine whether her verbal cognitive abilities were bolstered with Spanish. These tests were initially administered in English, and then items that Anna missed were readministered in Spanish. Although the complete test could not be administered due to her visual impairment, results of the Oral Vocabulary and Verbal Analogies tests (English) suggest that Anna's verbal cognitive abilities are within the Low range when compared to her age peers without a visual impairment. Readministration of items in Spanish did improve her scores somewhat, although some of the items that she answered incorrectly in English, she answered incorrectly in Spanish as well, often giving the same answer across languages. The items she was able to answer successfully in Spanish were words that are likely to be used in a home environment, where Spanish is the primary language. Overall, when compared to her age peers without a visual impairment, Anna's performance on these tasks indicated very limited proficiency regardless of which language was used to assess her abilities, indicating that such vocabulary tasks will be extremely difficult for her to manage.

Anna was also administered tasks of phonemic awareness in Spanish, which includes the knowledge and skills related to analyzing and synthesizing speech sounds. Her performance on the cluster indicated overall abilities in the High Average range when compared to her age peers without a visual impairment, indicating that her phonological processing abilities in her primary language are intact. Anna performed better on tasks requiring her to synthesize language sounds, or phonemes, to form a word than on tasks requiring her to complete a word when one or more phonemes were missing, but both abilities are well developed. Phonemic awareness is an important foundational linguistic ability in that it allows Anna to perceive and manipulate language sounds. Furthermore, a person with good phonemic awareness is able to recognize that words are composed of discrete segments of speech sounds, a necessary skill for becoming a proficient reader and speller.

To examine Anna's linguistic competency and vocabulary knowledge in English, she was presented with tasks requiring her to listen to a story and then recall the elements of that story (WJ III ACH Story Recall and Story Recall Delayed). Tasks of story recall provide a measure of expressive and receptive language skills as well as aspects of oral language such listening comprehension and meaningful memory. Anna's performance was in the Average range across both on the recall and delayed recall tasks, indicating that she is well able to attend to, comprehend, store, retrieve, and express details that she hears within narrative language.

In order to further examine Anna's receptive language abilities in English, she was presented with the WJ III ACH-Braille Oral Comprehension test, which required her to listen to a short passage and then provide the final word to complete it. Oral comprehension is a primarily receptive language task, which provides a measure of listening ability and language development as well as one's ability to access and make use of previously acquired knowledge, syntax, and context clues. Anna's performance was in the Low range. When examined in light of her Average performance on story recall tasks, it is apparent that Anna struggles with accessing specific vocabulary words as opposed to her broader comprehension abilities. Furthermore, the task demands are heavily reliant upon Anna's fund of acquired knowledge, which, as previously discussed, was in the Low range.

Memory and Learning

To assess Anna's memory skills related to verbal information (English), the California Verbal Learning Test, Children's Version (CVLT-C) was administered. The CVLT-C provides insights into the strategies and processes involved in her learning and recall of verbal material within the context of an everyday shopping task. Both recall and recognition of words are measured over a number of trials. Anna's ability to repeat a list of words the first time she heard it indicated a High Average initial memory span for auditory-verbal information. On her fifth learning attempt, her performance was Average. In addition, her total recall of the word list across the five learning trials was High Average compared to others her age.

The CVLT-C is also useful in providing information regarding Anna's learning characteristics. For example, one can determine whether Anna is using semantic or serial clustering strategies. Anna's use of semantic clustering was Low Average when compared to others her age; however, she did not overly use serial clustering (an ineffective learning strategy). Anna would likely benefit from learning

how to utilize more effective strategies for remembering verbal information, such as expanding her use of semantic clustering.

Another learning characteristic measured by the CVLT-C is Anna's learning style, which is determined by examining her ability to recall words from different regions of the list. Active learners tend to recall words from the more difficult regions of the list, that is, the beginning and middle, while passive learners are more likely to recall words from the end of the list. Anna's pattern of recall is indicative of an active learning style, which bodes well for her in the classroom in that she is likely attending to lectures, trying to put meaning to lessons, and retaining the information.

Anna's performance on short-delay tasks indicated Average abilities and suggests that category cueing aided her recall. Following a delay of about 20 minutes, Anna again demonstrated Average recall and benefitted from category cueing. Across all tasks, Anna's perseveration rate was mildly elevated, in that she had a slight tendency to repeat some of the words. Overall, Anna's ability to recognize information was about the same as her ability to recall it. Taken together, these findings suggest that Anna exhibited adequate encoding and retrieval skills in learning verbal information within the context of a stated category. Anna's performance indicated that she will benefit from the provision of category cues to organize her thinking with language and to prompt retrieval.

Anna's memory skills were also evaluated through the Working Memory Index on the WISC-IV, which measured her short-term auditory memory along with her ability to sustain attention, concentrate, and exert mental control. Anna's performance indicated overall working memory abilities in the Low range when compared to her same-age peers without a visual impairment (WMI = 77; 90% confidence interval = 70–83). She performed somewhat better on tasks where numbers were the only stimuli (Digit Span) than on tasks requiring a greater degree of information processing by incorporating numbers and letters simultaneously (Letter-Number Sequencing), with Low Average and Low abilities, respectively. In addition, her performance with numbers-only stimuli in Spanish also indicated abilities in the Average range when compared to her age mates (Numbers Reversed).

Anna's Low to Low Average performance on tasks of working memory will likely impact her ability to hold information in short-term memory while manipulating and attempting to transform it. Weaknesses in the mental control required by working memory may slow new learning and impede Anna's processing of complex information.

Anna will likely exhibit difficulties in the organization and storage of newly received information for generalization and use in subsequent academic activities.

Finally, Anna's Auditory Memory Span was assessed in English via the WJ III COG Memory for Words and Memory for Sentences. Auditory Memory Span provides a measure of Anna's ability to listen to and then immediately recall sequentially ordered, but noncontextual, information after one presentation. This type of memory is necessary for following directions, memorizing phone numbers, and otherwise holding on to verbal information that is being given when the sequence is important. When compared to others at her grade level without a visual impairment, Anna's performance was in the Low Average range, and lower on these tests than on the CVLT-C and on Story Recall. Anna appeared to perform better with memory tasks that incorporated a context that held meaning for her. The Memory for Sentences task, in this case, might be considered noncontextual because, although each sentence has meaning, the meaning does not necessarily relate to a context with which Anna has had experience. Additionally, each sentence is different, providing considerably less context than a story would. This may explain why Anna performed so much better on the Story Recall test. Surprisingly, Anna also scored within the Average range on the CVLT-C. Again, the provision of context may help to explain this higher score, as the words were presented within the format of a shopping list, a familiar task in Anna's everyday life. As well, sequence was not important. Results such as these indicate that Anna will find rote memory tasks to be very difficult unless they have a similarity in category.

ACADEMIC ASSESSMENT FINDINGS AND INTERPRETATIONS

Mathematics

Anna is currently working from a fourth-grade level text and exhibits difficulty understanding addition, subtraction, and other math concepts that are not language specific. Mrs. Delgado shared that at home, Anna is unable to identify money (i.e., coins) and has trouble reading and identifying her numbers in braille. The information gathered on this assessment indicated Anna's performance without a calculator. Aside from presentation of materials in braille, accommodations to testing included the use of an abacus where appropriate since sighted children are provided with scratch paper.

To assess Anna's familiarity with foundational math terminology (e.g., ordinal placement, quantity, distance), she was administered the Tactile Test of Basic Concepts, a tactile version of the Boehm Test of Basic Concepts. Anna was required to tactilely view a series of shapes and patterns along a plastic card and then answer questions related to the forms on the card. (e.g., "Put your finger on the rectangle with the dot at the top"). Anna demonstrated understanding of the majority of verbally based math concepts presented such as *top, center, middle, inside, over, farthest, around, below, nearest, right, left, pair, half, equal*, and *least*. In addition, she was able to consistently identify the following shapes: square, rectangle, circle, and triangle. She did not understand the following concepts: *skip, several, widest, most, between, matches, next to, side, medium-sized*, and *after*. The items Anna was unable to answer correctly appeared consistent across other assessment measures and teacher reports. The Number Series and Number Matrices tests (WJ III COG DS), which make up the Numerical Reasoning cluster, were brailled for this assessment.

Anna's performance on this cluster indicated overall performance in the Very Low range when compared to her age mates without a visual impairment. Numerical Reasoning provided a measure of Anna's fluid reasoning abilities, quantitative reasoning abilities, and mathematics knowledge. The Number Series tasks required Anna to determine a numerical sequence through identifying and applying an underlying rule. Anna was able to complete simple number series items where the missing number was next in the number line when counting up (e.g., 2, 3, 4, __). She was unable to successfully complete items requiring her to count backward e.g., 9, 8, 7, __) or those requiring her to count by 2s or 3s. Number Matrices tasks required Anna to determine a 2-dimensional numerical pattern and the relationship between/among numbers to complete an analogy. Anna was unable to complete any of the items on Number Matrices tasks. Based on her RPIs, Anna's proficiency is negligible, indicating that she will find numerical reasoning tasks to be impossible.

Anna was also administered the WJ III ACH-Braille Applied Problems test, which provided a measure of Anna's numerical reasoning and ability to apply math knowledge and skills. Anna was required to listen to the problem, sift through extraneous information, determine the procedure to be followed, and then perform relatively simple calculations. Anna was able to correctly identify coins and a dollar bill, add small amounts in pennies, and complete simple word problems when provided with raised graphics (e.g., I have 7 sticks; if I took away 5, how many would I have left?). Consistent with teacher reports, Anna did not demonstrate the ability to read a braille clock or thermometer, or to use her abacus independently. Overall, Anna's performance was in the Very Low range when compared to her age mates without a visual impairment. Her proficiency as measured by the RPI indicates negligible skills, implying that tasks of this nature will be impossible for her to complete independently. It is important to note that math reasoning tasks like this are heavily reliant on Anna's oral language abilities, as it requires her to move back and forth between verbal and tactile representations. When taking her low oral comprehension abilities in English and her low general information abilities in Spanish into consideration, it is difficult to pinpoint the root of Anna's very low performance in linguistically-laden aspects of mathematics.

Finally, Anna was given select sections of the Brigance Diagnostic Comprehensive Inventory of Basic Skills, Revised (CIBS-R) to further assess her mathematics skills. Although standard scores were not obtained, the information that was collected is valuable in describing the skills Anna possesses as well as those that she still needs to develop. Anna's overall performance indicated computational skills at the first-grade level and problem-solving skills in the first- to second-grade range of ability. Anna was able to read numbers to 9 with 100% accuracy, numbers to 99 with approximately 83% accuracy, and numbers to 999 with approximately 66% accuracy. Using her braillewriter, Anna was able to write numbers between 0 and 100. She demonstrated some understanding of ordinal numbers, indicated by her ability to identify the following: *first*, *last*, *third*, *fifth*, *second*, and *fourth*. She was *unable* to read meters and gauges or round numbers.

As part of the CIBS-R administration, Anna was also given tasks to gauge her knowledge of and fluency with addition and subtraction facts. Anna was only asked to read the item and respond orally in order to provide a more accurate measure of her fluency, unhindered by having to braille all of her answers. In addition, she knew facts for sums up to 6 with 80% accuracy, up to 8 with 70% accuracy, up to 10 with 80% accuracy, and up to 12 with 80% accuracy. With subtraction, Anna knew differences for minuends up to 6 with 70% accuracy and up to 8 with 60% accuracy. Anna's performance across both addition and subtraction facts was observed to be extremely slow with a lack of automaticity, as she responded slowly and counted on her fingers.

ADAPTIVE BEHAVIOR

The Vineland Adaptive Behavior Scales, Second Edition (Vineland-II) measures the personal and social skills of individuals from birth through adulthood. Because adaptive behavior refers to an individual's typical performance of the day-to-day activities required for personal and social sufficiency, these scales assess what a person actually does, rather than what he or she is able to do. The Vineland-II assesses adaptive behavior in three domains for Anna's age group: Communication, Daily Living Skills, and Socialization. It also provides a composite score that summarizes her performance across these domains.

According to Mrs. Delgado, Anna's performance across all three domains varied considerably, with scores in the Low, Moderately Low, and Adequate ranges of functioning. Based on Mrs. Delgado's perception of Anna, the area of communication emerged as a relative strength with abilities in the Adequate range of functioning. Mrs. Delgado reported that Anna's receptive and expressive skills are adequate, while her written communication appears much lower. Anna loves to read and can easily devote time and attention to reading or being read to; she is able to understand idioms in Spanish but not English, likes to tell people how to do things, can say her complete home address, and has expressed long-term goals such as studying to be a teacher or driving, once a special car for people with visual impairments is invented. Her written communication skills in the home environment are in marked contrast to her receptive and expressive oral lauguage strengths. Mrs. Delgado notes that although Anna can braille letters in order to write, she is unable to braille numbers. Furthermore, she cannot write her address or put things in alphabetical order.

Anna's next-highest area of ability, according to Mrs. Delgado, is in the Socialization domain, with scores in the Moderately Low range of performance. Mrs. Delgado notes that Anna's coping skills are adequate in that she is able to accept suggestions from others, apologize for unintended errors, and understand gentle teasing as humor; however, she has trouble keeping secrets and forgetting things that upset her. Anna's interpersonal relationships and play and leisure abilities were rated as Moderately Low and Low, respectively. Mrs. Delgado notes that Anna's only friends are the ones she has at school, as she does not socialize with the children in the neighborhood. She is able to take turns, follow the rules of simple games, share without being prompted to do so, and ask permission to use items belonging to another.

Anna's abilities in Daily Living Skills are noted to be her weakest area of ability, according to her mother.

Although Anna is independent in personal skills of daily living such as bathing and dressing, and community skills such as saving money, ordering meals for herself when told what is available, and using the speed dial on the telephone to make calls, she is considerably behind her age-peers in domestic skills. One of the primary reasons she is unable to complete many domestic skills is a lack of experience. Anna will occasionally fold clothes, but beyond that is not responsible for any other chores at home; her father expresses concerns regarding Anna's safety related to chores and her mother mentions that she babies Anna somewhat.

Isabel Duncan and Cathy Forsythe, Teachers of the Visually Impaired, also served as the raters on the Vineland. From the educational staff's perspective, Anna's area of relative strength is in Socialization as opposed to Communication. According to her teachers, Anna's areas of adaptive behavior are as follows: Communication and Daily Living Skills are within the Moderately Low range of functioning, while Socialization is Adequate.

SUMMARY

Anna is an 11-year-old youngster currently attending CSDB's Middle School for the Blind in Bakersfield, California. She has bilateral blindness secondary to ROP Grade V with complete bilateral retinal detachments. Anna is primarily a tactual learner, who also relies heavily on listening to get information. Her primary learning medium is braille and her secondary learning medium is auditory. She was referred for a psychoeducational evaluation to address a possible learning disability in the areas of language and/or math.

Results of current psychoeducational testing indicate that Anna's verbal abilities in English are in the Very Low range when compared to her peers without a visual impairment. Her verbal abilities in Spanish, however, indicate variable functioning based on the nature of the language task, ranging from Low to High Average. In addition, this evaluation found Anna's auditory memory to be within the Low and Low Average ranges across English and Spanish, indicating that tasks relying on her auditory memory will likely be difficult for her. Furthermore, Anna exhibits significant academic difficulty in the area of mathematics with performance in the Very Low range in tasks of calculation, application, and numerical reasoning. She demonstrated limited automaticity with single-digit addition and subtraction facts, indicating very limited overall proficiency and a weak number concept. According to her mother and her teachers, her strengths and weaknesses in

adaptive behaviors vary with her environment—home or school.

The primary language of Anna's home is Spanish. Anna has been exposed to English since she began receiving early intervention services at age 4 months. Overall results from bilingual psychoeducational testing indicate that Anna demonstrates a preference toward Spanish. Given this linguistic preference, Anna will likely struggle with many verbal tasks presented to her in the instructional setting where English is used. As was evident throughout this evaluation, her English-based performance is better when she does not need to supply specific English language vocabulary. Likewise, Anna is better able to categorize and determine relationships between items than express the meaning of individual words using either language. Anna is likely to exhibit more success on linguistically-based tasks when provided with context, when permitted to use open-ended responses to verbal queries, when new information is overtly linked to previously learned material, and when she is given many opportunities for practice and review.

While it is apparent that Anna's struggles with mathematics are compounded by her language limitations and her visual impairment, these factors cannot totally account for her weak math performance. Although Anna presents with deficits in the areas of math calculation and math reasoning, her low performance on tasks of math reasoning seems to be related to her low oral language and general linguistic abilities rather than to a learning disability per se. Therefore, while recognizing that Anna will struggle in math reasoning due to the linguistic underpinnings of such tasks, it is recommended that the team consider her as meeting the criteria of a student with a Specific Learning Disability in the area of Math Calculation only. The following recommendations are presented for team discussion.

RECOMMENDATIONS

1. Teach Anna math-related vocabulary, especially vocabulary used in word problems. List and review all words that indicate subtraction and addition (e.g., with addition: *add, altogether, and, both, how many, how much, in all, increased by, plus, sum, together, total*). Add a braille version of these word lists to her math notebook for use as an easy reference.

2. Anna was observed to use compensatory strategies such as finger counting when solving math problems. Due to the limited capacity of her working memory, it is difficult to hold on to the steps of the problem long enough to

work the calculation in this manner. Consequently, when focusing instruction on math reasoning skills and applications, allow Anna to use her calculator.

3. As part of Anna's math instruction, focus on increasing her knowledge of basic math facts.

   a. To help Anna increase her speed in math operations, provide drill on math facts using tactual stimuli such as flash cards with braille, computer programs, and when she can respond to a math fact within 3 seconds, worksheets. Eventually, move to timed tests. To add braille to the printed page, see this web site to create free flash cards: http://www.aplusmath.com/Flashcards/Flashcard_Creator.html.

   b. Administer daily timed addition or subtraction tests to see how many facts she can complete within 1 minute. Record and monitor her progress where she competes against her own best score.

   c. Anna needs to be given direct instruction in more efficient ways to calculate. For example, when given (6 + 3), she needs to be taught to "add on" instead of counting out each digit separately.

4. Encourage Anna to "chunk" information, that is, to group individual units of information into a smaller number of groups. For example, the number 1-3-5 could be remembered individually as three units or chunked as one unit of "one hundred thirty-five." Because the human memory has a limited capacity, it is suggested that material should be chunked into groups of approximately 5 +/− 2 units. This strategy can be used with lessons, directions, or other activities that will require Anna to use working memory.

5. Anna would likely benefit from learning more effective strategies for remembering verbal information. Specifically, teach Anna to think about the meanings of words when trying to remember them, and to recall words together that are close in meaning.

6. Anna is likely to exhibit more success on linguistically based tasks when provided with context that is meaningful to her. Therefore, Anna may benefit from having the content of lessons reviewed on different days, in order to ensure that this information is well encoded into her memory. In addition, encourage Anna to associate new material with previously learned material and elaborate on new concepts.

7. When asking Anna to answer questions verbally, she will likely perform better when she is not required to provide specific vocabulary. Reinforce vocabulary development with the specific terms after Anna provides her answer (e.g., If Anna's answer is "The girl, she had a job," reinforce and elaborate on this response with "Yes, Susie had a job as a cashier."). An alternative would be to provide Anna a different format to answer, as in presenting her with several options from which she must choose.

8. In order to further develop Anna's adaptive behavior skills in the area of daily living, give Anna chores to perform and teach her how to perform common household tasks. Anna has expressed interest in learning how to cook, which might serve as a springboard to developing skills of daily living.

WJ III NU Tests of Cognitive Abilities (including Diagnostic Supplement) (COG norms based on age 11-8; DS/ACH norms based on age 11-8)

CLUSTER/Test	GE	RPI	SS (68% Band)	Classification
NUMERICAL REASONING	1.2	3/90	58 (52–64)	Very Low
Number Series	1.2	1/90	56 (52–60)	Very Low
Number Matrices	<2.6	7/90	73 (65–82)	Very Low
Applied Problems*	1.5	1/90	56 (52–60)	Very Low
AUDITORY MEMORY SPAN	2.2	50/90	82 (77–86)	Low Average
Memory for Words	2.3	49/90	86 (79–92)	Low Average
Memory for Sentences	2.0	51/90	80 (75–86)	Low Average
LONG-TERM RETRIEVAL and ORAL LANGUAGE				
Retrieval Fluency	7.6	91/90	105 (99–111)	Average
Story Recall*	6.3	90/90	101 (92–109)	Average
Story Recall-Delayed*	8.9	91/90	103 (93–113)	Average
Oral Comprehension*	1.5	19/90	71 (66–76)	Low
*WJ III NU Tests of Achievement-Braille Adaptation.				

Batería III Woodcock-Muñoz NU Pruebas de habilidades cognitivas

CLUSTER/Test	GE	RPI	SS (68% Band)	Classification
PHONEMIC AWARE (*PERCEPCIÓN FONÉMICA*)	13.0	96/90	117 (111–123)	High Average
Sound Blending (Integración *de sonidos*)	16.3	99/90	122 (116–128)	Superior
Incomplete Words (Palabras *incompletes*)	5.6	89/90	99 (93–105)	Average
Numbers Reversed (*Inversión de números*)	4.8	80/90	80 (74–87)	Low/Low Average
General Information (*Información general*)	2.3	30/90	73 (67–78)	Low
Retrieval Fluency (*Fluidez de recuperación*)	3.3	86/90	84 (77–91)	Low Average

WISC-IV Summary of Performance: Composite Scores Summary

Scale	SS	PR	90% Confidence Interval	Description
Verbal Comprehension	67	1	63–75	Very Low
Working Memory	77	6	75–88	Low

Verbal Comprehension Subtest Score Summary

Subtest	Scaled Score	Percentile Rank
Similarities	5	5
Vocabulary	3	1
Comprehension	5	5
(Information)	4	2
(Word Reasoning)	5	5

Working Memory Subtest Score Summary

Subtest	Scaled Score	Percentile Rank
Digit Span	7	16
Letter-Number Sequencing	4	2
(Arithmetic)	5	5

Vineland-II Score Summary: Teacher Rating Form

(Raters: Isabel Duncan, Cathy Forsythe—Teachers of the Visually Impaired)

Domain	SS	90% Confidence Interval	PR	Adaptive Level
Communication	78	72–84	7	Moderately Low
Daily Living Skills	74	69–79	4	Moderately Low
Socialization	95	91–99	37	Adequate
Adaptive Behavior Composite	**80**	**76–84**	**9**	**Adequate**

Vineland-II Score Summary: Survey Interview Form

(Rater: Mrs. Delgado, Mother)

Domain	SS	90% Confidence Interval	PR	Adaptive Level
Communication	92	84–100	30	Adequate
Daily Living Skills	66	58–74	1	Low
Socialization	75	67–83	5	Moderately Low
Adaptive Behavior Composite	**75**	**69–81**	**5**	**Moderately Low**

CASE 33

Memory and Processing Assessments
A Report for Parents
Milton Dehn

This report was written mainly for the benefit of the parents because they initiated the assessment, and they were especially interested in trying to understand their child's learning difficulties. Consequently, there was an effort to explain cognitive processing and memory functions in a manner that the parents could readily understand. In order to accomplish this goal, the Learning, Memory, and Processing interpretation section is not organized on a test-by-test basis. Instead, data from several tests and informal methods are integrated from the perspective of an information-processing framework. One of the unique aspects of this report is a color-coded graphic that is used to illustrate the child's processing strengths and weaknesses. Another departure from traditional report writing is the summarizing of relevant information without reporting all the test scores involved.

PSYCHOLOGICAL REPORT

Name:	Jane Smalley
Date of Birth:	April 18, 1998
Age:	11 years, 9 months
School:	Grunewald Elementary School
Grade:	5
Primary Language:	English
Dates of Evaluation:	January 11 and 12, 2010
Evaluator:	Milton J. Dehn, Ph.D.

REASON FOR REFERRAL AND BACKGROUND INFORMATION

Jane was evaluated at the request of her parents, who are interested in obtaining a better understanding of her strengths and weaknesses and why she experiences learning difficulties. Jane struggles in oral language and in all areas of academic learning, except some aspects of mathematics. Although Jane reports that she likes to read, her parents report that reading is a concern. Homework is becoming more challenging for Jane, and her parents are concerned about how to maintain her school motivation and effort as she prepares to enter middle school in the fall.

Jane's learning challenges have been evident since before she entered school. As a preschooler she was diagnosed with delays in both receptive and expressive language development. It was noted in one of Jane's early language evaluations that, at times, it was difficult to understand her oral communication. (The difficulty was not due to articulation problems.) In an evaluation conducted with Jane when she was 4½ years old, the speech-language therapist, in referring to one of Jane's responses, reported that "her response did not appear to fit the question." Jane is still receiving speech-language therapy at school. In first grade, she was identified as having a learning disability and has been receiving services since that time. When she was administered the Stanford-Binet IQ test in first grade, Jane obtained a Full Scale IQ of 91, with approximately similar scores on the verbal and nonverbal scales. Her lowest score, an 86, was in working memory.

ASSESSMENT PROCEDURES

Brief interview

Review of special education records

Story Memory, Story Memory Recall, & Story Recognition from the Wide Range Assessment of Memory and Learning, Second Edition (WRAML-2)

Visuospatial Short-Term Memory Subtests from WISC-IV Integrated

Woodcock-Johnson III-NU Tests of Cognitive Abilities (WJ III COG)

Woodcock-Johnson III-NU Tests of Achievement (WJ III ACH)

School Motivation and Learning Strategies Inventory (SMALSI)

Conners' Parent Rating Scale, Revised

OBSERVATIONS

Jane was cooperative during two long testing sessions. She seemed to be making her best effort and performing up to her ability and skill levels. When she had difficulty comprehending some of the more complex test directions, the directions were repeated and paraphrased. During verbal portions of the testing, there were a few instances when it was apparent that Jane was having word retrieval problems. She would often try to explain the word she could not name. Her retrieval was slow even when retrieving a group of words in the same semantic category. Her oral communication difficulties emerged when she responded to an oral mathematics story problem with a response that had no logical connection to the question. During the one-on-one testing, her attention span seemed adequate and she persisted even on longer tasks.

RESULTS AND DISCUSSION

Cognitive testing was conducted with the WJ III COG (see attached Score Report). Jane's level of general intellectual functioning appears to be in the Low Average range, as indicated by her General Intellectual Ability (GIA) score of 85 (percentile rank of 16). Jane's verbal abilities, which are in the Low to Low Average range, are a significant individual weakness for her and are "pulling down" her overall score. Her fluid reasoning, visual-spatial processing, auditory processing, processing speed, auditory short-term memory, and phonological awareness are in the Low Average to Average range. Her verbal working memory and long-term retrieval are both Low Average (see Learning, Memory, and Processing subsection for details). Although Jane's overall performance in phonological and auditory processing is Average, her auditory closure ability (Incomplete Words) is in the Low Average range and significantly weaker than her Mid-Average Sound Blending score. Her processing speed performance is also inconsistent. She does better quickly processing the similarities and differences between real objects, based on their conceptual similarities, than between abstract symbols, based solely on visual similarities.

Learning, Memory, and Processing

This subsection will trace Jane's learning, processing, and memory functions in a flow of information from perception (input) to expression (output). After information is perceived (see Figure 1), the learner must focus attention on it if it is to be learned and remembered. The information is then briefly stored in short-term memory (STM). Short-term memory can be divided into auditory and visual-spatial components. Working memory, which is conscious processing of information, becomes involved along with short-term memory. When material is held and processed in short-term and working memory, there is more of an opportunity for the information to become encoded and stored in long-term memory. Working memory is also involved in the conscious retrieval of information from long-term memory. Long-term memory can

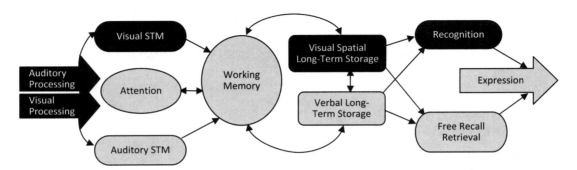

Figure 1   Jane's Processing and Memory Strengths and Weaknesses
Note: Relative strengths are black; relative weaknesses are gray.

be divided into verbal and visual-spatial storage. Retrieving information from long-term memory occurs through free recall or recognition. Regarding how these processes affect learning, auditory short-term memory span is related to vocabulary learning, and adequate working memory capacity is particularly necessary for reading comprehension, mathematics problem solving, and written expression. This analysis and summary of Jane's information-processing strengths and weaknesses are based on selective, cross-battery testing that included subtests from the WJ III COG, WRAML2, and the WISC-IV Integrated, as well as corroborating data from observations, interviews, and a review of records.

Jane's visuospatial perception appears to be average, as does her overall auditory perception and processing. At times, it appears that Jane is capable of adequately attending to incoming information. That is, she seems able to focus her attention and divide it (including filtering out distractions), but it's not clear how long she can sustain attention (see Attention subsection). Jane's ability to retain information in short-term memory is variable. Her visual-spatial short-term memory is average (see Table 1), whereas her overall ability to retain auditory content is in the Low Average range and an individual weakness for her (see Table 2). Her working memory capacity, which also controls attention and the implementation of strategies, appears to be in the Low Average range. When her short-term memory and working memory are put to work learning new information, she performs adequately as long as the learning task is structured, includes corrective feedback, and includes a visual component.

Jane's ability to encode auditory/verbal information into long-term memory seems to be a weakness. Her ability to store and retain newly learned verbal information in long-term memory is also below average. Fortunately, she appears to have good retention for the information that she is able to encode (learn). However, she has extreme difficulties with verbal retrieval, and this is the major hurdle in her processing of information. Retrieval, especially free recall, is very slow and difficult for her. She does better with cued recall, and even better with recognition. The fact that she can recognize information means that she knows and remembers it, in spite of the fact that she can't retrieve it very well on demand. Part of her retrieval difficulty may stem from not attaching cues or making associations during encoding. It's not clear how much of her verbal naming and expression difficulties are due to her verbal retrieval deficit, but the deficit clearly plays a role.

Table 1 WISC-IV Integrated Results

Subtest	Scaled Score*
Spatial Span Forward	9
Spatial Span Backward	11

*The scaled scores have a mean of 10 and a standard deviation of 3.

Table 2 WRAML2 Results

Subtest	Scaled Score*
Story Memory (auditory short-term memory)	7
Story Memory Recall (from verbal long-term memory)	7
Story Recognition	10

*The scaled scores have a mean of 10 and a standard deviation of 3.

Attention

Both of Jane's parents completed a Conners' Rating Scale, an instrument designed to screen for Attention-Deficit/ Hyperactivity Disorder (ADHD). There was agreement between the parents on all of the scales except hyperactivity (see Table 3). From these behavioral ratings provided by the parents, it appears that Jane's attention control problems are more of the Inattentive type than the Impulsive/ Hyperactive type. On the Inattention scale, Jane's scores are two standard deviations above the mean for a female her age. (Elevated scores indicate behaviors of concern.) On the mother's report, Jane also has Clinically Significant scores on the Hyperactivity and the ADHD Index. These results indicate that it is highly probable that Jane has ADHD. From the cognitive testing, attention problems are also indicated by her lower scores in processing speed, auditory short-term memory, and working memory.

Table 3 Conners' Parent Rating Scale

Scale	T Scores* (Mother)	T Scores (Father)
Oppositional	44	47
Cognitive Problems/ Inattention	70	73
Hyperactivity	74	60
Conners' ADHD Index	71	68

*T Scores have a mean of 50 and a standard deviation of 10.

Academic Skills

Jane's academic skills were tested with the WJ III ACH (see attached score report). Math is her highest skill area, whereas reading skills and written language are her weaknesses. Variability exists, however, across specific skills within each of these broad academic areas. Within reading, Jane does best with basic reading skills: phonetic decoding and fluency (speed). In contrast, reading comprehension is very challenging for her, whether it involves factual or inferential questions. Underlying her reading comprehension problems are inconsistent fluid reasoning, low working memory, poorly developed vocabulary, and difficulty retrieving information from long-term memory.

Within mathematics, Jane performs extremely well in calculation. Unfortunately, she has not figured out how to effectively apply her solid math foundations to math story problems. This relative weakness is related to the same processing factors that are affecting her reading comprehension. With written language, Jane's basic writing skills—spelling and editing—are well developed but she has difficulty expressing her ideas in writing, especially when more complex sentences are required.

Study Skills

Jane's study skills were assessed through the SMALSI (see Table 4), a self-report and self-rating scale. Some of Jane's scores seem to be unrealistically high, but at least the scores indicate that she knows what good study skills involve. Whether she uses them as frequently as she reports is questionable. Based on the scores obtained, it appears that she would benefit from instruction in reading comprehension strategies, writing strategies, and test-taking strategies. Jane's Below Average score in test-taking strategies is even more of a concern, given her difficulties with retrieval. All study skills taught to Jane need to take her memory strengths and weaknesses into account (see Recommendations section).

Table 4 SMALSI Results

Scale	Percentile
Study Strategies	46
Note-Taking/Listening Skills	82
Reading Comprehension Strategies	31
Writing Strategies	38
Test-Taking Strategies	10
Time Management/Organizational Strategies	62
Low Academic Motivation	10
Test Anxiety	51
Concentration/Attention Difficulties	49

RECOMMENDATIONS

1. Share this report with your family physician if you are interested in a more comprehensive evaluation for Attention-Deficit/Hyperactivity Disorder. To this end, the school psychologist should be able to document Jane's attention in school and how it affects her learning.

2. Request that the school psychologist or learning disabilities specialist observe Jane in the classroom and have a conversation with the classroom teacher to ascertain the type of attention problems Jane experiences in the classroom and the situations in which these are most likely to occur. This professional should then be able to make recommendations to increase Jane's attention that are specific to her needs.

3. Request that the learning specialist at Grunewald suggest reading comprehension strategies specific to the type of reading that Jane is doing in her class (e.g., narrative, expository). If Jane is able to organize textual information, it will be easier for her to retrieve it. The learning specialist can also suggest strategies for interpreting math word problems.

4. When helping Jane study for examinations, have her study in a manner that matches the format of the exam. To begin with, make her actually retrieve the material, not just review or repeat it. Try to phrase questions the way they will be phrased on the exam. When she can't retrieve the answer, provide a cue. Finally, give her practice with multiple-choice responding if the test will be in that format.

5. Jane's ability to retrieve factual information can be improved by helping her recall context clues associated with academic material. For example, when taking a test, teach Jane to think back about the circumstances that occurred when the tested material was being taught in class.

6. All of Jane's exams should be in a recognition format: true-false items, matching, or multiple choice. Because of her retrieval problems, free recall exams are unfair because she is not able to fully demonstrate the knowledge she has learned.

7. As tests in school become more challenging, she may need extended time due to her slower processing speed and slow retrieval.

8. In the classroom or home, when Jane is having difficulty retrieving, provide her with cues and prompts to support retrieval.

9. In the classroom or home, people communicating with Jane should consistently use the same terminology and phrasing when talking to her about instructions or concepts that are difficult for her to grasp.

10. Jane will need to learn effective study skills in order to compensate for her memory challenges. Such study skills include: organizational strategies, semantic clustering, self-testing, test-taking strategies, reading comprehension strategies, and written expression strategies.

11. Jane would benefit from learning a variety of memory strategies and visual mnemonics. In particular, she needs to learn strategies that allow her to process information more deeply, such as elaborative rehearsal, and strategies that attach cues during encoding, such as visual mnemonics.

12. Jane also needs to learn about her own memory functions (metamemory) and how she can monitor and regulate them.

Attention

The following recommendations for the teacher are often useful for students with attention problems:

1. Because Jane has difficulty retrieving verbal information and maintaining attention, she must work considerably harder and longer than her classmates to complete the same amount of work, lessening the quality of her work and causing stress. To offset this, reduce the amount of work assigned for homework in each area to the extent that Jane can complete her assignments in approximately the same amount of time other students are expected to spend. Examples of modified assignments are: solving the odd-numbered math problems instead of all the items, studying 10 spelling words instead of 20, and writing a half-page report instead of a whole page.

2. Make sure you have eye contact with Jane before speaking to her or giving oral instructions to the class.

3. Wherever possible, introduce new information by relating it to real-life examples or applications. Also, teaching scientific, literary, or historical events with stories (emphasizing the human challenges, conflicts, decision points, and drama) will increase Jane's (and other students') attention, thereby facilitating her retention of new information.

4. Divide Jane's in-class assignments into smaller, more manageable chunks. Give her one chunk at a time with instructions to hand each in as it is completed and pick up the next. Each time she hands in a portion of the work, provide reinforcement for completed work and for time on task. Examples for dividing the work are: Cut apart the major sections of a worksheet and give her one section at a time; place a piece of "sticky" paper over the bottom half of a worksheet; put a sticker on the bottom of every two pages of a story.

5. The use of technology such as videotapes, audiotapes, computer software/images, and computer speech programs that can read the on-screen print to Jane will enhance her engagement in academic tasks.

SCORE REPORT

Table of Scores

Woodcock-Johnson III NU Tests of Cognitive Abilities and Tests of Achievement, Version 3.0

Norms based on age 11-9

CLUSTER/Test	Raw	AE	EASY to DIFF	RPI	PR	SS (95% BAND)	GE
GIA (Ext)	–	9–4	7–10	11–6	73/90	15	85 (81–89)	3.9
THINKING ABILITY (Ext)	**–**	**9–10**	**7–4**	**16–0**	**85/90**	**29**	**92 (86–97)**	**4.4**
Sound Blending	20	11–11	8–9	18–1	90/90	51	100 (90–111)	6.8
Auditory Attention	38	11–9	7–6	>20	90/90	50	100 (85–115)	7.3
Picture Recognition	48–D	11–6	7–6	>25	90/90	49	99 (90–109)	6.1
Visual-Auditory Learning	13–E	10–2	7–3	>19	87/90	38	95 (86–105)	4.6
Spatial Relations	60–D	8–5	6–1	15–0	81/90	27	91 (82–99)	3.4
Analysis-Synthesis	23–E	10-7	8–5	14–2	86/90	42	97 (87–107)	5.3
Concept Formation	18–D	8–5	7–4	10–2	62/90	21	88 (80–96)	3.0

(Continued)

CLUSTER/Test	Raw	AE	EASY to DIFF		RPI	PR	SS (95% BAND)	GE
Retrieval Fluency	43	7–8	4–3	>30	84/90	8	79 (65–92)	2.3
VERBAL ABILITY (Ext)	–	**8–3**	**7–0**	**9–10**	**50/90**	**9**	**80 (72–87)**	**3.1**
COMP-KNOWLEDGE (Gc)	–	**8–3**	**7–0**	**9–10**	**50/90**	**9**	**80 (72–87)**	**3.1**
General Information	–	8–5	7–1	10–0	53/90	11	82 (71–92)	3.4
Verbal Comprehension	–	8–2	6–11	9–8	46/90	9	80 (71–88)	2.8
COG EFFICIENCY (Ext)	–	**10–1**	**8–11**	**11–8**	**74/90**	**25**	**90 (82–97)**	**4.7**
Memory for Words	17	11–4	9–2	15–4	88/90	47	99 (85–112)	6.2
Decision Speed	30	11–3	9–10	13–1	87/90	43	97 (89–106)	5.9
Numbers Reversed	10	8–2	7–2	9–10	55/90	20	87 (77–98)	3.0
Visual Matching	38–2	10–0	9–3	10–9	50/90	16	85 (77–93)	4.6
FLUID REASONING (Gf)	–	**9–3**	**7–9**	**11–11**	**76/90**	**26**	**90 (83–98)**	**3.8**
Analysis-Synthesis	23-E	10–7	8–5	14–2	86/90	42	97 (87–107)	5.3
Concept Formation	18-D	8–5	7–4	10-2	62/90	21	88 (80–96)	3.0
AUDITORY PROCESS (Ga)	–	**11–10**	**8–2**	**>25**	**90/90**	**51**	**100 (89–111)**	**7.0**
Sound Blending	20	11–11	8–9	18–1	90/90	51	100 (90–111)	6.8
Auditory Attention	38	11–9	7–6	>20	90/90	50	100 (85–115)	7.3
PHONEMIC AWARE	–	**9–9**	**6–10**	**15–9**	**85/90**	**31**	**92 (81–104)**	**4.2**
Incomplete Words	17	7–3	5–1	12–6	77/90	13	83 (68–98)	1.8
Sound Blending	20	11–11	8–9	18–1	90/90	51	100 (90–111)	6.8
SHORT-TERM MEM (Gsm)		**9–6**	**7–11**	**11–9**	**75/90**	**31**	**92 (82–102)**	**4.2**
Memory for Words	17	11–4	9–2	15–4	88/90	47	99 (85–112)	6.2
Numbers Reversed	10	8–2	7–2	9–10	55/90	20	87 (77–98)	3.0
WORKING MEMORY	–	**9–1**	**7–9**	**10–11**	**67/90**	**20**	**87 (79–96)**	**3.6**
Auditory Work Memory	17	10–0	8–6	11–11	76/90	30	92 (84–100)	4.4
Numbers Reversed	10	8–2	7–2	9–10	55/90	20	87 (77–98)	3.0
L-T RETRIEVAL (Glr)	–	**9–2**	**6–2**	**>22**	**85/90**	**21**	**88 (78–98)**	**3.5**
Retrieval Fluency	43	7–8	4–3	>30	84/90	8	79 (65–92)	2.3
Visual-Auditory Learning	13-E	10–2	7–3	>19	87/90	38	95 (86–105)	4.6
VIS-SPATIAL THINKING (Gv)	–	**9–9**	**6–8**	**22**	**86/90**	**34**	**94 (86–102)**	**4.6**
Picture Recognition	48-D	11–6	7–6	>25	90/90	49	99 (90–109)	6.1
Spatial Relations	60-D	8–5	6–1	15–0	81/90	27	91 (82–99)	3.4
PROCESS SPEED (Gs)	–	**10–5**	**9–6**	**11–7**	**72/90**	**25**	**90 (83–97)**	**5.0**
Visual Matching	38–2	10–0	9–3	10-9	50/90	16	85 (77–93)	4.6
Decision Speed	30	11–3	9–10	13–1	87/90	43	97 (89–106)	5.9
BROAD READING	–	**9–4**	**8–8**	**10–4**	**46/90**	**20**	**87 (84–91)**	**4.0**
Letter-Word Identification	48	9–2	8–7	9–11	34/90	21	88 (83–93)	3.8
Reading Fluency	43	10–3	9–6	11–1	56/90	30	92 (88–96)	4.8
Passage Comprehension	26	8–5	7–9	9–7	48/90	16	85 (78–92)	3.1
BASIC READING SKILLS	–	**9–2**	**8–6**	**10–3**	**52/90**	**26**	**90 (87–94)**	**3.9**
Word Attack	19	9–2	8–3	11–1	70/90	34	94 (89–98)	3.9
Letter-Word Identification	48	9–2	8–7	9–11	34/90	21	88 (83–93)	3.8
READING COMP	–	**8–8**	**7–11**	**9–11**	**54/90**	**13**	**83 (78–89)**	**3.2**
Passage Comprehension	26	8–5	7–9	9–7	48/90	16	85 (78–92)	3.1

CLUSTER/Test	Raw	AE	EASY to DIFF		RPI	PR	SS (95% BAND)	GE
Reading Vocabulary	–	8–11	8–0	10–4	59/90	18	86 (80–93)	3.5
BROAD MATH	**–**	**11–9**	**10–4**	**13–8**	**90/90**	**50**	**100 (94–106)**	**6.2**
Calculation	24	13–7	11–9	16–2	96/90	75	110 (99–121)	8.0
Math Fluency	85	12–6	10–0	16–2	92/90	62	104 (100–109)	7.1
Applied Problems	34	10–5	9–6	11–5	69/90	31	93 (87–99)	4.8
MATH CALC SKILLS	**–**	**13–2**	**11–1**	**16–2**	**95/90**	**73**	**109 (101–117)**	**7.6**
Calculation	24	13–7	11–9	16–2	96/90	75	110 (99–121)	8.0
Math Fluency	85	12–6	10–0	16–2	92/90	62	104 (100–109)	7.1
MATH REASONING	**–**	**9–11**	**8–11**	**11–0**	**63/90**	**24**	**89 (84–95)**	**4.3**
Quantitative Concepts	–	9–3	8–5	10–6	56/90	18	86 (77–95)	3.9
Applied Problems	34	10–5	9–6	11–5	69/90	31	93 (87–99)	4.8
BROAD WRITTEN LANG	**–**	**9–1**	**8–2**	**10–9**	**65/90**	**16**	**85 (79–91)**	**3.9**
Spelling	31	8–11	8–4	10–1	60/90	22	89 (81–96)	4.1
Writing Fluency	15	10–0	8–11	11–2	66/90	20	87 (77–97)	4.6
Writing Samples	8–C	8–0	7–1	10–4	69/90	7	77 (62–92)	2.3
BASIC WRITING SKILLS		**9–11**	**8–11**	**11–7**	**73/90**	**31**	**93 (88–98)**	**4.9**
Spelling	31	8–11	8–4	10–1	60/90	22	89 (81–96)	4.1
Editing	15	11–0	9–10	12–4	82/90	40	96 (89–103)	6.0
WRITTEN EXPRESSION	**–**	**9–3**	**8–0**	**11–0**	**67/90**	**13**	**83 (74–92)**	**3.8**
Writing Fluency	15	10–0	8–11	11–2	66/90	20	87 (77–97)	4.6
Writing Samples	8–C	8–0	7–1	10–4	69/90	7	77 (62–92)	2.3
ACADEMIC SKILLS	**–**	**10–2**	**9–2**	**11–8**	**74/90**	**33**	**93 (90–97)**	**4.8**
Calculation	24	13–7	11–9	16–2	96/90	75	110 (99–121)	8.0
Letter-Word Identification	48	9–2	8–7	9–11	34/90	21	88 (83–93)	3.8
Spelling	31	8–11	8–4	10–1	60/90	22	89 (81–96)	4.1
ACADEMIC FLUENCY	**–**	**10–6**	**9–5**	**11–10**	**76/90**	**29**	**92 (88–96)**	**5.1**
Reading Fluency	43	10–3	9–6	11–1	56/90	30	92 (88–96)	4.8
Writing Fluency	15	10–0	8–11	11–2	66/90	20	87 (77–97)	4.6
Math Fluency	85	12–6	10–0	16–2	92/90	62	104 (100–109)	7.1
ACADEMIC APPS	**–**	**9–2**	**8–2**	**10–8**	**62/90**	**17**	**86 (81–91)**	**3.7**
Passage Comprehension	26	8–5	7–9	9–7	48/90	16	85 (78–92)	3.1
Writing Samples	8–C	8–0	7–1	10–4	69/90	7	77 (62–92)	2.3
Applied Problems	34	10–5	9–6	11–5	69/90	31	93 (87–99)	4.8
Verbal Comprehension	–	8–2	6–11	9–8	46/90	9	80 (71–88)	2.8
Visual-Auditory Learning	13-E	10–2	7–3	>19	87/90	38	95 (86–105)	4.6
Spatial Relations	60–D	8–5	6–1	15–0	81/90	27	91 (82–99)	3.4
Sound Blending	20	11–11	8–9	18–1	90/90	51	100 (90–111)	6.8
Concept Formation	18–D	8–5	7–4	10–2	62/90	21	88 (80–96)	3.0
Visual Matching	38–2	10–0	9–3	10–9	50/90	16	85 (77–93)	4.6
Numbers Reversed	10	8–2	7–2	9–10	55/90	20	87 (77–98)	3.0
Incomplete Words	17	7–3	5–1	12–6	77/90	13	83 (68–98)	1.8
Auditory Work Memory	17	10–0	8–6	11–11	76/90	30	92 (84–100)	4.4

(Continued)

CLUSTER/Test	Raw	AE	EASY to DIFF		RPI	PR	SS (95% BAND)	GE
General Information	–	8–5	7–1	10–0	53/90	11	82 (71–92)	3.4
Retrieval Fluency	43	7–8	4–3	>30	84/90	8	79 (65–92)	2.3
Picture Recognition	48–D	11–6	7–6	>25	90/90	49	99 (90–109)	6.1
Auditory Attention	38	11–9	7–6	>20	90/90	50	100 (85–115)	7.3
Analysis-Synthesis	23–E	10–7	8–5	14–2	86/90	42	97 (87–107)	5.3
Decision Speed	30	11–3	9–10	13–1	87/90	43	97 (89–106)	5.9
Memory for Words	17	11–4	9–2	15–4	88/90	47	99 (85–112)	6.2
Form A of the following achievement tests was administered:								
Letter-Word Identification	48	9–2	8–7	9–11	34/90	21	88 (83–93)	3.8
Reading Fluency	43	10–3	9–6	11–1	56/90	30	92 (88–96)	4.8
Calculation	24	13–7	11–9	16–2	96/90	75	110 (99–121)	8.0
Math Fluency	85	12–6	10–0	16–2	92/90	62	104 (100–109)	7.1
Spelling	31	8–11	8–4	10–1	60/90	22	89 (81–96)	4.1
Writing Fluency	15	10–0	8–11	11–2	66/90	20	87 (77–97)	4.6
Passage Comprehension	26	8–5	7–9	9–7	48/90	16	85 (78–92)	3.1
Applied Problems	34	10–5	9–6	11–5	69/90	31	93 (87–99)	4.8
Writing Samples	8-C	8–0	7–1	10–4	69/90	7	77 (62–92)	2.3
Word Attack	19	9–2	8–3	11–1	70/90	34	94 (89–98)	3.9
Editing	15	11–0	9–10	12–4	82/90	40	96 (89–103)	6.0
Reading Vocabulary	–	8–11	8–0	10–4	59/90	18	86 (80–93)	3.5
Quantitative Concepts	–	9–3	8–5	10–6	56/90	18	86 (77–95)	3.9

DISCREPANCIES	STANDARD SCORES			DISCREPANCY		Significant at + or –1.00 SD (SEE)
	Actual	Predicted	Difference	PR	SD	
Intra-Cognitive						
COMP-KNOWLEDGE (Gc)	80	93	–13	13	–1.11	Yes
L-T RETRIEVAL (Glr)	88	91	–3	40	–0.26	No
VIS-SPATIAL THINK (Gv)	94	94	0	51	+0.02	No
AUDITORY PROCESS (Ga)	100	92	8	74	+0.64	No
FLUID REASONING (Gf)	90	92	–2	46	–0.10	No
PROCESS SPEED (Gs)	90	94	–4	40	–0.27	No
SHORT-TERM MEM (Gsm)	92	93	–1	49	–0.01	No
PHONEMIC AWARE	92	92	0	51	+0.03	No
WORKING MEMORY	87	92	–5	35	–0.38	No

DISCREPANCIES	STANDARD SCORES			DISCREPANCY		Significant at + or –1.00 SD (SEE)
	Actual	Predicted	Difference	PR	SD	
Intellectual Ability/Achievement Discrepancies*						
BROAD READING	87	89	–2	44	–0.14	No
BASIC READING SKILLS	90	90	0	51	+0.03	No
READING COMP	83	90	–7	26	–0.65	No
BROAD MATH	100	90	10	84	+0.98	No

DISCREPANCIES	STANDARD SCORES			DISCREPANCY		Significant at
	Actual	Predicted	Difference	PR	SD	+ or –1.00 SD (SEE)
MATH CALC SKILLS	109	91	18	92	+1.38	Yes
MATH REASONING	89	90	–1	48	–0.04	No
BROAD WRITTEN LANG	85	89	–4	35	–0.39	No
BASIC WRITING SKILLS	93	90	3	57	+0.18	No
WRITTEN EXPRESSION	83	90	–7	28	–0.57	No
*These discrepancies compare GIA (Ext) with Broad, Basic, and Applied ACH clusters.						

DISCREPANCIES	STANDARD SCORES			DISCREPANCY		Significant at
	Actual	Predicted	Difference	PR	SD	+ or –1.00 SD (SEE)
Predicted Achievement/Achievement Discrepancies*						
BROAD READING	87	86	1	57	+0.19	No
BASIC READING SKILLS	90	87	3	61	+0.29	No
READING COMP	83	87	–4	37	–0.34	No
BROAD MATH	100	86	14	92	+1.39	Yes
MATH CALC SKILLS	109	88	21	97	+1.94	Yes
MATH REASONING	89	86	3	65	+0.39	No
BROAD WRITTEN LANG	85	86	–1	44	–0.15	No
BASIC WRITING SKILLS	93	86	7	71	+0.56	No
WRITTEN EXPRESSION	83	88	–5	33	–0.45	No
*These discrepancies compare predicted achievement scores with Broad, Basic, and Applied ACH clusters.						

CASE 34

Oral and Written Language Influences on Academic and Social Functioning
A Whole Child Approach

Blanche Podhajski and Frances Ingram

Kyle Marshall's report illustrates why it is so important for evaluations to consider the whole child. It also underscores how traumatic early school experiences can be for children who have disabilities. This evaluation emphasizes the importance of integrating family history, early developmental history, and educational history with assessment data. It also demonstrates the importance of teaming across disciplines; parents, pediatricians, psychologists, and educators working together with evaluators offers the most robust opportunity for a unified intervention plan. In this situation, Kyle's pediatrician and psychotherapist had different perspectives on how to treat his anxiety. An objective eye can help offer direction. In this case, Kyle required explicit instruction in specific skills, combined with a supportive classroom environment in which he could feel comfortable.

Finally, every evaluator needs to be familiar with the influence of oral language on academic and social skills. Even if you are not a speech-language pathologist, it is critical to assess a child's listening comprehension and verbal expression. All too often, evaluations are done piecemeal: one report completed by the special educator, another by an SLP, a third by a psychologist without anyone integrating the findings. While team evaluations can be an excellent option, the outcome should reflect how core processing differences impact across different assessment areas. For Kyle, the contrast between his oral language and written language was significant and unusual. Typically, both spoken and written language are consistent because of difficulties with verbal expression. However, some children like Kyle who experience anxiety as well as language differences benefit from the structure and unlimited time available for language formulation when writing. Speaking is usually spontaneous and requires coming up with the correct pronunciation, vocabulary selection, syntax, and idea organization immediately. Writing can be more reflective, offering opportunities to plan what you would like to say and edit as you go. Comprehensively evaluating language across spoken and written domains in a cohesive fashion enlightens and facilitates true individualization of language interventions.

EVALUATION REPORT

Name:	Kyle Marshall
Date of Birth:	August 11, 1998
Age:	11 years, 11 months
Parents:	Kevin and Barbara Marshall
Address:	199 Harvest Lane
	Maplehurst, Vermont
School:	North Street School
Grade:	Entering 6th
Referred by:	Maureen Bevins, Special Educator
Dates of Evaluation:	July 21 and 22, 2010
Evaluators:	Blanche Podhajski, Ph.D., Frances Ingram, M.A.

REASONS FOR REFERRAL

Kyle was seen for a comprehensive psychoeducational evaluation on July 21 and 22, 2010, at the request of Maureen Bevins, special educator, in order to determine whether any cognitive, linguistic, or literacy difficulties are contributing to Kyle's high level of anxiety. In particular, concerns relative to whether he might be exhibiting a language processing deficit were raised. Kyle is presently on a 504 plan at school and his educational team is interested in learning more about how they can help Kyle find greater enjoyment and success from his school experiences.

RELEVANT BACKGROUND INFORMATION

Mrs. Marshall, who accompanied her son for this evaluation, provided relevant background information through both telephone and in-person interviews, as well as through completion of a child history form. She described Kyle as a "mellow baby" who slept well until 2 years of age, when he began having nightmares. She recalled that between 18 months and 2 years of age, Kyle and his family moved three times and that his father traveled considerably for business. She noted that Kyle was always a hypersensitive child. When she had to go on a business trip and left him with his grandparents for 2 days when he was 15 months of age, he was very detached from her on her return. Some degree of tactile defensiveness was also noted.

Kyle's speech and language development were noticeably delayed. He did not begin using two-word phrases until after the age of 2. According to Mrs. Marshall, Kyle "had his own language," and would repeat back what he had heard. He did not begin using complete sentences until approximately 3½ years of age.

Kyle entered Happy Times preschool when he was 3 years old. Although he did not interact with the other children, he enjoyed looking at books, and he did not experience an undue amount of separation anxiety from his mother. He threw temper tantrums, which were attributed to his being frustrated by his lack of communication skills. Fine-motor skills also were seriously underdeveloped. After 1 year at Happy Times, Kyle entered another preschool with 4- and 5-year-old children, the majority of whom were bigger physically and more advanced developmentally. Mr. and Mrs. Marshall then decided they would delay kindergarten for an additional year and have Kyle enroll in an early essential education program. It was during this year that Kyle's parents believe he experienced significant stress because of a mismatch with his teacher. According to his mother, Kyle was "soft spoken and shy" while his teacher was "loud and volatile." His anxiety increased significantly following this traumatic year.

Between kindergarten and second grade, Kyle had good educational experiences with teachers who understood his learning differences and anxiety. In third grade, he "fell apart" and began receiving psychotherapy. According to Mrs. Marshall, Kyle talked about his traumatic early education experiences throughout 2 years of therapy. In fifth grade, Kyle had a new teacher and completed standardized testing at the high end of proficiency. During fifth grade, however, he developed pneumonia and had to be taken from the school by ambulance. When he begins sixth grade this fall, Kyle will have his first male teacher, Jeffrey Case. Mrs. Marshall reports that Kyle is extremely excited about this new opportunity.

Mrs. Marshall questioned which came first: Kyle's anxiety or his difficulties with language processing and production. She indicated that Kyle hopes to become a writer and have his own computer. Although young emotionally, Kyle enjoys writing across a variety of topics, and she hopes that this will become a talent he can develop. Kyle's pediatrician has questioned whether he might benefit from a trial of medication to reduce his anxiety. His psychotherapist does not agree that Kyle needs medication since he has made such good progress in therapy.

Kyle is the older of Mr. and Mrs. Marshall's two children. His 9-year-old sister is described as a "very articulate," strong student. Family history is positive for learning problems, attention difficulties, and anxiety.

Mrs. Marshall reported that Kyle is "funny, bubbly, and talks nonstop" at home and with friends with whom he is comfortable. She continued that he is also a very sensitive, intuitive child who often withdraws in new situations.

PREVIOUS TESTING

Kyle's first evaluation occurred when he was 5 years of age and underwent an assessment to determine eligibility for special education regarding his receptive and expressive language skills, motor skills, sensory integration, and behavior. He was found eligible for early essential education in the area of motor and sensory integration. Although language scores were found to be within the Average range overall, subtest scores ranged from 7 to 12, with particular difficulties noted in recalling sentences, naming objects, and basic concepts.

Kyle was seen for a central auditory processing and oral motor evaluation at Central Children's Hospital in October 2004 when he was 6 years, 2 months old. Results revealed mild auditory processing difficulties and mild oral motor impairment (dyspraxia). Through Central Children's Hospital, Kyle received occupational therapy using sensory integration principles and techniques.

Because of persisting concerns regarding Kyle's difficulties with following directions, he was given the Woodcock-Johnson III Tests of Cognitive Abilities and Tests of Achievement at school. Results revealed his overall intellectual ability to be within the Average range, with comparable performance in language comprehension, cognitive processing, phonemic awareness, working memory, oral language, and academic skills. Given these age- and grade-appropriate performances, Kyle was not found eligible for special education services.

BEHAVIORAL OBSERVATIONS

Kyle was shy but cooperative as he accompanied the evaluators into the testing session. He is a blond, attractive boy, small in stature for his chronological age. Although polite throughout, Kyle's anxiety was apparent. He was painstakingly quiet and pensive, often needing to be asked to speak in a louder voice so his responses could be understood. Kyle appeared happier performing tasks that did not require verbal exchange. He would approach nonverbal activities in a reflective fashion, carefully analyzing his options and responding appropriately. Considerable latency of response was evident on language items, as were sound sequencing errors (e.g., aminals/animals). Despite Kyle's reticence, his motivation and effort extension during testing were good. Results obtained are felt to be a valid representation of Kyle's performance in an assessment situation but may be a minimal estimate of his overall potential.

DIAGNOSTIC EVALUATION PROCEDURES

Stern Center Questionnaires
Telephone interview with psychotherapist
Parent interview
Review of records

Wechsler Intelligence Scale for Children-Fourth Edition (WISC-IV)

Developmental Test of Visual-Motor Integration, Sixth Edition (Beery VMI)

Clinical Evaluation of Language Fundamentals, Fourth Edition (CELF-4)

Test of Word Reading Efficiency, Form A (TOWRE)

Woodcock-Johnson III Tests of Achievement, Form A (WJ III ACH)

Dynamic Indicators of Basic Early Literacy Skills (DIBELS)

Test of Written Language-IV (TOWL-4) (Spontaneous Writing Subtest)

Child Behavior Checklist (CBCL) and Teacher Report Form (TRF)

Test scores are reported as standard scores (SS) having a mean of 100 and a standard deviation of 15, and as subtest scaled scores (ScS) having a mean of 10 and a standard deviation of 3, unless otherwise noted. Test scores are also based on age norms unless otherwise noted.

DIAGNOSTIC EVALUATION RESULTS

Intellectual Functioning

In order to obtain an updated impression of Kyle's learning abilities, the Wechsler Intelligence Scale for Children, Fourth Edition was administered to him. Results revealed the following score profile.

WISC-IV INDEX/Subtest	Description	SS/ScS	Percentile
VERBAL COMPREHENSION	**Acquired verbal-related knowledge and verbal reasoning**	**100**	**50**
Similarities	Abstract verbal reasoning	11	63
Vocabulary	Word knowledge	11	63
Comprehension	Understanding of social conventions	9	37
PERCEPTUAL REASONING	**Nonverbal problem-solving ability with novel stimuli**	**108**	**70**
Block Design	Abstract visual-spatial reasoning	9	37
Picture Concepts	Nonverbal/abstract categorical reasoning	12	75
Matrix Reasoning	Visual information processing/abstract reasoning	13	84
WORKING MEMORY	**The ability to hold information in short-term memory to use or manipulate**	**91**	**27**
Digit Span	Short-term auditory memory; working memory	11	63
Letter-Number Sequencing	Working memory	6	9
PROCESSING SPEED	**Visual processing/fine-motor speed and accuracy**	**100**	**50**
Coding	Visual processing/fine-motor speed and accuracy	8	25
Symbol Search	Visual processing speed and accuracy	12	75

Kyle demonstrated average intelligence with strengths in nonverbal concept formation and visual scanning. He experienced the greatest difficulty with a working memory task, Letter-Number Sequencing, which involves holding information in memory in order to perform other mental operations. The significant difference between Kyle's performance on the two subtests that constitute the Working Memory composite may have been attributed to the increased manipulation challenges posed by the Letter-Number Sequencing task as opposed to the rote recall of Digit Span. Fine-motor speed and accuracy (Coding) were also in the Low Average range, consistent with Kyle's history of dyspraxia.

Oral Language

Given Kyle's history of delays in the acquisition and use of language, his receptive and expressive language abilities were measured using the CELF-4, with the following results.

CELF-4 Index/Subtest	SS/ScS	Percentile
Core Language	79	8
Receptive Language	83	14
Expressive Language	73	4
Concepts & Following Directions	9	37
Recalling Sentences	8	25
Formulated Sentences	5	5
Word Classes – Receptive	5	5
Word Classes – Expressive	4	2
Word Classes – Total	4	2
Understanding Spoken Paragraphs	9	37

Kyle's general language ability (Core Language) was significantly below average and well below the measured level of his verbal thinking abilities on cognitive assessment. Areas of personal strength, within the Average range, were found in Kyle's abilities to interpret spoken directions of increasing length and complexity involving concepts that required logical operations using visual stimuli (Concepts and Following Directions), and to listen to spoken paragraphs, think critically about them, and provide answers to content questions (Understanding Spoken Paragraphs). Kyle's ability to remember spoken sentences of increasing length and complexity (Recalling Sentences) was Low Average.

Kyle experienced considerable difficulty orally composing sentences when given a target word and picture prompt (Formulated Sentences), scoring Significantly Below Average. His greatest challenge on this subtest was formulating sentences using conjunctions, or words that connect parts of a sentence (e.g., *although*). Given Kyle's performance on this task, he might be expected to have difficulty producing semantically correct and complete sentences orally in the classroom and/or applying them in his writing. He also struggled in understanding and describing the relationships between words (Word Classes – Total), performing significantly below average in this area as well. A comparison between his performance on the CELF-4 Word Classes subtest and his higher score on the WISC-IV Similarities subtest, both of which tap associative thinking abilities, suggests that he may have found the Word Classes task especially challenging due to the greater number of items presented at one time and his difficulties with working memory.

Kyle's overall listening comprehension ability (Receptive Language) was Low Average, while his ability to express himself orally (Expressive Language) was Significantly Below Average. Although the difference between the two composite scores was not significant, the pattern of his score profile suggests somewhat better developed ability to understand what he listens to than to express himself orally.

Academics

Reading

Reading skills were assessed using three different standardized test measures. The Test of Word Reading Efficiency – Form B (TOWRE) was used to gauge Kyle's single-word reading efficiency. This test measures skills in recognizing familiar words as whole units or sight words and in sounding out nonwords quickly and accurately. He obtained the following scores.

TOWRE	SS	Percentile
Total Word Reading Efficiency	120	91
Sight Word Efficiency	114	82
Phonemic Decoding Efficiency	120	91

Kyle's skills in reading common sight words were High Average. His skills in decoding pronounceable printed nonwords with automaticity were within the High Average to Superior range. Kyle was asked to speak loudly and clearly ahead of time so the examiner could ascertain accuracy as he was quickly reading the words. He did a nice job increasing the volume of his voice while reading fluently through each task. Kyle's overall performance on this assessment was strong and reflected excellent word recognition and attack for sight words and phonetically regular words.

Kyle's reading fluency for connected text was assessed using the DIBELS. His skills in reading fifth-grade text on a timed trial (Oral Reading Fluency) were considered "low risk" for problematic reading outcomes. Kyle actually surpassed the Vermont Grade Expectations for the recommended range of oral reading fluency in grade five, reading 164 words correct per minute.

Kyle was also given several tests from the Woodcock-Johnson III Tests of Achievement – III (WJ III ACH) to assess his word identification and reading comprehension, with the following results.

WJ III ACH Cluster/Test	SS	Percentile
Brief Reading	95	37
Reading Comprehension	91	27
Letter-Word Identification	97	41
Passage Comprehension	93	31
Reading Vocabulary	91	28

Kyle's skills in reading words on an untimed assessment (Letter-Word Identification) were within the Average range. His skills in providing synonyms, antonyms, and analogies in response to target words that he read (Reading Vocabulary) were slightly weaker, at the low end of Average. Kyle's challenges in oral language, apparent on the Word Classes subtest of the CELF-4, likely impact his reading vocabulary skills. Kyle's reading comprehension, as measured on a task in which he read short passages and supplied a missing word in the passage, also fell at the lower end of Average. If Kyle is asked to respond to more open-ended comprehension questions following a reading assignment, such as summarizing or describing the main idea, it is possible that he would experience greater difficulty due to assessed weaknesses in oral language at the discourse level. While Kyle shows mild relative weaknesses in reading vocabulary and comprehension, his overall achievement level in reading (Brief Reading) is average.

Writing

Kyle's written language skills were evaluated with the Test of Written Language – Fourth Edition (TOWL-4) Form A, Spontaneous Writing subtests, using age-based norms. When shown a picture, provided with 5 minutes of planning

time, and then asked to write the best narrative that he could within 15 minutes, Kyle finished his story with 2 minutes to spare. His score profile follows (mean = 10, SD = 3).

TOWL-4	SS (ScS)	%ile
Contextual Conventions	(8)	16
Story Composition	(16)	>99
Spontaneous Writing	115	84

Writing is unquestionably an area of strength for Kyle and is in sharp contrast to his oral language abilities. Ideation and narrative language are strong despite persistent difficulties with the mechanics of writing. It is not surprising that Kyle enjoys writing and is considering it as a potential career goal. It may be that independent writing offers him the opportunity to organize his thoughts and formulate language less stressfully, thereby reducing anxiety and enabling him to communicate his ideas with greater facility and clarity.

Visual-Motor Integration

To assess Kyle's visual-motor integration skills, he completed the three subtests of the Developmental Test of Visual Motor Integration – Sixth Edition (Beery VMI). His score profile on this assessment follows.

Beery VMI	SS	Percentile
Visual-Motor Integration	95	37
Visual Perception	68	2
Motor Coordination	78	7

Although Kyle's overall visual-motor integration skills were assessed within the Average range, his performance was characterized by significant variability across the three subtests. Specifically, Kyle responded very quickly on the Visual Perception task, using only half the time allowed to match geometric forms by drawing a mark over them.

Observations of Kyle's approach to this task suggested that he scanned the forms quickly with minimal attention devoted to the detailed differences among the forms, which may have contributed to his extremely low score.

On the remaining two subtests, more complex fine-motor responses were required. For example, on the Motor Coordination subtest, Kyle had to trace forms with a pencil without going outside double-lined paths. His score was Significantly Below Average on this task. On the Visual-Motor Integration subtest, Kyle copied a developmental sequence of geometric forms to assess the extent to which he is able to integrate his visual and motor abilities. Kyle performed within the average range on this task. His stronger performance in Visual-Motor Integration was possibly a result of the task being administered without time constraints, whereas the Motor Coordination subtest was timed. On both subtests that involved copying or tracing, Kyle appeared to struggle with the activities, frequently sighing and grimacing. Overall results suggested that Kyle would be likely to experience difficulty with school-related tasks, such as copying printed information from a book or with handwriting, particularly under timed conditions. This performance is consistent with his longstanding history of dyspraxia.

Behavioral and Attention Measures

Mrs. Marshall completed the Child Behavior Checklist to obtain an impression of Kyle's social behavioral functioning. She endorsed behaviors that indicated Clinically Significant levels of anxiety and withdrawal. Mrs. Marshall reiterated longstanding concerns that Kyle was fearful, nervous, withdrawn, and shy. He worries and has difficulty getting to sleep at night. Although his mother describes Kyle as highly verbal at home, she reports that he is reluctant to talk elsewhere. She questioned how much of his verbal reticence results from his inability to understand oral and written directions. She continued that she is concerned that Kyle's social anxiety limits his ability to participate in academic and social activities.

SUMMARY AND RECOMMENDATIONS

Kyle is an almost 12-year-old boy entering sixth grade with a long history of language delay and anxiety. Evaluation results reveal average intelligence with strengths in nonverbal concept formation and visual scanning and relative weaknesses in working memory and visual-motor speed and accuracy.

Academically, Kyle demonstrated significant strengths in both word identification and written language. Oral language abilities were seriously below average and consistent with diagnosis of a Developmental Language Disorder, receptive and expressive type. The following of both oral and written directions is compromised by this condition, as is oral language formulation. While Kyle's severe anxiety can contribute to his difficulties with verbal expression, evaluation results strongly indicate that there is no question that there is an interaction between the two.

Kyle's oral language disorder and anxiety need to be addressed concomitantly. Toward this end, the following recommendations are offered:

1. It is fortunate that Kyle is about to begin a new school year and is looking forward to his new teacher. It will be important to ensure that this environment feels safe and comfortable to him. Mrs. Marshall indicated that both the school principal and Kyle's new teacher have been extremely supportive.

2. Capitalize on Kyle's strengths in written language to promote his increased oral language competence. Kyle would benefit from intensive speech-language therapy that can help him organize his ideas, select appropriate vocabulary, and generate varied sentences to communicate his ideas across different settings.

Geraldine Wallach has an excellent strategy to promote oral expression using different kinds of media:

- Have Kyle select a topic about which he wants to share some thoughts. The first vehicle for doing so would be by writing an article for a newspaper, which he could accompany with pictures, graphs, and charts.
- Next, have Kyle take that story and convert it for use on a television program, where he could still show the pictures, graphs, and charts, but now would need to have a script from which he could generate an oral presentation.
- Finally, encourage Kyle to present the same topic via radio, where his words would have to carry the entire message, since listeners cannot see pictures, graphs, and charts.

3. Encourage Kyle to participate in written language enrichment activities. This should be the school year in which he gets an article published in the local newspaper and/or writes his first book. The more comfortable Kyle becomes with a variety of expressive language skills and the more secure his environment, the better able he will be to increase his oral language output.

4. Take care to ensure that Kyle understands both spoken and written directions. Spend private time with him and request that he paraphrase what he thinks he needs to do.

5. Given Kyle's strong nonverbal reasoning, he will benefit from nonverbal aids such as flow charts within which to organize oral and written language. The software program Inspiration (http://www.inspiration.com) or the version for younger people, Kidspiration, might be helpful in this regard.

6. Use drawing as a way to relax, comprehend language, and formulate ideas. The program Visualizing and Verbalizing by Nanci Bell, available at http://www.lindamoodbell.com, would be an excellent intervention.

7. Encourage Kyle to engage in the mutual oral sharing of experiences, feelings, and concerns. Discuss with Kyle that all people wrestle with situations that pose stress or anxiety. Mutual journal writing is also advised.

8. Conversation starters as prompts for writing may be helpful and serve as a kind of activity icebreaker. www.teachers.net/Lesson Exchange: Journal Writing Ideas (Elementary, Reading/Writing) and www.rainforest-maths.com (writing link) are wonderful web sites to help generate writing.

9. Kyle has a strong support team that includes his parents, teachers, therapist, and pediatrician advocating for his educational and social success. Kyle's parents were advised to continue to be in close communication with them all as he begins this new school year.

10. Should Kyle's anxiety not decrease by the end of the first quarter, given all the changes in environment and educational interventions, Mr. and Mrs. Marshall might want to once again revisit the question of a trial of medication with Kyle's pediatrician. His psychotherapist's understandable reservations in this regard also should be taken into account.

It was a pleasure to evaluate Kyle. If there are any questions regarding this evaluation or report, please do not hesitate to contact us. We look forward to following Kyle's progress and would be happy to consult regarding any educational program needs throughout the school year.

CASE 35

Process Assessment of the Learner, 2nd Edition (PAL-II)

Comprehensive Assessment for Evidence-Based, Treatment-Relevant Differential Diagnosis of Dysgraphia, Dyslexia, Oral and Written Language Learning Disability (OWLLD), and Dyscalculia

Virginia Berninger

This case illustrates how a two-decade, multidisciplinary, programmatic research program, which validated assessment measures that were translated into nationally normed subtests and which also validated relationships between assessment measures and treatment, can be used for treatment-relevant, differential diagnosis of four common specific learning disabilities affecting reading, writing, and/or math achievement (Berninger, 2007a, 2007b, 2007c, 2008; Berninger, O'Donnell, & Holdnack, 2008; Berninger & O'Malley May, 2009). Such differential diagnosis differs from procedures for eligibility decisions for special education services, which are mandated in federal and state legal code and guarantee civil rights for free and appropriate education for students with educationally disabling conditions (Berninger & Holdnack, 2008).

To begin with, for research-supported reasons, neither a discrepancy between Full Scale IQs and cluster scores on achievement tests nor a Response to Intervention (RTI) alone without diagnostic testing is used. Rather, current cognitive functioning is assessed through verbal reasoning, which is the best predictor of academic achievement and thus scholastic aptitude, and sometimes through nonverbal reasoning in those with oral and written language disabilities (OWLLD). Differential diagnosis focuses mainly on identifying which research-supported phenotypes (behavioral expression of underlying genotypes and brain differences between children with and without specific learning

disabilities) are impaired (Berninger et al., 2006, 2008). Phenotypes may be specific to reading, writing, math, or related skills that contribute to problems in these skills and also provide instructional cues for remediating them (Berninger & O'Malley May, 2009). Children referred because they are not responding to instruction in general education are given evidence-based diagnostic assessment that pinpoints why they are having a problem, and test results are used to generate curriculum-relevant treatment plans and progress monitoring plans for evaluating whether the treatment is working or has to be modified through problem-solving consultation (see Berninger, 2000c).

This particular case was chosen to increase practitioner awareness that (a) many children overcome their early reading problems, but continue to have persisting writing problems especially in spelling and handwriting (Berninger, 2006; Berninger, Nielsen, et al., 2008); (b) many children with academic struggles have dysgraphia, dyscalculia, and comorbid dysgraphia and dyscalculia, which are often not identified and treated and may account for grade retention, school drop-out, and nongraduation due to inability to meet standards in writing (and thus complete written assignments and tests) and math; and (c) many students have difficulty with the writing rather than the thinking requirements of math. Technical terms are defined in the report, but readers may also consult a comprehensive glossary in Berninger (2007c).

PSYCHOLOGICAL ASSESSMENT REPORT

Name: Sarah Stein
Date of Birth: 7/7/1998
Age: 12-3
Parent: Ralph Stein
School: Beverly Middle School
Grade: 7
Handedness: Right
Place of Evaluation: University Brain, Education,
                     and Technology Center,
                     University of Washington
Date of Evaluation: 10/3/2010
Evaluator: Virginia W. Berninger, Ph.D.

REASON FOR REFERRAL

Sarah was referred at the beginning of seventh grade because of a past history of learning disabilities in reading and writing. Her father wondered whether she has overcome her learning disabilities sufficiently to succeed in middle school without specialized instruction.

FAMILY AND EDUCATIONAL BACKGROUND

Sarah, whose first language is English, lives with her father and brother. Her mother passed away 2 years ago. At the end of second grade, Sarah qualified for special education in reading, and an individualized education plan (IEP) was written so that she could receive specialized instruction in reading during third grade. Her father reported a family history of dyslexia.

In the annual review of her IEP in May 2007 at the end of fourth grade, a statement of adverse educational impact indicated that Sarah's learning disabilities significantly impact her ability to comprehend grade-level materials and write at grade level. However, according to an informal assessment in the review, she scored at the 80th percentile in reading comprehension. Her written expression problems were attributed to rate problems and it was noted that she was slow in producing written work. It was stated that her slowness in doing written work was not a handwriting problem. However, no standardized, normed measures of handwriting for letter formation accuracy, automatic, fast letter production, handwriting speed, or sustained handwriting over time were administered. She was given accommodations for the state high-stakes tests in reading, math, and science, but not in the area of writing. The recommended placement for services during fifth grade was the resource room. Measurable annual goals were defined for: (a) reading and reading comprehension skills, and (b) writing strategies (pre-writing, organization, answering questions, writing multiparagraph stories or reports, revising, editing for spelling, and completing work on time). Progress toward meeting those goals was to be assessed on the basis of inventories/surveys, rubrics, teacher-developed tests, and checklists/rating scales.

Sarah's father provided the examiner with the summary record of a district-administered test in spring of fourth grade and fall of fifth grade. Scaled scores with percentiles were reported, which indicated that at the end of fourth grade, Sarah had relative strengths in word recognition, reading vocabulary comprehension, math problem-solving skills, and written expression of ideas, which were all above the population mean. Relative weaknesses, which were below the population mean, were found in computation skills, computational rate, and writing rate. At the beginning of fifth grade, word recognition, reading vocabulary comprehension, and math problem solving remained relative strengths, but spelling, sentence writing, and the written expression composite were now below the population mean; also, math computation and computation rate continued to be areas of significant difficulty. According to her father, because Sarah made so much progress during fifth grade, she did not receive specialized instruction in the sixth grade, but he was under the impression that she still had an IEP and that it did not indicate what prior cognitive testing results might be. In seventh grade Sarah is taking Spanish at school. At the time of the parent feedback for this assessment, her father reported that Sarah enjoys learning Spanish but shows some difficulty in pronouncing words when presented visually.

BEHAVIORAL OBSERVATIONS

Sarah reported that she loves the seventh grade. In particular she likes art and science. She also enjoys language arts because it has a lot of reading and writing. She shared that she loves to read and does so before she goes to bed every evening. She does not, however, like all the math homework she gets. Math is her worst subject. Her math class is just before lunch and she is assigned to the last lunch period.

When asked about use of computers, Sarah reported that she does not use a laptop at school but does in completing writing assignments at home. Groups of children do, however, use computers at school to complete some class projects. She shared that she likes to use a mixture of handwriting and computer keyboarding.

When asked what she enjoyed the most during the session, she quickly volunteered that she liked the finger touches. When asked what she enjoyed the least, she explained that writing the story was difficult for her because there was a time limit and "My hand hurts when I write a lot really fast." Because of Sarah's very slow writing rate, it was not possible to administer all of the planned tests. These could be assessed in the future during progress monitoring as explained in the recommendations.

WRITING

Sarah mostly prints her letters when composing. On an alphabet writing task, when instructed to print lowercase letters from memory and in alphabetic order, Sarah made errors in letter form and case format. For example, she omitted the dot on the *j* and wrote a capital *K* and capital *M*. On a sentence copying task, three of the letters would not be identifiable out of word context: *h* which resembled an *n; i* which was not clearly distinguished from *l* (no clear gap between vertical line and dot); and *f* (only half of the horizontal cross-over stroke). Likewise, on a copy paragraph task, the following letters would not be identifiable out of word context (capital *J*, lowercase *h, a, f, u, n, e,* and *t*). In addition, she omitted some letters and an apostrophe. Difficulties were noted with forming the letters *f, h,* and *a* on the expressive orthographic coding task as well. Likewise, some numerals were not recognizable when she was asked to write numerals 1 to 26 in counting order. For example, she often did not make the horizontal line at a right angle with the vertical line in 4. In addition 5s often resembled 6s.

Sarah remained fully engaged in story writing during the 5 minutes allotted for each story prompt, with one exception. For the first story, she started sentences with capital letters and always punctuated sentences. On the second story, she used punctuation only once and produced no capital letters. For the expository writing task, she started each sentence with a capital letter, wrote long sentences with multiple clauses for each animal, but did not punctuate. The content of both of her stories and the expository report was interesting and age appropriate.

In summary, observation of Sarah's writing indicated that she has considerable difficulty with the aspects of handwriting that research shows contribute to problems in compositional fluency (amount written within a time limit): letter formation, especially as the writing requirements increased (for example, from writing alphabet letters from memory to copying a paragraph over a longer time interval). Also, she was less likely to punctuate and capitalize when writing for an extended amount of time. Likewise, she had difficulty with numeral formation. Observation of her writing across many tasks requiring production of letter forms and numeric forms led to the clinical hypothesis that Sarah may have undiagnosed dysgraphia, which may affect her written language production as well as written calculation. This clinical hypothesis was then tested with more formal assessment.

READING

Sarah's pseudoword decoding (English-like words that are pronounceable but have no corresponding semantic meaning in memory), which research has shown is one of the best behavioral indicators of underlying genetic basis for dyslexia, was analyzed for error patterns. Five errors occurred with a one-syllable, pseudoword analogue of words of Anglo Saxon origin, two errors with a two-syllable, pseudoword analogue of words of Anglo Saxon origin, and one error with a three-syllable, pseudoword analogue of words of Romance (French/Latin) origin. Error analysis showed that Sarah had more difficulty with decoding the unit of the pseudoword corresponding to a base than the unit corresponding to a real suffix attached to the pseudoword.

MATH

Because Sarah reported not liking math and because she never received specialized services in math, she was carefully observed while performing math tasks involving or related to computation. The following observations provide relevant information for her instructional needs in math during seventh grade:

a. Errors in numeral writing on tasks requiring coding of multiplace numbers in memory included writing a numeral she confused with a similar number in a different orientation (e.g., writing 9 for 6).

b. She had difficulty switching attention from one operation to another.

c. She was very persistent in trying to solve math computations but had difficulty with executing all the steps correctly; consequently, the final answer was incorrect.

d. She found it very difficult to self-monitor whether math computations were correct.

e. She knows her addition and subtraction facts for the most part, knows some multiplication facts, but knows few division facts.

f. She counts on her fingers when doing long division but not when doing the other computation operations.

g. She has been taught a very unusual approach to long division, which she could not apply to solve long division problems.

h. She could answer questions about place value more easily orally than in writing.

i. She understands place value for whole numbers to the left of the decimal point but not place value for decimals to the right of the decimal point.

At the same time, it is important to recognize that Sarah has the ability to deal with mathematical concepts. She appeared to really enjoy the part-whole concept and problem-solving tasks. She understands the relevance of the concepts of time and space to both math and science. For example, she spontaneously offered that in doing a science project, time could be an independent variable and space could be a "depending variable." She added that there can be multiple dimensions of time.

TESTS ADMINISTERED DURING TWO SESSIONS OF THREE HOURS EACH

WISC-IV Verbal Comprehension Composite (Index or Factor Score): Similarities, Vocabulary, and Comprehension

PAL-II Reading and Writing Diagnostic Battery subtests for reading, writing, and related process skills

PAL-II Math Diagnostic Battery subtests for math skills and related process skills

TEST RESULTS AND INTERPRETATION

See the Appendix for test scores for each measure administered. See the text that follows for interpretation of these results. The cognitive results are based on norms for age peers. The PAL-II test results are based on grade norms, which can be used for students during the current school grade or the first month of the next grade. For Sarah, who was tested during the first month of seventh grade, the sixth grade norms were used.

Cognitive Ability

Sarah's verbal reasoning fell in the Very Superior range. She scored as high as or higher than 99% of children in the standardization norming group for her age. Research shows that this measure is an excellent predictor of scholastic aptitude. Thus, Sarah can be expected to excel in content domains that rely greatly on verbal reasoning, that is, intellectual abilities that draw on language in learning and learning to learn and in expressing what is learned.

Reading and Reading-Related Skills

Sarah has overcome her earlier reading problems. Her oral decoding of pseudowords and real words fell at or above the population mean for sixth graders. Her silent reading comprehension skills ranged from Average for finding prefixes and suffixes in real words (differentiating spelling patterns that are and are not morphemes) to Superior for fluency or Very Superior for accuracy of sentence comprehension (integrating word identification and sentence syntax [grammar units that order and structure accumulating collections of words, e.g., clauses]) for sixth graders.

However, the process assessment identified residual phenotype markers (behavioral expression of underlying gene variants) consistent with partially compensated dyslexia (overcoming the impaired oral word decoding and reading but not necessarily the impaired spelling). Sarah scored considerably Below Average for sixth grade as well as discrepant from her Verbal IQ (Verbal Reasoning Composite) on both the Orthographic Composite (−1 SD) (storing and processing written words in working memory) and the Phonological Composite (−1 SD) (storing and processing spoken words in working memory). (See Figure 1 at the end of the Appendix.) In addition, her expressive orthographic skills (orthographic loop that links the orthographic word form in the mind's eye to the finger movements in writing a letter, letter group, or whole word by hand) were less well developed (−1⅓ SD) than her receptive orthographic coding (only orthographic word form in mind's eye) (−⅔ SD). Within the phonological profile, her phoneme awareness was at the mean for sixth grade, but syllable awareness (−1⅓ SD) (saying a multisyllabic word without a designated syllable) and rime awareness (−⅔ SD) (say a word without the part of a syllable remaining when the initial sound is deleted) were considerably underdeveloped for grade level and verbal ability. This pattern can occur if reading instruction emphasizes only phonics (correspondences between spelling units and phonemes) and not awareness of other phonological units such as syllables and rimes. At the same time, morphological coding of both spoken and written words into word parts that signal grammar (suffixes) and meaning (bases, prefixes, and suffixes) was consistently a strength (+1 SD) across two measures, as is typical in classic dyslexia without language learning problems beyond phonology. Likewise, Sarah had strengths in syntax coding (+1⅔ SD), silent sentence reading comprehension (range +1⅓ SD to + 2⅓ SD), and listening sentence comprehension in working memory (+2 SD). Again, these strengths are typical in classic dyslexia without language learning problems beyond phonology.

Writing and Writing-Related Skills

Sarah's writing profile meets the evidence-based criteria for dysgraphia. She shows evidence of difficulty in retrieving accurate letter forms from memory. On an alphabet writing task in which she had to write legible letters in alphabetic order, her total legibility was a relative weakness (−⅓ SD), but when she had to copy the letter form with a model present rather than rely on memory, it was a relative strength (+⅔ SD). The rate of legible letter production, however, was impaired both when writing letters from memory (−⅔ SD for the first 15 seconds and total time) and when copying from a model without memory retrieval requirements (−1⅔ SD for the first 15 seconds and −1 SD for the total time). Moreover, when she had to sustain the orthographic loop function in working memory over time from 30 seconds (mean for sixth grade) to 60 seconds (−⅓ SD) to 90 seconds (−⅔ SD), Sarah's total for accuracy in copying letters and punctuation steadily declined, indicative of difficulty in sustaining letter production over time, another characteristic of dysgraphia.

Collectively, these results documenting slow handwriting make it clear why Sarah reported that her hand hurts when she has to compose under time limits. Contrary to the fourth-grade assessment, slow handwriting rate does contribute to Sarah's writing difficulties. Consistent with research showing that slow legible letter production interferes with compositional fluency (number of words written within time limits), Sarah had a relative weakness (−⅔ SD) in number of words produced within time limits during both story writing and a composite based on story writing and narrative writing. Note that when spelling did not have handwriting requirements, her access to word-specific spellings was a relative strength whether accuracy or time was assessed (+⅔ SD). However, when spelling required handwriting, for example, during story writing or a composite based on story writing and essay writing, Sarah showed a relative (−⅔ SD) in spelling during timed composing.

When Sarah could read and take notes from source material and was given time for advanced planning, the quality (+⅓ SD) and organization (mean for sixth grade) of her essay writing was a relative strength. Likewise, her working memory for composing, which was scored for storage of content and processing to create coherent text but not for handwriting, was a relative strength (+1 SD).

The process assessment of writing-related skills identified the following relative weaknesses in hallmark phenotypes, which research has shown are associated with dysgraphia:

a. Orthographic coding, especially expressive orthographic coding (−1⅓ SD), which, like the number of legible consecutive alphabet letters during the first 15 seconds (−⅔ SD), assesses orthographic loop function.

b. Orthographic working memory storage and processing of written words and letters (letter retrieval from alphabet, −1 SD; identifying letters in written words in the mind's eye lacking any sound correspondence or one-to-one sound correspondence, −⅓ SD, and letters and words composite, (−⅔ SD).

c. Finger succession (planning, controlling, and executing sequential finger movements) (−⅔ SD) compared to executing repetitive, nonsequential finger movements (mean for sixth grade).

d. Timed cross-code integration of phonological naming codes and orthographic codes for single letters or high-frequency words that are not perfectly decodable on the basis of phonics, that is, phonological loop function (−⅔ SD).

e. Rapid automatic switching (RAS) between RAN for numerals and RAN for words (−1⅔ SD), that is, supervisory attention/executive function for switching attention.

Math and Math-Related Skills

Sarah's math profile meets the evidence-based criteria for dyscalculia. On the one hand, she exhibited relative strengths in math reasoning for math problem solving ($+1\frac{1}{3}$ SD), the math concept for part-whole relationships needed for fractions, mixed numbers, and measurement including telling time (part-whole concept composite $+\frac{2}{3}$ SD), and quantitative working memory ($+\frac{1}{3}$ SD). She also had a relative strength in explaining orally how to perform the calculation steps in addition, subtraction, and multiplication problems ($+1$ SD) and in placing numerals in correct places in two-dimensional grids for each of the operations (mean for sixth grade). However, she had relative weaknesses in:

a. Oral counting, which draws on the internal number line that underlies math fact

b. Learning and retrieval ($-\frac{2}{3}$ SD);

c. Expressing place value concepts in writing ($-1\frac{1}{3}$ to $-\frac{1}{3}$) compared to expressing them orally ($-\frac{1}{3}$ SD)

d. Timed written fact retrieval (range -3 to $-\frac{1}{3}$ SD)

e. Switching attention between operation signs ($-2\frac{1}{3}$ SD)

f. Completing all the steps of math calculation to arrive at the correct answer ($-1\frac{1}{3}$ SD)

g. Self-checking (monitoring) to find errors in written calculation (declined to complete this task, which was stressful for her)

Process assessment showed that these weaknesses may be related to the following math-related processes: (a) automatic legible numeral writing ($-\frac{1}{3}$ SD), (b) handwriting speed for numeral writing ($-1\frac{2}{3}$ SD), (c) coding multiplace numerals in working memory (-1 SD), a skill analogous to orthographic coding of written words and letters, (4) RAS ($-1\frac{2}{3}$ SD), and (5) self-monitoring of written calculation (not completed due to task difficulty).

Case Formulation

Sarah is twice exceptional. Her verbal reasoning falls in the Very Superior range, indicating that she is intellectually gifted. She also has specific learning disabilities: by history, dyslexia, and two additional specific learning disabilities identified in the current assessment—dysgraphia and dyscalculia. Her dyslexia appears to be compensated for, in that she has at least average scores for age in phonological decoding (pseudowords) and morphological decoding (real words). However, as is typical in partially compensated dyslexia, in which oral reading but not spelling problems are overcome, she still shows residual impaired phenotype markers in orthographic coding (e.g., especially in orthographic loop function) and phonological coding (e.g., syllables and rimes but not phonemes that are emphasized in phonics). Also, as is characteristic in dyslexia, she has relative strengths in morphology, syntax, and reading comprehension, which those with selective language impairment (also called language learning disability or oral and written language learning disability) do not, even after they respond to phonological decoding instruction, unless they receive and respond to treatment for the morphological and syntactic awareness problems.

Sarah's two other specific learning disabilities, dysgraphia and dyscalculia, according to the school records provided by her father, have not previously been diagnosed or treated (i.e., made a focus of specialized instruction with measurable goals in her IEP). Dysgraphia is an impairment in automatic legible letter writing, handwriting speed, and sustained handwriting over time, which in turn interferes with compositional fluency—the amount one can write within a time limit, rate of writing, ease of writing, ability to sustain writing over time, and accurate spelling during composing. Sarah's dysgraphia is reflected in her relative weaknesses in receptive and expressive orthographic coding (storing and analyzing letters in written words); switching attention among orthographic codes during automatic integration of naming/phonological and orthographic codes; planning, controlling, and executing timed sequential finger movements; and automatic retrieval and production of letters. Collectively, consistent with research, her dysgraphia is the result of impairment in the working memory architecture that supports handwriting during word spelling and text composing: (1) in the orthographic storage and processing unit; (2) in the orthographic loop from the contents of the orthographic unit in the mind's eye to the serial finger movements needed for producing the sequential strokes in letters, sequential letters in words, and sequential words in sentences and text; and (3) the executive functions for managing supervisory attention for automatic cross-code (phonological-orthographic) integration. (See Figure 1 at the end of the Appendix.) However, the content and quality of her compositions are a relative strength, probably because of her relative strengths in morphology and syntax and all aspects of working memory except letters and written words (i.e., orthographic working memory).

Sarah also has dyscalculia, a disorder in learning and retrieving math facts and in learning and applying the

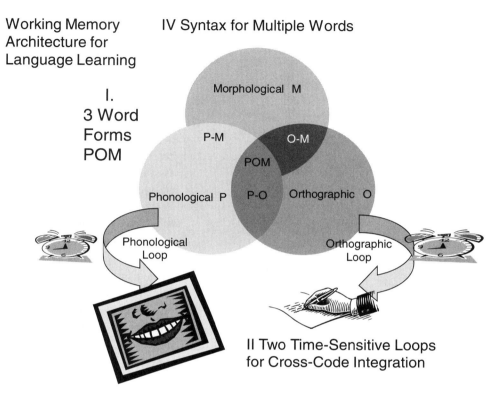

III Panel of Executive Functions
Inhibition, Flexible Set Switching, Sustained Task Maintenance,
Self-Monitoring, Self-Regulating Retrieval Fluency

Working Memory
Architecture for
Language Learning

IV Syntax for Multiple Words

I.
3 Word
Forms
POM

Morphological M

P-M   O-M

POM

Phonological P   P-O   Orthographic O

Phonological
Loop

Orthographic
Loop

II Two Time-Sensitive Loops
for Cross-Code Integration

Source: Berninger, V. (2007c). *Process Assessment of the Learner II User's Guide*. San Antonio, TX: Harcourt/PsyCorp. (CD format).

steps of calculation algorithms for the four basic arithmetic operations: addition, subtraction, multiplication, and division. Because both math fact fluency tasks and written paper-and-pencil calculation require writing the 10 numerals that represent an infinity of numbers according to place value rules for a specific base (in the case of conventional arithmetic, 10), Sarah's dysgraphia may also have contributed to her dyscalculia, consistent with research findings about math disability. Sarah showed a relative weakness in writing numerals legibly, automatically and quickly. Other relative weaknesses that may have contributed to her dyscalculia include oral counting, coding of numerals in working memory for multiplace numbers (an analogue of orthographic coding for written words), switching attention among operations, and self-monitoring. These relative weaknesses also point to hallmark impairments in the working memory architecture supporting math related to the orthographic loop (coding written numerals in

the mind's eye and producing them in writing through the hand) and executive functions of supervisory attention. At the same time, Sarah has relative strengths in understanding the part-whole concept, which underlies fractions, mixed numbers, telling time and other kinds of measurement, math problem solving, and oral explanation of steps of computation algorithms. She showed signs of being easily engaged in mathematical thinking, which is not the same as paper and pencil math calculation.

The process assessment showed that all of Sarah's specific learning disabilities—her compensated dyslexia with residual hallmark phenotypes and her previously undiagnosed and untreated dysgraphia and dyscalculia—can be explained within the conceptual framework of a working memory architecture (see Figure 1 at the end of the Appendix). This architecture has these components: (a) storage and processing units for spoken words, written words, and morphological structure of spoken and written words (base words and affixes); (b) the time-sensitive phonological loop and orthographic loop for connecting internal representations in the mind with the external world including learning environment; and (c) executive functions for supervisory attention and self-regulation of storage and processing in working memory. This working memory architecture supports the learning of both spoken and written language and then using language to learn.

Sarah still shows residual hallmark processing problems for (a) phonological and orthographic storage and processing for written words and for written numerals and multiplace numerals; (b) impaired phonological loop and orthographic loop function; and (c) executive functions for switching attention for time-sensitive, cross-code integration of phonological/name code and written letters, words, or numerals and self-monitoring of written calculations. Of diagnostic relevance, Sarah's working memory problems are specific to letters, written words, and single- and multiplace numerals. She has relative strengths in working memory involving syntax (listening or writing) and quantitative working memory.

RECOMMENDATIONS

1. Sarah should be nominated for the pull-out program that provides intellectual enrichment for the 2010–2011 school year. It is important that she receive recognition and nurturing for her exceptionally well-developed verbal reasoning skills.

2. The following instructional activities should be provided within the context of intellectually engaging writing and math activities rather than as isolated drill. The University of Washington Brain, Education, and Technology Center (UBET) lab teaching team invites Sarah to participate in the forthcoming after-school club, Erdös Multicultural Mathematicians Constructing, Conversing, and Writing. Erdös was the famous mathematician who loved only numbers and it was an honor to do math with him, which he only liked to do with others. These clubs will address the following and at the same time provide opportunities to engage in creating and solving oral and written math problems that include, but go beyond, arithmetic to algebra and other areas of math. The following activities will be used to emphasize the role of writing in learning and doing math, including writing equations:

a. Instructional activities for developing legible automatic letter writing and numeral writing, increasing handwriting speed for letters and numerals, improving letter and numeral retrieval from memory, and self-monitoring and reflecting on improving letter and numeral writing legibility for others.

b. Instructional activities for developing ability to hold letters, written words, single numerals, and multiplace numerals in working memory while analyzing their elements.

c. Review math facts for addition and subtraction and learn multiplication and division facts by anchoring the process for storage and retrieval in a visible number line initially, and an internalized number line eventually, but coupling it with writing numerals and written representation of the math facts (first goal accuracy, next goal fluency or speed).

   • Oral Counting with finger tapping along a masking tape number line

      Addition: Counting forward from first number by the quantity of the second number and note destination and record in writing.

      Subtraction: Counting backward from the first number by the quantity of the second number and note destination and record in writing.

      Multiplication: Fast forward addition by counting by a repeated constant increment (first number) for a certain number of times (second number) beginning at 0. Note destination and record in writing.

      Division: Fast backward subtraction counting by a repeated constant increment (second number) beginning at the first number. Note number of times moved backward by this increment until reaching 0 and record in writing.

   • Practice addition, subtraction, multiplication, and division facts in multimodal manner (input-output combinations: Look-Say, Look-Write, Listen-Say, Listen-Write).

   • Plot accuracy and time on growth graphs to have visible record of progress.

d. Learn the conventional computation procedures for long division.

e. Learn place value for the decimal system to right of the decimal point (concept, naming the places, and writing numbers involving decimals with and without zero as a placeholder).

3. Students with a history of problems in learning to read in their first language often struggle with learning to read in their second language. To help Sarah learn to read Spanish words, she might copy the written word, close her eyes and try to see the written word in her mind's eye, and then open her eyes and pronounce the word and explain its meaning. The act of writing may help her attend to the letters and letter patterns in the word, that is, its orthography, so that she gains a precise representation of it. Drawing on multiple codes may help her create a word-specific representation in memory that has links to orthography, phonology, morphology, and semantics. Also, for Spanish words that can be illustrated with a picture, a set of 3 × 5 cards with a picture of the word's meaning along with the written word may be helpful in practicing word pronunciation. In addition, an audio recording of the teacher or proficient speaker of Spanish might be made in which single words are pronounced in a series and Sarah views the printed word at the same time she hears the word spoken on tape.

4. Teach Sarah keyboarding skills and integrate these with the cognitive processes of written composing.

5. Follow-up testing:

   a. Complete testing was not possible at this initial assessment because of time limitations: WISC-IV subtests for Perceptual Organization, Working Memory, and Processing Speed Composites (Factor or Index Scores) and PAL-ll Finger Tip Writing, Visual Spatial Working Memory, Fact Retrieval—Listen and Say, and RAN Digits and Double Digits.

   b. Readminister writing and math measures on which Sarah demonstrated relative weaknesses, including Finding the Bug, which she could not complete, and evaluate whether she is showing progress in each of the skills. Also reevaluate the probes taken in each session to evaluate whether she is learning the taught skills.

   c. Guide Sarah in creating and periodically reviewing her math portfolio of games, puzzles, and problems she has created and/or solved.

6. The examiner is willing to meet with the multidisciplinary team and her father at Sarah's school to determine whether she still has an IEP and/or 504 accommodation plan and how her needs might best be met in seventh grade.

   a. For example, at school she might be allowed to use a laptop to complete written assignments. However, her writing should be monitored to ensure that use of the laptop helps Sarah write more quickly and effortlessly without sacrificing the quality of her written assignments and does in fact enhance completion of written assignments.

   b. Accommodations are needed for math homework as soon as possible so that Sarah does not lose interest in math and give up. For example, alternatives to writing answers might be considered (e.g., dictated audio recorded answers) and reducing homework to just the essential skills for practice or extending it to enrichment activities.

It was a pleasure working with Sarah and seeing how much she is enjoying school this year. We look forward to working with her in the after-school math club.

APPENDIX WITH TEST SCORES

(**Bold** indicates relative strengths and *italics* indicates relative weaknesses.)

Cognitive (Scale: Most average score for age [mean] = 100; unit of variation [standard deviation SD] = 15; 68% of population falls within + to −1 SD or 85 to 115)

WISC-IV Verbal Comprehension Index
         136   99th percentile

Reading (Scale: Most average score for age [mean] = 10; unit of variation [standard deviation SD] = 3; 68% of population falls within + to −1 SD or 7 to 13)

PAL-ll Reading Profile
   Oral Decoding:

   Phonological Decoding of Pseudowords

   Pseudoword Decoding Accuracy   11

   Pseudoword Decoding Rate   11

   Morphological Decoding of Real Words

   Morphological Decoding Accuracy   11

   Morphological Decoding Fluency   10

   Silent Reading for Meaning:

   Finding the True Fixes (single words) 10

   Sentence Sense (Reading Comprehension)

   Accuracy   17

   Fluency   14

Writing (Scale: Most average score for age [mean] = 10; unit of variation [standard deviation SD] = 3; 68% of population falls within + to −1 SD or 7 to 13)

PAL-II Writing Profile

Handwriting:

Alphabet Writing 15 sec	8*
Alphabet Writing Total Legible	9
Alphabet Writing Total Time	8
Copy Sentence 15 sec	5
Copy Sentence Total Legible	12
Copy Sentence Total Time	7
Copy Paragraph 30 sec	10*
Copy Paragraph 60 sec	9*
Copy Paragraph 90 sec	8* (Note decrease over time.)

Spelling and Composing:

Word Choice (no handwriting; word-specific)

Accuracy	12
Time	12

Narrative Fluency

# of words in 5 min	8
# correctly spelled words	8

Expository

Note Taking	10

Essay Writing

Quality	11
Organization	10

Cross-Genre Composing (Narrative and Expository):

Total # of Words	8
Total # Correctly Spelled Words	8
Total # Complete Sentences	9

PAL-II Related Processes for Reading and Writing

A. Three Storage and Processing Units for Words in Working Memory:

1. Orthographic Coding (Written Words)

Receptive Orthographic Coding	8*
Expressive Orthographic Coding	6*
Orthographic Coding Composite	7

2. Phonological Coding (Spoken Words)

Syllables	6
Phonemes	10
Rimes	8
Phonological Coding Composite	7

3. Morphological Coding (Bases and Suffixes Marking Meaning and Grammar of Written and Spoken Words)

Are They Related?	13
Does It Fit?	13

B. Storage and Processing Unit for Accumulating Spoken and/or Written Words in Working Memory:

Syntax Coding	15

C. More Working Memory during Language Tasks:

Orthographic storage and processing (letters and words):

Letter Retrieval from Alphabet	7
Letters in Written Words	9
Letters and Words Composite	8

Syntax storage and processing/production:

Sentences Listening	16
Sentences Writing	13

D. Rapid Automatic Naming (RAN) (timed cross-code [orthographic-phonological name] integration; phonological loop of working memory)

RAN letter	8
RAN letter groups	11
RAN word	8

E. Rapid Automatic Switching (RAS) (RAN under conditions of switching attention supervised by executive functions or supervisory attention in working memory)

RAS words and double digit numbers	5

F. Motor Planning by End Organ in Phonological Loop or Orthographic Loop:

Oral Motor Planning	11

(mouth—sequencing syllable production)

Finger Succession (Dominant, Nondominant)	8*

(hand-finger sequencing)

Finger Repetition (Dominant, Nondominant)	10

(hand-control motor output without finger sequencing)

*Note: Alphabet Writing 15 Seconds and Expressive Orthographic Coding assess orthographic loop. Receptive orthographic coding assesses orthographic without finger-motor part of orthographic loop. Finger Succession assesses sequential finger movements of orthographic loop. Copy Paragraph assesses sustained handwriting in working memory.

Math (Scale: Most average score for age [mean] = 10; unit of variation [standard deviation SD] = 3; 68% of population falls within + to −1 SD or 7 to 13)

PAL-ll Math Profile

Concepts and Math Reasoning:

Multistep Problem Solving	14

Part-Whole Relationships

Part-Whole Concepts	13
Part-Whole Fractions and	
Mixed Numbers	12
Part-Whole Time	11
Composite	12

Place Value

Oral	9
Written	6
Problem Response Written	9
Composite	8
Oral Counting	8

Calculation:

Fact Retrieval Fluency Look Write

addition	6
subtraction	4
switching + or −	3
multiplication	4
division	1
switching mult div	3

Computation Operations:

Spatial Alignment	10
Verbal Explanation	13
Problem Solution	6

PAL-ll Related Processes for Math

Automatic Numeral Writing	9
Total Legibility Numerals	12
Total Time for Numeral Writing	5
Numeric Coding	7
(multiplace numbers in working memory)	
Quantitative Working Memory	11

REFERENCES

Berninger, V. (2006). A developmental approach to learning disabilities. In I. Siegel & A. Renninger (Eds.), *Handbook of child psychology*, Vol. IV, *Child psychology and practice* (pp. 420–452). Hoboken, NJ: John Wiley & Sons.

Berninger, V. (2007a). *Process assessment of the learner, 2nd edition. Diagnostic for reading and writing* (PAL-II RW). San Antonio, TX: Pearson.

Berninger, V. (2007b). *Process assessment of the learner diagnostic for math (PAL-II-M)*. San Antonio, TX: Pearson.

Berninger, V. (2007c). *Process assessment of the learner II user's guide*. San Antonio, TX: Harcourt/PsyCorp. (CD format) ISBN 0158661818 Second Revision issued August 2008.

Berninger, V. (2008). Defining and differentiating dyslexia, dysgraphia, and language learning disability within a working memory model. In E. Silliman & M. Mody (Eds.), *Language impairment and reading disability-interactions among brain, behavior, and experience* (pp. 103–134). New York: Guilford Press.

Berninger, V., Abbott, R., Thomson, J., Wagner, R., Swanson, H. L., Wijsman, E., & Raskind, W. (2006). Modeling developmental phonological core deficits within a working-memory architecture in children and adults with developmental dyslexia. *Scientific Studies in Reading, 10*, 165–198.

Berninger, V., & Holdnack, J. (2008). Neuroscientific and clinical perspectives on the RTI initiative in learning disabilities diagnosis and intervention: Response to questions begging answers that see the forest and the trees. In C. Reynolds & E. Fletcher-Janzen (Eds.), *Neuroscientific and clinical perspectives on the RTI initiative in learning disabilities diagnosis and intervention* (pp. 66–81). Hoboken, NJ: John Wiley & Sons.

Berninger, V., Nielsen, K., Abbott, R., Wijsman, E., & Raskind, W. (2008). Writing problems in developmental dyslexia: Under-recognized and under-treated. *Journal of School Psychology, 46*, 1–21.

Berninger, V., O'Donnell, L., & Holdnack, J. (2008). Research-supported differential diagnosis of specific learning disabilities and implications for instruction and response to instruction (RTI). In A. Prifitera, D. Saklofske, & L. Weiss (Eds.), *WISC-IV clinical assessment and intervention* (2nd ed.) (pp. 69–108). San Diego, CA: Academic Press (Elsevier).

Berninger, V., & O'Malley May, M. (2009, revision submitted). Evidence-based diagnosis and treatment for specific learning disabilities involving impairments in written and/or oral language. For *Journal of Learning Disabilities* Special Issue on Cognitive and Neuropsychological Assessment Data That Inform Educational Intervention (guest editors B. Hale & D. Fuchs).

Berninger, V., Raskind, W., Richards, T., Abbott, R., & Stock, P. (2008). A multidisciplinary approach to understanding developmental dyslexia within working-memory architecture: Genotypes, phenotypes, brain, and instruction. *Developmental Neuropsychology, 33*, 707–744.

CASE 36

Math Problem Solving
Applying a Processing Model to LD Determination

Gail Cheramie, Linda Parks, and Ashley Schuler

The report on Randall represents a comprehensive reevaluation designed to investigate the referral issues and all areas of suspected disability. The evaluation follows a data-based problem-solving model where follow-up assessment occurs to rule in or rule out certain hypotheses (e.g., the academic assessment with the WJ III ACH is followed up with the WIAT-III in order to verify the deficit; certain clusters of the WJ III COG associated with math are administered to follow up on WISC-IV; and the Conners 3 is administered to follow up on the BASC-2).

Randall had already been identified as a student with a learning disability (LD) in math problem solving, and his parents had involved him in numerous hours of one-to-one tutoring. They were concerned that he was not making sufficient progress/catching up in math. This evaluation helped to identify and describe the processing deficits associated with the LD and facilitated understanding that such processes were interfering with Randall's ability to learn commensurate with age and grade expectations.

In order to determine the condition, Flanagan's operational definition of LD was applied where the following four questions were investigated and addressed:

1. The presence of a normative academic deficit despite adequate instruction and supplemental intervention.
2. The presence of cognitive strengths and weaknesses.
3. The cognitive deficits identified are directly associated to the academic deficits.
4. The presence of functional limitations.

In addition, exclusionary factors were ruled out at each level of investigation (e.g., academic deficits not due to lack of instruction or lack of supplemental intervention).

The parents were also concerned about Randall's difficulties with spelling and writing; these academic areas were also evaluated. While Randall showed weaknesses in these areas, he had not had specific intervention in this academic area and did not show deficits in language usually associated with written expression. He did display orthographic deficits associated with spelling. Although the team concluded that overall he did not qualify as having an LD in written expression, an intervention plan was still created.

The parents also mentioned a concern about dyslexia, and all areas required by the Texas Education Agency were assessed. While it was fairly clear Randall did not display a reading deficit, in order to form a conclusion that he did not display dyslexia consistent with our state's definition, an assessment of those areas was required.

A variety of instruments and assessment techniques were applied in this evaluation (e.g., review of records and previous assessments, interviews; cognitive and achievement tests; behavior rating scales; self-report measure). Throughout the evaluation, tests and other sources of data were used to serve as a database for making certain conclusions. The evaluation will be of interest for determining math LD, but also for conducting a comprehensive evaluation and meeting the Full and Individual Evaluation (FIE) requirements of IDEA.

COMPREHENSIVE EVALUATION

Name:	Randall Hosp
Date of Birth:	04/24/1997
Age:	12 years, 7 months
Gender:	Male
School:	Steinberg Elementary
Grade:	6
Date of Report:	11/24/2009
Evaluators:	Linda Hernandez Parks, M. A.; Ashley Schuler, M.A.; Gail M. Cheramie, Ph.D.

REASON FOR REFERRAL

Randall was referred for reevaluation by his mother due to concerns about his continued difficulties with math, writing, and spelling. Randall was previously evaluated at the University of Houston-Clear Lake (UH-CL) in December 2006. Evaluation results from UH-CL indicated that Randall displayed a learning disability (LD) in mathematics reasoning. Mrs. Hosp reported that the private school that Randall currently attends, Steinberg Elementary, does not have any special education teachers or services, but his teachers try to modify his schoolwork. In addition, Randall has been attending Sylvan Learning Center for additional math tutoring after school. Despite the modifications and additional tutoring, Mrs. Hosp reported that Randall is still displaying academic difficulties. The purpose of this evaluation is to determine the nature and extent of Randall's learning difficulties, as well as to identify strategies that will facilitate his academic progress.

PROCEDURES/TESTS ADMINISTERED

Review of Previous Evaluations and Educational Records 9/30–11/13/09

Behavior Assessment System for Children, Second Edition:

Structured Developmental History (BASC-2: SDH) 9/30/09

Parent Rating Scales (BASC-2: PRS) 9/30/09

Teacher Rating Scales (BASC-2: TRS) 11/4/09, 11/11/09

Self-Report of Personality (BASC-2: SRP) 9/30/09

Wechsler Intelligence Scale for Children, Fourth Edition (WISC-IV) 9/30/09

Woodcock-Johnson III NU: Tests of Cognitive Abilities (WJ III COG) 10/14 & 10/21

Woodcock-Johnson III NU Tests of Achievement (WJ III ACH) 10/14/09

Wechsler Individual Achievement Test-Third Edition (WIAT-III) 10/21/09

Gray Oral Reading Test-Fourth Edition (GORT-4) 10/28/09

Comprehensive Test of Phonological Processing (CTOPP) 10/28/09

Process Assessment of the Learner-Second Edition (PAL-II) 10/28/09

Receptive Coding, Expressive Coding, and Word Choice

AIMSweb Curriculum-Based Measurement: 10/28/09

Reading Fluency (R-CBM)

Conners 3rd Edition—Parent Assessment Report (Conners 3) 10/14/09

Student interview 10/14/09, 10/21/09

SCORES

The following abbreviations are used to represent score types.

Type of Score	Abbrev.	Mean	Standard Deviation
Standard score	SS	100	15
Scaled score	ScS	10	3
Percentile rank	PR	50	n/a
T score	TS	50	10
Age equivalent	AE	n/a	n/a
Relative proficiency index	RPI	Prediction of an individual's proficiency on a task similar to the one presented when a typical age/grade peer would be 90% proficient.	

BACKGROUND INFORMATION

Randall is a 12-year-old boy in the sixth grade at Steinberg Elementary. He currently lives with his biological mother and father and does not have any siblings. His father works in computer software development and his mother is an accountant. Randall participates in many activities with his family, including going to movies, playing games, taking trips, watching television, visiting with relatives, and going to church.

Mrs. Hosp reported that she was under a doctor's care during her pregnancy and was put on bed rest for 1½ months due to high blood pressure. At delivery, Randall's umbilical cord was wrapped around his neck, which caused his heart rate to fluctuate. He weighed 6 lbs. 10 oz. at birth. He reached all developmental milestones within age expectations. Mrs. Hosp reported that around the age of 1, Randall had a double hernia operation. She stated that Randall has never been a good sleeper and is often up throughout the night. He has no significant illnesses and is in good health despite year-round allergies. He is allergic to Cephzil (an antibiotic). He takes no medications on a regular basis. Lately, Randall has been complaining of headaches. Randall does wear glasses and had a recent visual examination this summer. There is no significant medical history in the parents.

Randall started daycare at the age of 2, attending 5 days a week for 7 hours each day. He attended Gateway Learning Center for pre-kindergarten and kindergarten. Since first grade Randall has attended Margaret Saunders Elementary. Mrs. Hosp reported that she and Mr. Hosp decided to have Randall repeat first grade due to concerns with his academic performance and maturity level. In his second year of first grade, he performed at an average level but in second grade his grades were inconsistent, and have remained inconsistent since. Currently, Mr. and Mrs. Hosp believe that Randall is still struggling to just get passing grades, especially in math, spelling, and writing, despite modifications given to him at school and his additional tutoring in math at Sylvan Learning Center.

Socially, Randall has friends and does not have problems relating to other children. Reportedly, Randall's behavior and socialization have been good throughout his educational history. Mrs. Hosp reported that she thinks Randall is usually the leader in group games. He is easily overstimulated in play (tends to get tired and wears himself out by continuing in activities) and gets upset when things are unfair. Mrs. Hosp also indicated that Randall has a short attention span when he is uninterested.

Mrs. Hosp described Randall as sweet, sensitive, kindhearted, and funny. He enjoys playing football, baseball, basketball, and video games, listening to music, and watching TV. He also enjoys Boy Scouts and church activities. Mrs. Hosp indicated that his most difficult behaviors are his typical teenage arguments. She also reported that Randall gets angry when he is overscheduled with activities that are not of his choosing. Mrs. Hosp hopes that Randall will go to college and subsequently do whatever makes him happy.

REVIEW OF PREVIOUS EVALUATIONS

Randall was initially evaluated in first grade (age 6-9) by Alliance Independent School District. The testing results indicated that Randall had a weakness in visual-motor integration, average intellectual and language functioning, and average to above average academic functioning. Scores on the various instruments were as follows: WISC-III SS: VIQ = 108, PIQ = 80, FSIQ = 94, VCI = 114, POI = 82, FDI = 84, & PSI = 96; Beery VMI SS = 73; WJ III ACH SS: Basic Reading = 106, Reading Comprehension = 100, Math Calculation = 118, Math Reasoning = 93, & Written

Expression = 91; PPVT-III SS = 119; EVT SS = 102; and TOLD:P SS = 100. Randall did not meet the criteria for special education in any disability classification.

Shortly after, at age 7-1, he was evaluated at UH for both vision (College of Optometry) and language (Department of Communication Disorders). The results of the evaluation indicated that Randall displayed classic signs of a learning disability in that he was not making expected progress due to a visual perceptual skill deficit. Criterion reference scores for listening, speaking, reading, and writing were also below level. Scores on the various instruments were as follows: K-BIT SS = 91; WRAT-3 SS: Reading = 108, Spelling = 106, Arithmetic = 97; WRMT-R SS: Visual Auditory Learning = 87, Word Identification = 111, Word Attack = 105, Word Comprehension = 98, Passage Comprehension = 93; TWS-3 SS: Predictable Words = 85, Unpredictable Words = 82; Spatial Awareness = 5.0 AE; Rutgers Drawing = 5.0 AE; PICAC Overall Communication = 12.62 (criterion score = 16); and Phonological Awareness = 5.0 AE. The academic skill area for the LD was not specifically identified. Recommendations included a home program and private tutoring.

Subsequently, at age 9-8, Randall was evaluated at UH-Clear Lake and identified as LD in math reasoning. Standard scores on the various instruments were as follows: WISC-IV: VCI = 96, PRI = 73, WMI = 94, PSI = 80; SB5: VIQ = 91; WJ III COG: Fluid Reasoning = 97 (Concept Formation = 91, Analysis-Synthesis = 105), Visual Spatial Thinking = 96 (Spatial Relations = 86, Picture Recognition = 107); WJ III ACH: Basic Reading = 96, Reading Comprehension = 92, Math Calculation = 98, Math Reasoning = 80, Broad Written Language = 83; WIAT-II: (Math Reasoning = 81 Written Expression = 98); Beery: VMI = 77; BASC-2 and CPT: no significant elevations; and RCMAS = average. Continued difficulties in visual-motor integration and visual perceptual tasks, including spatial and inductive reasoning, were identified as the processing deficits contributing to the LD in math.

BEHAVIORAL OBSERVATIONS

Randall was evaluated at UH-CL Psychological Services for four sessions, each lasting approximately 2 to 2½ hours. He was respectful, polite, and eager to begin each session. He consistently maintained eye contact and responded appropriately to questions. During the third session (10/21/09), Randall said he had a mild headache. During this session, he appeared to give up on test items easily (e.g., "I'm not sure") and required additional prompting to respond. When prompted, Randall did try to answer. Throughout the testing process, Randall attempted all tasks and appeared to put forth adequate effort. Overall, Randall was attentive, motivated, and cooperative. The results obtained in this evaluation are considered to be a valid estimate of Randall's levels of functioning in the areas assessed.

EVALUATION RESULTS: INTELLECTUAL/COGNITIVE

Wechsler Intelligence Scale for Children, Fourth Edition (WISC-IV)

The Wechsler Intelligence Scale for Children – Fourth Edition (WISC-IV) was administered on 9/30/09. The WISC-IV is used to assess the general thinking and reasoning skills of children and provides composite scores that represent intellectual functioning in four specific cognitive domains: Verbal Comprehension, Perceptual Reasoning, Working Memory, and Processing Speed. The WISC-IV also provides a Full-Scale composite score that represents the overall level of intellectual functioning. Randall's results are presented in the table following.

Randall's overall level of intellectual functioning fell in the Low Average range (FSIQ = 89) and is ranked at the 23rd percentile. This means that he is performing better than 23% of the population when compared to peers of the same age. However, due to discrepancies between the Processing Speed Index (PSI) and the other Index scores, Randall's composite score was also calculated using the General Ability Index (GAI). The GAI provides a summary score that is less sensitive to the influences of working memory and processing speed and is useful in assessing the effects of those processes on intellectual expression. Randall's GAI score fell in the Average range (GAI = 97) and is ranked at the 42nd percentile.

The Verbal Comprehension Index (VCI) involves the ability to provide categories for concrete and abstract concepts (e.g., In what way are ___ and ___ alike?), define words (e.g., What does ___ mean?), and apply social knowledge and judgment in answering questions (e.g., Why do people ___?). This index measures facility with language and acquired knowledge, and involves the ability to understand concepts and engage in verbal expression. Randall's Verbal Comprehension Index fell in the Average range; he displayed average skills on all subtests.

The Perceptual Reasoning Index (PRI) involves visual-spatial-motor integration (assembling blocks to match a design), categorical thinking with pictures (selecting pictures that form a group with a common characteristic), and analogic reasoning (identifying a missing part from a matrix pattern). Overall, Randall scored within the Average range on this Index. The WISC-IV Perceptual Reasoning Index measures

Wechsler Intelligence Scale for Children – Fourth Edition (WISC-IV)				
Scale	Index/IQ Score *	Percentile Rank	Confidence Interval**	Range
Verbal Comprehension	102	55	95–109	Average
Perceptual Reasoning	90	25	83–98	Average
Working Memory	91	27	84–99	Average
Processing Speed	80	9	73–91	Low Average
Full Scale IQ (FSIQ)	**89**	**23**	**84–94**	**Low Average**
General Ability Index (GAI)	**97**	**42**	**91–103**	**Average**
M = 100, SD = 15, **CI = 95%				

Subtest	Scaled Score*	Subtest	Scaled Score*
Similarities (S)	10	Block Design (BD)	7
Vocabulary (V)	11	Picture Concepts (PCn)	9
Comprehension (C)	11	Matrix Reasoning (MR)	9
Verbal Comprehension Index (VCI)	**102**	**Perceptual Reasoning Index (PRI)**	**90**
Digit Span (DSp)	7	Coding (Cd)	6
Letter-Number Sequencing (LNS)	10	Symbol Search (SS)	7
Working Memory Index (WMI)	**91**	**Processing Speed Index (PSI)**	**80**
*M = 10, SD = 3			

two types of processing—Fluid Reasoning and Visual-Spatial skills. Scores indicated that Randall exhibits a weakness in visual-spatial ability (Block Design). In the area of Fluid Reasoning, Randall's scores fell in the Average range. (In order to follow up on these processes, the WJ III COG was administered and those results are discussed below.)

The Working Memory Index (WMI) measures the ability to attend to, retain, and manipulate information in short-term memory to produce a result. Randall scored within the Average range on this Index, but the subtest scores constituting the Index fell in different ranges. Randall demonstrated a weakness on the Digit Span subtest (Low Average), which measures memory span and working memory. On this subtest, Randall was required to repeat a sequence of digits that were orally presented to him. On one portion, he was asked to repeat the sequence verbatim and the other portion required him to repeat the sequence of numbers in reverse order. Randall was able to retain four numbers on both the forward and backward sequence. Randall performed better on the Letter Number Sequencing subtest (Average), which requires divided attention. This subtest required Randall to reorder a series of numbers and letters that had been orally presented in random order. Randall was able to recall a series of four items (two letters and two numbers), which is consistent with the number of items he was able to recall on the Digit Span subtest. The higher score on Letter Number Sequencing is likely due to the structure of the test since there are more trials with fewer items. (In order to follow up on these processes, the WJ III COG was administered and the results are discussed below.)

The Processing Speed Index (PSI) measures the ability to perform a routine task quickly and efficiently. Randall's Index score fell within the Low Average range. He exhibited weaknesses on both Coding and Symbol Search. On the Coding subtest, Randall had to copy geometric shapes associated with numbers within a 2-minute time limit. This requires visual-motor integration. On the Symbol Search task, he had to use visual scanning and perceptual discrimination skills to determine if a target symbol was among a group of symbols. Thus, Randall's visual-perceptual and visual-motor integration skills are an area of weakness. Given that he also scored low on Block Design, he also has difficulty in perceptual-motor reproduction.

Woodcock-Johnson-III NU: Tests of Cognitive Abilities (WJ III COG)

To further investigate Randall's memory (short-term and working), fluid reasoning, ability to manipulate and transform visual stimuli, and ability to fluently and automatically perform cognitive tasks, several clusters were administered from the Woodcock-Johnson III NU: Tests of Cognitive Abilities (WJ III COG). Standard scores are listed in the table following.

Woodcock-Johnson III NU: Tests of Cognitive Abilities (WJ III COG)				
CLUSTER/Test	Standard Score*	Percentile Rank	Confidence Interval **	Range
Processing Speed (Gs)	**85**	**17**	**81–90**	**Low Average**
Visual Matching	82	11	76–87	Low Average
Decision Speed	94	36	89–100	Average
Short-Term Memory (Gsm)	**83**	**13**	**78–89**	**Low Average**
Numbers Reversed	81	10	75–87	Low Average
Memory for Words	91	27	84–97	Average
Working Memory	83	13	79–88	Low Average
Numbers Reversed	81	10	75–87	Low Average
Auditory Working Memory	91	27	86–95	Average
Visual-Spatial Thinking (Gv)	**83**	**13**	**78–88**	**Low Average**
Spatial Relations	76	5	72–80	Low
Picture Recognition	99	47	93–104	Average
Fluid Reasoning (Gf)	**74**	**4**	**70–78**	**Low**
Concept Formation	82	12	77–86	Low Average
Analysis-Synthesis	73	4	68–77	Low
*M = 100, SD = 15 **CI = 68%				

The Processing Speed cluster, composed of the Visual Matching and Decision Speed tests, measures the ability to perform automatic cognitive tasks, particularly when under pressure to maintain focused attention. On the Processing Speed cluster (Gs), Randall received a standard score of 82, which is in the Low Average range. The Visual Matching test measures the narrow ability of perceptual speed. On this test, Randall was asked to quickly find two numbers that are alike from a row of numbers. His score on this test was an 82, which is in the Low Average range. The Decision Speed test measures the narrow ability of speed of reasoning. On this test, Randall was asked to find two pictures that are the most alike from a row of pictures as quickly as possible. He received a standard score of 94 on this test, which is in the Average range. The Visual Matching test measures the same narrow ability as the Symbol Search subtest; both scores are low, which means that Randall has difficulty in the ability to rapidly search for and compare known visual symbols and patterns.

The Short-Term Memory cluster is composed of the Numbers Reversed, a measure of working memory, and the Memory for Words, a measure of memory span. On the Short-Term Memory cluster (Gsm), Randall received a standard score of 83, which is in the Low Average range. On the Numbers Reversed test, Randall was asked to repeat numbers that he heard by saying them backward. He received a standard score of 81 on this test, which is in the Low Average range. On the Memory for Words test, Randall was asked to repeat a series of unrelated words. On this test, he scored in the Average range with a standard score of 91. Thus, Randall's scores on Numbers Reversed and Digit Span are consistent and indicate that he has difficulty on tasks involving working memory. While he is able to recall input, he has difficulty performing mental operations on the information.

The Working Memory cluster, composed of the Numbers Reversed and Auditory Working Memory tests, measures the ability to hold information in immediate awareness while performing a mental operation on the information. Randall received a standard score of 83, which is in the Low Average range. Randall did perform better on the Auditory Working Memory test, which is similar to Letter Number Sequencing; thus, he does better on tasks of divided attention.

The Visual-Spatial Thinking cluster comprises the Spatial Relations and Picture Recognition tests. This cluster measures the ability to perceive, analyze, synthesize, and think with visual patterns, including the ability to store and recall visual representations. On the Visual-Spatial Thinking cluster, Randall received a standard score of 83, which is in the Low Average range, but significant differences existed between the tests. On the Spatial Relations test, Randall was asked to identify two or three pieces from a group that when joined would form a target shape. He scored in the Low range. On the Picture Recognition test, Randall was shown a set of similar pictures for 5 seconds and then was asked to look at a new set and identify the pictures he had just seen. Randall's score fell within the Average range on this test. These findings indicate that Randall has difficulty with spatial visualization, which is consistent with his performance on Block Design.

The Fluid Reasoning cluster contains the Concept Formation and the Analysis-Synthesis tests. It measures the ability to reason, form concepts, and solve problems using unfamiliar information or novel procedures. On the Fluid Reasoning cluster (Gf), Randall received a standard score of 74, which is in the Low range. On both the Concept Formation and Analysis-Synthesis tests, Randall was presented with a set of colored shapes and had to apply logical reasoning to solve the problems. Concept Formation requires inductive reasoning (ascertaining the rule that governs a problem), whereas Analysis-Synthesis requires deductive reasoning (following a set of steps to solve for a missing item). Randall had difficulty with both tasks. His performance on the fluid reasoning tasks on the WISC-IV was higher because the task involves verbal categorization, a relative strength for Randall. His higher score on Matrix Reasoning is likely due to the multiple-choice nature of the task. An analysis of the items indicates that Randall did experience difficulty on items that required taking multiple properties into consideration for problem solving (e.g., shape and position versus shape alone).

Given the results of the cognitive assessment, Randall has average skills in language processing and weaknesses in working memory, fluid reasoning, perceptual speed, and spatial visualization. These weaknesses are highly associated with difficulties in math achievement.

ACHIEVEMENT/EDUCATIONAL PERFORMANCE LEVELS

Grades

Mrs. Hosp provided copies of Randall's current sixth-grade report card from October 22, 2009. This was reviewed and his averages from the first quarter are as follows: English 73, Math 89, Science 80, Geography 93, Physical Education 100, Art 84, Computer 87, Bible Studies 99, Literature 91, and Beginning Band 100. A review of his English grades indicated that his low grade was due to poor performance on spelling tests and inconsistent performance on daily oral language assignments.

Sylvan Learning Center

Randall has been attending Sylvan for more than 2 years for math tutoring. Sylvan progress reports for Randall's fourth-grade year, based on the CAT-5 after 108 hours of tutoring, placed him at grade level in Math Computation but approximately a year behind in Math Concepts and Application. Toward the end of fifth grade, after 36 additional hours of tutoring, Math Concepts and Application remained approximately 1½ years below grade level.

Woodcock-Johnson III: Tests of Achievement (WJ III ACH)

Randall was administered the Woodcock-Johnson III Tests of Achievement (WJ III ACH) on October 14, 2009. The WJ III ACH measures academic skills in reading, math, and written language. The results obtained are presented in the following table.

Woodcock-Johnson III: Tests of Achievement (WJ III ACH)				
Cluster/Test	Standard Score*	Percentile	Confidence Interval**	Range
Basic Reading Skills	**94**	**34**	**92–96**	**Average**
Letter-Word Identification	97	42	94–100	Average
Word Attack	92	30	89–94	Average
Reading Comprehension	**100**	**50**	**96–103**	**Average**
Passage Comprehension	100	50	95–105	Average
Reading Vocabulary	100	50	96–103	Average
Math Calculation Skills	**109**	**73**	**105–113**	**Average**
Calculation	99	47	94–104	Average
Math Fluency	121	92	119–124	Superior
Math Reasoning	**85**	**16**	**82–88**	**Low Average**
Applied Problems	90	25	87–93	Low Avg/Avg
Quantitative Concepts	80	9	75–85	Low/Low Avg
Written Expression	**89**	**23**	**84–93**	**Low Average**
Writing Fluency	92	30	87–98	Average
Writing Samples	89	23	83–94	Low Average
Broad Written Language	**87**	**19**	**83–90**	**Low Average**
Spelling	87	19	83–90	Low Average

*M = 100, SD = 15
**68% level

The Basic Reading Skills cluster is a combination of the Letter-Word Identification and Word Attack tests, and provides a measure of reading decoding skills. The tests in this cluster measure sight vocabulary, phonics, and structural analysis. Randall's Basic Reading Skills score fell within the Average range. Although both test scores within this cluster are average, the Relative Proficiency Index (RPI) on the Word Attack test is 65/90 (meaning that when an average student of the same age as Randall shows 90% success on this task, Randall's expected proficiency would be 65%); this reflects poorly developed skills in decoding unfamiliar words. (Follow-up with the CTOPP was performed to assess phonological skills; these results are presented below.)

The Reading Comprehension cluster is a combination of the Passage Comprehension and Reading Vocabulary tests and provides a measure of comprehension, vocabulary, and reasoning. On the Passage Comprehension test,

Randall read a short passage/sentence with a word missing and had to determine the word through context. On the Reading Vocabulary test, Randall read words and provided synonyms, antonyms, and the missing words in analogies. Randall's Reading Comprehension standard score fell in the Average range with an RPI 90/90 (Average).

The Math Calculation Skills cluster is a measure of computational skills and automaticity with basic math facts and comprises the Calculation and Math Fluency tests. Randall's Math Calculation Skills standard score fell in the Average range with an RPI of 95/90 (Average). His ability to automatically solve basic math facts in the superior range.

The Math Reasoning cluster, which includes the Applied Problems and Quantitative Concepts tests, provides a measure of mathematical knowledge and reasoning. Randall's standard score in this cluster fell in the Low Average range with an RPI of 54/90 (Limited). This RPI indicates that Randall will find grade-appropriate tasks requiring math reasoning to be very difficult. The Applied Problems test involves solving math word problems by recognizing the operations to be applied and then applying such operations. Randall demonstrated difficulty when problems required multiple steps and operations. The Quantitative Concepts test requires knowledge of math symbols, concepts, and vocabulary, as well as the ability to comprehend number patterns. Randall had difficulty solving for a missing number in a sequence (e.g., 8 __ 24 32).

The Broad Written Language cluster provides a measure of written language achievement including spelling of single words, fluency of production, and quality of expression. This cluster comprises the Spelling, Writing Fluency, and Writing Samples tests. Randall's score on the Broad Written Language cluster fell in the Low Average range; his RPI was 72/90 (Limited to Average). The Spelling test required Randall to spell words from dictation. He spelled words phonetically; his RPI on this test was 57/90, indicating that his spelling proficiency is limited and that tasks requiring spelling are likely to be very difficult. On the Writing Fluency test, Randall was given three words and a picture and had to write simple sentences in a 7-minute time period. Randall scored within the Average range; his RPI was 80/90. An RPI of 80/90 indicates limited to average proficiency in speed of generating simple sentences with the result that Randall will perceive similar tasks to be difficult. The Writing Samples test measures the ability to convey ideas in writing and requires the production of meaningful written sentences in response to both oral and written directions. On this test, Randall constructed simple

sentences, and his lack of elaboration led to a lower point value. Several sentences had spelling errors, which are not penalized, and some word omissions.

Wechsler Individual Achievement Test-Third Edition (WIAT-III)

To further evaluate Randall's academic weaknesses, the WIAT-III subtests of Math Problem Solving, Spelling, Sentence Composition, and Essay Composition were administered. Results are presented in the table that follows.

Wechsler Individual Achievement Test-Third Edition (WIAT-III)			
Test	Standard Score*	Percentile	Range
Math Problem Solving	85	16	Low Average
Spelling	85	16	Low Average
Sentence Composition	81	11	Low Average
Essay Composition	99	48	Average
*M = 100, SD = 15			

Randall's score on the Math Problem Solving subtest of the WIAT-III is consistent with his score on the WJ III ACH Math Reasoning Cluster. Both were in the Low Average range. Randall had difficulties with comparisons and ordering/sequencing, making predictions, working with quantities less than a whole (fractions, decimals), solving problems with multiple steps using whole numbers, and solving problems involving time concepts.

Randall's Low Average Spelling test score on the WIAT-III is consistent with his WJ III ACH Spelling score. Randall spells words the way they sound and omits letters.

On the WIAT-III Sentence Composition test, there were two components. Randall had to combine simple sentences into compound and complex sentences (Sentence Combining) and write a sentence using a target word (Sentence Building). Randall combined sentences with the word "and," producing no complex sentences, and used incorrect punctuation and spelling. He scored in the Low Average range, similar to his performance on the WJ III ACH Writing Samples test. On the Essay Composition test, Randall wrote about his favorite game (baseball) and the overall score fell in the Average range. This score is based on two components, one involving word count and the other involving aspects of theme development and organization. The paragraph was composed of 82 words, which is average (SS = 99). Randall's theme development and organization also fell in the Average range (SS = 98) as his paragraph had an appropriate introduction and conclusion, had several reasons to support why baseball is his favorite game, and had a transition statement. The essay consisted of 11 simple sentences and only one paragraph. Although the time limit was 10 minutes, he finished in 6 minutes and declined to write any more. Randall's spelling within the paragraph was an area of difficulty and consistent with spelling assessments. In general, Randall has difficulty with writing in a complex manner. Previous assessments indicated that Randall's visual-motor integration is poorly developed; although his handwriting is legible, it appears quite labored. Dividing attention between legibility, retrieval of the spellings of words, and language production might well contribute to his difficulty with fluent expression of his thoughts in writing.

Randall's weakness in the academic area of math reasoning and his less developed written expression skills are consistent across both the WJ III ACH and WIAT-III. He is performing below age- and grade-level expectations in math reasoning and sentence construction.

Gray Oral Reading Test-Fourth Edition (GORT-4)

In order to investigate Randall's oral reading rate, accuracy, fluency, and comprehension, the GORT-4 was administered. The student is presented with a written story; the task is to read the story aloud and then verbally respond to five multiple-choice comprehension questions. Randall's Oral Reading Quotient was 88 (Low Average). His Average Rate (ScS 8) and Comprehension (ScS 9) scores were Average. Thus, he read the passages at a speed commensurate with age expectations and was able to answer the comprehension questions at an average level. Randall's Accuracy (ScS 7) was in the Low Average range. His miscues primarily involved omission of small words (e.g., *a, and*) and of plural *s*. Randall often self-corrected when he knew that he pronounced a word incorrectly. Thus, he is able to read words commensurate with expectations but omits words or word endings in text.

Comprehensive Test of Phonological Processing (CTOPP)

The CTOPP was administered to assess Randall's phonological processing. The CTOPP assesses phonological awareness, phonological memory, and rapid naming abilities. His scores are presented here.

Comprehensive Test of Phonological Processing				
Subtest/Composite	Scaled Score	Standard Score	Percentile	Range
Phonological Awareness		91	27	**Average**
Elision (EL)	8		25	Average
Blending Words (BW)	9		37	Average
Phonological Memory		109	73	**Average**
Memory for Digits (MD)	10		50	Average
Nonword Repetition	13		84	High Average
Rapid Naming		103	58	**Average**
Rapid Digit Naming	11		63	Average
Rapid Letter Naming	10		50	Average

On the three composites and six subtests of the Comprehensive Test of Phonological Awareness (CTOPP), Randall scored in the Average range on all but Nonword Repetition, on which he scored in the High Average range. The Phonological Awareness composite comprises the Elision and Blending Words subtests. On Elision, Randall was asked to repeat a word, omitting a specific sound (e.g., "Say gold without saying /g/."). For Blending Words, Randall was asked to listen to individual speech sounds (from a CD) and blend them to form a word (e.g., "What word do these sounds make: b-oi?" "Boy").

The Phonological Memory composite is composed of the Memory for Digits and Nonword Repetition subtests. Memory for Digits required that Randall repeat a series of numbers in the same order that he heard them. Randall was able to repeat six numbers. Nonword Repetition required that Randall repeat nonsense words exactly as he heard them. Randall was able to repeat words of up to six syllables.

The Rapid Naming composite comprises the Rapid Digit Naming and Rapid Letter Naming subtests. These subtests required Randall to read rows of numbers and letters, respectively, as fast as possible.

Based on Randall's performance on word reading tasks and phonological processing tasks, he has the phonological skills that underlie the reading process. Since his spelling is much below his reading, it is likely that Randall's difficulty is more attributable to orthographic processing. In order to investigate this hypothesis, several subtests from the PAL-II were administered.

Process Assessment of the Learner-Second Edition (PAL-II)

The PAL-II Receptive Coding, Expressive Coding, and Word Choice subtests were administered. Receptive Coding and Expressive Coding form the Orthographic Coding composite. Although Randall scored in the Average range on the composite (ScS 9), there was a significant difference between expressive and receptive skills. Expressive Coding (ScS 11) evaluates the ability to code whole written words into memory and reproduce the words or parts of the words in writing. Randall was asked to read a word, then write it, or part of it, from memory. Randall's Receptive Coding (ScS 7) fell in the Low Average range. Receptive Coding evaluates the ability to code whole written words into memory and then to segment each word into units of different size. The subtest asked Randall to read a word and then, from memory, decide if the next word or word part shown corresponded to the first word. It is likely that Randall's weak receptive coding affects the degree to which he can encode a whole word into memory. He continues to use phonological skills for decoding, leading to pronunciation errors, especially on irregular words. This was further confirmed by his performance on Word Choice, which measured Randall's accuracy in identifying the correctly spelled word among misspelled distracters. The Word Choice Fluency subtest measured Randall's rate and accuracy in completing the Word Choice subtest. His Below Average score

indicated that Randall had to slow down to be able to discern the correct word. Since the correct word cannot be chosen based solely on phonology, Randall's orthographic recognition skills appear to be less developed. He is not automatic in recognizing the spelling of common letter patterns.

Curriculum-Based Reading Measure

Randall's Reading Fluency skills were assessed using R-CBM Reading Fluency Probes from AIMSweb. The student is presented with a reading passage and is to read aloud for 1 minute. Randall's fluency on the grade-level probe was at the 75th percentile, with 159 words read correctly and 6 errors.

PARENT AND TEACHER RATING SCALES

Mrs. Hosp completed the Behavior Assessment System for Children – Second Edition: Parent Rating Scale (BASC-2: PRS); three of Randall's teachers at Steinberg Elementary completed the BASC-2: Teacher Rating Scale (TRS). The BASC-2: PRS and BASC-2: TRS are used to assess adaptive and maladaptive behavior in children and adolesents. The T scores for the raters appear in the following chart.

Behavior Assessment System for Children, Second Edition: Parent and Teacher Rating Scales				
		Teachers		
Scale	Mother	Math/Science	Geography	Language Arts
Hyperactivity	44	44	42	44
Aggression	40	46	44	44
Conduct Problems	41	43	43	45
Externalizing Problems	**41**	**44**	**43**	**44**
Anxiety	55	63*	42	42
Depression	50	48	45	42
Somatization	63*	43	43	43
Internalizing Problems	**57**	**52**	**42**	**41**
Attention Problems	63*	41	52	49
Learning Problems	–	48	48	48
School Problems	**–**	**44**	**50**	**48**
Atypicality	47	44	47	44
Withdrawal	41	44	52	44

(Continued)

Behavior Assessment System for Children, Second Edition: Parent and Teacher Rating Scales				
		Teachers		
Scale	Mother	Math/Science	Geography	Language Arts
Behavior Symptoms Index	**47**	**43**	**46**	**43**
Adaptability	55	56	51	49
Social Skills	47	67	53	57
Leadership	50	44	44	52
Activities of Daily Living	40*	–	–	–
Study Skills	–	63	49	47
Functional Communication	35*	51	46	48
Adaptive Skills	**45**	**57**	**48**	**51**

M = 50, SD = 10; Clinical Scales: 60–69 = At-Risk*; ≥70 = Clinically Significant**
Adaptive Scales: 31–40 = At-Risk*; ≤30 = Clinically Significant**; – Scale not on PRS/TRS

The BASC-2 measures a broad range of behaviors, including positive (adaptive) and negative (clinical) characteristics observed in the home and school settings. The Externalizing Problems composite is composed of the Aggression, Hyperactivity, and Conduct Problems scales. These scales measure acting-out, disruptive behaviors. Based on all raters, Randall does not exhibit these behaviors to an atypical degree.

The Internalizing Problems composite is characterized by behaviors that represent emotional distress and includes the scales of Anxiety, Depression, and Somatization. Although all raters' scores fell within the Average range on this composite, there were elevations in the At-Risk range in Somatization (Mrs. Hosp) and Anxiety (Math/Science teacher). Items endorsed by Mrs. Hosp on the Somatization scale indicate that Randall displays several health-related concerns such as headaches, stomach problems, and fears about getting sick. Items endorsed on the Anxiety scale by Randall's teacher indicate that he often worries (e.g., regarding performance in school).

The School Problems composite is made up of the Attention Problems and Learning Problems scales. This composite measures motivation, attention, and learning. All teachers' ratings fell within the Average range in this composite. Mrs. Hosp did report an elevation on the Attention Problems scale. Items endorsed on this scale indicate that Randall is easily distracted and has a short attention span.

The Behavior Symptoms Index reflects the overall level of problem behavior and includes the following scales: Hyperactivity, Aggression, Depression, Attention Problems, Atypicality, and Withdrawal. All raters' scores on this index fell within the Average range.

The Adaptive Skills composite includes Adaptability, Social Skills, Leadership, Activities of Daily Living, Study Skills, and Functional Communication. This composite reflects communication ability, organization, social skills, and overall daily living skills. On this composite, all raters' scores fell within the Average range. However, Mrs. Hosp's ratings of Randall fell in the At-Risk range for Activities in Daily Living and Functional Communication scales. Items endorsed by Mrs. Hosp describe Randall as needing to be reminded to brush his teeth, needing help to get up on time, and having difficulty writing messages that are clear and correct.

According to the BASC-2: PRS and TRS, Randall does not display any significant emotional or behavioral difficulties.

Conners-Third Edition: Parent Assessment Report (Conners 3-P)

Mrs. Hosp also completed the Conners – Third Edition (Conners 3-P). This is an assessment tool used to obtain parents' observations about their child. It is specifically designed to assess Attention-Deficit/Hyperactivity Disorder (ADHD) and its most common comorbid problems among children and adolescents. An analysis of her ratings revealed an acceptable response pattern and level of consistency. Randall's T scores are presented in the following table.

Based on these scores, Mrs. Hosp reported that Randall's inattention, hyperactivity/impulsivity, executive functioning, aggression, and peer relations are in the Average range. The Learning Problems score is elevated, indicating that Randall is experiencing academic struggles. Mrs. Hosp

Conners, Third Edition: Parent Assessment Report (Conners 3-P)		
Scale	T Score	Range
Inattention	58	Average
Hyperactivity/Impulsivity	43	Average
Learning Problems	72	Very Elevated
Executive Functioning	54	Average
Aggression	46	Average
Peer Relations	42	Average

indicated that Randall's problems seriously affect school-work or grades quite a bit. Specifically, she reported that Randall's spelling is poor, he often cannot grasp arithmetic, and that he often learns information as separate facts without "getting the big picture." This is consistent with Randall's previous assessments and current school grades. Randall does not display a profile consistent with ADHD.

Self-Report Measures

Randall completed the Behavior Assessment System for Children – Second Edition: Self-Report of Personality (BASC-2: SRP), a self-report measure designed to evaluate the personality and self-perceptions of children. An analysis of his ratings revealed an acceptable response pattern and level of consistency. The following table presents the T scores.

Behavior Assessment System for Children, Second Edition: Self-Report of Personality (BASC-2: SRP)			
Scale	T Score	Scale	T Score
Attitude to School	45	Attention Problems	47
Attitude to Teachers	43	Hyperactivity	46
Sensation Seeking	41	Inattention/ Hyperactivity	46
School Problems	41	Emotional Symptoms Index	42
Atypicality	41	Relations with Parents	54
Locus of Control	42	Interpersonal Relations	62
Social Stress	37	Self-Esteem	59
Anxiety	47	Self-Reliance	48
Depression	40	Personal Adjustment	58
Sense of Inadequacy	44		
Somatization	46		
Internalizing Problems	40		

M = 50, SD = 10; Clinical Scales: 60–69 = At-Risk*; ≥70 = Clinically Significant**;
Adaptive Scales: 31–40 = At-Risk*, ≤30 = Clinically Significant**

The School Problems composite includes the Attitude to School, Attitude to Teachers, and Sensation-Seeking scales. These scales are a broad measure of adaptation to school. On this composite, Randall rated himself in the Average range with no significant elevations on any of the scales within it. This indicates that Randall cares about school and believes that his teachers understand and care about him.

The Internalizing Problems composite includes Atypicality, Locus of Control, Social Stress, Anxiety, Depression, Sense of Inadequacy, and Somatization scales that correspond to behaviors indicating inward-directed distress. On this composite and all scales within it, Randall rated himself in the Average range.

The Inattention/Hyperactivity composite includes Attention Problems and Hyperactivity scales. Randall's scores on this composite and the scales within it fall in the Average range. Randall indicated that he does not have a short attention span and rarely has trouble sitting still.

The Emotional Symptoms Index is an indicator of emotional disturbance. It is composed of four scales from the Internalizing Problems composite (Social Stress, Anxiety, Depression, Sense of Inadequacy) and two scales from the Personal Adjustment composite (Self-Esteem and Self-Reliance). Randall rated himself within the Average range on this Index. Thus, there is no indication of emotional difficulties.

The Personal Adjustment composite consists of Relations with Parents, Interpersonal Relations, Self-Esteem, and Self-Reliance scales. Randall's scores in this composite all fall within the Average range. Randall feels that he gets along with his parents, is liked by his classmates, and feels good about himself.

STUDENT INTERVIEW

In several of the testing sessions, Randall was interviewed by the examiners. He was able to interact well and did not hesitate to answer any questions. In questions regarding school, Randall indicated that his favorite subjects are geography and science. He reports that he is generally doing well in school but has a bit of trouble with science and English. He also indicated that last year math gave him some trouble, but that he is doing well this year. When asked about his friends, Randall reported that he has a lot of friends and that they enjoy playing football, basketball, and video games. When asked about somatic concerns and complaints, he reported that he sometimes gets headaches and usually takes Tylenol for them. He indicated that he does not get stomachaches very often and has no other kind of body pain. When asked what he would wish for if given three wishes, Randall's responses involved aspirations in baseball. If he could be anything he wanted as an adult, Randall said he would be a professional baseball player for the Houston Astros.

SUMMARY AND CONCLUSIONS

Randall does not exhibit any significant emotional, behavioral, or attentional problems. His difficulties lie in the areas of cognitive processing and academic achievement.

Randall's overall level of intellectual functioning fell within the Low Average range (FSIQ = 89) when all dimensions of cognitive functioning are considered. However, his overall level of cognition fell in the Average range (GAI = 97) when working memory and processing speed were not included. Randall's verbal expression and language skills appear to be well developed.

Randall's cognitive processing deficits involve difficulty with working memory (this may be in part due to having to manipulate numbers mentally), fluid reasoning (using both inductive and deductive logic), perceptual speed (quickly processing abstract symbols and numbers), and visual-spatial skills (involving both spatial relations and visualization). Randall has difficulty holding information in immediate awareness while performing a mental operation on the information. However, as noted above, the working memory tasks involved numbers, and Randall did perform better on tasks involving words. Thus, the content of the items will likely have an impact on this process. Fluid reasoning is the ability to reason, form concepts, and solve problems using unfamiliar information or novel procedures. Randall exhibits weaknesses in both deductive and inductive reasoning. Consequently, he has difficulty with tasks that involve the ability to discover an underlying characteristic that governs a problem and the ability to start with rules and use steps to reach a solution [Example: A > B, B > C, what is the relationship between A and C?]. These processes involve difficulty in identifying relations and drawing inferences. Processing Speed is the ability to fluently and automatically perform cognitive tasks. Specifically, Randall exhibits difficulty in the ability to rapidly search for and compare known visual symbols or patterns (including numerical stimuli) presented side-by-

side or separated in a visual field. Visual Processing involves the ability to generate, perceive, analyze, synthesize, store, retrieve, manipulate, transform, and think with visual patterns and stimuli. Randall demonstrates difficulty with tasks that require the ability to mentally manipulate objects and visual patterns to see how they would appear under altered conditions.

An operational definition of a learning disability involves consistency between cognitive and academic deficits. (a) The student must display a significant normative deficit in an academic skill. Randall displays a deficit in Math Reasoning/Math Problem Solving (WJ III ACH = 85, RPI: 54/90; WIAT-III = 85). He is performing at beginning to mid-fourth grade level regarding these skills despite adequate instruction and extensive supplemental tutoring. (b) The student must display a significant normative deficit in a cognitive ability or process and display a pattern of strengths/assets and weaknesses/deficits in cognitive skills. For Randall, his assets are related to language processing and his cognitive deficits as noted above, are processing speed, working memory, visual-spatial processing, and fluid reasoning. (c) There must be an empirical or logical association between the cognitive deficit and the academic deficit. The specific deficits in cognitive areas that are associated with math include induction, general sequential reasoning/deduction, working memory, spatial processing, and perceptual speed. Fluid reasoning is related to mathematical activities at all ages. For example, figuring out how to set up math problems by using information in a word problem is important for math reasoning. (d) A functional impairment must exist. This is seen in Randall's lower grade equivalents in math reasoning. Randall has been previously identified as having a learning disability in math reasoning and has had tutoring in this area. His profile is still consistent with the presence of a learning disability in mathematics reasoning/problem solving.

Randall's performance in written expression, especially sentence construction and spelling, is also an area of weakness. He displayed difficulty in constructing complex sentences with details. He is able to produce simple and compound sentences. As writing demands became more involved and required more elaboration, Randall's performance declined. When constructing the essay on the WIAT-III, Randall wrote only simple sentences. However, he was able to write a sufficient amount and organize his thoughts to reflect an appropriate theme regarding the topic. Thus, the content of his writing is appropriate, but the mechanics and elaboration are lacking. Randall displays consistent difficulties in spelling, demonstrating a phonetic approach and some letter omissions. Although Randall did display weaknesses in sentence composition and spelling, his essay score fell in the Average range. While Randall does display a pattern of strengths and weaknesses in cognitive skills as noted above, his profile is not consistent with a learning disability in written expression. There is some overlap of narrow abilities (working memory and processing speed); however, those skills most associated with writing are linguistic and phonological, and Randall scored in the Average range in these areas. He did, however, have weaknesses in orthographic pattern recognition, which has contributed to spelling difficulties. It is concluded that Randall's difficulties in writing do not currently indicate a learning disability in the general area of written expression, but rather reflect specific weaknesses that will require appropriately focused and sufficiently intensive intervention. If, after intervention, Randall's skills in written expression do not improve, additional evaluation would be warranted.

Mrs. Hosp mentioned a concern regarding dyslexia. In order to determine whether Randall exhibits characteristics of dyslexia, the following domains required by the Texas Education Agency were assessed: Reading real and nonsense words in isolation, phonological awareness, rapid naming, reading fluency, reading comprehension, and written spelling. Except for spelling, Randall's scores on all tests assessing these domains fell within the Average range. Thus, Randall does not display a pattern associated with dyslexia according to the state of Texas guidelines. His difficulties in spelling are due to orthographic weaknesses and an intervention in this area is needed.

Randall has many positive characteristics that facilitate his functioning. Intellectually, he is performing in the Average range. His language skills and acquired knowledge are commensurate with his age. He is self-motivated and able to succeed in schoolwork; he participates in various after-school activities. Randall is sociable and gets along well with his peers, teachers, and parents and does not exhibit any behavior or emotional problems. His behavior is attentive and cooperative, and he is motivated to achieve. Given continued appropriate educational programming, specific skill intervention, and Randall's motivation, it is anticipated that he will be able to improve his academic achievement.

DIAGNOSTIC IMPRESSIONS

Axis I 315.1 Mathematics Disorder (Reasoning)

Based on the results of this evaluation, Randall displays a pattern of strengths and weaknesses that meet the criteria for a Learning Disability in math problem solving according to the Texas Education Agency guidelines.

RECOMMENDATIONS

General

1. The results of this evaluation should be shared with the appropriate school personnel—specifically the Math and English/Language Arts teachers. There may be specific interventions being offered in the school setting in which Randall could participate (e.g., before- or after-school tutoring or computer-based learning labs).

2. Computer-based programs for improving math reasoning and written expression would be appropriate. (Consult with Randall's teachers to ensure that there is consistency in the instructional goals and methods.)

Math

1. Randall needs to employ systematic problem-solving strategies when provided with reasoning/word problems. These should include techniques such as reading the problem carefully, gathering and reviewing all necessary information, and dividing the problem into distinct, manageable parts. Once a problem has been solved, he should check the solution for accuracy.

2. Randall will require explicit instruction in representing and solving the problem. In order to accomplish this, Randall can follow these steps:

   a. Read and reread the problem.

   b. Determine what operations need to be used (e.g., Harry weighed 250 lbs. He weighed 72 more lbs. than James. How much did James weigh?)

   c. Make a table, graph, or chart of the information provided (put 250 and 72 in an equation, such as H = 250 and J = 250–72, or J weighs 72 less than 250, then would know to subtract; J = ?)

   d. Perform the calculation.

   e. Arrive at the solution.

   f. Check the answer.

3. Randall will also need specific instruction in making inferences and logical deductions. (The Carsons went to Jack-in-the-Box and spent $20.75 for lunch. An adult meal cost $4.95 and lunch for a child cost $2.95. How many people are in the family? How many are children?). To solve such problems, prediction and estimation need to occur first based on obvious facts (e.g., try with 2 adults and 2 children, and then systematically worked from there. At first, $2 A + 2 C = 15.80$ and the total is 20.75, so $20.75 - 15.80 = 4.95$; therefore, there are 3 adults and 2 children).

4. Randall will profit from the use of cue cards to assist in math problem solving. These cards list a sequence of steps to follow, such as presented above, but each step may be more elaborated (e.g., visualize the problem, draw, use objects, restate the problem, explain problem in own words, identify what is known, identify what is unknown).

5. Provide tutoring/instruction in math problem solving using a variety of grade-level items, not just tutoring to keep up with his schoolwork. This will require working with a tutor who has specific expertise in math. Consultation with a math curriculum specialist would be appropriate.

6. One math reasoning program that Randall may benefit from is Plato Math Problem Solving. This computer program offers 57 hours of instruction and 19 interactive scenarios that encourage the student to apply mathematical concepts to solve multistep problems in a real-life context (http://www.plato.com/Post-Secondary-Solutions/Adult-Education/PLATO-Math-Problem-Solving.aspx).

Writing

1. Provide Randall with instruction in keyboarding and word processing skills to help him identify and correct spelling errors and increase productivity.

2. Randall would also benefit from strategies that would allow him to break various writing tasks into easier, more manageable parts. This will prevent him from becoming overwhelmed by a writing task, while also decreasing the demands that are placed on his working memory. Several strategies can aid in this process, such as the use of graphic organizers to assist with organization and elaboration. These visual supports organize content material in a way that makes it easier to understand. They highlight important concepts, facts, and key terms to show their relationships to each other, presenting abstract or implicit information in a concrete manner. Several types of organizers exist: hierarchical, conceptual, sequential, and cyclical.

   a. Hierarchical organizers highlight a main idea and subtopics in a linear fashion.

   b. Conceptual graphic organizers are often used to describe characters' actions and motivations. They begin with a concept, event, or idea, with subtopics branching out from the central theme.

   c. Sequential organizers illustrate chronological order as well as cause and effect. An example of this is a time line.

   d. Cyclical organizers, as their name suggests, illustrate a series of events that have no beginning, middle, or end (e.g., water cycle).

3. **POWER** is a mnemonic strategy that is used to help students proceed through the writing process in an organized, systematic manner. Teach and model each step of the mnemonic to Randall and provide practice in writing assignments. The POWER strategy includes the following steps:

   P – Plan: Discuss the basic format and type of writing required by the task, as well as determining the steps needed to complete the task.

   O – Organize: Identify and describe the parts of the task. Use visual or graphic organizers to aid in the organizational process.

   W – Write: Have the student write and elaborate on the ideas that were developed earlier.

   E – Edit: The student proofreads the finished product several times, and focuses on a different component of editing (capitalization, punctuation, spelling, etc.) each time the paper is read. Another mnemonic strategy that is helpful during this stage for editing is **COPS: C**apitalization, **O**rganization, **P**unctuation, **S**pelling.

   R – Revise: Have the student revise the writing, based on the editing that was previously completed.

4. Since Randall exhibited difficulty producing both complex and compound sentences, he may benefit from writing programs such as the University of Kansas Sentence Writing Strategy. This program will help Randall recognize and write 14 sentence patterns with four types of sentences: simple, compound, complex, and compound-complex (http://www.ku-crl.org/sim/strategies/sws_fundamentals.shtml).

Spelling

1. Randall would benefit from direct instruction in the common rules for letter patterns and exception/irregular spelling patterns.

2. Randall should spend between 10 and 15 minutes studying and practicing various common words that he misspells in his writing. Teach Randall how to use a Cover-Copy-Compare strategy: Give him a list of spelling words, an index card, and a blank sheet of paper. For each word on the spelling list, the student (1) copies the spelling list item onto a sheet of paper, (2) covers the newly copied word with the index card, (3) writes the spelling word again on the sheet (spelling it from memory), and (4) uncovers the copied word and checks to ensure that the word copied from memory is spelled correctly. If that word is spelled incorrectly, Randall repeats the sequence above until the word copied from memory is spelled correctly—then moves to the next word on the spelling list.

3. Randall would also benefit from strategies that will help him memorize the spellings of new words.

   a. Analyze for roots, prefixes, suffixes, and other patterns that will link the new word with previously learned words.

   b. Use of the "five senses" approach—listen to the word, speak the word, picture the word in your mind, write the word several times, and remember a sentence using the word correctly.

   c. Back-chaining—completing a word by filling in progressively more blank letters with each trial (e.g., *work, _ ork, _ _rk, _ _ _k, _ _ _ _*).

CASE 37

"Nonverbal" Learning Disabilities or Asperger's Syndrome?
Clarification Through Cognitive Hypothesis Testing

Lisa Hain and James Hale

Differential diagnosis remains a critical role for psychologists practicing in schools, especially when different subtypes of reading (Fiorello, Hale, & Synder, 2006), mathematics (Hale, Fiorello, Miller, Wenrich, Teodori, & Henzel, 2008), and psychosocial (Hain, Hale, & Kendorski, 2009) disability require comprehensive evaluation for identification and intervention purposes. This school neuropsychological report illustrates the use of the cognitive hypothesis testing (CHT) approach and the concordance-discordance model (C-DM) for establishing the diagnostic and intervention utility of cognitive and neuropsychological test results (see Fiorello, Hale, Decker, & Coleman, 2009; Hale & Fiorello, 2004; Hale et al., 2008; Miller & Hale, 2008).

CHT is based on the premise that nomothetic global or factor intelligence test scores are only sufficient for educational decision making when subtest profiles are relatively flat (i.e., not much scatter), but not sufficient to account for children with learning disabilities, Attention-Deficit/Hyperactivity Disorder, traumatic brain injury, and socioemotional disorders, where profile variability precludes global score interpretation (Fiorello, Hale, Holdnack, Kavanagh, Terrell, & Long, 2007; Fiorello, Hale, McGrath, Ryan, & Quinn, 2001; Hale, Fiorello, Kavanagh, Holdnack, & Aloe, 2007; Hale et al., 2008). For these children, idiographic examination requires detailed analysis of the intellectual data, with any hypotheses derived methodically evaluated with other data sources to further establish diagnostic specificity and empirically-based interventions (Hale & Fiorello, 2004).

Overcoming the limitations of traditional profile analysis (Hale et al., 2008), the CHT model begins with an overall theory of a child's presenting problem. The theory

is developed for children who have not shown adequate response to intervention (e.g., Hale, Kaufman, Naglieri, & Kavale, 2006), and should be based on background history, prior intervention attempts; observations; behavioral ratings; teacher, parent, and student interviews; curriculum-based measures; and other classroom data. If a cognitive and/or neuropsychological deficit is thought to be the cause of the problem, an intellectual/cognitive test is administered, scored, and interpreted. However, this measure only serves as a cognitive *screening* tool, and results are not considered sufficient for diagnostic or intervention purposes. Subsequent hypotheses regarding cognitive strengths and weaknesses are generated, evaluated, and authenticated using additional cognitive, behavioral, and/or neuropsychological measures that help validate or refute initial findings (Fiorello et al., 2009; Hale et al., 2008; Miller & Hale, 2008). After the concurrent and ecological validity of findings is established, the psychologist cannot only be more confident in diagnostic decision making, but can also use findings within the context of a subsequent collaborative problem-solving model to help teachers and parents design, implement, evaluate, and recycle interventions tailored to the child's academic and/or behavioral needs (Fiorello et al., 2009; Hale & Fiorello, 2004; Hale et al., 2008). CHT has been used to establish the treatment validity of cognitive and neuropsychological test results in children with reading (Fiorello et al., 2006), mathematics (Hale et al., 2006), attention (Reddy & Hale, 2007), and psychiatric (Hain, Hale, & Glass-Kendorski, 2009) disorders.

Insofar as the CHT model aids differential diagnosis and intervention design, the use of the concordance-discordance model (C-DM) (see Hale & Fiorello, 2004;

Hale et al., 2008) provides for the statistical evaluation of idiographic processing strengths and weaknesses between tests of cognitive functioning and academic achievement, and can aid in establishing whether a child has a specific learning disability (Fiorello et al., 2009; Hale et al., 2006). Described in detail elsewhere (Hale & Fiorello, 2004; Hale et al., 2008), the C-DM requires a *discordance* between a child's cognitive strength and cognitive weakness (establishes deficit in the basic psychological processes); a *discordance* between the cognitive strength and the academic deficit (establishes discrepant performance); and a *concordance* between the cognitive weakness and achievement deficit (establishes plausible explanation for poor achievement). To establish a child's specific learning disability using the C-DM, the cognitive and achievement standard scores and their reliability coefficients are needed for Standard Error of the Difference calculations (see Anastasi & Urbina, 1997).

The relationships between Cattell-Horn-Carroll (CHC) cognitive and neuropsychological processes (see Elliott et al., in press; Fiorello et al., 2006; Hale et al., 2008a; 2008b; McGrew & Wendling, in press) and academic achievement are now well established, and this can guide C-DM calculations. However, our model for comprehensive evaluation includes Response to Intervention (RTI) and other direct assessment and indirect informant report data sources. In addition, in many cases, moving beyond nomothetic summative intelligence test interpretation to idiographic formative interpretation of cognitive and neuropsychological tests requires the clinician to use scientific judgment and meticulous detective work (Miller & Hale, 2008) to ensure concurrent, ecological, and treatment validity of results (Fiorello et al., 2009; Hale et al., 2008). It is important to recognize that rigid or blind application of the C-DM to test data is extremely problematic. Careful psychological evaluation and disability determination require multiple data sources and informant report to ensure concurrent and ecological validity before determining whether a child has a specific learning disability or other disorder.

In the following case report, the CHT and C-DM approaches were used to establish the presence of what is often called a "nonverbal" learning disability, which apparently affected the child's right hemisphere visual-spatial and implicit language functioning (e.g., Bryan & Hale, 2001), as well as executive functions (e.g., Decker, Hill, & Dean, 2007). Although prior research has established a foundation for this disorder (see Rourke, 2008), debate over diagnosis and treatment continues, especially when subtypes are considered (Forrest, 2004; Hain et al., 2009).

We present the following school neuropsychological evaluation to demonstrate the utility of CHT and C-DM in differential diagnosis, the recognition of normative and idiographic strengths and weaknesses, the establishment of a specific learning disability, and the development of individual recommendations for intervention.

Given the complexity of school neuropsychological evaluations, it may be best to write the report for a professional audience. One could choose to write a school neuropsychological evaluation for lay people, and make sure it is understandable for all potential readers. However, this type of report may not be feasible or useful in many school settings, because it would need to be excessively long to convey the complexity of the child's functioning, or if succinct, leave out pertinent details. Instead of resolving this dilemma by choosing one type of report or another, we suggest the report should be succinct and professional. After the report is completed, we take the summary section of the report and paraphrase the content so it is in lay terminology. We put this revised summary content into the form of a letter to parents. Because it is based on the actual summary, it conveys the major points to the parents without overwhelming them. We also provide them with a copy of the written report. This technique, while somewhat more time consuming, is well received by parents, teachers, and other consumers.

SCHOOL NEUROPSYCHOLOGICAL EVALUATION

Name:	Erin Manley
Date of Birth:	8/13/96
Age:	12 years, 9 months
Dates of Evaluation:	3/30; 4/13; 4/20; 4/22/09
Evaluator:	Lisa A. Hain, Psy.D., NCSP
Supervising Consultant:	James B. Hale, Ph.D., ABSNP

INSTRUMENTS ADMINISTERED/ SOURCES OF INFORMATION

Wechsler Intelligence Scale for Children, Fourth Edition, Integrated (selected subtests) (WISC-IV Integrated)

Children's Auditory Verbal Learning Test-Second Edition (CAVLT-2)

Developmental Test of Visual-Motor Integration, Sixth Edition (Beery VMI)

Children's Memory Scale (CMS) (nonverbal subtests)

NEPSY-II (selected subtests)

Delis-Kaplan Executive Function System (D-KEFS) (selected subtests)

Comprehensive Assessment of Spoken Language (CASL) (Supralinguistic subtests)

Conners' Continuous Performance Test-II (CPT-II)

Woodcock-Johnson III NU Tests of Achievement, Third Edition (WJ III ACH) (selected subtests)

Gray Oral Reading Test-Fourth Edition (GORT-4)

Wechsler Individual Achievement Test-Third Edition (WIAT-III) (selected subtest)

Behavior Rating Inventory of Executive Function (BRIEF) (parent, teacher, self)

Child Behavior Checklist (CBCL) and Teacher Report Form (TRF)

Achenbach Youth Self-Report (YSR)

Conners' Teacher Rating Scale—Revised: Long Form (CTRS-R:L)

Conners' Parent Rating Scale—Revised: Long Form (CPRS-R:L)

Social Skills Improvement System (SSIS) (parent, self-report, teachers)

Children's Depression Inventory (CDI) (parent, self-report)

Piers-Harris Children's Self-Concept Scale, Second Edition (Piers-Harris 2)

Asperger Syndrome Diagnostic Scale (ASDS) (parent)

Classroom observation

Clinical interview (Child, Parent, Teacher)

Review of records

REASON FOR REFERRAL

Erin was referred for a school neuropsychological evaluation following a psychiatric evaluation that suggested she had symptoms suggestive of a "nonverbal learning disability" and associated social and emotional difficulties. This evaluation was undertaken to further clarify the nature of Erin's cognitive, academic, and psychosocial strengths and needs and to determine individual educational and psychosocial recommendations.

RELEVANT BACKGROUND INFORMATION

Medical/Developmental History

Erin's mother received appropriate medical care while pregnant and there was no known involuntary teratogen exposure, but the antidepressant Prozac was used as ordered before the pregnancy, and then after the first trimester. Although Erin was 3 weeks premature, a lengthy (72 hours total) induced labor following loss of amniotic fluid culminated in a uterine tear and subsequent emergency caesarian section. Surprisingly, Erin weighed 9 pounds at birth, suggesting possible undiagnosed gestational diabetes. Although APGARS were reportedly within normal limits, Erin was transferred to NICU and hospitalized for 5 days without further incident.

Throughout development, Erin experienced numerous illnesses, including ear infections with several myringotomies, bronchitis, allergic reactions, and chronic constipation (but reportedly not encopresis). On one occasion, Erin experienced a fever above 104 degrees for approximately 3 hours, which involved emergency treatment, but febrile seizures and head trauma were denied. Erin's complaints of headaches, stomachaches, muscle aches, and other somatic concerns have resulted in frequent school absences. Erin also experienced nightmares and night tremors as a young child, and she continues to have difficulty with initiation and duration of sleep. Erin has had regular pediatric checkups, dental visits, and hearing and vision tests, with all results within normal limits. According to her mother, Erin did not meet developmental milestones on time. The development of physical skills such as sitting, crawling, and reaching were attained later than most children, especially talking and walking, both of which occurred between 18 and 24 months. Additionally, Erin's fine- and gross-motor skills and social development were considered to be initially delayed, yet Erin caught up quickly, and her subsequent mental development in most areas was considered to be advanced thereafter.

Family/Social History

Erin is the only child of divorced parents who separated when she was an infant. Erin lives with her mother, and the relationship is described as positive and supportive. Her mother has worked with Erin intensely over the years to help her adjust academically and socially. Although Erin has regular visitation with her father, she reportedly feels conflicted over visitation and custody issues, and her relationship with him was described as "strained." Socially, Erin has struggled to develop peer relationships, and her mother described her as socially immature. Reportedly having no real friends and poor self-esteem, Erin has been teased, rejected, and verbally attacked by her peers. Additionally, her mother reported Erin frequently worries and has strong fears (e.g., death), and often appears anxious and tense, especially in new or unpredictable situations. Described as overly dependent, Erin copes by seeking adult affection and reassurance, and withdrawing from social exchanges with peers.

Academic/School History

Having been at home until kindergarten, Erin appeared to enjoy her academic success upon entering school, but she tended to play by herself and social difficulties were noted. Referred for a comprehensive evaluation in first grade, the school district's report indicated Erin had adequate verbal abilities and general information, but noted weaknesses in fluid reasoning, visual-spatial processing, and pragmatic language. As is typical in young children with this profile, Erin's achievement results were in the high average range. The occupational therapy evaluation revealed tactile sensitivity, somatosensory processing weaknesses, vestibular and proprioceptive difficulties, and praxis and motor planning deficits. The report concluded that she had a "generalized sensory integration dysfunction."

Under Section 504/ADA, Erin began receiving occupational therapy for handwriting and sensory concerns, and physical therapy for gross-motor difficulties. The third- and sixth-grade reevaluations led to similar recommendations for these related services. Additionally, the sixth-grade reevaluation noted the completion of a functional behavior analysis (FBA) due to behavioral concerns of the teaching team (i.e., not completing class work on time, needing a large amount of teacher assistance to complete even simple tasks, and a tendency to withdraw from social contacts). Results of the FBA indicated that Erin was displaying these behaviors as a function of avoidance or escape from schoolwork and social exchange and as a means of gaining individualized attention from the teacher. Erin also experienced physical symptoms of fears associated with personal or school problems and displayed a sad affect with thoughts of hurting herself. These led to a recent psychiatric evaluation, with subsequent diagnoses of Generalized Anxiety Disorder and Depression NOS, Zoloft® medication, and an Emotional Disturbance classification in the school.

The sixth-grade reevaluation recommendations included a home-school contract, systematic desensitization, social skills training, pragmatic language practice with the guidance counselor, and outpatient psychotherapy.

Currently, in seventh grade, Erin's Individualized Education Plan (IEP) suggests a need for behavioral support, counseling bi-weekly with the school psychologist, and working in a small group on social skills. She also continues to receive occupational therapy and a personal care aide who provides sensory breaks. She receives an itinerant level of special education support services for her learning needs.

CLASSROOM OBSERVATION

Erin was observed in math, Reading Plus, and science classes. A 15-minute systematic classroom observation revealed that Erin displayed high rates of academic engaged time and passive engaged time, with few instances of off-task motor or passive behaviors, and no off-task verbal behaviors. Off-task behaviors were more likely to occur when the class was taking a quiz, but she was not, because she had been absent when the instruction had occurred. Therefore, she was sitting quietly at her seat completing make-up work. Her off-task motor behaviors consisted of clasping her hands together and restless arm movements, followed by stretching across her desk, which occurred several times during the observational period. Before her reading class, Erin received a sensory break with her personal care aide and entered the classroom 10 minutes later than the other students because of her reported difficulty with transitions. Upon entering, Erin immediately approached the teacher for her independent seatwork assignment, which she completed easily. Peer interactions were positive but limited to task-specific questions about the assignment. In science class, Erin had high rates of participation, often raising her hand vigorously and providing correct answers when called on. Erin had numerous peer interactions because of the small group lab exercise. After the lab assignment, Erin transitioned quietly and efficiently to independent seatwork with no signs of frustration or noncompliance.

ASSESSMENT OBSERVATIONS

Erin presented as a talkative, pleasant youth with adequate health and hygiene. Rapport was easily established and Erin appeared motivated to put forth her best effort. Erin was an avid conversationalist, often speaking with the examiner about the many things going on in her life. Erin often asked about her performance, often wondering how high she was scoring and comparing herself to the performance of students in higher-grade levels. Erin performed better on auditory-based verbal tasks than she did on tasks involving visual-spatial-motor skills, and struggled with graphomotor (paper-and-pencil) reproduction. On tasks tapping language-based crystallized knowledge, Erin often replied quickly with accurate answers. On tasks tapping visual-spatial or fluid reasoning skills, Erin was less confident and did not persevere when items became difficult. Erin sometimes made off-task comments during administration of tasks she reported to be challenging or aversive, and used verbal mediation for some visual-spatial and written language tasks. She tended to use working memory processes to solve mathematical problems mentally rather than on paper. At times, Erin refused to attempt more difficult design-copy items, acknowledging that this was an area of weakness for her. Frustration tolerance overall appeared to be adequate, but frequent breaks were offered to encourage performance. These assessment observations suggest that the results are a reliable and valid estimate of Erin's overall level and pattern of cognitive, neuropsychological, academic, and behavioral functioning.

ASSESSMENT RESULTS AND CLINICAL IMPRESSIONS

Cognitive/Intellectual Functioning

To screen for cognitive and intellectual functioning, Erin was administered the WISC-IV core subtests and six supplemental (process) subtests. Erin was in the superior range for the Verbal Comprehension (VCI) factor and within the high average range for the Working Memory (WMI) factor, whereas her Processing Speed (PSI) and Perceptual Reasoning (PRI) factor scores were significantly lower, in the lower end of the average range. The difference between Erin's VCI and PRI (34 points) occurs in only .4% of standardization sample, and the difference between her VCI and PSI (31 points) occurs in only 2.6% of standardization sample. Because the significant differences between the factors suggested that a Full-Scale standard score (SS) was not valid, it is not reported. As these differences are quite rare, results suggest individual cognitive and neuropsychological processes must be further explored, and global composites may have limited utility.

An evaluation of Erin's pattern of performance revealed well-developed concordant/convergent thought processes (i.e., noting similarities among objects/words for categorical responding), local-detail processing (i.e., discriminating parts of objects and language details), and strong crystallized knowledge (i.e., information gained through experience and education). Although this may indicate auditory-verbal processing strengths, it is important to recognize that Erin's high performance is in part related to prior learning and achievement. Her explicit receptive and expressive language skills appeared to be well developed, with Erin providing quick and highly detailed answers. Her strong expressive vocabulary performance suggests good lexical-semantic knowledge, and her superior fund of factual knowledge likely led to competency on a verbal concept formation task that required concordant-convergent thought to determine categorical relationships among word pairs. When needing to provide lengthier statements regarding social knowledge and reasoning, and common sense problem solving, Erin performed in the superior range as well, indicating a good understanding of social conventions. Erin's auditory attention and immediate auditory sequential memory were average when she was asked to provide rote recall of digits in forward sequence. Her performance was in the high average range when asked to recite digits backward, sort and reorder random sequences of numbers and letters, and manipulate quantitative information when solving simple oral arithmetic problems, indicating good auditory-verbal working memory.

In contrast to her strong crystallized and explicit language skills, Erin's visual-spatial, global-holistic, novel problem solving, and processing speed skills were a relative weakness, albeit mostly in the average range. When asked to quickly scan and match simple abstract visual shapes and numbers, and use graphomotor (paper-and-pencil) skills to reproduce the shapes quickly and efficiently according to a template, Erin was in the average range. She was in the below average range on a task that required visual scanning and detection of abstract visual targets embedded within an array of distracter shapes, but she improved to an average level when provided with task structure. Erin showed relative difficulties, albeit mostly in the average range, on tasks tapping fluid reasoning, novel problem solving, visual-spatial concept formation, and global-holistic processing. Erin again displayed adequate concordant-convergent thought when asked to identify conceptual similarities among visually meaningful pictures. She was inconsistent with analyzing and completing visual matrix patterns, but still in the average range. Erin had difficulty with perceptual analysis and synthesis and part-whole relationships on a task that required manual reproduction of two-dimensional, geometric block patterns. Scoring below average on this task, Erin displayed configuration errors, a pattern that suggests visual-spatial-holistic processing deficits. Even when time limits were removed or a multiple-choice format was used, Erin's performance did not improve, suggesting that processing speed and/or motor skills were not factors in her poor performance.

Cognitive Hypothesis Testing

Given that subtest analysis without confirming evidence can be limited, cognitive hypothesis testing was conducted to examine Erin's relative weaknesses in visual-spatial-holistic and novel problem-solving skills. Auditory-explicit verbal skills, crystallized abilities, and concordant-convergent thought were not evaluated further, given her strengths in these areas; however, implicit, nonliteral language was evaluated further as this ability is commonly associated with visual-spatial-holistic and fluid/novel problem-solving skills.

Visual-Spatial-Holistic Processes, Visual-Motor Integration, and Motor Skills

On a spatial line orientation task that required Erin to examine a variety of two dimensional arrows pointing toward a center target, where there is little visual detail perception and no motor requirement, Erin's performance denoted difficulty with judging line and angle orientation, a problem inherent in children with visual-spatial-holistic processing deficits. On another task, Erin was presented with a picture of a large grid containing several abstract shapes that cannot be coded verbally, and was asked to recognize shapes outside the grid. As she was more successful on this mental rotation task, this suggests executive function can be used to help Erin overcome visual-spatial-holistic processing deficits.

Further analysis of visual-spatial-holistic processing can be accomplished using tasks that also require motor skills, as many children with this difficulty have considerable problems with integrating spatial perception with motor coordination, a function in part related to auditory-verbal-crystallized skills. On a simple task requiring visual perception and copying of abstract geometric shapes within a designated space with no time limits, Erin performed below expected levels. On a similar task that further delineates processing demands, Erin demonstrated a pattern of errors suggestive of motor and global deficits

in producing the general visual-spatial-gestalt or idea of the design stimulus. Problems with understanding figure-ground effects, part-whole relationships, and design orientation were evident. This suggests difficulty with analysis of abstract visual-spatial relationships among designs, and/or difficulty transferring this perceptual information onto paper using graphomotor or paper-and-pencil skills (visual-motor integration). Erin made a number of errors in line straightness, interruption (starts and stops), and overshoots (not stopping at end of line), and difficulties with fine-motor control (wavy lines). This could suggest poor sensory feedback to the motor system, a lack of motor precision or automaticity, or difficulty with integration of visual-spatial-tactile and motor functions.

To further assess motor functions without significant visual-spatial-tactile demands, several motor tasks were administered. On a task that required Erin to imitate hand/finger positions modeled by the examiner, Erin's performance suggested only mild weaknesses in visual perception and replication of simple movements, motor programming, and kinesthetic feedback. However, it is important to note that Erin demonstrated no weaknesses when using her right hand, which would be consistent with her strong auditory-verbal skills, but performance decreased when using the nondominant hand. On another task requiring Erin to draw a line with a pencil following a curving track as quickly and accurately as possible, Erin demonstrated graphomotor speed and accuracy at expected levels, but had a higher number of pencil lifts, suggesting difficulties with fluent pencil movement or coordination of visual feedback with ongoing simple motor performance. Observations of Erin revealed a unique pencil grasp in which she tilted the pencil forward away from her fingers and tended to write on a slant. Combined, these tasks suggest her fine-motor skills appear to be largely intact, especially in the dominant right hand, but her left-hand skills are less adequate. The left-hand motor problems, while commonly found in children with visual-spatial-holistic and perceptual-motor integration problems, are more related to executive and fluid reasoning difficulties, suggesting problems impact both perception and action, especially when tasks are novel, ambiguous, holistic, and/or complex. In contrast, perception and action when tasks are detailed, explicit, routinized, or automatic appear to be relatively easy for Erin.

Implicit Language and Pragmatics

Although Erin's expressive and receptive language skills appeared to be quite good (especially explicit language), implicit, nonliteral, and pragmatic language can be difficult for some individuals who have Erin's cognitive profile, and these difficulties interfere with social and adaptive functioning. In contrast to explicit language for which interpretation is straightforward, implicit language is indirect, ambiguous, and context dependent. Double meanings, idiom, sarcasm, metaphor, and humor are all examples of implicit language (Bryan & Hale, 2001). Erin performed below her explicit language strengths on measures of nonliteral and figurative language, as well as on the use of context skills to determine meanings, and had considerable difficulty in recognition and resolution of semantic and syntactic sentence ambiguity, consistent with her cognitive profile. These types of ambiguity often occur in multiple meanings and humorous context, the nonrecognition of which can hinder social judgment and relations. Relative to her explicit language strengths, Erin struggled with deciphering communicative intent, recognizing conversational topics, initiating conversation or turn-taking, adjusting communication to situational factors, and using language for expressing feelings, suggesting difficulty with language pragmatics. These relative weaknesses are important to consider, as they can interfere with Erin's success in ambiguous or dynamic social situations, and also lead to implicit or inferential comprehension difficulties when reading some types of literature, such as poetry.

Learning and Memory

Children with Erin's cognitive and neuropsychological profile tend to have excellent long-term memory once they learn the material but can have difficulty with encoding novel stimuli, or efficient retrieval from long-term memory. To further evaluate these possibilities, measures of word-list learning and visual-spatial memory were administered. On a list learning task that requires memorization and recall of words over five learning trials, Erin had no difficulty with encoding, organizing, and retrieving rote verbal information, demonstrating her strength in auditory-verbal long-term memory. Consistent with her previous visual processing of meaningful stimuli, and her implicit language performance, visual object recognition in the form of faces was fairly adequate. However, when Erin was shown a matrix containing dots in a pattern, and then asked to recall the location of them on the grid, immediately and after a delay, Erin's performance was severely deficient and suggests overall deficits in visual-spatial processing and abstract visual memory. Again, these hypothesis testing results suggest that not all visual processes are

equally impaired, with fairly adequate visual object recognition and implicit language relative to her visual-spatial-holistic and novel problem-solving deficits.

Attention, Working Memory, and Executive Function

Although preliminary evidence suggested only minor difficulty with attention, working memory, and executive function, these cognitive processes are often related to novel problem solving and visual-spatial-holistic processing, so it was important to examine these constructs further. A direct assessment of Erin's attentional processes was undertaken using a computer-based assessment of visual sustained attention and response inhibition, with discriminant function results indicating that Erin's profile was different from children with Attention-Deficit/Hyperactivity Disorder. Erin displayed few omission errors and her consistency of response was average, but she had some difficulty with response inhibition and reaction time, leading to several commission errors (i.e., responses to nontargets).

Erin performed well on working memory tasks, including the WISC-IV Arithmetic subtest, which is in part a measure of novel problem solving or fluid reasoning, areas that seem difficult for Erin. This suggests her mental manipulation of auditory-verbal information is well developed and fosters fluid reasoning. Contrasting visual-sequential rote memory and working memory revealed average performance for forward span, but low average performance when asked to repeat the sequence in reverse, both of which are considerably below her auditory-verbal working memory ability. These findings again suggest the visual-spatial nature of stimuli negatively influence working memory and fluid reasoning.

On measures of executive function with fewer visual-spatial requirements, Erin performed quite well. On tasks measuring word retrieval and fluency (i.e., generating words that start with a given letter or belong to a category), Erin performed exceptionally well, consistent with the word-list learning results discussed earlier. Additionally, she readily demonstrated skill at inhibiting an automatic verbal response in order to generate a conflicting response (naming the color of the ink a word was printed in, rather than the word), thereby suggesting good cognitive inhibition and decision skills. On a measure requiring graphomotor skills to draw lines alternating between numbers and letters (e.g., 1-A-2-B), which assesses flexibility of thinking, maintaining and shifting cognitive set, and visual-motor sequencing, Erin had little difficulty; however, on a subtest that required simple motor skills to trace lines, she was below average, again suggesting that visual-spatial-motor skills interfere with quick, efficient performance. Unlike verbal fluency, Erin's design fluency was quite poor. She had difficulty generating alternative line drawing combinations (i.e., connecting dots to form multiple designs without replicating) and had multiple rule violations, as if overwhelmed by this visual-spatial-generative task. She even commented that this task was the "hardest one I ever done."

A final area to consider in executive functions is self-regulation or response, and social judgment. As noted earlier, Erin had no difficulty with social judgment and common-sense problem solving on the WISC-IV subtest, but this task may be more related to general knowledge of societal expectations rather than social judgment and problem solving. Despite having good memory for faces as described earlier, Erin was challenged by a task that required the perception of emotions in pictures of children's facial expressions, with errors reflecting difficulties with the expressions of sadness, neutrality, and anger. On a task that requires understanding the perceptions, thoughts, and feelings of others, often referred to as theory of mind (belief, intention, deception, emotion, imagination, and pretending), Erin demonstrated no deficits in this regard, suggesting visual-spatial-holistic processing difficulties interfere with affect processing, and these problems likely secondarily affect executive function, fluid reasoning, social judgment, and common-sense decision making.

Academic Achievement

Selected tests from the WJ III Tests of Achievement were administered to gain insight into Erin's reading, written language, and mathematics skills. On the WJ III ACH, her performance was compared to students of similar age. To achieve this end, age-based standard scores and percentile ranks are used to describe Erin's level of academic functioning in these areas.

Clearly, Erin is functioning at or above academic levels for her age and grade, consistent with findings that prior learning and memory and acquired knowledge appear to be quite strong. Erin displayed good word reading, reading fluency, and explicit reading comprehension. Word attack skills were adequate, but lower than would be expected, and reflected possible orthographic (recognition of spelling patterns) difficulties. She performed well in stating antonyms and synonyms but had more difficulty with inference, implicit comprehension, and analogic rea-

soning, consistent with her cognitive profile. It should be noted that Erin used her good executive skills to recognize her difficulty here, commenting, "I'm not good at these." On the GORT-4, Erin's oral reading skills were assessed. Erin's rate, accuracy, fluency, and comprehension all fell in the high average range.

Although one might expect mathematics problems with Erin's cognitive profile, she performed quite well in this area, completing many age-appropriate items requiring advanced computation skills. However, it should be noted that Erin solved math tasks tapping problem solving and multistep problem solving without using the paper and pencil offered to her, again attesting to her adequate working memory and self-awareness to compensate for her visual-spatial-holistic processing weaknesses. Additionally, she had some minor difficulties with math word problems that required novel problem solving or fluid reasoning, albeit this pattern was not significant or consistent.

Erin had the most difficulty with measures of written expression, tasks that require multiple cognitive processes to be used simultaneously. Erin orally recited sentences before she wrote them; her sentence construction reflected good grammar but simplistic sentence structure. Some spelling and punctuation errors were noted, possibly reflecting difficulty with visual attention and orthography, which was also seen in her performance on the word attack test. Although Erin's writing sample had the required elements, it was generally concrete and straightforward. Noticeably missing was the advanced vocabulary and oral expression skills observed during the cognitive assessment, but the results were consistent with minor implicit language and pragmatic language difficulties.

Although Erin's academic achievement is solidly in the average range, this is primarily reflecting her prior learning, which is reportedly quite good. Her difficulties with visual-spatial-holistic processing, visual long-term and working memory, and fluid reasoning/novel problem solving will likely interfere with more advanced achievement. She may have difficulty attending to and/or comprehending complex concepts, translating spoken information into written notes, comprehending and expressing implicit information, and doing higher-level reasoning. As a result, the Concordance-Discordance Model (.01 level of significance) was used to determine if Erin has a specific learning disorder. With the WISC-IV Verbal Comprehension Index as her strength, and Perceptual Reasoning/Processing Speed as cognitive weaknesses, Erin was found to have reading and written language learning disorders. According to IDEA, this may not be interpreted as a learning disability by the multidisciplinary team given her average performance, but she certainly meets criteria for a specific learning disorder, thereby qualifying for an ADA/Section 504 plan for learning services.

Social-Emotional Functioning

According to the teachers, Erin is a polite and compliant girl who performs well on individual worksheets and/or brief assignments. She prefers verbally presented instructions and individual attention but can achieve during large-group instruction, depending on her "mood." Academic performance tends to be good to adequate, yet she has difficulty integrating material and understanding how disparate content is related. Occasionally, Erin has some difficulty with time on-task and work completion, which is in part due to avoidance behaviors and frequent absences. Yet, at other times, she will rush through assignments to be the first person to finish. She has difficulty with multistep assignments, written work, and lengthy tests. Cooperative learning groups are generally not effective, largely because of her social skills problems, aloofness, anxiety, and limited friendships. Erin sometimes complains, frets, paces, whines, and irritates classmates when in a "negative mood." When teased, Erin glares at others and can be verbally aggressive, but does so individually, and does not openly antagonize or provoke others in large group settings.

On teacher behavior ratings (TRF), Erin was rated in the average range with no reported psychopathology according to the reading and science teachers. However, the English teacher's ratings placed Erin's Total Problems, Internalizing, and Externalizing scores in the clinical range with the scores on the Anxious/Depressed, Social Problems, Delinquent Behavior, and Aggressive Behavior syndromes in the borderline clinical range. Given the reported attention and executive concerns, CTRS-R:L attention and BRIEF executive function rating scales were administered. Two of the teacher ratings revealed few difficulties except for clinical-range social problems; however, the English teacher's report indicated clinically elevated scores for oppositional behaviors, cognitive problems and inattention, hyperactivity, social problems, and emotional lability. She acknowledged difficulty with adjusting to task demands and self-monitoring, and also endorsed executive deficits in emotion modulation, initiating problem solving, sustaining working memory, and planning and organization. The teachers also reported social skills deficits on the SSIS, and in English class, a heightened level of problem behaviors.

The clinical interview with Erin's mother indicated a variety of problems. For language and cognitive skills, Erin sometimes becomes confused easily, uses immature speech, and has difficulty understanding multistep instructions and completing puzzles. Erin is reportedly disorganized and easily distracted, has difficulty planning and finishing projects, and, at times, seems listless or lacking energy. Motor problems include clumsiness and poor coordination (e.g., frequently bumping into things, trouble with balance). In terms of behavior, Erin can be argumentative, stubborn, and demanding, and has poor awareness of other children's feelings. She reportedly has poor hygiene, disregard for her appearance, and poor table manners. Most recently, Erin's somatic complaints have increased, and she has begun using sickness to avoid school.

Review of CBCL parent behavior ratings revealed difficulties with both internalizing and externalizing problems, with clinically significant ratings for the Anxious/Depressed, Somatic Complaints, Social Problems, and Thought Problems subscales, and for the *DSM-IV* areas of Affective Problems and Anxiety Problems. Erin's mother also rated Erin as having a clinically significant level of depression on the parent version of the CDI. For attention and executive concerns, parental CPRS-R:L attention and BRIEF executive ratings revealed social problems as the primary difficulty, but she also endorsed items suggestive of anxiety, psychosomatic behaviors, and an overall ADHD rating in the borderline clinical range for inattentive symptoms. On the BRIEF, parent ratings revealed Erin's difficulty with self-awareness and monitoring, with adjusting to novelty, and with changes in routine or task demands. Erin's mother reported Erin's difficulty with self-control, internalizing problems, and social functioning on the SSIS. According to parent ASDS ratings, Erin displays deficits in pragmatic nonliteral language, reading social cues, organization, using common-sense judgment, and transitioning during unplanned events. She has difficulty with fine-motor skills and appears clumsy and uncoordinated. ASDS ratings suggest Erin is *likely* to have an Autism Spectrum Disorder.

Erin's self-report ratings were very similar to those of her mother. She endorsed clinically significant levels for Anxious/Depressed, Withdrawn/Depressed, Social Problems, and Attention Problems. On the CDI and the Piers-Harris 2, Erin acknowledged a clinically significant level of depression with Negative Mood, Anhedonia, and Negative Self-Esteem. Erin noted difficulties with her peer group, being teased and rejected, and otherwise feeling different from others, negatively affecting her self-concept. Erin's

SSIS ratings were similar to those reported by her mother, with average social skills, but problem behaviors in the above average range. Erin reported that she lacks social engagement skills, and displays inattention, hyperactivity, and internalizing problems in the school setting.

As a result of these findings, Erin appears to have a cognitive, neuropsychological, and psychosocial profile that leads to several learning and social-emotional problems. In addition to "nonverbal" problems that lead to poor recognition of visual cues and prosody (vocal intonation, which may change the meaning of a statement or question) during social interactions, Erin's difficulty apparently extends to nonliteral, pragmatic language as well. Children with this profile often have poor self-awareness and self-management) and poor awareness of the environment (i.e., inattentive, forgetful, "spacey" behaviors). As a result, Erin demonstrates a significant impairment in social interaction, failure to develop peer and adult relationships appropriate to her developmental level, and a lack of social-emotional awareness and reciprocity. As children with similar profiles are comforted by routine and predictability, it is not surprising that Erin has a strong reaction to changes in routine and frequently becomes anxious or even displays panic behavior when unscheduled changes occur, thereby demonstrating an inflexible adherence to specific routines or rituals. Given these findings, it is apparent that Erin has considerable psychosocial difficulties and needs that warrant intensive psychosocial service delivery.

SUMMARY AND DIAGNOSTIC IMPRESSIONS

Erin is a 12-year, 9-month-old student who was referred for a school neuropsychological evaluation following her psychiatrist's recommendation for evaluation of a "nonverbal" learning disability. Erin has an extensive and rather remarkable history of intervention, beginning with treatment for birth and neonatal difficulties. Early developmental milestones were not met on time for physical, motor, and social skills. These weaknesses continued to be demonstrated throughout preschool and school-age years, culminating in the need for physical, occupational, and speech and language therapy. Erin has been evaluated numerous times by the school district and found eligible for special education services as a student with Other Health Impairment and Emotional Disturbance. Clinically, she is diagnosed with Generalized Anxiety Disorder and Depression NOS, for which she is currently taking Zoloft. In addition,

Erin has also received behavior support, counseling, and social skills through the school system.

Results of the current evaluation revealed Erin's cognitive and neuropsychological profile, which showed considerable variability, precluding interpretation of global composite scores. She displayed tremendous strengths in concordant-convergent thought, explicit receptive and expressive language, and crystallized/lexical-semantic knowledge. Erin has a strong fund of factual knowledge, solid vocabulary development, and strong verbal conceptual skills. Erin also demonstrated strong rote auditory-sequential memory skills, auditory-verbal working memory skills, and strong long-term memory encoding, storage, and retrieval for facts and details. These talents allow her to excel in many areas of academic achievement in which memorization of information is a critical component. Erin can readily convey this considerable knowledge base with explicit detail using her advanced expressive language skills.

In contrast to these advanced skills, Erin's visual-spatial-holistic processing and nonverbal reasoning skills are less well developed and in some cases impaired, which also affects her skill at processing information quickly and efficiently, especially when it is novel or complex. Subsequent cognitive hypothesis testing confirmed difficulty with visual-spatial, global/holistic, and discordant/divergent thought. This makes it difficult for Erin to integrate information and make novel or complex connections between disparate parts of her extensive knowledge base. This could explain her "sensory integration problem," because she has difficulty recognizing interrelationships and instead perceives information as disparate parts. These relative visual-spatial-global-holistic processing deficits affect multiple cognitive functions, including visual-spatial perception, perceptual analysis and synthesis, understanding of part-whole relationships, visual-spatial long-term memory, motor organization and planning, visual-motor integration, visual-spatial working memory, nonverbal concept formation, fluid reasoning/novel problem solving, and divergent-discordant thought. Difficulty with visual-spatial-global perception is most likely leading to graphomotor and constructional problems because these processes provide feedback to the motor system, which carries out the task.

Additionally, Erin may appear clumsy and uncoordinated, and have difficulty with gross-motor skills, and fine-motor skill in handwriting. These graphomotor deficits likely impact her written language, and Erin may appear more avoidant or aversive to tasks requiring these skills, especially considering the planning, organization, and novel problem-solving skills needed to produce written language. Although Erin presents with strengths in explicit language (expressive and receptive), she demonstrated some difficulty with implicit language, such as understanding ambiguity or multiple word meanings, and adaptive pragmatic language within a social context. For attention, memory, and executive functions, Erin's performance was mainly within normal limits, in contrast to reported difficulties in this area. She had some difficulty with attention on tasks, but this could be due to difficulty with orienting or selective attention, as she showed good sustained attention or vigilance. Erin did have some difficulty with response inhibition, but this could reflect need for accuracy and perfectionistic tendencies. Children with this profile can have difficulty with decision making, and rather than get bogged down with indecision, a quick response can be adaptive but can also lead to error.

Erin's mother and team of teachers report executive deficits in both monitoring of self and task monitoring, which likely is leading to her observed difficulties with completing assignments within specified time limits. Children like Erin tend to pay poor attention to themselves (i.e., poor self-awareness) and poor attention to the environment (i.e., inattentive, "spacey," and forgetful). However, these types of attention problems are qualitatively different, and have a different cause, than those found in children with ADHD, as the latter children have problems with executive control of attention. Erin does not appear to have this difficulty, and could actually benefit from an intervention using her executive control to better regulate her self-awareness and her attention to events in her environment.

Although Erin's academic achievement is solidly in the above average to average range, her difficulties with visual-spatial-holistic processing, visual long-term and working memory, fluid reasoning/novel problem solving, and discordant/divergent thought will likely interfere with more advanced achievement objectives and higher-order learning. She may have difficulty with quick and efficient processing of academic or social content, attending to and/or comprehending lectures, and translating spoken information into written notes. Weaknesses in comprehension and expression of implicit language may affect higher-level reasoning and inferential thought. Erin was found to have reading and written language learning disorders according to the Concordance-Discordance Model criteria, which is consistent with IDEA statutory requirements. However, this may not be interpreted as a learning disability by the multidisciplinary team, given her average performance in

these areas, even if the cognitive impairments are limiting her potential performance. She may have more difficulty in written language, mathematics word problems, and even reading comprehension as she progresses through school when rote learning and literal comprehension is no longer emphasized and higher-level thinking skills are needed to draw inferential conclusions, comprehend abstract concepts, and make predictions about academic content. Therefore, should the team decide against IDEA classification, Erin should be entitled to a Section 504/ADA plan and instructional accommodations, because her disability clearly interferes with major life activities including her academic and social functioning in school.

Children with "nonverbal" learning disorders (NVLD) often display social-emotional problems, particularly internalizing disorders, and have difficulty with regulating emotional systems, which is commensurate with Erin's prior diagnoses of Generalized Anxiety Disorder and Depression NOS. As was the case with Erin's profile, these children often display deficits in visual-spatial-global-holistic processing, discordant-divergent language, inferential thinking, novel problem-solving skills, and understanding implicit messages, metaphors, and humor, so both nonverbal *and* implicit verbal skills are affected. Children with these characteristics often have difficulty with novel problem solving and new learning, and can be confused by complex or ambiguous stimuli or situations. Erin may also show signs of neglect, such as poor hygiene and body awareness, and inattention to self and environment. Probably the most problematic result of these deficits, however, is that Erin is likely to miss the gist of social discourse, not only due to poor perception of nonverbal social cues, but also due to difficulty with following and responding to social language in an adaptive fashion (i.e., social reciprocity). This difficulty may contribute to the social skills problems she is experiencing in both peer and adult relationships. Although the term "nonverbal" learning disability is often understood as referring to a homogeneous group, this is incorrect; instead, it is likely that multiple subtypes exist.

Erin's neurocognitive profile is consistent with a subtype of NVLD, which has similar signs and symptoms to that of Asperger's Disorder, which affects both verbal and nonverbal skills and social relationships. Although some claim Asperger's Disorder is really high-functioning Autism, this is clearly not the case for Erin, who fits the profile of Asperger's Disorder of the NVLD type—with severe impairment in global-holistic, implicit language, and novel problem-solving skills, and relatively intact rote/automatic, detail-oriented, explicit verbal, and crystallized skills. As a result, specialized academic instruction and psychosocial intervention must be designed, implemented, evaluated, and modified as necessary to meet her cognitive, linguistic, motoric, academic, and psychosocial needs.

DIAGNOSTIC IMPRESSIONS

Axis I: Asperger's Disorder

Generalized Anxiety Disorder

Dysthymic Disorder

Learning Disorder

Axis II: Deferred

Axis III: No current significant medical problems reported

Axis IV: Psychosocial stressors, acute and chronic, moderate: school, peer relationships, family related psychosocial stressors

Axis V: GAF = 51

RECOMMENDATIONS

The following recommendations may be helpful for Erin and are not meant to be prescriptive. They should be taken into consideration by the multidisciplinary school team evaluation, and if implemented, they should be monitored and adjusted as necessary to ensure treatment efficacy.

1. The IEP team should consider this evaluation for IDEA eligibility classification under the Autism category. Children with Asperger's Disorder often have pronounced difficulty with internalizing disorders and social skills deficits, so while the Emotional Disturbance classification was not inaccurate, it does not reflect the complexity of cognitive, academic, and psychosocial needs of children with Asperger's Disorder.

2. Although Erin's neurocognitive profile likely leads to underachievement, and there was a discrepancy between her cognitive strengths and her reading and writing achievement, her academic scores were in the average range. There is clearly cognitive and neuropsychological interference with academic achievement, so the team may also want to determine IDEA eligibility and develop goals associated with her learning strengths and weaknesses. She certainly meets Section 504/ADA criteria for a child with a disability, and therefore requires the level of intensive services offered with an IEP.

3. Given Erin's incredibly strong skills in rote/automatic, detail-oriented, explicit verbal, and crystallized skills, it would be useful for her to receive supplemental or horizontal enrichment in academic areas that build on these strengths, such as social studies or history. In addition, she could provide class presentations or peer tutoring in these subject areas. She could help others in her classroom gain a better understanding of this information-laden content, or even tutor younger children who are struggling in these areas, which will likely foster self-esteem, peer and adult acknowledgment of her strengths, and interpersonal relationships.

4. Visual-spatial-holistic processing may be difficult for Erin, and she may benefit from teacher-organized worksheets, tests, and other materials. A step-by-step verbal approach to learning may be helpful. She could also benefit from gradual exposure to new concepts and linking those concepts to familiar or overlearned content. A strategy such as paired associative learning may be helpful where novel information can be linked with known information.

5. Erin needs considerable support in the areas of inferential and higher-order thinking. She would benefit from instruction in analyzing and synthesizing information and connecting disparate thoughts and information. Her level of responding tends to be somewhat concrete, so instructional efforts designed to help her flexibly brainstorm interrelationships among concrete parts, and then verbal labeling of higher-order connections, would be helpful.

6. Erin may have difficulty seeing the "big picture" and delaying gratification, which can lead to anxiety and impulsive responding or poor work completion due to perfectionistic tendencies. These tendencies interfere with quick, efficient performance because of fear of failure. Erin seems reluctant to complete or turn in assignments that are not correct in every possible detail, and each subsequent change she makes to better her work only creates additional doubt regarding the quality of her final product. Erin will need large multiple-step projects broken down into smaller, more manageable tasks, with initial focus on the parts of the project, followed by direct instruction on how to integrate those parts into a coherent whole.

7. Erin may require speech and language services focusing on implicit and pragmatic language competency. The interventions could focus on inferential skills, divergent language processing, understanding nonliteral and

ambiguous language, and the ability to use pragmatic, conversational speech appropriately with peers and adults. For instance, she could be given a list of meanings for a word, and then be taught to rank order them in terms of relevance to a given situation.

8. Difficulty with implicit language likely extends to reading comprehension as well. In reading and oral language, Erin may need explicit instruction in interpreting nonliteral language, such as metaphor, humor, sarcasm, ambiguity, and multiple-word meanings. Fostering flexible thinking and learning multiple methods of expressing words and sentences to convey different meanings may be helpful. Instruction in logic may be helpful for developing hypotheses regarding meaning, understanding relationships among content, using inferential thought, and drawing conclusions. Interpretation of poetry will likely be difficult for Erin, and extra care with these strategies will need to be taken to avoid frustration in this area.

9. Erin may also have difficulty with written expression, likely because she tends to be overly literal. Brainstorming ideas will be hard for her, so it will be important to help her identify what she knows, and how that knowledge may lead to more advanced conceptualizations. Explicit instruction on connecting parts (e.g., words) into meaningful wholes (e.g., sentences, paragraphs) would be helpful. She may need direct instruction on how to vary sentence structure, including modifying clauses, and providing adjectives and adverbs to provide richness in her written language output. After writing a sentence, she could be taught to flexibly modify the sentence, and add different words and clauses to convey different meanings. Encourage Erin to monitor, evaluate, and revise her writing.

10. Erin could also benefit from occupational therapy services designed to focus on sensory-motor integration, graphomotor coordination and speed, copying/note-taking skills, and general handwriting, but the focus should be on sensory feedback to the motor system. As copying tasks requiring near (book to paper) or far point (chalkboard to paper) translation may be difficult for Erin, providing her with teacher-made notes or another note-taking system may be warranted. She also will likely need explicit instruction on picking out key words and phrases so she doesn't attempt to copy everything from a passage or lecture. The use of a word processor may also be indicated, given her difficulty with fluent pencil control and aversion to writing tasks.

11. Erin must be given ample time to process sensory and academic information. With the additional weaknesses in processing speed, she will likely need extra time to complete tasks, especially tasks of a visual-spatial nature and those requiring writing skills. She may need extended time on assignments/testing when higher-order conceptual thinking is required. It would be important to provide differential reinforcement of quick, accurate performance, and self-monitoring of time to completion, to reduce the need for extended time accommodations.

12. Erin will need self-regulation and monitoring skills to guide her own thoughts and behaviors, especially those requiring task completion and those of a social nature.

   • Teachers can provide cues that will provide Erin with opportunities for self-monitoring of task performance and social behavior.

   • Erin may find it helpful to have video recording of her behavior and social encounters and then have these reviewed with her. This will allow Erin to see herself from another's perspective, and understand the perspectives of others. It would be important to discuss the videotape with the school psychologist or school counselor.

   • Erin may not consider the impact of her behavior in the immediate situation. It may be helpful or necessary to discuss or review her behavior following the situation and in private.

13. Erin would benefit from a research-based social skills curriculum with baseline measurement and progress monitoring of her social competence in the classroom and in group and/or individual sessions. She would benefit from learning to better discriminate and interpret facial expressions, body posture, and language prosody, as well as flexibly adjust to ongoing social communication with explicit pragmatics instruction. Erin may likely require verbal cues or reminders to increase visual attention to herself and her environment, both in the classroom and outside of school. She may need help in language formulation and use during social discourse.

14. Erin will likely benefit from intensive behavioral and psychotherapeutic interventions. She could benefit from a positive behavior management plan in classes such as English when avoidance behaviors are being displayed, and related psychological services for anxiety and affect regulation problems. Once medical evaluation has ruled out possible medical causes, somatic complaints should be addressed in the context of self-awareness and control. Additionally, systematic desensitization techniques and gradual exposure

to social and other anxiety-producing stimuli appear to be warranted. A cognitive-behavior therapy approach with skill focus, social skills homework, and role playing may be helpful, not only to foster social success, but to monitor affective and overall adjustment.

It has been our pleasure to work with Erin, her team of teachers, and her family in providing a school neuropsychological evaluation and recommendations for her educational and psychosocial programming. Please do not hesitate to contact us if we should be of further assistance regarding these assessment findings or intervention efforts.

SCORE SUMMARY SHEET

Wechsler Intelligence Scale for Children-Fourth Edition, Integrated

Scale	Composite Score	Percentile Rank	95% Confidence Interval	Qualitative Description
Verbal Comprehension (VCI)	128	97	120–133	Superior
Perceptual Reasoning (PRI)	94	34	87–102	Average
Working Memory (WMI)	116	86	107–122	High Average
Processing Speed (PSI)	97	42	88–106	Average
Full Scale (FSIQ)	112	79	–117	High Average

Verbal Comprehension Subtest Score Summary

Subtest	Scaled Score	Percentile Rank
Similarities	14	91
Vocabulary	14	91
Comprehension	16	98
(Information)	19	99.9

Perceptual Reasoning Subtest Score Summary

Subtests	Scaled Score	Percentile Rank
Block Design	6	9
Picture Concepts	11	63
Matrix Reasoning	10	50
(Picture Completion)	9	37

Working Memory Subtest Score Summary

Subtests	Scaled Score	Percentile Rank
Digit Span	12	75
Digit Span Forward	11	63
Digit Span Backward	12	75
(Spatial Span Forward)	9	37
(Spatial Span Backward)	8	25
Letter-Number Sequencing	14	91
(Arithmetic)	15	95

Processing Speed Subtest Scores Summary

Subtests	Scaled Score	Percentile Rank
Coding	9	37
Symbol Search	10	50
(Cancellation)	7	16
(Cancellation Random)	7	16
(Cancellation Structured)	9	37

Developmental Test of Visual-Motor Integration – 6

Standard Score = 82

Percentile Rank = 12th

Children's Auditory Verbal Learning Test – 2

Scale	Standard Score	Percentile Rank
Immediate Memory Span	105	63
Level of Learning	112	81
Interference Trial	89	23
Immediate Recall	107	68
Delayed Recall	118	88

Learning Trials	Learning Trial 1	Learning Trial 2	Learning Trial 3	Learning Trial 4	Learning Trial 5
Standard Score	115	96	117	104	115
Percentage	84	39	87	61	84

Comprehensive Assessment of Spoken Language

Scale	Standard Score
Nonliteral Language	105
Meaning from Context	109
Inference	108
Ambiguous Sentences	90
Pragmatic Judgment	97

NEPSY-II

Score Name	Scaled Scores	Percentile Ranks	Classification
Imitating Hand Position Total Score	7	16	Borderline
Imitating Hand Positions – Dominant Hand Score	–	–	At Expected Level
Imitating Hand Positions – Nondominant Hand Score	–	–	Borderline
Visuomotor Precision Total Completion Time	8	25	At Expected Level
Visuomotor Precision Total Errors	–	51–75	At Expected Level
Visuomotor Precision Combined Scaled Score	10	50	At Expected Level
Visuomotor Precision Pencil Lift Total	–	11–25	Borderline

Score Name	Scaled Scores	Percentile Ranks (%)	Classification
Affect Recognition Total Score	10	50	At Expected Level
Affect Recognition Total Happy (H) Errors	–	26–50	At Expected Level
Affect Recognition Total Sad (S) Errors	–	6–10	Below Expected Level
Affect Recognition Total Neutral (N) Errors	–	6–10	Below Expected Level
Affect Recognition Total Fear (F) Errors	–	51–75	At Expected Level
Affect Recognition Total Angry (A) Errors	–	11–25	Borderline
Affect Recognition Total Disgust (D) Errors	–	26–50	At Expected Level
Theory of Mind Total Score	–	>75	Above Expected Level
Theory of Mind–Verbal Score	–	>75	Above Expected Level

Score Name	Scaled Scores	Percentile Ranks	Classification
Arrows Total Score	4	2	Below Expected Level
Design Copying Process Total Score	6	9	Borderline

Score Name	Scaled Scores	Percentile Ranks	Classification
Design Copying Process Motor Score	1	0.1	Well Below Expected Level
Design Copying Process Global Score	8	25	At Expected Level
Design Copying Process Local Score	10	50	At Expected Level
DCP Global vs. Local Contrast Scaled Score	11	63	At Expected Level
Design Copying General Total Score	–	26–50	At Expected Level

Children's Memory Scale

Scale	Scaled Score	Percentile Rank
Dot Location		
Learning	9	37
Total Score	8	25
Long Delay	6	9
Faces		
Immediate	11	63
Delayed	15	95

Delis-Kaplan Executive Function System

Scale	Scaled Score
Trail Making Test	
Condition 1	10
Condition 2	11
Condition 3	11
Condition 4	10
Condition 5	7
Verbal Fluency	
Condition 1	13
Condition 2	14
Condition 3 Total Correct	17
Condition 3 Switching Accuracy	17
Design Fluency	
Condition 1	6
Condition 2	9
Condition 3	11
Total Correct	9
Color Word Interference	
Condition 1	14
Condition 2	13
Condition 3	14
Condition 4	11

Woodcock-Johnson III NU of Achievement (Age-Based Scores 12-8)

Test/Cluster	Standard Score	Percentile Rank	Classification
Letter Word Identification	104	60th	Average
Passage Comprehension	108	70th	Average
Word Attack	105	63rd	Average
Reading Vocabulary	103	58th	Average
Reading Fluency	127	97th	Advanced
Calculation	112	79th	Average
Applied Problems	105	63rd	Average
Quantitative Concepts	121	91st	Advanced
Math Fluency	114	82nd	Average/Advanced
Spelling	112	79th	Average/Advanced
Writing Samples	101	53rd	Average
Writing Fluency	105	63rd	Average
Academic Skills	**112**	**80th**	**Average/Advanced**
Academic Applications	**111**	**77th**	**Average/Advanced**
Academic Fluency	**119**	**90th**	**Advanced**

Gray Oral Reading Tests-Fourth Edition (GORT-4)

Scale	Scaled/Standard Score	Percentile Rank
Rate	13	84
Accuracy	14	91
Fluency	**14**	**91**
Comprehension	13	84
Oral Reading Quotient	**121**	**92**

REFERENCES

Anastasi, A., & Urbina, S. (1997). *Psychological testing* (7th ed.). Upper Saddle River, NJ: Prentice-Hall.

Fiorello, C. A., Hale, J. B., Holdnack, J. A., Kavanagh, J. A., Terrell, J., & Long, L. (2007). Interpreting intelligence test results for children with disabilities: Is global IQ relevant? *Applied Neuropsychology, 14*, 2–12.

Fiorello, C. A., Hale, J. B., McGrath, M., Ryan, K., & Quinn, S. (2001). IQ interpretation for children with flat and variable test profiles. *Learning and Individual Differences, 1*, 115–125.

Fiorello, C. A., Hale, J. B., & Snyder, L. E. (2006). Cognitive hypothesis testing and response to intervention for children with reading problems. *Psychology in the Schools, 4*, 835–853.

Forrest, B. J. (2004). The utility of math difficulties, internalized psychopathology, and visual-spatial deficits to identify children with the nonverbal learning disability syndrome: Evidence for a visuospatial disability. *Child Neuropsychology, 10*, 129–146.

Hain, L. A., Hale, J. B., & Kendorski, J. G. (2009). Comorbidity of psychopathology in cognitive and academic SLD subtypes. In S. G. Feifer & G. Rattan (Eds.), *Emotional disorders: A neuropsychological, psychopharmacological, and educational perspective* (pp. 199–234). Middletown, MD: School Neuropsych Press.

Hale, J. B., & Fiorello, C. A. (2004). *School neuropsychology: A practitioner's handbook.* New York, NY: Guilford Press.

Hale, J. B., Fiorello, C. A., Kavanagh, J. A., Holdnack, J. A., & Aloe, A. M. (2007). Is the demise of IQ interpretation justified? A response to special issue authors. *Applied Neuropsychology, 14*, 37–51.

Hale, J. B., Fiorello, C. A., Miller, J. A., Wenrich, K., Teodori, A., & Henzel, J. (2008). WISC-IV interpretation for specific learning disabilities identification and intervention: A cognitive hypothesis testing approach. In A. Prifitera, D. H. Saklofske, & L. G. Weiss (Eds.), *WISC-IV clinical assessment and intervention (2nd ed.)* (pp. 109–171). San Diego, CA: Elsevier Academic Press.

Hale, J. B., Kaufman, A., Naglieri, J. A., & Kavale, K. A. (2006). Implementation of IDEA: Integrating response to intervention and cognitive assessment methods. *Psychology in the Schools, 43*, 753–770.

McGrew, K. S., & Wendling, B. J. (in press). CHC cognitive-achievement relations: What we have learned from the past 20 years of research. *Psychology in the Schools.*

Miller, D., & Hale, J. B. (2008). Neuropsychological applications of the WISC-IV and WISC-IV Integrated. In A. Prifitera, D. H. Saklofske, & L. G. Weiss (Eds.), *WISC-IV clinical assessment and intervention (2nd ed.)* (pp. 445–495). San Diego, CA: Elsevier Academic Press.

Rourke, B. P. (2008). Neuropsychology as a (psycho) social science: Implications for research and clinical practice. *Canadian Psychology/Psychologie Canadienne, 49*, 35–41.

CASE 38

Applying a Multilevel Interpretive Framework with an Emphasis on the Assessment of Executive Functions

George McCloskey

Parents requested an evaluation because of concerns over Richard's lack of progress in acquiring basic academic skills and questions as to whether Richard's educational program was meeting his needs. The school district proposed an independent evaluation and the parents agreed to allow this psychologist to conduct the evaluation. The results of the evaluation as summarized in the following report were well received by the parents and their advocate, the school district staff, and Richard himself, who was apprised of the results in a separate meeting prior to the team meeting to discuss recommendations. Richard's mother was especially touched by what she read. In a meeting with the parents and advocate prior to the team meeting, she stated: "You really described our Richard and his struggles in this report; I cried when I read it; you helped us understand in a much deeper way both his needs and his potential and we thank you for the time you took to do this for Richard and for us."

The structure of Richard's report is one that I have worked out over the course of many years of experimenting with various formats. The report is structured to answer four important questions: What can Richard do well? What does Richard have difficulty doing? What needs to be done for Richard? Who can do what needs to be done for Richard? I have found that front-loading a summary that includes relevant background information, a listing of strengths and weaknesses, a concluding narrative that offers a comprehensive case conceptualization, and a listing of recommendations facilitates discussion of the report findings at a team meeting lasting less than an hour. Note that the recommendations are offered in three parts: (1) what the child can do for himself/herself; (2) what the parents can do; and (3) what school staff can do. This format helps to reinforce the need for effort by, and collaboration

among, all parties to effect positive change. The specific findings of the report are offered as an Appendix to the summary report. It is important to note that the sections included in the Appendix are organized by meaningful areas of cognition, behavior, and academic skill rather than by specific tests administered. This format enables maximum integration of information that belongs together to support clinical hypotheses regardless of the test from which it came.

Richard's case was a complicated one that defied simplistic interpretations based on the traditional intellectual and achievement test results that had been obtained in past evaluations. It demonstrates the need to employ an interpretive-level framework and to look beyond a global estimate of ability such as a Full-Scale IQ. Further, Richard's case shows the importance of delving much deeper than specific composite scores such as the Verbal Comprehension Index, Perceptual Reasoning Index, Working Memory Index, and Processing Speed Index to fully understand a child's cognitive strengths and weaknesses at the subtest cluster, individual subtest, and item levels. This case also demonstrates the benefits of gathering information with additional cognitive and academic measures in order to test hypotheses and more accurately characterize a child's mental capacities. Also illustrated in the report is the use of the process approach that emphasizes description of how a child performs a task and what such observations mean in terms of test score interpretation and hypothesis generation.

Although Richard demonstrated multiple difficulties, this report especially illustrates how various executive functions can enhance or inhibit performance. The report emphasizes the need to incorporate assessment of executive functions in clinical case work in order to characterize more effectively the child's cognitive capacities and understand the nature of difficulties the child may be experiencing.

The term *executive functions* refers to a diverse group of cognitive capacities that act in a coordinated way to direct perception, emotion, thinking, and motor activity. Executive functions are responsible for a person's ability to engage in purposeful, organized, strategic, self-regulated, and goal-directed behavior. As a collection of capacities that enable a person to direct and regulate his or her own thinking processes and actions, executive functions alert, or cue, a person to use other cognitive abilities such as reasoning, language, visual processing, and memory. Similarly, executive functions direct the performance of academic skills such as reading comprehension, math problem solving, and written expression.

Executive functions are not the mental capacities we use to perceive, feel, think, and act; rather, they are the capacities that direct or cue the engagement and use of the mental capacities that we use to perceive, feel, think, and act. It is helpful to think of executive functions as a set of independent but coordinated capacities rather than as a single unitary capacity. There is no guarantee that if one executive function is well developed that others will be well developed. Any person can have strengths and/or weaknesses in any one or more of the different executive functions at any given point in time. Assessment requires a multidimensional approach to identify the specific constellation of executive function strengths and weaknesses for any given child or adult.

A comprehensive model of executive functions (McCloskey, Perkins, & VanDivner, 2009) involves multiple levels of executive cueing of perceiving, feeling, thinking, and acting. At the lowest level, cues are provided for *self-activation*, that is, giving the command to wake up and engage a state of consciousness. Once awake, a person's *self-regulation* executive functions are involved in basic self-control of perceptions, emotions, thoughts, and behaviors. In the model used to interpret Richard's executive functioning, 29 specific self-regulation capacities were assessed. The specific names and descriptions of these executive functions are described in McCloskey and associates (2009). Additional executive function levels involve *self-realization* and *self-determination*. These executive functions direct a person's engagement with activities related to gaining an understanding of

personal strengths and weaknesses and how a person's behavior affects others, and developing a personal set of goals and long-term plans that motivate and drive behavior. Beyond these levels of self-control, an individual can engage in directive processes related to *self-generation*. These processes cue the active exploration of self-generation questions (Why do I do the things I do? What really motivates my choice of self-goals? What is the meaning of life?).

Assessment of children's executive functions focuses primarily on the *self-regulation* aspects of executive control. As children enter adolescence, *self-regulation* issues remain an important focus, but *self-determination* and *self-realization* capacities need to be addressed as well. *Self-generation* cues, if they emerge at all, tend to be addressed later in adulthood.

A child's demonstration of executive functions can vary greatly depending not only on the specific capacities required but also by domains of functioning and arenas of involvement. The domains of functioning highlight the distinctions among executive control of perception, emotion, thought, and action. The *intrapersonal arena* relates to the use of executive functions to regulate perception, emotion, thought, and action in relation to the inner workings of the person (perceptions of self, feelings about self, thoughts about self, actions toward self). The *interpersonal arena* reflects the use of executive functions to regulate perception, emotion, thought, and action in relation to other persons. The *environment arena* involves the use of executive functions to regulate perception, emotion, thought, and action in relation to objects and events in the surrounding environment. The *symbol system arena* reflects the use of executive functions to cue and direct perception, feeling, thought, and action involved with the systems used for communication, including reading, writing, and mathematics, especially as they apply to schoolwork.

Because of the multiple dimensions that can contribute to variability in the demonstration of executive functions, a multidimensional, multimethod approach is necessary to accurately characterize how a child is currently using, or not using, executive function capacities. The current assessment attempted to determine the effectiveness, or lack of effectiveness, of Richard's executive functions for the cueing and directing of perceiving, feeling, thinking, and acting in relation to self (intrapersonal), others (interpersonal), the world (environmental), and the cultural tools of communication (symbol system).

PSYCHOEDUCATIONAL EVALUATION REPORT

Name:	Richard Anderman
Date of Birth:	10/30/1997
Age:	13-1
School District:	Sunnyside
School:	Farling Middle
Grade:	7
Evaluation Dates:	11/27, 11/28, 12/04, 12/5, 12/11, 12/22/2009
Report Date:	1/30/2010
Evaluator:	George McCloskey, Ph.D.

REASON FOR REFERRAL/PURPOSE OF REPORT

Richard's parents requested an evaluation to assist in determining Richard's current profile of cognitive and behavioral strengths and weaknesses and to help clarify educational goals, as well as suggest the best instructional program for meeting educational goals.

BACKGROUND INFORMATION FROM PARENTS

The specific details of Richard's educational history are contained in various reports on file with the school district. Richard is currently enrolled in the seventh grade at Farling Middle School and receives his major academic coursework through the resource room program with speech therapy and occupational therapy on a weekly basis. His teachers indicate that he sometimes has difficulty working independently on assignments and can be somewhat impatient when he is required to wait for information about how to proceed on the assignments. Richard is being presented with content appropriate for seventh-grade students, but his low reading and writing skills sometimes make it difficult for him to fully engage in the learning of new material. Richard's teachers are making efforts to accommodate Richard's learning needs; he uses a computer for many assignments and has text-to-speech and speech-to-text options available for improving learning and classroom communication. Richard does not exhibit any behavior problems at school, but teachers have noted that Richard sometimes gets very frustrated with his limited academic success.

In an interview, Richard's parents related their desire to see Richard benefit as much as possible from his educational experiences. They see Richard in a realistic manner as a child with a number of strengths, such as good reasoning skills and good language comprehension and expression, but also as a child with some definite challenges that make it difficult for him to fully apply his cognitive capacities to demonstrate what he has learned. They are aware of Richard's speech impediment, which makes it difficult for others to consistently understand his speech, and the negative impact his speech problem can have on first impressions. Richard's parents expressed some concern with the kinds of homework assignments he brings home. They would like to see his homework focused more on the areas in which Richard requires the most remediation efforts, including basic reading and writing skill development. They are unsure whether Richard is receiving the kind of instruction they believe is necessary to help him improve his academic skills and prepare him for educational and/or work opportunities beyond high school. They see Richard as having good mechanical skills and would like to see him participate in a vocational training program that would provide him with opportunities to express his talents while working on strengthening his basic academic skills. Richard's parents did not express any concerns related to mental health issues, but like his teachers, they noted Richard's frustrations with his lack of academic success.

ASSESSMENT PROCEDURES

Richard was seen for an evaluation by Dr. George McCloskey, a consulting school psychologist, at the request of his parents and the Sunnyside School District. At the time of the evaluation, Richard was not taking any medication. He brought a pair of glasses with him to the sessions but did not wear them, stating that he does not wear them to read but only to see things at a distance.

Richard was administered the following measures over several days in a conference room at Farling Middle School:

Student interview
Delis Kaplan Executive Function System (D-KEFS) (selected subtest)
Children's Memory Scale (CMS) (selected subtest)
Woodcock-Johnson III NU Tests of Achievement (WJ III ACH) (selected subtests)

Woodcock-Johnson III NU Tests of Cognitive Ability (WJ III COG) (selected subtests)

Test of Word Reading Efficiency (TOWRE)

Wechsler Individual Achievement Test-Third Edition (WIAT-III) (selected subtests)

Wechsler Intelligence Scale for Children-Fourth Edition Integrated (WISC-IV Integrated)

Wisconsin Card Sorting Test—Revised and Expanded

Rey Complex Figure Test (RCFT)

Kaufman Adolescent and Adult Intelligence Test (KAIT) (selected subtests)

Process Assessment of the Learner-Second Edition (PAL-II) (selected subtests)

NEPSY-II: A Developmental Neuropsychological Assessment (selected subtests)

Richard also was administered the Clinical Evaluation of Language Functions (CELF-4) by the speech-language therapist on 11/30/2009. Results of the CELF-4 testing are incorporated into the interpretations of test performance provided in this report. In addition to the individual evaluation sessions, Richard's mother, father, speech therapist, and several teachers completed the Behavior Rating Inventory of Executive Function (BRIEF). Based on the assessments completed and the information gathered and interpreted, the following summary, conclusions, and recommendations are offered.

SUMMARY OF ASSESSMENT PERFORMANCE

Richard's Strengths

- Richard demonstrated a positive attitude, a warm and friendly demeanor, a good sense of humor, and effective social and interpersonal communication skills when interacting with the examiner.
- Richard typically performed in the Superior range when applying reasoning abilities with visually-presented nonverbal materials (e.g., blocks, picture designs).
- Richard typically performed in the Average range when applying reasoning abilities with orally-presented verbal information.
- Richard demonstrated adequately developed receptive language abilities that he used effectively to understand test directions and the content of verbal test items administered during the assessment. He engaged

in appropriate conversation with the examiner as long as the need to hold and manipulate a lot of information (i.e., working memory demands) was kept at a minimum.

- Richard demonstrated adequately developed expressive language abilities and expressive fluency when expressing his thoughts spontaneously in conversation and when responding to direct assessment questions.
- Richard demonstrated an Average to Above Average store of word meanings and verbal information related to topics typically learned in school.
- Richard demonstrated effective visual perception and discrimination abilities when dealing with basic nonverbal visual material such as pictures and geometric shapes, but these skills were not always applied effectively.
- Richard demonstrated effective use of fine-motor skills when handling materials if speed of performance was not a factor.
- Richard demonstrated the capacity for immediate attention to tasks and for sustained effort, at least for relatively short periods of time in the one-to-one context of the assessment situation.
- Richard demonstrated the capacity to use executive functions to cue the generation and application of reasoning strategies.
- Richard was much more effective with timed tasks when they emphasized reasoning with nonverbal information and did not emphasize attention to numerous small details. Overall, Richard appeared to perform much more effectively when tasks did not involve making fine discriminations between visual stimuli, such as reading words or attending to calculation operation signs and notation.
- The ratings provided by Richard's parents and teachers, the information offered by Richard's parents in an interview, and the observational and test data collected during the assessment sessions indicate that Richard usually has been effective in using executive functions to cue the use of perception, emotion, cognition, and action to deal effectively with other persons and the environment around him, maintain personal safety and hygiene routines, and, in many instances, learn and process information and solve problems in school and at home. None of the rating results indicated the presence of behavior problems or emotional disturbance either in the school setting or at home.

Richard's Challenges and Degree of Need

- Richard struggled with all tasks that required the use of working memory, that is, tasks that required him to hold and manipulate information in mind. These difficulties were especially evident when Richard was working with orally-presented information or written language. When tasks involved working memory demands, Richard was much less capable of demonstrating his good reasoning abilities.

- Richard demonstrated considerable difficulty in the ability to quickly attend to and register visual letter sequences and words in immediate memory and then hold them in working memory long enough to accurately reproduce them in writing. This difficulty has had a great impact on Richard's ability to initially register the spellings of words, as well as on his ability to store accurate representations of the correct spellings of words and reproduce them.

- Although the content of Richard's expressive language production was adequately developed, his unusual articulation pattern and frequently slurred speech often made it difficult to understand him. Listening to and comprehending what Richard was saying required a great deal of concentrated effort.

- Richard struggled greatly with tasks involving on-demand verbal fluency, that is, tasks that required him to exert executive function control over information retrieval processes (i.e., to cue and direct retrieval in specific ways) and quickly produce verbal responses that met a specific set of requirements (e.g., saying as many words as possible that begin with a specific letter). These results suggest that Richard is likely to have difficulties demonstrating what he knows when assessments use response formats that require verbal retrieval of highly specific responses.

- Although Richard demonstrated well-developed basic visual processing, when visual tasks required close attention to details, Richard tended to perform much less consistently, thereby reducing his overall level of success.

- Richard tended to work very slowly on most tasks; when responses were required within strict time limits or when bonus points were given for quick responses, Richard's performance dropped into the Low Average to Extremely Low ranges.

- Richard also struggled with all of the tasks that required him to rapidly link language processes with visual images, especially with orthography (i.e., printed letters and words). Consistent with his oral-motor production difficulties, Richard's oral reading and silent reading rates were extremely slow.

- Richard's reading comprehension skills are severely constrained by his extremely poor word recognition and word attack skills. Richard has trouble comprehending what he reads because he cannot recognize many of the words in grade-level texts. Additionally, although Richard is capable of comprehending what he reads, he has difficulty sustaining attention and holding information in his mind while reading, thereby reducing his ability to effectively process the information without rereading the material.

- Richard's lack of skill at recognizing words by sight, lack of consistent attention to the visual features of letters and words, lack of awareness that he did not recognize a word, and inability to apply decoding skills to sound out less familiar words all combined to produce very poor performance on all tasks requiring word reading.

- Although Richard demonstrated an adequate pencil grip and fine-motor control, his graphomotor (handwriting) production was typically very slow for all writing tasks and his letters were often poorly formed although still legible.

- Richard struggled noticeably in his efforts to spell words correctly, producing correct spellings for only a very limited number of high-frequency sight words. Richard's efforts to spell words he was not familiar with reflected significant deviations from what would be expected if he were effectively discriminating the sounds in the words; many of his spellings reflected significant disconnects between sound-to-letter translations or a limited understanding of sound-letter relationships.

- Richard struggled greatly in his efforts to produce grammatically correct phrases and sentences, earning scores in the Extremely Low range for all writing tasks.

- Richard had difficulty performing basic calculations mentally, without the aid of pencil and paper, and typically counted on his fingers to aid in addition and subtraction. The math calculations he attempted involved basic addition and subtraction, usually without regrouping. The multiplication and division items he attempted were simple facts. Richard did not demonstrate knowledge of multiplication or division calculation procedures or how to work with fractions or decimals.

- When attempting to solve math application problems, Richard made good use of his paper and pencil for many problems. This strategy enabled him to demonstrate his reasoning abilities much more than on any other academic task he attempted. He was successful with a number of problems involving time and money as well as subtraction and addition of quantities. Although Richard was effectively engaged in problem solving, his limited knowledge of calculation procedures beyond basic addition and subtraction greatly limited his overall success with this task. Richard earned his best academic score on math problem solving, although it was still within the Below Average range.

- Richard's strengths in executive functions are countered by a small but significant number of executive function difficulties primarily affecting his use of oral and written language abilities. These difficulties primarily affect Richard's processing of information and production of class work and homework. The specific self-regulation executive function difficulties that Richard demonstrated during the assessment and/or that were reported by Richard's parents and teachers involve:
  - Difficulty attending to visual details when initially processing information (especially words in print)
  - Difficulty directing quick, efficient retrieval of highly specific language
  - Difficulty gauging the amount of time and effort that academic tasks will require
  - Difficulty directing the pace of thought and action when thinking about or doing academic tasks
  - Difficulty judging the passage of time when thinking about or doing academic tasks
  - Difficulty monitoring thought and action when doing academic tasks

CONCLUSION

Richard's interactions with the examiner reflected a sincere, friendly, kind-hearted adolescent who is doing his best to stay engaged with school despite the significant challenges this poses. Although during formal individualized assessment Richard demonstrated well-developed cognitive capacities in many areas, including reasoning, language, visual processing, memory, and executive functions, he also displayed a number of cognitive difficulties that make it hard for him to profit from instruction.

Foremost of these problems is Richard's neurologically based speech impediment. Richard's normal speech production resembles the speech of a deaf person who has learned to talk without the ability to hear his own sound production and use it to monitor and correct articulation errors. Although Richard demonstrated superior reasoning abilities with many tasks involving visually presented nonverbal material and at least average reasoning abilities with orally presented verbal information, his significant speech articulation problems make it difficult to understand what he is saying. The unfortunate consequence of his limited intelligibility is that it gives the impression that Richard is not as mentally capable as he is.

Richard is aware of his speech difficulties and can exert some conscious control over his articulation when prompted to do so. It is important to realize, however, that people typically do not have to consciously engage executive functions to control speech production, but do so automatically. Any conscious executive control that Richard exerts over his speech production requires the use of additional mental resources and reduces his overall effectiveness with thought processing. Also, since this conscious monitoring is not a natural aspect of language processing, it is only natural for Richard to forget to do so and lapse into his poorly articulated speech production pattern.

Richard's working memory problems have a great impact on his receptive and expressive language usage. These working memory difficulties make it hard for him to understand oral directions beyond short sentences that are not overly complex in grammatical structure. They also make it difficult for Richard to think about this information or to work on problems without the aid of pencil and paper or visual images that he can frequently review to refresh the content he is attempting to hold in mind. Consequently, although Richard is monolingual, his profile of language strengths and weaknesses is best characterized by the language categories often used to distinguish two different sets of language competencies for bilingual children. Richard's difficulty with processing complex grammatical structures and abstract concepts that rely on good working memory capacities has produced a situation in which Richard's basic interpersonal communication skills (BICS) are much better developed than his cognitive academic language proficiency skills (CALPS). As a result, Richard is much more capable of participating in everyday conversations than he is in understanding and commenting on an academic lecture or in following detailed directions during classroom activities. It is important to note, however, that with frequent repetition of more complex directions, Richard was able to greatly improve his comprehension of grammatically complex or detailed instructions.

Complicating matters further for Richard is the fact that his processing speed tends to be very slow. Although he could perform some selected tasks quickly, generally his slow processing and production seem to extend to both oral information and visual material.

Richard's language, working memory, and processing speed problems are greatly impacting his attempts to learn academic material and produce school-related work. Although he has been receiving special education services since early elementary school, his rate of acquisition of reading, writing, and math skills has been very slow. Richard is at least average in his ability to reason with verbal information and comprehend spoken language. His knowledge of word meanings and fund of general information are average. Even with these good linguistic abilities, he had difficulty with all aspects of reading (i.e., sight recognition, decoding, oral and silent fluency, and comprehension). Writing was equally poor as Richard struggled with the spelling of most words beyond a few highly familiar words, as well as producing short, grammatically correct sentences. In math, Richard was capable of setting up math problems, but his limited knowledge of calculation procedures greatly reduced his effectiveness in solving them. He completed all academic tasks at a very slow pace.

Although Richard demonstrated effective use of many executive function capacities, his weakness in working memory and processing speed and his lack of academic skills make it very difficult for him to derive maximum benefit from the use of these executive functions. When there is little to direct, being able to do so is not a particularly noticeable strength. Contributing to his problems in learning and work production are a few important executive function difficulties. These include: inconsistent direction of attention to visual details, inconsistent direction of monitoring of work for errors, poor control of on-demand language retrieval, and poor ability to gauge and monitor time.

Readers of this report who are familiar with intelligence tests such as the WISC-IV must keep in mind that Richard's Full-Scale IQ of 88 is not an accurate estimate of his intellectual capabilities. The reasons are discussed extensively in the detailed addendum to this summary report.

Richard's unusual profile of cognitive strengths and weaknesses and his extreme academic deficiencies present a real challenge to educators charged with the task of preparing Richard for the future. The current testing indicates that despite his academic skill weaknesses, Richard has managed to store, and can effectively retrieve, general in-

formation and word associations and meanings. In other words, Richard is quite capable of learning many things despite his limited skill in reading, writing, and math. His academic deficiencies will continue to require focused direct instruction, but the methods used to deliver this instruction will need to be carefully selected with his working memory and processing speed difficulties in mind.

A concerted effort should be made to help Richard develop more automatic control of speech articulation so that his expressive language is more easily understood. An occupational or physical therapist should provide frequent instruction that addresses his oral-motor and graphomotor difficulties. Even if Richard's academic skill deficiencies are addressed, he will still require a great deal of support in the process of learning new material. Even though Richard cannot read grade-level texts, it does not mean that he is incapable of understanding and learning the concepts presented. The challenge will be in finding ways to help Richard get exposure to the information in the textbooks in a medium that enables him to use his strengths in reasoning while bypassing his weaknesses. While books on tape/CD are often a good backup strategy for poor readers requiring exposure to content, Richard's working memory difficulties are likely to make this resource less useful for him. In Richard's case, audiovisual media (e.g., videotapes) will more likely help him to learn new material. Given Richard's strengths with visual processing and weakness in working memory for oral information, instructional efforts will need to rely heavily on visual materials to support and enhance oral presentation of information.

Given Richard's unusual profile of cognitive strengths and weaknesses, extreme academic deficiencies, and speech impediment, it is not surprising that he finds school to be difficult and frustrating. For most children, the transition to adolescence is a time of increased self-consciousness as well as increased comparison of self to peers and intense comparison of self by peers. Richard is aware of his speech difficulties and academic deficiencies and of the impression that these make on his peers. When he finds himself in situations where his weaknesses are most apparent to others, his attempts to save face unfortunately appear to have the opposite effect on those around him.

When dealing with Richard in the educational environment, keep in mind that his cognitive and academic difficulties stem from real neurological deficits and are not simply a matter of choice or due to a lack of engagement. Although Richard needs to be held responsible for his actions, he should not be subjected to unduly negative consequences when his efforts do not meet desired standards. Accommodations will be necessary to enable Richard to effectively demonstrate what he has learned and to complete the tasks required of him at school. On days when Richard seems less than enthusiastic about taking on academic challenges, keep in mind the extent of his impairments. Creative efforts may be required to find ways to get him engaged and help him benefit from instruction.

To his credit, Richard seems to be aware of the fact that his cognitive challenges and academic deficiencies are not the full measure of who he is or what he can accomplish in life. When Richard is comfortable and does not feel vulnerable, he can be surprisingly adept at demonstrating his strengths and takes great pride in what he can accomplish. In his efforts during the assessment, Richard demonstrated a strength of will and spirit that will serve him well as he strives to find his place in society. A well-planned and well-executed educational program will be necessary in order to prepare him as effectively as possible for future career options. Although Richard may not develop reading, writing, or math skills commensurate with his grade-level placements, he is certainly capable of learning many skills and developing knowledge that will provide him with an opportunity to engage in meaningful full-time employment and possibly even education and training beyond high school.

Richard is a well-meaning, cognitively capable adolescent in many ways. Despite the difficulties he is experiencing with working memory, processing speed, and speech articulation, the likelihood is great that he will deal with these challenges in ways that enable him to express his talents, contribute to society, and lead a happy and meaningful life. This potential will be enhanced if he receives guidance and modeling of adaptive strategies from understanding parents and teachers and if appropriate accommodations are provided in the school setting.

RECOMMENDATIONS

Specific recommendations for addressing Richard's educational needs were discussed and recorded during a meeting on 1/20/2010 with the school-based multidisciplinary team, which included Richard and his parents and advocate. Helping Richard to reach his academic potential will require a collaborative effort involving Richard, his parents, and his teachers. Specific recommendations were as follows:

What Richard Can Do for Himself to Improve Mental Functions and Achieve Greater Academic Success

1. Maintain the desire to do well in school.
2. Continue to work with school staff in their efforts to help him improve his academic skills.
3. Continue to do assigned homework.
4. Continue to seek out sources of information about topics of great interest.
5. Maintain good sleep habits and a good sleep schedule.
6. Eat healthy foods.

What Richard's Parents Can Do to Help Him Improve Mental Functions and Achieve Academic Success

1. Continue to support Richard in his efforts to remain engaged with learning new material, completing assignments, and studying for tests.
2. Remind Richard of the importance of good sleep habits and a good diet for maximizing cognitive efficiency and mental clarity.
3. Continue to communicate with school staff to stay aware of what Richard is working on in his classes.
4. Continue to work with school staff to ensure that effective strategies for assisting Richard are developed and implemented in the school environment and that appropriate accommodations are provided.
5. Share this report with Richard's physician and ask if the physician can recommend someone to conduct an evaluation for Attention-Deficit/Hyperactivity Disorder.

What Teaching Staff Can Do to Help Richard Improve Mental Functions and Achieve Academic Success

Richard's unique combination of cognitive strengths and weaknesses will require a well-designed instructional program that includes the following elements:

1. Although work on Richard's speech difficulties should continue, there is some question as to the extent of progress that can be realized with such efforts. Given the unusual nature of Richard's language difficulties, consultation with a speech-language pathologist,

occupational therapist, or physical therapist who is highly knowledgeable in the area of developmental speech apraxia is recommended. With the proper type of software program that incorporates the use of visual elements and visual feedback (something akin to the Speechviewer III program that has been discontinued), meaningful gains in speech intelligibility should be possible. There is a real possibility, however, that Richard's articulation difficulties are not very amenable to change at this stage of brain development. Consequently, the effectiveness of interventions should be closely monitored. Interventions should incorporate visual materials to take advantage of Richard's visual processing strengths and interest in visual materials.

2. Instruction in reading should be balanced and include decoding skills development, fluency exercises, vocabulary building, and comprehension work. However, Richard's severe weakness in word attack and word recognition skills will need to be addressed with supplemental instructional activities and supplemental daily practice. As with instruction in the area of speech, reading instruction will need to incorporate visual elements as much as possible to help Richard learn as effectively as possible. Decoding skills should be taught through the use of visual supports such as Elkonin tiles, so that Richard can see the connection between phonology and orthography. Programs such as the Sonday System have such visually-based exercises built into the teaching lessons. A program such as Lexia could be used daily to provide Richard with the supplemental practice needed in applying the decoding rules he is learning through instructional lessons.

3. Richard's basic math skills are relatively poor; his application of quantitative thinking to solve problems is much better than his command of calculation procedures and operations. A software program that enables practice of calculation routines in support of problem solving might be an effective means of helping Richard improve his calculation skills.

4. Given Richard's expressive language difficulties and limited reading skills, technological options for assisting Richard in his efforts to learn information in the content areas and assist in efforts to improve his reading, writing, and mathematics should be explored. This likely will require consultation with an augmentative communication specialist.

5. Consistent with an assessment to provide Richard with technological assistance in learning, Richard would benefit greatly from the use of a laptop computer that could be used both in school and home. Use of a single technological platform for learning would enable Richard to achieve a greater level of independence with academic task completion as he becomes more familiar with software programs that are currently being used in school. Use of a laptop would allow for greater opportunities to practice skills likely to benefit Richard in school and work settings beyond high school and offer greater opportunities for transfer of skills across multiple settings.

6. Although Richard's reading and writing skills are very limited, his capacities for learning and higher-level thinking are much better developed. Richard's instructional program should continue to emphasize grade-level information in media that he can most effectively process. Due to Richard's weakness in working memory for auditory information, it is essential that teachers provide visual material to depict and support the concepts and skills they are introducing. The visual associations will allow him to refresh and maintain his thoughts, thereby increasing the likelihood that he will transfer the new learning to long-term storage and be able to retrieve it later.

7. As Richard gets older, career exploration activities will become increasingly important. Knowing the kinds of work that Richard is most interested in will help to orient his academic work in directions most likely to help him achieve his career goals. Currently, Richard is interested in engineering. By encouraging career exploration activities and incorporating associated activities into the instructional program, Richard's teachers can take advantage of his career interests to increase his engagement in learning basic academic skills.

8. Both Richard's parents and his teachers have noted his strong motivation to succeed in school despite the difficulties he is experiencing with the development of basic academic skills. They should praise and support his motivation and efforts to increase his basic skill levels.

APPENDIX TO REPORT: DETAILED DESCRIPTION AND INTERPRETATION OF ASSESSMENT RESULTS

General Observations Derived from Interview and Evaluation Session Behaviors

Richard worked with the psychologist on six separate occasions at Farling Middle School during the month of December 2009. His general demeanor varied greatly across these six sessions. On some days, Richard was in a good mood and readily engaged in conversation before starting assessment tasks; his energy level was good and he was especially attentive to tasks. Although a speech impediment was apparent, when Richard was in a good mood, he would readily engage in prolonged conversation and speak in a friendly, animated manner. On other days, Richard would report to the conference room and slump into a chair, avoiding eye contact and giving the impression that he would rather be somewhere else. On these days, he frequently yawned and was somewhat less forthcoming with verbal responses to conversation or questions. Regardless of his outward manner, Richard always complied with requests and appeared to be putting forth his best effort once he was engaged in a task. It was apparent, however, that Richard greatly enjoyed the challenge of tasks involving nonverbal, visual materials while only tolerating tasks involving oral directions, questions, and longer oral responses. On occasion, Richard expressed some frustration regarding his difficulty in clearly stating his ideas. Generally, he was more effective and at ease when working with a pencil and paper than when working on purely auditory tasks.

During all six sessions, Richard's oral speech was affected by difficulties with the pronunciation of various phonemes. In fact, as also noted in a prior speech evaluation, Richard's articulation pattern resembles that of a person with a severe hearing impairment who does not receive accurate auditory feedback regarding his own speech production. This speech pattern is quite puzzling as no physical cause has been identified and audiology reports indicate normal acuity.

In an interview after the assessment sessions, Richard appeared much more relaxed and was willing to share more personal information. Richard talked about the time he spends at his father's karate school on many weekday evenings. He likes to help out when he can and said that he is currently working on an advanced black belt level. Richard is interested in sports and plays soccer in a community league during the fall season each year. Although he said that he plays some video games, he is not that interested in game systems or computer gaming.

Richard stated that he likes school and, ideally, would like to continue his education beyond high school. He expressed a great interest in mechanical things and would like to pursue a career in engineering. Richard is aware of and quite frustrated with the difficulties he has with acquiring reading and writing skills; it is apparent that he would like to be a much better reader.

SUMMARY OF ASSESSMENTS OF COGNITIVE AND LINGUISTIC CAPACITIES

Score Ranges and Verbal Labels

Richard's performance on many of the tests administered are described as standard scores (SS), scaled scores (ScS), percentile ranks (PR), and/or verbal labels representing the range of the standard score or scaled score confidence interval. Standard scores have a mean of 100 and a standard deviation of 15. Scaled scores have a mean of 10 and a standard deviation of 3. The ranges and verbal labels are:

	SS	ScS
Extremely Low	<70	1–4
Low	70–79	5–6
Below Average	80–89	7
Average	90–110	8–12
Above Average	111–120	13
Superior	121–130	14–16
Very Superior	>130	17–19

Reasoning Abilities

Richard's performance with tasks that assessed reasoning abilities varied from Below Average to Superior, depending on the task demands. A clear pattern of strengths and weaknesses was evident from Richard's performance with all tasks that involved reasoning. As shown in the following table, Richard's reasoning abilities were more effective when working with nonverbal, visual materials than with oral information.

Reasoning with Nonverbal, Visual Material

Richard was exceptionally effective with the KAIT Logical Steps subtest, a complex task that requires the use of logic chains to solve problems depicted by visual diagrams. For example, given rules in diagram form about the location of "persons" on a staircase (Richard is always one step above Ann; Richard is always two steps above Bob), a question is posed: If Ann is on step 3, where is Bob? Each successive item in the series adds additional persons and rules for

Reasoning with Nonverbal, Visual Material				Reasoning with Orally Presented Verbal Information			
Subtest	SS	ScS	PR	Subtest	SS	ScS	PR
WCST % Conceptual Level Responses	127		96				
KAIT Logical Steps		15	95				
WJ III COG Concept Formation	122		93				
WISC-IV Picture Concepts		14	91				
				WJ III COG Verbal Comprehension	114		83
NEPSY-II Block Construction		12	75	KAIT Auditory Comprehension		12	75
WISC-IV Integrated Block Design No Time Bonus		11	63				
WISC-IV Matrix Reasoning		10	50	WISC-IV Similarities		10	50
				WISC-IV Comprehension		10	50
				CELF-4 Word Classes		10	50
WISC-IV Block Design (with Time Bonus)		9	37				
				WISC-IV Word Reasoning		6	9
Note: Tests in italics were administered by the speech therapist in a recent evaluation.							

their positions on the steps, and each item has to be solved within 30 seconds.

Although the instructions for this task are verbal, the associated visual diagrams appeared to clarify the nature of the task for Richard. As the items became more complex, Richard drew diagrams to support his reasoning. His use of this strategy enabled him to solve many of the most complex problems in relatively short periods of time. Richard's quick performance with this task was in great contrast to his difficulty with speed of performance in many less complex tasks.

In similar fashion, Richard effectively reasoned through the Wisconsin Card Sorting Test, a problem-solving task that requires a person to figure out the rule by which a set of cards (depicting visual patterns) is grouped and then complete the pattern. As the rules change, the person must recognize the change as well as the new pattern (Percent Conceptual Level Responses SS 127, 96th percentile).

Similar to his performance with the KAIT Logical Steps Subtest and the WCST, Richard performed in the Superior range with other tasks that emphasized reasoning with visual material, did not have strict time limits, and did not require him to use his hands to manipulate materials. Although these tasks involve visual stimuli, Richard was able to apply language concepts in completing some of them (e.g., WJ III COG Concept Formation, WISC-IV Picture Concepts).

An exception to this pattern of superior performance was the Average range score Richard earned on the WISC-IV Matrix Reasoning subtest. His lack of attention to relevant visual details caused him to respond incorrectly to two relatively easy items and greatly hampered his effectiveness with a number of the most complex items. Given the superior reasoning that he displayed with other untimed, motor-free tasks involving visual materials, it is highly likely that Richard's lack of attention to the most relevant visual details was the source of his relatively poor performance, rather than a lack of reasoning capacity.

When time limits were absent or minimized and Richard was required to manipulate tangible materials to solve problems, he earned scores in the higher end of the Average range (NEPSY-II Block Construction, WISC-IV Block Design no time bonus). When this type of task required speeded performance to earn points, Richard's performance dropped into the lower end of the Average range (WISC-IV Block Design with time bonus items). In all of his efforts with nonverbal visual materials, Richard's performance reflected a thoughtful, organized, strategic approach to task completion, with the only inefficiencies noted being his lack of attention to details on Matrix Reasoning, a behavior also apparent with other visual tasks that did not require much reasoning ability (discussed under Visual Processing).

Reasoning with Orally Presented Verbal Information

On reasoning tasks that presented information orally and that required oral responses, Richard performed in the average range with all but one of these tasks. His best performance was on the WJ III COG Verbal Comprehension test, although this test requires verbal reasoning (analogies) on only one of four subtests. The other subtests assessed Richard's capacity for retrieving word associations from long-term storage (antonyms, synonyms, and words corresponding to pictures).

Richard performed at the high end of the Average range on the KAIT Auditory Comprehension subtest, a task that required him to listen to short news stories and answer questions. The brief, highly contextual nature of these stories appeared to help Richard hold information in mind long enough to effectively apply his reasoning skills and produce many correct responses. Most tasks requiring verbal responses were performed at an Average level (WISC-IV Comprehension, Similarities, CELF-4 Word Classes).

In contrast to his average performance on most verbal tasks, Richard struggled with the WISC-IV Word Reasoning subtest (9th percentile), a task that required him to listen to a series of clues about the meaning of a word and then provide the word. He appeared to have difficulty holding the clues in mind while searching for a word that would fit all of them (items began with one clue, and then moved to two clues, and then three clues as they became more difficult). The working memory demands of this task appear to have greatly reduced Richard's ability to use reasoning to deduce the correct responses.

Language Abilities

The overall impression gleaned from conversation and interaction with Richard is that his interpersonal communication skills are adequately developed, but his unusual articulation pattern and frequently slurred speech make it difficult to understand him at times. Listening to and comprehending what Richard was saying required a great deal of concentrated effort. Nonetheless, it was apparent that Richard's comprehension of conversational language was effective, as were his responses to questions.

Formal assessment of receptive and expressive language and expressive production involving speed and fluency under timed conditions, however, resulted in a wide scatter of scores ranging from Superior to Extremely Low. The language processing weaknesses that Richard displayed are likely to significantly impact his classroom learning and demonstration of learning when the activities emphasize oral information and rapid oral responses.

Richard's performance with tasks primarily assessing receptive and/or expressive language or verbal fluency is summarized in the chart following. Note that some tasks assess both receptive and expressive language in that it is not possible to produce a coherent response if the stimuli are not comprehended adequately initially.

Receptive Language Tasks			Expressive Language Tasks		
Subtest	ScS	PR	Subtest	ScS	PR
			NEPSY-II Word Generation-Semantic	15	95
			CELF-4 Word Definitions	*13*	*84*
KAIT Auditory Comprehension	12	75	KAIT Auditory Comprehension	12	75
WISC-IV Comprehension	10	50	WISC-IV Comprehension	10	50
			WISC-IV Similarities	10	50
			WISC-IV Vocabulary	9	37
			CELF-4 Understanding Paragraphs	*9*	*37*
			CELF-4 Formulated Sentences	*7*	*16*
NEPSY-II Comprehension of Instructions	6	9	NEPSY-II Word Generation-Initial Letter	6	9
			NEPSY-II Inhibition – Inhibition Task	6	9
			CMS Sequences	5	5
			D-KEFS Color-Word Interference (CWI) Switching	5	5
			NEPSY-II Inhibition-Naming Task	4	2
CELF-4 Semantic Relationships	3	1	D-KEFS Color-Word Interference (CWI) – Inhibition Task	3	1
			NEPSY-II Inhibition – Switching Task	3	1
			CELF-4 Sentence Assembly	*2*	*1*
			D-KEFS CWI – Color Naming Task	1	<1
			D-KEFS CWI – Word Reading Task	1	<1

Note: Tests in *italics* were administered by the speech therapist in a recent evaluation.

Receptive Language Skills

Richard experienced no difficulties with comprehending instructions for tasks or following the examiner in conversation. The overall impression of Richard's comprehension of language in personal interactions was that of an adolescent with adequate capacities in this area, but when Richard was required to listen to oral information and demonstrate his comprehension, his scores varied from the upper end of Average to the Extremely Low range.

Richard's receptive language abilities were most evident on the KAIT Auditory Comprehension subtest. As mentioned in the section on Reasoning, Richard had no trouble comprehending the short news stories and frequently responded with well-reasoned answers reflecting his understanding of the content. Similarly, he understood the questions of the WISC-IV Comprehension subtest to an extent that enabled him to earn an Average score. Although Richard earned a slightly lower score on the CELF-4 Understanding Paragraphs subtest (administered in the speech evaluation), this might have been the result of the type of questions he was asked, the working memory demands of the longer passages, or the different norm groups, rather than difficulty with comprehension of the questions.

Richard performed poorly on the CELF-4 Semantic Relationships subtest (speech evaluation). This task required Richard to listen to sentences increasing in grammatical complexity and then select two sentences with the same meaning as the first from a list of options. To effectively perform this task, Richard had to process and hold verbal information in mind while considering the choices that were both read and shown to him in print. As was the case with Word Reasoning, Richard's poor performance was likely due to the working memory demands of this task and his inability to read the print to support his memory.

Expressive Language Skills

In conversation and responses to test questions from tasks such as the WISC-IV Similarities, Vocabulary, and Comprehension and KAIT Auditory Comprehension subtests, Richard demonstrated an effective command of grammar, syntax, and morphology and age-appropriate use of pragmatic language skills despite the fact that his speech was often hard to understand. When responding to test questions such as those that asked for explanations of rules and social conventions, similarities between words, and word meanings, Richard's responses earned him scores in the Average to Above Average ranges. In contrast, for tasks that restricted his sentence construction by specifying the words he had to use (e.g., "Make a sentence using the words …") (CELF-4 Formulated Sentences and Sentence Assembly), Richard's performance was considerably weaker, earning scores in the Below Average to Extremely Low range.

Basic Language Processes, Fluency, and Speed

On basic measures of expressive fluency and speed, Richard's performance typically was far below his demonstrated levels of conversational language production. One exception was his superior performance on the NEPSY-II Semantic Fluency task that required him to name as many things as he could within a given category in 60 seconds (e.g., articles of clothing, names of people). He also experienced no difficulties with the items of the CMS Sequences subtest that required him to retrieve words from highly automated sequences such as the numbers from 1 to 10, the alphabet, the days of the week, and the months of the year, sometimes even earning bonus points for speed of production.

On tasks requiring greater executive control of language production, Richard performed much less effectively. He had great difficulty with the NEPSY-II Initial Letter Naming task when given 60 seconds to provide as many words as possible that began with a specific letter. He had similar difficulty with tasks that assessed his speed of basic verbal production and his executive control of this production, earning scores in the Low to Extremely Low range on the various tasks of the NEPSY-II Inhibition Subtest and the D-KEFS Color-Word Interference Subtest. Richard was very slow when required to name colors, label objects, or read words as quickly as possible. Paradoxically, he performed somewhat better when the demand for executive function control over these rapid naming skills was required (e.g., Richard's scores on CWI-Inhibition and CWI- Inhibition/Switching, ScS 3 and 5, respectively, were relatively higher than his scores on CWI Color Naming and Word Reading, both ScS 1).

Although Richard had difficulty with all of these tasks, the fact that his performance increased substantially when executive control was required strongly suggests that deficiencies in basic oral-motor capacities or word retrieval are responsible for his problems with oral-motor production rather than his executive function capacities. Consequently, his executive function controls may be used to consciously direct these oral-motor capacities.

Memory for Orally Presented Verbal Information

Richard's performance on tasks requiring the use of memory processes varied greatly, depending on the task requirements and the type of memory processes that were demanded. For some of these tasks, Richard performed in the Superior range; on others he performed in the Below Average to Low ranges.

Immediate Encoding (Initial Taking-in of Information) and Working Memory

Beyond everyday conversation and listening to relatively short narrative passages, Richard experienced great difficulty initially registering, holding, and manipulating both meaningful (contextual) and non-meaningful (decontextual) oral information. Throughout these tasks, Richard found it difficult to register and hold onto long, complex sentences and sequences of unrelated bits of information such as a randomly ordered series of numbers. The chart following summarizes Richard's performance on tasks requiring initial registration and manipulation of material presented orally.

Contextually Meaningful Information			Decontextual, Nonmeaningful Information		
Subtest	ScS	PR	Subtest	ScS	PR
KAIT Auditory Comprehension	12	75			
CELF-4 Understanding Paragraphs	*9*	*37*			
NEPSY-II Narrative Memory Free Recall	8	25			
NEPSY-II Narrative Memory - Free and Cued Recall	8	25	WISC-IV Letter-Number Sequencing	8	25
			WISC-IV Digit Span Backward	7	16
			CELF-4 Formulated Sentences	*7*	*16*
NEPSY-II Comprehension of Instructions	6	9	NEPSY-II Phonological Processing	6	9
			CELF-4 Number Recall Backward	*6*	*9*
			WISC-IV Arithmetic	6	9
			CELF-4 Number Recall Forward	*5*	*5*
			CMS Sequences	5	5
CELF-4 Semantic Relationships	*3*	*1*	WISC-IV Digit Span forward	3	1
CELF-4 Recalling Sentences	*1*	*1*			

Note: Tests in *italics* were administered by the speech therapist in a recent evaluation.

Richard scored in the Low range when required to repeat random series of numbers exactly as he heard them as well as in reverse order. He also experienced difficulty when required to listen to a series of numbers and letters presented in random order, mentally rearrange them, and respond with the new organization. Nevertheless, his consistent success on items totaling three elements enabled him to score in the low end of the Average range.

Although Richard was able to quickly produce automated sequences such as the days of the week and months of the year, he was unable to adequately perform tasks that required him to hold and mentally manipulate information, especially when numbers were involved. Richard made errors when counting backward, when skip-counting, and when required to intersperse and recite letters and numbers. The cumulative effect of these difficulties resulted in a CMS Sequences score in the Low range (5th percentile).

As noted previously, Richard performed effectively when required to listen to short news stories and answer comprehension questions but was much less effective when working memory resources were strained by larger amounts of information presented at one time (e.g., CELF-4 Understanding Paragraphs, NEPSY-II Narrative Memory). Additional problems with working memory were evident in Richard's struggle with the items of the NEPSY-II Comprehension of Instructions subtest, and his Extremely Low scores on the CELF-4 Semantic Relationships and Recalling Sentences subtests. During the NEPSY-II Comprehension of Instructions subtest, Richard frequently asked to have the items repeated although he had been told that items could not be repeated. When directions were repeated, Richard was successful on many of the items. Although these items were scored as incorrect due to the scoring rules, it is important to recognize that when working on a task that strained his working memory resources, Richard's performance improved considerably with repetition.

Retrieval of Verbal Information from Long-Term Storage

In contrast to his struggles with tasks involving immediate registration of unrelated bits of information and tasks involving working memory, Richard performed in the Average to Above Average range on tasks requiring retrieval of information from long-term storage. These tasks included retrieving and expressing word meanings (CELF-4 Word Definitions, WISC-IV Vocabulary), antonyms and synonyms (WJ III COG Verbal Comprehension), and facts about history, geography, science, and other school-related subjects (WISC-IV Information).

Visual Processing

Richard's performance with tasks requiring visual processing varied greatly, depending on the task demands. He performed well with many tasks involving basic and complex visual processing that required minimal motor responses (e.g., pointing to a correct response, crossing out or checking response options), earning many scores in the Above Average to Superior range and a few in the Average range; however, when basic visual tasks required close attention to detail (NEPSY-II Arrows, PAL-II Receptive Coding), Richard performed much less consistently, missing easy items while getting harder items correct. On these tasks, his scores varied from the low end of the Average to the Low range. Additionally, Richard performed much less effectively when tasks involved time limits or awarded bonus points for quick responses (WISC-IV Block Design Multiple Choice, Symbol Search, and Coding).

Basic Visual Processing with Limited Motor Responses			
Subtest	SS	ScS	PR
WISC-IV Cancellation		15	95
Block Design Multiple Choice No Time Bonus		11	63
WJ III COG Spatial Relations	100		50
Block Design Multiple Choice (with time bonus)		8	25
WISC-IV Symbol Search (timed task)		7	16
NEPSY-II Arrows		7	16
PAL-II Receptive Coding		6	9
Complex Visual Processing with Limited Motor Responses			
KAIT Logical Steps		15	95
WJ III COG Concept Formation	122		93
WISC-IV Picture Concepts		14	91
WISC-IV Picture Completion		12	75
WISC-IV Matrix Reasoning		10	50
Visual Processing with Substantial Motor Activity			
NEPSY-II Block Construction		12	75
WISC-IV Block Design no Time Bonus		11	63
Rey Complex Figure Test – Copy Trial		53 (T Score)	63
Block Design (with time bonus)		9	37
PAL-II Alphabet Writing (timed task)		7	16
PAL-II Expressive Coding		5	5
WISC-IV Coding (timed task)		3	2

Richard also earned scores in the Average to High Average range when task responses involved a substantial amount of motor activity (e.g., continuous use of pencil and paper without involving handwriting, manipulating blocks to construct designs) and had either minimal or no time limits. As with the tasks described above, Richard's performance was significantly weaker, in the Low Average to Extremely Low range, on tasks requiring rapid responses and/or required printing of letters and words (WISC-IV Coding and PAL-II Copy A and Copy B).

Retrieval of Abstract Nonverbal Visual Material

Although Richard was able to effectively copy the Rey Complex Figure, he was less effective in his efforts to reconstruct the figure from memory three minutes later, earning a RCFT Immediate Recall score in the Low range.

Orthographic Processing (Visual Processing of Letters and Words)

Spelling ability is greatly enhanced when orthographic units (letters and letter clusters) are encoded effectively in memory. As spelling skill development progresses, orthographic units must be represented and stored and available for quick and efficient retrieval.

The PAL-II Receptive Coding task assessed how quickly Richard could register and encode written words into short-term visual-verbal memory. The initial items of this task required Richard to view a word for one second, then view another word and indicate whether or not the new word was the same as the first word. Later items of this task required him to view a word for one second, then view an isolated letter or letter cluster and indicate whether the letter/letter cluster appeared in the word and in the same order. Richard performed poorly on this task and scored in the Low range. His performance was compared to that of sixth-grade students because the PAL-II norms do not go above sixth grade. His errors were interspersed throughout the test, strongly suggesting that his low score was the result of an inability to consistently attend to the features of individual letters and words rather than difficulties with the initial registration of the visual information being presented.

The PAL-II Expressive Coding Task assessed Richard's ability to quickly register orthographic units in visual-verbal immediate memory and retrieve those units from immediate working memory to reproduce, in writing, a whole nonsense word or a specific letter/letter cluster from the nonsense word. Richard's performance on this task was in the Low range, compared to the sixth-grade group in the PAL-II standardization sample.

Richard demonstrated considerable weakness in the ability to quickly attend to and register visual letter sequences and words in immediate memory and then hold them in working memory long enough to accurately reproduce them in writing. This difficulty has a great impact on Richard's ability to initially register the spellings of words, as well as on his ability to store accurate representations of them in long-term memory for later retrieval.

Executive Functions

The term *executive functions* refers to a diverse group of cognitive capacities that act in a coordinated way to direct perception, emotion, thinking, and motor activity. Executive functions are responsible for a person's ability to engage in purposeful, organized, strategic, self-regulated, and goal-directed behavior. As a collection of capacities that enable a person to direct and regulate his or her own thinking processes and actions, executive functions alert, or cue, a person to use other cognitive abilities such as reasoning, language, visual processing, and memory. Similarly, executive functions direct the performance of academic skills such as reading comprehension, math problem solving, and written expression. This section describes the assessment findings regarding the development of Richard's executive functions.

Information from BRIEF Parent Ratings, Parent and Teacher Interviews, and Interviews with Richard

Richard's mother and father and several school staff members (current special education teacher and speech therapist, previous special education and reading teachers) all completed the Behavior Rating Inventory of Executive Function (BRIEF) to provide their perceptions of Richard's use of executive function processes in daily activities. The BRIEF ratings are negative indicators, that is, high scores indicate poor or ineffective functioning in a category. For example, for the Item "Makes Careless Errors" a rating of "Often" earns three points, while a rating of "Never" earns 1 point. Consequently, the higher a percentile rank for a scale, the greater the deficiency of behavior perceived by the rater.

Scores derived from the parents' and school staff's ratings are provided in a table at the end of this report. The information from the specific items of the BRIEF was integrated with information from parent and staff interviews to provide the following interpretation.

In terms of the four arenas of involvement, Richard is not reported as experiencing difficulties in dealing with the environment. Problems reported in the self-control/self-management area were relatively minimal and focused on some difficulties with impulsivity and emotional reactions. The greatest concerns were expressed in relation to handling symbol systems in the context of schoolwork; the most noticeable of these was difficulty monitoring for errors and sustaining concentration in academic tasks.

In domains of functioning, Richard is reported as experiencing some minor difficulties with emotional control in relation to others and to symbol systems. The few executive control problems reported mainly focused on the processing of perceptions (e.g., initial attention to details) and completing actions (e.g., slow rate of production) in the symbol system arena as directly related to schoolwork.

Specific items rated as problematic by parents and teachers included the following:

- Does not think before doing
- Interrupts others
- Reacts more strongly to situations than other children
- Has a short attention span
- Has good ideas but cannot get them on paper
- Written work is poorly organized
- Does not check work for mistakes
- Makes careless errors
- Has poor handwriting
- Work is sloppy

Richard's teachers also noted some interpersonal difficulties in classroom situations involving monitoring of behavior and interactions with others:

- Does not notice when his behavior causes negative reactions
- Does not realize that certain actions bother others
- Is unaware of his own behavior when in a group

Executive Function Evaluation During Assessment Sessions

To better understand the possible impact of any executive function difficulties on schoolwork, it was important to assess the use of executive functions in directing specific cognitive abilities such as reasoning, language, visual/spatial, memory, and graphomotor production. The results of this part of the assessment apply to Richard's use of executive functions to cue and direct other cognitive abilities as they would be used in school or in completing tasks at home, especially tasks involving reading, writing, listening, and speaking.

Executive Control of Basic Attention and Effort During Assessment Sessions

Richard demonstrated the ability to focus on and attend to tasks in the one-to-one context of the assessment session and did not require any prompts from the examiner in order to engage in tasks. Transitions from one task to another were accomplished smoothly without the need for prompting or redirecting. Richard demonstrated good capacity for engagement in tasks as he willingly involved himself in each new task and never asked for a break. Richard did have some difficulty with sustaining optimal levels of attention and effort for certain tasks, especially those that involved attention to many visual details simultaneously. Difficulties with sustained effort also were evident on prolonged reading and writing tasks.

Executive Direction of the Use of Reasoning Abilities During Assessment Sessions

As noted in the Reasoning section of this report, Richard was quite capable of reasoning with nonverbal, visual material and demonstrated effective cueing and strategy use to enhance task performance.

The best example of Richard's ability to effectively direct his reasoning capacities was his performance with the Wisconsin Card Sorting Test (WCST). Richard's quick adaptation to the task demands and his ability to quickly adjust to and anticipate the set shifts enabled him to earn Superior range scores on all of the indices of the WCST. The WCST employs a novel learning task in an open-ended, ambiguous problem-solving format. It assesses abstract reasoning abilities and self-regulation abilities, such as:

- Cueing the development of problem-solving strategies
- Consistent application of problem-solving strategies
- Cueing the flexible shifting of strategy application in response to changing information about the problem to be solved

The WCST requires persistence of problem solving over a prolonged period of time.

Executive Control of Retrieval and Production of Verbal Information During Assessment Sessions

Richard demonstrated average expressive language abilities when communicating his thoughts spontaneously and when responding to both open-ended and direct questions. As noted in the Language section of this report, Richard's expressive fluency was in the Superior range when asked to name things in categories. His verbal expression was hindered considerably, however, when he was required to exert greater executive control over his efforts to retrieve words that began with specific letters and he scored in the Low range. These results suggest that Richard is likely to have difficulty demonstrating his knowledge when assessments require responses that conform to a highly specific format and that require a high degree of executive control over information retrieval processes.

Richard also struggled with all of the tasks that required him to rapidly link language processes to visual images, especially with orthography (printed letters and words). Richard was exceedingly slow, scoring at or below the 1st percentile, with naming colors and reading words. He was also poor at controlling language processes when asked to inhibit impulsive responding and shift response set when reading (D-KEFS Inhibition and Inhibition Switching), tasks that require a high level of executive control. In these tasks, he scored in the Extremely Low to Low range.

These tasks directly reflect deficiencies in the control processes needed for reading fluency, that is, weaknesses in the type of multitasking and executive control necessary to effectively manage all of the cognitive processes required for reading words quickly and efficiently while extracting meaning from the text.

Executive Control of Speed of Production for Tasks During Assessment Sessions

As shown in the summary following, Richard was exceptionally poor at performing many tasks that imposed strict time limits for production of responses.

Subtest	SS	ScS	PR
KAIT Logical Steps (30-second time limit per item)		15	95
NEPSY-II Word Generation-Semantic (60 seconds per item)		15	95
WISC-IV Cancellation (45 seconds per item)		15	95
WISC-IV Picture Completion (20-second time limit per item)		12	75

Subtest	SS	ScS	PR
NEPSY-II Block Construction (liberal time limit per item; bonus points for fast completion for the most difficult items)		12	75
WISC-IV Block Design (liberal time limit per item; bonus points for fast completion for the most difficult items)		9	37
Block Design Multiple Choice (30-second limit per item with bonus point for response within 5 seconds)		8	25
WISC-IV Symbol Search (2-minute time limit)		7	16
PAL-II Alphabet Writing (15 seconds)		2 (Decile)	11–20
PAL-II Receptive Coding (stimuli of each item exposed for 1 second)		2 (Decile)	11–20
PAL-II Expressive Coding (stimuli of each item exposed for 1 second)		2 (Decile)	11–20
NEPSY-II Word Generation-Initial Letter (60 seconds per item)		6	9
NEPSY-II Inhibition-Inhibition Trial (scored by completion time)		6	9
D-KEFS CWI Inhibition/Switching (scored by completion time)		5	5
CMS Sequences (bonus points for speed of completion)		5	5
NEPSY-II Inhibition-Naming Trial (scored by completion time)		4	3
NEPSY-II Inhibition-Switching Trial (scored by completion time)		3	2
D-KEFS CWI Inhibition (scored by completion time)		3	2
WISC-IV Coding (2-minute time limit)		3	2
D-KEFS CWI Color Naming (scored by completion time)		1	1
D-KEFS CWI Word Reading (scored by completion time)		1	1
WJ III ACH Reading Fluency (3-minute time limit)	64		1
WJ III ACH Written Expression Fluency (7-minute time limit)	59		<1
WJ III ACH Math Fluency (3-minute time limit)	57		<1
TOWRE Sight Word Efficiency (45-second time limit)	<55		<1
TOWRE Phonemic Decoding Efficiency (45-second time limit)	<55		<1

Richard was effective in applying his reasoning abilities quickly to solve logic problems (KAIT Logical Steps), in searching for and marking all animal pictures on 11 × 17 pages filled with pictures of objects and animals, in generating lists of words according to given categories (e.g., clothing), in constructing designs using single color blocks, and in finding the missing detail in pictures of common objects and scenes. As the complexity or amount of detail of the visual designs increased, Richard's speed of completion of items decreased.

As the need for executive control of language production increased, Richard's language production became very slow. Performance also was extremely poor for any task that required the use of graphomotor skills for handwriting and/or the use of working memory. These tasks focused on language production on command, detailed visual processing and interpretation of the visual images, and graphomotor production. When these activities are the focus of instruction or assessment (which is the case most of the time), Richard is likely to require additional time to demonstrate what he knows and can do.

In contrast, Richard was much more effective with timed tasks when they emphasized reasoning with nonverbal information without emphasizing numerous small details. Overall, Richard is likely to perform much more effectively when tasks do not involve making fine discriminations among visual stimuli, such as reading words and attending to calculation operation signs and notation.

ACADEMIC FUNCTIONING

Richard was administered selected subtests from the WJ III ACH, WIAT-III, and the TOWRE to gain insight into his reading, writing, and math skill development and current level of functioning compared to students of the same age. For all of these tests, age-based standard scores and percentile ranks are used to describe his levels of academic functioning.

Reading

Word Recognition

Richard's word recognition skills were assessed using the WJ III ACH Letter/Word Identification test. The task involved reading words in a list one at a time. Richard identified only a few high-frequency words. Richard's errors illustrated a lack of attention to visual details that resulted in words with a somewhat similar appearance (e.g., *hate* for *hat, where* for *were, best* for *beside*). At no time did Richard slow down and attempt to sound out words using decoding strategies. Richard's limited sight word recognition, inconsistent attention to the visual features of letters and words, lack of awareness that he did not recognize a word, and inability to apply decoding skills to words resulted in a score in the Extremely Low range (SS 49, <1st percentile).

Both the TOWRE Phonemic Decoding Efficiency subtest and the WJ III ACH Word Attack test assessed Richard's facility with the rules of phonics, orthographic patterns, and structural analysis by requiring him to read lists of nonsense words (i.e., letters configured similarly to real words, such as *dreep*). Because these tasks used nonsense words, Richard was unable to depend on recognizing the words "by sight." Although the TOWRE is timed and Word Attack is not, Richard performed in the Extremely Low range on both, able to decode only a few CVC pattern words (TOWRE SS 55, PR < 1; Word Attack SS 68, PR 2).

Reading Speed and Reading Fluency

Richard's reading speed was assessed using the WJ III ACH Reading Fluency test, the TOWRE Sight Word Efficiency and Phonemic Decoding subtests, and the D-KEFS Word Reading task, and by timing Richard's passage reading on the WIAT-III Reading Comprehension subtest. These tests incorporated a variety of tasks, measuring the number of words (in lists) Richard read correctly, the amount of time it took him to read an entire list of words, and the number of simple sentences he read and understood (by indicating true or false) within a time limit. On all of these tests, Richard scored in the Extremely Low range.

Richard's silent reading rate on the passages of the WIAT-III Reading Comprehension subtest was extremely slow, varying from 18 to 40 words per minute. The mean oral reading rate for students in the winter of seventh grade is 136 correct words per minute (Hasbrouck & Tindal, 2006). Silent reading is usually faster. Overall, Richard's oral and silent reading rates were extremely slow.

Paragraph Reading Comprehension

The WIAT-III Reading Comprehension subtest required Richard to read paragraphs and answer questions. The paragraphs are composed primarily of high-frequency, easily read words so that comprehension rather than decoding is measured.

Richard appeared to have great difficulty with holding information in mind and integrating it while trying to respond to the questions. For nearly all of the questions, Richard reread sections of the passage before responding. Despite his Average performance on tasks involv-

ing reasoning with oral information and his Average to Above Average knowledge of word associations and word meanings, Richard had difficulty with most of the inferential comprehension questions, most likely a reflection of his limited word reading skills. As with his other reading skills, Richard's performance resulted in a score in the Extremely Low range (SS 56, PR 1).

Written Expression Skills

Richard's written expression skills were assessed using selected writing tasks of the WJ III ACH. He demonstrated a mature pencil grip and wrote in print rather than cursive. Sometimes his letters were poorly formed but legible and of appropriate size; he tended to leave large amounts of space between words.

The WJ III ACH Spelling test required Richard to write words from dictation. He was cooperative but struggled noticeably, spelling only a very limited number of high-frequency words correctly. Richard's spellings of other words deviated significantly from what would be expected if he were effectively discriminating the sounds; many of his spellings reflected significant difficulty in letter-sound association and a lack of knowledge of common spelling patterns. As with his reading scores, Richard's Spelling score was in the Extremely Low range (SS 58, PR < 1).

The WJ III ACH Writing Samples test required Richard to perform a variety of short writing tasks such as providing endings to sentences, providing the second sentence for a three-sentence paragraph, and describing events shown in pictures. The same spelling difficulties were evident in his responses in this test. Richard's difficulties producing grammatically correct phrases and sentences to complete these tasks resulted in a score in the Extremely Low range (SS 65, PR 1).

Richard's speed at formulating and writing simple sentences was assessed using the WJ III ACH Writing Fluency test. Based on a picture and three words for each item, Richard was to write as many sentences as possible in 7 minutes. Richard wrote an average of eight words per minute. His score, again, was in the Extremely Low range (SS 59, PR 1).

Math Problem Solving and Calculation

Richard's basic math skills were assessed using the WISC-IV Arithmetic subtest and the WJ III ACH Math Fluency, Calculation, and Applied Problems tests. Richard had difficulty performing basic calculations mentally, earning a score in the Low range on Arithmetic (SS 6, PR 9).

The WJ III ACH Math Fluency test assesses rapid retrieval of basic addition, subtraction, and multiplication facts within a 3-minute period. Richard made only two errors but worked slowly. His score was in the Extremely Low range (SS 57, PR < 1).

The Calculation test assessed Richard's ability to do math calculations with pencil and paper without time limits. Richard consistently used his fingers to calculate sums and attempted only basic addition and subtraction problems without regrouping and basic multiplication and division facts. He did not demonstrate knowledge of multiplication or division algorithms or how to work with fractions or decimals. His extremely limited calculation skills produced a score in the Low range (SS 79, PR 8).

The story problems on the WJ III ACH Applied Problems test required Richard to demonstrate a variety of skills including recognizing irrelevant data/numbers, determining the correct operation(s), and performing the necessary computations to solve the problems. For each item, the test easel shows a diagram of the elements of the problem and/or the wording of the problem as the examiner reads it aloud. The calculations were relatively simple, thereby emphasizing comprehension and analysis of the language of the problem and the ability to manipulate, convert, and compare data presented in different formats (e.g., fractions, decimals, percentages). This test is not timed and Richard made good use of the paper and pencil provided. It was apparent that this test enabled him to demonstrate his reasoning abilities much more than any other academic task throughout the assessment. Richard was successful with many problems involving time and money as well as subtraction and addition of quantities.

Although he was effectively engaged in problem solving, his inadequate knowledge of arithmetic algorithms beyond basic addition and subtraction greatly limited his overall success. Of the academic tests, Richard earned his highest score on this test, in the Below Average range (SS 87, PR 20).

TEST RESULTS

The following test results are organized by standard score (SS) or scaled score (ScS) ranges: Extremely Low (EL), Low (L), Below Average (BA), Average (A), Above Average (AA), Superior (S), and Very Superior (VS).

Wechsler Intelligence Scale for Children – Fourth Edition, Integrated (WISC-IV-Integrated)

Scales	SS	PR	EL	L	BA	A	AA	S	VS
Full Scale	88	21			88				
General Ability Index	102	55				102			
Indexes									
Verbal Comprehension (VCI)	98	45				98			
Perceptual Reasoning (PRI)	106	66				106			
Working Memory (WMI)	77	6		77					
Processing Speed (PSI)	73	4		73					

Note: Standard scores range from a low of 40 to a high of 160, with 100 as the average score.
Note: The Full Scale combines the core 10 subtests from all four Indexes; the GAI combines only the subtests of the Verbal Comprehension and the Perceptual Reasoning Indexes.

Verbal Comprehension Subtests	ScS	PR	EL	L	BA	A	AA	S	VS
Similarities (VCI)	10*	50*				10			
Comprehension (VCI)	10*	50*				10			
Vocabulary (VCI)	9*	37*				9			
Information	11	63				11			
Word Reasoning	6	9		6					
Perceptual Reasoning Subtests									
Picture Concepts (PRI)	14*	91*						14	
Matrix Reasoning (PRI)	10*	50*				10			
Block Design (PRI)	9*	37*				9			

(Continued)

Verbal Comprehension Subtests	ScS	PR	EL	L	BA	A	AA	S	VS
Block Design: No Time Bonus	11	63				11			
Block Design: Multiple Choice	8	25				8			
Block Design MC: No Time Bonus	11	63				11			
Working Memory Subtests									
Letter-Number Sequencing (WMI)	8*	25*				8			
Digit Span (WMI)	4*	2*	4						
Digit Span Forward	3	1	3						
Digit Span Backward	7	16			7				
Arithmetic	6	9		6					
Processing Speed Subtests									
Symbol Search (PSI)	7*	16*			7				
Coding (PSI)	3*	2*	3						
Cancellation	15	95						15	
Cancellation Random	14	91						14	
Cancellation Structured	13	84					13		

Note: Scaled scores range from a low of 1 to a high of 19, with 10 as the average score.
* Denotes Subtest Scores used in the calculation of the Index scores and the FSIQ. ( ) indicate the Index to which the subtest scores contribute.

Kaufman Adolescent and Adult Intelligence Test (KAIT)

Subtest	SS	PR	EL	L	BA	A	AA	S	VS
Auditory Comprehension	12	75				12			
Logical Steps	15	95						15	

Note: Standard scores range from a low of 40 to a high of 160, with 100 as the average score.

Woodcock-Johnson – III NU Edition Tests of Cognitive Abilities (WJ III COG)

	SS	PR	EL	L	BA	A	AA	S	VS
Verbal Comprehension	114	83					114		
Spatial Relations	100	49				100			
Concept Formation	122	93					122		

Note: Standard scores range from a low of 40 to a high of 160, with 100 as the average score.

Children's Memory Scale (CMS)

Attention and Concentration	ScS	PR	EL	L	BA	A	AA	S	VS
Sequences	5	5		5					

Note: Scaled scores range from a low of 1 to a high of 19, with 10 as the average score.

Delis-Kaplan Executive Function System (D-KEFS)

Color Word Interference Test	ScS	PR	EL	L	BA	A	AA	S	VS
Color Naming Speed	1	<1	1						
Word Reading Speed	1	<1	1						
Inhibition Speed	3	1	3						
Inhibition /Switching Speed	5	5		5					

Note: Scaled scores range from a low of 1 to a high of 19, with 10 as the average score.

Wisconsin Card Sorting Test (WCST)

Indexes	SS	PR	EL	L	BA	A	AA	S	VS
Total Errors Percentage	126	96						126	
% Perseverative Errors	127	96						127	

Indexes	SS	PR	EL	L	BA	A	AA	S	VS
% Nonperseverative Errors	122	93						122	
Percentage of Conceptual Level Responses	127	96						127	
Performance Characteristics	**Raw Score**	**Level**							
Categories (Sets) Completed	6	>16				Adequate			
Trials to Complete 1st Category	12	>16				Adequate			
Failure to Maintain Set	0	>16				Adequate			
Trials to Completion for Categories 1-6: 12, 12, 12, 11, 11, 12									

Note: Standard scores range from a low of 55 to a high of 145, with 100 as the average score. WCST scores are positively weighted; the higher the score, the better the performance.

NEPSY-II

Attention & Executive Functions	ScS	PR	EL	L	BA	A	AA	S	VS
Inhibition – Naming Time	4	2	4						
Inhibition – Inhibition Time	6	9		6					
Inhibition – Switching Time	3	1	3						
Inhibition Total Errors	8	25				8			
Language	**ScS**	**PR**							
Comprehension of Instructions	6	9		6					
Phonological Processing	6	9		6					
Word Generation – Semantic	15	95						15	
Word Generation – Initial Letter	6	9		6					
Memory and Learning	**ScS**	**PR**							
Narrative Memory – Free Recall	8	25				8			
Narrative Memory – Free & Cued Recall	8	25				8			
Visuospatial	**ScS**	**PR**							
Block Construction	12	75				12			

Note: Scaled scores range from a low of 1 to a high of 19, with 10 as the average score.

Rey Complex Figure Test (RCFT)

	T Score	PR	EL	L	BA	A	AA	S	VS
Copy Trial	53	63				53			
Immediate Recall	31	3	31						

Note: T scores range from a low of 20 to a high of 90, with 50 as the average score.

Behavior Rating Inventory of Executive Function (BRIEF)

T Scores and (Percentile Ranks)						
Scales	Mother	Father	Spec Ed 7th Grade Language Arts	Speech-Language Therapist	Spec Ed 5th–6th Grade Teacher	Spec Ed 4th–6th Reading Teacher
Inhibit	53 (74)	50 (68)	**78 (96)**	60 (85)	62 (88)	44 (45)
Shift	56 (75)	52 (65)	**79 (98)**	44 (50)	**87 (>99)**	63 (88)
Emotional Control	59 (84)	53 (70)	**88 (>99)**	48 (70)	**81 (>99)**	54 (81)
Initiate	47 (52)	47 (52)	57 (81)	42 (40)	57 (81)	42 (40)
Working Memory	56 (80)	47 (47)	64 (89)	64 (89)	62 (88)	43 (43)
Planning/Organize	51 (61)	49 (55)	60 (82)	51 (70)	64 (90)	49 (65)
Organize Materials	**66 (94)**	52 (65)	**70 (93)**	44 (55)	**70 (93)**	44 (55)
Monitor	63 (90)	54 (69)	**74 (96)**	**74 (96)**	**76 (97)**	48 (57)

Note: The BRIEF ratings are negative indicators, that is, high scores indicate a lack of functioning in a category. For example, for the Item "Makes Careless Errors" a rating of "Often" earns three points, while a rating of "Never" earns only 1 point. Since high ratings reflect a lack of functioning, the higher a percentile rank for a Scale or Index, the greater the deficiency of behavior perceived by the rater. Scores in bold print indicate problems occurring significantly more frequently than in age-peers.

ACADEMIC SKILLS

Test of Word Reading Efficiency (TOWRE)

	SS	PR	EL	L	BA	A	AA	S	VS
Sight Word Efficiency	<55	<1	<55						
Phonemic Decoding Efficiency	<55	<1	<55		·				

Note: Standard scores range from a low of 40 to a high of 160, with 100 as the average score.

Woodcock-Johnson III Tests of Achievement (WJ III ACH)

Reading Tests	SS	PR	EL	L	BA	A	AA	S	VS
Letter-Word Identification	49	<1	49						
Word Attack	68	2	68						
Reading Fluency	64	1	64						
Reading Vocabulary	80	9			80				
Writing Tests	**SS**	**PR**							
Spelling	58	<1	58						
Writing Samples	65	1	65						
Writing Fluency	59	1	59						
Math Tests	**SS**	**PR**							
Calculation	79	8		79					
Applied (Math) Problems	87	20			87				
Math Fluency	57	<1	57						

Note: Standard scores range from a low of 0 to over 200, with 100 as the average score.

Wechsler Individual Achievement Test-Third Edition (WIAT-III)

Reading Subtests	SS	PR	EL	L	BA	A	AA	S	VS
Reading Comprehension	56	<1	56						

Note: Standard scores range from a low of 40 to a high of 160, with 100 as the average score.

REFERENCES

Hasbrouck, J., & Tindal, G. A. (2006). Oral reading fluency norms: A valuable assessment tool for reading teachers. *Reading Teacher, 59,* 636–644.

McCloskey, G., Perkins, L. A., & VanDivner, B. (2009). *Assessment and intervention for executive function difficulties.* New York: Routledge Press.

The Assessment of "Nonverbal" Learning Disabilities

Christopher Nicholls

The best-understood reasons for a student to struggle in school involve language-based learning disabilities and attention disorders, bringing to mind the adage "If you hear hoof beats, think horses." Occasionally, however, the evaluation of learning difficulties reveals that we are dealing with a zebra! This realization was evident in the early writings of learning disability pioneers, including Marianne Frostig, Helmer Myklebust, and others who recognized that there are multiple developmental learning disorders. Given the primacy of reading as the key skill needed for success in school, however, research and clinical emphasis have been focused on the core language functions contributing to reading success, while explanations emphasizing visuospatial and perceptual-motor processes were often dismissed or minimized in their importance.

In the latter half of the 1980s, however, the work of Byron Rourke led to a renewed focus on learning disorders that focused primarily on competence in mathematics, written expression, reading comprehension (as opposed to decoding), and social interaction. Rourke's hypothesis was that these types of learning disabilities involved the "white matter" of the brain—the long tracks of axonal fibers that connect various regions of the brain. Rourke attempted to show that many neurodevelopmental disorders, including Asperger's Syndrome, Williams Syndrome, Turner Syndrome, and others, all shared similar cognitive characteristics.

Notably, Rourke suggested that these children exhibit "deficiencies in intermodal integration, problem-solving, and concept formation (especially in novel situations), and that they have profound difficulty in benefitting from experiences that do not mesh well with their only existing well-developed, over-learned descriptive system (i.e., natural language)" (Rourke, 1995, p. 19). Rourke's model thus became known as the "White Matter Model." Because there are a larger proportion of long white matter tracts in the right hemisphere as compared with the left, the "Nonverbal Learning Disability" syndrome became known as the "right hemisphere" category of learning disabilities.

As is common with a new taxonomic entity, researchers and clinicians first responded by "lumping" many diverse conditions under this "NLD" model, finding that the descriptions of challenges faced by such students closely matched many of the concerns brought to the office by parents who had often been seen by a multitude of prior professionals—all of whom seemed to have missed the key strengths and weaknesses of these children. Indeed, even the "nonverbal" aspect of the "syndrome" seemed, at times, to not reflect the primary difficulties their children were experiencing. Certainly, they had relative strengths in simple language, so to say that it was all "nonverbal" didn't seem right. The youngsters often seemed to have difficulties mainly with abstract language and inferential reasoning. Likewise, simply saying that "all math disorders are nonverbal" clearly isn't correct, as emerging research indicates that there are multiple subtypes of mathematics disorders, some of which are clearly based in language processing. Indeed, over the past few years, it has become quite fashionable among neuropsychologists to dismiss the entire Nonverbal Learning Disability Syndrome as not supported by our emerging knowledge of neuroanatomy and neurophysiology, leading to the pendulum swinging to the side of "splitters" who point out the unique features of various diagnoses, and how the "lumpers" must surely be wrong.

Research efforts currently under way are focusing on the possibility that there are subcategories within the NLD syndrome, with likely candidates including a primary visuospatial subtype, a primary social processing subtype, and a primary concept integration/frontal executive subtype. As the research for and against these new conceptualizations emerges, one hopes it will be accompanied by greater clarity in terms of diagnostic approaches and evidence-based recommendations for intervention. In the meantime, however, clinicians are encouraged to continue to be alert for the presentation of students who don't quite fit our tried and true approaches to SLD assessment, and to remain open to alternative explanations for what is often a puzzling presentation of symptoms. As an example of such a case presentation, the following psychoeducational evaluation is offered, in which a child who fits many features of the NLD syndrome is discussed.

PSYCHOEDUCATIONAL EVALUATION

Name:	Jim Paxton
Date of Birth:	12/20/1996
Age:	13-9
Parents:	Sue and Tom Paxton
Address:	9288 E. Main St, Springfield, AZ 85432
School:	Cordite Elementary
Grade:	7
Referred by:	Mother
Date of Evaluation:	9/3, 9/16, 9/17, 10/1/10
Evaluator:	Christopher J. Nicholls, Ph.D.

REASON FOR REFERRAL

Jim began the current academic year as a seventh-grade student at Cordite Elementary, having transferred from Monte Vista Elementary, where he was in a learning resource classroom (LRC) for three periods per day. Upon moving to Cordite, Jim's LRC placement was reduced from three to two periods per day, although he unofficially received services in an integrated math class where his special education teacher was teaching. Jim has also previously used the services of an instructional aide when he was attending school in New York; however, an aide has not been provided in Arizona. Recently, Jim's mother began to be concerned that "he wasn't keeping up" at Cordite, and during the course of the present evaluation, Jim was transferred to a private school, Maximize Learning Academy. Ricky, Jim's 15-year-old brother who has high functioning autism/Asperger's Disorder, also attends Maximize Learning Academy. Jim's mother reports that Jim needs a great deal of help with directions, has trouble following through on long-term plans or working on big projects, and often misunderstands the directions for assigned work. He also struggles with math, which is now at the level of algebra.

BACKGROUND INFORMATION

Jim's parents are married and live together; however, Jim's father was on a business trip on the dates of the current evaluation and was thus unavailable for interview. Jim was the third of four children born in the Paxton family; he has two older siblings, Cindy and Ricky, and a younger brother Bill. Cindy and Bill have had no academic difficulties. Jim was the product of a full-term pregnancy complicated by maternal hyperemesis, a severe form of morning sickness accompanied by unrelenting nausea and vomiting. Labor was induced and forceps were used during the delivery, which was complicated by the fact that Jim had his umbilical cord wrapped around his neck. He did not require neonatal resuscitation or specialized care, however, and was discharged with his mother.

Jim's early developmental history is characterized by feeding problems that resulted in a condition of failure to thrive. Jim's early motor milestones were mildly delayed, with walking at 14 months, first word use at 14 months, and speaking in phrases at 3 years of age. Mild delays in adaptive behavior skills were also noted; however, Jim has reportedly never lost a developmental skill once it was acquired. Mrs. Paxton feels that Jim was slow to develop speech, and that he demonstrated an unusual tone or pitch to his voice. Jim's speech was often difficult to understand, and he had a tendency to repeat questions rather than answer them. In the past, Jim did not demonstrate typical patterns of imitative behavior, for example, waving "bye-bye" or playing "patty-cake." He would not repeat things that were said to him, and at times seemed to ignore what was being said to him. Even at the present time, Jim reportedly often ignores sounds in his environment or is unpredictable in responding; sometimes he reacts and sometimes he doesn't. Jim has a history of avoiding looking at people when they are speaking with him, and he does not appear to use eye contact or visual exploration of his environment to any great degree. Jim also has an atypical pattern of emotional response, at times laughing for no obvious reason, and he has moods that change quickly or for no apparent reason. Jim often has a blank expression on his face and currently demonstrates little in the way of an emotional response to what is occurring around him.

Jim is followed by a pediatrician, Dr. Susan Milliron, and is also followed by Dr. Natasha Gorzanski for psychiatric care. Jim has been diagnosed as having an anxiety disorder, Attention-Deficit/Hyperactivity Disorder (ADHD), and a Pervasive Developmental Disorder (PDD). Currently, Jim takes the medications Lamictal, Provigil, Abilify, and Amantadine. His mother thinks his medications work "somewhat" because when he isn't taking them or they wear off, he is more hyperactive. When frustrated, he can become quite angry, and currently, his anxiety is quite high. Jim tells me that he thinks his medicines help him and that he isn't averse to taking medicines; he just doesn't know why he takes them.

Family history is significant for multiple neurological and psychiatric difficulties. Review of a background questionnaire completed by Jim's mother indicates that within the extended family there are diagnoses of substance abuse, schizophrenia, autism, ADHD, migraine headaches, anxiety, Alzheimer's disease, depression, dyslexia, speech/language delay, Obsessive-Compulsive Disorder, and Bipolar Disorder. There is also a history of diabetes, heart disease, strokes, and food allergies.

Discussion with Jim reveals that he doesn't really understand how he learns. He isn't sure if he learns best by listening or reading. He thinks he is good at math and basketball, and he enjoys riding dirt bikes. Jim also likes to play the violin and clarinet. He has one friend, Matthew, who goes to his school, but he says that his best friend is James, whom he has known for 4 years.

PRIOR EVALUATION FINDINGS

Jim was first evaluated through the Wylie Public Schools in May 2001, when he was 5 years of age. Administration of the Stanford-Binet Intelligence Scale, Fourth Edition, revealed Verbal Reasoning and Quantitative scores within the Average range, a Short-Term Memory score in the Low Average range, and a Visual Reasoning composite in the impaired range, with weaknesses both on the Pattern Analysis and the Copying subtests. Academic achievement testing, using the Woodcock-Johnson III Tests of Achievement (WJ III ACH), indicated impaired scores on measures of sight word reading and spelling, within the context of Average range performance on measures of quantitative

concepts and vocabulary. Jim was considered to have age-appropriate receptive and expressive language skills.

In October 2007, Jim was evaluated by Dr. Julie Fairchild. Results from the Wechsler Intelligence Scale for Children-Fourth Edition (WISC-IV) indicated a Full-Scale IQ score that was in the Borderline range, and scores within the Low Average range on measures of Verbal Comprehension, Perceptual Reasoning, and Working Memory. His lowest score was on the Processing Speed index, at the lowest end of the Borderline range. Academic achievement, as measured by the Wechsler Individual Achievement Test-Second Edition (WIAT-II), indicated Low Average scores on measures of sight word reading, spelling, and reading comprehension, along with Average scores on measures of mathematics and written expression. Fluency measures, using the WJ III ACH, were within the Average range. Neuropsychological evaluation procedures indicated better developed receptive than expressive language skills, with particular difficulties in the recall of verbal information and overall challenges in memory. Attention and concentration were impaired, with Jim performing poorly on a computerized measure of sustained attention. Additional concerns were noted in terms of an elevated level of anxiety. It was concluded that Jim had a learning disability, "language issues," a phonologically based reading disorder, symptoms of AD/HD, and indications of an explicit memory disorder.

Jim's most recent Individualized Education Program, dated November 9, 2009, documents that Jim was considered eligible for special education services within the Springfield Unified School District, under the categories of specific learning disability (SLD) and speech and language impairment (SLI). Administration of the WJ III ACH on November 5, 2009, indicated Average oral language skills but Low Average skills in listening comprehension. Academic skills and fluency were both within the Average range, but Jim's ability to apply these skills was in the Low Average range. Jim was found to perform in the High Average range in basic reading skills, the Average range in mathematics and written language, and within the Low Average range in the areas of reading comprehension and written expression.

BEHAVIORAL OBSERVATIONS

Jim was cooperative with testing but seemed to quickly become overwhelmed, seemed to shut down easily, and would often say, "This is too hard." Jim's grasp of his pencil involved a tripod grip; however, he leaned the shaft of the pencil away from his body in an awkward manner, causing him to have poor control of the pencil tip and difficulties in drawing certain shapes. In his approach to presented problems, Jim frequently seemed unsure as to how to begin a task or what strategy he should use to solve the problem. Particularly on tests that involved visual-spatial reasoning, Jim appeared to employ a random, trial-and-error strategy, and frequently said, "I don't get how to do this." Collectively, the results of the present evaluation are felt to be a valid appraisal of Jim's current status; however, Jim's information-processing difficulty lowers the reliability of many of the presented scores. Specifically, Jim appears to have a severe learning disability that impacts his ability to take standardized tests, and any decisions made solely on the basis of an analysis of summary test scores would be erroneous. The reader is encouraged to carefully consider interpretation of Jim's performance, described below.

TEST RESULTS AND INTERPRETATIONS

Jim's performance on the WISC-IV as well as his mother's description of his capabilities on the Adaptive Behavior Assessment System, Second Edition (ABAS-II), would lead one to conclude that Jim demonstrates an intellectual and developmental disability, due to summary scores that fall below the 2nd percentile for his age group. Such a conclusion would not only be inaccurate but would also misrepresent Jim. Jim's profile of test scores suggests a significant disorder of new learning affecting the integration of new information into conceptual categories, most likely reflective of primary challenges in the information analysis procedures typically attributed to the right hemisphere of the brain.

In other words, information that is presented for learning requires an initial analysis for meaningfulness, or perception. That information is then compared and contrasted at a somewhat higher level, involving pattern recognition, categorical analysis, and comparison with one's stored body of knowledge. New learning, therefore, is an active process that relies on stored bodies of information, but which requires the comparison of new information with one's knowledge base, the integration of parts in the whole, the development of appropriate problem-solving strategies, systematic application of information-processing procedures, and so forth. In comparison, one's ability to recall factual information from one's stores of knowl-

edge requires less active processing and more reliance on "automatic" procedures of memory retrieval. Individuals who are adept in this form of thinking can readily recall factual information that they have learned, and typically perform relatively more competently on tests that tap such automatic learning/recall. In most individuals, these complementary processes of entering new information into our current ways of thinking about the world, and changing our way of thinking about the world to adapt to new information, provide the opportunity for continued growth and development, and fluid management of the daily demands placed on us.

Jim, indeed, has good recall for well-learned information. His performance on the Peabody Picture Vocabulary Test-4, a measure of receptive vocabulary knowledge, was solidly within the Average range. Likewise, Jim was able to answer questions of a factual nature about the world, at a level equivalent to the 50th percentile of his age group. Jim, therefore, seems to be fully capable of recognizing words and pointing to pictures to reflect the meaning of words, as well as being able to answer specific questions about the world that require recall from long-term memory. Jim also scored well on a measure of mental arithmetic, in which he was asked to listen to orally presented word problems from daily life, and to perform simple calculations. His score on this subtest fell at the 63rd percentile, again indicating relatively competent application of automatic problem-solving procedures that he has overlearned. Collectively, these findings suggest that Jim's "crystallized intelligence" is intact and represents an area of strength within his learning profile.

In contrast, Jim's new learning and fluid reasoning skills are fairly severely impaired. Jim demonstrates fairly severe impairments in his ability to compare and contrast new information, particularly when such tasks require initial visual perception and shape discrimination, and attention to visual details. Jim appears to have great difficulty understanding visual/nonverbal information, which causes him to have difficulty holding that information in short-term memory, and he subsequently struggles to understand what to do with that information, or how to solve a problem for which explicit instructions are not provided. Difficulty processing complex information is also evident on verbal tasks, in that Jim appears to have trouble holding sequences of information within his short-term memory, and then analyzing that information and developing a good strategy to solve the problem. Thus, although Jim scored within the Average range on measures of simple recall of previously learned information, his abilities to make inferences, sequence information, make predictions as to what might happen in a certain situation, and solve "negative" questions (e.g. "why doesn't" or "why isn't") are fairly severely impaired. Jim therefore has to think at length about questions that are posed to him. His first task is to understand the nature of the question, even before he can begin to try to answer the question or solve the problem. Jim's speed of information processing is therefore quite low, and it takes him a fairly long period of time to work his way through directions and then tasks. This results in the appearance of difficulties with expressive language and motoric demonstration of his knowledge, which is further complicated by substantially impaired complex fine-motor coordination. In essence, Jim appears to have difficulties at both the input and output level of information processing and with higher-order thinking, as compared with relative competency in the recognition and expression of his knowledge about discrete facts.

The above conceptualization of Jim's learning style would predict that he would have academic strengths in areas that tap his knowledge of information to which he has had repeated exposures, and relatively greater difficulties on academic tasks that require him to solve unfamiliar problems or to extract understanding from novel information. This in fact was the case in his performance on the Wechsler Individual Achievement Test, Third Edition (WIAT-III). Jim scored at the 50th percentile on a measure of sight word reading, and within the Superior range, at the 91st percentile for his age group, in his capacity to decode nonsense words that conform to English spelling patterns. Jim also scored above his peers, at the 63rd percentile, on a measure of spelling. These findings suggest, once again, that Jim is fully competent in terms of his ability to recall information that he has "figured out" and learned at an automatic level. In contrast, his score on a measure of reading comprehension, in which he was to read short passages and answer questions about what he read, fell at the 5th percentile for his age group. Jim also scored well below expectancies for his age on measures of mathematical calculation, fluency, and reasoning, and in the Low Average range on measures of his ability to express his thoughts on paper. As suggested above, these types of tasks require Jim to analyze, integrate, and quickly solve problems that involve new information processing. These types of tasks reflect the difficulties Jim has in daily learning.

On an emotional/behavioral level, Jim's self-report of his current adaptation was essentially within normal lim-

its. Jim does not feel that he has substantial troubles with anxiety, depression, attention, or emotional control. He does admit that he has a great deal of frustration around schoolwork, and wishes that he could avoid school, quit school, and not have to be subjected to the pressures he experiences in that environment. Jim's mother's responses on a variety of questionnaires, nevertheless, indicate fairly severe concerns in several areas of adjustment. She reports that Jim presents with multiple symptoms consistent with his diagnosis of ADHD, with both hyperactive/impulsive as well as inattentive symptoms. She also feels that Jim has an elevated level of anxiety and demonstrates symptoms of generalized unhappiness. She feels that Jim engages in fairly atypical behaviors and that he has fairly substantial challenges in adaptive behavior.

Because his mother reported that Jim demonstrates symptoms consistent with a developmental social disorder, the Social Communication Questionnaire (Lifetime version), which looks at symptoms within the Autism Spectrum, was administered. Mrs. Paxton's responses indicated that Jim has a history of atypical behaviors such as repetitive use of odd phrases, confusion of personal pronouns, and a tendency to ask socially inappropriate questions. Jim has had some repetitive patterns of behavior, and has a history of failing to spontaneously interact with others on both a verbal and nonverbal level. Maternal responses to the Social Responsiveness Scale resulted in a score that was in the severe range and suggested severe interference in everyday social interaction tied to deficiencies in reciprocal social behavior. Scores of similar elevation are strongly associated with diagnoses of Autism, Asperger's Disorder, or more severe cases of Pervasive Developmental Disorder, Not Otherwise Specified. Maternal responses to the Pediatric and Early Adolescent Bipolar Disorder Symptoms Checklist indicated that Jim does have a tendency toward early-morning grouchiness, separation anxiety, and regression under stress. He is resistant toward rules, tends to blame others for his difficulties, and expresses feelings of worthlessness at times. Jim may be prone to rigid or inflexible thinking patterns, such as polarized "black or white" thinking. Significantly, Jim's mother does not describe symptoms of grandiose thinking, significant risk taking, precocious interest in sexuality, or times of manic activation, prompting me to conclude that the likelihood that Jim is demonstrating a Bipolar Disorder is low.

Most telling are Mrs. Paxton's responses to the Behavior Rating Inventory of Executive Function. On this questionnaire, she reported that Jim has severe challenges with behavioral regulation as well as meta-cognitive control. Jim has severe difficulties with mental flexibility in that he has great difficulty getting used to new situations, becomes upset in new situations, and has difficulty adapting to changes in his environment (e.g., teacher, classroom). He resists or has trouble accepting a different way to solve a problem and often will try the same approach to a problem over and over, even when it does not work. This is felt to be tied to Jim's difficulties with developing new strategies, and his overreliance on "tried and true" approaches to problem solving. Likely as a result of frustration he experiences when pressured, Jim tends to have angry or tearful outbursts that are intense but tend to end suddenly. In general, he becomes upset too easily, and his mood is easily influenced by the situation. Jim has difficulties with task initiation. He has trouble getting started on homework or chores, is not a self-starter, and lacks initiative. He has severe difficulties with working memory, has a short attention span, and has trouble concentrating on chores, schoolwork, and the like. If given three things to do, he typically will remember only the first or last, and he is often easily distracted by noises, activities, and events around him. Jim has trouble with chores or tasks that involve more than one step, and he needs help from adults to stay on task. He often forgets what he was doing, and if sent to get something will forget what he was supposed to get. Jim also has trouble with planning and organization. He seems to become overwhelmed by large assignments, does not plan ahead well for upcoming tests, and underestimates the time needed to complete something he begins. He therefore has trouble carrying out the actions needed to reach goals, and although he has good ideas, he has trouble getting them onto paper. Jim seems to have a poor understanding of his own strengths and weaknesses and is often unaware of how his behavior affects or bothers others.

IMPRESSIONS AND RECOMMENDATIONS

Taken collectively, the results of the present evaluation indicate that Jim is a 13-year-old boy who has a cognitive profile that is consistent with what has been termed the Nonverbal Learning Disability Syndrome. Although Jim's summary scale scores on standardized testing are quite low, these scores are not felt to be a good reflection of his learning potential. Indeed, Jim has some scores that

are well within the Average range, and his overall academic scores are above the level that would be expected on the basis of his intelligence test performance. It should therefore be understood that Jim has a severe nonverbal learning disability and is not intellectually or developmentally delayed. I do feel that Jim meets diagnostic criteria for High Functioning Autistic Disorder, based on his history of qualitative impairment in communication, challenges with social interaction, difficulties with novel problem solving, restricted patterns of interest, and difficulty with change/insistence on sameness. Many individuals who have Nonverbal Learning Disability Syndromes also meet diagnostic criteria for Autism Spectrum Disorders; however, current research thinking is not clear as to how these conditions overlap or are different. Jim does not demonstrate primary symptoms of a Bipolar Disorder at the current time, and although he certainly has symptoms of inattentiveness, impulsivity, and according to his mother an elevated activity level, ADHD does not completely capture the nature of his challenges. The following recommendations are offered:

1. Jim should be found eligible for services and governmental funding as a student with an Autistic Disorder. His mother is encouraged to pursue such services through the Division of Developmental Disabilities and the Social Security Administration. Consultation with Mr. Reginald Custer, 847-251-9876, regarding Jim's long-term planning is encouraged.

2. Jim and his parents are encouraged to learn more about the Nonverbal Learning Disability Syndrome. Although this conceptualization of children's learning problems is not without its critics, the model may serve as a useful approach to understanding Jim's challenges and coordinating a program of intervention. Information is available through several sources, including www.nldline.com, www.nldontheweb.org, www.nldbprourke.ca, and Jessica Kingsley Publishers (www.jkp.com). The book *Helping a Child with Nonverbal Learning Disorder or Asperger's Syndrome*, by Dr. Kathryn Stewart (New Harbinger Publications, Inc., www.newharbinger.com), may be particularly helpful.

3. Jim's mother is encouraged to share the current evaluation report with personnel at Maximize Learning Academy and request the development of a plan of instruction that will include accommodations and school assistance. Specifically, Jim would benefit from a daily study hall within which he could receive assistance with subject areas he finds difficult, as well as

supportive development of compensatory skills for his executive function difficulties and learning disability.

4. Jim will need specific training in "executive functions." These skills are associated with the development of organization, planning, goal setting and completion, working memory, and self-monitoring, as well as with emotional and behavioral self-regulation. A handout of one such strategy, involving the steps of "Goal, Plan, Do, Review," may be found in the Appendix.

5. Consider the development of a notebook of "strategies" to various problems, to which Jim can refer as he performs various tasks. For example, consider written algorithms for various math problems, and prompt Jim to first identify what kind of problem he is facing, to then refer to the algorithm, and finally use the algorithm in a step-by-step fashion to solve the problem. Have him check his work with a calculator. In writing, prompt him to develop an outline/plan for his work, which he then expands and integrates. By laminating such procedures and keeping them in a binder, Jim will have "reference" materials to help him solve problems as they come up, until such procedures are well established in his memory.

6. Provide Jim with specific training in activities to improve his short-term memory. A handout of strategies is provided in the Appendix; however, Jim will need to actively work to use these techniques in daily life. Jim would also benefit from a computer-based program designed to enhance short-term and working memory skills, entitled Cogmed Working Memory Training. Additional information about this program is available at www.cogmed.com.

7. Jim's difficulties with writing and motor skills suggest that he will need to develop keyboarding/typing skills in the very near future. Jim's reluctance to engage in written work may be bypassed if he were to feel more confident about getting his thoughts out, first, and then neatly written, second. Jim may learn best through an interactive computer software program such as "Type to Learn."

8. Consider providing Jim with a hand-held recorder into which he can verbally express his ideas, and then they can be transcribed. Also consider voice-recognition software, such as Dragon Naturally Speaking, to assist him with expressing his ideas while bypassing the necessity of writing. Indeed, Jim will fare best if all activities are approached from a verbal perspective, as opposed to visual, and from parts to whole rather than the converse. Although it will be important to provide Jim with the overall concept of a given task, he will need lots of practice with moving from details to the larger concept, and experience with variations on how a concept may be manifested.

9. Provide Jim with active social skills education and training that focuses upon helping him to understand sequences of interaction, and the relationships of verbal and nonverbal communication. Help him to develop "scripts" to follow in initiating contact with peers, and consider emphasizing the development of one or two close relationships rather than with larger groups.

10. Teach Jim specific stress-management skills and strategies. Many children with Jim's profile of cognitive skills often develop significant anxiety and depression as they enter adolescence, due to their uncertainty regarding subtle aspects of nonverbal communication. Jim would benefit from learning how to use deep breathing and progressive muscle relaxation to reduce his levels of tension, and how to use positive self-statements and affirmations to prevent the development of irrational thinking patterns. A focused program of cognitive behavioral therapy is recommended.

11. Personnel at Jim's school need to appreciate that his nonverbal learning disability may cause him to have trouble with the initiation and completion of assigned tasks, which is not the result of oppositional or defiant behavior. Indeed, Jim's challenges with task initiation are a specific manifestation of his educational disability, and he should never be disciplined or sent to detention for this behavior. Alternatively, Jim should be encouraged to ask for help when needed, and school personnel should prompt him/ask him if it is apparent that Jim is having difficulties with task initiation/completion.

Thank you for the opportunity to perform this evaluation.

TEST SCORES

> **Note:**
>
> These scores are provided for professional use only, by persons trained in psychological test theory, development, administration, scoring, and interpretation. A significant risk of misinterpretation of these scores exists. Please refer to the body of the report for interpretive information. If you have any questions about these scores, please speak with your psychologist.

Wechsler Intelligence Scale for Children-Fourth Edition

Scale/Subtest	SS	1	2	3	4	5	6	7	8	9	10	11	12	13	14	15	16	17	18	19
Full Scale	65			x																
Verbal Comprehension	75					x														
Similarities	6						x													
Vocabulary	5					x														
Picture Vocab Mult. Choice	6						x													
Comprehension	6						x													
Information	10										x									
Word Reasoning	6						x													
Perceptual Reasoning	59		x																	
Block Design	3			x																
Block Design Mult. Choice	6						x													
Picture Concepts	4				x															
Matrix Reasoning	3			x																
Picture Completion	3			x																
Working Memory	80						x													
Digit Span	6						x													
Digit Span Forward	7							x												
Digit Span Backward	5					x														
Letter-Number Sequencing	7							x												
Arithmetic	11												x							
Spatial Span Forward	5					x														
Spatial Span Backwards	1	x																		
Processing Speed	75					x														
Coding	4				x															
Symbol Search	7							x												
Cancellation	5					x														
Cancellation Random	5					x														
Cancellation Structured	6						x													

Peabody Picture Vocabulary Test-Fourth Edition

Scale/Subtest	SS/T	1	2	3	4	5	6	7	8	9	10	11	12	13	14	15	16	17	18	19
Receptive Vocabulary	94									x										

Kent Visual Perception Test

Scale/Subtest	SS/T	1	2	3	4	5	6	7	8	9	10	11	12	13	14	15	16	17	18	19
Discrimination	55	x																		
Copying	<60		<																	
Memory	66				x															

Test of Problem Solving-Third Edition

Scale/Subtest	SS/T	1	2	3	4	5	6	7	8	9	10	11	12	13	14	15	16	17	18	19
Making Inferences	63			x																
Sequencing	63			x																
Negative Questions	64			x																
Problem Solving	74				x															
Predicting	63			x																
Determining Causes	78					x														
Total Test	61			x																

Grooved Pegboard Test

Hand	time	1	2	3	4	5	6	7	8	9	10	11	12	13	14	15	16	17	18	19
Dominant	147	<<																		
Nondominant	135	<<																		

Wechsler Individual Achievement Test-Third Edition

Scale/Subtest	SS	1	2	3	4	5	6	7	8	9	10	11	12	13	14	15	16	17	18	19
Word Reading	99										x									
Reading Comprehension	74				x															
Pseudoword Decoding	116													x						
Numerical Operations	78						x													
Math Problem Solving	82							x												
Spelling	104											x								
Math Fluency-Addition	83							x												
Math Fluency-Subtraction	77						x													
Math Fluency-Multiplication	73					x														
Sentence Composition	86								x											
Essay Composition	88								x											

Adaptive Behavior Assessment System-Second Edition

Composite/Skill Area	SS	1	2	3	4	5	6	7	8	9	10	11	12	13	14	15	16	17	18	19
General Adaptive Composite	56		x																	
Conceptual	63			x																
Communication	3			x																
Functional Academics	5					x														
Self-Direction	2		x																	
Social	58		x																	
Leisure	3			x																
Social	1	x																		
Practical	50	<																		
– Community Use	2		x																	
– Home Living	1	x																		
– Health and Safety	6						x													
– Self-Care	2		x																	

REFERENCE

Rourke, B. (1995). Introduction: The NLD syndrome and white matter model. In B. P. Rourke, (Ed.), *Syndrome of nonverbal learning disabilities* (pp. 1–26). New York: Guilford Press.

CASE 40

Actively Involving an Adolescent in the Evaluation Process from Intake to Feedback

Promoting Positive Outcomes

Elizabeth Lichtenberger and Nadeen Kaufman

Mikaela McCarter is one of those young, well-behaved, female adolescents who has managed to progress through the school system without receiving enough academic support to provide the foundation necessary to succeed in high school. Her elementary schoolwork fell between "below average" and "average." Her parents have hired tutors for Mikaela since second grade, mostly with the goal of helping her get her homework done. When one of Mikaela's eighth-grade teachers casually mentioned to Mrs. McCarter that "maybe Mikaela has an attention disorder, because she seems to have such trouble focusing in class …," Mrs. McCarter followed through with a private assessment to see if that were true; it made sense to the whole family.

Because Mikaela was initially reluctant to come for the evaluation, having little hope that anything would change, the examiners made particular effort to keep her feeling involved, and in some control of what was described as "a joint partnership" to find meaningful help for her long school days. To maintain rapport at its highest level, the examiners believe it is essential to provide adolescents with separate intake interviews, separate feedback conferences, and separate case reports that will communicate best to each individual teenage client. Therefore, two case reports are included for this case, one with full information and recommendations (presented to Mikaela's parents), and one referred to as a "summary" written for Mikaela herself.

An evaluation can only succeed if the right people fully understand the recommendations and participate in translating the complex pages of information into action. With this in mind, the examiners discussed the case report and results with both Mr. and Mrs. McCarter, as well as all of her teachers. In addition to sharing information, the examiners responded to any perceived difficulties or questions that were raised. This personal effort can frequently create a real team who will strive to ensure that Mikaela can achieve her optimal performance for the rest of her high school career.

PSYCHOEDUCATIONAL EVALUATION

Name:	Mikaela McCarter
Date of Birth:	07/27/1995
Ages at Testing:	14-2, 14-4
School:	Pemberley High School Las Pulgas, California
Grade:	9
Dates of Evaluation:	10/01/2009, 10/15/2009, 12/02/2009
Evaluators:	Elizabeth O. Lichtenberger, Ph.D.; Nadeen L. Kaufman, Ed.D.

REASON FOR REFERRAL

Mikaela was referred for a psychoeducational evaluation by her parents, Margaret and Raymond McCarter, in order to determine the cause of Mikaela's academic struggles. Mikaela's parents have sent her to academic tutors on and off since second grade to help strengthen her foundational skills in math and reading. The most recent academic struggles that Mikaela has had, according to Mr. and Mrs.

McCarter and Mikaela, are in the areas of mathematics and "attention." Her sixth- through eighth-grade report cards from Darcy Middle School indicated difficulty in mathematics with letter grades ranging from C to D in pre-algebra and algebra. Mikaela and her parents agreed that she has some difficulty focusing her attention, and Mikaela's eighth-grade teacher suggested that she be assessed for Attention-Deficit/Hyperactivity Disorder (ADHD). As a result of the current evaluation, Mikaela hopes to better "direct her attention" and improve her ability "to learn." Mr. and Mrs. McCarter would like to learn methods for strengthening Mikaela's "building blocks for learning" and address her individual strengths and weaknesses in the academic realm.

BACKGROUND INFORMATION

Mikaela is a 14-year-old Caucasian adolescent female who is a native English speaker. She is the younger of two daughters. Her older sister, Brianna, is a 17-year-old senior in high school. A 17-year-old male friend of Brianna's is also currently residing with the McCarter family. Mr. and Mrs. McCarter have been married for 19 years and have resided in only one house in Las Pulgas, California, throughout Mikaela's lifetime. Both of Mikaela's parents are high school graduates, and both are currently employed full time. Her father is a veterinarian technician and her mother is a hair stylist. Mr. and Mrs. McCarter are the primary caregivers for Mikaela; however, her grandparents have also played a role in caring for Mikaela during her childhood.

Mrs. McCarter indicated that Mikaela was born in a hospital in Las Pulgas after an uncomplicated pregnancy. She stated that she did not use drugs, alcohol, or other medications while pregnant, but she was administered an epidural during her daughter's birth. Mrs. McCarter was in labor for 10 hours with Mikaela; her daughter was born full-term via a normal delivery, weighing 8 pounds, 9 ounces, and she was 20.5 inches in length. Mikaela did not require special medical attention during delivery or during the postnatal period. She was bottle-fed as an infant and weaned at 1 year. According to Mrs. McCarter, Mikaela's developmental milestones were met within the expected time frames.

Mikaela's medical history was also reported to be relatively unremarkable by Mrs. McCarter. Mikaela is in good health, as indicated by her last complete physical exam on 8/21/09. Her vision and hearing are within normal limits, and she has had no serious illnesses or hospitalizations.

The only medical issues reported for Mikaela are asthma symptoms and difficulty sleeping. Both Mrs. McCarter and Mikaela indicated that Mikaela has difficulty falling asleep, usually needs the television on to do so, and wakes up during sleep at least a couple of nights a week. Mikaela and her parents reported that she has a healthy diet, gets regular exercise, and ingests a minimal amount of caffeine (i.e., about two sodas a week). Mikaela's parents stated that she experimented with alcohol in July 2009, but they do not believe that she regularly uses alcohol or drugs. Mr. and Mrs. McCarter admitted that there is a history of alcoholism on both sides of Mikaela's family (paternal grandmother and maternal grandfather).

Mikaela's educational history began at age 3, when she was enrolled in preschool and attended twice a week. Her parents indicated that she responded well to the preschool environment. She attended kindergarten at age 5 and began first grade at Wickham Elementary School in Las Pulgas when she was 6 years old. Throughout her elementary education, Mikaela performed at the average to below average level, according to her report cards and standardized tests administered at school. The results of the Stanford Achievement Test (9th edition), showed that, in second grade, Mikaela was performing at the 2nd percentile in mathematics compared to a national sample of her peers. Her reading ability was at the 18th percentile, and language mechanics and spelling were at the 21st and 43rd percentiles, respectively. The Standardized Testing and Reporting (STAR) Performance Report indicated that in fifth, sixth, and seventh grades, Mikaela's abilities in mathematics continued to be in the "Below Basic" to "Far Below Basic" level (ranging from the 4th to 34th percentile compared to a national sample of her peers). However, her English-Language Arts skills were labeled "Basic" (e.g., Average), ranging from the 6th to 45th percentiles in Reading to the 20th to 23rd percentiles in Language.

Due to her identified difficulties in early elementary school, Mikaela was referred for a psychoeducational evaluation by her third-grade teacher, Mrs. Spiking, and the Student Study Team at Wickham Elementary School. The main concerns at the time of the referral for an evaluation were "math, writing, spelling, and dependence on an adult for one-on-one instruction." At the time of her evaluation in third grade, Mikaela was receiving help twice weekly from reading specialist Karen Larson, and was receiving hour-long tutoring sessions from Grace Quinley twice a week after school. Results of the psychoeducational evaluation conducted by the Las Pulgas Unified School District revealed that Mikaela did not meet the criteria for a Specific

Learning Disability and was therefore not eligible for special education services. However, the evaluation did reveal that her nonverbal reasoning ability and her visual-spatial abilities were in the Below Average range (on the Differential Abilities Scale and the Developmental Test of Visual Motor Integration). In contrast, the evaluation indicated that her academic abilities were in the Average range across all domains (on the Wechsler Individual Achievement Test and the Woodcock-Johnson III Tests of Achievement). Although Mikaela's psychoeducational evaluation in third grade indicated that her academic skills were within normal limits, her difficulties in mathematics continued and became more pronounced in sixth through eighth grade, when she attended Darcy Middle School. She received grades of C in sixth-grade math, D in seventh-grade Pre-Algebra, and D in eighth-grade Algebra. Mikaela's middle school report cards also indicated that she had more difficulty in science than in language arts and social studies, as she earned a C in seventh-grade Life Science and a C– in eighth-grade science. Her teachers commented that her low grades stemmed from missing and late assignments, as well as low test scores. Her stronger academic abilities were evident, however, in social studies and language arts where she earned Bs. Mikaela's middle school teachers indicated that she was a "pleasure to have in class," "she consistently participates," and she "has a good attitude."

At the end of eighth grade, one of Mikaela's teachers suggested that she obtain an evaluation for Attention-Deficit/Hyperactivity Disorder (ADHD). Thus, Mr. and Mrs. McCarter took Mikaela to the Las Pulgas Education and Learning Centers, where Hannah Lewis, Ph.D., administered a battery of tests to screen her for ADHD on June 27, 2009. In her summary of Mikaela's test results, Dr. Lewis concluded that Mikaela's abilities to shift her attention and maintain cognitive flexibility were in the Low Average to Average range. Her ability to take in, retain, and mentally manipulate information for brief periods of time was Below Average, and was suggestive of difficulty with working memory. Dr. Lewis's report indicated that Mikaela also has "mild difficulty" with her long-term memory. In addition, her performance on a computerized test of attention and impulsivity was "suggestive of an ADHD profile." Overall, Dr. Lewis concluded that the June 2009 evaluation "provides evidence of problems related to inattention and impulsivity."

Mikaela began attending ninth grade at Pemberley High School in September 2009. Her current course load includes the following academic subjects: English, Math, and Spanish. Mikaela also participates in the Advancement Via Individual Determination (AVID), an in-school academic support program. The AVID program is designed for students in grades 5 through 12 to prepare them for college eligibility and success. According to the AVID web site (www.avidonline.org), the program "places academically average students in advanced classes, and thereby levels the playing field for minority, rural, low-income, and other students without a college-going tradition in their families." Mikaela indicated that she liked her teacher for the AVID program, but she has had some difficulty getting her assignments in on time. She reported that she is currently having the most difficulty in Spanish, and is doing better in math this year than she did last year. She attributed this change in her math performance to the difference in teaching styles between this year's instructor and last year's.

Mikaela and her parents stated that Mikaela has always been "slower than other kids" in completing her schoolwork. She indicated that she sometimes spends from 4 to 7 hours on her homework, but has the television or music on during that period. On tests in school, she reported that she "goes blank" in Spanish or math, even if she has studied. Although she has received tutoring since second grade, neither Mikaela or her parents feel that it has helped her improve her academic skills tremendously. However, Mikaela stated that she is "fine with asking for help," and will often ask teachers for clarification, if necessary.

Mikaela and her parents both agree that she has strengths in the social realm. According to her parents, Mikaela has a good sense of humor, and is caring and sensitive. Mikaela indicated that she enjoys spending time with her friends, and she has a close-knit group of four "best friends." When asked about her strengths, she indicated that she is "hard-working" and that she will always "follow through."

BEHAVIORAL CHARACTERISTICS

Mikaela is an attractive, slim 14-year-old adolescent girl who has long blonde hair, which was fashionably styled. She was dressed casually and appropriately for each of the evaluation sessions. Rapport was easily established with Mikaela. She was friendly and openly responded to questions, although she did not offer much spontaneous conversation. During conversation, Mikaela's speech was clear and understandable, with no articulation difficulties. However, her spontaneous speech did include occasional grammatical errors, such as, "I could have went right here."

Mikaela was cooperative and motivated to put forth her best effort during the evaluation. Although many of the testing sessions lasted longer than 2 hours, Mikaela often refused breaks, and instead preferred to continue with the testing. She was motivated to work quickly when she knew she was being timed. For example, on timed tasks of modeling designs with triangles and of counting blocks, Mikaela worked rapidly through each task, but not in an impulsive manner. She commented positively after the timed tasks that she "likes working on puzzles" with her grandmother.

Mikaela's stamina to complete the testing was matched by her ability to maintain focused attention during the sessions. Although she had described herself as having difficulty with attention, she consistently maintained her focus during the tasks presented to her. Only during transitions between tasks did Mikaela look around the room and away from the testing materials and examiner. However, when tasks demanded increased attention or became more difficult for Mikaela, she exhibited more nervous energy. For example, she would shake her knees, chew on her rubber bracelet, or roll her bracelet on her leg. These small motor movements did not, however, detract from her ability to complete the tasks at hand.

Mikaela exhibited signs of anxiety and a lack of confidence on certain types of tasks. In addition to describing herself as having trouble with attention, Mikaela conveyed during the clinical interview that she has trouble in math. Thus, during mathematics tasks, Mikaela's anxiety and lack of confidence were evident with comments like, "Oh … fractions!" and with behaviors such as frowning with concentration. On a task that required her to remember a name that was paired with a picture of a fish, plant, or shell, Mikaela put her finger to her mouth and said, "I'm not good with names." Despite her uncertainty about her own skills, Mikaela persisted through all the tasks presented, even those that were quite challenging for her.

Mikaela frequently needed clarifications or repetitions of orally presented directions. Although she appeared to hear the directions adequately and would start the task, she seemed unsure of what to do. For example, on a task that required her to move a toy dog on a checkerboard-like grid to find the shortest route to the dog's bone, Mikaela was slow to understand the directions and had more difficulty than others her age understanding the nature of the task. This pattern of not understanding the directions was also noted on a memory task, which required the directions to be repeated to Mikaela. When mathematics problems were presented orally to her, Mikaela asked often for them to be repeated. Her frequent requests for repetition and clarification were indicative of the fact that tasks seemed to hold more ambiguity for Mikaela than the typical adolescent.

During challenging tasks, Mikaela implemented some compensatory strategies to try to solve the problem. For example, when working on mathematics problems, she counted on the fingers of her left hand while writing with her right hand. When working on building a model with triangles to match one shown on paper, she asked if she could hold up the triangles to the paper model for assistance. Her strategy for writing an essay involved writing, rereading her product to proof it, and then adding some words (with lines extending into the margin to show where they should be inserted). On a few tasks, she caught her own mistakes and then corrected herself.

Overall, Mikaela demonstrated a consistent level of motivation, effort, and focus during the examination sessions. Thus, the current results are thought to give a reliable and valid picture of Mikaela's current level of cognitive and academic functioning.

ASSESSMENT PROCEDURES

Clinical interview with Mr. and Mrs. McCarter

Clinical interview with Mikaela McCarter

Kaufman Assessment Battery for Children, Second Edition (KABC-II)

Kaufman Test of Educational Achievement, Second Edition (KTEA-II), Comprehensive Form A

Woodcock-Johnson – III NU Tests of Cognitive Ability (WJ III COG): Select tests

Woodcock-Johnson – III NU Tests of Achievement (WJ III ACH): Select tests

TEST RESULTS AND INTERPRETATION

Cognitive Abilities

Mikaela was administered the Kaufman Assessment Battery for Children-Second Edition (KABC-II) in order to obtain a comprehensive picture of her mental processing and cognitive abilities. The KABC-II is based on a double theoretical foundation, Luria's neuropsychological model and the Cattell-Horn-Carroll (CHC) psychometric theory. It offers five scales, each given a label that reflects both theoretical models: Sequential/Gsm, Simultaneous/Gv,

Learning/Glr, Planning/Gf, and Knowledge/Gc. (From the perspective of CHC theory: Gsm = short-term memory, Gv = visual processing, Glr = long-term storage and retrieval, Gf = fluid reasoning, and Gc = crystallized ability.)

Examiners are given the option of either selecting the Luria model or the CHC model of the KABC-II, based on the client's background and reason for referral. (Knowledge/Gc is excluded from the Luria model because measures of language ability and acquired knowledge may not provide fair assessment of some children's cognitive abilities, such as those who are from bilingual or non-mainstream backgrounds). Because English is the primary language spoken in Mikaela's home, and because she was referred for an assessment of learning problems, it is appropriate to use the CHC model of the KABC-II. The CHC model yields the Fluid Crystallized Index (FCI) as the global measure of general cognitive ability.

Mikaela's overall cognitive abilities were in the Average to Below Average range of intellectual functioning. With 90% confidence, her "true" FCI standard score is in the range from 83–91. She earned a KABC-II FCI of 87, ranking her overall cognitive processing abilities at the 19th percentile compared to other 14-year-olds. This score meaningfully represents her overall cognitive abilities because she performed consistently across the five cognitive domains assessed with the KABC-II.

Mikaela's short-term memory was in the Average range of functioning compared to that of her peers. This ability was evident from her standard score of 100 (50th percentile; 90% confidence interval of 92–108) on the Sequential/Gsm Index of the KABC-II. The tasks on the Sequential/Gsm scale required Mikaela to take in and hold information and then use it within a few seconds. Although Mikaela performed in the Average range of functioning and is Within Normal Limits, she appeared to become more anxious as the attention demands increased throughout the memory tasks. For example, on one task, the examiner said the names of a series of common objects and then Mikaela was asked to touch silhouettes of these objects in the same order as the examiner said the names. As the items increased in difficulty, an interference task (color naming) was introduced between the stimulus and response. When the interference task was introduced (and more concentration was necessary), Mikaela began to visibly shake her legs more. Because the interference task prevented her from mentally rehearsing the stimuli she had to remember, she appeared to have difficulty encoding the items. On other memory tasks, both visual and verbal, she exhibited similar signs of anxiety and effort as the difficulty of the tasks increased. However, throughout all of the memory

tasks, she persisted to the best of her ability, and ultimately her short-term memory proved to be a personal relative strength compared to her other cognitive abilities.

Mikaela's ability to actively process and manipulate information in memory (i.e., her working memory) was also assessed. The Working Memory tests from the Woodcock Johnson – Third Edition Tests of Cognitive Ability (WJ III COG) were administered to Mikaela. One working memory task required Mikaela to repeat lists of numbers in reverse order, and another task required her to listen to an unrelated series of digits and words, and then repeat the words followed by the numbers in the order in which they were presented. Like her short-term memory, her working memory was in the Average range, albeit in the low end of that range. She earned a standard score of 85 (16th percentile) on the WJ III COG Working Memory cluster. When the confidence interval is considered, her "true score" ranged from 78–92 with 90% confidence, indicating that her working memory abilities may fall in the Below Average to Average range of functioning. This level of ability is consistent with Dr. Lewis's assessment from June 2009 that found Mikaela's ability to take in, retain, and mentally manipulate information for brief time periods was Below Average, and was suggestive of difficulty with working memory. These difficulties in working memory were supported specifically by her Below Average performance on tasks requiring her to repeat digits forward and backward (16th percentile on WISC-IV Digit Span) and to remember a sequence of a series of letters and numbers (2nd percentile on WISC-IV Letter-Number sequencing). Thus, taken together these current and previous testing results are indicative of Mikaela's Below Average working memory skills.

Similar to her Average short-term memory and her Below Average to Average working memory abilities, Mikaela's long-term memory was also in the Average range. She earned a standard score of 89 (23rd percentile) on the Learning/Glr Index of the KABC-II. There is a 90% chance that her "true score" is between 83 and 95. The Learning/Glr Index involves storing and efficiently retrieving newly learned information. On tasks that make up this Index, Mikaela remained focused and attentive. In one of the long-term memory tasks, Mikaela was taught a word or concept associated with a particular symbol, and in another task, Mikaela was taught the nonsense names of a series of pictured fish, shells, and plants. Although Mikaela's anxiety increased somewhat as the memory and demands increased, she continued to maintain focused attention throughout these tasks. Her behavior on this task was in contrast with Mikaela's self-image of having poor attention skills. When required to recall information that she learned much earlier in the testing session, Mikaela also demonstrated abilities within the Average range (Delayed Recall standard score of 97; 42nd percentile). Thus, her ability to attend to and learn new information and recall it at a later time is Within Normal Limits compared to others her age.

Similar to her Average level abilities in short- and long-term memory, Mikaela's visual problem-solving ability and ability to reason out solutions to novel problems were in the Average range. The Simultaneous/Gv Index of the KABC-II required Mikaela to perceive, store, manipulate, and think with visual patterns. On the Simultaneous/Gv Index, she achieved a standard score of 89 (23rd percentile; true score 82–98), which is Within Normal Limits. One task that is part of the Simultaneous/Gv Index required Mikaela to move a toy dog to a bone on a checkerboard-like grid that contained obstacles (rocks and weeds) to find the "quickest" path—the one that takes the fewest moves. On this task, Mikaela often chose a "quick" path but not the "quickest." She typically "tested" the path with her finger, prior to actually moving the toy dog, indicating that she planned ahead, and was not impulsive on the visual and planning tasks. On tasks that required primarily novel problem solving and reasoning, Mikaela's performance was Within Normal Limits. She earned a standard score of 88 (21st percentile) on the Planning/Gf Index of the KABC-II. However, Mikaela's "true" score (79–99) on this Index has a good chance (90%) of falling between the Below Average and Average range of functioning. The Planning/Gf Index involves solving novel problems by using reasoning abilities such as induction and deduction. Mikaela was reflective in her approach to tasks that constituted the Planning/Gf Index. On a task that required her to best complete a story by placing the missing story cards in the correct location, she looked closely at each card before making her choice. Mikaela completed all items of the reasoning tasks in a timely manner but often looked hesitant after the items had been completed.

Mikaela's ability to remember information that she has acquired from her culture and daily experiences was also Within Normal Limits. She demonstrated the depth and breadth of her acquired knowledge on the KABC-II Knowledge/Gc Index, earning a standard score of 87 (19th percentile). However, when considering the confidence interval for her score, her abilities in this area ranged from a standard score of 80 to 94, which spans from the Below Average to Average range of ability (with 90% confidence). Mikaela's level of acquired knowledge is consistent with

her academic performance in school. Her grades in social studies, language arts, and science have been mainly Cs and Bs (although her mathematics grades have been lower). At times Mikaela appeared to have difficulty retrieving the particular word with which she wanted to answer, but she was able to recognize when questions addressed information that she remembered learning about previously. For example, in responding to a history-related question, she said, "like in fifth grade."

Academic Achievement Abilities

Further evidence of Mikaela's competence in acquired knowledge was demonstrated by her performance on the Kaufman Test of Educational Achievement-Second Edition (KTEA-II) Form A. This is a test of academic skills in several areas, including reading, math, oral language, and written language. Overall, on the KTEA-II, Mikaela earned a Comprehensive Achievement Composite (CAC) standard score of 85, which ranks her achievement at the 16th percentile (band of error, with 90% confidence, is 82–88) and corresponds to the Average range. This global score is virtually the same as her global score on the intelligence test, the KABC-II (FCI = 87), indicating that her overall intelligence and achievement are commensurate.

Similar to Mikaela's performance on tasks tapping her cognitive abilities, her skills on many of the academic tests were Within Normal Limits. Specifically, the following academic abilities were within the Average range for Mikaela:

- Reading, including word recognition (47th percentile), comprehension (30th percentile), and fluency (37th percentile—the rapid reading of real and nonsense words)
- Oral Expression (55th percentile—the ability to express one's ideas orally in a sensible, easily understood manner, using appropriate sentence structure, vocabulary, and grammar)
- Written Expression (47th percentile—the ability to express one's ideas in writing in a sensible, readable manner, using appropriate sentence structure, capitalization, punctuation, and grammar)
- Spelling (45th percentile)
- Oral Fluency (34th percentile—the ability to rapidly name words in a given category, such as "animals," and perform other rapid-naming tasks)

In contrast to her Average academic abilities, Mikaela performed at a Below Average level on the following academic areas:

- Mathematics Concepts and Applications (10th percentile—the ability to apply math principles to real-life situations and to understand a range of number concepts)

- Mathematics Computation (14th percentile—the ability to compute solutions to math problems printed in a booklet, assessing the operations of addition, subtraction, multiplication, and division; fractions and decimals; square roots; exponents; signed numbers; and algebra)

- Nonsense Word Decoding (10th percentile—the ability to apply phonics to decode invented "nonsense" words of increasing difficulty)

- Listening Comprehension (5th percentile—the ability to listen to passages on a CD and respond to literal and inferential questions about each passage)

Mikaela's Below Average scores on the two measures of math ability are consistent with the math difficulties she has experienced year after year in school. She performed at about the same level on the tests of Math Concepts and Applications and Math Computation, indicating that she has problems both with her computational skills and with her ability to figure out real-life problems. She also scored at the Below Average level on the reading task of Nonsense Word Decoding, indicating difficulties with the application of phonics. Her standard score of 81 (10th percentile) on this test is substantially lower than her score of 99 (47th percentile) on the Letter and Word Recognition test, indicating that Mikaela has well-developed ability in pronouncing words that she has already learned, but does not have facility in sounding out unfamiliar words. It is notable that even though her math achievement and reading decoding scores are Below Average and qualify as Normative Weaknesses, her standard scores on these tasks ranged from 81 to 84, which are not appreciably lower than her FCI of 87 (19th percentile).

The KTEA-II provides an analysis of a student's errors on each subtest, which helps identify specific areas that are weak relative to her peers and require remediation. Mikaela had considerable difficulty with fractions on both math subtests, as she failed 7 of 12 items attempted (the average ninth grader failed 1 to 3 items). She had special difficulties (1) adding or subtracting the numerator and denominator and (2) identifying equivalent fractions and finding the common denominator. She also had difficulty on the Math Computation subtest with items involving decimals and percents (which required knowledge of decimal place values and how to add, subtract, multiply, and divide decimals); she failed all four items, whereas

the average ninth grader passed all items. On the Math Computation subtest she also had particular difficulty with multiplication items (she failed 5 of 11, average = 0 to 2), and subtraction items, especially subtracting smaller from larger numbers in vertical columns. On Math Concepts and Applications, Mikaela had a weakness on items that involved time or money (e.g., telling time using an analog clock, finding dates on a calendar, using time schedules to find trip times, adding coin values, and making change; she failed four of nine items; average = 0).

Mikaela's lowest KTEA-II standard score was 75 on the test of Listening Comprehension (5th percentile, 90% confidence interval of 66–84). The error analysis indicated that she had special difficulty with items that measure *literal* comprehension (e.g., restating the speaker's intent or purpose, restating characters' actions or emotions, or relating factual information, when such information is specifically stated in the oral communication); she failed 12 of 39 literal items, compared to 3 to 8 for the average ninth grader. These error analyses suggest that she misses the gist of what she hears but is able to use common sense and reasoning to compensate, to some extent, on items that don't require her to recall specific facts.

The format of the Listening Comprehension subtest is similar to the format of Reading Comprehension (both present passages of comparable length and complexity that are followed by literal and inferential questions), permitting a direct comparison of a student's ability to derive meaning from information that is spoken or printed. Mikaela's Reading Comprehension standard score of 92 is significantly higher than her Listening Comprehension standard score of 75, emphasizing her much better ability to understand what she reads than what she hears. Even the error analysis produced different results, as Mikaela was able to perform in the Average range on Reading Comprehension *literal* items (she made 1 error on 26 such items, average = 1 to 2). Thus, when reading (which allows students to reread the passages, as necessary, to check on the facts), Mikaela is able to grasp the basic information as well as other ninth graders, but she is far below her peers when the information is presented orally and she gets only "one shot" at remembering it. But even on Reading Comprehension, Mikaela displayed a weakness relative to other ninth graders on *inferential* items (which require the reader to infer characters' actions, beliefs, and so forth, or the author's intentions, when such information is not directly stated in the passage); she failed 9 of 32 inferential items, where the average is 2 to 5 errors. Thus, Mikaela is able to understand the essence of the material that is printed (unlike material that is spoken), but she is weak, relative to her peers, when she needs to reason out what she has read.

The KTEA-II also provides comparable subtests to contrast a student's ability to express one's ideas via writing versus speaking. Mikaela demonstrated equal ability on the Written Expression and Oral Expression subtests (standard scores of 99 and 102, respectively). Furthermore, these were among Mikaela's best scores on the KTEA-II, ranking her at about the 50th percentile; also, both "Expression" subtests qualify as "relative strengths" for her compared to her overall CAC of 85 on the KTEA-II, denoting areas of integrity to call on when planning remedial activities. Nonetheless, the error analysis for Written Expression indicated one area that still requires attention— Punctuation (she made 14 errors on 22 items that measured her ability to apply the rules of punctuation when copying from dictation, composing new sentences and paragraphs, or editing sentences; average = 6–11 errors).

Overall, as demonstrated by her performance on the two "Comprehension" and two "Expression" subtests, Mikaela is able to express herself both in writing and orally, and to understand what she reads, but she has difficulty understanding what she hears. Her difficulty on Listening Comprehension not only contrasts to her ability to read and express herself in writing and in speech, but it also is in great contrast to her performance on a related skill on the KABC-II, recalling information that she was taught earlier in the testing session. Mikaela demonstrated abilities within the Average range on the KABC-II Delayed Recall tasks (standard score of 97 = 42nd percentile). Thus, her ability to attend to and learn new information and recall it at a later time is Within Normal Limits compared to others her age. So too is her immediate short-term memory for numbers and words (KABC-II Sequential/Gsm standard score = 100 = 50th percentile). However, when Mikaela is required to attend to and remember auditory stimuli that are longer in length, and that provide no chance for repetition (as on the KTEA-II Listening Comprehension subtest), she had much more difficulty. This difficulty was verified by administering a related task, Story Recall, on the WJ III Tests of Achievement. On that test, which required her to listen to stories that contained several details and then repeat as much of the story as she could remember, Mikaela again performed in the Below Average range, earning a standard score of 82 (12th percentile). Two key components were different on the achievement tasks of Listening Comprehension and Story Recall than on the KABC-II short-term and long-term memory tasks on which she scored in the

Average range. Specifically, she shows stronger abilities (and abilities within normal limits) when the stimuli are both auditory and visual, and when the stimuli are not as lengthy. Thus, she appears to benefit from stimuli presented in dual-modalities (verbal-visual) and with stimuli that are broken down into shorter segments.

To determine whether Mikaela's listening comprehension was related to the difficulties she experiences in hearing and remembering longer narratives (or directions), Mikaela was administered further tests from the WJ III Tests of Achievement. The results yielded similar results to what was noted on WJ III ACH Story Recall and KTEA-II Listening Comprehension. Namely, when Mikaela is provided with shorter auditory stimuli (e.g., WJ III ACH Oral Comprehension, which required her to listen to a short passage and supply the missing word using syntactic and semantic cues), she performed in the Average range with a standard score of 107 (69th percentile; 90% confidence interval = 99–115). In addition, when visual and auditory stimuli are relatively brief and paired together, her listening ability is also Within Normal Limits (standard score of 97 = 42nd percentile on WJ III ACH Understanding Directions).

Because of Mikaela's relative difficulty in the area of listening to and comprehending material presented in a long narrative fashion, her auditory processing abilities were assessed with the Auditory Processing cluster from the WJ III COG. Mikaela's auditory and attention skills were consistently in the Average range of functioning (Auditory Processing Composite standard score of 105 = 63rd percentile; 90% confidence interval of 96–114). One of the tasks that tapped her ability to process information auditorally required her to overcome the effects of auditory distortion in understanding oral language (i.e., she had to select which picture in a row was the one indicated by an audio recording while being distracted by background noise). Another auditory processing task required Mikaela to listen to a series of syllables or phonemes and then blend the sounds into a word. Mikaela had no problem maintaining a high level of focused attention throughout the auditory processing tasks.

SUMMARY AND DIAGNOSTIC IMPRESSIONS

Mikaela McCarter was referred by her parents for a psychoeducational evaluation to determine the cause of her academic difficulties that she has experienced in the areas of mathematics and "attention." Both the standardized group-administered tests at school and her academic grades have consistently indicated that she has struggled with mathematics from second to eighth grade. She is currently a 14-year-old ninth grader who has received remedial instruction in the form of tutoring on and off since third grade. Her history included a comprehensive psychoeducational assessment in third grade, which revealed that Mikaela did not meet the criteria for a learning disability (at that time, to diagnose a learning disability, her school district required a significantly large discrepancy between overall IQ and achievement). A brief assessment screening for the presence of ADHD at the end of eighth grade revealed that Mikaela had "problems related to inattention and working memory."

The results of the current assessment indicate Mikaela has specific cognitive processing deficits within the context of an otherwise Average-level cognitive profile. In fact, most of Mikaela's cognitive abilities are within normal limits. Specifically, the KABC-II and WJ III COG revealed that she has skills in the Average range of ability in the domains of short-term memory (50th percentile), visual processing (23rd percentile), novel problem solving (21st percentile), long-term memory (23rd percentile), acquired knowledge (19th percentile), and auditory processing (63rd percentile). Consistent with these intact areas of cognitive functioning are certain academic skills for Mikaela. In particular, she has Average-level abilities in recognizing words, reading comprehension, reading fluency, written and oral expression, spelling, and oral fluency. Her performance on KTEA-II tests tapping these domains showed these skills to range from the 30th to 55th percentiles.

In contrast to these cognitive abilities and academic skills that are within normal limits, Mikaela has specific cognitive and academic deficits that are consistent with her past patterns of performance. The WJ III COG (and previous WISC-IV) findings revealed that she has clear weaknesses in her working memory ability (4th to 16th percentile). This means that Mikaela has Below Average abilities to actively process and manipulate information in her memory. She also has a deficit in the domain of listening comprehension (5th percentile). Both tasks of working memory and listening comprehension demand active processing of auditory information, and Mikaela shows increased difficulty as the amount of information increases. Academically, she shows Below Average performance in mathematics computation (14th percentile), as well as mathematics applications (10th percentile), which

is completely consistent with her reported grades at school, and her belief that math is difficult for her.

It is likely that Mikaela's processing deficit in working memory is directly related to her deficit in mathematics, which is exacerbated by her poor listening comprehension. Often children with deficits in working memory struggle on tasks of mathematics. This consistency between her cognitive deficit, working memory, and her academic deficits in mathematics computation and application warrants a diagnosis of Mathematics Disability. Although Mikaela has received tutoring that included oral drill of mathematical facts (with no visual teaching aids), and lengthy oral description of how to solve mathematics problems, these methods of remediation have been unsuccessful due to her impaired listening comprehension ability and working memory deficits. The results of the current assessment revealed that Mikaela shows stronger abilities when two conditions are met: (1) stimuli are presented in dual modalities (i.e., both verbally and visually), and (2) stimuli are brief, not lengthy.

An additional area of difficulty for Mikaela academically is her ability to apply phonics to decode unfamiliar words (10th percentile). Although Mikaela does not have related difficulties in her ability to read whole words or to comprehend the meaning of text, her deficit in applying phonics to decode unfamiliar words may hamper her ability to learn new vocabulary and acquire knowledge of new concepts. Thus, she will benefit from remediation that will work on improving her phonics skills.

In addition to the referral concerns about her poor mathematics skills, her "attention" was another area of concern. During the current evaluation, Mikaela's behaviors indicated that she was motivated and cooperative. She consistently maintained focused attention but frequently needed clarifications or repetitions of orally presented directions (due to her listening comprehension deficits). Mikaela exhibited minor signs of anxiety and a lack of confidence for tasks related to mathematics and that required increased levels of attention. However, her behavior observed during the assessment sessions and her behaviors described in her academic and family history were inconsistent with symptoms of Attention-Deficit/Hyperactivity Disorder. She is not impulsive or inattentive, but she does have specific deficits in the area of working memory and listening comprehension.

Mikaela has sources of self-compensation that have helped her offset her areas of deficit. She has surrounded herself with a group of four best friends, which is a large enough group to always have at least one person to ask questions to (questions about what was just said, what was expected in class, namely, all the ambiguous areas of auditory information that Mikaela has trouble processing herself). The deficiencies in her working memory are also aided by this group, who accept Mikaela's needs and act nurturing and protective of her. No doubt the extended social group will transfer to a productive older adolescent style of "being" throughout high school and beyond.

RECOMMENDATIONS

Mathematics: School Interventions

1. Use interactive computer programs to keep Mikaela alert and motivated. Such interactive computer programs present information in visual-verbal modalities through the use of images, graphs, and animation, along with auditory information. Immediate feedback will promote new learning, in small steps, and provide for regular monitoring of progress. The visuals are especially important for abstract conceptual learning for Mikaela, such as those math concepts like fractions that she doesn't seem to internalize. One such software program that her teacher could consider to help Mikaela become more fluent in basic facts is FASTT Math™. More information can be found at http://www.tomsnyder.com/products/product.asp?SKU=FASFAS&Subject=Math.

2. Math calculation is a complex activity that involves recalling basic math facts, following procedures, working carefully, and checking one's work. Math calculation requires a careful (i.e., planful) approach to follow all of the necessary steps. For someone like Mikaela, who has trouble with math calculation, a technique that will help her approach the task planfully is likely to be useful.

Planning facilitation is a technique in which the teacher provides math problems for a group of students and, after they work on them, guides a discussion of the strategies they used, their effectiveness, and what they might do differently the next time. The teacher's role is as a facilitator, asking questions and guiding the discussion without offering suggestions. The discussion encourages students to be more reflective in their approach to problems. The teacher then provides a new set of problems to allow the students to experience working with a more thoughtful approach.

Information about how to implement the Planning Facilitation technique can be found in Planning Facilitation for Math Calculation, in *Helping Children Learn: Intervention Handouts for Use in School and at Home, Second Edition*. by Naglieri & Pickering (2010).

3. To help solidify Mikaela's knowledge of and fluency of basic math facts that are necessary for higher-level mathematics, she would benefit from being a peer tutor to someone in middle school who is struggling in math. The time she spends as a peer tutor should focus on fun math activities. Examples of such activities include board games like Equate, Flip 4, or Tally Rally (available at www.mindware.com).

Mathematics: Home Interventions

Practice new math skills with meaningful assignments, like recipes for the math skills that can be incorporated this way. A cooking assignment for homework will be appreciated by this family for whom elaborate dinners are a frequent party effort. Geometric concepts might be worked into gingerbread house or other structural edifices. Several other basic math skills can be practiced in a real-life setting also. Her documented errors with reading time, money, schedules, etc., can be worked into the planning and then the execution of a fun trip.

Listening Comprehension and Working Memory: School Intervention

1. Present all types of verbal information accompanied by visual stimuli that clearly illustrate the concept being taught. For example, use pictures, charts, graphs, semantic maps, and videotapes. Simultaneous visual-verbal presentation is necessary for Mikaela's comprehension and retention.

2. Mikaela should bring a digital voice recorder to class to record teachers' verbal directions and longer orally-presented lectures. Then, when necessary, she can play back the directions for clarification or transcribe the directions/lecture into written format.

3. Mikaela is more likely to remember the content of a lecture if she can devote her full attention to listening rather than dividing her attention between listening and note taking. To this end, provide her with a copy of the lecture notes or a copy of the notes of a student who is a particularly good note taker.

Listening Comprehension: Medical Intervention

To rule out the possibility that a subtle deficit in Mikaela's hearing is affecting her listening comprehension, a comprehensive audiological exam is recommended.

Homework

1. To get Mikaela to start internalizing a faster pace for schoolwork efforts, some assignments should be monitored for time. We saw her awareness of the stopwatch as a mechanism that led her to work faster. Some subjects on which she tends to work most slowly can be given a time limit, and whatever is finished by then is all that she is allowed to do that night in the specific subject. Her teachers can be more lenient at first with penalties, but she will not have missing or late assignments anymore, and she will eventually learn to pick up speed. Her homework hours should not be left open-ended anymore.

2. Mikaela has a good relationship with her grandparents, and she spends time with her grandmother on a regular basis. Perhaps her grandmother and she can read a novel out loud to each other, alternating chapters, so Mikaela will have practice with listening comprehension in an organized, socially reinforcing, "safe from criticism or judgment" format.

3. Vocabulary acquisition needs to be strengthened through homework, partly because Mikaela is not reading enough to acquire a broader fund of word knowledge on her own, and partly because her poor phonics skills prevent her from sounding out unlearned words easily. Computer programs designed for this purpose, as well as interactive games with her grandmother, may be beneficial.

Anxiety and Self-Concept Interventions

1. Mikaela's self-concept has been recently shaped to believe that she has ADHD. It may be more acceptable to appear distracted and unfocused than to have subtle, undiagnosed learning difficulties. Attempts to document the ADHD diagnosis have delayed a more productive problem-solving approach, and now a real set of strengths and weaknesses should be communicated to Mikaela so that she can keep on doing what's been right for her, helping her to compensate, but reduce the anxiety that comes into play when her working memory or listening comprehension are in high demand.

2. When Mikaela experiences anxiety (e.g., during tasks that call on her to function in her areas of weakness), she calms herself by increasing her motor activity. Thus, it would be worthwhile to plan such motor intervention as breaks during her lengthier homework sessions. This release of tension will aid her to keep focused on the uncomfortable tasks. These physical movement interventions may also help with Mikaela's sleep difficulties.

RESOURCES

Good starting points for mathematics intervention can be found at www.mathgoodies.com, www.sitesforteachers.com, and www.mathprojects.com, and in the following resources.

Kirby, J., & Williams, N. (1991). *Learning problems: A cognitive approach.* Toronto: Kagan & Woo Limited.

Naglieri, J. A. (1999). *Essentials of CAS assessment.* New York: John Wiley & Sons.

Naglieri, J. A., & Gottling, S. H. (1997). Mathematics instruction and PASS cognitive processes: An intervention study. *Journal of Learning Disabilities, 30,* 513–520.

Naglieri, J. A., & Johnson, D. (2000). Effectiveness of a cognitive strategy intervention to improve math calculation based on the PASS theory. *Journal of Learning Disabilities, 33,* 591–597.

Naglieri, J. A., & Pickering, E. B. (2010). Planning facilitation for math calculation. *Helping children learn: Intervention handouts for use in school and at home, Second Edition* Baltimore, MD: Paul H. Brookes Publishing.

Pressley, M., & Woloshyn, V. (1995). *Cognitive strategy instruction that really improves children's academic performance.* Cambridge, MA: Brookline Books.

PSYCHOMETRIC SUMMARY OF CURRENT TEST RESULTS

Age at test: 14 years, 2 months   Grade 9

Kaufman Assessment Battery for Children, Second Edition (KABC-II)

	Standard Score	Percentile Rank	90% Confidence Interval	Descriptive Category*
SEQUENTIAL/ *Gsm*	100	50	92–108	Average/ WNL
Number Recall	10	50		
Word Order	10	50		
(Hand Movements)	8	25		

(Continued)

	Standard Score	Percentile Rank	90% Confidence Interval	Descriptive Category *
SIMULTANEOUS/ *Gv*	89	23	82–98	Average/ WNL
Rover	8	25		
Triangles	7	16		
Block Counting	8	25		
(Gestalt Closure)	8	25		
LEARNING/*Glr*	89	23	83–95	Average/ WNL
Atlantis	9	37		
Rebus	7	16		
DELAYED RECALL	97	42		Average/ WNL
Atlantis Delayed	10	50		
Rebus Delayed	9	37		
PLANNING/*Gf*	88	21	79–99	Average/ WNL
Story Completion	9	37		
Pattern Reasoning	7	16		
KNOWLEDGE/*Gc*	87	19	80–94	Average/ WNL
Verbal Knowledge	8	25		
Riddles	7	16		
Expressive Vocabulary	7	16		
FLUID CRYSTALLIZED INDEX (FCI)	87	19	83–91	Average/ WNL

* WNL – Within Normal Limits

Woodcock Johnson – III NU Tests of Cognitive Ability (WJ III COG)

COMPOSITE Subtest	Score	Percentile Rank	90% Confidence Interval	Descriptive Category
AUDITORY PROCESSING (*Ga*)	105	63	96–114	Average/ WNL
Sound Blending	101	53	93–109	
Auditory Attention	110	75	96–124	
WORKING MEMORY	85	15	78–92	Average/ WNL
Numbers Reversed	86	17	77–94	
Auditory Working Memory	90	26	84–97	

*WNL – Within Normal Limits

Woodcock Johnson – III NU Tests of Achievement (WJ III ACH)

COMPOSITE Subtest	Score	Percentile Rank	90% Confidence Interval	Descriptive Category
ORAL LANGUAGE	91	28	84–98	Average / WNL
Story Recall	82	12	73–91	
Story Recall Delayed	93	32	–	
LISTENING COMPREHENSION	104	60	78–92	Average/ WNL
Oral Comprehension	107	69	99–115	
Understanding Directions	97	42	89–105	

* WNL – Within Normal Limits

Kaufman Test of Educational Achievement, Second Edition (KTEA-II) Comprehensive Form (Form A)

SCALE Subtest	Standard Score	Percentile Rank	90% Confidence Interval	Descriptive Category
Reading Composite	**95**	**16**	**90–100**	Average / WNL
Letter & Word Recognition*	99	47	95–103	
Reading Comprehension*	92	30	85–99	
Decoding Composite	**90**	**25**	**86–94**	Average / WNL
Letter & Word Recognition*	99	47	95–103	
Nonsense Word Decoding	81	10	75–87	
Reading Fluency Composite	**95**	**37**	**88–102**	Average / WNL
Word Recognition Fluency	89	23	79–99	
Decoding Fluency	103	58	95–111	
Mathematics Composite	**81**	**10**	**77–85**	Below Average/ Normative Weakness
Mathematics Concepts &Applications*	81	10	75–87	
Mathematics Computation*	84	14	79–89	

SCALE Subtest	Standard Score	Percentile Rank	90% Confidence Interval	Descriptive Category
Oral Language Composite	**86**	**18**	**78–94**	Average / WNL
Listening Comprehension*	75	5	66–84	
Oral Expression	102	55	90–114	
Oral Fluency Composite	**94**	**34**	**85–103**	Average / WNL
Associational Fluency	89	23	75–103	
Naming Facility/ RAN	103	58	95–111	
Written Language Composite	**98**	**45**	**92–104**	Average / WNL
Written Expression*	99	47	91–107	
Spelling	98	45	91–105	
Comprehensive Achievement Composite	**85**	**16**	**82–88**	Average / WNL

* WNL – Within Normal Limits
  Note: Subtests followed by an asterisk (*) are included in the
  Comprehensive Achievement Composite.

Wisconsin Card Sorting Test (WCST)

	Raw Score	T Score (mean = 50 SD = 10)	Percentile Rank
Trials Administered	**128**	–	–
Total Correct	**75**	–	–
Total Errors	53	39	13
% Errors	41	39	14
Perseverative Responses	32	39	13
% Perseverative Responses	25	39	14
Perseverative Errors	30	37	10
% Perseverative Errors	23	38	12
Non Perseverative Errors	23	42	21
% Non Perseverative Errors	18	43	23
Categories Completed	4	–	>16
Trials to Complete 1st Category	11	–	>16
Failure to Maintain Set	1	–	>16
Learning to Learn	–8.56	–	>16

PSYCHOMETRIC SUMMARY OF PREVIOUS TEST RESULTS

Age at Test: 13 years, 11 months   Grade 8

Wechsler Intelligence Scale for Children- Fourth Edition (WISC-IV)

SCALE Subtest	Standard Score	Percentile Rank	Descriptive Category
Working Memory Index	**74**	**4**	**Below Average/ Normative Weakness**
Digit Span	7	16	
Letter-Number Sequencing	4	2	

Conners' Continuous Performance Test-II (CPT-II)

	Value	T Score (mean = 50 SD = 10)	Description
Clinical Confidence Index *(likelihood overall performance is associated with ADHD)*	**57.4**	–	–
Omissions	25	65.16	Markedly Atypical
Commissions	27	61.44	Mildly Atypical
Hit Rate	350.6	39.55	A little Fast

REPORT FOR STUDENT

SUMMARY OF PSYCHOEDUCATIONAL EVALUATION

Name:	Mikaela McCarter
Date of Birth:	07/27/1995
Ages at Test:	14-2, 14-4
School:	Pemberley High School Las Pulgas, California
Grade:	9
Dates of Evaluation:	10/01/2009, 0/15/2009, 12/02/2009
Examiners:	Elizabeth O. Lichtenberger, Ph.D.; Nadeen L. Kaufman, Ed.D.

REFERRAL AND BACKGROUND

Mikaela, you came in for an assessment so we could help you determine the cause of the academic difficulties that you have experienced in the areas of mathematics and attention. Since second grade, your grades and scores on group tests at school have consistently indicated that you have struggled with mathematics. Although you have been receiving tutoring on and off since third grade, you feel that you are still struggling in school. When you were in third grade you completed an assessment that concluded you did not meet the criteria for a learning disability. However, at that time, to diagnose a learning disability, your school district's criteria required a "significant discrepancy between overall IQ and achievement." Later, at the end of eighth grade, a brief assessment revealed that you had "problems related to both inattention and working memory."

SUMMARY OF TEST RESULTS: COGNITIVE AND ACADEMIC

Intact Abilities

The results of the current assessment indicate that, although you do have a few areas of particular difficulty, most of your abilities to think, learn, and process information are average, or comparable to those of other teenagers your age. We have described your performance on the

tests in a score called percentiles. This number tells you the percentage of students your age who scored the same as or lower than you did on a particular test. For example, the 63rd percentile means that you did as well as or better than 63% (63 out of 100) of 14-year-olds. Specifically, the tests that you took revealed that you have skills in the Average range in the following areas:

- Your ability to remember things in the short term, or over a few minutes (50th percentile)
- Your ability to remember things long term (23rd percentile)
- Your ability to understand and think about material that is shown to you visually (23rd percentile)
- Your ability to solve new or unusual problems (21st percentile)
- Your ability to gain knowledge from school or your environment (19th percentile)
- Your ability to recognize and work with the individual sounds in words (63rd percentile)

These abilities are sometimes given the general label *cognitive abilities.*

Many of your academic skills are at the same level as these cognitive abilities, which are similar to most 14-year-olds' abilities. In particular, your academic skills are in the Average range in the following areas:

- Your ability to recognize words in print, comprehend what you read, and read quickly
- Your ability to express yourself clearly in writing and spell correctly
- Your ability to express yourself clearly and with ease when you are talking

Your performance on the academic tests that you took showed these school-related skills were as good as or better than 30 to 55 percent of other 14-year-olds (30th to 55th percentiles).

Areas of Weakness

In contrast to your good cognitive abilities and academic skills, two areas are more challenging for you. Some of the tests revealed that you have particular trouble with one type of memory, called *working memory.* This means that, compared to others your age, your ability to hold information in your mind and while you actively work with it is not as strong as it is for other 14-year-olds. This may cause you to forget some information while you're working with it or to get mixed up when you have several steps to follow to complete a math problem. You also have a weakness in your ability to understand information that you hear, particularly if it is a lot of information and there is nothing for you to look at that is related to it, such as pictures. Your listening comprehension skills are better than only about 5% of teenagers your age.

On school-related tests, you showed particular difficulty with computing answers to math problems, such as multiplication and division of whole numbers, and adding and subtracting fractions. Your score was in the 14th percentile, meaning that you did better than 14 percent of 14-year-olds. You also had a particular weakness in solving story problems and in using math in everyday situations (10th percentile). Your performance on the math tests we gave you is completely consistent with your grades at school, as well as your concerns regarding your math skills.

How the Skills and Weaknesses Interact

It is likely that your difficulty in working memory is what is causing your problems with math; this is true of many people who have weaknesses in working memory. Also, your difficulty understanding information that is told, but not shown, to you adds to that difficulty. Although you have received tutoring that included oral drill of math facts and lengthy oral descriptions of how to solve math problems, you told us that this type of tutoring didn't help you very much. The results of our assessment shows that (a) you are much more likely to understand, remember, and be able to work with new information if the person explaining it also uses pictures, drawings, videos, or something else you can see, and (b) if it is presented in short chunks.

A weakness in a cognitive ability, such as yours in working memory, which is related to a specific difficulty in some academic area, is called a learning disability. It means that, overall, you have a good capacity to learn but that one or more particular ways of remembering or using information does not work well for you. Consequently, you have a mathematics learning disability.

An additional area of difficulty for you academically is your ability to use phonics to sound out unfamiliar words.

Although you are able to read the words that you have learned as whole words and you understand what you read (as long as you can read all of the words), your limited knowledge of phonics makes it harder for you to figure out new or unfamiliar words. If you cannot learn new words through reading, it will be harder for you to learn new vocabulary and gain knowledge or new concepts. Thus, you will benefit from learning more about basic reading skills, such as how to break longer words into syllables to make them easier to pronounce.

Evaluation of Attention

In addition to the concerns you had about your poor math skills, both you and your parents had concerns about your attention. Sometimes people with weaknesses in working memory and listening comprehension *seem* like they have attention problems, and this may be true of you in some circumstances, but you do not have a disability in the area of attention or what is referred to as Attention-Deficit/Hyperactivity Disorder (ADHD). During the current evaluation, you were motivated and cooperative. Although you frequently needed clarification or repetition of oral directions (due to your weaknesses in listening comprehension and working memory), you consistently maintained focused attention. You exhibited some signs of anxiety (or nervousness) and a lack of confidence on tasks related to math that required you to increase your level of attention; however, your behavior during the testing and your behaviors described in your academic and family history are not consistent with symptoms or a diagnosis of ADHD.

Additional Skill Areas: Interpersonal

You have sources of self-compensation and support that have helped you balance out your areas of difficulty. For example, you have surrounded yourself with four best friends, which is a large enough group to always have at least one person to ask questions of (such as what was just said, what was expected in class—namely, information that you might miss or forget when you hear it). The trouble you have with your working memory is also aided by this group of friends, who accept your needs and act nurturing and protective of you. No doubt this extended social group will help you in growing into "your own" as a mature young woman throughout high school and beyond.

RECOMMENDATIONS

Mikaela, we suggest the following recommendations to help you with the difficulties that you have been experiencing.

Mathematics: School Interventions

1. Ask your teacher to help you find computer programs that you can work with to learn and memorize new math skills and concepts. It should have a verbal explanation as well as images, graphs, and/or animation to help you "see" what it is teaching. The visuals are especially important for learning abstract concepts, such as fractions, that you seem to have difficulty grasping. The program should present just a small amount of information at a time, give you immediate feedback as to whether or not your answers are right, and evaluate your input so that it reteaches what you don't yet understand and moves on when you do.

2. You should also use computer programs for drill on math facts so that you are continuously active and are continuously getting feedback from the program. One such software program that your teacher could consider to help you become more fluent in basic facts is FASTT Math™. More information can be found at http://www.tomsnyder.com/products/product.asp?SKU=FASFAS&Subject=Math.

3. In the report for your parents and teachers, we have recommended a technique called "Planning Facilitation" to help you and your classmates think more carefully about what you are doing when you are doing math work. Your teacher needs to be the one to lead this technique.

4. To help solidify your knowledge of basic math facts and your ability to recall them quickly, we have suggested that you be allowed to tutor a middle school student who is having trouble in math. During this time, you would do fun math activities that would help both of you. If your teacher sets this up, he will help you find activities that would be appropriate. Some games that we suggest are board games like Equate, Flip 4, or Tally Rally (available at www.mindware.com).

5. At home, work with whoever cooks in your house to do the math to change the amounts in recipes to fit your family. Or you can choose a recipe, change the amounts of ingredients, and cook it yourself (e.g., double the recipe for chocolate chip cookies, then make them). There are many other ways to practice math at home, such as going shopping with a parent and practicing counting money and making sure you have received the correct change when paying for your purchases. Plan a trip on a bus by reading the bus schedule and figuring out how much time you will need to go through each step of your trip so you can figure out the total time it will take.

Listening Comprehension and Working Memory: School Interventions

1. If you feel comfortable doing this (you can ask a parent to accompany you), schedule a meeting with your teachers and explain that you will understand all types of verbal information much better if the teachers present it along with visual information that clearly illustrates the skill or concept they are teaching. For example, pictures, charts, graphs, semantic maps, and videotapes will make learning much easier for you.

2. Also explain to the teachers that you are more likely to remember the content of a lecture if you can devote your full attention to listening rather than trying to listen and take notes at the same time. If they will give you a copy of their lecture notes or allow another student (who is a particularly good note taker) to make a copy for you, you are likely to understand the material much better.

3. Try bringing a digital voice recorder to class to record anything you think you may not remember or, possibly, understand later. This could include the teachers' explanations of assignments, especially long assignments with multiple deadlines. You could also record a lecture and then take notes while you listen to it later.

Listening Comprehension: Medical Intervention

Just to make sure that your problem in listening comprehension is not caused by problems in hearing, we suggested that your parents take you to have your hearing checked.

Homework

1. Your homework is taking you too much time to get through. When you were aware of being timed on our tests, you worked faster and still worked effectively. We recommend that you place a time limit on some of your assignments and set a timer. If you are aware that you have a limited time, you are more likely to increase

and maintain your focus on the assignment and finish it more quickly.

2. Your listening comprehension might improve if you practice listening to well-organized and enjoyable information. One way to do this is by sharing reading aloud with your grandmother. Choose a book you are both interested in and take turns reading chapters to each other. Alternatively, if your friends are interested you might have "reading parties" where you take turns reading aloud a book you have all agreed on, or each person can read a part of a book or poems that are favorites.

3. You can build your vocabulary in other ways besides reading. Look for computer software that teaches new vocabulary, especially programs that use pictures and animation to depict the meanings of words.

Anxiety and Self-Concept Interventions

When you experience anxiety, such as during tasks that you know will be difficult for you, you tend to calm yourself by increasing your movement (e.g., shaking your legs). When you know you are going to have a lengthy homework assignment, plan for breaks at specific times and plan to do something active, such as walking your dog or jogging around the block. This physical release of tension will help you keep focused on more difficult tasks, and the physical activity may also help with your sleep difficulties.

We have really enjoyed the opportunity to work with you. Please feel free to call us if you have any additional questions that were not answered during our conference.

CASE 41

A Comprehensive Evaluation
of a High School Student
When Social-Emotional Functioning and Specific
Learning Disabilities Interact

Toby Laird

The following report for Jamie describes a complex initial evaluation for special education eligibility. The results indicated that a constellation of factors including specific cognitive weaknesses, such as memory, academic deficiencies, and various social-emotional problems (social anxiety and feelings of inadequacy) were interacting in a way that substantially impeded his ability to be successful in the general education curriculum. The intended audience for this report was a Multidisciplinary Education Team at a public charter school composed of several general education teachers, a special education teacher, a school administrator, the student, and the student's parents.

Although the comprehensive details of the assessment findings and interpretation are placed in the "results" section of the report, the most critical elements, starting with the student's strengths and progressing to areas of concern, are presented immediately after the reason for referral. The purpose of this organization is so that the reader will have immediate access to the most critical information, such as the type of instruction with which Jamie would be expected to learn most effectively and areas of strengths and weaknesses, including academics, cognitive processing, adaptive behaviors, and social-emotional characteristics. Also included are recommendations for special education eligibility and instructional programming. The overarching goal of this report was to provide a comprehensive picture of how this student would be expected to function in a variety of domains so that the Multidisciplinary Education Team would be able to make informed decisions regarding the development of an Individualized Education Program that would alter

Jamie's pattern of consistent failure and allow him to capitalize on his strengths.

Name:	Jamie C. Yazzie
Date of Birth:	July 19, 1995
Age:	14-7
Ethnicity:	Native American
Language:	English
School:	Cedar Falls Academy Primary Home and School
Grade:	9.7
Examiner:	Toby D. Laird, Ph.D.
Evaluation Date:	March 17, 2010

REASON FOR REFERRAL

Jamie is a ninth-grade student who was referred by his multidisciplinary team for a psychoeducational evaluation due to academic concerns stemming from poor work completion, as well as difficulties with staying organized and keeping up with the pace of his classes. Teachers and parents have also expressed concern regarding Jamie's disengagement from academic tasks and high levels of anxiety. This evaluation will provide information regarding Jamie's learning strengths and challenges, along with social/emotional data, in order to gain an understanding of his school difficulties. Recommendations will be provided to assist in the development of the most appropriate educational plan for his academic success.

SUMMARY AND DIAGNOSTIC IMPRESSIONS

This section provides a summary of the findings of this evaluation, diagnostic impressions, and recommendations. Following are sections that provide more in-depth information regarding Jamie's background and important details of Jamie's test performance.

Jamie is a polite, creative, and soft-spoken ninth-grade student who enjoys playing basketball and video games, as well as visiting his grandmother on the Navajo Reservation and helping her care for her animals. Although he is not sure what he would like to study, Jamie stated during an interview that he thinks he would like to attend college some day. However, he also remarked that he wasn't sure that he would end up actually pursuing a college degree because he finds school to be very challenging. When asked to elaborate about his school difficulties, he expressed concern regarding the pace of his core academic courses and his ability to take notes effectively. He further noted that the content covered in math and biology was too hard. Information provided by Jamie's educational team indicated that he typically is a quiet student in class, but he can interact socially with other peers when he chooses to do so. It was also reported that Jamie benefits from a high degree of individualized attention in order to assist him with task persistence, organizing his time, and developing self-advocacy skills.

Jamie's cognitive testing revealed that he possesses relative strengths in the following areas: comprehension of vocabulary and connected oral language, verbal inductive reasoning, visual-spatial thinking, visual memory, and processing speed. Areas in which Jamie exhibited relative processing weaknesses were auditory memory span and working memory. He demonstrated severe weaknesses in retrieving verbal labels and words from long-term memory, especially under time constraints. Collectively, these abilities have been shown to be critical for academic achievement in a variety of areas.

Results of academic testing showed specific academic deficiencies that can be related to his processing weaknesses. Jamie's standard score in general reading ability was in the Below Average range. His RPIs indicated that his proficiency in reading decoding and comprehension is limited to the extent that the likelihood of his success in tasks similar to those assessed would be 53% to 54%, respectively, when a typical age peer would be 90% successful. His calculation skills and ability to retrieve arithmetic facts efficiently are barely above this level, and his proficiency in application of these skills to practical problems is considerably more limited: 24% compared with typical age peers who would be 90% proficient.

Social-emotional data obtained from Jamie, his mother, and his general education English teacher gave the impression that he has adaptive strengths related to his ability to interact successfully with peers outside of the school environment and adapt to difficult or changing environmental conditions. It was also evident that he does not exhibit hyperactive/impulsive behaviors in the classroom. Jamie, however, reported in an interview that he often experiences intense anxiety at school that clouds his ability to think and inhibits his capacity to relax. Specifically, he stated that he worries excessively about tests and the potential of having to speak in front of other students in the class (social and performance anxiety). He also reported intense feelings of inadequacy regarding his ability to successfully perform a wide variety of tasks, with a rating that exceeded 93% of what typical students his age report. In addition, Jamie's mother reported behaviors consistent with elevated levels of anxiety, and his teacher's ratings indicated that he frequently disengages from classroom activities, struggles to take initiative to explain his needs to others, and has exhibited clinically significant difficulties with establishing and maintaining interpersonal relationships in his English class.

ELIGIBILITY AND RECOMMENDATIONS

Based on the findings of this evaluation, the following recommendations are offered to the Cedar Falls Academy multidisciplinary team.

Eligibility

1. Provide Jamie with special education services and accommodations in the general education classroom as an intellectually capable student with a primary IDEA diagnosis of Emotional Disability. This recommendation is based on findings suggesting that Jamie's emotional distress (i.e., anxiety and feelings of inadequacy) is inhibiting his ability to apply his intellectual and academic strengths in a manner that will allow him to be successful in school without support. Specifically,

he has exhibited inappropriate types of behavior and feelings under normal circumstances, extreme school-related anxiety (e.g., test anxiety that clouds his ability to think clearly), and an inability to build or maintain satisfactory interpersonal relationships with peers and/or teachers in the school environment.

2. Identify Jamie as a student with a Specific Learning Disability as a secondary area of eligibility. Specific areas of need are basic reading skills, reading comprehension, written expression, mathematics calculation, and mathematics problem solving. This recommendation was established after examining specific processing and academic weaknesses, in comparison to Jamie's other considerable strengths, which do not seem to be primarily due to an educational disadvantage or his emotional disability.

Anxiety

1. It is strongly recommended that Jamie and his mother seek community-based psychological and psychiatric treatment services, along with in-school counseling services, as part of a comprehensive treatment program to address his mental health needs (i.e., school-related and social anxiety), develop and maintain pro-social behaviors, and foster opportunities for school-related success.

2. Due to Jamie's anxiety and feeling of "differentness," all specialized instruction should take place outside of the classroom, although working in a small group of students with similar needs in a private area might be beneficial.

Academic Instruction

1. If Jamie is to develop his academic skills so that he can be successful in high school and have options open for college and career, he must be able to understand what he reads, write in a coherent and articulate fashion, and apply math skills in practical situations. He cannot learn these higher-level skills without the basics. Consequently, he requires intensive instruction from a learning disabilities specialist who can provide a structured and systematic approach in teaching:

   - Phonics, syllabication, and structural analysis for reading and spelling
   - Reading comprehension strategies

   - Expository writing following the six traits of writing (http://thetraits.org)
   - Automatic retrieval of arithmetic facts, arithmetic algorithms, and translation of practical math problems into the necessary computation

2. To facilitate the previous recommendation, the learning disabilities specialist or educational diagnostician at Cedar Falls should conduct an in-depth assessment of Jamie's reading skills to identify areas of concern and inform the planning of interventions.

3. Using text at his instructional level, teach Jamie how to make mental images of any material he is reading. Visualization improves comprehension by helping the reader to retain the information read (as images) in memory as he assimilates the meaning, to associate the new information with information he knows already, and to recognize when he does not understand.

4. Provide Jamie with instruction and practice in key-boarding skills and use of a word processing program. Proficient word processing will make it easier and more palatable for him to express his thoughts in writing, check his spelling, revise, and edit.

5. To aid with spelling, buy Jamie a pocket-sized electronic spell-checker, such as the Franklin Spelling Ace. He will have to make more of an effort to spell words as they sound but if he can come close, the spell-checker will provide the correct spelling or some possibilities from which he can select the word he was trying to spell.

6. Ensure that Jamie has full mastery of the prerequisite math skills before introducing new math concepts. In addition to directly teaching the new skill/concept and its relationship to known skills/concepts, engage Jamie in activities that will help him build a sequential bridge between the new and the known. Jamie plans to sign up for the afternoon Math Lab. Ms. Larsen, the math teacher, will administer the Key Math-3 to Jamie and will use this information to develop a specific program and materials from the Key Math Essential Resources.

7. To enhance Jamie's memory of information and concepts, when planning lessons, include visual examples (i.e., pictures, web-diagrams, charts) and demonstrations as often as possible to support the verbal presentation. Although Jamie's language skills are adequate, the use of visual imagery should help him to understand and consolidate new concepts. The better he grasps a concept, the easier it will be for him to retrieve it later and work with it.

Accommodations

1. Jamie's team should consider reducing his current course load to mitigate his feelings of being overwhelmed by the pace of in-class demands. Scheduling a daily study hall where Jamie could receive direct instruction/support on his assigned work from a teacher at school would also be beneficial. The goal of reducing his course load is not to limit his overall exposure to the general curriculum but to modify the quantity and variety of information that he is required to master at any one time.

2. Since Jamie reported difficulties with taking notes, help him to arrange with another student, who takes good class notes, to make a copy of his/her notes for each class session. This will allow Jamie to listen carefully to the lecture and to participate in class discussion. Make sure that Jamie is comfortable with this arrangement before setting it up. It might also be beneficial to permit Jamie to tape-record all class lectures so that he may play them back at a slower pace later and take notes. Due to the time this will take, however, it would need to be accompanied with a reduction in homework.

3. Because Jamie's ability to hold many pieces of information in memory and work with them is somewhat compromised, the teachers can make it easier for him to hold on to information long enough to process or work with it by doing the following:

   - Present information in shorter segments interspersed by an activity or discussion designed to help students process the information.
   - Emphasize the conceptual underpinnings of new math and science formulas and ensure that he understands each part of a multistep process before moving on to the next.
   - Break down complex instructions and assignments into simpler, sequential steps.

BACKGROUND INFORMATION

Developmental/Medical/Family History

Although a complete social and developmental history questionnaire was not obtained at the time of this evaluation, Jamie's mother reported that he generally attained all of his developmental milestones within the expected time frames and has never experienced any significant illnesses or injuries that resulted in excessive school absences or would be expected to interfere with his ability to learn. (Refer to Jamie's MET Report from 4/7/2010 for additional information.)

Performance in the General Curriculum

Information provided by Jamie's educational team indicated that he typically is a quiet student in class but has demonstrated the capacity to interact socially with other students when he chooses to do so. It was also reported that Jamie benefits from a high degree of individualized attention in order to assist him with task persistence, organizing his time, and developing self-advocacy skills. Jamie has substantially struggled to complete his work in a timely manner for the majority of the year, and his grades since 2/13/2010 were reflective of that fact. Specifically, Jamie earned all Ds and Fs with the exception of his art class where he earned an A. (Refer to Jamie's MET Report from 4/7/2010 for additional information.)

Standardized Test Results and Vision and Hearing Screening

Jamie's MET report from 4/7/2010 stated that he had recently passed both vision and hearing screenings.

Effects of Culture, Educational Disadvantage, and Limited English Proficiency

Jamie is a Native American student whose primary language is English, suggesting that the standardization samples of the psychometric instruments used in this evaluation were appropriate. Also, nonverbal, low verbal, and memory/speed subtests were specially selected to assess processing and reasoning abilities in a manner that would be less biased for culturally and linguistically diverse children. Further, Jamie's attendance at the Cedar Falls Academy has been satisfactory and there have been no assistive devices required in his general school program other than what is typically used for students in his grade, such as keyboard training. Although his records indicated that he has experienced a fairly recent school change, the specific processing weaknesses he exhibited would not be affected by changing schools. Consequently, environmental or educational disadvantage are ruled out as primary causes of any academic or language delays identified.

Classroom Observations (See Appendix)

ASSESSMENT FINDINGS AND INTERPRETATION

Testing Observations

Jamie arrived at the testing location with a guarded attitude toward the evaluation process. He presented with a blunted affect and did not engage in any spontaneous speech for approximately the first 10 minutes of the interview. During this time he responded to questions from the examiner with one- or two-word responses after waiting as long as 10 seconds to respond. However, after the purpose of the evaluation was explained to him and he learned that it would not negatively impact his school grades, Jamie appeared to relax somewhat and was able to more comfortably discuss his interests. When testing commenced, Jamie demonstrated the ability to effectively modulate his attention in a one-on-one situation, but he frequently required verbal encouragement to persist on challenging tasks. He responded positively to praise and encouragement, and it is the examiner's opinion that the results provide a valid representation of Jamie's cognitive abilities and academic skills.

Measures Used

Differential Ability Scales, Second Edition (DAS-II)

Differential Ability Scales, Second Edition—Diagnostic Supplement (selected subtests)

Woodcock-Johnson III NU Tests of Cognitive Abilities (selected subtests) (WJ III COG)

Woodcock-Johnson III NU Tests of Achievement Form A (WJ III ACH)

Behavioral Assessment System for Children, Second Edition—Self-Report (BASC-2)

Behavioral Assessment System for Children, Second Edition—Parent (BASC-2)

Behavioral Assessment System for Children, Second Edition—Teacher (BASC-2)

Behavioral observations

Record review

Educational interview (student, teacher, parent)

Score Interpretation

The following table depicts the range of and percentile ranks associated with each verbal label and the percentage of individuals who score within each category.

Std. Score	Range	% people	Percentiles
<70	Lower Extreme	2%	2nd & below
70–79	Well Below Average	7%	3rd to 8th
80–89	Below Average	16%	9th to 24th
90–109	Average	50%	25th to 74th
110–119	Above Average	16%	75th to 90th
120–129	Well Above Average	7%	91st to 97th
>130	Upper Extreme	2%	98th & above

Cognitive Results

When relative processing weaknesses suppress intelligence test results, one is justified in computing a measure of ability that is less affected by the nature of a person's learning difficulty. If this is not done, a processing weakness associated with an individual's learning inconsistencies confounds a clear understanding of their overall cognitive abilities, academic achievement, and the relationship between these measures. In Jamie's case, his performance on the Differential Ability Scales, Second Edition (DAS-II) and WJ III Tests of Cognitive Abilities (WJ III COG) revealed relative strengths in processing and recall of visual-spatial information, speed of processing visual symbols, comprehension of oral language, and verbal reasoning. Areas of relative weakness were short-term memory and working memory; areas of severe weakness were associative memory and retrieval of words from long-term memory. Due to these discrepant abilities, integrating Jamie's subtest scores into a global estimate of intelligence would yield an inaccurate representation of his overall intelligence. Instead, his processing abilities should be interpreted individually (see below) to understand how he approaches academic tasks and interacts with the world.

When examining Jamie's oral language skills on the DAS-II Verbal Ability cluster and the WJ III Verbal Ability and Oral Language clusters, his performance exceeded 32% to 34% of students his age, and fell within the Average range. This indicates that Jamie possesses an age-appropriate knowledge of vocabulary, the ability to use language to express that knowledge, and comprehension of oral language. He was also adept at a task in which he was asked orally to identify abstract relationships between concepts. His performance surpassed 42% of same-aged peers nationally. This form of verbal inductive reasoning is important for academic achievement in numerous subject areas.

On the Nonverbal Reasoning Cluster of the DAS-II, Jamie's performance exceeded 37% of students his age, within the Average range of functioning. Within this cluster, Jamie displayed a balance of skills and was able to satisfactorily integrate individual visual details in order to identify a larger pattern (visual inductive reasoning). In addition, Jamie demonstrated an age-appropriate capacity to identify sequential patterns in sets of numbers. This form of sequential and quantitative reasoning is critical for achievement in the areas of mathematical calculation and mathematical reasoning.

Jamie's standard score of 101 on the Spatial cluster of the DAS-II exceeded 53% of students his age, within the Average range. Visual-spatial thinking was an area of relative strength for Jamie. He excelled when asked to accurately draw the key features of previously viewed images from memory; his performance surpassed 73% of same-aged peers. These visual-spatial abilities entail visually perceiving and synthesizing spatial information, as well as creating accurate mental representations of 3-dimensional images. This type of processing has been shown to be important for some forms of advanced mathematical functioning (e.g., geometry), science concepts, and artistic expression, and can assist a student with encoding information from short-term memory storage into long-term memory storage.

Jamie was administered two diagnostic subtests from the DAS-II to specifically assess his immediate visual memory and ability to retain visual information over an extended time period. When processing visual information from memory over a short time period, Jamie's performance exceeded 73% of students his age, at the upper limit of the average range. In addition, when asked to recall that same visual information at a later time, his performance surpassed 76% of his peers, in the Above Average range. These data suggest that Jamie is skilled at visually encoding and retaining images. It will be crucial to capitalize on these abilities in his instructional program by using frequent visual examples and demonstrations along with opportunities for verbal discussions.

After evaluating Jamie's immediate visual memory and long-term storage ability, he was administered three diagnostic subtests from the DAS-II to assess his auditory memory span and working memory ability. Auditory memory span refers to the number of orally presented units of information

a person can encode and recall immediately. Jamie's auditory memory span was found to exceed 27% of students his age, which constitutes a relative weakness in comparison to his other abilities and skills. Working memory is different than short-term memory span because it requires more than rote recall. Specifically, working memory involves encoding information into short-term memory, mentally manipulating that information in some fashion, and then producing an accurate response. Because Jamie performed well on one working memory task, which included the visualization of body parts (Recall of Sequential Order, PR 46), and relatively poorly on one that required the rearrangement of digits (Digits Backward, PR 24), an additional working memory test was given, the results of which also indicated a relative weakness (WJ III COG Numbers Reversed, PR 29, RPI 73/90). These results suggest that Jamie will find tasks requiring mental transformation of numbers difficult, whereas memory tasks that incorporate visualization of tangible objects will be easier.

Finally, Jamie was administered a battery of diagnostic tests from the WJ III COG to assess his ability to retrieve verbal labels and words from long-term storage with or without a visual prompt, especially under time constraints. Jamie's performance on these tasks ranged from the lower extreme to well below average, suggesting that he experiences considerable difficulty with retrieval of newly learned words for visual symbols and rapid recall of known words. His RPIs on these three tests also predicted difficulty with these types of tasks.

Processing speed refers to the speed and accuracy with which individuals process visual symbols and details. This ability has been shown to be correlated with basic skills in reading, math, and writing. Jamie's performance on tests measuring processing speed surpassed 73% of students his age across the country. It appears that Jamie's processing speed is only compromised when it involves rapid verbal retrieval, despite his average overall verbal reasoning.

Achievement Results

Results of achievement testing using the Woodcock-Johnson III (WJ III ACH) showed that Jamie exhibits specific academic deficiencies that could be related to his processing weaknesses. Looking at the area of reading, although Jamie's standard score on basic reading skills is in the Below Average range, his RPI of 53/90 predicts that he will find decoding and acquiring new sight words considerably more difficult than would be expected from the standard score alone. Results regarding reading comprehension were similar. Considering the previous results of age-appropriate oral language, poor basic reading skills, and significantly weak word retrieval, two hypotheses come to mind regarding Jamie's difficulty with text comprehension. First, it is likely that he is unable to read some of the words necessary to understand the text. Second, this particular test required him to read one or two sentences and supply the missing word. Given his difficulty with word retrieval, he may have had some difficulty retrieving the specific word he intended to use. Jamie's RPI (78/90) on the test of Reading Fluency suggested that his proficiency in reading simple sentences with speed and comprehension is relatively better, an outcome that may, at least in part, be due to the support of meaningful context.

In the area of math, Jamie's ability to do calculations and retrieve simple math facts exceeded 21% and 7% of students his age, respectively, within the Below Average and Well Below Average ranges. His proficiency in these skills is likely to be 69% compared with age peers' 90%. Further, Jamie experienced significant difficulty (RPI 24/90) when attempting to apply his knowledge of mathematics to solving real-world problems. He had particular difficulty handling problems that required multiple steps and rational numbers, such as decimals and fractions. Although his approach to many of the problems was sound, he made errors on the algorithms and, occasionally, on renaming.

With respect to writing, Jamie's overall performance exceeded 17% of same-aged peers and fell within the Below Average range. Within this cluster, Jamie demonstrated similar levels of performance (SS and RPI) in spelling, composing age-level sentences that conveyed creative ideas with sufficient detail, and speed of generating simple sentences.

Social/Emotional Functioning

The BASC-2 is an instrument designed to provide information that may assist in understanding social-emotional and/or behavioral difficulties in children. Scaled scores in the Clinically Significant range (T = 70+ for Clinical Scales, T = <31 for Adaptive Scales) suggest social-emotional and/or behavioral maladjustment that require extensive intervention. Scaled scores in the At-Risk range (T = 60–69 for Clinical Scales, T = 31–40 for Adaptive Scales) indicate behaviors that warrant monitoring but may not be severe enough to require formal intervention, depending on the degree to which they interfere with a student's academic or social functioning.

On the BASC-2 Self-Report, Jamie identified an adaptive strength with regard to his capacity to successfully interact with others when he chooses to do so. He did not report concerns regarding sustained attention or engaging in hyperactive/impulsive behaviors. Jamie did not report a depressed mood or concerns related to generalized anxiety outside of the normal limits for someone of his age. His ratings, however, did place him in the At-Risk range regarding his ability to make decisions, solve problems, be dependable, and successfully perform a variety of tasks despite putting forth substantial effort. Further, a review of Jamie's content scales revealed that he reported problems with test anxiety exceeding 94% of students his age, and that he experiences extended periods of heightened arousal and difficulty relaxing. In addition to these findings, Jamie talked at length about how he cannot relax the night before a test and is almost always excessively nervous about the possibility that the teacher may call on him in class and ask him to speak in front of the other students. (One validity scale indicated that Jamie's ratings may represent an attempt to minimize the severity of his social-emotional difficulties within his daily functioning.)

Jamie's mother completed the BASC-2 Parent Report. Her ratings also suggested adaptive strengths with respect to Jamie's ability to successfully interact with others and build interpersonal relationships, as well as his ability to adapt to difficult or changing environmental conditions and effectively communicate his needs to others. Further, her ratings did not suggest elevated concerns with respect to hyperactivity, distractibility, or sustained depressed mood. Her ratings did, however, place Jamie in the At-Risk range regarding his tendency to worry or exhibit behaviors consistent with excessive nervousness, his ability to perform simple daily tasks with speed and efficiency, and his capacity to take the initiative in solving difficult problems or getting people to work together effectively. (All validity scales fell within the acceptable range.)

On the BASC-2 Teacher Report, Jamie's general education English teacher expressed relative strengths when considering his ability to adapt to changing or difficult environmental conditions in the classroom, and did not report elevated levels of generalized anxiety, depression, or distractibility. Her ratings did, however, suggest Clinically Significant concerns regarding his ability to effectively build or maintain interpersonal relationships in the school environment, as well as the frequency with which he chooses not to actively participate in class activities. In an interview, Jamie clarified that the reason he often chooses not to participate in classroom discussions or other activities is because he does not want to draw attention to himself in front of other students. (All validity scales fell within the acceptable range.)

PSYCHOMETRIC SUMMARY

Differential Ability Scales, Second Edition (DAS-II)

COMPOSITE/Subtest	SS	T Score	Percentile	Range
VERBAL ABILITY	94		34	Average
Word Definitions		46	34	
Verbal Similarities		48	42	
NONVERBAL REASONING	95		37	Average
Sequential & Quantitative Reasoning		47	38	
Matrices		47	38	
SPATIAL	101		53	Average
Pattern Construction		46	34	
Recall of Designs		56	73	
WORKING MEMORY	93		32	Average
Recall of Sequential Order		49	46	Average
Recall of Digits Backward		43	24	Below Average
DIAGNOSTIC SUBTESTS				
Recall of Objects – Immediate		56	73	Average
Recall of Objects – Delayed		57	76	Above Average`
Recall of Digits Forward		41	18	Below Average

Woodcock-Johnson III COG and ACH

Woodcock-Johnson III Normative Update Tests of Cognitive Abilities and Tests of Achievement (Form A), WJ III NU Compuscore and Profiles Program, Version 3.0. Norms based on age 14-8

CLUSTER/Test	W	AE	Proficiency	RPI	SS (68% Band)	PR
COG EFFICIENCY (Ext)	515	13–11	Average	88/90	97 (93–102)	43
Visual Matching	526	17–1	Avg to Adv	95/90	109 (103–116)	74
Decision Speed	517	>19	Average	94/90	106 (101–111)	65
Numbers Reversed	509	11–6	Lmtd to Avg	73/90	92 (86–98)	29
Memory for Words	507	11–6	Lmtd to Avg	79/90	94 (87–102)	36
L-T RETRIEVAL (Glr)	495	7–7	Lmtd to Avg	73/90	67 (62–72)	1
Visual-Auditory Learning	495	8–0	Lmtd to Avg	72/90	76 (71–82)	6
Retrieval Fluency	494	6–8	Lmtd to Avg	74/90	58 (50–65)	0.3
PROCESS SPEED (Gs)	522	18–10	Average	94/90	109 (104–114)	72
Visual Matching	526	17–1	Avg to Adv	95/90	109 (103–116)	74
Decision Speed	517	>19	Average	94/90	106 (101–111)	65
SHORT-TERM MEM (Gsm)	508	11–6	Lmtd to Avg	76/90	92 (87–97)	30
Numbers Reversed	509	11–6	Lmtd to Avg	73/90	92 (86–98)	29

(continued)

CLUSTER/Test	W	AE	Proficiency	RPI	SS (68% Band)	PR
Memory for Words	507	11–6	Lmtd to Avg	79/90	94 (87–102)	36
COGNITIVE FLUENCY	501	10–8	Lmtd to Avg	76/90	81 (78–84)	10
Decision Speed	517	>19	Average	94/90	106 (101–111)	65
Retrieval Fluency	494	6–8	Lmtd to Avg	74/90	58 (50–65)	0.3
Rapid Picture Naming	491	8–4	Limited	42/90	76 (74–78)	6
ORAL LANGUAGE (Std)	503	11–9	Average	86/90	93 (88–98)	32
Story Recall	501	10–9	Average	86/90	92 (85–99)	30
Understanding Directions	505	12–4	Average	86/90	95 (90–101)	38
LISTENING COMP	509	12–8	Average	86/90	96 (92–100)	39
Understanding Directions	505	12–4	Average	86/90	95 (90–101)	38
Oral Comprehension	513	12–11	Average	86/90	97 (93–102)	43
BROAD READING	507	11–1	Limited	58/90	85 (82–87)	15
Letter-Word Identification	514	11–1	Limited	40/90	86 (83–89)	18
Reading Fluency	508	12–9	Lmtd to Avg	78/90	91 (87–95)	28
Passage Comprehension	500	9–8	Limited	54/90	81 (76–87)	11
BRIEF READING	507	10–7	Limited	47/90	83 (81–86)	13
Letter-Word Identification	514	11–1	Limited	40/90	86 (83–89)	18
Passage Comprehension	500	9–8	Limited	54/90	81 (76–87)	11
BASIC READING SKILLS	509	10–9	Limited	53/90	88 (85–90)	21
Letter-Word Identification	514	11–1	Limited	40/90	86 (83–89)	18
Word Attack	505	10–3	Limited	66/90	91 (88–94)	28
BROAD MATH	505	10–5	Limited	54/90	78 (75–81)	7
Calculation	517	11–9	Lmtd to Avg	69/90	88 (83–93)	21
Math Fluency	499	10–3	Lmtd to Avg	69/90	78 (75–80)	7
Applied Problems	498	9–6	Very Limited	24/90	80 (77–84)	10
BRIEF MATH	507	10–6	Limited	46/90	79 (75–83)	8
Calculation	517	11–9	Lmtd to Avg	69/90	88 (83–93)	21
Applied Problems	498	9–6	Very Limited	24/90	80 (77–84)	10
MATH CALC SKILLS	508	11–3	Lmtd to Avg	69/90	82 (78–86)	12
Calculation	517	11–9	Lmtd to Avg	69/90	88 (83–93)	21
Math Fluency	499	10–3	Lmtd to Avg	69/90	78 (75–80)	7
BROAD WRITTEN LANG	508	11–5	Lmtd to Avg	71/90	86 (82–89)	17
Spelling	513	11–9	Lmtd to Avg	70/90	90 (86–94)	25
Writing Fluency	509	11–5	Lmtd to Avg	68/90	87 (81–92)	19
Writing Samples	502	10–11	Lmtd to Avg	74/90	88 (82–93)	21
BRIEF WRITING	508	11–5	Lmtd to Avg	72/90	87 (83–91)	19
Spelling	513	11–9	Lmtd to Avg	70/90	90 (86–94)	25

CLUSTER/Test	W	AE	Proficiency	RPI	SS (68% Band)	PR
Writing Samples	502	10–11	Lmtd to Avg	74/90	88 (82–93)	21
WRITTEN EXPRESSION	505	11–3	Lmtd to Avg	71/90	85 (81–90)	16
Writing Fluency	509	11–5	Lmtd to Avg	68/90	87 (81–92)	19
Writing Samples	502	10–11	Lmtd to Avg	74/90	88 (82–93)	21
ACADEMIC SKILLS	515	11–6	Limited	60/90	85 (82–88)	16
Letter-Word Identification	514	11–1	Limited	40/90	86 (83–89)	18
Spelling	513	11–9	Lmtd to Avg	70/90	90 (86–94)	25
Calculation	517	11–9	Lmtd to Avg	69/90	88 (83–93)	21
ACADEMIC FLUENCY	505	11–7	Lmtd to Avg	72/90	83 (80–86)	13
Reading Fluency	508	12–9	Lmtd to Avg	78/90	91 (87–95)	28
Writing Fluency	509	11–5	Lmtd to Avg	68/90	87 (81–92)	19
Math Fluency	499	10–3	Lmtd to Avg	69/90	78 (75–80)	7
ACADEMIC APPS	500	9–9	Limited	50/90	77 (73–80)	6
Passage Comprehension	500	9–8	Limited	54/90	81 (76–87)	11
Writing Samples	502	10–11	Lmtd to Avg	74/90	88 (82–93)	21
Applied Problems	498	9–6	Very Limited	24/90	80 (77–84)	10
TOTAL ACHIEVEMENT	507	10–11	Limited	61/90	81 (79–83)	10

Visual-Auditory Learning	495	8–0	Lmtd to Avg	72/90	76 (71–82)	6
Visual Matching	526	17–1	Avg to Adv	95/90	109 (103–116)	74
Numbers Reversed	509	11–6	Lmtd to Avg	73/90	92 (86–98)	29
Retrieval Fluency	494	6–8	Lmtd to Avg	74/90	58 (50–65)	0.3
Decision Speed	517	>19	Average	94/90	106 (101–111)	65
Memory for Words	507	11–6	Lmtd to Avg	79/90	94 (87–102)	36
Rapid Picture Naming	491	8–4	Limited	42/90	76 (74–78)	6
Letter-Word Identification	514	11–1	Limited	40/90	86 (83–89)	18
Reading Fluency	508	12–9	Lmtd to Avg	78/90	91 (87–95)	28
Story Recall	501	10–9	Average	86/90	92 (85–99)	30
Understanding Directions	505	12–4	Average	86/90	95 (90–101)	38
Calculation	517	11–9	Lmtd to Avg	69/90	88 (83–93)	21
Math Fluency	499	10–3	Lmtd to Avg	69/90	78 (75–80)	7
Spelling	513	11–9	Lmtd to Avg	70/90	90 (86–94)	25
Writing Fluency	509	11–5	Lmtd to Avg	68/90	87 (81–92)	19
Passage Comprehension	500	9–8	Limited	54/90	81 (76–87)	11
Applied Problems	498	9–6	Very Limited	24/90	80 (77–84)	10
Writing Samples	502	10–11	Lmtd to Avg	74/90	88 (82–93)	21
Word Attack	505	10–3	Limited	66/90	91 (88–94)	28
Oral Comprehension	513	12–11	Average	86/90	97 (93–102)	43

(continued)

| VARIATIONS | STANDARD SCORES | | | VARIATION | | |
	Actual	Predicted	Difference	PR	SD	Significant at + or –1.50 SD (SEE)
Intra-Achievement (Std)						
BROAD READING	85	87	–2	39	–0.27	No
BROAD MATH	78	90	–12	13	–1.11	No
BROAD WRITTEN LANG	86	87	–1	44	–0.16	No
ORAL LANGUAGE (Std)	93	87	6	69	+0.50	No

*Note: Proficiency ranges (e.g., limited, average, advanced) are associated with the Relative Proficiency Index (RPI), not standard scores. RPIs show the individual's level of proficiency (accuracy, speed, or whatever skill has been measured by the test) at the level at which peers are 90% proficient.

BASC-2: Self-Report

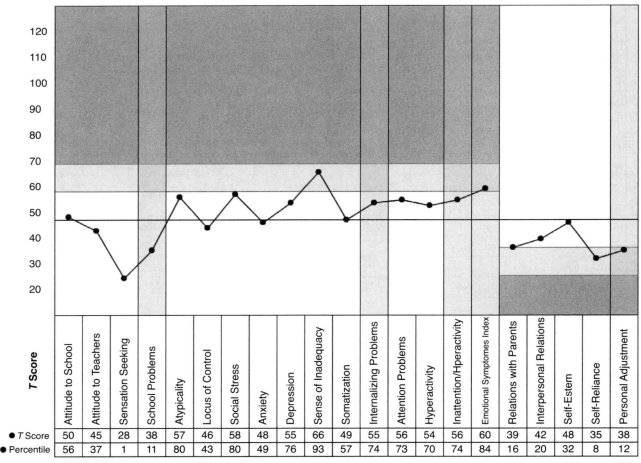

● = General - Combined Sex

Figure 1

BASC-2: Parent Report

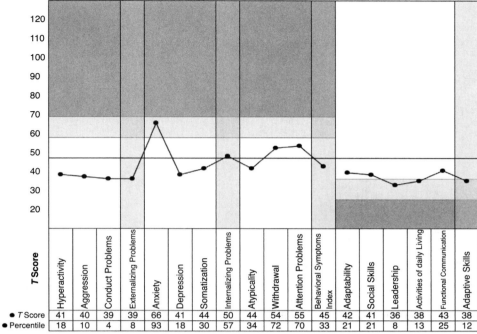

	Hyperactivity	Aggression	Conduct Problems	Externalizing Problems	Anxiety	Depression	Somatization	Internalizing Problems	Atypicality	Withdrawal	Attention Problems	Behavioral Symptoms Index	Adaptability	Social Skills	Leadership	Activities of daily Living	Functional Communication	Adaptive Skills
● *T* Score	41	40	39	39	66	41	44	50	44	54	55	45	42	41	36	38	43	38
● Percentile	18	10	4	8	93	18	30	57	34	72	70	33	21	21	8	13	25	12

● = General - Combined Sex

Figure 2

BASC-2: Teacher Report

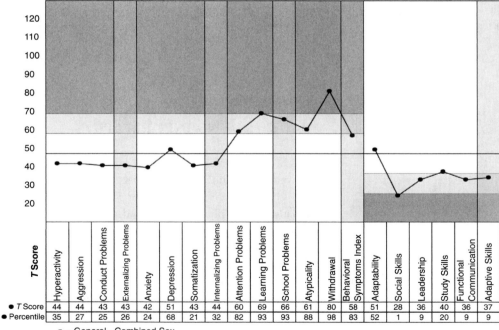

	Hyperactivity	Aggression	Conduct Problems	Externalizing Problems	Anxiety	Depression	Somatization	Internalizing Problems	Attention Problems	Learning Problems	School Problems	Atypicality	Withdrawal	Behavioral Symptoms Index	Adaptability	Social Skills	Leadership	Study Skills	Functional Communication	Adaptive Skills
● *T* Score	44	44	43	43	42	51	43	44	60	69	66	61	80	58	51	28	36	40	36	37
● Percentile	35	27	25	26	24	68	21	32	82	93	93	88	98	83	52	1	9	20	9	9

● = General - Combined Sex

Figure 3

CASE 42

ADHD: To Be or Not to Be?

That Was the Question

Ron Dumont

The following report is an example of a "cross-battery" assessment that uses the WISC-IV and WJ III to assess a student with Attention-Deficit/Hyperactivity Disorder (ADHD). A major question to be answered was whether this student, besides being identified as a student with ADHD, might also be a student with a comorbid learning disability. The report is written in a "parent friendly" way, avoiding, as much as possible, the use of numbers within the narrative. Instead, the student's results are communicated using the classification labels associated with the obtained scores.

PSYCHOEDUCATIONAL EVALUATION

Name:	Kate Wilhelm
Date of Birth:	05/09/1995
Age:	14-8
Grade:	9.4
Date of Testing:	01/11/2010
Evaluator:	Ron Dumont, Ed.D., NCSP

REASON FOR REFERRAL

Kate was referred for evaluation by her mother and father, Mrs. and Mr. Wilhelm, who stated that Kate has recently been having some problems at school. Mrs. Wilhelm noted that Kate was diagnosed in second grade with Attention-Deficit/Hyperactivity Disorder (ADHD) for which she is currently prescribed Concerta. Mrs. Wilhelm stated that the problems associated with ADHD

have led to a point where Kate is becoming increasingly overwhelmed by her schoolwork—particularly in learning a foreign language. She noted that Kate is impulsive and easily distracted; she has low self-esteem, low frustration tolerance, and she often gives up quickly on tasks she finds difficult. She also stated that Kate may have difficulties with aspects of organization. The Wilhelms wished to know if Kate has learning disabilities that are affecting her school performance, as well as to better understand Kate's learning style, strengths, and weaknesses. They also requested strategies that could be employed by a counselor to help Kate recognize her abilities and to understand the potential impact of her difficulties with attention. When interviewing Kate, she said that she thought she was "a smart kid" who was "trying hard" at school although she felt at times "confused by the questions that [my] teachers ask."

BACKGROUND INFORMATION

Kate is a 14-year-old female who resides with her parents, Mr. and Mrs. Wilhelm. Kate attends Wheeler High School and is in the ninth grade. Both of her parents are professionals. Mrs. Wilhelm reported no problems or concerns during her pregnancy with Kate. There were no reported complications during birth, and Kate's developmental milestones were reached within normal limits. Kate has done well in school but has recently received tutoring to improve her skills in the area of mathematics, specifically geometry. Her mother reported that Kate has had a "tough adjustment to high school" and this has resulted in several "meltdowns" where Kate appears to become overwhelmed by school demands.

TESTS ADMINISTERED

Wechsler Intelligence Scale for Children-Fourth Edition (WISC-IV)

Selected tests from:

Woodcock-Johnson III NU Tests of Achievement (WJ III ACH) (Form A)

Woodcock-Johnson III NU Tests of Cognitive Abilities (WJ III COG)

Behavior Assessment System for Children-Second Edition (BASC-2)

    Self-Report Form

    Parent Report

TESTING OBSERVATIONS

Kate was tested over two sessions. Her appearance was neat and she presented as a friendly, polite young woman. Rapport was easily established and she appeared comfortable and confident regarding testing. Kate was inquisitive about many aspects of the testing, and often sought feedback about her performance on the tasks. She did not appear anxious or fidgety at any time during testing. On rare occasions, some of the tasks seemed to cause her frustration. For example, on several math problems that included extraneous information, she verbally noted this and asked, "Why do they bother with all these extraneous facts?" To her credit, despite any frustration that she seemed to feel, Kate maintained focus throughout the session. During each session, a break was given for her to walk around and to have a drink.

Kate was typically very quick to understand the individual task demands (at times attempting to begin a task before the directions had been completed), and also quick to respond to questions asked of her. Although her responses to verbal items were often given quickly, they typically were not only correct but thorough and long. On several nonverbal, timed tasks, Kate made comments about the timing and appeared to try to "beat the clock" in an attempt to do well. Even on several untimed tasks, Kate also appeared to try to finish the tasks quickly. When items became difficult and took Kate longer, she seemed to become a bit stressed, asking "Is there more time?" and "Should I keep going—Is this timed?" She appeared most relaxed on tasks that were straightforward and in which there was little, if any, ambiguity in the directions. When instructions were less structured and more ambiguous, Kate attempted to impose her own control. When in doubt, Kate asked many questions to ensure that she knew exactly what was expected. These types of requests imply that Kate has the need for as well as the ability to create organization and structure to complete tasks.

ASSESSMENT OF COGNITIVE FUNCTIONING

Both the obtained scores and the range of scores on the Cognitive and Achievement tests are described using the following terms:

Very Superior	131 and above
Superior	121 to 130
High Average	111 to 120
Average	90 to 110
Low Average	80 to 90
Low	70 to 79
Very Low	69 and below

Acquired Knowledge

Acquired knowledge, which is based on prior learning and experience, should be immediately available for recall and processing. Kate's acquired knowledge was assessed in two areas: crystallized ability, defined as abstract language development and breadth and depth of knowledge of a culture; and quantitative knowledge, defined as general information about numerical concepts and mathematical quantities.

Overall, Kate performed in the Superior range on tasks assessing crystallized ability and quantitative knowledge. She had no difficulty explaining how two different objects or concepts could be alike; giving oral definitions of words; answering oral questions regarding social and practical situations; and answering oral, "trivia"-style general information questions. Her lowest score was on a task in which she was trying to guess a word from a series of clues. (It must be noted that her score, although "low" for Kate, was perfectly average and does not denote a difficulty. This was also the last task after close to 2 hours of assessment and may therefore reflect her energy level and motivation, rather than her linguistic abilities.)

Kate also performed in the Superior range on tasks assessing quantitative knowledge. She had no difficulty solving verbally presented math application problems without the use of paper and pencil.

Higher-Level Processing

Above and beyond acquired knowledge, one must employ higher-level processing, or thinking abilities, to carry out novel learning or problem solving. This domain includes a variety of cognitive abilities that require processing information, rather than simply recalling it. The abilities within this domain are fluid reasoning, long-term retrieval, and visual processing. Because Kate's functioning within this domain is varied, each of these areas will be considered separately.

New learning may involve novel reasoning and problem solving, known as fluid reasoning. Kate's performance varied on the different abilities assessed within this area. She performed in the High Average range on a task assessing deductive reasoning ability (Analysis-Synthesis). On two tasks of inductive reasoning, one visual in nature (Matrix Reasoning) and one verbal in nature (Picture Concepts), Kate performed in the Superior range on the visual task, but only in the Average range on the verbal task. This finding may suggest that Kate may reason effectively if presented with the rules and guidelines from which to draw her conclusions. However, she may experience *relative* difficulty solving problems that require her to use verbal skills to discover and apply underlying information, or when the rules for solving problems are not explicitly stated. Again, the scores that Kate obtained on these tasks were all Average and above. The "lower" score on the Picture Concepts task is well within the Average range and should not be considered to be a problem area.

Learning new information requires the ability to store information in long-term memory and retrieve it fluently at a later time. Kate's performance did not differ regardless of the skill area assessed by the tasks. She obtained scores in the High Average range on tasks requiring her to retrieve previously learned information, such as the names for common items and words in a semantic category. On tasks requiring Kate to use associative memory, in which new material is learned and remembered by linking it to previously learned information, Kate was also found to function in the High Average range. This finding suggests that Kate is adequately able to retrieve information already stored in long-term memory and assimilate new information into her knowledge store.

The processing of some tasks involves visual processing, which is the ability to analyze and synthesize visual-spatial information and manipulate visual shapes. Kate performed in the Average range. She demonstrated adequate ability to process, recall, and manipulate visual-spatial information. The ability to visualize adequately is helpful for conceptualizing information and for mathematical problem solving. This particular area was one of Kate's weaker areas (although still within the Average range).

Lower-Level Processing

Learning is also influenced by an individual's lower-level processing, the ability to automatically process information in an efficient manner. Two distinct influences on automatic information processing—short-term memory and processing speed—were measured. If either of these areas is impaired, the efficiency of both automatic tasks, as well as higher-level skills, can be reduced.

Short-term memory is the ability to hold information and use it within a few seconds; it includes auditory memory span and working memory. Processing speed is the ability to do simple tasks quickly, requiring focused attention. Kate was found to function in the Average range in both of these areas. Thus, her lower-level processing skills are adequate to allow higher-level thinking to proceed without interference.

Cognitive Impressions

Overall, Kate's cognitive ability was found to be in the High Average to Superior range of functioning. Her cognitive factor scores were all Average or above, with the majority of skills being High Average to Superior. Generally, her lower scores were in lower-level processing areas. It is important to note two aspects of Kate's performance in these areas. First, because Kate's scores in these areas were all within the Average range, the differences between these lower-level processing tasks and the higher-level reasoning tasks are less important. Secondly, the reason for the differences between the higher- and lower-level abilities may actually have more to do with the nature of the tasks rather than with Kate's cognitive abilities. Research has shown that when children with superior higher-level abilities are administered tasks of lower-level skills, a large difference may exist between the person's abilities on the two types of tasks. Kate's "lower scores" on the Processing Speed and Short-Term Memory factors may also be related to her Attention-Deficit/Hyperactivity Disorder (ADHD).

It is not at all uncommon for children identified as having ADHD to perform lower on these types of tasks when compared to the higher-level tasks.

One other comment regarding Kate's cognitive function relates to her "Average" ability in the area of visual-spatial processing. Visual-spatial skills have been defined as the ability to "see with the mind's eye." It is the ability to place, and hold in one's memory, a visual image and then to manipulate that image. This particular aspect of cognitive skill has been found to relate to the understanding of higher-level math concepts, in particular the area of geometry. Although this ability is in the Average range for Kate, it is lower than all of her other higher-level abilities. One wonders if Kate might become frustrated at her inability to quickly and easily grasp concepts that involve these visual-spatial abilities, particularly when Kate finds things to be so easy in the verbal and nonverbal problem-solving realms.

ASSESSMENT OF ACADEMIC FUNCTIONING

Kate's academic skills were assessed in a number of areas including reading, writing ability, and math using selected tests of the Woodcock-Johnson III NU Tests of Achievement (WJ III ACH).

Reading

Kate's reading ability was assessed in the areas of basic reading and reading comprehension. She demonstrated Superior ability to decode and recognize words (Letter-Word Identification). Kate read words aloud from a list with extremely good accuracy for her age. She relied more on instant recognition with familiar words and used phonetic decoding strategies to attack unfamiliar words, resulting in automatic reading vocabulary that was exceedingly strong. She did try to sound out some unfamiliar words, some successfully and some not. This finding indicates that Kate's word recognition skills are adequate for comprehension. Kate's ability to quickly (fluently) read and understand sentences (Reading Fluency) was also found to be in the Superior range. Her ability to comprehend written material (Passage Comprehension) was not as strong as her accuracy in reading words aloud from a list. Although her comprehension score was below both the decoding and fluency scores, it still remained within the Average range. The WJ III ACH assesses comprehension by having Kate read a short passage with one important word left out. Kate was to "fill in the blank" with an appropriate single word. Interestingly, on one item, the passage read is actually complete and understandable despite having a word missing. Kate read the passage and remarked "It doesn't need a word," which was correct, except the directions required her to come up with a word that would fit. She responded, "I can't think of a word." Her comprehension was intact on this item but she could not supply another word.

Written Language

In the area of written language skills, Kate demonstrated High Average ability in basic mechanics (Spelling). For spelling items, her mistakes on harder items were generally phonemically correct and close approximations to the target word. Kate demonstrated Average ability to communicate in written form (Writing Samples). This test had Kate writing sentences according to specific directions. On this task, spelling does not count on most items. Although her responses to all items administered were correct and earned points, Kate seldom obtained maximum credit for items. Her writing was clear and to the point but seldom included any elaboration or details.

Mathematics

Kate's mathematical skills were assessed in three areas: math fluency, math calculation, and mathematical reasoning. Kate had no difficulty quickly recalling basic addition, subtraction, and multiplication facts (Math Fluency), scoring in the Superior range. Fluency in basic mathematical operations depends on thorough learning, which automates the process. When given unlimited time, Kate performed in the High Average range on math computation (Math Calculation). She was able to correctly perform most simple addition, subtraction, multiplication, and division problems, making only two errors in this area. On one simple multiplication problem, she quickly wrote an incorrect response. Several problems later she noticed her error and asked if she could correct it. When she did so, she got the right answer. On a division problem, Kate quickly wrote in an incorrect answer and did not notice her error. She was able to do several algebraic problems, a square root problem, and a problem involving finding the slope and y-intercept when given the equation for a line. Her basic age- and grade-appropriate math knowledge base seems intact. Kate also performed in the Superior range on untimed mathematical reasoning tasks (Applied Problems).

She had no difficulty with these verbally framed math application problems presented to her both orally and in writing. As long as she had the necessary computational skill, she understood the problems and solved them correctly. Although Kate was provided with a pencil and scrap paper, she chose to do the vast majority of the problems in her head, relying on her skill and memory to come up with the correct answer. Kate's apparent ease with some of the math problems and her preference for performing the computations in her head did not hinder her on this test. However, it seemed clear that as the problems became more difficult, Kate's performance may have improved with the use of paper and pencil.

Academic Achievement Impressions

Overall, Kate's academic achievement is strong and consistent with, and in fact usually better than, her same-age peers. Once again, as in the cognitive areas, Kate's scores ranged from Average to Superior with no significant problems in reading, writing, or mathematic skills.

ASSESSMENT OF SOCIAL-EMOTIONAL FUNCTIONING

To assess her current perceptions of her own abilities and functioning, Kate and her mother were asked to complete the Behavior Assessment System for Children, Second Edition (BASC-2). The BASC-2 is a multidimensional tool that measures many aspects of behavior and personality, both positive and negative. Clinically significant scores indicate a high level of maladaptive behavior in that particular area (i.e., behavior that is dramatically different from the average behavior of same-age peers). At-risk scores indicate behaviors more severe than about two-thirds of the general population, but not yet severe enough to be considered clinically significant. At-risk scores may indicate a developing or potential problem, but not to the extent of requiring formal diagnosis or treatment.

Self-Report

Kate independently completed a BASC-2 self-report of personality for adolescents. The Emotional Symptoms Index (ESI) of the BASC-2 provides a general level of functioning based on the various scales measured by the checklist. Kate's ESI fell within the Average range and did not indicate a pervasive emotional or behavioral disturbance. Both the "lie scale" and "faking good" scales were not elevated,

suggesting that these results are valid representations of Kate's self-perception.

The School Maladjustment domain comprises the following three areas: attitude to school, attitude to teachers, and sensation seeking ("tendency to take risks, to like noise, and to seek excitement"). Kate's attitude toward school fell within the Average range and indicated that Kate associates normal feelings and general satisfaction with school settings. She does not perceive teachers as being overly negative, as her attitude toward teachers was also Average. Kate's ratings of her behaviors/feelings indicate sensation seeking within the Clinically Normal range. The School Maladjustment composite score was within the Average range.

The Clinical Maladjustment area is made up of the following scales: Atypicality (tendency toward odd behaviors, extreme mood swings), Locus of Control (belief that there are external forces in control), Somatization (tendency to complain about physical ailments), Social Stress (anxiety regarding interpersonal relationships, feeling left out), and Anxiety (worrisome, nervous feelings). Kate's self-ratings fell within the Average range in all areas.

The difference between Kate's School Maladjustment and her Clinical Maladjustment is considered to be statistically nonsignificant. This indicates that any attitude or stress that Kate perceives with regard to school-related aspects of her life are equal to her general perceptions of her attitudes toward clinical aspects of life (e.g., social stress, anxiety).

The Personal Adjustment composite contains the following scales: Relations with Parents, Interpersonal Relations, Self-Esteem, and Self-Reliance. Kate's report of her behaviors and feelings were all within the Average range. The overall composite score was within the Average range.

Parent Report

On the BASC-2 Parent Rating Scales, Mrs. Wilhelm's ratings placed Kate's ESI within the At-Risk range. The Externalizing Problems domain comprises the following three areas: Hyperactivity, Aggression, and Conduct Problems. Mrs. Wilhelm's ratings of Kate's aggression and conduct were both within Normal range, while the hyperactivity rating was in the Clinically Significant range.

The Internalizing Problems area is made up of the following scales: Anxiety (worrisome, nervous feelings), Depression (feelings of unhappiness, sadness, and stress), Somatization (tendency to complain about physical ailments), and Social Stress (anxiety regarding interpersonal relationships, feeling left out). Mrs. Wilhelm's ratings of Kate fell within the Average range in all areas.

The additional scales, not included in any separate composite score, are as follows: Atypicality (the tendency to behave in ways that are immature, considered "odd"), Withdrawal (the tendency to evade others to avoid social contact), and Attention Problems (the tendency to be easily distracted and unable to concentrate more than momentarily). Mrs. Wilhelm's ratings of Kate fell within the Average range with the single exception of the Attention Problems scale, rated as Clinically Significant. The rating for the Adaptive Skills composite was within the Average range.

Overall, Mrs. Wilhelm's ratings of her daughter are consistent with Kate's previous diagnosis as a child with ADHD. Only the individual Hyperactive and Attentional scales were elevated, and each of these raised the Externalizing and BSI composites into the Clinically Significant range.

ATTENTION-DEFICIT/ HYPERACTIVITY DISORDER

The BASC-2 PRS-A contains items related to *DSM-IV* criteria for ADHD diagnosis. Not surprisingly, the ratings for Kate tended to be relatively high on the items related to Attention Problems and Hyperactivity. Listed below are *all* the items related to the *DSM-IV* criteria, regardless of their responses. Items related to attention are listed first, followed by those related to hyperactivity.

Attention

4. Forgets things	Almost Always
36. Has short attention span	Often
47. Completes work on time	Sometimes
68. Has trouble concentrating	Often
79. Listens to directions	Sometimes
99. Completes homework from start to finish without taking a break	Never
110. Is easily distracted	Often

Hyperactivity

8. Needs too much supervision	Sometimes
19. Is restless during movies	Never
29. Acts without thinking	Often
40. Throws a tantrum	Sometimes
51. Cannot wait to take turn	Sometimes
61. Interrupts parents when they are on the phone	Often
72. Taps foot or pencil	Sometimes
83. Is overly active	Often
103. Interrupts others when they are speaking	Often
114. Fiddles with things while at meals	Often

CONCLUSION

Results from both the cognitive and academic assessment indicate that Kate is an adolescent who excels in many areas. Her cognitive abilities are generally well above average, with her lowest cognitive abilities (visual-spatial processing and processing speed) being solidly in the Average range. Academically, Kate's abilities ranged again from Average to Superior, with her lowest (yet Average) academic areas being in reading comprehension and written expression. Overall, Kate views herself as average emotionally and did not endorse any aspect of her emotional functioning to a degree that would raise concerns. In contrast, Mrs. Wilhelm rated Kate's functioning in the Clinically Significant range, but the two areas endorsed (attention problems and hyperactivity) are consistent with what might be expected for a child identified as having ADHD.

Regarding her scholastic difficulties, the current evaluation found no evidence to suggest a learning disability. Learning disabilities are typically defined as "disorders in a basic psychological process" that impact a person in academic areas. Each of the cognitive processes assessed during this evaluation were found to be in the Average to Superior range, and similar results were found in the academic achievement areas. It would therefore appear that any difficulties that Kate is experiencing at school are not the result of a learning disability. It may be that because Kate is so bright and has had little trouble in the past learning academically oriented materials that she expects all aspects of her schooling to come as easily. It is not uncommon for bright children to become frustrated when they encounter a new topic or subject that does not come easily to them.

Couple Kate's approach to tasks (e.g., quick, somewhat impulsive, verbally oriented, and with a need for clear guidelines) with some of her ADHD symptoms (forgetful, short attention span, distractibility) and the result can contribute to some problems in school.

Counseling should focus on helping Kate understand the impact that her ADHD might have on her when it comes to learning new material, as well as learning organizational and study skills to assist her with her school work. Kate should learn to evaluate her work for levels of difficulty and apply different strategies to the more difficult areas than those she uses with easier, rote material. Below is a list of suggestions that may be useful for Kate and her teachers.

RECOMMENDATIONS

Organization of Materials and Assignments

For the Parents

1. Set up Kate's notebook in the following manner:
   a. Choose a 3-ring binder that has pockets and holders for pens, erasers, and other school supplies, as well as a transparent pocket in which to display a card with Kate's name and phone number in case it is lost.
   b. Insert a folder with inside pockets. Label the front cover HOMEWORK. On the inside, label the left pocket "Not finished" and the right, "Finished." Any papers given out in class—related to assignments—are to be placed in the Not Finished pocket and all completed assignments in the Finished pocket until they are handed in.
   c. Buy an assignment book that has room to write assignments for each subject on two facing pages and that has a month-to-month calendar in it. All assignments should be written daily on the appropriate page. Use the monthly calendar to fill in assignment deadlines as well as intermediate deadlines and work sessions for long-term projects. Color in school breaks and special events.
   d. Put tabbed dividers of different colors in the notebook, one for each subject. Plastic dividers are easier to handle and are more durable than paper dividers.
   e. In the back of the binder, include a section for blank notebook paper.
2. At home, if necessary, check Kate's assignment book, make sure the assignments are completed, and make sure she puts the assignment in the "Finished" pocket of the homework folder.

3. Help Kate set up a file system at home. Place files, each one labeled with the name of a class/subject, in a file drawer, file box, or accordion file. Periodically, go through the notebook with Kate and pull out the papers that no longer need to be kept in the notebook. File these, by subject, in the corresponding file. Kate will then have these papers to refer back to if necessary and the number of papers in the notebook is more manageable.

For the Teachers

1. With a note from parents attesting that Kate has put time and effort into an assignment, be flexible with deadlines without penalties.
2. If Kate is spending excessive amounts of time on homework or completing unfinished class assignments at home, decrease the length of her assignments. Her assignments should take no longer than other students are expected to spend. Examples include reducing the length of written reports and assigning fewer math problems or spelling words.
3. When possible, assign one task at a time and break academic tasks into clearly designated stages and steps with time lines for each step. Better yet, teach Kate how to analyze long-term assignments and set intermediate deadlines.
4. Incorporate a study hall into Kate's daily schedule toward the end of the day so that she can use that time to begin her homework while a teacher is available to provide whatever organizational help is necessary.

Improving Learning Behaviors in the Classroom

1. As much as possible, use teaching activities that encourage active responding such as discussion, board work, and cooperative learning in small groups.
2. If Kate tends to respond impulsively during class, help her to stop and think before answering. With Kate, create a visual signal, such as placing your finger beside your cheek, to remind her to slow down and think before responding.
3. If Kate appears to have difficulty paying attention in class, seat her near the teacher. Avoid seating her near distracting stimuli such as windows, doors, AC units, heaters, and high traffic areas.
4. Keep classroom noise, such as unnecessary student chatting, to a minimum.

Giving Instructions

1. Make sure you have Kate's attention before giving directions. Eye contact is important.
2. To avoid misunderstandings, write assignments on the board and designate a specific time for students to write them in their assignment books. Make sure that Kate does so.

3. Do not include any irrelevant information during oral directions. Keep directions concise and simple.

Foreign Language

Discuss with the school counselor whether or not a waiver of the foreign language requirement would be a significant disadvantage to Kate when she applies to college. If not, consider waiving this requirement for high school graduation.

Scores and Classifications for the Cognitive Domains, Factors, and Skills Assessed

	Factor	Skill Areas Assessed	Test	Subtest	Scaled Score	Average Factor Score	Classification
Acquired Knowledge	Crystallized Ability	Lexical Knowledge General Knowledge Language Development	WJ III COG WISC-IV	Verbal Comprehension Similarities Comprehension Information Vocabulary Word Reasoning	128 120 130 140 125 100	124	Superior
	Quantitative Knowledge	Quantitative Reasoning	WISC-IV	Arithmetic	125	125	Superior
High-Level Processing and Reasoning	Fluid Reasoning	Deductive Reasoning Inductive Reasoning	WJ III COG WISC-IV	Analysis-Synthesis Matrix Reasoning Picture Concepts	114 125 95	111	High Average
	Long-Term Storage and Retrieval	Word Finding & Retrieval Associative Memory & Learning	WJ III COG	Retrieval Fluency Visual-Auditory Learning Visual-Auditory Learning delayed	116 117 129	121	Superior
	Visual Processing	Visualization Spatial Relations Flexibility of Closure	WJ III COG WISC-IV	Spatial Relations Block Design Picture Completion	114 100 95	103	Average
Low-Level Processing	Short-Term Memory	Working Memory Memory Span	WISC-IV	Digit Span Backward Letter Number Sequencing Digit Span Forward	110 115 105	110	Average
	Processing Speed	Perceptual Speed Rate of Test Taking	WISC-IV	Symbol Search Cancellation Coding	110 90 100	100	Average

Scores and Classifications for the Achievement Areas and Skills Assessed

Academic Area	Skill Areas Assessed	WJ III ACH Test	Standard Score	Range
Reading	Reading Decoding	Letter-Word Identification	122	Superior
	Reading Comprehension	Passage Comprehension	98	Average
	Fluency	Reading Fluency	141	Superior
Writing Ability	Spelling	Spelling	113	High Average
	Written Expression	Writing Samples	103	Average
Mathematics	Calculation	Calculation	116	High Average
	Fluency	Math Fluency	120	High Average
	Reasoning	Applied Problems	122	Superior

Scores and Classification for the Parent and Self-Reports of the BASC-2

Parent Report			Self Report		
Hyperactivity	72	Clinically Significant	Attitude to School	56	Average
Aggression	57	Average	Attitude to Teachers	55	Average
Conduct Problems	55	Average	Sensation Seeking	46	Average
Anxiety	56	Average	Atypicality	41	Average
Depression	55	Average	Locus of Control	50	Average
Somatization	52	Average	Somatization	45	Average
			Social Stress	49	Average
Atypicality	50	Average	Anxiety	47	Average
Withdrawal	54	Average			
Attention Problems	76	Clinically Significant	Depression	55	Average
Social Skills	47	Average			
Leadership	43	Average	Relations with Parents	52	Average
			Interpersonal Relations	49	Average
Externalizing Problems	63	At-Risk	Self-Esteem	46	Average
Internalizing Problems	55	Average	Self-Reliance	46	Average
Behavior Symptoms Index	65	At-Risk			
Adaptive Skills	45	Average	School Maladjustment	53	Average
			Clinical Maladjustment	46	Average
			Personal Adjustment	51	Average
			Emotional Symptoms Index	49	Average

Terms used in this report for describing the *T* scores on the BASC-2 are:

Adaptive Scales	Clinical Scales	*T* Score Range
Very High	Clinically Significant	70 and above
High	At-Risk	60–69
Average	Average	41–59
At-Risk	Low	31–40
Clinically Significant	Very low	30 and below

TEST DESCRIPTIONS

Wechsler Intelligence Scale for Children-Fourth Edition (WISC-IV)

The WISC-IV is an individual test that does not require reading or writing. Verbal subtests are oral questions requiring oral answers. Perceptual Reasoning subtests are nonverbal problems, some of which are timed and one of which allows bonus points for extra fast work. Working Memory subtests require remembering data (e.g., repeating dictated digits) or remembering and mentally manipulating data (e.g., repeating dictated digits in reverse order). Processing Speed subtests measure speed on fairly simple paper-and-pencil tasks. Two supplemental subtests (no more than one per scale) can be substituted for standard subtests in total scores if absolutely necessary. Process subtests are never used for calculating total scores. Subtest scores and total scores are based on the scores of the 2,200 children originally tested in a very carefully designed, nationwide sample, but still must be interpreted very cautiously for any individual, especially one who may have somewhat unusual patterns of strengths and weaknesses. As with any test, influences such as anxiety, motivation, fatigue, rapport, and experience may invalidate test scores.

Standard Verbal Subtests

- Similarities: explaining how two different things (e.g., horse and cow) or concepts (e.g., hope and fear) could be alike. Scoring is 2-1-0, according to the quality of the responses.
- Vocabulary: giving oral definitions of words. Scoring is 2-1-0, according to the quality of the responses.
- Comprehension: oral questions of social and practical understanding. Scoring is 2-1-0, based on quality.

Supplemental Verbal Subtests

- Information: oral, "trivia"-style, general information questions. Scoring is pass/fail.

- Word Reasoning: trying to guess a word from a series of clues.

Standard Perceptual Reasoning Subtests

- Block Design**: copying small geometric designs with four or nine larger plastic cubes. The most difficult items offer bonus points for speed.
- Picture Concepts: choosing one picture from each of two or three rows so that the selected pictures all illustrate the same concept.

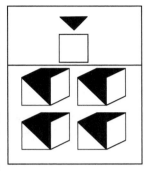

- Matrix Reasoning: completing logical arrangements of designs with missing parts; multiple-choice.

Supplemental Perceptual Reasoning Subtest

- Picture Completion*: identifying missing parts removed from pictures.

Perceptual Organization Process Subtest

- Block Design subtest by norms without bonuses for speed; pass/fail scoring only.

Standard Working Memory Subtests

- Digit Span: repeating dictated series of digits (e.g., 4 1 7 9) forwards and other series backwards. Series begin with two digits and keep increasing in length, with two trials at each length.
- Letter-Number Sequencing: repeating dictated series of letters and digits (e.g., 4 3 R 9 B) in numerical, then alphabetical order (e.g., 3 4 9 B R).

Supplemental Working Memory Subtest

- Arithmetic*: oral, verbally-framed math applications problems without paper. Scoring is pass/fail.

Working Memory Process Subtests

- Digit Span has additional scores for digits forward and backward raw scores (1 point for each series recalled correctly) and also for the greatest number of digits recalled forward and the greatest number recalled backward (e.g., 3 9 2 7 = four digits).

Standard Processing Speed Subtests

- Coding A**: marking rows of shapes with different lines according to a code as quickly as possible for 2 minutes (under age 8).

1	2	3	4	5	6	7	8	9
⊥	↑	>	↔	Π	∩	∅	∴	↓

- Coding B**: transcribing a digit-symbol code as quickly as possible for 2 minutes (eight and older).

3	7	4	1	2	9	6	5	2	1	4

- Symbol Search**: deciding if target symbols appear in a row of symbols and marking Yes or No accordingly.

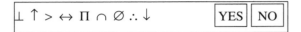

⊥ ↑ > ↔ Π ∩ ∅ ∴ ↓   YES NO

Supplemental Processing Speed Subtest

- Cancellation: speed of marking all the animals among pictures of many things.

Processing Speed Process Subtests

- Cancellation: separate scores for one page on which the pictures are scattered randomly and one on which the pictures are arranged in rows.

*time limit **time limit and bonuses for speed

Woodcock-Johnson III NU Tests of Cognitive and Achievement Abilities (WJ III)

Unlike many individual ability tests, the WJ III Cognitive Ability tests are explicitly designed to assess a student's abilities on many specific Cattell-Horn-Carroll (CHC) "cognitive factors," not just to provide a total score. Each of seven tests in the Standard Battery is designed to measure one factor. The Extended Battery offers seven more tests to make two for each factor. There are three Standard Battery and three Extended Battery tests that contribute to additional Clinical Clusters. Tests can also be combined into a General Intellectual Ability (GIA) score of 7 or 14 tests and into several cognitive categories. The WJ III ACH measures a great many aspects of academic achievement with a wide variety of relatively brief tests. Many of these achievement tests can be used with the WJ III COG tests to assess a student's abilities on many specific CHC "cognitive factors." Examiners are permitted to select the tests they need to assess abilities in which they are interested for a particular student. The WJ III was normed on 8,818 children and adults (4,783 in grades kindergarten through 12) in a well-designed, national sample. The same persons also provided norms for the WJ III ACH tests, so the ability and achievement tests can be compared directly, and cognitive and achievement tests can be combined to measure CHC factors.

Listed below are the factors and tests administered:

Woodcock-Johnson III Tests of Cognitive Abilities (WJ III COG)

Comprehension-Knowledge (Gc)

- Verbal Comprehension. Naming pictures, giving antonyms or synonyms for spoken words, and completing oral analogies.

Long-Term Retrieval (Glr) [Note: "Long-term" can be as short as several minutes.]

- Visual-Auditory Learning. The student is taught rebus symbols for words and tries to "read" sentences written with those symbols.
- Visual-Auditory Learning – Delayed. The student tries again to "read" sentences written with the rebuses learned in Visual-Auditory Learning. There are norms from one half-hour to 8 days. This is an additional measure of Glr.
- Retrieval Fluency. The student tries to name as many things as possible in 1 minute in each of three specified categories (e.g., fruits).

Visual Processing (Gv)

- Spatial Relations. The student tries to select by sight alone, from many choices, the fragments that could be assembled into a given geometric shape.

Fluid Reasoning (Gf)

- Analysis-Synthesis. The student tries to solve logical puzzles involving color codes similar to mathematical and scientific symbolic rules.

Woodcock-Johnson III Tests of Achievement (WJ III ACH)

Reading (Grw)

- Letter-Word Identification: naming letters and reading words aloud from a list.
- Reading Fluency: speed of reading sentences and answering "yes" or "no" to each.

- Passage Comprehension: orally supplying the missing word removed from each sentence or very brief paragraph (e.g., "Woof," said the _____, biting the hand that fed it.").

Writing (Grw)

- Spelling: writing letters and words from dictation.
- Writing Samples: writing sentences according to directions; many items include pictures; spelling does not count on most items.

Mathematics (Gq)

- Calculation: involves arithmetic computation with paper and pencil.
- Math Fluency: speed of performing simple calculations for 3 minutes.
- Applied Problems: oral, math "word problems," some with illustrations or printed instructions, solved with paper and pencil.

BASC-2 Parent Rating Composites and Scales

Externalizing Problems

- Aggression: tendency to act in a hostile manner (either verbal or physical) that is threatening to others
- Hyperactivity: tendency to be overly active, rush through work or activities, and act without thinking
- Conduct problems: tendency to engage in antisocial and rule-breaking behavior, including destroying property

Internalizing Problems

- Anxiety: tendency to be nervous, fearful, or worried about real or imagined problems
- Depression: feelings of unhappiness, sadness, and stress that may result in an inability to carry out everyday activities (or may bring on thoughts of suicide)
- Somatization: tendency to be overly sensitive to and complain about relatively minor physical problems and discomforts

School Problems

- Attention problems: tendency to be easily distracted and unable to concentrate more than momentarily

Other Problems

- Atypicality: tendency to behave in ways that are immature, considered "odd," or commonly associated with

psychosis (such as experiencing visual or auditory hallucinations)
- Withdrawal: tendency to evade others to avoid social contact

Adaptive Skills

- Adaptability: ability to adapt readily to changes in the environment
- Leadership: skills associated with accomplishing academic, social, or community goals, including, in particular, the ability to work well with others
- Social skills: skills necessary for interacting successfully with peers and adults in home, school, and community settings
- Study skills: skills that are conducive to strong academic performance, including organizational skills and good study habits

Behavior Symptoms Index

- Aggression - Hyperactivity - Anxiety - Depression - Attention - Problems - Atypicality

BASC-2 Student Rating Composites and Scales

Clinical Maladjustment

- Anxiety: feelings of nervousness, worry, and fear; the tendency to be overwhelmed by problems
- Atypicality: the tendency toward gross mood swings, bizarre thoughts, subjective experiences, or obsessive-compulsive thoughts and behaviors often considered "odd"
- Locus of control: the belief that rewards and punishments are controlled by external events or other people
- Social stress: feelings of stress and tension in personal relationships; a feeling of being excluded from social activities
- Somatization: the tendency to be overly sensitive to, experience, or complain about relatively minor physical problems and discomforts

School Maladjustment

- Attitude toward school: feelings of alienation, hostility, and dissatisfaction regarding school
- Attitude toward teachers: feelings of resentment and dislike of teachers; beliefs that teachers are unfair, uncaring, or overly demanding

- Sensation seeking: the tendency to take risks, to like noise, and to seek excitement

Other Problems

- Depression: feelings of unhappiness, sadness, and dejection; a belief that nothing goes right
- Sense of inadequacy: perceptions of being unsuccessful in school, unable to achieve one's goals, and generally inadequate

Personal Adjustment

- Relations with parents: a positive regard toward parents and a feeling of being esteemed by them

- Interpersonal relations: the perception of having good social relationships and friendships with peers
- Self-esteem: feelings of self-esteem, self-respect, and self-acceptance
- Self-reliance: confidence in one's ability to solve problems; a belief in one's personal dependability and decisiveness

Emotional Symptoms Index

- Anxiety-Social Stress-Depression-Sense of Inadequacy-Interpersonal Relations-Self-Esteem

CASE 43

Assessing an Adolescent English Language Learner
Teasing Apart the Threads of Two Languages
Deborah Rhein

Assessing non-native speakers of English for a possible language disorder is much more complex than simply testing the speaker in the dominant language. That was the practice years ago, when the organization of linguistic knowledge in the bilingual brain was less understood. It is also more complex than simply using a good standardized instrument in both languages and evaluating the scores. These instruments yield valuable information and should be part of the process, but they present unique challenges when used with bilingual speakers.

If all one wished from the results of an evaluation were the ability to compare broad aspects of one person's linguistic knowledge to that of peers, then it would be sufficient to test in one language and report the results. It would be possible to say that a student is three standard deviations below monolingual English-speaking peers in the areas of Expressive Language or Language Content. Such a statement, however, may not imply disability but rather that the student is still in the process of acquiring English. In addition, even if the student's scores were significantly below average in both languages, it would not necessarily mean that he has a language disorder. Before one can understand why the assessment of bilingual speakers is so complex, it is imperative to explore a core assumption inherent in standardized assessment instruments.

The goal of most language evaluations is not simply to establish a benchmark for linguistic skill, but rather to make a determination about a person's learning abilities. That assumes that the person being tested has had adequate opportunity to learn that which he is being tested on. That assumption can be a major pitfall when assessing bilingual speakers unless the evaluator can establish that there has been adequate opportunity to learn at least one language.

One problem, however, is determining what constitutes an adequate opportunity to learn a language.

In addition, establishing that there was adequate opportunity to learn a language is a necessary but not sufficient condition for understanding language development. The evaluator must also consider whether there has been adequate opportunity to maintain the skills in the language, because first language loss can occur when such opportunities are not present. The resulting low scores in both the first and second languages can mimic a language learning disability (Kohnert, 2007). Thus, the evaluator must also determine whether or not there has been sufficient opportunity to acquire, maintain, and develop skills in each language. This is precisely why case history becomes a vital part of the assessment process. The interpretation of the scores of the following report would have been different if there had not been such strong evidence of support in the first language.

Another consideration when assessing bilingual speakers is the linguistic level being assessed. Cummins (1980) differentiated an informal level of language, such as one might use in a social conversation, from academic language, the language needed to understand, speak, read, and write about subject area content material. Cummins stated an English Language Learner (ELL) could acquire the first level of language, termed Basic Interpersonal Communication Skills (BICS), in approximately 2 years, whereas it takes approximately 5 to 7 years to acquire the more advanced level of language, Cognitive-Academic Language Proficiency (CALP). Cummins explained the importance of assessing language at the academic level, as well as the basic level, because the linguistic demands in an academic environment are very different than the linguistic demands of everyday interaction (Cummins, 1980, 2000). In the following case, the student, Esteban, did not appear to perform adequately in either language at the academic level.

In a bilingual language evaluation, a language sample in each language should be obtained in the contexts in which the student is likely to use that language (Patterson & Rodriguez, 2005). Ideally, the student would be recorded interacting with family and peers without his knowledge, in order to obtain an untainted language sample. With small children, this is often accomplished by having the main caregiver collect the language sample at home. With an older student, this is more problematic. Additional complications exist when assessing an adolescent. By that age, most students have had such varied exposure to and opportunity to use both languages that it is very difficult to get a language sample of both receptive and expressive language and to do so in all of the different contexts in which the student typically uses language. Thus, the odds are likely that it will be possible to sample only one or two of the relevant contexts. Here again, a comprehensive case history can help fill in gaps for areas not sampled. In the following case, attempts were made to meet that standard in the school setting, by obtaining the sample while Esteban interacted with friends in each language.

The following report is an example of the factors that should be addressed when assessing a bilingual student, as well as an attempt to meet the demands of the efficiency required of evaluators who work in a busy school district. To this end, the school social worker obtained consent to evaluate from Esteban's mother, then interviewed her to obtain a detailed case history. The bilingual evaluator reviewed the written report of the case history and then called the mother for clarification and elaboration regarding specific points. In the case of an older student, the case history may also include portfolio samples of classwork.

A further consideration when assessing bilingual students is the decision of whether to include normative data derived from monolingual students. Because these norms alone should never be used to determine the existence of a disability, most clinicians opt out of reporting them and just use the tests as criterion-based instruments. Although this is an ethical choice, there is a real loss when discarding the normative data. Normative data can and should be used to document the educational disadvantage of a student who receives no classroom support as he continues to acquire English. Unfortunately, this is often the case after a student is classified as Fully English Proficient. In addition, comparing normative scores in *both* languages can be useful in determining if there is a similar pattern of relative strengths and weaknesses across languages, and in ascertaining the likelihood of a language disorder. This use is demonstrated in the following report.

Finally, an important point regarding the writing of reports addressing the linguistic skills of a bilingual student concerns the background knowledge of the intended audience. Often, a referral for a speech and language evaluation is made by a professional who needs the information to obtain a more comprehensive view of the child's difficulties and needs. In this case, as with the current evaluation, the report is written for the referring professional. Like most professional reports, the report may be read by professionals from a wide variety of disciplines. Unlike most professional reports, its intended readers are unlikely to have background knowledge of second language acquisition issues. Consequently, they may not understand the reason that test score interpretation is so dependent on the information obtained from the case history. Thus, when writing a report regarding the language evaluation of a bilingual student, more explanation is needed than when writing reports on monolingual children; and, because most bilingual clinicians do not include the normative data based on the monolingual English sample, the explanation must be even more extensive if that data are to be used. In that case, the evaluator bears a significant responsibility to ensure that the reported scores will not be misinterpreted or misused.

BILINGUAL SPEECH-LANGUAGE EVALUATION

Name:	Esteban Garcia
Date of Birth:	07/02/95
Age:	14-9
School:	Rio Vistoso Middle School
Grade:	9
School Year:	2009–2010
Test Dates:	04/02 and 04/09/2010
Report Date:	04/15/2010
Evaluator:	Deborah Rhein, Ph.D.

REASON FOR REFERRAL

Esteban Garcia is a bilingual male, age 14-9, who was referred by his Language Arts teacher, Mrs. Martinez, for a bilingual speech-language evaluation to rule out the possibility of a language learning disability.

BACKGROUND INFORMATION

Education

Esteban attends Rio Vistoso Middle School and is in the ninth grade. He entered kindergarten as an English Language Learner and was enrolled in a bilingual program, which he attended through fourth grade. At the end of fourth grade, his family moved to another district where he received pull-out English as a Second Language (ESL) services. He continued to receive ESL services until eighth grade when he received the designation of Fully English Proficient (FEP) and English support services were discontinued.

Information collected from his other teachers support the observations of Mrs. Martinez that Esteban doesn't engage in class, he doesn't have an answer when called on, and he doesn't appear to understand oral directions. She reported that he frequently watches the other students before attempting any in-class assignments, that he seldom completes homework or in-class assignments, and that when he does, he frequently does not follow the instructions correctly. Esteban is performing best in math, except on word problems. All of his teachers suggested that he may have been exited from ESL services too early and that he doesn't appear to have the English vocabulary or reading skills to handle grade-level work.

Home Language Use

When his mother, a Spanish speaker, was interviewed, she stated that she believed Esteban was more proficient in English than Spanish, but that he appears fluent in both languages. She said that Spanish is the main language of the adults at home, but that the children often speak English. She reported that the family watches television and listens to the radio in both languages. Esteban is the third of eight children, all of whom still live at home. Both of his parents attended school in Mexico until the eighth grade; both read and write in Spanish. While there is no history of any language or learning problems, Esteban's mother reported that Esteban's father was slow at learning to read and, unlike her, never reads the Spanish-language newspaper.

Developmental History

Esteban's mother provided the following developmental history. Esteban achieved all developmental milestones at age-appropriate times and his medical history was generally unremarkable except for frequent ear infections in early childhood. He had pressure equalization tubes inserted when he was 4 years old. His speech remained "baby-like" for a longer period than his siblings, but he was always intelligible to family and friends. He was never referred for a speech or language evaluation and, by the end of second grade, his speech was commensurate with that of his siblings. He was always a very quiet child and spoke less often than his siblings, although this was never a concern because Esteban's father is also a quiet person.

His mother also reported that Esteban was slow in acquiring reading skills, which were taught in Spanish, but that by the end of third grade, he was reading well in Spanish. Since he left the bilingual program, she hasn't helped him with homework, so she doesn't know how well he reads in English. She noted that his sister, who is 1 year younger, frequently helps him with his homework.

Self-Assessment

When interviewed, Esteban stated that English is his preferred language, that he uses English in the classroom, and that the majority of his education has been in this language. However, he uses both languages with friends at school and at home, sometimes speaking English with his siblings, but usually speaking Spanish with his parents. He stated that he doesn't like schoolwork and finds school difficult, but considers himself an average student. On a rating scale of 1–5 (1-lowest and 5-highest), he gave himself the following ratings for his academic skills in English: spelling-3, reading-3, and writing-3. He stated he was unable to rate his academic skills in Spanish, since it has been many years since he has done any academic work in that language.

TESTING OBSERVATIONS

At the beginning of the evaluation, Esteban appeared apprehensive and quiet, answering with short responses. While he was cooperative, he said that the evaluation made him uncomfortable and that he did not want to return the following week for the assessment in Spanish. Despite the fact that he did not want to participate in the assessment, he seemed motivated to do his best.

Tests/Procedures/Measures

Clinical Evaluation of Language Fundamentals, Fourth Edition (CELF-4)

Clinical Evaluation of Language Fundamentals, Fourth Edition Spanish (CELF-4 Spanish)

Expressive One-Word Picture Vocabulary Test Spanish-Bilingual Edition (EOWPVT-SPE)

Receptive One-Word Picture Vocabulary Test Spanish-Bilingual Edition (ROWPVT-SPE)

Written language sample—English/Spanish

Verbal language sample—English/Spanish

Hearing screening

Oral-peripheral screening

TEST RESULTS/INTERPRETATION

Hearing

A pure-tone hearing screening was conducted as part of the evaluation. Results indicated normal hearing bilaterally.

Oral-Peripheral Screening

A brief oral-peripheral screening was conducted. Results indicated that the structures and functions of the speech mechanisms (e.g., mouth, lips, tongue) were adequate for normal speech.

Voice, Articulation, and Fluency

A perceptual screening of voice, articulation, and fluency indicated all were functioning normally and in the appropriate range for age and gender.

Clinical Evaluation of Language Fundamentals-4

The Clinical Evaluation of Language Fundamentals-4 (CELF-4) was administered to determine Esteban's expressive and receptive language abilities in English. The scores represent Esteban's linguistic functioning within the domains of expressive and receptive language (i.e., listen-ing and speaking) and the language components of semantics, syntax, morphology, and pragmatics. Both Spanish and English versions of the CELF-4 have composite standard score (SS) means of 100, with a standard deviation (SD) of 15, whereas the individual subtests have scaled score (ScS) means of 10, with a standard deviation of 3. In the field of speech and language, standard scores between 85 and 115 (±1 SD) are considered to be within the average range; scores between 78 and 84 (−1 to −1.5 SD) are borderline (i.e., normalcy/disorder is indeterminate); and scores below 78 (<1.5 SD) indicate a disorder.

For reporting purposes, subtest raw scores have been converted to standard scores. In the English-language edition, standard scores compare Esteban's language performance to that of monolingual English-speaking age peers. In the Spanish-language edition, Esteban's performance is compared to that of bilingual age peers representative of the people of Hispanic origin who are living in the United States. The subtest scores are combined to create index scores that measure a specific construct and are statistically more robust. The Core Language score is a measure of general language ability. The CELF-4 manual recommends consideration of the Core Language score as the first step in determining a language disorder and analysis of these and supplementary tests to determine the nature of the disorder, if one appears to be present.

Language: English Assessments

The table below describes Esteban's performance on the indexes and subtests of the CELF-4 when compared with that of English-speaking monolingual age peers. In Esteban's case, it is necessary to consider the limitations of such comparisons. Low scores in a second language are not necessarily an indication of a language disorder, but rather are useful in documenting the extent of disadvantage created by the incomplete acquisition of English. The results inform the need for modifications and/or accommodations when a student is required to function in a class conducted in monolingual English.

CELF-4 English			
Index/Subtest	SS/ScS	PR	English Norms
Core Language	70	2	compared with monolingual English peers
Recalling Sentences	4		compared with monolingual English peers
Formulated Sentences	4		compared with monolingual English peers
Word Classes—Total	6		compared with monolingual English peers
Word Definitions	6		compared with monolingual English peers

CELF-4 English Index/Subtest	SS/ScS	PR	English Norms
Receptive Language	80	9	compared with monolingual English peers
Word Classes—Receptive	7		compared with monolingual English peers
Understanding Spoken Paragraphs	6		compared with monolingual English peers
Semantic Relationships	7		compared with monolingual English peers
Expressive Language	65	1	compared with monolingual English peers
Recalling Sentences	4		compared with monolingual English peers
Formulated Sentences	4		compared with monolingual English peers
Word Classes—Expressive	5		compared with monolingual English peers
Language Content	76	5	compared with monolingual English peers
Word Definitions	6		compared with monolingual English peers
Understanding Spoken Paragraphs	6		compared with monolingual English peers
Sentence Assembly	6		compared with monolingual English peers
Language Memory	66	1	compared with monolingual English peers
Recalling Sentences	4		compared with monolingual English peers
Formulated Sentences	4		compared with monolingual English peers
Semantic Relationships	7		compared with monolingual English peers
Working Memory	66	1	compared with monolingual English peers
Number Repetition	4		compared with monolingual English peers
Familiar Sequences	4		compared with monolingual English peers
RAN	atypical		compared with monolingual English peers

Score Comparisons

When compared to monolingual English peers, Esteban's Core Language score of 70 places him 2 standard deviations below the mean. There is a significant difference, however, between his Receptive Language index, in the borderline range, and his Expressive Language index, in the disordered range. The score difference between the Expressive and Receptive Language indexes is significant at the .05 level. All other language indices in English are at least 1.5 standard deviations below monolingual peers.

It is important to reiterate that when non-native speakers of English obtain low scores on standardized tests, it does not necessarily indicate they have a disorder. While Esteban's index scores indicate the possibility of a language disorder, these results are not conclusive. They do, however, indicate that Esteban is greatly in need of accommodations and modifications in his classroom.

The subtest scores were analyzed for patterns of relative strengths and weaknesses so that these could be compared for similarities and differences with his subtest profile in Spanish. When compared to monolingual peers, Esteban scored at least 1 standard deviation below the mean on every subtest but two, in which he obtained scores in the lower end of the average range. He scored more than 2 standard deviations below the mean on four subtests: Recalling Sentences, Formulated Sentences, Number Repetition, and Familiar Sequences. Task performance on these four subtests relies heavily on auditory memory and, in the case of an English language learner like Esteban, limited vocabulary in English could also contribute to his low scores. However, because Number Repetition and Familiar Sequences have highly controlled vocabulary, language differences are less likely to contribute to Esteban's poor performances on these tests. Thus, while these results must be interpreted with caution, there are some indications that Esteban may have some underlying processing problems.

Rapid Automatized Naming—English

Rapid Automatized Naming (RAN) tests assess a person's speed and accuracy in naming very familiar visual prompts, in this case, colors and shapes. His rating for accuracy was "typical" but for speed, "atypical." In other words, he was slow but accurate.

English: Reading, Narrative, Peer Interaction, and Writing

Observation of Esteban reading a paragraph of an age-appropriate story in English indicated that he is a slow reader and has not reached automaticity for many common English words (e.g., *many, reason, decision*). He frequently sounded out the initial part of a word, then said the whole word. His reading was marked by pausing to decode at least one word in every sentence. As a result, he did not exhibit any variations of intonation during the oral reading.

Esteban's speech prosody was monotone during both spontaneous and structured oral tasks. Esteban was shown a picture card illustrating a variety of action and content and he was asked to describe what was happening. His verbal description consisted of 16 utterances ranging from 1 to 8 words (e.g., "a dog," "water," "another boat," "a guy in uh, in uh almost like a car"). Due to his limited responses, he needed prompting to facilitate further discussion of the picture. Esteban was asked to write about the same picture and needed an example carrier phrase to get started (e.g., "There is …"). Esteban used this carrier phrase to produce eight simple sentences (e.g., "There is a rat walking on the rope."). His written sentences contained both syntactic and spelling errors. His handwriting was legible and punctuation and capitalization appropriate at the beginning and end of sentences.

In order to obtain a naturalistic language sample, Esteban was recorded interacting with a friend who is a monolingual English speaker. From their conversation, a 100-utterance language sample in English was obtained and analyzed using Damico's (1985) discourse analysis and Retherford's guidelines (2000).

Damico's discourse analysis looks for topic maintenance, clarity, coherence, and cohesion in the overall interaction. Although Esteban's utterances were short, with occasional code-switching to Spanish, he appeared able to use most conventions for discourse. The exceptions were his overuse of nonspecific vocabulary (60% of his utterances contained at least one nonspecific word such as "thing," or "stuff"), combined with poor referencing for nonspecific and deictic words (i.e., words that specify a spatial, temporal, or identity relationship from the perspective of the participants, such as "here," "this," or "then"). Deictic words are significant in the analysis of pragmatic skills because their effective use requires the speaker to consider what information his conversational partner requires to derive the intended meaning. For example, Esteban said, "The thing over there" without specifying what the "thing" was and where "there" existed. His friend seemed to know what Esteban was referring to, so that may have been a frequent topic between friends and thus did not need prior referencing. Esteban's use of nonspecific vocabulary and poor referencing could be due to limited vocabulary in English or to a possible language disorder. It is also important to note that the language sample was limited to language that meets the criteria for Cummins' Basic Interpersonal Communication Skills (BICS), although attempts were made to obtain a language sample on a more complex linguistic task to ascertain Esteban's Cognitive Academic Language Proficiency (CALP) (Cummins, 1980, 2000). Because Esteban responded with short responses or no responses during the CALP-level activities, the sample was insufficient and could not be analyzed. Thus, the conclusions from his discourse in English is that he appeared to know and be able to use most discourse conventions at a BICS level but was not proficient at CALP.

Retherford's guidelines (2000) were used to calculate the Type-Token Ratio (TTR) for the analysis of semantic skills. TTR is a ratio derived from the number of novel words used in a language sample (i.e., words used only once) by the total number of words. A low TTR is indicative of a limited vocabulary. The completed analysis identified a ratio of .43. This result is a typical score for monolingual English children between 3 and 8 years old. Within the 100 utterances, Esteban used 455 words, of which 196 were novel. Consequently, 259 of the words were repeated, indicating a limited vocabulary sample in English, and which is consistent with the results of his standardized testing in English and the observation of his overuse of nonspecific vocabulary in the English language sample.

Spanish Assessments

Use of the CELF-4 Spanish edition in assessments of bilingual students in the United States is a more appropriate choice than many other instruments because it was normed on bilingual English/Spanish speakers residing in the United States. Thus, this normative data are more comparable to Esteban's experience than an instrument normed on Spanish speakers in Spanish-dominant countries. However, because the opportunities to acquire and maintain skills in Spanish differ among bilingual speakers residing in the United States, even use of these norms must be interpreted with some caution. If sufficient evidence were available that Esteban has had adequate opportunity to learn and maintain skills in his first language, then low scores could be indicative of a language disorder. The table below describes Esteban's performance on the indexes and tests of the CELF-4 Spanish edition compared to bilingual age peers.

CELF-4 Spanish			
INDEX SCORE	**SS/ScS**	**PR**	**Norms**
Core Language	79	8	compared with bilingual peers
Recalling Sentences	6		compared with bilingual peers
Formulated Sentences	6		compared with bilingual peers
Word Classes—Total	8		compared with bilingual peers
Word Definitions	6		compared with bilingual peers
Receptive Language	87	19	compared with bilingual peers
Word Classes—Receptive	10		compared with bilingual peers
Understanding Spoken Paragraphs	6		compared with bilingual peers
Semantic Relationships	4		compared with bilingual peers
Expressive Language	79	19	compared with bilingual peers
Recalling Sentences	6		compared with bilingual peers
Formulated Sentences	6		compared with bilingual peers
Word Classes—Expressive	7		compared with bilingual peers
Language Content	82	12	compared with bilingual peers
Word Definitions	6		compared with bilingual peers
Understanding Spoken Paragraphs	6		compared with bilingual peers
Language Memory	76	5	compared with bilingual peers
Recalling Sentences	6		compared with bilingual peers
Formulated Sentences	6		compared with bilingual peers
Working Memory	67	1	compared with bilingual peers
Number Repetition	5		compared with bilingual peers
Familiar Sequences	4		compared with bilingual peers
RAN	atypical		compared with bilingual peers

A review of Esteban's case history indicates that his early acquisition of Spanish was well supported. He attended a bilingual program from kindergarten until fourth grade, and began reading and writing in Spanish. In addition, at home he speaks in Spanish with the adults and, at times, watches television and listens to the radio in Spanish. He has both Spanish-dominant and English-dominant friends and communicates with both.

As noted previously, the CELF-4 Spanish manual suggests consideration of the Core Language score as the first step in making a determination of a language difference versus a disorder. Esteban's Core Language standard score of 79 is borderline. Esteban's performance on the Receptive Language index was in the lower end of the Average range and his Expressive Language index was borderline; however, the difference was not statistically significant. Esteban's performance on Language Content was borderline, and on Language Memory and Working Memory was in the Disordered range. Again, no statistically significant difference existed between Language Content and Language Memory.

Esteban's subtest scores indicate average performance on Word Classes—Receptive, Word Classes—Expressive, and Word Classes—Total in Spanish. His scores fell within the borderline range for Recalling Sentences, Formulated Sentences, Word Definitions, and Understanding Spoken Paragraphs. His scores for Number Repetition and Familiar Sequences are very low and fell within the Disordered range.

The Pragmatics Profile of the CELF-4 is a checklist describing social language skills in three areas: Rituals and Conversational Skills; Asking For, Giving, and Responding to Information; and Nonverbal Communication Skills. Most behaviors were observed during the evaluation or when Esteban was with friends; the few items not observed were scored following an interview with his teachers and friends. Other than not asking for clarification and not following reminders well, Esteban met the criterion score for his age and demonstrated age-appropriate pragmatic language skills in general.

Rapid Automatized Naming – Spanish

Esteban's performance on the RAN task in Spanish mirrored his performance in English. His score was "typical" for errors (accurate) and "atypical" for time (slower than the criterion).

Spanish: Reading, Narrative, Peer Interaction, and Writing

Esteban was observed reading an age-appropriate paragraph in Spanish. Esteban appeared to read with even less ease in Spanish than he did in English. Again, attempts were made to obtain a discourse sample in Spanish using academic language. A brief passage from a Spanish textbook was read to Esteban and he was asked to summarize the material. He was then asked questions about the passage that required him to draw inferences about the situation. Esteban responded with two- to three-word answers (e.g., *hay una persona," "blanco y negro"*). Esteban's summary did not contain complete sentences and was limited to naming and simple phrases; he did not draw inferences. Compared to his academic responses in English, his Spanish appeared more limited.

In order to obtain a more naturalistic language sample in Spanish, Esteban was taped interacting with a friend who speaks little English. A 100-utterance sample was obtained, transcribed, and analyzed. Esteban's TTR of .65 in Spanish was higher than his TTR of .43 in English and most likely represents greater vocabulary knowledge in Spanish. This increased TTR in Spanish is consistent with his increased receptive and expressive vocabulary scores (Word Classes) on the CELF-4 Spanish.

A brief writing sample in Spanish was obtained by presenting a picture and asking Esteban to write a description of the events depicted. Initially, Esteban could not write anything. When asked if he wanted to verbally state what was occurring, he said he could not and asked if he could do the task in English. He was then presented with a few examples in Spanish. With the examples in front of him, Esteban wrote more of the clinician's ideas than his own. His writing contained seven sentences with errors suggesting that he has difficulty with sentence structure, spelling, and capitalization in Spanish. This indicates overall weakness in the areas of semantics and syntax, which could be the result of lack of current familiarity with reading and writing in Spanish. Esteban's productions in English, while also limited, were more elaborate than his reading, speaking, and writing samples in Spanish.

CELF-4: Table of Score Comparisons: English and Spanish

INDEX SCORE	English			Spanish		
	SS/ScS	PR	Norms	SS/ScS	PR	Norms
Core Language	70	2	monolingual English peers	79	8	bilingual peers
Recalling Sentences	4		monolingual English peers	6		bilingual peers
Formulated Sentences	4		monolingual English peers	6		bilingual peers
Word Classes—Total	6		monolingual English peers	8		bilingual peers
Word Definitions	6		monolingual English peers	6		bilingual peers
Receptive Language	80	9	monolingual English peers	87	19	bilingual peers
Word Classes—Rec.	7		monolingual English peers	10		bilingual peers
Understanding Spoken Paragraphs	6		monolingual English peers	6		bilingual peers
Semantic Relationships	7		monolingual English peers	n/a		
Expressive Language	65	1	monolingual English peers	79	19	bilingual peers
Recalling Sentences	4		monolingual English peers	6		bilingual peers
Formulated Sentences	4		monolingual English peers	6		bilingual peers
Word Classes—Exp.	5		monolingual English peers	7		bilingual peers
Language Content	76	5	monolingual English peers	82	12	bilingual peers
Word Definitions	6		monolingual English peers	6		bilingual peers
Understanding Spoken Paragraphs	6		monolingual English peers	6		bilingual peers
Sentence Assembly	6		monolingual English peers	n/a		

INDEX SCORE	English			Spanish		
	SS/ScS	PR	Norms	SS/ScS	PR	Norms
Language Memory	66	1	monolingual English peers	76	5	bilingual peers
Recalling Sentences	4		monolingual English peers	6		bilingual peers
Formulated Sentences	4		monolingual English peers	6		bilingual peers
Semantic Relationships	7		monolingual English peers	n/a		
Working Memory	66	1	monolingual English peers	67	1	bilingual peers
Number Repetition	4		monolingual English peers	5		bilingual peers
Familiar Sequences	4		monolingual English peers	4		bilingual peers
RAN	atypical		monolingual English peers	atypical		bilingual peers

DISCUSSION

Esteban demonstrates a mixed profile of skills. His standard scores in Spanish place his general language (Core Language) functioning in the borderline range, while his performance on the same index in English is lower. In contrast, his performance on the language samples and the other informal measures indicated better performance in English. One possible explanation for the difference is the contextual constraints; the evaluation took place at school, where Esteban is accustomed to speaking English.

Because Esteban's Core Language score in Spanish is borderline, it is not clear that he has a general language learning disability. Analysis of his performance on the subtests in both languages indicates that he appears to have some patterns of relative strengths and weaknesses across languages. For example, he scored highest in both English and Spanish on receptive vocabulary (Word Classes – Receptive), whereas the lowest scores he obtained in both languages were on the two subtests that make up the Working Memory Index (Number Repetition and Familiar Sequences). These subtests are least susceptible to language weaknesses due to their highly controlled, high-frequency vocabulary. Additionally, although Language Memory is relatively higher in Spanish than in English, both index scores are in the Disordered range.

Although test scores comparing Esteban's performance to monolingual English speakers must be interpreted with caution, scores in the Disordered range on both memory indexes, across both languages, suggests an underlying processing problem that requires further evaluation. In addition, Esteban's performance on the RAN task did not meet the criteria for speed in either language, possibly indicating slow processing of visual input or slow word retrieval. Reading research indicates that poor performance on RAN tasks is correlated with difficulties in acquiring basic reading skills

and reading fluency. Consequently, weaknesses in memory and in rapid automatized naming might be contributing to Esteban's difficulty in acquiring reading skills, even when the instruction was in Spanish. Further, teachers' reports of his inability to follow directions in class may be related to memory issues; however, his borderline performance in both languages on Understanding Spoken Paragraphs raises the possibility of an auditory processing disorder. Esteban's oral language samples in both languages indicate that he is an effective communicator at the BICS level but does not have CALP-level language skills.

Regardless of a determination of disability, Esteban's test scores and performance on informal assessments in English clearly place him at significant disadvantage in the classroom. He clearly needs modifications and classroom-based interventions to fully participate in the classroom learning environment.

SUMMARY AND ELIGIBILITY STATEMENT

At this time, it is not possible to make a clear determination regarding whether or not Esteban has a language disorder. He presents with borderline skills in Spanish, which could be the result of a language learning disability or the result of attrition due to a lack of Spanish language support for the past several years. Because there is evidence that his early learning opportunities in Spanish were supported, this borderline performance is less likely to be the result of first language attrition and more likely to be evidence of a language learning disability.

Dynamic assessment, or diagnostic teaching, of his ability to learn deficient language-related skills would be the best way to confirm or rule out a language disorder.

Dynamic assessment involves assessing a narrow parameter of language to establish a baseline, involving Esteban in 2 weeks of intervention targeting that area of language, and retesting him at the end of the 2 weeks. If he demonstrates significant gains, then his language deficits are more likely to be due to educational disadvantages than an innate language-learning disability. If he does not show significant improvement, the post-treatment results will help confirm the suspected language-learning disorder.

Additionally, formal and informal test results coincide with teacher reports to suggest weaknesses in the memory and rapid automatized naming. These require further evaluation.

RECOMMENDATIONS

1. Perform a dynamic assessment of Esteban's language learning ability targeting the following abilities: (a) following three-step directions; (b) orally summarizing a paragraph of grade-level content; (c) drawing inferences from situations; and (d) retelling an event with appropriate prior referencing. The dynamic assessment should be conducted bilingually with explanations and clarifications in both languages.

2. Separate from the questions of disability is the issue that his skills in English place him at significant disadvantage in the general education classroom. Esteban requires modifications and additional scaffolding to ensure his ability to participate in the classroom. This evaluator will assist the teachers in designing and implementing a plan to help increase Esteban's involvement and successful functioning in the classroom, as well as ways of assessing these improvements.

3. As soon as possible, conduct a comprehensive bilingual psychoeducational evaluation to confirm or rule out significant weaknesses in memory, RAN, reading, and writing. Refer Esteban to an educational audiologist with expertise in evaluating for central auditory processing disorders.

4. Classroom/teacher(s) accommodations: Ensure that Esteban understands directions for daily academic class assignments by providing them to him in written form; encourage classroom participation by allowing Esteban to demonstrate knowledge through nonlinguistic means, such as hands-on projects rather than written reports.

5. Regardless of decisions regarding eligibility, a Response to Intervention plan needs to be developed and implemented immediately. The following are examples of classroom-based interventions that are appropriate for Esteban: systematic instruction in English morphology and sentence structure, instruction in study skills and note-taking, writer's workshop for creating and editing written work, systematic spelling study of high-frequency words, and reading comprehension strategy instruction. Esteban should read short passages from his textbooks, summarize the main ideas, and receive feedback from a more proficient reader.

While additional assessment is necessary to make a final determination of disability, the final decision should be made in conjunction with the parents and the multidisciplinary assessment team.

REFERENCES

Cummins, J. (1980). The cross-linguistic dimensions of language proficiency: Implications for bilingual education and the optimal age issue. *TESOL Quarterly, 14,* 175–187.

Cummins, J. (2000). *Language, power and pedagogy: Bilingual children in the crossfire.* Clevedon, England: Multilingual Matters.

Damico, J. S. (1985). Clinical discourse analysis: A functional approach to language assessment. In C. S. Simon (Ed.), *Communication skills and classroom success* (pp. 165–204). San Diego, CA: College-Hill Press.

Kohnert, K. (2007). *Language disorders in bilingual children and adults.* San Diego, CA: Plural Publishing.

Patterson, J. L., & Rodriguez, B. L. (2005). Designing assessments for multilingual children. In M. J. Ball (Ed.), *Clinical sociolinguistics* (pp. 230–241). Oxford, England: Blackwell.

Retherford, K. S. (2000). *Guide to analysis of language transcripts* (3rd ed). Greenville, SC: Super Duper Publications.

Neuropsychological Evaluation of an Adolescent with Moderate Mental Retardation

The Importance of Making an Accurate Diagnosis

Janice Sammons and Judith Kroese

Robert, a 14-year-old adolescent, was diagnosed by the school psychologist as a student with a specific learning disability. He was also determined to need special education services in the moderate mental retardation self-contained classroom. Although Robert's diagnostic results clearly supported an intellectual disability, the school psychologist reported that he did not want to "label" Robert with mental retardation so that Robert "would not feel bad about himself."

State and federal agencies provide services and programs to eligible individuals with developmental disabilities (e.g., Supplemental Security Income). In addition, the individual's disability must result in substantial functional limitations in three or more major life activities. Robert's parents sought benefits from state and federal agencies to meet his special needs in self-care, receptive and expressive language learning, and mobility, as well as his future capacity for independent living and economic self-sufficiency. When these state and federal programs reviewed Robert's current disability diagnosis, they determined he was ineligible based on the school's diagnosis of a specific learning disability. This inability to receive additional support placed a heavy burden on Robert's family, which made it difficult for his needs to be addressed appropriately.

The following report provides a current neuropsychological evaluation of Robert, including his present level of functioning and corrected diagnosis. In addition, this report documents Robert's developmental history and prior neuropsychological evaluation results, and compares him to his prior levels of functioning.

NEUROPSYCHOLOGICAL EVALUATION

Name:	Robert Perrin
Date of Birth:	April 6, 1995
Age:	14-9
Parents:	Lisa and Carl Perrin
Grade:	8
Date of Evaluation:	January 20, 2010
Evaluators:	Janice Sammons, Ph.D.
	Judith M. Kroese, Ph.D., CCC-SLP

REASON FOR REFERRAL

Robert was referred for evaluation by his physician, Dr. Cynthia Clift, to determine his present levels of cognitive impairment and compare his current level of functioning to his previous neuropsychological evaluation in 2005. Results from the 2005 evaluation are included in the Summary of Test Results of this report for comparison; however, not all tests from the 2005 evaluation were re-administered. Robert's parents are also seeking Department of Developmental Disabilities (DDD) services to help Robert meet his current needs.

BACKGROUND INFORMATION

Robert is a 14-year-old boy now in middle school receiving special education services in a classroom for individuals with moderate mental retardation. He lives with his mother, stepfather, and two older sisters. The Perrins provided background information, in addition to previous reports from Dr. Jennifer Owel (Neuropsychological evaluation report 2005) and Dr. Ronald Babur (Pediatric evaluation report 2010).

Robert was born prematurely at 35 weeks' gestation via caesarian section. He weighed 5 pounds, 15 ounces, and was 49.8 cm in length. His Apgar scores were 8 and 9 at 1 and 5 minutes, respectively. His mother reported that Robert was hospitalized in the neonatal intensive care unit, requiring ventilator support before he was transferred to the nursery. Early development was delayed. Robert walked at around 3 years of age and motor problems persisted. Speech development was also late; at age 4 or 5, he began using more than one word.

Robert's medical history was significant for seizure disorder and psychiatric disorders. Seizures are currently being treated with Depakote. As of 1/20/2010, he was also taking the following medications: Atenolol, Cogentin, Clozaril, Ativan, and BuSpar, and nutritional supplements, vitamin E and folic acid. Previous reports and parent interview also indicated an earlier diagnosis of Bipolar Disorder and a history of aggressive behaviors toward self, others, and animals. He has demonstrated some suicidal behaviors in the past at around the age of 6. As previously reported (Neuropsychological Evaluation 2005), Robert has had two episodes of neuroleptic malignant syndrome (NMS) associated with Risperdal, requiring hospitalization in 2005. Mrs. Perrin reported that the family has worked with Robert's doctor to reduce his dosages with some success. Severe separation anxiety was also noted. During the current evaluation, Robert requested that his mother stay with him during the remainder of testing (after 2 hours of testing one-on-one with the examiner).

In the past few years, Robert's neuromuscular control has deteriorated. Three or four years ago, Robert could print his name neatly, but now he can only write his name using very large letters. Robert has always struggled to brush his teeth independently and at this time is unable to maintain his arm upright to brush. Robert enjoys playing with remote control cars and he used to be able to use smaller remote controls, but he now has to be given larger controls for manipulation. He used to enjoy playing with a Game Boy, but he is no longer able to manipulate the controls. In the past, Robert was able to ride a bike, but he is no longer able to do so. Formerly, he was able to walk all around the neighborhood, but he currently needs a wheelchair because he gets so fatigued. His speech has always been difficult to understand, but his parents report they can now understand about 50 percent of what he says. Finally,

Robert has always been messy and eats too fast, but now he is unable to find his mouth. When he is chewing, food falls out of his mouth. He has always drooled and continues to drool. In the past, when he was off medication, the decline in his motor skills was worse. Robert's earlier episodes of NMS in addition to the quantity and combinations of medications may be related to his drooling.

A neuropsychological evaluation was conducted in September 2005 at Children's Research Center, in which Robert's current level of functioning was determined in the following areas: intellectual functioning, academic achievement, language functioning, memory, sensory, perceptual, motor abilities, and psychosocial functioning. He was diagnosed with Mild Mental Retardation and Cognitive Disorder. In regard to school testing conducted by the school psychologist a few days after the neuropsychological evaluation, Dr. Owel noted a cautionary interpretation of several of the exact subtests that were readministered to Robert, due to practice effects, which may have spoiled the school's testing results.

Educational History

Per the school's most recent 3-year reevaluation report, Robert was receiving special education services under the category of Specific Learning Disability (SLD) and Emotional Disability (ED). He began receiving special education services in preschool under the category of Preschool Moderately Delayed (PDM). Before entering kindergarten, he was dismissed from special education; however, due to behavior problems in kindergarten, he was identified under the category of Other Health Impairment (OHI). Robert repeated kindergarten and was placed in Residential Treatment Care (RTC) and began attending the in-house school under the category of ED. He also received services in speech, occupational, and physical therapy.

Previous school testing reports indicated a WISC-IV Verbal Comprehension Index score within the Low Average range; however, the remaining three composite scores were within the Severely Impaired range, and no adaptive behavior was reported. Academic testing 3 years earlier on the Woodcock-Johnson III Tests of Achievement (WJ III ACH) provided Broad Reading, Math, and Written Language cluster scores; however, no subtest scores were provided. An Academic Fluency cluster standard score of 51 was reported; however, Robert's basic academic skills are currently inadequate to obtain any academic fluency measures at the time of this report. No Full-Scale IQ score was available for the school evaluation in 2005, in which it appeared that all cognitive processing composite scores were obtained. This is not explained. School testing in 2003 obtained a Full-Scale IQ of 71, which is considered to be in the Borderline range.

Robert's current special education teacher, Ms. Mallory Miller, described Robert's present level of functioning: Robert participates in a class for individuals in the sixth, seventh, and eighth grades who have needs at the moderate mental retardation (MOMR) level. In addition, Robert has a one-to-one aide. In describing his academic ability, she noted that he is unable to correctly identify letters of the alphabet consistently. Writing is often illegible due to poor fine-motor skills. He can add simple problems using manipulatives, but only at the single-digit level. He cannot tell time but is learning to identify money and its value. He can read about 50 words, mostly safety and survival words. Behaviorally, Robert, at times, will become agitated and act inappropriately. After calming down, he usually apologizes. He seeks attention from adults only and does not interact much with classmates. He has difficulty following directions and following along with the class. Robert needs assistance with dressing skills, cannot tie his shoes, and needs assistance putting on his shoes. He also needs daily reminders to wash his hands after using the restroom and before eating. In the 3 years Ms. Miller has been working with Robert, he has not shown much improvement, is working at the same level academically, and has difficulty retaining any learning, even with the assistance of his aide.

OBSERVATIONS AND IMPRESSIONS

Robert was seen for two formal testing sessions on 1 day (morning and afternoon). He consistently attended to tasks presented and appeared to do his best; however, as tasks became more difficult, he became more restless. At times, he rested his head on the table as he completed tasks. Other times, he exhibited excessive body movements. Throughout the testing session, he had poor eye contact, did not initiate conversation with the examiner, and drooled constantly. His speech was characterized by poor articulation, slurring, and reduced volume. He did, however, take notice of the examiner's mechanical pencil. On several appropriate tasks, Robert used the mechanical pencil and bargained to earn the pencil for "keeps" by attending to each task required and doing his best work. (He took the mechanical pencil with him at the end of the testing sessions.) Robert was able to test one-on-one with the examiner for 2 hours. At that time, Robert requested that his mother stay with him during testing, and he continued to complete tasks administered with his mother in the room.

TESTS ADMINISTERED

Beery-Buktenica Developmental Test of Visual-Motor Integration-Sixth Edition (Beery VMI)

Behavior Assessment System for Children, Second Edition (BASC-2) Parent Rater Forms

California Verbal Learning Test—Children's Edition (CVLT-C)

Delis Kaplan Executive Function System (D-KEFS)

Grooved pegboard

Vineland Adaptive Behavior Scales, Second Edition (Vineland-II)

Wechsler Intelligence Scale for Childrens-Fourth Edition (WISC-IV)

Woodcock-Johnson III NU Tests of Achievement (WJ III ACH)

Parent interview

Review of records

TEST RESULTS AND INTERPRETATION

Intellectual Functioning

Testing results in the area of overall intellectual ability revealed that Robert is functioning in the Severely Impaired range compared to his age peers (WISC-IV FSIQ SS = 43, <1st percentile). Although somewhat stronger than other abilities, he demonstrated severe impairment on verbal tasks, such as providing definitions for terms, describing general vocabulary concepts, and describing similarities between two general objects or concepts (WISC-IV Verbal Comprehension Index, 1st percentile). Robert also demonstrated severe impairment on nonverbal tasks (WISC-IV Perceptual Reasoning Index, <1st percentile). His processing speed fell in the Severely Impaired range (WISC-IV Processing Speed Index, <1st percentile). These timed tasks, requiring visual-motor integration, were difficult for him to complete, and are discussed further in the Visual Processing and Visual-Motor Coordination section of this report. He refused to continue with one of the tasks (WISC-IV Coding), which he was unable to do. He did complete another comparable task in which the interest level and recognition of figures was within his ability (WISC-IV Cancellation). When compared with his 2005 performance, Robert's cognitive ability is lower, particularly in the areas of verbal comprehension, working memory, and overall ability.

Attention and Executive Functioning

Robert's attention and executive functioning abilities were assessed through a behavioral rating scale and additional tests that assessed different facets of cognitive abilities. His mother completed rating scales as part of this evaluation (BASC-2 Adolescent Parent Rater Form). These scales, in part, are designed to assess his attention abilities, as well as other areas discussed in a later section. On the Clinical scales, T scores 60–69 are considered "at risk" while scores of 70 and above are considered "clinically significant." On the Adaptive scales, scores 30–39 are considered "at risk" while scores below 30 are considered "clinically significant."

In the area of attention, Mrs. Perrin rated Robert in the clinically significant range (BASC-2 Attention Problems T score = 76). Based on school and developmental history, as well as interviews with his mother, it appears that Robert's attentional issues are, at times, problematic, and warrant regular monitoring for intervention.

Executive functioning directs the flow of thinking, manages thinking while learning is occurring, and keeps track of the information that is being learned and processed. Robert's performance was severely impaired on executive functioning tasks. Robert was unable to follow directions without considerable prompting and cueing. Number sequencing in a dot-to-dot tracing format was severely impaired <1st percentile). Robert was unable to complete several tasks. He was unable to sequence the alphabet correctly and could not alternate his attention between numbers and letters when completing a similar tracing task.

Memory and Learning

Robert's overall abilities in memory and learning were severely impaired. His ability to immediately repeat verbal information presented fell in the severely impaired range (WISC-IV Digit Span < 1st percentile). On a verbal learning and memory measure, the first and the final trials of learning a list of 16 items was severely impaired (<1st percentile). After a brief distraction, both spontaneous and cued recall continued to be greatly impaired (<1st percentile); after a 20-minute delay, Robert was unable to recall any items (<1st percentile).

Visual Processing and Visual-Motor Coordination

Visual processing is the ability to perceive, analyze, synthesize, and think with visual patterns. It includes the ability to store and recall visual representations. Visual-motor coordination requires the integration of visual processing and the motor system (transferring information from the visual system to the motor system quickly and easily). On tasks in which Robert had to perceive and copy patterns, his performance was within the severely impaired range (Beery VMI <1st percentile). His ability to perceive visual figures (and identify similar figures) was severely impaired (Beery VMI Visual Perception <1st percentile) as well as his ability to use fine-motor skills in following patterns (Beery VMI Motor Integration <1st percentile). Overall, his abilities in visual processing and visual-motor tasks are severely impaired.

Oral Language

Oral language encompasses syntax, semantics, phonology, and pragmatics, both receptive and expressive. Robert's ability in the area of language semantics (meaning) was assessed by asking him to provide vocabulary definitions and conceptual similarities between words. His performance fell in the borderline range (WISC-IV Similarities 5th percentile, Vocabulary 2nd percentile). His ability to provide concepts based on his understanding of general principles and social situations was in the Severely Impaired range (WISC-IV Comprehension < 1st percentile). Robert's conversational language appeared significantly below age-typical peers, and he exhibited poor articulation, slurring, and reduced volume. Throughout the testing, he was unable to perceive nonverbal cues or make inferences and, at times, had difficulty following direct instructions (e.g., when directed to stop a task, the materials had to be taken away because he would continue). These perseverative-like behaviors occurred on a few isolated, highly motivating tasks, and were, therefore, not considered generally problematic.

Academic Achievement

Robert demonstrated severe impairment across all academic skills. He was evaluated in basic academic skills including letter and word recognition and word reading, forming (copying) simple figures and writing letters and words, and completing basic calculation problems (e.g., counting ducks and pennies, and subtracting objects). Similar to the results of academic testing in 2005, Robert identified some letters but could not read any words. Also similar to his performance in 2005, he correctly added single-digit problems (forming most numbers in reverse) but was unable to complete subtraction problems. In writing tasks, he was able to form a few letters but with great difficulty, and most of his attempted letters were illegible.

Adaptive Skills

Robert's mother completed rating scales as part of this evaluation (BASC-2 Adolescent Parent Rater Form) as described earlier in this report. In addition, as part of the interview, Mrs. Perrin responded to questions to complete an additional adaptive behavioral rating scale (Vineland-II). Robert's overall adaptive skills fell within the Severely Impaired range (Vineland-II Adaptive Behavior Composite <1st percentile). Furthermore, although most of his skills appear to be within the same range, Robert exhibited a relative strength in receptive and expressive language skills, which are needed for communication with other people. The tasks included defining vocabulary words and responding to questions. While these relative strengths are important to identify so that Robert can build on them, it is important to note that his overall abilities in communication fell in the Moderately Impaired range (Vineland-II Communication Domain <1st percentile). Daily living skills fell in the Severely Impaired range (Vineland-II Daily Living Skills Domain <1st percentile). This is consistent with earlier reports (2004) of significant impairments in communication, self-care, and overall functioning.

Social-Emotional Functioning

Attentional problems were addressed earlier in this report but additional externalizing problems as rated as by Mrs. Perrin were in the At-Risk to Clinically Significant range (Hyperactivity T score = 97; Conduct Problems T score = 73; Aggression T score = 68). Furthermore, Mrs. Perrin rated internalizing problem areas in the Clinically Significant range (Depression T score = 73; Somatization T score = 71). She rated areas of Atypicality (T score = 76) and Withdrawal (T score = 84) in the Clinically Significant range. Overall, Robert's social and emotional functioning are Severely Impaired. Furthermore, results from the interview-based rating on Robert's socialization skills indicated a level of Moderate Impairment (Vineland-II Socialization Domain <1st percentile), similar to impairment reported in 2004.

SUMMARY AND CONCLUSIONS

Robert is a 14-year-old adolescent with a history of developmentally delayed characteristics, seizure disorder, Bipolar Disorder, and declines in function. He lives with his parents and brother and currently participates in a special education classroom for individuals with Moderate Mental Retardation. Robert's cognitive abilities, academic abilities, and adaptive skills are severely impaired compared to his age-peers although currently he is receiving special education services under the category of Specific Learning Disability and Emotional Disability. Based on his current levels of performance in the areas of intellectual functioning, academics, and adaptive ability, Robert meets the diagnostic criteria for Moderate Mental Retardation and does not meet the criteria for a student with a Specific Learning Disability

Impairments in processing speed, memory, and learning are within the moderate to severe levels. Visual perception, fine-motor integration, and visual-motor integration are also impaired. Adaptive skills, including communication, daily living skills, and socialization are far below age-expected levels. Robert exhibits problems in the areas of attention, hyperactivity, conduct problems, and aggression, which all fell in the At-Risk to Clinically Significant ranges and warrant monitoring for intervention. He exhibited problems in the areas of separation anxiety, which may include areas of depression, somatization, atypicality, and withdrawal, based on clinically significant results on the behavior rating scales completed by his mother. When comparing him to his age-peers, Robert is moderately to severely impaired, functioning statistically lower than he was in 2005. Although the cause of the decline in his motor skills is unknown, it is possible that it is related to the NMS or to the medications he is currently taking. His physician, Dr. Cynthia Clift, who referred him for this evaluation, will continue to investigate the cause of this decline, as well as additional medical factors that may be influencing Robert's academic development.

Impressions

Axis I:	Bipolar Disorder (prior diagnosis)
Axis II:	Moderate Mental Retardation
Axis III:	Seizure Disorder, motor impairments, enuresis (prior diagnosis)

RECOMMENDATIONS

1. Results from this evaluation should be copied and discussed with Dr. Cynthia Clift and Dr. Ronald Babur. Given the diagnosis of moderate mental retardation, application for services from the Department of Developmental Disabilities should be pursued. Occupational, physical, and speech therapy are needed, and evaluations for current strengths and needs may also be addressed.

2. Robert's current special education placement appears to be appropriate to address his current needs. In addition, continued services in speech, occupational, and physical therapy should continue at maximum levels.

3. Robert's current special education category does not fit his profile. Robert is functioning at the moderate mental retardation range in all areas including cognitive functioning, academic abilities, and adaptive skills, including communication, daily living skills, and socialization. It is highly recommended that the school's multidisciplinary team meet to address this incongruity.

4. Before he turns 16 years old, the MET/IEP team should consider a transitional plan for Robert. Resources and ideas for developing an appropriate transition plan for Robert include the following:

   - Arizona Department of Education Exceptional Student Services @ http://www.ade.az.gov/ess/Special-Projects/transition/
   - Transition from School to Adult Life, Ages 14–22 @ http://www.disabilityworks.org/default.asp?contentID=61
   - Designing Individualized Education Program (IEP) Transition Plans @ http://www.ericdigests.org/2001-4/iep.html

Robert was a pleasure to work with. If you have any questions about these findings or this report, please do not hesitate to contact us.

SUMMARY OF TEST RESULTS

Score Interpretation

Type of Score*	Low Average Range	Average Range	High Average Range
Percentiles (%ile)	9–24	25–75	76–91
Subtest Scaled Scores (ss)	6–7	8–12	13–14
Quotients & Standard Scores (SS)	80–89	90–110	111–120

Type of Score*	Clinically Significant Range	At-Risk Range	Within Average Range
T Scores Clinical Scales (e.g., BASC-2)	70–above	60–69	59–below
T Scores Adaptive Scales (e.g., BASC-2)	29–below	30–39	40–above

1. Some slight variations in categories of "low average," "average," and "high average" occur across tests.
2. T Scores (from BASC-2) do not fall under typical Low Average to High Average ranges.

Beery-Buktenica Developmental Test of Visual-Motor Integration, Sixth Edition (Beery VMI)

Tests	Standard Score	Percentile	2004 Percentile
Visual-Motor Integration	58	0.6	1
Visual Perceptual	48	0.05	1
Motor Integration	<45	<0.02	

California Verbal Learning Test-Children's Edition (CVLT-C)

Subtests	Z Score	Percentile	2005 Percentile
Trial 1 Free Recall	−3.0	≤0.1	7
Trial 5 Free Recall	−3.5	≤0.1	31
Trials 1–5	20 (T Score)	≤0.1	
List B Free Recall	−2.0	2	
Short-Delay Free Recall	−3.5	≤0.1	
Long-Delay Free Recall	−3.0	≤0.1	
Short-Delay Cued Recall	−4.0	≤0.1	
Long-Delay Cued Recall	−4.0	≤0.1	

Behavior Assessment System for Children, Second Edition (BASC-2): Parent Report

Composite Scores:	T Scores Mother	Significance Level
Clinical Scales:		
Hyperactivity	97	Clinically Significant
Aggression	68	At-Risk
Conduct Problems	73	Clinically Significant
Externalizing Problems	82	Clinically Significant
Anxiety	41	
Depression	73	Clinically Significant
Somatization	71	Clinically Significant
Internalizing Problems	64	At-Risk
Atypicality	76	Clinically Significant
Withdrawal	84	Clinically Significant
Attention Problems	76	Clinically Significant
Behavioral Symptoms Index	87	Clinically Significant
Adaptive Scales:		
Adaptability	22	Clinically Significant
Social Skills	31	At-Risk
Leadership	25	Clinically Significant
Activities of Daily Living	20	Clinically Significant
Functional Communication	24	Clinically Significant
Adaptive Skills	20	Clinically Significant

Grooved Pegboard

No normative scores available. Robert was unable to complete the motor task (using one hand to pick up peg, place in hole, and continue without help of other hand) due to poor fine-motor ability.

Delis Kaplan Executive Function System (D-KEFS)*

Subtests	Scaled Score	Percentile
Trail Making Test		
Condition 1: Visual Scanning	1	<0.1
Condition 2: Number Sequencing	1	<0.1
Condition 3: Letter Sequence	1	<0.1
Condition 4: Number-Letter Switching	1	<0.1
Condition 5: Motor Speed	6	9

*Scores should be interpreted with caution as not all parts of the test were administered. Extra time was allowed as Robert was unwilling to stop the task at time limit.

Wechsler Intelligence Scale for Children-Fourth Edition (WISC-IV)

Verbal Comprehension Subtests	Scaled Score	Percentile	2005 Results Percentile
Similarities	5	5	16
Vocabulary	4	2	2
Comprehension	2	<1	16 (Information)
Perceptual Reasoning Subtests			
Block Design	1	≤0.1	<1
Picture Concepts	2	<1	1 (Pic Complet)
Matrix Reasoning	1	≤0.1	2
Working Memory Subtests			
Digit Span	1	≤0.1	1
Letter-Number Sequence	1	≤0.1	2 (Arithmetic)
Processing Speed Subtests			
Cancellation	1	≤0.1	<1
Symbol Search	1	≤0.1	<1

Composite Scores	Standard Score (95% Confidence Interval)	Percentile	2005 Percentile
Verbal Comprehension Index (VCI)	63 (58–72)	1	6
Perceptual Reasoning Index (PRI)	47 (44–59)	<0.1	<1
Working Memory Index (WMI)	50 (46–62)	<0.1	1
Processing Speed Index (PSI)	50 (47–65)	<0.1	<1
Full-Scale IQ (FSIQ)	43 (40–50)	<0.1	<1

Woodcock-Johnson III Normative Update Tests of Achievement (WJ III ACH)

Composite Scores and Individual Test Scores	Standard Score for Age	%ile for Age	2005 Grade-Based Percentile
Brief Reading	1	<0.1	<1
Letter-Word Identification	1	<0.1	
Passage Comprehension	1	<0.1	
Brief Math	17	<0.1	
Calculation	19	<0.1	5
Applied Problems	46	<0.1	
Academic Skills	1	<0.1	
Spelling	8	<0.1	

Vineland Adaptive Behavior Scales, Second Edition (Vineland-II), Parent Form

Skill Area	Standard Score	Scaled Score	Percentile	Adaptive Level
Adaptive Behavior Composite	41		<1	Moderate Deficit
Communication Domain	49		<1	Moderate Deficit
Receptive		6		
Expressive		6		
Written		5		
Daily Living Skills Domain	35		<1	Moderate Deficit
Personal		1		
Domestic		4		
Community		3		
Socialization Domain	43		<1	Moderate Deficit
Interpersonal Relationships		4		
Play & Leisure Time		2		
Coping Skills		5		

CASE 45

The Impact of Slow Processing Speed
on Performance

Jane McClure

Whereas the issue underlying the request for psychoeducational testing is not unusual in this case (i.e., Andrea has little if any difficulty understanding concepts presented to her in school, but has great difficulty completing assignments and tests in the time that it takes her classmates), the degree of discrepancy between her processing speed and other areas of functioning is unusual. The discrepancy is so unusual, in fact, that it occurs in less than 1 percent of the population. Thus, this case provides a clear demonstration of the impact of extremely slow processing speed not only on academic performance but also on other areas of cognitive functioning. In this way, the report is illustrative of a common presenting problem, although the degree of processing deficiency is atypical.

Another area of interest in this case is the description of ways in which the examiner arrived at a diagnosis, ruling out the most obvious (but incorrect) interpretations of some test results by explaining how they were impacted by other factors. The beginning professional often has difficulty with this aspect of differential diagnosis; thus, this report may provide insights not otherwise considered. For example, Andrea's extremely low scores on a continuous performance test might have led an evaluator to suspect Attention-Deficit/Hyperactivity Disorder (ADHD), although a diagnosis would never be made on the basis of one test; however, an explanation of how Andrea's extremely slow performance on this test impacted her other scores caused the evaluator to state that the scores on the Conners' Continuous Performance Test (CPT) needed to be interpreted with caution and in light of all the other assessment data. In the end, ADHD was not diagnosed.

The final aspect of particular interest in this case is the way in which various areas of functioning are assessed and then corroborated by additional measures. Assembling this kind of comprehensive battery of tests is an example of "best practices" for school psychologists and diagnosticians, demonstrating how an evaluator can gain increasing confidence in a hypothesis when results from different measures provide consistent data. Similarly, testing observations and relevant background information are incorporated into the interpretation of the test results.

PSYCHOEDUCATIONAL EVALUATION

Name:	Andrea Baker
Date of Birth:	August 5, 1995
Age:	14 years, 10 months
School:	Fisher High School
Grade:	10 (Fall 2010)
Current Medications:	none reported
Dates of Evaluation:	June 21 and 22, 2010
Evaluator:	Jane McClure, Ph.D.

BACKGROUND INFORMATION AND REASON FOR REFERRAL

Andrea is a 14-year-old female who was referred for a psychoeducational evaluation to assess her current levels of functioning. Her parents requested testing to better understand her cognitive strengths and weaknesses and determine if she qualifies for extended time accommodations in school and on standardized tests. Despite a history of success in school, Andrea has always had trouble finishing tests on time and is always the last one in her class to complete testing. She was recently denied admission to an honors science class because she was unable to finish the admission test in the allotted time and therefore earned a low score. (Andrea was later granted admission to this class on appeal, due to the recommendations of her classroom teachers.) Andrea is highly motivated and does well on tests when she is provided with additional time.

Developmental and Medical History

Andrea is the youngest of her parents' four children. She was the product of an uncomplicated pregnancy and delivery. She weighed 6 lbs., 10 oz. at birth and went home after 1 day in the hospital. Her medical history is unremarkable, and she is currently reported to be in good health.

Andrea's mother reports that she reached physical and language developmental milestones within expected time frames. She had colic as a baby, which sometimes woke her in the middle of the night. Now, she is a very sound sleeper who "can sleep anywhere and immediately, and is hard to wake up." She had temper tantrums as a toddler—"five or six a day"—and her mother had to physically hug her to calm her. Her mother also stated that Andrea is "very energetic, and then crashes completely."

There is no history of head trauma or seizures. Andrea's last vision and hearing exams were in June 2009, and the results were normal. Andrea's family history is positive for ADHD in her father, as well as for both auditory and visual processing problems in her brother, and Prader-Willi syndrome in a paternal aunt. Andrea's parents report that there is no known history of substance use.

Educational Background

According to her parents, Andrea was the oldest child in her preschool class and the only one who went to kindergarten the following year. She loved the school aspect of kindergarten, although she did not make friends easily. She enjoyed first, second, and third grades, and had good friends by then. In grades four through six, Andrea's parents described her as a hardworking and excellent student. She was, however, always the last one to finish school exams and state testing. Her mother also commented that it took her excessive time to complete her homework assignments, especially writing assignments, which she seemed to agonize over, sometimes complaining, "I just can't figure out how to say what I want to say." She continued to receive primarily As and some Bs in grades seven through nine but had increasing difficulty finishing

math and science tests in the time provided, and the time needed for homework increased as well. Although she would take frequent breaks from her homework and get up and move around, she was conscientious about completing her assignments. Her mother also reported that she has some organizational problems, such as leaving materials for school at home or leaving materials needed for homework at school.

Previous Evaluations

Andrea has not been evaluated previously.

Social-Emotional

Andrea lives with her parents and an older sister. She has an older brother and sister who attend college. Andrea's mother describes her as "very passionate, lovable, affectionate, happy, and likable." She reports that Andrea is somewhat anxious and has some emotional ups and downs. Her motivation for school and for athletics is very strong, and she is a consistently hard worker. Andrea wants to please and has good abilities. Her parents see, however, that she "sometimes lacks confidence and needs lots of reassurance." Overall, they describe her as "a great kid."

Andrea does not like to be alone and also has a fear of spiders. She is reportedly well able to express her feelings. She has certain routines that she likes to follow. Andrea has strong attachments to her parents and siblings and has many close friends. She is extremely active and plays two competitive sports at a time all year. She also enjoys art and music.

TESTS ADMINISTERED

Wechsler Intelligence Scale for Children-Fourth Edition (WISC-IV)

Woodcock-Johnson III NU Tests of Cognitive Abilities (WJ III COG)—Selected Tests

Children's Memory Scale (CMS)

Wisconsin Card Sorting Test—Computer Version 4-Research Edition (WCST:CV4)

Comprehensive Test of Phonological Processing (CTOPP)—Rapid Naming Tests

Woodcock-Johnson III NU Tests of Achievement (WJ III ACH, Form A)—Selected Tests

Nelson-Denny Reading Test (NDRT)

Integrated Visual & Auditory Continuous Performance Test (IVA+Plus)

Conners' Rating Scales—Revised (CRS-R)

Rey Complex Figure Test (RCFT)

BEHAVIORAL OBSERVATIONS

Andrea arrived for testing casually and appropriately dressed. She was cooperative throughout testing and readily answered questions asked of her. On some subtests (e.g., Block Design on the WISC-IV), she appeared to be unsure of herself, as she checked and rechecked her work. Generally, she worked very slowly through nearly all tests administered to her. The visual-motor and processing speed subtests were particularly difficult for her. She was more fidgety than is usual for a student her age, but she attended to the tasks and was not impulsive. The test results are felt to be an accurate assessment of Andrea's current level of functioning.

TEST RESULTS

Different tests use different verbal labels to explain score ranges. To establish consistency among the tests used in this assessment, the following verbal labels and score ranges will be used for all tests and composites or clusters. When score ranges are discussed, the Average range comprises the middle 68% of scores obtained by people of the same age or grade in the norming sample. For standard scores (SS), the mean is 100 and the standard deviation is 15. In this report, standard scores of 90 to 110 are considered Average, 80 to 89 are Below Average, 70 to 79 are Low, and any score below 70 is Very Low. Scores of 111

to 120 are Above Average, 121 to 130 are Superior, and above 130 are Very Superior.

Scaled scores (ScS) have a mean of 10 and a standard deviation of 3. Scores between 8 and 12 are considered Average, scores of 6 and 7 are Below Average, and scores of 13 and 14 are Above Average.

Percentile ranks (PR) have a mean of 50. A percentile rank indicates the percentage of people in the norming sample, at the individual's age or grade, who scored at or below the individual's score. For example, Andrea's percentile rank of 91 on the WISC-IV Digit Span subtest means that 91% of people of age 14-10 (14 years, 10 months) in the norming sample obtained a score the same as or lower than Andrea's.

A group of subtests that measures a similar ability may be called an index, factor, cluster, or composite, depending on the test administered.

Cognitive/Perceptual

Wechsler Intelligence Scale for Children-IV (WISC-IV)

The WISC-IV was administered in order to assess Andrea's information processing abilities. The WISC-IV measures four components of cognitive processing: verbal comprehension (learned knowledge), perceptual reasoning (nonverbal problem-solving skills), working memory (the ability to hold information in one's mind while performing cognitive tasks), and processing speed (speed of cognitive processing).

Andrea obtained a Full-Scale IQ standard score of 98 (SS: 93–103) with scores on the four indexes varying from the Very Low range to the Above Average range. The Perceptual Reasoning, Working Memory, and Verbal Comprehension Indices spanned the Average to Above Average ranges. Her scores on Verbal Comprehension

	SS	95% CI	ScS	%
Verbal Comprehension	112	105–118		79
Similarities			12	75
Vocabulary			14	91
Comprehension			11	63

	SS	95% CI	ScS	%
Perceptual Reasoning	104	96–111		61
Block Design			8	25
Matrix Reasoning			14	91
(Picture Completion)			8	25
Picture Concepts			10	50

	SS		ScS	%
Working Memory	110	102–117		75
Digit Span			14	91
Letter-Number Sequencing			10	50

	SS		ScS	%
Processing Speed	56	52–70		0.2
Coding			1	0.1
Symbol Search			3	1

and Perceptual Reasoning indicated that her nonverbal reasoning abilities are comparable to her verbal reasoning abilities. Because Andrea's Processing Speed score was severely discrepant from her other index scores, in the Very Low range, her Full-Scale IQ score does not provide a valid description of her general intellectual abilities. Therefore, the individual Index scores, rather than the Full-Scale IQ, should be used when considering Andrea's intellectual potential as well as her cognitive strengths and weaknesses. Each index and its subtests are discussed below.

Andrea's Verbal Comprehension Index percentile rank of 79 indicates Above Average verbal thinking abilities. She scored in the Average range on the Comprehension test, a task requiring her to answer questions about social rules and scenarios. She exhibited Above Average abstract verbal reasoning on the Similarities test, a task requiring her to explain how pairs of words are alike, and Superior knowledge of word meanings on Vocabulary.

Andrea's Perceptual Reasoning score was 104, indicating Average ability to solve nonverbal problems using spatial reasoning and abstract thinking. She had most success on Matrix Reasoning (PR 91), an untimed test during which she mentally manipulated designs in order to complete abstract nonverbal patterns. Her lowest scores (PR 25) were on Block Design, a timed task during which she had to analyze a visual pattern and reproduce it with colored blocks, and Picture Completion, a task requiring her to determine what part was missing from pictures, again under time pressure. She was accurate on these tasks but did not earn bonus points for speed. Her score on Picture Concepts, a task requiring her to determine concepts from groups of pictures, was Average (PR 50). It is noteworthy that Andrea's scores on the two timed tests were at the lower end of the Average range, whereas her performance on Matrix Reasoning, which is untimed, was in the Above Average to Superior range.

As with her Verbal Comprehension score, Andrea's Working Memory score fell in the Average to Above Average range. She scored in the Superior range on Digit Span, composed of a simple short-term memory task and a working memory task. Her score on Letter-Number Sequencing, a working memory task involving both numbers and letters, was Average. Andrea's performance on these tasks shows that she can mentally manipulate and reorganize bits of auditory information in order to perform simple tasks. Her lower score on the Letter-Number Sequencing test, a more complicated task than the Digit

Span test, suggests that adding complexity to a task may make it more difficult for Andrea to process and retain the information. The lower score, however, does not represent a normative weakness.

Andrea's Processing Speed percentile rank of 0.2 reveals Very Low functioning in this area. Only two people out of a thousand would score as low as or lower than she did. The discrepancies between her Processing Speed score and her other index scores are so unusual that they occur in less than 1 percent of the population. Her scores on both processing speed tests were in the Very Low range. Symbol Search is a visual scanning test requiring a simple motor response (i.e., marking a square to indicate *yes* or *no*); Coding is a paired-associate learning task involving the use of a key to quickly draw symbols to match numbers. On Coding, she tracked the key with her finger to find each number and the associated symbol, said the number aloud, and then drew the symbol in the appropriate place. Completing each item was a slow, deliberate process for her, and it was obvious that she was not learning the number-symbol relationships as she went along. Additionally, the more refined and complex motor component appeared to further erode her already deficient visual scanning ability. Andrea's severely impaired performance on these tasks suggests that her rote visual and visual-motor processing speed is extremely slow and clearly inconsistent with her higher-level reasoning abilities.

Woodcock-Johnson III NU Tests of Cognitive Abilities

Andrea was administered selected tests from the WJ III COG. The WJ III COG measures an ability that was not assessed by the WISC-IV, specifically her automatic access to known words and verbal labels. Rapid Picture Naming required her to name pictures of common objects as quickly as she could. Her Very Low score (PR 1) is significantly lower than her WISC-IV Verbal Reasoning and Perceptual Reasoning scores, indicating a significant weakness in her ability to access or retrieve specific words on demand. In contrast, she scored in the Average range on Retrieval Fluency (PR 45), a task that required her to name items from a given category in a 60-second time frame. Although both tests are time limited and require retrieval of single, familiar words from long-term storage, Rapid Picture Naming requires retrieval of specific words, whereas Retrieval Fluency gives one a category but then allows considerable flexibility in acceptable responses. Accordingly, Andrea may have significant difficulty with efficient retrieval of *specific* words in a timed format.

Other tests on the WJ III COG reinforced her performances on certain WISC-IV indices. Her Working Memory cluster score was in the High Average range (PR 80). Her score on the Pair Cancellation, a test of visual processing speed, was in the Very Low range (PR 0.4).

Her score on Auditory Attention was in the first percentile, possibly due to the requirement of speed of response. Auditory Attention requires the individual to quickly identify one of four pictures to match a word that is spoken against a background of gradually increasing noise. The recording proceeds at a brisk pace and may not be paused; consequently, although the test is not time limited, it is not self-paced either.

Comprehensive Test of Phonological Processing (CTOPP)

To confirm Andrea's weakness in rapid naming, Rapid Naming subtests of the CTOPP were administered. In separate tasks, Andrea was asked to scan and name a series of letters and digits as fast as she could. The ability to quickly and automatically access this type of information has been found to be a critical aspect of fluent reading. As with the WJ III COG Rapid Picture Naming test, Andrea's score on the CTOPP Rapid Naming composite was in the Very Low range, below the first percentile. This is far below expectation, based on Andrea's Average to Above Average verbal and nonverbal reasoning abilities as measured by the WISC-IV. The significant discrepancy between her thinking skills and her ability to access specific words quickly has ramifications for her achievement in academic areas, especially in fluency in academic skills, in retrieval of known information, and, consequently, in the effort required to produce academic work quickly.

Attention

Attention plays an important role in determining the amount of information a person is able to take in, process, and learn. In order to assess Andrea's ability to attend, the Integrated Visual and Auditory-Plus Continuous Performance Test (IVA+Plus) was administered. The IVA+PLUS is a computerized test designed to assess attention and control of response, and to aid in the diagnosis of Attention-Deficit/Hyperactivity Disorder. It measures one's ability to shift responses to a boring, repetitive visual and auditory task. Andrea was required to click a device when she saw or heard the number one and not click when she saw or heard the number two.

All of Andrea's standard scores on the IVA+PLUS were extremely low, ranging from 0 to 34. Consequently, a working diagnosis of Attention-Deficit/Hyperactivity Disorder, Combined Type was indicated by the IVA+PLUS test data; however, Andrea's Auditory and Visual Speed scores were so Low (PR 1) that further analysis was required. Such slow recognition reaction times indicated extreme difficulty in her ability to perceive and rapidly respond to auditory and visual stimuli. Most likely, it was her slow processing speed rather than poor attention that impacted her performance on the other areas of the IVA+PLUS as well. Overall, the results of the IVA+PLUS must be interpreted with caution and a diagnosis of ADHD cannot be made without review of data from other sources.

Andrea's parents completed the Conners' Parent Rating Scale – Revised. Independently, they both gave her clinically elevated scores in the scales of Hyperactivity and Anxious/Shy. Andrea's mother also gave her clinically elevated scores in Psychosomatic, *DSM-IV*: Inattentive, *DSM-IV*: Hyperactive-Impulsive, and *DSM-IV*: Total. Andrea's father rated her within the normal range on all of these scales. Two of Andrea's teachers also completed teacher rating forms. One teacher gave her a clinically elevated score for Perfectionism. The other teacher did not endorse any areas as being problematic. As noted previously, during this evaluation, Andrea was noticeably fidgety but her attention to task and ability to stay focused were average. She did not exhibit signs of perfectionism.

Overall, based on objective testing (CMS, below), observations made by this examiner, and information provided by Andrea's parents and teachers, Andrea does not meet criteria for the diagnosis of ADHD. Andrea's parents see the same level of activity that was noted during this evaluation; however, this could also be the result of high energy level and enthusiastic temperament. In any case, there is not sufficient consistency in the reports to satisfy the diagnostic criteria for ADHD.

Learning and Memory

Children's Memory Scale (CMS)

The CMS (which has been statistically linked to the WISC-IV, allowing comparisons of scores) was administered in order to further assess Andrea's memory and learning ability. The CMS provides information about immediate and delayed visual and auditory memory, as well as concentration and attention. Although Andrea's visual memory scores are in the Average range and her verbal memory scores are in the Below Average range, the discrepancy between these scores does not approach statistical significance. Consequently, her memory abilities appear to be fairly even across modalities (auditory vs. visual) and time (immediate vs. delayed). However, Andrea's auditory memory skills are significantly lower than her WISC-IV Verbal Comprehension Index score.

Analysis of her behaviors on these tests and the tasks involved provide insight into her processing of verbal information. Both tests in the Verbal Immediate and Verbal Delayed composites required her to recall newly learned information (i.e., stories and word pairs). Asked to listen to and then retell a story, she related the details in a somewhat "shotgun" fashion, going back several times to reorganize the information. On Word Pairs, although her learning *rate* was similar to that of her age peers, the number of words she was able to repeat back was lower. Consequently, it is unclear if her difficulty was in learning the word associations or in retrieving them. It is possible that she had difficulty in easily accessing the specific words she needed to adequately respond to the word pairs and to formulate an adequate retelling of the stories. The tests on the Attention/Concentration composite required Andrea to repeat a series of digits or a very familiar list, such as the alphabet, forwards and backwards. When repeating the sequences in reverse, Andrea appeared to try to visualize them and then name them in reverse order. Although she scored well on both tests, her performance with numbers was significantly better ($p > .05$) than her performance with words.

Rey Complex Figure Test (RCFT)

Andrea also completed the RCFT, a test requiring her to copy a complex geometric design, and then draw it from memory. Her visual-motor coordination was good, and she demonstrated good visual-spatial construction skills. She copied the design in the standard amount of time; her otherwise very slow processing speed did not interfere. On trials of immediate and delayed recall, Andrea showed Average to Below Average memory in drawing the designs, scoring at the 34th and 21st percentiles, respectively. On the recognition portion of the test, she scored at the 14th percentile, so it appears that cuing (i.e., asking her to recognize the part that she had seen previously) did not help

her. Overall, Andrea's performance on this test indicates adequate visual-motor integration and relatively weak visual memory skills for visual designs. This pattern was also observed in her difficulty learning the symbols to match the numbers on the WISC-IV Coding subtest.

Higher-Order Cognition/Executive Functions

The Wisconsin Card Sorting Test – Computer Version 4 (WCST:CV4) was also administered. The WCST:CV4 is a measure of abstract reasoning and the ability to develop and maintain an appropriate problem-solving strategy across changing conditions. Andrea was asked to sort a series of cards on a computer according to various categories.

Andrea's scores on the WCST:CV4 were in the Average to Superior ranges, compared to scores of other adolescents her age. She easily learned the task and she conceptualized the sorting principles as she progressed. Over time, she learned from past mistakes, demonstrated good accuracy, and completed all of the categories. When her WCST:CV4 performance is compared with her scores on the WISC-IV Perceptual Reasoning scale, her scores were comparable to her Superior score on the (untimed) Matrix Reasoning subtest and significantly higher than her scores on the timed subtests. This is further substantiation that it is primarily processing speed that limits Andrea's ability to perform at a level consistent with her nonverbal reasoning skills.

Overall, Andrea's profile indicates strengths in verbal reasoning, processing of and reasoning with visual-spatial information (e.g., designs), and short-term memory and working memory, as long as speed is not required. Areas of weakness are rate of processing visual symbols, speed of retrieving specific words from memory, and memory for visual designs.

Educational

The Woodcock-Johnson III NU Tests of Achievement (WJ III ACH) were administered in order to assess the amount of information that Andrea has been able to learn and acquire from school and other sources. Andrea's reading comprehension skills were also assessed using the Nelson-Denny Reading Test (NDRT).

Oral Language

Andrea scored in the higher end of the Average range on the WJ III ACH Listening Comprehension cluster (PR 57) and significantly lower on the Oral Expression cluster (PR 18). The Listening Comprehension cluster includes Oral Comprehension (listening to a brief passage and filling in the missing word) and Understanding Directions (listening to syntactically complex sentences and pointing to objects in a picture based on the instructions). Neither has a time limit. Her performance on this cluster indicates that her comprehension of brief discourse is age appropriate and that her comprehension of and memory for complex syntax are intact. The Oral Expression cluster includes Story Recall (retelling stories read to her) and Picture Vocabulary (naming pictured objects). She scored in the Below Average range on both, similar to her scores on the CMS verbal memory tasks. Again, she appeared to have some difficulty organizing her retelling of the stories. On the vocabulary task, some of her error responses were close but not exact.

Reading

According to the WJ III ACH results, Andrea's ability to decode unfamiliar words was Average (PR 45). Her word identification (PR 76) and comprehension of brief passages (PR 73) were in the Average to Above Average range. Her performance on Passage Comprehension (PR 73) was the same as her performance on Oral Comprehension. Both tests are structured similarly, with the only difference being that one is oral and the other is read. Andrea's performance on all of these tests was consistent with intellectual expectation. In contrast, she earned a significantly lower score on Reading Fluency (PR 9), a time-limited test requiring her to read simple sentences as quickly as possible and decide if each was true. She was accurate but worked very slowly. Clearly, Andrea's slow processing speed and retrieval of words hinder her ability to read quickly and effortlessly even in simple text.

Andrea also completed the Comprehension section of the Nelson-Denny Reading Test (NDRT). Her reading comprehension and reading rate on this test were consistent with her reading performance on the WJ III ACH. She read a series of passages and answered multiple-choice questions. Her comprehension score was Average (PR 52) and her reading rate was Below Average (PR 23). Within the 20-minute time limit, she completed only 25 of the 38 questions, although she answered 23 of them correctly. When given 12 additional minutes to complete the test, she answered 13 more questions, missing only one.

Overall, Andrea is capable of reading at a level commensurate with her high verbal ability (WISC-IV Verbal Comprehension), as long as she has enough time to work through material at her own pace. Her weaknesses in naming speed and processing speed impact her reading fluency, making tests that require reading particularly taxing for her. She needs more time than expected to process written material and express her understanding of it.

Writing

On the writing tests of the WJ III ACH, Andrea's performance was Above Average on the Spelling test (PR 89) and Average to Above Average on Writing Samples (PR 74). Andrea's spelling errors demonstrate that she uses a phonetic approach to spelling when she does not know the correct spelling of a word; all of her errors were phonetically accurate. Writing Samples required Andrea to write one-sentence responses to oral prompts; her ideas and sentence formulation were very good. On both tests, her performance was consistent with her verbal ability. Writing Fluency is a time-limited test requiring Andrea to write a simple sentence incorporating three given words. Her performance was in the Low range (PR 4), comparable to her performance on Reading Fluency. Although the sentence requirements were simple, her production speed was very slow.

Math

Consistent with her overall pattern of performance, Andrea demonstrated strong higher-level math skills during untimed tests but had difficulty when speed was a factor. She scored in the High Average range on Calculation (PR 82), which required her to solve a series of computation problems, and on Applied Problems (PR 86), during which she completed word problems that were read to her. In contrast, Andrea scored in the Below Average to Average range on Math Fluency (PR 28), a timed test requiring rapid retrieval of basic math facts. Her slow perceptual speed impairs her ability to have the effortless and immediate access to math facts that one would expect from someone of her level of intelligence and educational background.

Academic Skills

Overall, Andrea's scores on academic testing indicate that whenever time is a factor she scores below intellectual expectation. She has a specific weakness in fluency across all academic areas. While her basic skills are High Average to Superior (Academic Skills, PR 90), and her ability to apply those skills to more complex tasks is comparable (Academic Applications, PR 84), Andrea's weaknesses in speed of processing visual symbols and rapid naming are so severe that her Academic Fluency score was in the Low range (PR 5). Thus, the evidence of her functional limitation on her *rate* of performing academic tasks is clearly evident in these achievement test results.

SUMMARY

Andrea is a nearly 15-year-old female who was seen for a psychoeducational evaluation to assess her current level of functioning. She will begin her sophomore year at Fisher High School in the fall. Andrea has a history of slow reading and difficulty finishing assignments, school exams, and standardized tests. She and her parents are hoping to better understand why academic tasks take Andrea a longer time than expected, especially since she doesn't have difficulty understanding the material and can do very well as long as she has sufficient time.

Significant scatter is present in Andrea's intellectual profile. On this assessment, her verbal reasoning skills were Above Average, her working memory was Average to Above Average, and her nonverbal thinking abilities ranged from High Average/Superior on an untimed task to Below Average/Average range on timed tasks. In contrast, Andrea's visual processing speed (the ability to recognize and identify visual symbols) and rapid naming speed (the ability to access and retrieve specific words from memory quickly) are extremely weak. Consequently, Andrea's fluency in academic areas is substantially lower than expected and significantly discrepant from her other cognitive and achievement scores. Her pattern in all areas— reading, writing, and math—was accurate but slow. In academic skills and applications in which speed was not a factor or, as in the case of the NDRT, when the time limit was removed, Andrea scored solidly in the Above Average range.

Results of testing do not support a diagnosis of ADHD. Although the IVA+PLUS results suggested ADHD due to extremely slow response times, Andrea's scores are most likely attributable to her slow processing speed, rather than difficulty sustaining attention. Based on interviews, clinical observations, and her parent and teacher rating scales, she does not have a global attention problem. However, her personality style may lead others to wonder if she is focused and attentive, because she tends to be vivacious and energetic. Also, in the past, some of her teachers have assumed that perfectionism has led to her slow work rate.

She did not exhibit any signs of perfectionism, such as erasing and rewriting, during this evaluation. Andrea appears to have a very healthy balance between wanting to do as well as she can and accepting the fact that she cannot get everything right. Her slow processing and inability to access specific words *quickly and on demand*, however, affect the speed at which she can complete tasks and tests.

DIAGNOSES

DSM-IV-TR Diagnosis

Axis I: 315.9   Learning Disorder Not Otherwise Specified: visual and auditory processing deficits leading to extremely slow information processing overall

Axis II: V71.09   No Diagnosis on Axis II

IDEA 2004 Diagnosis

Learning disability in reading fluency, written expression (speed only), and basic math skills (speed only).

RECOMMENDATIONS

Andrea qualifies for accommodations as a student with a specific learning disability. The appropriate team should convene to develop an Individualized Educational Plan (IEP) for her that includes the following accommodations and academic interventions.

1. Because of her extremely slow processing speed and significant underachievement on timed tests, she should be given unlimited time on untimed tests and double time on time-restricted tests, unless the intention of the test is to assess performance rate rather than knowledge. Andrea demonstrated during this evaluation that she is patient and willing to expend the necessary extra effort to produce work at a level commensurate with her intelligence if she has sufficient time.

2. Andrea would benefit from specific strategies to increase reading fluency. Improved reading fluency would not only permit her to reduce the amount of time that her assignments require but, as she develops more automaticity, she would have more cognitive attention

available to better understand and think critically about what she is reading.

3. Provide Andrea with specific writing strategies for organizing her ideas and information in a variety of types of documents, such as narratives, research reports, and persuasive essays. In addition to improving her writing, use of strategies will increase her efficiency so she can complete assignments in a more timely fashion.

4. Due to the effect of her slow processing on her ability to rapidly access math facts, Andrea should be permitted to use a calculator for assignments and tests when the focus is on the higher-level aspects of math. Without this accommodation, Andrea will use a great deal of cognitive attention and working memory in doing basic computation rather than having these cognitive resources available for the conceptual aspect of problem solving.

5. Because of her slow writing fluency and slow retrieval of specific words from long-term storage, Andrea is likely to have considerable difficulty listening to a lecture and taking notes at the same time. Make provisions to provide her with a copy of another student's notes or with a copy of the teacher's lecture notes.

6. Start teaching Andrea self-advocacy skills so that she can explain her learning disability to her teachers, explain the accommodations that she needs, and the reasons for those accommodations. To this purpose, also include her as an active participant in her IEP meetings.

SUMMARY PROFILE

Wechsler Intelligence Scale for Children – Fourth Edition

Woodcock-Johnson III NU Tests of Cognitive Abilities

Cluster	SS	68% Band	PR	RPI
Working Memory	113	109–117	80	97/90
Numbers Reversed	116	111–121	86	99/90
Auditory Working Memory	104	99–108	59	93/90
Broad Attention	89	85–92	22	79/90
Numbers Reversed	116	111–121	86	99/90
Auditory Working Memory	104	99–108	59	93/90
Auditory Attention	66	57–75	1	65/90
Pair Cancellation	61	58–63	0.4	7/90

Comprehensive Test of Phonological Processing

Composite	SS	ScS	PR
Rapid Naming	64		1
Subtests			
Rapid Digit Naming		5	5
Rapid Letter Naming		3	1

Integrated Visual and Auditory-Plus Continuous Performance Test

	SS
Full Scale Response Control Quotient	17
Auditory	25
Visual	34
Full Scale Attention Quotient	14
Auditory	27
Visual	26
Sustained Auditory Attention Quotient	0
Sustained Visual Attention Quotient	0

Factor Indices/Subtests	SS	ScS	PR			SS	ScS	PR
Full Scale IQ	98		45					
Verbal Comprehension	112		79		**Perceptual Reasoning**	104		61
Similarities		12	75		Block Design		8	25
Vocabulary		14	91		Matrix Reasoning		14	91
Comprehension		11	63		Picture Concepts		10	50
					(Picture Completion)		8	25
Working Memory	110		75		**Perceptual Speed**	56		0.2
Digit Span		14	91		Coding		1	0.1
Letter-Number Sequencing		10	50		Symbol Search		3	1

Wisconsin Card Sorting Test – Revised and Expanded

Scale	Score	PR
Total Number	116	86
Perseverative Responses	121	92
Perseverative Errors	121	92
Nonperseverative Errors	107	68
Percent Conceptual Level Responses	120	91
Scale		
Number of Categories Completed		>16*
Trials to Complete 1st Category		>16*
Failure to Maintain Set		>16*
Learning to Learn		>16*
*Highest percentile given		

Children's Memory Scale

Indexes	SS	95% Band	PR
General Memory	89	81–98	23
Attention/Concentration	128	118–138	97
Learning	91	81–101	27
Visual Immediate	100	84–116	50
Visual Delayed	100	85–115	50
Verbal Immediate	82	72–92	12
Verbal Delayed	88	79–97	21

Rey Complex Figure Test

Scale	T Score	PR
Copy	n/a	>16
Time to Copy	n/a	>16
Immediate Recall	46	34
Delayed Recall	42	21
Recognition	39	14

Woodcock-Johnson III NU Tests of Achievement

Cluster/Test	SS	68% Band	PR	RPI
Oral Language	**94**	**91–98**	**35**	**85/90**
Oral Comprehension	106	101–110	64	95/90
Understanding Directions	98	92–103	43	88/90
Story Recall	86	79–93	17	83/90
Picture Vocabulary	88	84–93	22	62/90
Listening Comprehension	**103**	**98–107**	**57**	**92/90**
Oral Comprehension	106	101–110	64	95/90
Understanding Directions	98	92–103	43	88/90
Oral Expression	**86**	**82–90**	**18**	**73/90**
Story Recall	86	79–93	17	83/90

Cluster/Test	SS	68% Band	PR	RPI
Picture Vocabulary	88	84–93	22	62/90
Broad Reading	**101**	**98–104**	**52**	**91/90**
Letter-Word Identification	110	106–115	76	97/90
Reading Fluency	80	76–83	9	51/90
Passage Comprehension	109	104–114	73	96/90
Brief Reading	**112**	**107–116**	**78**	**97/90**
Letter-Word Identification	110	106–115	76	97/90
Passage Comprehension	109	104–114	73	96/90
Basic Reading Skills	**105**	**101–109**	**63**	**94/90**
Word Attack	98	95–102	45	87/90
Letter-Word Identification	110	106–115	76	97/90
Broad Written Language	**101**	**97–106**	**53**	**91/90**
Spelling	118	114–123	89	99/90
Writing Samples	110	103–116	74	95/90
Writing Fluency	74	69–80	4	35/90
Brief Writing	**117**	**113–122**	**88**	**98/90**
Spelling	118	114–123	89	99/90
Writing Samples	110	103–116	74	95/90
Broad Math	**113**	**110–115**	**80**	**97/90**
Calculation	114	109–119	82	98/90
Applied Problems	116	113–119	86	99/90
Math Fluency	91	89–94	28	84/90
Brief Math	**117**	**114–120**	**87**	**99/90**
Calculation	114	109–119	82	98/90
Applied Problems	116	113–119	86	99/90
Academic Skills	**119**	**115–122**	**90**	**98/90**
Academic Fluency	**75**	**72–79**	**5**	**58/90**
Academic Applications	**115**	**112–118**	**84**	**98/90**

Nelson-Denny Reading Test

Scale	PR	GE
Reading Rate	23	N/A
Comprehension	52	11.3
Extended Time Comprehension	85	15.6

CASE 46

Falling Through the Cracks
An Adolescent with a Severe Reading Disability

Bashir Abu-Hamour, Annmarie Urso, and Nancy Mather

This report illustrates a case of a bright, bilingual student with a severe reading disability who was not accurately diagnosed until his second year of high school and who never received special education services. He was enrolled in the gifted and talented program in early elementary school and then dropped when he could not keep up with the reading. His mother expressed concerns regarding his reading development from first grade on but was not aware that she was allowed to make a formal referral for services. Although Miguel was finally referred for an evaluation in the sixth grade, the cognitive testing was insufficient, academic testing was not conducted, and no recommendations or interventions were developed. The examiner recommended further testing in Spanish, thus making the assumption that Miguel was still an English language learner. If in doubt, he should have made the recommendation that Miguel be assessed for English proficiency. Miguel is fully proficient in both Spanish and English. His difficulties with behavior and subsequent frustration stemmed from his inability to perform any of the reading or writing tasks that were being presented to him in his classes. An interesting finding of this evaluation was that his difficulty learning to read stemmed from weaknesses in memory and rapid symbol perception, rather than in aspects of phonological processing. In contrast, both his oral language and mathematical abilities are average or above. Miguel requires intensive one-to-one instruction to learn to read and spell, as well as accommodations for low literacy levels in all of his high school classes.

The WJ III Developmental Zone and Instructional Zone Worksheets appended to this report provide a quick visual overview of Miguel's proficiency in cognitive and language abilities and in academic skills compared with his age peers. The Developmental and Instructional Zones are based on the Relative Proficiency Index (RPI). Distinct from the standard score, which simply indicates the *position* of a score on the

bell curve as influenced by the standard deviation, the RPI is a qualitative measure that predicts a person's *proficiency* in tasks similar to the one used in the assessment. (An explanation of the development and interpretation of the RPI is available on the Riverside Publishing Company web site, www.riverpub.com/products/wjIIIComplete/resources.html.)

For intervention after this evaluation, Miguel was provided tutoring in basic reading and writing skills from a group of graduate students in a university class in instructional methods for students with learning disabilities. Five different students rotated meeting with him each day for 12 weeks, using a systematic, synthetic phonics program, the *Phonic Reading Lessons: Skills and Practice* (Kirk, Kirk, Minskoff, Mather, & Roberts; Roberts & Mather, 2007). After 3 months of instruction, Miguel's reading was assessed on curriculum-based probes. From a starting point of 25 correct words per minute (cwpm) on first-grade reading material, Miguel had progressed to 75 cwpm on third-grade level materials.

DIAGNOSTIC EVALUATION REPORT

Name:	Miguel Laguna
Date of Birth:	09/13/1994
Age:	15 years, 4 months
Parent:	Delia Laguna
Languages:	English and Spanish
School:	Sterling Art Academy
Grade:	9.4
Test Dates:	01/11, 01/14, and 01/18/2010
Evaluators:	Bashir Abu-Hamour, Ph.D.
	Annmarie Urso, Ph.D.
	Nancy Mather, Ph.D.

REASON FOR REFERRAL

Miguel was referred for an evaluation by his teacher, Ms. Jane Simon, because of his extreme difficulties in learning basic and reading and writing skills. Ms. Simon stated that "Miguel is very much a beginning reader; his reading behaviors are similar to someone who is just learning to read and amazingly low for someone of his level of intelligence." The purposes of this evaluation were to determine what factors are affecting Miguel's reading and writing development, what level of support is needed, and what instructional methodologies and technologies would be most effective for addressing his educational needs.

BACKGROUND INFORMATION

Miguel is a 15-year-old Hispanic male. Because of his good artistic ability, he is enrolled in a charter school that integrates art into a general academic curriculum. He is currently living with his biological mother. According to interviews with his mother and teacher, and a review of school records, Miguel's mother was born in Mexico and has been living in Sierra Vista for 24 years. She received a G.E.D. 5 years ago and currently works for a landscaping business. Miguel also has an 18-year-old sister who is studying architecture at a university.

Mrs. Laguna reported that her pregnancy with Miguel was normal and that he reached his early developmental milestones within normal limits. Although Miguel has been struggling with reading and writing since the first grade, and his mother has regularly expressed concern to his teachers, no systematic reading interventions were ever provided. Miguel admitted that he is often embarrassed in school because of his limited reading ability. Despite this, he stated that he likes school and attends regularly. He said that his favorite sport is football and that he likes spending time with friends. He also enjoys doing landscape work with his mother.

A review of Miguel's school records indicated that he attended Franklin Elementary School from kindergarten through fifth grade and was never retained. In first grade, Miguel was in the school's gifted program but was dropped from the program in the middle of second grade when he could not do the reading necessary for many of the projects. In contrast to his reading skills, math and art have always been areas of strength. Teachers also report that Miguel has good social skills, is cooperative, and has a positive attitude toward school and others. He expresses himself clearly and communicates well with his teachers and peers. Prior to this evaluation, Miguel's hearing and visual acuity were tested by his primary care doctor and found to be normal.

PREVIOUS TESTING

In sixth grade, Miguel was referred for a psychological evaluation by the Child Study Team at Mercer Middle School to determine eligibility for exceptional education services. On 3/20/2007, James Barker, the school psychologist, administered the Universal Nonverbal Intelligence Test (UNIT). Miguel's scores placed him in the average range of intellectual functioning and no processing deficits were identified. A summary of the UNIT results is presented below:

Scale	Standard Score	Percentile Rank	Classification
Memory Quotient	100	50	Average
Reasoning Quotient	109	73	Average
Symbolic Quotient	103	58	Average
Nonsymbolic Quotient	106	66	Average
Full-Scale IQ	105	63	Average

Formal academic testing was not done but a review of curriculum-based measurements (CBM) indicated that Miguel was considerably delayed in reading and written language skills. Conversely, the CBM results suggested that his math skills were similar to those of other children in his grade. Recommendations were made for further testing in Spanish and the development of a behavioral intervention plan, because of teachers' reports that Miguel was not participating in class discussions and rarely completed his work in school or at home. The evaluation team noted that assistive technology was not needed.

TESTS ADMINISTERED

Woodcock-Johnson III Tests of Cognitive Ability (WJ III COG): Tests 1–7, 11–17

Woodcock-Johnson III Diagnostic Supplement (WJ III DS): Tests 26–27

Woodcock-Johnson III Tests of Achievement (WJ III ACH): Tests 1–15, 20–21

CBM for reading: Correct Words per Minute (CWPM)

CBM for spelling: Number of Correct Letter Sequences (CLS)

Test of Irregular Word Reading Efficiency (TIWRE)

Rapid Automatized Naming and Rapid Alternating Stimulus Tests (RAN/RAS)

Wide Range Assessment of Memory and Learning, Second Edition (WRAML 2)

TESTING OBSERVATIONS

Miguel was told that the purpose of testing was to find the best way to teach him how to read. He asked, "So after the testing is done, is someone going to teach me how to read?" then muttered to himself, "Yeah, right." He was told that, through a special program at the university, students in the graduate program in learning disabilities would provide individual tutoring at least three times a week. Throughout testing, Miguel appeared to try his best on most of the tests administered. When he was able to accomplish the tasks, he remained attentive and cooperative. Overall, he was careful and slow in considering his responses. When reading and writing tasks became too difficult, he yawned and became less engaged but responded when encouraged to try his best. In contrast, Miguel's conversational proficiency was advanced for his grade level. By the end of the third session, he seemed tired and less motivated than he had been in the first session. He yawned and then asked, "When will this testing be finished?" These test results are believed to be a valid representation of Miguel's current cognitive abilities and academic achievement.

TEST RESULTS

The WJ III COG, WJ III DS, and WJ III ACH were scored according to age norms. Because these batteries are co-normed, direct comparisons can be made among Miguel's cognitive and achievement scores. These comparisons help determine the presence and significance of any strengths and weaknesses among his abilities. These tests provide measures of Miguel's specific cognitive and oral language abilities, as well as his academic achievement. The WRAML 2 was also scored according to age norms. Results are reported as standard scores and scaled scores. Miguel's performance is compared to his age peers using standard score (SS) ranges:

SS Range	<69	70–79	80–89	90–110	111–120	121–130	>130
Verbal Label	Very Low	Low	Low Average	Average	High Average	Superior	Very Superior

His proficiency on specific tasks is described by Relative Proficiency Index (RPI) levels:

RPI Range	Level of Proficiency
0–3	Negligible
3–24	Very Limited
24–67	Limited
67–82	Limited to Average
82–95	Average
95–98	Average to Advanced
98–100	Advanced
100	Very Advanced

Percentile ranks and descriptive ratings are provided for the RAN/RAS tests and the TIWRE. Results from the CBM measurements for reading (CWPM) and spelling (CLS) are also provided.

The WJ III measures broad abilities within different areas of cognition. Each broad ability, represented by a cluster score, is composed of at least two narrow abilities, represented by the individual test scores. When Miguel's performance on the narrow abilities within a broad ability are similar, only the cluster score is discussed. In instances where the scores of the component tests in a cluster are significantly dissimilar, the individual test scores are discussed. Results from both the cognitive abilities and achievement clusters are ordered from the strongest to the weakest areas.

Cognitive Abilities

Based on the tests of the WJ III COG, Miguel's General Intellectual Ability – Extended (GIA) score fell in the lower end of the Average range (SS 91, SS ± 1 SEM = 89–93). Due to the wide variation in Miguel's scores on the tests that make up the GIA, this score does not provide a good estimate of Miguel's intelligence or learning potential.

Fluid Reasoning

Miguel's standard score on the Fluid Reasoning cluster was in the High Average range. Based on the RPI, compared to typical 15-year-olds, his proficiency was Advanced in using logical reasoning to solve increasingly complex problems presented as visual patterns. The two tests of this cluster measure different aspects of fluid reasoning. His deductive reasoning was Average to Advanced. The task required him to use given rules to work through problems in a step-by-step fashion. His inductive reasoning was advanced. This task required him to consider multiple elements within two sets of drawings and ascertain the rule for their separation. In both tests, the rules become increasingly complex and the types of problems change. Thus, these tests also require flexibility in shifting one's mindset.

WJ III COG Cluster/Tests	RPI	Proficiency	SS (±1 SEM)
FLUID REASONING	98/90	Advanced	117 (111–124)
Concept Formation	99/90	Advanced	123 (114–131)
Analysis-Synthesis	95/90	Average to Advanced	107 (100–114)

Oral Language

The WJ III ACH Oral Language-Extended cluster provides a broad sample of linguistic competence, including expressive vocabulary, comprehension of syntactically complex verbal directions, and comprehension and recall of narrative information ranging in length from a single sentence to paragraph-length stories. Miguel's proficiency in all of the oral language tests except Picture Vocabulary was Average to Advanced. In contrast, his proficiency in naming pictured objects was Limited to Average and his standard score was significantly lower than his other scores. Miguel's lower vocabulary performance is most likely a reflection of his limited exposure to reading vocabulary. His RPI indicates that when average age peers are 90% successful in their ability to name pictures, Miguel is likely to be 75% successful.

WJ III ACH Cluster/Tests	RPI	Proficiency	SS (±1 SEM)
ORAL LANGUAGE – Ext.	94/90	Average	109 (104–113)
Story Recall	95/90	Average to Advanced	118 (110–125)
Understanding Directions	97/90	Average to Advanced	117 (108–125)
Picture Vocabulary	75/90	Limited to Average	93 (88–97)
Oral Comprehension	97/90	Average to Advanced	111 (106–116)

Visual-Spatial Thinking

Results of the WJ III Visual-Spatial Thinking cluster indicated that Miguel can think with visual patterns, such as perceiving part/whole relationships in designs and mentally manipulating pieces of a pattern to match a complete design. In addition, his recognition memory for details in pictures was within the Average range.

WJ III COG Cluster/Tests	RPI	Proficiency	SS (±1 SEM)
VISUAL-SPATIAL THINKING	93/90	Average	106 (102–111)
Spatial Relations	94/90	Average	107 (102–112)
Picture Recognition	92/90	Average	103 (98–109)

Processing Speed

Processing speed reflects speed and efficiency in performing simple cognitive tasks, influencing the ability to make repeated routines automatic. Perceptual speed is narrower, the ability to rapidly identify similarities and differences among visual symbols, such as letters or numbers. Overall, considering both the standard scores and the RPIs, Miguel was more successful in rapidly scanning and matching pictures based on their *conceptual* similarities (e.g., Which two objects are most alike?) than on matching symbols based solely on their *visual* similarities (e.g., 12 21 45 78 21). This finding suggests that Miguel will have difficulty on age-level tasks requiring rapid recognition and comparison of symbols, such as letter and number patterns.

WJ III COG Cluster/Tests	RPI	Proficiency	SS (±1 SEM)
PROCESSING SPEED	83/90	Average	90 (85–95)
Visual Matching	77/90	Limited to Average	87 (81–93)
Decision Speed	87/90	Average	96 (90–102)
PERCEPTUAL SPEED	76/90	Limited to Average	85 (75–91)
Visual Matching	77/90	Limited to Average	87 (81–93)
Cross Out	74/90	Limited to Average	87 (79–95)

Auditory Processing and Phonemic Awareness

Miguel's standard scores and RPIs on two tests of phonemic awareness were in the Average range, indicating that Miguel can perceive and manipulate the individual sounds in words to come up with other words. Good phonemic awareness is critical for the acquisition of reading skills. In contrast, Miguel's ability to discriminate speech sounds in the presence of background noise, despite normal hearing acuity, was in the Low range. His RPI suggested that Miguel will have difficulty when trying to listen to speech in the presence of competing noise. Miguel stated that he has not noticed any difficulty hearing and understanding what a teacher says in the classroom or hearing his friends across the table from him in the cafeteria.

WJ III COG and ACH Cluster/Tests	RPI	Proficiency	SS (±1 SEM)
AUDITORY PROCESSING	84/90	Average	92 (87–98)
Sound Blending	91/90	Average	100 (96–105)
Auditory Attention	75/90	Limited to Average	77 (68–86)
Sound Awareness	87/90	Average	96 (89–103)

WJ III COG Cluster/Tests	RPI	Proficiency	SS (±1 SEM)
SHORT-TERM MEMORY	30/90	Limited	78 (74–83)
Numbers Reversed	34/90	Limited	81 (75–87)
Memory for Words	26/90	Limited	80 (73–86)
AUDITORY MEMORY SPAN	25/90	Limited	73 (68–78)
Memory for Words	26/90	Limited	80 (73–86)
Memory for Sentences	24/90	Limited	69 (64–75)

Comprehension-Knowledge

Comprehension-Knowledge is a measure of the breadth and depth of language-based knowledge. It includes the expression of common knowledge and vocabulary knowledge, and reasoning with word meanings. Miguel's standard score was in the Low Average range. His RPI indicates that knowledge of vocabulary and common information, such as where one would find certain objects and what they are used for, are areas of difficulty for Miguel. When average age peers are 90% successful, Miguel is expected to be 70% successful on tasks requiring vocabulary knowledge and 62% successful on tasks requiring common knowledge. Miguel's inability to read (discussed below) and his subsequent lack of exposure to reading materials are likely major factors contributing to his limited vocabulary and general knowledge.

WJ III COG Cluster/Tests	RPI	Proficiency	SS (±1 SEM)
COMPREHENSION-KNOWLEDGE	70/90	Limited to Average	88 (85–92)
Verbal Comprehension	76/90	Limited to Average	92 (88–96)
General Information	62/90	Limited	86 (81–91)

Short-Term Memory

The Short-Term Memory and Auditory Memory Span clusters assess the ability to hold information in mind for a few seconds to a minute. An example is remembering a phone number long enough to walk across the room and dial it or remember the directions that the teacher gives regarding a reading assignment while finding the right page and the questions to answer. Miguel's performance on this cluster was in the Low range. His RPI of 30/90 suggests that on tasks requiring short-term memory, specifically without a meaningful context, Miguel's proficiency would likely be 30%, which is limited proficiency compared with the 90% proficiency of typical students his age. A memory weakness of this type can affect almost all new learning of academic skills as well as more complex tasks involving following verbal directions, reading comprehension, and written expression.

Working Memory

Working memory is the ability to hold information in immediate awareness while performing a mental operation on it. Due to the discrepancy between the two tests of working memory on the WJ III COG, Miguel was administered the two tests that make up the Working Memory composite of the WRAML2. Miguel's scores on both tests were in the Low range, confirming that Miguel has significant difficulty in maintaining discrete items in memory while manipulating or transforming them.

WJ III COG Cluster/Tests	RPI	Proficiency	SS (±1 SEM)
WORKING MEMORY	56/90	Limited	83 (79–88)
Auditory Working Memory	n/a	n/a	n/a
Numbers Reversed	34/90	Limited	81 (75–87)

WRAML-2 Composite/Tests	SS	ScS
WORKING MEMORY	73	
Verbal Working Memory		4
Symbolic Working Memory		5

Long-Term Retrieval

Miguel's scores on the two tests of WJ III Long-Term Retrieval cluster were significantly discrepant. Visual-Auditory Learning is a test of paired-associate learning. Miguel was taught to associate common words (e.g., red, where) with novel symbols and then to "read" a story "written" in the symbols. Although his standard score bordered the Low Average and Average ranges, the RPI indicated that Miguel would be almost as proficient as his peers in this type of task. Given the difficulty Miguel had on other memory tests, it is likely that both the visual symbols and the story context supported his ability to recall the words associated with the symbols. In contrast, Miguel had considerable difficulty on Retrieval Fluency, retrieving known words from long-term memory to fit a given category (e.g., "Name as many types of clothing as you can"). This time-limited task requires speed of recall but differs from other word-retrieval tasks in that it allows the subject flexibility in choosing among the words he knows rather than having to find the "right" word. Miguel's responses did not suggest difficulty with word retrieval; the words he chose were specific and accurate, but slow. Miguel's Very Low standard score indicates poor efficiency in retrieving information from long-term memory. He is predicted to be 65% successful when typical age peers are 90% successful on similar tasks.

WJ III COG Cluster/ Tests	RPI	Proficiency	SS (±1 SEM)
LONG-TERM RETRIEVAL	76/90	Limited to Average	71 (65–77)
Visual-Auditory Learning	84/90	Average	90 (83–97)
Retrieval Fluency	65/90	Limited	40 (32–49)

Rapid Automatized Naming (RAN), Rapid Alternating Stimuli (RAS)

Miguel demonstrated weaknesses on all measures of RAN and RAS. RAN tasks require the subject to name a series of visually-presented digits, letters, colors, or pictured objects as quickly as possible, whereas RAS tasks have a mixture of symbols (e.g., letters and numbers). Research in acquisition of reading skills indicates that RAN is related to the developmental of basic reading and spelling skills. Distinct from phonological skills, it appears to predict a person's facility with orthographic processing, the ability to perceive, store, and recall familiar letter combinations (words and word parts) as immediately recognizable visual patterns, as well as reading rate and fluency. All of Miguel's RAN/RAS scores were in the Low range, placing him within the lowest 5% of his age peers.

Test	Age Equivalent	Grade Equivalent	Percentile Rank	Standard Score	Descriptive Rating
Objects	7–9	3.2	6	77	Poor
Colors	7–9	2.7	5	76	Poor
Numbers	6–3	1.2	5	75	Poor
Letters	6–3	1.2	5	75	Poor
2-Set Letters & Numbers	6–9	2.0	5	76	Poor
3-Set Letters, Numbers, & Colors	7–0	2.4	6	77	Poor

Academic Achievement

Miguel's academic skills were assessed in reading, writing, and math using selected tests of the Woodcock-Johnson III NU Tests of Achievement (WJ III ACH) and qualitative analysis of expository writing samples. In addition, his performance was analyzed on the Test of Irregular Word Reading Efficiency (TIWRE) which measures the ability to read words with irregular spelling patterns, and on CBM measures for reading and spelling.

Broad Math

Miguel's mathematics skills were assessed in three areas: math computation, automaticity of math facts, and practical application of math knowledge. Standard scores and RPIs indicated that math computation and practical application were Average for his age. His proficiency in solving math facts of addition, subtraction, and multiplication rapidly, however, was Limited. His standard score, in the Low range, was significantly lower than that of the other two tests. During the math tests, Miguel sometimes counted on his fingers, used hatch marks, and drew small diagrams to help him with computation, reinforcing the finding of limited math fact knowledge.

WJ III ACH Cluster/ Tests	RPI	Proficiency	SS (±1 SEM)
BROAD MATH	88/90	Average	97 (94–100)
Calculation	89/90	Average	99 (94–104)
Applied Problems	96/90	Average to Advanced	105 (102–107)
Math Fluency	67/90	Limited	77 (74–79)

Phoneme-Grapheme Knowledge

The Phoneme-Grapheme cluster represents the ability to use phonics and orthographic knowledge (knowledge of the spelling patterns of the language) to read and spell unfamiliar words. Miguel's standard score on this cluster was in the Very Low range. Miguel's RPIs indicated that his proficiency in reading nonsense words that follow regular phonics and orthographic patterns was Negligible. On the initial words, he said each sound slowly and then attempted to blend them but came up with a different word. His proficiency in spelling similarly structured nonsense words was limited; he had difficulty sequencing sounds and made errors on frequently seen spelling patterns (e.g., suffixes *-ed*, *-ble*). Although his proficiency on the two tasks differed somewhat, both indicated that he will have severe difficulty reading and spelling words he does not already know.

WJ III ACH Cluster/ Tests	RPI	Proficiency	SS (±1 SEM)
PHONEME-GRAPHEME KNOWLEDGE	11/90	Very Limited	57 (53–61)
Word Attack	3/90	Negligible	67 (63–70)
Spelling of Sounds	37/90	Limited	67 (61–72)

Broad Reading

The tests of the Broad Reading cluster assess three reading skills: word identification, reading fluency, and reading comprehension. Miguel's performance on all three tests was in the Very Low range. On the Reading Fluency test, where he was to read simple sentences quickly and decide if they were true or false, his score reflected both slow reading and incorrect responses. When reading lists of real words, Miguel consistently guessed and did not appear to attempt to use phonics to sound them out. Fewer than 1 in 1,000 students of his age would score as low or lower on word identification tasks. Miguel's low score on Passage Comprehension is due to his weak decoding skills; he cannot understand the text because he cannot read the words. Miguel's Passage Comprehension RPI of 0/90 predicts that on classroom tasks requiring age-appropriate reading, he would have no success. Because his proficiency in reading is negligible, grade-level reading tasks would be impossible for him.

WJ III ACH Cluster/Tests	RPI	Proficiency	SS (±1 SEM)
BROAD READING	0/90	Negligible	27 (24–30)
Letter-Word Identification	0/90	Negligible	14 (11–18)
Reading Fluency	10/90	Very Limited	60 (56–64)
Passage Comprehension	3/90	Negligible	48 (43–53)

Test of Irregular Word Reading Efficiency (TIWRE)

Miguel scored significantly below average on the TIWRE, with a grade equivalent of K.2. His score indicates that he will find irregular words (i.e., words containing atypical spelling patterns, such as *does*) extremely difficult to read. His percentile rank of >0.1 indicates that less than 1 out of 1,000 students would score as low or lower than he did.

Curriculum-Based Measurements for Reading

Curriculum-Based Measurements for reading were administered using probes appropriate for first grade. This task combines both word accuracy and rate of reading, and the results are reported as correct words per minute (CWPM). At first-grade level, the median CWPM is 25. Miguel's CWPM for the three probes were 25, 24, and 26.

Broad Written Language

Miguel's written language skills were assessed in three areas: spelling, writing fluency, and written expression. Although his scores were not similar enough to discuss as a cluster, all were in the Very Low range. Miguel's standard score and RPI on the Spelling test and qualitative analysis of his responses indicated that his knowledge of phonics, spelling rules, and orthographic patterns was Negligible. Further, his writing was slow and laborious. On the Writing Fluency test, he was required to generate and write simple sentences as rapidly as possible. He worked slowly and, for many items, could not come up with a sentence at all. The Writing Samples test measures skill in generating and writing phrases or sentences in response to a variety of demands. Miguel's answers were generally acceptable but lacked elaboration and details. Some of his responses could not be credited because they contained spellings that were nonphonetic and could not be deciphered. Miguel's RPIs indicated that he would find classroom writing assignments to be extremely difficult to impossible. This finding is supported by analysis of his classroom writing samples, which are short, contain indecipherable spelling, and lack detail.

WJ III ACH Cluster/Tests	RPI	Proficiency	SS (±1 SEM)
BROAD WRITTEN LANGUAGE	5/90	Very Limited	44 (40–48)
Spelling	0/90	Negligible	31 (25–36)
Writing Fluency	18/90	Very Limited	66 (60–72)
Writing Samples	54/90	Limited	78 (72–83)

Curriculum-Based Measurements for Spelling

On 12 orally dictated spelling words, administered in English class, Miguel's score was 35 out of 68 Correct Letter Sequences (CLS). This score indicates Very Limited ability to spell words at the first-grade level. Examples of Miguel's spelling errors were *yaiol* for *while* and *awy* for *away*.

WJ III Discrepancy and Variation Procedures

On the WJ III, intraindividual discrepancies are computed to show the likelihood of a person obtaining a particular cluster score, given the cluster score against which it is being compared. Of 15-year-olds who scored similarly to Miguel on the GIA and Oral Language clusters, less than 1 in 1,000 would have scored as low as he did on the reading and writing clusters. The variation procedures are computed to show a person's significant strengths and weaknesses. On the WJ III COG, the Fluid Reasoning factor is a strength. In fact, when Miguel's Fluid Reasoning is compared to his other cognitive abilities, only 3 out of 1,000 people would have a score as high. In contrast, when both Long-Term Retrieval and Auditory Memory Span are compared to his other cognitive abilities, only 1 out of 100 and 4 out of 100 people would have scores as low. On the WJ III ACH, when his Oral Language abilities are compared to his reading, writing, and math performance, only 1 out of 1,000 people would score as high. When both his reading and writing abilities are compared to the other three areas of achievement, less than 1 out of 1,000 people would obtain scores as low.

SUMMARY AND CONCLUSIONS

Miguel is presently a 15-year-old Hispanic male who attends Sterling Art Academy. He is fluent in both English and Spanish. He was referred for an evaluation by his teacher because of his severe difficulties with reading and writing. Because of the wide variation in the scores that make up the GIA, this score is not a valid estimate of Miguel's general capacity for learning.

Miguel has a strength in fluid reasoning, the ability to use inductive and deductive logic for problem solving, and in phonemic awareness, the ability to perceive and work with the individual sounds in words. He has average abilities in working with visual-spatial tasks such as mentally manipulating pieces of abstract designs and remembering details in pictures. He also demonstrated average ability to find conceptual similarities among pictures. In contrast, Miguel has weaknesses in perceptual speed (the ability to scan and discriminate among visual symbols rapidly), in general knowledge, and in discriminating speech sounds in competing noise. More severe weaknesses were found in short-term memory, in working memory (the ability to work with and transform the information held in short-term memory), and in the ability to retrieve well-known words from long-term storage rapidly. Despite severe weaknesses in short-term memory and working memory, Miguel was able to retain and follow complex directions and to remember word-symbol associations long enough to use them to "read" a story made up of the symbols. Additionally, Miguel was able to remember brief stories long enough to retell them. Analysis of these tasks indicates that Miguel's recall of verbal information is significantly aided when the information is supported by visual material and when in-

formation is presented in a meaningful context, such as a story. He has considerably more difficulty learning and retaining isolated pieces of information or facts by rote.

With the exception of vocabulary knowledge, Miguel's oral language abilities, including comprehension of meaningful information from a sentence to a paragraph-length story, and instructions incorporating complex syntax are advanced. His knowledge of vocabulary was limited, likely due to the fact that he does not read and so, does not encounter new vocabulary unless he hears it spoken.

Based on the current test results, Miguel's only academic strength is in practical application of math knowledge. His ability to do computation is average for his age but he is limited in his knowledge of math facts, which slows down and complicates his efforts in solving problems. Miguel has severe weaknesses in all reading skills including word attack, word identification, fluency, and comprehension. He also has severe weaknesses in spelling and in speed of generating and writing sentences.

Analysis

Reading

Most likely, Miguel's severely limited reading fluency and comprehension are directly caused by his inability to recognize the words on the page. Typically, good readers have a strong foundation in phonemic awareness and learn easily to perceive and manipulate the sounds of spoken words. As they learn to associate the sounds with letters (phonics), they begin to sound out new words. After sounding out the same word repeatedly, it becomes a sight word. In other words, the reader recognizes the visual pattern as a whole and instantaneously recalls the oral equivalent of the word. Miguel cannot sound out new words and so has not built a base of sight words. His almost nonexistent decoding skill is most likely caused by his severe memory weaknesses, inefficient retrieval of verbal information from long-term memory, and slow perceptual speed. Despite his facility with phonemic awareness, limitations in memory and retrieval would interfere with his ability to learn the sounds of letters, retrieve those that he had learned, and hold them in memory long enough to blend them into a known word. Slow processing speed would impede his perception and assimilation of frequently seen letter combinations and, consequently, his translation of the words he had managed to sound out into sight words. Based on his average to advanced oral language performance, Miguel's reading comprehension should increase as he learns to decode the words and develops some fluency. His vocabulary will increase also as he reads more, although at this point he requires direct instruction to help him catch up. Due to his limited memory and perceptual speed, Miguel is likely to need comprehension strategies to help him process and retain information from text as he approaches high school reading material.

Writing

The same problems, as well as limited exposure to text, have likely prevented Miguel from recognizing, assimilating, and then retrieving common letter patterns when he tries to spell words. Although, when directed to do so, he is able to segment a syllable into its sounds, most often he does not know the correct letters to represent the sounds (e.g., *yaiol* for *while*). When trying to articulate his thoughts on paper, spelling the words becomes a bottleneck, as the process is slow, arduous, and unsuccessful. Additionally, Miguel demonstrated difficulty formulating sentences to express his thoughts. Since his oral expression appears to be at least age appropriate, this difficulty may be related to the complexity of the writing process and his difficulty with basic writing skills.

Math

Similarly, poor short-term memory, working memory, retrieval, and perceptual speed would make it difficult for Miguel to memorize and then efficiently retrieve math facts. His average and above performance in calculation and practical application suggests that he understands the concepts and the algorithms associated with addition and subtraction of fractions and decimal numbers but has not yet learned more advanced computation of rational numbers, negative numbers, or basic algebra. His progress in math will be increasingly impeded by lack of automatic access to the facts, most immediately in working with rational numbers and algebra.

Diagnostic Impressions

The results of this evaluation indicate that Miguel has a specific reading disability that has impeded his development of basic reading and writing skills. Additionally, the cognitive weaknesses contributing to his reading and writing disabilities have also affected his ability to retain and quickly retrieve math facts. Miguel has never received long-term, systematic instruction to address any of these cognitive or academic weaknesses. If proper instruction, including sufficient intensity and frequency, is provided before Miguel decides to give up, he is likely to make steady progress in all of these areas.

EDUCATIONAL RECOMMENDATIONS

Speech Discrimination

1. Miguel's difficulty in discriminating speech sounds in competing noise may have been an anomaly caused by factors other than hearing or auditory processing, such as attention. Nevertheless, his hearing should be tested again by an educational audiologist. Request that the evaluation include speech sound discrimination in both quiet and noise. If Miguel has significant difficulty on these tests, the audiologist may make a recommendation for further testing, therapy, accommodations, and/or amplification.

2. Until the audiological evaluation is completed, it would be prudent to provide accommodations for Miguel similar to those used for a student with a mild hearing loss. Explain to Miguel that although he is not aware of it, he may be missing information that other people hear. To help minimize that possibility, the following accommodations should be provided until the hearing evaluation is completed.

   a. In the classroom, seat Miguel away from ambient noise such as the air conditioner, the window, or the door to the hallway. Additionally, seat him close to where the teacher will be giving directions or lecturing.

   b. When giving directions to the class, stand relatively close to Miguel and make sure he is looking at your face.

Reading and Spelling

1. Due to the combination of Miguel's cognitive weaknesses and the severity of his reading and spelling problems, he requires a highly structured and systematic approach to reading and spelling instruction. As he has received no intervention to this point, and has only a few more years to learn what others have had 10 years to learn, he should receive intensive, daily instruction in sound-symbol association, syllable division, morphology, vocabulary, and comprehension strategies. The principles that have been shown to be effective in instruction for students with specific reading disabilities are as follows:

   a. Use multisensory instruction, incorporating multiple activities that will allow Miguel to use hearing, vision, and manipulation of objects such as letter tiles, syllable cards, and tokens.

   b. Use a systematic and cumulative program in which skills are presented in graduated steps, from simple to complex, with Miguel achieving mastery before the next skill is introduced. Practice assignments on the current skill incorporate previously learned skills, providing sufficient practice for Miguel to develop automaticity.

c. Provide direct instruction: Explicitly teach Miguel the skills and concepts you expect him to learn. Make no assumptions about what he knows or has learned.

d. Use a program that teaches reading and spelling simultaneously so that for every skill or rule that Miguel learns for reading, he learns the associated spelling rule. For example, when he learns to read *ck*, he learns that *ck* is used in spelling one-syllable words when /k/ follows a short vowel sound and ends the word.

e. Use diagnostic teaching: While teaching, continuously assess Miguel's comprehension, retention, and application of previously learned skills and concepts. Reteach and incorporate reinforcement in future lessons for any that he misunderstands or has forgotten.

f. Teach both synthetic and analytic methods of working with oral and written language. For example, blending individual sounds or syllables into a word (synthesis) is necessary for reading; analyzing a word into its component sounds or syllables is necessary for spelling.

The Wilson Reading System is one evidenced-based program that incorporates these principles and was specifically designed for older students and adults with dyslexia (http://www.WilsonLanguage.com). For a review of other evidence-based methods of reading/spelling instruction, see the web site of the Florida Center for Reading Research (www.fcrr.edu).

2. At first, devote most of Miguel's reading instructional time to focusing on reading decoding skills, spelling skills, and vocabulary development. Reading comprehension strategies can be taught as oral comprehension strategies. As his reading level increases, guide him to apply the comprehension skills he has learned to reading.

3. Teach sight words from one of the lists of the words most frequently used in reading materials, such as *1,000 Instant Words* (Fry, 1994). Available from Teacher Created Materials, 6421 Industry Way, Westminister, CA, 92683, (800) 662-4321. [See Appendix for the first 300: Instant Words.]

4. To support Miguel's ability to retain sight words, use the modified Fernald method. Important elements of these methods are repeatedly tracing the word while saying it, writing it from memory, and frequent reinforcement. [See Appendix: Fernald Method for Reading and Spelling: Modified.]

5. Use reading speed drills as needed to help Miguel develop instant recognition of letter patterns such as common letter combinations (e.g., *sh, ing, tion*), syllable patterns, and sight words. The same 6 items are printed in random order over 10 rows. The goal is for Miguel to read 60 items within 60 seconds.

Oral/Reading Vocabulary

To effectively handle the tasks of school and adult life, Miguel must greatly increase both the breadth of his vocabulary and the depth in terms of related meanings (e.g., antonyms, synonyms, multiple meanings). Teach new words and their meanings explicitly and in context. Use a variety of activities that involve active learning. Avoid passive activities, such as asking him to look words up in the dictionary. He is unlikely to retain words learned out of context.

Written Expression

Miguel will not be able to write any assignment until his spelling is closer to phonetically correct. Any spell-checker needs a phonetic approximation of the intended word to provide possible correct spellings. For now, Miguel should be provided with and trained to use voice recognition software so that he can see on the computer screen the words he is saying. Alternatively, he should be able to tape-record his answers to assignments or be provided with a scribe to write down his answers.

Math

In discussion with Miguel, make a decision as to whether or not he will learn the math facts he does not yet know or use a calculator for all computation. Make sure that Miguel understands the advantages and disadvantages inherent in either decision. If he decides to try to learn the math facts, the following instructional recommendations are offered. Whether or not he chooses to learn the math facts, he should learn to do the algorithms without the calculator.

1. Mental organization of math facts reduces memory demands and facilitates retrieval. Teach math facts in a sequence and using an instructional approach in which each new set of facts is related to facts or processes Miguel already knows. Suggestions for instructional sequences are attached to this report.

2. To develop retention and efficient retrieval of math facts, Miguel will require frequent drill and practice. Reinforcement can be provided through commercial programs such as Great Leaps Math (Mercer, Mercer, & Campbell, 2002) (www.greatleaps.com) and online games that provide immediate feedback. A variety of interactive games to reinforce multiplication facts may be found on www.multiplication.com. Timez Attack is an especially appealing video game (www.bigbrainz.com).

3. Because Miguel has not developed automatic recall of math facts and algorithms, provide him with a calculator to use in all activities focused on mathematical reasoning. This will allow him to concentrate on the reasoning process without diverting attention to the more mechanical aspects of the task.

ACCOMMODATIONS AND MODIFICATIONS

Testing

1. Administer all tests, other than reading tests, orally. Miguel's reading and writing skills are such that he cannot independently understand what a test is asking or demonstrate his knowledge if he has to do it in writing. This includes word problems on math tests. So as not to embarrass Miguel, provide a private area for testing.

2. Do not have Miguel do timed tests, written or oral. Provide him as much time as he needs to complete a test. If extra time cannot be made available, reduce the number of problems he is expected to do.

Homework and In-Class Assignments

Due to his severe reading and writing disabilities, Miguel must spend considerably more time than his peers in completing his assignments, and the level of effort is exhausting. Reduce the amount of work in each area assigned for homework so that he can complete his assignment in approximately the same amount of time other students are expected to spend. Examples of modified assignments are: solving the odd-numbered math problems instead of all the items, studying 10 spelling words instead of 20, and writing a half-page report instead of a whole page.

Technology

Miguel would be able to keep up with classroom reading assignments and would be more successful in writing assignments if he had access to and training in using technology. The following technological accommodations are recommended:

1. Provide Miguel training in keyboarding skills and use of a word processing program so that he can access the other technological accommodations that are only available on a computer.

2. The most effective and comprehensive accommodation for reading, writing, study skills, and test-taking would be use of Kurzweil 3000. Kurzweil 3000 (www.kurzweiledu.com) is a highly flexible software program that allows a student access to the same content as his peers. It reads aloud, at a speed set by the user, any print that can be put into electronic form. To facilitate the user following along, the sentence being read is highlighted in one color and the word being read is highlighted in another. Within the content, the user may highlight important text, look up definitions and synonyms, and take teacher-made tests. For writing, the software includes graphic organizers, writing templates, and word prediction and spell-check programs. The user may have his writing read to him as he types and/or when he has completed any segment of the work, allowing him to monitor for errors and make revisions.

3. Alternatively, provide Miguel access to and training in using a screen-reading program with a voice synthesizer that simulates the prosody of normal speech so that Miguel can have the computer read to him any text that he can get online. Additionally, provide Miguel with a good word prediction program, such as Co-Writer, to alleviate the severe spelling problems that impede his writing.

4. Provide Miguel with taped versions of his classroom textbooks. Because Miguel has been identified as having learning disabilities that interfere with reading, recorded books may be obtained from Recording for the Blind & Dyslexic (RFB&D). It is best to find out what books will be needed and order them as far ahead of time as possible. If RFB&D does not have them on CD/DVD already, they may choose to record them. Novels on CD are also available at public libraries.

5. For independent reading, to aid in spelling, and to support new vocabulary that he finds in his reading, provide Miguel with an electronic speaking dictionary and spell-checker such as those developed by Franklin Learning Resources. As Miguel improves in phonetic spelling of words, the spell-checker will become more useful to him in giving him choices of the correct spelling. Available from: Franklin Learning Resources, 122

Burrs Road, Mt. Holly, NJ 08060, phone: (800) 525-9673, web site: http://www.franklin.com.

6. Audiotape classes that depend mainly on lecture so that Miguel can review the material at home. He will not be able to read notes provided by the teacher or taken by another student.

REFERENCES

Kirk, S. A., Kirk, W. D., Minskoff, E., Mather, N., & Roberts, R. (2007). *Phonic reading lessons: Skills.* Novato, CA: Academic Therapy.

Roberts, R., & Mather, N. (2007). *Phonic reading lessons: Practice.* Novato, CA: Academic Therapy.

Table of Scores

Woodcock-Johnson III Normative Update Tests of Cognitive Abilities (including Diagnostic Supplement) and Tests of Achievement (Form A)

WJ III NU Compuscore and Profiles Program, Version 3.0

Norms based on age 15-4

Bolded cluster names indicate that the confidence bands of the tests that comprise the cluster overlap, thus allowing interpretation of the broad cluster.

CLUSTER/Test	Raw	W	AE	Proficiency	RPI	SS (68% Band)	GE
GIA (Ext)	–	511	13–0	average	82/90	91 (89–93)	7.7
FLUID REASONING (Gf)	–	**531**	**>19**	**advanced**	**98/90**	**117 (111–124)**	**>17.8**
Concept Formation	39–E	541	>18–8	advanced	99/90	123 (114–131)	>17.8
Analysis-Synthesis	28–E	521	>20	average	95/90	107 (100–114)	13.4
VERBAL ABILITY (Ext)	–	**513**	**12–4**	**lmtd to avg**	**70/90**	**88 (85–92)**	**6.9**
COMP-KNOWLEDGE (Gc)	–	**513**	**12–4**	**lmtd to avg**	**70/90**	**88 (85–92)**	**6.9**
Verbal Comprehension	–	514	13–0	lmtd to avg	76/90	92 (88–96)	7.6
General Information	–	512	11–10	limited	62/90	86 (81–91)	6.4
VIS-SPATIAL THINK (Gv)	–	**512**	**>24**	**average**	**93/90**	**106 (102–111)**	**15.6**
Spatial Relations	74–D	514	>25	average	94/90	107 (102–112)	16.7
Picture Recognition	52–D	510	18–7	average	92/90	103 (98–109)	13.0
PROCESS SPEED (Gs)	–	**512**	**13–4**	**average**	**83/90**	**90 (85–95)**	**7.9**
Visual Matching	45–2	512	12–5	lmtd to avg	77/90	87 (81–93)	7.0
Decision Speed	35	512	14–4	average	87/90	96 (90–102)	8.9
PERCEPTUAL SPEED	–	**511**	**12–5**	**lmtd to avg**	**76/90**	**85 (79–91)**	**7.0**
Visual Matching	45–2	512	12–5	lmtd to avg	77/90	87 (81–93)	7.0
Cross Out	23	510	12–5	lmtd to avg	74/90	87 (79–95)	7.0
AUDITORY PROCESS (Ga)	–	**506**	**12–4**	**average**	**84/90**	**92 (87–98)**	**6.9**
Sound Blending	23	515	15–8	average	91/90	100 (96–105)	10.2
Auditory Attention	34	496	7–10	lmtd to avg	75/90	77 (68–86)	2.5
AUDITORY MEM SPAN	–	**486**	**7–3**	**limited**	**25/90**	**73 (68–78)**	**1.9**
Memory for Words	15	487	7–7	limited	26/90	80 (73–86)	2.3
Memory for Sentences	38	484	6–10	limited	24/90	69 (64–75)	1.5
SHORT-TERM MEM (Gsm)	–	**492**	**8–5**	**limited**	**30/90**	**78 (74–83)**	**3.1**
Memory for Words	15	487	7–7	limited	26/90	80 (73–86)	2.3
Numbers Reversed	11	496	9–3	limited	34/90	81 (75–87)	3.9

CLUSTER/Test	Raw	W	AE	Proficiency	RPI	SS (68% Band)	GE
WORKING MEMORY	–	504	10–7	limited	56/90	83 (79–88)	5.2
Numbers Reversed	11	496	9–3	limited	34/90	81 (75–87)	3.9
Auditory Working Memory	22	512	12–6	lmtd to avg	76/90	91 (87–95)	7.1
ASSOCIATIVE MEMORY	**–**	**500**	**10–6**	**average**	**86/90**	**92 (88–97)**	**5.1**
Visual-Auditory Learning	11–E	502	10–11	average	84/90	90 (83–97)	5.5
Memory for Names	54–C	499	9–11	average	88/90	96 (91–101)	4.6
L-T RETRIEVAL (Glr)	–	496	8–0	lmtd to avg	76/90	71 (65–77)	2.7
Visual-Auditory Learning	11–E	502	10–11	average	84/90	90 (83–97)	5.5
Retrieval Fluency	26	491	5–4	limited	65/90	40 (32–49)	K.1
COG EFFICIENCY (Ext)	–	502	10–3	limited	59/90	78 (74–82)	4.9
Visual Matching	45–2	512	12–5	lmtd to avg	77/90	87 (81–93)	7.0
Decision Speed	35	512	14–4	average	87/90	96 (90–102)	8.9
Memory for Words	15	487	7–7	limited	26/90	80 (73–86)	2.3
Numbers Reversed	11	496	9–3	limited	34/90	81 (75–87)	3.9
COGNITIVE FLUENCY	–	494	8–8	limited	57/90	66 (62–69)	3.3
Decision Speed	35	512	14–4	average	87/90	96 (90–102)	8.9
Retrieval Fluency	26	491	5–4	limited	65/90	40 (32–49)	K.1
Rapid Picture Naming	75	480	6–5	v limited	15/90	63 (61–65)	1.1
ORAL LANGUAGE (Ext)	–	520	22	average	94/90	109 (105–113)	13.0
Understanding Directions	–	523	>21	avg to adv	97/90	117 (108–126)	>18.0
Oral Comprehension	28	530	>30	avg to adv	97/90	111 (106–116)	14.6
Story Recall	–	511	>20	avg to adv	95/90	118 (110–125)	>13.3
Picture Vocabulary	29	517	13–5	lmtd to avg	75/90	93 (88–97)	8.0
LISTENING COMP	**–**	**526**	**>30**	**avg to adv**	**97/90**	**115 (110–120)**	**>18.0**
Understanding Directions	–	523	>21	avg to adv	97/90	117 (108–126)	>18.0
Oral Comprehension	28	530	>30	avg to adv	97/90	111 (106–116)	14.6
ORAL EXPRESSION	–	514	14–9	average	89/90	98 (94–102)	9.3
Story Recall	–	511	>20	avg to adv	95/90	118 (110–125)	>13.3
Picture Vocabulary	29	517	13–5	lmtd to avg	75/90	93 (88–97)	8.0
BROAD READING	–	449	6–11	negligible	0/90	27 (24–30)	1.6
Reading Fluency	16	479	7–5	v limited	10/90	60 (56–64)	2.2
Passage Comprehension	19	469	7–2	negligible	3/90	48 (43–53)	1.9
Letter-Word Identification	22	400	6–6	negligible	0/90	14 (11–18)	1.2
BRIEF READING	–	434	6–10	negligible	0/90	20 (17–23)	1.5
Passage Comprehension	19	469	7–2	negligible	3/90	48 (43–53)	1.9
Letter-Word Identification	22	400	6–6	negligible	0/90	14 (11–18)	1.2
BASIC READING SKILLS	–	434	6–10	negligible	0/90	33 (30–36)	1.5
Word Attack	8	468	7–4	negligible	3/90	67 (63–70)	2.0
Letter-Word Identification	22	400	6–6	negligible	0/90	14 (11–18)	1.2
PHON/GRAPH KNOW	**–**	**478**	**7–4**	**v limited**	**11/90**	**57 (53–61)**	**2.0**
Spelling of Sounds	19	488	7–5	limited	37/90	67 (61–72)	2.1
Word Attack	8	468	7–4	negligible	3/90	67 (63–70)	2.0

(*continued*)

CLUSTER/Test	Raw	W	AE	Proficiency	RPI	SS (68% Band)	GE
BROAD WRITTEN LANG	–	475	7–6	v limited	5/90	44 (40–48)	2.2
Writing Samples	13–C	495	9–3	limited	54/90	78 (72–83)	3.9
Writing Fluency	12	489	8–7	v limited	18/90	66 (60–72)	3.3
Spelling	17	442	6–7	negligible	0/90	31 (25–36)	1.3
BRIEF WRITING	–	468	7–3	negligible	3/90	39 (34–43)	1.9
Writing Samples	13–C	495	9–3	limited	54/90	78 (72–83)	3.9
Spelling	17	442	6–7	negligible	0/90	31 (25–36)	1.3
WRITTEN EXPRESSION	–	492	8–11	limited	34/90	67 (62–72)	3.6
Writing Samples	13–C	495	9–3	limited	54/90	78 (72–83)	3.9
Writing Fluency	12	489	8–7	v limited	18/90	66 (60–72)	3.3
BROAD MATH	–	523	14–6	average	88/90	97 (94–100)	9.1
Applied Problems	48	539	18–1	avg to adv	96/90	105 (102–107)	12.5
Calculation	26	530	14–10	average	89/90	99 (94–104)	9.4
Math Fluency	66	500	10–6	limited	67/90	77 (74–79)	5.1
BRIEF MATH	**–**	**535**	**16–8**	**average**	**93/90**	**103 (100–105)**	**11.3**
Calculation	26	530	14–10	average	89/90	99 (94–104)	9.4
Applied Problems	48	539	18–1	avg to adv	96/90	105 (102–107)	12.5
MATH CALC SKILLS	–	515	12–9	lmtd to avg	80/90	90 (86–94)	7.3
Calculation	26	530	14–10	average	89/90	99 (94–104)	9.4
Math Fluency	66	500	10–6	limited	67/90	77 (74–79)	5.1
ACADEMIC SKILLS	–	458	7–5	negligible	0/90	29 (26–32)	2.0
Calculation	26	530	14–10	average	89/90	99 (94–104)	9.4
Letter-Word Identification	22	400	6–6	negligible	0/90	14 (11–18)	1.2
Spelling	17	442	6–7	negligible	0/90	31 (25–36)	1.3
ACADEMIC FLUENCY	–	489	8–6	limited	27/90	58 (55–61)	3.2
Math Fluency	66	500	10–6	limited	67/90	77 (74–79)	5.1
Writing Fluency	12	489	8–7	v limited	18/90	66 (60–72)	3.3
Reading Fluency	16	479	7–5	v limited	10/90	60 (56–64)	2.2
ACADEMIC APPS	–	501	9–11	limited	49/90	75 (71–78)	4.6
Applied Problems	48	539	18–1	avg to adv	96/90	105 (102–107)	12.5
Writing Samples	13–C	495	9–3	limited	54/90	78 (72–83)	3.9
Passage Comprehension	19	469	7–2	negligible	3/90	48 (43–53)	1.9
BRIEF ACHIEVEMENT	–	460	7–7	negligible	0/90	40 (37–42)	2.2
Applied Problems	48	539	18–1	avg to adv	96/90	105 (102–107)	12.5
Spelling	17	442	6–7	negligible	0/90	31 (25–36)	1.3
Letter-Word Identification	22	400	6–6	negligible	0/90	14 (11–18)	1.2
Verbal Comprehension	–	514	13–0	lmtd to avg	76/90	92 (88–96)	7.6
Visual-Auditory Learning	11–E	502	10–11	average	84/90	90 (83–97)	5.5
Spatial Relations	74–D	514	>25	average	94/90	107 (102–112)	16.7
Sound Blending	23	515	15–8	average	91/90	100 (96–105)	10.2
Concept Formation	39–E	541	>18–8	advanced	99/90	123 (114–131)	>17.8
Visual Matching	45–2	512	12–5	lmtd to avg	77/90	87 (81–93)	7.0

CLUSTER/Test	Raw	W	AE	Proficiency	RPI	SS (68% Band)	GE
Numbers Reversed	11	496	9–3	limited	34/90	81 (75–87)	3.9
Auditory Working Memory	22	512	12–6	lmtd to avg	76/90	91 (87–95)	7.1
General Information	–	512	11–10	limited	62/90	86 (81–91)	6.4
Retrieval Fluency	26	491	5–4	limited	65/90	40 (32–49)	K.1
Picture Recognition	52–D	510	18–7	average	92/90	103 (98–109)	13.0
Auditory Attention	34	496	7–10	lmtd to avg	75/90	77 (68–86)	2.5
Analysis-Synthesis	28–E	521	>20	average	95/90	107 (100–114)	13.4
Decision Speed	35	512	14–4	average	87/90	96 (90–102)	8.9
Memory for Words	15	487	7–7	limited	26/90	80 (73–86)	2.3
Rapid Picture Naming	75	480	6–5	v limited	15/90	63 (61–65)	1.1
Memory for Names	54–C	499	9–11	average	88/90	96 (91–101)	4.6
Cross Out	23	510	12–5	lmtd to avg	74/90	87 (79–95)	7.0
Memory for Sentences	38	484	6–10	limited	24/90	69 (64–75)	1.5
Letter-Word Identification	22	400	6–6	negligible	0/90	14 (11–18)	1.2
Reading Fluency	16	479	7–5	v limited	10/90	60 (56–64)	2.2
Story Recall	–	511	>20	avg to adv	95/90	118 (110–125)	>13.3
Understanding Directions	–	523	>21	avg to adv	97/90	117 (108–126)	>18.0
Calculation	26	530	14–10	average	89/90	99 (94–104)	9.4
Math Fluency	66	500	10–6	limited	67/90	77 (74–79)	5.1
Spelling	17	442	6–7	negligible	0/90	31 (25–36)	1.3
Writing Fluency	12	489	8–7	v limited	18/90	66 (60–72)	3.3
Passage Comprehension	19	469	7–2	negligible	3/90	48 (43–53)	1.9
Applied Problems	48	539	18–1	avg to adv	96/90	105 (102–107)	12.5
Writing Samples	13–C	495	9–3	limited	54/90	78 (72–83)	3.9
Word Attack	8	468	7–4	negligible	3/90	67 (63–70)	2.0
Picture Vocabulary	29	517	13–5	lmtd to avg	75/90	93 (88–97)	8.0
Oral Comprehension	28	530	>30	avg to adv	97/90	111 (106–116)	14.6
Spelling of Sounds	19	488	7–5	limited	37/90	67 (61–72)	2.1
Sound Awareness	40	508	14–3	average	87/90	96 (89–103)	8.8

VARIATIONS	STANDARD SCORES			VARIATION		Significant at + or − 1.50 SD (SEE)
	Actual	Predicted	Difference	PR	SD	
Intra-Cognitive (Ext)						
COMP-KNOWLEDGE (Gc)	88	93	−5	33	−0.43	No
L-T RETRIEVAL (Glr)	71	96	−25	1	−2.27	Yes
VIS-SPATIAL THINK (Gv)	106	93	13	86	+1.06	No
AUDITORY PROCESS (Ga)	92	94	−2	45	−0.13	No
FLUID REASONING (Gf)	117	88	29	99.7	+2.72	Yes
PROCESS SPEED (Gs)	90	95	−5	36	−0.35	No
SHORT-TERM MEM (Gsm)	78	95	−17	7	−1.47	No
WORKING MEMORY	83	95	−12	17	−0.97	No
PERCEPTUAL SPEED	85	94	−9	24	−0.71	No
AUDITORY MEM SPAN	73	95	−22	4	−1.77	Yes
ASSOCIATIVE MEMORY	92	96	−4	39	−0.29	No

VARIATIONS	STANDARD SCORES			VARIATION		Significant at + or − 1.50 SD (SEE)
	Actual	Predicted	Difference	PR	SD	
Intra-Achievement (Std)						
BROAD READING	27	89	−62	<0.1	−7.01	Yes
BROAD MATH	97	71	26	99	+2.43	Yes
BROAD WRITTEN LANG	44	84	−40	<0.1	−4.21	Yes
ORAL LANGUAGE (Std)	121	67	54	>99.9	+4.61	Yes

DISCREPANCIES	STANDARD SCORES			DISCREPANCY		Significant at − 1.50 SD (SEE)
	Actual	Predicted	Difference	PR	SD	
Intellectual Ability/Achievement Discrepancies*						
BROAD READING	27	93	−66	<0.1	−6.93	Yes
BASIC READING SKILLS	33	94	−61	<0.1	−5.66	Yes
BROAD MATH	97	94	3	63	+0.34	No
MATH CALC SKILLS	90	95	−5	34	−0.41	No
BROAD WRITTEN LANG	44	94	−50	<0.1	−5.02	Yes
WRITTEN EXPRESSION	67	94	−27	0.4	−2.68	Yes
ORAL LANGUAGE (Ext)	109	93	16	97	+1.81	No
ORAL EXPRESSION	98	94	4	66	+0.42	No
LISTENING COMP	115	93	22	99	+2.18	No
BRIEF READING	20	94	−74	<0.1	−7.15	Yes
BRIEF MATH	103	94	9	79	+0.81	No
BRIEF WRITING	39	94	−55	<0.1	−5.07	Yes

*These discrepancies compare WJ III GIA (Ext) with Broad, Basic, Brief, and Applied ACH clusters.

DISCREPANCIES	STANDARD SCORES			DISCREPANCY		Significant at − 1.50 SD (SEE)
	Actual	Predicted	Difference	PR	SD	
Oral Language/Achievement Discrepancies*						
BROAD READING	27	106	−79	<0.1	−7.56	Yes
BASIC READING SKILLS	33	105	−72	<0.1	−5.95	Yes
BROAD MATH	97	105	−8	27	−0.62	No
MATH CALC SKILLS	90	104	−14	15	−1.02	No
BROAD WRITTEN LANG	44	105	−61	<0.1	−5.07	Yes
WRITTEN EXPRESSION	67	105	−38	<0.1	−3.24	Yes
BRIEF READING	20	106	−86	<0.1	−7.80	Yes
BRIEF MATH	103	105	−2	42	−0.21	No
BRIEF WRITING	39	105	−66	<0.1	−5.39	Yes

*These discrepancies compare Oral Language (Ext) with Broad, Basic, Brief, and Applied ACH clusters.

DISCREPANCIES	STANDARD SCORES			DISCREPANCY		Significant at + or − 1.50 SD (SEE)
	Actual	Predicted	Difference	PR	SD	
Predicted Achievement/Achievement Discrepancies*						
BROAD READING	27	91	−64	<0.1	−6.93	Yes
BASIC READING SKILLS	33	92	−59	<0.1	−5.54	Yes
BROAD MATH	97	94	3	64	+0.35	No
MATH CALC SKILLS	90	93	−3	41	−0.23	No
BROAD WRITTEN LANG	44	92	−48	<0.1	−4.90	Yes
WRITTEN EXPRESSION	67	94	−27	0.4	−2.69	Yes
ORAL LANGUAGE (Ext)	109	103	6	71	+0.56	No
ORAL EXPRESSION	98	103	−5	36	−0.37	No
LISTENING COMP	115	102	13	88	+1.15	No
BRIEF READING	20	92	−72	<0.1	−7.27	Yes
BRIEF MATH	103	95	8	76	+0.70	No
BRIEF WRITING	39	92	−53	<0.1	−4.97	Yes
*These discrepancies compare predicted achievement scores with Broad, Basic, Brief, and Applied ACH clusters.						

Developmental Zone Worksheet
WJ III Tests of Cognitive Abilities and Diagnostic Supplement

Based on Relative Proficiency Indexes

Cognitive Factor/Clusters Cognitive Tests	Extremely Difficult 3/90 to 24/90	Very Difficult 24/90 to 67/90	Difficult 67/90 to 82/90	Appropriate 82/90 to 89/90	Appropriate 90/90 to 95/90	Easy 95/90 to 98/90	Very Easy 98/90 & above
Comprehension-Knowledge (Gc)							
Verbal Comprehension			O				
General Information		O					
Long-Term Retrieval (Glr)							
Visual-Auditory Learning				O			
Retrieval Fluency		O					
Visual-Spatial Thinking (Gv)					●		
Spatial Relations							
Picture Recognition							
Auditory Processing (Ga)							
Sound Blending					O		
Auditory Attention			O				
Fluid Reasoning (Gf)							
Concept Formation							O
Analysis-Synthesis						O	
Processing Speed (Gs)							
Visual Matching (2)			O				
Decision Speed				O			
Perceptual Speed (Gs)			●				
Visual Matching (2)							
Cross Out							

(continued)

Cognitive Factor/Clusters Cognitive Tests	Extremely Difficult 3/90 to 24/90	Very Difficult 24/90 to 67/90	Difficult 67/90 to 82/90	Appropriate 82/90 to 89/90	90/90 to 95/90	Easy 95/90 to 98/90	Very Easy 98/90 & above
Short-Term Memory (*Gsm*)		●					
Numbers Reversed							
Memory for Words							
Auditory Memory Span (*Gsm*)		●					
Memory for Words							
Memory for Sentences							
Phonemic Awareness (*Ga*)							
Sound Blending					○		
Incomplete Words							
(Sound Awareness – ACH)				○			

Note: Solid circles on the zone worksheets indicate that the component tests were in the same RPI range so that only the broader category is marked. Open circles indicate that the component tests were not the same so that the range is marked for each one.

Instructional Zone Worksheet
WJ III Tests of Achievement

Based on Relative Proficiency Indexes

Achievement Clusters Achievement Tests	Impossible 0/90 to 3/90	Extremely Difficult 3/90 to 24/90	Very Difficult 24/90 to 67/90	Difficult 67/90 to 82/90	Appropriate 82/90 to 89/90	90/90 to 95/90	Easy 95/90 to 98/90	Very Easy 98/90 & above
Oral Expression								
Story Recall					○			
Picture Vocabulary				○				
Listening Comprehension							●	
Broad Reading								
Letter-Word Identification	○							
Reading Fluency			○					
Passage Comprehension	○							
Basic Reading	●							
Broad Written Language								
Spelling	○							
Writing Fluency			○					
Writing Samples				○				
Phoneme/Grapheme								
Word Attack	○							
Spelling of Sounds				○				
(Sound Awareness)					○			
Broad Math								
Math Calculation					○			
Math Fluency				○				
Applied Problems							○	

Note: Solid circles on the zone worksheets indicate that the component tests were in the same RPI range so that only the broader category is marked. Open circles indicate that the component tests were not the same so that the range is marked for each one.

CASE 47

A Multiple Measures Approach to Assessing
a Student Who Is Deaf

Lisa Coyner

This case may be interesting to evaluators who have had limited opportunities to assess students who are deaf or hard of hearing, because Samantha's profile is not atypical or uncommon for a student with an educationally significant hearing loss. Samantha is profoundly deaf and communicates primarily through American Sign Language (ASL). She has had itinerant and resource support, as well as a full-time interpreter in her core subjects. Although she has a fluent language base (i.e., ASL) and has limited ability to hear with which she developed some phonemic awareness skills, she has not developed the English language skills needed to successfully participate in the general education curriculum. She still requires significant support and explicit teaching from a teacher trained to work with students who are deaf or hard of hearing. In addition to this support, she also needed, but did not receive, ongoing explicit instruction in reading and study skills specifically focused on the needs of a student who is deaf.

PSYCHOEDUCATIONAL EVALUATION

Name:	Samantha Sechrist
Date of Birth:	6/30/1994
Age:	15-6
Ethnicity:	Caucasian
Primary Language:	American Sign Language (ASL)
School:	Westview High School
Grade:	9
Report Date:	12/15/2009
Evaluator:	Lisa S. Coyner, Ph.D.

REASON FOR REFERRAL

Samantha was referred by her educational team to obtain current information pertaining to her nonverbal reasoning abilities and academic skills. In a child study meeting, several of her teachers wondered if Samantha may have a learning disability. They raised concerns regarding her ability to retain and retrieve information that she has learned; therefore, her short-term visual memory skills will also be assessed as part of this evaluation. Her team has also requested any strategies or recommendations that may help Samantha improve her academic performance.

BACKGROUND INFORMATION

Family

Samantha lives at home with her mother, Mary Sechrist, her older sister, and two younger siblings. Mr. Sechrist passed away 3 years ago after suffering a heart attack in 2006. Ms. Sechrist indicated that his illness and subsequent death were very difficult for the entire family. Two of Samantha's siblings have also had individual education plans to address reading concerns. Ms. Sechrist is a billing coordinator, and the primary language in their home is English, although some sign language is also used.

Development and Health

Ms. Sechrist reported that she contracted an infection at 23 weeks' gestation with Samantha and was hospitalized for approximately a week. At 24 weeks, Samantha was born weighing 1 lb., 11½ oz. Samantha was in the hospital for 4 months. According to Ms. Sechrist, she was on a ventilator for 2 months and given high doses of gentamya-cin. Samantha also had eye surgery to correct retinopathy of prematurity. She was brought home on oxygen and re-mained on it for several months.

Samantha's developmental milestones were generally delayed. She didn't crawl until she was almost a year old and started walking very shortly after. Ms. Sechrist re-ported that Samantha has been very healthy, and, other than seasonal allergies, she has had no other chronic health concerns.

When Samantha was in third grade, she received a cochlear implant (CI). Ms. Sechrist stated that Saman-tha stopped using her CI when she was in eighth grade. Samantha stated that she did not like wearing it, that she couldn't understand spoken language anyway, and that she was deaf.

Samantha gets along well with her siblings and her mother. Ms. Sechrist noted that Samantha's social interac-tions with peers and other adults are similar to that of her age mates. She reported that Samantha's abilities to attend and communicate are similar to her age mates who are also deaf. Samantha is physically coordinated and active, able to manage her anger, and willingly accepts discipline. Her ability to work independently and her social maturity are below those of her age peers without a hearing impair-ment.

Samantha is independent in all activities of daily living. Ms. Sechrist noted that Samantha is able to tell time, count money, and make small purchases, and that she is very adept at texting and using the videophone and Skype to communicate with her signing friends. She stated that she had some concerns about how Samantha would cope with an emergency, as well as her ability to communicate with unfamiliar people in the community.

Samantha will complete household chores if she is asked and usually completes her homework. Samantha enjoys reading magazines. According to Ms. Sechrist, she is interested in health, fitness, the environment, makeup, clothes, boys, and texting. Ms. Sechrist also reported that Samantha is a kind, loving, strong, athletic, smart, and funny young woman who is good with kids and animals.

School

All of Samantha's education has been in Prescott, Arizona. She was initially enrolled in a preschool program at High-land Elementary School. Since then, she has always had an ASL interpreter with her in all of her classes. At her mother's request, Samantha repeated kindergarten. Her

first year of kindergarten was at Laura Kinsey Elementary School. For her second year she transferred to Townsend Elementary School, where she stayed until middle school. Samantha attended Tolleson Middle School for seventh and eighth grade where she was involved in a program that used advanced technology. She and her classmates had two teachers for their core subjects. This program allowed the teachers to integrate the curriculum, pro-vide project-based learning, and identify each student's strengths and needs. They noted that Samantha was a curi-ous student who wanted to learn about the world around her. She worked better in small groups and with one-to-one instructional support. They also reported that Samantha was always caring and kind to others. Academically, she faced significant challenges in their classes. Her academic struggles became more evident as the course content be-came increasingly difficult. During these times, Saman-tha's attention span seemed to become shorter and she was more easily distracted. Samantha seemed to struggle with remembering content from one day to the next, as well as applying what she learned in one class to another. For example, Samantha had difficulty creating a bar graph in her science class, although she had previously seemed to master this skill in her math class. They also noted that Samantha frequently had difficulty solving problems with multiple steps or following multistep directions, and that even following a sequence of no more than three things created confusion.

Samantha is currently a freshman at Westview High School. She attends four general education classes with support from interpreters and a teacher of the deaf, Betsy McMillan. Samantha works individually with Ms. Mc-Millan during fifth period. Ms. McMillan has also noted similar concerns with Samantha's learning (i.e., she strug-gles to remember information presented on several con-secutive days, as well as to recall information believed to be previously learned). Ms. McMillan noted that Samantha has not consistently maintained her planner and does not always inform her about extended projects.

PREVIOUS ASSESSMENTS

In December 2002, Dr. Linn Jenkins, learning disabili-ties specialist, conducted informal observations and diagnostic teaching with Samantha who, at that time, did not have a CI and, with her hearing aids, had some usable hearing and speech. Dr. Jenkins noted that Sa-mantha had developed some good skills in phonemic awareness and the use of phonics. She reported that Samantha did not fully understand how to use a phonetic system and, like most deaf students, relied heavily on trying to remember the (visual) letter patterns of printed words, albeit without a system for that either. Dr. Jenkins indicated that the apparent unevenness of Samantha's progress in reading and writing might suggest only that she required a more explicit and systematic instructional approach and not that she had a learning disability. She stated that at that point, Samantha's hearing impairment, limited phonics skills and orthographic awareness, and weak grasp of the reading-spelling principles and patterns were the more likely causes of her academic difficulties. Dr. Jenkins recommended specific teaching strategies to be used with Samantha and suggested that if she did not make good progress with a more systematic and focused approach, the question of a learning disability might be revisited.

TESTS ADMINISTERED

Wechsler Intelligence Scale for Children-Fourth Edition (WISC-IV)

Perceptual Reasoning Index

Processing Speed Index

Wechsler Scale of Nonverbal Ability (WNV)

Spatial Span Subtest

Picture Arrangement Subtest

Wide Range Assessment of Memory and Learning, Second Edition (WRAML-2)

Visual Memory

Visual Recognition

Kaufman Test of Educational Achievement, Second Edition (KTEA-II)

Reading Composite

Math Composite

Wechsler Individual Achievement Test-Third Edition (WIAT-III)

Math Fluency – Addition

Math Fluency – Subtraction

Math Fluency – Multiplication

These tests provide measures of Samantha's specific cognitive abilities with relative strengths and weaknesses described within this report as well as her academic skills in reading and mathematics. Her performance in each assessment task is compared to age peers using a standard score range. However, the age peers used for comparative purposes were individuals without a significant hearing loss; results, therefore, should be interpreted with caution.

Samantha's ethnic and racial background was considered prior to test selection and interpretation of test results; neither was found to be the primary factor in her need for special education. Samantha has received special education services as a student with a hearing impairment since she was in preschool. The evaluator is a fluent ASL signer whose primary role is the evaluation of students who are deaf or hard of hearing; thus, communication between Samantha and the evaluator was direct, without use of an interpreter. All assessments were conducted in her primary language, American Sign Language (ASL).

CLASSROOM OBSERVATIONS

Samantha was observed on October 9, 2009, during her pre-algebra class. Throughout the lesson, Samantha appeared attentive and engaged. Her teacher, Gina Maurone, had a summary of her lesson prepared for Samantha's interpreter. Samantha worked diligently on the worksheet; when Ms. Maurone went over the work with the entire class using an Elmo overhead projector, Samantha followed the discussion and indicated that she had gotten three of the four problems correct. Ms. Maurone gave Samantha a copy of all of the correct answers she had projected using the Elmo. Ms. Maurone then reviewed the homework from the previous day. Samantha had not been there, and when she asked what she was to do, Ms. Maurone walked over to her and identified each problem Samantha was to complete. Ms. Maurone then went over what the students needed to know for a test the following day. Samantha's full attention appeared to be on her interpreter, and after the review Ms. Maurone gave Samantha the notes she had projected on the Elmo. During instruction of new material, Samantha correctly answered a question posed to her by Ms. Maurone. When the class was given an independent assignment, Samantha got right to work. Ms. Maurone circulated around the class as they worked, and Samantha appeared to remain focused on her work. After the students had completed their independent work, Ms. Maurone reviewed the answers, and Samantha reported that she had derived the correct answer for three of the four problems.

TESTING OBSERVATIONS AND INTERVIEW WITH SAMANTHA

Samantha was a pleasant and cooperative test participant. She attempted all tasks presented to her and asked for clarification when needed. Samantha was careful to scan all of the materials before providing a response, and as tasks became more challenging she was persistent in her attempts to determine the correct answer. When asked what she liked to do for fun, she reported that she enjoyed hanging out with her family and friends, playing volleyball, and working out. She was unable to identify a career path or what she would like to do once she completed high school. Samantha is right-handed. She appeared competent in her ability to grasp concepts and express her ideas in ASL.

Samantha was asked about her apparent difficulty remembering procedures she had learned and not following through on directions. She stated that she thinks that she is just not very organized. With new information that the teacher is presenting, she said that it's hard to see what the teachers are writing or drawing on the board, or the graphic information (she signed "pictures" and "graphs") they are discussing and still get all of what the interpreter is signing. She feels that she often has to make a decision to watch one or the other so she "kind of gets it" and can do it right then because the teacher is there to help, but is somewhat hazy on it later. She stated that it's the same when they are working independently on worksheets in class. Although she may have understood the teacher's lecture, she doesn't always understand everything written on the worksheet. Responding to a series of questions about what specifically she did not understand, it seems that there are words that she does not recognize, and there are words that she thinks she knows but the meaning doesn't make sense in the context—"so maybe it's a different word. I don't know." Asked why she doesn't request help from the teacher, she said she'd be embarrassed.

COGNITIVE TESTING RESULTS AND DISCUSSION

Wechsler Intelligence Scale for Children–Fourth Edition

The Wechsler Intelligence Scale for Children-Fourth Edition (WISC-IV) is used to assess the general think-ing and reasoning skills of individuals from the ages of 6 to 16. Samantha was administered six subtests of the WISC-IV from which her composite scores were derived. She was administered only the subtests contained within the Perceptual Reasoning and Processing Speed scales due to her severe hearing impairment. Therefore, these results focus on Samantha's cognitive abilities in the narrow domains of perceptual reasoning and visual processing speed.

Samantha's nonverbal reasoning abilities as measured by the Perceptual Reasoning Index (PRI) were in the Average range and above those of approximately 25% of her age peers without a hearing impairment. The Perceptual Reasoning Index is designed to measure fluid reasoning in the perceptual domain with tasks that assess nonverbal concept formation, visual perception and organization, simultaneous processing, visual-motor coordination, learning, and the ability to separate figure and ground in visual stimuli. Samantha performed comparably on the perceptual reasoning subtests contributing to the PRI, suggesting that her visual-spatial reasoning and perceptual-organizational skills are similarly developed.

Samantha's ability in rapid processing of simple or routine visual material without making errors was also in the Average range when compared to her age mates without a hearing impairment. She performed better than approximately 42% of her peers on processing speed tasks.

Wechsler Scale of Nonverbal Ability

Samantha was also presented with two subtests from the Wechsler Scale of Nonverbal Ability (WNV). The WNV is an individually administered battery of tests designed to measure the general cognitive ability of examinees ages 4 through 21 years. This test was developed so that general ability could be measured using a multi-subtest, comprehensive format that eliminates or minimizes verbal content. Pictorial directions were developed to communicate the demands of the subtests with little or no verbal instructions.

Samantha's performance on the Spatial Span subtest was within the Average range when compared to her age peers without a hearing impairment. Samantha's performance on the Picture Arrangement subtest of the WNV was well below that of her age peers without a hearing impairment. On the Picture Arrangement subtest, Samantha was asked to arrange cards illustrating an event in an order that makes sense and tells a story. This subtest is primarily a nonverbal reasoning test that may be viewed as a measure of planning ability. Anticipation, visual organization, and temporal sequencing may also be assessed.

Wide Range Assessment of Memory and Learning, Second Edition

The Wide Range Assessment of Memory and Learning-2 (WRAML-2) is an individually administered test battery designed to assess memory ability. Samantha's performance on short-term visual memory tasks was commensurate with her age peers without a hearing impairment. Her performance on the Design Memory Recognition task was within the High Average range, whereas her performance on the Picture Memory Recognition task was within the Average range. On the Design Memory Recognition task, Samantha was provided with 46 geometric shapes or groupings of shapes, half of which were previously seen on the Design Memory subtest, and was asked to state whether or not she had seen the design before. Similarly, on the Picture Memory subtest, Samantha was asked to view 44 picture elements, and then mark either yes or no depending on whether she believed she had previously seen the picture element.

Academic Testing Results and Discussion

The Kaufman Test of Educational Achievement, Second Edition (KTEA-II), and one test from the Wechsler Individual Achievement Test-Third Edition (WIAT-III), were used to assess Samantha's academic skills in reading and mathematics. Samantha's basic reading skills when compared to her age peers without a hearing impairment were found to be within the Below Average range. Her reading comprehension and math reasoning skills were measured well below her age peers without a hearing impairment. However, Samantha's math computation skills were comparable to her age peers without a hearing impairment. Samantha stated, "I'm getting better in math." Her performance on the Math Fluency tests of the WIAT-III suggests that when compared to her grade peers, Samantha's rate of retrieval of math facts (addition, subtraction, and multiplication) is not sufficiently developed. Addition and subtraction were Below Average and multiplication was Well Below Average. It is important to note that although Samantha's performance on these tasks was slower than that of her age peers, she made only a few errors on multiplication and none at all on addition and subtraction.

SUMMARY

Samantha is a 15-year-old student who continues to demonstrate an educationally significant hearing impairment. She received a cochlear implant when she was in third grade and discontinued using it during the 2007–2008 school year, identifying herself as deaf (culturally as well as functionally). Samantha has received special education services as a student with a hearing impairment since she was a preschooler; she is currently a freshman at Westview High School. Samantha attends four general education classes with an ASL interpreter. She also receives individual instruction and support from Ms. McMillan, teacher of the deaf.

Current testing indicates that Samantha's overall nonverbal reasoning and visual processing skills are within the Average range when compared to her age peers without a hearing impairment. Her short-term visual memory skills are commensurate with those of her age peers. Samantha's performance on a visual recognition task of abstract designs was somewhat better than her recognition of previously presented pictures, but the difference was not significant. Samantha's performance on one nonverbal reasoning task was below that of her age peers. This subtest, Picture Arrangement, assesses planning ability, visual organization, and temporal sequencing.

Test results indicated that Samantha's overall reading abilities and math reasoning skills are well below those of her age peers. Her math calculation abilities were within the Average range and commensurate with those of her age peers. Although her math fluency skills were found to be below that of others her age, she made few errors, and only on multiplication, suggesting that she is accurate but slower than her age peers when solving simple computations.

With the exception of slow math fluency, all of Samantha's academic challenges appear to be in areas that are heavily English language loaded. It is the experience of this evaluator working with students who have educationally significant hearing impairments that Samantha's academic profile is similar to other students her age who are deaf and is not suggestive of a specific learning disability. However, Samantha does need direct instruction to improve her word identification skills, and to learn reading comprehension and organizational strategies.

APPROACHES TO MANAGEMENT

Accommodations

1. When the teacher intends to discuss/explain visual information (e.g., chart, graph, picture, written words), direct the students' attention to it and then count to 30 (less if the information is very simple, more if more complex) before you start to talk. This will give Samantha time to focus her attention on the visual information before she has to turn her gaze away from it to watch the interpreter. Alert the class that you will be doing this every time this situation arises. This is a difficult routine to establish, so you might enlist the students' help by establishing a signal that anyone can give you if you start to talk before giving sufficient "look time."

2. Each teacher should consider having a private meeting with Samantha and Ms. McMillan periodically to discuss ways to make it easier for her to access the information in class.

Organization

1. Teach Samantha how to effectively maintain and use her school planner. Initially, Samantha's planner should be checked each day by Ms. McMillan and her mother to ensure that her homework is being noted and completed.

2. Assist Samantha in breaking down large projects into manageable chunks. Help her identify reasonable time lines for completing each portion of a project and put these on the calendar section of her planner.

Reading

Samantha needs direct instruction to improve her word identification skills and her reading comprehension.

1. Guide Samantha to develop orthographic awareness by helping her recognize the letter patterns that are frequently seen in written English. The object is for Samantha to perceive common letter patterns as chunks, rather than as a string of individual letters. For example, once she automatically recognizes *pr*, *ea*, and *ch*, she is likely to perceive the word *preach* as having only three elements rather than six. As her inventory of chunks increases, she will perceive new words as having fewer, and more familiar, elements, facilitating both recognition and retrieval. Provide instruction and reinforcement of letter patterns until recognition and retrieval are automatic.

2. To further aid Samantha in developing orthographic awareness, teach her the difference between vowels and consonants, what syllables are, and that each syllable has at least one vowel. Generally, except for final, silent e, each vowel or vowel combination that is separated from another vowel/vowel combination by consonants represents a syllable. The ability to recognize the number of syllables in a word gives a clue to its length and facilitates chunking the words for easier recognition of word parts. Make sure that Samantha learns that there are no words without vowels in English and that all syllables have at least one vowel.

3. To learn new sight words and spelling words, teach Samantha to use LSFW (Look-Sign-Fingerspell-Write) or other study methods that depend on revisualization of the word without a model (no copying) after initial study. If Samantha has difficulty retaining the words, use one of the modifications, such as incorporating a tracing step. (See the Appendix for a more in-depth description of this procedure: Look-Sign-Fingerspell-Write.)

4. Create multiple opportunities for Samantha to encounter new words and previously learned words in a variety of reading materials and to write them many times within meaningful but structured writing assignments.

5. Use computer programs whenever possible for drill and practice to enhance Samantha's attention to the principle or skill being reinforced. Make sure, however, that the programs used directly address the skill she is learning and that the auditory components of the program are not necessary for her to benefit from its use.

6. When teaching any reading comprehension skill, teach the concept first in ASL, Samantha's primary communication mode. For example, when teaching identification of the main idea, present stories or expository information in sign, and conduct activities and discussion regarding the main idea in ASL. When Samantha can watch a signed presentation and paraphrase the main idea, provide reading passages at her independent reading level, and practice expressing the main idea.

7. Teach Samantha some simple comprehension strategies such as paraphrasing the main idea of a story or recognizing expository text structures. Use graphic organizers to illustrate the latter. Examples of expository structures include: sequence (main idea and details that must be given in a specific order), cause/effect (topic sentence and details telling why), and descriptive (topic sentence and description of attributes). As she learns

these strategies, the use of the computer program Inspiration might enhance her interest in working out the organizational structure of a reading passage or writing assignment (www.inspiration.com).

Content Areas

1. As Samantha depends on visual learning, to the extent possible, when planning lessons, think in terms of replacing sound with vision. Make every effort to provide visual representations of concepts and information that she needs to learn. This includes the use of videotapes and computer software. For example, computer software is available that provides explanations along with 3-dimensional views of geometry concepts, photosynthesis, and historical events. Make frequent use of graphic organizers, such as using a timeline to show events in temporal relationship or a two-column table to show comparison/contrast. These techniques will also enhance the interest value and learning of the other students.

2. Teach Samantha a study technique for learning and recalling conceptual information using index cards as study materials. On one side of the index card, print the word for the target concept. On the other side of the card, provide examples of the concept using pictures, pictures of the signs, or printed words. For example, if photosynthesis were printed on one side of the card, a diagram of the process could be drawn on the other; if attitude were written on one side, the other could have pictures or signs illustrating willing, cheerful, angry, and rude. Samantha can read the word on the card, try to explain the meaning to herself, and then check by turning the card over. Conversely, she can look at the picture/sign side of the card and sign or spell the word that names the concept.

Math

1. Samantha knows her math facts but needs to develop automaticity in recalling them while doing more complex computation. Provide drill and practice through computer software that can be programmed to specific facts. Provide regular timed fact drills and have her keep a chart of the number she completes and her accuracy so that she can see her improvement.

2. Request that Samantha's math teacher work with her individually for one or two sessions (with the interpreter) to investigate the reason(s) that she is having such difficulty understanding and solving math word problems. Various reasons could include difficulty reading/understanding the words, understanding the syntax of the sentences, figuring out what she is to do with the information, and translating the problem into computation.

SCORE ADDENDUM

WISC-IV Composite Score Summary

Composite	Composite Score*	Percentile Rank	95% Standard Score Confidence Interval*
Perceptual Reasoning Index	90	25	83–98
Processing Speed Index	97	42	88–106
*Standard Score Mean = 100; standard deviation = 15			

WISC-IV Subtest Score Summary

Subtest	Scaled Score**	Percentile Rank
Perceptual Reasoning		
Block Design	7	16
Picture Concepts	10	50
Matrix Reasoning	8	25
Processing Speed		
Coding	8	25
Symbol Search	11	63
**Scaled score mean = 10; standard deviation = 3		

WNV

Subtest	T Score*	Percentile Rank
Spatial Span	54	66
Picture Arrangement	30	2
*T score mean = 50; standard deviation = 10		

WRAML2

Summary Data	Composite Score*	Percentile Rank	68% Standard Score Confidence Interval*
Visual Memory Index	91	27	87–96
Visual Recognition Index	103	58	92–112
*Standard Score Mean = 100; standard deviation = 15			

WRAML-2 Subtest Score Summary

Subtest	Scaled Score*	Percentile Rank
Visual Memory		
Design Memory	8	25
Picture Memory	9	37
Attention and Concentration		
Finger Windows	8	25
Visual Recognition		
Design Recognition	14	98
Picture Memory Recognition	10	50
*Scaled score mean = 10; standard deviation = 3		

WIAT-III

Test	Standard Score*	Percentile Rank	90% Standard Score Confidence Interval*
Math Fluency – Addition	87	19	78–92
Math Fluency – Subtraction	83	13	77–87
Math Fluency – Multiplication	78	7	73–83
*Standard score mean = 100; standard deviation = 15			

KTEA-II

Summary Data	Composite Score*	Percentile Rank	90% Standard Score Confidence Interval*
Reading Composite	72	3	67–77
Letter & Word Recognition	77	6	73–81
Reading Comprehension	69	2	62–76
Math Concepts & Applications	67	1	61–73
Math Computation	92	30	87–97
*Standard score mean = 100; standard deviation = 15			

CASE 48

Comprehensive Assessment of an Attention-Based Learning Problem
Capturing the Relevance of "Psychological Vital Signs"
Thomas Brunner

No two people have the exact same learning problem, partly because the way they learn is significantly affected by their unique personalities. Capturing the unique way a person is experiencing, expressing, and coping with a learning problem demands assessment of his or her personality. To assess personality, one should recognize that a vast body of literature indicates that humans experience both transient feelings (i.e., "state-like" emotions) and more enduring, relatively stable predispositions (i.e., trait-like qualities). More than 30 years ago, Dr. Charles Spielberger, an authority on personality assessment, began constructing measures designed around this "state-trait" distinction, which has become widely accepted. Additionally, Spielberger recognized the importance of evaluating the experience, expression, and control of core personality attributes. A long history of literature, dating back to the writing of Charles Darwin, identifies anger, anxiety, and sadness as core human attributes, which Spielberger termed, collectively, "psychological vital signs." Tying this into modern-day assessment, Spielberger, Reheiser, Owen, and Sydeman (2004) identified these three emotions as worthy of detailed evaluation. They found that evaluating these phenomena in terms of their facets, which could be broken down into measurable dimensions, can greatly enhance the evaluator's grasp of the psychological dynamics related to overall learning and general functioning. In this way, a truly comprehensive assessment identifies emotional states and personality traits related to the learning problem, as well as detecting problematic emotional or behavioral conditions.

Comprehensive assessment, at its best, is the result of a fusion between two historically distinct yet complementary approaches: categorical and dimensional. Categorical assessment focuses on determining whether someone manifests enough qualities/symptoms, based on a diagnostic checklist, to fall into a category, such as that of ADHD. The categorical approach serves important purposes, such as recognition of an aggregate of symptoms that may suggest a widely prevalent and well-researched condition. However, the categorical approach has potential pitfalls. For example, an evaluator may view inattentiveness as a significant contributor to a person's difficulty in learning and be inclined to diagnose ADHD. The subsequent assumption is that treatment of ADHD will alleviate the learning problem. Meanwhile, a myriad of other cognitive/personality/clinical factors that could be contributing to the learning problem would be missed. Thus, sole reliance on a categorical style of assessment can result in a narrow focus, with little recognition of the need to assess the full spectrum of intensity of a particular characteristic.

The value of an evaluation that includes a dimensional facet is that it endeavors to determine the precise degree to which a person has developed an academic skill (e.g., phonemic awareness), behavioral quality (e.g., acting out), and/or emotional state or personality trait (e.g., angry temperament). The dimensional approach can produce an individualized understanding of a person's functioning through a score profile that represents precise measurements of characteristics. The goal of the dimensional approach is to place someone along a measurable continuum as precisely as possible. This approach may reveal a significant level of a quality (high or low) that, while not placing the person into a currently defined category, yields significant information that must be integrated into the overall conceptualization. For example, an evaluator conducting a risk assessment might recognize that while a child falls short of qualifying for a clinical or learning problem category, the child may have a strong tendency to hide or suppress anger. Since suppressed anger can lead to explosive outbursts, a dimensional approach can provide for early intervention to those who may be at high risk for harming others. Consequently, we best serve our clients by conducting a comprehensive evaluation that includes a dimensional facet, thus revealing the levels of various characteristics relevant to the problem.

There is additional value to complementing the categorical approach with the dimensional approach. To understand this, we must first recognize that it is fairly common for psychologists assessing learning problems to administer broad rating scales to identify problematic social-emotional and behavioral issues. This makes sense since an overwhelming body of literature states that learning problems do not "travel alone" and often are joined by emotional or behavioral problems. However, broad rating scales can fall prey to the same problems incurred by a categorical approach. For example, many of these broad screenings are designed to help the evaluator place the most focus on scale scores above a certain cutoff (e.g., T score > 65), rather than placing emphasis on measurement of the intensity of a characteristic along its full continuum. This is understandable because broad scales may focus on screening, rather than on assessment of the multiple facets of core emotions such as anger. In contrast, dimensional measures that assess conceptually-defined and empirically-validated facets of anger (for example) determine "significance" of each score in relation to the scores representing other facets of the same emotion. For example, with "multi" dimensional measures such as the State-Trait Anger Expression Inventory-2 Child and Adolescent (STAXI-2 C/A), even an average range score indicating the frequency with which a child expresses anger outwardly could be considered "significant" when compared to a very high score on a scale assessing the frequency with which he suppresses anger. Multidimensional measures like the STAXI-2 C/A do not use generic cutoffs; instead, significance is derived by comparison to other facet scores.

The following report demonstrates the combined use of a categorical and dimensional approach to evaluate learning/emotional/behavioral issues within the framework of a comprehensive evaluation. A thorough explanation of the referral problem and the formulation of focused recommendations are achieved, in part, by recognizing the influence that emotions such as anger can have on behavior.

PSYCHOEDUCATIONAL EVALUATION

Name:	Glenn Wagner
Date of Birth:	4/2/1994
Age:	15-9
Ethnicity:	White, Not Hispanic
Grade:	10.4
Dates of Assessment:	1/12/10, 1/13/10, 1/26/10, 1/27/10
Report Date:	2/7/2010
Examiner:	Thomas M. Brunner, Ph.D.

REFERRAL INFORMATION

Glenn is a 15-year-old, right-handed Caucasian male who was referred by his parents for a psychoeducational evaluation. The current assessment was requested to evaluate his present levels of academic functioning, as well as to determine how his general psychological functioning might relate to his learning difficulties. Specific issues of concern were: avoidance of homework, poor academic performance, distractibility, and low motivation. Mrs. Wagner brought Glenn to the office for each meeting.

PROCEDURES

Administration of standardized battery of psychoeducational/psychological tests

Clinical/academic interview with Glenn

Developmental/academic/clinical interview with Glenn's mother

DSM-IV-based interview with Glenn and his mother and father (separate interviews)

Interview of English teacher, Ms. James

TESTS ADMINISTERED

Child Report Measures

Behavior Assessment System for Children, Second Edition, Self-Report of Personality-Adolescent (BASC-2, SRP-A)

Behavior Rating Inventory of Executive Function – Self-Report (BRIEF-SR)

Children's Depression Inventory (CDI)

Florida Obsessive Compulsive Inventory (FOCI)

Multidimensional Anxiety Scale for Children (MASC)

State-Trait Anger Expression Inventory-2, Child and Adolescent (STAXI-2 C/A)

Wechsler Intelligence Scale for Children-Fourth Edition (WISC-IV)

Woodcock-Johnson III NU Tests of Achievement, Standard Battery (WJ III ACH)

Parent Report Measures

Behavior Assessment System for Children, Second Edition, Parent Rating Scales-Adolescent (BASC-2, PRS-A)

Behavior Rating Inventory of Executive Function, Parent Form (BRIEF)

Teacher Report Measures

Behavior Assessment System for Children, Second Edition, Teacher Rating Scales-Adolescent (BASC-2, TRS-A)

Behavior Rating Inventory of Executive Function, Teacher Form (BRIEF)

BACKGROUND INFORMATION

Glenn lives with his mother, father, and a younger sister, age 10. Mrs. Wagner is a dental hygienist and Mr. Wagner is a mechanical engineer. Glenn's sister is reported to be an average student. Both parents came for an interview prior to Glenn's evaluation. Mrs. Wagner stated that she is not aware of any learning, emotional, or behavioral problems in her family history. As a teenager, Mr. Wagner struggled with depression, which he later assumed was a stage that most teenagers go through. He noted also that throughout his life he has tended to become distracted easily, which affects his work efficiency.

Developmental History

Glenn's parents provided information regarding his developmental history. Glenn met all developmental milestones on time. His medical history has been unremarkable except that he has severe headaches that have no identifiable pattern. His parents believe these are stress induced.

Psychological/Behavioral History

Glenn's parents characterized his basic temperament with these descriptors: quiet, caring, sensitive, moody, low energy, verbally impulsive, and off task. They noted that he "holds his feelings inside." As a toddler and into his school years, Glenn appeared to be average in his level of activity, but they noted that he was easily distracted ("his father's child"), frequently lost things or couldn't find things that his parents found easily for him (e.g., butter in the refrigerator, a favorite shirt in the closet, papers in his backpack), and was generally disorganized.

The Wagners stated that Glenn has age-appropriate social skills but tends to lose track of conversations with his parents and peers. Glenn has trouble keeping friends, and his parents said this is due to his problems with remembering to call them or to show up for activities he has arranged with them. They identified no problems with basic daily living skills.

Glenn's parents perceive him as having low frustration tolerance and generalized anger that is moderate in intensity. They first noticed these problems when Glenn was in fourth grade. At that time, he began to "shut down" when he felt criticized or overwhelmed, broke eye contact, refused to talk, and put his head down. These behaviors gradually increased in frequency; they now occur almost daily, especially when he is faced with school-related challenges, such as completing homework or studying for tests. The Wagners estimated that sometime in sixth grade, Glenn began to seem depressed. In eighth grade, he began to exhibit some compulsive behaviors, including picking his skin and needing to have his hair look "just right" to the point that he had emotional "meltdowns" if any hairs were out of place.

General Educational History

Glenn is currently a high school sophomore. He was never retained and has had good attendance. He does not receive special education services or any accommodations or modifications to the curriculum. In elementary school, teachers did mention that he was inattentive and that he often did not turn in his homework, but they also commented on how bright he was. Nobody suggested that he should be evaluated, and the parents assumed that his behaviors were "just Glenn." His grades throughout elementary and middle school have been inconsistent, varying from poor to above average. Some teachers have observed that Glenn seemed to absorb and retain information well when he was paying attention but often forgot information, particularly if it was information that required rote memorization or instructions for tasks. Currently, as noted above, Glenn avoids doing homework, his academic performance is poor, and he is not motivated.

Current Classroom Functioning

Ms. James, Glenn's science teacher, was interviewed because Glenn reported that he likes science but still faces the same difficulties he is having in his other courses. Glenn's current grade is an "F" in this class. Ms. James said this grade is due to problems with daily homework completion and test scores, but she was unable to identify any other reasons for his low grades. She reported that she and Glenn have a "lukewarm" relationship. Her general impression of him was that he is an "unmotivated, sweet, but very fidgety boy who at times bounces off the walls." When asked about his motivation on a scale of 1 to 10 (1 is minimum, 10 is maximum), she rated his level of academic motivation as a 1. She has had several one-on-one talks with him about his poor performance, and his response has been that he does not care about school.

Ms. James reported she has made several calls home throughout the year, and after these calls his performance improves for a few days. She said that his general reputation among teachers is that he is unmotivated academically but seems to be relatively good-hearted and is usually socially appropriate, although at times he makes a disrespectful comment or seems verbally impulsive. Ms. James perceives that he is seen by his peers as the class clown who can be "goofy." She estimates that Glenn is on task about 60% of the time with consistent prompting. Without prompting, she believes he would be on task about 30% of the time. She stated that he does respond to her redirection. When Glenn is off-task, he is either staring blankly, talking to friends, or "clowning around." Ms. James has not been able to identify any particular learning problems because his work production has been too low for her to evaluate. Based on the few written assignments he has turned in, however, she estimates that he is

generally meeting grade-level expectations in his written expression. On a scale of 1 to 10, Ms. James perceives his general mood (10 is joyous, 1 is severe depression) as a 4. She perceives Glenn as quiet, sometimes irritable, but not anxious.

Review of Records

Glenn's academic transcripts were reviewed, and over the last 2 years of high school, his grades have ranged from Cs to Fs. The school counselor reported that there is no history of disciplinary problems or referrals.

BEHAVIORAL OBSERVATIONS

Glenn made good eye contact and his affect was upbeat and positive. He also was open and friendly. Glenn's speech quality was within normal limits. His interaction style could be characterized as quiet and well mannered.

Glenn was on task approximately 60% of the time during one-on-one testing. He had particular difficulty staying focused during the working memory and processing speed tasks; he stared blankly for a few seconds, then brought himself back to the task at hand. When distracted at other times, he was easily redirected. When focused on a task, Glenn's speed of responding to questions was average and his responses appeared careful. On tasks that he found particularly difficult, Glenn became frustrated, gave up easily, and would not guess.

The results of this evaluation are believed to be a valid estimate of Glenn's current level of functioning, although Glenn's potential is probably not well represented due to his inattentiveness.

TESTING CONSIDERATIONS AND ENVIRONMENT

Testing was done over two sessions of 3 hours each in a private office with no outside distractions. Glenn takes no medications except occasionally aspirin for his headaches. He reported that his sleep had been normal before each testing session. He did not appear to have any test anxiety, and his teacher and parents did not perceive this as a problem. No language difficulties were noted. No modifications to the standardized testing procedures were made.

ASSESSMENT RESULTS

Attention/Concentration

The Behavior Rating Inventory of Executive Functioning (BRIEF) is a multidimensional measure of attention. The BRIEF has multiple forms such that youth, parents, and teachers can complete questionnaires, producing a consistent set of scores that allows comparisons across informants. The BRIEF was administered to Glenn, his mother and father, and two teachers (Ms. James and his English teacher, Mr. Cunningham). Four of the five response sets (all except Mr. Wagner, where there were no significant elevations) produced across-the-board convergence indicating clinically significant scores (T > 70) on the Initiate, Inattention, Working Memory Emotional Control, Plan/Organize, and Monitoring scales. The Inhibit and Organization of Materials scales were not significantly elevated. When these results were reviewed with Mr. Wagner, he and his wife agreed that since he has his own ADHD-like behaviors, that he probably answered many of the questions with lower endorsements. Review of the answer sheets confirmed this perception.

Intellectual Functioning

The Wechsler Intelligence Scale for Children-Fourth Edition (WISC-IV) was administered to assess Glenn's general level of intellectual functioning. His profile of scores is displayed in the Appendix to this report. Glenn's Full-Scale IQ (FSIQ) score of 96 (39th percentile) fell in the Average range of performance. Using a 95% confidence interval, his IQ on retesting is estimated to fall between the standard scores of 91 and 101. Due to significant discrepancies among the four Index scores, the FSIQ does not provide an accurate representation of his intellectual abilities. Glenn's Verbal Comprehension Index score was in the mid-Average range, his Perceptual Reasoning Index in the lower end of the Average range, and his Working Memory Index score was significantly Below Average, in the Borderline range. The Processing Speed Index was comprised of two widely varying subtest scores, with one score in the lower end of the Average range and the other in the Very Superior range. Thus, the tests within this index provide different estimates of Glenn's speed of processing visual information. As noted previously, on the Coding subtest (processing speed) and both Working Memory subtests, Glenn seemed to lose focus intermittently. Consequently, his poor performance on these tasks was likely mediated by limited attention. Given Glenn's difficulties with attention and concentration, he is likely to perform inconsistently on tasks with similar requirements. Although it is not uncommon for people with attention problems to vary widely on their performance on tests assessing the same abilities, depending on their level and consistency of attention at the time, other reasons for these differences, such as emotional factors, must be ruled out.

Academic Achievement

The Woodcock-Johnson III NU Tests of Achievement, Standard Battery (WJ III ACH) was administered to assess Glenn's general level of academic achievement. Scores were based on age 15 years, 9 months. Glenn's profile of scores is displayed in the Appendix.

Glenn's performance, in general, on the tests of oral language, reading, writing, and math were in the mid-range to higher end of the Average range, with some notable strengths. His ability to immediately recall details of stories that were told to him bordered the Average to High Average range; the number of details he could recall after a delay was in the Superior to Very Superior range, indicating that his ability to retain narrative information is particularly strong. Additionally, his performance on fluency tests was significantly higher than his performance on basic and applied academic skills. His reading ability (i.e., word recognition and comprehension of brief passages) was in the mid-Average range but his reading fluency was significantly higher, in the High Average range. Similarly, his math calculation and problem-solving abilities were in the mid-Average range compared to his Superior ability to quickly retrieve math facts. Glenn scored in the higher end of the Average range in spelling and writing fluency, and speed of writing simple sentences. It is possible that Glenn's one exceptionally high processing speed score is indicative of his general processing speed ability, and that this supported his speed in completing the timed academic tasks. As well, Glenn seemed to involve himself in the challenge of completing as many items as possible within the time limits, especially since the tasks are designed to be easy. He did appear to be on task and involved for the three fluency tests.

Glenn's one area of apparent difficulty was on the Writing Samples test, in which his performance was in the Low Average range. On this test, each item required him to write one good sentence in response to specific instructions that changed from item to item. Review of his responses indicated that, on some items, he did not follow directions. Although he appeared to be listening to the directions, some of his responses were off topic. Consequently, it appears that his poor performance was due to inattention, rather than to writing difficulty. As noted above, Glenn's English teacher reported that when he does turn work in, his written work appears to be on grade level. Based on his performance on the academic tests, Glenn does not appear to have a learning disability.

Similar to results of Glenn's cognitive tests, this achievement profile should not necessarily be considered as an estimate of Glenn's potential, but rather an estimate of his current levels of functioning. His performance on the fluency tests is clearly a strength.

Social-Emotional Functioning

The BASC-2 is a measure that screens for a wide range of common emotional/behavioral problems. Multiple forms make it possible to compare responses across informants. Glenn, his parents, and two teachers (Ms. James and his English teacher, Mr. Cunningham) completed the BASC-2. All five response sets produced across-the-board convergence indicating clinically significant scores (T > 80) on the Depression and Attention Problems scales. Review of the critical items on Glenn's self-report revealed endorsement of the following items: I feel like my life is getting worse and worse (Often); I feel sad (Often); and I hate school (Often).

The State Trait Anger Expression Inventory–2, Child and Adolescent (STAXI-2 C/A) was used to assess how Glenn experiences, expresses, and controls anger while accounting for both temporary "state-like" qualities as well as more enduring "trait-like" aspects. Glenn's anger profile is displayed in the Appendix. The following is a description of the STAXI-2 C/A scales and subscales.

Description of the STAXI-2 C/A Scales and Subscales

Scale/Subscale	Description
State Anger (S-Ang)	Measures the intensity of angry feelings and the extent to which a youth feels like expressing anger at a particular time.
State Anger-Feelings (S-Ang/F)	Measures the intensity of the angry feelings a youth is currently experiencing.
State Anger-Expression (S-Ang/VP)	Measures the intensity of current feelings related to verbal or physical expressions of anger.
Trait Anger (T-Ang)	Measures how often angry feelings are experienced over time.

Scale/Subscale	Description
Trait Anger-Temperament (T-Ang/T)	Measures the disposition to experience anger without specific provocation.
Trait Anger-Reaction (T-Ang/R)	Measures the frequency with which angry feelings are experienced in situations that involve frustration and/or negative evaluation.
Anger Expression-Out (AX-O)	Measures how often angry feelings are expressed in verbally or physically aggressive behavior.
Anger Expression-In (AX-I)	Measures how often angry feelings are experienced but not expressed (e.g., suppressed).
Anger Control (AC)	Measures how often a youth tries to control the inward or outward expression of angry feelings.

Glenn's profile of scores suggests that at the time of testing, he was not experiencing anger, as his State Anger scores were in the Average range. In contrast, review of the scales assessing Glenn's general experience of anger over time revealed a concerning pattern. His score on the Trait Anger-Temperament scale was in the 74th percentile, indicating that Glenn tends to experience anger to a significant degree without specific provocation. While the 75th percentile is generally considered a level of significance, the ultimate determinant of this score is derived by its comparison to other scores. In contrast, Glenn's score on the Trait Anger-Reaction subscale is considerably lower, in the 23rd percentile. This combination of scores suggests that while Glenn tends to experience anger frequently across a variety of situations, he does not generally experience anger in situations that involve frustration or negative evaluation (e.g., being criticized). It may be that he tends to suppress anger, and thus, the more accurate way of describing his low Trait Anger-Reaction subscale score would be that he is not aware of the anger he is experiencing. This hypothesis would be corroborated by a significantly higher Anger-In score.

It may be that Glenn tends to internalize anger, particularly when he is criticized, which is both counterintuitive and uncommon. This pattern is likely to be found in people who have low self-esteem, who expect to be criticized because they know they fall short of their own and others' expectations in some way. Often, these respondents have problems with depression and tend to have some sort of impairment in general functioning.

Glenn's Anger Expression-In score was in the 99th percentile, suggesting that Glenn must put a great deal of energy into suppressing his anger instead of expressing it outward. In contrast, Glenn's Anger Expression-Out score was in the 45th percentile, indicating that he very strongly favors an internalizing style of anger control. Overall, what is of particular concern is that since Glenn has such a high degree of generalized anger, he must expend considerable energy holding his anger inside. People with this type of anger profile are at risk for developing both mental health conditions (such as depression or anxiety) and medical conditions such as hypertension. When this anger profile was reported to his mother and his science teacher, both people agreed that the results captured his anger style.

The Multidimensional Anxiety Scale for Children (MASC) is a self-report measure of anxiety. The validity scale did not detect a concerning pattern of responses. There was a clinical elevation on the Performance Fears (T = 75) subscale. When Glenn was asked about this, he reported that since seventh grade, he has felt worried when he must present in front of a class or group because of his awareness of his problems with focus, his low self-esteem, and a previous experience of being bullied. Glenn reported he is concerned he will say something that is "stupid" and that he will be mocked by his peers. The other MASC scales were not significantly elevated.

The Florida Obsessive Compulsive Inventory (FOCI) was used as a screening measure to detect any regularly recurring thoughts or compulsive behaviors that might interfere with general functioning. Glenn reported being bothered by the following thoughts: harm coming to a loved one (3x/week), burglary of house (3x/week), and excessive grooming (6x/day). He reported he perceived having moderate control over these obsessions/compulsions and stated these take up about 30 minutes of his time each day.

The Children's Depression Inventory (CDI) is a self-report measure administered to screen for common cognitive/affective and/or somatic symptoms associated with depressive tendencies that are also reflected in the *DSM-IV* criteria. Glenn's responses to this measure produced a "much above average" elevation on the Negative Mood scale and on the Total score. Numerous concerning endorsements were made, indicating low self-esteem, low energy, and difficulty with generating energy to complete schoolwork.

STRUCTURED CLINICAL INTERVIEW

A structured clinical interview was conducted with Glenn and then independently with his mother and father. Based on convergence of Glenn's and his mother's responses to

diagnostically based symptom checklists, Glenn clearly met criteria for ADHD/Primarily Inattentive Type.

Structured interviews were also conducted to see if Glenn met criteria for Obsessive-Compulsive Disorder and/or a unipolar depressive spectrum condition. Although he fell short of a diagnosis in both areas, his OCD and depressive spectrum tendencies impair the quality of his life and thus necessitate treatment.

Interview with Glenn

Glenn was interviewed to assess for relevant personal/clinical information. The following information was significant. Glenn reported that he recalls being in trouble "a lot" as a young child, as far back as first grade. He remembers often feeling frustrated because he felt like he was trying his best to behave but felt like "I could not help myself." When asked to elaborate, he said he felt like he could not focus on one thing, and that his mother was often angry with him because he was not paying attention. Over time, Glenn said he became angry that his efforts were not recognized. By middle school, he was often angry. However, Glenn said that he recalls feeling like he was always trying very hard to hold his anger in because he knew that if he expressed it, he would get into even more trouble. Glenn admitted that he began to feel like a burden to his parents by fifth grade, because he knew that when they argued with each other it was often because he had misbehaved in school.

Glenn recalled that the next major event in his life was in seventh and eighth grade, when he was bullied. He believes he became an easy target since his peers knew he was not likely to retaliate even when they taunted him. Moreover, since Glenn sometimes made comments without thinking, he would say things that were easy to make fun of. Due to this bullying, Glenn reported he had thoughts about wanting to kill a few students who were consistently annoying him. He reported that these thoughts lasted for only a week, that he never attempted to hurt anyone, denied any other episodes of homicidal ideation, and reported there is no chance he would ever hurt anyone. He reported he never told anyone about these thoughts and that he felt very guilty about having had them. Nevertheless, Glenn said he still carries a large amount of generalized anger and feels like he could unleash a significant amount of anger that has "built up."

On a 10-point scale (10 is "joyous," 1 is "suicidal"), Glenn said his current mood tends to be anywhere from a 4 to a 5. He said he felt totally unprepared for high school and now he feels like he is trying to "catch up." He said that he understands information easily when he is focused, but that he is able to focus some of the time. He also reported that he experiences significant anxiety, especially in social situations and during tests. Glenn said that this anxiety began around seventh grade, when he felt his self-esteem began to sink as he realized how different he was from other students. He said that in earlier grades, he simply associated with other students having similar problems, but that by seventh grade, he realized his problems were not going away.

SUMMARY AND CONCLUSIONS

Glenn is a 15-year-old boy who was referred by his parents for a psychoeducational evaluation. The current assessment was requested to evaluate the level of Glenn's academic functioning, as well as to how his general psychological functioning might relate to his learning difficulties. Based on the information obtained during the course of this evaluation, no educational, environmental, economic, cultural, and/or ethnic difference is considered to be a significant factor influencing the data gathered. This evaluation is considered to provide a valid representation of Glenn's current level of functioning. Anyone working with Glenn must have an understanding of his difficulties and how they manifest within his personality. Simply looking at a diagnosis or recommendations is not sufficient to understand how to work with him effectively.

Attention and Concentration

Before one looks at any estimates of intelligence, it is important to first look at whether there is data to suggest a person may have consistent problems with attention and/or concentration, as intelligence is somewhat dependent on one's ability to absorb information by attending to and/or focusing on environmental stimuli.

Integration of direct and teacher-based observation, structured clinical interview, and results of parent, teacher, and self-report questionnaires consistently indicate clinically significant problems with attention and concentration. Glenn met criteria for a diagnosis of ADHD/Primarily Inattentive Type. Since emotional factors appear to be exacerbating his attention problems, it is important that he receive both academic accommodations and therapeutic treatment.

Intellectual Functioning

The WISC-IV was administered to assess Glenn's general level of intellectual functioning. Glenn's FSIQ score fell in the Average range, but with significant discrepancies among the Indexes. Glenn's profile was indicative of those with inattentive type ADHD. He had significant difficulties on the Working Memory subtests. It is quite possible that his ADHD, anxiety, and depression were factors contributing to his low Working Memory score. It is clear that this cognitive profile does not represent Glenn's potential.

Academic Achievement

Results of the WJ III ACH indicated that Glenn's performance across all the broad academic domains was commensurate or roughly commensurate with expectations based on age-level standards, except in the area of written expression. However, Glenn's difficulties in this area appeared to be due to his difficulty sustaining attention and following the directions. In this way, his difficulties provided corroborating data for the ADHD diagnosis and did not support the presence of a writing disability. His English teacher confirmed that Glenn is a capable writer. Glenn demonstrated significant strengths in automatic recall of math facts, reading fluency, and long-term memory for narrative information.

OVERALL IMPRESSION

Overall, Glenn presents as a sensitive and moody adolescent who has been struggling in school for a long time. It is understandable that he is seen as unmotivated, as he himself recognizes his disengagement with his education.

Clearly, Glenn's difficulties are driven by a combination of cognitive and emotional factors that began in kindergarten with inattentiveness. Around fourth grade, Glenn became angry frequently. Glenn's anger profile suggests that he internalizes anger, and it is likely that this tendency contributed to his developing a depressive disposition in fifth grade. While there is no diagnostic category to capture the significance of Glenn's anger style, the degree to which Glenn seems to hold anger in does predispose him (based on empirical research on anger) to develop problems with depression as well as medical problems. Contributors to Glenn's anger likely include frustration with his inattentiveness and low academic performance. Glenn's anger requires treatment. A common pattern seen in those who lash out with explosive and damaging anger is that, previously, they internalized anger for long periods of time until the accumulation was beyond their psychological control.

Around seventh grade, Glenn developed some performance anxiety. His current fears of being up in front of others may stem from ongoing experiences of negative feedback regarding his lack of focus over many years. A year later, in eighth grade, Glenn developed some compulsive behaviors that helped him to cope with his distress.

On a positive note, Glenn appears to have a strong base of intellectual, language, and academic skills. It is noteworthy that even given his chronic problems, he has remained at academic level in many ways. Once Glenn receives appropriate treatment, he is likely to develop further areas of strength. Glenn's parents are highly invested in his success, and there are many well-researched treatments for his problems. An aggressive and integrated treatment and educational plan need to be developed. The goals of this plan should be to help him become more confident and engaged.

CLINICAL/DIAGNOSTIC IMPRESSION

Axis I: Attention-Deficit/Hyperactivity Disorder (ADHD), Primarily Inattentive Type

Rule Out Depression Spectrum Disorder

Rule Out Obsessive-Compulsive Disorder (OCD)

Axis II: Deferred

Axis III: Deferred

Axis IV: Low self-esteem; poor educational experiences; obsessive-compulsive tendencies; generalized anger and low mood

Axis V: Deferred

SPECIAL EDUCATION

Based on his diagnosis of ADHD, Primarily Inattentive Type, Glenn qualifies for consideration of special education services at his high school. By law, he may qualify via the category of Other Health Impaired (OHI), with the consent of his school team, or he would qualify for an accommodation plan under Section 504 of the Rehabilitation Act of 1973.

RECOMMENDATIONS

Reassessment

Once Glenn receives appropriate treatment for his cognitive and emotional problems, cognitive and academic achievement should be retested to get a more valid measure of his potential.

Working Memory, Depression, and Obsessions

1. A systematic, evidence-based working memory training program should be considered regarding the effect of Glenn's inattention on working memory tasks. Research regarding one such program, called CogMed (www.cogmed.com), should be reviewed and considered.

2. For depression, consider therapeutic treatment for Glenn's low self-esteem, low energy, and negative attitude about school. Possible treatment approaches are Cognitive-Behavioral Therapy and Acceptance and Commitment Therapy. Both of these treatments assist a person in understanding the relationship among thoughts, feelings, and behavior. People learn to minimize the effect of negative thinking on how they feel, while learning ways to catch themselves when they are exhibiting a depressive cognitive style.

3. Consider therapeutic treatment of Glenn's compulsions. One evidence-based technique is Exposure Response Prevention (ERP). ERP is a process in which a person is taught to handle a recurring problematic thought or feeling by responding to it with a competing, healthier behavior.

4. Glenn would benefit from coaching regarding how to better handle public presentations since they tend to be a regular part of academic assignments. Until his confidence increases, he should be given alternative assignments rather than having to make oral presentations in class.

Building Emotional Intelligence

Glenn appears to cope with troublesome thoughts by internalizing his feelings. Boys often lack the emotional language to describe how they are feeling, and thus, it would be beneficial for Glenn to learn the vocabulary that will allow him to express his feelings.

Medication

1. Share this report with a psychiatrist who will discuss with Glenn and his parents the benefits and possible side effects of medication. Medication is likely to help Glenn improve his attention and ability to concentrate substantially. Also discuss the potential need for medication to treat the depression, though it is not at a diagnostic level yet.

2. If medication is prescribed, explain the reason to Glenn, what effect it is expected to have (e.g., allow him to pay attention if he tries), what it cannot do (e.g., make him pay attention if he does not try), and the possible side effects. Involve him as much as possible in the decision to take the medication and in monitoring and discussing how it is working.

3. Before Glenn starts a trial of medication, initiate teacher completion of a rating chart composed of a few behaviors that are problems in the classroom and that are likely to respond to medication (e.g., pays attention while teacher is talking, socializes only when appropriate, work shows appropriate level of thought), a question about time of the day when medication benefits appear to have worn off, and comments. Have the teachers continue to chart behaviors and share the results with you so that you can share them with the physician), until the optimal dosage and dosage times are established. It is often best to do this by e-mail rather than expect Glenn to take the rating charts from teacher to teacher or to bring them home.

4. In establishing the correct dosage and times of medication, discuss with the doctor your concern that Glenn has a steady level of medication throughout the day, to include homework time, after-school or extracurricular sports, and social time with friends.

Parent Guidance

1. The Wagners should call the school to request a meeting to discuss providing Glenn with a 504 Accommodation Plan. At the meeting, share the findings of this report so that teachers understand the emotional dynamics and pressures Glenn is living with and discuss the recom-

mended accommodations. It may be that more emphasis should be placed on long-term skill building rather than solely on grades, at least in the immediate future, as effective intervention is begun. The overall intent is to help Glenn regain interest in his education and increase his engagement in both school and social activities.

2. If possible, hire a tutor to act as an academic coach with responsibility for teaching Glenn organizational skills, such as time management and materials management, directly and explicitly, with modeling, guided practice and reinforcement, and independent practice and monitoring. Having a tutor for this type of work will ease the conflict between Glenn and you regarding homework.

3. Before beginning nightly homework, help Glenn review all assignments, estimate the time each will take, prioritize them, and then list them in order on an index card. As he finishes an assignment, have him cross it off the list.

4. Provide Glenn with a separate folder to use to transport homework to and from school. Have him place new assignments on one side of the folder and completed assignments on the other side to be handed in on the next day.

5. Consider joining a support group for parents of adolescents with ADHD. For information about groups in your area, contact CHADD, 800-233-4050, http://www.chadd.org/findchap.htm.

6. Help Glenn learn as much about ADHD as possible from reliable sources such as www.chadd.org and encourage him to consider how it affects him. Also, look for videotapes that explain ADHD in adolescents and adults. Explore the availability of an education and support group for adolescents in Glenn's age range. The purpose would be to increase his understanding of ADHD, teach him how to advocate for himself and set up situations for success, and help him recognize that he is not unique in having this condition.

7. Develop a school schedule for Glenn in which one class (e.g., elective, foreign language) is replaced with a study hall or a second study hall to allow for tutorial support and in-school homework time. This reduces the problem of Glenn doing homework after school when he may be cognitively exhausted and is without the benefit of medication.

8. Ask Glenn if he's interested in a device such as the WatchMinder-2, a watch that signals the wearer to do certain activities at preset times (e.g., MEDS, COPY HMWK, DO CHORES) throughout the day. As a

training device, the WatchMinder-2 may also be programmed to vibrate at regular intervals to signal Glenn to do certain behaviors such as ask himself if he is actively working (http://www.watchminder.com).

School Accommodations/Modifications

Instruction

1. Seat Glenn close to where you often stand in the classroom so that you can help him remain on task or return to task. Your proximity will help Glenn stay involved in teacher-directed and interactive tasks and make it easier for you to make frequent contact and provide feedback during independent work.

2. Prior to a lecture, write an outline on the board and review it with the class. Not only does this provide a vital framework for the information that will be presented, it will also allow Glenn to reorient himself if his attention wanders during the lecture.

3. As much as possible, when presenting information, use accompanying visual images such as pictures, graphics (e.g., webs, charts, graphs), and videotapes. Enhancing auditory information may be as simple as drawing a sketch on the board to illustrate concepts such as contrasts, similarities, levels of importance, and cause-effect. Use numbers and/or colors to differentiate sections of information.

Homework and Assignments

1. Always write homework assignments on the board and then give students time to write them in their assignment calendars. Make sure that Glenn does this.

2. Reduce the amount of work Glenn is required to do for homework. Because his ability to focus and maintain concentration is compromised, it will take him longer than most students to do the same amount of work. Reducing his assignments will make it more likely that he will attempt and complete them.

3. Because Glenn forgets to turn in completed homework, remind him daily to turn in his homework and specify that he is to do it right then.

Thank you for the opportunity to participate in Glenn's care. I look forward to providing further assistance in the creation of an appropriate counseling plan.

APPENDIX: SCORES

Wechsler Intelligence Scale for Children-Fourth Edition

Composite Scores Summary

Scale	Composite Score	Percentile Rank	95% Confidence Interval	Qualitative Description
Verbal Comprehension (VCI)	100	50	93–107	Average
Perceptual Reasoning (PRI)	92	30	85–100	Average
Working Memory (WMI)	74	4	68–84	Borderline
Processing Speed (PSI)	121	92	110–127	Superior
Full Scale (FSIQ)	96	39	91–101	Average

Verbal Comprehension Subtest Scores Summary

Subtests	Scaled Score	Age Equiv.	Percentile Rank
Similarities	10	15–6	50
Vocabulary	10	15–10	50
Comprehension	11	16–6	63

Perceptual Reasoning Subtest Scores Summary

Subtests	Scaled Score	Age Equiv.	Percentile Rank
Block Design	10	16–2	50
Picture Concepts	7	10–2	16
Matrix Reasoning	9	12–10	37

Working Memory Subtest Scores Summary

Subtests	Scaled Score	Age Equiv.	Percentile Rank
Digit Span	5	8–2	5
Letter-Number Sequencing	6	8–10	9

Processing Speed Subtest Scores Summary

Subtests	Scaled Score	Age Equiv.	Percentile Rank
Coding	8	13–2	25
Symbol Search	19	>16–10	99.9

Composite Score Differences

Discrepancy Comparisons	Scaled Score 1	Scaled Score 2	Diff.	Critical Value	Sig. Diff. Y/N	Base Rate
VCI – PRI	100	92	8	10.59	N	25.8%
VCI – WMI	100	74	26	10.59	Y	3.6%
VCI – PSI	100	121	-21	11.38	Y	11%
PRI – WMI	92	74	18	11.75	Y	12.4%
PRI – PSI	92	121	-29	12.46	Y	2.9%
WMI – PSI	74	121	-47	12.46	Y	0.8%

Base Rate by Overall Sample
Statistical Significance (Critical Values) at the .05 level.

Subtest Score Differences

Discrepancy Comparisons	Scaled Score 1	Scaled Score 2	Diff.	Critical Value	Sig. Diff. Y/N	Base Rate
Digit Span – Letter-Number Seq.	5	6	–1	2.83	N	47.1%
Coding – Symbol Search	8	19	–11	3.55	Y	0.2%
Similarities – Picture Concepts	10	7	3	3.36	N	19.5%

Statistical Significance (Critical Values) at the .05 level.

Woodcock-Johnson III NU Tests of Achievement: Standard Battery

Table of Scores

Woodcock-Johnson III Normative Update Tests of Achievement (Form A)

WJ III NU Compuscore and Profiles Program, Version 3.0 Norms based on age 15-9

CLUSTER/Test	AE	Proficiency	RPI	SS (68% Band)	PR
ORAL LANGUAGE	17–6	average	92/90	105 (100–111)	64
Story Recall	>21	average	93/90	110 (102–118)	75
Understanding Directions	15–10	average	92/90	102 (96–108)	55
(Story Recall – Delayed)	>21	avg to adv	97/90	131 (122–141)	98
BROAD READING	20	average	95/90	107 (104–110)	67
Letter-Word Identification	15–0	average	85/90	97 (94–101)	43
Passage Comprehension	16–11	average	91/90	101 (96–107)	53

CLUSTER/Test	AE	Proficiency	RPI	SS (68% Band)	PR
Reading Fluency	>30	advanced	99/90	117 (114–120)	87
BRIEF READING	15–4	average	89/90	99 (96–102)	47
Letter-Word Identification	15–0	average	85/90	97 (94–101)	43
Passage Comprehension	16–11	average	91/90	101 (96–107)	53
BROAD WRITTEN LANG	15–2	average	89/90	99 (95–102)	46
Spelling	19	average	94/90	104 (100–108)	61
Writing Samples	10–2	limited	63/90	82 (76–88)	11
Writing Fluency	>21	avg to adv	95/90	109 (102–116)	72
BRIEF WRITING	13–8	average	84/90	94 (90–98)	34
Spelling	19	average	94/90	104 (100–108)	61
Writing Samples	10–2	limited	63/90	82 (76–88)	11
WRITTEN EXPRESSION	13–9	average	85/90	95 (90–99)	36
Writing Samples	10–2	limited	63/90	82 (76–88)	11
Writing Fluency	>21	avg to adv	95/90	109 (102–116)	72
BROAD MATH	>30	avg to adv	96/90	108 (106–111)	71
Calculation	>23	average	94/90	104 (99–108)	60
Applied Problems	16–11	average	93/90	102 (99–105)	55
Math Fluency	>25	advanced	98/90	127 (125–130)	97
BRIEF MATH	17–8	average	93/90	103 (100–105)	57
Calculation	>23	average	94/90	104 (99–108)	60
Applied Problems	16–11	average	93/90	102 (99–105)	55
MATH CALC SKILLS	>24	avg to adv	97/90	113 (110–116)	81
Calculation	>23	average	94/90	104 (99–108)	60
Math Fluency	>25	advanced	98/90	127 (125–130)	97
ACADEMIC SKILLS	16–4	average	92/90	102 (99–105)	55
Letter-Word Identification	15–0	average	85/90	97 (94–101)	43
Calculation	>23	average	94/90	104 (99–108)	60
Spelling	19	average	94/90	104 (100–108)	61
ACADEMIC FLUENCY	>24	advanced	98/90	119 (116–122)	90
Reading Fluency	>30	advanced	99/90	117 (114–120)	87
Writing Fluency	>21	avg to adv	95/90	109 (102–116)	72
Math Fluency	>25	advanced	98/90	127 (125–130)	97
ACADEMIC APP	14–4	average	86/90	96 (92–99)	39
Passage Comprehension	16–11	average	91/90	101 (96–107)	53
Writing Samples	10–2	limited	63/90	82 (76–88)	11
Applied Problems	16–11	average	93/90	102 (99–105)	55

VARIATIONS	STANDARD SCORES			VARIATION		Significant at + or − 1.50 SD (SEE)
	Actual	Predicted	Difference	PR	SD	
Intra-Achievement (BRIEF)						
BRIEF READING	99	99	0	50	+0.01	No
BRIEF MATH	103	97	6	68	+0.46	No
BRIEF WRITING	94	101	−7	26	-0.64	No

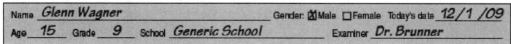

STAXI-2 C/A

Profile Form

Thomas M. Brunner, PhD
Charles D. Spielberger, PhD

Name _Glenn Wagner_ Gender: ☒ Male ☐ Female Today's date _12/1/09_
Age _15_ Grade _9_ School _Generic School_ Examiner _Dr. Brunner_

STAXI-2 C/A Percentile Profile

	S-Ang	S-Ang/F	S-Ang/VP	T-Ang	T-Ang/T	T-Ang/R	AX-O	AX-I	AC	
%ile	53	66	61	43	73	23	45	99	65	%ile
Raw score	12	7	5	17	9	8	8	14	12	Raw score

Normative table used: _Males Ages 15-18 years_

STAXI-2 C/A *T*-Score Profile

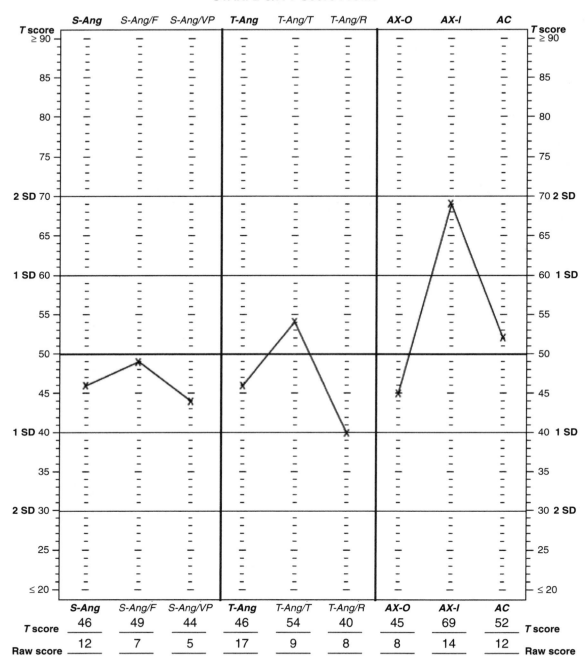

	S-Ang	S-Ang/F	S-Ang/VP	T-Ang	T-Ang/T	T-Ang/R	AX-O	AX-I	AC	
T score	46	49	44	46	54	40	45	69	52	*T* score
Raw score	12	7	5	17	9	8	8	14	12	Raw score

Normative table used: *Males Ages 15-18 years*

REFERENCE

Spielberger, C. D., Reheiser, E. C., Owen, A. E., & Sydeman, S. J. (2004). Measuring the psychological vital signs of anxiety, anger, depression, and curiosity in treatment planning and outcome assessment. In M. E. Maruish (Ed.), *The use of psychological tests for treatment planning and outcome assessment* (3rd ed.) (pp. 421–447). Hillsdale, NJ: Erlbaum.

CASE 49

Psychoeducational Assessment of a Juvenile
Offender in a Correctional Setting

Christina Vasquez and Richard Morris

The research literature has reported that juvenile offenders residing in detention and correctional settings are often found to have a special education diagnosis, with the most frequent diagnosis being emotional disability followed by the diagnosis of specific learning disability (e.g., Morris & Morris, 2006). These youth, as well as those not having a special education diagnosis, are required by state and, in many cases, federal law to have the opportunity to receive a free and appropriate education until they reach a specific age. For example, in the case of those youth who qualify for special education services under the eligibility criteria listed in the Individuals with Disabilities Education Improvement Act (IDEA, 2004), they must have the opportunity to receive special education services until their 22nd birthday—including being evaluated on a regular basis with regard to the appropriateness of their educational placement and educational remediation plan (IDEA, 2004; Morris & Thompson, 2008).

Assessing the cognitive, emotional, and academic strengths and needs of juvenile offenders who reside in detention and correctional settings presents several potential challenges for psychologists and diagnosticians. The major reason for this is the fact that, in most cases, psychoeducational evaluations of these juveniles are conducted under conditions that are not consistent with the standardization of the tests being used. For example, most standardized tests that measure cognition, achievement, and behavior do not include in the general norm or clinical norm sample population youth who are currently incarcerated. Further, the test results achieved by youth in detention or correctional settings may not be representative of the results that they would have achieved had they been tested in a general education setting under conditions that were consistent with the standardization conditions. Such skewing of test results could take place in either a negative or positive direction, depending on the extent to which particular tests were administered under nonstandardized conditions.

In addition to norming and standardization issues, the environmental conditions under which psychoeducational evaluations take place in detention and correctional settings versus general education settings could further have an effect on the test results. For example, a psychologist, speech pathologist, or other diagnostician may be required to test a youth with a corrections officers present in the testing room, or the evaluator may be required to hold in her or his hand a "panic button" during all testing sessions in case something untoward happens during the testing. In addition, testing may need to take place in a room that has undraped windows that provide no privacy and which are in direct view of officers, staff, and other inmates who may pass by the room. Steel doors may also close loudly on a regular basis during testing as well as alarms sounding that indicate correctional officers or other personnel have entered or exited a cell block. Moreover, emergency alarms may sound that indicate a "lock down" situation, in which case the testing would be interrupted immediately and the psychologist or diagnostician would be quickly escorted out of the cell block with no information being provided regarding when such testing might be resumed.

Some youth might also be tested while in shackles or handcuffed to a chair or desk. This would necessitate, in some cases, the omission of testing a youth on subtests or tests that require the free use of both hands (e.g., the Block Design subtest on the Wechsler Intelligence Scale for Children-IV; the Design Memory subtest and Spatial Addition subtest on the Wechsler Memory Scale-IV).

These latter testing circumstances could further skew test results and the accompanying test interpretations. A youth's criminal history and/or history of the nature of his or her interactions with court and detention personnel may also affect his or her willingness to establish rapport with the test examiner due, for example, to issues of mistrust on the part of the youth regarding how the test results will be used in the future. Finally, a youth's stress and related emotionality regarding an upcoming (or just completed) judicial hearing, institutional or cell block transfer, or other mental and emotional preoccupations may influence test results.

These are just some of the many potential issues that need to be considered when administering and scoring psychoeducational tests, as well as in interpreting test results. Some of these issues are highlighted in the following case example involving the psychoeducational assessment of a juvenile offender.

Case Description

The following case illustrates the need to consider various factors that may impact the validity of the results obtained during a psychoeducational evaluation that focused on assessing a youth's cognitive, academic, and emotional strengths and needs. The juvenile offender, Jeff, is an eleventh grader who is serving a court-ordered sentence for aggravated assault on a police officer and drug possession. Because Jeff is to be released within 6 months, his education team wanted to know his current cognitive, academic, and emotional strengths and needs. According to the principal at the correctional center's school, Jeff does not intend to continue in school once he is released. Thus, information from the psychoeducational assessment is needed to provide the school's educational staff with more detailed information as to how the team can best serve Jeff's academic and transitional needs once he is released back into the community.

PSYCHOEDUCATIONAL REPORT

Name:	Jeff Carsons
Date of Birth:	10/09/1992
Age:	17-2
Ethnicity:	Caucasian
Primary Language:	English
Home Language:	English
School:	Correctional Center
Grade:	11
Hearing Screening:	09/09/2009
Vision Screening:	09/09/2009
Date of Evaluation:	12/09/2009
Date of Report:	12/20/2009
Examiners:	Christina Vasquez, Ed.S.
	Richard Morris, Ph.D.

REASON FOR REFERRAL

Jeff was referred for a psychoeducational evaluation by the principal at the correctional center in order to evaluate his strengths and needs in terms of his cognitive, academic, and emotional functioning as they apply to his current education and the planning of his education transition back into the community.

BACKGROUND HISTORY

The following background information was obtained from the correctional center's school records and medical records and from a social history interview with Jeff.

According to school records, Jeff attended kindergarten at Ridgewood Elementary School, first grade at Springfield Elementary School, and part of second grade at Anderson Elementary School, at which point he transferred to Homestead Elementary School until fifth grade. Jeff attended Northpoint Middle School in sixth grade, where he was diagnosed as having a specific learning disability in reading, written expression, and math. Jeff continued to attend Northpoint through eighth grade. During ninth grade, Jeff was caught selling drugs and sentenced to the Arlington Correctional Facility; he was released to the community after 2 months and court-ordered to attend public school. During tenth grade, he was sentenced for aggravated assault and drug possession and was incarcerated in a state correctional center. When Jeff was released in April 2009, he did not enroll in school and remained out of school from April 2009 until September 2009 when he was arrested for robbery and sentenced again to the state correctional center. Although Jeff is considered to be in the eleventh grade, he has never attended a public high school and has the credits of a beginning ninth grade student.

Before his most recent incarceration, Jeff was living with his foster parents in Salt Lake City. Jeff is the youngest of eight children with one older biological sister still living in the foster home. Jeff states that he feels his biological and foster parents have given up on him since his first incarceration at the Arlington Correctional Facility. Jeff has been incarcerated in the state correctional center since September 2009.

EVALUATION PROCEDURE

Jeff's racial, cultural, primary language, and educational background were considered prior to the selection of psychoeducational tests and in the scoring and interpretation of test results. In this regard, the following assessments were used:

Review of school and medical records

Social history interview

Wechsler Adult Intelligence Scale-Fourth Edition (WAIS-IV)

Woodcock-Johnson III NU Tests of Achievement, (WJ III ACH)

Wechsler Memory Scale-Fourth Edition (WMS-IV)

Minnesota Multiphasic Personality Inventory-Adolescent (MMPI-A)

Jeff comes from a household where English is the only language spoken. Thus, there is no indication that language would be a factor to consider when analyzing Jeff's test results.

The examiners do not believe that Jeff's race or culture negatively affected his performance. There is evidence to suggest that Jeff's test scores may not be a true reflection of his ability because of Jeff's history of not attending a public high school, his past and present incarcerations, and the current testing environment.

BEHAVIORAL OBSERVATIONS

Jeff was willing to participate in the assessment process. Although Jeff had never previously met the examiners, rapport was established easily. Jeff did not provide any information unless asked and appeared reserved during the majority of the testing sessions. His eye contact was normal and he appeared focused during all tasks despite both visual and auditory distractions within the correctional center's environment. Jeff indicated to the examiner whenever he felt fatigued or needed to take a break. One observation that was consistent throughout the testing was that if Jeff was unsure of an answer he would give up and state, "I have no idea." In addition, when Jeff was presented with a challenging math task, he would state, "I hate math" or "I can't do math."

At the time of the test administration, Jeff was waiting to hear from his lawyer regarding the status of an upcoming adjudication hearing concerning a second crime that Jeff allegedly committed.

There were both auditory and visual interruptions throughout the testing process. This occurred on both the cognitive and achievement tests. Specifically, Jeff's ability to listen and store information during various auditory memory tasks may have been negatively affected by the frequent auditory distractions that were present during the administration of the test. Visual and auditory distractions also occurred during several other timed subtests, which may have affected Jeff's ability to follow oral directions.

In the opinion of the examiners, the environmental conditions under which the current evaluation was conducted influenced the test results at the following level: moderate to severe. In addition to the environmental disruptions, the testing occurred in a corrections setting that is not consistent with the conditions under which the cognitive, academic, and emotional assessment instruments were standardized. The reader should, therefore, consider these limitations in reviewing the overall findings and recommendations contained in this report.

TEST RESULTS

Cognitive Testing

Wechsler Adult Intelligence Scale–Fourth Edition (WAIS-IV)

Jeff was administered the WAIS-IV, a standardized, individually administered test measuring an individual's overall cognitive abilities. His scores are included in the following table:

(Composite Scores: Mean = 100, Standard Deviation = 15)

(Subtest Scores: Mean = 10, Standard Deviation = 3)

Composite	Standard Score	Percentile Rank	95% Confidence Interval	Qualitative Description
Verbal Comprehension	84	13	78–89	Low Average
Perceptual Reasoning	108	73	102–115	Average
Working Memory	93	30	86–99	Average
Processing Speed	93	30	84–101	Average
Full-Scale IQ	93	32	89–97	Average

Subtest	Standard Score/ Scaled Score	Percentile Rank
Verbal Comprehension Index	**84**	**13**
Similarities	8	25
Vocabulary	7	16
Information	6	9
Perceptual Reasoning Index	**108**	**73**
Block Design	15	95
Visual Puzzles	9	37
Matrix Reasoning	11	63
Working Memory Index	**93**	**30**
Digit Span	7	16
Arithmetic	10	50
Processing Speed Index	**93**	**30**
Coding	7	16
Symbol Search	10	50

Jeff earned a Full-Scale IQ (FSIQ) score of 93, placing him in the Average range of overall cognitive functioning. His current performance placed him in the 32nd percentile as compared to his same-age peers. On the Verbal Comprehension Index (VCI), Jeff earned a score of 84, which is in the Low Average range, performing in the 13th percentile as compared to his same-age peers. Jeff's scores on the subtests that constitute the VCI were not significantly different. It should be noted that the two subtests that Jeff scored lower on are weighted heavily on knowledge accrued through school and exposure to one's environment. Because Jeff missed school frequently, changed schools multiple times, and never attended a public high school, such factors may have contributed to his relative low scores. However, Jeff was able to perform relatively well in describing how two things are similar but had difficulty when the two items had a commonality that were outside of concrete explanation.

Jeff earned a score of 108 on a measure of nonverbal reasoning, the Perceptual Reasoning Index (PRI), which was in the Average range. Although Jeff's PRI subtest scores were Average or above, there was a significant difference between his scores on the Block Design and Visual Puzzles subtests. This may be indicative of Jeff performing to the best of his ability when visual information can be manipulated and there are minimal stimuli from which to differentiate. Nevertheless, Jeff's perceptual reasoning ability is a strength in his overall cognitive capabilities.

The Working Memory Index (WMI) measures an individual's ability to temporarily retain information in memory, perform an operation with it, and then produce a result. Jeff performed in the Average range on this composite, with no significant differences in the subtest scores. In general, Jeff performed well but seemed to have difficulty in maintaining strategies that would help him retain larger amounts of information that were given to him.

The Processing Speed Index (PSI) measures the ability to quickly and correctly scan, sequence, or discriminate simple visual information. Both of the tasks that constitute this measure are timed. Jeff performed in the Average range with no significant differences between the subtests that make up the PSI; however, Jeff was able to work more quickly when he was able to scan stimuli rather than reproduce symbols in a motoric manner.

Achievement Testing

The WJ III ACH is an individually administered standardized test of achievement. Jeff was administered the WJ III ACH and his scores are included in the following tables.

Woodcock-Johnson III NU Tests of Achievement (WJ III ACH)

Cluster	Standard Score	Age Equivalent	Grade Equivalent	Qualitative Description
Brief Achievement	74	10–5	5.1	Low
Broad Reading	75	10–11	5.5	Low
Broad Math	74	9–6	5.4	Low
Broad Written Language	81	9–11	6.4	Low Average
Math Calculation Skills	72	10–8	5.2	Low
Written Expression	88	12–11	7.5	Low Average
Academic Fluency	80	12–3	6.8	Low Average
Cluster Scores: Mean = 100, SD = 15				

Subtest	Standard Score	Age Estimate	Grade Estimate	Qualitative Description
Letter-Word Identification	71	10-0	4.7	Low
Reading Fluency	85	13-1	7.7	Low Average
Passage Comprehension	84	10-9	5.4	Low Average
Calculation	71	10-2	4.7	Low
Math Fluency	81	12-2	6.8	Low Average
Applied Problems	82	11-1	5.7	Low Average
Spelling	76	10-5	5.1	Low
Writing Fluency	84	11-5	6	Low Average
Writing Samples	92	16-6	11	Average

Test Scores: Mean = 100, SD = 15

Jeff's Brief Achievement score of 74 placed him in the Low range of academic functioning when compared to his same-age peers. His individual academic scores spanned from the Low to Low Average range with the exception of one Average score, which was in Written Expression. Jeff's performance on Broad Reading was in the Low range, which suggests that his performance is equivalent to that of a youth at the age of 10 years, 11 months or at fifth- to sixth-grade reading level. Such a score would suggest that Jeff is not proficient enough to benefit from grade-level instruction and material.

Jeff's Broad Math performance was in the Low range of functioning, which places his performance equivalent to that of a youth of 9 years, 6 months. Within the three tests that constitute Broad Math, Jeff performed best on Applied Problems, which focuses on real-life math problem-solving skills. Jeff's basic computational skills were a weakness but may be strengthened with tutoring to solidify the foundational rules of mathematics.

Jeff's Broad Written Language was in the Low Average range, which translates into writing skills at an age equivalent of 9 years, 11 months. Jeff's writing samples displayed poor spelling, incorrect use of punctuation, and minimal elaboration or expression of an idea.

In general, Jeff's academic scores reflect overall low achievement in reading, writing, and math in relation to his age peers. These scores may be the result of numerous factors. One factor that must be considered is that Jeff has a diagnosis of a learning disability in each of these areas. Second, school records indicate a high frequency of school transfers and absences, which can affect progress in fundamental academic skills. Third, the age/grade equivalent scores in all areas correlate positively to the time in which Jeff began to show conduct problems in his life. Fourth, the setting in which these tests were administered may have affected Jeff's true academic performance as described previously. Also, Jeff was preoccupied with meeting with his lawyer and was distracted by every person walking by. Last, Jeff has never been consistently enrolled in school so his instructional opportunities have been limited. With such a large number of extraneous factors potentially affecting Jeff's cognitive and academic profile, the obtained scores should be interpreted with caution.

Memory

Wechsler Memory Scale-Fourth Edition (WMS-IV)

Index	Index Score	Percentile Rank	95% Confidence Interval	Qualitative Description
Auditory Memory	96	37	89–101	Average
Visual Memory	106	70	102–113	Average
Visual Working Memory	95	34	87–102	Average
Immediate Memory	100	50	94–106	Average
Delayed Memory	102	66	99–112	Average

The Auditory Memory Index (AMI) is a measure of Jeff's ability to listen to oral information, repeat it immediately, and then recall the information after a 20- to 30-minute delay. Compared to other individuals his age, Jeff's auditory memory capacity is in the Average range.

On the Visual Memory Index (VMI), a measure of memory for visual details and spatial location, Jeff performed in the Average range (VMI = 106, 95% confidence interval = 102–113). Jeff's visual memory capacity exceeds that of approximately 70% of individuals in his age group and is a relative strength.

Compared to individuals with similar auditory memory capacity, Jeff's visual memory performance is in the High Average range (75th percentile), indicating no significant difference between his levels of visual and auditory memory functioning. Within immediate memory, Jeff exhibited a strength on the Visual Reproduction I subtest. He displayed a weakness on the Logical Memory I subtest. Logical Memory I required Jeff to recall specific details of information presented orally in a story format after only a single exposure. This subtest measures the ability to recall verbal information that is conceptually organized and semantically related immediately after hearing it.

On Visual Reproduction I, Jeff was required to view a series of designs and to draw each one from memory immediately after seeing it. This subtest measures recall for visual information, including the details and relative spatial relationship among elements of a drawing (Visual Reproduction I scaled score = 12). Within delayed memory, Jeff exhibited a strength on the Visual Reproduction II subtest.

Personality

Minnesota Multiphasic Personality Inventory-Adolescent Version (MMPI-A)

In regard to the validity of the test, Jeff responded to the items in a defensive manner and attempted to present himself in a favorable light. Thus, the findings suggest that the resulting MMPI-A may underestimate his present symptoms and overestimate his psychological adjustment. In this regard, the results suggest that Jeff appears to have little insight into any psychological difficulties that he may have, and may be reluctant to accept psychological explanations for his problems. He is not likely to seek psychological treatment for his problems and would not be very open to behavioral change if treatment were imposed on him.

His two highest MMPI-A clinical scales, Pd and Pa, which are clearly elevated above other scales, are the fourth most frequent well-defined two-point scale elevations among adolescents in psychiatric or alcohol/drug treatment units. His elevated score on the Disconstraint scale may indicate high risk-taking, impulsivity, and irresponsibility. Within the Psychopathic Deviate subscales, the Authority Problems scale was significantly elevated, which is consistent with Jeff's history of delinquency.

SUMMARY AND RECOMMENDATIONS

Jeff is a 17-year-old Caucasian male in the eleventh grade, attending school in a county correctional center. He was referred for a psychoeducational evaluation by the principal at the correctional center in order to evaluate his strengths and needs in terms of his cognitive, academic,

and emotional functioning as they apply to his current education and the planning of his transition back into the community. In this regard, Jeff was administered the WAIS-IV to determine his current level of cognitive and intellectual functioning. His Full-Scale IQ score of 93 indicated that he is functioning in the Average range. He also performed in the Average range on Perceptual Reasoning, Working Memory, and Processing Speed. In Verbal Comprehension, Jeff scored in the Low Average range, which may be a reflection of his absences in school or lack of enrollment in school, as well as his diagnosis of a learning disability.

Jeff's overall academic achievement indicated that he is performing in the Low to Low Average range across all academic areas. Such discrepancy between these scores and his cognitive scores may be a reflection of Jeff's learning disability, his frequent moves throughout his elementary years, his extended history of incarceration status, and his frequent absences.

On the personality assessment, Jeff's scores on the validity scale reflected a potential inhibition of his true scores. Jeff's profile represents an individual who has issues with authority and has great difficulty with trust. In general, Jeff sees himself in a positive light and may perceive many negative incidents in his life as the responsibility of others. Nevertheless, Jeff seems to be aware of his faults and has career goals that he wants to work toward.

It is also important to note that the conditions under which the testing occurred are considered to be outside of standardized procedures. Further, because Jeff is incarcerated, one should consider the impact that emotional stress he may be experiencing has on his test results.

RECOMMENDATIONS

Based on the present evaluation results, the following recommendations are made:

1. Provide academic instruction with visual and hands-on activities that is closer to the grade level at which Jeff is functioning successfully, rather than the grade in which he is enrolled.

2. Encourage individuals closest to Jeff to approach him in a positive and sensitive manner. Verbally reinforce him for positive behaviors. Maintaining a consistent, positive, and supportive environment is important for Jeff's emotional state and maturity. Also, focus on reinforcing positive behaviors rather than attending to negative behaviors.

3. Assign Jeff small jobs or responsibilities that make him feel important and needed in the pod, in the classroom context, or at work. These tasks should be clearly stated, and completion of such tasks should be rewarded with immediate verbal praise. Jeff must see "jobs" as genuine involvement, not as chores or punishment.

4. Those closest to Jeff can help him by verbally praising him ("Great job!"; "That looks terrific!") for his successes and accomplishments.

5. Place emphasis on Jeff's positive accomplishments. It might be beneficial for him to keep a daily record of his successes or accomplishments. This record could be written in a journal or discussed on a daily basis to reinforce his progress.

6. Teach Jeff positive coping statements to use when encountering difficult situations or experiencing failure (e.g., "Oh, I made a mistake. Next time I'll be more careful and try harder.")

7. Jeff may benefit from significant others and/or caregivers working with him to establish realistic goals and keep a record of goals that are accomplished. Emphasize realistic expectations.

8. Jeff should consider completing a career interest inventory to help guide him in his future educational and career endeavors. This testing should be arranged by his educational transition planning team. Career fields that would best fit Jeff's profile should include those that will allow him to work with his hands with job duties that are concrete, explicit, and concise. Since Jeff does well in the area of visuospatial/visuomotor reasoning, and has good auditory and memory skills, he should be encouraged to pursue tasks/jobs involving spatial reasoning.

9. Jeff may profit from counseling that would help him develop his interpersonal social skills, regain trust of others, and learn to identify and regulate his internal emotional states.

REFERENCES

Individuals with Disabilities Improvement Education Act of 2004. (2005). P.L. 108–446, §601, 118 Stat. 2647.

Morris, K., & Morris, R. J. (2006). Disability and juvenile delinquency: Issues and trends. *Disability and Society, 21*, 613–627.

Morris, R., & Thompson, K. (2008). Juvenile delinquency and special education laws: Policy implementation issues and directions for future research. *The Journal of Correctional Education, 59*, 173–190.

CASE 50

When the Child with Specific Learning Disabilities Grows Up

Nicole Ofiesh

Michael Skriverson's case is a good example of what can happen to a child with a specific learning disability (SLD) over time. He comes from a middle-class family who has done everything they can to understand and support his educational challenges. Three themes run through this report that are regularly seen among veteran educators, but that may be misunderstood by individuals new to the field. First, is the double-edged sword that occurs when individuals with SLD receive the intense, prescriptive intervention they need. Often, as in the case of Michael, the intensive tutoring diminishes the aptitude-achievement discrepancy and then the student does not qualify for special education services, even when processing problems are still apparent. Individuals who receive the type of help that Michael did at the William Arthur School often make significant gains in basic skills, but the automatic application of these skills is difficult to remediate in the face of the kinds of processing problems that are described in the report. Educators and clinicians must truly understand the strengths and limitations of the cognitive and academic tests that they administer and realize that even when a discrepancy does not exist, a child can still have significant difficulty acquiring information and applying acquired skills.

Related to this is the issue of the provision of test accommodations that are regularly granted under the Americans with Disabilities Act to individuals with SLD, based on the severity of their disability as portrayed in their diagnostic test profile. Michael's broad reading scores are in the Average to Low Average range. Does this mean that he is not impaired by his disability? To the contrary, when his broad reading scores are evaluated with respect to the amount of early intervention he has received, his cognitive processing scores, the individual tests on the WJ III ACH that make up the broad achievement scores (note the RPI scores), and

the results of the Nelson-Denny Reading Test (NDRT), a multipassage reading test, he is indeed impaired. A thorough analysis of this case clearly indicates that Michael is an individual with SLD that impacts his learning in a substantial manner. The differences noted between the WJ III ACH Reading Fluency and the NDRT also illustrate how important it is for evaluators to consider the differences in the demands of the tests they administer. The WJ III ACH Reading Fluency test is a 3-minute timed reading test with simple, short sentences. The NDRT requires much more sustained effort, and even though the timed reading portion is only one minute long, it requires the individual to move through a longer passage of text.

Moreover, there is a tendency for individuals new to the field to rely only on cluster scores for the final interpretation of skills; a practice that can mask the true nature of a child's learning abilities. This practice is usually supported because many school districts prefer to use these scores in a discrepancy formula. However, without a careful analysis of the tests that make up a cluster, students who need services can be mistakenly denied. Take, for example, Michael's WJ III ACH Reading Comprehension cluster, which is Low Average, but not Below Average according to the normal curve. This cluster is made up of the two tests, Reading Vocabulary and Passage Comprehension. Skilled clinicians understand that those two tests assess an individual's reading comprehension in very different ways. Both ways are important for academic success, and when a significant discrepancy is observed between two subtests that constitute a cluster, the clinician must consider: (a) the basis for that discrepancy, (b) how it will affect the individual, and (c) what can be done to support the individual. This aspect of the case is discussed in more detail in the report.

The third theme that runs through this case is that of the impact of early reading difficulties. Dr. Keith Stanovich used the term the "Matthew Effect" to refer to children who lost critical ground in the growth of their reading vocabulary simply because their reading disability prevented them from reading and learning new words. He noted that without the ongoing and constant exposure to print, these children would always be at a loss in terms of their breadth of vocabulary. In short, the more you read, the more words you learn; and the more you don't, the fewer you learn. This is exactly what has happened to Michael. Not only did his early difficulty with decoding impact his vocabulary, it hampered his ability to use language to support reading comprehension, math applications, and in short, his ability to reason using language.

EDUCATIONAL EVALUATION

Name:	Michael Skriverson
Date of Birth:	12/18/1992
Age:	17-4
Sex:	Male
Parents:	Mary Jane and Raymond Skriverson
School:	St. Nicholas Academy Teacher (Homeroom) Ms. Panos
Grade:	11.7
Date of Testing:	04/11/2010, 4/13/2010
Date of Report:	05/04/2010
Examiner:	Nicole Ofiesh, Ph.D.

REASON FOR REFERRAL

Michael was referred for an evaluation by the Academic Services Liaison at his school to update the achievement portion of his records. Michael attends St. Nicholas Academy, a private school, and receives accommodations through the PACE Program, which administers services and accommodations to students with learning disabilities.

BACKGROUND

Michael is a 17-year-old eleventh grader at St. Nicholas Academy who lives at home with both parents and his younger sister. English is the only language spoken in the home. Michael began to show difficulties with learning in kindergarten and first grade. He was diagnosed with a learning disability and received special education services in second and third grade at a local public school. He made minimal gains and was referred by his teacher to the William Arthur School, a private school for children with learning disabilities that emphasizes a multisensory approach to the language arts (i.e., Slingerland method). Michael entered William Arthur School in fourth grade and made considerable gains. By sixth grade, his parents considered placing him in another school, but he was no longer eligible for special education services in the public school when tested by the local school district. The school psychologist told his parents that the school's academic testing of Michael indicated average achievement scores in reading, writing, and math. Despite these scores, his parents and teachers continued to see evidence of the disability in terms of Michael's lack of automaticity in applying basic academic skills. As a result, his parents decided to keep Michael at the William Arthur School through eighth grade. While Michael was an eighth grader, thorough psychoeducational testing was conducted at this clinic and he was given a DSM diagnostic code of 315.9, Learning Disorder Not Otherwise Specified (related to executive functioning skills). After eighth grade, he and his parents decided Michael should attend St. Nicholas Academy because of the strong reputation of the PACE Program.

Mrs. Skriverson reported that Michael gets along well with others, including his sister and other adults, and is well liked at school. She noted that Michael's transition to St. Nicholas Academy went well and both parents report that he is doing fairly well there, as long as accommodations are in place. The most critical accommodation has been extended time on standardized and classroom tests, as well as reading and writing assignments. Without accommodations, though, they said the speed with which he can perform is noticeably deficient and he tends to fall behind academically. On the intake form, Mrs. Skriverson noted that Michael has trouble concentrating and staying on task and received a D in geometry.

Medical history is insignificant and, other than occasional ear infections, Michael is a healthy young man. Michael has a paternal family history of attentional problems and a maternal family history of dyslexia. His younger sister shows no signs of attention or learning problems.

Michael has a strong interest in athletics but currently does not participate in school sports so that he can place greater attention on his academic work. He has played football and taken karate in the past. He enjoys riding motorcycles and duck hunting.

TESTS ADMINISTERED

Woodcock-Johnson III NU Tests of Cognitive Ability (WJ III COG)

Woodcock-Johnson III NU Tests of Achievement (WJ III ACH)

Nelson-Denny Reading Test, Form G (NDRT)

TEST SESSION OBSERVATIONS

Michael's conversational proficiency seemed typical for his age level. He was exceptionally cooperative throughout the examinations; his activity level seemed typical for his age. He appeared at ease, comfortable, and attentive to the tasks. During administration of the WJ III COG and WJ III ACH, Michael responded slowly and carefully to test questions. Michael generally persisted with difficult tasks. Given his cooperation and motivation, the test results are considered to be a valid representation of his current skills in the areas tested.

SUMMARY OF ACADEMIC FUNCTIONING

The WJ III ACH evaluates academic performance in a variety of ways. These include the analysis of an individual's reading, writing, and math functioning in: (1) basic academic skills (i.e., reading words, calculating math, and spelling words), (2) application of those skills (i.e., comprehending written sentences, solving math word problems, and writing sentences) and, (3) the fluency with which he can apply basic skills (i.e., correct and timely processing of reading, math, and writing). Any breakdown in one or more of these areas impacts the other. Though not entirely discrete, basic skills are usually mastered in early elementary school, followed by the application of those basic skills to acquire breadth and depth of knowledge and think critically, with increasing proficiency in their fluent application. Overall, the findings suggest that while Michael's performance in basic skills and the application of those skills ranges from Low to Average, the cognitive processing problems that interfered with his early mastery of basic academic skills still persist. Because of intensive intervention, the residual evidence of his learning disability now manifests in terms of his slow speed in the application of the basic academic skill. Math calculation

skills are still very low. The basic disorder that appears to interfere with Michael's problems in reading, writing, and math seems to be orthographic in nature and associated with the automatic interpretation of abstract symbols (i.e., letters and numbers and their associated meanings). This can be seen on the four WJ III COG Processing Speed tests (Visual Matching, Decision Speed, Rapid Picture Naming, and Pair Cancellation). All were Below to Low Average compared to age peers. Additional evidence of orthographic problems was noted through an analysis of Michael's spelling errors. The following discussion details Michael's performance in reading, writing, and math and how this disorder impacts these areas.

Reading

On the Letter-Word Identification test, Michael was required to read a list of words of increasing difficulty without context. He demonstrated good mastery of sight vocabulary and was able to read words such as "proficient" and "pneumonia." He had difficulty with and missed longer multisyllabic words such as "serendipitous," "heterogeneous," "cotillion," and "perseverance." On the Word Attack test, which measures Michael's ability to apply structural analysis, phonics, and knowledge of word patterns in order to read unknown words, he performed similarly. These tests constitute Michael's Basic Reading Skills, which were Average. This means that Michael has an average sight vocabulary compared to age peers and has also learned strategies to pronounce unfamiliar words.

Michael's ability to apply these basic skills and comprehend what he reads was measured by the Passage Comprehension and Reading Vocabulary tests. While performance on the Passage Comprehension test was Average, indicating that Michael can use contextual cues to supply missing words, his performance on Reading Vocabulary was noticeably discrepant with all other reading tests, placing him in the Low Average range. Careful consideration of the Relative Proficiency Index (RPI) helps to illustrate Michael's level of difficulty with reading vocabulary. When Michael's peers perform with 90% success on tasks that require a good fund of vocabulary, he can be expected to perform with 52% success. Achievement on the Reading Vocabulary test is related to basic reading skills; therefore, his achievement in this area is noteworthy. Low performance in this area could be a function of limited basic reading skills (which he struggled with in elementary school), limited word comprehension, or both. In contrast, on the Passage Comprehension test, his RPI was 90/90.

While this is an important reading comprehension skill, this average proficiency does not guarantee that Michael will be able to succeed with reading material that is new or nonroutine—exactly the type of reading material he will encounter in high school and college.

Because Michael also showed substantial difficulty with appropriate word choice on the Writing Samples subtest (see writing section below) and the Quantitative Concepts test, it appears that part of the manifestation of his disability is difficulty with word comprehension. It is likely that this is a direct result of his early problems learning to read. In other words, during the time typical readers would be increasing their word knowledge, Michael was still learning to identify words. Evidence of this early struggle to read can still be observed on his performance on the Rapid Picture Naming test, as efficient lexical access is a strong predictor of early reading ability. On this test, Michael scored below the 1st percentile.

Testing indicates that Michael's reading fluency is in the Low Average range, which reflects his lack of automaticity with word reading. While he can read and comprehend, it takes him longer than his peers. Moreover, the WJ III ACH Reading Fluency test measures the fluent reading and comprehension of very simple sentences, which do not match the level of multisyllabic words and syntactic complexity that he encounters in high school level texts. More advanced reading is measured by the NDRT. On this test, Michael's overall performance ranged from the 1st to 8th percentile on all subtests, including Reading Rate. Thus, Michael's overall reading scores suggest that he has learned strategies to identify words and comprehend what he reads; however, he does not read "automatically" or fluently. This characteristic of his reading problem is typically seen in older students with reading-based learning disabilities who have received intensive intervention. This situation is not uncommon and speaks to his parents' observations that Michael does fairly well in school as long as accommodations are in place.

Writing

Michael's basic writing skills in terms of spelling and sentence formation are Low Average to Average. On the Spelling test, he was able to spell complex, multisyllabic words but missed words that were clearly age and grade appropriate, such as *organization*, which he spelled *orginizaesion*. His errors suggested that his phonological skills are intact, as nearly all attempts were phonetically correct. For example, he spelled *hokes* for *hoax*, *bazar* for *bizarre*,

leejin for *legion*, and *unasumean* for *unassuming*. These errors suggest good phonological abilities but difficulty with orthographic processing. Additionally, on many sentences in the Writing Fluency and Writing Samples tests, Michael had incorrect or missing punctuation, including periods. All of these characteristics indicate that writing is not an automatic or consistent process for Michael. His writing fluency was lower than his skills and application. Based on the RPI, when Michael's peers perform with 90% success in fluent writing, he can be expected to show only 66% success.

Math

Michael's academic functioning in math indicates that he still struggles with the basic skills associated with math (i.e., calculation, quick fact retrieval), but his overall intellectual ability has enabled him to apply concepts slightly beyond his basic skills. However, this struggle slows the process of applying these skills. In fact, there was a statistically significant discrepancy between his ability to apply math skills and the speed with which he can calculate. This pattern of low skills, slightly higher application, and very low fluency parallels the pattern seen across both reading and writing. Noteworthy is his Low Average performance on the Quantitative Concepts test, as it speaks to the challenges that were noted on the Reading Vocabulary test. Low performance on the Quantitative Concepts test is often seen as a function of limited vocabulary and insufficient concept development, or both, because the test taker must use conceptual language to help solve math problems rather than simply calculate an algorithm or apply a calculation to a word problem. Limited vocabulary and insufficient concept development can be a direct result of early reading problems.

SUMMARY

Overall, the findings suggest that Michael's academic performance and related learning processes indicate a learning disability that now manifests itself in the inefficient application of basic skills. Math calculation skills are still very low. The results of this testing indicate cognitive processing problems that persist and seem to be associated with the nonautomatic and dysfluent interpretation of abstract symbols (i.e., letters and numbers and their associated meanings). Despite the fact that his basic skills in reading, writing, and math are in the Low

Average to Average range, it is an arduous process for Michael to apply these skills to acquire new knowledge, build on existing knowledge, and demonstrate newly learned information. He has developed excellent strategies, to his own credit and to the credit of his teachers, and due to his parents' tenacity in finding an educational setting that can capitalize on his strengths and teach him effective learning strategies. Accommodations and a thoughtful analysis of available postsecondary settings will remain an important aspect of Michael's future educational planning.

RECOMMENDATIONS

The following recommendations are suggested:

1. Continue enrollment in the PACE program in order to receive test and instructional accommodations and specialized learning strategies.

2. Provide extended time on all standardized exams at approximately 2.0 times the standard administration (speeded tests ranged from below the 1st percentile to the 19th percentile).

3. Provide a basic four-function calculator as an accommodation on all tests that involve math and do not measure basic calculation skills.

4. Allow use of a spell-checker as an accommodation on all classroom and standardized tests where spelling is not the construct being measured.

5. Have all textbooks placed on a recorded audio device. These can be accessed via your educational institution through Recordings for the Blind and Dyslexic (www.rfbd.org).

6. Consider instruction in textbook comprehension through mapping programs such as Inspiration (www.inspiration.com), SQ4R, and similar strategies.

7. Have Michael confer with this education specialist to develop a clear understanding of his strengths and weaknesses and how they impact his processing of information. This is important in order for him to begin to self-advocate for the required accommodations that he will need in the future.

8. Michael should begin to consider postsecondary programs that offer strong support programs for students with SLD. The guidance counselor at St. Nicholas

Academy will help with transition planning. A good resource to consult would be *Peterson's Colleges for Students with Learning Disabilities or AD/HD.*

TABLE OF SCORES

Woodcock-Johnson III NU Tests of Cognitive Abilities and Tests of Achievement (Form A) Normative Update WJ III NU Compuscore and Profiles Program, Version 3.0

Norms based on age 17-4

CLUSTER/Test	PR (68% Band)	SS	RPI
COG EFFICIENCY (Std)	34 (23–46)	94	83/90
PROCESS SPEED (Gs)	9 (5–14)	79	69/90
COGNITIVE FLUENCY	1 (1–2)	67	59/90
BRIEF ACHIEVEMENT	38 (32–44)	95	83/90
TOTAL ACHIEVEMENT	29 (25–33)	92	81/90
BROAD READING	41 (35–48)	97	86/90
BROAD MATH	24 (18–30)	89	77/90
BROAD WRITTEN LANG	25 (18–33)	90	78/90
BRIEF READING	42 (34–50)	97	86/90
BASIC READING SKILLS	37 (30–45)	95	82/90
READING COMP	22 (15–30)	88	75/90
BRIEF MATH	32 (24–41)	93	80/90
MATH CALC SKILLS	14 (9–21)	84	71/90
MATH REASONING	27 (20–34)	91	73/90
BRIEF WRITING	33 (24–43)	94	83/90
WRITTEN EXPRESSION	21 (13–31)	88	75/90
ACADEMIC SKILLS	31 (25–38)	93	79/90
ACADEMIC FLUENCY	18 (13–24)	86	75/90
ACADEMIC APPS	39 (31–49)	96	86/90

Woodcock-Johnson III NU Tests of Cognitive Abilities

CLUSTER/Test	PR (68% Band)	SS	RPI
Visual Matching	10 (5–19)	81	66/90
Numbers Reversed	55 (43–66)	102	92/90
Incomplete Words	62 (45–78)	105	93/90
Retrieval Fluency	53 (39–67)	101	90/90
Decision Speed	11 (6–20)	82	72/90
Rapid Picture Naming	<1 (<1 – <1)	59	11/90
Pair Cancellation	13 (10–16)	83	53/90

Woodcock-Johnson III NU Tests of Achievement

CLUSTER/Test	PR (68% Band)	SS	RPI
Letter-Word Identification	39 (31–47)	96	81/90
Reading Fluency	42 (34–51)	97	86/90
Calculation	26 (16–38)	90	74/90
Math Fluency	7 (5–10)	78	69/90
Spelling	38 (28–48)	95	83/90
Writing Fluency	17 (9–28)	86	66/90
Passage Comprehension	49 (35–63)	100	90/90
Applied Problems	44 (36–52)	98	85/90
Writing Samples	33 (21–48)	94	83/90
Word Attack	40 (31–50)	96	83/90
Picture Vocabulary	49 (39–60)	100	90/90
Reading Vocabulary	14 (10–20)	84	52/90
Quantitative Concepts	14 (8–23)	84	55/90

Nelson-Denny Reading Test: Form G/Grade 11: Spring Norms	Percentile Rank	Grade Equivalent
Vocabulary	8	6.9
Comprehension	2	4.1
Total Test	3	4.5
Reading Rate	1	–

CASE 51

A Comprehensive Evaluation of a High-Functioning Secondary Student with Dyslexia

Chris Coleman

This report, while largely straightforward, raises certain issues that may be of interest to school psychology students, diagnosticians, and other practitioners. First, it uses a diagnostic model for learning disabilities that requires evidence not only of significant underachievement, but also of cognitive processing deficits that plausibly explain the underachievement. Second, it reflects a comprehensive approach to assessment in which an extensive battery of cognitive, language, achievement, and social-emotional measures is administered regardless of the referral question. Third, the report provides an example of a score profile generated by a high-functioning adolescent with learning disabilities—a profile in which the extent of underachievement may be masked by several factors, including: (1) compensatory abilities/strategies, (2) the trend of regression to the mean with repeated testing, and (3) the fact that cognitive processing deficits can impact ability scores as well as academic skills. Finally, this report describes a certain subtype of reading disability that is sometimes referred to as double-deficit dyslexia.

COMPREHENSIVE EVALUATION

Name:	Ella Perin
Date of Birth:	12/18/1992
Age:	17-9
School:	Newton Graham High School
Dates of Evaluation:	9/18/ and 9/20/2010
Evaluator:	Chris Coleman, M.A.

DIAGNOSTIC SUMMARY AND RECOMMENDATIONS

Sources of Information

Clinical interview; client self-report questionnaires; parent questionnaire; consultation with/letters from Doris Perin (mother); transcript from high school (2010); psychoeducational reports from Terra Firma Unified School District (1998, 2002); IEP documentation (1998–2009); Iowa Test scores (1998); PSAT scores (2007); submitted writing samples; and tests administered.

Tests Administered

Beck Anxiety Inventory (BAI)
Beck Depression Inventory (BDI)
Delis-Kaplan Executive Function System (D-KEFS)
Gray Oral Reading Test-Fourth Edition (GORT-4)
Peabody Picture Vocabulary Test, Fourth Edition (PPVT-4)
Rey Complex Figure Test and Recognition Trial (RCFT)
Wechsler Adult Intelligence Scale-Fourth Edition (WAIS-VI)
Wechsler Memory Scale-Third Edition (WMS-III)
Woodcock-Johnson III NU Tests of Achievement (WJ III AC)
Woodcock-Johnson III NU Tests of Cognitive Abilities (WJ III COG)

Diagnosis

Learning Disabilities
(*DSM-IV* Reading Disorder [315.00], Disorder of Written Expression [315.2])

544

Strengths

Ella exhibited cognitive strengths in the following areas:

- Verbal abilities: including verbal reasoning, listening comprehension, vocabulary, and word fluency
- Learning and memory: the ability to encode and retain verbal or visual information)
- Pragmatics: social awareness and the ability to establish and maintain good interpersonal relationships

Academic strengths included reading comprehension, although decoding problems significantly affected her speed on reading tasks.

Deficits

Ella demonstrated cognitive and linguistic deficits in the following areas:

- Phonemic awareness: the ability to identify language sounds and distorted words, as well as the ability to repeat, retain, and manipulate made-up words
- Orthographic awareness: speed and accuracy in matching printed numbers/letters, sensitivity to the details of printed words, and retention of spelling patterns
- Working memory: the ability to mentally hold and manipulate pieces of information
- Visual-spatial/constructional abilities: perception and analysis of shapes, angles, etc., as well as construction of designs/patterns, such as arranging blocks or drawing

These deficits contribute to academic underachievement in reading (decoding and functional rate), as well as aspects of written expression (spelling and proofreading).

SUMMARY OF RESULTS

Reason for Referral

Ella is currently starting her senior year at Newton Graham High School. She has a well-documented history of learning disabilities impacting literacy skills (e.g., 2 years of pre-kindergarten speech therapy, continuing difficulty with basic aspects of reading and writing). Through most of her academic career, she has been eligible for special education services including tutoring and accommodations (e.g., extra time for exams/projects, no penalty for spelling errors). She has been a conscientious student who has always tried to compensate for her learning difficulties. Ella has done well in high school (weighted GPA = 4.10) and would like to help others by becoming a special education teacher.

The primary purpose of this report is to establish whether or not Ella is eligible for academic accommodations for disabilities, as allowed by the Georgia Board of Regents and in accordance with Regents' guidelines for diagnosing learning disorders. A secondary purpose is to aid Ella in understanding her cognitive and language functioning and her academic performance. The report begins with a summary of findings, a list of suggested accommodations that would be appropriate in current and future courses as well as on high-stakes tests such as state graduation exams, and a list of general recommendations. Pertinent background information follows. A psychometric summary (a list of all tests and Ella's scores) can be found at the end of this report.

Diagnostic Findings

The results of the evaluation supported a continued diagnosis of learning disabilities as defined by the Georgia Board of Regents (evidence of both underachievement and associated processing deficits). Ella's pattern of difficulties, which includes underachievement in literacy skills, is commonly referred to as dyslexia. The *DSM-IV* codes to describe her learning disabilities would be 315.00 (Reading Disorder) and 315.2 (Disorder of Written Expression). Ella does not meet the diagnostic criteria for ADHD (neither she nor her mother endorsed any *DSM-IV* symptoms as being significant in the past year) or any other psychological disorder.

Behavioral Observations

Ella's evaluation was conducted at the Regents' Center for Learning Disorders (RCLD) at the University of Georgia on September 18 and 20. On both occasions, she appeared healthy and comfortably dressed. Ella made eye contact with clinicians, answered all questions asked of her, participated pleasantly in conversations, and maintained polite and friendly interactions with others. On occasion, she made self-deprecating comments (e.g., "I have a bad memory"), but they did not suggest that she is overly harsh toward or critical of herself. Clinicians enjoyed working with Ella and appreciated her positive attitude, sense of humor, considerate nature, strong work ethic, and persistence on challenging tasks.

Ella was administered the Beck Depression Inventory (BDI-II) and the Beck Anxiety Inventory (BAI). Her responses indicated that she was experiencing minimal symptoms of depressed mood and mild symptoms of anxiety during the days leading up to and including the full day of testing. Some of the items she endorsed were related to asthma and fatigue. She also noted that she has some important decisions to make about the future; in addition to applying to several colleges, she was just offered a full-time position in her church for the coming year. Behaviorally, nothing in Ella's deportment suggested that she was in emotional distress. She presented as a resilient, mature, and modest young woman with a clever sense of humor and excellent interpersonal skills.

Strengths

On the WAIS-IV, Ella's performance yielded an estimated ability score in the Average to High Average range (General Ability Index [GAI] = 68th percentile; confidence interval [CI] = 58th–77th percentile). Due to the nature of her learning disabilities (which affected scores on several WAIS-IV subtests), that score likely represents a low estimate of her intellectual ability. Relative to the GAI, Ella exhibited the following impressive strengths:

- Verbal abilities: Ella's scores were generally above average on tests of verbal reasoning (WAIS-IV Similarities = 95th percentile; Comprehension = 99th percentile), listening comprehension (WJ III ACH Listening Comprehension Cluster = 74th percentile; Memory for Sentences = 90th percentile), vocabulary (PPVT-4 = 91st percentile), and word fluency (D-KEFS Category Fluency = 95th percentile; WJ III COG Rapid Picture Naming = 95th percentile). Strong verbal abilities may well be the best asset a college student can possess.
- Learning and memory: On the WMS-III, Ella demonstrated superior ability to learn and retain new information (General Memory Index = 93rd percentile). She did well with various types of information (i.e., verbal or visual) and formats (e.g., associative and contextual). The only memory task on which she struggled was visual-spatial/constructional in nature (RCFT, Immediate Recall = 4th percentile; discussed further below).
- Pragmatics: Ella's social awareness, interpersonal skills, poise, and maturity were well beyond what would typically be expected of a high school senior. In addition to being considerate and articulate, she was able to weather frustration and discuss sensitive topics (e.g., learning problems) with grace and humor.

Academically, Ella had a relative strength in reading comprehension (GORT-4 Comprehension = 75th percentile). Ella's performance was particularly impressive given the fact that she demonstrated what has been referred to as "double-deficit" dyslexia (i.e., problems with both the visual and auditory abilities that underlie literacy). Despite her compensatory efforts on certain reading measures, it should not be inferred that she is not entitled to accommodations on reading comprehension tasks, as her decoding and functional reading rate scores were well below expectations.

Cognitive Deficits

Some individuals with learning disabilities demonstrate difficulty processing auditory information; others demonstrate difficulty processing certain types of visual information. Ella performed well below expectations in sub-areas of both modalities. The cognitive/linguistic deficits below are listed in order of probable effect on academic skills and school performance:

- Phonological awareness: Ella demonstrated age-appropriate abilities on certain low-level phonological awareness tasks (i.e., rhyming and syllabication). However, she performed below expectations on several tests of phonemic awareness requiring auditory discrimination, identification of slightly distorted words, and repetition/manipulation of made-up words (e.g., WJ III COG Sound Blending = 35th percentile; Phonological Segmentation z-score = -1.5). Qualitative evidence of her compromised ability to "hear sounds right" was also noted on tasks designed to measure other abilities (e.g., misperceiving words and letters spoken in isolation). Deficits in phonology often cause literacy problems, particularly with regard to spelling-sound correspondences (WJ III ACH Phoneme/Grapheme Knowledge cluster = 15th percentile).
- Orthographic awareness: Across clerical scanning tasks (i.e., looking at rows of stimuli and circling the two matching items in each row as quickly as possible), there was a notable difference between Ella's speed and accuracy with pictures (e.g., WAIS-IV Symbol Search = 50th percentile) and printed numbers/letters (e.g., WJ III COG Visual Matching = 13th percentile). Her performance on the Colorado Perceptual Speed Task (e.g., xqpx: xqqx xqpk xqpx xpqx) was well below average on all three trials (z = -2, -1.5, -6). Notably, she was no faster with pronounceable clusters (e.g., *klaf*) than unpronounceable ones. Individuals demonstrating this pattern usually

possess poor processing of the details of printed words, resulting in spelling and decoding underachievement.

- Working memory: Ella performed below expectations on tests of her ability to mentally hold and manipulate multiple pieces of information (e.g., WAIS-IV Working Memory Index = 30th percentile). For example, she was unable to consistently repeat more than three numbers in a reverse order. Working memory problems can affect performance on complex tasks such as reading comprehension and written expression.
- Visual-spatial/constructional abilities: Ella's perception and analysis of visual-spatial information, as well as her construction of designs/patterns, were areas of weakness (e.g., WAIS-IV Block Design = 25th percentile; Figure Weights = 9th percentile). This weakness may help explain her dislike of geometry and possibly her reported tendency to be "clumsy." It also seemed to limit her ability to reproduce (from memory) a complex geometric figure she had copied a few minutes before (RCFT Immediate Recall = 4th percentile).

Effects of Learning Disabilities

The above deficits have resulted in underachievement (25 or more standard score points below her estimated verbal ability) in the following areas:

- Reading decoding: Ella's decoding skills were below expectations with both real words (e.g., GORT-4 Accuracy = 9th percentile; WJ III ACH Letter-Word Identification = 27th percentile) and pseudowords (WJ III ACH Word Attack = 6th percentile).
- Functional reading rate: Although Ella tries to compensate for decoding problems by skipping words she does not recognize, her speed was compromised on an oral reading measure (GORT-4 Rate = 25th percentile). She made numerous mistakes, even on passages featuring common words and basic sentence structures.
- Spelling: Ella's spelling skills were below expectations with both real words and pseudowords (WJ III ACH Spelling = 22nd percentile; Spelling of Sounds = 36th percentile).
- Proofreading: Ella had great difficulty identifying and correcting errors in typewritten sentences (WJ III ACH Editing = 8th percentile). Additionally, her spontaneous writing contained frequent mistakes related to spelling and word usage (e.g., *Immigrants comming to America do not always speak English.; It has been debated by many government officals weather or not this diverse*

systeme…should continue.). These errors sometimes affected the clarity and persuasiveness of her arguments.

Other Areas Assessed

In addition to the strengths and weaknesses described above, Ella demonstrated intact abilities in the following areas:

- Psychomotor speed: efficiency on clerical tasks such as scanning rows of pictures and circling a certain sequence of pictures in each row.
- Nonverbal reasoning: the ability to make logical inferences based on visual information (e.g., predicting the next shape in an abstract sequence of shapes).
- Executive functions: cognitive "self-management" abilities such as sustained attention, organization, planning, and self-monitoring.
- Higher-level written expression skills: ideation, argumentation, cohesion, and organization in writing.
- Math skills: proficiency on calculation and math reasoning tasks.

The results of this evaluation suggest that although learning disabilities will slow her progress, Ella has the intellectual ability, positive attitude, and persistence to succeed in college. She is encouraged to use all the resources available to her (see the accommodations and recommendations below) in order to obtain equal access to classroom information, implement supplementary learning strategies (including the use of assistive technologies), and make the most of her education. It was a pleasure to work with Ella.

SPECIFIC ACCOMMODATIONS

1. The following modifications would be appropriate to assist Ella in her current and future courses. Unless otherwise specified, the reasons for each modification are indicated by the following abbreviations: PHON = phonemic awareness deficit; OA = orthographic awareness deficit; WM = working memory deficit; and VS = visual-spatial/constructional deficit.
   - Extended time (1.5x) for all tests (PHON, OA, WM, VS)
   - Speech-to-text technology for tests requiring written responses (i.e., fill-in-the-blank, short-answer, and/or essay) (PHON, OA)

- Use of a word-processor with a spell-checking program (PHON, OA)
- Use of a hand-held electronic spell checker or spelling dictionary (PHON, OA)
- During tests, access to a reader and/or proofreader (PHON, OA, WM)
- Permission to use a calculator (OA, WM)
- Permission to use an instructor-approved word bank during tests (PHON, OA)
- Permission to write directly on tests; proctor should transfer responses to scantron form (VS)
- Written instructions for all assignments/tests (PHON, WM)
- Use of a note taker and/or tape recorder during lectures (PHON, OA, WM)
- Seating in front of classroom (PHON, VS)
- Exemption from reading aloud in class (PHON, OA)
- Access to textbooks and other required readings in alternative formats (e.g., audiotape, CD, access to scan-and-read computer programs) (PHON, OA)
- Waiver of foreign language requirement (PHON, WM, OA)
- Priority registration (due to the combination of deficits)
- Up to two (2) additional semesters in Developmental Studies if needed (PHON, OA, WM, VS)

2. It is recommended that Ella request the following modifications when she sits for standardized tests, such as the ACT or SAT:
- Extended time (1.5x) for all portions of the exam
- Use of a word-processor and spell-checking program/tool for written portions
- Test administrator/proctor to read her prose aloud exactly as written while she makes corrections to it
- Proctor to transfer answers to scantron form

GENERAL RECOMMENDATIONS

1. It is recommended that Ella work with her college service provider on class selection, optimal use of accommodations, and exploration of assistive technologies. (Also see next recommendation.)
2. Ella should explore assistive technologies that might reduce the difficulty of tasks such as reading and writing

(e.g., word prediction and dictation programs, hand-held spelling tools, and text-to-speech software). She may wish to consult with Tools for Life (http://www.gatfl.org), a nonprofit organization in Atlanta that provides personalized advice about available technologies.

3. Ella may want to obtain a free membership to Recordings for the Blind and Dyslexic (RFB&D), a nonprofit organization that offers thousands of book titles on tape/CD. To find out more, she can call RFB&D's toll-free number (1-800-221-4792) or visit their web site (http://www.rfbd.org). Note: This would be a student membership to access audiobooks for pleasure reading; it will be the responsibility of Ella's college to purchase an institutional RFB&D membership in order to provide course textbooks and other required readings in alternative formats.

BACKGROUND INFORMATION

Family/Social History

Ella has been raised in the Atlanta area. She resides with her parents, Frank and Doris Perin. Frank is a college graduate who works as a business manager; Doris is a law school graduate who works as an attorney. Ella has an older sister (Emma, 19, a college sophomore at George Washington University) and a fraternal twin sister, Rosa. Rosa has learning disabilities that are similar to Ella's; no one else in the immediate family has experienced learning difficulties. The family history was reportedly negative for mental health disorders, seizure disorders, and chronic illnesses. Socially, Ella reported good relations with her family and with friends. She is well-liked at school, active in her church, and popular with those she knows through volunteer and religious programs. Ella also leads a group that puts on puppet shows for children.

Birth/Developmental/Medical History

Mrs. Perin reported that there were no difficulties for her 38-week pregnancy with Ella and Rosa, although she was not expecting twins. No delivery or perinatal complications were noted, and Ella was the heavier of the two girls (6 lbs., 4 oz.; Apgar = 8). Regarding developmental milestones, Ella sat alone at 6 months of age, said her first word at 11 months, and walked alone at 14 months. Because her early speech was difficult to understand (she "dropped middle and final consonants," "her sister was her translator"), Ella received 2 years of pre-K speech therapy. Ella reported that she experienced feelings of low mood and anxiousness during 8th grade (a taxing year academically), but that she is "usually pretty positive."

Childhood illnesses included chicken pox and pneumonia. A prior report noted that Ella experienced medical problems related to Epstein-Barr virus (2000), which led to asthma and allergies that have persisted into adolescence. She noted that while the allergies have diminished, the asthma has gotten worse. She is currently prescribed steroids and although she does not often need to use her inhaler, she finds that it is generally "harder to breathe" than when she was younger. Due to frequent migraines, Ella participated in an MRI scan (date unspecified; normal results). She continues to get headaches and has noticed that they seem related to light and reading. Ella denied any history of seizures, hospitalizations, blows to the head, loss of consciousness, or other cognitive risk factors. In a letter, Mrs. Perin reported that Ella's vision and hearing screenings have always been normal; she wears glasses to improve her distance vision. Ella denied use of tobacco, alcohol, or other recreational drugs. She drinks caffeinated sodas on occasion.

Psychiatric/Psychological Treatment History

Ella has never participated in therapy or counseling.

Previous Testing

The Perins noticed Ella's learning problems very early, as she received 2 years of speech therapy before starting kindergarten. To confirm continued eligibility for special education services, she has participated in testing regularly throughout her compulsory schooling. Two full reports were available.

In December 1999, Ella (who was nearly 7) participated in an evaluation with Dr. Randall Pierce, NCSP, of Clayton County Schools. Dr. Pierce administered the WISC-III (Verbal Comprehension = SS 122, Perceptual Organization = SS 113, Freedom From Distractibility = SS 96, Processing Speed = SS 99, Full-Scale IQ = SS 114), the Draw-A-Person Test (SS 92), and the Wepman Auditory Discrimination Test (16th percentile). Ella's achievement was assessed through several measures. Oral expression, listening comprehension, math calculation, and math reasoning skills were found to be "adequate." Ella's scores were well below expectations in basic reading (WRAT-R = SS 72; PIAT-R = SS 86), reading comprehension (PIAT-R = SS 82), and spelling (WRAT-3 = SS 78; PIAT-R = SS 82). These low

scores were attributed to "... a pattern of specific processing deficits in visual-spatial, auditory discrimination, and symbolic-sequential memory skills. Test results also suggest a pattern of weak attention/concentration which is an impediment to cognitive processing." Although an anxiety screener revealed no clinical problems (RCMAS = 14th percentile), Ella "...acknowledged feeling some academic pressure, sensitivity, and physiological concerns which may place her at risk for future problems." Access to special education services was recommended.

In April 2007, Ella participated in a triennial reevaluation with Dr. Sheryl K. Posner, Ed.S., of John Henry County Schools. Dr. Posner administered: the DAS (Verbal Ability = SS 134, Nonverbal Reasoning Ability = SS 86, Spatial Ability = SS 87, General Conceptual Ability = SS 103), the Draw-A-Person Test (standard score not provided, but described as "significantly lower" than expectations), and the VMI (SS 86). Regarding academic skills, Ella's standard scores on the WJ III Achievement tests were as follows: Letter-Word Identification = 89; Passage Comprehension = 98; Calculation = 99; Applied Problems = 110; Spelling = 73; Writing Samples = 113. Dr. Posner concluded that a specific learning disability was still apparent. It was also noted that "social/emotional indicators were not evident at this time."

Academic History

Ella has always attended public schools in the Atlanta area. In elementary school, she had difficulty spelling, reading, telling time, reading measurements, learning the sounds of letters, and writing in cursive. In high school, she has struggled primarily with algebra (learning formulas) and spelling. After 3 years in special education classes, Ella was transitioned to general education classes but continued to receive tutoring and specific accommodations (i.e., extended time on tests/projects and no penalties for spelling errors). In high school, she has taken honors/AP classes in some subjects (particularly English and science) and has earned all As and Bs (weighted GPA = 4.10). She is on schedule to graduate in 2011 and is in the process of applying to several colleges.

Academic Skills

Ella was asked to describe her academic skills. She explained that she continues to have trouble with spelling but generally does well in higher-level aspects of written expression (e.g., organizing ideas and developing an argument). Her spelling errors are usually sufficiently phonetic that a computer spell-check will suggest the correct word.

Regarding reading, Ella still needs to reread sentences or passages at times in order to understand them or because she has inadvertently skipped a line. She feels that her comprehension and retention are good, her reading rate is "about the same as my friends," and her decoding is not as problematic as it used to be. Interestingly, she sometimes makes mistakes when reading sheet music (she plays the clarinet in the school band) and is much more effective at playing tunes from memory. (She said that she is better with music sounds than language sounds.) Regarding math, Ella reported a tendency to make "simple mistakes" (e.g., 2 × 3 = 5) even though she knows most of the multiplication tables and has intact calculation skills ("I actually like fractions"). She noted that some higher-level concepts are "hard at first," but that she is typically able to catch up. Ella disliked Spanish classes, which she took for two years. She described the situation as "a shame—I always wanted to learn Spanish" but she found the aural aspects were too difficult. Ella could not hear the differences between similar-sounding words, could not spell or use word endings effectively, and could not speak very well. She noted that even when conversing in English, she does not "hear sounds right" and sometimes has to ask people to repeat things. Across most subjects, Ella reports that she "tests badly" (partly due to nervousness) and sometimes she needs extra time on tests.

Current Symptoms

Ella described herself as a positive and spiritual person and denied difficulties related to mood, concentration, memory, or social relationships. She also denied problems with sleep (4 to 5 hours per night during the week, more on weekends), although she has started to have nightmares during the past year (e.g., in a recent dream, her sister's hip was broken). Regarding health, the combination of asthma and Ella's busy schedule means that she "gets tired a lot." She also noted with humor that, like her mother and sister, she is "incredibly klutzy" (e.g., re-breaking an ankle during marching band practice). Regarding college, she wrote, "I don't believ [sic] I'll need much help in collage [sic] besides an occassional [sic] time extension."

Goals/Interests

Ella plans to become a special education teacher in an elementary school. In addition to working hard academically, she participates in student government (class president), church events, youth groups, and children's groups. (As noted earlier, she organizes and puts on puppet shows.)

Ella also enjoys reading articles on the Internet. When asked to describe her strengths, she wrote the following: "I have always been very good at compensating for my disabilities. Also, I've got good social skills so I've got friends who are willing to help me in my work."

PSYCHOLOGICAL AND EDUCATIONAL INSTRUMENT SUMMARY

Unless otherwise indicated, Standard Scores (SS) have a mean of 100 and standard deviation of 15; WAIS-IV, WMS-III, and D-KEFS subscales (ScS) have a mean of 10 and standard deviation of 3; T scores have a mean of 50 and standard deviation of 10. On the WAIS-IV, WMS-III, and WJ III, 90% confidence intervals were used.

Cognitive Processing

	SS (ScS)	Percentile	Conf Band
WAIS-IV Indexes			
Verbal Comprehension	122	93	86–96
Perceptual Reasoning	92	30	20–45
Working Memory	92	30	20–45
Processing Speed	92	30	18–50
Full Scale Intelligence Quotient	101	53	45–61
General Ability Index	107	68	58–77
WAIS-VI Subtests			
Block Design	(8)	25	
Similarities	(15)	95	
Digit Span	(9)	37	
Matrix Reasoning	(10)	50	
Vocabulary	(14)	91	
Arithmetic	(8)	25	
Symbol Search	(10)	50	
Visual Puzzles	(8)	25	
Information	(13)	84	
Coding	(7)	16	
Figure Weights	(6)	9	
Comprehension	(17)	99	

WJ III COG Clusters			
Verbal Ability	104	61	42–79
Thinking Ability	92	30	21–40

	SS (ScS)	Percentile	Conf Band
Cognitive Efficiency	80	9	4–18
Auditory Processing (Ga)	97	41	23–61
Fluid Reasoning (Gf)	91	27	18–40
Processing Speed (Gs)	88	21	13–32
Visualization	98	46	25–66
WJ III COG Tests			
1. Verbal Comprehension	104	61	
2. Visual-Auditory Learning	96	39	
3. Spatial Relations	94	35	
4. Sound Blending	94	35	
5. Concept Formation	92	30	
6. Visual Matching 2	85	15	
7. Numbers Reversed	83	12	
14. Auditory Attention	103	59	
15. Analysis-Synthesis	92	29	
16. Decision Speed	95	36	
18. Rapid Picture Naming	125	95	
20. Pair Cancellation	83	13	
27. Memory for Sentences	119	90	
28. Block Rotation	105	63	

Rey Complex Figure Test			
Copy	NA	>16	
Short Delay	T=33	4	
Long Delay	T=33	4	

WMS-III Indexes			
Auditory Immediate	111	77	61–86
Visual Immediate	112	79	53–88
Immediate Memory	114	82	66–90
Auditory Delayed	111	77	55–87
Visual Delayed	129	97	86–99
Auditory Recog. Delayed	110	75	45–87
General Memory	122	93	81–96
Working Memory	96	39	23–61

WMS-III Subtests			
Logical Memory I – Recall	(11)	63	
Faces I – Recognition	(9)	37	
Verbal Paired Assoc. I – Recall	(13)	84	
Family Pictures I – Recall	(15)	95	
Mental Control	(12)	75	
Letter-Number Sequencing	(10)	50	
Digit Span	(7)	16	

	SS (ScS)	Percentile	Conf Band
Spatial Span	(9)	37	
Logical Memory II – Recall	(12)	75	
Faces II – Recognition	(14)	91	
Verbal Paired Assoc. II – Recall	(12)	75	
Family Pictures II – Recall	(15)	95	
Auditory Recognition – Delayed	12	75	

D-KEFS			
Verbal Fluency Test			
Letter Fluency	(9)	37	
Category Fluency	(14)	91	
Category Switching: Total Correct Responses	(15)	95	
Category Switching: Total Switching Accuracy	(15)	95	
Color-Word Interference Test			
1. Color Naming	(12)	75	
2. Word Reading	(12)	75	
3. Inhibition	(7)	16	
4. Inhibition/Switching	(10)	50	
Inhibition vs. Color Naming	(5)	5	
Inhibition/Switching vs. Naming & Reading	(8)	25	
Inhibition/Switching vs. Inhibition	(13)	84	
Tower Test			
Total Achievement Score	(8)	25	

ACHIEVEMENT

	SS	Percentile
WJ III Achievement		
Clusters		
Broad Math	98	46
Basic Reading Skills	85	16
Math Calculation Skills	100	49
Math Reasoning	98	43
Basic Writing Skills	82	11
Academic Skills	92	30
Academic Fluency	103	59
Phoneme/Grapheme Knowledge	84	15

(continued)

	SS	Percentile
WJ III Achievement		
Tests		
1. Letter-Word Identification	91	27
2. Reading Fluency	103	57
5. Calculation	101	53
6. Math Fluency	98	43
7. Spelling	88	22
8. Writing Fluency	108	71
10. Applied Problems	97	43
13. Word Attack	77	6
16. Editing	78	8
18. Quantitative Concepts	98	45
20. Spelling of Sounds	95	36
WRAT4		
Reading	93	32
NDRT		
Reading Comprehension:		
Timed	NA	48
Reading Rate	NA	64
GORT-4		
Rate	8	25
Accuracy	6	9
Comprehension	12	75

ORAL LANGUAGE

	SS	Percentile	Conf Band
WJ III ACH			
Listening Comprehension Cluster	110	74	53–90
4. Understanding Directions	109	72	
15. Oral Comprehension	108	70	
PPVT-4	120	91	

SOCIAL-EMOTIONAL

	Raw Score
BDI-II Composite	Total = 12 (minimal)
BAI Composite	Total = 12 (mild)

TEST INSTRUMENTS

Adult AD/HD Observation Form

Adult AD/HD Self-Report Checklist (ADHD-SR)

Adult AD/HD Significant Other Behavior Observation Checklist (ADHD-SO)

Adult Reading History Questionnaire

Beck Anxiety Inventory (BAI)

Beck Depression Inventory – Second Edition (BDI-II)

Delis Kaplan Executive Function System (D-KEFS)

Gray Oral Reading Test – Fourth Edition (GORT-4)

Nelson Denny Reading Test (NDRT)

Peabody Picture Vocabulary Test – Fourth Edition (PPVT-4)

Phonological/Orthographic Battery (Informal Tests)

Reading and Media Habits Questionnaire

Rey Complex Figure Test (RCFT)

Wechsler Adult Intelligence Scale – Fourth Edition (WAIS-IV)

Wechsler Memory Scale – Third Edition (WMS-III)

Wide Range Achievement Test 4 (WRAT4)

Woodcock-Johnson III NU Tests of Cognitive Ability (WJ III COG, Selected Subtests)

Woodcock Johnson III NU Tests of Achievement (WJ III ACH, Selected Subtests)

Writing Samples

CASE 52

Use of Nonverbal Cognitive Assessment to Distinguish Learning Disabilities from Second Language Learning Difficulties

Sherry Bell

Often, teachers and parents are puzzled when students fail to make academic progress commensurate with their peers. If students have been exposed to effective instruction but continue to struggle academically, it is important to determine if the student has a disability that negatively impacts learning. However, practitioners must be cognizant of and adhere to best practices when considering a disability for a student who is an English language learner or ELL (that is, for whom English is not the first language). The Individuals with Disabilities Education Improvement Act (IDEA, 2004) requires nondiscriminatory assessment. For ELL students, this means using assessment tools that are culturally and linguistically fair. (These same considerations apply for students from minority cultures, who have hearing impairments, or who are unwilling to speak in public.)

In order to provide appropriate instruction, educators need information about the cognitive abilities of struggling students. Instructional pacing should be determined, in part at least, by the cognitive capabilities of a student. For example, if a student from a non-English speaking family fails to progress relative to peers with a similar background, we might suspect a learning disability or limited general intellectual functioning. For most students, language is considered to be a window on intelligence; consequently, traditional language-loaded cognitive tests are typically used to rule out limited general cognitive ability (or more specific cognitive limitations such as weaknesses in auditory processing, processing speed, or working memory that may contribute to a specific learning disability) as the primary reason for limited progress. For students with limited English language skills, those who are hard of hearing, or those who refuse to talk, however, the choices are limited. Ti's case illustrates the use of a nonverbal test, the Universal Nonverbal Intelligence Test (UNIT), to determine general cognitive

ability of a student with English as a second language. The UNIT was used in conjunction with the Woodcock-Johnson III (WJ III) to consider Ti's general intellectual ability, as well as her cognitive academic language proficiency. In this case, scores from the UNIT and the WJ III indicate some relative cognitive weaknesses that help explain Ti's lack of academic progress and difficulties with mathematics.

PSYCHOLOGICAL REPORT

Name:	Ti Nguyen
Date of Birth:	12/18/1991
Age:	17-11
Sex:	Female
School:	Center High School
Grade:	11.3
Dates of Testing:	11/4/2009, 11/18/2009, 11/25/2009, 12/02/2009
Examiner:	Sherry Mee Bell, Ph.D.

REASON FOR REFERRAL AND BACKGROUND INFORMATION

Ti was referred for an assessment by her school counselor at Center High School (CHS). Ti is of Vietnamese ethnicity and has lived in the United States for 5 years. Her first language is Vietnamese and both Vietnamese and English are spoken in the home. Her father is an engineer who works in a local electronics company; her mother is unemployed. Ti has an older brother and a younger sister who are both strong students. Her brother attends an area university on a partial academic scholarship. The school counselor reports that Ti has had difficulty, relative to her siblings and other Vietnamese peers, in adapting to the CHS curriculum. In October 2008, her performance on the PLAN, a high school aptitude test, yielded an overall score at the 3rd percentile. Other scores were: English, 1st percentile; Reading, 31st percentile; Math, 3rd percentile; and Science Reasoning, 35th percentile.

Ti's parents provided medical and social history. Ti was the result of a normal pregnancy and has had no significant health problems. Her parents noted, however, that she met developmental milestones (walking and talking) a little later than her siblings. The family moved to the United States in the summer of 2004. Several extended family members also live in the area; the Nguyens attend a local church with other native Vietnamese families. They have also participated in English classes in the evening. Ti and her siblings studied English in Vietnam but did not speak English with any frequency until moving to the States. Ti's father is highly fluent in English, and her mother uses English in conversation relatively well. Ti's parents are concerned about her slow academic progress; they indicated she studies at home several hours each night and on the weekends. Ti participates in soccer and church activities.

ASSESSMENT PROCEDURES AND INSTRUMENTS

Universal Nonverbal Intelligence Test (UNIT)
Woodcock-Johnson III NU Tests of Cognitive Ability (WJ III COG) and Achievement (WJ III ACH)
Record review
Interviews
Classroom observation

CLASSROOM OBSERVATION

Ti was observed in her eleventh-grade geometry class with 23 students on 11/04/09 from 9:45 A.M. to 10:15 A.M. The classroom was arranged in a traditional manner with the teacher at the front of the room and students seated in rows. Ti sat in the second seat in the middle row. In general, students were attentive as the teacher explained the assignment orally and wrote on a whiteboard. Ti was attentive throughout the lesson, watching the teacher and writing in her notebook. When the teacher asked for student responses,

Ti did not volunteer and the teacher did not call on her to respond. Following the observation, the teacher noted that Ti is always quiet and attentive and does her homework, apparently with some help from parents. She tends to do better on homework than on in-class assignments and has difficulty on tests. Her class average is currently a low C.

RELEVANT TEST BEHAVIORS

Ti is average in size for her chronological age with long, dark hair and attractive features. She was cooperative and pleasant during the assessment sessions and seemed to put forth good effort despite some obvious initial anxiety. Ti spoke softly and her speech was intelligible. Ti presented as timid and hesitant to attempt tasks or to respond if unsure of the answer or solution. She was often slow to respond and worked slowly on most tasks. She responded well to encouragement, smiled, and appeared to relax as the assessment progressed. Given apparent good rapport and effort, the following results are considered accurate and valid.

ASSESSMENT RESULTS

The UNIT is a multidimensional, nonverbal test designed to measure intellectual abilities while minimizing the confounding factor of language. On the UNIT, Ti achieved the following scores:

	ScS	SS	PR		ScS	SS	PR
Memory Scale		85	16	**Symbolic Scale**		100	50
Symbolic Memory	8			Symbolic Memory	8		
Spatial Memory	7			Analogic Reasoning	12		
Reasoning Scale		100	50	**Nonsymbolic Scale**		85	16
Analogic Reasoning	12			Spatial Memory	7		
Cube Design	8			Cube Design	8		
Full-Scale IQ		91	27				

The standard scores (SS) have a mean of 100 and a standard deviation of 15. The subtest scores (scaled scores, ScS) have a mean of 10 and a standard deviation of 3.

Percentile ranks (PR) have a mean of 50; standard deviations do not apply.

Ti obtained a Full-Scale IQ score of 91. The range of scores from 86 to 98 is believed to capture her true score with 90 percent confidence. Ti's Full-Scale score is in the low end of the Average range and suggests Average to Low Average cognitive abilities with relative weaknesses in memory and nonsymbolic reasoning. Ti demonstrated a relative strength (High Average range) on Analogic Reasoning, a symbolic reasoning task that does not require hands-on performance or speed. This subtest measures the ability to discern relationships among related ideas and/or objects. Results suggested mild weaknesses in the other cognitive areas tapped by the UNIT. Ti's performance on tasks assessing memory, both symbolic and spatial, were in the Low Average range. She also performed in the Low Average range on a hands-on, timed task of nonverbal reasoning (Cube Design).

Ti's cognitive abilities were further assessed by administration of selected tests from the WJ III NU Tests of Cognitive Abilities (WJ III NU COG). In addition, academic achievement was assessed by the WJ III Tests of Achievement (WJ III ACH). WJ III NU standard scores have the same mean and standard deviation as the UNIT, simplifying comparisons of Ti's test performance. Ti's WJ III scores are presented in the Appendix.

Summary of WJ III Cognitive and Academic Performance

Ti's overall intellectual ability, as measured by the WJ III General Intellectual Ability (GIA, Extended), was in the Low Average range, approximately one-half a standard deviation lower than her Full-Scale IQ score on the (nonverbal) UNIT. Ti's performance on the WJ III cognitive tasks varied considerably (from the Average range to the Low range) but her performance on the UNIT cognitive tasks was less variable (ranging from High Average to Low Average). The variability in Ti's performance on tasks that constitute the WJ III GIA limits its appropriateness for representing her general ability.

Cognitive

Ti's long-term retrieval, visual-spatial processing, short-term memory, and working memory standard scores were in the Average range when compared to others at her age level. Her fluid reasoning, auditory processing, and phonemic awareness scores were in the Low Average range. Her scores on the clusters of Verbal Ability (acquired knowledge and language comprehension), Processing Speed (speed and

efficiency in performing automatic or simple cognitive tasks), and Cognitive Fluency (ease and speed in performing simple to complex cognitive tasks) were in the Low range. Additionally, when her Verbal Ability score was compared with her Thinking Ability and Cognitive Efficiency scores, Ti demonstrated a significant weakness in verbal ability. Although not included in this comparison, Ti's score on the Oral Language cluster was also in the Low range.

Some of Ti's cognitive ability clusters were composed of scores that were so discrepant that the broader ability could not be interpreted. These included Broad Attention (the ability to focus attention on relevant stimuli) and Executive Processes (the ability to plan, monitor, and arrive at solutions to problems).

Academic

Ti's oral language skills were significantly low when compared to the range of scores obtained by others at her age level. Ti's overall level of achievement was Low Average and generally commensurate with the estimates of her intellectual ability from the UNIT. She displayed considerable variability, however, among her academic skills.

When compared to others at her age level, Ti's standard scores were Average in basic reading skills but Low Average in passage comprehension. Although she demonstrated a relative strength in spelling (Average), her written expression was in the Low Average range. Her math reasoning (solving practical problems and demonstrating comprehension of math concepts) was Low Average and her math calculation skills Very Low. When her cluster scores for the four achievement areas were compared with the predicted scores, Ti demonstrated a significant strength on the WJ III ACH Broad Written Language cluster and a significant weakness on the Broad Mathematics cluster. In general, mathematics is challenging for Ti. She performed relatively strongest on tasks measuring math concepts. That is, she recognizes mathematical signs and can complete number series patterns. She can add money and calculate the amount needed to buy items costing less than $10.00; also, she can add time using an analog clock. However, her math operations skills are weak, and her retrieval of math facts is slow. On the untimed test of math calculations, she worked slowly and missed some easier items before completing more complex ones, suggesting she has forgotten some previously learned skills. On the timed test of simple math facts (1-digit addition, subtraction, and multiplication), she made only one error but worked extremely slowly.

Because English is Ti's second language, her cognitive-academic language proficiency (CALP) was calculated for selected WJ III tests. Experts estimate that it takes students 5 to 7 years to acquire a level of second-language proficiency that will facilitate academic success. That is, the cognitive-academic language proficiency necessary to perform the academic tasks associated with reading, writing, and test taking requires 5 to 7 years to fully develop. WJ III CALP scores range from 1 (negligible) to 5 (advanced). Generally, 3 is considered Limited and 4 is Average. Ti's CALP scores fell between 3 and 4. Her Verbal Ability cluster CALP score was 3; Oral Language, Broad Reading, and Written Expression cluster scores were 3.5. Her Broad Written Language CALP score (4) fell within the Average range. Her relatively higher performance on the Broad Written Language cluster was due to her relatively stronger performance on the spelling test.

Ability/Achievement Comparisons

To help determine if any ability/achievement discrepancies existed, comparisons were made between Ti's cognitive and achievement scores. When compared to her overall intellectual ability (WJ III COG GIA-Extended), Ti's achievement was significantly lower than predicted in the areas of Broad Mathematics and Math Calculation Skills. Based on a mix of the cognitive tasks associated with and most relevant to performance in a particular academic area, her achievement was significantly lower than predicted in the areas of Broad Mathematics, Math Calculation Skills, and Oral Language.

SUMMARY

Results indicated that Ti's overall intellectual abilities are in the lower end of the Average to the Low Average range as assessed by both the UNIT and the WJ III COG. She demonstrated cognitive weaknesses (relative to same-age peers) in verbal comprehension and expression, processing speed, cognitive fluency, and auditory processing. Ti's relatively weaker performance on several tests of the WJ III is likely due to the fact that English is her second language; she has been an English speaker for only 5 years. Consequently, the UNIT estimate may be a more accurate indicator of her general cognitive ability. Ti demonstrated a relative strength on tasks measuring visual-spatial thinking on the WJ III COG. She performed in the High Average range on the UNIT task assessing ability to perceive relationships among visually presented stimuli. Her performance on two visual memory tasks from the UNIT, however, was weaker.

Ti's academic achievement ranged from Average to Low, with relative strengths in written language skills, especially spelling. Her basic reading skills (sight and nonsense word reading) were Average but reading comprehension was Low Average, as was reading fluency.

It is not uncommon for English language learners to master basic reading and writing skills, but to continue to struggle with higher-level linguistic abilities involving the acquisition of vocabulary, and reading and listening comprehension. Ti's oral language development in English is significantly low, likely influenced by the fact she has been speaking English for only 5 years. She does not appear to have fully developed the deep vocabulary knowledge required for cognitive academic language proficiency (i.e., to read, write, solve problems, and think efficiently about academic concepts in English).

Ti's limited English exposure probably contributed to her weaker performance on some of the WJ III Cognitive tests (e.g., Verbal Comprehension, General Information, Rapid Picture Naming). Ti's difficulties in basic math skills are less likely to be language-related and are presumably related to her slow processing speed and relatively weak fluid reasoning skills. She exhibited difficulty, however, across all areas of math, including math reasoning. Although limited language exposure may have had some influence on math reasoning, poor calculation skills and weak retrieval of math facts are more likely to be the foundational deficits.

Assessment results should help inform educational planning and services for Ti. Her pattern of scores indicates intraindividual cognitive and academic variation, which suggests that she may meet system or state criteria for identification under the category of Specific Learning Disabilities. Specifically, Ti's pattern of scores suggests learning disabilities affecting mathematics calculation and mathematics problem solving. Slow processing speed is frequently associated with poor performance in basic math skills. These results should be reviewed by the school support team.

RECOMMENDATIONS

1. Regardless of special education eligibility, Ti needs extra instruction and support in mathematics. Goals should focus on improving automatic retrieval of math facts, computation, and math problem solving.

2. Practice in retrieval of basic math facts using computer software may be used to help Ti acquire automaticity

with math facts. Brief practice sessions daily are recommended rather than longer and/or less frequent sessions.

3. Build on Ti's current math knowledge to teach new facts or concepts. For example, explicitly teach math facts families in addition/subtraction and multiplication/division. Also, teach her to use what she knows to solve an unknown (e.g., if $8 \times 8 = 64$, 8×9 must be 8 more than 64).

4. Because Ti's understanding of quantitative concepts is stronger than her other math skills, she should benefit from strategies that help her understand relationships among numbers. For example, explicitly teach her the relationships between the operations (e.g., between addition and multiplication and between subtraction and division).

5. Additionally, after Ti learns a specific algorithm, computer software can be used to provide interactive practice with the related computation. Teach algorithms with simple examples that illustrate the procedure and provide ample repetition and reinforcement of the procedures.

6. Use of visual and concrete examples in math should be helpful. Ti might benefit from having example problems on a card or piece of paper that she can keep handy in her notebook. She might benefit from using a pocket math facts chart and/or a small number line.

7. Ensure that Ti understands the math vocabulary used in class and in her texts. Preteaching essential terms and having her write them with a visual cue or simple example should be helpful.

8. When Ti's father assists her with math at home, he should discuss the math concepts in both Vietnamese and English to see if the use of her most familiar language allows her to learn more effectively.

9. Teach Ti how to use a calculator for solving complex, multistep problems and word problems. Allow her to use a calculator in class, on final exams, and on group-administered standardized tests.

10. Due to her slow processing speed, Ti would likely benefit from extended time on tests (both classroom and standardized tests) and on assignments, in all academic areas.

11. Ti should benefit from continued exposure to English language in a variety of contexts and to academic instruction in English at an appropriate level. Ti's teachers would likely benefit from routine consultation by the school system's instructor for English Language Learners.

12. It will be important to provide Ti with small group or individual tutoring that teaches vocabulary and concepts using familiar examples. She might also benefit from using graphic organizers (using meaningful stimuli) to develop vocabulary and concepts, as well as explicit teaching of reading comprehension strategies (comprehension monitoring, question generation and answering, and understanding text structure).

13. The results of this evaluation should be shared with the school counselor who will assist in planning for Ti's postsecondary education. As her current academic performance indicates that she may have difficulty experiencing success in a traditional university program, alternative options (e.g., vocational training, a small specialized junior college) should be discussed.

TABLE OF SCORES

Woodcock-Johnson III Normative Update Tests of Cognitive Abilities and Tests of Achievement (Form A)
WJ III NU Compuscore and Profiles Program, Version 3.0
Norms based on age 17-11

CLUSTER/Test	Raw	W	AE	Proficiency	RPI	SS (68% Band)	CALP
GIA (Ext)	–	509	12–2	Limited	67/90	82 (80–84)	–
VERBAL ABILITY (Ext)	–	509	11–5	Limited	41/90	76 (72–80)	3
COMP-KNOWLEDGE (Gc)	–	509	11–5	Limited	41/90	76 (72–80)	3
Verbal Comprehension	–	502	10–3	Limited	29/90	74 (69–78)	–
General Information	–	515	12–6	Limited	53/90	82 (76–87)	–
THINKING ABILITY (Ext)	–	506	12–10	Average	83/90	90 (87–92)	–
Picture Recognition	53-D	512	>20	Average	92/90	103 (97–109)	–

(continued)

CLUSTER/Test	Raw	W	AE	Proficiency	RPI	SS (68% Band)	CALP
Spatial Relations	72-D	510	>25	Average	91/90	101 (97–106)	–
Visual-Auditory Learning	9-E	504	12–9	Average	87/90	94 (88–101)	–
Retrieval Fluency	65	503	11–11	Average	86/90	85 (79–91)	–
Sound Blending	20	506	11–9	Lmtd to Avg	70/90	87 (81–92)	–
Auditory Attention	37	501	9–10	Average	82/90	86 (77–95)	–
Concept Formation	30-E	512	13–5	Lmtd to Avg	77/90	92 (89–96)	–
Analysis-Synthesis	23-E	501	10–4	Limited	60/90	84 (79–90)	–
COG EFFICIENCY (Ext)	–	513	13–4	Lmtd to Avg	77/90	89 (85–93)	–
Numbers Reversed	17	534	>26	Avg to Adv	95/90	105 (100–109)	–
Memory for Words	17	507	11–6	Lmtd to Avg	70/90	91 (84–99)	–
Visual Matching	43-2	509	11–6	Limited	56/90	77 (71–82)	–
Decision Speed	30	503	11–3	Lmtd to Avg	67/90	79 (73–84)	–
L-T RETRIEVAL (Glr)	–	503	12–5	Average	86/90	91 (85–96)	–
Visual-Auditory Learning	9-E	504	12–9	Average	87/90	94 (88–101)	–
Retrieval Fluency	65	503	11–11	Average	86/90	85 (79–91)	–
VIS-SPATIAL THINK (Gv)	–	511	>24	Average	92/90	103 (98–107)	–
Picture Recognition	53-D	512	>20	Average	92/90	103 (97–109)	–
Spatial Relations	72-D	510	>25	Average	91/90	101 (97–106)	–
AUDITORY PROCESS (Ga)	–	504	11–2	Lmtd to Avg	77/90	85 (80–90)	–
Sound Blending	20	506	11–9	Lmtd to Avg	70/90	87 (81–92)	–
Auditory Attention	37	501	9–10	Average	82/90	86 (77–95)	–
FLUID REASONING (Gf)	–	507	11–8	Lmtd to Avg	69/90	87 (84–91)	–
Concept Formation	30-E	512	13–5	Lmtd to Avg	77/90	92 (89–96)	–
Analysis-Synthesis	23-E	501	10–4	Limited	60/90	84 (79–90)	–
PROCESS SPEED (Gs)	–	506	11–5	Limited	62/90	76 (72–80)	–
Visual Matching	43-2	509	11–6	Limited	56/90	77 (71–82)	–
Decision Speed	30	503	11–3	Lmtd to Avg	67/90	79 (73–84)	–
SHORT-TERM MEM (Gsm)	–	520	16–1	Average	87/90	98 (94–103)	–
Numbers Reversed	17	534	>26	Avg to Adv	95/90	105 (100–109)	–
Memory for Words	17	507	11–6	Lmtd to Avg	70/90	91 (84–99)	–
PHONEMIC AWARE	–	504	11–7	Lmtd to Avg	78/90	87 (82–92)	–
Incomplete Words	22	503	11–2	Average	84/90	91 (84–98)	–
Sound Blending	20	506	11–9	Lmtd to Avg	70/90	87 (81–92)	–
WORKING MEMORY	–	524	16–6	Average	88/90	98 (94–102)	–
Numbers Reversed	17	534	>26	Avg to Adv	95/90	105 (100–109)	–
Auditory Working Memory	23	515	13–2	Lmtd to Avg	72/90	89 (85–93)	–
BROAD ATTENTION	–	513	13–5	Lmtd to Avg	77/90	87 (84–91)	–
Numbers Reversed	17	534	>26	Avg to Adv	95/90	105 (100–109)	–
Auditory Working Memory	23	515	13–2	Lmtd to Avg	72/90	89 (85–93)	–
Auditory Attention	37	501	9–10	Average	82/90	86 (77–95)	–
Pair Cancellation	59	503	11–0	Limited	35/90	77 (75–79)	–

CLUSTER/Test	Raw	W	AE	Proficiency	RPI	SS (68% Band)	CALP
COGNITIVE FLUENCY	–	500	10–3	Limited	65/90	72 (69–75)	–
Retrieval Fluency	65	503	11–11	Average	86/90	85 (79–91)	–
Decision Speed	30	503	11–3	Lmtd to Avg	67/90	79 (73–84)	–
Rapid Picture Naming	95	494	9–0	Limited	35/90	73 (70–75)	–
EXEC PROCESSES	–	505	11–9	Lmtd to Avg	70/90	80 (77–83)	–
Concept Formation	30-E	512	13–5	Lmtd to Avg	77/90	92 (89–96)	–
Planning	–	500	9–3	Average	88/90	85 (75–95)	–
Pair Cancellation	59	503	11–0	Limited	35/90	77 (75–79)	–
ORAL LANGUAGE (Std)	–	496	8–10	Lmtd to Avg	70/90	73 (68–78)	3.5
Understanding Directions	–	493	8–9	Limited	55/90	76 (71–81)	–
Story Recall	–	498	9–1	Lmtd to Avg	81/90	82 (75–89)	–
TOTAL ACHIEVEMENT	–	514	12–6	Limited	63/90	83 (81–84)	–
BROAD READING	–	520	13–9	Lmtd to Avg	69/90	89 (86–91)	3.5
Letter-Word Identification	68	548	16–9	Average	87/90	98 (95–102)	–
Reading Fluency	57	507	12–8	Limited	56/90	84 (81–87)	–
Passage Comprehension	31	505	10–9	Limited	58/90	83 (78–88)	–
BROAD MATH	–	503	10–2	Limited	31/90	68 (65–71)	–
Calculation	18	503	10–1	V Limited	22/90	71 (66–76)	–
Math Fluency	54	496	9–4	Limited	47/90	63 (61–65)	–
Applied Problems	37	509	10–7	Limited	25/90	81 (78–85)	–
BROAD WRITTEN LANG	–	520	14–7	Average	84/90	94 (90–97)	4
Spelling	47	536	23	Average	93/90	103 (99–107)	–
Writing Fluency	22	513	12–5	Lmtd to Avg	71/90	88 (82–93)	–
Writing Samples	13-D	509	13–2	Lmtd to Avg	80/90	91 (86–96)	–
BASIC READING SKILLS	–	531	15–4	Average	82/90	96 (93–98)	–
Word Attack	26	513	12–3	Lmtd to Avg	76/90	94 (90–97)	–
Letter-Word Identification	68	548	16–9	Average	87/90	98 (95–102)	–
MATH CALC SKILLS	–	500	9–10	Limited	33/90	63 (59–67)	–
Calculation	18	503	10–1	V Limited	22/90	71 (66–76)	–
Math Fluency	54	496	9–4	Limited	47/90	63 (61–65)	–
MATH REASONING	–	518	12–2	Limited	52/90	84 (81–87)	–
Applied Problems	37	509	10–7	Limited	25/90	81 (78–85)	–
Quantitative Concepts	–	527	13–10	Lmtd to Avg	77/90	92 (87–97)	–
WRITTEN EXPRESSION	–	511	12–9	Lmtd to Avg	76/90	88 (84–92)	3.5
Writing Samples	13-D	509	13–2	Lmtd to Avg	80/90	91 (86–96)	–
Writing Fluency	22	513	12–5	Lmtd to Avg	71/90	88 (82–93)	–
ACADEMIC SKILLS	–	529	14–3	Lmtd to Avg	75/90	90 (88–93)	–
Spelling	47	536	23	Average	93/90	103 (99–107)	–
Letter-Word Identification	68	548	16–9	Average	87/90	98 (95–102)	–
Calculation	18	503	10–1	V Limited	22/90	71 (66–76)	–
ACADEMIC FLUENCY	–	506	11–8	Limited	58/90	77 (74–80)	–
Writing Fluency	22	513	12–5	Lmtd to Avg	71/90	88 (82–93)	–

(continued)

CLUSTER/Test	Raw	W	AE	Proficiency	RPI	SS (68% Band)	CALP
Reading Fluency	57	507	12–8	Limited	56/90	84 (81–87)	–
Math Fluency	54	496	9–4	Limited	47/90	63 (61–65)	–
ACADEMIC APPS	–	508	11–2	Limited	55/90	78 (74–81)	–
Writing Samples	13-D	509	13–2	Lmtd to Avg	80/90	91 (86–96)	–
Passage Comprehension	31	505	10–9	Limited	58/90	83 (78–88)	–
Applied Problems	37	509	10–7	Limited	25/90	81 (78–85)	–

CLUSTER/Test	Raw	W	AE	Proficiency	RPI	SS (68% Band)	CALP
Verbal Comprehension	–	502	10–3	Limited	29/90	74 (69–78)	–
Visual-Auditory Learning	9-E	504	12–9	Average	87/90	94 (88–101)	–
Spatial Relations	72-D	510	>25	Average	91/90	101 (97–106)	–
Sound Blending	20	506	11–9	Lmtd to Avg	70/90	87 (81–92)	–
Concept Formation	30-E	512	13–5	Lmtd to Avg	77/90	92 (89–96)	–
Visual Matching	43-2	509	11–6	Limited	56/90	77 (71–82)	–
Decision Speed	30	503	11–3	Lmtd to Avg	67/90	79 (73–84)	–
Incomplete Words	22	503	11–2	Average	84/90	91 (84–98)	–
Auditory Working Memory	23	515	13–2	Lmtd to Avg	72/90	89 (85–93)	–
General Information	–	515	12–6	Limited	53/90	82 (76–87)	–
Retrieval Fluency	65	503	11–11	Average	86/90	85 (79–91)	–
Picture Recognition	53-D	512	>20	Average	92/90	103 (97–109)	–
Auditory Attention	37	501	9–10	Average	82/90	86 (77–95)	–
Analysis-Synthesis	23-E	501	10–4	Limited	60/90	84 (79–90)	–
Decision Speed	30	503	11–3	Lmtd to Avg	67/90	79 (73–84)	–
Memory for Words	17	507	11–6	Lmtd to Avg	70/90	91 (84–99)	–
Rapid Picture Naming	95	494	9–0	Limited	35/90	73 (70–75)	–
Planning	–	500	9–3	Average	88/90	85 (75—95)	–
Pair Cancellation	59	503	11–0	Limited	35/90	77 (75–79)	–

CLUSTER/Test	Raw	W	AE	Proficiency	RPI	SS (68% Band)	CALP
Letter-Word Identification	68	548	16–9	Average	87/90	98 (95–102)	–
Reading Fluency	57	507	12–8	Limited	56/90	84 (81–87)	–
Story Recall	–	498	9–1	Lmtd to Avg	81/90	82 (75–89)	–
Understanding Directions	–	493	8–9	Limited	55/90	76 (71–81)	–
Calculation	18	503	10–1	V Limited	22/90	71 (66–76)	–
Math Fluency	54	496	9–4	Limited	47/90	63 (61–65)	–
Spelling	47	536	23	Average	93/90	103 (99–107)	–
Writing Fluency	22	513	12–5	Lmtd to Avg	71/90	88 (82–93)	–
Passage Comprehension	31	505	10–9	Limited	58/90	83 (78–88)	–
Applied Problems	37	509	10–7	Limited	25/90	81 (78–85)	–
Writing Samples	13-D	509	13–2	Lmtd to Avg	80/90	91 (86–96)	–
Word Attack	26	513	12–3	Lmtd to Avg	76/90	94 (90–97)	–
Quantitative Concepts	–	527	13–10	Lmtd to Avg	77/90	92 (87–97)	–

VARIATIONS	STANDARD SCORES			VARIATION		Significant at + or –1.50 SD (SEE)
	Actual	Predicted	Difference	PR	SD	
Intra-Cognitive (Std)						
VERBAL ABILITY (Std)	74	95	–21	2	–1.96	Yes

VARIATIONS	STANDARD SCORES			VARIATION		Significant at
	Actual	Predicted	Difference	PR	SD	+ or −1.50 SD (SEE)
THINKING ABILITY (Std)	92	87	5	70	+0.53	No
COG EFFICIENCY (Std)	94	90	4	65	+0.39	No
Intra-Achievement (Std)						
BROAD READING	89	81	8	84	+0.99	No
BROAD MATH	68	88	−20	3	−1.81	Yes
BROAD WRITTEN LANG	94	80	14	93	+1.50	Yes
ORAL LANGUAGE (Std)	73	87	−14	10	−1.29	No

VARIATIONS	STANDARD SCORES			VARIATION		Significant at
	Actual	Predicted	Difference	PR	SD	+ or −1.50 SD (SEE)
Intellectual Ability/Achievement Discrepancies*						
BROAD READING	89	89	0	51	+0.04	No
BASIC READING SKILLS	96	90	6	70	+0.54	No
BROAD MATH	68	89	−21	3	−1.93	Yes
MATH CALC SKILLS	63	91	−28	1	−2.26	Yes
MATH REASONING	84	88	−4	35	−0.38	No
BROAD WRITTEN LANG	94	89	5	68	+0.48	No
WRITTEN EXPRESSION	88	90	−2	42	−0.19	No
ORAL LANGUAGE (Std)	73	88	−15	8	−1.44	No

*These discrepancies compare WJ III GIA (Std) with Broad, Basic, and Applied ACH clusters.

VARIATIONS	STANDARD SCORES			VARIATION		Significant at
	Actual	Predicted	Difference	PR	SD	+ or −1.50 SD (SEE)
Predicted Achievement/Achievement Discrepancies*						
BROAD READING	89	79	10	87	+1.12	No
BASIC READING SKILLS	96	84	12	88	+1.15	No
BROAD MATH	68	84	−16	6	−1.59	Yes
MATH CALC SKILLS	63	85	−22	3	−1.85	Yes
MATH REASONING	84	84	0	49	−0.02	No
BROAD WRITTEN LANG	94	81	13	91	+1.36	No
WRITTEN EXPRESSION	88	83	5	70	+0.52	No
ORAL LANGUAGE (Std)	73	93	−20	4	−1.81	Yes

*These discrepancies compare predicted achievement scores with Broad, Basic, and Applied ACH clusters.

VARIATIONS	STANDARD SCORES			VARIATION		Significant at
	Actual	Predicted	Difference	PR	SD	+ or −1.50 SD (SEE)
GIA Std/Cognitive						
COMP-KNOWLEDGE (Gc)	76	88	−12	10	−1.31	No
L-T RETRIEVAL (Glr)	91	88	3	60	+0.26	No
VIS-SPATIAL THINK (Gv)	103	91	12	84	+0.99	No
AUDITORY PROCESS (Ga)	85	90	−5	33	−0.43	No
FLUID REASONING (Gf)	87	87	0	53	+0.07	No
PROCESS SPEED (Gs)	76	91	−15	12	−1.20	No
SHORT-TERM MEM (Gsm)	98	88	10	87	+1.13	No
PHONEMIC AWARE	87	90	−3	40	−0.25	No
WORKING MEMORY	98	88	10	87	+1.13	No
COGNITIVE FLUENCY	72	92	−20	6	−1.55	Yes

CASE 53

The Enduring Nature of Specific Learning Disability
A College Freshman with a Specific Reading Disability

Barbara Wendling

Perhaps the most important lesson to be learned from Tory's report is that specific learning disabilities endure. No matter how bright Tory is, no matter how many intact abilities she has, no matter how hard she works, she continues to struggle with specific academic areas. Her learning difficulties were apparent by second grade and they are still apparent 12 years later. Tory may learn to compensate for her specific learning disabilities, but they will not disappear.

Another lesson to be learned from this case is the need for quality early intervention. The signs were there; Tory was well aware that something was "wrong" with her. The second-grade teacher was supportive and accommodating, but Tory did not get the instruction she needed. Even after years in special education, she did not obtain the skills needed to decode words or to recognize high-frequency words. Understanding Tory's learning disabilities and then prescribing and providing appropriate instruction were and still are critical elements necessary for improving her learning experiences.

Several examples in Tory's report illustrate the importance of considering all levels of score information when interpreting test performance. On certain tests, Tory's standard scores are in the Average range, but her proficiency on the tasks is actually limited. In some cases the reverse is true: low standard scores but average proficiency. The Relative Proficiency Index (RPI) provides an opportunity to look at Tory's proficiency, or functionality, on the task, irrespective of her relative standing in the norm reference group.

Finally, Tory demonstrates the importance of practitioners being aware of the characteristics of specific learning disabilities. She exhibits classic characteristics of dyslexia. Knowledge of the cognitive correlates of reading combined with quantitative and qualitative information lead to good diagnostic conclusions. This understanding is essential when looking for a pattern of strengths and weaknesses that suggests the presence of a specific learning disability.

> **Note:**
>
> While there is a great deal of instructional information that could be garnered from the results of this evaluation, the purpose of the evaluation was to document the presence of a learning disability so that Tory would be eligible for accommodations at college. Therefore, instructional implications were not included.

LEARNING DISABILITIES EVALUATION

Name:	Tory Marten
Date of Birth:	12/15/90
Age:	19-1
Sex:	Female
Parents:	Gina and Keith Marten
School:	Greenwood College
Grade:	13.0
Dates of Testing:	1/16/2010, 1/17/2010
Evaluator:	Barbara J. Wendling, M.A.

REASON FOR EVALUATION

Tory's parents requested a private evaluation to help determine their daughter's present performance in reading, as well as to determine whether or not she has a specific reading disability. Although Tory was identified as having dyslexia in third grade and received special education services throughout elementary and middle school, she was exited from special education when she entered high school. This was done on the advice of the school counselor who told Tory's parents that she would have a better chance of being accepted by the college of her choice if she was not receiving special education services. This left Tory without any support services or a 504 plan during high school, as well as when she entered college. With extraordinary effort, Tory did complete high school, but her parents are very concerned about her ability to handle the increased academic demands of college. The college Tory is attending requires a current evaluation to determine whether or not she is eligible for any accommodations that may be granted to students with disabilities.

BACKGROUND INFORMATION

Currently, Tory is a freshman at Greenwood College and will be starting again in fall 2010. She dropped out during the fall 2009 semester because of feelings of anxiety over her inability to handle the academic demands. Tory recalls that school was fun in kindergarten and first grade, but that things changed in second grade. She was placed in the lowest reading group, which turned out not to be low enough. A new, lower group was formed just for her. The school conducted a full individual evaluation while Tory was in second grade. Although she exhibited significant discrepancies between her intelligence score and basic reading, reading comprehension, and written expression scores, the school determined Tory did not need special services at that time because the second-grade teacher felt she could accommodate Tory's needs in the general education classroom.

In third grade, the teacher reported that Tory was an extremely bright, articulate child who frequently seemed nervous in the academic setting and lacked confidence. Tory's math skills were very strong but her reading skills were described as significantly below level. In addition, her handwriting was a concern. Tory had difficulty with letter formation, pencil control, and writing speed. During her third-grade year, her parents had her tested at the Child Development Center of a local hospital. The conclusion of that evaluation was that Tory had dyslexia. At this point, the school found her to be eligible for special education and provided her with services until she reached high school.

Even with special education services, Tory felt as though she was struggling just to keep up. She describes her educational experience as "hanging on by her fingernails." Tory expects a great deal from herself and says that "failure is not an option." Her internal drive to succeed and willingness to work extra hard have gotten her through to this point.

Tory reports that she still transposes letters and numbers and has trouble sounding out words. She reports that she even forgot "how" to sound out a word recently when reading to a young child. She misspells simple words like "again," spelling it as "agian." When she comes to a word she doesn't know, she does make an attempt to read it. She tries to determine if she has seen or heard the word she is trying to decode. Clearly, she relies on her oral language and her store of learned words to assist her reading. If she cannot read the word, she skips it and moves on, trying to preserve meaning. In addition, Tory states that she has to read assignments three or four times to really comprehend the text. She spends many hours a night just trying to keep up with class work.

Tory's favorite academic area is mathematics. It is also the area in which she has experienced the most success in her school career thus far. Tory loves children and it is her goal to become a math teacher.

DEVELOPMENTAL AND FAMILY HISTORY

Information regarding Tory's developmental and family history was obtained via review of prior evaluations and an interview with her parents. Her mother reports that pregnancy and birth were uneventful and that Tory passed all developmental milestones within normal limits. Tory's family is intact and she is the youngest of three children. Both parents are college graduates with professional careers. Her sister is a college graduate and her brother is a senior in college. Both siblings had difficulty learning to read in the early grades but were not evaluated for learning disabilities and never received special education services. The father reports that he never enjoyed reading or writing and that he still experiences difficulty with spelling, preferring to do everything on the computer to make use of the spell-checking feature.

ASSESSMENT/EVALUATION PROCEDURES

Woodcock-Johnson III NU Tests of Cognitive Abilities (WJ III COG) (Tests 1–9 and 11–18) 1/16/2010

Woodcock-Johnson III NU Tests of Achievement
(WJ III ACH) (Tests 1–11, 13, 17, 20, 21) 1/17/2010
Informal reading sample
Review of previous evaluations

Tory was administered a set of tests from the Wood-cock-Johnson III Normative Update (WJ III NU). The WJ III NU is composed of two batteries: the Tests of Cognitive Abilities (WJ III COG) and the Tests of Achievement (WJ III ACH). The WJ III COG is a comprehensive battery of individually administered tests measuring different cognitive/intellectual abilities. The WJ III ACH is a comprehensive battery of individually administered tests measuring oral language, reading, written language, mathematics, and academic knowledge. Because the tests were normed on the same population, direct comparisons can be made among Tory's cognitive abilities and achievement scores. These comparisons can help determine the presence and significance of any strengths and weaknesses among her abilities. Further, the pattern of relationships between Tory's cognitive abilities and academic performance can be explored. The WJ III was selected based on the reasons for the evaluation. The tests were scored using grade norms, which provided the most relevant comparison group for this evaluation.

BEHAVIORAL OBSERVATIONS

Tory was very cooperative and personable during both testing sessions. She appeared at ease, comfortable, and attentive. Rapport was easily established and maintained. During testing, she was focused and took great care in responding. As items became more difficult, she persisted until she was sure she did not know the answer, at which point she would often say, "I have no idea." The present results represent a reliable and valid estimate of Tory's current level of cognitive and academic functioning in the areas assessed.

ASSESSMENT/EVALUATION FINDINGS

Results from the WJ III COG are presented first, followed by the achievement findings. Scores that are discussed include standard scores, percentile ranks, relative proficiency indexes, and instructional zones (achievement tests only). Standard scores (SS) are norm-referenced scores that have a mean of 100 and a standard deviation of 15. The Average

range for the WJ III is defined as standard scores from 90 to 110. The standard scores in the report may appear with the +/–1 standard error of measurement (SEM) or range of standard scores, shown in this manner (SS = 110; 105–115). Including the +/–1 SEM increases the likelihood that Tory's true score is represented. Because grade norms were used, the standard scores show Tory's performance relative to other college freshmen attending 4-year colleges or universities. Percentile ranks (PR) indicate the percent of grad peers that scored the same as or lower than Tory on the task. Percentile ranks range from 0.1 to 99.9 on the WJ III. The Average range is defined as percentile ranks from 25 to 75. The relative proficiency index (RPI) is a criterion-referenced score indicating proficiency or functionality on a task compared to average grade peers. It is expressed as an index, for example, RPI 10/90. The top number in the index ranges from 0–100 and reflects Tory's proficiency on the task. The bottom number in the index is fixed at 90 and reflects the average proficiency level of grade peers. RPIs of 75/90 or lower indicate Tory's proficiency on the task is well below the average grade peer's proficiency and that grade-level materials and expectations would be difficult for Tory to manage.

Intellectual/Cognitive Testing

Tory's General Intellectual Ability (GIA) standard score of 99 fell within the Average range and provides an estimate of her general intelligence. The GIA is composed of seven distinctly different cognitive abilities. Her performance on these seven abilities showed significant variation so a better estimate of her ability for academic learning may be Comprehension-Knowledge, a measure of verbal ability or crystallized intelligence (SS 110, PR 74). Tory's results from the WJ III NU Tests of Cognitive Abilities are presented and reviewed below. Her performance is compared to grade peers, other college freshmen attending a 4-year college or university.

Comprehension-Knowledge

Tory's performance on Comprehension-Knowledge, which includes measures of verbal ability and acquired knowledge, was in the Average to High Average range (SS = 110; 105–115). The task demands for both tests within this cluster include oral presentation of the items by the examiner and require oral responses from Tory. She found these verbal tasks manageable to easy and should be able to handle grade-level oral tasks with no problem. Comprehension-Knowledge is an important ability for academic success. Tory has the necessary verbal abilities

Cluster/Test	Standard Score (+/–1 SEM)	PR	Relative Proficiency Index (RPI)	RPI Implication (will find grade-level tasks to be)
GIA-EXTENDED	**99 (97–101)**	**47**	**89/90**	**Manageable**
COMPREHENSION-KNOWLEDGE	**110 (105–115)**	**74**	**95/90**	**Easy**
Verbal Comprehension	104 (98–111)	62	93/90	Manageable
General Information	113 (107–120)	81	97/90	Easy
LONG-TERM RETRIEVAL	**104 (98–111)**	**61**	**92/90**	**Manageable**
Visual-Auditory Learning	108 (103–114)	71	95/90	Easy
Retrieval Fluency	81 (74–88)	11	86/90	Manageable
VISUAL-SPATIAL THINKING	**114 (108–121)**	**83**	**96/90**	**Easy**
Spatial Relations	103 (98–108)	57	92/90	Manageable
Picture Recognition	124 (112–135)	94	98/90	Easy
AUDITORY PROCESSING	**82 (76–87)**	**11**	**74/90**	**Difficult**
Sound Blending	88 (83–93)	22	70/90	Difficult
Auditory Attention	78 (68–88)	7	77/90	Difficult
PROCESSING SPEED	**84 (81–87)**	**14**	**41/90**	**Very Difficult**
Visual Matching 2	83 (79–87)	13	32/90	Very Difficult
Decision Speed	85 (81–89)	16	51/90	Very Difficult
FLUID REASONING	**108 (101–115)**	**69**	**94/90**	**Manageable**
Concept Formation	100 (94–106)	50	90/90	Manageable
Analysis-Synthesis	120 (106–133)	91	96/90	Easy
SHORT-TERM MEMORY	**100 (94–106)**	**50**	**90/90**	**Manageable**
Numbers Reversed	91 (86–96)	28	67/90	Very Difficult
Memory for Words	109 (103–116)	73	98/90	Easy
COGNITIVE FLUENCY	**87 (85–89)**	**19**	**62/90**	**Very Difficult**
Retrieval Fluency	81 (74–88)	11	86/90	Manageable
Decision Speed	85 (81–89)	16	51/90	Very Difficult
Rapid Picture Naming	90 (88–92)	25	42/90	Very Difficult
PHONEMIC AWARENESS 3	**90 (86–94)**	**25**	**81/90**	**Difficult**
Sound Blending	88 (83–93)	22	70/90	Difficult
Incomplete Words	111 (100–123)	77	94/90	Manageable
Sound Awareness (ACH)	88 (83–93)	21	71/90	Difficult
WORKING MEMORY	**95 (92–99)**	**38**	**83/90**	**Manageable**
Numbers Reversed	91 (86–96)	28	67/90	Very Difficult
Auditory Working Memory	102 (97–108)	57	92/90	Manageable

and acquired knowledge to succeed, especially when no reading is involved.

Long-Term Retrieval

Long-Term Retrieval, the ability to store and retrieve information through an associative memory process, was in the Average range (SS = 104; 98–111). However, Tory's performance on the two tests composing this cluster varied. Visual-Auditory Learning, an associative memory task, was solidly in the Average range (SS = 108; 103–114) while Retrieval Fluency, a measure of ideational fluency, fell in the Low to Low Average range (SS = 81; 74–88).

Even with these Low to Low Average standard scores, Tory's proficiency on Retrieval Fluency was not impaired as noted by her RPI of 86/90. This indicates that college freshmen were not that variable on this task, so even with low relative standing, Tory is not that far from Average. Because Retrieval Fluency has an element of speed (e.g., name as many pieces of clothing as you can in 1 minute) and Visual-Auditory Learning does not, this may be a possible explanation for the differences noted.

Visual-Spatial Thinking

Visual-Spatial Thinking (SS = 114; 108–121), the ability to analyze, manipulate, and recall visual stimuli, was in the Average to Superior range and is related to higher-level math achievement. Picture Recognition, a measure of visual memory for drawings, was a superior area for Tory, which illustrates her good attention to visual detail. She scored at the 94th percentile with an RPI of 98/90, indicating that these types of visual memory tasks are easy for her. This strength may be related to Tory's interest and success in mathematics.

Auditory Processing

Auditory Processing (SS = 82; 76–87), the ability to analyze, discriminate, and manipulate sounds, is an important ability related to reading. This area was a normative weakness (SS < 85) for Tory and she finds these tasks difficult (RPI 74/90). To explore this area further, additional tests were administered in order to obtain the Phonemic Awareness 3 cluster. Phonemic awareness, a component of auditory processing, is highly related to acquiring basic reading and spelling skills. Tory's performance on two of the tests, Sound Awareness and Sound Blending, fell in the Low Average to Average range (SS = 88; 83–93). Her RPIs for both of these tests indicate she will find grade-level phonemic awareness tasks difficult. Tory's intact verbal and reasoning abilities aided her on the Incomplete Words task, which presents real words with one or more phonemes missing. It is essentially an auditory cloze task, and Tory was able to guess the complete word without too much difficulty. When Tory has to process the individual sounds by blending, deleting, substituting, or discriminating sounds, she has greater difficulty. These weaknesses are directly related to her reading and spelling difficulties.

Fluid Reasoning

Fluid Reasoning, the ability to reason and solve novel problems, was solidly in the Average to High Average range (SS = 108; 101–115). This ability is related to math

achievement and to reading comprehension and written expression. On one of the Fluid Reasoning tests, Analysis-Synthesis, a measure of deductive reasoning, Tory scored at the 91st percentile and her RPI of 96/90 indicates advanced proficiency compared to grade-peers. This strength helps explain Tory's affinity for math, which is her favorite academic area. Her reasoning abilities compare favorably to those of other college freshmen.

Processing Speed

Tory scored in the Low Average range (SS = 84; 81–87) for Processing Speed. She found both tasks, Visual Matching and Decision Speed, very difficult. On the Visual Matching test, a perceptual speed task related to basic reading skills, Tory demonstrated limited proficiency (RPI 32/90). To explore Tory's speed-related issues, additional tests were administered to obtain the Cognitive Fluency cluster, which includes aspects of rapid naming and semantic speed. These abilities are related to reading and spelling. Tory's performance fell in the Low Average range (SS = 87; 85–89) and was consistent with her performance in Processing Speed. On the Rapid Picture Naming test, although Tory's standard score was Average (SS = 90), her RPI of 42/90 indicates that rapid retrieval of words from long-term storage is very difficult for her. A slow rate in rapid automatized naming has been linked to reading difficulties.

Short-Term Memory

Short-Term Memory, the ability to hold information in immediate awareness and use it within a few seconds, fell in the Average range (SS = 100; 94–106). Although both tests in this cluster were in the Average range, Tory's proficiency on the memory span task, Memory for Words, was advanced (RPI 98/90), whereas her proficiency on the working memory task, Numbers Reversed, was limited (RPI 67/90). It is important to note that Tory recalled all the numbers presented but did not always repeat them in the exact reverse sequence required. To examine working memory further, the Auditory Working Memory test was administered. Tory scored in the Average range (SS = 102; 97–108). It appears that Tory has adequate memory span and working memory.

Review of Intracognitive Variations

When Tory's performance on the seven cognitive abilities is analyzed using the intracognitive variation procedure, she demonstrates significant and unusual weaknesses in Auditory Processing and Processing Speed. Not only are these two cognitive abilities weak for Tory when compared to the performance of other college freshmen, but they are also weak when compared to Tory's own performance on the other cognitive abilities. Based on her performance on the other cognitive clusters, only 3 out of 100 college freshmen with the same predicted score would obtain a score as low or lower on Auditory Processing, and only 7 out of 100 would score as low or lower on Processing Speed. These significant weaknesses help explain the academic difficulties Tory has experienced throughout her school career. Auditory Processing has a causal and reciprocal relationship with reading and spelling; normal auditory processing facilitates the acquisition of reading and spelling skills, and the acquisition of these skills helps to develop auditory processing further. Consequently, a weakness in auditory processing both impedes the acquisition of reading and spelling skills and, in turn, its own developmental course. A deficit in processing speed directly impacts the ability to develop fluency and automaticity in these skills.

Cognitive Testing Summary

The results of the cognitive testing provide evidence of cognitive processing difficulties in auditory processing and processing speed, both of which are directly related to Tory's difficulties in reading and writing. Furthermore, Tory has many intact abilities, including comprehension-knowledge, fluid reasoning, long-term retrieval, visual-spatial thinking, and short-term memory. These abilities, combined with her high motivation and work ethic, help explain why she has experienced success in mathematics and also how she has managed to survive in school. These results also help illuminate the reasons why Tory has difficulty understanding her learning problems. Tory has good knowledge, language, reasoning, memory, and visual skills, so her difficulty with reading is unexpected and confusing to her. She feels she "should" be able to do it, but no matter how hard she tries, it is a struggle.

Variations	Standard Scores			Variation		Significant at +/–1.50 SD
	Actual	Predicted	Difference	PR	SD	
Intracognitive						
Comp-Knowledge (Gc)	110	99	+11	81	+0.89	No
L-T Retrieval (Glr)	104	99	+ 5	70	+0.51	No
Vis-Spatial Think (Gv)	114	98	+16	90	+1.30	No
Auditory Process (Ga)	82	103	–21	3	–1.84	Yes
Fluid Reasoning (Gf)	108	99	+ 9	84	+0.98	No
Process Speed (Gs)	84	102	–18	7	–1.50	Yes
Short-Term Memory (Gsm)	100	100	0	49	–0.01	No

Achievement Testing

Tory's performance in Broad Reading (SS = 89; 87–91) and Broad Written Language (SS = 86; 82–90) was in the Low Average to Average range, whereas Broad Math (SS = 108; 104–111) was in the Average to High Average range. In all cases, her performance on basic skills was lower than her performance on the higher-level academic areas of reading comprehension, written expression, and math reasoning. Her oral language performance was solidly in the Average range. When viewed across the academic areas of reading, writing, and math, Tory's performance was lowest on measures of fluency that require speed and automaticity. Her proficiency on these tasks was limited compared to the proficiency of

average college freshmen. Tory's results from the WJ III NU Tests of Achievement are presented in the following chart.

Oral Language

Tory's performance on oral language tasks fell in the Average range (SS = 97; 92–103). She should find grade-level oral language demands manageable. This supports the Comprehension-Knowledge results obtained during the cognitive evaluation. These verbal abilities provide an important foundation for learning. Therefore, Tory's difficulties with reading and writing are unexpected. In addition, English is Tory's only language so there are no second language issues to consider.

CLUSTER/Test	Standard Score (+/–1 SEM)	PR	Relative Proficiency Index (RPI)	RPI Implication (will find grade level task)
BROAD READING	**89 (87–91)**	**23**	**57/90**	**Very Difficult**
Letter-Word Identification	84 (80–89)	15	57/90	Very Difficult
Reading Fluency	88 (87–90)	22	10/90	Extremely Difficult
Passage Comprehension	107 (100–114)	67	94/90	Manageable
BASIC READING	**85 (82–88)**	**16**	**57/90**	**Very Difficult**
Letter-Word Identification	84 (80–89)	15	57/90	Very Difficult
Word Attack	85 (80–89)	15	60/90	Very Difficult
READING COMPREHENSION	**113 (108–118)**	**81**	**96/90**	**Easy**
Passage Comprehension	107 (100–114)	67	94/90	Manageable
Reading Vocabulary	112 (108–116)	79	97/90	Easy
PHONEME/GRAPHEME KNOWLEDGE	**80 (76–84)**	**9**	**59/90**	**Very Difficult**
Word Attack	85 (80–89)	15	60/90	Very Difficult
Spelling of Sounds	82 (77–86)	11	58/90	Very Difficult
BROAD WRITTEN LANGUAGE	**86 (82–90)**	**18**	**74/90**	**Difficult**
Spelling	85 (81–89)	16	57/90	Very Difficult
Writing Fluency	83 (78–87)	12	50/90	Very Difficult
Writing Samples	119 (105–132)	89	95/90	Manageable
WRITTEN EXPRESSION	**90 (84–95)**	**25**	**81/90**	**Difficult**
Writing Fluency	83 (78–87)	12	50/90	Very Difficult
Writing Samples	119 (105–132)	89	95/90	Manageable
BROAD MATH	**108 (104–111)**	**70**	**94/90**	**Manageable**
Calculation	111 (105–117)	77	96/90	Easy
Math Fluency	91 (88–94)	27	84/90	Manageable
Applied Problems	110 (106–115)	75	97/90	Easy
BASIC MATH SKILLS	**103 (99–107)**	**58**	**92/90**	**Manageable**
Calculation	111 (105–117)	77	96/90	Easy
Math Fluency	91 (88–94)	27	84/90	Manageable
ORAL LANGUAGE	**97 (92–103)**	**43**	**88/90**	**Manageable**
Story Recall	103 (97–110)	59	91/90	Manageable
Understanding Directions	95 (89–101)	37	85/90	Manageable
ACADEMIC SKILLS	**89 (85–93)**	**23**	**78/90**	**Difficult**
Letter-Word Identification	84 (80–89)	15	57/90	Very Difficult
Spelling	85 (81–89)	16	57/90	Very Difficult
Calculation	111 (105–117)	77	96/90	Easy
ACADEMIC FLUENCY	**86 (84–88)**	**17**	**45/90**	**Very Difficult**
Reading Fluency	88 (87–90)	22	10/90	Extremely Difficult
Writing Fluency	83 (78–87)	12	50/90	Very Difficult
Math Fluency	91 (88–94)	27	84/90	Manageable
ACADEMIC APPLICATIONS	**111 (107–115)**	**76**	**96/90**	**Easy**
Passage Comprehension	107 (100–114)	67	94/90	Manageable
Writing Samples	119 (105–132)	89	95/90	Manageable
Applied Problems	110 (106–115)	75	97/90	Easy

Reading

Tory's Reading Comprehension was in the High Average range (SS = 113; 108–118). Tory's comprehension is aided by her good oral language skills, knowledge base, and reasoning abilities. However, when reading was timed or decontextualized (e.g., words in lists, rather than in passages), her performance declined. On Basic Reading Skills, comprised of tests of word identification and word attack, Tory's performance was in the Low Average range (SS = 85; 82–88). She had difficulty reading both real and nonsense words. Tory's errors on real words typically resulted in words that were not real, especially when reading multisyllabic words. She appeared to focus on specific letter strings and ignore others within the word. When reading phonically regular nonsense words, Tory's errors demonstrated a lack of knowledge of the phonological and orthographic rules of English. For example, she read words that had two vowels together—signaling a long vowel sound—as short vowels. She did not know how to pronounce certain phonic elements, such as "ph," when they occurred at the beginning of a word. Her proficiency on these tasks was limited compared to grade peers, indicating that decoding grade-level materials will be very difficult for her.

In addition, Tory's proficiency on Reading Fluency, a timed test, was very limited (RPI 10/90). She will find grade-level reading tasks that are timed or need to be performed under time constraints extremely difficult. Tory was accurate on the items she completed but she worked slowly. She also demonstrated lack of fluency on an oral reading of a college-level passage from one of her textbooks. Her rate was 70 words per minute with 12 errors and 4 self-corrections. As a point of reference, the oral reading rate for an average eighth-grade student is between 133 and 151 words per minute. The errors Tory made were a mix of mispronunciations, substitutions, deletions, and additions. For example, she substituted the word "use" for "utility," omitted the ending on "intellectual" reading it as "intellect," and changed "included" to "includes."

Her performance on Phoneme/Grapheme Knowledge (SS = 80; 76–84), the ability to encode and decode nonsense words, was at the 9th percentile, with limited proficiency compared to average grade peers. The task of reading or spelling nonsense words requires the application of phonological and orthographic abilities, both of which are problematic for Tory.

Written Language

Tory obtained scores in the Low Average to Average range on Broad Written Language (SS = 86; 82–90) and Written Expression (SS = 90; 84–95), with Spelling (SS = 85; 81–89) in the Low Average range. Again, just as with reading, Tory's performance in written language was characterized by higher scores on higher-level tasks and lower scores on timed or lower-level basic skills tasks. On the Writing Samples test, a task scored on the quality of the ideas expressed, without penalties for spelling errors, Tory's score was in the High Average to Superior range (SS = 119; 105–132). Her strengths in oral language and reasoning assisted her on this type of task. However, on Writing Fluency, a timed task requiring rapid production of simple sentences, Tory's score was in the Low to Low Average range (SS = 83; 78–87). Although she received a point for every sentence she wrote, she completed only 22 of 40 items during the 7-minute time limit. Tory's spelling was in the Low Average range and was characterized by errors in both phonology and orthography. Looking at her errors on the Writing Samples test, Tory demonstrated a lack of knowledge about the rules that govern English spelling. She did not double the consonant when writing the past tense of "trip" or "stop," spelling these words as "triped" and "stoped." Other examples of errors included "exallent" for "excellent" and "vechile" for "vehicle."

Mathematics

Mathematics was Tory's strongest academic area. The Broad Math cluster was in the Average to High Average range (SS = 108; 104–111). There are three tests in this cluster: Calculation, Applied Problems, and Math Fluency. Again, Tory's performance was better when time limits were not involved, as evidenced by her significantly higher scores on the two untimed tests, Calculation (SS = 111; 105–117) and Applied Problems (SS = 110; 106–115). Math Fluency, a timed test requiring the rapid retrieval of simple addition, subtraction, and multiplication facts, was her lowest score (SS = 91; 88–94). Her performance was accurate but slow. Because math was not an area of concern for Tory, only the tests that constitute the Broad Math cluster were administered. Two of those three tests, Calculation and Math Fluency, create the Basic Math Skills cluster so that is reported as well. Tory's performance on Basic Math Skills was in the Average range (SS = 103; 99–107), with the timed test, Math Fluency, lower than the untimed Calculation test, as noted previously.

Cross-Academic Clusters

The cross-academic clusters, Academic Skills, Academic Fluency, and Academic Applications, evaluate performance across reading, writing, and math. An examination of those three clusters illustrates that Tory primarily struggles with basic skills and fluency but not with application of those skills to higher-level tasks. This is a common characteristic of individuals with a specific learning disability. Further, by examining the tests within the Academic Skills and Academic Fluency clusters, it is apparent that Tory has difficulty with skills and fluency related to reading and writing but not related to math. For example, in the Academic Skills cluster (SS = 89; 85–93), Tory's performance on Letter-Word Identification (SS = 84; 80–89) and Spelling (SS = 85; 81–89) was in the Low Average range. However, her performance on Calculation (SS = 111; 105–117) was in the Average to High Average range. While struggling with reading and spelling skills, Tory finds math skills easy. This pattern of problems in specific academic areas while other areas are intact is another characteristic of a specific learning disability.

Achievement Testing Summary

The results of the achievement testing reveal normative weaknesses (SS < 85) in the areas of basic reading, spelling, and writing fluency. In addition, Tory has many intact academic areas, especially in mathematics, but also in reading comprehension and oral language. In general, Tory has more difficulty with basic skills and fluency than she does with higher-level tasks. Because her oral language is adequate, it is not the reason for her learning difficulties.

SUMMARY OF FINDINGS

Tory will soon be reentering Greenwood College. She is a polite, friendly, and intellectually curious young woman. She has a history of reading and writing difficulties, including a diagnosis of dyslexia in third grade. Results from past evaluations, her history, and the present evaluation confirm that Tory is an individual with dyslexia, a type of specific learning disability. She demonstrates overall intellectual abilities in the Average range. Her verbal, reasoning, visual-spatial, and long-term retrieval abilities were all in the Average to High Average range, and her short-term memory abilities were in the Average range. These intact abilities help explain her strong performance in mathematics, reading comprehension, and written expression. In contrast, she has significant weaknesses in auditory processing and processing speed. These deficits are related to and help explain her academic limitations in decoding, spelling, and fluency with basic skills. This pattern of strengths and weaknesses suggests the presence of specific learning disabilities.

Her pattern of difficulties indicates a lack of automaticity when working with phonological or orthographic information (i.e., the accurate and automatic identification of printed words and the letter patterns that comprise them). Her basic reading skills were lower than expected given her intellectual ability, verbal ability, and educational background. Her spelling was also below expectation. Qualitatively, many of her incorrect attempts violated basic English spelling principles. Given her pattern of cognitive abilities, her difficulties with decoding and spelling are best explained by deficits in phonological and orthographic processing, as well as her slow naming and processing speed.

Because Tory is not able to decode and spell nearly as many words as are in her oral vocabulary, she is much slower to complete reading and writing assignments than others of her ability and educational level. Compared to her peers, when reading a text she does not recognize as many words quickly and automatically. In addition, her sounding out of unfamiliar or unrecognized words is slow and often inaccurate, taking up cognitive resources that should be available for comprehension and critical thinking. These same problems affect Tory's writing. She has to focus on the basic skills (e.g., letter formation, which letters spell which sounds, what sequence of sounds are in a word), which then reduces her speed and the quantity of work she can complete within a given time frame.

Despite her extraordinary efforts, Tory's learning disabilities limit her access to classroom and textbook information and interfere with her ability to demonstrate what she knows. Tory has the ability and motivation to succeed. Her strengths help her compensate for her specific weaknesses. However, advanced reading and writing tasks are time-consuming and difficult for her. In order to benefit from her future postsecondary experiences, Tory should be encouraged to use all available resources. In addition, Tory should be entitled to the accommodations allowed for individuals with specific learning disabilities.

RECOMMENDATIONS AND ACCOMMODATIONS

The following accommodations would assist Tory in her future courses. The reasons for each accommodation are based on Tory's significant weaknesses in auditory processing, orthographic processing, and processing speed.

1. Provide Tory with extra time for in-class writing and reading assignments.

2. Permit use of a tape/digital recorder during lectures.

3. Provide access to textbooks and required readings on CDs.

4. Allow extended time for exams (double time).

5. Allow use of a computer for writing assignments and exams.

6. If necessary, allow Tory to take exams in a separate room.

7. Allow access to assistive technology.

Tory would benefit from work with a learning disability specialist or an academic coach to help her understand her specific weaknesses and develop strategies that will help her to take advantage of her strengths. In addition, Tory should be encouraged to advocate for herself, creating and requesting accommodations to facilitate her learning experience.

CASE 54

Comprehensive Evaluation of a Hard of Hearing High School Student in a Rural Setting

Kelly Metz

The following evaluation was conducted by a teacher of students who are deaf or hard of hearing (D/HH teacher). The purpose of the evaluation was to contribute data and recommendations for the student's 3-year evaluation and reinstate services for his hearing impairment. In conducting the evaluation, the examiner has attempted to avoid some errors that are commonly made when evaluating D/HH students.

Common Errors to Avoid

One error that is commonly made by evaluators is to place too much or too little emphasis on the educational impact of the student's hearing loss. Some evaluators make the erroneous assumption that a mild or unilateral hearing loss has *no* educational implications. At other times evaluators assume that *all* of a student's difficulties can be attributed to his or her hearing loss without considering the possibility of concurrent disabilities or learning problems. In this case, the examiner points out the impact of the student's hearing loss, as well as discussing other factors contributing to his delays such as his excessive absences and below average cognitive abilities.

Other common errors have to do with not using the student's amplification equipment (hearing aids or FM system) during the evaluation process, not conducting an equipment check prior to each evaluation session, and not stating in the evaluation report whether or not the equipment was used and if it was functioning optimally. I address this issue within the report under the heading of "Accommodations." One further error is not requiring the student to repeat the auditory stimulus prior to responding to a test item; this must be done to ensure that the student has heard the stimulus item correctly. This is especially important when dictating sounds or words for the student to spell. It is absolutely essential if administering a pseudo-word (nonsense word) spelling test.

Unique Challenges in a Rural Setting

Evaluating and serving special-needs students in a rural setting poses some unique challenges. While this is the case for all special-needs students, it is especially true when working with a low-incidence population such as D/HH students. First, the same continuum of placement services and resources available in a metropolitan area are generally not available in a rural setting. Self-contained classes designed specifically for D/HH students who need more intensive instruction than can be provided in a resource setting are often unavailable. Further, recruiting highly qualified teachers and therapists to a rural setting can be difficult. Additionally, teachers and therapists in a rural area may have less access to training in instructional approaches for children with special needs. An itinerant D/HH teacher may not be able to provide an optimal level of service time due to the travel time involved in serving students in a rural area. These challenges influence the recommendations that an evaluator is able to make. For example, the minimum service time recommended for this student was actually the maximum amount of time that the itinerant D/HH could devote to this case. Given the degree of this student's delays, if he were in an urban area with greater accessibility to services, I would have recommended at least an hour a day of direct instruction from the D/HH teacher, or possibly placement in a self-contained classroom for hard-of-hearing students.

Another unique challenge in a rural setting is that oversight of special education programs and services by state or federal agencies may be more lax than they are in more affluent metropolitan areas. For example, although it is required by law to provide educational services to students with disabilities until the student reaches the age of 22, this district does not adhere to this policy. Additionally, parents in a rural setting may be less knowledgeable about their rights and therefore less able or willing to advocate for their child or to hold the district accountable for progress.

What do these challenges mean for the evaluator? In addition to placement and service recommendations being limited to what can reasonably be provided in the rural setting, knowing that these students are not likely to get all the services necessary for optimal progress in school, the evaluator also has the responsibility to provide a quite comprehensive evaluation and to provide knowledgeable recommendations. For this particular student, I made recommendations keeping in mind the student's needs, as well as the skills and resources of the school staff and the availability of resources.

Rationale for Assessment Procedures

- The Screening Instrument for Targeting Educational Risk was chosen for the purpose of obtaining the general education teachers' perspectives on how this student was functioning in comparison to his classmates and to elicit concerns from the general education teachers. Ideally, this instrument should have been completed by all of his general education teachers; however, as is often the case, only one teacher complied with this request.
- An audiological evaluation is necessary for determining eligibility for HI services and must be updated annually.
- The Ling Six Sound Test, along with an equipment check of any amplification devices, should be conducted prior to evaluating any deaf or hard of hearing student. Additionally, the evaluator needs to specifically state whether or not these devices were used.
- A student interview was conducted to establish rapport prior to testing and to elicit student concerns about the type of services and support that the student would like to receive from the D/HH teacher.
- The Woodcock-Johnson III NU Tests of Achievement was chosen because it was appropriate for the student's age (19), and because the examiner's manual provides guidelines for its use with individuals with hearing impairments.

- Diagnostic teaching was conducted to get additional information about specific skill mastery and to see how the student would respond to certain types of instruction.

EVALUATION REPORT FOR HEARING IMPAIRMENT

Name:	Russell Thompson
Date of Birth:	9/14/1990
Age:	19-3
Ethnicity:	Native American
Parent:	Josephina Ramsey
School:	Cortez High School
Grade:	12-3
Dates of Evaluation:	12/9–11/2009
Evaluator:	Kelly Metz, M.Ed.

Assessment Team

Kelly Metz: Teacher for the deaf and hard of hearing (D/HH teacher)

Jessica Gibbs: Educational audiologist

Gloria Wainwright: School psychologist

James Barker: Shop teacher

REASON FOR REFERRAL

In accordance with the reauthorization of the Individuals with Disabilities Education Act, the multidisciplinary team has met and determined that Russell's three-year reevaluation should indeed be conducted and a complete battery of assessments administered. His last reevaluation was conducted almost 4 years ago on February 14, 2006. Russell only attended school for about 1 month at the beginning of his junior year; therefore, he was not in school at the time his 3-year reevaluation would have been due.

STATEMENT OF RACIAL/ETHNIC AND ECONOMIC STATUS

It is this team's consensus that this evaluation was not negatively impacted by racial/ethnic, economic, or environmental factors. Although Russell's poor school attendance could constitute an educational disadvantage due to a lack of continuous instruction, this disadvantage alone cannot account for the degree and severity of his overall delays.

ASSESSMENT PROCEDURES

File Review

Screening Instrument for Targeting Educational Risk (SIFTER)

Consultation with teachers

Complete audiological evaluation

Ling Six Sound Test

Student interview

Woodcock-Johnson III NU Tests of Achievement (WJ III ACH)

Diagnostic teaching

CONSIDERATIONS AND ACCOMMODATIONS

In consideration of Russell's hearing impairment, all testing was done in a quiet, one-to-one setting. He has an in-the-ear (ITE) hearing aid for his left ear, which was worn for all testing and was in good working order. A Ling Six Sound Test was conducted prior to testing. The Ling Six Sounds are speech sounds that broadly represent the speech spectrum from 250–8,000 Hz. The six phonemes, which are [ah], [oo], [ee], [s], [sh], and [m], target the low, middle, and high frequency sounds. The test was conducted by using an acoustic screen to cover the examiner's mouth, then producing the sounds in random order, two times each, for Russell to repeat. Russell was able to repeat the sounds with 100% accuracy.

Because of his hearing impairment, some tests on the WJ III that are normally administered via CD were administered via live voice in order to provide the best sound quality and to allow for use of speech reading along with listening. Russell was cooperative for all tasks and activities requested of him. Results of this evaluation are thought to be representative of a reasonable effort on Russell's part and therefore provide an accurate picture of his present abilities.

BACKGROUND INFORMATION

Russell lives with his mother, two younger brothers (ages 6 and 9), and a younger sister (age 15) on the Juan Carlos Apache reservation in Decimo Springs, New Mexico. Ms. Wainwright, the school psychologist, conducted an interview with Russell's mother, who related the following information. Russell has sporadic contact with his father who, she thinks, might distract him from his primary

responsibility, which she feels is school. Ms. Ramsey speaks Apache to her children because she wants them to stay in touch with their heritage. The children speak Apache to her most of the time and all of the time to their grandparents, but they speak only English with each other. She reported that Russell's command of Apache is not good and is sometimes unintelligible but that he is respectful and makes an effort to speak to his elders in Apache. There is often a lot of noise and bustle around the house with so many children, and Russell usually does not take part in conversations. Although she and his siblings make an effort to remember to face him when they speak to him, they often forget. Because she did not know that Russell had a hearing impairment, he did not receive early intervention outreach services. She stated that although she thinks school is important, it doesn't seem to be doing Russell any good and he has lost any sense of its usefulness to him. When he dropped out, he told her, "I never going to learn anything there." She encourages him to go to school but cannot make him do so. He recently returned to school because he decided that he needed a high school diploma to get a decent job.

Developmental and Health History

Russell was born 3 weeks prematurely with congestive heart failure. He was hospitalized at 4 months of age for an 8-month period due to heart surgery and recovery. Developmental milestones were documented in a May 1997 comprehensive evaluation report conducted by the New Mexico Agency for Deaf and Blind Education (NMADB) team. Various developmental milestones were delayed. Russell sat at 18 months, walked at 24 months, and spoke his first words at 30 months. Russell was diagnosed with a mild (left ear) to moderate (right ear) conductive hearing loss and was fitted for a hearing aid to the left ear in July 1996, at age 6. Results from an October 2000 comprehensive evaluation report written by the teacher of the deaf and hard of hearing indicated that Russell's hearing aid use in the primary grades was inconsistent. Russell has microtia/atresia of the right ear and a misshapen pinna on the left side. (Microtia is a birth deformity of the ear. Atresia is an absence or underdevelopment of the ear canal and middle ear structures.)

Educational History

Russell has attended the Juan Carlos Unified School District for his entire academic career, beginning with the district preschool program in 1993. He was retained in first grade. Based on the 1997 NMADB team evaluation and recommendations, he began receiving special education services as a student with a hearing impairment in September 1997, soon after he was diagnosed. At that time he was found to have significantly below average ability in visual-motor integration, preacademic achievement, and adaptive behavior skills. Russell has continued to receive resource support from site-based special education staff throughout his academic career. Additionally, he received services from the itinerant teacher for the deaf and hard of hearing from NMADB throughout his elementary years and for the first year and a half of high school. He was discontinued from HI services by NMADB midway through his sophomore year due to excessive absences followed by a period of absence of more than 10 days. During his junior year, he attended school only from August 11 through September 24. In spite of this extended period of absence from school, he is now classified as a senior. His attendance this year has been good, with only three documented absences so far this semester.

Audiological Evaluation

An audiological evaluation was conducted by educational audiologist Jessica Gibbs on 12/3/2009. Findings indicated that Russell has a bilateral, moderate-to-mild conductive hearing loss. He wears an in-the-ear hearing aid in his left ear. Ms. Gibbs recommended that Russell should continue to receive ongoing audiological and otological management through Juan Carlos Indian Medical Center. Ms. Gibbs recommended preferential seating, minimizing background noise, and the use of visual aids as classroom accommodations. She recommended that the multidisciplinary team review the existing data to determine if he would also benefit from use of an FM system to improve the signal-to-noise ratio during large group instruction.

SCREENING INSTRUMENT FOR TARGETING EDUCATIONAL RISK (SIFTER)

The SIFTER was completed by Russell's shop teacher, Mr. Barker, who has Russell for a construction class. This instrument requires the respondent to rate the student in five different areas affecting school performance, resulting in a "pass," "marginal pass," or "fail" in each area. Russell passed in Social Behavior and failed in Academics, Attention, Communication, and Class Participation. Mr. Barker commented that Russell has difficulty understanding oral language, that he has a short

attention span, and that he will wander about the room unless he is provided with continuous cues to stay on task. He commented that attendance has been a problem but that it is improving. He reported that since moving from the classroom into the shop and working on projects, Russell is showing increased interest and is beginning to make progress. He also stated that Russell never has attitude problems.

Russell's resource teacher, Mr. Kinard, was consulted. He did not express any concerns at this time. Russell's hearing loss was explained to him and he was given a spare pack of hearing aid batteries to keep in the resource room.

ACHIEVEMENT TESTING

Russell was administered various tests from Form A of the Woodcock-Johnson III NU Tests of Achievement (WJ III ACH). Norms are based on his grade placement of 12.3. Results are reported as standard scores (SS) with a 68% confidence interval (CI), grade equivalents (GE), relative proficiency indexes (RPI), and the proficiency levels associated with the RPI. Standard scores have a mean of 100 and a standard deviation of 15; the GE indicates the grade level for which the mean W score matched Russell's W score. (The W score is a transformation of the raw score.) The RPI indicates the likelihood that Russell will be successful on a task similar to that used in the test when his average grade peers are 90% successful. His proficiency is described by the associated verbal labels. Caution should be used in interpreting these scores, as students with hearing impairments were not included in the norming sample. Consequently, Russell's performance is compared to his grade peers without an educationally significant hearing impairment.

The following are verbal labels associated with standard score ranges and proficiency descriptors associated with RPI ranges.

SS Range	Verbal Label
<70	Very Low
70–79	Low
80–89	Low Average
90–110	Average
111–120	High Average
121–130	Superior
>130	Very Superior

RPI Range	Level of Proficiency
0/90–3/90	Negligible
3/90–24/90	Very Limited
24/90–67/90	Limited
67/90–82/90	Limited to Average
82/90–95/90	Average
95/90–98/90	Average to Advanced
98/90–100/90	Advanced
100/90	Very Advanced

Oral Language

Russell's primary mode of communication is aural/oral. His primary language is English, although Apache is also spoken in the home. Results from the WJ III ACH Oral Language Standard Battery cluster were as follows.

Cluster/Test	SS (CI 68%)	RPI	Proficiency Level	GE
Oral Language (Std)	30 (23–36)	17/90	**Very Limited**	< K.0
Story Recall	33 (20–45)	37/90	Limited	< K.0
Understanding Directions	36 (31–42)	7/90	Very Limited	K.1
Oral Comprehension	62 (57–67)	8/90	Very Limited	1.9

Russell's standard score of 30 on the Oral Language cluster fell in the Very Low range in comparison to his same-grade peers. His RPI of 17/90 predicts that Russell would have a 17% success rate on oral language tasks for which his grade peers would have a 90% success rate. This means that tasks involving oral language will be extremely difficult for Russell. The Story Recall test requires the student to listen to a short story and then repeat it back to the examiner, recalling as many details as possible. Russell's performance on this test fell in the Limited range of proficiency, indicating that understanding and recalling narrative information will be very difficult. The Understanding Directions test requires the subject to point to objects in pictures after listening to directions of increasing length and complexity. Russell's proficiency on this test was Very Limited. An analysis of errors on this task indicated that Russell is able to recall up to three directions in sequence; however, he missed items that required comprehension of spatial adjectives, such as tallest, top, bottom, and middle. The Oral Comprehension test requires the individual to listen to a short phrase or passage, and then fill in a missing word. The items begin with simple analogies and associations, progressing to more complex passages. Russell's proficiency level on this test was Very Limited. Although Russell stated that he could hear the items clearly, his limited vocabulary made it difficult for him to comprehend many of them and he could not supply the missing words.

Reading

Russell's performance on the Broad Reading cluster fell in the Very Low range in comparison to his grade peers. His RPI of 1/90 indicates that, generally, on reading tasks, Russell would be 1% proficient when his grade peers would be 90% proficient. This means that reading tasks in the general education classroom will be impossible for Russell to do without significant modifications. Russell's scores on the tests in this cluster were as follows:

Cluster/Test	SS (CI 68%)	RPI	Proficiency Level	GE
Broad Reading Cluster	35 (32–38)	1/90	**Negligible**	**2.3**
Letter-Word Identification	34 (30–38)	0/90	Negligible	2.4
Word Attack	55 (50–60)	1/90	Negligible	1.7
Passage Comprehension	47 (41–53)	6/90	Very Limited	2.3
Reading Fluency	58 (55–61)	5/90	Very Limited	2.2

Russell's proficiency on the Letter-Word Identification test was Negligible (RPI = 0/90). An analysis of his errors revealed that he has mastered only primary level, high-frequency sight words. When items progressed beyond that level, he usually did not attempt to try to pronounce the words. The Word Attack test requires the subject to read nonsense words. This test measures the person's ability to decode words phonetically. Russell's proficiency on this test was also Negligible. An error analysis of his responses indicated that Russell was able to consistently decode consonant-vowel-consonant (CVC) words and some consonant blends. He was not able to decode consonant digraphs, vowel digraphs, or diphthongs. He also has not mastered the long vowel sound of the vowel-consonant-silent /e/ syllable (CVCe). Russell's proficiency on the Passage Comprehension and Reading Fluency tests was Very Limited. Overall, he demonstrated greater proficiency with sight words than with phonics skills. His reading fluency rate and reading comprehension performance were commensurate with his sight word decoding ability.

Based on the results of this test, Russell is, essentially, a nonreader.

Written Expression

Russell's performance on the Brief Writing cluster fell in the Very Low range in comparison to his same-grade peers. His RPI of 6/90 indicates that Russell would have a 6% success rate on writing tasks that average grade-peers would be able to do with 90% success. Consequently, writing tasks in the general education classroom will be extremely difficult for Russell to complete without significant modifications. Russell's scores for the tests in this cluster were as follows:

Cluster/Test	SS (CI 68%)	RPI	Proficiency Level	GE
Brief Writing	**40 (35–45)**	**6/90**	**Very Limited**	**2.4**
Writing Samples	34 (25–42)	9/90	Very Limited	2.0
Spelling	57 (52–61)	3/90	Negligible	2.7

The Writing Samples test measures the subject's ability to express ideas in writing; however, most of these items (except for the beginning items) are not scored for spelling or punctuation. Russell's performance on this task was in the Very Limited range. Russell was able to generate simple sentences that consistently began with a capital letter and sometimes ended with a period. Words that were misspelled indicated difficulty both with phonological and orthographic processing. The Spelling test requires the subject to spell both phonically regular and irregular words. Russell's performance in this area was Very Limited and demonstrated that he could spell only a limited number of primary grade words. On one item he correctly spelled a homophone for the word. On another item, which he could not spell, he chose to write a synonym with an easier spelling. Although the synonym was still spelled incorrectly, it would have been discernible in context. He smiled when he noticed the examiner saw his altered response. For the most part Russell did not attempt to spell any words that he was unsure of; however, his use of a synonym on the final word indicated some ability to be strategic.

Mathematics

Russell's performance on the Broad Math cluster fell in the Very Low range in comparison to his same-grade peers. His RPI of 3/90 indicates that when average grade peers would have 90% success, Russell would have only 3% success. This means that math tasks in the general

education classroom will be extremely difficult, if not impossible, for Russell to complete without modifications. His scores on the tests in this cluster were as follows:

Cluster/Test	SS (CI 68%)	RPI	Proficiency Level	GE
Broad Math	**47 (44–50)**	**3/90**	**Very Limited**	**2.6**
Calculation	51 (44–57)	4/90	Very Limited	3.2
Math Fluency	33 (20–45)	37/90	Limited	5.2
Applied Problems	36 (31–41)	0/90	Negligible	1.7

Although Russell is functioning significantly below grade level in mathematics, this area is a relative strength for him, particularly for Calculation and Math Fluency. However, he scored lower on Applied Problems, which is a measure of math reasoning and includes functional math skills such as time and money concepts.

In addition to administering the standardized tests, the examiner also did some diagnostic teaching in math, focusing on the topics of fractions and money. An analysis of Russell's errors on these tests, as well as his performance during the diagnostic teaching session, revealed the following:

- He was able to do single-digit addition and subtraction, and paid attention to the signs if given mixed problems.

- He could do simple 1-digit multiplication problems but was not consistently accurate.

- He demonstrated some knowledge of regrouping for addition, subtraction, and simple 2-digit by 1-digit multiplication; however, he was not consistently accurate. He did not attempt any long division.

- Given fractions to add or subtract, he did not know that the value of the denominator doesn't change.

- Given portions of a figure shaded to represent simple fractions (e.g., ½, ⅔, ¾), initially, he was unable to identify these at all. After about 10 minutes of instruction, he could correctly identify the fraction indicated. The next day he was still able to identify the fractions indicated by the shaded figures without additional review or teaching.

- He was able to tell time to the hour.

- He was able to identify coins and state their value; however, he was not initially able to count coins at all. Given $4.86, after about 15 minutes of instruction and three to four repetitions of modeling by the examiner, Russell was finally able to count this amount of change.

COGNITIVE PERFORMANCE AND ADAPTIVE BEHAVIOR

The school psychologist administered the following assessments in December 2009: Comprehensive Test of Nonverbal Intelligence, Second Edition (CTONI-2), selected subtests of the Wechsler Adult Intelligence Scale-Fourth Edition (WAIS-IV), and the Adaptive Behavior Assessment System – Second Edition (ABAS-II). Russell's cognitive scores were more than 2 standard deviations below the mean, indicating intellectual ability well below average. His adaptive behavior skills, while also below average, were better than expected based on his cognitive test results. For additional information about Russell's cognitive ability, please refer to the psychoeducational evaluation report by Gloria Wainwright, M.A., dated 12/9/2009.

STUDENT INTERVIEW

When asked what job he would like to have when he graduates, Russell replied that he wants to work at the casino. There was a note in his file indicating that he had expressed an interest in being a security guard; however, when given a list of occupations at the casino (e.g., waiter, bus boy, maintenance, security), he did not indicate a preference for any particular job. At the end of the test session, Russell was told that the next day he should come prepared to tell the examiner the following two things: (a) What job do you want to do after high school? (b) What do you most want to learn with the time you have left in school? When asked to repeat back what he needed to be prepared to discuss tomorrow, he was unable to do so, even after several repetitions of the information. The information was written down for him to read (following modeling) and he was able to do this.

He did come prepared the following day. When asked about a job, this time he responded "security." When asked what a security guard does, he said, "Walk around." When asked why the security guard walks around, he shrugged his shoulders and indicated that he did not know. It appears that someone providing vocational counseling may have steered Russell toward security, but it does not seem to be his idea, as he does not know what a security guard does and could not choose it from a list of possible jobs when initially interviewed. In any case, given his lack of interpersonal communication skills, this may not be the best career choice for Russell. A more obtainable goal may be something along the lines of a bus boy or something in housekeeping or grounds maintenance; however, even for these jobs, he needs to improve his communication skills and will likely need some vocational training.

When asked what he most wants to learn in the time he has left in school, he replied, "Math." When asked specifically what math skills he wants to improve, he commented, "Money." This is certainly a valid goal as the diagnostic teaching session revealed that he is not able to consistently count change to $5.00.

SUMMARY

Russell is a 19-year-old male with a bilateral moderate-to-mild conductive hearing loss. He has an in-the-ear-hearing aid for his left ear. He has a history of inconsistent hearing aid use and poor school attendance. Although he did not attend school for the second half of his sophomore year or for his entire junior year, he is currently classified as a senior. He is very delayed in all aspects of language and academics, which is commensurate with his below average cognitive ability. His overall academic functioning is at about a second-grade level, with relative strengths in the areas of math calculation and adaptive behavior skills. He is not sure what he wants to do when he graduates but thinks he would like to work at the casino. He needs to improve both his basic interpersonal communication skills and his functional academic skills in order to successfully enter the workforce in any capacity.

IMPLICATIONS FOR INSTRUCTION

Accommodations

In light of Russell's hearing impairment, he needs the following accommodations in all of his classes in order to access the general education curriculum:

1. Use of his personal hearing aid for all academic classes. A listening check should be performed daily. Russell's resource teacher or a paraprofessional can be taught how to do a listening check of his hearing aid using a listening stethoscope, or alternatively staff can be taught how to do a Ling Six Sound Test. Either of these tasks can be done in 2 to 3 minutes.
2. Preferential seating near and in good view of the speaker, favoring his left ear, which, when aided, is his better ear.
3. Liberal use of visual aids to support comprehension.

4. Frequent checking for understanding, using open-ended questions.

5. Directions repeated and simplified as needed.

Modifications

In light of Russell's significant language and academic delays, he will need the following modifications in order to function successfully in general education classes:

1. He will need below-grade-level reading material for content area classes. Even if the material is read to him, it still would need to be below grade level in order for him to comprehend the information. His instructional reading level is about second grade, as is his oral comprehension level. Refer to the instructional strategies below for sources of developmentally appropriate reading material for addressing grade-level content topics.

2. He will need a reduced amount of target vocabulary and a reduced number of standards or objectives to master for all general education classes.

3. Written work will need to be reduced. He may need the opportunity for alternative responses to written tasks such as multiple choice rather than short answer tests.

4. He may need modified grading procedures for written assignments such as credit for correct letter sequences on spelling words or credit for correct writing sequences on written tasks rather than "all-or-none" grading for whole words or complete sentences or paragraphs.

5. He should be taught to use and should be able to use a calculator for computation tasks. Tasks involving math reasoning will have to be modified to about a beginning second-grade level.

Instructional Strategies

Functional Academics

With his academic career coming to an end, Russell should be guided to choose an appropriate job objective soon so that academic instruction can be focused on functional academic tasks that will support success in his chosen occupation, such as learning job-related vocabulary and communication skills.

Reading

1. While Russell needs to improve all aspects of reading (sight words, phonics, fluency, comprehension), his phonic skills are below that of his sight word reading ability, fluency, and comprehension, which are at about mid-second grade level. It is necessary to improve his phonic skills in order to improve his overall reading ability. Phonics instruction needs to be explicit and systematic. An example of a program that meets these criteria is Phonics for Reading by Curriculum Associates. Although there is no research documenting the effectiveness of this program, it was developed by incorporating evidence-based research practices. This is an age-neutral program that can be implemented with older students or adults. It is a teacher-directed, systematic phonics program that can be implemented in 40 minutes a day either individually or in small groups of up to 10 students. It is an inexpensive program that does not require a great deal of lesson planning or training to implement. It can be implemented by a tutor, aide, or volunteer with minimal training. Free online training is offered at: http://www.curriculumassociates.com/professional-development/subjects.asp?subject=phonics. There are three levels of the program. Level 2 would be appropriate for Russell.

2. Quick Reads, published by Pearson, is a fluency program that also incorporates elements of vocabulary and comprehension. This program consists of a series of short stories on nonfiction topics that are high-interest low-vocabulary. Each story is followed by a variety of written comprehension activities. Graphs are provided for charting fluency progress. Due to the fact that the stories are nonfiction, this program provides a source of material for content area teachers to find below-grade-level reading material on the same topic that is currently being studied in the general education curriculum.

3. Another potential source of below-grade-level reading material related to topics in content area classes are stories from the Reading A–Z web site (www.readinga-z.com). Although this web site includes fictional stories from a variety of genres, it also includes quite a few nonfiction stories. It is often possible to find stories related to a variety of science and social studies topics at two to three different grade levels, allowing the teacher to truly differentiate instruction.

4. An additional source of developmentally appropriate reading material that cannot be overlooked is that of material adapted by the teacher. Teachers can write a simple summary of target concepts from the current unit of study. While this may sound like a daunting task, keep in mind that this would not need to be a large amount of material since the amount of content

to be mastered has to be greatly reduced for Russell anyway. Additionally, this only needs to be done when other sources of below-grade-level material have been exhausted.

5. Russell should continue to expand his bank of sight words, which will also lead to increased fluency and therefore increased comprehension. Use a variety of games and drills for sight word acquisition and use charting and rewards to motivate Russell. Functional sight words such as environmental print or job-related vocabulary should not be overlooked.

Written Expression

Given the short amount of time Russell has left in school, writing instruction should be geared to functional life or job-related writing tasks. Functional writing tasks that should be addressed include activities like filling out a job application or writing a check.

Math

Russell stated math as the area he most wishes to improve on in the time he has left in school, specifically money skills. The following strategies are recommended for improving Russell's overall math skills:

1. Teach him to use a calculator (if he does not already know how to do so) and give him opportunities to practice using it with real-world application activities such as using grocery store ads to calculate how much money he needs to purchase items on a shopping list.

2. Use real money to teach functional skills such as counting out the correct amount of money for a purchase or counting change received. Practice counting by 5s and 10s, in order to be able to count dimes and nickels. Drill

and practice counting out change using modeling and repetition.

SUMMARY AND RECOMMENDATIONS

A Multidisciplinary Evaluation Team (MET) meeting should be convened to review the results of this evaluation. The following educational and instructional interventions are suggested regarding Russell's qualification for HI services:

1. Russell qualifies for services as a student with a hearing impairment. See attached audiological evaluation.

2. Russell would benefit from services from the itinerant teacher for the deaf and hard of hearing for a minimum of 2 hours a month to address the following areas of need:

   • Hearing aid care and maintenance

   • Direct instruction in basic interpersonal communication skills

   • Direct instruction in vocabulary related to vocational goals

   • Consultation services for general education teachers to address necessary accommodations and modifications

   • Consultation services for special education staff to address functional academic skills

Russell is a polite young man. It was a pleasure to work with him. Feel free to call me if I may be of further assistance or if you have any questions regarding these results or recommendations.

CASE 55

Assessment of a Cognitively Capable Student Who Is Struggling to Succeed in College

Andrew Shanock

This is a case of a college sophomore, Annie, who has average cognitive ability but both her anxiety and self-doubt are interfering with her academic success and ability to meet college demands. Growing up, she always thought that she could do better academically and that she was not as talented as her friends and peers. Compounding this belief was Annie's willingness to take ownership of her perceived failures but to give credit to others for her successes. For example, if she had a tutor help her prepare for two tests, only one of which she passed, she believed that it was the tutor's assistance that allowed her to pass one and her own lack of ability that caused her to fail the other. Annie believed that she had a cognitive processing deficit and thus was not as capable as her peers, which, in turn, heightened her anxiety and self-doubt.

This report illustrates several important points regarding assessments. First, it supports the power of data to help a person better understand himself or herself in an objective manner. By knowing specifically one's cognitive strengths and weaknesses, one feels empowered to address one's own learning issues. In this case, Annie's test performance and strategies clearly indicated a person who works well under pressure, has good short-term and long-term retrieval skills, can reason effectively, and has a good knowledge base from which to work. If Annie were asked about any of these skills prior to the assessment, she would have said that, outside of her knowledge base, her skills and abilities were significantly weaker than that of others. Imagine what it must be like for Annie, with her high level of anxiety, to attempt to be a part of a study group or participate in a classroom activity. Then, when she makes an error or only partially understands a concept or procedure, she uses this random data to support her belief that her own limited abilities are impacting her success.

It should be apparent that de-emphasizing general intelligence (*g*) and emphasizing broad and narrow cognitive abilities better assist the school psychologist in understanding the client, as well as in developing recommendations. In this case, the overall *g* was not a concern. In fact, it was Annie's belief that she was "smart" but could not show it that was heightening her anxiety and lowering her self-esteem. If the only results were that her overall intellect was normal, she would have received no solace and would likely have been further depressed. By seeing objective data indicating that all of the cognitive abilities she suspected to be weak were actually adequately developed, a huge obstacle was eliminated regarding her ability to believe in herself and in her own capabilities. Now, instead of having to overcome both anxiety and a processing deficit, she has only to address the anxiety—and this, in itself, helped reduce her anxiety.

Another function the report can serve is how one can use Cattell-Horn-Carroll (CHC) theory to assist in tailoring the assessment to the referral question. All too often school psychologists use the same test battery or batteries without thinking about why the student is to be assessed in the first place. Be it a fifth grader who has a reading issue, a first grader with a writing issue, or a high school student who is struggling in math, each will be administered the same set of tests, without consideration of what would be a more tailored, targeted assessment. In this case, the student's short-term memory and long-term retrieval were assessed in greater detail than other cognitive areas. CHC Cross-Battery principles helped in the selection of the core battery and the subtests that would provide a focused and comprehensive assessment that could be completed in a timely manner.

Lastly, this report contains several examples of how to explain various cognitive abilities in layman terms, helping readers improve their understanding of what is being discussed. Often, those administering cognitive assessments are so familiar with the language and concepts that they forget what it was like when they were first learning the new terminology. Although it makes sense to the writer, the reader is quickly lost and skips to the summary. When the reader finds the conclusions, he or she looks for the one sentence that sums up the whole report. Using metaphors and real-life examples to explain the various cognitive functions provides the reader with a basis for comprehending and interpreting the information.

PSYCHOEDUCATIONAL EVALUATION

Name:	Annie Steven
Date of Birth:	06/06/1990
Age:	19-7
Date of Evaluation:	01/07/2010
Evaluator:	Andrew Shanock, Ph.D.

REASON FOR REFERRAL AND BACKGROUND INFORMATION

Ms. Annie Steven referred herself for an evaluation because of increasing difficulty with her college coursework. Ms. Steven wondered if she had learning disabilities or some other type of problem that was affecting her performance. Ms. Steven is currently a sophomore at Wakefield College and enrolled in the Speech and Language program.

She expressed concern in regard to her ability to remember information, especially during exams. On tests, Ms. Steven explained that she often forgets material that she has repeatedly studied. She has trouble organizing her thoughts and when she comes across a question for which she does not immediately know the answer, it affects her confidence and increases her anxiety.

In high school, Ms. Steven received some test accommodations, including additional time and taking tests outside the classroom. She passed all of her state exams. No significant medical history was reported. Ms. Steven has taken medication in the past for anxiety.

Ms. Steven discussed her study habits and stated that she needs deadlines to push her to complete the work or prepare for a test. She has difficulty breaking down tasks into smaller parts and addressing these parts over time. Although she understands that "cramming" for a test has not been an effective approach, she also believes that if she attempts to spread out her studying, she will forget the initial information, and therefore have to re-study the information later on anyway. Ms. Steven prefers to study alone rather than in study groups. She thinks that in study groups, she will take more than give, which would be unfair to the group.

Ms. Steven's professors reported that she appears to be a hard worker who wants to succeed. However, she often does not advocate for herself or approach the professors if she is having difficulty understanding various concepts. The professors also indicated that Ms. Steven seems to be having the most trouble applying key concepts to more abstract assignments. Ms. Steven appears to need things repeatedly reviewed and to be taken through step-by-step to understand and retain more complex concepts.

ASSESSMENT TECHNIQUES

This assessment used the Cattell-Horn-Carroll (CHC) Cross Battery approach to develop the most useful information about Ms. Steven's cognitive abilities. The CHC Cross-Battery approach is defined as a method of psychoeducational assessment that is grounded in contemporary research and theory. More specifically, it allows practitioners to measure a wider range (or a more selective but in-depth range) of abilities than can be represented by a single intelligence battery. Subtests were selected from various test batteries and reorganized to help define Ms. Steven's abilities and to investigate strengths and weaknesses within each area. Assessments included the Woodcock-Johnson III NU Tests of Cognitive Abilities and Tests of Achievement (WJ III COG, WJ III ACH), the Wechsler Adult Intelligence Scale-Fourth Edition (WAIS-IV), the Clinical Evaluation of Language Fundamentals, Fourth Edition (CELF-4), and the Comprehensive Test of Phonological Processing (CTOPP). A majority of the subtests measured Ms. Steven's memory skills. Other techniques included clinical observation, a review of the records, and an interview.

Results are reported as scaled scores (ScS), which have a mean of 10 and a standard deviation of 3, and standard scores (SS), which have a mean of 100 and a standard deviation of 15. The standard score ranges used in this report are described by the following verbal labels: Average (90 to 109) and High Average (110 to 119). The Average range incorporates the middle 50% of scores obtained by people of Ms. Steven's age in the norm sample. All of Ms. Steven's scores were within the Average or High Average range.

COGNITIVE ASSESSMENT RESULTS

Ms. Steven's overall cognitive ability, as indicated by the WJ III COG, was found to be within the High Average range (standard score of 113; 80th percentile rank). This indicates that Ms. Steven performed as well as or better than 80% of individuals her age in the norming sample. There is a 68% chance that her true abilities fell between the Average and Superior ranges (SS of 108 to 121). A great majority of Ms. Steven's scores fell within the Average range, indicating that her cognitive abilities assessed are adequately developed. Her background knowledge, reasoning skills, and memory all appear to be within the Average and High Average ranges.

ited a general understanding but was not a specific definition. Yet, when asked to expand on her initial response, she could provide a more detailed and specific answer.

Ms. Steven showed good verbal reasoning skills, performing within the High Average range when comparing words. She was able to find both concrete and abstract connections. In some cases, she talked her way through to an answer by defining both words and then coming up with the concept by describing their similarity. On one test, Ms. Steven was read a list of four words and was asked to state which two were similar and her reasoning. Ms. Steven often asked for the list to be repeated prior to responding. After stating the two words, Ms. Steven would sigh and take a few moments to explain her reasoning, and many of her answers were correct.

Cluster	Test Battery	Test/Subtest Name	Standard Score	Confidence Interval (68%)	PR	Classification
Crystallized Knowledge			**106**	**101–111**	**65**	**Average**
Breadth and depth of acquired cultural knowledge and its effective application	WAIS-IV	Similarities	110	103–117	75	High Average
	WAIS-IV	Vocabulary	110	103–117	75	High Average
	WJ III COG	General Information	94	87–101	35	Average
	WJ III COG	Verbal Comprehension	97	90–104	43	Average
	CELF-4	Word Classes	110	103–117	75	High Average
	CELF-4	Semantic Relationships	115	108–122	84	High Average

Crystallized Knowledge

Crystallized intelligence, one's breadth and depth of knowledge of a culture and previously learned concepts, is highly correlated with most academic areas. Crystallized intelligence is useful in games such as Jeopardy or Trivial Pursuit, but on a larger scale, it is the knowledge of facts and procedures acquired throughout our life span. Ms. Steven's overall knowledge base was found to be within the Average range (SS 106; PR 65).

Ms. Steven exhibited a strong vocabulary. Throughout most of the subtests, Ms. Steven would take a few moments prior to responding and sometimes stated slight frustration in not being able to recall the definition or come up with an answer immediately. Her overall performance was within the High Average range. However, on many of the items, Ms. Steven's first response was one that exhib-

In contrast, Ms. Steven had some difficulty when she had to complete a four-part verbal analogy. She was able to quickly solve A:B = C:D analogies (e.g., water is to ocean as sand is to desert), but was initially confused and unsure of how to attack an A:C = B:D analogy (e.g., water is to sand as ocean is to desert). After a few questions, Ms. Steven figured out how to work that format. So although she initially had difficulty, she was able to come up with an effective problem-solving technique and apply it to the remaining problems.

Overall, Ms. Steven's general knowledge was an area of relative strength. She was often hesitant in her approach. In discussing her response style, Ms. Steven acknowledged that she often does not feel confident in her knowledge base and becomes unsure of how to answer. Still, she exhibited good problem-solving skills that allowed her to effectively demonstrate her knowledge.

Fluid Reasoning

Cluster	Test Battery	Test Name	Standard Score	Confidence Interval (68%)	PR	Classification
Fluid Reasoning			**118**	**113–123**	**88**	**High Average**
Use of inductive and deductive reasoning to solve novel problems	WJ III COG	Concept Formation	123	116–130	94	Superior
	WJ III COG	Analysis-Synthesis	103	96–110	57	Average

Fluid intelligence involves novel reasoning and problem solving, is assumed to depend minimally on previous learning experience, and is highly related to academic areas such as math and reading comprehension. These tasks measure inductive and deductive reasoning skills. Inductive reasoning is the ability to ascertain a rule, generalization, or conclusion based on multiple observations or examples, similar to the way a detective puts together clues to solve a crime). Deductive or sequential reasoning is the ability to start with stated rules and take steps to reach a solution, similar to an "if-then" statement. The subtests involved single to multistep problem solving using colored shapes. For both tasks, Ms. Steven was provided with corrective feedback. If correct, she was told so; if she was incorrect, she would be given the correct answer but no further assistance. She had to use the feedback to assist with solving the subsequent problems. Ms. Steven's performance in this area varied (Average to Superior), but her reasoning skills appeared to be well developed.

On the deductive reasoning task, Ms. Steven was provided with a key that showed how combinations of certain colors "equaled" one color. Ms. Steven was required to use the key to find the missing color in problems (similar to an algebraic problem) that became gradually more complex. Ms. Steven's responses were quick and accurate when, on initial items, she needed to simply refer to the key. Where she started to struggle is when, on the more complex problems, she had to find an alternate way to come up with an answer. Her organization was seemingly logical but was not in accordance to the structure or the rules of the task. In the classroom, this is similar to the student who may combine unlike terms (e.g., $5x^2 + x$ does not equal $5x^3$). More to the point, similar to her difficulties solving verbal analogies, Ms. Steven appeared to have trouble shifting her thinking and modifying her problem-solving approach.

Ms. Steven had a much stronger performance on the inductive reasoning task in which she was asked to identify the characteristic that identified the main difference (i.e., the rule) that differentiated one group of colored shapes from another. Here again, the problems increased in complexity, reflecting an increasing number of characteristics that differentiated the two groups. Ms. Steven took her time with these items, repeatedly reviewing the problem before responding. She was consistently correct as the items increased in complexity and difficulty, indicating that she was flexible in her thinking and attentive to detail. Her problem-solving method, however, could stay relatively the same.

For both tasks, Ms. Steven stated that she liked the corrective feedback because it let her know if she was "doing things right." She indicated that it increased her confidence and assurance on how she was attacking the problems.

Processing Speed

Ms. Steven's processing speed, which is the ability to perform tasks fluently and automatically, especially when under time pressure to maintain focused attention and concentration, was also within the Average range (SS 102; PR 56). The tasks are generally easy and most people would get all items correct if the tests were not highly speeded. On one subtest, Ms. Steven was asked to identify two pictured objects that were most alike within a row of six pictured items. On the other subtest, Ms. Steven had to circle identical numbers within rows of similar-looking numbers (e.g., 40, 41, 14, 44, 41). Although she performed within the Average range on both tasks, Ms. Steven had a slightly stronger performance on the latter. It is possible that, in comparison to the former, the latter task was clear and concrete, which may have relieved some anxiety that occurs when doing a speeded task.

Cluster	Test Battery	Subtest Name	Test Score	Confidence Interval (68%)	PR	Classification
Processing Speed			**102**	**97–107**	**56**	**Average**
Ability to perform simple tasks quickly and fluently	WJ III COG	Decision Speed	96	89–103	40	Average
	WJ III COG	Visual Matching	106	99–113	65	Average

Visual-Spatial Thinking

Cluster	Test Battery	Test Name	Standard Score	Confidence Interval (68%)	PR	Classification
Visual-Spatial Thinking			97	92–102	42	Average
Ability to analyze, synthesize, and manipulate visual patterns/stimuli	WJ III COG	Spatial Relations	103	96–110	57	Average
	WJ III COG	Picture Recognition	93	86–100	33	Average

Visual-spatial thinking is the ability to analyze, synthesize, and manipulate visual stimuli. Although research has indicated that visual-spatial thinking has little impact on academic areas such as reading and math, it may be important with hands-on, detailed tasks. Ms. Steven's overall performance (SS 97; PR 42) and individual subtest performances were within the Average range, indicating adequately developed skills in this area. She ably identified various pieces (from a choice of five options) that form a complete shape. This is similar to seeing which puzzle pieces go together without touching them. In comparison, Ms. Steven had some trouble applying her attentiveness to detail when placed under time pressure. Similar to looking at a police lineup, Ms. Steven was presented with a pictured object or objects, and then had to pick out the target object(s) from an array of similar-looking items. For this visual memory subtest, Ms. Steven had trouble adequately splitting her attention among all of the target items. She would spend too much time on one, thus missing out on the details of the others. This type of planning appears analogous to Ms. Steven's procedure for studying for classes.

Short-Term Memory

Short-term memory, which is the ability to hold information in immediate awareness and then use it within a few seconds, has been found to have a relationship with reading, math, and written expression. Ms. Steven's overall performance was found to be within the Average range (SS 102; PR 53). The two primary abilities within short-term memory are memory span and working memory. Memory span is the ability to attend to and immediately recall sequentially ordered elements in the correct order after they are presented only once. A common example is immediately attempting to repeat a phone number you have just been told. On these tasks, Ms. Steven repeated the series at a deliberate, steady pace. She was able to repeat sequences of seven items in length. Working memory is the ability to temporarily store and mentally manipulate information. Examples include attempting to recite the alphabet backwards or doing long division without pencil and paper. Ms. Steven's performance on both working memory and memory span tasks were within the Average range.

Ms. Steven used her strong memory span to assist her performance on working memory tasks. She often repeated the series a few times before attempting to reorganize it. When Ms. Steven made an error, she was readily able to correct it as she could retrieve the entire series to "check" her answer. So, not only could she reorganize a seven-item sequence, but she could still maintain and work with the original sequence to correct and finalize

Cluster	Test Battery	Test/Subtest Name	Test Score	Confidence Interval (68%)	%ile	Classification
Short-Term Memory		**Cluster Average =**	102	97–107	55	**Average**
Ability to hold info in immediate awareness and then use it within a few seconds	WAIS-IV	Digit Span (MS/WM)	100	93–107	50	Average
	WJ III COG	Numbers Reversed (WM)	104	97–111	62	Average
	CELF-4	Recalling Sentences (MS)	115	108–122	84	High Average
	CELF-4	Familiar Sequence (MS)	95	88–102	38	Average
	WJ III COG	Aud Working Memory (WM)	106	99–113	65	Average
	WJ III COG	Memory for Words (MS)	100	93–107	50	Average
	WJ III ACH	Understanding Directions (WM)	127[a]	120–134	97	Superior
MS = Memory Span; WM = Working Memory [a] Considered an outlier and not included in overall cluster average.						

her answer. Ms. Steven's strongest performance was on a working memory task in which she had to review a detailed picture of a scene, listen to a series of instructions, and then point to various items in the order specified. As the complexity of the instructions increased, the order in which items were mentioned was different from the sequence in which she was to point to them (e.g., point to the ball after you point to the table); additionally, the number of items to which she had to attend steadily increased. Eventually, Ms. Steven had to follow "if-then" statements in which she was required to review the picture and decide whether or not to point to certain objects.

Although Ms. Steven appeared to be at relative ease while attempting each task, she later revealed that she was unsure of herself and felt she had done poorly. She was surprised that she did so well; she seemed to give greater weight to the items she thought she got wrong than on those she thought she got right.

Long-Term Retrieval

Long-term retrieval is the ability to store, consolidate, and then retrieve information through association. Ms. Steven's performance in this area was found to be within the Average range (SS 103; PR 57) on tasks requiring her to learn novel associations, to quickly name familiar picture cues, or to recall the details of brief narratives that were read to her. She performed in the High Average range when asked to recall details about the stories after a delay.

Ms. Steven performed in the Average range when "reading" novel visual symbols representing common words (associative memory). The task is similar to identifying words based on their shape (whole word), context, and word prediction. For this task, Ms. Steven was presented four or five new "words" after reading "sentences" containing previously presented "words." The evaluator corrected Ms. Steven if she "misread" a symbol. Ms. Steven would typically miss at least one word from each new presentation. She seemed to benefit from corrective feedback, as she rarely misread a symbol twice. She "read" many of the sentences smoothly and contextually. Ms. Steven was able to hold and retrieve much of the information throughout the subtests.

Ms. Steven showed further success when recalling familiar, stored words under time pressure. On the game show Jeopardy, for example, all the contestants have a great knowledge base, but the person who can recall the information the quickest gets the opportunity to answer.

She ably recalled and stated names of things within a category, such as items that are square. Her responses were organized and smoothly paced. Ms. Steven had similar success when she had to name familiar pictured items rapidly.

Ms. Steven also performed adequately when recalling various details and general themes of brief oral passages. She was able to recall specific names, remember numerical information, and restate the passage in the correct sequence. Later in the session, and after several nonrelated tasks were completed, Ms. Steven easily retold the details of these passages. This would be akin to recalling information from a classroom lecture.

Cluster	Test Battery	Test/Subtest Name	Standard Score	Confidence Interval (68%)	PR	Classification
Long-Term Retrieval			**103**	**98–108**	**57**	**Average**
Ability to store, consolidate, and then retrieve information through association	WJ III COG	Vis-Auditory Learning	102	95–107	55	Average
	WJ III COG	Vis-Aud Learning-Delayed	106	99–113	65	Average
	WJ III COG	Rapid Picture Naming	104	97–111	62	Average
	CTOPP	Rapid Naming	100	93–107	50	Average
	WJ III ACH	Story Recall	104	97–111	62	Average
	WJ III ACH	Story Recall-Delayed	114	107–121	83	High Average
	WJ III COG	Retrieval Fluency	100	93–107	50	Average
	CELF-4	Understanding Paragraphs	95	88–102	38	Average

Social-Emotional Functioning

Behavior Assessment System for Children, Second Edition

	T Score	Percentile
Composites		
Externalizing Problems	58	81
Internalizing Problems	69	95
Emotional Symptoms	59	83
Personal Adjustment	*52*	*54*
Scales		
Hyperactivity	60	85
Locus of Control	43	31
Social Stress	52	60
Anxiety	70	96
Depression	49	63
Somatization	66	92
Atypicality	45	43
Sensation Seeking	44	30
Attention Problems	73	98
Alcohol Abuse	43	24
School Maladjustment	47	45
Sense of Inadequacy	67	93
Relation With Parents	*59*	*81*
Interpersonal Relations	*52*	*51*
Self-Esteem	*52*	*45*
Self-Reliance	*44*	*25*
T Score classifications: Average: 41–59, At-Risk: 60–69, Clinically Significant: > 69 For italicized scales: At-Risk: 30–40, Clinically Significant: < 30		

Ms. Steven completed the Behavior Assessment System for Children, Second Edition (BASC-2), Self-Report College form, which presents multiple-choice questions regarding her perception of her moods, behaviors, self-worth, and interpersonal relationships. Ms. Steven rated a majority of social-emotional functioning categories to be well within the Average range. For example, Ms. Steven indicated that she likes herself and is reliable. However, she rated her ability to be successful within the At-Risk range. She rated her anxiety and level of attentiveness to be within the Clinically Significant range. Her answers indicated a high level of indecisiveness, tendency to be easily bothered by "little things," and propensity to worry. These feelings appear to decrease her ability to attend as her stress and worry about various issues impede her concentration skills. Her lack of confidence and limited ability to plan seem to be confirmed through conversations with Ms. Steven. She acknowledged that she needs guidance as to which materials to study; without it, she may attempt to study all of the information, which overwhelms her before she even starts the process. Ms. Steven stated that she has great difficulty getting work done early but can get it done when deadlines are set. Although she was unsure as to what is a typical level of anxiety regarding tests and studying, she feels that she is much more nervous prior to a test than her peers; this, in turn, negatively affects her self-confidence and increases her anxiety. Through the discussions, it became evident that Ms. Steven takes full responsibility when she does poorly on an assignment or test but takes little credit when she receives a high grade. For example, she commented that the only reason that she passed her Regents exams was because her brother helped her study.

SUMMARY

Ms. Steven was self-referred because she is having difficulty maintaining her grades at the college level. The results of this evaluation indicate that her cognitive abilities are all within the Average range or higher. She exhibited good problem solving, general knowledge, short-term memory, long-term retrieval, and the ability to work under time pressure. At times during the assessment, Ms. Steven was hesitant or unsure of her answers. As we reviewed her test results, Ms. Steven was surprised at her performance, as she believed that she was well below the norm, especially in terms of her memory abilities.

Ms. Steven's difficulties within the college classroom appear to be due to her perceptions of her abilities and her inability to internalize her successes at the same level as she does her failures. There are reasonable steps that Ms. Steven can take to reduce her anxiety and collect data to better provide a more realistic picture of her skills. From the results of this evaluation, it does not appear that Ms. Steven has a learning disability or requires additional accommodations or modifications. However, she should share this report with her professors (at the beginning of a semester) to discuss possible alternate means of assessment for class assignments and tests.

Ms. Steven is hardworking and has a strong desire to be a speech-language pathologist. She enjoys her classes and is excited about learning more. With some counseling and reasonable self-initiated interventions, she should have more opportunities to exhibit her strong abilities and enthusiasm in her classes and profession.

RECOMMENDATIONS

1. Hire an academic coach for weekly meetings. The coach will help you stay on track with your assignments and help you organize your study and assignment schedule.

2. Seek counseling at the Wakefield College Counseling Center. It is a free service for students. It would be good for you to schedule regular meetings with a counselor to help you learn ways to appreciate your successes, recognize your strengths, and increase your level of self-confidence.

3. Talk to an academic counselor at Student Support Services and request that she/he help you find a tutor who has specific expertise in teaching study skills and test-taking strategies. Working with an academic coach and learning these skills and strategies are likely to be very effective in allowing you to learn the information expected and demonstrate your knowledge on assignments and tests with significantly reduced anxiety.

Until the above recommendations can be put into place, the following recommendations regarding study skills and test-taking strategies are offered:

1. You may benefit from learning first-letter mnemonic strategies to help you remember and recall facts and information. For this to be effective, the information to be recalled must be both familiar and meaningful.

2. You may feel anxious when taking tests. To help reduce your stress, it would be beneficial to learn specific test-taking strategies, such as reading over the entire test before starting, outlining the answers to essay questions, and reading all multiple-choice answers before selecting a response. After finishing a test, review which strategies you used, which ones were beneficial, and how to modify the way you attack a test accordingly.

3. When reading content area textbooks, read the questions at the end of the chapter first so that you know which information is important and can look for the answers as you read. You should then turn chapter subheadings into questions and read to find the answers.

4. You may enhance your writing by learning how to create brief outlines prior to writing an essay. Try creating semantic maps or graphic organizers that will provide simple visual anchors/cues to assist in the writing process. A useful program for this purpose is Inspiration (www.inspiration.com).

5. Helpful websites for further educational strategies include: www.nild.net; www.ldonline.org; and www.schoolpsychology.net. Although these websites deal primarily with learning disabilities, they do offer strategies that can be helpful for anyone. Other useful web sites in this regard are Study Guides and Strategies (http://www.studygs.net) and Strategies for Success (http://www.accd.edu/sac/history/keller/ACCDitg/SSindex.htm).

6. Make appointments to meet with your professors during office hours on a regular basis (once a month) to review your performance and ask any questions you may have. As the semester progresses, you can better determine in which classes you are having difficulty and need more assistance.

7. You will greatly benefit if you keep your academic advisor regularly apprised of your progress. This will allow the advisor to readily advocate for you when needed.

8. Attempt to increase the number of study group participations with each semester (e.g., one in the fall, two in the spring). When joining a group, suggest that each member have an assigned topic to work on. This will allow you to focus on one topic and exhibit expertise, thus allowing you to give and take in equal measure.

CASE 56

Making the Most of One's Strengths: When Verbal Intelligence and Dedication to Succeed Overcome Late Identification

Michael E. Gerner

For many years during her schooling, Ms. Sawyer struggled to keep pace in class and showed considerable problems with mathematics. Although taking notes in class and mathematics were very difficult for her, she was verbally expressive and her reading and writing skills were adequate. Most significantly, she was a well-behaved student who internalized the problems she endured with the result she was never referred or evaluated until high school. The original referral was not initiated in the schools, but rather it was made to an outside evaluator at the request of her parents who were very concerned about her high levels of anxiety and low self-esteem.

Ms. Sawyer's academic problems at school contributed to maladaptive anxiety, stress, and low self-esteem. Despite her best efforts and dedication to achieve, she had to endure the chronic difficulty of keeping pace in the classroom, low math performance, and the pressure and confusion of performing below her peers in certain areas and never understanding why. After the school reviewed the evaluator's report and granted accommodations, she was able to succeed in her classes and graduate; but by this time, she had failed a number of math classes and had developed severe levels of stress and anxiety. The ball, however, was again dropped when she applied for admission to a university. The admissions committee did not consider her special needs and refused admission. It was not until yet another evaluation that she was finally admitted to the university and granted appropriate accommodations. She graduated with a double major and a 3.1 GPA and, after 1 year in the Peace Corps, is applying to graduate school.

This case illustrates several factors to consider:

- The importance of understanding and accommodating learning differences early in schooling, even when they do not involve a reading and/or writing disability.

- The "invisibility" of anxiety and attention problems in a well-behaved, polite, and highly motivated girl who may fall "under the radar screen" of educators.

- The possible development of an anxiety disorder as a consequence of misunderstanding a student's individual differences and failing to provide appropriate accommodations in school.

- The frequency with which a learning disability is manifested by deficits in processing speed and cognitive efficiency (i.e., recall, sequencing, and quick processing of details), rather than verbal intelligence.

- The ability to overcome many challenges through personal resolve and dedication demonstrated by this courageous and talented young woman. There are likely many individuals who would not have been able to overcome the problems she endured. Without identification, intervention, and parental involvement, they would be "casualties of the educational system" who are never able to actualize their abilities or talents.

- The academic problems caused by the interaction of attention problems, processing deficits, and anxiety rather than by one factor alone.

- The necessity of a recent evaluation (within 3 years) when transitioning from high school to college.

Finally, the format of this report is intended to point out the importance of:

- Discussing and emphasizing strengths first in a presentation of evaluation findings.

- Providing justification for recommendations by including a rationale for each.

- The need to include a *DSM-IV-TR* diagnosis for post-secondary institutions and test agencies.
- Placing "Conclusions and Recommendations," the most important elements, at the beginning of a report rather than at the end.

PSYCHOEDUCATIONAL REPORT

Name:	Angie A. Sawyer
Date of Birth:	September 9, 1984
Age:	25
Ethnicity:	Caucasian, Non-Hispanic
Status/School:	Bachelor's Degree 2008, University of Southern Utah
Current Work:	Peace Corps, India
Evaluation Date:	July 27, 2010
Evaluator:	Michael E. Gerner, Ph.D., P.C.

SUMMARY AND RECOMMENDATIONS

Reason for Referral

Ms. Sawyer has had well-documented educational problems since early elementary school, but has received educational accommodations only since her sophomore year in high school. Granted appropriate accommodations in college, she earned a Bachelor of Arts degree with a dual major in Anthropology and Spanish. She is currently teaching English in India as a Peace Corps volunteer. Ms. Sawyer is dedicated to continuing her education and plans to apply to a graduate school program in International Studies. The purpose of this evaluation was to update information concerning her individual strengths and weaknesses for educational planning.

Summary and Conclusions

Ms. Sawyer is likely to be successful in a graduate program and in employment due to her verbal intelligence, good reading comprehension and written expression, desire to succeed, and persistence in pursuing her goals. Her ability to understand concepts and advanced vocabulary in spoken language exceeded 58% of adults her age across the United States. She surpassed 81% in written expression and 65% in spatial relations. Ms. Sawyer is dedicated to achieving her educational/career objectives; she is adaptable and enjoys living and working in different countries and cultures. Her successes include graduating with a 3.19 cumulative grade point average in college and receiving excellent job performance ratings in her work as a Peace Corps volunteer. Moreover, background information and current test performance strongly support the conclusion that Ms. Sawyer is an individual who shows trustworthiness, high moral standards, and resilience in the face of adversity. Although she only surpassed 26% of college seniors in reading comprehension, this test was administered, as standardized, with time constraints, a factor that imposes significant limitations on Ms. Sawyer's ability to perform to her level of capability.

In contrast to these considerable strengths, Ms. Sawyer demonstrated significant weaknesses in short-term memory, rote processing speed, and general cognitive efficiency. She exceeded only 3% of adults her age in the first area and less than 1% of adults her age in the other two. Cognitive efficiency involves both immediate memory and the ability to complete simple, routine tasks quickly and accurately. Within the current test setting, her weakness in cognitive efficiency was the major factor contributing to her difficulties in almost all of the other measures, cognitive and academic.

The interaction of these cognitive weaknesses have contributed to the development of a specific learning disability in mathematics. On this testing, Ms. Sawyer's math calculation skills, automaticity of math fact retrieval, and ability to apply those skills surpassed only 19%, 1%, and 18% of same-age adults, respectively.

Additionally, Ms. Sawyer's history and this evaluation support a diagnosis of Attention-Deficit/Hyperactivity Disorder (ADHD)—Inattentive type. Associated characteristics were clinically significant and surpassed 98% of women her age on the Achenbach DSM-Oriented Scales for Women 18–59. A clinical interview, in conjunction with background information, also revealed that anxiety continues to be a significant issue when she is under time pressure and does not have accommodations for tests. Her anxiety regarding these issues is complicated by her ADHD. The interaction of her weak cognitive efficiency, ADHD, and anxiety significantly affects her personal organization, efficiency, ability to learn and apply mathematics skills, and performance in all test situations and academic situations in which there are time constraints. More specifically, she is substantially less efficient in the presence of distractions, when she must carry out routine or systematic tasks rapidly, and when she must recall and sequence auditory details or complete detailed academic tasks under time pressure. Consequently, she requires considerably more time than her peers for study and review of detailed information. Additionally, as Ms. Sawyer's auditory memory is well below average, she is unable to take lecture notes as she attends to a lecture.

The central issues of concern for Ms. Sawyer have never been her intelligence or high-order reasoning abilities. Given Ms. Sawyer's success in her undergraduate career, graduating with a 3.19 GPA with dual majors in Anthropology and Spanish, she is well able to handle the demands of university coursework when provided the appropriate accommodations, despite her significant learning disability in mathematics, ADHD, and anxiety. Nevertheless, these learning issues have contributed to high levels of personal stress and anxiety, especially when accommodations are either inadequate or absent. Furthermore, her difficulties erode her self-confidence when she feels that she is performing below her intellectual ability.

A clinical interview, self-report personality measures, test results, and background information support the impression of a verbally and intellectually competent individual with a mathematics disability and weaknesses in cognitive efficiency, complicated by Attention-Deficit/Hyperactivity Disorder and anxiety.

Recommendations

Ms. Sawyer's ADHD, anxiety, slow processing speed, and limited auditory memory span interact to cause maladaptive levels of stress and performance well below her level of knowledge and intellectual sophistication in classes, tests, and all other academic situations if she does not have appropriate accommodations. The following recommendations and rationales supporting them are offered to Ms. Sawyer's future student disability services program and the Graduate Record Examination Committee:

1. Ms. Sawyer should be eligible for testing and program accommodations by the Graduate Record Examination (GRE) Committee and her future disability student services department.

   Rationale: Ms. Sawyer's educational history, behavioral manifestations, personality profile, and current evaluation results indicate that she is eligible for accommodations under Section 504 of the Rehabilitation Act and the Americans with Disabilities Act. Learning and taking tests, specifically under time constraints, is a major

life function that is significantly negatively affected by ADHD, processing deficits, and anxiety.

2. Ms. Sawyer should be granted time extensions of 1.5 (time and one-half) on each section of the GRE. She should take the GRE in a quiet, private room with permission to use a calculator on the mathematics portion of the test.

   Rationale: Ms. Sawyer requires these accommodations so that her slow processing, immediate memory weaknesses, math learning disability, distractibility, and anxiety do not impede her ability to demonstrate her knowledge or true competence in her chosen field of study.

3. In graduate school, Ms. Sawyer should:

   a. Have time extensions on course tests, semester exams, and any other high-stakes tests.

      Rationale: Ms. Sawyer's weakness in processing speed, retrieval of information under time constraints, and attentional difficulties make it impossible for her to demonstrate her knowledge in the same amount of time that is usual for her peers.

   b. Be assigned a note-taker or a complete set of lecture notes for classes.

      Rationale: Due to the combination of difficulties caused by her weak processing speed and immediate memory, attentional difficulties, and anxiety, Ms. Sawyer cannot attend to the information in a lecture and take notes simultaneously. Throughout her undergraduate program, this accommodation proved highly successful.

   c. Have permission to use a voice recorder during class.

      Rationale: Due to the effects of her multiple learning difficulties, Ms. Sawyer is likely to miss information during class lectures and discussions. A recording will allow her to listen to the lecture/discussion later, stopping it as necessary.

   d. Be provided oral testing as a backup to written testing whenever her performance is substandard or marginal, even with test modifications (i.e., extended time; quiet, private room).

      Rationale: As her ADHD, processing deficits, and anxiety may significantly impact performance on any formal assessment, oral testing can determine if lack of knowledge, test anxiety, processing speed, or the disruptive effects of her ADHD prevented adequate performance. As well, oral testing would help to keep her better structured and organized, and help her modulate disruptive feelings of stress and anxiety. Although her written expression is well developed as a channel through which she can demonstrate her knowledge, distractions and time constraints must be carefully controlled.

e. Be permitted to use a calculator in mathematics and on any test that involves mathematics calculation and quantitative problem solving. In math classes or math-related classes, instructors are encouraged to consider additional accommodations such as permitting a reference sheet for any formula(e) that may be required. Additionally, a course substitution/waiver for mathematics should be permitted when possible. In the event Ms. Sawyer must take a statistics course, course accommodations need to made where comprehension of design principles and study design are emphasized without requiring mastery of the quantitative procedures or methods to execute the statistical tests independently.

Rationale: Ms. Sawyer has the ability to design studies with relevant research questions; however, her problems are application and execution of mathematics methods, her longstanding mathematics disability, and the drastically slower speed and efficiency of her math calculation and quantitative problem solving. Processing speed and working memory are cognitive abilities directly related to mathematics performance, and these abilities are significant weaknesses for Ms. Sawyer. Difficulty with math has been observed throughout Ms. Sawyer's educational history and has been diagnosed as a learning disability in the current evaluation.

4. Ms. Sawyer is encouraged to consult with a medical professional to consider medication to address her attention deficit and its interaction with high levels of test and performance anxiety. This must not in any way be considered a substitute for the necessary accommodations described above, but it could be a helpful adjunct to program and test modifications/accommodations. The intent is to reduce her acute distractibility and feelings of personal stress, tedium, and anxiety that erode her ability to concentrate as well as to better actualize her learning abilities over longer durations.

The following current diagnoses, based on the *Diagnostic and Statistical Manual of Mental Disorders, Fourth Edition* (*DSM-IV-TR*) is made:

AXIS I:	314.00 Attention-Deficit/Hyperactivity Disorder, Inattentive Type
	315.9 Learning Disability NOS (Rote Processing Speed)
	315.1 Mathematics Disorder
AXIS II:	V71.09 No Diagnosis or Condition on Axis II
AXIS III:	Migraines, past report of hearing problems
AXIS IV:	Educational problems; need for accommodations at university; anxiety as a complicating influence on timed tests and in situations where accommodations are absent or incomplete
AXIS V:	GAF 65

Ms. Sawyer is an intellectually sophisticated, talented, and dedicated individual who has made impressive academic attainments when appropriate accommodations have been made. For example, she earned a 3.19 cumulative GPA in a BA with dual majors in Anthropology and Spanish. Moreover, she has demonstrated the effort, motivation, and resolve to fully apply herself and spend long hours of study and preparation in her undergraduate classes. Ms. Sawyer's successful participation in Peace Corps and her openness and sensitivity to other cultures also are laudable personal attributes. Ms. Sawyer has strong capabilities for success in a variety of fields; however, in academic environments and formal test situations, accommodations are necessary and justified to best assess her knowledge. The recommendations, findings, and conclusions of this evaluation are based on the background information, behavioral observations, clinical interview, self-report of personality, and test data that follow.

MEDICAL/DEVELOPMENTAL/ EDUCATIONAL HISTORY

Please see Ms. Sawyer's Comprehensive Psychoeducational Evaluation (10/23/99) by Jolene R. Duncan, Ph.D. when she was a sophomore in high school, and her Psychoeducational Evaluation by Sean Weaver, Ph.D., ABPP (8/1/04). Ms. Sawyer was born in Mexico and was adopted by her parents when she was 3 months old. Little is known about her biological parents or the first few months of her life.

The following information is based on the background information provided in the previous reports. In early childhood, Ms. Sawyer displayed language delays, had a 35 dB conductive hearing loss in one ear due to otitis media, and was myopic. Throughout her childhood and adolescence, she was provided language therapy, which was helpful to her.

Ms. Sawyer experienced considerable problems throughout elementary school, but it was not until she was a sophomore in high school that she was first evaluated by an outside evaluator at the request of her parents. It was difficult for her to process information quickly and she had problems with mathematics. Despite her best efforts, Ms. Sawyer endured chronic difficulty keeping pace in the classroom, extremely low math performance, and the pressure and confusion of performing below her peers without understanding why. Her academic problems contributed to anxiety, stress, and low self-esteem. Dr. Duncan's evaluation confirmed average verbal intelligence and a significant impairment in processing speed. A primary effect of the processing speed weakness was that Ms. Sawyer took significantly longer than other people to process both visual and auditory information. Mathematics continued to be tremendously difficult; she needed to take Algebra I three times and Geometry twice. In high school, she received counseling due to migraines, frequent nightmares, anxiety, and depression, and was prescribed, at different times, Elavil, Prozac, Celexa, and Lithium. She also had a trial on Ritalin for attention problems.

With accommodations and support, Ms. Sawyer graduated high school. After initially being rejected by the University of Southern Utah (USU) as not meeting the academic criteria, she appealed the decision on the grounds that she had a learning disability. The results of Dr. Weaver's evaluation (8/1/04) were that Ms. Sawyer had significant information-processing problems, a mathematics disability, and concomitant anxiety and depression. He also noted personality characteristics that were clear assets, including trustworthiness, high moral standards, and resilience in the face of adversity. Dr. Weaver rendered the following diagnostic impressions:

AXIS I: 315.9 Learning Disability Not Otherwise
          Specified
          315.1 Mathematics Disorder

296.32 Major Depression, Chronic, Moderate

300.02 Generalized Anxiety Disorder

AXIS II: V71.09 No Diagnosis or Condition on Axis II

AXIS III: Migraines, hearing impairment

AXIS IV: College entry

AXIS V: GAF 55

Dr. Weaver concluded that given Ms. Sawyer's genuine desire to graduate from USU, she deserved to be accepted and provided with accommodations, saying, "a college education could transform her life." Substantiating this impression, Ms. Sawyer was subsequently admitted to USU, was granted appropriate accommodations, and earned a 3.19 cumulative GPA and a Bachelor's of Arts degree in the dual majors of Anthropology and Spanish.

RULE-OUT CONSIDERATIONS

Ms. Sawyer has regularly attended school throughout her educational career. She has not experienced economic disadvantage; cultural difference and environmental factors could not account for her relative weaknesses or emotional challenges. In addition, educational disadvantage stemming from a differing curriculum or missed schooling was not present.

CLINICAL INTERVIEW AND ACHENBACH ADULT SELF-REPORT

In a clinical interview, Ms. Sawyer was asked about her strengths and challenges. She proved to be articulate and self-perceptive in her responses. Regarding her strengths, she reported that she likes literature, is compassionate, is dedicated to achieving her educational/career goals, is pretty adaptable, and enjoys living and working in different countries and cultures. She also described herself as kind and, although she needs time to get close to people, is a lasting and valued friend. In addition, Ms. Sawyer said that she does not get angry easily and sticks by her convictions. Ms. Sawyer noted that mood stability is no longer an issue and she feels she is basically a happy person. Although she worries about school and sometimes about things in general, she has learned to manage her anxieties more effectively. In fact, problems with anxiety are no longer generalized, but specific to test and performance anxiety when there are time pressures and distractions. Academically, she understands written material and can communicate her understanding orally or in writing, as long as there are no time limits. In the interview, it was apparent that Ms. Sawyer is an intelligent and capable person who is open to new experiences and different cultures, and has general knowledge, verbal reasoning, and communication skills that are competitive with her peers.

Ms. Sawyer stated that her challenges are mathematics, note-taking, distractibility, and anxiety. She still sees her mathematics knowledge as exceptionally weak, and far below her other abilities. She reported that her distractibility and anxiety increase dramatically when she is under stress to quickly complete academic tasks, take class notes, or complete tests.

Ms. Sawyer stated clearly that feeling rushed or that there is insufficient time do a task has a major negative impact on her functioning; she becomes increasingly anxious and her performance significantly deteriorates. As compensations, Ms. Sawyer takes time to consider, evaluate, and organize an approach to any situation. On tests with time limits or administered in a large room with many other students and distractions, her anxiety and distractibility combine to seriously affect her ability to concentrate and perform. During classroom lectures, when students are expected to take notes, she is unable to keep pace with the instructor and quickly falls so far behind that she misses much information.

Ms. Sawyer expressed that she is appreciative of the accommodations USU provided her during her undergraduate career. She was granted extended time, provided a note-taker, permitted to tape-record classes, and use a calculator; the mathematics requirement was waived, and she was allowed to take her tests in a private room. Ms. Sawyer typically worked 3 to 6 hours per evening on schoolwork, entirely dedicating herself to her studies, which left essentially no time for other pursuits.

In addition to the clinical interview, Ms. Sawyer also completed the Achenbach Adult Self-Report, rating herself along a variety of dimensions. She reported very supportive relationships with her family, positive associations with friends, and no aggressive, rule-breaking, or intrusive behaviors. She also expressed a realistic assessment of her personal assets and challenges associated with her attentional problems and the demands of formal education. She somewhat underreported anxiety due to the considerable personal coping skills she has developed, although in the clinical interview it was apparent that anxiety remains a significant influence in situations where accommodations are either insufficient or absent.

Ms. Sawyer's responses on the Achenbach produced clinically significant ratings in the domain of Attention-Deficit/Hyperactivity Disorder-Inattentive Type, which surpassed 98% of adults her age. Items she endorsed included trouble concentrating for long periods of time, forgetful, poor at details, loses things, and impulsive. She rated as "somewhat true" that she is impatient, disorganized, and rushes into things. She is also fearful (specifically of loud and sudden noises) and "somewhat" nervous and anxious. On the other hand, Ms. Sawyer indicated that she is adaptable, funny, semi-outgoing with those she knows well, loyal, and she would do anything for a trusted friend.

BEHAVIORAL OBSERVATIONS

Throughout testing, Ms. Sawyer was cooperative and consistently put forth her best effort. The results are judged to be a reliable and valid reflection of her current cognitive abilities, achievement levels, and processing domains. She was persistent in her attempt to complete all aspects of the evaluation, although some aspects of the processing tests were not only tedious for her, but took excessive time. Even in the highly controlled test setting, she was frequently distracted by small sounds, such as the tape player button being pressed, the turning of a page, or a slight shuffle of papers.

MEASURES

Wechsler Adult Intelligence Scale-Fourth Edition (WAIS-IV), Verbal Comprehension Index

Woodcock-Johnson III NU Tests of Cognitive Ability (WJ III COG)

Woodcock-Johnson III NU Tests of Achievement (WJ III ACH)

Nelson-Denny Reading Test, Form G: Reading Vocabulary, Comprehension and Reading Rate

Achenbach Adult Self-Report for Ages 18–59 (ASR)

Behavioral Observations

Clinical Interview

Record Review

INTERPRETATION

Evaluation Design and Test Considerations

The Wechsler Adult Intelligence Scale-Fourth Edition (WAIS-IV), Verbal Comprehension Index was administered because it is a reliable measure of verbal intelligence in an expressive format without time constraints. In addition, the Woodcock-Johnson III NU Tests of Cognitive Ability, Diagnostic Supplement, and Tests of Achievement were selected because they operationalize advancements in cognitive science for the assessment of intelligence. Considerable factor-analytic evidence has been amassed indicating that human cognitive abilities are made up of at least 9 or 10 broad cognitive areas and over 70 narrow abilities, many of which can be reliably assessed. The Woodcock-Johnson III assesses fluid intelligence, crystallized/verbal intelligence, short-term memory, visual-spatial thinking, auditory processing, long-term retrieval, processing speed, quantitative knowledge, reading and writing, and other discrete cognitive areas.

Understanding the Scores in This Report

The following table depicts the standard score ranges, the associated verbal labels, the percentile ranks associated with each range, and the percent of individuals who score within each category. There is error in any test, so standard scores are typically bounded by confidence intervals of several points, using the standard error of measurement.

Std. Score	Range	% people	Percentiles
<70	Lower Extreme	2%	2nd & below
70–79	Well Below Average	7%	3rd to 8th
80–89	Below Average	16%	9th to 24th
90–109	Average	50%	25th to 74th
110–119	Above Average	16%	75th to 90th
120–129	Well Above Average	7%	91st to 97th
>130	Upper Extreme	2%	98th & above

RESULTS

Cognitive Abilities

In reviewing these results, it is important to remember that an intelligence test does not measure global or innate intelligence. An intelligence test is an estimate of scholastic aptitude, or the type of ability and reasoning required in traditional academic work. Many characteristics, such as creativity, mechanical aptitude, divergent thinking, personal adaptability, social intelligence, interpersonal understanding, wisdom (self-knowledge), and common-sense reasoning, are absent or not well represented on an intelligence test.

Ms. Sawyer's performance on the WAIS-IV Verbal Comprehension Index surpassed 58% of adults her age in the United States. Her verbal reasoning and ability to express her ideas are assets for learning, particularly when Ms. Sawyer is provided sufficient time to consider the information provided and respond without time pressure. Her vocabulary and general knowledge are competitive with her peers.

In addition, Ms. Sawyer's visual-spatial thinking, assessed on the WJ III COG, was in the Average range, indicating that she is able to integrate complex visual elements into an overall pattern. Her scores on the two tests that measure this ability, however, were significantly different. On the Spatial Relations test, which was untimed, her score surpassed 65% of adults her age, whereas her score on the Picture Recognition test surpassed only 17% of her age peers. A likely reason for the difference is that the latter test is time-restricted, allowing the stimuli to be exposed for only 5 seconds, which may have been insufficient to allow Ms. Sawyer to grasp the visual details before answering.

Cognitive fluency and rote processing speed relate to one's speed in handling tasks with relatively easy demands and recognizing minor similarities and differences among visual symbols. On the Processing Speed cluster, only 3 in 1,000 adults her age would have scored as low as or lower than Ms. Sawyer; only 1 in 100 would score as low as or lower than she did on the Cognitive Fluency cluster. Consider as well that Ms. Sawyer was functioning within optimal conditions of low stress and an absence of distractions.

The Long-Term Retrieval cluster of the WJ III COG assesses the ability to learn, store, and retrieve newly learned associations and words stored in long-term memory. Ms. Sawyer's performance on this cluster surpassed less than 1% of adults her age. Of the two tests in the cluster, one (Visual-Auditory Learning) involves exposing a set of visual symbols only long enough to teach a word to associate with each. Then the individual is asked to "read" a story composed of the symbols. The other test requires the individual to name as many words as possible within a given category in 1 minute. Additionally, Ms. Sawyer scored above only 1% of her peers on another test (Rapid Picture Naming) that required rapid retrieval of known words from long-term memory, this time naming pictures of common objects. Again, the tests on which she had considerable difficulty involved time limits or the rapid presentation of details.

Test results indicated that Ms. Sawyer has significant difficulty with auditory memory span, short-term memory, and working memory. Her scores on these clusters/tests surpassed only 8%, 3%, and 3% of her peers, respectively. As a result of her low processing speed and memory, Ms. Sawyer's overall cognitive efficiency, the capacity of the cognitive system to process information automatically, surpassed less than 1% of adults her age overall. Consequently, trying to track, recall, and mentally manipulate details is Ms. Sawyer's greatest challenge; this has significantly affected her speed and efficiency in doing detailed academic work throughout her school career.

Ms. Sawyer's performance in all of these abilities is clearly well below the sophistication of her verbal intelligence and general knowledge, which exceeded 58% of her peers nationally.

Academic Achievement

Results of the WJ III ACH verified that without time constraints, Ms. Sawyer has well-developed writing skills, in contrast to mathematics skills and fluency, which were labored and weak. In written expression, Ms. Sawyer scored beyond 81% of adults her age on the Brief Writing cluster, which combines spelling and written expression, without time limits. Her scores were similarly high on both tests. Ms. Sawyer required excessive time, however, on the test of written expression, to consider the task demands and write individual sentences. Under time pressure, her score would have been significantly lower. She was able to earn an average score on the Writing Fluency test; however, as each item on this test provided a picture and most of the words, and the sentences were to be simple and short, her score was more a measure of her effort under optimal conditions, rather than the writing fluency she would need for more complex content.

Ms. Sawyer's math calculation skills, as measured by the WJ III ACH Calculation test, surpassed only 19% of students her age nationally but required con-

siderably more time than usual to achieve even this level of success. Her performance on the Math Fluency test, which involved timed retrieval of single-digit addition, subtraction, and multiplication facts, exceeded only 1% of her age peers. Again, this performance was under optimal conditions with no distractions and reduced anxiety. On both tests, the time needed to work through the problems was a significant factor. On Applied Problems, a test that involves solving word problems, her score exceeded only 18% of her peers.

On the Nelson-Denny Reading Test, Ms. Sawyer's performance was compared with second-semester seniors at 4-year colleges and universities, the highest normative level provided. Ms. Sawyer exceeded 26% of this group on the Comprehension section but was not able to finish within the time limits. She completed 30 of 38 items and, on the items she completed, made only two errors. Again, under test conditions that should be optimal to alleviate her distractibility and anxiety, the effect of time constraints on her reading comprehension was evident. Even though she did not complete over one-quarter of the items, she still performed in the Average range (albeit marginally) compared to college seniors. Yet, when tested on the Verbal Comprehension Index of the WAIS-IV, her verbal reasoning, vocabulary, and general information, all of which underlie reading comprehension, were firmly within the Average range. Regarding vocabulary knowledge, on the WAIS-IV, Ms. Sawyer surpassed 75% of her age peers; on the Nelson-Denny, she exceeded 50% of college seniors. Interestingly, the number of words Ms. Sawyer read within the first minute of the Comprehension test gave her a reading rate score that surpassed 69% of college seniors. She commented, however, that she was reading as fast as she could to cover as much content as possible within the time limit. Consequently, this result is considered spuriously high in light of her actual performance reading the rest of the longer Comprehension passages. Ms. Sawyer's overall performance on the Nelson Denny exceeded 35% of college seniors, which was somewhat attenuated by her Comprehension score, again negatively influenced by time constraints. On the WJ III ACH Reading Fluency test, reading single sentences with simple sentence structure, one-by-one, and under optimal conditions (i.e., no distractions in a private test setting), she exceeded 45% of her age-peers.

This concludes the Interpretation section of Ms. Sawyer's psychometric test results. Please note that the Recommendations resulting from this evaluation follow the Reason for Referral and the Summary and Conclusions section that introduces the report.

PSYCHOMETRIC SUMMARY

Wechsler Adult Intelligence Scale – Fourth Edition, Verbal Comprehension Index

Subtest/Index	Percentile	Scaled Score/ Standard Score
Similarities Subtest	37	9
Information Subtest	63	11
Vocabulary Subtest	75	12
Verbal Comprehension Index	**58**	**103**

Woodcock-Johnson III NU Tests of Cognitive Abilities (including Diagnostic Supplement) and Tests of Achievement (Form A)

WJ III NU Compuscore and Profiles Program, Version 3.0
Norms based on age 25–10

CLUSTER/Test	Raw	W	AE	*Proficiency	RPI	SS (68% Band)	PR
VIS-SPATIAL THINK (Gv)	–	507	14–3	Average	86/90	95 (91–99)	37
VIS-SPA THINK 3 (Gv3)	–	506	13–0	Average	84/90	94 (91–97)	35
COG EFFICIENCY (Ext)	–	486	7–9	V Limited	13/90	61 (58–65)	0.5
PROCESS SPEED (Gs)	–	486	8–0	V Limited	16/90	59 (56–62)	0.3
SHORT-TERM MEM (Gsm)	–	485	7–7	V Limited	10/90	71 (66–75)	3
L-T RETRIEVAL (Glr)	–	490	6–5	Limited	59/90	60 (57–63)	0.4
COGNITIVE FLUENCY	–	493	8–5	Limited	46/90	62 (60–65)	1
AUDITORY MEM SPAN	–	490	7–11	Limited	27/90	79 (75–82)	8
BROAD MATH	–	511	11–6	Limited	45/90	82 (80–84)	11
BROAD WRITTEN LANG	–	536	>28	Avg to Adv	96/90	110 (106–113)	74
BRIEF MATH	–	518	11–11	Limited	44/90	85 (83–88)	17
MATH CALC SKILLS	–	509	11–5	Limited	54/90	77 (73–80)	6
BRIEF WRITING	–	543	>30	Advanced	98/90	113 (110–116)	81
WRITTEN EXPRESSION	–	526	>24	Average	93/90	105 (100–110)	63
ACADEMIC FLUENCY	–	515	14–2	Lmtd to Avg	78/90	91 (88–93)	27
Visual-Auditory Learning	32–D	478	5–6	Limited	30/90	67 (65–70)	2
Retrieval Fluency	59	501	10–7	Average	83/90	83 (79–88)	13
Spatial Relations	75–D	515	>25	Average	94/90	106 (101–111)	65
Picture Recognition	45–D	498	9–2	Lmtd to Avg	69/90	86 (82–90)	17
Numbers Reversed	9	483	7–6	V Limited	6/90	71 (67–76)	3
Memory for Words	15	487	7–7	V Limited	18/90	80 (74–85)	9
Memory for Sentences	41	493	8–4	Limited	37/90	82 (78–86)	12
Visual Matching	28–2	483	7–9	V Limited	6/90	59 (56–63)	0.3
Decision Speed	23	490	8–5	Limited	36/90	65 (61–70)	1
Rapid Picture Naming	87	488	7–10	V Limited	18/90	66 (64–68)	1
Visual Closure	35	506	11–8	Lmtd to Avg	79/90	95 (92–98)	37

(continued)

CLUSTER/Test	Raw	W	AE	*Proficiency	RPI	SS (68% Band)	PR
Reading Fluency	71	524	17–2	Average	87/90	98 (96–101)	45
Spelling	54	557	>30	Advanced	99/90	111 (108–114)	77
Writing Fluency	26	523	15–5	Average	88/90	98 (94–103)	45
Writing Samples	17–E	529	>30	Avg to Adv	96/90	110 (105–115)	75
Calculation	23	520	12–4	Limited	62/90	87 (82–91)	19
Math Fluency	59	497	9–9	Limited	46/90	63 (61–66)	1
Applied Problems	39	515	11–7	Limited	27/90	86 (84–88)	18

*Note 1: Proficiency ranges (e.g., limited, average, advanced) are associated with RPI scores, not standard scores. RPIs are interpreted as: When the typical student performs at 90% proficiency, this student can be expected to perform at 98%, 69%, or 45% proficiency or whatever the number is to the left of the slash. RPIs are more sensitive to the difficulty level of the items comprising the test. Sometimes apparent differences exist between standard scores and RPIs because RPIs are not influenced by the standard deviation as standard scores are. The best method is to consider both standard scores (ranked position) and RPIs (proficiency with reference to item/task difficulty).

Nelson-Denny Reading Test, Form G

Subtest	Standard Score	Percentile Rank	Grade Equivalent
Vocabulary	100	50th	16.7
Comprehension	90	26th	14.4
Total Test	94	36th	15.6
Reading Rate	108	69th	

ID: BA Anthropology, Spanish Gender: Female Date Filled: 07/27/2010 Clinician: Michael E. Gerner, Ph.D., P.C. Informant: Self

Name: Angie A. Sawyer Age: 25 Birth Date: 10/09/1984 Agency: *Consulting Psychologists* Relationship: Self

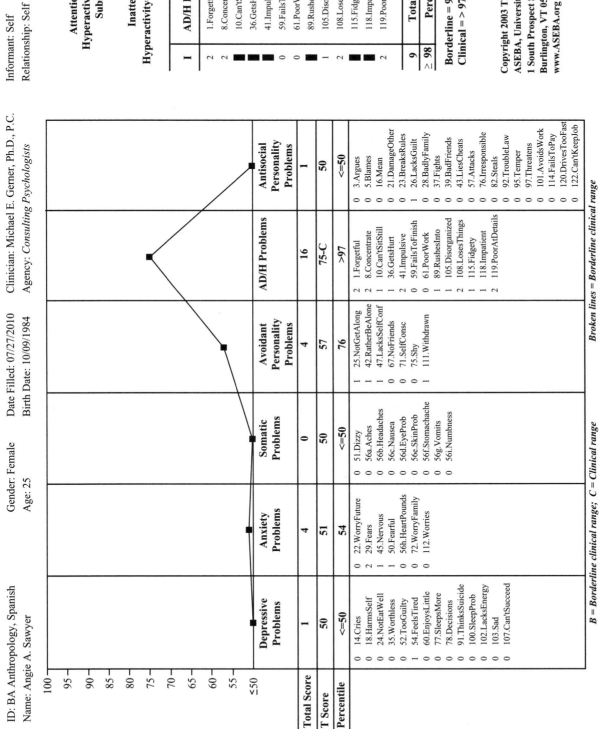

Attention Deficit/ Hyperactivity Problems Subscales:

Inattention (I)
Hyperactivity-Impulsivity (H-I)

I		AD/H Problems	H-I
2		1.Forgetful	▬▬
2		8.Concentrate	▬▬
▬▬		10.Can'tSitStill	1
▬▬		36.GetsHurt	1
2		41.Impulsive	2
0		59.FailsToFinish	▬▬
0		61.PoorWork	▬▬
▬▬		89.RushesInto	1
1		105.Disorganized	▬▬
2		108.LosesThings	▬▬
		115.Fidgety	1
		118.Impatient	1
2		119.PoorAtDetails	▬▬
9		**Total Score**	**7**
≥ 98		**Percentile**	95

Borderline = 93rd–97th %ile
Clinical = > 97th %ile

Copyright 2003 T.M. Achenbach
ASEBA, University of Vermont
1 South Prospect St.
Burlington, VT 05401-3456
www.ASEBA.org

	Depressive Problems	Anxiety Problems	Somatic Problems	Avoidant Personality Problems	AD/H Problems	Antisocial Personality Problems
Total Score	1	4	0	4	16	1
T Score	50	51	50	57	75-C	50
Percentile	<=50	54	<=50	76	>97	<=50
	0 14.Cries	0 22.WorryFuture	0 51.Dizzy	1 25.NotGetAlong	2 1.Forgetful	0 3.Argues
	0 18.HarmsSelf	0 29.Fears	0 56a.Aches	0 42.RatherBeAlone	2 8.Concentrate	0 5.Blames
	0 24.NotEatWell	1 45.Nervous	0 56b.Headaches	1 47.LacksSelfConf	0 10.Can'tSitStill	0 16.Mean
	0 35.Worthless	1 50.Fearful	0 56c.Nausea	0 67.NoFriends	1 36.GetsHurt	0 21.DamageOther
	0 52.TooGuilty	0 56h.HeartPounds	0 56d.EyeProb	0 71.SelfConsc	2 41.Impulsive	0 23.BreaksRules
	1 54.FeelsTired	0 72.WorryFamily	0 56e.SkinProb	0 75.Shy	0 59.FailsToFinish	1 26.LacksGuilt
	0 60.EnjoysLittle	0 112.Worries	0 56f.Stomachache	1 111.Withdrawn	0 61.PoorWork	0 28.BadlyFamily
	0 77.SleepsMore		0 56g.Vomits		1 89.RushesInto	0 37.Fights
	0 78.Decisions		0 56i.Numbness		1 105.Disorganized	0 39.BadFriends
	0 91.ThinksSuicide				2 108.LosesThings	0 43.LiesCheats
	0 100.SleepProb				1 115.Fidgety	0 57.Attacks
	0 102.LacksEnergy				1 118.Impatient	0 76.Irresponsible
	0 103.Sad				2 119.PoorAtDetails	0 82.Steals
	0 107.Can'tSucceed					0 92.TroubleLaw
						0 95.Temper
						0 97.Threatens
						0 101.AvoidsWork
						0 114.FailsToPay
						0 120.DrivesTooFast
						0 122.Can'tKeepJob

B = Borderline clinical range; C = Clinical range   Broken lines = Borderline clinical range

Figure 1   ASR/18–59—DSM-Oriented Scales for Women Aged 18–35

CASE 57

Use of the Stanford-Binet Fifth Edition in a Brain Injury Case

Gale Roid and Krystle Edwards

This report was written mainly for three audiences: (1) the parents of the college student in the case study, (2) the other professionals working with the student, and (3) the future readers of the report in the learning-resource center or disability-services office of a future college. Communication with the college offices is important for implementation of possible learning accommodations for the student if and when she returns to college.

Also, the case study provides an example of a community college student with a history of severe head injury, exploring the connections between brain imaging data and test data—a challenging area of assessment that has shown enormous progress in recent years. Rather than the past method of relating specific brain "locations" (e.g., temporal lobe) to behavior, the modern trend is to connect the findings from various "brain scans" to thinking, learning, speech, and other behaviors related to daily functioning, schoolwork, and employment. First, we will define some of the brain imaging techniques, as a background for the case presentation. Even if the reader does not expect to interpret brain imaging results by herself or himself, it will be important to have a basic knowledge of the terminology and use of brain-scan information in assessment reports by colleagues or in referral files. The reader should note the severity of the student's head injury and compare it to recent findings and evaluations.

Purpose of the Case Study

The special education category of traumatic brain injury (TBI) represents a small but important part of the population of students nationally. TBI has been included in the Individuals with Disabilities Education Improvement Act (IDEA, 2004) and, thus, requires testing under the general assessment guidelines of IDEA to identify "strengths and weaknesses" in the student's profile of capabilities. Also, various cognitive disorders are specified in *DSM-IV-TR* (American Psychiatric Association, 2000) where causes such as brain injury and evidence such as deficits in intellectual functioning (from standardized tests) are included in the diagnostic criteria.

EVALUATION OF TRAUMATIC BRAIN INJURY

Name:	Jan Wagner
Date of Birth:	February 10, 1976
Age:	33 years, 6 months
Primary Language:	English
Grade:	13
Dates of Evaluation:	July 23 and 30, 2009
Evaluators:	Gale Roid, Ph.D., Krystle Edwards, B.S.

REASON FOR REFERRAL AND BACKGROUND INFORMATION

Jan, a female patient, aged 33, suffered a traumatic brain injury (TBI) in a car accident when she was 20 years of age and was referred for a comprehensive evaluation by the psychologist who has been providing therapy and guidance for her since her accident. The reason for referral was to establish a new benchmark of her performance in hopes of seeing progress and recovery of function. Jan suffered an impaled left temporal lobe from debris that flew into her automobile and struck her head. Following the injury she remained in the ICU for several weeks. On the fourth day, she suffered a stroke that caused paralysis. Physicians speculated that she might not survive and a speech therapist believed she would not regain her ability to speak.

In this case study, the student's past records from physicians, specialists in brain injury, and the referring psychologist were analyzed along with new test data. Initial assessments of her general intellectual functioning after the accident showed a borderline level of functioning (IQ scores in the low 70s). Some records were obtained 5 years post injury showing that intellectual function had begun to increase, but an attempt to restart her college studies proved unsuccessful and she had to drop out of school again. Brain scans (taken 7 years post injury) were also available in her files and these were examined in comparison to past and current psychological reports of assessments administered.

Jan currently lives with her mother and her aunt, and has been seen for several years by the attending psychologist at the clinic where the current testing occurred. She has shown progress in speech and motor function. In terms of employment since withdrawing from college, she has worked in the food-service industry (mostly washing dishes) and has done volunteer work. Jan would like to return to college but only if she can be successful.

ASSESSMENT PROCEDURES

Clearly, in all cases involving a background of developmental delays in brain function, injuries, or diseases affecting the brain, or various environmental sources of damage to the neurological system, clinical evaluation using cognitive, achievement, and behavioral assessments become important for diagnosis, treatment, and monitoring.

For these reasons, the case study presented here focuses on a variety of evidence from intellectual, achievement, and behavioral measures. Choices among the many measures available for cases involving brain or neurological involvement would include:

1. Measures known to be sensitive to brain dysfunction, such as measures of memory, particularly verbal versus visual memory and working memory (the ability to sort or highlight portions of input stimuli and transform them) (Baddeley, 1986).

2. Measures often used by neuropsychologists (see Lezak, 1995); hence, based on clinical experience and research that shows the effectiveness of certain measures

with this type of case, such as tests with "hands-on" manipulative materials, or tasks known to discriminate between various disorders.

3. Measures based on cognitive or neurological theories that are known to relate to brain function or neuropsychological research, such as theories that include memory, attention, or executive process elements (e.g., Delis-Kaplan Executive Function System; Delis, Kaplan, & Kramer, 2001).

4. Measures expected to be effective that are not too long, tedious, or threatening to individuals with brain injury, such as measures with a "game-like" feel and known "examinee friendliness" (e.g., nonverbal portions of the Stanford-Binet, Fifth Edition [SB5], Roid, 2003b).

5. For busy clinicians with heavy case loads or difficulties getting insurance coverage for long testing sessions— and for clients who have short attention span—measures with efficiency (a lot of information in a short time), such as abbreviated forms of SB5 or Wechsler scales, and selected subtests of any test instead of the full battery.

6. For purposes of treatment planning and school learning for student- and career/work-skills, measures of practical and academic skills are often needed. The most widely used measures are individual achievement tests such as the Woodcock-Johnson III NU Tests of Achievement (WJ III ACH), Wechsler Individual Achievement Test—Third Edition (WIAT-III), Wide Range Achievement Test 4 (WRAT4), Peabody Individual Achievement Test-R (PIAT-R), KeyMath3, and Kaufman Test of Educational Achievement-II (KTEA-II)

7. Brain scans or injury records whenever available.

Measures

Intake interview (50 minutes) by the examiner

Review of referral psychologist's records, brain scans, and physician reports

Adaptive Behavior Assessment System, Second Edition (ABAS-II) Adult Form: completed by mother

Achenbach Adult Self Report (ASEBA), Ages 18–59

Conners' Continuous Performance Test (CPT)

Stanford-Binet Intelligence Scale, Fifth Edition (SB5)

Wechsler Individual Achievement Test-Second Edition (WIAT-II): Oral Expression

Wechsler Memory Scale-Third Edition (WMS-III)

Wechsler Adult Intelligence Scale-Fourth Edition (WAIS-IV): Processing Speed subtests

Woodcock-Johnson III NU Tests of Achievement (WJ III ACH): selected subtests

Debriefing session with attending psychologist, mother, and student

OBSERVATIONS

Jan was a hardworking and cooperative test subject during two rather lengthy sessions. She seemed to be seriously interested in doing a good job and showing what she was (or was not) capable of doing. She was diligent in trying to compensate for the speech and attention difficulties produced by her past injury. She often had difficulty finding the "right words" to use, and this limitation was slightly frustrating to her. Sometimes her limitations with quick responding and rapid speech became obvious during timed tasks, and she realized her performance was slow.

Jan reports enjoyment of her volunteer work at a local hospital where she shares her brain-injury story with patients who have driving-related accidents. Also, she likes to give verbal encouragement to less fortunate people she meets. During her work days (3 days a week), she has little time for anything but going to work, getting home, and going to bed. She reports that her mother is her "best friend" but she is quite strict. She doesn't report having any other friends, getting phone calls, or engaging in activities on the weekend (except picking up mail, TV, and watching her pet).

RESULTS AND DISCUSSION

Brain Imaging Records

Jan was referred to a medical clinic specializing in brain imaging 7 years after her initial accident (age 27) by her attending psychologist for purposes of planning additional interventions. The clinic employed SPECT scanning methods as compared to other types of brain imaging. SPECT (single photon emission computed tomography) scans (Amen Clinic, 2009) are used to determine areas of the brain that work well and those that are lower or higher in activity while the individual is performing a task. In contrast, MRI (magnetic resonance imaging) analyses produce an anatomical image by tracking the interaction between radio waves and a strong magnetic field. Another method, CT (computerized tomography) scanning, uses beams of X-rays to view a two-dimensional image through the body (Carlson, 2007). Positron emission tomography (PET) scans are also used to measure the metabolic activity of brain regions.

For this evaluation, several SPECT scans were conducted with Jan in resting versus active conditions. SPECT scans, as compared to MRIs and CT scans, use blood flow and activity levels to determine brain functioning.

For the scans described in this report (see Figures 1 and 2), two contrasting activity levels and surface views are shown—resting and active brain activity with the view downward on the top of the brain and the view from the left side. One pair of scans (Figure 1) was collected while Jan

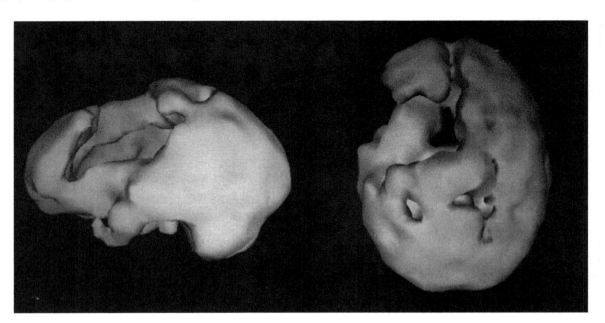

Figure 1 Black-and-White Version of the SPECT Brain Scan Results for the Case Study of Jan: Resting State.

was in a resting state, and a second pair (Figure 2) while she was involved in a computerized attention task (Conners' Continuous Performance Test). Figure 2 (active state) shows some smooth areas on the scan that indicate effective activity that falls within 55% of the brain's maximum blood flow (mental activity) level as well as some bumps and "holes." Figure 1, in the resting state, particularly shows bumpy and rough textures or even absent areas ("holes") that indicate areas of lower blood flow and mental activity that are below the 55% blood flow (oxygen metabolism) level. Lighter or darker shades on the resulting images indicate decreased or increased activity for that area. For more extensive information on brain imaging techniques in assessment, the reader should consult Gregory (2007), Carlson (2007), or the Amen Clinic web site.

Technical Details of the Brain Imaging Results[1]

Jan suffered damage directly to the left temporal lobe (see both the top and side images in the resting state in Figure 2). The SPECT scans show bumpy and absent areas (a rather large "hole") of significantly decreased neural activity in approximately a 2-inch radius of the temporal lobe. The area of decreased activity also extends upward to the medial transverse line. The scans indicate that decreased activity is generalized from the primary motor cortex to the

---

[1] The authors of this report are including results by neurologists, but any errors of interpretation or transcription are their own. Prediction of test results or behavior from brain imaging should be seen as hypotheses and not necessarily factual.

frontal lobes and the temporal lobe. The area of damage in the left hemisphere, indicated here, is often involved in processing positive emotions and speech; the right hemisphere plays a greater role in expressing emotions. There is also evidence of asymmetrical distribution of neurotransmitters in the cerebral cortex (bumpy or absent sections on both right and left). The physician commented that he notices that dopamine are more prominent in the left hemisphere. Dopamine contributes to attention, movement, and learning processes carried out by the brain (Carlson, 2007). Jan showed severe deficits in speech fluency. The ability to produce and comprehend speech is most often associated with the left cerebral hemisphere where the missing sections and bumpiness are most pronounced in the resting images (Figure 1), although the "active/attentive" scans in Figure 2 also show missing sections and roughness.

COGNITIVE ABILITIES

Cognitive testing included two of the major batteries used to assess intellectual abilities.

Stanford-Binet, Fifth Edition (SB5)

The SB5 subtest, Factor Index, and IQ scores are shown in Table 1. Nonverbal Working Memory (scaled score [ScS] of 4, 2nd percentile nationally) was found to be a notable weakness, significantly and practically lower than the average of the 10 SB5 subtests. This may show that Jan has

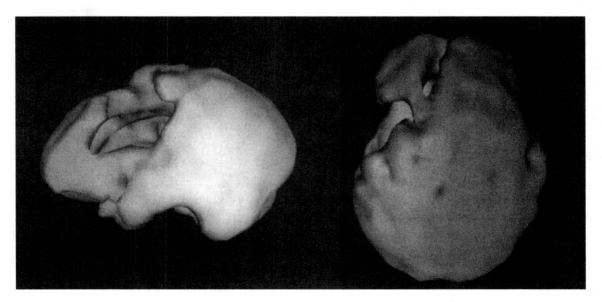

Figure 2   Black-and-White SPECT Scan for Active State in Case Study of Jan.

a relative weakness in retaining and sorting through visual information held in short-term memory. Nonverbal Visual-Spatial skills (e.g., puzzle completion, discriminating and forming visual images, quick assembly of puzzle pieces) was also quite low (ScS 5, 5th percentile). Jan was aware that certain tasks were difficult for her. For example, on the SB5 Visual-Spatial subtest (the tangram-style puzzles), she commented that assembling puzzles was difficult for her, but that she would try anyway.

Verbal Fluid Reasoning (ScS 13, 84th percentile) was an important strength, significantly and practically higher than the average of the 10 subtests. This may show that Jan is relatively more proficient with identifying and describing relationships between illustrated objects or printed words and sentences. Scatter among the subtests was 9 points (Verbal Fluid Reasoning 13 versus Nonverbal Working Memory [tapping blocks] which was 4). This discrepancy is considered to reflect true differences in ability

(statistically significant and occurring in only about 15% of the general population).

In terms of the five major factor indexes on the SB5, Jan showed both strengths and weaknesses on these composite scores that combine one nonverbal and one verbal subtest in each index. Jan scored above average on Fluid Reasoning (standard score [SS] of 106)—the ability to solve novel problems with both visual and verbal information. This above average score, and the lack of scores below 80, showed some significant recovery of function compared to her previous records showing borderline performance in nearly all areas (scores in the low 70s range). She was relatively low in three other areas—Knowledge, Visual-Spatial, and Working Memory. Knowledge (SS 83, 13th percentile nationally) involves breadth of vocabulary and the ability to identify and explain oddities in pictures and to solve word problems. Visual-Spatial ability (SS 82, 12th percentile) includes the ability to solve puzzle-like

Table 1   Scoring Results for Jan on the Stanford-Binet Intelligence Scales, Fifth Edition

IQ and Factor Index Score Results					
	Sum of Scaled Scores	**Standard Score**	**95% Confidence Intervals (CI)**		
			Percentile	**SS CI**	**Percentile CI**
IQ Scores					
Full-Scale IQ (FSIQ)	79	86	18	82–90	12–25
Nonverbal IQ (NVIQ)	35	81	10	76–88	5–21
Verbal IQ (VIQ)	44	92	30	86–98	18-45
Factor Index Scores					
Fluid Reasoning (FR)	22	106	66	97–113	42–81
Knowledge (KN)	14	83	13	76–92	5–30
Quantitative Reasoning (QR)	16	89	23	82–98	12–45
Visual-Spatial (VS)	14	82	12	75–91	5–27
Working Memory (WM)	13	80	9	74–90	4–25

Note: The sum of scaled scores is transformed into a normalized standard score with a mean of 100 and a standard deviation of 15.

Subtest Scores						
	Nonverbal Scores			**Verbal Scores**		
	Raw	**Scaled**	**%ile**	**Raw**	**Scaled**	**%ile**
Fluid Reasoning	21	9	37	22	13	84
Knowledge	21	8	25	36	6	9
Quantitative Reasoning	21	9	37	17	7	16
Visual-Spatial	17	5	5	22	9	37
Working Memory	16	4	2	20	9	37

Note: All scaled scores are normalized raw scores with mean of 10 and a standard deviation of 3.

constructions and reason with spatial information (e.g., explaining directions in space using north, south, east, and west or pictorial cues). Finally, Jan scored low in Working Memory (SS 80, 9th percentile) indicating difficulty in sorting and transforming both verbal and visual information in short-term memory—a deficit often associated with brain injuries, learning disabilities, attention deficits, and other neurological conditions.

Wechsler Adult Intelligence Scale, Fourth Edition (WAIS-IV)

Another indicator of the effects of neurological deficits, the ability to process information quickly and efficiently (processing speed), is measured well in the WAIS-IV by two subtests—Symbol Search and Coding. Symbol Search involves quick visual attention and decision making to determine presence/absence of certain printed symbols. Jan had a low score of 6 (9th percentile nationally). Also, Coding, the ability to quickly complete the clerical task of converting numbers and symbols using a printed key, showed a similarly low scaled score of 6—1.33 standard deviations below the national average. Together, these two subtests combine to measure general processing speed, showing a very low standard score of 79, at the 8th percentile. Because this score is more than 20 points lower than Jan's Fluid Reasoning standard score (106), it signals a true deficit that is often associated with attention and learning difficulties and with general difficulty handling the rapid flow of information in modern society and, particularly, in college-level classrooms and activities. Continuing improvement in Jan's functioning combined with further

training and tutoring can restore some of this function. (See Recommendations below.)

LEARNING AND MEMORY

Wechsler Memory Scale (WMS-III)

Memory for information is clearly an important mental ability, and good memory helps students succeed in college-level education or specialized training. This subsection traces Jan's memory functions in the major area of concern based on low scores from the SB5, visual memory (pictures, perceptions, and illustrations). Both visual composite indexes were low on the WMS-III (see Table 2); Visual Immediate Memory (Faces and Family Pictures, SS 78) at the 7th percentile nationally was low and not significantly higher than Visual Delayed Memory (SS 75) at the 5th percentile. The scores in Table 2 show that Jan has difficulty recalling things she sees, such as pictures and illustrations, if she has to recall all the information (rather than just recognize a part of it or a clue). Jan did much better, however, with recognition memory (Faces I, ScS 8) and she improved further on delayed recognition (Faces II, ScS 10). When required to recall pictures, her performance was particularly low (Family Pictures I, ScS 5, and Family Pictures II, ScS 2, compared to Faces II, ScS 10). She showed a strength in delayed visual recognition (identifying 37 of the 48 Faces) especially in comparison to her low visual-motor ability (Nonverbal Working Memory, ScS 4) and processing speed (WAIS-IV Processing Speed subtests ScS 6). Her performance on delayed recognition of visual material shows that she has some intact visual abilities. This suggests

Table 2   Notable Strengths and Weaknesses in Memory Function on WMS-III

Subtest	Scaled Score*	Percentile	Indexes	Standard Score	Percentile
Faces I (Recognition total)	8	25	Visual Immediate Memory	78	7
Faces II (Delayed recognition)	10	50	Visual Delayed Memory	75	5
Family Pictures I (Recall total score)	5	5			
Family Pictures II (Delayed recall)	2	0.4			
Word List I (Immediate 1st recall)	11	63			
Word List I (Learning slope)	5	5			
Word List II (Delayed recall)	8	25			
*The scaled scores have a mean of 10 and a standard deviation of 3.					

a possible accommodation in future college or training—to have exams that are multiple-choice or matching rather than ones that require free-recall answers or essays.

Given that Jan has some speech and vocabulary deficits, it was also important to examine her memory for words. On the WMS-III Word List, Jan's delayed recall was considerably lower than her immediate recall. Her visual learning was certainly better than verbal learning, given that the number of faces she recognized after a delay (Faces II). was more than the number she recognized immediately (Faces I). She showed some strength in immediate learning of Word List I (6 of 12 words) but her Learning Slope (progression of words learned on multiple trials) was below average (ScS 5). Again, Jan certainly needs additional practice and strategies to assist with verbal and memory retrieval to function successfully in a post-secondary educational setting.

ACHIEVEMENT AND ACADEMIC SKILLS

Table 3 (based on age norms) and Table 4 (based on 2-year college norms) show a complete report of various scores from both the Woodcock-Johnson III NU Tests of Achievement (WJ III ACH) and one from the Woodcock-Johnson III NU Tests of Cognitive Abilities (WJ III COG). Differences in normative scores according to the reference group should not be surprising, but they do signal a caution to evaluators that interpretation is often influenced and dependent on the choice and appropriateness of the normative reference group.

WJ III ACH Oral Language

Because of her obvious speaking difficulties, tests of listening and understanding directions (administered via audio recording) were given. As shown in Table 3, Oral Language was at a below average level (SS 81, Second) using the age-based norms, but extremely low when compared with college students (SS 63). Story Recall was also very low (age-based norms: SS 79; 2-year-college norms: SS 71) meaning that Jan is likely to have difficulty recalling things that the instructors say in class. Story Recall-Delayed also showed a wide variation depending on the reference group (age-based 72, college-based 86).

Understanding Directions (following complex instructions) (SS 83 by age norms) was also low compared to college students (SS 70). These weaknesses in understanding and recalling verbal information suggest that Jan will need accommodations (e.g., recording of classroom lectures) if she is to succeed in further education or training.

Jan also obtained very low scores on the WJ III COG Rapid Picture Naming (age-based 73, college-based 70). This difficulty with retrieving verbal labels quickly is consistent with her slow and somewhat dysfluent speech.

WJ III ACH Broad Reading

Jan reports great difficulty with mathematics, but her reading level was not previously documented. All three of the WJ III ACH standard battery reading tests (in Table 3) were administered, with standard scores as follows: Letter-Word Identification: age-based SS 94, college-based

Table 3

Woodcock-Johnson III Normative Update Tests of Cognitive Abilities and Tests of Achievement (Form A)

WJ III NU Compuscore and Profiles Program, Version 3.1

Norms based on age 33-6

CLUSTER/Test	Raw	W	AE	EASY	to	DIFF	RPI	SS (68% Band)	GE
ORAL LANGUAGE (Std)	–	490	7–7	5–9		10–6	59/90	81 (78–84)	2.3
BROAD READING	–	520	13–8	11–7		16–4	51/90	91 (89–92)	8.2
BRIEF READING	–	530	15–4	12–10		23	63/90	94 (93–96)	9.8
Rapid Picture Naming (WJ III COG)	85	487	7–6	5–11		9–9	16/90	73 (71–74)	2.2
Letter-Word Identification	66	542	15–7	13–9		19	49/90	94 (92–95)	10.1
Reading Fluency	44	499	10–10	8-8		13–0	30/90	82 (80–84)	5.4
Story Recall	–	494	7–4	4–3		14–2	75/90	79 (72–85)	2.0
Understanding Directions	–	487	7–8	6–5		9–7	40/90	83 (80–87)	2.4
Passage Comprehension	36	518	14–8	11–5		>30	75/90	95 (93–98)	9.2
Story Recall-Delayed	–	494	6–2	4–4		>29	76/90	72 (61–82)	K.9

Table 4

Woodcock-Johnson III Normative Update Tests of Cognitive Abilities and Tests of Achievement (Form A); WJ III NU Compuscore and Profiles Program, Version 3.1; Norms based on grade 13.3 (2-year college)

CLUSTER/Test	Raw	W	AE	EASY	to DIFF	RPI	SS (68% Band)	GE
ORAL LANGUAGE (Std)	–	490	7–7	K.5	5.1	62/90	63 (57–70)	2.3
BROAD READING	–	520	13–8	6.2	10.9	76/90	91 (88–93)	8.2
BRIEF READING	–	530	15–4	7.4	13.0	88/90	98 (95–101)	9.8
Rapid Picture Naming	85	487	7–6	K.7	4.4	22/90	70 (68–72)	2.2
Letter-Word Identification	66	542	15–7	8.3	13.0	85/90	97 (94–101)	10.1
Reading Fluency	44	499	10–10	3.3	7.6	38/90	75 (72–79)	5.4
Story Recall	–	494	7–4	<K.0	8.8	77/90	71 (61–80)	2.0
Understanding Directions	–	487	7–8	1.1	4.2	45/90	70 (64–76)	2.4
Passage Comprehension	36	518	14–8	6.0	16.2	90/90	100 (95–105)	9.2
Story Recall-Delayed	–	494	6–2	<K.0	13.0	83/90	86 (77–94)	K.9

SS 97; Reading Fluency: age-based SS 82, college-based SS 75; and Passage Comprehension: age-based SS 95, college-based SS 100. The result is a Broad Reading score of 91 (both age- and college-based). Although reading is a relative strength for Jan, her low score in reading fluency (speed of reading sentences) suggests that she will require additional time for reading, and will likely benefit from methods designed to increase her reading speed.

WIAT-II

The WIAT-II includes a series of individually administered achievement tests that provide an alternate measure of Jan's oral and listening skills. The composite score, Oral Language, showed a standard score of 85, at the 16th percentile, very similar to the WJ III ACH age-based Oral Language score. The WIAT-II composite consists of two parts: Listening Comprehension (SS 72) and Oral Expression (SS 99). Jan's Oral Expression score (SS 99) was considerably higher than her Listening Comprehension score (SS 72), indicating a possible strength. Within Oral Expression, the Visual-Passage Retelling (stories depicted by a picture stimulus) showed a lower level of skill than the Giving Directions (spoken directions for common daily activities) portion of the scale. Thus, the visual-ability deficits she showed on SB5 may be reflected here in the visual retelling tasks. These findings suggest that Jan will have difficulty with tasks involving verbal comprehension and memory, and is likely to benefit from both accommodations and instruction in strategies. Her limitations regarding slow responses and speech became obvious during timed tasks, and she realized her performance

was slow. On the Word Fluency tasks each of the WIAT-II, for example, she could come up with only a few responses and she knew this was inadequate. Given her past difficulties with expressive speech, it was remarkable to hear her clear explanation of all the steps in "making a sandwich" on the Oral Expression subtest. She fully explained each step in clear language.

RATING SCALES

Achenbach Adult Self-Report

Among the items marked "very true or often true," Jan reported thoughts and feelings of worthlessness, being lonely, worried about her future, acting impulsively, difficulty managing money, and rushing into things. However, she also reported several positive attributes such as being fair to others, helping others, asserting her rights, being responsible to family, enjoying people, being honest, and working up to her ability. Thus, she showed two sides that may reflect different levels of self-confidence depending on the situation.

ABAS-II Adult Rating (Mother's Report)

Jan's mother reported very high levels of adaptive behavior for Self-Care, Community Use (except calling a repairman or using the library), Home Living (except making minor repairs, cooking complex foods, or maintenance of home and car), and Communication (except answering complex questions or having realistic career goals). She expressed more concerns about Jan in the Social and Leisure areas, and some areas of Communication. In the comments section, she reported concerns regarding Jan's functioning under stress, her excessive eagerness to provide help to people on the street in an urban setting, and some challenges with others in the home (e.g., an ill relative).

SUMMARY

Jan's overall cognitive level remains below average but with evidence of recovery of function. Her delayed recall memory is near the deficient level, regarding both visual and verbal recall. Her reading level, fluid reasoning, and delayed recognition memory, however, seem to be near average, and are encouraging given the severity of her past brain injury.

Possible Diagnoses

Language Disorder or Cognitive Dysfunction due to TBI

RECOMMENDATIONS FOR JAN

1. Take an aptitude and interest inventory at the local community college and, with the results, talk with a career counselor about technical training either at the community college or at a technical school. Your goals for successful employment are more likely to be met in this course of postsecondary work than with a liberal arts degree from a 4-year college. Steer away from careers that emphasize the need for rapid recognition, learning, and recall of visual details and the need to make quick decisions based on these.

2. Prior to starting school, register with the department that provides services for students with disabilities. They will work with you to establish accommodations and provide you with a letter to your teachers describing the accommodations. Our recommendations for accommodations are as follows:

   - Extended time on tests involving reading and writing due to slow reading speed and difficulty with word retrieval

   - Use of a calculator for math classes and science classes that involve math

   - A note-taker to relieve you from having to attend to listening to the instructor and taking notes simultaneously

   - Permission to use a voice recorder to record lectures and discussions to listen to later

   - Flexibility with assignment due dates if you are having difficulty, although you will have to alert your instructors ahead of the due date if you will need extra time

   - An academic coach to help you stay on top of your assignments and organize your time

3. Join study groups for classes when they are available.

4. Request help from disability resources at your school to obtain a tutor for any classes that you find difficult. You are likely to need help in math and math-related courses (e.g., economics) due to your difficulty in verbal quantitative reasoning. In math, the support of visual information is likely to be helpful if your tutor can help you to learn to take advantage of verbal working memory by talking through concepts and processes.

5. Pursue a more in-depth reading evaluation at the community college or through a private learning disabilities or reading specialist to find out more specifically which reading skills you need to work on and the best methods for doing so. It would be advisable for you to work with a learning disabilities specialist for tutoring, as your tutor will need to understand the cognitive difficulties that you have, such as slow processing speed, and modify the techniques accordingly.

6. Consult with a speech-language pathologist regarding therapy to improve your speed of word retrieval and dysfluent speech.

7. For the following recommendations, it would be best to work with a learning disabilities specialist or a speech-language pathologist so that she/he can help you determine which techniques will be most effective for you to use independently:

   a. You appear to be able to learn verbal information by rote but need considerably extra time and repetitions to do so. Memory strategies would be a more efficient way to learn information that needs to be memorized but is not meaningfully interrelated. Other areas in which you should pursue specialized tutoring are study strategies and test-taking strategies. Very effective strategies have been developed in all of these areas, but you are most likely to benefit from them if you have a tutor working with you to select those that are needed for specific courses, assignments, and tests. In the meantime, the following is a good source of a wide range of study strategies: www.studygs.net.

b. Because your ability to work with verbal information mentally (i.e., manipulate it while holding it in memory) is significantly better than your nonverbal working memory, and your ability to express your ideas and logical reasoning are strong, experiment with talking yourself through problems that are presented in a visual form. This would be helpful not only for solving problems, but also for going back to recheck your solutions.

c. Because your verbal working memory and verbal visual-spatial ability are considerably stronger than your nonverbal working memory and nonverbal visual-spatial ability, you are likely to understand visual-spatial information (e.g., maps, designs, schematics) better if you talk through each part and their relationships to each other. More generally, as much as possible, transfer any visual information that you must work with/interpret into verbal information. For example, ask people to give you verbal directions to places rather than drawing you a map.

8. To increase your general knowledge of the world, spend some of your free time watching documentaries in the areas of history, geography, animal science, human anatomy, astronomy, other cultures, or any other area of study. Choose one area and stick with that for a while so that you learn some in-depth information about the subject. This will help you increase your knowledge of the world in the easiest way possible. These types of documentaries are available on many cable TV channels (e.g., History, Discovery, Animal Planet) as well as in the public library, the community college library, and video stores.

9. Your limited social relationships outside of your family appear to be a concern, as you state that you are lonely and have few friends. Your mother suggested increasing interactions with other women in the activity you attend together. You might also consider joining one club at school or in the community, such as a hiking club, to help you begin to socialize with others and become more comfortable in social interactions.

REFERENCES

Amen Clinic (2009). Information on SPECT scans retrieved from the Amen Clinic web site: http://www.amenclinics.com/clinics/information/the-science-behind-brain-spect-imaging/ November 7, 2009. American Psychiatric Association. (2000). *Diagnostic and Statistical Manual of Mental Disorders* (4th ed., Text Revision). Washington, D.C.: Author.

Baddeley, A. D. (1986). *Working memory.* Oxford, England Clarendon Press.

Carlson, N. R. (2007). *Physiology of behavior* (9th ed.). Boston, MA: Allyn & Bacon.

Delis, D. C., Kaplan, E., & Kramer, J. H. (2001). *Delis-Kaplan Executive Function System.* San Antonio, TX: Psychological Corporation.

Donders, J. (1993). Memory functioning after traumatic brain injury in children. *Brain Injury, 7,* 431–437.

Gregory, R. J. (2007). *Psychological testing* (5th ed.). Boston, MA: Allyn & Bacon.

Roid, G. H. (2006, March). *Linking cognitive assessment with SB5 to instruction and intervention.* Mini-skills workshop paper presented at the meetings of the National Association of School Psychologists, Anaheim, CA.

Psychoeducational Evaluation of an Adult for LD and ADHD

Integrating Neuropsychological Measures into Cross-Battery Assessment

Catherine Fiorello

This report illustrates several important issues about the assessment of adults. One is the importance of a good history and the solicitation of collateral reports. Gathering as much information as possible about past and current functioning is particularly important with adults, who have learned coping strategies on their own and may be compensating in ways they are not even aware of. Additionally, because current school observations and teacher ratings were not possible, information and ratings were solicited from a work supervisor.

This report also illustrates my use of graphs to convey functioning levels. I find that a visual presentation is easier for clients to understand than numbers. Of course, I include actual scores in an appendix. Whenever I assess an adult, I graph both age and grade norms when available. Most of my adult evaluations are for accommodations in postsecondary settings, so a comparison with grade peers is important. I also do this whenever an individual's age and grade placement may not correspond, as in cases when a child has been retained. Although legal eligibility for accommodations under the ADA depends on age peer comparisons only (an adult must be impaired compared to typical adults, not educational or professional peers, to be considered disabled), it is important for adult clients to understand how their performance will compare to that of their classmates.

For older adolescents and adults, I use informal measures of reading and writing to supplement standardized testing. This allows me to assess strategies and performance on longer assignments, which are more typical of the requirements in secondary and postsecondary educational settings.

This report also demonstrates my inclusion of neuropsychological measures within an overall Cattell-Horn-Carroll (CHC) framework. As this case included concerns regarding ADHD symptoms, measures of aspects of executive functioning were an important part of the evaluation.

Note: Appreciation is expressed to Celeste M. Malone, M.S., M.Ed. for her assistance in formatting this report.

PSYCHOEDUCATIONAL EVALUATION REPORT

Name:	Sarah Hines
Year of Birth:	1961
Age:	49 years
Sex:	Female
Address:	86 Yonkers Place
Evaluation Dates:	7/6,71/13, 7/20/2010
Report Date:	August 3, 2010
Examiner:	Catherine A. Fiorello, Ph.D.

REASON FOR REFERRAL

Sarah requested an evaluation to aid in obtaining accommodations at work and at school if she decides to enroll in a Master's degree program. She has been previously identified as having Attention-Deficit/Hyperactivity Disorder (ADHD), but also wished an evaluation for possible learning disabilities.

HISTORY

Sarah is one of eight children. Her parents are still alive, and her mother, Mrs. Hines, provided some information about Sarah's childhood symptoms. She indicated that Sarah "always seemed to be on the go." She also noted some difficulty with excessive talking, not being able to play quietly, and losing things. Sarah did not, however, have school problems. One of Sarah's sisters, Marie, also rated her behavior, indicating significant difficulties with attention, hyperactivity, and impulsivity that led to problems in family, school, leisure, work, and social activities. Marie, however, is 10 years younger than Sarah so she could not provide information on her childhood. Sarah herself recalls symptoms including hyperactivity and impulsivity that were somewhat problematic in social relationships and hindered her ability to complete chores. A childhood friend, Laura Simon, indicated significant difficulties with attention, hyperactivity, and impulsivity that became more evident with time and interfered with family and social relationships.

Sarah has typically earned good grades in school despite difficulties with reading and writing. She earned her Associates degree from the Chapel Community College and her Bachelor's degree from Stanton College. She describes her college career as characterized by doing well on tests and using her own strategies (such as recording information on a cassette and repeatedly reviewing it) to complete work that was difficult for her. She noted particular difficulties with organizing her work and "putting it in my own words." Sarah reads very slowly and must reread repeatedly to comprehend. When under time pressure, she has trouble remembering what she has learned. She attempted to refer herself to the learning lab at both colleges but was turned down because her grades were too high.

Sarah's family members also have a history of learning and behavioral difficulties, including ADHD (a brother and his two sons), possible learning disabilities (a sister and a niece), anxiety and mood swings (her father), and panic attacks (her mother). She described her mother as being very social, and although her father was social while she was growing up, she now describes him as asocial and reclusive. Both parents are described as not "talking about feelings or things," and her mother may minimize problems.

Sarah's medical history is notable for allergies and migraine headaches. She is currently being treated for gallstones. She is not currently taking any medications but has previously been treated with Zoloft for sleep difficulties and premenopausal symptoms (discontinued due to lethargy) and Ritalin for attention difficulties (improved her attention and ability to read, but discontinued due to agitation). Sarah has never slept much but reports that recently she is having more difficulty sleeping. Her appetite varies, and she has gained weight with stress but was able to lose it through participation in Weight Watchers. Sarah uses reading glasses but otherwise has normal vision and hearing.

Sarah has been married and divorced twice. She described a history of mood difficulties during her first marriage, and reported having three panic attacks about 10 years ago during marital stress and separation, but reported no current psychological problems.

Sarah has two grown sons. The younger son moved in with his father during his teens, when he was described as rebellious and angry. The older son had been diagnosed with ADHD inattentive type and dysthymia (i.e., mild chronic depression).

Currently, Sarah works as a behavior consultant at a school. She is described as very hardworking, and has a good sense of children's behavioral cues, situational factors, and developmentally appropriate strategies. She struggles, however, to organize and present her ideas orally and finds writing extraordinarily difficult and time consuming. Her supervisor, Dr. Zimmerman, notes that Sarah always completes her tasks and meets her deadlines but that she does so at great personal cost. Sarah completes a great deal of written work at home after work, and her inability to complete it with ease undermines her confidence.

BEHAVIORAL OBSERVATIONS

Sarah appeared comfortable with the examiner. She worked extremely hard, was very cooperative, and persisted with difficult tasks. She spoke rapidly and with somewhat pressured speech. She showed difficulty with organization, both with her physical possessions and in presenting her history. She was able to work on the varied tasks of the assessment with minimal breaks but was noted to fidget and tap her leg while working. Sarah was very motivated and interested in the assessment, and often commented on specific strengths or strategies she had used to solve a problem. Because of Sarah's excellent attention and effort, these results are felt to be a valid evaluation of her current functioning.

ASSESSMENT RESULTS AND INTERPRETATION

Tests Administered

Wechsler Adult Intelligence Scale–Fourth Edition (WAIS-IV)

Woodcock-Johnson III NU Tests of Cognitive Abilities (WJ III COG)

Woodcock-Johnson NU Tests of Achievement (WJ III ACH)

Nelson-Denny Reading Test (NDRT)

Conners' Continuous Performance Test–II

Wisconsin Card Sorting Test–64

Brown Attention-Deficit Disorder Scales (BADDS)

Barkley and Murphy Clinical Workbook rating scales

Informal reading and writing tasks.

Test Results

Sarah's Full-Scale score on the WAIS-IV fell in the Average range, indicating that she scored as well as or better than 47% of people her age in overall intellectual functioning. Scores from the tests administered have been combined into clusters to describe Sarah's strengths and weaknesses more fully.

Higher-level processing and reasoning, often referred to as thinking ability, consists of four clusters. Sarah scored at the upper end of the Average range on the Fluid Reasoning cluster, novel tasks requiring reasoning skills. Sarah scored in the Average range on Long-Term Memory and Retrieval, another high-level processing cluster. She had somewhat weaker skills in narrative memory, remembering a story presented once, which is often a weakness for adults with ADHD. Sarah scored in the High Average range on Auditory Processing, specifically the ability to manipulate the phonemes of spoken language, which is a prerequisite skill for learning decoding (reading) and encoding (spelling) skills. She showed more variability in Visual Processing, the ability to solve problems by using visual-spatial skills. Sarah was lower, at the bottom of the Average range, on a task requiring analysis and synthesis of visual designs using blocks, having difficulty with orientation of the blocks, and on a timed task in which she had to choose the pieces needed to complete a visual puzzle. She performed in the Average range, however, when she just had to point out (rather than move) the pieces that went together to solve a visual puzzle, and performed Well Above Average using paper and pencil to trace complex designs. Although her spatial orientation abilities appear to be relatively weak, her visual processing skills vary depending on the processing demands of the task. Overall, Sarah is at least Average in the high-level processing skills necessary for learning.

Low-level processing refers to underlying skills that support learning. Two areas of low-level processing were assessed. Sarah's performance on the Processing Speed cluster, her ability to perform simple cognitive tasks quickly, was in the Average to High Average range. Because Sarah's processing speed on pure cognitive tasks is at least average, any difficulties with reading speed may derive from her attentional difficulties. The other area of low-level processing assessed was Short-Term Memory, or the ability to hold information in mind briefly while processing it. Sarah scored in the Average range in this area overall but had more difficulty with some aspects of working memory, tasks in which she had to hold information in mind and use it rather than just recalling it by rote. For example, she was easily able to repeat a string of digits in order but had more difficulty when asked to repeat them in reverse order. In addition, although Sarah's math skills are quite strong, when asked to solve problems in her head, requiring the use of working memory, her performance was significantly worse.

Executive functions are those cognitive functions where the frontal lobes control other processes in the brain, as an executive controls the workers in a company. Executive functions are often impaired in people with ADHD, so specific tests of these functions were administered. On relatively brief, novel tasks, Sarah was able to plan ahead, use appropriate strategies to solve problems, and remain focused. She showed good attention, flexibility, and ability to profit from feedback. When presented with a computerized task of longer duration (14 minutes), however, she had great difficulty remaining focused, responding correctly, and refraining from responding impulsively. Her responses on this task were highly abnormal for her age and showed clear signs of ADHD. Sarah was also asked to rate her own everyday behaviors in various areas of executive functions. She reported significant difficulties overall, consistent with ADHD, and noted particular difficulties with sustaining attention and concentration, sustaining energy and effort on long tasks, getting organized and activated to start work, and using working memory and accessing recall in everyday tasks.

Acquired knowledge and achievement, which are most dependent on exposure and instruction, were also assessed. Sarah has been exposed to a strong learning environment, so she would be expected to have adequate achievement. The first cluster is Crystallized Ability, or verbal ability, which includes language development and general knowledge. Sarah scored in the Average range in this area. The next three clusters target academic achievement in reading, writing, and math.

Sarah's basic reading skills were Average, indicating that she can read and decode adequately for her age. Her skills were also Average compared to other college graduates.

Sarah's reading fluency varied depending on the specific task. When asked to read short sentences quickly and comprehend them, she scored in the High Average range for her age and in the Average range for college graduates. When asked to read long passages silently, her speed was Low Average for her age and Well Below Average for college graduates. When asked to read long passages aloud, her speed (130 words per minute) was Significantly Below Average for a college student (age norms are not available for this measure). Sarah's reading rate, overall, is significantly poor for her age, as well as for her educational level. This lack of fluency is not linked to any primary difficulty in basic reading skills, processing speed, or memory, but appears to be a reflection of her attentional difficulties. She is unable to remain focused on the text for any length of time, and must continuously refocus her attention.

Sarah's reading comprehension was in the Average range for her age, and Low Average for college graduates, when given very short passages to read and complete. However, when given longer passages (from high school and college level texts), her comprehension fell to the bottom of the Average range for her age, and to the Significantly Below Average range for college graduates. Her score fell at the 4th percentile for college graduates, indicating severe difficulties.

Sarah's spelling skills were in the Average range for her age and grade. Her writing fluency (writing simple sentences quickly given several words) and written expression (writing sentences to meet certain requirements) were both Average. However, when Sarah was asked to read a passage and summarize it in writing, she took a very long time, completed several sets of notes and rough drafts, and ultimately produced a short, somewhat inaccurate, summary of the passage. She took over 12 minutes to read a one-page passage and take notes, about 11 minutes to write a first draft, and an additional 10 minutes to rewrite her two-paragraph summary. Although there are no age or grade norms available for this task, she was not able to demonstrate writing abilities, such as taking notes and organizing a brief essay, that are required at the secondary and postsecondary levels.

Sarah's basic math skills were Average for her age and grade. Her fluency of solving basic math calculations was Significantly Above Average for her age and Well Above Average for her grade. Her ability to solve real-life math problems was Average for her age and grade. Sarah expressed that math has always been a strength, and she displayed no difficulties in this area.

SUMMARY

Sarah is a motivated, hardworking adult who meets criteria for the diagnosis of Attention-Deficit/Hyperactivity Disorder. Although academic weaknesses exist, they appear to stem from problems with attention, rather than specific learning disabilities. In addition to the core symptoms of inattention, impulsivity, and hyperactivity, she experiences difficulty with memory, organization, and fluency affecting oral language, reading, and writing production. Although Sarah can focus for relatively brief periods of time to plan and produce academic work, longer tasks are extraordinarily difficult for her. When compared to adults her own age, Sarah has average overall cognitive functioning but clinically significant impairment in attention, impulse control, and silent and oral reading rate. In addition, in comparison to others who have completed 4 years of college, she is clinically significantly impaired in oral language comprehension and memory, oral and silent reading rate, and reading comprehension. She also demonstrates skills below the mastery level for college graduates in oral and written math calculation, word decoding, and reading cloze procedures. Informal reading and writing activities reveal extraordinary difficulty organizing and completing written work of any length, although she can complete brief (one-sentence) writing tasks at an appropriate level for her age and grade.

RECOMMENDATIONS

1. Sarah may wish to consult a physician with knowledge of adult attention-deficit disorders (neurologist or psychiatrist) about the possibility of medical management of her ADHD. She has expressed that a trial of Ritalin in the past greatly improved her focus but was discontinued due to side effects. There are many more medications available for adults now, and a physician would be able to explore these options with her.

2. A number of books have been designed to teach coping strategies to adults with ADHD. Three particularly helpful ones are:
   - Dr. Edward Hallowell and Dr. John Ratey: *Driven to Distraction* (Touchstone)

- Dr. Lynn Weiss: *The Attention Deficit Disorder in Adults Workbook* (Taylor)
- Judith Kolberg and Dr. Kathleen Nadeau: *ADD-Friendly Ways to Organize Your Life* (Brunner-Routledge)

3. Because sustained reading is difficult for Sarah, she may wish to investigate the availability of videotapes on adult ADHD. Possible web sites for videos and other resources are www.chadd.org (CHADD: Children and Adults with ADHD) and www.help4adhd.org (National Resource Center on ADHD).

4. Sarah may wish to pursue obtaining accommodations at work under the Americans with Disabilities Act (ADA). Information about the ADA may be found at: http://www.usdoj.gov/crt/ada/adahom1.htm. Accommodations may include such things as scheduled time each day when Sarah is assigned to a closed office to work on paperwork without distractions, being able to provide information orally to another staff member to type and organize, providing forms to be completed rather than producing written work or plans from scratch each time, and providing recorded books in content areas

she needs to review. Extended time alone is unlikely to be effective because Sarah may lose focus and still not complete the work. Structure in addition to extended time will more likely be effective.

5. If Sarah chooses to continue her education, she may wish to pursue obtaining accommodations at school under the ADA as well. However, even with accommodations, Sarah's skill levels may be below the expected levels for graduate students in oral language (listening and remembering), reading, and writing. Accommodations for school may include such things as a reduced course load, recorded books, producing written work via dictation or tape, and extended time in a quiet area for testing and other evaluations.

6. If Sarah chooses to continue her education, she should explore whether the university has academic coaches available to help her with organizational skills such as staying on top of her workload, meeting due dates, planning study time, and strategies for studying that are active rather than passive (e.g., creating questions to answer while reading, writing brief notes in the margins of her text, highlighting different types of information in different colors).

Summary of Scores

Cognitive

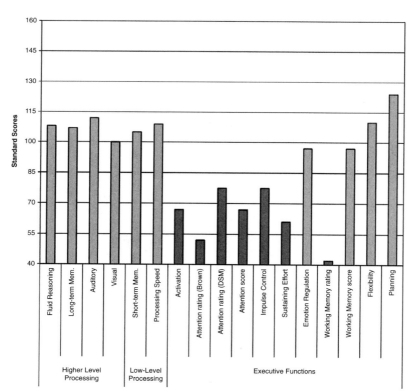

Figure 1

Academic

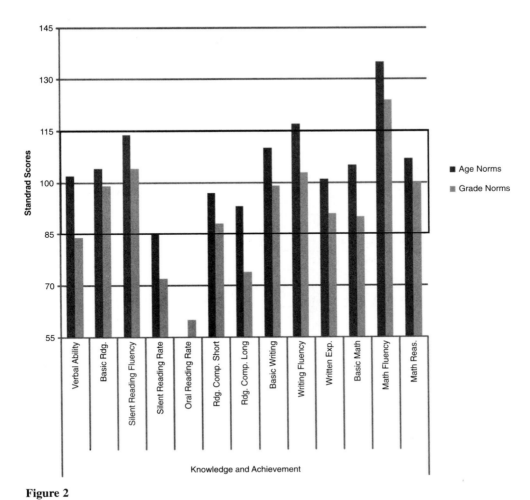

Figure 2

Summary of Scores Using the Cattell-Horn-Carroll Model

	Factor	Test	Subtest Name	Subtest Score	Converted Score	Average Score	Level of Performance	Description
Higher-Level Processing and Reasoning	Gf	WAIS-IV	Figure Weights	11	105	107	Avg.	Fluid Reasoning
		WAIS-IV	Matrix Reasoning	13	115			
		WJ III COG	Concept Formation	101	101			
		WJ III COG	Analysis-Synthesis	107	107			
	Glr	WJ III COG	V-A Learning	107	107	103	Avg.	Long-Term Retrieval
		WJ III COG	V-A Delayed	107	107			
		WJ III COG	Story Recall (SR)	97	97			
		WJ III COG	SR Delayed	95	95			
		WJ III COG	Retrieval Fluency	108	108			
	Ga	WJ III COG	Sound Blending	111	111	112*	High Avg.	Auditory Processing
		WJ III COG	Incomplete Words	110	110			
	Gv	WAIS-IV	Block Design	8	90	90	Avg.	Visual Processing
		WAIS-IV	Visual Puzzles	8	90			
		WJ III COG	Spatial Relations	110	110	110	High Avg	
		WJ III COG	Planning	124	124	124	Well Above	

(continued)

	Factor	Test	Subtest Name	Subtest Score	Converted Score	Average Score	Level of Performance	Description
Low-Level Processing	Gsm	WAIS-IV	Digit Span	10	100	105	Avg.	Short-Term Memory
			Digits Forward	11	105			
			Digits Backward	7	85			
		WAIS-IV	L-N Sequencing	12	110			
	Gs	WAIS-IV	Digit Symbol: Coding	14	120	109	Avg.	Processing Speed
		WAIS-IV	Symbol Search	10	100			
		WJ III COG	Pair Cancellation	108	108			
Acquired Knowledge and Achievement	Gc	WAIS-IV	Vocabulary	12	110	102	Avg.	Crystallized Ability (verbal, knowledge)
		WAIS-IV	Similarities	9	95			
		WAIS-IV	Information	11	105			
		WAIS-IV	Comprehension	10	100			
		WJ III ACH	Understanding Directions	102	102			
	Gq	WAIS-IV	Arithmetic	7	85	85	Low Av	Quantitative Ability and Math Achievement
		WJ III ACH	Calculation	105	105	105	Avg.	
		WJ III ACH	Math Fluency	135	135	135	Signif. Above	
		WJ III ACH	Applied Probs.	107	107	107	Avg.	
	Grw	WJ III ACH	Letter-Word ID	106	106	105*	Avg.	Literacy Skills— Reading
		WJ III ACH	Word Attack	103	103			
		WJ III ACH	Rdg. Fluency	114	114	114	High Avg.	
		NDRT	Reading Rate	175	85	85	Low Avg.	
		ORF	Oral Reading Rate		60[a]	60	Signif. Below	
		WJ III ACH	Passage Comp.	97	97	97	Avg.	
		NDRT	Comprehension	93	93	93	Avg.	
	Grw	WJ III ACH	Spelling	110	110	110	High Avg.	Literacy Skills— Writing
		WJ III ACH	Writing Fluency	117	117	117	Above	
		WJ III ACH	Writing Samples	101	101	101	Avg.	

Converted scores are standard scores with a mean of 100 and a standard deviation of 15; Average range is 85–115.

* Indicates cluster scores from norms, not a calculated average. All other cluster scores are averages.

a Indicates college norms; all other scores are based on age norms.

APPENDIX OF TEST SCORES

WAIS-IV

Index/Score	Standard Score*	Percentile	Classification
Verbal Comprehension	103	58	Average
Perceptual Organization	98	45	Average
Working Memory	97	42	Average
Processing Speed	111	77	High Average
Full-Scale Score	104	61	Average

WJ III COG

Test/Cluster	Standard Score	Percentile	Classification
Concept Formation	101	53	Average
Analysis-Synthesis	107	68	Average
FLUID REASONING	104	61	Average
Visual-Auditory Learning	107	68	Average
Visual-Auditory Learning Delay	107	69	Average
Retrieval Fluency	108	70	Average
LONG-TERM RETRIEVAL	108	71	Average
Sound Blending	111	76	High Average
Incomplete Words	110	74	High Average
PHONEMIC AWARENESS	112	79	High Average
Spatial Relations	110	75	High Average
Pair Cancellation	108	70	Average
Planning	124	95	Well Above Avg.
EXECUTIVE PROCESSES	108	71	Average

Wisconsin Card Sorting Test-64

Score	Raw Score	Standard Score	T Score**	Percentile	Classification
Number Correct	56				
Errors	8	110	57	75	Normal
Perseverative Errors	6	91	44	27	Normal
Non-perseverative Errors	2	114	59	82	Normal
Conceptual Level Responses	52	99	49	47	Normal
Categories Completed	5			>16	Normal
Trials to Complete First Category	11			>16	Normal
Failure to Maintain Set	0				Normal
Learning to Learn	0			>16	Normal

*All standard scores have a mean of 100 and a standard deviation of 15; Average range is 85–115.
**All T scores have a mean of 50 and a standard deviation of 10.

Conners' Continuous Performance Test-II

Score indicated client matches ADHD sample with 99.9% probability.

WJ III ACH

Test/Cluster	Age SS	Age %ile	Class	Grade SS	Grade %ile	Class	RPI
Story Recall	97	41	Avg.	82	12	Below Avg.	82/90
Story Recall-Delayed	95	37	Avg.	76	5	Well Below Avg.	81/90
Understanding Directions	102	54	Avg.	88	21	Low Avg.	76/90
ORAL LANGUAGE	100	50	Avg.	84	14	Below Avg.	79/90
Letter-Word ID	106	66	Avg.	104	60	Avg.	94/90
Word Attack	103	59	Avg.	94	34	Avg.	79/90
BASIC READING	105	64	Avg.	99	46	Avg.	88/90
Reading Fluency	114	83	High Avg.	104	60	Avg.	98/90
Passage Comprehension	97	41	Avg.	88	22	Low Avg.	73/90
Spelling	110	74	High Avg.	99	46	Avg.	88/90
Writing Fluency	117	88	Above Avg.	103	57	Avg.	92/90
Writing Samples	101	53	Avg.	91	28	Avg.	85/90
WRITTEN EXPRESSION	115	84	High Avg.	99	47	Avg.	89/90
Calculation	105	62	Avg.	90	26	Avg.	71/90
Math Fluency	135	99	Signif. Above Avg.	124	95	Well Above Avg.	99/90
MATH CALCULATION	119	90	Above Avg.	104	60	Avg.	93/90
Applied Problems	107	67	Avg.	100	50	Avg.	90/90

Nelson-Denny Reading Test

Test	Raw Score	Age SS*	Percentile	Grade SS	Percentile	Classification
Reading Rate	137 wpm	(175*) 85	16	72	3	Well Below Avg.
Compre-hension		(188*) 93	32	74	4	Well Below Avg.

*Nelson-Denny Scaled Scores, mean = 200, standard deviation of 25

Oral Reading Fluency

Correct Words per Minute	College Standard Score	Percentile	Classification
130 wpm	60	<1	Signif. Below Avg.

BADDS—Self-Report

Subtest	T Score	Classification
Activation	72	Clinical Range
Attention	82	Clinical Range
Effort (Sustained Effort)	76	Clinical Range
Affect (Emotions)	52	Normal
Memory (Working Memory)	89	Clinical Range
TOTAL SCORE	79	Clinical—ADD Highly Probable

Barkley Symptom Rating Scales

Scale	Symptoms Endorsed	Score	Range
Self-Report (General)			
Inattentive	7		Clinical
Hyperactive/ Impulsive	6		Clinical
Total Score		38	Clinical
Scale	Symptoms Endorsed	Score	Range
Self-Report (Work)			
Inattentive	7		Clinical
Hyperactive/ Impulsive	6		Clinical
Other Report (Mother)			
Inattentive	0		Normal
Hyperactive/ Impulsive	1		Normal
Other Report (Sister)			
Inattentive	9		Clinical
Hyperactive/ Impulsive	8		Clinical
Other Report (Friend since childhood)			
Inattentive	6		Clinical
Hyperactive/ Impulsive	6		Clinical
Other Report (Work Supervisor)			
Inattentive	3		Normal
Hyperactive/ Impulsive	3		Normal

Appendix A: Table of Reports

Age	Name	Diagnosis	Tests Used in the Current Evaluations	Evaluator(s)
3-11	Erik Templeton	Autism	ADI–R, ADOS	Sally Logerquist, Ph.D.
4-3	Susie Waterhouse	Language and memory deficits due to seizure disorder	BASC–2, Miller Neuropsychological Processing Concerns Checklist, NEPSY, WPPSI–III	Marshall Andrew Glenn, Ph.D.
5-1	Anthony Oscar	Receptive/Expressive Language Disorder	CASL, TOLD:P–4	Dale A. Bailey, M.A., CCC–SLP
5-8	Brandon Weiss	Speech–Language Disorder	ADOS, CARS, Leiter–R, PLS–3, SS/LS, TACL–3, WJ III ACH, WJ III COG	Stephen M. Camarata, Ph.D., CCC–SLP Mary N. Camarata, M.S., CCC–SLP
6-4	Clara Mays	Attention-Deficit/Hyperactivity Disorder, emotional control, Speech–Language Disorder	BASC–2, Beery VMI, CSRPI, KABC–II, KTEA–II	Randy W. Kamphaus, Ph.D. Tara C. Raines, Psy.S.
6-6	Trevor Martinelli	Attention	CRS–R, SB5	Eva M. Prince, Ed.S.
6-11	Isaac Hartman	Learning Disability (basic reading and writing skills), Attention-Deficit/Hyperactivity Disorder	WJ III ACH, WJ III COG, WJ III DS	James M. Creed, M.Ed.
7-9	Alondra Torres	Language Disorder, Autism Spectrum Disorder	ATEC, BASC–2, Bateria III, CARS, CBM, KFD, KTEA–II, OWLS, Roberts–2, UNIT, WISC–IV Integrated, WJ III COG	Brigid Garvin, M.Ed.
7-10	Rebekah Washington	Gifted, Expressive Language Disorder	TNL, WJ III ACH, WJ III COG	Aimee Yermish, Psy.D.
7-11	Ralph Benigno	Learning Disability (basic reading and writing skills)	DAS–II, WIAT–III	Colin D. Elliott, Ph.D.
8-1	Sabrina Jones	Learning Disability (basic reading and writing skills), Attention-Deficit/Hyperactivity Disorder, emotional factors	BASC–2, CRS–R, BRIEF, KABC–II, WJ III COG	James Hanson, M.Ed.
8-3	Dakota Briones	Learning Disability (basic reading and writing skills), secondary emotional factors	CASL, CTOPP, PAT–2, QRI–5, WJ III ACH, WJ III COG, WJ III DS	Lynne E. Jaffe, Ph.D.
8-4	Maria Ayala	Cultural and linguistic factors	C–LIM, WJ III ACH, WJ III COG	Samuel O. Ortiz, Ph.D.
8-5	Ben Tarantino	Learning Disability (basic reading and math skills, written expression, oral expression)	CAS, CTOPP, KTEA–II	Jack A. Naglieri, Ph.D.
8-11	David Sylvester	Brain injury and cognitive disorder caused by perinatal stroke	Beery VMI, CAS, CBRS, EVT–2, GDS, MVPT–3, Purdue Pegboard, PPVT–IV, Social Communication Questionnaire, TOMAL–2, WISC–IV, WJ III ACH	Sam Goldstein, Ph.D. Sean Cunningham, M.S.

(continued)

Age	Name	Diagnosis	Tests Used in the Current Evaluations	Evaluator(s)
8-11	Tanya Rubens	Learning Disability (basic reading, writing, and math skills), Attention-Deficit/Hyperactivity Disorder	BASC–2, TOC, TOSWRF, WJ III ACH, WJ III COG	Nancy Mather, Ph.D.
9-0	Brianna Zimmerman	Learning Disability (math)	Beery VMI, GORT–4, PAL–II, WISC–IV	Steven G. Feifer, D.Ed.
9-2	Fulanito Fulano	Adjustment Disorder with Disturbance of Conduct, Attention-Deficit/Hyperactivity Disorder, Learning Disorder NOS	BASC–2, CAT, CTMT, RIAS	Tara C. Raines, Psy.S. Cecil Reynolds, Ph.D.
9-2	Sara Post	Learning Disability (math), Speech Articulation	CAS, WISC–IV, WJ III ACH	Tulio M. Otero, Ph.D. Jack A. Naglieri, Ph.D.
9-3	Brayden Moats	High Functioning Autism, Speech–Language Disorder, Attention-Deficit/Hyperactivity Disorder	DAS–II, WIAT–III	Joel S. Hanania, Ph.D.
9-8	Thomas MacAloon	Learning Disability (basic reading and writing skills)	BASC–2, KTEA–II, WJ III ACH, WJ III COG	Dawn Flanagan, Ph.D. Vincent Alfonso, Ph.D.
9-9	Olivia Firek	Learning Disability (math)	CBM, WJ III ACH, WJ III COG, WJ III DS	Ed Schultz, Ph.D.
9-10	Maggie Moore	Specific Learning Disability (Reading)	DAS–II, TOSWRF, WIAT–III	Donna Rury Smith, Ed.D.
9-11	Marty Vinson	Pervasive Developmental Disorder NOS	NEPSY–II, UNIT	R. Steve McCallum, Ph.D.
10-3	Lupita Thalgott	Math difficulties	BASC–2, D–KEFS, KeyMath–R, PAL–II, WJ III ACH, WJ III COG	John Garruto, D. Ed..
10-8	Aaron Demers	Blind, inconsistent cognitive abilities	DAS–II, RIAS, Vineland–II, WJ III ACH–Braille	Kimberly Morris, Ph.D.
10-11	Page Smith	Asperger's Syndrome	ASDS, BASC–2, Bender Gestalt II, BRIEF, CTMT, GADS, KADI, Kinetic Drawing System, KTEA–II, RIAS	Elaine Fletcher–Janzen, Ed.D.
11-3	Lucille Miller	Intellectual Disability	GORT–4, WIAT–III, WJ III COG	Melissa M. King, M.Ed. Mary C. Wright, M.A.
11-4	Bobby Johnson	Severe Conduct Disorder	BASC–2, Bender Gestalt II, BRIEF, KABC–II, KTEA–II	Elaine Fletcher–Janzen, Ed.D.
11-5	John West	Learning Disability (math)	CBM, WISC–IV, WJ III ACH, WJ III COG, WJ III DS	Robert Misak, M.A., M.Ed.
11-6	Larry Robeson	Emotional Disorder	CVLT–C, D–KEFS, KABC–II, KTEA–II, M–PACI, NEPSY–II, RAN/RAS, Rorschach, TOC, TOWL–4, WJ III ACH, WJ III COG	Mitchel D. Perlman, Ph.D.
11-8	Anna Delgado	Visual impairment, ELL, math difficulties, adaptive behavior	Bater'a III, BVAT, CIBS–R, CVLT–C, TTBC, Vineland–II, WISC–IV, WJ III ACH, WJ III COG, WJ III DS	Sarah Gaines, Psy.S.
11-9	Jane Smalley	Learning Disability (reading comprehension, written expression, math problem solving), Language Disorder	CRS–R, SMALSI, WISC–IV Integrated, WJ III ACH, WJ III COG, WRAML2	Milton J. Dehn, Ph.D.
11-11	Kyle Marshall	Receptive and Expressive Language Disorder, severe anxiety	Beery VMI, CBCL, CELF–4, CTOPP, DIBELS, GORT–4, Stern Center Questionnaire, TOWL–4, TOWRE, WISC–IV, WJ III ACH	Blanche Podhajski, Ph. D., CCC–SLP Frances Ingram, M.A.
12-3	Sarah Stein	Gifted, Learning Disability (basic reading, writing, and math skills)	PAL–II, WISC–IV	Virginia W. Berninger, Ph.D.

Age	Name	Diagnosis	Tests Used in the Current Evaluations	Evaluator(s)
12-7	Randall Hosp	Learning Disability (math problem–solving), difficulties in written expression	BASC–2, BRIEF, Conners 3–P, CTOPP, GORT–4, PAL–II, R–CBM, WIAT–III, WISC–IV, WJ III ACH, WJ III COG	Gail M. Cheramie, Ph.D. Linda Hernandez Parks, M.A. Ashley Schuler, M.A.
12-9	Erin Manley	Asperger's Disorder/Nonverbal Learning Disorder, Generalized Anxiety Disorder, Dysthymic Disorder	ASDS, Beery VMI, BRIEF, CASL, CAVLT–2, CBCL, CDI, CMS, CPT II, CRS–R, D–KEFS, GORT–4, NEPSY–II, Piers–Harris 2, SSIS, WIAT–III, WISC–IV, WJ III ACH	Lisa A. Hain, Psy.D. James B. Hale, Ph.D.
13-1	Richard Goldstein	Neurologically based speech impediment/executive function weakness	BRIEF, CELF–4, CMS, D–KEFS, KAIT, NEPSY–II, PAL, RCFT, TOWRE, WCST, WIAT–III, WISC–IV, WJ III ACH, WJ III COG	George McCloskey, Ph.D.
13-9	Jim Paxton	Nonverbal Learning Disorder	ABAS–II, BRIEF, PPVT–4, SCQ, WIAT–III, WISC–IV	Christopher J. Nicholls, Ph.D.
14-2	Mikaela M.	Learning Disability (math), difficulties with receptive language	KABC–II, KTEA–II, WJ III ACH, WJ III COG	Liz Lichtenberger, Ph.D. Nadeen Kaufman, Ed.D.
14-7	Jamie Yazzie	Learning Disability (basic reading, writing, and math skills, reading comprehension, written expression, math problem solving), Emotional Disorder	BASC–2, DAS–II, WJ III ACH, WJ III COG	Toby D. Laird, Ph.D.
14-8	Kate Wilhelm	Attention-Deficit/Hyperactivity Disorder	BASC–2, WISC–IV, WJ III ACH, WJ III COG	Ron Dumont, Ed.D.
14-9	Esteban Garcia	ELL, possible primary language disorder	CELF–4 English and Spanish, EOWPVT–SPE, ROWPVT–SPE	Deborah Rhein, Ph.D.
14-9	Robert Perrin	Intellectual Disability	BASC–2, Beery VMI, CVLT–C, D–KEFS, Grooved Pegboard, Vineland–II, WISC–IV, WJ III ACH	Janice Sammons, Ph.D. Judith M. Kroese, Ph.D., CCC–SLP
14-10	Andrea Baker	Learning Disability (reading fluency, written expression/fluency, math fluency)	CMS, CRS–R, CTOPP, IVA+Plus, NDRT, RCFT, WCST–R, WISC–IV, WJ III ACH, WJ III COG	Jane McClure, Ph.D.
15-4	Miguel Laguna	Learning Disability (basic reading skills, written expression/fluency, math facts)	CBM, RAN/RAS, TIWRE, WJ III ACH, WJ III COG, WJ III DS, WRAML2	Bashir Abu-Hamour, Ph.D. Annmarie Urso, Ph.D. Nancy Mather, Ph.D.
15-6	Samantha Sechrist	Deaf, academic difficulties	KTEA–II, WIAT–III, WISC–IV, WNV, WRAML2	Lisa S. Coyner, Ph.D.
15-9	Glenn Wagner	Attention-Deficit/Hyperactivity Disorder, emotional difficulties	BASC–2, BRIEF, CDI, FOCI, MASC, STAXI–2 C/A, WISC–IV, WJ III ACH	Thomas M. Brunner, Ph.D.
17-2	Jeff Carsons	Delinquent, behavior and academic problems	MMPI–A, WAIS–IV, WJ III ACH, WMS–IV	Christina Vasquez, Ed.S. Richard Morris, Ph.D.
17-4	Michael Skriverson	Learning Disability (reading fluency, reading comprehension, written expression/fluency, basic math skills)	NDRT, WJ III ACH, WJ III COG	Nicole Ofiesh, Ph.D.
17-7	Ella Perin	Learning Disability (basic reading skills, written expression)	Adult ADHD Observation Form, Attention-Deficit/Hyperactivity Disorder–SR, Attention-Deficit/Hyperactivity Disorder–SO, BAI, BDI–II, D–KEFS, GORT–4, NDRT, PPVT–4, Phonological/Orthographic Battery (informal tests), Reading and Media Habits Questionnaire, RCFT, WAIS–IV, WJ III ACH, WJ III COG, WMS–III. WRAT4	Chris Coleman, M.A.

(continued)

Age	Name	Diagnosis	Tests Used in the Current Evaluations	Evaluator(s)
17-11	Ti Nguyen	ELL, Learning Disability (basic math skills, math problem solving)	UNIT, WJ III ACH, WJ III COG	Sherry Mee Bell, Ph.D.
19-1	Tory Marten	Learning Disability (basic reading and writing skills)	WJ III ACH, WJ III COG	Barbara J. Wendling, M.A.
19-3	Russell Thompson	Hearing Impairment, low cognitive abilities	Ling Six Sound Test, SIFTER, WJ III ACH	Kelly Metz, M.Ed.
19-7	Annie Stevens	Anxiety, low self–concept	CELF–4, CTOPP, WJ III ACH, WJ III COG	Andrew Shanock, Ph.D.
25	Angie Sawyer	Attention-Deficit/Hyperactivity Disorder, Learning Disability, (basic math skills, math problem olving) anxiety	ASR, NDRT, WAIS–IV, WJ III ACH, WJ III COG	Michael E. Gerner, Ph.D.
33	Jan Guilford	Language Disorder or Cognitive Dysfunction due to Traumatic Brain Injury	ABAS, ASR, CPT, SB5, WAIS–IV, WIAT–II, WJ III ACH, WMS–III	Gale H. Roid, Ph.D. Krystle Edwards, B.A.
49	Sarah Hines	Attention-Deficit/Hyperactivity Disorder	BADDS, Barkley and Murphy Clinical Workbook Rating Scales, CPT II, NDRT, WAIS–IV, WCST–64, WJ III ACH, WJ III COG	Catherine A. Fiorello, Ph.D.

Appendix B: Guidelines for Writing Assessment Reports

An outline is often helpful in structuring reports, although the nature of each assessment will ultimately determine the information that is included. Different evaluators use different types of identifying information and headings. The following outline may be useful as a starting point.

Identifying Information in the Report Heading

- Student's name, date of birth, age, and grade
- Testing and report (optional) date(s)
- Evaluator's name
- School, parents' names, teachers' names (optional)
- Ethnicity (optional)

Reason for Referral

- Identify the person who referred the student and that person's role or relationship to the student.
- State the specific concerns of the referral source and the purpose of the evaluation, such as the specific questions to be answered.
- Remember that the reason for referral is the reason for testing. The assessment results should help clarify the concerns on which the referral is based and answer the referral question(s).
- Be concise. This section can usually be written in one short paragraph.

Background Information

- Describe the current family constellation, living situation, and relevant family history. Include familial history of learning/behavioral problems or other problems that might be relevant to the referral concerns.
- Discuss any pertinent birth, developmental, and medical history. Before testing, make sure that the student

has had a recent vision and hearing screening so as to rule out any sensory problems.
- Include behavioral, social, and emotional history at school and at home if the reason for the referral includes behavioral/social concerns.
- Review relevant educational history, such as multiple school changes, school settings (e.g., public, private, religious, discovery learning), academic grades, special services, and retentions.

Classroom Observations

- For students in an elementary or secondary school, a classroom observation may be required by the local educational agency. For referrals involving behavioral, attentional, or social concerns, a classroom observation should always be done.
- Describe the number of students, teachers, and instructional aides in the classroom.
- Describe the class activity and the general class involvement with the task.
- Describe the task on which the student was working; the student's attention, level of motor activity, effort, task success, and general behavior; and whether the student required individual teacher attention.

Previous Evaluations and Results

- Summarize the findings of past medical (including vision and hearing), psychological, and educational evaluations.
- Discuss any prior interventions (e.g., school-based tutoring, RTI intervention, speech-language therapy) and their effectiveness.

Tests Administered

- List the full names of the tests, rating scales, or other assessment tools used, including the form or edition, followed by the acronym in parentheses. Test publishers provide specific acronyms for their tests in the manuals. Use those and do not make one up (e.g., correct: Vineland-II; incorrect: VABS-2). The test can then be referred to by its initials throughout the remainder of the report.

- If you administered only selected subtests, state the name of the test followed by the names of the subtests administered.

- List any informal assessment procedures and people interviewed (e.g., student, teachers, parents, outside counselor, or tutor).

Assessment Procedures Used

- State adherence to or exceptions to best assessment practices (e.g., ethnicity and race considered in test selection; educational disadvantage or other exclusionary factors were not primary factors in test results; tests were administered in the student's primary language). Describe any modifications to standardized administration. Describe any cautions or limitations that may affect interpretation of the findings (e.g., normative sample was not based primarily on students with similar characteristics, such as a sensory impairment; student's performance may have been negatively affected by impulsivity and attentional difficulties).

- State the type of norms used (e.g., age, grade).

- Explain how the scores used are interpreted, such as the meaning of the percentile rank or relative proficiency index.

- If verbal descriptors for score ranges are used, list the lower and upper limit of each score range and the associated descriptor (e.g., SS 90–109: Average). Many report writers capitalize these verbal descriptors, whereas some do not. Whichever style you select, stay consistent throughout the report.

- Maintain consistency in use of score ranges throughout the report or explain when changing to different ranges and descriptors (e.g., cognitive/academic standard score descriptors vs. *T*-score ranges and developmental classifications for adaptive behavior scales).

Behaviors during Testing

- Describe general observations concerning the student's behavior in the testing situation, such as response style (e.g., impulsive to reflective) as well as involve-

ment and motivation throughout the test. Include the student's activity level, attention, and general attitude toward testing.

- Note the student's verbal communication skills.

- Briefly describe the student's response to success, failure, and feedback but save comments relevant to specific tests or tasks for the "Results" section.

- Cite specific examples if possible, such as "he rocked back and forth in his chair frequently during the assessment procedure," or "she looked out the window and avoided eye contact with the examiner." Do not label the behavior (e.g., "John was hyperactive during testing") and do not interpret the intent (e.g., "John's discomfort in the testing session was apparent as he avoided eye contact.")

Reporting Scores

- Report scores in text; include them in a table within the body of the associated section of the document, or attach them in tables at the end.

- Report the scores in ranges when possible and state the level of confidence (e.g., 68% confidence interval).

Results and Interpretation

- Analyze, interpret, and integrate data in this section. Consider findings from a variety of sources (e.g., test results, response-to-intervention data, curriculum-based measurement probes, classroom work samples, diagnostic teaching, high-stakes testing).

- When test scores within a scale, factor, or cluster differ significantly, do not use the broader score to represent the ability assessed. Attempt to explain the reason or reasons for the differences and interpret the narrow abilities. Discrepant scores within a cluster may require further testing to investigate/confirm the results.

- Separate sections for cognitive, academic, and behavioral information. Within these, separate paragraphs for each subtopic. Subtopics do not have to be organized by the cognitive/academic areas tested. Use whatever organization will communicate the results in the most understandable fashion (e.g., strengths/weaknesses, answering referral questions).

- For each area of performance to be discussed:
  - Organize the discussion as follows: total test scores; composites, clusters, or factors; tests and subtests;

and qualitative information (comments, information from error analysis).

- If the individual tests of a composite or cluster score are significantly discrepant, I do not discuss the broad ability; instead, discuss the narrow abilities and attempt to explain the reasons for these differences.
- Make a general statement about the student's performance followed by more specific comments.
- Include discussion of results of response/error analysis indicating specific cognitive/academic difficulties and provide specific examples to document a clinical interpretation. Do not include actual test items in examples; make up similar items and errors.
- Include the student's behaviors and comments regarding performance on specific tests or types of tasks (e.g., "I never can figure these out." "These types of tests make my eyes hurt." "I hear it but then it just disappears.").

Summary and Conclusions

- Briefly restate the referral concern and specific questions.
- Briefly summarize test results and, in doing so, answer the referral question(s).
- Briefly explain the cause-effect relationship, if any, among the cognitive, academic, and behavioral results.
- Add any pertinent information regarding the student's functioning that was not addressed in the referral concerns.
- Do not include information in this section that was not introduced in the body of the report.
- Include statement of diagnosis or refer to multidisciplinary team for consideration of next step.

Recommendations

- Make recommendations specific to the referral question and/or to the findings, if different from the referral question.

- In most instances, if working with a multidisciplinary team within a school system, do not state whether a student does or does not have a specific educational classification (e.g., learning disabilities, intellectual disability) unless this has been determined previously by the team. Instead, make a recommendation that the team will consider eligibility for special services during the meeting.
- Further testing. Recommend further testing to yield more specific information, if necessary, or to address problems that have become evident as a result of the evaluation but were not included in the referral concern (e.g., a student referred for reading problems performs poorly on oral language tests).
- Instruction. Provide and explain realistic and practical interventions based on the student's strengths and weaknesses. Include a brief explanation regarding the rationale for the recommendation.
- Attach outlines of strategies recommended or more detailed explanations of instructional techniques, if available (optional).

General Suggestions

- Use third person (e.g., "the examiner" or "the evaluator") or first person "I." Be consistent.
- Use formal language but avoid jargon. Attempt to use terminology that will be familiar to the reader.
- Capitalize names of tests, subtests, factors, and clusters so that they can be distinguished from the general ability (e.g., spelling vs. the Spelling subtest). Make sure to edit your report carefully.

Adapted from: Mather, N., & Jaffe, L. E. (2002). *Woodcock-Johnson III: Reports, recommendations, and strategies.* Hoboken, NJ: John Wiley & Sons.

Appendix C: Test Acronyms

ABAS-II	Adaptive Behavior Assessment System – Second Edition
AD/HD-SO	Adult AD/HD Significant Other Behavior Observation Checklist (ADHD-SO)
AD/HD-SR	Adult AD/HD Self-Report Checklist (ADHD-SR)
ADI-R	Autism Diagnostic Interview, Revised
ADOS	Autism Diagnostic Observation Schedule
ASDS	Asperger Syndrome Diagnostic Scale
ASR	Adult Self-Report
ATEC	Autism Treatment Evaluation Checklist – Spanish Version
BADDS	Brown Attention-Deficit Disorder Scales
BAI	Beck Anxiety Inventory
No acronym	Barkley and Murphy Clinical Workbook Rating Scales
BASC-2	Behavior Assessment System for Children, Second Edition
Batería III	Batería III Woodcock-Munoz Pruebas de habilidades cognitivas
BDI-II	Beck Depression Inventory, Second Edition
Beery VMI	Beery-Buktenica Developmental Test of Visual-Motor Integration, 5th Edition
Beery VMI	Beery-Buktenica Developmental Test of Visual-Motor Integration, 6th Edition
Bender-Gestalt II	Bender Visual-Motor Gestalt Test, Second Edition
BRIEF	Behavior Rating Inventory of Executive Function
BVAT	Bilingual Verbal Ability Tests Normative Update
CARS	Childhood Autism Rating Scale
CAS	Cognitive Assessment System
CASL	Comprehensive Assessment of Spoken Language
CAT	Children's Apperception Test
CAVLT-2	Children's Auditory Verbal Learning Test–2
CBCL	Child Behavior Checklist & Teacher Report Form
CBM	Curriculum Based Measures
CCTT	Children's Color Trails Test
CDI	Children's Depression Inventory
CELF-4	Clinical Evaluation of Language Fundamentals, Fourth Edition
CELF-4 Spanish	Clinical Evaluation of Language Fundamentals, Fourth Edition Spanish
C.H.A.P.S.	Children's Auditory Performance Scale
CIBS-R	Brigance Comprehensive Inventory of Basic Skills-Revised
C-LIM	Culture-Language Interpretive Matrix
CMS	Children's Memory Scale

Conners CBRS	Conners Comprehensive Behavior Rating Scales
Conners 3	Conners 3rd Edition
CPST	Colorado Perceptual Speed Test
CPT	Conners' Continuous Performance Test
CPT II	Conners' Continuous Performance Test II
CRS-R	Conners' Rating Scale – Revised
CSRPI	Children's Self-Report and Projective Inventory
CTMT	Comprehensive Trail-Making Test
CTONI-2	Comprehensive Test of Nonverbal Intelligence, Second Edition
CTOPP	Comprehensive Test of Phonological Processing
CVLT-C	California Verbal Learning Test-Children's Version
DAP	Draw-A-Person Test
DAS-II	Differential Ability Scales, Second Edition
DIBELS	Dynamic Indicators of Basic Early Literacy Skills
D-KEFS	Delis-Kaplan Executive Function System
DP-3	Developmental Profile-3
DTVP-2	Developmental Test of Visual Perception, Second Edition
EOWPVT-SPE	Expressive One-Word Picture Vocabulary Test Spanish-Bilingual Edition
EVT-2	Expressive Vocabulary Test-2
No acronym	Fisher's Auditory Problems Checklist
FOCI	Florida Obsessive Compulsive Inventory
GADS	Gilliam Asperger's Disorder Scale
GDS	Gordon Diagnostic System
GORT-4	Gray Oral Reading Test – Fourth Edition
HFDT	Human Figure Drawing Test
HSQ	Home Situations Questionnaire
IVA+Plus	IVA + Plus Continuous Performance Test
KABC-II	Kaufman Assessment Battery for Children, Second Edition
KADI	Krug Asperger's Disorder Index
KAIT	Kaufman Adolescent and Adult Intelligence Test
KBIT-2	Kaufman Brief Intelligence Test, Second Edition
(No acronym)	Kent Visual Perception Test
KeyMath-R	KeyMath-Revised: A Diagnostic Inventory of Essential Mathematics
KeyMath 3	KeyMath3 Diagnostic Assessment
KFD	Kinetic Family Drawing
KTEA-II	Kaufman Test of Educational Achievement, Second Edition
Leiter-R	Leiter International Performance Scale – Revised
No acronym	Ling Six Sound Test
MASC	Multidimensional Anxiety Scale for Children
No acronym	Miller Neuropsychological Processing Concerns Checklist
MMPI-A	Minnesota Multiphasic Personality Inventory-Adolescent
M-PACI	Millon Pre-Adolescent Clinical Inventory
MSE	Mental Status Exam

(continued)

MVPT- 3	Motor-Free Visual Perception Test, Third Edition
NDRT	Nelson-Denny Reading Test
No acronym	NEPSY
NEPSY-II	NEPSY-Second Edition
NNAT	Naglieri Nonverbal Ability Test
OWLS	Oral and Written Language Scales
PAL-II	Process Assessment of the Learner – Second Edition
PAT-2	Phonological Awareness Test 2
No acronym	Pediatric and Early Adolescent Bipolar Disorder Symptoms Checklist
Piers-Harris 2	Piers-Harris Children's Self-Concept Scale, Second Edition
PLS-4	Preschool Language Scale, Fourth Edition
PPVT-4	Peabody Picture Vocabulary Test, Fourth Edition
No acronym	Purdue Pegboard Test
QRI-5	Qualitative Reading Inventory, Fifth Edition
RAN/RAS	Rapid Automatized Naming and Rapid Alternating Stimulus Tests
R-CBM	AIMSweb Curriculum-Based Measurement: Reading Fluency
RCFT	Rey Complex Figure Test and Recognition Trial
RIAS	Reynolds Intellectual Assessment Scales
Roberts-2	Roberts Apperception Test for Children: 2
Rorschach	Rorschach Inkblot Test
ROWPVT-SPE	Receptive One-Word Picture Vocabulary Test, Spanish-Bilingual Edition
(No acronym)	RSEC School Self-Rating Scale
(No acronym)	Social Attributes Checklist
SB5	Stanford-Binet Intelligence Scales, Fifth Edition
SCQ	Social Communication Questionnaire
SIFTER	Screening Instrument for Targeting Educational Risk
SMALSI	School Motivation and Learning Strategies Inventory
SSIS	Social Skills Improvement System
SS/LS	Spontaneous Speech and Language Sample
STAXI-2 C/A	State-Trait Anger Expression Inventory–2 Child and Adolescent
(No acronym)	Stern Center Questionnaires
TAAS	Test of Auditory Analysis Skills
TACL-3	Test of Auditory Comprehension of Language-Third Edition
TAKS	Texas Assessment of Knowledge and Skills
TAPS-R	Test of Auditory Perceptual Skills-Revised
TEKS	Texas Essential Knowledge and Skills
TIWRE	Test of Irregular Word Reading Efficiency
TNL	Test of Narrative Language
TOC	Test of Orthographic Competence
TOLD-P:4	Test of Language Development-Primary: Fourth Edition
TOMAL-2	Test of Memory and Learning, Second Edition
TOPS	Test of Problem Solving, Third Edition

TOSWRF	Test of Silent Word Reading Fluency
T.O.V.A.	Test of Variables of Attention
TOWL-2	Test of Written Language-Second Edition
TOWL-3	Test of Written Language-Third Edition
TOWL-4	Test of Written Language-Fourth Edition
TOWRE	Test of Word Reading Efficiency
TTBC	Tactile Test of Basic Concepts
UNIT	Universal Nonverbal Intelligence Test
Vineland-II	Vineland Adaptive Behavior Scales, Second Edition
WAIS-IV	Wechsler Adult Intelligence Scale-Fourth Edition
WCST	Wisconsin Card Sorting Test – Revised and Expanded
WCST:CV4	Wisconsin Card Sorting Test Computer Version 4 – Research Edition
WCST-64	Wisconsin Card Sorting Test – 64 Card Version
WIAT-II	Wechsler Individual Achievement Test – Second Edition
WIAT-III	Wechsler Individual Achievement Test – Third Edition
WISC-IV	Wechsler Intelligence Scale for Children – Fourth Edition
WISC-IV Integrated	Wechsler Intelligence Scale for Children – Fourth Edition, Integrated
WJ III ACH	Woodcock- Johnson III NU Tests of Achievement
WJ III ACH – Braille	Woodcock-Johnson III NU Tests of Achievement – Braille Adaptation
WJ III COG	Woodcock-Johnson III NU Tests of Cognitive Abilities
WJ III DS	Woodcock-Johnson III NU Tests of Cognitive Abilities Diagnostic Supplement
WMS-III	Wechsler Memory Scale-Third Edition
WMS-IV	Wechsler Memory Scale-Fourth Edition
WNV	Wechsler Scale of Nonverbal Ability
WPPSI-III	Wechsler Preschool and Primary Scale of Intelligence – Third Edition
WRAML2	Wide Range Assessment of Memory and Learning, Second Edition
WRAT4	Wide Range Achievement Test 4
YSR	Achenbach Youth Self-Report